THE OXFORD COLOUR SPELLING DICTIONARY

£ 6.99

D1150438

NORTH LEAMINGTON
SIXTH FORM CV32 5SF
LEARNING RESOURCES
CENTRE, BINSWOOD

WITHDRAWN

WITHDRAWN

The Oxford Colour Spelling Dictionary

Edited by
Maurice Waite

CLARENDON PRESS • OXFORD

1996

Oxford University Press, Walton Street, Oxford OX2 6DP

Oxford New York
Athens Auckland Bangkok Bombay
Calcutta Cape Town Dar es Salaam Delhi
Florence Hong Kong Istanbul Karachi
Kuala Lumpur Madras Madrid Melbourne
Mexico City Nairobi Paris Singapore
Taipei Tokyo Toronto

and associated companies in
Berlin Ibadan

Oxford is a trade mark of Oxford University Press

Published in the United States by
Oxford University Press Inc., New York

© Oxford University Press 1986, 1995, 1996

First Edition of the Oxford Spelling Dictionary 1986
Second Edition 1995
Published in paperback as the Oxford Colour Spelling Dictionary 1996

All rights reserved. No part of this publication may be reproduced,
stored in a retrieval system, or transmitted, in any form or by any means,
without the prior permission in writing of Oxford University Press.
Within the UK, exceptions are allowed in respect of any fair dealing for the
purpose of research or private study, or criticism or review, as permitted
under the Copyright, Designs and Patents Act, 1988, or in the case of
reprographic reproduction in accordance with the terms of the licences
issued by the Copyright Licensing Agency. Enquiries concerning
reproduction outside these terms and in other countries should be
sent to the Rights Department, Oxford University Press,
at the address above

This book is sold subject to the condition that it shall not, by way
of trade or otherwise, be lent, re-sold, hired out or otherwise circulated
without the publisher's prior consent in any form of binding or cover
other than that in which it is published and without a similar condition
including this condition being imposed on the subsequent purchaser

British Library Cataloguing in Publication Data
Data available

Library of Congress Cataloging in Publication Data
Data available

ISBN 0–19–860030–5

10 9 8 7 6 5 4 3 2 1

Printed in Hong Kong

Preface

This volume contains the full text of the second edition of the *Oxford Spelling Dictionary*, which has been completely re-edited and considerably enlarged by the addition of not only more headwords but also all inflections. The coverage is based on that of the *Concise Oxford Dictionary* (Ninth Edition, 1995) and the *Oxford English Reference Dictionary* (1995), with further items included on grounds of spelling difficulty or possible confusion. This edition also includes a large number of compounds written as two words (see the Introduction for the categories covered).

American spellings are now included, and both they and their British equivalents are labelled and cross-referred to each other to enable the book to be used for adapting texts to either British or American usage.

Another major innovation in this edition is the use of computerized collections of English (the British National Corpus and the Oxford Dictionary Department's own body of citations) in identifying new words for inclusion and in comparing the frequencies of variant spellings. The recommended spelling of a word is not always simply that found most frequently, because other factors are also taken into account, such as the number and type of sources using each variant.

The recommended word divisions shown have been completely revised in the light of modern practice and represent an attempt to find the most unobtrusive solutions. They are based on a combination of etymological and phonological considerations, since overstrict adherence to either principle can result in misleading or inelegant divisions, such as *auto-nomous* and *lung-ing* or *profi-teer* and *overwa-ter.*

I am indebted to Rosamund Moon for her contribution to the planning of the project before I became involved.

M. J. W.

Editorial Staff

Editor
Maurice Waite

Adviser on word division
Judith Scott

Assistant editor and keyboarder
Susan Wilkin

Chief Editor, Current English Dictionaries
Patrick Hanks

Contents

Introduction

I. SPELLING

Indicators

Various indicators are given to help the reader spell a word correctly, especially when there are others with which it could be confused. These are referred to after the symbol ⚠, which can be taken to mean 'Do not confuse with…'. The indicators are of the following types:

1. Sense indicators, e.g.

> **hare** (animal. ⚠ hair)
> **hair** (on head etc. ⚠ hare)

These are not complete definitions, nor do they always cover all parts of speech, as they are intended to be merely enough to enable the reader to choose the correct spelling of a word, often giving no more than a single quality or feature which distinguishes one thing from another.

2. Word-class (or part-of-speech) labels, e.g.

> **double fault** *noun*
> **double-fault** *verb*

3. Subject-field labels, e.g.

> **bailor** (*Law.* ⚠ bailer, baler)

4. Brief descriptions of people, places, institutions, etc., e.g.

> **Pavarotti, Luciano** (Italian tenor)
> **Delhi** (capital of India)

Spelling recommendations

When there is variation in the spelling of a word, e.g. *judg(e)ment*, the use of one spelling is normally recommended, thus:

> **judgment** (use judgement)

No preference is normally given among variants which differ more than slightly in pronunciation and are therefore treated as synonyms, e.g. *brontosaur/brontosaurus* or *archil/orchil*.

A non-recommended spelling is normally entered with a cross-reference to the recommended spelling, as with *judgment* above, but if it is also the recommended or only spelling of a different word, it is not mentioned as being a non-recommended variant, since the purpose of this book is not to provide a record of all existing variants. For example, although *weepy*, besides meaning 'tearful', is a non-recommended spelling of *weepie*, meaning 'a sentimental or emotional film, play, etc.', the two words are simply entered thus:

> **weepie** (film etc. ⚠ weepy)
> **weepy** (tearful. ⚠ weepie)

Variants which differ only in the matter of accents, apostrophes, or capital letters, or whether they are written hyphenated, as two words, or as one, e.g. *fete*, *Holarctic*, and *back-up* (as opposed to the recommended *fête*, *holarctic*, and *backup*) are not normally shown, since they would almost always be adjacent to the recommended forms and there are very large numbers of particularly the last type.

When an inflection has different spellings which are pronounced identically, the first one given is recommended. For example, in

> **cue**
> > **cues**
> > **cued**
> > **cueing** *or* **cuing**

cueing is recommended, and in

> **bureau**
> > **bureaux** *or* **bureaus**

bureaux is recommended.

Capital initial letters

Many pairs of words with capital and lower-case initials are given if each refers to a very different person or thing, e.g.

> **Balaclava** (battlefield, Crimea)
> **balaclava** (helmet)

> **Felicity** (name)
> **felicity** (happiness)

> **Pentagon** (US defence HQ)
> **pentagon** (five-sided figure)

However, when the capitalized form refers merely to a particular example of the person or thing in question, e.g. *the Queen* or *the Renaissance*, it is not normally entered.

Compounds

This dictionary contains large numbers of compound expressions written as one word or with a hyphen, so that the reader is left in no doubt as to the recommended form. ('Syntactic' hyphenated compounds, such as *mud-spattered* or *assembly-line* in *assembly-line workers*, being almost unlimited in number, are only given if they are extremely common, e.g. *high-street* in *high-street shops*, or if there could be doubt about another aspect of their spelling.)

In addition, compounds that are written as separate words are given if

1. there is evidence of variation in their use, as with, e.g., *street lamp*, which is also, but not so frequently, written as *street-lamp*;

2. they are of a construction that might suggest that they are written as one word or with a hyphen, e.g. *chess player*;

3. they could be confused with particular single-word or hyphenated compounds, e.g. *all together* (compare *altogether*) or *way in* (compare *weigh-in*); or

4. the predominant form has recently changed, resulting in a different recommendation from that in earlier Oxford publications, e.g. *horse race*.

In this book, hyphens introduced because a word is divided at the end of a line are printed sloping (‐), while 'permanent' hyphens, as in *eighty-first*, are always printed horizontally, even at the end of a line.

British and American spellings

The labels *Br.* and *Am.* are recommendations as to which spelling to use in British and American English respectively, e.g.

> **pretence** *Br.* (*Am.* pretense)
> **pretense** *Am.* (*Br.* pretence)

They are not to be taken as indications of the currency of the different spellings; *pretence* is in fact used in both British and American English but is labelled *Br.* as it is the only British spelling and is not the predominant American spelling.

Words that are found only in British or American English, such as *blowlamp* and *preppy*, are not labelled as such.

-ise and *-ize*

The verbal ending *-ize* has been in general use since the 16th century; it is favoured in American use, while, in Britain, both *-ize* and *-ise* are acceptable, provided that their use is consistent. The preferred style of Oxford University Press in academic and general books published in Britain is *-ize*, and this book therefore lists words showing such variation thus:

> **nationalise** *Br.* (use nationalize)
> **nationalize**
>
> **organiser** *Br.* (use organizer)
> **organizer**

Note that a number of verbs ending in *-ise* or *-ize* do not have alternative spellings, such as *televise* and *capsize*.

Transliterations

Alternative transliterations of foreign names are entered thus:

> **Tsinghai** (= Qinghai)

indicating that they are acceptable but at the same time showing which spelling to use to ensure consistency with other names.

Inflections

Inflections are given in the order:

> noun plural and/or 3rd person singular of the present tense
> past tense
> present participle
> past participle
> comparative adjective
> superlative adjective

If the noun plural and the 3rd person singular of a word that is both a noun and a verb have the same form, it is given only once, e.g.

> **break**
>   **breaks**
>   **broke**
>   **breaking**
>   **broken**

(If it is different, the noun and the verb are given separate entries for the sake of clarity.)

If the past tense and the past participle have the same form, it is given only once, in the position for the past tense, e.g.

> **deal**
>   **deals**
>   **dealt**
>   **dealing**

If all the inflections of a word are regular, e.g. *calms*, *calmed*, *calming*, *calmer*, *calmest*, then only the endings are given, thus:

> **calm** +s +ed +ing +er +est
> **claim** +s +ed +ing
> **cold** +s +er +est

II. WORD DIVISION

'Word division' means the splitting of a word at the end of a line of print or writing, with a hyphen added at the end of the first part, and the second part taken over to the next line. (It is often called 'hyphenation', but that term is also used to refer to the use of 'permanent' hyphens in compounds such as *pay-bed* and *over-abundant*.)

In handwriting and typing, it is safest (and often neatest) not to divide words at all; however, in word-processing and typesetting that is justified (i.e., with the lines expanded to make the right-hand ends align vertically, as in this Introduction), the overall appearance may well be better if a word is divided than if it is taken over to the next line and the remaining words are spaced out.

Where to divide

The vertical bar (|) indicates a 'preferred' division point, at which a word can be divided under almost any circumstances, while a broken vertical bar (¦) indicates a 'secondary' division point, at which a word is best divided only in narrow-measure work (i.e., narrow columns of type, as, for example, in newspapers and some dictionaries). A word containing both kinds should be divided at a preferred point if possible.

The division indicators have both relative and absolute value: for instance, a secondary division point in a word which also contains a preferred point, such as **con¦tent|ment** (*con-tentment*), may be a better division than that indicated by a secondary point that is the only point in a short word, such as **hag¦gle**, but it is given secondary status because it is not as good as the preferred division (*content-ment*).

Every word division should, ideally, be vetted by eye as a check that it is both the best division possible and better than not dividing at all: for instance, even a 'preferred' division may be quite unnecessary at the end of a wide line if the word spaces are not too large. Furthermore, the recommendations in this or any other book should not be regarded as inviolable rules; the typesetter or proof-reader should occasionally feel free to depart from them if the circumstances warrant it.

Division of regular inflections

In regular inflections (shown as **+ing** etc.—see p. xii), the endings are separable as follows:

+ed: only in narrow-measure work and then only if the word is of at least six letters and the ending is pronounced as a separate syllable, e.g. *bleat-ed* or *part-ed*; compare *ended* and *calmed*.

+ing: always, if the word is of more than six letters, e.g. *calm-ing* or *sharpen-ing*, but otherwise only in narrow-measure work, e.g. *buy-ing*.

+er: only in narrow-measure work and then only if the word is of at least six letters, e.g. *calm-er* or *sharp-er*; compare *odder*.

+est: always, if the word is of more than six letters, as in *calm-est* or *shallow-est*, but otherwise only in narrow-measure work, e.g. *odd-est*.

The above rules are all qualified by those for the division of hyphenated compounds given on p. xiv; thus, e.g., *self-seeded* and *self-seeding* should not normally be divided before *-ed* and *-ing* respectively, and *co-presented* and *co-presenting* should be divided at those points normally only in narrow-measure work.

Division of hyphenated compounds

A hyphenated compound, such as *after-effect*, can be divided at the hyphen under almost any circumstances; the only proviso is that, because it could then appear to be a divided solid word, care should be taken that no confusion can arise as a result, as it might with, e.g., *re-cover* (meaning 'cover again'), which could be mistaken for *recover* (meaning 'reclaim' etc.).

Additionally, hyphenated compounds are shown with secondary division points at least six letters after the hyphen, e.g. **self-govern¦ment**. Finally, in order to avoid very bad spacing, one could divide either (*a*) the second element at a point fewer than six letters after the hyphen or (*b*) the first element, in each case following, whenever possible, the recommendations for the elements as words on their own. The most important consideration in doing so would be to avoid producing an unacceptably obtrusive or misleading result, such as *scab-bard-fish*.

Personal names

Some writers and typesetters prefer not to divide personal names at all, and some prefer to do so only in narrow-measure work. The personal names included in this dictionary are shown with both preferred and secondary division points so that, if they are divided, the best point at which to do so can be chosen, but they are identified as the names of people, e.g.

Mac|ken¦zie, Alex|an¦der (Scottish explorer)

so that it is possible to avoid dividing them if one wishes.

Note on Proprietary Terms

This dictionary includes some words which are, or are asserted to be, proprietary names or trade marks. Their inclusion does not imply that they have acquired for legal purposes a non-proprietary or general significance, nor is any other judgement implied concerning their legal status. In cases where the editor has some evidence that a word is used as a proprietary name or trade mark this is indicated by the label *Propr.*, but no judgement concerning the legal status of such words is made or implied thereby.

Aa

a *indefinite article*
aa (lava)
Aachen (city,
  Germany)
Aal|borg (city,
  Denmark)
Aalst (town,
  Belgium)
Aalto, Alvar
  (Finnish architect)
aard|vark +s
aard|wolf

  aard|wolves
Aar|gau (canton,
  Switzerland)
Aar|hus (city,
  Denmark)
Aaron (*Bible*; name)
Aaron's beard
Aaron's rod
aas|vogel +s
Ab (Jewish month)
aba +s
abac +s
abaca +s
aback
aba|cus

  aba|cuses *or*
  abaci
Aba|dan (port,
  Iran)
Abad|don
abaft
Aba|kan (city,
  Russia)
aba|lone +s
aban|don +s +ed
  +ing
aban|don|ee +s
aban|don|er +s
aban|don|ment +s
abase

  abases
  abased
  abas|ing
abase|ment
abash

  abashes
  abashed
  abash|ing
abash|ment
abask
abat|able
abate

  abates
  abated
  abat|ing
abate|ment

aba|tis
  plural aba|tis *or*
  aba|tises
aba|tised
abat|tis (use
  abatis)
  plural abat|tis *or*
  abat|tises
ab|at|toir +s
ab|ax|ial
abaya +s
Abba (Swedish pop
  group)
abba +s (garment;
  use aba)
ab|bacy

  ab|ba|cies
Abbas, Fer|hat
  (Algerian
  nationalist leader)
Ab|basid +s
ab|ba|tial
Abbe, Ernst
  (German
  physicist)
abbé +s
ab|bess

  ab|besses
  (nun. ⚠ abyss)
Abbe|vil|lian
abbey +s
abbot +s
ab|bot|ship +s
ab|bre|vi|ate

  ab|bre|vi|ates
  ab|bre|vi|ated
  ab|bre|vi|at|ing
ab|bre|vi|ation +s
ab|bre|vi|atory
ABC Is|lands
  (Aruba, Bonaire,
  and Curaçao,
  Netherlands
  Antilles)
ab|dic|able
ab|di|cate

  ab|di|cates
  ab|di|cated
  ab|di|cat|ing
ab|di|ca|tion +s
ab|di|ca|tor +s
ab|do|men +s
ab|dom|inal +s
ab|dom|in|al|ly
ab|dom|in|ous
ab|duct +s +ed
  +ing
ab|duc|tion +s
ab|duct|or +s
Abduh,
  Mu|ham|mad

Abduh (*cont.*)
  (Egyptian
  reformer)
Abdul Hamid II
  (Sultan of Turkey)
Ab|dul|lah, Sheikh
  Mu|ham|mad
  (Kashmiri leader)
Ab|dul|lah ibn
  Hus|sein
  (Jordanian king,
  1946–51)
Abdul Rah|man,
  Tunku (Malayan
  statesman)
Abe
abeam
abe|ce|dar|ian +s
abed
Abel (*Bible*; name)
Abel, Niels
  Hen|rik
  (Norwegian
  mathematician)
Abel|ard, Peter
  (French scholar)
abele +s
abelia +s
abel|ian
Abeo|kuta (city,
  Nigeria)
Aber|deen (city,
  Scotland)
Aber|deen, Lord
  (British prime
  minister)
Aber|deen Angus
  Aber|deen
  An|guses
Aber|deen|shire
  (former county,
  Scotland)
Aber|do|nian +s
Aber|fan (town,
  Wales)
Aber|nethy
  Aber|neth|ies
ab|er|rance
ab|er|rancy
ab|er|rant
ab|er|ra|tion +s
Aber|yst|wyth
  (city, Wales)
abet

  abets
  abet|ted
  abet|ting
abet|ment
abet|ter +s
abet|tor +s *Law*
abey|ance
abey|ant

abhor

  ab|hors
  ab|horred
  ab|hor|ring
ab|hor|rence
ab|hor|rent
ab|hor|rent|ly
ab|hor|rer +s
abid|ance
abide

  abides
  abided *or* abode
  abid|ing
abid|ing|ly
Abi|djan (port, the
  Ivory Coast)
Abi|gail (name)
abi|gail +s
abil|ity

  abil|ities
ab ini|tio
abio|gen|esis
abio|gen|ic
abio|gen|ic|al|ly
abi|ogen|ist +s
Abi|ola, Mos|hood
  (Nigerian
  politician)
abi|ot|ic
ab|ject
ab|jec|tion
ab|ject|ly
ab|ject|ness
ab|jur|ation +s
ab|jure

  ab|jures
  ab|jured
  ab|jur|ing
Ab|khaz
  plural Ab|khaz
Ab|khazi
  plural Ab|khazi *or*
  Ab|kha|zis
Ab|khazia
  (territory,
  Georgia)
Ab|khaz|ian +s
ab|late

  ab|lates
  ab|lated
  ab|lat|ing
ab|la|tion +s
ab|la|tival
ab|la|tive +s
ab|la|tive|ly
ab|laut +s
ablaze
able

  abler
  ablest
able-bodied

abled
able|ism
ablism (use
  ableism)
abloom
ablush
ab|lu|tion +s
ab|lu|tion|ary
ably
ab|neg|ate
  ab|neg|ates
  ab|neg|ated
  ab|neg|at|ing
ab|neg|ation +s
ab|neg|ator +s
Abner
ab|nor|mal
ab|nor|mal|ity
  ab|nor|mal|ities
ab|nor|mal|ly
ab|nor|mity
  ab|nor|mities
ABO (blood-group
  system)
Abo +s (*offensive*;
  use Aborigine or
  Aboriginal)
aboard
abode +s
abol|ish
  abol|ishes
  abol|ished
  abol|ish|ing
abol|ish|er +s
abol|ish|ment
abo|li|tion
abo|li|tion|ism
abo|li|tion|ist +s
abo|ma|sum
  abo|masa
A-bomb +s
Abo|mey (town,
  Benin)
abom|in|able
abom|in|able|ness
abom|in|ably
abom|in|ate
  abom|in|ates
  abom|in|ated
  abom|in|at|ing
abom|in|ation +s
abom|in|ator +s
ab|oral
Abo|ri|ginal +s
  (indigenous
  Australian;
  language; *may
  cause offence* when
  used of one
  person; use
  Aborigine)

abo|ri|ginal +s
  (indigenous;
  person)
abo|ri|gin|al|ity
abo|ri|gin|al|ly
Abo|ri|gine +s
  (indigenous
  Australian; *may
  cause offence* in
  plural; use
  Aboriginals)
abo|ri|gine +s
  (indigenous
  person)
aborn|ing
abort +s +ed +ing
abor|ti|fa|cient +s
abor|tion +s
abor|tion|ist +s
abort|ive
abort|ive|ly
abort|ive|ness
Abou|kir Bay (off
  Egypt)
abou|lia
aboulic
abound +s +ed
  +ing
about
about-face
  about-faces
  about-faced
  about-facing
about-turn +s +ed
  +ing
above
above-mentioned
ab ovo
abra|ca|dabra
ab|rade
  ab|rades
  ab|raded
  ab|rad|ing
ab|rader +s
Abra|ham (*Bible*;
  name)
Abra|hams,
  Har|old (British
  sprinter)
Abram
abra|sion +s
abra|sive
abra|sive|ly
abra|sive|ness
ab|re|act +s +ed
  +ing
ab|re|ac|tion +s
ab|re|act|ive
abreast
abridg|able
abridge
  abridges

abridge (*cont.*)
  abridged
  abridg|ing
abridge|ment +s
abridger +s
abroach
abroad
ab|ro|gate
  ab|ro|gates
  ab|ro|gated
  ab|ro|gat|ing
ab|ro|ga|tion +s
ab|ro|ga|tor +s
ab|rupt
ab|rup|tion
ab|rupt|ly
ab|rupt|ness
Ab|ruzzi (region,
  Italy)
ab|scess
  ab|scesses
  ab|scessed
ab|scisic
ab|scissa
  ab|scis|sas *or*
  ab|scis|sae
ab|scis|sion +s
ab|scond +s +ed
  +ing
ab|scond|er +s
ab|seil +s +ed
  +ing
ab|seil|er +s
ab|sence +s
ab|sent
ab|sen|tee +s
ab|sen|tee|ism
ab|sent|ly
absent-minded
absent-minded|ly
absent-
  minded|ness
ab|sent|ness
ab|sinth (plant)
ab|sinthe +s
  (drink)
absit omen
ab|so|lute +s
ab|so|lute|ly
ab|so|lute|ness
ab|so|lu|tion
ab|so|lut|ism
ab|so|lut|ist +s
ab|solve
  ab|solves
  ab|solved
  ab|solv|ing
ab|solver +s
ab|sorb +s +ed
  +ing
ab|sorb|abil|ity
ab|sorb|able

ab|sorb|ance
ab|sorb|ed|ly
ab|sorb|ency
  ab|sorb|en|cies
ab|sorb|ent +s
ab|sorb|er +s
ab|sorb|ing|ly
ab|sorp|tion
ab|sorp|tive
ab|sorp|tive|ness
ab|squatu|late
  ab|squatu|lates
  ab|squatu|lated
  ab|squatu|lat|ing
ab|stain +s +ed
  +ing
ab|stain|er +s
ab|ste|mi|ous
ab|ste|mi|ous|ly
ab|ste|mi|ous|ness
ab|sten|tion +s
ab|sten|tion|ism
ab|ster|gent +s
ab|ster|sion +s
ab|ster|sive
ab|stin|ence +s
ab|stin|ency
ab|stin|ent
ab|stin|ent|ly
ab|stract +s +ed
  +ing
ab|stract|ed|ly
ab|stract|ed|ness
ab|strac|tion +s
ab|strac|tion|ism
ab|strac|tion|ist +s
ab|stract|ly
ab|stract|ness
ab|stract|or +s
ab|struse
ab|struse|ly
ab|struse|ness
ab|surd
ab|surd|ism
ab|surd|ist +s
ab|surd|ity
  ab|surd|ities
ab|surd|ly
ab|surd|ness
ABTA (Association
  of British Travel
  Agents)
Abu Dhabi (state
  and capital, UAE)
Abuja (capital of
  Nigeria)
Abu|kir Bay (use
  Aboukir Bay)
abu|lia (use
  aboulia)
Abu Musa (island,
  Persian Gulf)

abun|dance +s
abun|dant
abun|dant¦ly
abuse
  ab¦uses
  ab¦used
  ab¦us¦ing
ab¦user +s
Abu Sim¦bel
  (ancient site,
  Egypt)
abu|sive
abu|sive¦ly
abu|sive|ness
abut
  abuts
  abut|ted
  abut|ting
abut|ment +s
abut|ter +s
abuzz
abysm +s
abys|mal
abys|mal¦ly
abyss
  abysses
  (chasm.
  ⚠ abbess)
abys|sal
Abys|sinia (former
  name of Ethiopia)
ab¦zyme +s
aca¦cia +s
Aca|deme (in
  'groves of
  Academe')
aca|deme +s (the
  world of learning)
aca|demia
aca|dem¦ic +s
aca|dem¦ic|al +s
aca|dem¦ic|al¦ly
acad¦em|ician +s
aca|demi|cism
Acad|émie
  fran|çaise
acad¦em|ism
Acad|emy (of
  Plato)
acad|emy
  acad|emies
  (place of study)
Aca¦dia (Nova
  Scotia, Canada)
Aca|dian +s (of
  Nova Scotia.
  ⚠ Akkadian,
  Arcadian)
acan¦tho|
      ceph¦alan +s
acan¦tho|ceph¦alid
  +s

acan|thus
  acan|thuses
a cap|pella
Aca|pulco (resort,
  Mexico)
acari|cide +s
aca¦rid +s
acar|ology
acarp|ous
ACAS (Advisory,
  Conciliation, and
  Arbitration
  Service)
acata|lec¦tic +s
acaus¦al
Ac¦ca|dian +s (use
  Akkadian.
  ⚠ Acadian,
  Arcadian)
ac¦cede
  ac|cedes
  ac|ceded
  ac|ced¦ing
  (take up office;
  agree. ⚠ exceed)
ac¦cel¦er|ando
  ac¦cel¦er|andos or
  ac¦cel¦er|andi
ac¦cel¦er|ate
  ac¦cel¦er|ates
  ac¦cel¦er|ated
  ac¦cel¦er|at¦ing
ac¦cel¦er|ation +s
ac¦cel¦era|tive
ac¦cel¦er|ator +s
ac¦cel¦er|om¦eter
  +s
ac¦cent +s +ed
  +ing
ac¦cent¦or +s
ac|cen|tual
ac|cen|tual¦ly
ac|cen¦tu|ate
  ac|cen|tu|ates
  ac|cen|tu|ated
  ac|cen|tu|at¦ing
ac|cen|tu|ation +s
ac¦cept +s +ed
  +ing (receive.
  ⚠ except)
ac¦cept|abil¦ity
ac¦cept|able
ac¦cept|able|ness
ac¦cept|ably
ac¦cept|ance +s
ac¦cept|ant
ac¦cep|ta|tion +s
ac¦cept¦er +s
  (generally)
ac¦cept¦or +s
  *Commerce and
  Science*

ac¦cess
  ac|cesses
  ac|cessed
  ac|cess|ing
ac¦ces¦sary (use
  accessory)
  ac¦ces|sar¦ies
ac¦ces|si|bil¦ity
  ac¦ces|si|bil¦ities
ac¦cess|ible
ac¦cess|ibly
ac¦ces|sion +s +ed
  +ing
ac¦ces|sit (in
  'proxime
  accessit')
ac¦ces|sor¦ial
ac¦ces|sor|ise *Br.*
  (use accessorize)
  ac¦ces|sor|ises
  ac¦ces|sor|ised
  ac¦ces|sor|is¦ing
ac¦ces|sor|ize
  ac¦ces|sor|izes
  ac¦ces|sor|ized
  ac¦ces|sor|iz¦ing
ac¦ces|sory
  ac¦ces|sor¦ies
ac¦ciac|ca|tura
  ac¦ciac|ca|turas
  or ac¦ciac|ca|ture
ac¦ci|dence +s
ac¦ci|dent +s
ac¦ci|den¦tal +s
ac¦ci|den¦tal¦ly
accident-prone
ac¦ci|die
ac¦cip|iter +s
ac¦claim +s +ed
  +ing
ac¦claim|er +s
ac¦clam|ation +s
ac¦climat|ation
ac¦cli|mate
  ac¦cli|mates
  ac¦cli|mated
  ac¦cli|mat¦ing
ac¦cli|ma|tion
ac¦cli|ma|tisa|tion
  Br. +s (use
  acclimatization)
ac¦cli|ma|tise *Br.*
  (use acclimatize)
  ac¦cli|ma|tises
  ac¦cli|ma|tised
  ac¦cli|ma|tis¦ing
ac¦cli|ma|tiza|tion
  +s
ac¦cli|ma|tize
  ac¦cli|ma|tizes
  ac¦cli|ma|tized
  ac¦cli|ma|tiz¦ing

ac¦clivi|tous
ac¦cliv|ity
  ac¦cliv|ities
ac¦coll|ade +s
ac¦com|mo¦date
  ac¦com|mo¦dates
  ac¦com|mo¦dated
  ac¦com|
      mo¦dat¦ing
ac¦com|
      mo¦dat¦ing¦ly
ac¦com|mo¦da¦tion
  +s
ac¦com|
    mo¦da¦tion¦ist +s
ac¦com|pani¦ment
  +s
ac¦com|pan¦ist +s
ac¦com|pany
  ac¦com|pan¦ies
  ac¦com|pan¦ied
  ac¦com|pany|ing
ac¦com|plice +s
ac¦com|plish
  ac¦com|plishes
  ac¦com|plished
  ac¦com|plish|ing
ac¦com|plish|ment
  +s
ac¦cord +s +ed
  +ing
ac¦cord|ance
ac¦cord|ant
ac¦cord|ant¦ly
ac¦cord|ing¦ly
ac¦cor|dion +s
ac¦cor|dion|ist +s
ac¦cost +s +ed
  +ing
ac¦couche|ment +s
ac¦couch|eur +s
  male
ac¦couch|euse +s
  female
ac¦count +s +ed
  +ing
ac¦count|abil¦ity
  ac¦count|
      abil¦ities
ac¦count|able
ac¦count|able|ness
ac¦count|ably
ac¦count|ancy
ac¦count|ant +s
ac¦cou¦ter *Am.* +s
  +ed +ing
ac¦cou¦ter|ment
  Am. +s
ac¦coutre *Br.*
  ac|coutres
  ac|coutred
  ac|cout¦ring

ac|coutre|ment *Br.*
+s
Accra (capital of
Ghana)
ac|credit +s +ed
+ing
ac|credit|ation +s
ac|crete
  ac|cretes
  ac|creted
  ac|cret|ing
ac|cre|tion +s
ac|cre|tive
ac|crual +s
ac|crue
  ac|crues
  ac|crued
  ac|cru|ing
ac|cul|tur|ate
  ac|cul|tur|ates
  ac|cul|tur|ated
  ac|cul|tur|at|ing
ac|cul|tur|ation
ac|cul|tur|ative
ac|cu|mu|late
  ac|cu|mu|lates
  ac|cu|mu|lated
  ac|cu|mu|lat|ing
ac|cu|mu|la|tion
  +s
ac|cu|mu|la|tive
ac|cu|mu|la|tive|ly
ac|cu|mu|la|tor +s
ac|cur|acy
  ac|cur|acies
ac|cur|ate
ac|cur|ate|ly
ac|cur|sed
ac|curst (*archaic*
  accursed)
ac|cusal
ac|cus|ation +s
ac|cusa|tival
ac|cusa|tive +s
ac|cusa|tive|ly
ac|cusa|tor|ial
ac|cusa|tory
ac|cuse
  ac|cuses
  ac|cused
  ac|cus|ing
ac|cuser +s
ac|cus|ing|ly
ac|cus|tom +s +ed
  +ing
ace
  aces
  aced
  acing
acedia

Acel|dama (field
  near ancient
  Jerusalem)
acel|lu|lar
aceph|al|ous
acer +s
acerb
acerb|ic
acerb|ic|al|ly
acerb|ity
  acerb|ities
aces|cence
aces|cent
acet|abu|lum
  acet|abula
acetal
acet|al|de|hyde
acet|amino|phen
acet|ate +s
acet|ic
acet|one +s
acet|ous
acetyl
acetyl|chol|ine
acetyl|ene
acetyl|ide
acetyl|sali|cyl|ic
Achaea (district,
  ancient Greece)
Achaean +s
Achae|men|ian +s
Achae|menid +s
acharne|ment
Acha|tes
  plural Acha|tes
ache
  aches
  ached
  ach|ing
Achebe, Chinua
  (Nigerian writer)
achene +s
Acher|nar (star)
Ache|son, Dean
  (American
  statesman)
Acheu|lean +s
Acheu|lian +s (use
  Acheulean)
achiev|able
achieve
  achieves
  achieved
  achiev|ing
achieve|ment +s
achiever +s
achil|lea
Achil|les *Greek
  Mythology*
Achil|les heel +s
Achil|les ten|don
  +s

Achi|nese
  plural Achi|nese
ach|ing|ly
achiral
achon|dro|pla|sia
achon|dro|pla|sic
  +s
achon|dro|plas|tic
  +s
achro|mat +s
achro|mat|ic
achro|mat|ic|al|ly
achro|ma|ti|city
achro|ma|tism
achron|ical (use
  acronychal)
achron|ic|al|ly
  (use
  acronychally)
achy
acid +s
acid-free *attributive*
acid head +s
acid house
acid|ic
acid|ifi|ca|tion
acid|ify
  acid|ifies
  acid|ified
  acid|ify|ing
acid|im|eter +s
acid|im|etry
acid|ity
acid|ly
acid|ness
acido|phil +s
acido|phile +s
acido|phil|ic
acid|oph|ilus
acid|osis
  acid|oses
acid|otic
acid test +s
acidu|late
  acidu|lates
  acidu|lated
  acidu|lat|ing
acidu|la|tion
acidu|lous
aci|nus
  acini
ack
ack-ack
ackee +s
ack emma
ac|know|ledge
  ac|know|ledges
  ac|know|ledged
  ac|know|ledg|ing
ac|know|ledge|
                able

ac|know|ledge|
                ment +s
ac|know|ledg|
  ment +s (use
  acknowledge-
  ment)
aclin|ic
acme +s
acne
acned
aco|lyte +s
Ac|on|cagua
  (volcano, Andes)
acon|ite +s
acon|it|ic
acon|it|ine
acorn +s
acoty|ledon +s
acoty|led|on|ous
acous|tic
acous|tic|al
acous|tic|al|ly
acous|ti|cian +s
acous|tics
ac|quaint +s +ed
  +ing
ac|quaint|ance +s
ac|quaint|ance|
                  ship
ac|quest +s
ac|qui|esce
  ac|qui|esces
  ac|qui|esced
  ac|qui|es|cing
ac|qui|es|cence
ac|qui|es|cent
ac|qui|es|cing|ly
ac|quir|able
ac|quire
  ac|quires
  ac|quired
  ac|quir|ing
ac|quire|ment +s
ac|quirer +s
ac|qui|si|tion +s
ac|quisi|tive
ac|quisi|tive|ly
ac|quisi|tive|ness
ac|quit
  ac|quits
  ac|quit|ted
  ac|quit|ting
ac|quit|tal +s
ac|quit|tance +s
Acre (town, Israel)
acre +s
acre|age +s
acred
acrid
ac|rid|ine
ac|rid|ity
ac|rid|ly

acri|fla|vine
acri|mo|ni|ous
acri|mo|ni|ous|ly
acri|mony
acro|bat +s
acro|bat|ic
acro|bat|ic|al|ly
acro|bat|ics
acro|gen +s
ac|rogen|ous
ac|ro|meg|al|ic +s
ac|ro|meg|aly
acrony|cal (use
　acronychal)
acrony|cal|ly (use
　acronychally)
acrony|chal
acrony|chal|ly
acro|nym +s
acrop|etal
acrop|et|al|ly
acro|pho|bia
acro|pho|bic +s
Acrop|olis (in
　Athens)
acrop|olis
　(generally)
　acrop|olises or
　acrop|oles
across
ac|ros|tic +s
Acrux (star)
acryl|ic +s
acrylo|ni|trile
act +s +ed +ing
act|abil|ity
act|able
Ac|taeon *Greek*
　Mythology
actin
ac|tinia
　ac|tiniae
ac|tin|ic
ac|tin|ide +s
ac|tin|ism
ac|tin|ium
ac|tin|oid +s
ac|tin|om|eter +s
ac|tino|morph|ic
Ac|tino|
　　　　my|cet|ales
ac|tino|my|cete +s
ac|tion +s +ed
　+ing
ac|tion|able
ac|tion|ably
Ac|tion Di|recte
action-packed
Ac|tium (battle off
　Greece)
ac|ti|vate
　ac|ti|vates

ac|ti|vate (*cont.*)
　ac|ti|vated
　ac|ti|vat|ing
ac|ti|vation
ac|ti|va|tor +s
ac|tive
ac|tive|ly
ac|tive|ness
ac|tiv|ism
ac|tiv|ist +s
ac|tiv|ity
　ac|tiv|ities
actor +s
actor-manager +s
ac|tress
　ac|tresses
ac|tressy
ac|tual +s
ac|tu|al|isa|tion *Br.*
　(use
　actualization)
ac|tu|al|ise *Br.* (use
　actualize)
　ac|tu|al|ises
　ac|tu|al|ised
　ac|tu|al|is|ing
ac|tu|al|ity
　ac|tu|al|ities
ac|tu|al|iza|tion
ac|tu|al|ize
　ac|tu|al|izes
　ac|tu|al|ized
　ac|tu|al|iz|ing
ac|tu|al|ly
ac|tu|ar|ial
ac|tu|ari|al|ly
ac|tu|ary
　ac|tu|ar|ies
ac|tu|ate
　ac|tu|ates
　ac|tu|ated
　ac|tu|at|ing
ac|tu|ation
ac|tu|ator +s
acu|ity
acu|leate +s
acu|men
acu|min|ate
　acu|min|ates
　acu|min|ated
　acu|min|at|ing
acu|pres|sure
acu|punc|ture
acu|punc|tur|ist +s
acushla +s
acu|tance
acute
　acuter
　acut|est
acute|ly
acute|ness
acyclo|vir

acyl +s
ad +s
　(advertisement.
　△ add)
Ada (computer
　language; name)
adage +s
ada|gio +s
Adam (*Bible*; name)
Adam, Rob|ert
　(Scottish
　architect)
ad|am|ance
ad|am|ant +s
ad|am|ant|ine
ad|am|ant|ly
Ad|am|ite +s
Adams, Ansel
　(American
　photographer)
Adams, John
　(American
　president)
Adams, John
　Couch (English
　astronomer)
Adams, John
　Quincy
　(American
　president)
Adam's ale
Adam's apple +s
Adam's Bridge
　(series of shoals
　between Sri Lanka
　and India)
Adam's Peak
　(mountain, Sri
　Lanka)
Adana (town,
　Turkey)
adapt +s +ed +ing
adapt|abil|ity
adapt|able
adapt|able|ness
adapt|ably
adap|ta|tion +s
adapt|er *Am.* +s
　(*Br.* adaptor)
adap|tive
adap|tive|ly
adap|tive|ness
adap|tor *Br.* +s
　(*Am.* adapter)
Adar (Jewish
　month)
adat
ad|ax|ial
ad cap|tan|dum
　vul|gus

add +s +ed +ing
　(put together.
　△ ad)
Ad|ams, Jane
　(American
　reformer)
addax
　ad|daxes
ad|den|dum
　ad|denda
adder +s
adder's tongue +s
ad|dict +s +ed
　+ing
ad|dic|tion +s
ad|dict|ive
Ad|ding|ton,
　Henry (British
　prime minister)
Addis Ababa
　(capital of
　Ethiopia)
Ad|di|son, Jo|seph
　(English writer)
Ad|di|son,
　Thomas (English
　physician)
Ad|di|son's
　dis|ease
add|ition +s
　(adding;
　something added.
　△ edition)
add|ition|al
add|ition|al|ity
add|ition|al|ly
addi|tive +s
addle
　ad|dles
　ad|dled
　ad|dling
Addo (national
　park, South Africa)
add-on +s *noun and
　adjective*
ad|dress
　ad|dresses
　ad|dressed
　ad|dress|ing
ad|dress|ee +s
ad|dress|er +s
Ad|dresso|graph
　+s *Propr.*
ad|duce
　ad|duces
　ad|duced
　ad|du|cing
ad|du|cible
ad|duct +s +ed
　+ing
ad|duc|tion +s
ad|duct|or +s

Adel|aide (city, Australia; name)
Adele
Ad|élie Coast (= Adélie Land)
Ad|élie Land (part of Antarctica)
Adel|ine
Aden (port, South Yemen)
Aden, Gulf of (part of Arabian Sea)
Aden|auer, Kon|rad (German statesman)
ad|en|ine
ad|en|oid|al
ad|en|oid|al|ly
ad|en|oids
ad|en|oma
    ad|en|omas or
    ad|en|omata
adeno|sine
adept +s
adept|ly
adept|ness
ad|equacy
ad|equate
ad|equate|ly
ad eun|dem
à deux
ad fin.
ad|here
    ad|heres
    ad|hered
    ad|her|ing
ad|her|ence
ad|her|ent +s
ad|he|sion +s
ad|he|sive +s
ad|he|sive|ly
ad|he|sive|ness
ad|hibit +s +ed +ing
ad|hib|ition +s
ad hoc
ad hom|inem
adia|bat|ic +s
adia|bat|ic|al|ly
adi|an|tum +s
adieu
    adieus or adieux
Adi Granth (Sikh scripture)
ad in|fin|itum
ad in|terim
adios
adi|po|cere
adi|pose
adi|pos|ity

Adi|ron|dack Moun|tains (in USA)
Adi|ron|dacks (= Adirondack Mountains)
Adis Abeba (use Addis Ababa)
adit +s
Adi|vasi +s
ad|ja|cency
ad|ja|cent
ad|jec|tival
ad|jec|tival|ly
ad|jec|tive +s
ad|join +s +ed +ing
ad|journ +s +ed +ing
ad|journ|ment +s
ad|judge
    ad|judges
    ad|judged
    ad|judg|ing
ad|judge|ment +s
ad|judg|ment +s (use adjudgement)
ad|ju|di|cate
    ad|ju|di|cates
    ad|ju|di|cated
    ad|ju|di|cat|ing
ad|ju|di|ca|tion +s
ad|ju|di|ca|tive
ad|ju|di|ca|tor +s
ad|junct +s
ad|junct|ive +s
ad|junct|ive|ly
ad|jur|ation +s
ad|jura|tory
ad|jure
    ad|jures
    ad|jured
    ad|jur|ing
ad|just +s +ed +ing
ad|just|abil|ity
ad|just|able
ad|just|er +s
ad|just|ment +s
ad|ju|tage +s
ad|ju|tancy
ad|ju|tan|cies
ad|ju|tant +s
Ad|ju|tant Gen|eral +s
ad|ju|vant +s
Adlai
Adler, Al|fred (Austrian psychologist and psychiatrist)

Ad|ler|ian +s
ad lib
ad libs
ad libbed
ad lib|bing
ad lib|itum
ad litem
adman
    admen
ad|mass
ad|meas|ure
    ad|meas|ures
    ad|meas|ured
    ad|meas|ur|ing
ad|meas|ure|ment +s
admin
ad|min|icle +s
ad|min|icu|lar
ad|min|is|ter +s +ed +ing
ad|min|is|trable
ad|min|is|trate
    ad|min|is|trates
    ad|min|is|trated
    ad|min|is|trat|ing
ad|min|is|tra|tion +s
ad|min|is|tra|tive
ad|min|is|tra|tive|ly
ad|min|is|tra|tor +s
ad|min|is|tra|tor|ship +s
ad|min|is|tra|trix
    female
    ad|min|is|tra|trixes or
    ad|min|is|tra|tri|ces
ad|mir|able
ad|mir|ably
ad|miral +s
Ad|miral's Cup
ad|miral|ship +s
Ad|mir|alty (department)
ad|mir|alty Law
Ad|mir|alty Is|lands (part of Papua New Guinea)
ad|mir|ation
ad|mire
    ad|mires
    ad|mired
    ad|mir|ing
ad|mirer +s
ad|mir|ing|ly
ad|mis|si|bil|ity
ad|mis|sible

ad|mis|sion +s
ad|mis|sive
admit
    ad|mits
    ad|mit|ted
    ad|mit|ting
ad|mit|table
ad|mit|tance
ad|mit|ted|ly
admix
    ad|mixes
    ad|mixed
    ad|mix|ing
ad|mix|ture +s
ad|mon|ish
    ad|mon|ishes
    ad|mon|ished
    ad|mon|ish|ing
ad|mon|ish|ment +s
ad|mon|ition +s
ad|moni|tory
ad nau|seam
ad|nom|inal
Ad|nya|matha|nha
ado
adobe
ado|les|cence
ado|les|cent +s
Ado|nis Greek Mythology
Ado|nis blue +s
adopt +s +ed +ing
adopt|ee +s
adopt|er +s
adop|tion +s
adop|tive
adop|tive|ly
ador|able
ador|ably
ad|or|ation
adore
    adores
    adored
    ador|ing
adorer +s
ador|ing|ly
adorn +s +ed +ing
adorn|ment +s
Adorno, Theo|dor (German philosopher)
adown
ad per|sonam
Adrar des Iforas (massif, Sahara)
ad rem
ad|renal
ad|rena|lin
ad|rena|line (use adrenalin)

ad|reno|cor|tico| troph|ic
ad|reno|cor|tico| troph|in
ad|reno|cor|tico| trop|ic
Adrian (man's name)
Adrian IV (born Nicholas Breakspear, English pope)
Adri|anne (woman's name)
Adri|at|ic
Adri|at|ic Sea (part of Mediterranean)
Adri|enne
adrift
adroit
adroit|ly
adroit|ness
ad|sci|ti|tious
ad|sorb +s +ed +ing
ad|sorb|able
ad|sorb|ate +s
ad|sorb|ent +s
ad|sorb|tion (use adsorption)
ad|sorp|tion
ad|sorp|tive
ad|suki +s (use adzuki)
adsum
aduki +s
adu|late
adu|lates
adu|lated
adu|lat|ing
adu|la|tion
adu|la|tor +s
adu|la|tory
Adul|lam|ite +s
adult +s
adul|ter|ant +s
adul|ter|ate
adul|ter|ates
adul|ter|ated
adul|ter|at|ing
adul|ter|ation
adul|ter|ator +s
adul|ter|er +s
adul|ter|ess
adul|ter|esses
adul|ter|ine
adul|ter|ous
adul|ter|ous|ly
adul|ter|ous|ness
adul|tery
adul|ter|ies
adult|hood

adult|ly
ad|um|brate
ad|um|brates
ad|um|brated
ad|um|brat|ing
ad|um|bra|tion
ad|um|bra|tive
ad val|orem
ad|vance
ad|vances
ad|vanced
ad|van|cing
ad|vance|ment +s
ad|van|cer +s
ad|van|tage
ad|van|tages
ad|van|taged
ad|van|ta|ging
ad|van|ta|geous
ad|van|ta|geous|ly
ad|vect +s +ed +ing
ad|vec|tion
ad|vec|tive
Ad|vent (of Christ; season)
ad|vent +s (generally)
Ad|vent|ism
Ad|vent|ist +s
ad|ven|ti|tious
ad|ven|ti|tious|ly
ad|ven|ture
ad|ven|tures
ad|ven|tured
ad|ven|tur|ing
ad|ven|turer +s
ad|ven|ture|some
ad|ven|tur|ess
ad|ven|tur|esses
ad|ven|tur|ism
ad|ven|tur|ist +s
ad|ven|tur|ous
ad|ven|tur|ous|ly
ad|ven|tur|ous| ness
ad|verb +s
ad|ver|bial +s
ad|ver|bi|al|ly
ad ver|bum
ad|ver|sar|ial
ad|ver|sary
ad|ver|sar|ies
ad|ver|sa|tive +s
ad|ver|sa|tive|ly
ad|verse
ad|verse|ly
ad|verse|ness
ad|ver|sity
ad|ver|sities
ad|vert +s +ed +ing

ad|ver|tise
ad|ver|tises
ad|ver|tised
ad|ver|tis|ing
ad|ver|tise|ment +s
ad|ver|tiser +s
ad|ver|tor|ial +s
ad|vice +s noun
ad|vis|abil|ity
ad|vis|able
ad|vis|ably
ad|vise
ad|vises
ad|vised
ad|vis|ing verb
ad|vised|ly
ad|viser +s
ad|visor +s (use adviser)
ad|vis|ory
ad|vo|caat +s
ad|vo|cacy
ad|vo|cate
ad|vo|cates
ad|vo|cated
ad|vo|cat|ing
ad|vo|cate|ship +s
ad|vo|ca|tory
ad|vow|son
Ady|gea (republic, Russia)
ady|tum
adyta
adz (use adze)
adzes
adzed
adz|ing
adze
adzes
adzed
adz|ing
ad|zuki +s
ae|dile +s
ae|dile|ship +s
Ae|gean
Ae|gean Sea (part of Mediterranean)
aegis
ae|gises
Ae|gis|thus Greek Mythology
aegro|tat +s
Aelf|ric (Anglo-Saxon monk and writer)
Ae|neas Greek and Roman Mythology
Ae|neid (epic poem)

ae|olian Br. (Am. eolian)
Ae|olian Is|lands (ancient name for the Lipari Islands)
Ae|ol|ic Br. (Am. Eolic)
Ae|olus Greek Mythology
aeon +s
aepy|or|nis
aepy|or|nises
aer|ate
aer|ates
aer|ated
aer|at|ing
aer|ation
aer|ator +s
aer|en|chyma
aer|ial +s (radio etc.; in the air. △ areal, ariel)
aeri|al|ist +s
aeri|al|ity
aeri|al|ly
aerie +s (use eyrie)
aeri|form
aero|batic
aero|bat|ics
aer|obe +s
aer|ob|ic
aer|ob|ic|al|ly
aer|obics
aero|biolo|gist +s
aero|biol|ogy
aero|drome +s
aero|dy|nam|ic
aero|dy|nam|ic| al|ly
aero|dy|nami|cist +s
aero|dy|nam|ics
aero-engine +s
aero|foil +s
aero|gram +s (use aerogramme)
aero|gramme +s
aero|lite +s
aero|logic|al
aer|olo|gist +s
aer|ology
aero|mag|net|ic
aero|naut +s
aero|naut|ic
aero|naut|ic|al
aero|naut|ic|al|ly
aero|naut|ics
aer|onomy
aero|plane Br. +s
aero|sol +s
aero|space

aero|stat +s
aero|tow +s +ed
  +ing
aero|train +s
Aer|tex *Propr.*
aer|ugin|ous
Aes|chi|nes
  (Athenian orator
  and statesman)
Aes|chyl|ean
Aes|chylus (Greek
  dramatist)
Aes|cu|la|pian
Aesir *Norse
  Mythology*
Aesop (Greek
  storyteller)
aes|thete *Br.* +s
  (*Am.* esthete)
aes|thet|ic *Br.* (*Am.*
  esthetic)
aes|thet|ic|al|ly *Br.*
  (*Am.* esthetically)
aes|thet|ician *Br.*
  +s (*Am.*
  esthetician)
aes|theti|cism *Br.*
  (*Am.* estheticism)
aes|thet|ics *Br.*
  (*Am.* esthetics)
aes|tival *Br.* (*Am.*
  estival)
aes|tiv|ate *Br.*
  aes|tiv|ates
  aes|tiv|ated
  aes|tiv|at|ing
  (*Am.* estivate)
aes|tiv|ation *Br.*
  (*Am.* estivation)
ae|ta|tis
ae|ther (use ether)
aetio|logic *Br.* (*Am.*
  etiologic)
aetio|logic|al *Br.*
  (*Am.* etiological)
aetio|logic|al|ly *Br.*
  (*Am.*
  etiologically)
aeti|ology *Br.* (*Am.*
  etiology)
Afar
  plural **Afar** *or*
  Afars
  (people; language)
afar (at or to a
  distance)
af|fa|bil|ity
af|fable
af|fably
af|fair +s
af|fairé (busy)

af|faire (*de cœur*)
  af|faires (*de cœur*)
af|fect +s +ed +ing
  (have an effect on;
  feign. △ effect)
af|fect|ation +s
af|fect|ed|ly
af|fect|ing|ly
af|fec|tion +s
af|fec|tion|al
af|fec|tion|al|ly
af|fec|tion|ate
af|fec|tion|ate|ly
af|fect|ive
  (concerning
  emotion.
  △ effective)
af|fect|ive|ly (as
  regards emotion.
  △ effectively)
af|fect|iv|ity
  (emotional
  susceptibility.
  △ effectivity)
af|fen|pin|scher +s
af|fer|ent
af|fi|ance
  af|fi|ances
  af|fi|anced
  af|fi|an|cing
af|fi|ant +s
af|fiche +s
af|fi|da|vit +s
af|fili|ate
  af|fili|ates
  af|fili|ated
  af|fili|at|ing
af|fili|ation +s
af|fined
af|fin|ity
  af|fin|ities
af|firm +s +ed
  +ing
af|firm|able
af|firm|ation +s
af|firma|tive
af|firma|tive|ly
af|firma|tory
af|firm|er +s
affix
  af|fixes
  af|fixed
  af|fix|ing
af|fix|ture
af|fla|tus
af|flict +s +ed +ing
af|flic|tion +s
af|flict|ive
af|flu|ence
af|flu|ent
af|flu|en|tial
af|flu|ent|ly

af|flux
  af|fluxes
af|force
  af|forces
  af|forced
  af|for|cing
af|ford +s +ed
  +ing
af|ford|abil|ity
af|ford|able
af|ford|ably
af|for|est +s +ed
  +ing
af|for|est|ation
af|fran|chise
  af|fran|chises
  af|fran|chised
  af|fran|chis|ing
af|fray +s
af|freight|ment
af|fri|cate +s
af|fright +s +ed
  +ing
af|front +s +ed
  +ing
af|fu|sion
Af|ghan +s (of
  Afghanistan;
  hound)
af|ghan +s
  (blanket; shawl)
af|ghani +s
  (Afghan currency)
Af|ghani|stan
afi|cion|ado +s
afield
afire
aflame
af|la|toxin +s
afloat
afoot
afore
afore|men|tioned
afore|said
afore|thought
a for|ti|ori
afoul
afraid
A-frame +s
afreet +s
afresh
afric
Af|rica
Af|ri|can +s
Af|ri|cana
African-American
  +s
Af|ri|can|der +s
Af|ri|can|ise *Br.*
  (use Africanize)
  Af|ri|can|ises

Af|ri|can|ise (*cont.*)
  Af|ri|can|ised
  Af|ri|can|is|ing
Af|ri|can|ism
Af|ri|can|ist +s
Af|ri|can|ize
  Af|ri|can|izes
  Af|ri|can|ized
  Af|ri|can|iz|ing
Af|ri|kaans
Af|rika Korps
  (German army
  force)
Af|ri|kan|der +s
  (use Africander)
Af|ri|kaner +s
  (person)
af|ri|kaner +s
  (sheep; cattle;
  gladiolus)
afrit +s (use afreet)
Afro +s
Afro-American +s
Afro-Asian +s
Afro-Asiat|ic
Afro-Caribbean +s
Afro|cen|tric
Afro-Indian +s
af|ror|mo|sia +s
aft
after
after|birth +s
after|burn|er +s
after|care
after|damp
after|deck +s
after-dinner
  attributive
after-effect +s
after|glow +s
after|grass
after-hours
  attributive
after-image +s
after|life +s
after|light
after|mar|ket +s
after|math +s
after|most
after|noon +s
after|pains
af|ters
after-sales
after-school
  attributive
after|shave +s
after|shock +s
after|taste +s
after|thought +s
after|ward
after|wards
after|word +s

Aga +s (stove)
Propr.
aga +s (Muslim
    chief)
Aga¦dir (port,
    Morocco)
again
against
Aga Khan +s
agal +s
agama +s
Aga|mem¦non
    (Mycenaean king)
agam¦ic
agamo|gen¦esis
agamo|gen¦et¦ic
agamo|spermy
ag¦am|ous
aga|pan¦thus
    aga|pan¦thuses
agape +s (gaping;
    fellowship; feast)
aga|pem¦one
agar
agar-agar
agar¦ic
Agar|tala (city,
    India)
Agas|siz, Louis
    (Swiss-born
    zoologist etc.)
agate +s
Aga¦tha
agave +s
agaze
agba
age
    ages
    aged
    age¦ing
age group +s
age¦ism
age¦ist +s (showing
    age-discrimination;
    person. △ agist)
age|less
age-long
agency
    agen|cies
agenda +s
agen|dum
    agenda
agent +s
agent-general
    agents-general
agen|tial
agent
    pro|voca|teur
    agents
    pro|voca|teurs
age-old

age range +s
age-related
Aggie
ag¦giorna|mento
ag¦glom¦er|ate
    ag¦glom¦er|ates
    ag¦glom¦er|ated
    ag¦glom¦er|at¦ing
ag¦glom¦er|ation
    +s
ag¦glom¦era|tive
ag¦glu¦tin|ate
    ag¦glu¦tin|ates
    ag¦glu¦tin|ated
    ag¦glu¦tin|at¦ing
ag¦glu¦tin|ation +s
ag¦glu¦tin|ative
ag¦glu|tinin +s
ag¦grand|ise *Br.*
    (use aggrandize)
    ag¦grand|ises
    ag¦grand|ised
    ag¦grand|is¦ing
ag¦grand|ise|ment
    Br. (use
    aggrandizement)
ag¦grand|iser *Br.*
    +s (use
    aggrandizer)
ag¦grand|ize
    ag¦grand|izes
    ag¦grand|ized
    ag¦grand|iz¦ing
ag¦grand|ize|ment
    +s
ag¦grand|izer +s
ag¦gra|vate
    ag¦gra|vates
    ag¦gra|vated
    ag¦gra|vat¦ing
    ag¦gra|vat¦ing|ly
    ag¦gra|va¦tion +s
ag¦gre|gate
    ag¦gre|gates
    ag¦gre|gated
    ag¦gre|gat¦ing
ag¦gre|ga¦tion +s
ag¦gre|ga¦tive
ag¦gres|sion +s
ag¦gres|sive
    ag¦gres|sive|ly
    ag¦gres|sive|ness
ag¦gres|sor +s
ag¦grieve
    ag¦grieves
    ag¦grieved
    ag¦griev|ing
ag¦griev|ed¦ly
aggro
aghast
Aghios Niko|laos
    (port, Crete)

agile
agile¦ly
agil|ity
agin
Agin|court (battle
    site, France)
aging (use ageing)
agio +s
agio|tage
agism (use ageism)
agist +s +ed +ing
    (feed livestock.
    △ ageist)
agist|ment
agi|tate
    agi|tates
    agi|tated
    agi|tat¦ing
agi|tated¦ly
agi|ta¦tion +s
agi|tato
agi|ta¦tor +s
agit|prop
aglet +s
agley
aglow
agma +s
ag¦nail +s
ag¦nate +s
ag¦nat¦ic
ag¦na¦tion
Agnes (Roman
    saint; patron saint
    of Bohemia;
    name)
Agnesi, Maria
    Gae|tana (Italian
    mathematician)
Agni *Hinduism*
agno|lotti
ag|no¦men +s
ag|no¦sia
ag|nos¦tic +s
ag|nos¦ti|cism
Agnus Dei
ago
agog
agogic
ago¦gics
à gogo
agon¦ic
ag¦on|ise *Br.* (use
    agonize)
    ag¦on|ises
    ag¦on|ised
    ag¦on|is¦ing
ag¦on|is¦ing¦ly *Br.*
    (use agonizingly)
agon|ist +s
ag¦on|is¦tic
ag¦on|is¦tic|al¦ly

ag¦on|ize
    ag¦on|izes
    ag¦on|ized
    ag¦on|iz¦ing
    ag¦on|iz¦ing¦ly
agony
ag|onies
agora|phobe +s
agora|pho¦bia
agora|pho¦bic +s
agouti +s
Agra (city, India)
ag¦ra|phon
    ag¦ra|pha
agrar¦ian +s
agree
    agrees
    agreed
    agree|ing
agree|able
agree|able|ness
agree|ably
agree|ment +s
agri|busi¦ness
agri|busi¦ness|
    man
agri|busi¦ness|
    men
agri|chem¦ical +s
Agric|ola, Ju¦lius
    (Roman general)
agri|cul¦tural
agri|cul¦tur|al¦ly
agri|cul¦ture +s
agri|cul¦tur|ist +s
agri|mony
    agri|monies
Agrippa, Mar¦cus
    Vip|san¦ius
    (Roman general)
agro|chem¦ical +s
agro|for¦est¦ry
agro|nom¦ic
agro|nom¦ic¦al
agro|nom¦ic|al¦ly
agro|nom¦ics
agrono|mist +s
agron|omy
aground
Aguas|cali¦en¦tes
    (state and state
    capital, Mexico)
ague +s
agued
aguish
Agul|has, Cape (in
    South Africa)
Agul|has Cur|rent
    (off E. Africa)
aguti +s (use
    agouti)
ah *interjection.* △ are

aha
Ahag|gar
  Moun|tains (in
  Algeria)
ahead
ahem
ahimsa
ahis|tor|ic
ahis|tor|ic|al
Ah|mada|bad (city,
  India)
ahoy
Ah|ri|man
  (Zoroastrian evil
  spirit)
à huis clos
ahull
Ahura Mazda
  (Zoroastrian god)
Ahvaz (town, Iran)
Ahwaz (use Ahvaz)
ai +s
aid +s +ed +ing
  (help)
Aidan (Irish
  missionary and
  saint; name)
aide +s (assistant)
aide-de-camp
  aides-de-camp
aide-mémoire
  aides-mémoires
  or aides-mémoire
Aids (= acquired
  immune
  deficiency
  syndrome)
Aids-related
aig|let +s (use
  aglet)
aig|rette +s
Aigues-Mortes
  (town, France)
ai|guille +s
ai|guill|ette +s
ai|kido
ail +s +ed +ing (be
  ill. △ ale)
ai|lan|thus
  ai|lan|thuses
Ai|leen
ail|eron +s
ail|ment +s
Ailsa
ai|luro|phile +s
ai|luro|phobe +s
ai|luro|pho|bia
ai|luro|pho|bic
aim +s +ed +ing
Aimée
aim|less
aim|less|ly

aim|less|ness
Ains|ley
ain't
Ain|tab (former
  name of
  Gaziantep)
Ain|tree
  (racecourse,
  England)
Ainu
  plural Ainu or
  Ainus
aioli
air +s +ed +ing
  (gas; tune; breeze
  etc. △ e'er, ere,
  heir)
air bag +s
air|base +s
air-bed +s
air|borne
air brake +s
air|brick +s
air bridge +s
air|brush
  air|brushes
  air|brushed
  air|brush|ing
Air|bus Propr.
Air Chief Mar|shal
  +s
Air Com|mo|dore
  +s
air-conditioned
air-condition|er +s
air-condition|ing
air-cooled
air|craft
  plural air|craft
air|craft car|rier
  +s
air|craft|man
  air|craft|men
air|craft|woman
  air|craft|women
air|crew +s
air cush|ion +s
air|drop
  air|drops
  air|dropped
  air|drop|ping
Aire|dale +s
airer +s
air fare +s
air|field +s
air|flow +s
air|foil +s
air force +s
air|frame +s
air|freight
air|glow
air|gun +s

air|head +s
air host|ess
  air host|esses
air|ily
airi|ness
air-jacket +s
air|less (lacking air.
  △ heirless)
air|less|ness
air|lift +s +ed +ing
air|line +s
air|liner +s
air|lock +s
air|mail +s +ed
  +ing
air|man
  air|men
Air Mar|shal +s
air mile +s (unit of
  distance)
Air Miles (points
  exchangeable for
  free air travel)
  Propr.
air|miss
  air|misses
air|mo|bile +s
Air Of|ficer +s
air|plane +s
air|play +s
air|port +s
air raid +s
air-raid shel|ter
  +s
air|screw +s
air-sea rescue +s
air|ship +s
  (aircraft.
  △ heirship)
air show +s
air|sick
air|sick|ness
air|side
air|space
air|speed
air|stream +s
air|strip +s
air|tight
air|time
Air Vice-Marshal
  +s
air|wave attributive
air|waves noun
air|way +s
air|woman
  air|women
air|worthi|ness
air|worthy
Airy, George
  Bid|dell (English
  astronomer and
  geophysicist)

airy
  air|ier
  airi|est
airy-fairy
aisle +s (passage.
  △ I'll, isle)
aisled
ait +s (island.
  △ ate, eight)
aitch
  aitches
aitch|bone +s
Ait|ken, Max
  (Lord
  Beaverbrook)
Aix-en-Provence
  (city, France)
Aix-la-Chapelle
  (French name for
  Aachen)
Aiz|awl (city, India)
Ajac|cio (city,
  Corsica)
Aj|anta Caves (in
  India)
ajar
Ajax Greek
  Mythology
Ajman (emirate
  and city, UAE)
Ajmer (city, India)
Akbar the Great
  (Mogul emperor
  of India)
akee +s (use
  ackee)
Akela +s
Akhe|na|ten
  (pharaoh)
Akhe|na|ton (use
  Akhenaten)
Akhe|taten
  (ancient capital of
  Egypt)
Akh|mat|ova,
  Anna (Russian
  poet)
ak|hund +s
akimbo
akin
Akkad (city and
  ancient kingdom,
  Mesopotamia)
Ak|ka|dian +s (of
  Akkad.
  △ Acadian,
  Arcadian)
Akko (port, Israel)
Ak-Mechet (former
  name of
  Simferopol)
Akron (city, USA)

Aksai Chin (region, Himalaya)

Aksum (town, Ethiopia)

Akur|eyri (city, Iceland)

akva|vit (use aquavit)

Al (name)

à la

Ala|bama (state, USA)

Ala|baman +s

ala|bas|ter

ala|bas|trine

à la carte

alack

alack-a-day

alac|rity

Alad|din

Alad|din's cave +s

Alad|din's lamp +s

Ala|goas (state, Brazil)

Alain-Fournier (French novelist)

Ala|mein *in full* El Ala|mein (battle site, Egypt)

Alamo, the (mission and siege, USA)

à la mode

Alan *also* Allan, Allen, Alun

Alana *also* Al¦anna, Alan|nah

Åland Is|lands (in Gulf of Bothnia)

ala|nine

Al¦anna *also* Alana, Alan|nah

Alan|nah *also* Alana, Al¦anna

Alar (plant growth regulator) *Propr.*

alar (of wings)

Alar|cón, Pedro An|tonio de (Spanish writer)

Alar|cón y Men|doza, Juan Ruiz de (Spanish playwright)

Al¦aric (king of Visigoths)

alarm +s +ed +ing

alarm clock +s

alarm|ing|ly

alarm|ism

alarm|ist +s

al¦arum +s

alas

Alas|dair *also* Alas|tair, Alis|dair, Alis|tair

Al¦aska (state, USA; in 'baked Alaska')

Al¦aska, Gulf of (part of NE Pacific)

Alas|tair *also* Alas|dair, Alis|dair, Alis|tair

Al¦as|tor +s

alate

alb +s

Al¦ba|cete (province and city, Spain)

al¦ba|core *plural* al¦ba|core

Alba Iulia (city, Romania)

Alban (British saint)

Al¦ba|nia

Al¦ba|nian +s

Al¦bany (city, USA)

al¦bata

al¦ba|tross al¦ba|trosses

al¦bedo +s

Albee, Ed¦ward (American dramatist)

al¦beit

Al¦bena (resort, Bulgaria)

Al¦bers, Josef (German-born artist)

Al¦bert (name)

Al¦bert, Lake (former name of Lake Mobutu Sese Seko)

Al¦bert, Prince (husband of Queen Victoria)

al¦bert +s (watch-chain)

Al¦berta (province, Canada)

Al¦berti, Leon Bat|tista (Italian architect, painter, etc.)

Al¦ber|tus Mag¦nus (medieval saint)

al¦bes|cent

Albi (town, France)

Al¦bi|gen|ses

Al¦bi|gen|sian +s

al¦bin|ism

al¦bino +s

Al¦bi|noni, Tom¦aso (Italian composer)

al¦bin|ot|ic

Al¦bi¦nus (alternative name for Alcuin)

Al¦bion (England; Britain)

Ål¦borg (use Aalborg)

Al¦bu|feira (town, Portugal)

album +s

al¦bu|men (white of egg)

al¦bu|min (protein)

al¦bu|min|oid

al¦bu|min|ous

al¦bu|min|uria

Al¦bu|quer¦que (city, USA)

Al¦bu|quer¦que, Al|fonso de (Portuguese statesman)

al¦bur|num

Al|caeus (Greek poet)

al¦ca|hest (use alkahest)

al¦caic

Al¦calá de He|nares (city, Spain)

al|calde +s

Al|ca|traz (island, USA)

Al|ces|tis *Greek Mythology*

al|chem¦ic

al¦chem|ic¦al

al¦chem|ise *Br.* (use alchemize)

al¦chem|ises

al¦chem|ised

al¦chem|is¦ing

al¦chem|ist +s

al¦chem|ize

al¦chem|izes

al¦chem|ized

al¦chem|iz¦ing

al¦chemy

al¦cher|inga

Al¦ci|bi¦ades (Athenian general and statesman)

alcid +s

Al¦cock, John Wil|liam (English aviator)

al¦co|hol +s

alcohol-free

al¦co|hol¦ic +s

al¦co|hol|ism

al¦co|hol|om|eter +s

al¦co|hol|om¦etry

Al¦cott, Lou¦isa May (American novelist)

al¦cove +s

Al¦cuin (English theologian)

Al|dabra (island group, Indian Ocean)

Al¦deb|aran (star)

Alde|burgh (town, England)

al¦de|hyde +s

al¦de|hydic

al dente

alder +s

al¦der|man al¦der|men

al¦der|man¦ic

al¦der|man¦ry

al¦der|man|ship

Al¦der|mas|ton (village, England)

Al¦der|ney (Channel Island; cattle)

al¦der|per|son +s

Al¦der|shot (town, England)

al¦der|woman al¦der|women

Al¦dine

Aldis lamp +s

Al¦diss, Brian (English writer)

al|dos|ter|one

Al¦dous

al¦drin

Aldus Manu|tius (Italian printer)

ale +s (beer. △ ail)

alea|tor¦ic

alea|tory

Alec *also* Alick (name)

alec +s (in 'smart alec')

ale|cost

Alecto *Greek Mythology*
alee
ale¦gar
ale|house +s
Ale|khine, Alex¦an¦der (Russian-born chess player)
Alek¦san¦dro|pol (former name of Gyumri)
Alek¦san¦drovsk (former name of Zaporizhzhya)
Alem|bert, Jean le Rond d' (French philosopher and mathematician)
alem|bic +s
alem¦bi¦cated
alem¦bi¦ca¦tion
Alen|tejo (region and former province, Portugal)
aleph +s
Al¦eppo (city, Syria)
alert +s +ed +ing
alert¦ly
alert|ness
Aletsch|horn (mountain, Switzerland)
aleuron
aleur|one
Aleut +s
Aleu|tian Is|lands (off Alaska)
Aleu|tians (= Aleutian Islands)
A level +s
ale|wife
ale|wives
Alex *also* Alix
Alexa
Alex¦an¦der (Russian emperors and Scottish kings)
Alex¦an¦der, Har¦old (British field marshal)
Alex¦an¦der Archi|pel¦ago (island off Alaska)
Alex¦an¦der Nev¦sky (Russian hero)

alex¦an¦ders (plant)
Alex¦an¦der tech|nique
Alex¦an¦der the Great (Macedonian king)
Alex¦an¦dra
Alex¦an|dretta (former name of Iskenderun)
Alex¦an¦dria (port, Egypt; name)
Alex¦an|drian +s
alex¦an|drine +s (line of verse)
alex¦an|drite (mineral)
Alex¦an¦dro|pol (former name of Gyumri)
alexia
alexin
alex|ine (use alexin)
alexi|phar¦mic
Alexis
al|fal¦fa
Al Fatah (Palestinian organization)
Al|fonso (Spanish kings)
Al¦fred
Al¦fred the Great (king of Wessex)
al|fresco
Alf¦vén, Hannes Olof Gösta (Swedish theoretical physicist)
alga
   algae
algal
Al|garve (province, Portugal)
al¦ge|bra +s
al¦ge¦bra¦ic
al¦ge¦bra¦ic¦al
al¦ge¦bra¦ic¦al¦ly
al¦ge¦bra¦ist +s
Al|ge|ciras (port and resort, Spain)
Alger
Al|geria
Al|ger¦ian +s
Al|ger|non
al¦gi|cide
algid
al¦gid|ity

Al|giers (capital of Algeria)
al¦gin|ate +s
al¦gin¦ic
alg¦oid
Algol (star; computing language)
al¦go|lag¦nia
al¦go|lag¦nic
al¦go|logic¦al
al¦golo|gist +s
al|gology
Al¦gon|quian +s
Al¦gon|quin +s
al¦go|rithm +s
al¦go|rith¦mic
al¦go|rith¦mic|al¦ly
al¦gua|cil +s
al¦gua|zil +s (use alguacil)
Al¦ham|bra (palace, Granada)
Al¦ham|bresque
Ali, Mu¦ham|mad (American boxer)
alias
   aliases
Ali Baba
alibi
   ali¦bis
   ali|bied
   alibi|ing
Ali|cante (port, Spain)
Alice
Alice-in-Wonder¦land *attributive*
Alice Springs (town, Australia)
Ali¦cia
Alick *also* Alec
ali|cyc¦lic
al¦id|ade +s
alien +s
alien|abil¦ity
alien|able
alien|age
alien|ate
   alien|ates
   alien|ated
   alien|at¦ing
alien|ation
alien|ator +s
alien|ism
alien|ist +s
alien|ness
ali|form
Ali|garh (city, India)

Ali|ghieri, Dante (Italian poet)
alight +s +ed +ing
align +s +ed +ing
align|ment +s
alike
ali|ment +s
ali|men¦tal
ali|men¦tary
ali|men|ta¦tion
ali|mony
Alinda
Aline (name)
A-line (flared)
ali|phat¦ic
ali|quot +s
Alis|dair *also* Alas|dair, Alas|tair, Alis|tair
Ali|son *also* Al|lison
Al|issa
Alis|tair *also* Alas|dair, Alas|tair, Alis|dair
alive
alive|ness
Alix *also* Alex
aliz|arin
Al Jizah (Arabic name for Giza)
al|ka|hest
al|kali
   al¦ka|lis *Br.*
   al¦ka|lies *Am.*
al¦kali|fy
   al¦kali|fies
   al¦kali|fied
   al¦kali¦fy|ing
al¦kal|im¦eter +s
al¦kal|im¦etry
al¦ka|line
al¦ka|lin|ity
al¦kal|oid +s
al¦kal|osis
   al¦kal|oses
al¦kane +s
al¦ka|net +s
al¦kene +s
alkie +s (use alky)
alky
   alk¦ies
alkyd +s
alkyl +s
al¦kyl|ate
   al¦kyl|ates
   al¦kyl|ated
   al¦kyl|at¦ing
al¦kyne +s
all (everything, everyone, etc.
   ⚠ awl, orle)
alla breve

alla cap|pella
Allah *Islam*
Al|lah|abad (city, India)
all-America +s
all-American
Allan *also* Alan, Allen, Alun
al|lan|toic
al|lan|tois
   al|lan|to|ides
all-around
   attributive
allay +s +ed +ing
All Blacks
all-clear +s *noun*
all comers
all-day *attributive*
Al|lecto (use Alecto)
al|le|ga|tion +s
al|lege
   al|leges
   al|leged
   al|leging
   al|leged|ly
Al|le|ghen|ies (= Allegheny Mountains)
Al|le|gheny Moun|tains (in USA)
al|le|giance +s
al|le|gor|ic
al|le|gor|ic|al
al|le|gor|ic|al|ly
al|le|gor|isa|tion *Br.* (use allegorization)
al|le|gor|ise *Br.* (use allegorize)
   al|le|gor|ises
   al|le|gor|ised
   al|le|gor|is|ing
al|le|gor|ist +s
al|le|gor|iza|tion
al|le|gor|ize
   al|le|gor|izes
   al|le|gor|ized
   al|le|gor|iz|ing
al|le|gory
   al|le|gor|ies
al|le|gretto +s
al|legro +s
allel +s
al|lele +s
al|lel|ic
al|lelo|morph +s
al|lelo|morph|ic
al|le|luia +s
alle|mande +s
all-embracing

Allen *also* Alan, Allan, Alun
Allen (key, screw) *Propr.*
Allen, Woody (American film director, writer, and actor)
Al|lenby, Vis|count (British soldier)
all-encompass|ing
Al|lende, Sal|va|dor (Chilean statesman)
Al|len|stein (German name for Olsztyn)
al|ler|gen +s
al|ler|gen|ic
al|ler|gic
al|ler|gist +s
al|lergy
   al|ler|gies
al|le|vi|ate
   al|le|vi|ates
   al|le|vi|ated
   al|le|vi|at|ing
al|le|vi|ation
al|le|via|tive
al|le|vi|ator +s
al|le|vi|atory
alley +s
alley cat +s
al|ley|way +s
All Fools' Day
All Hal|lows
al|li|aceous
al|li|ance +s
al|li|cin
Allie *also* Ally
al|lied
Al|lier (river, France)
al|li|ga|tor +s
all-import|ant
all in (tired)
all-in (complete)
all-inclusive
all-in-one +s
   adjective and noun
all-in wrest|ling
Al|lison *also* Ali|son
al|lit|er|ate
   al|lit|er|ates
   al|lit|er|ated
   al|lit|er|at|ing
al|lit|er|ation +s
al|lit|era|tive
al|lium +s
all-night *attributive*

Alloa (town, Scotland)
al|loc|able
al|lo|cate
   al|lo|cates
   al|lo|cated
   al|lo|cat|ing
al|lo|ca|tion +s
al|lo|ca|tor +s
al|lo|cu|tion +s
al|loch|thon|ous
al|lo|dial +s
al|lo|dium +s
al|logamy
allo|graft +s
allo|morph +s
allo|morph|ic
allo|path +s
allo|path|ic
al|lop|ath|ist +s
al|lop|athy
allo|pat|ric
allo|phone +s
allo|phon|ic
allo|poly|ploid +s
all-or-nothing *attributive*
allo|saur +s
allo|saurus
   allo|saur|uses
allot
   al|lots
   al|lot|ted
   al|lot|ting
al|lot|ment +s
allo|trope +s
allo|trop|ic
allo|trop|ic|al
al|lot|ropy
al|lot|tee +s
all-out *attributive*
all-over *attributive*
allow +s +ed +ing
al|low|able +s
al|low|ably
al|low|ance +s
al|low|ed|ly
alloy +s +ed +ing
all-party *attributive*
all-pervad|ing *attributive*
all-pervasive
all-powerful
all-purpose
all ready (entire number of people or things in a state of readiness. △ already)
all right *adjective, adverbial, and interjection*

all-right *attributive*
all-round *attributive*
all-rounder +s
All Saints' Day
all-seater *attributive*
all|seed
all-share *attributive*
All Souls' Day
all|spice
All|ston, Wash|ing|ton (American painter)
all-ticket *attributive*
all-time
all to|gether (all at once; all in one. △ altogether)
al|lude
   al|ludes
   al|luded
   al|lud|ing
   (refer indirectly. △ elude, illude)
all-up *attributive*
al|lure
   al|lures
   al|lured
   al|lur|ing
al|lure|ment +s
al|lu|sion +s (indirect reference. △ illusion)
al|lu|sive (containing an allusion. △ elusive, illusive)
al|lu|sive|ly (in an allusive way. △ elusively, illusively)
al|lu|sive|ness (allusive nature. △ elusiveness, illusiveness)
al|lu|vial
al|lu|vion
al|lu|vium
   al|lu|via *or*
   al|lu|vi|ums
all-weather *attributive*
all-wheel
Ally (name)
ally
   al|lies
   al|lied
   ally|ing
allyl +s
Alma

Alma-Ata (former name of Almaty)
al¦ma|can¦tar +s (use almucantar)
Al¦ma|gest (Ptolemy's treatise)
al¦ma|gest +s (generally)
Alma Mater +s
al|manac +s
Al¦man|ach de Gotha
Al¦man|ack (in 'Oxford Almanack', 'Whittaker's Almanack')
al¦man|dine +s
Alma-Tadema, Law|rence (Dutch-born British painter)
Al¦maty (capital of Kazakhstan)
Al|mería (town, Spain)
al|mighty
al|mirah +s
Al¦mir|ante Brown (city, Argentina)
Al¦mo|had +s
Al¦mo|hade +s (use Almohad)
al|mond +s
al|mon¦er +s
al|mon¦ry
Al|mora|vid +s
Al|mora|vide +s (= Almoravid)
al|most
alms (charity. △ arms)
alms|house +s
alms|man
alms|men
al¦mu|can¦tar +s
aloe +s
alo|et¦ic
aloe vera
aloft
alogic¦al
alogic|al¦ly
aloha
alone
alone|ness
along
along|shore
along|side
aloof
aloof¦ly
aloof|ness

alo|pe¦cia
Alor Setar (city, Malaysia)
Alost (French name for Aalst)
aloud (audibly. △ allowed)
alow (below, in a ship)
Aloy|sius
alp +s (mountain)
al¦paca +s
al¦par|gata +s
al¦pen|horn +s
al¦pen|stock +s
alpha +s
al¦pha|bet +s
al¦pha|bet¦ic
al¦pha¦bet|ic¦al
al¦pha¦bet|ic|al¦ly
al¦pha¦bet|isa¦tion Br. (use alphabetization)
al¦pha¦bet|ise Br. (use alphabetize)
al¦pha¦bet|ises
al¦pha¦bet|ised
al¦pha¦bet|is¦ing
al¦pha¦bet|iza¦tion
al¦pha¦bet|ize
al¦pha¦bet|izes
al¦pha¦bet|ized
al¦pha¦bet|iz¦ing
Alpha Cen|tauri (star)
alpha|numer¦ic
alpha|numer|ic¦al
alpha test +s +ed +ing
Al¦pine (of Alps or downhill skiing)
al¦pine (of high mountains)
Al¦pin|ist +s
Alps (mountain range, Europe; also in names of other ranges)
al|ready (beforehand; as early or as soon as this. △ all ready)
al|right (use all right or all-right)
Al¦sace (region, France)
Al|sa¦tian +s
al¦sike
also
also-ran +s
al¦stroe|me¦ria +s

Altai (territory, Russia)
Al¦taic
Altai Moun|tains (central Asia)
Al¦tair (star)
Al¦ta|mira (site of cave paintings, Spain; town, Brazil)
altar +s (table in church. △ alter)
al¦tar|piece +s
Altay (use Altai)
alt|azi¦muth +s
Alt|dor¦fer, Al|brecht (German painter)
Alte Pi¦na¦ko|thek (museum, Munich)
alter +s +ed +ing (change. △ altar)
al¦ter|able
al¦ter|ation +s
al¦tera|tive
al¦ter|cate
al¦ter|cates
al¦ter|cated
al¦ter|cat¦ing
al¦ter|ca¦tion +s
alter ego +s
al¦ter|nance
al¦ter|nant +s
al¦ter|nate
al¦ter|nates
al¦ter|nated
al¦ter|nat¦ing
al¦ter|nate¦ly
al¦ter|na¦tion +s
al¦ter|na¦tive +s
al¦ter|na¦tive¦ly
al¦ter|na¦tor +s
Al¦thea
alt|horn +s
al|though
Al¦thus|ser, Louis (French philosopher)
Al¦thus¦ser|ean +s (use Althusserian)
Al¦thus¦ser|ian +s
al¦tim|eter +s
al¦ti|plano +s
al¦ti|tude +s
al¦ti|tud¦inal
alto +s
alto|cumu¦lus
alto|cumuli

al|together (totally; in total. △ all together)
alto-relievo +s
alto-rilievo +s (use alto-relievo)
alto|stra¦tus
al¦tri|cial +s
al¦tru|ism
al¦tru|ist +s
al¦tru|is¦tic
al¦tru|is¦tic|al¦ly
alum
alu|mina
alu¦min|isa|tion Br. (use aluminization)
alu¦min|ise Br. (use aluminize)
alu¦min|ises
alu¦min|ised
alu¦min|is¦ing
alu|min¦ium Br.
alu¦min|iza|tion
alu¦min|ize
alu¦min|izes
alu¦min|ized
alu¦min|iz¦ing
alu¦mino|sili¦cate +s
alu|mi¦num Am.
alumna
alum|nae female
alum|nus
alumni male
Alun also Alan, Allan, Allen
Alvar
Al|varez, Luis Wal|ter (American physicist)
al¦veo|lar +s
al¦veo|late
al¦veo|lus
al|veoli
Alvin
al|ways
alys|sum +s
Alz|heim¦er's dis|ease
am
ama¦da|vat +s
ama¦dou
amah +s (maid. △ armor, armour)
amain
Amal +s
Amalfi (resort, Italy)

amal|gam +s
amal|gam|ate
    amal|gam|ates
    amal|gam|ated
    amal|gam|at|ing
amal|gam|ation
    +s
Amal|thea (*Greek Mythology*; moon of Jupiter)
Amanda
amanu|en|sis
    amanu|en|ses
Amapá (state, Brazil)
am|ar|anth
am|ar|anth|ine
am|ar|etto
    am|ar|etti
    (liqueur; biscuit. △ *amoretto*)
Amarna, Tell el- (site of Akhetaten, Egypt)
amar|yl|lis
    amar|yl|lises
amass
    amasses
    amassed
    amass|ing
amass|er +s
Ama|ter|asu
ama|teur +s
ama|teur|ish
ama|teur|ish|ly
ama|teur|ish|ness
ama|teur|ism
Amati +s
ama|tive
ama|tory
am|aur|osis
    am|aur|oses
am|aur|ot|ic
amaze
    amazes
    amazed
    amaz|ing
amaze|ment
amaz|ing|ly
amaz|ing|ness
Amazon +s
    (region, S. America; legendary female warrior)
amazon +s (strong, athletic woman)
amazon ant +s
Ama|zo|nas (state, Brazil)
Ama|zonia (region, S. America)

Ama|zon|ian
am|bas|sador +s
ambassador-at-large
    ambassadors-at-large
am|bas|sador|ial
am|bas|sa|dor|ship +s
am|bas|sadress
    am|bas|sadresses
am|batch
    am|batches
Am|bato (town, Ecuador)
amber
am|ber|gris
am|ber|jack
    plural am|ber|jack or am|ber|jacks
am|bi|ance +s (use ambience)
ambi|dex|ter|ity
ambi|dex|trous
ambi|dex|trous|ly
ambi|dex|trous|ness
am|bi|ence +s
am|bi|ent
am|bi|gu|ity
    am|bi|gu|ities
am|bigu|ous
am|bigu|ous|ly
am|bigu|ous|ness
ambi|son|ics
am|bit +s
am|bi|tion +s
am|bi|tious
am|bi|tious|ly
am|bi|tious|ness
am|biva|lence +s
am|biva|lency
am|biva|lent
am|biva|lent|ly
ambi|ver|sion
ambi|vert +s
amble
    am|bles
    am|bled
    am|bling
am|bler +s
am|bly|opia
am|bly|opic
ambo
    ambos or am|bo|nes
Am|boina (= Ambon)
Am|boi|nese
    plural Am|boi|nese

Ambon (island and port, Indonesia)
am|boyna
Am|brose (Roman saint; name)
am|bro|sia
am|bro|sial
am|bro|sian
ambry
    am|bries
ambs-ace
am|bu|lance +s
am|bu|lant
am|bu|la|tory
    am|bu|la|tor|ies
am|bus|cade
    am|bus|cades
    am|bus|caded
    am|bus|cad|ing
am|bush
    am|bushes
    am|bushed
    am|bush|ing
ameba *Am.*
    amebas or amebae
    (*Br.* amoeba)
ame|bean *Am.* (*Br.* amoebean)
ameb|ia|sis *Am.*
    ameb|ia|ses
    (*Br.* amoebiasis)
ameb|ic *Am.* (*Br.* amoebic)
ameb|oid *Am.* (*Br.* amoeboid)
ameer +s (use amir)
Am|elia
ameli|or|ate
    ameli|or|ates
    ameli|or|ated
    ameli|or|at|ing
ameli|or|ation
ameli|ora|tive +s
ameli|or|ator +s
amen +s
amen|abil|ity
amen|able
amen|able|ness
amen|ably
amend +s +ed +ing (improve. △ emend)
amend|able
amende
    hon|or|able
    amendes
    hon|or|ables
amend|er +s
amend|ment +s

Amen|ho|tep (pharaohs)
amen|ity
    amen|ities
Ameno|phis (Greek name for Amenhotep)
amen|or|rhea *Am.*
amen|or|rhoea *Br.*
ament +s
amen|tia
amen|tum
    amenta
Amer|asian +s
amerce
    amerces
    amerced
    amer|cing
amerce|ment +s
amer|ci|able
Amer|ica +s
Ameri|can +s
Ameri|cana
Ameri|can|isa|tion *Br.* (use Americanization)
Ameri|can|ise *Br.* (use Americanize)
    Ameri|can|ises
    Ameri|can|ised
    Ameri|can|is|ing
Ameri|can|ism +s
Ameri|can|iza|tion
Ameri|can|ize
    Ameri|can|izes
    Ameri|can|ized
    Ameri|can|iz|ing
Amer|ica's Cup
ameri|cium
Amer|ind +s
Amer|in|dian +s
Amer|in|dic
Ames|lan (= American sign language)
ameth|yst +s
ameth|yst|ine
Amex (= American Stock Exchange)
Amex (= American Express) *Propr.*
Am|har|ic
ami|abil|ity
ami|able
ami|able|ness
ami|ably
ami|an|thus
am|ic|abil|ity
am|ic|able
am|ic|able|ness
am|ic|ably

amice +s
ami¦cus curiae
　amici curiae
amid
amide +s
amid|done
amid|ship
amid|ships
amidst
Am¦iens (city,
　France)
amigo +s
Amin, Idi
　(Ugandan soldier
　and head of state)
Am¦in|divi
　Is¦lands (now
　part of
　Lakshadweep
　Islands)
amine +s
amino +s
amino acid +s
amir +s (title of
　some Muslim
　rulers. △ emir)
Amir|ante Is¦lands
　(in Indian Ocean)
amir|ate +s
　(position or
　territory of an
　amir. △ emirate)
Amis, Kings|ley
　and Mar¦tin
　(British writers)
Amish
amiss
ami|tosis
ami|trip¦tyl|ine
amity
Amman (capital of
　Jordan)
am|meter +s
ammo
Ammon (= Amun)
am¦mo|nia
am¦mo|niac
am¦mo|ni|ac¦al
am¦mo|ni|ated
am¦mon|ite +s
am¦mo|nium
am¦mu|ni¦tion +s
am|nesia
am|nesiac +s
am|nesic +s
am|nesty
　am|nes¦ties
　am|nes¦tied
　am¦nesty|ing
amnio +s
　(= amniocentesis)

am¦nio|cen¦tesis
am¦nio|cen¦teses
am¦nion
　amnia or
　am|nions
am¦ni|ote +s
am¦ni|ot¦ic
amoeba Br.
　amoe|bas or
　amoe|bae
　(Am. ameba)
amoe|bean Br.
　(Am. amebean)
amoeb|ia¦sis Br.
　amoeb|ia¦ses
　(Am. amebiasis)
amoeb|ic Br. (Am.
　amebic)
amoeb|oid Br. (Am.
　ameboid)
amok
among
amongst
amon¦til|lado +s
amoral
amor¦al|ism
amor¦al|ist +s
amor¦al|ity
amor¦al|ly
amor|etto
　amor|etti
　(Cupid.
　△ amaretto)
am|or|ist +s
Am|or|ite +s
amor|oso +s
am|or|ous
am|or|ous¦ly
am|or|ous|ness
amorph|ous
amorph|ous¦ly
amorph|ous|ness
amort|isa|tion Br.
　(use
　amortization)
amort|ise Br. (use
　amortize)
amort|ises
amort|ised
amort|is¦ing
amort|iza|tion
amort|ize
amort|izes
amort|ized
amort|iz¦ing
Amos Bible
amount +s +ed
　+ing
amour +s
amour|ette +s
amour propre

Amoy (alternative
　name for Xiamen)
amp +s
am|pel|op¦sis
　plural
　am|pel|op¦sis
am|per|age +s
Am¦père, André-
　Marie (French
　physicist)
am¦pere +s (unit)
am|per|sand +s
am|phet|amine +s
Am|phibia
am|phib|ian +s
am|phibi|ous
am|phibi|ous¦ly
amphi|bole +s
am|phibo|lite +s
amphi|bology
　amphi|bolo¦gies
amphi|brach +s
amphi|brach¦ic
am|phic|tyon +s
am|phic|ty|on¦ic
am|phic|ty|ony
am|phig|am|ous
amphi|gouri +s
amphi|mic¦tic
amphi|mixis
　amphi|mixes
amphi|oxus
　amphi|oxi
amphi|path¦ic
amphi|pod +s
am|phip¦ro|style
　+s
am|phis|baena +s
amphi|theater Am.
　+s
amphi|theatre Br.
　+s
Amphi|trite Greek
　Mythology
am|phit¦ryon
am|phora
　am|phorae or
　am|phoras
ampho|ter¦ic
ampi|cil¦lin
ample
amp¦ler
amp|lest
ample|ness
amp¦li|fi|ca¦tion
amp¦li|fier +s
amp¦lify
　amp¦li|fies
　amp¦li|fied
　amp¦li|fy¦ing
amp¦li|tude
amply

am|poule +s
amp|ster +s
am|pulla
　am|pul¦lae
am|pu|tate
　am|pu|tates
　am|pu|tated
　am|pu|tat¦ing
am|pu|ta¦tion +s
am|pu|ta¦tor +s
am|pu|tee +s
Am¦rit|sar (city,
　India)
amster +s (use
　ampster)
Am¦ster|dam
　(capital of the
　Netherlands)
am¦trac +s
　(amphibious
　vehicle)
Am|track (use
　Amtrak)
Am¦trak (US
　railway) Propr.
am¦trak +s
　(amphibious
　vehicle; use
　amtrac)
amuck (use amok)
Amu Darya (river,
　central Asia)
amu¦let +s
Amun Egyptian
　Mythology
Amund|sen, Roald
　(Norwegian
　explorer)
Amur (river, NE
　Asia)
amuse
　amuses
　amused
　amus¦ing
amuse|ment +s
amus|ing¦ly
Amy
amyg|dale +s
amyg¦dal|oid +s
amyl
amyl|ase
amyl|oid
amyl|op¦sin
Amy¦tal Propr.
an indefinite article
ana +s
Ana|bap¦tism
Ana|bap¦tist +s
ana¦bas
ana|basis
　ana|bases
ana|bat¦ic

ana|bi|osis
  ana|bi|oses
  ana|bi|ot|ic
ana|bol|ic
an|ab|ol|ism
ana|branch
  ana|branches
ana|chron|ic
an|achron|ism +s
ana|chron|is|tic
ana|chron|is|tic|
      al|ly
ana|co|lu|thic
ana|co|lu|thon
  ana|co|lu|tha
    Br. (use
    anacoluthon)
ana|conda +s
Anac|reon (Greek
  poet)
anac|re|on|tic
ana|cru|sis
  ana|cru|ses
anad|ro|mous
an|aemia *Br.* (*Am.*
  anemia)
an|aemic *Br.* +s
  (*Am.* anemic)
an|aer|obe +s
an|aer|obic
an|aes|the|sia *Br.*
  (*Am.* anesthesia)
an|aes|the|si|ology
  Br. (*Am.*
  anesthesiology)
an|aes|thet|ic *Br.*
  +s (*Am.*
  anesthetic)
an|aes|thet|ic|al|ly
  Br. (*Am.*
  anesthetically)
an|aes|the|tisa|
  tion *Br.* (use
  anaesthetization.
  Am.
  anesthetization)
an|aes|the|tise *Br.*
  (use
  anaesthetize)
  an|aes|the|tises
  an|aes|the|tised
  an|aes|the|tis|ing
  (*Am.* anesthetize)
an|aes|the|tist *Br.*
  +s (*Am.*
  anesthetist)
an|aes|the|tiza|
  tion *Br.* (*Am.*
  anesthetization)
an|aes|the|tize *Br.*
  an|aes|the|tizes
  an|aes|the|tized
  an|aes|the|tiz|ing
  (*Am.* anesthetize)

ana|glyph +s
ana|glyph|ic
Ana|glypta +s
  Propr.
an|ag|nor|isis
  an|ag|nor|ises
ana|goge +s
ana|gogic
ana|gogic|al
ana|gram +s
ana|gram|mat|ic
ana|gram|
      mat|ic|al
ana|gram|ma|tise
  Br. (use
  anagrammatize)
ana|gram|
      ma|tises
ana|gram|
      ma|tised
ana|gram|
      ma|tis|ing
ana|gram|ma|tize
ana|gram|
      ma|tizes
ana|gram|
      ma|tized
ana|gram|
      ma|tiz|ing
Ana|heim (city,
  USA)
anal
ana|lecta
ana|lects
ana|lep|tic +s
an|al|gesia
an|al|gesic +s
anal|ly
ana|log +s
  Computing
ana|log *Am.* (*Br.*
  analogue)
ana|logic
ana|logic|al
ana|logic|al|ly
analo|gise *Br.* (use
  analogize)
  analo|gises
  analo|gised
  analo|gis|ing
analo|gist +s
analo|gize
  analo|gizes
  analo|gized
  analo|giz|ing
analo|gous
analo|gous|ly
ana|logue *Br.* +s
  (*Am.* analog)
ana|logy
  ana|lo|gies
anal re|ten|tion

anal-retentive +s
anal
  re|ten|tive|ness
ana|lys|able *Br.*
  (*Am.* analyzable)
an|aly|sand +s
ana|lyse *Br.*
  ana|lyses
  ana|lysed
  ana|lys|ing
  (*Am.* analyze)
ana|lyser *Br.* +s
  (*Am.* analyzer)
an|aly|sis
  an|aly|ses
ana|lyst +s (person
  who analyses.
  △ annalist)
ana|lyt|ic
ana|lyt|ic|al
ana|lyt|ic|al|ly
ana|lyz|able *Am.*
  (*Br.* analysable)
ana|lyze *Am.*
  ana|lyzes
  ana|lyzed
  ana|lyz|ing
  (*Br.* analyse)
ana|lyzer *Am.* +s
  (*Br.* analyser)
an|am|nesis
  an|am|neses
ana|morph|ic
ana|mor|phosis
  ana|mor|phoses
ana|nas
an|an|drous
An|angu
  plural An|angu
Ananias *Bible*
ana|paest +s
ana|paes|tic
ana|phase +s
anaph|ora +s
ana|phor|ic
an|aphro|dis|iac
  +s
ana|phyl|actic
ana|phyl|axis
  ana|phyl|axes
anap|tyc|tic
anap|tyxis
  anap|tyxes
an|arch +s
an|arch|ic
an|arch|ic|al
an|arch|ic|al|ly
an|arch|ism
an|arch|ist +s
an|arch|is|tic
an|archy
Ana|sazi

Ana|sta|sia
ana|stig|mat +s
ana|stig|mat|ic
anas|to|mose
  anas|to|moses
  anas|to|mosed
  anas|to|mos|ing
anas|to|mosis
  anas|to|moses
anas|tro|phe +s
anath|ema +s
anath|ema|tise *Br.*
  (use
  anathematize)
  anath|ema|tises
  anath|ema|tised
  anath|ema|tis|ing
anath|ema|tize
  anath|ema|tizes
  anath|ema|tized
  anath|ema|tiz|ing
Ana|to|lia
  (peninsula forming
  most of Turkey)
Ana|to|lian +s
ana|tom|ical
ana|tom|ic|al|ly
anato|mise *Br.* (use
  anatomize)
  anato|mises
  anato|mised
  anato|mis|ing
anato|mist +s
anato|mize
  anato|mizes
  anato|mized
  anato|miz|ing
anat|omy
  anat|omies
anatta
anatto (use
  annatto)
An|ax|ag|oras
  (Greek
  philosopher)
Anaxi|man|der
  (Greek
  philosopher and
  astronomer)
An|ax|im|enes
  (Greek
  philosopher)
an|bury
  an|bur|ies
an|ces|tor +s
an|ces|tral
an|ces|tral|ly
an|ces|tress
  an|ces|tresses
an|ces|try
  an|ces|tries

An|chises *Greek and Roman Mythology*
an|chor +s +ed +ing
An|chor|age (city, USA)
an|chor|age +s
an|chor|ess
  an|chor|esses
an|choret +s
an|chor|et|ic
an|chor|ite +s (recluse. △ ankerite)
an|chor|it|ic
an|chor|man
  an|chor|men
an|chor|per|son
  an|chor|per|sons *or* an|chor|people
an|chor plate +s
an|chor|woman
  an|chor|women
an|chovy
  an|cho|vies
an|chusa +s
an|chy|lose (use ankylose)
  an|chy|loses
  an|chy|losed
  an|chy|los|ing
an|chy|losis (use ankylosis)
an|cien ré|gime
  an|ciens ré|gimes
an|cient +s
an|cient|ly
an|cient|ness
an|cil|lary
  an|cil|lar|ies
ancon
  an|co|nes *or* an|cons
An|cona (port, Italy)
An|cyra (ancient name for Ankara)
and
An|da|lu|cia (Spanish name for Andalusia)
An|da|lu|sia (region, Spain)
An|da|lu|sian +s
An|da|man and Nico|bar Is|lands (off India)
an|dante +s
an|dan|tino +s
An|dean

An|der|sen, Hans Chris|tian (Danish writer)
An|der|son, Carl David (American physicist)
An|der|son, Eliza|beth Gar|rett (English physician and feminist)
An|der|son, Mar|ian (American contralto)
Andes (mountain range, S. America)
an|des|ite +s
An|dhra Pra|desh (state, India)
and|iron +s
An|dorra
An|dor|ran +s
Andre, Carl (American sculptor)
André
An|drea
An|drea del Sarto (Italian painter)
An|dreas
An|drew (name, but merry andrew)
An|drew (Apostle and saint)
An|drew, Prince (Duke of York)
An|drews, Julie (English actress and singer)
An|drews, Thomas (Irish chemist)
An|drić, Ivo (Yugoslav writer)
an|dro|cen|tric
an|dro|cen|trism
An|dro|cles (legendary Roman slave)
an|droe|cium
  an|droe|cia
an|dro|gen +s
an|dro|gen|ic
an|dro|gyne +s
an|drogy|nous
an|drogyny
an|droid +s
An|drom|ache *Greek Mythology*

An|drom|eda (*Greek Mythology;* constellation)
An|dro|pov (former name of Rybinsk)
An|dro|pov, Yuri (Soviet statesman)
an|ec|dot|age
an|ec|dotal
an|ec|dotal|ist +s
an|ec|dot|al|ly
an|ec|dote +s
an|ec|dot|ic
an|echo|ic
An|eirin *also*
  An|eurin
anele
  aneles
  aneled
  anel|ing (anoint. △ anneal)
an|emia *Am.* (*Br.* anaemia)
an|emic *Am.* +s (*Br.* anaemic)
anemo|graph +s
anemo|graph|ic
an|emom|eter +s
anemo|met|ric
an|emom|etry
anem|one +s
an|emoph|il|ous
anen|ceph|al|ic +s
anen|ceph|aly
anent
an|er|oid +s
an|es|the|sia *Am.* (*Br.* anaesthesia)
an|es|the|si|ology *Am.* (*Br.* anaesthesiology)
an|es|thet|ic *Am.* +s (*Br.* anaesthetic)
an|es|thet|ic|al|ly *Am.* (*Br.* anaesthetically)
an|es|the|tist *Am.* +s (*Br.* anaesthetist)
an|es|the|tiza|tion *Am.* (*Br.* anaesthetization)
an|es|the|tize *Am.* (*Br.* anaesthetize)
  an|es|the|tizes
  an|es|the|tized
  an|es|the|tiz|ing
An|eurin *also* An|eirin
an|eurin (vitamin)
an|eur|ysm +s

an|eur|ys|mal
anew
an|frac|tu|os|ity
an|frac|tu|ous
an|gary
Angel (name)
angel +s
An|gela
An|gel|eno +s
Angel Falls (in Venezuela)
angel|fish
  plural angel|fish *or* angel|fishes
an|gel|ic
An|gel|ica (name)
an|gel|ica
an|gel|ic|al
an|gel|ic|al|ly
An|gel|ico, Fra (Italian painter)
An|gel|ina
An|ge|lou, Maya (American writer)
angel-shark +s
angels-on-horseback
an|gelus
anger +s +ed +ing
An|gers (city, France)
An|ge|vin +s
An|gharad
Angie
an|gina
an|gio|gram +s
an|gi|og|raphy
an|gi|oma
  an|gi|omas *or* an|gi|omata
angio|plasty
angio|sperm +s
angio|sperm|ous
Ang|kor (ancient city, Cambodia)
Angle +s (people)
angle
  an|gles
  an|gled
  an|gling (*Geometry;* fish)
angle|dozer +s
angle-iron +s
angle|poise +s *Propr.*
an|gler +s
angler-fish
  plural angler-fish
Angle|sey (island, Wales)
An|glian +s
An|gli|can +s

An|gli|can|ism
an|glice
An|gli|cisa|tion *Br.*
   (use
   Anglicization)
An|gli|cise *Br.* (use
   Anglicize)
An|gli|cises
An|gli|cised
An|gli|cis|ing
An|gli|cism +s
An|gli|ciza|tion
An|gli|cize
   An|gli|cizes
   An|gli|cized
   An|gli|ciz|ing
An|glist +s
An|glis|tics
Anglo +s
Anglo-American
   +s
Anglo-Catholic +s
Anglo-
   Catholi|cism
Anglo|cen|tric
Anglo-French
Anglo-Indian +s
Anglo-Irish
Anglo-Latin
Anglo|mania
Anglo|maniac +s
Anglo-Norman +s
Anglo|phile +s
Anglo|phobe +s
Anglo|pho|bia
anglo|phone +s
Anglo-Saxon +s
An|gola
An|gora (former
   name of Ankara)
an|gora +s (goat;
   wool)
An|gos|tura
   (former name of
   Ciudad Bolívar)
an|gos|tura (plant;
   Angostura Bitters)
An|gos|tura
   Bit|ters *Propr.*
an|grily
angry
   an|grier
   an|gri|est
angst
angst-ridden
Ång|ström,
   An|ders Jonas
   (Swedish
   physicist)
ang|strom +s (unit)
An|guilla (island,
   West Indies)

an|guine
an|guish
   an|guishes
   an|guished
   an|guish|ing
an|gu|lar
an|gu|lar|ity
an|gu|lar|ly
Angus (former
   county, Scotland;
   name)
an|gwan|tibo +s
an|he|dral
an|hinga +s
Anhui (province,
   China)
An|hwei (= Anhui)
an|hyd|ride +s
an|hyd|rite
an|hyd|rous
ani +s (bird)
an|icon|ic
ani|cut +s
anile
an|il|ine
anil|ity
anima
an|im|ad|ver|sion
   +s
an|im|ad|vert
   +ed +ing
ani|mal +s
ani|mal|cu|lar
ani|mal|cule +s
ani|mal|isa|tion
   Br. (use
   animalization)
ani|mal|ise *Br.* (use
   animalize)
   ani|mal|ises
   ani|mal|ised
   ani|mal|is|ing
ani|mal|ism
ani|mal|ist +s
ani|mal|is|tic
ani|mal|ity
ani|mal|iza|tion
ani|mal|ize
   ani|mal|izes
   ani|mal|ized
   ani|mal|iz|ing
anima mundi
ani|mate
   ani|mates
   ani|mated
   ani|mat|ing
ani|mated|ly
ani|ma|teur +s
ani|ma|tion +s
ani|ma|tor +s
anima|tron +s
anima|tron|ic

anima|tron|ics
animé
ani|mism
ani|mist +s
ani|mis|tic
ani|mos|ity
   ani|mos|ities
ani|mus
anion +s
an|ion|ic
anise
ani|seed
an|is|ette
an|iso|trop|ic
an|iso|trop|ic|al|ly
an|isot|ropy
Anita
Anjou (former
   province, France;
   wine)
An|kara (capital of
   Turkey)
an|ker|ite (mineral.
   △ anchorite)
ankh +s
ankle +s
ankle-biter +s
ankle-bone +s
ankle-deep
ankle sock +s
ank|let +s
an|ky|lo|saur +s
an|ky|lose
   an|ky|loses
   an|ky|losed
   an|ky|los|ing
an|ky|losis
   an|ky|loses
Ann *also* Anne
Anna (name)
anna +s (former
   Indian and
   Pakistani
   currency)
An|naba (port,
   Algeria)
annal +s
an|nal|ist +s
   (writer of annals.
   △ analyst)
an|nal|is|tic
an|nal|is|tic|al|ly
An|nap|olis (city,
   USA)
An|na|purna
   (mountain ridge,
   Himalayas)
an|nates
an|natto
Anne *also* Ann

Anne (saint; mother
   of the Virgin
   Mary)
Anne (queen of
   England and
   Scotland)
Anne, Prin|cess
   (the Princess
   Royal)
Anne of Cleves
   (wife of Henry
   VIII of England)
an|neal +s +ed
   +ing (toughen.
   △ anele)
an|neal|er +s
an|nect|ent
an|nelid +s
an|nel|id|an
An|nette
annex
   an|nexes
   an|nexed
   an|nex|ing
   verb
an|nex|ation +s
an|nexe +s *noun*
an|ni|cut +s (use
   anicut)
Annie
An|ni|goni, Pietro
   (Italian painter)
an|ni|hi|late
   an|ni|hi|lates
   an|ni|hi|lated
   an|ni|hi|lat|ing
an|ni|hi|la|tion
an|ni|hi|la|tion|
      ism
an|ni|hi|la|tor +s
an|ni|ver|sary
   an|ni|ver|sar|ies
Anno|bón (island,
   Gulf of Guinea)
Anno Dom|ini
an|no|tat|able
an|no|tate
   an|no|tates
   an|no|tated
   an|no|tat|ing
an|no|ta|tion +s
an|no|ta|tive
an|no|ta|tor +s
an|nounce
   an|nounces
   an|nounced
   an|noun|cing
an|nounce|ment
   +s
an|noun|cer +s
annoy +s +ed +ing
an|noy|ance +s

an|noy|er +s
an|noy|ing|ly
an|noy|ing|ness
an|nual +s
an|nu|al|ise Br.
   (use annualize)
   an|nu|al|ises
   an|nu|al|ised
   an|nu|al|is|ing
an|nu|al|ize
   an|nu|al|izes
   an|nu|al|ized
   an|nu|al|iz|ing
an|nu|al|ly
an|nu|it|ant +s
an|nu|ity
   an|nu|ities
annul
   an|nuls
   an|nulled
   an|nul|ling
an|nu|lar
an|nu|lar|ly
an|nu|late
an|nu|lated
an|nu|la|tion
an|nu|let +s
an|nul|ment +s
an|nu|lus
   an|nuli
an|nun|ci|ate
   an|nun|ci|ates
   an|nun|ci|ated
   an|nun|ci|at|ing
An|nun|ci|ation (of
   birth of Christ;
   festival)
an|nun|ci|ation +s
   (generally)
an|nun|ci|ator +s
annus hor|ri|bilis
annus mira|bilis
anoa +s
an|odal
anode +s
an|odic
ano|dise Br. (use
   anodize)
   ano|dises
   ano|dised
   ano|dis|ing
ano|diser Br. +s
   (use anodizer)
ano|dize
   ano|dizes
   ano|dized
   ano|diz|ing
ano|dizer +s
ano|dyne +s
ano|esis
   ano|eses
ano|etic

anoint +s +ed
   +ing
anoint|er +s
anole +s
anom|al|is|tic
anom|al|ous
anom|al|ous|ly
anom|al|ous|ness
anom|al|ure +s
anom|aly
   anom|al|ies
anom|ic
an|omie
anomy (use
   anomie)
anon (soon)
anon.
   (= anonymous)
an|on|aceous
ano|nym +s
ano|nym|ity
an|onym|ous
an|onym|ous|ly
anoph|eles
   plural anoph|eles
an|oph|thal|mia
ano|rak +s
an|or|ec|tic +s
an|or|exia
   (ner|vosa)
an|or|exic +s
an|or|ex|ic|al|ly
an|ortho|site +s
an|ortho|sit|ic
an|os|mia
an|os|mic +s
an|other
an|otherie (use
   anothery)
an|othery
Anouilh, Jean
   (French writer)
ANOVA (= analysis
   of variance)
an|ovu|lant +s
an|ox|ae|mia
an|oxia
an|oxic
An|schluss (of
   Austria)
an|schluss (other
   unification)
An|selm (Italian-
   born saint)
an|ser|ine
An|shan (city,
   China)
an|swer +s +ed
   +ing
an|swer|abil|ity
an|swer|able
an|swer|phone +s

ant +s +ed +ing
   (insect)
an't (= am not;
   have not.
   △ aren't, aunt)
ant|acid +s
An|taeus Greek
   Mythology
an|tag|on|isa|tion
   Br. (use
   antagonization)
an|tag|on|ise Br.
   (use antagonize)
   an|tag|on|ises
   an|tag|on|ised
   an|tag|on|is|ing
an|tag|on|ism +s
an|tag|on|ist +s
an|tag|on|is|tic
an|tag|on|is|tic|
      al|ly
an|tag|on|iza|tion
an|tag|on|ize
   an|tag|on|izes
   an|tag|on|ized
   an|tag|on|iz|ing
an|them +s
An|takya (Turkish
   name for Antioch)
An|tall, Jo|zsef
   (Hungarian
   statesman)
An|talya (port,
   Turkey)
An|tana|na|rivo
   (capital of
   Madagascar)
Ant|arc|tic
Ant|arc|tica
ant-bear +s
ante
   antes
   anted
   ante|ing
   (stake. △ anti)
ant|eat|er +s
ante-bellum
ante|ce|dence
ante|ce|dent +s
ante|ce|dent|ly
ante|cham|ber +s
ante|chapel +s
ante|date
   ante|dates
   ante|dated
   ante|dat|ing
ante|di|lu|vian +s
ante|lope +s
ante-mortem
ante|mun|dane
ante|natal

an|tenna
   an|ten|nae
   Zoology
an|tenna +s
   (aerial)
an|ten|nal
an|ten|nary
ante|nup|tial
ante|pen|dium
   ante|pen|dia
ante|pen|ult +s
ante|pen|ul|ti|
      mate +s
ante-post
ante|pran|dial
an|ter|ior
an|ter|ior|ity
an|teri|or|ly
ante-room +s
An|thea
ant|heap +s
ant|he|lion
   ant|he|lia
an|thel|min|thic
   +s
an|thel|min|tic +s
an|them +s
an|the|mion
   an|the|mia
An|the|mius of
   Tralles (Greek
   mathematician,
   engineer, and
   artist)
an|ther +s
an|ther|al
an|ther|id|ium
   an|ther|idia
ant|hill +s
an|tholo|gise Br.
   (use anthologize)
   an|tholo|gises
   an|tholo|gised
   an|tholo|gis|ing
an|tholo|gist +s
an|tholo|gize
   an|tholo|gizes
   an|tholo|gized
   an|tholo|giz|ing
an|thol|ogy
   an|tholo|gies
An|thony also
   An|tony
An|thony (Egyptian
   saint)
An|thony of
   Padua
   (Portuguese saint)
an|tho|zoan +s
an|thra|cene
an|thra|cite
an|thra|cit|ic

an¦thrac|nose
an¦thrax
an¦thro¦po|cen¦tric
an¦thro¦po|cen¦tric|
    al¦ly
an¦thro¦po|
    cen¦trism
an¦thro¦po|
    gen¦esis
an¦thro¦po|gen¦ic
an¦thro¦pogeny
an¦thro¦pog¦raphy
an¦thro¦poid +s
an¦thro¦po|logic¦al
an¦thro¦po|logic¦
    al¦ly
an¦thro¦polo|gist
    +s
an¦thro¦pol¦ogy
an¦thro¦po|met¦ric
an¦thro¦pom¦etry
an¦thro¦po|
    morph¦ic
an¦thro¦po|
    morph¦ic|al¦ly
an¦thro¦po|morph|
    ise Br. (use
    anthropomorph-
    ize)
an¦thro¦po|morph|
    ises
an¦thro¦po|morph|
    ised
an¦thro¦po|morph|
    is¦ing
an¦thro¦po|morph|
    ism
an¦thro¦po|morph|
    ize
an¦thro¦po|morph|
    izes
an¦thro¦po|morph|
    ized
an¦thro¦po|morph|
    iz¦ing
an¦thro¦po|
    morph¦ous
an¦thro¦ponymy
an¦thro|
    popha¦gous
an¦thro|poph¦agy
an¦thro¦poso¦phy
anti +s (against;
    opposer. ⚠ ante)
anti-abortion
    attributive
anti-abortion¦ist
    +s
anti-aircraft
anti-apartheid
    attributive
an¦tiar +s

anti|bac¦ter¦ial
An¦tibes (resort
    and port, France)
anti|bi¦osis
anti|bi¦oses
anti|bi¦ot¦ic +s
anti|body
anti|bodies
antibody-negative
antibody-positive
antic +s
anti|cath¦ode +s
anti-choice
Anti|christ +s
anti|chris¦tian
an¦tici|pate
    an¦tici|pates
    an¦tici|pated
    an¦tici|pat¦ing
an¦tici|pa¦tion
an¦tici|pa¦tive
an¦tici|pa¦tor +s
an¦tici|pa¦tory
anti|cler¦ic¦al
anti|cler¦ic¦al|ism
anti|cli¦mac¦tic
anti|cli¦mac¦tic|
    al¦ly
anti|cli¦max
    anti|cli¦maxes
anti|clinal
anti|cline +s
anti|clock|wise
anti|coagu|lant +s
anti|codon +s
anti-commun¦ist
    +s
anti|con¦sti|
    tu¦tion|al
anti|con¦vul¦sant
    +s
anti|cyc¦lone +s
anti|cyc¦lon¦ic
anti|depres|sant
    +s
anti|diur¦et¦ic +s
anti|dotal
anti|dote +s
anti-
    establish¦ment
    attributive
anti-fascist +s
anti|freeze +s
anti-g
anti|gen +s
anti|gen¦ic
An¦tig¦one *Greek
    Mythology*
anti-govern¦ment
    attributive
anti-gravity

An|tigua (town,
    Guatemala)
An|tigua
    Gua¦te|mala
    (= Antigua)
An|ti¦guan +s
anti-hero
    anti-heroes
anti|his¦ta|mine
anti-
    inflam¦ma¦tory
anti-inflation
    attributive
anti-Jacobin +s
anti|knock
Anti-Lebanon
    Moun|tains (in
    Near East)
An¦til|lean +s
An¦til¦les (islands,
    Caribbean)
anti-lock
anti|log +s
anti|log¦ar¦ithm +s
an|tilogy
an|tilo¦gies
anti|macas|sar +s
anti|mal¦ar¦ial
anti|masque +s
anti|mat¦ter
anti|metab¦ol¦ite
    +s
anti|mon¦arch|
    ic¦al
anti|monial
anti|mon¦ic
anti|moni|ous
an|tim¦ony
    (chemical
    element.
    ⚠ antinomy)
anti|node +s
anti|nomian +s
anti|nomian|ism
anti|nomy
    anti|nomies
    (contradiction
    between laws.
    ⚠ antimony)
anti|novel +s
anti-nuclear
An¦tioch (city,
    Turkey)
An¦tioch (city,
    ancient Phrygia)
An¦tio|chus
    (Seleucid kings)
anti|oxi¦dant +s
anti|par¦ticle +s
anti|pasto
    anti|pasti *or*
    anti|pas¦tos

anti|path¦et¦ic
anti|path¦et¦ic|al
anti|path¦et¦ic|
    al¦ly
anti|path¦ic
an|tip¦athy
    an|tip¦athies
anti-person¦nel
anti|per¦spir¦ant
    +s
anti|phlo¦gis|tic
anti|phon +s
an|tiph¦on|al
an|tiph¦on|al¦ly
an|tiph¦on|ary
    an|tiph¦on|ar¦ies
an|tiph¦ony
    an|tiph¦on|ies
anti|podal
anti|pode
An|tipo|dean +s
    (Australasian)
an|tipo|dean +s
    (generally)
An|tipo|des
    (Australasia)
an|tipo|des
    (generally)
anti|pole +s
anti|pope +s
anti|pro¦ton +s
anti|prur¦it¦ic
anti|pyr¦et¦ic +s
anti|quar¦ian +s
anti|quar¦ian|ism
anti|quary
    anti|quar¦ies
anti|quated
an|tique
    an|tiques
    an|tiqued
    an|tiquing
an|tiquity
    an|tiqui¦ties
anti-racism
anti-racist +s
anti-roll bar +s
an¦tir|rhinum +s
anti|sab¦bat|ar¦ian
    +s
Anti|sana (volcano,
    Ecuador)
anti|scor¦bu¦tic +s
anti|scrip¦tural
anti-Semite +s
anti-Semitic
anti-Semitism
anti|sep¦sis
anti|sep¦tic +s
anti|sep¦tic|al¦ly
anti|serum
    anti|sera

anti|social
anti|social|ly
anti|stat|ic
anti|stat|ic|al|ly
an|tis|tro|phe
anti|stroph|ic
anti-tank *attributive*
anti-terror|ist
attributive
anti|tet|anus
anti|the|ism
anti|the|ist +s
an|tith|esis
  an|tith|eses
anti|thet|ic
anti|thet|ic|al
anti|thet|ic|al|ly
anti|toxic
anti|toxin +s
anti|trade +s
anti|trini|tar|ian
anti|trust *attributive*
anti|type +s
anti|typ|ical
anti|ven|ene +s
anti|venin +s
anti|viral
anti|virus
  anti|viruses
anti|vivi|sec|tion|
         ism
anti|vivi|sec|tion|
         ist +s
ant|ler +s
ant|lered
ant-lion +s
An|to|fa|gasta
  (port and region,
  Chile)
An|toine
An|toin|ette
Anton
An|tonia
An|to|nine +s
An|to|ni|nus Pius
  (Roman emperor)
an|tono|ma|sia
An|tony *also*
  An|thony
An|tony of Padua
  (use Anthony of
  Padua)
ant|onym +s
ant|onym|ous
an|tral
An|trim (district,
  Northern Ireland)
an|trum
  antra
antsy

An|tung (former
  name of
  Dandong)
Ant|werp (port and
  province,
  Belgium)
Anu|bis *Egyptian
  Mythology*
Anura|dha|pura
  (city, Sri Lanka)
anur|an +s
anus
  anuses
anvil +s
anx|iety
  anx|ieties
anxio|lyt|ic
anx|ious
anx|ious|ly
anx|ious|ness
any
Anya|oku,
  Elea|zar
  (Nigerian
  diplomat)
any|body
any|how
any|more *Am.
  adverb (Br.* any
  more)
any more *Br.
  adverb (Am.*
  anymore)
any|one (anybody)
any one (any single
  one)
any|place
  (anywhere)
any road (anyway)
any|thing
any|time *Am.
  adverb (Br.* any
  time)
any time *Br.* adverb
  (*Am.* anytime)
any|way
any|ways
any|where
any|wise
Anzac +s
  (Australian or
  New Zealander,
  especially a
  soldier)
Anzus (= Australia,
  New Zealand, and
  United States)
ao dai +s
A-OK (= all systems
  OK)
A-okay (use A-OK)

Aor|angi (region
  and mountain,
  New Zealand)
aor|ist +s
aor|is|tic
aorta +s
aor|tic
Aosta (city, Italy)
Aotea|roa (Maori
  name for New
  Zealand)
aou|dad +s
à ou|trance
Aou|zou Strip
  (region, Chad)
apace
Apa|che +s
  (American Indian)
apa|che +s (street
  ruffian)
ap|an|age +s
apart
apart|heid
apart|ment +s
apart|ness
apa|thet|ic
apa|thet|ic|al|ly
ap|athy
apa|tite +s
apato|saurus
  apato|saur|uses
ape
  apes
  aped
  aping
apeak
Apel|doorn (town,
  the Netherlands)
ape|like
Apel|les (painter to
  Alexander the
  Great)
ape|man
  ape|men
Ap|en|nines
  (mountain range,
  Italy)
ap|erçu +s
aperi|ent +s
aperi|odic
aperi|od|icity
aperi|tif +s
aper|ture +s
apery
  aper|ies
apet|al|lous
APEX (Association
  of Professional,
  Executive,
  Clerical, and
  Computer Staff)

Apex (airline ticket
  system)
apex
  apexes *or* api|ces
  (point)
ap|fel|stru|del +s
aphaer|esis
  aphaer|eses
apha|sia
apha|sic +s
ap|he|lion
  ap|he|lia
aph|esis
  aph|eses
aphet|ic
aphet|ic|al|ly
aphid +s
aphis
  aphi|des
apho|nia
aph|ony
aph|or|ise *Br.* (use
  aphorize)
  aph|or|ises
  aph|or|ised
  aph|or|is|ing
aph|or|ism +s
aph|or|ist +s
aph|or|is|tic
aph|or|is|tic|al|ly
aph|or|ize
  aph|or|izes
  aph|or|ized
  aph|or|iz|ing
aph|ro|dis|iac +s
Aph|ro|dis|ias
  (ancient city,
  Turkey)
Aph|ro|dite *Greek
  Mythology*
aphyl|lous
Apia (capital of
  Western Samoa)
apian
api|ar|ian
api|ar|ist +s
api|ary
  api|ar|ies
ap|ical
ap|ic|al|ly
api|ces
api|cul|tural
api|cul|ture
api|cul|tur|ist
apiece
Apis *Egyptian
  Mythology*
apish
apish|ly
ap|ish|ness
ap|la|nat +s
ap|la|nat|ic

apla|sia
aplas|tic
aplenty
aplomb
apnea *Am.*
ap¦noea *Br.*
Apoca|lypse *Bible*
apoca|lypse +s
(generally)
apoca|lyp¦tic
apoca|lyp¦tic|al
apoca|lyp¦tic|al¦ly
apo|carp¦ous
apo|chro¦mat +s
apo|chro¦mat¦ic
apoc|ope +s
apo|crine
Apoc|rypha *Bible*
apoc|rypha
(spurious writings)
apoc¦ryph¦al
apoc¦ryph|al¦ly
apo¦dal
apo|dic¦tic
apo|dict¦ic|al¦ly
apo|dosis
apo|doses
apo|dous
apo|gean
apo¦gee +s
apo|laus¦tic
apol¦it¦ical
apol¦it¦ic|al¦ly
Apol¦lin|aire,
Guil|laume
(French writer)
Apol¦lin|ar¦ian +s
Apol¦lin|aris (early
bishop)
Apollo (*Greek
Mythology*;
American space
programme)
Apol¦lo|nian
Apol¦lon¦ius of
Perga (Greek
mathematician)
Apol¦lon¦ius of
Rhodes (Greek
poet)
Apol¦lyon (the
Devil)
apolo|get¦ic
apolo|get¦ic|al¦ly
apolo|get¦ics
apo|lo¦gia +s
apolo|gise *Br.* (use
apologize)
apolo|gises
apolo|gised
apolo|gis¦ing
apolo|gist +s

apolo|gize
apolo|gizes
apolo|gized
apolo|giz¦ing
apo|logue +s
apol|ogy
apolo|gies
apo|lune +s
apo|mic¦tic
apo|mixis
apo|phat¦ic
apoph|thegm *Br.*
+s (*Am.*
apothegm.
maxim.
⚠ apothem)
apoph|theg¦mat¦ic
Br. (*Am.*
apothegmatic)
apoph|theg¦mat¦ic|
al¦ly *Br.* (*Am.*
apothegmatic-
ally)
apo|plec¦tic
apo|plec¦tic|al¦ly
apo|plexy
apo|plex¦ies
apop|tosis
apop|totic
aporia +s
apo|sem¦at¦ic
apo|sio|pesis
apo|sio|peses
apos|tasy
apos|tas¦ies
apos|tate +s
apos|tat¦ical
apos¦ta|tise *Br.*
(use apostatize)
apos¦ta|tises
apos¦ta|tised
apos¦ta|tis¦ing
apos¦ta|tize
apos¦ta|tizes
apos¦ta|tized
apos¦ta|tiz¦ing
a pos¦teri|ori
*adjective and
adverb*
Apos¦tle +s *Bible*
apos¦tle +s (leader;
representative)
apostle-bird +s
Apos¦tles' Creed
apostle|ship +s
Apos¦tle spoon +s
apos¦to|late +s
apos¦tol¦ic +s
apos¦tol|ic|al
apos¦tol|ic|al¦ly
apos|tro|phe +s
apos|troph¦ic

apos¦tro|phise *Br.*
(use
apostrophize)
apos¦tro|phises
apos¦tro|phised
apos¦tro|phis¦ing
apos¦tro|phize
apos¦tro|phizes
apos¦tro|phized
apos¦tro|phiz¦ing
apoth|ecar¦ies'
measure +s
apoth|ecar¦ies'
weight +s
apoth|ecary
apoth|ecar¦ies
apo|thegm *Am.* +s
(*Br.* apophthegm.
maxim.
⚠ apothem)
apo|theg¦mat¦ic
Am. (*Br.*
apophthegmatic)
apo|theg¦mat¦ic|
al¦ly *Am.* (*Br.*
apophthegmatic-
ally)
apo|them +s
(*Geometry.*
⚠ apophthegm,
apothegm)
apothe|osis
apothe|oses
apotheo|sise *Br.*
(use apotheosize)
apotheo|sises
apotheo|sised
apotheo|sis¦ing
apotheo|size
apotheo|sizes
apotheo|sized
apotheo|siz¦ing
apo|tro¦paic
app +s
(= application)
appal *Br.*
ap¦pals
ap|palled
ap|pall¦ing
(*Am.* appall)
Ap¦pa|lach¦ian +s
Ap¦pa|lach¦ian
Moun|tains (in
USA)
Ap¦pa|lach¦ians
(= Appalachian
Mountains)
ap¦pall *Am.*
ap|palls
ap|palled
ap¦pall¦ing
(*Br.* appal)

ap¦pal|ling¦ly
Ap¦pa|loosa +s
ap¦pan|age +s (use
apanage)
ap|parat +s
ap¦par¦at|chik
ap¦par¦at|chiks *or*
ap¦par¦at|chiki
ap¦par|atus
plural ap¦par|atus
or ap¦par|atuses
ap¦par|atus
criti|cus
ap|parel
ap|parels
ap|par¦elled *Br.*
ap|par¦eled *Am.*
ap|parel|ling *Br.*
ap|parel|ing *Am.*
ap¦par|ent
ap|par¦ent¦ly
ap¦par|ition +s
ap|pari|tor +s
ap¦peal +s +ed
+ing
ap|peal|able
ap|peal|er +s
ap¦peal|ing¦ly
ap¦pear +s +ed
+ing
ap¦pear|ance +s
ap¦pease
ap|peases
ap|peased
ap|peas|ing
ap|pease|ment
ap|peaser +s
Appel, Karel
(Dutch painter)
ap¦pel|lant +s
ap¦pel|late
ap¦pel|la¦tion +s
ap¦pel¦la¦tion
con|trôlée
ap¦pel¦la¦tion
d'ori|gine
con|trôlée
ap¦pel|la¦tive +s
ap¦pend +s +ed
+ing
ap¦pend|age +s
ap¦pend|ant +s
ap¦pend|ec¦tomy
ap¦pend|
ec¦tomies
ap¦pen¦di|
cec¦tomy
ap¦pen¦di|
cec¦tomies
ap¦pen¦di|citis

ap|pen|dix
  ap|pen|di|ces *or*
  ap|pen|dixes
ap|per|ceive
  ap|per|ceives
  ap|per|ceived
  ap|per|ceiv|ing
ap|per|cep|tion +s
ap|per|cep|tive
ap|per|tain +s +ed
  +ing
ap|pe|tence +s
ap|pe|tency
  ap|pe|ten|cies
ap|pe|tent
ap|pe|tise *Br.* (use
  appetize)
  ap|pe|tises
  ap|pe|tised
  ap|pe|tis|ing
ap|pe|tiser *Br.* +s
  (use appetizer)
ap|pe|tis|ing|ly *Br.*
  (use appetizingly)
ap|pe|tite +s
ap|pe|ti|tive
ap|pe|tize
  ap|pe|tizes
  ap|pe|tized
  ap|pe|tiz|ing
ap|pe|tizer +s
ap|pe|tiz|ing|ly
Ap|pian Way
  (road, Roman
  Italy)
ap|plaud +s +ed
  +ing
ap|plause
apple +s
apple-cart +s
apple-cheeked
apple|jack +s
apple juice +s
apple-pie bed +s
apple-pie order
Apple|ton,
  Ed|ward (English
  physicist)
apple tree +s
ap|pli|ance +s
ap|plic|abil|ity
ap|plic|able
ap|plic|ably
ap|pli|cant +s
ap|pli|ca|tion +s
ap|pli|ca|tor +s
ap|plier +s
ap|pli|qué
  ap|pli|qués
  ap|pli|quéd
  ap|pli|qué|ing

apply
  ap|plies
  ap|plied
  ap|ply|ing
ap|pog|gia|tura +s
ap|point +s +ed
  +ing
ap|point|ee +s
ap|point|er +s
ap|point|ive
ap|point|ment +s
ap|port +s +ed
  +ing
ap|por|tion +s +ed
  +ing
ap|por|tion|able
ap|por|tion|ment
ap|po|site
ap|po|site|ly
ap|po|site|ness
ap|pos|ition +s
ap|pos|ition|al
ap|prais|able
ap|prais|al +s
ap|praise
  ap|praises
  ap|praised
  ap|prais|ing
ap|praisee +s
ap|praise|ment +s
ap|praiser +s
ap|prais|ing|ly
ap|prais|ive
ap|pre|ciable
ap|pre|ciably
ap|pre|ci|ate
  ap|pre|ci|ates
  ap|pre|ci|ated
  ap|pre|ci|at|ing
ap|pre|ci|ation +s
ap|pre|cia|tive
ap|pre|cia|tive|ly
ap|pre|cia|tive|
            ness
ap|pre|ci|ator +s
ap|pre|ci|atory
ap|pre|hend +s
  +ed +ing
ap|pre|hen|si|
          bil|ity
ap|pre|hen|sible
ap|pre|hen|sion +s
ap|pre|hen|sive
ap|pre|hen|sive|ly
ap|pre|hen|sive|
           ness
ap|pren|tice
  ap|pren|tices
  ap|pren|ticed
  ap|pren|ticing
ap|pren|tice|ship
  +s

ap|prise
  ap|prises
  ap|prised
  ap|pris|ing
  (inform)
ap|prize
  ap|prizes
  ap|prized
  ap|priz|ing
  (esteem highly;
  praise)
appro
ap|proach
  ap|proaches
  ap|proached
  ap|proach|ing
ap|proach|abil|ity
ap|proach|able
ap|pro|bate
  ap|pro|bates
  ap|pro|bated
  ap|pro|bat|ing
ap|pro|ba|tion
ap|pro|ba|tive
ap|pro|ba|tory
ap|pro|pri|ate
  ap|pro|pri|ates
  ap|pro|pri|ated
  ap|pro|pri|at|ing
ap|pro|pri|ate|ly
ap|pro|pri|ate|ness
ap|pro|pri|ation +s
ap|pro|pri|ation|ist
  +s
ap|pro|pria|tive
ap|pro|pri|ator +s
ap|prov|al +s
ap|prove
  ap|proves
  ap|proved
  ap|prov|ing
ap|prov|ing|ly
ap|proxi|mate
  ap|proxi|mates
  ap|proxi|mated
  ap|proxi|mat|ing
ap|proxi|mate|ly
ap|proxi|ma|tion
  +s
ap|proxi|ma|tive
ap|pur|ten|ance +s
ap|pur|ten|ant
après-ski
apri|cot +s
April (month;
  name)
April Fool +s
April Fool's Day
a pri|ori
apri|or|ism
apron +s
ap|roned

apron|ful +s
apron strings
apro|pos
apse +s
ap|sidal
apsis
  ap|si|des
apt +er +est
ap|ter|ous
ap|teryx
  ap|ter|yxes
ap|ti|tude +s
aptly
apt|ness
Apu|leius (Roman
  writer)
Apu|lia (region,
  Italy)
Aqaba (port,
  Jordan)
Aqaba, Gulf of
  (part of Red Sea)
aqua
aqua|cul|ture
aqua for|tis
aqua|lung +s
aqua|mar|ine +s
aqua|naut +s
aqua|plane
  aqua|planes
  aqua|planed
  aqua|plan|ing
aqua regia
aqua|relle +s
Aquar|ian +s
aqua|rist +s
aquar|ium
  aqua|ria *or*
  aquar|iums
Aquar|ius
  (constellation;
  sign of zodiac)
aqua|tic +s
aqua|tics
aqua|tint +s
aqua|vit
aqua vitae
aque|duct +s
aque|ous
aqui|fer +s
Aquila
  (constellation)
aqui|le|gia +s
aquil|line
Aqui|nas, Thomas
  (Italian saint)
Aqui|taine (region,
  France)
Arab +s
Ara|bella
ar|ab|esque
  ar|ab|esques

ar¦ab¦esque (*cont.*)
  ar¦ab¦esqued
  ar¦ab¦esquing
Ara¦bia
Ara¦bian +s
Arab¦ic (language)
arab¦ic (numerals;
  in 'gum arabic')
arab¦ica +s
Arabi¦cise *Br.* (use
  Arabicize)
  Arabi¦cises
  Arabi¦cised
  Arabi¦cis¦ing
Arabi¦cism +s
Arabi¦cize
  Arabi¦cizes
  Arabi¦cized
  Arabi¦ciz¦ing
ar¦abis
Ar¦ab¦ism +s
Arab-Israeli
  attributive
Arab¦ist +s
ar¦able
Araby (Arabia)
Ara¦cajú (port,
  Brazil)
Arachne *Greek
  Mythology*
arach¦nid +s
arach¦nid¦an +s
arach¦noid +s
arach¦no¦phobe +s
arach¦no¦pho¦bia
Ara¦fat, Yas¦ser
  (Palestinian
  leader)
Ara¦fura Sea (north
  of Australia)
Ara¦gon (region,
  Spain)
arak (use arrack)
Ara¦kan (former
  name of Rakhine)
Ar¦al¦dite *Propr.*
Aral Sea (in central
  Asia)
Ara¦maean +s
Ara¦maic
Aran (knitwear.
  △ Arran)
Ar¦anda
  plural Ar¦anda *or*
  Ar¦an¦das
Aran Is¦lands (off
  the Republic of
  Ireland. △ Arran)
Ara¦nyaka +s
  Hinduism
ara¦paima +s

Ara¦rat, Mount
  (two volcanic
  peaks, Turkey)
aration¦al
Arau¦can¦ian +s
arau¦caria +s
Ara¦wak
  plural Ara¦wak
arb +s
ar¦ba¦lest +s
ar¦bi¦ter +s
ar¦bi¦ter
  ele¦gan¦tiae
ar¦bi¦ter
  ele¦gan¦ti¦arum
ar¦bi¦trage
  ar¦bi¦trages
  ar¦bi¦traged
  ar¦bi¦tra¦ging
ar¦bi¦trager +s (use
  arbitrageur)
ar¦bi¦tra¦geur +s
ar¦bi¦tral
ar¦bi¦tra¦ment +s
ar¦bi¦trar¦ily
ar¦bi¦trari¦ness
ar¦bi¦trary
ar¦bi¦trate
  ar¦bi¦trates
  ar¦bi¦trated
  ar¦bi¦trat¦ing
ar¦bi¦tra¦tion +s
ar¦bi¦tra¦tor +s
ar¦bi¦tra¦tor¦ship
  +s
ar¦bi¦tress
  ar¦bi¦tresses
arb¦last +s
arbor +s (spindle.
  △ arbour)
arbor *Am.* +s
  (bower. *Br.*
  arbour)
ar¦bor¦aceous
Arbor Day
ar¦bor¦eal
ar¦bored *Am.* (*Br.*
  arboured)
ar¦bor¦eous
ar¦bor¦es¦cence
ar¦bor¦es¦cent
ar¦bor¦etum
  ar¦bor¦eta *or*
  ar¦bor¦etums
ar¦bori¦cul¦tural
ar¦bori¦cul¦ture
ar¦bori¦cul¦tur¦ist
  +s
ar¦bor¦isa¦tion *Br.*
  (use arborization)
ar¦bor¦iza¦tion
arbor vitae

ar¦bour *Br.* +s (*Am.*
  arbor. bower.
  △ arbor)
ar¦boured *Br.* (*Am.*
  arbored)
arbo¦virus
  arbo¦viruses
Arbus, Diane
  (American
  photographer)
Ar¦buth¦not, John
  (Scottish
  physician and
  writer)
ar¦bu¦tus
  ar¦bu¦tuses
arc +s +ed +ing
  (curve. △ ark)
ar¦cade +s
  ar¦caded
Ar¦ca¦dia (district,
  Greece; pastoral
  paradise)
Ar¦ca¦dian +s (of
  Arcadia.
  △ Acadian,
  Akkadian)
Ar¦ca¦dian¦ism
ar¦cad¦ing
Ar¦cady (pastoral
  paradise)
ar¦cane
ar¦cane¦ly
ar¦canum
  ar¦cana
Arc de Tri¦omphe
  (in Paris)
arch
  arches
  arched
  arch¦ing
Ar¦chaean *Br.* (*Am.*
  Archean)
arch¦aeo¦logic
arch¦aeo¦logic¦al
arch¦aeo¦logic¦
        al¦ly
archae¦olo¦gise *Br.*
  (use
  archaeologize)
  archae¦olo¦gises
  archae¦olo¦gised
  archae¦olo¦gis¦ing
archae¦olo¦gist +s
archae¦olo¦gize
  archae¦olo¦gizes
  archae¦olo¦gized
  archae¦olo¦giz¦ing
archae¦ology
arch¦aeo¦mag¦net¦
        ism

archae¦op¦teryx
  archae¦
      op¦ter¦yxes
ar¦chaic
ar¦cha¦ic¦al¦ly
ar¦cha¦ise *Br.* (use
  archaize)
  ar¦cha¦ises
  ar¦cha¦ised
  ar¦cha¦is¦ing
archa¦ism +s
archa¦ist +s
archa¦is¦tic
archa¦is¦tic¦al¦ly
ar¦cha¦ize
  ar¦cha¦izes
  ar¦cha¦ized
  ar¦cha¦iz¦ing
Arch¦an¦gel (port,
  Russia)
arch¦an¦gel +s
arch¦an¦gel¦ic
arch¦bishop +s
arch¦bish¦op¦ric
  +s
arch¦deacon +s
arch¦deacon¦ry
  arch¦deacon¦ries
arch¦deacon¦ship
  +s
arch¦dio¦cesan
arch¦dio¦cese +s
arch¦ducal
arch¦duch¦ess
  arch¦duch¦esses
arch¦duchy
  arch¦duch¦ies
arch¦duke +s
Ar¦chean *Am.* (*Br.*
  Archaean)
arche¦go¦nium
  arche¦go¦nia
arch-enemy
  arch-enemies
archeo¦logic *Am.*
  (*Br.*
  archaelologic)
archeo¦logic¦al
  Am. (*Br.*
  archaeological)
archeo¦logic¦al¦ly
  Am. (*Br.*
  archaeologically)
arche¦olo¦gist *Am.*
  +s (*Br.*
  archaeologist)
arche¦olo¦gize *Am.*
  arche¦olo¦gizes
  arche¦olo¦gized
  arche¦olo¦giz¦ing
  (*Br.*
  archaeologize)

arche|ology *Am.*
(*Br.* archaeology)
Arch|er, Jef|frey
(British writer and
politician)
Arch|er, the
(constellation;
sign of zodiac)
arch|er +s
arch|er fish
plural arch|er fish
arch|ery
arche|typal
arche|typ|al|ly
arche|type +s
arche|typ|ical
Archi|bald
archi|diac|onal
archi|diac|on|ate
+s
Ar|chie *also* Archy
archi|epis|copal
archi|epis|cop|ate
+s
ar|chil +s
Ar|chilo|chus
(Greek poet)
archi|man|drite +s
Archi|me|dean +s
Archi|me|des
(Greek
mathematician
and inventor)
Archi|me|des'
principle
archi|pel|ago +s
Archi|penko,
Alex|an|der
Por|fir|ye|vich
(Russian-born
American
sculptor)
Archi|piél|ago de
Colón (official
Spanish name for
the Galapagos
Islands)
archi|tect +s +ed
+ing
archi|tec|ton|ic
archi|tec|ton|ics
archi|tec|tural
archi|tec|tur|al|ly
archi|tec|ture +s
archi|trave +s
arch|ival
arch|ive +s
arch|iv|ist +s
archi|volt +s
arch|lute +s
arch|ly

arch|ness
ar|chon +s
ar|chon|ship +s
arch-rival +s
arch|way +s
Archy *also* Ar|chie
arc lamp +s
arc light +s
ar|cology
    ar|colo|gies
Arc|tic (north polar
    region)
arc|tic +s (very
    cold; overshoe)
Arc|turus (star)
ar|cu|ate
arcus sen|ilis
arc weld|ing
Arden, Eliza|beth
(Canadian-born
American
businesswoman)
ar|dency
Ar|dennes (region,
NW Europe)
ar|dent
ar|dent|ly
Ard|na|mur|chan
(peninsula,
Scotland)
ardor *Am.* +s
ar|dour *Br.* +s
ar|du|ous
ar|du|ous|ly
ar|du|ous|ness
are +s (in 'we are'
etc.; unit. △ ah)
area +s
areal (pertaining to
area. △ aerial,
ariel)
area|way +s
areca +s
areg (plural of erg,
'sand dunes')
arena +s
ar|en|aceous
Ar|endt, Han|nah
(German-born
American
philosopher)
aren't (are not.
△ an't, aunt)
areola
    areo|llae
areo|lar
Are|opa|gus (hill;
ancient Athenian
council)
Are|quipa (city,
Peru)

Ares (*Greek
Mythology.*
△ Aries)
arête +s
ar|gala +s
ar|gali
plural ar|gali
(sheep)
ar|gent
ar|gent|ifer|ous
Ar|gen|tina
Ar|gen|tine +s (of
Argentina;
Argentinian)
ar|gen|tine
(containing silver)
Ar|gen|tin|ian +s
argil
ar|gil|la|ceous
ar|gin|ine +s
Ar|give
Argo (constellation)
Argo (Jason's ship)
argol +s
argon
Ar|go|naut +s
(companion of
Jason)
ar|go|naut +s (sea
animal)
Argos (city, ancient
Greece. △ Argus)
ar|gosy
    ar|gos|ies
argot +s
ar|gu|able
ar|gu|ably
argue
    ar|gues
    ar|gued
    ar|gu|ing
ar|guer +s
ar|gufy
    ar|gu|fies
    ar|gu|fied
    ar|gu|fy|ing
ar|gu|ment +s
ar|gu|men|ta|tion
ar|gu|men|ta|tive
ar|gu|
    men|ta|tive|ly
ar|gu|men|ta|tive|
    ness
ar|gu|men|tum e
si|len|cio
Argus (*Greek
Mythology.*
△ Argos)
argus
    ar|guses
(butterfly;
pheasant)

Argus-eyed
ar|gute
ar|gute|ly
argy-bargy
    argy-bargies
    argy-bargied
    argy-bargying
Ar|gyll|shire
(former county,
Scotland)
Århus (use Aarhus)
aria +s
Ari|adne (name;
Greek Mythology)
Arian +s (of Arius.
△ Aryan)
Ar|ian|ism
arid
arid|ity
arid|ly
arid|ness
Ariel (spirit in *The
Tempest*; moon of
Uranus; name)
ariel +s (gazelle.
△ areal, aerial)
Ari|elle
Aries
(constellation;
sign of zodiac.
△ Ares)
aright
aril +s
aril|late
Arion (Greek poet
and musician)
ari|oso +s
Ari|osto,
Ludo|vico (Italian
poet)
arise
    arises
    arose
    aris|ing
    arisen
aris|ings
Ar|is|tar|chus
(Greek
astronomer; Greek
librarian and
commentator)
Ar|is|ti|des
(Athenian
statesman and
general)
Ar|is|tip|pus (two
Greek
philosophers)
ar|is|toc|racy
    ar|is|toc|ra|cies
ar|is|to|crat +s
ar|is|to|crat|ic

ar¦is¦to¦crat¦ic¦
al¦ly
Ar¦is¦topha¦nes
(Greek dramatist)
Ar¦is¦to¦tel¦ian+s
Ar¦is¦totle(Greek
philosopher)
Arita
arith¦met¦ic
arith¦met¦ic¦al
arith¦met¦ic¦al¦ly
arith¦met¦ician+s
Arius(Christian
theologian and
heretic)
Ari¦zona(state,
USA)
Ar¦juna Hinduism
ark+s (Judaism;
also in 'Noah's
Ark'. ⚠ arc)
Ar¦kan¦sas(state,
USA)
Ark¦wright,
Rich¦ard(English
inventor and
industrialist)
Ar¦lene
Arles(city, France)
Ar¦lette
Ar¦ling¦ton
(national
cemetery,
Virginia; city,
Texas)
Arlon(town,
Belgium)
arm+s +ed +ing
ar¦mada+s
ar¦ma¦dillo+s
Ar¦ma¦ged¦don
Ar¦magh(district,
Northern Ireland)
Ar¦mag¦nac+s
(area, France;
brandy)
ar¦ma¦ment+s
ar¦ma¦ment¦arium
ar¦ma¦ment¦aria
Ar¦mani, Gior¦gio
(Italian couturier)
ar¦ma¦ture+s
arm¦band+s
arm¦chair+s
Armco+s (crash
barrier) Propr.
arme blanche
armes blanches
Ar¦menia
Ar¦me¦nian+s (of
Armenia.
⚠ Arminian)

arm¦ful+s
arm¦hole+s
ar¦mi¦ger+s
ar¦mi¦ger¦ous
ar¦mil¦lary
ar¦mil¦lar¦ies
arm in arm
Ar¦mi¦nian+s (of
Arminius.
⚠ Armenian)
Ar¦mi¦nian¦ism
Ar¦mi¦nius(Dutch
theologian)
ar¦mis¦tice+s
arm¦less
arm¦let+s
arm¦load+s
arm¦lock+s +ed
+ing
ar¦moire+s
armorAm. +s +ed
+ing (Br. armour.
⚠ amah)
ar¦mor¦erAm. +s
(Br. armourer)
ar¦mor¦ial+s
ar¦mor¦ist+s
armor-plateAm.
(Br. armour-
plate)
armor-platedAm.
(Br. armour-
plated)
armor-platingAm.
(Br. armour-
plating)
ar¦mory
ar¦mor¦ies
(heraldry.
⚠ armoury)
ar¦mory Am.
ar¦mor¦ies
(arsenal; weapons.
Br. armoury)
ar¦mour Br. +s +ed
+ing (Am. armor.
⚠ amah)
ar¦mour¦er Br. +s
(Am. armorer)
armour-plate Br.
(Am. armor-plate)
armour-plated Br.
(Am. armor-
plated)
armour-plating Br.
(Am. armor-
plating)
ar¦moury Br.
ar¦mour¦ies
(Am. armory.
arsenal.
⚠ armory)

arm¦pit+s
arm¦rest+s
arms(weapons.
⚠ alms)
Arm¦strong,
Edwin How¦ard
(American
electrical
engineer)
Arm¦strong, Louis
(American jazz
musician)
Arm¦strong, Neil
(American
astronaut)
arm-twisting
arm-wrestling
army
ar¦mies
Arne, Thomas
(English
composer)
Arn¦hem(town, the
Netherlands)
Arn¦hem Land
(peninsula,
Australia)
ar¦nica
Arno(river, Italy)
Ar¦nold
Ar¦nold, Mat¦thew
(English writer)
aroid+s
aroma+s
aroma¦thera¦
peut¦ic
aroma¦ther¦ap¦ist
+s
aroma¦ther¦apy
aro¦mat¦ic+s
aro¦mat¦ic¦al¦ly
aroma¦ti¦city
aroma¦tisa¦tion Br.
(use
aromatization)
aroma¦tise Br. (use
aromatize)
aroma¦tises
aroma¦tised
aroma¦tis¦ing
aroma¦tiza¦tion
aroma¦tize
aroma¦tizes
aroma¦tized
aroma¦tiz¦ing
arose
around
arous¦able
arousal
arouse
arouses

arouse(cont.)
aroused
arous¦ing
arouser+s
Arp, Jeanalso
Hans
(French painter,
sculptor, and
poet)
ar¦peg¦gio+s
arque¦bus
arque¦buses
ar¦rack
ar¦raign
ar¦raigns
ar¦raigned
ar¦raign¦ing
ar¦raign¦ment+s
Arran(island,
Scotland. ⚠ Aran)
ar¦range
ar¦ranges
ar¦ranged
ar¦ran¦ging
ar¦range¦able
ar¦range¦ment+s
ar¦ran¦ger+s
ar¦rant
ar¦rant¦ly
Arras(town,
France)
arras
ar¦rases
(tapestry. ⚠ arris)
Arrau, Clau¦dio
(Chilean pianist)
array+s +ed +ing
ar¦rear+s
ar¦rear¦age+s
ar¦rest+s +ed +ing
ar¦rest¦able
ar¦rest¦ation
ar¦rest¦er+s
ar¦rest¦ing¦ly
ar¦rest¦ment+s
Ar¦rhen¦ius,
Svante Au¦gust
(Swedish chemist)
ar¦rhyth¦mia+s
arrière-pensée
+s
arris
ar¦rises
(Architecture.
⚠ arras)
ar¦rival+s
ar¦rive
ar¦rives
ar¦rived
ar¦riv¦ing
ar¦riv¦isme
ar¦riv¦iste+s

ar¦ro|gance
ar¦ro|gancy
ar¦ro|gant
ar¦ro|gant|ly
ar¦ro|gate
  ar¦ro|gates
  ar¦ro|gated
  ar¦ro|gat|ing
ar¦ro|ga¦tion
ar¦ron|disse|ment
  +s
Arrow, Ken|neth
  Jo¦seph
  (American
  economist)
arrow +s +ed +ing
arrow-grass
ar¦row|head +s
ar¦row|root
arrow slit +s
arrow-worm +s
ar¦rowy
ar¦royo +s
arse *Br.* +s (*coarse
  slang; Am.* ass)
arse|hole *Br.* +s
  (*coarse slang; Am.*
  asshole)
arse-licker *Br.* +s
  (*coarse slang; Am.*
  ass-licker)
arse-licking *Br.*
  (*coarse slang; Am.*
  ass-licking)
ar¦senal +s
ar¦senic
ar¦sen|ic|al
ar¦seni|ous
arses (plural of arse
  and arsis)
ars¦ine
arsis
  arses
arson
ar¦son|ist +s
ars|phen¦am¦ine
  +s
arsy-versy
Art (name)
art +s (creative skill
  etc.; in 'thou art')
Ar¦taud, An¦tonin
  (French actor etc.)
Ar¦ta|xer¦xes
  (Persian kings)
art deco
arte|fact +s
arte|fac¦tual
artel
  ar¦tels or ar¦teli
Ar¦te|mis (*Greek
  Mythology*; name)

ar¦te|misia +s
ar¦ter¦ial
ar¦teri¦al|isa¦tion
  Br. (use
  arterialization)
ar¦teri¦al|ise *Br.*
  (use arterialize)
ar¦teri¦al|ises
ar¦teri¦al|ised
ar¦teri¦al|is|ing
ar¦teri¦al|iza¦tion
ar¦teri¦al|ize
  ar¦teri¦al|izes
  ar¦teri¦al|ized
  ar¦teri¦al|iz|ing
ar¦teri|ole +s
ar¦terio|scler|osis
  ar¦terio|scler|oses
ar¦terio|scler|ot¦ic
ar¦ter|itis
ar¦tery
  ar¦ter|ies
ar¦te|sian
Artex *Propr.*
art form +s
art¦ful
art¦ful|ly
art¦ful|ness
art his¦tor|ian +s
art-historical
art his|tory
arth|rit¦ic +s
arth|ritis
arthro|pod +s
Ar¦thur
Ar¦thur (legendary
  king of Britain)
Ar¦thur, Ches¦ter
  Alan (American
  president)
Ar¦thur|ian +s
artic +s
ar¦ti|choke +s
art|icle
  art|icles
  art|icled
  art|ic¦ling
ar¦ticu|lacy
ar¦ticu|lar
ar¦ticu|late
  ar¦ticu|lates
  ar¦ticu|lated
  ar¦ticu|lat¦ing
ar¦ticu|late|ly
ar¦ticu|late|ness
ar¦ticu|la¦tion +s
ar¦ticu|la¦tor +s
ar¦ticu|la¦tory
ar¦ti|fact +s (use
  artefact)
ar¦ti|fac¦tual (use
  artefactual)

ar¦ti|fice +s
ar¦tifi|cer +s
ar¦ti|fi¦cial
ar¦ti|fi¦cial|ise *Br.*
  (use artificialize)
ar¦ti|fi¦cial|ises
ar¦ti|fi¦cial|ised
ar¦ti|fi¦cial|is|ing
ar¦ti|fi¦ci¦al|ity
ar¦ti|fi¦ci¦al|ities
ar¦ti|fi¦cial|ize
ar¦ti|fi¦cial|izes
ar¦ti|fi¦cial|ized
ar¦ti|fi¦cial|iz¦ing
ar¦ti|fi¦cial|ly
ar¦til¦ler|ist +s
ar¦til|lery
  ar¦til|ler¦ies
ar¦til¦lery|man
  ar¦til¦lery|men
arti|ness
artio|dac¦tyl +s
ar¦ti|san +s
ar¦ti|san|ate
art¦ist +s (painter)
ar¦tiste +s
  (performer)
art|is¦tic
art|is¦tic|al|ly
art|is¦try
art|less
art|less¦ly
art|less|ness
art nou|veau
Ar¦tois (region,
  France)
artsy-fartsy
art|work +s
arty
  art¦ier
  arti|est
arty-crafty
arty-farty
Aruba (island,
  Caribbean)
aru|gula
arum +s
Ar¦un|achal
  Pra|desh (state,
  India)
Ar¦unta (= Aranda)
  plural Ar¦unta *or*
  Ar¦un|tas
arvo +s
Arya|bhata I
  (Indian
  astronomer and
  mathematician)
Aryan +s (peoples;
  language.
  △ Arian)
aryl +s

as *preposition and
  conjunction*
as
  asses
  (Roman coin)
Asa
asa|foe¦tida
Asan|sol (city,
  India)
As¦ante (Twi name
  for Ashanti)
as|best|ine
as|bes¦tos
as|bes¦tos|ine
as|bes|tosis
As¦ca|lon (ancient
  city, Israel, site of
  Ashqelon)
as|carid +s
as|caris
  as|cari|des
  (worm. △ askari)
as|cend +s +ed
  +ing
as¦cend|ancy
  as|cend|an¦cies
as¦cend|ant +s
as¦cend¦er +s
As¦cen|sion (of
  Christ)
as¦cen|sion
  (generally)
As¦cen¦sion|al
As¦cen¦sion|tide
as¦cent +s (climb.
  △ assent)
as¦cen¦tion|ist +s
as¦cer|tain +s +ed
  +ing
as¦cer|tain|able
as¦cer|tain|ment
as|cesis
  as|ceses
as¦cet|ic +s
as¦cet|ic|al|ly
as¦ceti|cism
As¦cham, Roger
  (English scholar)
as¦cid|ian +s
ASCII (= American
  Standard Code for
  Information
  Interchange)
as|ci¦tes
  plural as|ci¦tes
As|cle¦piad +s
As|cle¦pius *Greek
  Mythology*
as|cor¦bic
Ascot (racecourse,
  England)
ascrib|able

ascribe
ascribes
ascribed
ascrib|ing
ascrip|tion +s
asdic
ASEAN
(= Association of
South East Asian
Nations)
ase|ity
asep|sis
asep|tic
asex|ual
asexu|al|ity
asexu|al|ly
As|gard *Norse Mythology*
ASH (= Action on
Smoking and
Health)
ash
ashes
ashamed
ashamed|ly
Ash|anti (region,
Ghana)
Ash|anti
plural Ash|anti
(people)
ash blonde +s
ash|can +s
Ash|croft, Peggy
(English actress)
Ash|dod (port,
Israel)
Ash|down, Paddy
(British politician)
Ashe, Ar|thur
(American tennis
player)
ashen
ashen-faced
Asher *Bible*
ashet +s
Ash|ga|bat (capital
of Turkmenistan)
Ash|ke|lon (ancient
Philistine city, site
of modern
Ashqelon)
Ash|ken|azi
Ash|ken|azim
Ash|ken|az|ic
Ash|ken|azy,
Vlad|imir
(Russian-born
Icelandic pianist)
ash-key +s
Ash|kha|bad
(use
Ashgabat)

ash|lar
ash|lar|ing
Ash|ley (name)
Ash|ley, Laura
(Welsh fashion
and textile
designer)
Ash|molean
Mu|seum (in
Oxford)
Ash|more and
Car|tier Is|lands
(in Indian Ocean)
ashore
ash|pan
ash|plant +s
Ash|qe|lon (resort,
Israel)
ash|ram +s
ash|rama +s
Hinduism
Ash|ton,
Fred|erick
(British dancer
and
choreographer)
ash|tray +s
Ashur (alternative
name for Assur)
Ashur|bani|pal
(Assyrian king)
ash|wood
ashy
ash|ier
ashi|est
Asia
Asia Minor
Asian +s
Asi|at|ic +s
(*offensive* when
used of people;
prefer Asian)
A-side +s
aside +s
Asi|mov, Isaac
(Russian-born
American writer)
as|in|ine
as|in|in|ity
Asir Moun|tains
(in Saudi Arabia)
ask +s +ed +ing
askance
as|kari
plural as|kari or
as|karis
(E. African soldier
or policeman.
△ ascaris)
asker +s
askew
aslant

asleep
Aslef (= Associated
Society of
Locomotive
Engineers and
Firemen)
AS level +s
aslope
As|mara (capital of
Eritrea)
As|mera
(alternative name
for Asmara)
aso|cial
aso|cial|ly
Asoka (Indian
emperor)
asp +s
as|para|gine
as|para|gus
as|par|tame
as|par|tic
as|pect +s
as|pect|ed
as|pect|ual
Aspen (city, USA)
aspen +s (tree)
as|per|gil|lum
as|per|gilla or
as|per|gil|lums
as|per|ity
as|perse
as|perses
as|persed
as|pers|ing
as|per|sion +s
as|per|sor|ium
as|per|soria
as|phalt
as|phalt|er +s
as|phal|tic
as|pho|del +s
as|phyxia
as|phyx|ial
as|phyxi|ant +s
as|phyxi|ate
as|phyxi|ates
as|phyxi|ated
as|phyxi|at|ing
as|phyxi|ation
as|phyxi|ator +s
aspic
as|pi|dis|tra +s
as|pir|ant +s
as|pir|ate
as|pir|ates
as|pir|ated
as|pir|at|ing
as|pir|ation +s
as|pir|ation|al
as|pir|ator +s

as|pire
as|pires
as|pired
as|pir|ing
as|pirin
plural as|pirin or
as|pir|ins
as|plen|ium
asquint
As|quith, Her|bert
Henry (British
prime minister)
ass
asses
(donkey)
ass *Am.*
asses
(*coarse slang*
buttocks; *Br.* arse)
Assad, Hafiz al-
(Syrian Baath
statesman)
as|sa|gai +s (use
assegai)
assai
as|sail +s +ed +ing
as|sail|able
as|sail|ant +s
Assam (state, India;
tea)
As|sam|ese
plural As|sam|ese
as|sas|sin +s
as|sas|sin|ate
as|sas|sin|ates
as|sas|sin|ated
as|sas|sin|at|ing
as|sas|sin|ation +s
as|sas|sin|ator +s
as|sault +s +ed
+ing
as|sault|er +s
as|sault|ive
assay +s +ed +ing
as|say|able
as|se|gai +s
as|sem|blage
as|sem|ble
as|sem|bles
as|sem|bled
as|sem|bling
as|sem|bler +s
as|sem|bly
as|sem|blies
as|sem|bly line +s
as|sem|bly|man
as|sem|bly|men
as|sent +s +ed
+ing (agree.
△ ascent)

as|sent|er +s
(person who
assents)
as|sen|tient
as|sent|or +s (in
nomination of
candidate)
as|sert +s +ed
+ing
as|sert|er +s (use
assertor)
as|ser|tion +s
as|sert|ive
as|sert|ive|ly
as|sert|ive|ness
as|sert|or +s
asses (plural of as
and ass)
asses' bridge
as|sess
   as|sesses
   as|sessed
   as|sess|ing
as|sess|able
as|sess|ment +s
as|ses|sor +s
as|ses|sor|ial
asset +s
asset-strip
   asset-strips
   asset-stripped
   asset-stripping
asset-stripper +s
as|sev|er|ate
   as|sev|er|ates
   as|sev|er|ated
   as|sev|er|at|ing
as|sev|er|ation +s
ass|hole Am. +s
   (coarse slang; Br.
   arsehole)
as|sibi|late
   as|sibi|lates
   as|sibi|lated
   as|sibi|lat|ing
as|sibi|la|tion
as|si|du|ity
as|sidu|ous
as|sidu|ous|ly
as|sidu|ous|ness
as|sign +s +ed
   +ing
as|sign|able
as|sig|na|tion +s
as|sign|ee +s
as|sign|er +s
as|sign|ment +s
as|sign|or +s Law
as|sim|il|able
as|simi|late
   as|simi|lates

as|simi|late (cont.)
   as|simi|lated
   as|simi|lat|ing
as|simi|la|tion +s
as|simi|la|tion|ist
   +s
as|simi|la|tive
as|simi|la|tor +s
as|simi|la|tory
As|sisi (town, Italy)
as|sist +s +ed +ing
as|sist|ance
as|sist|ant +s
as|sist|er +s
as|size +s
ass-kissing Am.
ass-licker Am. +s
   (coarse slang; Br.
   arse-licker)
ass-licking Am.
   (coarse slang; Br.
   arse-licking)
as|so|ci|abil|ity
as|so|ci|able
as|so|ci|ate
   as|so|ci|ates
   as|so|ci|ated
   as|so|ci|at|ing
as|so|ci|ate|ship
   +s
as|so|ci|ation +s
as|so|ci|ation|al
As|so|ci|ation
   Foot|ball
as|so|ci|ation|ist
   +s
as|so|cia|tive
as|so|ci|ator +s
as|so|cia|tory
as|soil +s +ed +ing
as|son|ance +s
as|son|ant +s
as|son|ate
   as|son|ates
   as|son|ated
   as|son|at|ing
as|sort +s +ed
   +ing
as|sorta|tive
as|sort|ment +s
as|suage
   as|suages
   as|suaged
   as|sua|ging
as|suage|ment
as|sua|ger +s
As
   Su|lay|man|iyah
   (full name of
   Sulaymaniyah)
as|sum|able

as|sume
   as|sumes
   as|sumed
   as|sum|ing
   as|sumed|ly
As|sump|tion (of
   Virgin Mary)
as|sump|tion +s
   (act of assuming
   etc.)
as|sump|tive
Assur (ancient city-
   state of
   Mesopotamia)
as|sur|able
as|sur|ance +s
as|sure
   as|sures
   as|sured
   as|sur|ing
   as|sured|ly
   as|sured|ness
as|surer +s
As|syria
As|syr|ian +s
As|syri|olo|gist +s
As|syri|ology
astable
As|taire, Fred
   (American dancer
   etc.)
As|tarte Semitic
   Mythology
astat|ic
as|ta|tine
aster +s
as|ter|isk
   as|ter|isks
   as|ter|isked
   as|ter|isk|ing
as|ter|ism
As|terix (cartoon
   character)
astern
as|ter|oid +s
as|ter|oid|al
as|the|nia
as|then|ic +s
as|theno|sphere
asthma
asth|mat|ic +s
asth|mat|ic|al|ly
Asti +s (wine)
astig|matic
astig|ma|tism
as|tilbe +s
astir
Asti spu|mante
Aston, Fran|cis
   Wil|liam (British
   physicist)

as|ton|ish
as|ton|ishes
as|ton|ished
as|ton|ish|ing
as|ton|ish|ing|ly
as|ton|ish|ment +s
Astor, Nancy
   (Lady Astor,
   American-born
   British politician)
as|tound +s +ed
   +ing
as|tound|ing|ly
astrad|dle
As|traea (Roman
   Mythology;
   asteroid)
as|tra|gal +s
as|trag|alus
   as|trag|ali
As|tra|khan (city,
   Russia)
as|tra|khan (fleece)
as|tral
astray
As|trid
astride
astrin|gency
   astrin|gen|cies
astrin|gent +s
astrin|gent|ly
astro|biol|ogy
astro|bot|any
astro|chem|is|try
astro|dome +s
astro|hatch
   astro|hatches
as|troid +s
astro|labe +s
as|trol|oger +s
astro|logic
astro|logic|al
astro|logic|al|ly
as|trol|ogy
astro|naut +s
astro|naut|ic|al
astro|naut|ics
as|tron|omer +s
astro|nom|ic
astro|nom|ic|al
astro|nom|ic|al|ly
as|tron|omy
astro|phys|ic|al
astro|physi|cist +s
astro|phys|ics
Astro'Turf Propr.
As|tur|ias (region,
   Spain)
As|tur|ias,
   Ma|nuel Ángel
   (Guatemalan
   writer)

as¦tute
as¦tute¦ly
as¦tute¦ness
Asun¦ción (capital of Paraguay)
asun¦der
Asur (use Assur)
asura +s
Aswan (city and dam, Egypt)
asy¦lum +s
asym¦met¦ric
asym¦met¦ric¦al
asym¦met¦ric¦al¦ly
asym¦metry
 asym¦met¦ries
asymp¦tom¦at¦ic
asymp¦tote +s
asymp¦tot¦ic
asymp¦tot¦ic¦al¦ly
asyn¦chron¦ous
asyn¦chron¦ous¦ly
asyn¦det¦ic
asyn¦deton
 asyn¦deta
at
At¦ab¦rine Propr.
Ata¦cama Des¦ert (in Chile)
Ata¦lanta Greek Mythology
at¦ar¦ac¦tic
at¦ar¦axia
at¦ar¦axic
at¦ar¦axy
Ata¦türk, Kemal (Turkish general and statesman)
at¦av¦ism
at¦av¦is¦tic
at¦av¦is¦tic¦al¦ly
ataxia
ataxic
ataxy
at bat +s Baseball
ate (past tense of eat. △ ait, eight)
A-team +s
At¦eb¦rin Propr.
atel¦ier +s
a tempo
Aten Egyptian Mythology
Atha¦basca, Lake (in Canada)
Atha¦bas¦can +s (use Athapaskan)
Atha¦na¦sian +s
Athan¦as¦ius
Atha¦pas¦kan +s
Atharva-veda
 Hinduism

athe¦ism
athe¦ist +s
athe¦is¦tic
athe¦is¦tic¦al
athel¦ing +s
Athel¦stan (Anglo-Saxon king)
athem¦at¦ic
Athen¦aeum (temple; London club)
athen¦aeum Br. +s (institution; library. Am. atheneum)
Athe¦ne Greek Mythology
athen¦eum Am. +s (institution; library. Br. athenaeum)
Athen¦ian +s
Ath¦ens (capital of Greece)
ath¦ero¦scler¦osis
 ath¦ero¦scler¦oses
ath¦ero¦scler¦ot¦ic
Ather¦ton Table¦land (in Australia)
athirst
ath¦lete +s
ath¦lete's foot
ath¦let¦ic
ath¦let¦ic¦al¦ly
ath¦leti¦cism
ath¦let¦ics
at-home +s noun
Athos, Mount (in Greece)
athwart
atilt
At¦kin¦son, Harry (New Zealand prime minister)
At¦lanta (city, USA)
At¦lan¦tean +s
at¦lan¦tes
At¦lan¦tic (Ocean)
At¦lan¦ti¦cism
At¦lan¦ti¦cist +s
At¦lan¦tis (legendary island)
Atlas Greek Mythology
atlas
 at¦lases (book; bone)
Atlas Moun¦tains (in N. Africa)
atman

at¦mos¦phere +s
at¦mos¦pher¦ic
at¦mos¦pher¦ic¦al
at¦mos¦pher¦ic¦al¦ly
at¦mos¦pher¦ics
atoll +s
atom +s
atom bomb +s
atom¦ic
atom¦ic¦al¦ly
atom¦ic¦ity
atom¦isa¦tion Br. (use atomization)
atom¦ise Br. (use atomize)
atom¦ises
atom¦ised
atom¦is¦ing
atom¦iser Br. +s (use atomizer)
atom¦ism
atom¦ist +s
atom¦is¦tic
atom¦is¦tic¦al¦ly
atom¦iza¦tion
atom¦ize
atom¦izes
atom¦ized
atom¦iz¦ing
atom¦izer +s
atom smash¦er +s
atomy
 atom¦ies
Aton (use Aten)
atonal
aton¦al¦ity
aton¦al¦ly
atone
 atones
 atoned
 aton¦ing
atone¦ment +s
atonic
atony
atop
atra¦bili¦ous
At¦reus Greek Mythology
at¦rial
at¦rium
 atria or at¦riums
atro¦cious
atro¦cious¦ly
atro¦cious¦ness
atro¦city
 atro¦ci¦ties
at¦ro¦phy
 at¦ro¦phies
 at¦ro¦phied
 at¦ro¦phy¦ing
at¦ro¦pine

At¦ro¦pos Greek Mythology
at¦ta¦boy
at¦tach
 at¦taches
 at¦tached
 at¦tach¦ing
at¦tach¦able
at¦taché +s
at¦taché case +s
at¦tach¦er +s
at¦tach¦ment +s
at¦tack +s +ed +ing
at¦tack¦er +s
at¦tain +s +ed +ing
at¦tain¦abil¦ity
at¦tain¦able
at¦tain¦able¦ness
at¦tain¦der +s
at¦tain¦ment +s
at¦taint
At¦ta¦lid +s
attar +s
at¦tem¦per +s +ed +ing
at¦tempt +s +ed +ing
at¦tempt¦able
At¦ten¦bor¦ough, David (British naturalist)
At¦ten¦bor¦ough, Rich¦ard (British film director etc.)
at¦tend +s +ed +ing
at¦tend¦ance +s
at¦tend¦ant +s
at¦tend¦ee +s
at¦tend¦er +s
at¦ten¦tion +s
at¦ten¦tion¦al
at¦ten¦tive
at¦ten¦tive¦ly
at¦ten¦tive¦ness
at¦tenu¦ate
 at¦tenu¦ates
 at¦tenu¦ated
 at¦tenu¦at¦ing
at¦tenu¦ation
at¦tenu¦ator +s
at¦test +s +ed +ing
at¦test¦able
at¦test¦ation
at¦test¦or +s
Attic (of Attica; language)
attic +s (room in roof)

At¦tica
(promontory,
Greece)
at¦ti¦cism
At¦tila (king of the
Huns)
at¦tire
  at¦tires
  at¦tired
  at¦tir¦ing
Attis *Anatolian
Mythology*
at¦ti¦tude +s
at¦ti¦tu¦dinal
at¦ti¦tu¦din¦ise *Br.*
(use attitudinize)
  at¦ti¦tu¦din¦ises
  at¦ti¦tu¦din¦ised
  at¦ti¦tu¦din¦is¦ing
at¦ti¦tu¦din¦ize
  at¦ti¦tu¦din¦izes
  at¦ti¦tu¦din¦ized
  at¦ti¦tu¦din¦iz¦ing
Att¦lee, Clem¦ent
(British prime
minister)
atto|meter *Am.* +s
atto|metre *Br.* +s
at¦tor|ney +s
Attorney-General
  Attorneys-
  General *or*
  Attorney-
  Generals
at¦torney|ship +s
at¦tract +s +ed
  +ing
at¦tract|able
at¦tract|ant +s
at¦trac¦tion +s
at¦tract|ive
at¦tract|ive¦ly
at¦tract¦ive|ness
at¦tract¦or +s
at¦trib|ut|able
at¦trib|ut|able|
           ness
at¦trib|ut|ably
at¦tri|bute +s *noun*
at¦trib|ute
  at¦trib|utes
  at¦trib|uted
  at¦trib|ut|ing
  verb
at¦tri|bu|tion +s
at¦tribu|tive
at¦tribu|tive¦ly
at¦trit
  at¦trits
  at¦trit|ted
  at¦trit|ting
at¦tri|tion

at¦tri|tion|al
at¦tune
  at¦tunes
  at¦tuned
  at¦tun|ing
At¦wood,
  Mar|ga|ret
  (Canadian writer)
atyp|ical
atyp|ic|al¦ly
au¦bade +s
au|berge +s
au¦ber|gine +s
Au|beron
Aub¦rey (name)
Aub¦rey, John
  (English
  antiquarian and
  writer)
au¦brie|tia +s
au¦burn +s
Au¦bus|son +s
  (town, France;
  tapestry)
Auck|land (city,
  New Zealand)
au cour|ant
auc|tion +s +ed
  +ing
auc|tion|eer +s
auc|tion|eer|ing
auc|tion house +s
au|da¦cious
au|da¦cious|ly
au|da¦cious|ness
au|da¦city
Auden, W. H.
  (British poet)
Au|den|arde
  (French name for
  Oudenarde)
Audh (use Oudh)
audi|bil¦ity
aud|ible
aud|ible|ness
aud|ibly
audi|ence +s
aud|ile +s
audio +s
audio-animatron
  +s
audio-
  animatron¦ic
  Propr.
Audio-
  Animatron¦ics
  Propr.
audio cas|sette +s
audi|olo¦gist +s
audi|ology
audi|om¦eter +s
audi|om¦etry

audio|phile +s
audio|tape +s
audio typ|ist +s
audio-visual
audit +s +ed +ing
au|di¦tion +s +ed
  +ing
audi|tive
au|dit¦or +s
audi|tor¦ial
audi|tor¦ium
  audi|tor¦iums *or*
  audi|toria
audi|tory
Audra
Aud¦rey
Au¦du|bon, John
  James (American
  naturalist and
  artist)
Auer von
  Wels|bach, Carl
  (Austrian chemist)
au fait
au fond
Au¦gean
Au¦geas *Greek
  Mythology*
auger +s (tool.
  ⚠ augur)
aught (anything.
  ⚠ ought)
aug¦ite +s
aug¦ment +s +ed
  +ing
aug¦men|ta¦tion +s
aug|men|ta¦tive
aug¦ment¦er +s
Au¦gra|bies Falls
  (in South Africa)
au grand séri|eux
au gra¦tin
Augs|burg (city,
  Germany)
augur +s +ed +ing
  (portend;
  interpreter of
  omens. ⚠ auger)
au|gural
au|gury
  au|gur|ies
Au¦gust +s (month)
au¦gust (venerable)
Au¦gusta (cities,
  USA; name)
Au¦gust|an +s
Au¦gust|ine (Italian
  saint)
Au¦gust|ine +s
  (friar)

Au¦gust|ine of
  Hippo (N. African-
  born saint)
Au¦gust|in¦ian +s
au|gust¦ly
au|gust|ness
Au¦gus|tus (Roman
  emperor; name)
auk +s (bird. ⚠ orc)
auk|let +s
auld
auld lang syne
aulic
aum¦bry
  aum|bries
au nat|urel
Aung San
  (Burmese
  nationalist leader)
Aung San Suu Kyi
  (Burmese political
  leader, daughter of
  Aung San)
aunt +s (parent's
  sister. ⚠ an't,
  aren't)
Auntie (= BBC)
auntie +s (aunt)
Aunt Sally
  Aunt Sal|lies
  (game)
aunty (use auntie)
  aunt|ies
au pair +s
aura
  auras *or* aurae
aural (of the ear.
  ⚠ oral)
aur|al¦ly
Aur|ang|zeb
  (Mogul emperor
  of Hindustan)
aure|ate
Aur|elia
Aur|elian (Roman
  emperor)
aur|elian +s
  (lepidopterist)
Aur|elius, Mar¦cus
  (Roman emperor)
aure|ola +s
aure|ole +s
aureo|my¦cin
au re|voir +s
Auric, Georges
  (French
  composer)
auric (of trivalent
  gold)
aur|icle +s
aur¦ic|ula +s
aur¦icu|lar

aur'icu'lar'ly
aur'icu'late
aur'if'er'ous
Aur'iga
(constellation)
Aur'ig'na'cian +s
auri'scope +s
aur'ist +s
aur'ochs
plural aur'ochs
Aur'ora (*Roman
Mythology*; name)
aur'ora
  aur'oras *or*
  aur'orae
  (atmospheric
  lights)
aur'ora aus'tralis
aur'ora bor'ealis
aur'oral
Ausch'witz
  (concentration
  camp, Poland)
aus'cul'ta'tion
aus'cul'ta'tory
au séri'eux
aus'pi'cate
  aus'pi'cates
  aus'pi'cated
  aus'pi'cat'ing
aus'pice +s
aus'pi'cious
aus'pi'cious'ly
aus'pi'cious'ness
Aus'sie +s
Aus'ten, Jane
  (English novelist)
aus'tere
  aus'terer
  aus'terest
aus'tere'ly
aus'ter'ity
  aus'ter'ities
Aus'ter'litz (battle
  site, Czech
  Republic)
Aus'tin (city, USA;
  name)
Aus'tin +s (friar)
Aus'tin, Her'bert
  (British car maker)
Aus'tin, John
  (English jurist)
Aus'tin, John
  Lang'shaw
  (English
  philospher)
Aus'tral (of
  Australia or
  Australasia)
aus'tral (southern)
Austra'lasia

Austra'la'sian +s
Aus'tra'lia
Aus'tra'lian +s
Aus'tra'li'ana
Aus'tra'lian'ise *Br.*
  (use
  Australianize)
  Aus'tra'lian'ises
  Aus'tra'lian'ised
  Aus'tra'lian'is'ing
Aus'tra'lian'ism
  +s
Aus'tra'lian'ize
  Aus'tra'lian'izes
  Aus'tra'lian'ized
  Aus'tra'lian'iz'ing
Aus'tra'lian Rules
Austral'oid +s
aus'tralo|
        pith'ecine +s
Aus'tralo|pith'ecus
Aus'tria
Austria–Hungary
Aus'trian +s
Austro-Hungar'ian
Austro|nes'ian +s
aut|arch'ic
aut|arch'ic'al
aut|archy (absolute
  sovereignty.
  ⚠ autarky)
aut|ark'ic
aut|ark'ic'al
aut|ark'ist +s
aut|arky (self-
  sufficiency.
  ⚠ autarchy)
au'teur +s
au'teur'ism
au'teur'ist
au'then'tic +s
au'then'tic'al'ly
au'then'ti'cate
  au'then'ti'cates
  au'then'ti'cated
  au'then'ti'cat'ing
au'then'ti'ca'tion
  +s
au'then'ti'ca'tor
  +s
au'then'ti'city
author +s +ed
  +ing
author|ess
  author|esses
au'thor'ial
au'thor'isa'tion *Br.*
  (use
  authorization)
au'thor'ise *Br.* (use
  authorize)
  au'thor'ises

au'thor'ise (*cont.*)
  au'thor'ised
  au'thor'is'ing
au'thori'tar'ian +s
au'thori'tar'ian|
         ism
au'thori'ta'tive
au'thori'ta'tive'ly
au'thori'ta'tive|
         ness
au'thor'ity
  au'thor'ities
au'thor'iza'tion
au'thor'ize
  au'thor'izes
  au'thor'ized
  au'thor'iz'ing
author|ship
aut'ism
aut'is'tic
auto +s
auto|bahn +s
auto|biog'raph'er
  +s
auto|bio'graph'ic
auto|bio'graph|
        ic'al
auto|biog'raphy
  auto|
      biog'raph'ies
auto|cade +s
auto|car +s
auto|cata|lyst +s
auto|ceph'al'ous
au'toch'thon
  au'toch|thons *or*
  au'toch|thones
au'toch'thon'al
au'toch'thon'ic
au'toch'thon'ous
auto|clave +s
auto|code +s
auto'toc'racy
  au'toc'ra'cies
auto|crat +s
auto|crat'ic
auto|crat'ic'al'ly
auto|cross
auto|cue +s Propr.
auto|cycle +s
auto-da-fé +s
auto|didact +s
auto|didac'tic
auto-erotic
auto-eroticism
auto-erotism
auto|focus
au'tog'am'ous
au'tog'amy
auto|gen'ic
au'togen'ous
auto|giro +s

auto|graft +s
auto|graph +s +ed
  +ing
auto|graph'ic
aut'og'raphy
auto|gyro +s (use
  autogiro)
auto|harp +s
auto|immune
auto|immun'ity
auto|intoxi'ca'tion
au'toly'sis
auto|lyt'ic
auto|mat +s
auto|mate
  auto|mates
  auto|mated
  auto|mat'ing
auto|mat'ic +s
auto|mat'ic'al'ly
auto|ma'ti'city
auto|ma'tion
au'toma|tisa'tion
  Br. (use
  automatization)
au'toma|tise *Br.*
  (use automatize)
  au'toma|tises
  au'toma|tised
  au'toma|tis'ing
au'toma|tism
au'toma|tiza'tion
auto|ma'tize
  auto|ma'tizes
  auto|ma'tized
  auto|ma'tiz'ing
au'toma|ton
  au'toma|tons *or*
  au'tom|ata
auto|mo'bile +s
auto|mo'tive
auto|nomic
au'tono|mist +s
au'tono|mous
au'tono|mous'ly
au'ton|omy
  au'ton|omies
auto|pilot +s
auto|pista +s
auto|poly|ploid +s
auto|poly|ploidy
aut|opsy
  aut|op'sies
  aut|op'sied
  aut|opsy|ing
auto|radio|graph
auto|radio|
      graph'ic
auto|radi|og'raphy
auto|rotate
  auto|rotates

auto|rotate (*cont.*)
  auto|rotated
  auto|rotat|ing
auto|rota|tion +s
auto|route +s
auto|strada
  auto|stra|das
auto-suggestion
auto|tel|ic
au|tot|omy
auto|toxic
auto|toxin +s
auto|troph|ic
auto|type +s
aut|oxi|da|tion
au|tumn +s
au|tum|nal
Au|vergne (region, France)
aux|an|ometer +s
aux|il|iary
  aux|il|iar|ies
auxin +s
Av (alternative name for Ab)
Ava
ava|da|vat +s
avail +s +ed +ing
avail|abil|ity
  avail|abil|ities
avail|able
avail|able|ness
avail|ably
ava|lanche
  ava|lanches
  ava|lanched
  ava|lanch|ing
Ava|lon (in Arthurian Legend)
avant-garde +s
avant-gardism
avant-gardist +s
Avar +s
avar|ice
avar|icious
avar|icious|ly
avar|icious|ness
avast
ava|tar +s
avaunt
Ave +s (prayer)
ave +s (welcome; farewell)
Ave|bury (village and ancient monument, England)
avenge
  avenges
  avenged
  aven|ging
aven|ger +s

avens
  plural avens
aven|tur|ine
av|enue +s
aver
  avers
  averred
  aver|ring
aver|age
  aver|ages
  aver|aged
  aver|aging
aver|age|ly
aver|ment
Aver|nus (lake, Italy)
Aver|roës (Islamic philosopher)
averse
aver|sion +s
aver|sive
avert +s +ed +ing
avert|able (use avertible)
avert|ible
Avery
Avesta
Aves|tan
Aves|tic +s
av|go|lem|ono
avian +s
avi|ary
  avi|ar|ies
avi|ate
  avi|ates
  avi|ated
  avi|at|ing
avi|ation
avi|ator +s
avia|trix
  avi|at|ri|ces
  female
Avi|cenna (Islamic philosopher and physician)
avi|cul|ture
avi|cul|tur|ist +s
avid
avid|ity
avid|ly
Avie|more (resort, Scotland)
avi|fauna
avi|faunal
Avi|gnon (city, France)
Ávila, Ter|esa of (Spanish saint)
avi|on|ics
avit|amin|osis
  avit|amin|oses
aviz|an|dum

avo|cado +s
avo|ca|tion
avo|cet +s
Avo|gadro, Ama|deo (Italian physicist)
avoid +s +ed +ing
avoid|able
avoid|ably
avoid|ance
avoid|er +s
avoir|du|pois
Avon (county and rivers, England)
avouch
  avouches
  avouched
  avouch|ing
avouch|ment +s
avow +s +ed +ing
avow|able
avow|al +s
avow|ed|ly
Avril
avul|sion
avun|cu|lar
AWACS
  plural AWACS
  (= airborne warning and control system)
Awadh (= Oudh)
await +s +ed +ing
awake
  awakes
  awoke
  awak|ing
  awoken
awaken +s +ed +ing
award +s +ed +ing
award|er +s
award-winning
  attributive
aware
aware|ness
  aware|nesses
awash
away
awe
  awes
  awed
  awing
aweary
aweigh
awe-inspir|ing
awe|some
awe|some|ly
awe|some|ness
awe|stricken
awe|struck
awful

aw|ful|ly
aw|ful|ness
awheel
awhile
awk|ward
awk|ward|ly
awk|ward|ness
awl +s (tool. Δ all, orle)
awn +s
awned
awn|ing +s
awoke
awoken
AWOL (= absent without leave)
awry
aw-shucks
  adjective
ax *Am.*
  axes
  axed
  axing
axe *Br.*
  axes
  axed
  axing
axe-breaker +s
axel +s (skating movement. Δ axil, axle)
axe|man *Br.*
axe|men
  (*Am.* axman)
axes (plural of ax, axe, and axis)
axial
axi|al|ity
axi|al|ly
axil +s (angle between leaf and stem. Δ axel, axle)
ax|illa
  ax|il|lae
ax|il|lary
axio|logic|al
axi|olo|gist +s
axi|ology
axiom +s
axio|mat|ic
axio|mat|ic|al|ly
Axis (German alliance)
axis
  axes
axle +s (spindle connecting wheels. Δ axel, axil)
axled

axle-tree +s
axman *Am.*
  axmen
  (*Br.* axeman)
Ax|min|ster +s
  (town, England;
  carpet)
axo|lotl +s
axon +s
axono|met|ric
Axum (use Aksum)
ay +s (yes; vote;
  use aye. △ eye, I)
Aya|cucho (city,
  Peru)
ayah +s (nurse.
  △ ire)
aya|tol|lah +s
Aya|tol|lah
  Kho|meini
  (Iranian Shiite
  Muslim leader)
Ayck|bourn, Alan
  (English
  playwright)
aye +s (yes; vote.
  △ eye, I)
aye (always. △ eh)
aye aye (*Nautical*
  yes)
aye-aye +s (lemur)
Ayer, A. J. (English
  philosopher)
Ayers Rock (in
  Australia)
Ayles|bury +s
  (town, England;
  duck)
Ay|mara
  plural Ay|mara *or*
  Ay|maras
Ayr (town,
  Scotland)
Ayr|shire +s
  (former county,
  Scotland; cattle)
Ayub Khan,
  Mu|ham|mad
  (Pakistani soldier
  and president)
ayur|veda
ayur|vedic
Azad Kash|mir
  (state, Pakistan)
aza|lea +s
Aza|nia (South
  Africa)
azeo|trope +s
azeo|trop|ic
Azer|bai|jan
Azer|bai|jani +s
Azeri +s

azide +s
azido|thy|mid|ine
Azi|kiwe, Nnamdi
  (Nigerian
  statesman)
Azil|ian
azi|muth +s
azi|muth|al
azine +s
azo dye +s
azoic
Azores (island
  group, N. Atlantic)
Azov, Sea of
  (north of Black
  Sea)
Az|rael
Aztec +s
azuki +s
azure +s
azy|gous
Az Zarqa
  (alternative name
  for Zarqa)

Bb

....

baa
  baas
  baaed *or* baa'd
  baa|ing
  (bleat. △ bah, bar,
  barre)
Baade, Wal|ter
  (German-born
  physicist)
Baader-Meinhof
  (terrorist group)
Baa|gan|dji
Baal (ancient god)
baa-lamb +s
Baal|bek (town,
  Lebanon)
Baal|ism
baas
  baases
baas|skap
Baath|ism
Baath|ist +s
Baath Party (Arab
  political party.
  △ Bath)
baba +s (in 'rum
  baba')
baba|coote +s
Bab|bage, Charles
  (English
  mathematician)
Bab|bitt +s (metal;
  complacent
  business man)
Bab|bitt, Mil|ton
  (American
  composer)
bab|bitt +s
  (bearing-lining)
Bab|bitt|ry
bab|ble
  bab|bles
  bab|bled
  bab|bling
babble|ment
bab|bler +s
bab|bling +s
babe +s
Babel, Tower of
  Bible
babel (scene of
  confusion)
Babi +s
babi|roussa +s
  (use babirusa)
babi|rusa +s
Bab|ism

Bab|ist +s
  (adherent of
  Babism. △ Barbie)
ba|boon +s
Ba|bru|isk (city,
  Belarus)
Babs
babu +s
Babur (Mogul
  emperor of India)
ba|bushka +s
Babu|yan Is|lands
  (in Philippines)
baby
  ba|bies
  ba|bied
  baby|ing
baby blue +s *noun
  and adjective*
baby-blue
  attributive
baby boom +s
baby boom|er +s
baby boun|cer +s
baby buggy
  baby bug|gies
  Propr.
baby-doll *adjective*
baby face +s
baby-faced
Baby|gro +s *Propr.*
baby|hood
baby|ish
baby|ish|ness
Baby|lon (ancient
  city, Middle East;
  white society)
Baby|lonia
  (ancient region,
  Middle East)
Baby|lon|ian +s
baby's breath
  (plant)
baby|sit
  baby|sits
  baby|sat
  baby|sit|ting
baby|sit|ter +s
baby-snatch|er +s
baby talk
baby walk|er +s
Ba|call, Lauren
  (American
  actress)
Ba|cardi +s *Propr.*
bac|ca|laur|eate
  +s
bac|carat
bac|cate
Bac|chae *Greek
  Mythology*
bac|chanal +s

Bac¦chan¦alia
  (Roman festival)
bac¦chan¦alia
  (general revelry)
Bac¦chan¦al¦ian +s
bac¦chant
  bac¦chants *or*
  bac¦chan¦tes
  male
bac¦chante +s
  female
bac¦chan¦tic
Bac¦chic
Bac¦chus *Greek*
  Mythology
baccy
  bac¦cies
Bach, Jo¦hann
  Se¦bas¦tian
  (German
  composer)
bach¦elor +s
bach¦elor¦hood
bach¦elor's
  but¦tons
bach¦elor¦ship
ba¦cil¦lary
ba¦cil¦li¦form
ba¦cil¦lus
  ba¦cilli
back +s +ed +ing
back¦ache +s
back¦bar +s
back¦beat +s
back¦bench
  back¦benches
back¦bench¦er +s
back¦bite
  back¦bites
  back¦bit
  back¦bit¦ing
  back¦bit¦ten
back¦biter +s
back¦blocks
back¦board +s
back boil¦er +s
back¦bone +s
back-breaking
back-channel
  adjective
back¦chat
back¦cloth +s
back¦comb +s +ed
  +ing
back¦coun¦try
back-crawl
back cross
  back crosses
  back crossed
  back cross¦ing
back¦date
  back¦dates

back¦date (*cont.*)
  back¦dated
  back¦dat¦ing
back door +s *noun*
back-door *adjective*
back¦down +s
back¦draft +s
back¦drop +s
back¦er +s
back¦field
back¦fill +s +ed
  +ing
back¦fire
  back¦fires
  back¦fired
  back¦fir¦ing
back¦flip +s
back-formation +s
back¦gam¦mon
back¦ground +s
back¦hand +s
back¦hand¦ed
back¦hand¦er +s
back¦hoe +s
back¦ing +s
back¦lash
  back¦lashes
back¦less
back¦light
back¦list +s
back¦lit
back¦log +s
back¦mark¦er +s
back¦most
back num¦ber +s
back¦pack +s +ed
  +ing
back¦pack¦er +s
back pas¦sage +s
back-pedal
  back-pedals
  back-pedalled *Br.*
  back-pedaled *Am.*
  back-pedalling
  Br.
  back-pedaling
  Am.
back-projec¦tion
back¦rest +s
back room +s *noun*
back-room
  attributive
Backs (in
  Cambridge)
back¦scat¦ter¦ing
back-scratch¦er +s
back-scratch¦ing
back seat +s
back-seat driver
  +s
back¦sheesh (use
  baksheesh)

back¦side +s
back¦sight +s
back slang
back¦slap¦ping
back¦slash
  back¦slashes
back¦slide
  back¦slides
  back¦slid
  back¦slid¦ing
  back¦slid¦den *or*
  back¦slid
back¦slider +s
back¦space
  back¦spaces
  back¦spaced
  back¦spa¦cing
back¦spin
back¦stage
back¦stair
back¦stairs
back¦stay +s
back¦stitch
  back¦stitches
  back¦stitched
  back¦stitch¦ing
back¦stop +s
back¦street +s
back¦stroke
back talk
back to back
  adverbial
back-to-back +s
  adjective and noun
back to front
back-to-nature
back¦track +s +ed
  +ing
back-up +s
back¦veld +s
back¦veld¦er +s
back¦ward
back¦ward¦ation
back¦ward¦ness
back¦wards
back¦wash
back¦water +s
back¦woods
back¦woods¦man
  back¦woods¦men
backy
  back¦ies
  (use baccy)
back¦yard +s
bac¦lava (use
  baklava)
Ba¦co¦lod (city,
  Philippines)
Bacon, Fran¦cis
  (English
  statesman and
  philosopher)

Bacon, Fran¦cis
  (Irish painter)
Bacon, Roger
  (English
  philosopher etc.)
bacon +s
Ba¦con¦ian +s
bac¦teria (plural of
  bacterium)
bac¦ter¦ial
bac¦teri¦cidal
bac¦teri¦cide +s
bac¦terio¦logic¦al
bac¦terio¦logic¦
  al¦ly
bac¦teri¦olo¦gist +s
bac¦teri¦ology
bac¦teri¦oly¦sis
  bac¦teri¦oly¦ses
bac¦terio¦lyt¦ic
bac¦terio¦phage +s
bac¦terio¦stasis
  bac¦terio¦stases
bac¦terio¦stat +s
bac¦terio¦stat¦ic
bac¦ter¦ium
  bac¦teria
Bac¦tria (region,
  central Asia)
Bac¦trian
bad
  worse
  worst
  (inferior; harmful;
  etc. ⚠ bade)
bad
  bad¦der
  bad¦dest
  (*slang* excellent.
  ⚠ bade)
bad¦ass
  bad¦asses
bad¦die +s (use
  baddy)
bad¦dish
baddy
  bad¦dies
bade (*archaic* past
  tense of bid.
  ⚠ bad)
Baden (town,
  Austria)
Baden-Baden
  (town, Germany)
Baden-Powell,
  Rob¦ert (English
  soldier and
  founder of the Boy
  Scouts)
Baden-
  Württem¦berg
  (state, Germany)

Bader, Doug|las
(British airman)
badge
  badges
  badged
  badg|ing
badger +s +ed +ing
Ba|dian +s
bad|in|age
Bad Lands (region,
  USA)
bad|lands
  (generally)
badly
bad|min|ton
bad mouth *noun*
bad-mouth +s +ed
  +ing *verb*
bad|ness
Badon Hill
  (battlefield,
  England)
bad-tempered
bad-tempered|ly
Bae|deker +s
Baer, Karl von
  (German biologist)
Bae|yer, Adolph
  von (German
  chemist)
Baez, Joan
  (American folk
  singer)
Baf|fin, Wil|liam
  (English explorer)
Baf|fin Bay
  (between Canada
  and Greenland)
Baf|fin Is|land (off
  Canada)
baf|fle
  baf|fles
  baf|fled
  baf|fling
baf|fle board +s
baffle|ment
baffle-plate +s
baf|fler +s
baf|fling|ly
BAFTA (= British
  Association of
  Film and
  Television Arts)
bag
  bags
  bagged
  bag|ging
Ba|ganda (people)
ba|garre +s
ba|gasse
baga|telle +s

Bage|hot, Wal|ter
  (English
  economist and
  political journalist)
bagel +s
bag|ful +s
bag|gage +s
bag|gily
bag|gi|ness
baggy
  bag|gier
  bag|gi|est
Bagh|dad (capital
  of Iraq)
bag lady
  bag la|dies
bag|man
  bag|men
bagnio +s
bag|pipe +s
bag|piper +s
bag|pip|ing
ba|guette +s
bag|wash
  bag|washes
bag|worm +s
bah (*interjection.*
  △ baa, bar, barre)
Baha'i +s
Ba|ha'ism
Ba|ha'ist +s
Ba|ha'ite +s
Ba|ha|mas
Ba|ha|mian +s
Ba|hasa
  In|do|nesia
Baha Ullah
  (Persian founder
  of Baha'ism)
Ba|ha|wal|pur
  (city, Pakistan)
Bahia (state, Brazil;
  former name of
  Salvador)
Bahía Blanca
  (port, Argentina)
Bah|rain
Bah|raini +s
baht
  plural baht
Ba|hutu (plural of
  Hutu)
baign|oire +s
Bai|kal, Lake (in
  Siberia)
Bai|ko|nur (space
  launch site,
  Kazakhstan)
bail +s +ed +ing
  (security for
  prisoner; secure
  release of;

bail (*cont.*)
  crosspiece on
  cricket stumps;
  bar on typewriter;
  bar in stable; hold
  up to rob; scoop
  water. △ bale)
bail|able
bail|ee +s *Law*
bail|er +s (scoop
  for water.
  △ bailor, baler)
Bai|ley (shipping
  area)
Bai|ley, David
  (English
  photographer)
bai|ley +s (part of
  castle)
Bai|ley bridge +s
bai|lie +s (Scottish
  magistrate)
bail|iff +s
baili|wick +s
bail|ment
bail|or +s (*Law.*
  △ bailer, baler)
bail|out +s *noun*
bails|man
  bails|men
bain-marie
  bains-marie
Bai|ram (Muslim
  festival)
Baird, John Logie
  (Scottish pioneer
  of television)
bairn +s
Bair|rada (region,
  Portugal)
bait +s +ed +ing
  (in hunting or
  fishing; harass;
  torment. △ bate)
baize +s
Baja Cali|for|nia
  (peninsula,
  Mexico)
Bajan +s
bajra
bake
  bakes
  baked
  bak|ing
bake|house +s
Bake|lite *Propr.*
Baker, Janet
  (English mezzo-
  soprano)
Baker, Jo|seph|ine
  (American dancer)
baker +s

Baker day +s
baker's dozen +s
bakery
  baker|ies
Bake|well, Rob|ert
  (English livestock
  expert)
Bake|well tart +s
Bakh|tin, Mikh|ail
  (Russian critic)
bak|ing pow|der
bak|ing soda
bak|lava
bak|sheesh
Bakst, Léon
  (Russian painter
  and designer)
Baku (capital of
  Azerbaijan)
Ba|ku|nin,
  Mikh|ail (Russian
  revolutionary)
Bala (lake, Wales)
Bala|clava
  (battlefield,
  Crimea)
bala|clava +s
  (helmet)
bala|laika +s
Bal|ance, the
  (constellation;
  sign of zodiac)
bal|ance
  bal|ances
  bal|anced
  bal|an|cing
bal|ance|able
bal|an|cer +s
bal|ance sheet +s
bal|ance wheel +s
Bal|an|chine,
  George (Russian-
  born American
  ballet dancer and
  choreographer)
bal|anda +s (use
  balander)
bal|an|der +s
balas-ruby
  balas-rubies
bal|ata +s
Bala|ton, Lake (in
  Hungary)
Bal|boa (port,
  Panama)
Bal|boa, Vasco de
  (Spanish explorer)
bal|boa +s
  (Panamanian
  currency)
Bal|brig|gan
  (fabric)

Bal¦con, Mi¦chael (film producer)
bal¦con|ied
bal¦cony
  bal¦con|ies
bald +s +ed +ing +er +est
bal¦da|chin +s
bal¦da|quin +s (use baldachin)
Bal¦der *Norse Mythology*
bal¦der|dash
bald-faced
bald|head +s
bald-headed
baldie +s (use baldy)
bald|ish
bald|ly
bald|money +s
bald|ness
bald|pate +s
bal|dric +s
Bald|win (name)
Bald|win, James (American novelist)
Bald|win, Stan|ley (British prime minister)
baldy
  bald|ies
Bâle (French name for Basle)
bale
  bales
  baled
  bal¦ing
(bundle; evil, destruction, etc.; in 'bale out' (of aircraft). △bail)
Ba¦le|ar¦ic Is¦lands (off E. Spain)
Ba¦le|ar¦ics (= Balearic Islands)
ba|leen
bale|ful
bale|ful¦ly
bale|ful|ness
Ba¦len|ciaga, Cris¦tó|bal (international couturier)
baler +s (machine for making bales. △bailer, bailor)
Bal|four, Ar¦thur (British prime minister)

Bali (island, Indonesia)
Bali|nese
  plural Bali|nese
balk +s +ed +ing (use baulk)
Bal¦kan
Bal¦kan|isa¦tion *Br.* (use Balkanization)
Bal¦kan|ise *Br.* (use Balkanize)
  Bal¦kan|ises
  Bal¦kan|ised
  Bal¦kan|is¦ing
Bal¦kan|iza¦tion
Bal¦kan|ize
  Bal¦kan|izes
  Bal¦kan|ized
  Bal¦kan|iz¦ing
Bal¦kans, the (group of countries, SE Europe)
Bal¦khash, Lake (use Balqash)
Bal¦kis (queen of Sheba)
balky
  balk|ier
  balk|iest
(use baulky)
ball +s +ed +ing (sphere; dance. △bawl)
bal¦lad +s
bal|lade +s
bal|lad|eer +s
ballad-monger +s
bal|lad¦ry
  bal¦lad|ries
Bal¦la|dur, Édou|ard (French statesman)
ball-and-socket *attributive*
Bal¦la|rat (town, Australia)
bal|last +s
ball-bearing +s
ball|boy +s
ball|cock +s
bal¦ler|ina +s
Bal¦le|steros, Sev¦eri|ano (Spanish golfer)
bal¦let +s
bal¦let dan¦cer +s
bal¦let|ic
bal¦leto|mane +s
bal¦leto|mania

Bal¦lets Russes (ballet company)
ball-flower +s
ball game +s
ball|girl +s
ball gown +s
bal|lista
  bal|lis¦tae
bal|lis¦tic
bal|lis¦tic|al¦ly
bal|lis¦tics
bal|locks (*coarse slang*; use bollocks)
bal¦lon d'essai
  bal¦lons d'essai
bal|loon +s +ed +ing
bal¦loon|ist +s
bal¦lot +s +ed +ing
bal¦lot box
  bal¦lot boxes
bal¦lot paper +s
ball|park +s
ball-pen +s
ball|point +s
ball-race +s
ball|room +s
ball|room dan¦cing
balls-up +s *noun* (*coarse slang*)
ballsy
ball valve +s
bally
bally|hoo
Bally|mena (town, Northern Ireland)
bally|rag
  bally|rags
  bally|ragged
  bally|rag|ging
balm +s (ointment; plant. △barm)
balm|ily
balmi|ness
bal|moral +s (cap; boot)
Bal|moral Cas¦tle (in Scotland)
balmy
  balm|ier
  balmi|est
(soothing. △barmy)
bal|ne¦ary
bal¦neo|logic¦al
bal¦ne|olo¦gist +s
bal¦ne|ology
ba|lo¦ney +s

BALPA (= British Air Line Pilots Association)
Bal¦qash, Lake (in Kazakhstan)
balsa
bal¦sam +s
bal¦sam¦ic
bal¦sam|ifer|ous
balsa wood
Balt +s
Bal¦tha¦sar (one of the Magi; name)
Balti +s
Bal¦tic (sea, N. Europe)
Bal¦ti|more (city, USA)
Bal¦ti|stan (region, Himalayas)
Ba¦luchi +s
Ba¦luchi|stan (region, W. Asia; province, Pakistan)
bal¦us|ter +s
bal¦us|trade +s
bal¦us|traded
bal¦us|trad¦ing
Bal¦zac, Hon¦oré de (French novelist)
bama +s
Bam¦ako (capital of Mali)
bam|bino
  bam|bi¦nos *or* bam|bini
bam¦boo +s
bam¦boo¦zle
  bam¦boo¦zles
  bam¦boo¦zled
  bam¦booz¦ling
bam¦boozle|ment
bam¦booz¦ler +s
Ba¦mian (province and city, Afghanistan)
ban
  bans
  banned
  ban|ning
(prohibit; prohibition; curse. △banns)
Ba¦naba (in W. Pacific)
banal
ban¦al|ity
  ban¦al|ities
ban|al¦ly
ba¦nana +s

ban|ausic
Ban|bury cake +s
banc (*Law* in 'in banc'. ⚠ bank)
band +s +ed +ing
Banda, Hast|ings (Malawian statesman)
ban|dage
  ban|dages
  ban|daged
  ban|da|ging
Band-Aid +s *Propr.*
ban|danna +s
Ban|da|ra|naike, Siri|mavo (Sri Lankan prime minister)
Ban|dar Lam|pung (city, Indonesia)
Ban|dar Seri Be|ga|wan (capital of Brunei)
Banda Sea (in Indonesia)
band|box
  band|boxes
ban|deau
  ban|deaux
ban|der|illa +s
ban|derol +s (use banderole)
ban|der|ole +s
bandi|coot +s
ban|dit
  ban|dits *or*
  ban|ditti
ban|dit|ry
Band|jar|masin (use Banjarmasin)
band|lead|er +s
band|mas|ter +s
ban|dog +s
ban|do|leer +s (use bandolier)
ban|do|lier +s
band|pass
  band|passes
band|saw +s
bands|man
  bands|men
band|stand +s
Ban|dung (city, Indonesia)
band|wagon +s
band|width +s
bandy
  ban|dies
  ban|died
  bandy|ing

bandy (*cont.*)
  ban|dier
  ban|di|est
bandy-legged
bane +s
bane|berry
  bane|berries
bane|ful
bane|ful|ly
Banff (towns, Scotland and Canada)
Banff|shire (former county, Scotland)
bang +s +ed +ing (sound; fringe; strike; etc. ⚠ bhang)
Banga|lore (city, India)
bang|er +s
Bang|kok (capital of Thailand)
Ban|gla|desh
Ban|gla|deshi +s
ban|gle +s
Ban|gor (towns, Wales and Northern Ireland)
bang|tail +s
Ban|gui (capital of the Central African Republic)
bang-up *adjective*
ban|ian +s (use banyan)
ban|ish
  ban|ishes
  ban|ished
  ban|ish|ing
ban|ish|ment +s
ban|is|ter +s
Ban|jar|masin (port, Indonesia)
banjo +s
ban|jo|ist +s
Ban|jul (capital of the Gambia)
bank +s +ed +ing
bank|abil|ity
bank|able
bank bill +s
bank book +s
bank card +s
bank|er +s
bank|er's card +s
bank|er's order +s
bank|note +s
bank|roll +s +ed +ing
bank|rupt +s +ed +ing

bank|rupt|cy
  bank|rupt|cies
Banks, Jo|seph (English naturalist)
bank|sia +s
ban|ner +s
ban|nered
ban|neret +s
Ban|nis|ter, Roger (English athlete)
ban|nis|ter +s (use banister)
ban|nock +s
Ban|nock|burn (battlefield, Scotland)
banns (of marriage)
ban|quet +s +ed +ing
ban|quet|er +s
ban|quette +s
ban|shee +s
ban|tam +s
ban|tam|weight +s
ban|ter +s +ed +ing
ban|ter|er +s
Ban|ting, Fred|erick (Canadian surgeon)
Bantu
  plural **Bantu** *or* **Ban|tus**
Ban|tu|stan +s
ban|yan +s
ban|zai
bao|bab +s
Bao|tou (city, China)
bap +s
bap|tise *Br.* (use baptize)
  bap|tises
  bap|tised
  bap|tis|ing
bap|tism +s
bap|tis|mal
Bap|tist +s (denomination)
bap|tist +s (person who baptizes)
bap|tist|ery
  bap|tist|er|ies
bap|tist|ry (use baptistery)
  bap|tist|ries
bap|tize
  bap|tizes
  bap|tized
  bap|tiz|ing

Bar, the (barristers collectively)
bar
  bars
  barred
  bar|ring
(rod; counter; room in pub; obstruction; section of music; unit of pressure; fasten; prohibit; except. ⚠ baa, bah, barre)
Bar|ab|bas *Bible*
bara|thea +s
Barb (= Broadcasters' Audience Research Council)
barb +s +ed +ing (projection; hurtful remark)
Bar|ba|dian +s
Bar|ba|dos (state, Caribbean)
Bar|bara
bar|bar|ian +s
bar|bar|ic
bar|bar|ic|al|ly
bar|bar|isa|tion *Br.* (use barbarization)
bar|bar|ise *Br.* (use barbarize)
  bar|bar|ises
  bar|bar|ised
  bar|bar|is|ing
bar|bar|ism +s
bar|bar|ity
  bar|bar|ities
bar|bar|iza|tion
bar|bar|ize
  bar|bar|izes
  bar|bar|ized
  bar|bar|iz|ing
Bar|ba|rossa, Fred|erick (German king)
bar|bar|ous
bar|bar|ous|ly
bar|bar|ous|ness
Bar|bary
Bar|bary Coast (area, NW Africa)
bar|ba|stelle +s
bar|be|cue
  bar|be|cues
  bar|be|cued
  bar|be|cu|ing
barbed wire *Br.* (*Am.* barbwire)

bar¦bel +s (fish;
  part of fish)
bar¦bell +s
  (weights)
Bar¦ber, Sam¦uel
  (American
  composer)
bar¦ber +s
bar¦berry
  bar|berries
barber-shop
  (singing)
bar¦ber's pole +s
bar¦ber's shop +s
  (place)
bar¦bet +s (bird)
bar¦bette +s (gun
  platform)
bar¦bi|can +s
bar¦bie +s
  (= barbecue)
Bar¦bie doll +s
  (doll; young
  woman. △ Babi)
  Propr.
Bar¦bi|rolli, John
  (English
  conductor)
bar¦bi|tal
bar¦bi|tone
bar¦bit|ur|ate +s
bar¦bi|tur¦ic
Bar¦bi|zon School
  (French painters)
barb|less
bar¦bola
Bar|bour +s
  (jacket) *Propr.*
Bar|bour, John
  (Scottish poet)
Bar|buda (island,
  West Indies)
Bar|budan +s
barb|ule +s
barb|wire *Am.* (*Br.*
  barbed wire)
Barca, Pedro
  Cal|derón de la
  (Spanish writer)
bar¦car|ole +s
bar¦car|olle +s (use
  barcarole)
Bar¦ce|llona (city,
  Spain)
bar¦chan +s
Bar|clay (name.
  △ Barkly,
  Berkeley)
Bar-Cochba
  (Jewish rebel)
bar code +s *noun*

bar-code
bar-codes
bar-coded
bar-coding
  verb
Bar¦coo
bard +s
bard¦ic
bard|ol¦atry
Bar¦dot, Bri|gitte
  (French actress)
bardy
  bar|dies
bare
  bares
  bared
bar¦ing
barer
bar¦est
  (naked; mere;
  uncover; etc.
  △ bear)
bare|back
Bare|bones
  Par|lia|ment
bare|faced
bare|faced¦ly
bare|faced|ness
bare|foot
bare|foot¦ed
bar¦ège +s
bare|head¦ed
Ba|reilly (city,
  India)
bare-knuckle
  adjective
bare-knuckled
bare¦ly
bare|ness
Bar|ents, Wil|lem
  (Dutch explorer)
Bar|ents Sea (part
  of Arctic Ocean)
barf +s +ed +ing
bar¦fly
  bar|flies
bar¦fly jump|ing
bar|gain +s +ed
  +ing
bar|gain
  base|ment +s
bar|gain¦er +s
barge
  barges
  barged
bar¦ging
barge|board +s
bar¦gee +s
Bar|gello
barge|man
  barge|men
barge|pole +s

Bari (city, Italy)
bar|illa +s
Bari|sal (port,
  Bangladesh)
bar¦ite *Am.* (*Br.*
  barytes)
bari|tone +s
bar¦ium
bark +s +ed +ing
  (cry of dog; on
  tree trunk.
  △ barque)
bar|keep +s
bar|keep¦er +s
bar¦ken|tine *Am.*
  +s (*Br.*
  barquentine)
Bark¦er, George
  (English poet)
bark¦er +s
Barkly Table|land
  (plateau,
  Australia)
bar¦ley +s
bar¦ley|corn +s
bar¦ley|mow +s
bar¦ley sugar
bar¦ley water
bar¦ley wine
bar|line +s
barm (froth; yeast.
  △ balm)
bar|maid +s
bar|man
  bar¦men
barm|brack +s
Bar|me|cide +s
bar|mily
barmi|ness
bar mitz|vah +s
barmy
  bar|mier
  bar|miest
  (crazy. △ balmy)
barn +s
Bar|na|bas
  (Apostle and saint;
  name)
Bar|naby
bar|nacle +s
bar|nacled
Bar|nard,
  Chris|tiaan
  (South African
  surgeon)
Bar|nardo,
  Thomas (English
  philanthropist,
  founder of 'Dr
  Barnardo's
  homes')

Bar|naul (city,
  Russia)
barn|brack +s
Bar¦ney (name)
bar¦ney +s
  (quarrel)
barn owl +s
Barns|ley (town,
  England)
barn|storm +s +ed
  +ing
barn|storm¦er +s
Bar¦num, Phin|eas
  T. (American
  showman)
barn|yard +s
Bar|oda (former
  state, India;
  former name of
  Vadodara)
baro|graph +s
bar|om¦eter +s
baro|met|ric
baro|met|ric¦al
baro|met|ric|al¦ly
bar|om¦etry
baron +s
  (nobleman.
  △ barren)
bar|on|age
bar|on|ess
  bar|on|esses
bar|onet +s
bar|on|et|age
bar|on|et|cy
  bar|on|et|cies
bar|on|ial
bar¦ony
  bar|on|ies
bar|oque
baro|recep|tor +s
bar|ouche +s
bar per|son +s
bar¦quan|tine +s
  (use barquentine)
barque +s (ship.
  △ bark)
bar¦quen|tine *Br.*
  +s (*Am.*
  barkentine)
Bar|qui|si|meto
  (city, Venezuela)
Barra (Scottish
  island)
bar|rack +s +ed
  +ing
barrack-room
  attributive
bar|racks
bar|rack square +s
bar|ra|couta
  plural

bar¦ra|couta (*cont.*)
  bar¦ra|couta *or*
  bar¦ra|cou¦tas
  (long thin food
  fish; loaf)
bar¦ra|cuda +s
  (large voracious
  fish)
bar¦rage +s
bar¦ra|mundi
  plural
  bar¦ra|mundi *or*
  bar¦ra|mun¦dis
Bar¦ran|quilla
  (city, Colombia)
bar¦ra|tor +s
bar¦ra|trous
bar¦ra|try
barre +s (*Ballet.*
  ⚠ baa, bah, bar)
barré *Music*
bar¦rel
  bar¦rels
  bar¦relled *Br.*
  bar¦reled *Am.*
  bar¦rel|ling *Br.*
  bar¦rel|ing *Am.*
barrel-chested
bar¦rel|ful +s
bar¦rel organ +s
barrel-vaulted
bar¦ren +er +est
  (infertile.
  ⚠ baron)
bar¦ren|ly
bar¦ren|ness
bar¦ret +s (cap)
Bar¦rett,
  Eliza|beth
  (English poet, wife
  of Robert
  Browning)
bar¦rette +s
  (hairslide)
bar¦ri|cade
  bar¦ri|cades
  bar¦ri|caded
  bar¦ri|cad¦ing
Bar¦rie, James M.
  (Scottish writer.
  ⚠ Barry)
bar¦rier +s
bar¦rio +s
bar¦ris|ter +s
barrister-at-law
  barristers-at-law
bar room +s
bar¦row +s
bar¦row boy +s
Barrow-in-
  Furness (town,
  England)

bar¦row|load +s
Barry (name)
Barry, Charles
  (English architect.
  ⚠ Barrie)
Barry|more
  (American
  theatrical family)
Bar¦sac +s (region,
  France; wine)
bar stool +s
Bart (name)
Bart. (= Baronet)
bar¦tend¦er +s
bar¦ter +s +ed
  +ing
bar¦ter¦er +s
Barth, John
  (American writer)
Barth, Karl (Swiss
  theologian)
Barthes, Ro¦land
  (French
  semiotician)
Bar¦tholo|mew
  (Apostle and
  saint)
bar¦ti|zan +s
bar¦ti|zaned
Bar¦tók, Béla
  (Hungarian
  composer)
Bar¦to¦lom|meo,
  Fra (Florentine
  painter)
Bart's (St
  Bartholomew's
  Hospital, London)
Bar¦uch *Bible*
baryon +s
bary|on¦ic
Bar¦ysh|nikov,
  Mikh|ail (Latvian-
  born American
  ballet dancer)
bary|sphere +s
ba¦ryta
bar¦yte (use barite)
ba|ry¦tes
ba|ryt¦ic
basal
bas¦alt +s
bas¦alt¦ic
bas|cule +s
  (bridge)
base
  bases
  based
  bas¦ing
  baser
  bas¦est
  (foundation;

base (*cont.*)
  establish;
  cowardly; impure.
  ⚠ bass)
base|ball +s
base|ball play¦er
  +s
base|board +s
base|born
base camp +s
base|head +s
BASE jump +s +ed
  +ing
BASE jump¦er +s
Basel (German
  name for Basle)
base|less
base|less|ness
base|line +s
base|load +s
base|man
  base|men
base|ment +s
base metal +s
base|ness
bas|enji +s
base|plate +s
base rate +s
bases (plural of
  base and basis)
bash
  bashes
  bashed
  bash|ing
bash|ful
bash|ful¦ly
bash|ful|ness
bashi-bazouk +s
Bash|kir
  plural Bash|kir *or*
  Bash|kirs
Bash|kiria
  (republic, Russia)
Bash|kor¦to|stan
  (alternative name
  for Bashkiria)
basho
  plural basho *or*
  bashos
BASIC *Computing*
basic +s
ba|sic|ally
Basic Eng|lish
bas|icity
bas¦ici|ties
ba|sid|ium
  ba|sidia
Basie, Count
  (American jazz
  musician)
Basil (early saint;
  name)

basil +s (herb)
basi|lar
Bas¦il|don (town,
  England)
ba|sil|ica +s
ba|sili|can
Ba|sili|cata (region,
  Italy)
basi|lisk +s
basin +s
basi|net +s
  (headpiece.
  ⚠ bassinet)
basin|ful +s
ba|sip|etal
ba|sip|et|al¦ly
basis
  bases
bask +s +ed +ing
  (laze in the sun
  etc. ⚠ basque)
Bas¦ker|ville, John
  (English printer)
bas¦ket +s
bas¦ket|ball +s
bas¦ket case +s
  (*offensive*)
bas¦ket|ful +s
Bas¦ket Maker +s
  (American Indian)
basket-maker +s
  (maker of baskets)
basket-making
bas¦ket¦ry
bas¦ket weave
bas¦ket|work
Basle (city,
  Switzerland)
bas|mati
baso|phil +s
baso|phile +s
baso|phil¦ic
Ba|so|tho
Basque +s (people;
  language)
basque +s (bodice.
  ⚠ bask)
Basra (port, Iraq)
bas-relief +s
bass
  basses
  (voice; double
  bass; low pitch.
  ⚠ base)
bass
  plural bass *or*
  basses
  (fish. ⚠ base)
Bas|sein (port,
  Burma)
Basse-Norman¦die
  (region, France)

bas|set +s
Basse|terre (capital
of St Kitts and
Nevis)
Basse-Terre
(island and city,
Guadeloupe)
basset-horn +s
basset-hound +s
bassi (plural of
basso)
bas|sinet +s
(cradle; pram.
△ basinet)
bass|ist +s
basso
bas|sos or bassi
bas|soon +s
bas|soon|ist +s
basso pro|fundo
basso pro|fun|dos
or bassi pro|fundi
basso-relievo +s
basso-rilievo +s
(use basso-
relievo)
bass play|er +s
Bass Strait
(channel between
Australia and
Tasmania)
bass|wood
bast
bas|tard +s
bas|tard|isa|tion
Br. (use
bastardization)
bas|tard|ise Br.
(use bastardize)
bas|tard|ises
bas|tard|ised
bas|tard|is|ing
bas|tard|iza|tion
bas|tard|ize
bas|tard|izes
bas|tard|ized
bas|tard|iz|ing
bas|tardy
baste
bastes
basted
bast|ing
Bas|tet Egyptian
Mythology
Bas|tia (port,
Corsica)
Bas|tille (in Paris)
bas|tille +s
(fortress)
bas|tin|ado +s
noun

bas|tin|ado
bas|tin|adoes
bas|tin|adoed
bas|tin|ado|ing
verb
bas|tion +s
ba|suco
Ba|su|to|land
(former name of
Lesotho)
bat
bats
bat|ted
bat|ting
Bata (town,
Equatorial Guinea)
Batan Is|lands
(part of the
Philippines)
ba|tata +s
Bat|avia (former
name of Djakarta)
Bat|avian +s
batch
batches
batched
batch|ing
Bat|dam|bang (use
Battambang)
bate +s (rage.
△ bait)
bat|eau
bat|eaux
bated (in 'with
bated breath')
bat|el|leur +s
Bates, Alan
(English actor)
Bates, Henry
(English
naturalist)
Bates, H. E.
(English writer)
Bates|ian
Bate|son, Wil|liam
(English
geneticist)
Bath (city, England.
△ Baath)
bath +s +ed +ing
Bath bun +s
bath chair +s
Bath chap +s
bath cube +s
bathe
bathes
bathed
bath|ing
bather +s
bath|et|ic
bath|house +s

bath|ing cos|tume
+s
bath|ing suit +s
bath mat +s
batho|lith +s
Bath Oli|ver +s
Propr.
bath|om|eter +s
bathos
bath|ot|ic
bath|robe +s
bath|room +s
bath salts
Bath|sheba Bible
bath|tub +s
Bath|urst (former
name of Banjul)
bath|water
ba|thym|eter +s
bathy|met|ric
ba|thym|etry
bathy|scaphe +s
bathy|sphere +s
batik +s
Bat|ista,
Ful|gen|cio
(Cuban soldier
and dictator)
bat|iste +s
Bat|man (fictional
character)
bat|man
bat|men
(military
attendant)
baton +s (stick
used by
conductor, relay
runner, or drum
major or as
symbol of
authority;
truncheon.
△ batten)
Baton Rouge (city,
USA)
baton round +s
bat|ra|chian +s
bats|man
bats|men
bats|man|ship
Ba|tswana (plural
of Tswana)
bat|tal|ion +s
Bat|tam|bang
(region and city,
Cambodia)
bat|tels (college
account at Oxford
University.
△ battles)

Bat|ten, Jean
(New Zealand
aviator)
bat|ten +s +ed
+ing (strip of
wood used for
fastening.
△ baton)
Bat|ten|berg +s
(cake)
bat|ter +s +ed
+ing
bat|ter|er +s
bat|ter|ing ram +s
bat|tery
bat|ter|ies
battery-operated
battery-powered
Bat|ti|ca|loa (city,
Sri Lanka)
bat|tily
bat|ti|ness
bat|tle
bat|tles
bat|tled
bat|tling
(fight. △ battels)
battle|axe +s
battle|bus
battle|buses
battle|cruiser +s
battle-cry
battle-cries
battle|dore +s
battle|dress
battle|field +s
battle|ground +s
battle|group +s
battle-hardened
battle|ment +s
battle|ment|ed
bat|tler +s
bat|tle royal
bat|tles royal
battle-scarred
battle|ship +s
battle-weary
bat|tue +s
batty
bat|tier
bat|ti|est
Batwa (plural of
Twa)
bat|wing attributive
bat|woman
bat|women
bau|ble +s
Bau|cis Greek
Mythology
baud
plural **baud** or
bauds

baud (*cont.*)
(*Computing* unit of
speed. △ bawd,
board, bored)
Baude|laire,
Charles (French
poet)
Bau|haus
baulk +s +ed +ing
baulk|er +s
baulki|ness
baulky
  baulk|ier
  baulki|est
baux|ite
baux|it|ic
bav|ard|age
Bav|aria (state,
Germany)
Bav|ar|ian +s
bawd +s
  (prostitute.
  △ baud, board,
  bored)
bawd|ily
bawdi|ness
bawdy
  bawd|ier
  bawdi|est
bawdy house +s
bawl +s +ed +ing
  (yell. △ ball)
bawl|er +s
Bax, Ar|nold
  (English
  composer)
Bax|ter (name)
Bax|ter, James
  (New Zealand
  poet)
bay +s +ed +ing
  (inlet of sea; tree;
  window; recess;
  compartment;
  colour; horse;
  howl. △ bey)
bay|ad|ère
Bay|ard, Pierre
  (French soldier)
bay|berry
  bay|berries
Bay|eux (town,
  France; tapestry)
Bay|kal, Lake (use
  Baikal)
Bay|ko|nur (use
  Baikonur)
bay leaf
  bay leaves
Bay|lis, Lil|ian
  (English theatre
  manager)

bay|onet
bay|on|ets
bay|on|et|ed *or*
bay|on|et|ted
bay|on|et|ing *or*
bay|on|et|ting
bayou +s
Bay|reuth (town,
  Germany)
bay tree +s
bay win|dow +s
Baz
ba|zaar +s
bazoo +s
ba|zooka +s
ba|zuco (use
  basuco)
B-cell +s
bdel|lium
be
  am
  are
  is
  was
  were
  being
  been
Bea (name)
beach
  beaches
  beached
  beach|ing
  (shore. △ beech)
beach ball +s
Beach Boys, the
  (American pop
  group)
beach|comb|er +s
beach|front
beach|head +s
Beach-la-mar
beach|side
beach|wear
Beachy Head
  (headland,
  England)
bea|con +s
bead +s +ed +ing
bead|ily
beadi|ness
bea|dle +s
beadle|ship +s
bead-moulding
beads|man
  beads|men
bead|work
beady
  bead|ier
  beadi|est
beady-eyed

bea|gle
  bea|gles
  bea|gled
  beag|ling
Bea|gle Chan|nel
  (off S. America)
beag|ler +s
beak +s
beaked
Bea|ker (people)
bea|ker +s
  (drinking vessel)
beaky
Beale, Doro|thea
  (English
  educationist)
be-all and end-all
beam +s +ed +ing
beam-compass
  beam-compasses
beam-ends
beam|er +s
Bea|mon, Bob
  (American athlete)
beamy
  beam|ier
  beami|est
bean +s (vegetable.
  △ been)
bean|bag +s
bean-counter +s
bean curd
bean|ery
  bean|er|ies
bean|feast +s
beanie +s
beano +s
bean|pole +s
bean sprout +s
bean|stalk +s
bear +s (animal.
  △ bare)
bear
  bears
  bore
  bear|ing
  borne
  (carry; exert;
  tolerate; etc.
  △ bare)
bear
  bears
  bore
  bear|ing
  born
  (give birth to.
  △ bare)
bear|abil|ity
bear|able
bear|ably
bear-baiting

bear|berry
  bear|berries
beard +s +ed +ing
beardie +s
beard|less
Beard|more
  Gla|cier (in
  Antarctica)
Beards|ley,
  Aub|rey (English
  painter)
bear|er +s
bear|gar|den +s
bear-hug +s
bear|ing +s
bearing-rein +s
bear|ish
bear mar|ket +s
Béarn|aise
bear|pit +s
bear's breech
bear's ear +s
bear's foot +s
bear|skin +s
Beas (river, India)
beast +s
beastie +s
beast|ings (use
  beestings)
beast|li|ness
beast|ly
  beast|lier
  beast|li|est
beat
  beats
  beat
  beat|ing
  beaten
  (hit; rhythm; etc.
  △ beet)
beat|able
beat|er +s (person
  or thing that beats.
  △ beta)
bea|tif|ic
bea|tif|ic|al|ly
be|ati|fi|ca|tion
be|atify
  be|ati|fies
  be|ati|fied
  be|ati|fy|ing
be|ati|tude +s
Beatles, the
  (British pop
  group)
beat|nik +s
Bea|ton, Cecil
  (English
  photographer)
Bea|trice (woman
  loved by Dante;
  name)

Bea|trix
Beatty, David
(British admiral)
Beatty, War|ren
(American actor)
beat-up *adjective*
Beau (man's name.
△Bo)
beau
beaux *or* beaus
(dandy. △bo,
bow)
Beau|bourg
(building, Paris)
Beau|fort scale
Beau|fort Sea (part
of Arctic Ocean)
beau geste
beaux gestes
beau idéal
beaux idéals
Beau|jo|lais
plural Beau|jo|lais
(district, France;
wine)
Beau|jo|lais
Nou|veau
Beau|mar|chais,
Pierre de (French
dramatist)
Beau|maris (town,
Wales)
beau monde
Beau|mont,
Fran|cis (English
dramatist)
Beaune +s (town,
France; wine)
beaut +s (excellent;
beautiful. △butte)
beaut|eous
beaut|ician +s
beau|ti|fi|ca|tion
beau|ti|fier +s
beau|ti|ful
beau|ti|ful|ly
beaut|ify
beau|ti|fies
beau|ti|fied
beau|ti|fy|ing
beauty
beaut|ies
beauty spot +s
Beau|voir,
Sim|one de
(French writer)
beaux (plural of
beau)
beaux arts
Bea|ver +s (junior
Scout)

bea|ver
plural bea|ver *or*
bea|vers
(animal)
bea|ver +s +ed
+ing (armour;
bearded man;
work)
bea|ver|board
Bea|ver|brook,
Lord (Canadian-
born British
politician and
newspaper
proprietor)
bebop
be|bop|per +s
be|calm +s +ed
+ing
be|came
be|cause
béch|amel
bêche-de-mer
plural bêche-de-
mer *or* bêche-de-
mers
Bech|stein,
Fried|rich
(German piano-
builder)
Bech|uana|land
(former name of
Botswana)
Beck, Jeff (English
rock musician)
beck +s
Beck|en|bauer,
Franz (German
footballer)
Becker, Boris
(German tennis
player)
Becket, St
Thomas à
(English
archbishop)
becket +s
Beck|ett, Sam|uel
(Irish writer)
Beck|ford,
Wil|liam (English
writer)
Beck|mann, Ernst
Otto (German
chemist)
Beck|mann, Max
(German painter)
beckon +s +ed
+ing
Becky
be|cloud +s +ed
+ing

be|come
be|comes
be|came
be|com|ing
be|come
be|com|ing|ly
be|com|ing|ness
Bec|querel,
Antoine-Henri
(French physicist)
bec|querel +s
(unit)
bed
beds
bed|ded
bed|ding
be|dab|ble
be|dab|bles
be|dab|bled
be|dab|bling
bedad
bed and
break|fast +s
noun
bed-and-breakfast
+s +ed +ing *verb*
be|daub +s +ed
+ing
be|daz|zle
be|daz|zles
be|daz|zled
be|daz|zling
be|dazzle|ment
bed|bug +s
bed|cham|ber +s
bed|clothes
bed|cover +s
bed-covering +s
bed|dable
bed|der +s
beddy-byes
Bede, The
Ve|ner|able
(English monk and
writer)
be|deck +s +ed
+ing
bed|eguar
bedel +s
bed|ell +s (use
bedel)
be|devil
be|devils
be|dev|illed *Br.*
be|dev|iled *Am.*
be|dev|il|ling *Br.*
be|dev|il|ing *Am.*
be|devil|ment
bedew +s +ed
+ing
bed|fast
bed|fel|low +s

Bed|ford (town,
England)
Bed|ford|shire
(county, England)
bed|head +s
bed-hop
bed-hops
bed-hopped
bed-hopping
be|dight
bedim
be|dims
be|dimmed
be|dim|ming
be|dizen +s +ed
+ing
bed|jacket +s
bed|lam +s
bed|linen
Bed|ling|ton
(terrier)
bed|maker +s
Bed|ouin
plural Bed|ouin
bed|pan +s
bed|plate +s
bed|post +s
be|drag|gle
be|drag|gles
be|drag|gled
be|drag|gling
bed|rest
bed|rid|den
bed|rock +s
bed|roll +s
bed|room +s
Beds.
(= Bedfordshire)
bed|side +s
bed|sit +s
bed|sit|ter +s
bed-sitting room
+s
bed|skirt +s
bed|sock +s
bed|sore +s
bed|spread +s
bed|stead +s
bed|straw
bed|table +s
bed|time +s
Bed|uin (use
Bedouin)
plural Beduin
bed-wetter +s
bed-wetting
bee +s
Beeb
bee-bread
beech
beeches
(tree. △ beach)

Beecham,
  Thomas (English
  conductor)
beech-fern +s
beech mar¦ten +s
beech|mast
  plural beech|mast
beech|wood
beechy
bee-eater +s
beef
  plural beef *or*
  beeves
  (meat; cattle)
beef +s +ed +ing
  (complaint;
  complain)
beef|alo
  plural beef|alo *or*
  beef|aloes
beef|bur¦ger +s
beef|cake +s
beef cat¦tle
beef|eater +s
beef|heart
beef|ily
beefi|ness
beef|steak +s
beef tea
beef|wood +s
beefy
  beef|ier
  beefi|est
bee|hive +s
bee-keeper +s
bee-keeping
bee|line +s
Be¦el¦ze¦bub *Bible*
bee-master +s
been (past
  participle of be.
  △bean)
beep +s +ed +ing
beep¦er +s
beer +s (drink.
  △bier)
Beer|bohm, Max
  (English writer)
beer cel¦lar +s
beer en¦gine +s
beer gar¦den +s
beer hall +s
beer|house +s
beer|ily
beeri|ness
beer mat +s
Beer|sheba (town,
  Israel)
beery
  beer|ier
  beeri|est
beest|ings

bees|wax
bees|wing
beet +s (vegetable.
  △beat)
Beet|hoven,
  Lud¦wig van
  (German
  composer)
Bee|tle +s
  (Volkswagen)
  Propr.
bee¦tle
  bee¦tles
  bee¦tled
beet|ling
  (insect; game;
  scurry; tool;
  projecting; to
  project. △betel)
beetle-browed
beetle-crusher +s
Bee|ton, Mrs
  (Isa|bella)
  (English cookery
  writer)
beet|root
  plural beet|root *or*
  beet|roots
beeves
be|fall
  be|falls
  be|fell
  be|fall|ing
  be|fallen
befit
  be¦fits
  be¦fit|ted
  be¦fit|ting
  be¦fit|ting¦ly
befog
  be¦fogs
  be|fogged
  be|fog|ging
be¦fool +s +ed
  +ing
be¦fore
Be¦fore Christ
be¦fore|hand
be¦foul +s +ed
  +ing
be|friend +s +ed
  +ing
be|fud¦dle
  be|fud¦dles
  be|fud¦dled
  be|fud¦dling
be|fuddle|ment
beg
  begs
  begged
  beg|ging
begad

began
beget
  be¦gets
  begot
  or begat *archaic*
  be¦get|ting
  be¦got|ten
be¦get|ter +s
beg|gar +s
beg|gar|li|ness
beg|gar¦ly
beggar-my-
  neighbour
beg|gary
Begin,
  Men|achem
  (Israeli prime
  minister)
begin
  be¦gins
  began
  be¦gin|ning
  begun
be¦gin|ner +s
be¦gin|ner's luck
be¦gin|ning +s
be|gird
  be|girds
  be|girt
  be|gird|ing
be|gone *interjection*
be|go¦nia +s
be|gorra
begot
be|got|ten
be|grime
  be|grimes
  be|grimed
  be|grim¦ing
be|grudge
  be|grudges
  be|grudged
  be|grudg¦ing
be|grudg¦ing¦ly
be|guile
  be|guiles
  be|guiled
  be|guil¦ing
be|guile|ment
be|guiler +s
be|guil¦ing¦ly
be|guine +s
Begum (title of
  Muslim woman)
begum +s (high-
  ranking Muslim
  lady)
begun
be¦half
Behan, Bren|dan
  (Irish dramatist)

be¦have
  be|haves
  be|haved
  be|hav¦ing
be|hav¦ior *Am.* +s
be|hav¦ior|al *Am.*
be|hav¦ior|al|ist
  Am. +s
be¦hav¦ior|al¦ly
  Am.
be|hav¦ior|ism *Am.*
be|hav¦ior|ist *Am.*
  +s
be|hav¦ior|is¦tic
  Am.
be|hav¦iour *Br.* +s
be|hav¦iour|al *Br.*
be|hav¦iour|al|ist
  Br. +s
be|hav¦iour|al¦ly
  Br.
be|hav¦iour|ism *Br.*
be|hav¦iour|ist *Br.*
  +s
be|hav¦iour|is¦tic
  Br.
be¦head +s +ed
  +ing
be¦head|ing +s
be|held
be|he¦moth +s
be|hest +s
be¦hind
be¦hind|hand
behind-the-scenes
  attributive
Behn, Aphra
  (English writer)
be¦hold
  be|holds
  be¦held
  be¦hold|ing
be|holden
be|hold|er +s
be|hoof
be|hoove *Am.*
  be|hooves
  be|hooved
  be|hoov¦ing
be|hove *Br.*
  be¦hoves
  be¦hoved
  be|hov¦ing
Behr|ens, Peter
  (German
  architect)
Behr|ing, Emil
  von (German
  immunologist)
Bei¦der|becke, Bix
  (American jazz
  musician)

beige+s
bei¦gel+s (use
  bagel)
Beijing(capital of
  China)
being+s
Beira(region,
  Portugal; port,
  Mozambique)
Bei¦rut(capital of
  Lebanon)
be¦jab¦bers
be¦ja¦bers
Béjart, Maur¦ice
  (French
  choreographer)
be¦jew¦eled Am.
be¦jew¦elled Br.
Bekaa(valley,
  Lebanon)
Bel(= Baal)
bel+s (10 decibels.
  △ bell, belle)
be¦la¦bor Am. +s
  +ed +ing
be¦la¦bour Br. +s
  +ed +ing
Bela¦fonte, Harry
  (American singer)
Bela¦rus
Bela¦rus¦sian +s
  (use Belorussian)
bellated
be¦lated¦ly
be¦lated¦ness
Belau (= Pelau)
belay +s +ed +ing
belaying-pin +s
bel canto
belch
  belches
  belched
  belch¦ing
belch¦er+s
bel¦dam +s
bel¦dame +s (use
  beldam)
be¦lea¦guer +s +ed
  +ing
Belém (city, Brazil)
bel¦em¦nite +s
bel es¦prit
  beaux es¦prits
Bel¦fast (capital of
  Northern Ireland)
bel¦fry
  bel¦fries
Bel¦gae
Bel¦gaum (city,
  India)
Bel¦gian +s

Bel¦gian Congo
  (former name of
  Zaire)
Bel¦gic
Bel¦gium
Bel¦gorod(city,
  Russia)
Bel¦grade(capital
  of Serbia)
Bel¦gra¦via(area,
  London)
Bel¦gra¦vian +s
Be¦lial
belie
  be¦lies
  be¦lied
  be¦ly¦ing
be¦lief+s
be¦liev¦abil¦ity
be¦liev¦able
be¦liev¦ably
be¦lieve
  be¦lieves
  be¦lieved
  be¦liev¦ing
be¦liever +s
Be¦linda
Beli¦sar¦ius
  (Roman general)
Be¦li¦sha(beacon)
be¦lit¦tle
  be¦lit¦tles
  be¦lit¦tled
  be¦lit¦tling
be¦little¦ment
be¦lit¦tler+s
be¦lit¦tling¦ly
Be¦li¦tung (island,
  Indonesia)
Be¦lize
Be¦lize City (city,
  Belize)
Be¦li¦zian +s
Bell, Alex¦an¦der
  Gra¦ham
  (Scottish inventor
  of the telephone)
Bell, Ger¦trude
  (English traveller
  and scholar)
bell +s +ed +ing
  (object that rings;
  cry of stag; etc.
  △ bel, belle)
Bella
bella¦donna
bell¦bird +s
bell-bottom +s
bell-bottomed
bell¦boy +s (page
  in hotel or club)

bell-buoy+s
  (warning device)
Belle(name)
belle+s (woman.
  △ bel, bell)
belle époque
  belles époques
belle laide
  belles laides
Bel¦ler¦ophon
  Greek Mythology
belles-lettres
bell¦let¦rism
bell¦let¦rist+s
bell¦let¦ris¦tic
bell¦flower+s
bell-founder+s
bell-glass
  bell-glasses
bell¦hop +s
bel¦li¦cose
bel¦li¦cos¦ity
bel¦li¦ger¦ence
bel¦li¦ger¦ency
bel¦li¦ger¦ent
bel¦li¦ger¦ent¦ly
Bel¦lings¦hau¦sen
  Sea (part of SE
  Pacific)
Bel¦lini, Gen¦tile,
  Gio¦vanni, and
  Ja¦copo
  (Venetian
  painters)
Bel¦lini, Vin¦cenzo
  (Italian composer)
bell jar+s
bell¦man
  bell¦men
bell metal
Bel¦loc, Hil¦aire
  (British humorist)
Bel¦low, Saul
  (American
  novelist)
bel¦low+s +ed
  +ing
bell pull +s
bell push
  bell pushes
bell-ringer +s
bell-ringing
Bell Rock (off
  Scotland)
Bell's palsy
bell tent +s
bell tower +s
bell-wether +s
belly
  bel¦lies
  bel¦lied
  belly¦ing

belly¦ache
  belly¦aches
  belly¦ached
  belly¦ach¦ing
belly¦acher+s
belly¦band+s
belly but¦ton+s
belly dance+s
belly dan¦cer+s
belly dan¦cing
belly¦flop
  belly¦flops
  belly¦flopped
  belly¦flop¦ping
belly¦ful+s
belly land¦ing
belly laugh+s
Bel¦mondo, Jean-
  Paul(French
  actor)
Bel¦mo¦pan
  (capital of Belize)
Belo Hori¦zonte
  (city, Brazil)
be¦long+s +ed
  +ing
be¦long¦ing¦ness
be¦long¦ings
Belo¦rus¦sia
  (alternative name
  for Belarus)
Belo¦rus¦sian +s
Belo¦stok (Russian
  name for
  Białystok)
be¦loved
below (under.
  △ billow)
below-the-line
  attributive
Bel Paese Propr.
Bel¦sen
  (concentration
  camp, Germany)
Bel¦shaz¦zar
  (Babylonian king)
belt +s +ed +ing
belt and braces
Bel¦tane
belt drive +s
belt¦er+s
belt¦man
  belt¦men
belt¦way +s
be¦luga +s
bel¦ve¦dere +s
be¦ly¦ing (present
  participle of belie)
be¦med¦aled Am.
be¦med¦alled Br.
be¦mire
  be¦mires

be¦mire (*cont.*)
  be¦mired
  be¦mir¦ing
be¦moan +s +ed
  +ing
be¦muse
  be¦muses
  be¦mused
  be¦mus¦ing
be¦mused¦ly
be¦muse¦ment
Ben
Ben¦ares (former
  name of
  Varanasi)
Ben¦bec¦ula
  (Scottish island)
Ben Bella, Ahmed
  (Algerian
  statesman)
bench
  benches
  benched
  bench¦ing
bench¦er +s
bench¦mark +s
  +ed +ing
bench seat +s
bench war¦rant +s
bend
  bends
  bent
  bend¦ing
bend¦able
bend¦ed
bend¦er +s
Ben¦digo (town,
  Australia)
bendi¦ness
bend sin¦is¦ter
  bends sin¦is¦ter
bendy
  bend¦ier
  bendi¦est
be¦neath
Bene¦di¦cite
  (canticle)
bene¦di¦cite +s
  (blessing; grace)
Bene¦dict
Bene¦dic¦tine +s
  (monk or nun)
Bene¦dic¦tine
  (liqueur) *Propr.*
bene¦dic¦tion +s
bene¦dic¦tory
Bene¦dic¦tus
bene¦fac¦tion +s
bene¦fac¦tor +s
bene¦fac¦tress
  bene¦fac¦tresses
bene¦fice +s

bene¦ficed
be¦nefi¦cence
be¦nefi¦cent
be¦nefi¦cent¦ly
bene¦fi¦cial
bene¦fi¦cial¦ly
bene¦fi¦ciary
  bene¦fi¦ciar¦ies
bene¦fici¦ation
bene¦fit
  bene¦fits
  bene¦fit¦ed *or*
  bene¦fit¦ted
  bene¦fit¦ing *or*
  bene¦fit¦ting
Bene¦lux
  (= Belgium, the
  Netherlands, and
  Luxembourg)
Ben¦en¦den
  (school, England)
Beneš, Ed¦vard
  (Czechoslovak
  statesman)
Benet¦ton,
  Lu¦ciano and
  Giuli¦ana (Italian
  clothing store
  founders)
be¦nevo¦lence
be¦nevo¦lent
be¦nevo¦lent¦ly
Ben¦gal (region,
  India)
Ben¦gali +s
Ben¦ghazi (port,
  Libya)
Ben¦guela (port,
  Angola)
Ben¦guela
  Cur¦rent (off SW
  Africa)
Ben-Gurion,
  David (Israeli
  statesman)
Beni¦dorm
  (Spanish resort)
be¦night¦ed
be¦night¦ed¦ness
be¦nign
be¦nig¦nancy
be¦nig¦nant
be¦nig¦nant¦ly
be¦nig¦nity
  be¦nig¦nities
be¦nign¦ly
Benin
Benin, Bight of
  (off W. Africa)
Be¦nin¦ese
  plural Be¦nin¦ese
beni¦son +s

Ben¦ja¦min (*Bible*;
  name)
Ben¦late *Propr.*
Ben¦nett, Alan
  (English writer)
Ben¦nett, Ar¦nold
  (English writer)
Ben Nevis
  (mountain,
  Scotland)
benni
Be¦noni (city, South
  Africa)
bent +s
Ben¦tham,
  Jer¦emy (English
  philosopher)
Ben¦tham¦ism
Ben¦tham¦ite +s
ben¦thic
ben¦thos
ben¦ton¦ite
ben tro¦vato
bent¦wood
be¦numb +s +ed
  +ing
Benxi (city, China)
Benz, Karl
  (German car
  maker)
Ben¦ze¦drine *Propr.*
ben¦zene
  (substance
  obtained from
  coal tar)
ben¦zene ring +s
ben¦zen¦oid
ben¦zin (use
  benzine)
ben¦zine
  (substance
  obtained from
  petroleum)
benzo¦di¦azep¦ine
  +s
ben¦zoic
ben¦zoin
ben¦zol
ben¦zole (use
  benzol)
benzo¦quin¦one
ben¦zoyl
ben¦zyl
Beo¦wulf
  (legendary
  Scandinavian
  hero)
be¦queath +s +ed
  +ing
be¦queather +s
be¦quest +s

be¦rate
  be¦rates
  be¦rated
  be¦rat¦ing
Ber¦ber +s
Ber¦bera (port,
  Somalia)
ber¦beris
ber¦ceuse +s
Berch¦tes¦gaden
  (town, Germany)
be¦reave
  be¦reaves
  be¦reaved *or*
  be¦reft
  be¦reav¦ing
be¦reave¦ment +s
be¦reft
Bere¦nice (Egyptian
  queen; name)
beret +s (cap.
  △ berry, bury)
Berg, Alban
  (Austrian
  composer)
berg +s (ice.
  △ burg)
ber¦ga¦masque +s
Ber¦gamo (city,
  Italy)
ber¦ga¦mot +s
Ber¦gen (city,
  Norway)
Ber¦ger, Hans
  (German
  psychiatrist)
Ber¦gerac +s
  (region, France;
  wine)
Ber¦gerac, Cyr¦ano
  de (French soldier
  and writer)
Ber¦gius,
  Fried¦rich
  (German industrial
  chemist)
Berg¦man,
  Ing¦mar (Swedish
  film and theatre
  director)
Berg¦man, Ing¦rid
  (Swedish actress)
berg¦schrund +s
Berg¦son, Henri
  (French
  philosopher)
berg wind +s
Beria, Lav¦renti
  (head of Soviet
  secret police)
be¦rib¦boned
beri¦beri

Ber|ing, Vitus
(Danish navigator
and explorer)
Ber|ing Sea (part of
N. Pacific)
Ber|ing Strait
(between Siberia
and Alaska)
Berio, Lu|ciano
(Italian composer)
berk +s
Berke|leian +s
Berke|ley (city and
university, USA.
⚠ Barkly)
Berke|ley, Busby
(American
choreographer.
⚠ Barclay)
Berke|ley, George
(Irish philosopher
and bishop.
⚠ Barclay)
ber|ke|lium
Berks.
(= Berkshire)
Berk|shire (county,
England)
Ber|lin (capital of
Germany)
Ber|lin, Ir|ving
(American song
writer)
ber|lin +s
(carriage)
Ber|lin|er +s
Ber|lioz, Hec|tor
(French
composer)
berm +s
Ber|muda (country;
rig; shorts)
Ber|mudan +s
Ber|mu|das
(= Bermuda
shorts)
Ber|mu|das, the
(= Bermuda)
Ber|muda
Tri|angle (area of
W. Atlantic)
Ber|mu|dian +s
Bern (German
name for Berne)
Ber|na|dette also
Ber|nar|dette
(name)
Ber|na|dette
(French saint)
Ber|na|dotte,
Folke (Swedish
statesman)

Ber|na|dotte, Jean
(French soldier)
Ber|nard (French
saint; name)
Ber|nard, Claude
(French
physiologist)
Ber|nar|dette also
Ber|na|dette
Ber|nard of
Clair|vaux
(French saint)
Berne (capital of
Switzerland)
Bern|hardt, Sarah
(French actress)
Ber|nice
Ber|nini,
Gian|lor|enzo
(Italian sculptor)
Ber|noulli (Swiss
family of
mathematicians
and scientists)
Bern|stein, Basil
(English
sociologist and
educationist)
Bern|stein,
Leon|ard
(American
composer etc.)
Berra, Yogi
(American
baseball player)
Berry (former
province, France)
Berry, Chuck
(American singer
and songwriter)
berry
ber|ries
ber|ried
berry|ing
(fruit. ⚠ beret,
bury)
ber|serk
ber|serk|er +s
Bert also Burt
berth +s +ed +ing
(bed; place for
ship. ⚠ birth)
Ber|tha (name)
ber|tha +s (collar;
cape)
Ber|til|lon,
Al|phonse
(French
criminologist)
Ber|to|lucci,
Ber|nardo (Italian
film director)

Ber|tram
Ber|trand
Ber|wick|shire
(former county,
Scotland)
Berwick-upon-
Tweed (town,
England)
Beryl (name)
beryl +s (precious
stone)
beryl|lium
Ber|ze|lius, Jöns
(Swedish chemist)
Bes *Egyptian
Mythology*
Be|san|çon (city,
France)
Bes|ant, Annie
(English writer
and politician)
be|seech
be|seeches
be|seeched *or*
be|sought
be|seech|ing
beset
be|sets
beset
be|set|ting
be|set|ment
be|side
be|sides
be|siege
be|sieges
be|sieged
be|sieging
be|sieger +s
be|slaver +s +ed
+ing
be|slob|ber +s +ed
+ing
be|smear +s +ed
+ing
be|smirch
be|smirches
be|smirched
be|smirch|ing
besom +s
be|sot|ted
be|sought
be|span|gle
be|span|gles
be|span|gled
be|span|gling
be|spat|ter +s +ed
+ing
be|speak
be|speaks
be|spoke
be|speak|ing
be|spoken

be|spec|tacled
be|sprin|kle
be|sprin|kles
be|sprin|kled
be|sprink|ling
Bess
Bess|arabia
(region, Moldova
and Ukraine)
Bess|arab|ian +s
Bes|sel, Fried|rich
Wil|helm
(German
astronomer)
Bes|semer, Henry
(English engineer
and inventor;
process;
converter)
Bes|sie also Bessy
Bessy also Bes|sie
Best, Charles
Her|bert
(Canadian
physiologist)
Best, George (Irish
footballer)
best
bests
best|ed
best|ing
(superlative of
good)
bes|tial
bes|tial|ise Br. (use
bestialize)
bes|tial|ises
bes|tial|ised
bes|tial|is|ing
bes|ti|al|ity
bes|ti|al|ities
bes|tial|ize
bes|tial|izes
bes|tial|ized
bes|tial|iz|ing
bes|ti|al|ly
bes|tiary
bes|tiar|ies
be|stir
be|stirs
be|stirred
be|stir|ring
best-known
be|stow +s +ed
+ing
be|stow|al +s
be|stow|ment
be|strew
be|strews
be|strewed
be|strew|ing

be|strew (*cont.*)
  be|strewed *or*
  be|strewn
be|stride
  be|strides
  be|strode
  be|strid|ing
  be|strid|den
best-seller +s
best-selling
Bet *also* Bette
  (name)
bet
  bets
  bet *or* bet|ted
  bet|ting
  (wager)
beta +s (Greek
  letter. △ beater)
beta block|er +s
beta decay
be|take
  be|takes
  be|took
  be|tak|ing
  be|taken
Beta|max *Propr.*
beta par|ticle +s
beta ray +s
beta rhythm +s
beta test +s +ed
  +ing
be|ta|tron +s
beta waves
betel +s (leaf.
  △ beetle)
Betel|geuse (star)
betel-nut +s
bête noire
  bêtes noires
Beth
Bethan
Beth|any
bethel +s
be|think
  be|thinks
  be|thought
  be|think|ing
Beth|le|hem (town,
  Israel)
Beth|une, Henry
  Nor|man
  (Canadian
  surgeon)
be|tide
be|times
bêt|ise +*s*
Betje|man, John
  (English poet)
be|token +s +ed
  +ing

bet|ony
  bet|onies
be|took
be|tray +s +ed
  +ing
be|tray|al +s
be|tray|er +s
be|troth +s +ed
  +ing
be|troth|al +s
Betsy
Bette *also* Bet
bet|ter +s +ed
  +ing
bet|ter|ment
better-off *attributive*
Bet|ter|ton,
  Thomas (English
  actor)
Betti, Ugo (Italian
  writer)
Bet|tina
bet|ting shop +s
bet|tor +s (use
  better)
Betty
be|tween
be|twixt
Beu|lah
Beu|then (German
  name for Bytom)
Bevan, An|eurin
  (Nye) (British
  politician. △ Bevin)
beva|tron
bevel
  bevels
  bev|elled *Br.*
  bev|eled *Am.*
  bev|el|ling *Br.*
  bev|el|ing *Am.*
bev|er|age +s
Bev|er|idge,
  Wil|liam (British
  economist)
Bev|er|ley *also*
  Bev|erly
  (name)
Bev|er|ley (town,
  England)
Bev|erly *also*
  Bev|er|ley
  (name)
Bev|erly Hills (city,
  USA)
Bevin, Er|nest
  (British
  statesman.
  △ Bevan)
bevvy
  bev|vies
  (drink)

bevy
  bev|ies
  (flock)
be|wail +s +ed
  +ing
be|wail|er +s
be|ware
be|whis|kered
Bew|ick, Thomas
  (English artist and
  engraver)
Bew|ick's swan +s
be|wigged
be|wil|der +s +ed
  +ing
be|wil|der|ing|ly
be|wil|der|ment
be|witch
  be|witches
  be|witched
  be|witch|ing
be|witch|ing|ly
bey +s (Ottoman
  governor. △ bay)
be|yond
bez|ant +s
bezel +s
be|zique +s
be|zoar +s
B-film +s
Bhag|avad|gita
bhaji +s
bhakti
bhang (drug.
  △ bang)
bhangra
bharal +s
Bha|rat|pur (bird
  sanctuary, India)
Bhav|nagar (port,
  India)
Bhoj|puri
Bho|pal (city,
  India)
Bhu|ba|nes|war
  (city, India)
Bhu|tan
Bhu|tan|ese
  plural Bhu|tan|ese
Bhutto, Bena|zir
  and Zul|fikar
  (Pakistani prime
  ministers)
bi +s (= bisexual.
  △ buy, by, bye)
Bi|afra
Bi|af|ran +s
Bia|łys|tok (city,
  Poland)
Bi|anca

bi|an|nual (half-
  yearly.
  △ biennial)
bi|an|nu|al|ly (half-
  yearly.
  △ biennially)
Biar|ritz (resort,
  France)
bias
  biases
  biased *or* biassed
  bias|ing *or*
  bias|sing
bias-ply
bi|ath|lete +s
bi|ath|lon +s
bi|axial
bib
  bibs
  bibbed
  bib|bing
bib|ber +s
bib-cock +s
bibe|lot +s
Bible (Christian or
  Jewish scriptures)
bible +s (generally)
Bible-basher +s
Bible-bashing
Bible belt
Bible-puncher +s
Bible-punching
Bible-thumper +s
Bible-thumping
bib|lical
bib|lic|al|ly
bibli|og|raph|er +s
bib|lio|graph|ic
bib|lio|graph|ic|al
bib|lio|graph|ic|
      al|ly
bibli|og|ra|phise
  Br. (use
  bibliographize)
  bibli|og|ra|phises
  bibli|og|ra|phised
  bibli|
     og|ra|phis|ing
bibli|og|ra|phize
  bibli|og|ra|phizes
  bibli|og|ra|phized
  bibli|
     og|ra|phiz|ing
bibli|og|raphy
  bibli|og|raph|ies
bib|lio|mancy
bib|lio|mania
bib|lio|maniac +s
bib|lio|phil +s
bib|lio|phile +s
bib|lio|phil|ic
bibli|oph|ily

bib¦lio¦pole +s
bibli¦op¦oly
bibu¦lous
bibu¦lous¦ness
bi¦cam¦eral
bi¦cam¦eral¦ism
bi¦carb
bi¦car¦bon¦ate +s
bice +s
bi¦cen¦ten¦ary
  bi¦cen¦ten¦ar¦ies
bi¦cen¦ten¦nial +s
bi¦ceph¦al¦ous
bi¦ceps
  plural bi¦ceps
bicker +s +ed +ing
bick¦er¦er +s
bicky
  bick¦ies
bi¦color *Am.* +s
bi¦col¦ored *Am.*
bi¦col¦our *Br.* +s
bi¦col¦oured *Br.*
bi¦con¦cave
bi¦con¦vex
bi¦cul¦tural
bi¦cus¦pid +s
bi¦cus¦pi¦date
bi¦cycle
  bi¦cycles
  bi¦cycled
  bi¦cyc¦ling
bi¦cyc¦ler +s
bi¦cyc¦lic
bi¦cyc¦list +s
bid
  bids
  bid
  or bade *archaic*
  bid¦ding
  bid
  or bid¦den *archaic*
bid¦dabil¦ity
bid¦dable
bid¦der +s
bid¦ding prayer +s
Biddy (name)
biddy
  bid¦dies
  (woman)
bide
  bides
  bided
  bid¦ing
bidet +s
bi¦dir¦ec¦tion¦al
bid¦on¦ville +s
Bie¦der¦meier
Biele¦feld (city,
  Germany)
bi¦en¦nia

bi¦en¦nial +s (two-
  yearly.
  △ biannual)
bi¦en¦ni¦al¦ly (two-
  yearly.
  △ biannually)
bi¦en¦nium
  bi¦en¦ni¦ums *or*
  bi¦en¦nia
bier +s (coffin-
  stand. △ beer)
Bierce, Am¦brose
  (American writer)
bier¦wurst
biff +s +ed +ing
bif¦fin +s
bifid
bif¦ida (in 'spina
  bifida')
bi¦focal +s
bi¦fur¦cate
  bi¦fur¦cates
  bi¦fur¦cated
  bi¦fur¦cat¦ing
bi¦fur¦ca¦tion
big
  big¦ger
  big¦gest
bigam¦ist +s
bigam¦ous
big¦amy
Big Dip¦per
  (constellation)
big dip¦per +s
  (switchback)
Big¦foot
  Big¦feet
  (creature)
big¦gie +s
big¦gish
big-head +s
big-headed
big-headed¦ness
big-hearted
big¦horn +s
bight +s (inlet;
  loop. △ bite, byte)
big-league
  attributive
big-name *attributive*
big¦ness
bigot +s
big¦ot¦ed
big¦ot¦ry
  big¦ot¦ries
big-timer +s
big¦wig +s
Bihar (state, India)
Bi¦hari +s
bijou (small and
  elegant)

bijou
  bi¦joux
  (jewel)
bi¦jou¦terie
bike
  bikes
  biked
  bik¦ing
biker +s
bikie +s
Bi¦kini (atoll, W.
  Pacific)
bi¦kini +s
  (garment)
bikky (use bicky)
  bik¦kies
Biko, Steve (South
  African black
  activist)
bi¦la¦bial
bi¦lat¦eral
bi¦lat¦eral¦ism
bi¦lat¦eral¦ly
Bil¦bao (city, Spain)
bil¦berry
  bil¦berries
bilbo
  bil¦bos *or* bil¦boes
  (sword)
bil¦boes (ankle
  shackles)
Bil¦dungs¦roman
  Bil¦dungs¦romane
bile
bile duct +s
bilge
  bilges
  bilged
  bil¦ging
bilge keel +s
bilge water
bil¦har¦zia
bil¦har¦zia¦sis
bil¦iary
bi¦lin¦gual +s
bi¦lin¦gual¦ism
bili¦ous
bili¦ous¦ness
bili¦ru¦bin
bilk +s +ed +ing
bilk¦er +s
Bill (name)
bill +s +ed +ing
bill¦able
billa¦bong +s
bill¦board +s
bil¦let +s +ed +ing
billet-doux
  billets-doux
bil¦let¦ee +s
bil¦let¦er +s
bill¦fold +s

bill¦head +s
bill¦hook +s
bill¦iard
bill¦iards
Bil¦lings¦gate
  (market, London)
bil¦lion +s
bil¦lion¦aire +s
bil¦lion¦air¦ess
  bil¦lion¦air¦esses
bil¦lionth +s
Bil¦li¦ton
  (= Belitung)
Bill of Rights
bil¦lon
bil¦low +s +ed
  +ing (wave.
  △ below)
bil¦lowy
bill¦post¦er +s
bill¦post¦ing
bill¦stick¦er +s
Billy (name)
billy
  bil¦lies
  (billycan; billy
  goat)
billy¦can +s
billy¦cart +s
billy goat +s
billy-o
billy-oh (use
  billy-o)
bi¦lob¦ate
bi¦lobed
bil¦tong
bi¦manal
bim¦an¦ous
bim¦bashi +s
bimbo +s
bi-media
bi¦met¦al¦lic
bi¦met¦al¦lism
bi¦met¦al¦list +s
bi¦mil¦len¦ary
  bi¦mil¦len¦ar¦ies
bi¦modal
bi¦month¦ly
  bi¦month¦lies
bin
  bins
  binned
  bin¦ning
bin¦ary
  bin¦ar¦ies
bin¦ate
bin¦aural
bind
  binds
  bound
  bind¦ing
bind¦er +s

bind|ery
  bind|er|ies
bindi-eye
bind|ing +s
bind|weed +s
bine +s
bin-end +s
Binet, Al|fred
  (French
  psychologist)
Binet–Simon (test)
binge
  binges
  binged
  binge|ing *or*
  bin|ging
bin|gie +s (use
  bingy)
bin|gle +s
bingo +s
bingy
  bin|gies
bin liner +s
bin|man
  bin|men
bin|nacle +s
Bin|nie
bin|ocu|lar
bin|ocu|lars
bi|no|mial +s
bi|no|mi|al|ly
bi|nom|inal
bint +s
bin|tur|ong +s
bio|assay +s
bio|cen|ology *Am.*
  (*Br.*
  biocoenology)
bio|cen|osis *Am.*
  bio|cen|oses
  (*Br.* biocoenosis)
bio|cen|ot|ic *Am.*
  (*Br.* biocoenotic)
bio|ceram|ic +s
bio|chem|ical +s
bio|chem|ist +s
bio|chem|is|try
bio|chip +s
bio|cide +s
bio|coen|ology *Br.*
  (*Am.*
  biocenology)
bio|coen|osis *Br.*
  bio|coen|oses
  (*Am.* biocenosis)
bio|coen|ot|ic *Br.*
  (*Am.* biocenotic)
bio|com|pati|
          bil|ity
bio|com|pat|ible
bio|com|put|ing
bio|con|trol

bio|degrad|abil|ity
bio|degrad|able
bio|deg|rad|ation
bio|diver|sity
bio|ener|get|ic
bio|ener|get|ics
bio|energy
bio|engin|eer +s
bio|engin|eer|ing
bio|ethi|cist +s
bio|eth|ics
bio|feed|back
bio|flavon|oid
bio|gas
bio|gen|esis
bio|gen|et|ic
bio|gen|ic
bio|geo|graph|ic
bio|geo|graph|ic|al
bio|geog|raphy
biog|raph|er +s
bio|graph|ic
bio|graph|ic|al
biog|raphy
  biog|raph|ies
bio|haz|ard +s
Bioko (island,
  Equatorial Guinea)
bio|logic|al
bio|logic|al|ly
biolo|gist +s
biol|ogy
  biol|ogies
bio|lu|min|
        es|cence
bio|lu|min|es|cent
bio|mass
  bio|masses
bio|mater|ial +s
bio|mathe|mat|ics
biome +s
bio|mech|an|ics
bio|med|ical
bio|medi|cine
bio|met|ric
bio|met|ric|al
bio|met|ri|cian +s
bio|met|rics
bi|om|etry
bio|morph +s
bio|morph|ic
bi|onic
bi|on|ic|al|ly
bi|on|ics
bio|nomic
bio|nom|ics
bio|phys|ic|al
bio|physi|cist +s
bio|phys|ics
bio|pic +s
bi|opsy
  bi|op|sies

bio|rhythm
bio|rhyth|mic
bio|rhyth|mic|
         al|ly
bio|scope +s
bio|sen|sor +s
bio|sphere +s
bio|syn|thesis
  bio|syn|theses
bio|syn|thet|ic
biota
bio|tech|nolo|gist
  +s
bio|tech|nol|ogy
  bio|tech|nolo|gies
bi|ot|ic
bio|tin
bio|tite +s
bi|par|tisan
bi|par|tisan|ship
bi|part|ite
biped +s
bi|pedal
bi|pedal|ism
bi|pedal|ity
bi|phenyl +s
bi|pin|nate
bi|plane +s
bi|po|lar
bi|po|lar|ity
birch
  birches
birch-bark
birch|en
birch-rod +s
birch|wood
bird +s +ed +ing
bird bath +s
bird|brain +s
bird|brained
bird|cage +s
bird call +s
bird|er +s
bird-fancier +s
bir|die
  bir|dies
  bir|died
  birdy|ing
bird|lime
bird-nesting
bird|seed
Birds|eye,
  Clar|ence
  (American
  inventor of frozen
  food)
bird's-eye (plant)
bird's-eye view
bird's-foot +s
  (plant)
bird's-nesting
bird's nest soup

bird|song
bird-strike +s
bird table +s
bird|watch|er +s
bird|watch|ing
bi|refrin|gence
bi|refrin|gent
bi|reme +s
bi|retta +s
Bir|gitta (Swedish
  name for St
  Bridget)
biri|ani +s
Bir|ken|head (port,
  England)
Bir|ming|ham
  (cities, England
  and USA)
biro +s *Propr.*
birth +s +ed +ing
  (being born.
  △ berth)
birth con|trol
birth|day +s
birth|mark +s
birth|place +s
birth rate +s
birth|right +s
birth|stone +s
birth|weight
Birt|wistle,
  Har|ri|son
  (English
  composer)
biry|ani +s (use
  biriani)
Bis|cay (shipping
  area)
Bis|cay, Bay of
  (between France
  and Spain)
bis|cotti
bis|cuit +s
bis|cuity
bise +s (wind)
bi|sect +s +ed
  +ing
bi|sec|tion +s
bi|sect|or +s
bi|sex|ual +s
bi|sexu|al|ity
bish
  bishes
Bish|kek (capital of
  Kyrgyzstan)
Bisho (town, South
  Africa)
bishop +s
bish|op|ric +s
bisk +s (use
  bisque)
Bis|lama

Bis|marck (city, USA)

Bis|marck, Otto, Prince of (German statesman)

Bis|marck Archi|pel|ago (Papua New Guinea)

Bis|marck Sea (part of W. Pacific)

bis|muth

bison
plural bison

bisque +s

Bis|sa|gos Is|lands (off W. Africa)

Bis|sau (capital of Guinea-Bissau)

bis|sex|tile +s

bi|stable

bis|ter *Am.* +s (*Br.* bistre)

bis|tort

bis|toury
bis|tour|ies

bistre *Br.* +s (*Am.* bister)

bis|tro +s

bi|sul|fate *Am.* +s

bi|sul|phate *Br.* +s

bit
bits
bit|ted
bit|ting
(small part; tool; part of bridle; *Computing*; past tense of bite. △ bitts)

bitch
bitches
bitched
bitch|ing

bitch|ily

bitchi|ness

bitchy
bitch|ier
bitchi|est

bite
bites
bit
bit|ing
bit|ten
(cut with teeth; etc. △ bight, byte)

biter +s

bite-size

bite-sized

Bi|thynia (ancient region, Asia Minor)

bit|ing|ly

bit|map
bit|maps
bit|mapped
bit|map|ping

bit part +s

bit|ser +s (use bitzer)

bit|ter +s +er +est

bitter-apple +s

bit|ter|ling +s

bit|ter|ly

bit|tern +s

bit|ter|ness

bitter-sweet

bit|tily

bit|ti|ness

bitts (*Nautical.* △ bit)

bitty
bit|tier
bit|ti|est

bitu|men

bi|tu|min|isa|tion *Br.* (use bituminization)

bi|tu|min|ise *Br.* (use bituminize)
bi|tu|min|ises
bi|tu|min|ised
bi|tu|min|is|ing

bi|tu|min|iza|tion

bi|tu|min|ize
bi|tu|min|izes
bi|tu|min|ized
bi|tu|min|iz|ing

bi|tu|min|ous

bit|zer +s

bi|va|lent *Chemistry*

biva|lent +s *Biology*

bi|valve +s

biv|ouac
biv|ouacs
biv|ou|acked
biv|ou|ack|ing

bivvy
biv|vies

bi|week|ly
bi|week|lies

bi|year|ly

biz

bi|zarre

bi|zarre|ly

bi|zarre|ness

bi|zar|rerie

Bi|zerta (port, Tunisia)

Bi|zerte (use Bizerta)

Bizet, Georges (French composer)

Bjerk|nes, Vil|helm (Norwegian geophysicist and meteorologist)

blab
blabs
blabbed
blab|bing

blab|ber +s +ed +ing

blab|ber|mouth +s

Black, Jo|seph (Scottish chemist)

black +s +ed +ing +er +est (colour; person)

black|amoor +s

black and blue

Black and Tans

black and white

black|ball +s +ed +ing

black|berry
black|berries

black|berry|ing

black|bird +s

black|board +s

black|boy +s (tree)

black|buck
plural black|buck

Black|burn (town, England)

black|cap +s (bird)

black|cock
plural black|cock or black|cocks

black|cur|rant +s

black|en +s +ed +ing

Black|ett, Pat|rick (English physicist)

black-eye bean +s

black-eyed bean +s

black-eyed Susan +s

black|face (sheep; make-up)

black|fel|low +s

black|fish
plural black|fish

black|fly
plural black|fly or black|flies

Black|foot
plural Black|foot or Black|feet

Black For|est gat|eau

Black For|est gat|eaus or Black For|est gat|eaux

black|guard +s

black|guard|ly

black|head +s

black|ish

black|jack +s

black|lead +s +ed +ing

black|leg
black|legs
black|legged
black|leg|ging

black|list +s +ed +ing

black|ly

black|mail +s +ed +ing

black|mail|er +s

Black Maria +s

black mar|ket +s

black mar|ket|eer +s

black mar|ket|eer|ing

black mass
black masses

Black|more, R. D. (English writer)

black|ness

black|out +s

Black|pool (city, England)

black power

black|shirt +s (fascist)

black|smith +s

black spot +s

Black|stone, Wil|liam (English jurist)

black|thorn +s

black|top +s

black|water fever

blad|der +s

blad|der|wort

blad|der|wrack

blade +s

blade-bone +s

bladed

blae|berry
blae|berries

blag
blags
blagged
blag|ging

blag|ger +s
blague
bla|gueur +s
blah
blah-blah
blain +s
Blair (name)
Blair, Tony
  (Scottish
  politician)
Blaise
Blake (name)
Blake, Peter
  (English painter)
Blake, Wil|liam
  (English artist and
  poet)
blakey +s
blam|able *Am.* (*Br.*
  blameable)
blame
  blames
  blamed
  blam|ing
blame|able *Br.*
  (*Am.* blamable)
blame|ful
blame|ful|ly
blame|less
blame|less|ness
blame|worthi|ness
blame|worthy
blanch
  blanches
  blanched
  blanch|ing
Blan|chard, Jean
  (French
  balloonist)
Blanche
blanc|mange +s
blanco
  blan|coes
  blan|coed
  blanco|ing
bland +er +est
bland|ish
  bland|ishes
  bland|ished
  bland|ish|ing
bland|ish|ment +s
bland|ly
bland|ness
blank +s +ed +ing
  +er +est
blan|ket +s +ed
  +ing
blan|ket|weed
blank|ety
blank|ness
blanky
blan|quette +s

Blan|tyre (city,
  Malawi)
blare
  blares
  blared
  blar|ing
blar|ney
blasé
blas|pheme
  blas|phemes
  blas|phemed
  blas|phem|ing
blas|phemer +s
blas|phem|ous
blas|phem|ous|ly
blas|phemy
  blas|phemies
blast +s +ed +ing
blast|er +s
blast-furnace +s
blast-hole +s
blast-off +s *noun*
blas|tula
  blas|tu|lae *or*
  blas|tu|las
bla|tancy
bla|tant
bla|tant|ly
blather +s +ed
  +ing
blather|skite +s
Blaue Reit|er, Der
  (German painters)
Bla|vat|sky,
  Ma|dame
  (Russian
  spiritualist)
blax|ploit|ation
blaze
  blazes
  blazed
  blaz|ing
blazer +s
blaz|ing|ly
blazon +s +ed
  +ing
blaz|on|ment
blaz|on|ry
bleach
  bleaches
  bleached
  bleach|ing
bleach|er +s
bleach|ing
pow|der +s
bleak +er +est
bleak|ly
bleak|ness
blear
blear|ily
bleari|ness

bleary
blear|ier
bleari|est
bleary-eyed
bleat +s +ed +ing
bleat|ing|ly
bleb +s
bleed
  bleeds
  bled
  bleed|ing
bleed|er +s (*coarse
  slang*)
bleep +s +ed +ing
bleep|er +s
blem|ish
  blem|ishes
  blem|ished
  blem|ish|ing
blench
  blenches
  blenched
  blench|ing
blend +s +ed +ing
  (mix; mixture)
blende +s (metal
  sulphide)
blend|er +s
Blen|heim
  (battlefield,
  Germany)
Blen|heim Or|ange
  +s (apple)
Blen|heim Pal|ace
  (in England)
blenny
  blen|nies
blent
bleph|ar|itis
Blér|iot, Louis
  (French aviator)
bles|bok
  plural bles|bok
bles|buck +s
bless
  blesses
  blessed
  bless|ing
bless|ed|ly
bless|ed|ness
bless|ing +s
blest (*poetic
  =* blessed)
blether +s +ed
  +ing
blether|skate +s
  (use blatherskite)
blew (past tense of
  blow. △ blue)
blew|its
  plural blew|its

Bligh, Wil|liam
  (captain of *The
  Bounty*)
blight +s +ed +ing
blight|er +s
Blighty
  (= England)
bli|mey
Blimp (in 'Colonel
  Blimp')
blimp +s (airship;
  barrage balloon;
  camera cover)
blimp|ery
blimp|ish
blind +s +ed +ing
  +er +est
blind|er +s
blind|fold +s +ed
  +ing
blind|ing|ly
blind|ly
blind man's buff
blind|ness
blind side
blind stitch *noun*
blind-stitch
  blind-stitches
  blind-stitched
  blind-stitch|ing
  verb
blind|worm +s
blink +s +ed +ing
blink|er +s +ed
  +ing
blip
  blips
  blipped
  blip|ping
Bliss, Ar|thur
  (English
  composer)
bliss
  blisses
  blissed
  bliss|ing
bliss|ful
bliss|ful|ly
bliss|ful|ness
blis|ter +s +ed
  +ing
blis|tery
blithe
  blither
  blith|est
blithe|ly
blithe|ness
blith|er|ing
blithe|some
Blitz, the (on
  London in 1940)

blitz
  blitzes
  blitzed
  blitz|ing
  (generally)
blitz|krieg +s
Blixen, Karen
  (Danish writer)
bliz|zard +s +ing
bloat +s +ed +ing
bloat|er +s
blob
  blobs
  blobbed
  blob|bing
bloc +s (group of
  governments etc.
  △ block)
Bloch, Er|nest
  (Swiss-born
  composer)
block +s +ed +ing
block|ade
  block|ades
  block|aded
  block|ad|ing
block|ader +s
blockade-runner
  +s
block|age +s
block|board +s
block|bust|er +s
block|bust|ing
block|er +s
block|head +s
block|head|ed
block|head|ing
block|house +s
block|ish
block|ish|ly
block|ish|ness
block|ship +s
bloc vote +s (use
  block vote)
Blod|wen
Bloem|fon|tein
  (judicial capital of
  South Africa)
Blok, Alex|an|der
  (Russian poet)
bloke +s
blond +s *male*
blonde +s *female*
Blon|del (minstrel)
Blon|din, Charles
  (French tightrope-
  walker)
blond|ness
Blood
  plural Blood *or*
  Bloods
  (American Indian)

blood +s +ed +ing
  (body fluid)
blood-and-
  thunder
blood bank +s
blood|bath +s
blood-borne
blood brother +s
blood cell +s
blood clot +s
blood-curdling
blood donor +s
blood-heat
blood|hound +s
blood|ily
bloodi|ness
blood|less
blood|less|ly
blood|less|ness
blood|let|ting
blood|line +s
blood|lust
blood money
blood poi|son|ing
blood pres|sure
blood red +s *noun*
  and adjective
blood-red
  attributive
blood|shed
blood|shot
blood sport +s
blood|stain +s
blood|stained
blood|stock
blood|stone +s
blood|stream +s
blood|suck|er +s
blood|suck|ing
blood sugar
blood test +s
blood|thirst|ily
blood|thirsti|ness
blood|thirsty
blood|thirst|ier
blood|thirsti|est
blood ves|sel +s
blood|worm +s
blood-wort +s
bloody
  blood|ies
  blood|ied
  bloody|ing
  blood|ier
  bloodi|est
Bloody Mary +s
bloody-minded
bloody-minded|ly
bloody-
  minded|ness
bloom +s +ed +ing
bloom|er +s

bloom|ery
  bloom|er|ies
Bloom|field,
  Leon|ard
  (American
  linguist)
Blooms|bury
  (district, London;
  group of writers)
bloop|er +s
Blos|som (name)
blos|som +s +ed
  +ing (flower)
blos|somy
blot
  blots
  blot|ted
  blot|ting
blotch
  blotches
  blotched
  blotch|ing
blotchy
  blotch|ier
  blotchi|est
blot|ter +s
blot|ting paper
blotto
blouse
  blouses
  bloused
  blous|ing
blouson +s
blow
  blows
  blew
  blow|ing
  blown
  (all senses except
  'curse')
blow
  blows
  blowed
  blow|ing
  (curse)
blow-ball +s
blow-by-blow
  attributive
blow-drier +s (use
  blow-dryer)
blow-dry
  blow-dries
  blow-dried
  blow-drying
blow-dryer +s
blow|er +s
blow|fish
  plural blow|fish
blow|fly
  blow|flies
blow|gun +s
blow|hard +s

blow|hole +s
blowi|ness
blow job +s (*coarse
  slang*)
blow|lamp +s
blown
blow-out +s *noun*
blow|pipe +s
blow|torch
  blow|torches
blow-up +s *noun*
blowy
  blow|ier
  blowi|est
blowz|ily
blowzi|ness
blowzy
  blowz|ier
  blowzi|est
blub
  blubs
  blubbed
  blub|bing
blub|ber +s +ed
  +ing
blub|ber|ing|ly
blub|bery
blu|chers
bludge
  bludges
  bludged
  bludg|ing
bludg|eon +s +ed
  +ing
bludger +s
blue
  blues
  blued
  blu|ing *or* blue|ing
  bluer
  blu|est
  (colour;
  depressed.
  △ blew)
Blue|beard
  (fictional wife-
  murderer)
blue|bell +s
blue|berry
  blue|berries
blue|bird +s
blue-black
blue-blooded
blue|bot|tle +s
blue-chip *attributive*
blue-collar
  attributive
blue-eyed
Blue|fields (port,
  Nicaragua)
blue|fish
  plural blue|fish

blue|grass
blue-green+s
blue|gum
blue|ish(use
  bluish)
blue|jacket+s
Blue John
  (mineral)
Blue|man|tle
blue|ness
blue-pencil
  blue-pencils
  blue-pencilled Br.
  blue-penciled Am.
  blue-pencil|ling
  Br.
  blue-pencil|ing
  Am.
  verb
blue|print+s +ed
  +ing
blue|stock|ing+s
blue|stone+s
bluesy
bluet+s
blue|throat+s
blue tit+s
Blue Vin|ney
bluey+s
bluff+s +ed +ing
bluff|er+s
bluff|ly
bluff|ness
blu|ish
Blum, Léon
  (French
  statesman)
Blu|men|bach,
  Jo|hann (German
  physiologist)
Blun|den,
  Ed|mund
  (English writer)
blun|der+s +ed
  +ing
blun|der|buss
blun|der|busses
blun|der|ing|ly
blunge
  blunges
  blunged
  blun|ging
blun|ger+s
Blunt, An|thony
  (English art
  historian and
  Soviet spy)
blunt+s +ed +ing
  +er +est
blunt|ly
blunt|ness

blur
  blurs
  blurred
  blur|ring
blurb+s
blurry
blur|rier
blur|ri|est
blurt+s +ed +ing
blush
  blushes
  blushed
  blush|ing
blush|er+s
blush|ful
blus|ter+s +ed
  +ing
blus|tery
B-lympho|cyte+s
Bly|ton, Enid
  (English writer)
B-movie+s
B.Mus. (= Bachelor
  of Music)
B'nai B'rith
  (Jewish
  organization)
Bo (woman's name.
  △ Beau)
bo+s (interjection;
  form of address to
  man. △ beau,
  bow)
boa+s (snake;
  feather stole.
  △ Boer)
Boa|di|cea (use
  Boudicca)
boar
  plural boar or
  boars
  (pig. △ Boer,
  boor, bore)
board+s +ed +ing
  (timber; go on
  board ship, train,
  etc. △ baud,
  bawd, bored)
board|er+s
  (person who
  boards. △ border)
board game+s
board|ing house
  +s
board|ing ken|nel
  +s
board|ing school
  +s
board|room+s
board|sail|er+s
  (use boardsailor)
board|sail|ing+s

board|sail|or+s
board|walk+s
boart+s (use bort
  diamond.
  △ bought)
Boas, Franz
  (American
  anthropologist)
boast+s +ed +ing
boast|er+s
boast|ful
boast|ful|ly
boast|ful|ness
boast|ing|ly
boat+s +ed +ing
boat|build|er+s
boat-building
boatel+s (use
  botel)
boat|er+s
boat|ful+s
boat-hook+s
boat|house+s
boatie+s
boat|load+s
boat|man
  boat|men
boat people
boat race+s
boat|swain+s
boat|swain's chair
  +s
boat-train+s
boat|yard+s
Boa Vista (town,
  Brazil)
Boaz
Bob (name, but
  'bob's your uncle')
bob
  bobs
  bobbed
  bob|bing
bob|ber+s
Bob|bie also Bobby
bob|bin+s
bob|bin lace
bob|ble+s
bob|bly
Bobby also Bobbie
  (name)
bobby
  bob|bies
bobby-dazzler+s
bobby-pin+s
bobby socks Br.
bobby sox Am.
bobby-soxer+s
bob|cat+s
bobo|link+s

Bo|bru|isk (use
  Babruisk)
bob|sled+s
bob|sled|ding
bob|sleigh+s
bob|stay+s +ed
  +ing
bob|tail+s
boc|age
Boc|cac|cio,
  Gio|vanni (Italian
  writer and
  humanist)
Boc|cher|ini, Luigi
  (Italian composer)
Boche+s (offensive
  German soldier.
  △ bosh)
Bochum (city,
  Germany)
bock+s
bod+s
bo|da|cious
bode
  bodes
  boded
  bod|ing
bode|ful
bo|dega+s
bode|ment+s
Bode's law
bodge
  bodges
  bodged
  bodg|ing
bodgie+s
Bodh|gaya (village,
  India)
Bodhi|sat|tva+s
bod|ice+s
bodice-ripper+s
bodice-ripping
bodi|less
bod|ily
bod|kin+s
Bod|leian Lib|rary
  (in Oxford)
Bod|ley
  (= Bodleian
  Library)
Bo|doni,
  Giam|bat|tista
  (Italian painter)
Bod|rum (town,
  Turkey)
body
  bod|ies
  bod|ied
  body|ing
body bag+s
body blow+s
body|build|er+s

body-building
body-check
   body-checks
   body-checked
   body-checking
body color *Am.* +s
body col|our *Br.*
  +s
body|guard +s
body lan|guage
body-line *attributive*
body louse
  body lice
body pier|cing
body-popping
body scan|ner +s
body-snatch|er +s
body-snatch|ing
body stock|ing +s
body|suit +s
body wall +s
body warm|er +s
body wave +s
body weight
body|work
Boe|otia (region, Greece)
Boe|otian +s
Boer +s (Afrikaner. △boa, boar, boor, bore)
Bo|eth|ius (Roman statesman and philosopher)
bof|fin +s
Bo|fors gun +s
bog
  bogs
  bogged
  bog|ging
bogan +s
Bo|garde, Dirk (British actor)
Bo|gart, Hum|phrey (American actor)
bog|bean +s
bogey +s +ed +ing (in golf; evil spirit; nasal mucus. △bogie)
bo|gey|man
  bo|gey|men
bog|gi|ness
bog|gle
  bog|gles
  bog|gled
  bog|gling
boggy
  bog|gier
  bog|gi|est

bogie +s (wheeled undercarriage. △bogey)
bogle +s
Bo|gotá (capital of Colombia)
bog|trot|ter +s (*offensive*)
bogus
bogus|ness
bogy (use bogey)
  bogies
bogy|man (use bogeyman)
  bogy|men
Bo Hai (inlet, China)
bohea +s
Bo|he|mia (region, Czech Republic)
Bo|he|mian +s (from Bohemia)
bo|he|mian +s (unconventional)
bo|he|mian|ism
boho +s
Bohol (island, Philippines)
Bohr, Niels (Danish physicist)
boil +s +ed +ing
Boi|leau, Nico|las *in full* Boileau-Despré|aux (French critic and writer)
boil|er +s
boiler|maker +s
boiler-plate +s
boil|ing point +s
Boise (city, USA)
bois|ter|ous
bois|ter|ous|ly
bois|ter|ous|ness
Bo|kassa, Jean (Central African dictator)
Bo|khara (= Bukhoro)
Bok|mål
boko +s
bolas
  plural bolas (missile. △bolus)
bold +er +est
bold|face *Printing*
bold|ly
bold|ness
Boldre|wood, Rolf (Australian writer)

bole +s (trunk of tree; clay. △boll , bowl)
bo|lec|tion +s
bol|ero +s
bol|etus
  bol|eti *or* bol|etuses
Bo|leyn, Anne (wife of Henry VIII of England)
Bol|ger, James (New Zealand prime minister)
Bol|ing|broke (surname of Henry IV of England)
Bol|in|ger, Dwight (American linguist)
Bolí|var, Simón (Venezuelan patriot and statesman)
boli|var +s (Venezuelan currency)
Bo|livia
Bo|liv|ian +s
bo|liv|iano +s
Böll, Hein|rich (German writer)
boll (seed-vessel. △bole , bowl)
Bol|land|ist +s
bol|lard +s
Bol|lin|ger +s (champagne) *Propr.*
bol|lock +s +ed +ing (*coarse slang*)
bol|lock|ing +s (*coarse slang*)
bol|locky (*coarse slang*)
boll-weevil +s
Bol|ogna (city, Italy)
bol|ogna (= Bologna sausage)
Bol|ogna saus|age +s
Bol|ognese
bol|om|eter +s
bolo|met|ric
bol|om|etry
bo|lo|ney +s (use baloney)
Bol|shevik +s
Bol|shev|ism

Bol|shev|ist +s
Bol|shie +s (Bolshevik)
bol|shie (rebellious; left-wing)
bol|shi|ness
Bol|shoi (Ballet; Theatre)
Bol|shy
  Bol|shies (use Bolshie)
bol|shy (use bolshie)
bol|ster +s +ed +ing
bol|ster|er +s
bolt +s +ed +ing
bolt|er +s
bolt-hole +s
Bol|ton (town, England)
bolt-on +s *noun and adjective*
Boltz|mann, Lud|wig (Austrian physicist)
bolus
  bo|luses (ball of food etc. △bolas)
Bol|zano (province and city, Italy)
bomb +s +ed +ing (explosive device. △*bombe*)
bom|bard +s +ed +ing (attack)
bom|barde (musical instrument)
bom|bard|ier +s
bom|bard|ment +s
bom|bardon +s
bom|bas|ine +s (use bombazine)
bom|bast
bom|bas|tic
bom|bas|tic|al|ly
Bom|bay (city, India)
bom|baz|ine +s
bombe +*s* (dessert. △bomb)
bombed-out *adjective*
bomb|er +s
bomb|ing +s
bomb-maker +s
bomb-making
bom|bora +s
bomb|proof

bomb|shell +s
bomb|sight +s
(device in aircraft)
bomb-site +s (area
destroyed by
bomb)
Bon, Cape (in
Tunisia)
bona fide
bona fides
plural bona fides
Bon|aire (island,
Netherlands
Antilles)
bon|anza +s
Bona|parte,
Na|po|leon
(French emperors)
bona va|can|tia
Bona|ven|tura
(Italian saint)
bon-bon +s
bonce +s
Bond, James
(fictional British
agent)
bond +s +ed +ing
bond|age
bond|ager +s
bond|hold|er +s
Bondi (resort,
Australia)
bondi +s (weapon)
bonds|man
bonds|men
bond|stone +s
bond-washing
Bône (former name
of Annaba)
bone
  bones
  boned
  bon|ing
bone china
bone dry
bone|fish
plural bone|fish
bone|head +s
bone|head|ed
bone idle
bone lazy
bone|less
bone|meal
bone-oil
boner +s
bone-setter +s
bone|shaker +s
bone-yard +s
bon|fire +s
Bon|fire Night
bongo
plural bongo *or*

bongo (*cont.*)
  bon|gos
(antelope)
bongo +s (drum)
Bon|hoef|fer,
  Diet|rich
(German
theologian)
bon|homie
bon|hom|ous
boni|er
(comparative of
bony)
boni|est
(superlative of
bony)
Boni|face (Anglo-
Saxon saint)
boni|ness
Bon|ing|ton, Chris
(English
mountaineer)
bon|ism
bon|ist +s
Bon|ita
bon|ito +s
bonk +s +ed +ing
bonk|er +s
bonk|ers
bon mot
  bons mots
Bonn (city,
Germany)
Bon|nard, Pierre
(French artist)
bonne bouche
  bonne bouches or
  bonnes bouches
bon|net +s
bon|net|ed
bon|net|head +s
Bon|nie (name)
Bon|nie Prince
  Char|lie (Charles
Edward Stuart, the
'Young
Pretender')
bon|nily
bon|ni|ness
bonny
  bon|nier
  bon|ni|est
(attractive etc.)
bon|sai +s
bon|spiel +s
bont|bok
  plural bont|bok *or*
  bont|boks
bon|te|bok
  plural bon|te|bok
  or bon|te|boks

bonus
  bo|nuses
bon viv|ant
  bon viv|ants *or*
  bons viv|ants
bon viv|eur
  bon viv|eurs *or*
  bons viv|eurs
bon voy|age
bony
  boni|er
  boni|est
bonze +s
bon|zer
boo +s +ed +ing
boob +s +ed +ing
boo|boo +s
boo|book +s
booby
  boo|bies
booby-hatch
  booby-hatches
booby trap +s
  noun
booby-trap
  booby-traps
  booby-trapped
  booby-trapping
  verb
boo|dle
boof|head +s
boo|gie
  boo|gies
  boo|gied
  boo|gie|ing
boogie-woogie
boo|hoo +s +ed
  +ing
book +s +ed +ing
book|able
book|bind|er +s
book|bind|ing +s
book|case +s
book|end +s
book|er +s
Book|er Prize +s
book|ie +s
book|ing +s
book|ing clerk +s
book|ing hall +s
book|ing of|fice +s
book|ish
book|ish|ness
book|keep|er +s
book|keep|ing
book|land
book|let +s
book|list +s
book-louse
  book-lice
book|maker +s
book|mak|ing

book|man
book|men
book|mark +s
book|mark|er +s
book|mobile +s
book|plate +s
book-rest +s
book|sell|er +s
book|shelf
  book|shelves
book|shop +s
book|stall +s
book|store +s
booksy
book-trough +s
book|work
book|worm +s
Boole, George
(English
mathematician)
Bool|ean +s
boom +s +ed +ing
boom|er +s
boom|er|ang +s
  +ed +ing
boom|let +s
boom|slang +s
boom town +s
boon +s
boon|dock +s
boon|dog|gle
  boon|dog|gles
  boon|dog|gled
  boon|dog|gling
Boone, Dan|iel
(American
pioneer)
boong +s (*offensive*)
boon|ies, the
boor +s (rude
person. △ Boer)
boor|ish
boor|ish|ly
boor|ish|ness
boost +s +ed +ing
boost|er +s
boot +s +ed +ing
boot|black +s
boot|boy +s
bootee +s (shoe.
  △ booty)
Bo|ötes
(constellation)
boot-faced
Booth, Wil|liam
and Cath|er|ine
(founders of the
Salvation Army)
booth +s
Boothia, Gulf of
(off Canada)

Boothia
Pen|in|sula (in
Canada)
boot|jack +s
boot|lace +s
Boo|tle (town,
England)
boot|leg
boot|legs
boot|legged
boot|leg|ging
boot|leg|ger +s
boot|less
boot|lick|er +s
boot|maker +s
boot|strap
boot|straps
boot|strapped
boot|strap|ping
boot-tree +s
booty (plunder.
△ bootee)
booze
boozes
boozed
booz|ing
boozer +s
booze-up +s
booz|ily
boozi|ness
boozy
booz|ier
boozi|est
bop
bops
bopped
bop|ping
bo-peep
Bophu|tha|tswana
(former homeland,
South Africa)
bop|per +s
bora +s
Bora-Bora (island,
French Polynesia)
bor|acic
bor|age
borak
bor|ane +s
Borås (city,
Sweden)
bor|ate +s
borax
Bor|azon
bor|bo|ryg|mic
bor|bo|ryg|mus
bor|bo|rygmi
Bor|deaux
plural Bor|deaux
(city, France;
wine)
bor|del +s

bor|dello +s
Bor|der, Allan
(Australian
cricketer)
bor|der +s +ed
+ing (edge.
△ boarder)
Bor|der col|lie +s
bor|der|er +s
bor|der|land +s
bor|der|line +s
Bor|ders (region,
Scotland)
Bor|der ter|rier +s
Bor|det, Jules
(Belgian
bacteriologist and
immunologist)
Bor|done, Paris
(Venetian painter)
bord|ure +s
bore
bores
bored
bor|ing
(make hole; hole;
wave; past tense
of bear. △ boar,
Boer)
bor|eal
bor|ea|lis (in
'aurora borealis')
bored (fed up.
△ baud, bawd,
board)
bore|dom
bore|hole +s
borer +s
Borg, Björn
(Swedish tennis
player)
Bor|ges, Jorge
Luis (Argentinian
writer)
boric
bor|ing +s
bor|ing|ly
bor|ing|ness
Boris
Born, Max
(German
physicist)
born (in 'to be born'
etc. △ borne,
bourn)
born-again
attributive
borne (past
participle of bear.
△ born, bourn)
borné (narrow-
minded)

Born|ean +s
Bor|neo (island,
Malay
archipelago)
Born|holm (island,
Baltic Sea)
Born|holm
dis|ease
Boro|bu|dur
(monument, Java)
Boro|din,
Alek|sandr
(Russian
composer)
Boro|dino (battle
site, Russia)
boro|fluor|ide
boron
bo|ro|nia +s
boro|sili|cate
bor|ough +s
(British town; US
municipal
corporation;
division of New
York; Alaskan
county. △ burgh)
Boro|vets (resort,
Bulgaria)
Bor|ro|mini,
Fran|cesco
(Italian architect)
Bor|row, George
(English writer)
bor|row +s +ed
+ing
bor|row|er +s
bor|row|ing +s
borsch
Bor|stal +s
bort +s (diamond.
△ bought)
bortsch
bor|zoi +s
Bosan|quet,
Ber|nard (English
cricketer)
bosc|age
Bosch,
Hier|ony|mus
(Dutch painter)
Bose, Sat|yen|dra
Nath (Indian
physicist)
Bose, Jag|dis
Chan|dra (Indian
physicist and plant
physiologist)
bosh (nonsense.
△ Boche)
bosie +s

bosk|age (use
boscage)
Bos|kop (town,
South Africa)
bosky
bosk|ier
boski|est
bo's'n +s (use
bosun)
Bos|nia (region,
Bosnia–Herzegovina)
Bosnia–Herzegov|ina
Bos|nian +s
bosom +s
bos|omy
boson +s
Bos|phorus
(= Bosporus)
Bos|porus
(between Black
Sea and Sea of
Marmara)
BOSS (= Bureau of
State Security)
boss
bosses
bossed
boss|ing
bossa nova +s
boss-eyed
boss|ily
bossi|ness
boss-shot +s
bossy
boss|ier
bossi|est
bossy-boots
Bos|ton (town,
England; city,
USA)
bosun +s
Bos|well, James
(biographer of Dr
Johnson)
Bos|well|ian +s
Bos|worth Field
(battlefield,
England)
bot +s
bo|tan|ic
bo|tan|ic|al
bo|tan|ic|al|ly
bot|an|ise Br. (use
botanize)
bot|an|ises
bot|an|ised
bot|an|is|ing
bot|an|ist +s
bot|an|ize
bot|an|izes
bot|an|ized
bot|an|iz|ing

Bot¦any(wool)
bot¦any
  bot|anies
  (study of plants)
Bot¦any Bay(on
  SE coast of
  Australia)
bo|targo
  bo¦tar|goes
botch
  botches
  botched
  botch|ing
botch¦er+s
botel+s
bot¦fly
  bot|flies
both
Botha, Louis
  (South African
  soldier and
  statesman)
Botha, P. W.
  (South African
  statesman)
Botham, Ian
  (English cricketer)
bother+s +ed
  +ing
both¦er|ation
both¦er|some
bothie+s (use
  bothy)
Both|nia, Gulf of
  (part of Baltic Sea)
Both|well, James
  (Earl of Bothwell,
  husband of Mary
  Queen of Scots)
bothy
  both¦ies
bo tree+s
botry|oid¦al
Bot|swana
bott+s (use bot)
bott-fly (use
  botfly)
  bott-flies
Bot¦ti|celli,
  San¦dro
  (Florentine
  painter)
bot¦tle
  bot¦tles
  bot¦tled
  bot¦tling
bot¦tle bank+s
bottle-brush
  bottle-brushes
bottle-feed
  bottle-feeds

bottle-feed(cont.)
  bottle-fed
  bottle-feeding
bottle|ful+s
bot¦tle green+s
  noun and adjective
bottle-green
  attributive
bottle|neck+s
bottle|nose
  plural bottle|nose
bottle-nosed
bot|tler+s
bottle-washer+s
bot¦tom+s +ed
  +ing
bot¦tom|less
bot¦tom|most
bot¦tom¦ry
  bot¦tom|ries
  bot¦tom|ried
  bot¦tom|ry|ing
bottom-up
  attributive
botu|lism
Bou|cher,
  Fran|çois(French
  artist)
Bou|cher de
  Perthes, Jacques
  (French
  archaeologist)
bou¦clé
Bou|dicca(queen
  of the Iceni)
bou|doir+s
bouf|fant+s
Bou¦gain|ville
  (island, Solomon
  Islands)
Bou¦gain|ville,
  Louis de(French
  explorer)
bou¦gain|vil¦lea
  +as
Bou¦gain|vil¦lian
  +s
bough+s (limb of
  tree. △ bow)
bought (past tense
  and past participle
  of buy. △ bort)
bought¦en
bou¦gie+s
bouil¦la|baisse
bouilli
bouil|lon+s
boul|der+s (rock.
  △ bolder)
boul|der clay
boul|dery

boule(French
  bowls)
boule+s (Greek
  council)
boule(inlay; use
  buhl)
boules(French
  bowls; use boule)
boule|vard+s
Bou|lez, Pierre
  (French composer
  and conductor)
Boulle, André-
  Charles(French
  cabinet-maker)
boulle(inlay; use
  buhl)
Bou|logne in full
  Boulogne-sur-
  Mer
  (port, France)
Boult, Ad¦rian
  (English
  conductor)
boult+s +ed +ing
  (use bolt)
Boult|ing, John
  and Roy(British
  film producers and
  directors)
Boul|ton,
  Mat¦thew
  (English engineer)
bounce
  bounces
  bounced
  boun|cing
bounce-back+s
  noun and
  attributive
boun|cer+s
boun|cily
boun|ci|ness
bouncy
  boun|cier
  boun|ci|est
bound+s +ed +ing
bound|ary
  bound|ar¦ies
bound¦en
bound¦er+s
bound|less
bound|less|ness
boun|teous
boun|teous|ness
boun|ti|ful
boun|ti|ful¦ly
Bounty (mutiny
  ship)
bounty
  boun|ties
bounty hunt¦er+s

bou|quet+s
bou|quet garni
  bou|quets gar|nis
Bour|baki
Bour|bon+s
  (French dynasty;
  biscuit;
  reactionary)
bour|bon+s
  (whisky)
Bour¦bon|nais
  (former province,
  France)
bour|don+s
bour|geois
  plural bour|geois
bour|geoisie+s
Bour|guiba, Habib
  ben Ali(Tunisian
  statesman)
Bourke-White,
  Mar|ga¦ret
  (American
  photojournalist)
bourn+s (stream;
  goal; limit.
  △ born, borne)
bourne+s (goal;
  limit; use bourn)
Bourne|mouth
  (resort, England)
bour|rée+s
Bourse(Paris Stock
  Exchange)
bourse+s (money
  market)
bous|tro|phedon
bout+s
bou|tique+s
bou|ton|nière+s
Bou¦vet Is|land (in
  S. Atlantic)
bou|zouki+s
bo|vate+s
bo|vine
bo|vine¦ly
Bov¦ril Propr.
bov¦ver
Bow, Clara
  (American
  actress)
bow+s +ed +ing
  (incline head or
  body; front of
  ship. △ bough)
bow+s +ed +ing
  (knot; ribbon; in
  archery; for violin
  etc. △ beau, bo)
bow-compass
  bow-compasses

bowd¦ler|isa¦tion
Br. (use
bowdlerization)
bowd¦ler|ise Br.
(use bowdlerize)
bowd¦ler|ises
bowd¦ler|ised
bowd¦ler|is¦ing
bowd¦ler|ism
bowd¦ler|iza¦tion
bowd¦ler|ize
bowd¦ler|izes
bowd¦ler|ized
bowd¦ler|iz¦ing
bowel +s
Bowen, Eliza|beth
(Irish-born writer)
bower +s +ed +ing
bower-anchor +s
bower|bird +s
bower-cable +s
bow¦ery
bow¦er|ies
bow¦fin +s
bow|head +s
Bowie, David
(English rock
singer and actor)
bowie +s
bowl +s +ed +ing
(basin; ball; etc.
△bole, boll)
bow-legged
bow-legs
bowl¦er +s
bowl¦er hat +s
noun
bowler-hat
bowler-hats
bowler-hatted
bowler-hatting
verb
bowl|ful +s
bow|line +s
bowl|ing alley +s
bowl|ing crease
+s
bowl|ing green +s
bow¦man
bow¦men
bow¦saw +s
bow¦ser +s
bow|shot
bow|sprit +s
Bow Street (in
London)
bow|string
bow|strings
bow|stringed or
bow|strung
bow|string|ing
bow tie +s

bow win|dow +s
bow-wow +s
bow|yang +s
bow¦yer +s
box
boxes
boxed
box¦ing
Box and Cox
box-bed +s
box|calf
box|calves
box|car +s
Boxer +s (member
of Chinese secret
society)
boxer +s (in
boxing; dog)
box file +s
box¦ful +s
box-haul +s +ed
+ing
Box¦ing Day
box¦ing glove +s
box kite +s
box of|fice +s noun
box-office adjective
box pleat +s
box|room +s
box spring +s
box|wood +s
boxy
box¦ier
box|est
boy +s (male child.
△buoy)
boyar +s
Boyce, Wil|liam
(English
composer)
Boy|cott,
Geof|frey
(English cricketer)
boy|cott +s +ed
+ing
Boyd, Ar¦thur
(Australian artist)
Boyer, Charles
(French actor)
boy|friend +s
boy|hood
boy¦ish
boy|ish¦ly
boy|ish|ness
Boyle, Rob¦ert
(Irish scientist)
Boyle's law
Boyne (river,
Republic of
Ireland)
boyo +s
Boys' Bri|gade

Boy Scout +s
(former name for
a Scout)
boy¦sen|berry
boy¦sen|berries
Boz (pseudonym of
Charles Dickens)
bozo +s
B.Phil. (= Bachelor
of Philosophy)
B-picture +s
bra +s
Bra|bant (former
duchy, NW
Europe)
Brab|ham, Jack
(Australian racing
driver)
brace
braces
braced
bra¦cing
brace|let +s
bracer +s
bra|chial
bra¦chi|ate
bra¦chi|ates
bra¦chi|ated
bra¦chi|at¦ing
bra|chi|ation
bra¦chi|ator +s
bra|chio|pod +s
bra|chio|saurus
bra|chio|
saur¦uses or
bra¦chio|sauri
bra|chis¦to|chrone
+s
bra|chy|ceph¦al¦ic
bra|chy|ceph¦al|
ous
bra|chy|ceph¦aly
bra|chyl¦ogy
bra|chylo¦gies
bra|cing|ness
brack +s
bracken +s
bracket +s +ed
+ing
brack|ish
brack|ish|ness
bract +s
brac|teal
brac|te|ate +s
Brad (name)
brad +s (nail)
brad|awl +s
Brad|bury,
Mal|colm
(English novelist)

Brad|bury, Ray
(American science
fiction writer)
Bra|den
Brad|ford (city,
England)
Brad|ley (name)
Brad|ley, James
(English
astronomer)
Brad|man,
Don|ald
(Australian
cricketer)
Brad|shaw +s
Brady
brady|car¦dia
brae +s (hill.
△bray)
Brae|mar (town,
Scotland)
brag
brags
bragged
brag|ging
Braga (city,
Portugal)
Bra|ganza (city,
Portugal; dynasty)
Bragg, Wil|liam
and Law|rence
(English
physicists)
brag|ga|do¦cio
brag|gart +s
brag|ger +s
brag|ging¦ly
Brahe, Tycho
(Danish
astronomer)
Brahma Hinduism
brahma +s (fowl)
Brah|man +s
(Hindu supreme
being; member of
highest Hindu
class. △Brahmin)
Brah|mana
Brah|man¦ic
Brah|man|ic¦al
Brah|man|ism
Brah|ma|putra
(river, S. Asia)
brah|ma|putra +s
(fowl)
Brah|min +s
(superior person.
△Brahman)
Brahms,
Jo|han¦nes
(German
composer)

braid+s +ed +ing
braid¦er+s
brail+s +ed +ing
(haul up)
Bräila(city, Romania)
Braille(writing for the blind)
Brain, Den¦nis (English horn player)
brain+s +ed +ing
brain|box
    brain|boxes
brain|child
    brain|chil¦dren
brain-damaged
brain-dead
brain death
brain drain+s
Braine, John (English writer)
brain fever
braini|ness
brain|less
brain|pan+s
brain|power
brain|stem+s
brain|storm+s
    +ed +ing
brains trust+s
brain-teaser+s
brain trust+s
brain|wash
    brain|washes
    brain|washed
    brain|wash|ing
brain|wave+s
brain|work
brainy
    brain|ier
    braini|est
braise
    braises
    braised
    brais|ing
    (cook. △ braze)
brake
    brakes
    braked
    brak¦ing
    (slow down; device for slowing; estate car; crushing instrument; thicket; bracken; archaic past tense of break △ break)
brake block+s
brake drum+s

brake|less
brake|man
    brake|men
brake shoe+s
brakes|man
    brakes|men
brake|van+s
Bra¦mah, Jo¦seph (English inventor)
Bra|mante, Do¦nato(Italian architect)
bram¦ble
    bram¦bles
    bram¦bled
    bram|bling
bram|bling+s
bram¦bly
Bram|ley+s
Bram|ley's seed|ling+s
bran
Bran|agh, Ken|neth(English actor and director)
branch
    branches
    branched
    branch|ing
bran|chia
bran|chiae
bran|chial
bran|chi¦ate
branch|let+s
branch|like
branchy
Bran|cusi, Con¦stan|tin (Romanian sculptor)
brand+s +ed +ing
Bran¦den|burg (state, Germany)
brand¦er+s
bran|dish
    bran|dishes
    bran|dished
    bran|dish|ing
    bran|dish|er+s
brand|ling+s
brand new
Brando, Mar¦lon (American actor)
Bran|don
Brands Hatch (motor-racing circuit, England)
Brandt, Bill (British photographer)

Brandt, Willy (German statesman)
brandy
    bran|dies
brandy ball+s
brandy but¦ter
brandy snap+s
brank-ursine
brant+s
bran tub+s
Braque, Georges (French painter)
Brase|nose(Oxford college)
brash
brash¦ly
brash|ness
Bra|silia(city, Brazil)
Bra¦şov(city, Romania)
brass
    brasses
    brassed
    brass|ing
brass|age
bras|sard+s
brassed off
bras|serie+s
Bras|sey, Thomas (English engineer)
bras|sica+s
brassie+s (golf club)
bras|siere+s
brass|ily
brassi|ness
Brassó (Hungarian name for Braşov)
brass-rubbing
brass|ware
brassy
    brass|ier
    brassi|est
    (like brass)
brassy (golf club; use brassie)
brass|ies
brat+s
Brati|slava (capital of Slovakia)
brat pack+s
brat pack¦er+s
brat¦tice+s
bratty
brat|wurst+s

Braun, Karl (German physicist)
Braun, Wern¦her von(German rocket designer)
Braun|schweig (city, Germany)
bra|vado
brave
    braves
    braved
    brav¦ing
    braver
    brav¦est
brave¦ly
brave|ness
bravery
bravo+s (cry of approval)
bravo
    bra|voes or bra¦vos (desperado)
bra|vura
braw
brawl+s +ed +ing
brawl¦er+s
brawn
brawni|ness
brawny
    brawn|ier
    brawni|est
Bray (in 'The Vicar of Bray')
bray+s +ed +ing (cry of donkey; crush. △ brae)
braze
    brazes
    brazed
    braz¦ing
    (solder. △ braise)
bra|zen+s +ed +ing
brazen-faced
bra|zen¦ly
bra|zen|ness
bra|zier+s
bra|ziery
bra¦zier|ies
Bra|zil
bra¦zil+s (nut; wood)
Bra¦zil|ian+s
Bra¦zil nut+s
Bra¦zil wood+s
Braz¦za|ville (capital of the Republic of the Congo)

breach
　breaches
　breached
　breach|ing
　(break; failure; etc.
　⚠ breech)
bread +s +ed +ing
　(loaf etc.; coat
　with breadcrumbs.
　⚠ bred)
bread-and-butter
　attributive
bread|bas|ket +s
bread bin +s
bread|board +s
bread|crumb +s
bread|fruit
　plural bread|fruit
　or bread|fruits
bread|line
breadth +s
breadth|ways
breadth|wise
bread|win|ner +s
break
　breaks
　broke
　break|ing
　broken
　(shatter; make or
　become
　inoperative; etc.
　⚠ brake)
break|able +s
break|age +s
break|away +s
　noun and
　attributive
break-dancing
break|down +s
　noun
break|er +s
break|fast +s +ed
　+ing
break|fast|er +s
break-in +s noun
break|ing point +s
break-line +s
break|neck
break-off +s noun
　and attributive
break|out +s noun
break|point +s
　Computing
break point +s
　(Tennis;
　interruption)
Break|spear,
　Nich|olas
　(English pope,
　Adrian IV)

break|through +s
　noun
break-up +s noun
　and attributive
break|water +s
Bream, Ju|lian
　(English classical
　guitarist and
　lutenist)
bream
　plural bream
　(fish)
breast +s +ed +ing
breast|bone +s
breast|feed
　breast|feeds
　breast|fed
　breast|feed|ing
breast-high
breast|less
breast-pin +s
breast|plate +s
breast pocket +s
breast|stroke
breast|sum|mer
　+s
breast|work +s
breath +s noun
breath|able
breath|alyse Br.
　breath|alyses
　breath|alysed
　breath|alys|ing
breath|alyser Br.
　+s
breath|alyze Am.
　breath|alyzes
　breath|alyzed
　breath|alyz|ing
breath|alyzer Am.
　+s Propr.
breathe
　breathes
　breathed
　breath|ing
　verb
breather +s
breath|ily
breathi|ness
breathing-space
　+s
breath|less
breath|less|ly
breath|less|ness
breath|tak|ing
breath|tak|ing|ly
breath test +s
breathy
　breath|ier
　breathi|est
brec|cia +s

brec|ci|ate
　brec|ci|ates
　brec|ci|ated
　brec|ci|at|ing
brec|ci|ation
Brecht, Ber|tolt
　(German
　dramatist)
Breck|nock|shire
　(alternative name
　for Breconshire)
Brecon (town,
　Wales)
Brecon Bea|cons
　(hills, Wales)
Brecon|shire
　(former county,
　Wales)
bred (past tense
　and past participle
　of breed.
　⚠ bread)
Breda (town, the
　Netherlands)
breech
　breeches
　breeched
　breech|ing
　(part of gun;
　buttocks; put into
　breeches.
　⚠ breach)
breech birth +s
breech-block +s
breeches (trousers)
Breeches Bible
breeches-buoy +s
breech-loader +s
breech-loading
breed
　breeds
　bred
　breed|ing
breed|er +s
breed|ing ground
　+s
breeks
breeze
　breezes
　breezed
　breez|ing
breeze-block +s
breeze|less
breeze|way +s
breez|ily
breezi|ness
breezy
　breez|ier
　breezi|est
Bre|genz (city,
　Austria)

Bre|men (state and
　city, Germany)
brems|strahl|ung
Bren +s (= gun)
Brenda
Bren|dan (Irish
　saint)
Bren|del, Al|fred
　(Austrian pianist)
Bren gun +s
Bren|nan
Bren|ner Pass (in
　the Alps)
Brent (name)
brent +s (goose)
brent-goose
　brent-geese
Brescia (city, Italy)
Bres|lau (German
　name for
　Wrocław)
Bres|son, Rob|ert
　(French film
　director)
Brest (port, France;
　city, Belarus)
Brest-Litovsk
　(former name of
　Brest, Belarus)
breth|ren
Bre|ton +s
Bre|ton, André
　(French writer)
Brett
bret|zel +s
Breu|ghel (use
　Bruegel or
　Brueghel)
Breuil, Henri
　(French
　archaeologist)
breve +s
brevet
　brev|ets
　brev|et|ed or
　brev|et|ted
　brev|et|ing or
　brev|et|ting
bre|vi|ary
　bre|vi|ar|ies
brev|ity
　brev|ities
brew +s +ed +ing
brew|er +s
brew|ery
　brew|er|ies
Brew|ster, David
　(Scottish
　physicist)
brew|ster +s
brew-up +s noun

Brezh|nev,
  Leo|nid (Soviet
  statesman)
Brian *also* **Bryan**
Brian Boru (Irish
  king)
Bri|and, Aris|tide
  (French
  statesman)
Bri|ansk (use
  Bryansk)
briar +s (use **brier**)
Bri|ard +s
brib|able
bribe
  bribes
  bribed
  brib|ing
briber +s
brib|ery
  brib|er|ies
bric-a-brac
brick +s +ed +ing
brick|bat +s
brick-built
brick-field +s
brick|field|er +s
brickie +s
  (bricklayer.
  ⚠ bricky)
brick|lay|er +s
brick|lay|ing
brick red +s *noun
  and adjective*
brick-red *attributive*
brick|work +s
bricky (made of
  many bricks.
  ⚠ brickie)
brick|yard +s
bri|dal (of bride.
  ⚠ bridle)
bri|dal|ly
Bride (Irish saint)
bride +s
bride|groom +s
bride price +s
brides|maid +s
bride|well +s
Bridge, Frank
  (English
  composer)
bridge
  bridges
  bridged
  bridg|ing
bridge|able
bridge-builder +s
bridge-building
bridge-deck +s
bridge|head +s

Bridge of Sighs (in
  Venice)
Bridges, Rob|ert
  (English poet)
Bridget *also* **Brigid,
  Brigit**
Bridget (Irish and
  Swedish saints)
Bridge|town
  (capital of
  Barbados)
bridge|work
Bridg|man, Percy
  Wil|liams
  (American
  physicist)
bri|die +s
bridle
  bridles
  bridled
  brid|ling
  (for horse; bring
  under control.
  ⚠ bridal)
bridle path +s
bridle|way +s
bri|doon +s
Brie (cheese)
brief +s +ed +ing
  +er +est
brief|case +s
brief|less
brief|ness
brier +s
brier rose +s
bri|ery
brig +s
bri|gade
  bri|gades
  bri|gaded
  bri|gad|ing
briga|dier +s
briga|dier gen|eral
  +s
briga|low +s
brig|and +s
brig|and|age
brig|an|dine +s
brig|and|ish
brig|and|ism
brig|and|ry
brig|an|tine +s
Briggs, Henry
  (English
  mathematician)
Brig|ham
Bright, John
  (English political
  reformer)
bright +er +est
bright|en +s +ed
  +ing

bright-eyed
bright|ish
bright|ly
bright|ness
Brighton (town,
  England)
Bright's dis|ease
bright|work
Brigid *also* **Bridget,
  Brigit**
Brigit *also* **Bridget,
  Brigid**
Bri|gitte
brill
  plural **brill**
  (fish; brilliant)
bril|liance
bril|liancy
bril|liant +s
bril|liant|ine
bril|li|ant|ly
brim
  brims
  brimmed
  brim|ming
brim|ful (use brim-
  full)
brim-full
brim|less
brim|stone
brim|stony
brin|dle
brin|dled
Brind|ley, James
  (British canal
  builder)
brine
  brines
  brined
  brin|ing
bring
  brings
  brought
  bring|ing
bring-and-buy +s
bring|er +s
brini|ness
brin|jal +s
Brink, André
  (South African
  writer)
brink
brink|man|ship
brinks|man|ship
briny
  brini|er
  brini|est
brio
bri|oche +s
Bri|ony *also*
  Bry|ony

bri|quet +s (use
  briquette)
bri|quette +s
Bris|bane (city,
  Australia)
brisk +er +est
brisk|en +s +ed
  +ing
bris|ket +s
brisk|ness
bris|ling (fish)
bris|tle
  bris|tles
  bris|tled
  brist|ling
  (stiff hair etc.)
bristle|cone pine
  +s
bristle|tail +s
bristle|worm +s
brist|ly
Bris|tol (city,
  England)
Bris|tol fash|ion
Bris|tols
Brit +s
Brit|ain
Bri|tan|nia
Bri|tan|nic
Briti|cism +s
Brit|ish
Brit|ish
  Col|um|bia
  (province,
  Canada)
Brit|ish|er +s
Brit|ish Hon|duras
  (former name of
  Belize)
Brit|ish|ism +s
  (use Briticism)
Brit|ish|ness
Briton +s
Brit|tany (region,
  France; name)
Brit|ten,
  Ben|ja|min
  (English
  composer)
brit|tle
brittle-bone
  disease
brittle|ly
brittle|ness
brittle-star +s
brit|tly
Brit|ton|ic
britzka +s
Brno (city, Czech
  Republic)
bro (= brother)

broach
  broaches
  broached
  broach|ing
  (pierce; raise
  subject; spire; a
  spit. ⚠ brooch)
broad +s +er +est
broad|band
broad-based
broad bean +s
broad-brush
broad|cast
  broad|casts
  broad|cast *or*
  broad|cast|ed
  broad|cast|ing
broad|cast|er +s
Broad Church
broad|cloth
broad|en +s +ed
  +ing
broad|leaved
broad|loom +s
broad|ly
broad-minded
broad-minded|ly
broad-
  minded|ness
Broad|moor
  (secure hospital,
  England)
Broads, the
  (region, England)
broad|sheet +s
broad|side +s
broad|sword +s
broad|tail +s
Broad|way (in New
  York)
broad|way +s
  (broad road)
broad|wise
Brob|ding|nag
  (imaginary
  country)
Brob|ding|nag|ian
  +s
bro|cade
  bro|cades
  bro|caded
  bro|cad|ing
broc|coli
broch +s (tower.
  ⚠ brock)
bro|chette +s
bro|chure +s
brock +s (badger.
  ⚠ broch)
Brocken
  (mountain,
  Germany)

brocket +s
bro|derie an|glaise
Brod|sky, Jo|seph
  (Russian-born
  American poet)
brogue +s
broil +s +ed +ing
broil|er +s
broil|er house +s
broke
broken
broken-down
  adjective
broken-hearted
Broken Hill (town,
  Australia; former
  name of Kabwe)
broken|ness
broken-winded
broker +s
broker|age +s
broker-dealer +s
brok|ing
brolga +s
brolly
  brol|lies
bro|mate +s
Brom|berg
  (German name for
  Bydgoszcz)
brome +s
bro|melia +s
bro|meliad +s
bro|mic
brom|ide +s
brom|ine
brom|ism
bronc +s
bron|chi
bron|chia
bron|chial
bron|chi|olar
bron|chi|ole +s
bron|chit|ic +s
bron|chitis
bron|cho|cele +s
bron|cho|di|la|tor
  +s
bron|cho|
    pneu|mo|nia
bron|cho|scope +s
bron|chos|copy
bron|chus
  bron|chi
bronco +s
bronco|bust|er +s
Brontë, Anne,
  Char|lotte, and
  Emily (English
  writers)
bron|to|saur +s

bron|to|saurus
bron|to|saur|uses
  or bron|to|sauri
Bron|wen
Bronx, the
  (borough, New
  York)
bronze
  bronzes
  bronzed
  bronz|ing
Bronze Age
bronzy
brooch
  brooches
  (ornamental
  fastening.
  ⚠ broach)
brood +s +ed +ing
brood|er +s
brood|ily
broodi|ness
brood|ing|ly
brood mare +s
broody
  brood|ier
  broodi|est
Brook, Peter
  (English stage and
  film director)
brook +s +ed +ing
Brooke (name)
Brooke, Ru|pert
  (English poet)
Brook|lands
  (motor-racing
  circuit, England)
brook|let +s
brook|lime
Brook|lyn
  (borough, New
  York)
Brook|ner, Anita
  (English novelist)
brook|weed
broom +s +ed
  +ing (brush;
  shrub. ⚠ brume)
broom|rape +s
broom|stick +s
brose
broth +s
brothel +s
brother
  broth|ers *or in
  religious use*
  breth|ren
brother ger|man
  broth|ers ger|man
brother|hood +s
brother-in-law
  brothers-in-law

broth|er|li|ness
broth|er|ly
brother uter|ine
  broth|ers uter|ine
brougham +s
brought
brou|haha +s
Brou|wer,
  Adri|aen (Flemish
  painter)
brow +s
brow|beat
  brow|beats
  brow|beat
  brow|beat|ing
  brow|beat|en
brow|beat|er +s
browed
Brown, Ar|thur
  Whit|ten
  (Scottish aviator)
Brown,
  Cap|abil|ity
  (English landscape
  gardener)
Brown, Ford
  Madox (British
  painter)
Brown, George
  Mac|kay
  (Scottish writer)
Brown, James
  (American singer)
Brown, John
  (American
  abolitionist)
brown +s +ed
  +ing +er +est
brown-bagger +s
Browne, Thomas
  (English
  physician)
browned off
brown|field
  attributive
Brown|ian +s
Brownie +s
  (former name for
  a Brownie Guide)
brownie +s
  (goblin; cake)
Brownie Guide +s
Brownie Guider
  +s
brownie point +s
Brown|ing,
  Eliza|beth
  Bar|rett and
  Rob|ert (English
  poets)
Brown|ing +s
  (gun)

brown|ish
brown|ness
brown-nose
  brown-noses
  brown-nosed
  brown-nosing
Brown Owl +s
  (Brownie Guide
  leader)
brown owl +s
  (bird)
Brown|shirt +s
brown|stone +s
browny
browse
  browses
  browsed
  brows|ing
browser +s
Bruce
Bruce, Rob|ert the
  (Scottish king)
Bruce, James
  (Scottish explorer)
Bruce, James (Earl
  of Elgin)
bru|cel|losis
bru|cite
Bruck|ner, Anton
  (Austrian
  composer)
Brue|gel, Pieter
  ('the Elder' and
  'the Younger',
  Flemish artists)
Brue|gel, Jan
  (Flemish artist)
Brue|ghel (use
  Bruegel)
Bruges (city,
  Belgium)
Bruin (bear)
bruise
  bruises
  bruised
  bruis|ing
bruiser +s
bruit +s +ed +ing
  (spread rumour.
  ⚠ brut, brute)
Brum
  (= Birmingham)
brumby
  brum|bies
brume (mist.
  ⚠ broom)
Brum|ma|gem
Brum|mell, Beau
  (English dandy)
Brum|mie +s

Brummy (use
  Brummie)
  Brum|mies
bru|mous
brunch
  brunches
  brunched
  brunch|ing
Brundt|land, Gro
  Har|lem
  (Norwegian
  stateswoman)
Bru|nei (sultanate,
  Borneo)
Bru|neian +s
Bru|nel, Marc
  Isam|bard and
  Isam|bard
  King|dom
  (English
  engineers)
Bru|nel|les|chi,
  Fi|lippo
  (Florentine
  architect)
bru|net +s (use
  brunette)
bru|nette +s
Brun|hild *Germanic
  Legend*
Bruno (German-
  born French saint;
  name)
Bruno, Gior|dano
  (Italian
  philosopher)
Bruns|wick
  (English name for
  Braunschweig)
brunt
brush
  brushes
  brushed
  brush|ing
brush|fire +s
brush|less
brush|like
brush-off +s *noun*
brush stroke +s
brush-up +s *noun*
brush|wood
brush|work
brushy
brusque
  brusquer
  brusquest
brusque|ly
brusque|ness
brus|querie
Brus|sels (capital of
  Belgium)
Brus|sels sprout
  +s

brut (of wine.
  ⚠ bruit, brute)
bru|tal
bru|tal|isa|tion *Br.*
  (use
  brutalization)
bru|tal|ise *Br.* (use
  brutalize)
  bru|tal|ises
  bru|tal|ised
  bru|tal|is|ing
bru|tal|ism
bru|tal|ist
bru|tal|ity
  bru|tal|ities
bru|tal|iza|tion
bru|tal|ize
  bru|tal|izes
  bru|tal|ized
  bru|tal|iz|ing
bru|tal|ly
brute +s (brutal
  person; etc.
  ⚠ bruit, brut)
brute force
bru|tish
bru|tish|ly
bru|tish|ness
Bru|tus (supposed
  ancestor of the
  British)
Bru|tus, Lu|cius
  Jun|ius
  (legendary
  founder of the
  Roman Republic)
Bru|tus, Mar|cus
  Jun|ius (Roman
  senator)
brux|ism
Bryan *also* **Brian**
Bry|ansk (city,
  Russia)
Bryl|creem *Propr.*
Bryl|creemed
Bryn|ner, Yul
  (American actor)
bryo|logic|al
bry|olo|gist +s
bry|ology
Bry|ony *also*
  Bri|ony (name)
bry|ony
  bry|onies
  (plant)
bryo|phyte +s
bryo|phyt|ic
bryo|zoan +s
bryo|zo|ology
Bry|thonic
B side +s (second
  team)

B-side +s (of
  record etc.)
bub +s
bubal
bub|ble
  bub|bles
  bub|bled
  bub|bling
bub|ble bath +s
bubble|gum
bub|bly
  bub|blier
  bub|bli|est
bubbly-jock +s
Buber, Mar|tin
  (Austrian-born
  Israeli
  philosopher)
bubo
  bu|boes
bu|bon|ic
bu|bono|cele +s
buc|cal (of the
  cheek or mouth.
  ⚠ buckle)
buc|can|eer +s
  +ed +ing
buc|can|eer|ish
buc|cin|ator +s
Bu|ce|llas (region,
  Portugal)
Bu|ceph|alus
  (Alexander the
  Great's horse)
Buchan,
  Alex|an|der
  (Scottish
  meteorologist)
Buchan, John
  (Scottish writer
  and statesman)
Bu|chanan, James
  (American
  president)
Bu|cha|rest (capital
  of Romania)
Buchen|wald
  (concentration
  camp, Germany)
Buch|man|ism
Buch|man|ite +s
Buch|ner, Ed|uard
  (German organic
  chemist)
buck +s +ed +ing
buck|bean +s
buck|board +s
buck|er +s
bucket +s +ed
  +ing
bucket|ful +s
bucket shop +s

buck|eye +s
buck-horn
buck-hound +s
Buck|ing|ham
    Pal|ace (in
    London)
Buck|ing|ham|
    shire (county,
    England)
Buck|land,
    Wil|liam (English
    geologist)
buckle
    buckles
    buckled
    buck|ling
    (fastener; fasten;
    crumple; make an
    effort. △ buccal)
buck|ler +s
Buck|ley's
    (chance)
buck|ling +s
buck|min|ster|
        ful|ler|ene
bucko
    buck|oes
buck-passing
buck|ram
buck rare|bit
Bucks.
    (= Buckingham-
    shire)
Buck's Fizz
buck|shee
buck|shot
buck|skin +s
buck|thorn +s
buck-tooth
    buck-teeth
buck-toothed
buck|wheat
bucky|ball +s
bu|col|ic
bu|col|ic|al|ly
bud
    buds
    bud|ded
    bud|ding
Buda|pest (capital
    of Hungary)
Bud|dha (founder
    of Buddhism)
Buddh Gaya
    (= Bodhgaya)
Bud|dhism
Bud|dhist +s
Bud|dhis|tic
Bud|dhis|tic|al
bud|dleia +s
buddy
    bud|dies

buddy (cont.)
    bud|died
    buddy|ing
Budge, Don
    (Australian tennis
    player)
budge
    budges
    budged
    budg|ing
budg|eri|gar +s
budget +s +ed
    +ing
budget|ary
budgie +s
Bud|weis (German
    name for Ceské
    Budějovice)
Buena|ven|tura
    (port, Colombia)
Bue|nos Aires
    (capital of
    Argentina)
buff +s +ed +ing
Buf|falo (city, USA)
buf|falo
    plural buf|falo or
    buf|fa|loes
Buf|falo Bill
    (nickname of
    William Cody,
    American
    showman)
buf|fer +s
buf|fet +s +ed
    +ing
buffle|head +s
buffo +s
Buf|fon, Georges-
    Louis, Comte de
    (French naturalist)
buf|foon +s
buf|foon|ery
buf|foon|ish
buff-stick +s
bug
    bugs
    bugged
    bug|ging
bug|aboo +s
Bu|ganda (former
    kingdom, E.
    Africa)
bug|bear +s
bug-eyed
bug|ger +s +ed
    +ing (coarse slang)
bugger-all (coarse
    slang)
bug|gery
Bug|gins's turn

buggy
    bug|gies
    bug|gier
    bug|gi|est
bugle
    bu|gles
    bu|gled
    bu|gling
bugle call +s
bugle-horn +s
bu|gler +s
bu|glet +s (small
    bugle)
bug|let +s (small
    bug in program)
bu|gloss
    bu|glosses
buhl +s (inlay.
    △ boule)
build
    builds
    built
    build|ing
build|er +s
build|ers'
    mer|chant +s
build|ing +s
build-up +s noun
built-in +s adjective
    and noun
built-up adjective
Bu|jum|bura
    (capital of
    Burundi)
Bu|khara
    (= Bukhoro)
Bu|kha|rin,
    Niko|lai (Soviet
    political leader)
Bu|khoro (city,
    Uzbekistan)
Buko|vina (region,
    SE Europe)
Bu|kow|ski,
    Charles
    (American writer)
Bula|wayo (city,
    Zimbabwe)
bulb +s
bul|bil +s (small
    bulb)
bulb|ous
bul|bul +s (bird)
Bul|ga|kov,
    Mikh|ail (Russian
    writer)
Bul|ga|nin,
    Niko|lai (Soviet
    political leader)
Bul|gar +s
bul|gar (wheat)
Bul|garia

Bul|gar|ian +s
bulge
    bulges
    bulged
    bul|ging
bul|ghur (use
    bulgar)
bul|gur (use
    bulgar)
bulgy
    bul|gier
    bul|gi|est
bu|lima|rexia
bu|lima|rex|ic +s
bu|limia
    (ner|vosa)
bu|lim|ic +s
bulk +s +ed +ing
bulk-buy +s +ed
    +ing verb
bulk buy|ing noun
bulk|head +s
bulk|ily
bulki|ness
bulky
    bulk|ier
    bulki|est
Bull, the
    (constellation;
    sign of zodiac)
bull +s +ed +ing
bul|lace +s
bul|late
bull|dog +s
bull|dog clip +s
bull|doze
    bull|dozes
    bull|dozed
    bull|doz|ing
bull|dozer +s
bul|let +s
bullet-headed
bul|letin +s
bul|letin board +s
bul|let|proof
bull-fiddle +s
bull|fight +s
bull|fight|er +s
bull|fight|ing
bull|finch
    bull|finches
bull|frog +s
bull|head +s
bull-headed
bull-headed|ness
bull|horn +s
bul|lion
bull|ish
bull|ish|ly
bull|ish|ness
bull mar|ket +s
bull-nose

bull-nosed
bul|lock +s
bul|locky
bul|lock|ies
bul|ring +s
Bull Run (river and
  battlefield, USA)
bull-running
bull's-eye +s
bull|shit (coarse
  slang)
bull|shit|ter +s
  (coarse slang)
bull-terrier +s
bull|trout +s
bully
  bul|lies
  bul|lied
  bully|ing
bully boy +s
bully|rag
  bully|rags
  bully|ragged
  bully|rag|ging
bul|rush
  bul|rushes
Bult|mann,
  Ru|dolf (German
  theologian)
bul|wark +s
Bulwer-Lytton,
  Ed|ward (English
  writer and
  statesman)
bum
  bums
  bummed
  bum|ming
bum|bag +s
bum-bailiff +s
bum|ble
  bum|bles
  bum|bled
  bum|bling
bumble-bee +s
bumble|dom
bumble-puppy
  bumble-puppies
bum|bler +s
bum|boat +s
bum|boy +s
bumf
bumi|putra
  plural bumi|putra
  or bumi|pu|tras
bum|malo
  plural bum|malo
bum|mer +s
bump +s +ed +ing
bump|er +s
bumph (use bumf)
bump|ily

bumpi|ness
bump|kin +s
bump-start +s +ed
  +ing
bump|tious
bump|tious|ly
bump|tious|ness
bumpy
  bump|ier
  bumpi|est
bum's rush
bum-sucker +s
  (coarse slang)
bum-sucking
  (coarse slang)
bun +s
Buna Propr.
Bun|bury (town,
  Australia)
bunch
  bunches
  bunched
  bunch|ing
bunchy
bunco
  bun|coes
  bun|coed
  bunco|ing
bun|combe (use
  bunkum)
bun|der +s
Bun|des|bank
Bun|des|rat
Bun|des|tag
bun|dle
  bun|dles
  bun|dled
  bund|ling
bund|ler +s
bundo|bust
bun fight +s
bung +s +ed +ing
bun|ga|low +s
bun|gee +s
bun|gee jump|ing
bung-hole +s
bun|gle
  bun|gles
  bun|gled
  bun|gling
bun|gler +s
Bunin, Ivan
  (Russian poet)
bun|ion +s
bunk +s +ed +ing
bunk bed +s
bun|ker +s +ed
  +ing
Bun|ker Hill
  (battlefield, USA)
bunk|house +s
bun|kum

bunny
  bun|nies
Bun|sen, Rob|ert
  (German chemist;
  burner)
bunt +s +ed +ing
bun|tal +s
Bun|ter, Billy
  (fictional
  schoolboy)
bunt|ing
bunt|line +s
Bunty
Bu|ñuel, Luis
  (Spanish film
  director)
bunya +s
bunya bunya +s
Bun|yan, John
  (English religious
  writer)
bun|yip +s
Buona|parte
  (Italian name for
  Bonaparte)
Buon|ar|roti,
  Mi|chel|an|gelo
  (Italian artist)
buoy +s +ed +ing
  (float; etc. △ boy)
buoy|age
buoy|ancy
  buoy|an|cies
buoy|ant
buoy|ant|ly
bup|pie +s
bur +s (clinging
  seed case; catkin.
  △ burr)
burb +s
Bur|bage,
  Rich|ard (English
  actor)
Bur|bank (city,
  USA)
Bur|berry
  Bur|berries
  Propr.
bur|ble
  bur|bles
  bur|bled
  burb|ling
bur|bler +s
bur|bot +s
bur|den +s +ed
  +ing
bur|den|some
bur|dock +s
bur|eau
  bur|eaux or
  bur|eaus

bur|eau|cracy
  bur|eau|cra|cies
bur|eau|crat +s
bur|eau|crat|ic
bur|eau|crat|ic|
  al|ly
bur|eau|crat|
  isa|tion Br. (use
  bureaucrat-
  ization)
bur|eau|crat|ise
  Br. (use
  bureacratize)
bur|eau|crat|ises
bur|eau|crat|ised
bur|eau|crat|
  is|ing
bur|eau|crat|
  iza|tion
bur|eau|crat|ize
bur|eau|crat|izes
bur|eau|crat|ized
bur|eau|crat|
  iz|ing
buret Am. +s
bur|ette Br. +s
burg +s (town.
  △ berg)
bur|gage +s
Bur|gas (port,
  Bulgaria)
bur|gee +s
Bur|gen|land
  (state, Austria)
bur|geon +s +ed
  +ing
bur|ger +s (food.
  △ burgher)
Bur|gess,
  An|thony
  (English novelist
  and critic)
Bur|gess, Guy
  (British Soviet
  spy)
bur|gess
  bur|gesses
  (citizen; governor)
burgh +s (former
  Scottish borough.
  △ borough)
bur|ghal (of a
  burgh. △ burgle)
bur|gher +s
  (citizen. △ burger)
Burgh|ley,
  Wil|liam Cecil
  (English
  statesman)
burg|lar +s
burg|lari|ous

burg¦lar¦ise *Br.*
(use **burglarize**)
  burg¦lar¦ises
  burg¦lar¦ised
  burg¦lar¦is¦ing
burg¦lar¦ize
  burg¦lar¦izes
  burg¦lar¦ized
  burg¦lar¦iz¦ing
burg¦lary
  burg¦lar¦ies
bur¦gle
  bur¦gles
  bur¦gled
  burg¦ling
  (commit burglary.
  △ burghal)
burgo|mas¦ter +s
Bur¦gos (town,
  Spain)
Bur¦goyne, John
  (English general
  and writer)
bur¦grave +s
Bur¦gundy (region,
  France)
bur¦gundy
  bur¦gun|dies
  (wine; colour)
bur¦hel +s (use
  bharal)
bur¦ial +s
bur¦ial ground +s
burin +s
burk +s (use berk)
burka +s
Burke, Ed¦mund
  (British writer and
  politican)
Burke, John (Irish
  genealogist)
Burke, Rob¦ert
  O'Hara (Irish
  explorer)
Burke, Wil|liam
  (Irish body-
  snatcher)
Bur|kina (Faso) (in
  W. Africa)
Bur|kinan +s
Bur|kin|ese
  plural Bur¦kin|ese
Bur|kitt's
  lymph|oma
burl +s
bur¦lap
bur|lesque
  bur|lesques
  bur|lesqued
  bur|lesquing
bur|lesquer +s
bur¦li|ness

Bur¦ling|ton (city,
  Canada)
burly
  bur|lier
  bur¦li|est
Burma
Bur¦man +s
Burm|ese
  plural Burm|ese
burn
  burns
  burned *or* burnt
  burn|ing
Burne-Jones,
  Ed¦ward (English
  painter and
  designer)
burn¦er +s
bur¦net +s
Bur¦nett, Fran|ces
  Hodg¦son
  (English-born
  American
  novelist)
Bur¦ney, Fanny
  (English novelist)
Burn|ham (scale)
burning-ghat +s
burning-glass
  burning-glasses
burn|ing¦ly
bur|nish
  bur|nishes
  bur|nished
  bur|nish|ing
bur|nish¦er +s
Burn|ley (town,
  Lancashire)
bur|noose *Am.* +s
bur|nous *Br.*
  bur|nouses
burn-out *noun*
Burns, Rob¦ert
  (Scottish poet)
burnt
burnt-out *adjective*
bur oak +s
burp +s +ed +ing
bur|pee +s
Burr, Aaron
  (American
  statesman)
burr +s +ed +ing
  (rough edge;
  rough sounding of
  r; drill; rock; on
  antler. △ bur)
Burra, Ed¦ward
  (English painter
  and designer)
burra|wang +s

Bur¦ren, the
  (region, Republic
  of Ireland)
bur¦rito +s
burro +s (donkey.
  △ burrow)
Bur|roughs, Edgar
  Rice (American
  writer)
Bur|roughs,
  Wil|liam
  (American writer)
bur¦row +s +ed
  +ing (hole; dig.
  △ burro)
bur|row¦er +s
Bursa (city,
  Turkey)
bursa
  bur¦sae *or* bur¦sas
bur¦sal
bur¦sar +s
bur¦sar|ial
bur¦sar|ship
bur|sary
  bur¦sar|ies
bur|sitis
burst
  bursts
  burst
  burst|ing
burst|proof
Burt *also* Bert
bur|then +s
Bur¦ton, Rich|ard
  (Welsh actor;
  English explorer)
bur¦ton +s
Burton-upon-
  Trent (town,
  England)
Bur|undi
Bur¦und|ian +s
bur wal|nut
Bury (town,
  England)
bury
  bur¦ies
  bur¦ied
  bury|ing
  (inter. △ beret,
  berry)
Bur¦yat
Burya|tia (republic,
  Russia)
Bury St Ed|munds
  (town, England)
bus
  buses
  (vehicle;
  Computing.
  △ buss)

bus
  bus¦ses *or* buses
  bussed *or* bused
  buss|ing *or*
  bus¦ing
  (convey by bus.
  △ buss)
bus¦bar +s
bus¦boy +s
busby
  bus|bies
bus driver +s
Bush, George
  (American
  president)
bush
  bushes
  bushed
  bush|ing
bush|baby
  bush|babies
bush basil
bush|buck +s
bushel +s
bushel|ful +s
bush|fire +s
bu|shido
bush|ily
bushi|ness
Bush|man
  Bush|men
  (in South Africa)
bush|man
  bush|men
  (in Australia)
bush|mas¦ter +s
bush|ran¦ger +s
bush|veld
bush|whack +s
  +ed +ing
bush|whack¦er +s
bushy
  bush|ies
  bush|ier
  bushi|est
busily
busi|ness
  busi|nesses
  (trade; work; etc.
  △ busyness)
busi|ness|like
busi|ness|man
busi|ness|men
busi|ness per¦son
busi|ness people
busi|ness|woman
busi|ness|women
busk +s +ed +ing
busk¦er +s
bus|kin +s
bus|kined
busk|ing

bus|man
  bus|men
bus|man's
  holi|day +s
Bu|soni,
  Fer|ruc|cio
  (Italian composer
  and conductor)
Buss, Fran|ces
  (English
  educationist)
buss
  busses
  bussed
  buss|ing
  (kiss. △ bus)
bus shel|ter +s
bus sta|tion +s
bus stop +s
bust
  busts
  bust|ed *or* bust
  bust|ing
bus|tard +s
bus|tee +s
bust|er +s
bus|tier +s (bodice)
bust|ier
  (comparative of
  busty)
busti|ness
bus|tle
  bus|tles
  bus|tled
  bust|ling
bust|ler +s
bust-up +s *noun*
busty
  bust|ier
  busti|est
busy
  busies
  busied
  busy|ing
  busier
  busi|est
busy bee +s
busy|body
  busy|bod|ies
busy Liz|zie +s
busy|ness (being
  busy. △ business)
but +s
  (*conjunction,*
  preposition,
  and adverb;
  room; also in 'but
  me no buts'.
  △ butt, butte)
bu|ta|di|ene

but and ben
  (rooms in house)
bu|tane
butch
  butches
butcher +s +ed
  +ing
butcher-bird +s
butcher|ly
butcher meat
butcher's (look)
butcher's broom
  +s
butcher's meat
butch|ery
  butch|er|ies
Bute (island,
  Scotland)
Bute, Earl of
  (Scottish
  statesman)
Bu|the|lezi,
  Man|go|su|thu
  (Zulu leader and
  politican)
butle (use buttle)
  butles
  butled
  but|ling
But|ler, Reg
  (English sculptor)
But|ler, Sam|uel
  (English poet;
  English novelist)
but|ler +s
But|lin's (holiday
  camp)
butt +s +ed +ing
  (push; cask;
  target; end;
  buttocks; fish.
  △ but, butte)
butte +s (hill.
  △ beaut, but,
  butt)
butt-end +s
but|ter +s +ed
  +ing
butter-and-eggs
but|ter|ball +s
butter-bean +s
but|ter|bur +s
butter-cream
but|ter|cup +s
but|ter|fat
butter-fingers
  plural butter-
  fingers
but|ter|fish
  plural but|ter|fish
  or but|ter|fishes

but|ter|fly
  but|ter|flies
butter-icing
but|teri|ness
but|ter knife
  but|ter knives
but|ter|milk
but|ter|nut +s
but|ter|scotch
but|ter|wort +s
but|tery
  but|ter|ies
but|tie +s
but|tle
  but|tles
  but|tled
  but|tling
but|tock +s
but|ton +s +ed
  +ing
button-back
  adjective
but|ton|ball tree
  +s
button-down
  adjective
but|ton|hole
  but|ton|holes
  but|ton|holed
  but|ton|hol|ing
but|ton|hook +s
but|ton|less
but|tons (page-
  boy)
button-through
  adjective
but|ton|wood +s
but|tony
but|tress
  but|tresses
  but|tressed
  but|tress|ing
butts (shooting
  range)
butt weld
butty
  but|ties
butty-gang +s
butyl
bu|tyr|ate +s
bu|tyr|ic
buxom
bux|om|ly
bux|om|ness
Bux|te|hude,
  Diet|rich (Danish
  musician and
  composer, in N.
  Germany)
buy
  buys
  bought

buy (*cont.*)
  buy|ing
  (purchase. △ bi,
  by, bye)
buy-back +s *noun*
  and adjective
buyer +s
  (purchaser.
  △ byre)
buyer's mar|ket
  +s
buy-in +s *noun*
buy|out +s *noun*
buzz
  buzzes
  buzzed
  buzz|ing
buz|zard +s
buzz|er +s
buzz-saw +s
buzz|word +s
bwana +s
by (*preposition and
  adverb.* △ bi, buy,
  bye)
Byatt, A. S.
  (English writer)
Byb|los (ancient
  port, Lebanon)
by-blow +s
Byd|goszcz (port,
  Poland)
bye +s (*Sport;*
  goodbye. △ bi,
  buy, by)
bye-bye *interjection*
bye-byes (sleep)
bye-law +s (use by-
  law)
by-election +s
Byelo|rus|sia (use
  Belorussia)
Byelo|rus|sian (use
  Belorussian)
by-form +s
by|gone +s
by-lane +s
by-law +s
by|line +s
by|name +s
by|pass
  by|passes
  by|passed
  by|pass|ing
by|path +s
by|play +s
by-product +s
Byrd, Rich|ard
  (American
  explorer)

Byrd, Wil|liam
  (English
  composer)
Byrds, the
  (American rock
  group)
byre +s (barn.
  △ buyer)
by|road +s
Byron (name)
Byron, Lord
  (English poet)
Byron|ic
bys|sin|osis
bys|sus
  bys|suses or byssi
by|stand|er +s
by-street +s
byte +s (Computing.
  △ bight, bite)
Bytom (city,
  Poland)
byway +s
by|word +s
by-your-leave
  noun
By|zan|tine +s
By|zan|tin|ism
By|zan|tin|ist +s
By|zan|tium
  (ancient Istanbul)

Cc

Caaba (use Kaaba)
cab +s
cabal +s
Ca|bala (Judaism;
  use Kabbalah)
ca|bala +s
  (generally; use
  cabbala)
Cab|al|ism
  (Judaism; use
  Kabbalism)
cab|al|ism
  (generally; use
  cabbalism)
Cab|al|ist +s
  (Judaism; use
  Kabbalist)
cab|al|ist +s
  (generally; use
  cabbalist)
Cab|al|is|tic
  (Judaism; use
  Kabbalistic)
cab|al|is|tic
  (generally; use
  cabbalistic)
ca|bal|lero +s
ca|bana +s
caba|ret +s
cab|bage +s
cab|bage palm +s
cab|bage white +s
cab|bagy
Cab|bala (Judaism;
  use Kabbalah)
cab|bala +s
  (generally)
Cab|bal|ism
  (Judaism; use
  Kabbalism)
cab|bal|ism
  (generally)
Cab|bal|ist +s
  (Judaism; use
  Kabbalism)
cab|bal|ist +s
  (generally)
Cab|bal|is|tic
  (Judaism; use
  Kabbalistic)
cab|bal|is|tic
  (generally)
cab|bie +s (use
  cabby)
cabby
  cab|bies
cab driver +s
caber +s

Cab|er|net +s
Cab|er|net Franc
  +s
Cab|er|net
  Sau|vi|gnon +s
cabin +s +ed +ing
cabin boy +s
Cab|inda (enclave,
  Angola)
Cab|inet +s
  (government)
cab|inet +s
  (furniture)
cab|inet|maker +s
cab|inet|mak|ing
cab|in|et|ry
cable
  cables
  cabled
  cab|ling
cable car +s
cable|gram +s
cable-laid
cable-laying
cable tele|vi|sion
cable TV
cable|way +s
cab|man
  cab|men
cabo|chon +s (but
  en cabochon)
ca|boo|dle
ca|boose +s
Ca|bora Bassa
  (lake,
  Mozambique)
Cabot, John and
  Se|bas|tian
  (Venetian
  explorers)
cab|ot|age
cabo|tin +s male
cabo|tine +s female
cab|ri|ole +s
cab|ri|olet +s
ca'|canny
cacao +s
cacha|lot +s
cache
  caches
  cached
  cach|ing
  (store. △ cash)
cach|ec|tic
cache pot +s
cachet +s
cach|exia
cach|exy
cach|in|nate
  cach|in|nates
  cach|in|nated
  cach|in|nat|ing

cach|in|na|tion
cach|in|na|tory
cacho|long +s
cachou +s
  (lozenge.
  △ cashew)
ca|chu|cha +s
ca|cique +s
ca|ciqu|ism
cack-handed
cack-handed|ly
cack-handed|ness
cackle
  cackles
  cackled
  cack|ling
caco|dae|mon +s
  (use cacodemon)
caco|demon +s
caco|dyl
caco|dyl|ic
caco|epy
caco|ethes
cac|og|raph|er +s
caco|graph|ic
caco|graph|ic|al
cac|og|raphy
caco|ology
  caco|olo|gies
caco|mis|tle +s
cac|oph|on|ous
cac|oph|ony
  cac|oph|onies
cac|ta|ceous
cac|tal
cac|tus
  cacti or cac|tuses
ca|cu|min|al
cad +s
ca|das|tral
ca|da|ver +s
ca|da|ver|ic
ca|da|ver|ous
Cad|bury, George
  and Rich|ard
  (British
  manufacturers and
  reformers)
cad|die
  cad|dies
  cad|died
  caddy|ing
  (in golf. △ caddy)
cad|dis
  cad|dises
caddis-fly
  caddis-flies
cad|dish
  (dishonourable.
  △ Kaddish)
cad|dish|ly
cad|dish|ness

caddis-worm +s
caddy
  cad¦dies
  (box for tea.
   ⚠ caddie)
ca¦dence +s
ca¦denced
ca¦dency
ca¦den¦tial
ca¦denza +s
cadet +s
ca¦det¦ship +s
cadge
  cadges
  cadged
  cadg¦ing
cadger +s
cadi +s (Muslim
  judge. ⚠ cardy)
Cadiz (city, Spain)
Cad¦mean (victory)
cad¦mium
Cad¦mus Greek
  Mythology
cadre +s
ca¦du¦ceus
  ca¦du¦cei
  Greek and Roman
  Mythology
ca¦du¦city
ca¦du¦cous
cae¦cal Br. (Am.
  cecal)
cae¦cil¦ian +s
cae¦citis Br. (Am.
  cecitis)
cae¦city Br. (Am.
  cecity)
cae¦cum Br.
  caeca
  (Am. cecum)
Caed¦mon (English
  poet)
Caen (city, France)
Cae¦no¦zoic (use
  Cenozoic)
Caer¦nar¦fon (city,
  Wales)
Caer¦nar¦von
  (English spelling
  of Caernarfon)
Caer¦nar¦von¦shire
  (former county,
  Wales)
Caer¦philly (town,
  Wales; cheese)
Cae¦sar +s (Roman
  emperor)
Cae¦sa¦rea (ancient
  port, Israel)

Cae¦sa¦rea
  Maz¦aca (former
  name of Kayseri)
Cae¦sar¦ean Br. +s
  (Am. Cesarean)
Cae¦sa¦rea
  Phil¦ippi (city,
  ancient Palestine)
Cae¦sar¦ian Br. +s
  (use Caesarean.
  Am. Cesarean)
Cae¦sar's wife
cae¦si¦ous
cae¦sium Br. (Am.
  cesium)
caes¦ura +s
caes¦ural
ca¦fard
café +s
café au lait
café-bar +s
café noir
cafe¦teria +s
cafe¦tière +s
caff +s
caf¦feine
Cafod (= Catholic
  Fund for Overseas
  Development)
caf¦tan +s (use
  kaftan)
Ca¦gayan Is¦lands
  (in the
  Philippines)
Cage, John
  (American
  composer)
cage
  cages
  caged
  ca¦ging
cage bird +s
cagey
  cagi¦er
  cagi¦est
ca¦gey¦ness (use
  caginess)
cagi¦ly
cagi¦ness
Cagli¦ari (capital of
  Sardinia)
Cag¦ney, James
  (American actor)
ca¦goule +s
cagy
  cagi¦er
  cagi¦est
ca¦hoots
cai¦man +s (use
  cayman)

Cain (Bible; in 'raise
  Cain'. ⚠ cane)
Caine, Mi¦chael
  (English actor)
Caino¦zoic (use
  Cenozoic)
ca¦ique +s
cairn +s
cairn¦gorm +s
  (mineral)
Cairn¦gorm
  Moun¦tains (in
  Scotland)
Cairn¦gorms
  (= Cairngorm
  Mountains)
Cairo (capital of
  Egypt)
cais¦son +s
Caith¦ness (former
  county, Scotland;
  glass)
cai¦tiff +s
Cait¦lín
ca¦jole
  ca¦joles
  ca¦joled
  ca¦jol¦ing
ca¦jole¦ment
ca¦joler +s
ca¦jolery
Cajun +s
cake
  cakes
  caked
  cak¦ing
cake-hole +s
cake¦walk +s
Cala¦bar (port,
  Nigeria; bean)
cala¦bash
  cala¦bashes
cala¦boose +s
cala¦brese
Ca¦lab¦ria (region,
  Italy)
Ca¦lab¦rian +s
Cal¦ais (port,
  France)
cala¦manco
  cala¦man¦coes
cala¦man¦der +s
cala¦mares (Greek
  dish)
cala¦mari (Italian
  dish)
cala¦mary
  cala¦mar¦ies
  (animal)
cala¦mine
cala¦mint +s
ca¦lami¦tous

ca¦lami¦tous¦ly
ca¦lam¦ity
  ca¦lam¦ities
Ca¦lam¦ity Jane
  (American horse-
  rider and
  markswoman)
ca¦lando
ca¦lash
  ca¦lashes
cal¦ca¦neum
  cal¦ca¦nea
cal¦ca¦neus
  cal¦ca¦nei
cal¦car¦eous
cal¦ceo¦laria
  plural
  cal¦ceo¦laria or
  cal¦ceo¦lar¦ias
cal¦ceo¦late
cal¦ces (plural of
  calx)
cal¦ci¦cole +s
cal¦cif¦erol
cal¦cif¦er¦ous
cal¦cif¦ic
cal¦ci¦fi¦ca¦tion
cal¦ci¦fuge +s
cal¦cify
  cal¦ci¦fies
  cal¦ci¦fied
  cal¦ci¦fy¦ing
cal¦cin¦ation
cal¦cine
  cal¦cines
  cal¦cined
  cal¦cin¦ing
cal¦cite
cal¦cium
cal¦crete
calc-sinter
calc¦spar
calc-tuff +s
cal¦cul¦abil¦ity
cal¦cul¦able
cal¦cul¦ably
cal¦cu¦late
  cal¦cu¦lates
  cal¦cu¦lated
  cal¦cu¦lat¦ing
cal¦cu¦lated¦ly
cal¦cu¦lat¦ing¦ly
cal¦cu¦la¦tion +s
cal¦cu¦la¦tive
cal¦cu¦la¦tor +s
cal¦cu¦lous
  Medicine adjective
cal¦cu¦lus
  cal¦culi
  Medicine noun

cal¦cu¦lus
  cal¦cu¦luses
  Mathematics
Cal¦cutta (port,
  India)
cal¦dar¦ium
  cal¦dar¦iums *or*
  cal¦daria
Cal¦de¦cott, Ralph
  (English artist)
Cal¦der,
  Alex¦an¦der
  (American artist
  and sculptor)
cal¦dera +s
Cal¦derón de la
  Barca, Pedro
  (Spanish writer)
cal¦dron +s (use
  cauldron)
Caleb
Cale¦do¦nian +s (of
  Scotland; Scottish
  person; geology)
cale¦fa¦cient +s
cale¦fac¦tory
  cale¦fac¦tor¦ies
cal¦en¦dar +s
  (almanac)
cal¦en¦der +s
  (press)
ca¦len¦dric
ca¦len¦dric¦al
cal¦ends
cal¦en¦dula +s
cal¦en¦ture
calf
  calves
calf¦hood
calf¦ish
calf-length
  adjective
calf¦like
calf love
calf¦skin
Cal¦gary (city,
  Canada)
Cali (city,
  Colombia)
Cali¦ban (in *The
  Tempest*)
cali¦ber *Am.* +s (*Br.*
  calibre)
cali¦bered *Am.* (*Br.*
  calibred)
cali¦brate
  cali¦brates
  cali¦brated
  cali¦brat¦ing
cali¦bra¦tion +s
cali¦bra¦tor +s

cali¦bre *Br.* +s (*Am.*
  caliber)
cali¦bred *Br.* (*Am.*
  calibered)
ca¦li¦ces (plural of
  calix)
ca¦li¦che
cal¦icle +s
cal¦ico
  cali¦coes *Br.*
  cali¦cos *Am.*
Cali¦cut (port,
  India)
Cali¦for¦nia (state,
  USA)
Cali¦for¦nian +s
cali¦for¦nium
Ca¦lig¦ula (Roman
  emperor)
cali¦pash
  cali¦pashes
cali¦pee +s
cali¦per +s (use
  calliper)
ca¦liph +s
ca¦liph¦ate +s
cal¦is¦then¦ic (use
  callisthenic)
cal¦is¦then¦ics (use
  callisthenics)
calix (use calyx)
  ca¦lixes *or*
  ca¦li¦ces
calk *Am.* +s +ed
  +ing (*Br.* caulk
  stop up. △ cork)
calk¦er +s *Am.* (*Br.*
  caulker. person
  who calks.
  △ corker)
call +s +ed +ing
  (shout; telephone;
  visit; name; etc.
  △ caul)
calla +s
Cal¦laghan, James
  (British prime
  minister)
Cal¦lao (port, Peru)
Cal¦las, Maria
  (American-born
  Greek soprano)
call box
  call boxes
call-boy +s
call¦er +s
call-girl +s
cal¦lig¦raph¦er +s
cal¦li¦graph¦ic
cal¦lig¦raph¦ist +s
cal¦lig¦raphy

Cal¦lil, Car¦men
  (Australian
  publisher)
Cal¦lima¦chus
  (Hellenistic poet)
call¦ing +s
call¦ing card +s
Cal¦liope *Roman
  Mythology*
cal¦liope +s
cal¦li¦per +s
cal¦li¦py¦gian
cal¦li¦py¦gous
cal¦lis¦then¦ic
cal¦lis¦then¦ics
Cal¦listo (*Greek
  Mythology*; moon
  of Jupiter)
cal¦lop
  plural cal¦lop
cal¦los¦ity
  cal¦los¦ities
cal¦lous *adjective*
  (unfeeling.
  △ callus)
cal¦lous *noun* (use
  callus)
  cal¦louses
cal¦lous¦ly
cal¦lous¦ness
call-out +s *noun*
call-over +s *noun*
cal¦low
cal¦low¦ly
cal¦low¦ness
call sign +s
cal¦luna +s
call-up +s
cal¦lus
  cal¦luses
  (hard skin.
  △ callous)
calm +s +ed +ing
  +er +est
calma¦tive +s
calm¦er +s (person
  who calms.
  △ Kama, karma)
calm¦ly
calm¦ness
calo¦mel +s
Calor gas *Propr.*
cal¦oric +s
cal¦orie +s
calorie-free
  adjective
cal¦or¦if¦ic
cal¦or¦if¦ic¦al¦ly
cal¦or¦im¦eter +s
cal¦ori¦met¦ric
cal¦or¦im¦etry

cal¦ory (use
  calorie)
  cal¦or¦ies
ca¦lotte +s
calque +s
cal¦trap +s (use
  caltrop)
cal¦trop +s
Calum
calu¦met +s
ca¦lum¦ni¦ate
  ca¦lum¦ni¦ates
  ca¦lum¦ni¦ated
  ca¦lum¦ni¦at¦ing
ca¦lum¦ni¦ation
ca¦lum¦ni¦ator +s
ca¦lum¦ni¦atory
ca¦lum¦ni¦ous
cal¦umny
  cal¦um¦nies
  cal¦um¦nied
  cal¦um¦ny¦ing
Cal¦va¦dos (region,
  France)
cal¦va¦dos (drink)
Cal¦vary
  (Jerusalem)
calve
  calves
  calved
  calv¦ing
  (give birth to a
  calf. △ carve)
calves (plural of
  calf)
Cal¦vin (name)
Cal¦vin, John
  (French Protestant
  theologian)
Cal¦vin, Mel¦vin
  (American
  biochemist; cycle)
Cal¦vin¦ise *Br.* (use
  Calvinize)
  Cal¦vin¦ises
  Cal¦vin¦ised
  Cal¦vin¦is¦ing
Cal¦vin¦ism
Cal¦vin¦ist +s
Cal¦vin¦is¦tic
Cal¦vin¦is¦tic¦al
Cal¦vin¦ize
  Cal¦vin¦izes
  Cal¦vin¦ized
  Cal¦vin¦iz¦ing
Cal¦vino, Italo
  (Italian writer)
calx
  cal¦ces
  (metal oxide.
  △ calques)
Ca¦lypso

ca|lypso +s
calyx
    ca|ly|ces or
    ca|lyxes
cal|zone
    cal|zoni or
    cal|zones
Cam (river,
    England)
cam +s (device)
cama|rad|erie
Cam|argue, the
    (region, France)
cama|rilla +s
cama|ron +s
Cam|bay, Gulf of
    (Arabian Sea)
cam|ber +s
Cam|ber|well
    Beauty
    Cam|ber|well
    Beau|ties
cam|bial
cam|bist +s
cam|bium
    cam|bia or
    cam|biums
Cam|bo|dia
Cam|bo|dian +s
Cam|brian +s
    (Welsh; Geology)
cam|bric +s
Cam|bridge (cities,
    England and USA)
Cam|bridge blue
    +s noun and
    adjective
Cambridge-blue
    attributive
Cam|bridge|shire
    (county, England)
Cam|by|ses
    (Persian king and
    soldier)
cam|cord|er +s
came (past tense of
    come. △ kame)
camel +s
cam|el|back
cam|el|eer +s
camel-hair +s
cam|el|lia +s
cam|elo|pard +s
Cam|elot
    Arthurian Legend
cam|el|ry
    cam|el|ries
camel's-hair +s
Cam|em|bert +s
    (village, France;
    cheese)
cameo +s

cam|era +s
cam|era lu|cida +s
cam|era|man
    cam|era|men
cam|era ob|scura
    +s
camera-ready
cam|era-work
cam|er|lingo +s
Cam|eron
Cam|eron, Julia
    Mar|ga|ret
    (English
    photographer)
Cam|eron
    High|lands
    (resort, Malaysia)
Cam|er|oon (in W.
    Africa)
Cam|er|oon|ian +s
Cam|er|oun
    (French name for
    Cameroon)
cami|knick|ers
Cam|illa
cam|ion +s
cami|sole +s
Cam|ões, Luis de
    (Portuguese poet)
camo|mile
Cam|orra
cam|ou|flage
    cam|ou|flages
    cam|ou|flaged
    cam|ou|fla|ging
camp
    camps
    camped
    camp|ing
    camp|er
    camp|est
cam|paign +s +ed
    +ing
cam|paign|er +s
Cam|pa|nia
    (region, Italy)
Cam|pa|nian +s
cam|pa|nile +s
cam|pan|olo|ger
    +s
cam|pano|logic|al
cam|pan|olo|gist
    +s
cam|pan|ology
cam|pan|ula +s
cam|panu|late
camp bed +s
Camp|bell,
    Don|ald (English
    holder of water-
    speed record)

Camp|bell,
    Mal|colm
    (English racing
    driver)
Camp|bell, Mrs
    Pat|rick (English
    actress)
Camp|bell, Roy
    (South African
    poet)
Camp|bell,
    Thomas (Scottish
    poet)
Campbell-
    Banner|man,
    Henry (British
    statesman)
Camp David (in
    USA)
Cam|peachy wood
Cam|peche (state,
    Mexico)
camp|er +s
camp|fire +s
camp fol|low|er +s
camp|ground +s
cam|phor
cam|phor|ate
    cam|phor|ates
    cam|phor|ated
    cam|phor|at|ing
cam|phor|ic
camp|ily
Cam|pi|nas (city,
    Brazil)
campi|ness
Cam|pion,
    Ed|mund
    (English saint)
cam|pion +s
Campo|basso (city,
    Italy)
Campo Grande
    (city, Brazil)
camp-on noun
camp|site +s
cam|pus
    cam|puses
campy
    camp|ier
    campi|est
cam|pylo|bacter
    +s
CAMRA
    (= Campaign for
    Real Ale)
cam|shaft +s
Camu|lo|dunum
    (Roman name for
    Colchester)
Camus, Al|bert
    (French writer)

cam|wood
can (auxiliary verb
    be able)
can
    cans
    canned
    can|ning
    (tin; put in tin)
Cana (town,
    Galilee)
Ca|naan
    (= Palestine)
Ca|naan|ite +s
Can|ada (in N.
    America.
    △ Kannada)
Can|adian +s
ca|naille
canal +s
Cana|letto,
    Gio|vanni
    (Venetian painter)
can|al|isa|tion Br.
    (use canalization)
can|al|ise Br. (use
    canalize)
    can|al|ises
    can|al|ised
    can|al|is|ing
can|al|iza|tion
can|al|ize
    can|al|izes
    can|al|ized
    can|al|iz|ing
canal|side
can|apé +s
can|ard +s
Can|ar|ese (use
    Kanarese)
    plural Can|ar|ese
Can|ar|ies
    (= Canary
    Islands)
can|ary
    can|ar|ies
canary-colored
    Am.
canary-coloured
    Br.
can|ary creep|er
    +s
can|ary grass
Can|ary Is|lands
    (off African coast)
can|ary yel|low +s
    noun and adjective
canary-yellow
    attributive
can|asta +s (card
    game)
can|as|ter +s
    (tobacco)

Can|av|eral, Cape (US space centre)
Can|berra (capital of Australia)
can|can +s
can|cel
  can|cels
  can|celled *Br.*
  can|celed *Am.*
  can|cel|ling *Br.*
  can|cel|ing *Am.*
can|cel|er *Am.* +s
can|cel|late
can|cel|lated
can|cel|la|tion +s
can|cel|ler *Br.* +s
can|cel|lous
Can|cer (constellation; sign of zodiac)
can|cer +s
Can|cer|ian +s
can|cer|ous
can|croid +s
Can|cún (resort, Mexico)
Can|dace *also* Can|dice
can|dela +s
can|de|la|brum
  can|de|la|bra
can|des|cence
can|des|cent
Can|dice *also* Can|dace
can|did
Can|dida (name)
can|dida +s (fungus)
can|di|dacy
  can|di|da|cies
can|di|date +s
can|di|da|ture +s
can|did|ly
can|did|ness
can|dle
  can|dles
  can|dled
  cand|ling
candle|hold|er +s
candle|light
candle|lit
Candle|mas
candle|power
cand|ler +s
candle|stick +s
candle|wick +s
can-do *adjective*
Can|dolle, Augustin-Pyramus de (Swiss botanist)

can|dor *Am.*
cand|our *Br.*
Candy (name)
candy
  candies
  can|died
  candy|ing (confectionery)
candy|floss
candy stripe +s
candy-striped
candy|tuft
  plural candy|tuft
cane
  canes
  caned
  can|ing (stick; to hit with a cane. ⚠ Cain)
cane-brake +s
caner +s
cane sugar
Canes Ve|nat|ici (constellation)
cane toad +s
cane-trash
ca|nine +s
can|ing +s
Canis Major (constellation)
Canis Minor (constellation)
can|is|ter +s (container. ⚠ canaster)
can|ker +s +ed +ing
can|ker|ous
can|ker|worm +s
Can|more, Mal|colm (Malcolm III of Scotland)
canna +s (plant. ⚠ canner)
can|na|binol
can|na|bis
can|na|bis resin
can|nel
can|nel|loni
can|nel|ure +s
can|ner +s (person who cans. ⚠ canna)
can|nery
  can|ner|ies
Cannes (resort, France)
can|ni|bal +s
can|ni|bal|isa|tion *Br.* (use cannibalization)

can|ni|bal|ise *Br.* (use cannibalize)
  can|ni|bal|ises
  can|ni|bal|ised
  can|ni|bal|is|ing
can|ni|bal|ism
can|ni|bal|is|tic
  can|ni|bal|is|tic|al|ly
can|ni|bal|iza|tion
can|ni|bal|ize
  can|ni|bal|izes
  can|ni|bal|ized
  can|ni|bal|iz|ing
can|ni|kin +s
can|nily
can|ni|ness
Can|ning, George (British prime minister)
Can|niz|zaro, Stan|is|lao (Italian chemist)
can|non +s +ed +ing (gun; *Billiards*; *Mechanics.* ⚠ canon)
can|non|ade
  can|non|ades
  can|non|aded
  can|non|ad|ing
can|non ball +s
cannon-bit +s
cannon-bone +s
can|non fod|der
can|not
can|nula
  can|nu|lae *or* can|nu|las
can|nu|late
  can|nu|lates
  can|nu|lated
  can|nu|lat|ing
canny
  can|nier
  can|ni|est
canoe
  ca|noes
  ca|noed
  ca|noe|ing
ca|noe|ist +s
canon +s (rule; member of cathedral chapter; *Music.* ⚠ cannon)
cañon +s (use canyon)
ca|non|ess
  ca|non|esses
ca|non|ic
ca|non|ic|al +s

ca|non|ic|al|ly
ca|noni|cate +s
can|on|icity
can|on|isa|tion *Br.* +s (use canonization)
can|on|ise *Br.* (use canonize)
  can|on|ises
  can|on|ised
  can|on|is|ing
can|on|ist +s
can|on|iza|tion
can|on|ize
  can|on|izes
  can|on|ized
  can|on|iz|ing
canon law
canon regu|lar
  canons regu|lar
can|on|ry
  can|on|ries
ca|noo|dle
  ca|noo|dles
  ca|noo|dled
  ca|nood|ling
can-opener +s
Ca|no|pic
Ca|no|pus (*Greek Mythology*; star)
can|opy
  can|opies
  can|opied
  can|opy|ing
can|or|ous
Ca|nova, An|tonio (Italian sculptor)
canst
cant +s +ed +ing
can't (= cannot)
can|ta|bile +s
Can|tab|ria (region. Spain)
Can|tab|rian +s
Can|ta|bri|gian +s (of Cambridge or Cambridge University)
can|tal
can|ta|loup +s (use cantaloupe)
can|ta|loupe +s
can|tan|ker|ous
can|tan|ker|ous|ly
can|tan|ker|ous|ness
can|tata +s
can|ta|trice +*s*
cant-dog +s
can|teen +s
can|ter +s +ed +ing

Can¦ter¦bury (city, England)
can¦ter¦bury
  can¦ter¦buries (furniture)
Can¦ter¦bury bell +s (plant)
Can¦ter¦bury Plains (region, New Zealand)
can¦thari¦des
cant-hook +s
can¦thus
  can¦thi
can¦ticle +s
can¦ti¦lena +s
can¦ti¦lever
  can¦ti¦levers
  can¦ti¦levered
  can¦ti¦lever¦ing
can¦til¦late
  can¦til¦lates
  can¦til¦lated
  can¦til¦lat¦ing
can¦til¦la¦tion
can¦tina +s
cant¦ing arms
can¦tle +s
canto +s
Can¦ton (city, China)
can¦ton +s +ed +ing (subdivision of country; *Heraldry*)
can¦ton¦al
Can¦ton¦ese *plural* Can¦ton¦ese
can¦ton¦ment +s
Can¦tor, Georg (Russian-born mathematician)
can¦tor +s
can¦tor¦ial
can¦toris
cant¦rail +s
can¦trip +s
Can¦uck +s (*usually offensive*)
Can¦ute (use Cnut)
can¦vas
  can¦vases (cloth. △ canvass)
canvas-back
can¦vass
  can¦vasses
  can¦vassed
  can¦vass¦ing (solicit. △ canvas)
can¦vass¦er +s
can¦yon +s
can¦zonet +s

can¦zon¦etta +s
caou¦tchouc +s
cap
  caps
  capped
  cap¦ping
cap.
  caps. (= capital letter)
cap¦abil¦ity
  cap¦abil¦ities
Capa¦blanca, José (Cuban chess player)
cap¦able
cap¦ably
cap¦acious
cap¦acious¦ly
cap¦acious¦ness
cap¦aci¦tance +s
cap¦aci¦tate
  cap¦aci¦tates
  cap¦aci¦tated
  cap¦aci¦tat¦ing
cap¦aci¦ta¦tive
cap¦aci¦tive (use capacitative)
cap¦aci¦tor +s
cap¦acity
  cap¦aci¦ties
ca¦pari¦son +s +ed +ing
cape +s
Cape ... (see Agulhas, Bon, etc.)
Cape Bre¦ton Is¦land (in Canada)
Cape Col¦ony (former name of Cape Province)
Cape Col¦ored *Am.* +s
Cape Col¦oured *Br.* +s
caped
Cape doc¦tor +s
Cape Dutch
Cape goose¦berry
  Cape goose¦berries
Cape John¦son Depth (in W. Pacific)
Čapek, Karel (Czech writer)
cap¦elin +s
Ca¦pella (star)
caper +s +ed +ing
cap¦er¦cail¦lie +s

cap¦er¦cail¦zie +s (use capercaillie)
caper¦er +s
cape¦skin
Capet, Hugh (French king)
Cap¦etian +s
Cape Town (legislative capital of South Africa)
Cape Ver¦dean +s
Cape Verde Is¦lands (off coast of Senegal)
cap¦ful +s
cap¦ias
ca¦pil¦lar¦ity
ca¦pil¦lary
  ca¦pil¦lar¦ies
cap¦ital +s
cap¦ital gain +s
cap¦ital gains tax
capital-intensive
cap¦it¦al¦isa¦tion *Br.* (use capitalization)
cap¦it¦al¦ise *Br.* (use capitalize)
  cap¦it¦al¦ises
  cap¦it¦al¦ised
  cap¦it¦al¦is¦ing
cap¦it¦al¦ism
cap¦it¦al¦ist +s
cap¦it¦al¦is¦tic
cap¦it¦al¦is¦tic¦al¦ly
cap¦it¦al¦iza¦tion
cap¦it¦al¦ize
  cap¦it¦al¦izes
  cap¦it¦al¦ized
  cap¦it¦al¦iz¦ing
cap¦it¦al¦ly
capi¦ta¦tion +s
Cap¦itol (in ancient Rome or Washington DC)
Ca¦pit¦ol¦ine (hill, ancient Rome)
ca¦pitu¦lar
ca¦pitu¦lary
  cap¦itu¦lar¦ies
ca¦pitu¦late
  ca¦pitu¦lates
  ca¦pitu¦lated
  ca¦pitu¦lat¦ing
ca¦pitu¦la¦tion +s
ca¦pitu¦la¦tor +s
ca¦pitu¦la¦tory
ca¦pit¦ulum
  ca¦pit¦ula
cap¦lin +s (use capelin)

cap'n (= captain)
capo +s
Capo di Monte (porcelain)
capon +s
Ca¦pone, Al (American gangster)
ca¦pon¦ier +s
ca¦pon¦ise *Br.* (use caponize)
  ca¦pon¦ises
  ca¦pon¦ised
  ca¦pon¦is¦ing
ca¦pon¦ize
  ca¦pon¦izes
  ca¦pon¦ized
  ca¦pon¦iz¦ing
capot
  ca¦pots
  ca¦pot¦ted
  ca¦pot¦ting
capo tasto +s
Ca¦pote, Tru¦man (American writer)
ca¦pote +s
Cap¦pa¦do¦cia (ancient name of region of Asia Minor)
Cap¦pa¦do¦cian +s
cap¦ping +s
cap¦puc¦cino +s
Capra, Frank (Italian-born American film director)
Capri (island, Italy)
cap¦ric
ca¦pric¦cio +s
ca¦pric¦ci¦oso +s *Music*
ca¦price +s
ca¦pri¦cious
ca¦pri¦cious¦ly
ca¦pri¦cious¦ness
Cap¦ri¦corn (constellation; sign of zodiac)
Cap¦ri¦corn¦ian +s
Cap¦ri¦cor¦nus (constellation; use Capricorn)
cap¦rine
cap¦ri¦ole
  cap¦ri¦oles
  cap¦ri¦oled
  cap¦ri¦ol¦ing
Capri pants
Ca¦pris
Ca¦privi Strip (in Namibia)

cap rock
cap|roic
caps. (= capital
    letters)
Cap|sian +s
cap|sicum +s
cap|sid +s
cap|sizal
cap|size
    cap|sizes
    cap|sized
    cap|siz|ing
cap sleeve +s
cap|stan +s
cap|stone +s
cap|su|lar
cap|su|late
cap|sule +s
cap|su|lise Br. (use
    capsulize)
    cap|su|lises
    cap|su|lised
    cap|su|lis|ing
cap|su|lize
    cap|su|lizes
    cap|su|lized
    cap|su|liz|ing
cap|tain +s +ed
    +ing
Cap|tain Cook|er
    +s
cap|tain|cy
    cap|tain|cies
captain-general
    +s
cap|tain|ship +s
cap|tion +s +ed
    +ing
cap|tious
cap|tious|ly
cap|tious|ness
cap|tiv|ate
    cap|tiv|ates
    cap|tiv|ated
    cap|tiv|at|ing
cap|tiv|at|ing|ly
cap|tiv|ation
cap|tive +s
cap|tiv|ity
    cap|tiv|ities
cap|tor +s
cap|ture
    cap|tures
    cap|tured
    cap|tur|ing
cap|turer +s
Capu|chin +s
    (friar; cloak and
    hood)
capu|chin +s
    (monkey; pigeon)
capy|bara +s

car +s (vehicle.
    △carr, ka)
Cara
cara|bin|eer +s
    (soldier.
    △karabiner)
cara|bin|iere
    cara|bin|ieri
cara|cal +s (lynx.
    △karakul)
Cara|calla (Roman
    emperor)
cara|cara +s
Ca|ra|cas (capital
    of Venezuela)
cara|cole
    cara|coles
    cara|coled
    cara|col|ing
Ca|ract|acus (use
    Caratacus)
cara|cul +s (use
    karakul)
ca|rafe +s
Caraljás (region,
    Brazil)
ca|ram|bola +s
cara|mel +s
cara|mel|isa|tion
    Br. (use
    caramelization)
cara|mel|ise Br.
    (use caramelize)
    cara|mel|ises
    cara|mel|ised
    cara|mel|is|ing
    cara|mel|iza|tion
    cara|mel|ize
    cara|mel|izes
    cara|mel|ized
    cara|mel|iz|ing
ca|ran|gid +s
cara|pace +s
carat +s (unit of
    weight for jewels.
    △caret, carrot,
    karat)
carat Br. +s
    (measure of purity
    for gold. Am.
    karat. △caret,
    carrot)
Ca|rat|acus (British
    chieftain)
Cara|vag|gio
    (Italian painter)
cara|van
    cara|vans
    cara|vanned
    cara|van|ning
cara|van|ette +s
cara|van|ner +s

cara|van|sary (use
    caravanserai)
cara|van|sar|ies
cara|van|serai +s
cara|vel +s
cara|way
carb +s
car|ba|mate +s
car|bide +s
car|bie +s
car|bine +s
carbo|hy|drate +s
car|bol|ic
car bomb +s
car|bon +s
car|bon|aceous
car|bon|ade +s
    (use carbonnade)
car|bon|ado +s
car|bon|ara
car|bon|ate
    car|bon|ates
    car|bon|ated
    car|bon|at|ing
car|bon|ation
car|bon black
car|bon copy
    car|bon cop|ies
car|bon cycle +s
car|bon dat|ing
car|bon fiber Am.
    +s
car|bon fibre Br.
    +s
carbon-14
car|bon|ic
Car|bon|ifer|ous
    Geology
car|bon|ifer|ous
car|bon|isa|tion Br.
    (use
    carbonization)
car|bon|ise Br. (use
    carbonize)
    car|bon|ises
    car|bon|ised
    car|bon|is|ing
    car|bon|iza|tion
    car|bon|ize
    car|bon|izes
    car|bon|ized
    car|bon|iz|ing
car|bon|nade +s
car|bon paper
carbon-12
car|bonyl +s
car-boot sale +s
car|bor|un|dum
carb|oxyl +s
carb|ox|yl|ate +s
carb|ox|yl|ic
car|boy +s

car|bun|cle +s
car|bun|cu|lar
car|bur|ation
car|buret
    car|bur|ets
    car|bur|et|ted Br.
    car|bur|et|ed Am.
    car|bur|et|ting Br.
    car|bur|et|ing Am.
car|bur|etor Am.
    +s
car|bur|et|tor Br.
    +s
car|bur|isa|tion Br.
    (use
    carburization)
car|bur|ise Br. (use
    carburize)
    car|bur|ises
    car|bur|ised
    car|bur|is|ing
    car|bur|iza|tion
    car|bur|ize
    car|bur|izes
    car|bur|ized
    car|bur|iz|ing
carby (use carbie)
car|bies
car|ca|jou +s
car|case +s (use
    carcass)
car|cass
    car|casses
Car|cas|sonne
    (city, France)
Car|chem|ish
    (ancient city,
    Syria)
car|cino|gen +s
car|cino|gen|esis
car|cino|gen|ic
car|cino|gen|ic|
    al|ly
car|cino|gen|icity
car|cin|oma
    car|cin|omata or
    car|cin|omas
car|cin|omat|ous
card +s +ed +ing
car|da|mom
Car|da|mom
    Moun|tains (in
    Cambodia)
car|dan joint +s
car|dan shaft +s
card|board +s
card-carrying
card|er +s
card game +s
card|hold|er +s
car|diac

car¦die +s (use
  cardy . cardigan.
  △cadi)
Car¦diff (capital of
  Wales)
car¦di¦gan +s
Car¦di¦gan Bay (off
  Wales)
Car¦di¦gan¦shire
  (former county,
  Wales)
Car¦din, Pierre
  (French couturier)
car¦din¦al +s
car¦din¦al¦ate +s
car¦din¦al flower
  +s
car¦din¦al¦ly
car¦din¦al¦ship +s
card index
  card in¦dexes
card¦ing wool
car¦dio¦gram +s
car¦dio¦graph +s
car¦di¦og¦raph¦er
  +s
car¦di¦og¦raphy
car¦di¦oid +s
car¦di¦olo¦gist +s
car¦di¦ology
car¦dio¦
      my¦op¦athy
  car¦dio¦
      my¦op¦athies
car¦dio¦
      pul¦mon¦ary
car¦dio¦vas¦cu¦lar
car¦doon +s
card¦phone +s
card-playing
card-sharp +s
card-sharper +s
card table +s
card vote +s
cardy
  car¦dies
  (cardigan. △cadi)
care
  cares
  cared
  car¦ing
car¦een +s +ed
  +ing
car¦een¦age
car¦eer +s +ed
  +ing
career-best +s
car¦eer¦ism
car¦eer¦ist +s
care¦free
care¦free¦ness

care¦ful
care¦ful¦ly
care¦ful¦ness
care¦giver +s
care¦less
care¦less¦ly
care¦less¦ness
carer +s
ca¦ress
  ca¦resses
  ca¦ressed
  ca¦ress¦ing
ca¦ress¦ing¦ly
caret (omission
  mark. △carat ,
  carrot , karat)
care¦taker +s
Carew, Thomas
  (English poet)
care¦worn
Carey *also* **Cary**
  (name)
Carey, George
  (English
  archbishop)
car¦ezza (use
  karezza)
car¦fare +s
car¦fax
  car¦faxes
car¦ful +s
cargo
  car¦goes
car¦hop +s
Caria (ancient
  region, SW Asia)
cari¦ama +s
Car¦ian +s
Carib +s
Carib¦bean +s
Carib¦bean Sea
cari¦bou
  plural cari¦bou
cari¦ca¦tural
cari¦ca¦ture
  cari¦ca¦tures
  cari¦ca¦tured
  cari¦ca¦tur¦ing
cari¦ca¦tur¦ist +s
CARICOM
  (= Caribbean
  Community and
  Common Market)
car¦ies
  plural car¦ies
car¦il¦lon +s
Ca¦rina (name)
ca¦rina +s *Biology*
car¦in¦al
car¦in¦ate
Car¦in¦thia (state,
  Austria)

Car¦in¦thian +s
cari¦oca +s
cario¦gen¦ic
cari¦ole +s (use
  carriole)
cari¦ous
car¦jack +s +ed
  +ing
car¦jack¦er +s
cark¦ing
  (burdensome)
Carl *also* **Karl**
  (name)
carl +s (man)
Carla
carl¦ine +s
Car¦lisle (city,
  England)
car¦load +s
Car¦lo¦vin¦gian +s
Car¦low (county
  and city, Republic
  of Ireland)
Carls¦bad (German
  name for Karlovy
  Vary)
Carl¦ton
Carly
Car¦lyle, Thomas
  (Scottish writer)
car maker +s
car¦man
  car¦men
Car¦mar¦then
  (town, Wales)
Car¦mar¦then¦
  shire (former
  county, Wales)
Car¦mel (name)
Car¦mel, Mount
  (group of
  mountains, Israel)
Car¦mel¦ite +s
Car¦men
Car¦michael,
  Hoagy (American
  jazz musician)
Car¦mina Bur¦ana
car¦mina¦tive +s
car¦mine +s
Car¦naby Street
  (in London)
Car¦nac (village,
  France.
  △Karnak)
carn¦age
car¦nal
car¦nal¦ise *Br.* (use
  carnalize)
  car¦nal¦ises

car¦nal¦ise *(cont.)*
  car¦nal¦ised
  car¦nal¦is¦ing
car¦nal¦ity
car¦nal¦ize
  car¦nal¦izes
  car¦nal¦ized
  car¦nal¦iz¦ing
car¦nal¦ly
Car¦nap, Ru¦dolf
  (German-
  American
  philosopher)
car¦nas¦sial +s
car¦na¦tion +s
car¦nauba +s
Carné, Mar¦cel
  (French film
  director)
Car¦negie,
  An¦drew (Scottish
  entrepreneur and
  philanthropist)
car¦nel¦ian +s
car¦net +s
car¦ni¦val +s
Car¦niv¦ora
car¦ni¦vore +s
car¦niv¦or¦ous
car¦niv¦or¦ous¦ly
car¦niv¦or¦ous¦
        ness
Car¦not, Nico¦las
  (French scientist)
car¦no¦tite
carny
  car¦nies
  car¦nied
  carny¦ing
carob +s
carob tree +s
Carol *also* **Car¦ole,**
  Caryl
  (name)
carol
  carols
  car¦olled *Br.*
  car¦oled *Am.*
  car¦ol¦ling *Br.*
  car¦ol¦ing *Am.*
  (song. △carrel)
Car¦ole *also* **Carol,**
  Caryl
  (name)
Caro¦lean +s
car¦ol¦er *Am.* +s
  (*Br.* caroller)
Caro¦lina, North
  and South (states,
  USA)
Caro¦line (of the
  time of Charles I

Caro|line (*cont.*)
   or II of England;
   name)
Caro|line Is|lands
   (in W. Pacific)
Caro|lines
   (= Caroline
   Islands)
Caro|lin|gian +s
car|ol|ler *Br.* +s
   (*Am.* caroler)
Caro|lyn
carom +s +ed +ing
car|ot|ene
ca|rot|en|oid
Ca|roth|ers,
   Wal|lace
   (American
   chemist)
ca|rotid +s
ca|rousal +s
   (drinking party)
ca|rouse
   ca|rouses
   ca|roused
   ca|rous|ing
car|ou|sel *Br.* +s
   (merry-go-round;
   conveyor. *Am.*
   carrousel)
ca|rouser +s
carp +s +ed +ing
   (find fault)
carp
   plural carp
   (fish)
Car|pac|cio,
   Vit|tore (Italian
   painter)
car|pac|cio (food)
car|pal +s (bone.
   △ carpel)
car park +s
Car|pa|thian
   Moun|tains (in E.
   Europe)
car|pel +s (part of
   flower. △ carpal)
car|pel|lary
Car|pen|taria,
   Gulf of (on N
   coast of Australia)
car|pen|ter +s
car|pen|try
carp|er +s
car|pet +s +ed
   +ing
carpet-bag +s
carpet-bagger +s
car|pet bomb|ing
car|pet|ing +s
car|pet slip|per +s

car|pet sweep|er
   +s
car|phol|ogy
car phone +s
car|pol|ogy
car|port +s
car|pus
   carpi
Carr, Emily
   (Canadian painter)
carr +s (marsh.
   △ car, ka)
Car|racci (Italian
   family of painters)
car|rack +s
car|ra|geen
car|ra|geenan
car|ra|gheen (use
   carrageen)
Car|rara (town,
   Italy)
Car|rel, Alexis
   (French surgeon
   and biologist)
car|rel +s (cubicle.
   △ carol)
Car|reras, José
   (Spanish tenor)
car|riage +s
car|riage clock +s
carriage-dog +s
car|riage|way +s
car|rick bend +s
Carrick-on-
   Shannon (town,
   Republic of
   Ireland)
Car|rie
car|rier +s
car|rier bag +s
car|rier pi|geon +s
car|ri|ole +s
car|rion
car|rion crow +s
carrion-eater +s
carrion-eating
Car|roll, Lewis
   (English writer)
car|ron|ade +s
car|rot +s
   (vegetable.
   △ carat, caret,
   karat)
car|roty
car|rou|sel *Am.* +s
   (*Br.* carousel)
carry
   car|ries
   car|ried
   carry|ing
   (convey. △ karri)
carry-all +s

carry|cot +s
carrying-on
   carryings-on
   noun
carrying trade
carry-on +s *noun*
carry-out +s
carry-over +s
carry-through
   adjective
carse +s
car|sick
car|sick|ness
Car|son, Kit
   (American
   frontiersman)
Car|son, Ra|chel
   (American
   zoologist)
Car|son City (city,
   USA)
cart +s +ed +ing
   (unpowered
   vehicle; convey.
   △ kart, khat,
   quart)
cart|age
Car|ta|gena (ports,
   Spain and
   Colombia)
carte (*Fencing;* use
   quart. △ cart,
   kart, khat)
carte blanche
car|tel +s
car|tel|isa|tion *Br.*
   (use
   cartelization)
car|tel|ise *Br.* (use
   cartelize)
   car|tel|ises
   car|tel|ised
   car|tel|is|ing
car|tel|iza|tion
car|tel|ize
   car|tel|izes
   car|tel|ized
   car|tel|iz|ing
Car|ter, An|gela
   (English writer)
Car|ter, El|li|ott
   Cook (American
   composer)
Car|ter, Jimmy
   (American
   president)
car|ter +s
Car|te|sian +s
Car|tes|ian|ism
cart|ful +s
Car|thage (ancient
   city, Africa)

Car|tha|gin|ian +s
cart|horse +s
Car|thu|sian +s
Car|tier, Jacques
   (French explorer)
Cartier-Bresson,
   Henri (French
   photographer)
Car|tier Is|lands
   (in Indian Ocean)
car|til|age +s
car|ti|la|gin|oid
car|ti|la|gin|ous
Cart|land,
   Bar|bara (English
   writer)
cart|load +s
carto|gram +s
car|tog|raph|er +s
carto|graph|ic
carto|graph|ic|al
carto|graph|ic|
   al|ly
car|tog|raphy
carto|mancy
car|ton +s
car|toon +s
car|toon|ing
car|toon|ish
car|toon|ist +s
car|toon strip +s
car|toony
car|touche +s
cart|ridge +s
cart|ridge belt +s
cart|ridge paper
cart road +s
cart track +s
car|tu|lary
   car|tu|lar|ies
cart|wheel +s +ed
   +ing
Cart|wright,
   Ed|mund
   (English inventor)
cart|wright +s
car|uncle +s
car|un|cu|lar
Ca|ruso, En|rico
   (Italian tenor)
carve
   carves
   carved
   carv|ing
   (cut; slice.
   △ calve)
car|vel +s
carvel-built
car|ven
Car|ver *Am.* +s
   (rush-seated chair)

car|ver +s (person
who carves; knife;
dining chair with
arms. △ cava,
kava)
car|very
car|ver|ies
carve-up +s noun
carv|ing +s
carv|ing fork +s
carv|ing knife
carv|ing knives
car wash
car washes
Cary also Carey
(name)
Cary, Joyce
(English novelist)
cary|atid
cary|atides or
cary|atids
Caryl also Carol,
Car|ole
cary|op|sis
cary|op|ses
Casa|blanca (city,
Morocco)
Ca|sals, Pablo
(Spanish cellist
and composer)
Casa|nova +s
(philanderer)
cas|bah +s (use
kasbah)
cas|cade
cas|cades
cas|caded
cas|cad|ing
Cas|cade Range
(mountains, N.
America)
Cas|cais (resort,
Portugal)
cas|cara
(sag|rada)
case
cases
cased
cas|ing
case|book +s
case-bound
case-harden +s
+ed +ing
case his|tory
case his|tor|ies
ca|sein
ca|sein|ogen
case knife
case knives
case law
case|load +s
case|mate +s

Case|ment, Roger
(Irish nationalist)
case|ment +s
ca|se|ous
case-shot
case study
case studies
case|work
case|work|er +s
Casey also Casy
Cash, Johnny
(American singer)
cash
cashes
cashed
cash|ing
(money. △ cache)
cash|able
cash and carry
cash book +s
cash box
cash boxes
cash card +s
cash crop +s
cash desk +s
cash dis|pen|ser
+s
cashew +s (nut.
△ cachou)
cashew apple +s
cashew nut +s
cash flow +s
cash|ier +s +ed
+ing
cash-in +s noun
cash|less
cash|mere (wool.
△ Kashmir)
cash|point +s
cash regis|ter +s
cas|ing +s
ca|sino +s
cask +s (box.
△ casque)
cas|ket +s
Cas|lon, Wil|liam
(English
typographer)
Cas|par also
Cas|per
(name)
Cas|par (one of the
Magi)
Cas|per also
Cas|par
(name)
Cas|pian Sea (in
central Asia)
casque +s (helmet;
helmet-like
structure. △ cask)

Cas|san|dra (Greek
Legend; name)
cas|sata +s
cas|sa|tion +s
cas|sava +s
Casse|grain
(telescope)
cas|ser|ole
cas|ser|oles
cas|ser|oled
cas|ser|ol|ing
cas|sette +s
cas|sette play|er
+s
cas|sia +s
Cas|sie
cas|sin|gle +s
Propr.
Cas|sini (moon of
Saturn)
Cas|sini,
Gio|vanni
Do|men|ico
(Italian-born
astronomer)
Cas|sio|peia
(constellation)
cas|sis
cas|sit|er|ite +s
Cas|sius (Roman
general)
cas|sock +s
cas|socked
cas|sou|let +s
cas|so|wary
cas|so|war|ies
cast
casts
cast
cast|ing
(throw etc.
△ caste, karst)
Cas|talia (sacred
spring, Mount
Parnassus)
Cas|ta|lian
cas|ta|net +s
cast|away +s
caste +s (social
class. △ cast,
karst)
caste|ism
Cas|tel Gan|dolfo
(in Italy)
cas|tel|lan +s
cas|tel|lated
cas|tel|la|tion +s
caste mark +s
cast|er +s (person
or machine that
casts. △ castor)
cast|er sugar

cas|ti|gate
cas|ti|gates
cas|ti|gated
cas|ti|gat|ing
cas|ti|ga|tion
cas|ti|ga|tor +s
cas|ti|ga|tory
Cas|tile (region,
Spain)
Cas|tile soap
Cas|til|ian +s
Castilla-La
Mancha
(province, Spain)
Castilla-León
(region, Spain)
cast|ing +s
cast iron noun
cast-iron adjective
cas|tle
cas|tles
cas|tled
cast|ling
Castle|bar (town,
Republic of
Ireland)
Castle|reagh,
Rob|ert (British
statesman)
cast net +s
cast-off +s adjective
and noun
Cas|tor (Greek
Mythology; star)
cas|tor +s
(perforated jar;
wheel; oily
substance.
△ caster)
cas|tor ac|tion
cas|tor oil
cas|tor oil plant
cas|tor sugar (use
caster sugar)
cas|trate
cas|trates
cas|trated
cas|trat|ing
cas|tra|tion +s
cas|tra|tive
cas|trato
cas|trati
cas|tra|tor +s
cas|tra|tory
Cas|tries (capital of
St Lucia)
Cas|tro, Fidel
(Cuban
statesman)
Cas|tro|ism
cas|ual +s
casu|al|ly

casu|al|ness
casu|alty
  casu|al|ties
casu|ar|ina +s
casu|ist +s
casu|is|tic
casu|is|tic|al
casu|is|tic|al|ly
casu|is|try
casus belli
Casy *also* Casey
cat
  cats
  cat|ted
  cat|ting
cata|bol|ic
cata|bol|ic|al|ly
ca|tab|ol|ism
cata|chre|sis
  cata|chre|ses
cata|chres|tic
cata|chres|tic|al
cata|clasis
  cata|clases
cata|clas|tic
cata|clysm +s
cata|clys|mal
cata|clys|mic
cata|clys|mic|al|ly
cata|comb +s
cata|di|op|tric
ca|tad|rom|ous
cata|falque +s
Cata|lan +s
cata|lase +s
cata|lec|tic
cata|lepsy
  cata|lep|sies
cata|lep|tic
cata|log *Am.* +s
  +ed +ing
cata|log|er *Am.* +s
cata|logue *Br.*
  cata|logues
  cata|logued
  cata|loguing
cata|loguer *Br.* +s
cata|logue
  rai|sonné
  cata|logues
  rai|son|nés
Cata|lo|nia (region, Spain)
cat|alpa +s
cata|lyse *Br.*
  cata|lyses
  cata|lysed
  cata|lys|ing
cata|lyser *Br.* +s
cata|ly|sis
  cata|ly|ses

cata|lyst +s
cata|lyt|ic
cata|lyze *Am.*
  cata|lyzes
  cata|lyzed
  cata|lyz|ing
cata|ma|ran +s
cata|mite +s
cata|moun|tain +s
cata|nan|che +s
cat-and-dog
  adjective
Cat|ania (port, Sicily)
cata|plec|tic
cata|plexy
  cata|plex|ies
cat|ar|act +s
ca|tarrh +s
ca|tar|rhal
cat|ar|rhine
ca|tas|trophe +s
cata|stroph|ic
cata|stroph|ic|al|ly
ca|tas|troph|ism
ca|tas|troph|ist +s
cata|to|nia
cata|ton|ic +s
ca|tawba +s
cat|bird +s
cat|boat +s
cat burg|lar +s
cat|call +s
catch
  catches
  caught
  catch|ing
catch|able
catch-all +s
catch-as-catch-can
catch crop +s
catch|er +s
catch|fly
  catch|flies
catch|ily
catchi|ness
catch|line +s
catch|ment
catch|penny
  catch|pen|nies
catch|phrase +s
catch-points
catch|pole +s
catch-22
catchup +s (sauce)
catch-up *noun and attributive*
catch|weight +s

catch|word +s
catchy
  catch|ier
  catchi|est
cat door +s
cate +s
cat|ech|et|ic
cat|ech|et|ic|al
cat|ech|et|ic|al|ly
cat|ech|et|ics
cat|ech|ise *Br.* (use catechize)
  cat|ech|ises
  cat|ech|ised
  cat|ech|is|ing
cat|ech|iser *Br.* +s (use catechizer)
cat|ech|ism +s
cat|ech|is|mal
cat|ech|ist +s
cat|ech|ize
  cat|ech|izes
  cat|ech|ized
  cat|ech|iz|ing
cat|ech|izer +s
cat|echol|amine +s
cat|echu +s
cat|echu|men +s
cat|egor|ial
cat|egoric
cat|egor|ic|al
cat|egor|ic|al|ly
cat|egor|isa|tion *Br.* +s (use categorization)
cat|egor|ise *Br.* (use categorize)
  cat|egor|ises
  cat|egor|ised
  cat|egor|is|ing
cat|egor|iza|tion +s
cat|egor|ize
  cat|egor|izes
  cat|egor|ized
  cat|egor|iz|ing
cat|egory
  cat|egor|ies
ca|tena
  ca|tenae
ca|ten|ary
  ca|ten|ar|ies
cat|en|ate
  cat|en|ates
  cat|en|ated
  cat|en|at|ing
cat|en|ation +s
cater +s +ed +ing
cat|eran +s
cater-cornered
cater|er +s

cat|er|pil|lar +s (larva)
cat|er|pil|lar track +s *Propr.*
cat|er|waul +s +ed +ing
cat|fish
  plural cat|fish
cat flap +s
cat|gut
Cath *also* Kath
Cathar
  Cath|ars *or* Cath|ari
Cath|ar|ine *also* Cath|er|ine, Cath|ryn, Kath|ar|ine, Kath|er|ine, Kath|ryn
Cath|ar|ism
Cath|ar|ist +s
cath|ar|sis
  cath|ar|ses
cath|ar|tic +s
cath|ar|tic|al|ly
Ca|thay (poetic or historical name of China)
cat|head +s
cath|ec|tic
cath|edra (in 'ex cathedra')
cath|edral +s
Cather, Willa (American novelist)
Cath|er|ine *also* Cath|ar|ine, Cath|ryn, Kath|ar|ine, Kath|er|ine, Kath|ryn
Cath|er|ine (Russian empress)
Cath|er|ine de' Med|ici (French queen)
Cath|er|ine of Alex|an|dria (early saint)
Cath|er|ine of Ara|gon (wife of Henry VIII of England)
Cath|er|ine wheel +s
cath|eter +s
cath|et|er|ise *Br.* (use catheterize)
  cath|et|er|ises

cath¦et¦er¦ise
  (*cont.*)
  cath¦et¦er¦ised
  cath¦et¦er¦is¦ing
cath¦et¦er¦ize
  cath¦et¦er¦izes
  cath¦et¦er¦ized
  cath¦et¦er¦iz¦ing
cath¦etom¦eter +s
cath¦exis
  cath¦exes
Cathie *also* Cathy,
  Kathie, Kathy
Cath¦leen *also*
  Kath¦leen
cath¦odal
cath¦ode +s
cath¦ode ray +s
cath¦ode ray tube
  +s
cath¦od¦ic
Cath¦olic +s (in
  religious senses)
cath¦olic (universal
  etc.)
cath¦olic¦al¦ly (use
  catholicly)
Cath¦oli¦cise *Br.*
  (use Catholicize)
  Cath¦oli¦cises
  Cath¦oli¦cised
  Cath¦oli¦cis¦ing
  (make or become
  a Roman Catholic)
cath¦oli¦cise *Br.*
  (use catholicize)
  cath¦oli¦cises
  cath¦oli¦cised
  cath¦oli¦cis¦ing
  (make or become
  catholic)
Cath¦oli¦cism
cath¦ol¦icity
Cath¦oli¦cize
  Cath¦oli¦cizes
  Cath¦oli¦cized
  Cath¦oli¦ciz¦ing
  (make or become
  a Roman Catholic)
cath¦oli¦cize
  cath¦oli¦cizes
  cath¦oli¦cized
  cath¦oli¦ciz¦ing
  (make or become
  catholic)
cath¦olic¦ly
cath¦oli¦con +s
Cath¦ryn *also*
  Cath¦ar¦ine,
  Cath¦er¦ine,
  Kath¦ar¦ine,

Cath¦ryn (*cont.*)
  Kath¦er¦ine,
  Kath¦ryn
Cathy *also* Cathie,
  Kathie, Kathy
cat-ice
Cati¦line (Roman
  nobleman and
  conspirator)
cat¦ion +s
cat¦ion¦ic
cat¦kin +s
cat-lap
cat¦lick +s
cat¦like
cat¦mint
cat¦nap
  cat¦naps
  cat¦napped
  cat¦nap¦ping
cat¦nip
Cato (Roman
  statesman and
  orator)
cat-o'-nine-tails
  plural cat-o'-nine-
  tails
cat¦op¦tric
cat¦op¦trics
Cat¦rin
Ca¦tri¦ona
cat's cra¦dle +s
Cats¦eye +s (on
  road) *Propr.*
cat's-eye +s
  (precious stone;
  marble)
cat's-foot +s
Cats¦kill
  Moun¦tains (in
  USA)
cat's-paw +s
cat's py¦ja¦mas
cat's-tail +s
cat¦suit +s
cat¦sup +s
cat's whis¦ker +s
cat¦tery
  cat¦ter¦ies
cat¦tily
cat¦ti¦ness
cat¦tish
cat¦tish¦ly
cat¦tish¦ness
cat¦tle
cat¦tle cake +s
cattle-dog +s
cat¦tle grid +s
cat¦tle guard +s
cattle¦man
  cattle¦men
cattle-plague

cat¦tle stop +s
catt¦leya +s
catty
  cat¦tier
  cat¦ti¦est
catty-cornered
Ca¦tul¦lus (Roman
  poet)
cat¦walk +s
Cau¦ca¦sian +s
Cau¦cas¦oid +s
Cau¦casus
  (mountain range,
  Georgia)
Cauchy,
  Au¦gus¦tin Louis
  (French
  mathematician)
cau¦cus
  cau¦cuses
cau¦dal (of or like a
  tail. △ chordal)
caud¦al¦ly
caud¦ate (having a
  tail. △ chordate,
  cordate)
cau¦dillo +s
caught (past tense
  and past participle
  of catch. △ court)
caul +s (amnion.
  △ call)
caul¦dron +s
cauli¦flower +s
caulk *Br.* +s +ed
  +ing (*Am.* calk.
  stop up. △ cork)
caulk¦er +s *Br.*
  (*Am.* calker.
  person who
  caulks. △ corker)
caus¦able
causal
caus¦al¦ity
caus¦al¦ly
caus¦ation
causa¦tive +s
causa¦tive¦ly
cause
  causes
  caused
  caus¦ing
'cause (= because)
cause and ef¦fect
cause cé¦lèbre
  causes cé¦lèbres
cause¦less
causer +s
caus¦erie +s
cause¦way +s
causey +s
caus¦tic

caus¦tic¦al¦ly
caus¦ti¦cise *Br.* (use
  causticize)
  caus¦ti¦cises
  caus¦ti¦cised
  caus¦ti¦cis¦ing
caus¦ti¦city
caus¦ti¦cize
  caus¦ti¦cizes
  caus¦ti¦cized
  caus¦ti¦ciz¦ing
caus¦tic soda
caut¦er¦isa¦tion *Br.*
  (use
  cauterization)
caut¦er¦ise *Br.* (use
  cauterize)
  caut¦er¦ises
  caut¦er¦ised
  caut¦er¦is¦ing
caut¦er¦iza¦tion
caut¦er¦ize
  caut¦er¦izes
  caut¦er¦ized
  caut¦er¦iz¦ing
caut¦ery
  caut¦er¦ies
cau¦tion +s +ed
  +ing
cau¦tion¦ary
cau¦tious
cau¦tious¦ly
cau¦tious¦ness
Cau¦very (river,
  India)
cava +s (wine.
  △ carver, kava)
Ca¦vafy,
  Con¦stan¦tine
  (modern Greek
  poet)
cav¦al¦cade +s
Cava¦lier +s (in
  English Civil War)
cava¦lier +s
cava¦lier¦ly
cav¦alry
  cav¦al¦ries
cav¦al¦ry¦man
  cav¦al¦ry¦men
Cavan (county,
  Republic of
  Ireland)
cava¦tina +s
cave
  caves
  caved
  cav¦ing
  (hollow; explore
  caves; collapse)
cave (beware)
cav¦eat +s

cav¦eat emp¦tor
cave bear +s
cave dwell¦er +s
cave-in +s
cave¦like
Cav¦ell, Edith
. (English nurse)
cave¦man
  cave¦men
Cav¦en¦dish,
  Henry (English
  scientist)
cave paint¦ing +s
caver +s
cav¦ern +s
cav¦erned
cav¦ern¦ous
cav¦ern¦ous¦ly
cav¦es¦son +s
ca¦vetto
  ca¦vetti
cav¦iar +s
cavi¦are +s (use
  caviar)
cavil
  cavils
  cav¦illed
  cav¦il¦ling
cav¦il¦ler +s
cavi¦ta¦tion
cav¦ity
  cav¦ities
cav¦ity wall +s
ca¦vort +s +ed
  +ing
Ca¦vour, Cam¦illo
  di (Italian
  statesman)
cavy
  cavies
caw +s +ed +ing
  (bird's cry. △ cor,
  core, corps)
Caw¦ley, Evonne
  (Australian tennis
  player)
Cawn¦pore (former
  name of Kanpur)
Cax¦ton, Wil¦liam
  (English printer)
cay +s
Cay¦enne (capital
  of French Guiana)
cay¦enne +s
  (pepper)
Cay¦ley, Ar¦thur
  (English
  mathematician)
Cay¦ley, George
  (British
  aeronautics
  pioneer)

cay¦man +s
  (alligator)
Cay¦man Is¦lands
  (in Caribbean)
Cay¦mans
  (= Cayman
  Islands)
Ca¦yuga
  plural Ca¦yuga or
  Ca¦yu¦gas
CD play¦er +s
CD-ROM +s
cea¦no¦thus
Ceará (state, Brazil)
cease
  ceases
  ceased
  ceas¦ing
cease¦fire +s
cease¦less
cease¦less¦ly
Ceau¦şescu,
  Nico¦lae
  (Romanian
  statesman)
Cebu (island and
  city, Philippines)
cecal Am. (Br.
  caecal)
Cecil
Ce¦ci¦lia (Roman
  saint; name)
Cecily
ce¦citis Am. (Br.
  caecitis)
ce¦city Am. (Br.
  caecity)
cecum Am.
  ceca
  (Br. caecum)
cedar +s (tree.
  △ seeder)
ce¦darn
cedar¦wood
cede
  cedes
  ceded
  ced¦ing
  (give up. △ seed)
cedi +s (Ghanaian
  currency.
  △ seedy)
ce¦dilla +s
Ced¦ric
Cee¦fax Propr.
cei¦lidh +s
ceil¦ing +s (upper
  surface of room.
  △ sealing)
cela¦don +s
cel¦an¦dine +s
celeb +s

Cel¦ebes (former
  name of
  Sulawesi)
cele¦brant +s
cele¦brate
  cele¦brates
  cele¦brated
  cele¦brat¦ing
cele¦bra¦tion +s
cele¦bra¦tor +s
cele¦bra¦tory
ce¦leb¦rity
  ce¦leb¦rities
ce¦ler¦iac
ce¦ler¦ity
cel¦ery
  cel¦er¦ies
cell¦esta +s
Céleste
cel¦este +s
ce¦les¦tial
ce¦les¦ti¦al¦ly
Celia
ce¦liac Am. (Br.
  coeliac)
celi¦bacy
celi¦bate +s
cell +s (prison;
  Biology. △ sell)
cel¦lar +s
  (basement.
  △ seller)
cel¦lar¦age
cel¦lar¦er +s
cel¦laret +s
cel¦lar¦man
  cel¦lar¦men
cell block +s
celled
Cel¦lini,
  Ben¦ve¦nuto
  (Florentine
  goldsmith and
  sculptor)
cell¦ist +s
cell-like
Cell¦net Propr.
cello +s
cel¦lo¦phane Propr.
cell¦phone +s
cel¦lu¦lar
cel¦lu¦lar¦ity
cel¦lu¦late
cel¦lu¦la¦tion
cel¦lule +s
cel¦lu¦lite
cel¦lu¦litis
cel¦lu¦loid +s
cel¦lu¦lose
  cel¦lu¦los¦ing
cel¦lu¦los¦ic
cel¦lu¦lous

celom Am. (Br.
  coelom)
Cel¦sius
  (temperature
  scale)
Cel¦sius, An¦ders
  (Swedish
  astronomer)
Celt +s (people.
  △kelt)
celt +s (implement.
  △kelt)
Cel¦tic
Cel¦ti¦cism +s
cem¦balo +s
ce¦ment +s +ed
  +ing
ce¦men¦ta¦tion
ce¦ment¦er +s
ce¦men¦ti¦tious
ce¦ment mixer +s
ce¦men¦tum
cem¦et¦ery
  cem¦et¦er¦ies
ceno¦bite Am. +s
  (Br. coenobite)
ceno¦bit¦ic¦al Am.
  (Br. coenobitical)
ceno¦taph +s
Ceno¦zoic
cense
  censes
  censed
  cens¦ing
  (to perfume.
  △ sense)
cen¦ser +s (vessel
  for incense.
  △ censor, sensor)
cen¦sor +s +ed
  +ing (cut film etc.;
  Roman
  magistrate.
  △ censer, sensor)
cen¦sor¦ial
cen¦sori¦al¦ly
cen¦sori¦ous
cen¦sori¦ous¦ly
cen¦sori¦ous¦ness
cen¦sor¦ship
cen¦sur¦able
cen¦sure
  cen¦sures
  cen¦sured
  cen¦sur¦ing
  (criticize;
  criticism)
cen¦sus
  cen¦suses
  cen¦sused
  cen¦sus¦ing

cent +s (monetary
  unit (not of
  Estonia); in 'per
  cent'. △ scent,
  sent)
cen¦tal +s
cen|taur +s
Cen|taurus
  (constellation)
cen|taury
  cen¦taur|ies
  (plant)
cen|tavo +s
Cent|com
cen¦ten|ar¦ian +s
cen¦ten¦ary
  cen¦ten|ar¦ies
cen¦ten|nial +s
cen¦ter *Am.* +s +ed
  +ing (*Br.* centre)
cen¦ter back *Am.*
  +s (*Br.* centre
  back)
cen¦ter bit *Am.* +s
  (*Br.* centre bit)
cen¦ter|board *Am.*
  +s (*Br.*
  centreboard)
cen¦ter|fold *Am.* +s
  (*Br.* centrefold)
cen¦ter for|ward
  Am. +s (*Br.* centre
  forward)
cen¦ter half *Am.*
  cen¦ter halves
  (*Br.* centre half)
cen¦ter line *Am.* +s
  (*Br.* centre line)
cen¦ter|most *Am.*
  (*Br.* centremost)
cen¦ter|piece *Am.*
  +s (*Br.*
  centrepiece)
cen¦ter spread *Am.*
  +s (*Br.* centre
  spread)
cen¦ter stage *Am.*
  (*Br.* centre stage)
cen¦tes¦im¦al
cen¦tes¦im|al¦ly
cen¦tésimo +s
centi|grade
centi|gram +s
centi|liter *Am.* +s
centi|litre *Br.* +s
cent|ime +s
centi|meter *Am.* +s
centi|metre *Br.* +s
centimetre-gram-
  second (system)
cen|timo +s
centi|pede +s

cento +s
cen|tral
cen¦tral|isa¦tion
  Br. (use
  centralization)
cen¦tral|ise *Br.* (use
  centralize)
  cen¦tral|ises
  cen¦tral|ised
  cen¦tral|is¦ing
cen¦tral|ism
cen¦tral|ist +s
cen¦tral|ity
cen¦tral|iza¦tion
cen¦tral|ize
  cen¦tral|izes
  cen¦tral|ized
  cen¦tral|iz¦ing
cen¦tral|ly
Centre (region,
  France)
centre *Br.*
  centres
  centred
  cen¦tring *or*
  centre|ing
  (*Am.* center)
centre-back *Br.* +s
  (*Am.* center back)
centre bit *Br.* +s
  (*Am.* center bit)
centre|board *Br.*
  +s (*Am.*
  centerboard)
centre|fold *Br.* +s
  (*Am.* centerfold)
centre for|ward *Br.*
  +s (*Am.* center
  forward)
centre half *Br.*
  centre halves
  (*Am.* center half)
centre|ing *Br.* +s
  (use centring. *Am.*
  centering)
centre line *Br.* +s
  (*Am.* center line)
centre|most *Br.*
  (*Am.* centermost)
centre|piece *Br.* +s
  (*Am.* centerpiece)
centre spread *Br.*
  +s (*Am.* center
  spread)
centre stage *Br.*
  (*Am.* center
  stage)
cen|tric
cen|tric¦al
cen¦tri¦city
cen¦tri¦fu¦gal
cen¦tri¦fu¦gal¦ly

cen¦tri¦fu¦ga¦tion
cen¦tri¦fuge
  cen¦tri¦fuges
  cen¦tri¦fuged
  cen¦tri¦fu¦ging
cen|tring *Br.* +s
  (*Am.* centering)
cen¦tri|ole +s
cen¦tri|pet¦al
cen¦tri|pet¦al¦ly
cen|trism
cen|trist +s
cen|tro|mere +s
cen|tro|some +s
cen|tu¦ple
  cen|tu¦ples
  cen|tu¦pled
  cen|tu¦pling
cen|tur|ion +s
cen|tury
  cen|tur¦ies
cep +s
ceph|al¦ic
ceph|al|isa¦tion
  (use
  cephalization)
ceph|al|iza¦tion
Cepha|lonia
  (island, Greece)
ceph¦alo|pod +s
ceph¦alo|thorax
  ceph|alo|
  thor¦aces *or*
  ceph|alo|
        thor¦axes
ce|pheid +s
Ce|pheus (*Greek
  Mythology*;
  constellation)
cer|am¦ic +s
cer¦ami|cist +s
cer|am¦ics
cer¦am|ist +s
Ceram Sea (part of
  W. Pacific)
cer|as|tes
  plural cer|as|tes
cer|as|tium +s
Cer|berus *Greek
  Mythology*
cer|caria
  cer|cariae
cer|cus
  cerci
  (*Zoology.*
  △ circus)
cere +s (swelling at
  base of bird's
  beak. △ sear, seer,
  sere)

cer|eal +s (grain
  used for food.
  △ serial)
ce¦re|bel¦lar
ce¦re|bel¦lum
  ce¦re|bel¦lums *or*
  cere|bella
cere|bral
cere|bral¦ly
cere|brate
  cere|brates
  cere|brated
  cere|brat¦ing
cere|bra¦tion
cere|bro|spinal
cere|bro|vas¦cu¦lar
cere|brum
  ce¦re|bra
cere|cloth +s
cere|ment +s
cere|mo¦nial +s
cere|mo¦ni¦al|ism
cere|mo¦ni¦al|ist
  +s
cere|mo¦ni¦al|ly
cere|mo¦ni|ous
cere|mo¦ni|ous¦ly
cere|mo¦ni|ous|
           ness
cere|mony
  cere|monies
Cer|en|kov, Pavel
  (Soviet physicist)
Cer|en|kov
  ra|di|ation
Ceres (*Roman
  Mythology*;
  asteroid)
cer|esin
cer¦ise +s
cer|ium
cer|met
CERN (European
  Council (or
  Organization) for
  Nuclear Research)
cer|og|raphy
cero|plas¦tic
cert +s
cer|tain
cer|tain¦ly
cer|tainty
  cer|tain|ties
Cert. Ed.
  (= Certificate in
  Education)
cer¦ti|fi¦able
cer¦ti|fi¦ably
cer¦tifi|cate
  cer¦tifi|cates
  cer¦tifi|cated
  cer¦tifi|cat¦ing

cer|ti|fi|ca|tion +s
cer|tify
  cer|ti|fies
  cer|ti|fied
  cer|ti|fy|ing
cer|ti|or|ari
cer|ti|tude +s
ceru|lean
ceru|men
ceru|min|ous
cer|use
Cer|van|tes,
  Mi|guel (Spanish
  writer)
cer|velat +s
cer|vical
cer|vine
cer|vix
  cer|vi|ces
Ce|sar|ean Am. +s
  (Br. Caesarean)
ce|sar|evitch
  (eldest son of
  Russian emperor;
  use tsarevich)
Ce|sar|ewitch
  (horse race)
Ce|sar|ian Am. +s
  (use Cesarean. Br.
  Caesarean)
ces|ium
České
  Budě|jo|vice
  (city, Czech
  Republic)
cess
  cesses
  (tax, levy; also in
  'bad cess to')
ces|sa|tion +s
cess|er
ces|sion (ceding;
  territory ceded.
  △session)
ces|sion|ary
  ces|sion|ar|ies
cess|pit +s
cess|pool +s
cest|ode +s
cest|oid +s
cet|acean +s
cet|aceous
ce|tane
cet|eris pari|bus
Cetus
  (constellation)
Ceuta (enclave,
  Morocco)
Cé|vennes
  (mountain range,
  France)

Cey|lon (former
  name of Sri
  Lanka)
Cey|lon|ese
  plural Cey|lon|ese
Cé|zanne, Paul
  (French painter)
cha (use char)
Chab|lis
  plural Chab|lis
Chab|rier, Al|exis
  Em|man|uel
  (French
  composer)
Chab|rol, Claude
  (French film
  director)
cha-cha
  cha-chas
  cha-chaed or cha-
  cha'd
  cha-chaing
cha-cha-cha
  cha-cha-chas
  cha-cha-chaed or
  cha-cha-cha'd
  cha-cha-chaing
Chaco (plain, S.
  America)
cha|conne +s
Chad (country;
  name)
Chad, Lake (in
  central Africa)
cha|dar +s (use
  chador)
Chad|ian +s
Chad|ic
cha|dor +s
Chad|wick, James
  (English physicist)
chae|tog|nath +s
chaeto|pod +s
chafe
  chafes
  chafed
  chaf|ing
chafer +s
chaff +s +ed +ing
chaff-cutter +s
chaf|fer +s +ed
  +ing
chaf|fer|er +s
chaf|finch
  chaf|finches
chaffi|ness
chaffy
chaf|ing dish
  chaf|ing dishes

Cha|gall, Marc
  (Russian-born
  painter)
Cha|gas' dis|ease
Cha|gas's dis|ease
  (use Chagas'
  disease)
Cha|gos
  Archi|pel|ago (in
  Indian Ocean)
chag|rin
Chain, Er|nest
  (British
  biochemist)
chain +s +ed +ing
chain armor Am.
chain ar|mour Br.
chain gang +s
chain gear +s
chain|less
chain let|ter +s
chain link +s
  adjective and noun
chain mail
chain re|ac|tion +s
chain|saw +s
chain-smoke
  chain-smokes
  chain-smoked
  chain-smoking
chain-smoker +s
chain stitch
chain store +s
chain-wale +s
chain wheel +s
chair +s +ed +ing
chair-bed +s
chair-borne
chair-car +s
chair|lady
  chair|ladies
chair|lift +s
chair|man
  chair|men
chair|man|ship +s
chair|per|son +s
chair|woman
  chair|women
chaise +s
chaise longue
  chaise longues or
  chaises longues
chaise lounge +s
Chaka (use Shaka)
chakra +s
cha|laza
  cha|lazae
Chal|ce|don
  (ancient city, Asia
  Minor)
Chal|ce|don|ian +s
chal|ce|don|ic

chal|ced|ony
  chal|ced|onies
Chal|cis (town,
  Euboea, Greece)
chal|co|lith|ic
chal|co|pyr|ite
Chal|dea (part of
  Babylonia)
Chal|dean +s
Chal|dee +s
  (language; native
  of Chaldea)
cha|let +s
Cha|lia|pin,
  Fyo|dor
  Ivan|ovich
  (Russian singer)
chal|ice +s (goblet.
  △challis)
chalk +s +ed +ing
chalk|board +s
chalkie +s
chalki|ness
chalk pit +s
chalk-stone
chalk-stripe +s
chalk-striped
chalky
  chalk|ier
  chalki|est
chal|lah
  chal|lahs or
  chal|lot
chal|lenge
  chal|lenges
  chal|lenged
  chal|len|ging
chal|lenge|able
chal|len|ger +s
Chal|len|ger Deep
  (in N. Pacific)
chal|len|ging|ly
chal|lis (cloth.
  △chalice)
cha|lyb|eate
chamae|phyte +s
cham|ber +s
cham|bered
Cham|ber|lain,
  Jo|seph (British
  statesman)
Cham|ber|lain,
  Nev|ille (British
  prime minister)
Cham|ber|lain,
  Owen (American
  physicist)
cham|ber|lain +s
cham|ber|lain|ship
cham|ber|maid +s
cham|ber music
cham|ber pot +s

Cham|bers,
    Wil|liam
    (Scottish
    architect)
Cham|ber|tin +s
    (wine)
Cham|béry (town,
    France)
cham|bray +s
    (cloth)
cham|bré (brought
    to room
    temperature)
cha|meleon +s
cha|mele|on|ic
cham|fer +s +ed
    +ing
cham|ois
    plural cham|ois
chamo|mile (use
    camomile)
Cham|onix (ski
    resort, France)
champ +s +ed
    +ing
Cham|pagne (area,
    France)
cham|pagne +s
    (wine)
Champagne-
    Ardenne
    (administrative
    region, France)
cham|paign +s
    (open country)
cham|pen|oise (in
    'méthode
    champenoise')
cham|pers
cham|per|tous
cham|perty
    cham|per|ties
cham|pion +s +ed
    +ing
Cham|pion of
    Eng|land
cham|pion|ship +s
Cham|plain, Lake
    (in N. America)
Cham|plain,
    Sam|uel de
    (French explorer
    and statesman)
champ|levé
Cham|pol|lion,
    Jean-François
    (French
    Egyptologist)
Champs Élysées
    (street, Paris)
chance
    chances

chance (*cont.*)
    chanced
    chan|cing
chan|cel +s
chan|cel|lery
    chan|cel|ler|ies
chan|cel|lor +s
chan|cel|lor|ship
    +s
chance-medley +s
    (Law)
chan|cer +s
Chan|cery (Lord
    Chancellor's
    court)
chan|cery
    chan|cer|ies
Chan Chan (ruined
    city, Peru)
Chan-chiang
    (= Zhanjiang)
chan|cily
chan|ci|ness
chan|cre +s
chan|croid
chancy
    chan|cier
    chan|ci|est
chan|de|lier +s
Chan|di|garh
    (territory and city,
    India)
Chand|ler,
    Ray|mond
    (American writer)
chand|ler +s
chand|lery
    chand|ler|ies
Chan|dra|sekhar,
    Su|brah|
    man|yan (Indian-
    born American
    astronomer)
Cha|nel, Coco
    (French couturière
    and perfumer)
Chan|gan (former
    name of Xian)
Chang-chiakow
    (= Zhangjiakou)
Chang|chun (city,
    China)
change
    changes
    changed
    chan|ging
change|abil|ity
change|able
change|able|ness
change|ably
change|ful

change|ful|ness
change|less
change|less|ly
change|less|ness
change|ling +s
change|over +s
chan|ger +s
change-ringer +s
change-ringing
chan|ging room +s
Chang|sha (city,
    China)
Cha|nia (port,
    Crete)
chan|nel
    chan|nels
    chan|nelled *Br.*
    chan|neled *Am.*
    chan|nel|ling *Br.*
    chan|nel|ing *Am.*
chan|nel|ise *Br.*
    (use channelize)
    chan|nel|ises
    chan|nel|ised
    chan|nel|is|ing
chan|nel|ize
    chan|nel|izes
    chan|nel|ized
    chan|nel|iz|ing
chan|son +s
chan|son de geste
    chan|sons de geste
chant +s +ed +ing
chant|er +s
chan|ter|elle +s
chant|eur +s *male*
chant|euse +s
    female
chan|ti|cleer +s
Chan|tilly (lace;
    cream)
chan|try
    chan|tries
chanty (use
    shanty)
chan|ties
Cha|nuk|kah (use
    Hanukkah)
Cha|nute, Oc|tave
    (Franco-American
    aviation pioneer)
chaol|ogy
Chao Phraya
    (river, Thailand)
Chaos *Greek*
    Mythology
chaos (confusion)
cha|ot|ic
cha|ot|ic|al|ly
chap
    chaps

chap (*cont.*)
    chapped
    chap|ping
chapa|rajos
chap|ar|ral +s
cha|patti +s
chap|book +s
chape +s
chapeau-bras
    chapeaux-bras
chapel +s
chap|el|ry
    chap|el|ries
chap|eron +s +ed
    +ing (use
    chaperone)
chap|er|on|age
chap|er|one
    chap|er|ones
    chap|er|oned
    chap|er|on|ing
chap-fallen
chap|lain +s
chap|lain|cy
    chap|lain|cies
chap|let +s
chap|let|ed
Chap|lin, Char|lie
    (British actor)
Chap|man,
    George (English
    writer)
chap|man
    chap|men
chap|pal +s
Chap|pa|quid|dick
    (island, USA)
Chap|pell, Greg
    (Australian
    cricketer)
chap|pie +s
    (person)
chappy (chapped)
chaps
    (= chaparajos)
chap|stick +s
chap|ter +s
char
    chars
    charred
    char|ring
    (burn;
    charwoman; tea)
char
    plural char
    (fish)
chara|banc +s
chara|cin +s
char|ac|ter +s
char|ac|ter|ful
char|ac|ter|ful|ly

char¦ac¦ter¦
  isa¦tion *Br.* +s
  (use
  characterization)
char¦ac¦ter¦ise *Br.*
  (use characterize)
  char¦ac¦ter¦ises
  char¦ac¦ter¦ised
  char¦ac¦ter¦is¦ing
char¦ac¦ter¦is¦tic
  +s
char¦ac¦ter¦is¦tic¦
        al¦ly
char¦ac¦ter¦
        iza¦tion +s
char¦ac¦ter¦ize
  char¦ac¦ter¦izes
  char¦ac¦ter¦ized
  char¦ac¦ter¦iz¦ing
char¦ac¦ter¦less
char¦ac¦ter¦ology
cha¦rade +s
charas
char¦broil +s +ed
  +ing
char¦coal +s
Char¦cot, Jean-
  Martin (French
  neurologist)
char¦cu¦terie
chard +s
  (vegetable.
  △ charred)
Char¦don¦nay +s
  (grape; wine)
Char¦ente (river,
  France)
charge
  charges
  charged
  char¦ging
charge¦able
charge card +s
charge-coupled
chargé d'af¦faires
  chargés
    d'af¦faires
charge¦hand +s
charge nurse +s
char¦ger +s
charge sheet +s
chari¦ly
chari¦ness
char¦iot +s
char¦iot¦eer +s
cha¦risma
  cha¦ris¦mata
cha¦ris¦mat¦ic +s
cha¦ris¦mat¦ic¦
        al¦ly

Cha¦risse, Cyd
  (American
  actress)
char¦it¦able
char¦it¦able¦ness
char¦it¦ably
Char¦ity (name)
char¦ity
  char¦ities
  (help for needy)
cha¦ri¦vari +s
char¦lady
  char¦ladies
char¦la¦tan +s
char¦la¦tan¦ism
char¦la¦tan¦ry
Charle¦magne
  (ruler of Franks)
Char¦lene
Charle¦roi (city,
  Belgium)
Charles (British,
  French, Spanish
  and Swedish
  kings)
Charles, Prince
  (Prince of Wales)
Charles' Law
  Chemistry
Charles Mar¦tel
  (Frankish ruler)
Charles's Law (use
  Charles' Law)
Charles's Wain
  (constellation)
Charles¦ton (cities,
  USA)
charles¦ton +s
  (dance)
char¦ley horse
Char¦lie (name)
char¦lie +s (fool)
char¦lock
Char¦lotte (city,
  USA; name)
char¦lotte +s
  (dessert)
Char¦lotte Ama¦lie
  (capital of the US
  Virgin Islands)
Char¦lotte Dun¦das
  (steamship)
char¦lotte russe
Char¦lotte¦town
  (city, Canada)
Charl¦ton, Bobby
  and Jack (English
  footballers)
charm +s +ed +ing
Char¦maine
charm brace¦let
  +s

charm¦er +s
charm¦euse
Char¦mian
charm¦ing
charm¦ing¦ly
charm¦less
charm¦less¦ly
charm¦less¦ness
char¦nel +s
char¦nel house +s
Charo¦lais
  plural **Charo¦lais**
Char¦ol¦lais (use
  Charolais)
  plural **Char¦ol¦lais**
Cha¦ron (*Greek
  Mythology*; moon
  of Pluto)
char¦poy +s
charr (use char)
  plural **charr**
chart +s +ed +ing
chart¦bust¦er +s
char¦ter +s +ed
  +ing
char¦ter¦er +s
char¦ter mem¦ber
  +s
char¦ter party
  char¦ter par¦ties
Chart¦ism
Chart¦ist +s
Char¦tres (city,
  France)
char¦treuse +s
chart-topper +s
chart-topping
char¦woman
  char¦women
chary
  chari¦er
  chari¦est
Cha¦ryb¦dis *Greek
  Legend*
chase
  chases
  chased
  chas¦ing
chaser +s
Cha¦sid (use
  Hasid)
  Cha¦sid¦im
Cha¦sid¦ism (use
  Hasidism)
chasm +s
chas¦mic
chassé
  chas¦sés
  chas¦séd
  chas¦sé¦ing
  (step)
chasse +*s* (liqueur)

chas¦seur +s
chas¦sis
  plural **chas¦sis**
chaste (pure etc.
  △ chased)
chaste¦ly
chas¦ten +s +ed
  +ing
chas¦ten¦er +s
chaste¦ness
chaste-tree +s
chas¦tise
  chas¦tises
  chas¦tised
  chas¦tis¦ing
chas¦tise¦ment +s
chas¦tiser +s
Chas¦tity (name)
chas¦tity (being
  chaste; simplicity)
chas¦uble +s
chat
  chats
  chat¦ted
  chat¦ting
cha¦teau
  cha¦teaux
Cha¦teau¦bri¦and,
  François-René
  (French writer and
  diplomat)
cha¦teau¦bri¦and
  +s (steak)
chat¦elaine +s
Chat¦ham (town,
  England)
Chat¦ham Is¦lands
  (in SW Pacific)
chat¦line +s
chat show +s
chat¦tel +s
chat¦ter +s +ed
  +ing
chat¦ter¦box
  chat¦ter¦boxes
chat¦ter¦er +s
Chat¦ter¦ton,
  Thomas (English
  poet)
chat¦tery
chat¦ti¦ly
chat¦ti¦ness
chatty
  chat¦tier
  chat¦tiest
chat-up +s *adjective
  and noun*
Chat¦win, Bruce
  (Australian writer)
Chau¦cer,
  Geof¦frey
  (English writer)

Chau|cer|ian +s
chaud-froid +s
chauf|feur +s +ed
+ing (*male driver;
verb* drive.
△ shofar)
chauf|feuse +s
female
Chau|liac, Guy de
(French physician)
chaul|moo|gra +s
chau|tau|qua +s
chau|vin|ism +s
chau|vin|ist +s
chau|vin|is|tic
chau|vin|is|tic|
al|ly
Cha|vín
cheap +er +est
(inexpensive.
△ cheep)
cheap|en +s +ed
+ing
cheapie +s
cheap|ish
cheap|jack +s
cheap|ly
cheap|ness
cheapo
Cheap|side (street,
London)
cheap|skate +s
cheat +s +ed +ing
cheat|er +s (person
who cheats.
△ cheetah)
cheat|ing|ly
Cheb|ok|sary (city,
Russia)
Che|chen
plural Che|chen *or*
Che|chens
Chech|nya
(republic, Russia)
check +s +ed +ing
(verify; stop, slow;
act of verifying,
stopping or
slowing; pattern;
Chess. △ cheque)
check *Am.* +s
(*Banking. Br.*
cheque)
check|able
check|book *Am.* +s
(*Br.* chequebook)
check|er +s
(person or thing
that checks;
cashier.
△ chequer)

check|er *Am.* +s
+ed +ing (pattern.
Br. chequer)
check|er|berry
check|er|berries
check|er|board -
Am. +s (*Br.*
chequerboard)
check|er|man
check|er|men
check|ers (game)
check-in +s *noun
and attributive*
check|ing
ac|count +s
check|list +s
check|mate
check|mates
check|mated
check|mat|ing
check|out +s
check|point +s
check-rein +s
check|room +s
check sum +s
check-up +s *noun*
check valve +s
check|weigh|man
check|weigh|men
Ched|dar (village,
England; cheese)
cheek +s +ed +ing
cheek|bone +s
cheek|ily
cheeki|ness
cheeky
cheek|ier
cheeki|est
cheep +s +ed +ing
(bird's cry.
△ cheap)
cheer +s +ed +ing
cheer|ful
cheer|ful|ly
cheer|ful|ness
cheer|ily
cheeri|ness
cheerio +s
cheer|lead|er +s
cheer|less
cheer|less|ly
cheer|less|ness
cheer|ly
cheery
cheer|ier
cheeri|est
cheese
cheeses
cheesed
chees|ing
cheese|board +s
cheese|bur|ger +s

cheese|cake +s
cheese|cloth +s
cheese-cutter +s
cheesed
cheesed-off
attributive
cheese-fly
cheese-flies
cheese-head +s
cheese|maker +s
cheese|mak|ing
cheese-mite +s
cheese|mon|ger +s
cheese-paring +s
cheese plant +s
cheese-skipper +s
cheese straw +s
cheese|wood +s
cheesi|ness
cheesy
chees|ier
cheesi|est
chee|tah +s
(animal.
△ cheater)
chef +s
chef-d'œuvre
chefs-d'œuvre
Che|foo (former
name of Yantai)
Cheka (Soviet
organization)
Chek|hov, Anton
(Russian writer)
Chek|hov|ian
Che|kiang
(= Zhejiang)
chela
che|lae
(claw)
chela +s (Buddhist
novice; pupil)
che|late
che|lates
che|lated
che|lat|ing
che|la|tion
chel|icera
chel|icerae
chel|icer|ate +s
Chel|lean
Chelms|ford (city,
England)
che|lo|nian +s
Chel|sea (district,
London)
Chel|sea ware
Chel|ten|ham
(town, England)
Chel|ya|binsk
(city, Russia)
chem|ical +s

chem|ical|ly
chemi|lu|min|
es|cence
chemi|lu|min|
es|cent
che|min de fer
che|mins de fer
(gambling game)
che|mise +s
chemi|sorp|tion
chem|ist +s
chem|is|try
chem|is|tries
Chem|nitz (city,
Germany)
chemo
(= chemotherapy)
chemo|recep|tor
+s
chemo|syn|thesis
chemo|tac|tic
chemo|taxis
chemo|ther|ap|ist
+s
chemo|ther|apy
chem|ur|gic
chem|urgy
Che|nab (river,
India and Punjab)
Chen-chiang
(= Zhenjiang)
Cheng|chow
(= Zhengzhou)
Chengdu (city,
China)
che|nille +s
cheong|sam +s
Cheops (pharaoh)
cheque *Br.* +s (*Am.*
check. *Banking.*
△ check)
cheque|book *Br.*
+s (*Am.*
checkbook)
cheque card *Br.* +s
chequer *Br.* +s +ed
+ing (*Am.*
checker. pattern.
△ checker)
chequer|board *Br.*
+s (*Am.*
checkerboard)
che|quered
Che|quers (home
of British prime
minister)
che|quers *Br.* (in
'Chinese
chequers'.
△ checkers. *Am.*
checkers)
Cher (river, France)

Cher (American singer and actress)

Cher|bourg (port, France)

Cher|en|kov, Pavel (Soviet physicist; use Cerenkov)

Cher|en|kov ra|di|ation (use Cerenkov radiation)

Cher|epo|vets (city, Russia)

Che|rida

cher|ish
  cher|ishes
  cher|ished
  cher|ish|ing

cher|ish|able

Cher|kassy (port, Ukraine)

Cher|kessk (city, Russia)

Cher|nenko, Kon|stan|tin (Soviet president)

Cher|ni|gov (port, Ukraine)

Cher|niv|tsi (city, Ukraine)

Cher|no|byl (city, Ukraine)

Cher|no|reche (former name of Dzerzhinsk)

Cher|nov|tsy (Russian name for Chernivtsi)

cher|no|zem

Chero|kee +s

che|root +s

Cherry (name)

cherry
  cher|ries
  (fruit)

cherry laurel
  plural cherry laurel

cherry-pick
  cherry-picks
  cherry-picked
  cherry-picking

cherry pick|er +s

cherry pie +s

cherry plum +s

cherry red +s *noun and adjective*

cherry-red *attributive*

cherry to|mato
  cherry to|ma|toes

cherry tree +s

cher|ry|wood +s

Cher|son|ese (ancient name for Thracian or Gallipoli peninsula)

cher|son|ese (other peninsula)

chert +s

cherty

cherub
  cher|ubs *or*
  cher|ubim

cher|ub|ic

cher|ub|ic|al|ly

Cheru|bini, Luigi (Italian composer)

cher|vil

Cher|well, Lord (German-born British physicist)

Cheryl

Chesa|peake Bay (in USA)

Chesh|ire (county, England; cheese; cat)

Chesil Beach (in England)

chess

chess|board +s

ches|sel +s

chess|man
  chess|men

chess piece +s

chess play|er +s

chest +s

Ches|ter (city, England)

Ches|ter|field (town, England)

ches|ter|field +s (sofa)

Ches|ter|ton, G. K. (English writer)

chest|ily

chesti|ness

chest|nut +s

chest voice +s

chesty
  chest|ier
  chesti|est

Ches|van (use Hesvan)

chet|nik +s

Chetu|mal (port, Mexico)

che|val glass
  che|val glasses

Che|va|lier, Maur|ice (French singer and actor)

cheva|llier +s

che|vet +s

Chev|iot +s (sheep)

chev|iot (wool)

Chev|iot Hills (in England)

Chev|iots (=Cheviot Hills)

chèvre +s (cheese)

chev|ron +s

chev|ro|tain +s

chev|ro|tin +s (use chevrotain)

chevy
  chev|ies
  chev|ied
  chevy|ing

chew +s +ed +ing

chew|able

chew|er +s

chewi|ness

chew|ing gum

chewy
  chew|ier
  chewi|est

Chey|enne (city, USA)

Chey|enne
  plural Chey|enne (American Indian)

Cheyne–Stokes (respiration)

chez

chi +s (Greek letter)

chi|ack +s +ed +ing

Chi|ang Kai-shek (Chinese leader)

Chi|ang|mai (city, Thailand)

Chi|anti +s (region, Italy; wine)

Chi|apas (state, Mexico)

chiaro|scuro +s

chi|asma
  chi|as|mata
  chi|as|mus
  chi|asmi
  chi|as|tic

Chiba (city, Japan)

Chib|cha
  plural Chib|cha

Chib|chan

chi|bouk +s

chi|bouque +s (use chibouk)

chic
  chic-er
  chic-est
  (stylish)

Chi|cago (city, USA)

Chi|cago|an +s

chi|cane
  chi|canes
  chi|caned
  chi|can|ing

chi|can|ery
  chi|can|er|ies

Chi|cano +s

Chi|chén Itzá (in Mexico)

Chi|ches|ter (city, England)

Chi|ches|ter, Fran|cis (English yachtsman)

chi|chi

Chi|chi|mec
  plural Chi|chi|mec

chick +s (young bird)

chicka|dee +s

chick|en +s +ed +ing

chicken-and-egg *adjective*

chick|en feed

chicken-hearted

chick|en|pox

chick|en wire

chick|ling +s

chick|pea +s

chick|weed +s

chi|cle (chewing-gum ingredient)

chic|ly (stylishly)

chic|ness

chic|ory
  chic|or|ies

chide
  chides
  chided *or* chid
  chid|ing
  chided *or* chid|den

chider +s

chid|ing|ly

chief +s

chief|dom +s

chief|ly

Chief of Staff
  Chiefs of Staff

chief|tain +s

chief|tain|cy
  chief|tain|cies

chief|tain|ship +s

chiff|chaff +s

chif|fon +s
chif|fon|ier +s
chig|ger +s
chi|gnon +s
chi|goe +s
Chi|hli, Gulf of
(alternative name
for Bo Hai)
Chi|hua|hua (state
and city, Mexico)
chi|hua|hua +s
(dog)
chil|blain +s
chil|blained
child
chil|dren
child|bear|ing
child|bed
child|birth
child|care
child-centered Am.
child-centred Br.
Childe (in 'Childe
Harold' etc.)
Chil|der|mas
Chil|ders, Er|skine
(Irish nationalist)
child|hood +s
child|ish
child|ish|ly
child|ish|ness
child|less
child|less|ly
child|less|ness
child|like
child|mind|er +s
child|proof
child-rearing
chil|dren
child's play
Chile (in S.
America)
chile +s (food. use
chili Am. chilli Br.
△ chilly)
Chil|ean +s
chili +s Am. (food.
Br. chilli. △ chilly)
chil|iad +s
chili|asm
chili|ast +s
chili|as|tic
chill +s +ed +ing
chill|er +s
chilli Br.
chil|lies or
chil|lis
(food. Am. chili
△ chilly)
chilli con carne
chil|li|ness
chill|ing|ly

chill|ness
chill|some
chilly
chill|ier
chilli|est
(cold. △ chili,
chilli)
Chil|pan|cingo
(city, Mexico)
Chil|tern Hills
(England)
Chil|tern
Hun|dreds
Chil|terns
(= Chiltern Hills)
chi|maera +s (use
chimera)
Chim|bo|razo
(mountain,
Ecuador)
chime
chimes
chimed
chim|ing
chimer +s
chi|mera +s
(monster)
chi|mere +s (robe)
chi|mer|ic
chi|mer|ic|al
chi|mer|ic|al|ly
chimi|changa +s
chim|ney +s
chim|ney breast
+s
chim|ney piece +s
chim|ney pot +s
chim|ney stack +s
chim|ney sweep
+s
chimp +s
chim|pan|zee +s
Chimu
plural Chimu
Chin (Hills, in
Burma)
Chin (Chinese
dynasty; = Jin)
Ch'in (Chinese
dynasty; = Qin)
chin +s (part of
face)
China (country)
china +s (ceramic
ware)
china|graph +s
China|man
China|men
(offensive when
used of a person)
China|town +s
china|ware

chinch
chinches
chin|cher|in|chee
+s
chin|chilla +s
chin-chin
Chin|dit +s
Chin|dwin (river,
Burma)
chine
chines
chined
chin|ing
(backbone; ridge;
ravine; on ship)
chiné (mottled)
Chi|nese
plural Chi|nese
Ching (in 'I Ching')
Ch'ing (Chinese
dynasty; = Qing)
Chin Hills (in
Burma)
Chink +s (offensive
Chinese)
chink +s +ed +ing
(crack; ringing
sound)
Chin|kiang
(= Zhenjiang)
Chinky
Chink|ies
(offensive)
chin|less
chino +s
chi|nois|erie
Chi|nook
plural Chi|nook
(American Indian)
chi|nook +s (wind;
salmon)
chin|strap +s
chintz
chintzes
chintz|ily
chintzi|ness
chintzy
chintz|ier
chintzi|est
chin-up +s noun
chin|wag
chin|wags
chin|wagged
chin|wag|ging
chin|wags
chi|ono|doxa +s
Chios (Greek
island)
chip
chips

chip (cont.)
chipped
chip|ping
chip|board +s
chip|munk +s
chipo|lata +s
Chip|pen|dale,
Thomas (English
cabinet-maker;
style of furniture)
chip|per
chip|pie +s (use
chippy)
chip|pi|ness
chip|ping +s
chippy
chip|pies
Chips (carpenter)
chip shot +s
Chirac, Jacques
(French
statesman)
chiral
chir|al|ity
chi-rho
Chi|rico, Gior|gio
de (Italian
painter)
chir|og|raphy
chiro|mancy
Chiron (Greek
Mythology;
asteroid)
chir|opo|dist +s
chir|opody
chiro|prac|tic
chiro|prac|tor +s
chir|op|teran +s
chir|op|ter|ous
chirp +s +ed +ing
chirp|er +s
chirp|ily
chirpi|ness
chirpy
chirp|ier
chirpi|est
chirr +s +ed +ing
chir|rup
chir|rups
chir|ruped
chir|rup|ling
chir|rupy
chisel
chis|els
chis|elled Br.
chis|eled Am.
chis|el|ling Br.
chis|el|ing Am.
chis|el|er Am. +s
chis|el|ler Br. +s
Chişi|nău (capital
of Moldova)

chi-square (test)
Chis|wick (in London)
chit +s
chi¦tal
chit-chat
  chit-chat
  chit-chatted
  chit-chatting
chi¦tin
chi¦tin|ous
chi¦ton +s
Chit¦ta|gong (city, Bangladesh)
chit¦ter|ling +s
chitty
  chit|ties
chiv
  chivs
  chivved
  chiv|ving
chiv¦al|ric
chiv¦al|rous
chiv¦al|rous|ly
chiv|alry
  chiv¦al|ries
chive +s
chivvy
  chiv|vies
  chiv|vied
  chivvy|ing
Chka|lov (former name of Orenburg)
chla|mydia
  chla|mydiae
chla|myd¦ial
chlamy¦do|mo|nas
Chloe
chlor|acne
chlor¦al
chlor|am¦pheni|col
chlor|ate +s
chlor|ella +s
chlor¦ic
chlor|ide +s
chlor¦in|ate
  chlor¦in|ates
  chlor¦in|ated
  chlor¦in|at¦ing
chlor¦in|ation
chlor¦in|ator +s
chlor|ine +s
Chloris
chlor|ite +s
chlor|it¦ic
chloro|fluoro|car¦bon +s
chloro|form +s +ed +ing

Chloro|my¦cetin Propr.
chloro|phyll
chloro|phyl¦lous
chloro|plast +s
chloro|quine
chlor|osis
  chlor|oses
chlor|ot¦ic
chlor|ous
chlor|pro¦maz|ine
choc +s (chocolate. △chock)
choc-a-bloc (use choc-a-block)
choca|hol¦ic +s (use chocoholic)
choccy
  choc|cies
chocho +s
choc ice +s
chock +s +ed +ing (wedge. △choc)
chock-a-block
chocker
chock-full
chock|stone +s
choco|hol¦ic +s
choc|olate +s
choc|olate box
  choc|olate boxes noun
chocolate-box attributive
choc|olate brown +s noun and adjective
chocolate-brown attributive
choc|olatey
Choc|taw
  plural Choc|taw or Choc|taws
choice
  choices
  choicer
  choicest
choice¦ly
choice|ness
choir +s (singers; part of church. △quire)
choir|boy +s
choir|girl +s
choir|man
  choir|men
choir|mas¦ter +s
choir stall +s
choke
  chokes
  choked
  chok¦ing

choke|berry
  choke|berries
choke chain +s
choke-cherry
  choke-cherries
choke-damp
choker +s
chokey +s (use choky)
choki¦ly
choki|ness
choko +s
choky
  chokies
  choki¦er
  choki|est (prison; causing choking)
chol|an¦gi|og¦raphy
chole|cal¦cif¦erol
chole|cyst|og¦raphy
choler (anger; bile. △collar)
chol|era
chol¦er|aic
chol|er¦ic
chol¦er|ic|al¦ly
chol|es|terol
choli +s (bodice. △coaly, coley)
cho¦li|amb +s
cho¦li|am¦bic
cho¦line +s
cholla +s
chomp +s +ed +ing
Chom|skian +s
Chom|sky, Noam (American linguist)
chon|drite +s
chon¦dro|cra¦nium +s
Chong|jin (port, North Korea)
Chong|qing (city, China)
choo-choo +s
chook +s
chookie +s
choose
  chooses
  chose
  choos|ing
  chosen
chooser +s
choos|ily
choosi|ness

choosy
  choos|ier
  choosi|est
chop
  chops
  chopped
  chop|ping
chop-chop
Cho¦pin, Fréd|éric (Polish composer and pianist)
chop|per +s
chop|pily
chop|pi|ness
chop|ping block +s
choppy
  chop|pier
  chop¦pi|est
chop|stick +s
chop suey +s
choral (of a choir or chorus)
chor|ale +s (hymn tune; choir. △corral)
chor|al¦ly
chord +s (in music or mathematics. △cord)
chord¦al (of a chord. △caudal)
Chord|ata
chord|ate +s (animal. △caudate, cordate)
chord|ing (playing etc. of chords. △cording)
chore +s
cho¦rea
choreo|graph +s +ed +ing
chore¦og|raph¦er +s
choreo|graph¦ic
choreo|graph¦ic|al
choreo|graph¦ic|al¦ly
chore¦og|raphy
chore¦olo|gist +s
chore¦oll|ogy
chori|am¦bic
chori|am¦bus
  chori|ambi
chor¦ic
chor|ine +s
chor|ion +s
chori|on¦ic
chor|is|ter +s
chor|og|raph¦er +s

choro|graph¦ic
choro|graph¦ic|
al¦ly
chor|og¦raphy
chor|oid +s
choro|logic¦al
choro|logic¦al¦ly
chor|olo¦gist +s
chor|ology
chor¦tle
  chor¦tles
  chor¦tled
  chort|ling
chorus
  chor¦uses
  chor¦used
  chor¦us|ing
chorus girl +s
chorus-master +s
chose
chosen
Chou (= Zhou)
Chou En-lai
  (= Zhou
  Enlai)
chough +s (crow.
  ⚠ chuff)
choux (pastry; bun.
  ⚠ shoe)
chow +s (food;
  dog. ⚠ ciao)
chow-chow +s
chow|der +s
chow¦ki|dar +s
chow mein
chre¦ma¦tis¦tic
chre¦ma¦tis¦tics
chres|tom¦athy
  chres|tom¦athies
Chré|tien de
  Troyes (French
  poet)
Chris
chrism (oil)
chrisom +s (robe)
chrisom-cloth +s
Chris|sie
Christ (title)
Christa also Krista
Christa|bel
Christa|delph¦ian
  +s
Christ|church
  (city, New
  Zealand)
chris¦ten +s +ed
  +ing
Chris¦ten|dom
chris¦ten¦er +s
chris¦ten|ing +s
Christ|hood

Chris|tian +s
  (follower of Christ;
  name)
Chris|tian,
  Fletch¦er (Bounty
  mutineer)
Chris|ti¦ana
Chris|ti¦ania
  (former name of
  Oslo)
Chris|tian|isa¦tion
  Br. (use
  Christianization)
Chris¦tian|ise Br.
  (use Christianize)
  Chris¦tian|ises
  Chris¦tian|ised
  Chris¦tian|is¦ing
Chris|tian|ity
Chris|tian|iza¦tion
Chris|tian|ize
  Chris¦tian|izes
  Chris¦tian|ized
  Chris¦tian|iz¦ing
Chris|tian|ly
Chris|tian name
  +s
Chris|tian Sci|ence
Chris|tian
  Sci¦en|tist +s
Chris|tie +s Skiing
Chris|tie, Aga¦tha
  (English writer)
Chris|tie, Lin|ford
  (Jamaican-born
  British sprinter)
Chris|tina
Chris|tine
Christ|in¦gle +s
Christ|like
Christ|ly
Christ|mas
  Christ|mases
Christ|mas Is|land
  (in Indian Ocean;
  also former name
  of Kiritimati)
Christ|massy
Christ|mas tide
Christ|mas time
Christ|ol¦atry
Chris|to|logic¦al
Christ|ology
Christ|oph¦any
Chris|to¦pher
  (legendary saint;
  name)
Christ's Hos|pital
  (school, England)
Christy
  Chris|ties

Christy (cont.)
  (Skiing; use
  Christie)
chroma
chro|mate +s
chro|mat¦ic
chro¦mat¦ic|al¦ly
chro¦mati|cism
chro¦ma|ti¦city
chro¦ma|tid +s
chro¦ma|tin
chro¦ma|tism
chro¦mato|gram
  +s
chro¦mato|graph
  +s
chro¦ma|to|
     graph¦ic
chro¦ma|to|
    graph¦ic|al¦ly
chro¦ma|tog¦raphy
chro¦ma|top¦sia
chrome
  chromes
  chromed
  chrom¦ing
chrome lea¦ther
  +s
chrome-moly
chrome steel
chro|mic
chro¦min|ance
chro¦mite +s
chro|mium
chromium-plate
  chromium-plates
  chromium-plated
  chromium-
    plating
  noun and verb
chromo +s
chromo|
    dy¦nam¦ics
chromo|litho|
     graph +s
chromo|
  lith¦og¦raph¦er
  +s
chromo|litho|
     graph¦ic
chromo|
  lith¦og¦raphy
chromo|somal
chromo|some +s
chromo|sphere +s
chromo|spheric
chron|ic
chron¦ic|al¦ly
chron|icity
chron|icle
  chron|icles

chron|icle (cont.)
  chron|icled
  chron|ic¦ling
chron|ic¦ler +s
chrono|gram +s
chrono|gram|
     mat¦ic
chrono|graph +s
chrono|graph¦ic
chrono|olo¦ger +s
chrono|logic¦al
chrono|logic¦al¦ly
chro|nolo¦gisa|
  tion Br. (use
  chronologization)
chron|olo¦gise Br.
  (use
  chronologize)
chron|olo¦gises
chron|olo¦gised
chron|olo¦gis¦ing
chron|olo¦gist +s
chro|nolo¦giza|
     tion
chron|olo¦gize
  chron|olo¦gizes
  chron|olo¦gized
  chron|olo¦giz¦ing
chron|ology
  chron|olo¦gies
chron|om¦eter +s
chrono|met¦ric
chrono|met¦ric¦al
chrono|met¦ric|
     al¦ly
chron|om¦etry
chrono|scope +s
chrys|alid +s
chrys|alis
  chrys|al¦ises or
  chrys|al¦ides
chrys|anth +s
  (= chrys
  anthemum)
chrys|an¦the¦mum
  +s
chrys|ele¦phant|
     ine
chryso|beryl +s
chryso|lite +s
chryso|prase +s
Chrys|os¦tom,
  John (early saint)
chryso|tile
Chrys|tal also
  Crys|tal
chthon|ian
chthon¦ic
chub
  plural chub or
  chubs
  (fish)

Chubb +s (lock)
Propr.
chub|bily
chub|bi|ness
chubby
  chub|bier
  chub|bi|est
Chubu (region, Japan)
chuck +s +ed +ing
chucker-out +s
chuckle
  chuckles
  chuckled
  chuck|ling
chuckle|head +s
chuckle|head¦ed
chuck|ler +s
chuck|wagon +s
chud|dar +s (use chador)
chuff +s +ed +ing (make a puffing sound; delighted. △ chough)
chug
  chugs
  chugged
  chug|ging
Chu|goku (region, Japan)
chu¦kar +s (partridge)
Chuk|chi Sea (part of Arctic Ocean)
chukka +s (in polo)
chukka boot +s
chuk|ker +s (use chukka)
chum
  chums
  chummed
  chum|ming
chum|mily
chum¦mi|ness
chummy
  chum|mier
  chum¦mi|est
chump +s
chun|der +s +ed +ing
Chung|king (= Chongqing)
Chung-shan (= Zhongshan)
chunk +s +ed +ing
chunk|ily
chun|ki|ness
chunky
  chunk|ies
  chunk|ier
  chunki|est

Chun|nel (= Channel Tunnel)
chun|ter +s +ed +ing
chu|patty (use chapatti)
chu|pat¦ties
Chu¦qui|saca (former name of Sucre)
Church (body of Christians)
church
  churches
  churched
  church|ing (building; service; bring to church)
church|goer +s
church|going
Church|ill, Caryl (English writer)
Church|ill, Win|ston (British prime minister)
Church¦ill|ian
churchi|ness
church|man
  church|men
church|man|ship
Church|ward, George (English railway engineer)
church|war¦den +s
church|woman
  church|women
churchy
  church|ier
  churchi|est
church|yard +s
chur|inga +s
churl +s
churl|ish
churl|ish¦ly
churl|ish|ness
churn +s +ed +ing
churr +s +ed +ing (use chirr)
chur¦ras|caria +s
chur|rasco +s
Chur¦ri|guer|esque
chute +s (sloping channel or slide. △ shoot)
chut¦ist +s
chut|ney +s
chutz|pah
Chu|vashia (republic, Russia)

chy¦ack +s +ed +ing (use chiack)
chyle
chyl|ous
chyme
chym|ous
chy¦pre +s
cia|batta
  cia|bat¦tas or
  cia|batte
ciao (hallo; goodbye. △ chow)
ci¦bor|ium
  ci|boria
ci¦cada
  ci¦ca|das or
  ci¦ca|dae
cica|trice +s
cica|tri¦cial
cica¦trisa|tion *Br.* (use cicatrization)
cica|trise *Br.* (use cicatrize)
  cica|trises
  cica|trised
  cica|tris¦ing
cica|trix
  cica|tri¦ces
cica¦triza|tion
cica|trize
  cica|trizes
  cica|trized
  cica|triz¦ing
Ci¦cely (name)
ci¦cely
  ci¦cel|ies (plant)
Ci¦cero (Roman statesman and writer)
ci¦cer|one
  ci¦cer|oni
Ci¦cero|nian
cich|lid +s
Cid, El (Spanish warrior)
cider +s
cider press
  cider presses
ci-devant
cig +s (= cigarette)
ci¦gala +s
cigar +s
cig|aret +s (use cigarette)
cig¦ar|ette +s
cig¦ar|ette end +s
cig¦ar|illo +s

ciggy
  cig|gies (= cigarette)
cilia (plural of cilium. △ sillier)
cil|iary
cili|ate
cili|ated
cili|ation
cil¦ice +s
Cil|icia (ancient name of part of Asia Minor)
Cil|ician +s
cil¦ium
  cilia
cill +s (use sill)
cim|ba¦lom +s
Cim|mer|ian +s
cinch
  cinches
  cinched
  cinch|ing
cin|chona +s
cin|chon¦ic
cin|chon|ine
Cin¦cin|nati (city, USA)
cinc|ture
  cinc|tures
  cinc|tured
  cinc|tur|ing
cin|der +s
Cin|der|ella +s (in fairy story; neglected person)
cin|dery
Cindy *also* **Sindy**
cine|aste +s
cine-camera +s
cin|ema +s
cinema-goer +s
cinema-going
Cinema|Scope *Propr.*
cine|ma|theque +s
cine|mat¦ic
cine|mat¦ic|al¦ly
cine|mato|graph +s
cine¦ma| tog¦raph|er +s
cine|mato| graph¦ic
cine|mato| graph¦ic|al¦ly
cine|ma|tog|raphy
cinéma-vérité
cine|phile +s
cin¦er|aria +s (plant)

cin|er|arium +s
(place for cinerary
urns)
cin|er|ary
cin|er|eous
ciné-vérité
Cin|gal|ese
plural Cin|gal|ese
cin|gu|lum
cin|gula
cin|na|bar +s
cin|na|mon
cinq +s (use
cinque)
cinque +s (5 on dice.
△ sink)
cin|que|cen|tist +s
cin|que|cento
cinque|foil +s
Cinque Ports (in
England)
Cin|tra (use Sintra)
cion *Am.* +s (use
scion)
ci|pher +s +ed
+ing
cipo|lin
circa
cir|ca|dian
Cir|cas|sian +s
Circe *Greek Legend*
Cir|ce|an
cir|cin|ate
cir| citer
cir|cle
cir|cles
cir|cled
circ|ling
circ|ler +s
circ|let +s
cir|clip +s
circs
(= circumstances.
△ cirques)
cir|cuit +s +ed
+ing
circuit-breaker +s
cir|cu|it|ous
cir|cu|it|ous|ly
cir|cu|it|ous|ness
cir|cuit|ry
cir|cuit|ries
cir|cu|lar +s
cir|cu|lar|isa|tion
Br. (use
circularization)
cir|cu|lar|ise *Br.*
(use circularize)
cir|cu|lar|ises
cir|cu|lar|ised
cir|cu|lar|is|ing
cir|cu|lar|ity
cir|cu|lar|ities

cir|cu|lar|iza|tion
cir|cu|lar|ize
cir|cu|lar|izes
cir|cu|lar|ized
cir|cu|lar|iz|ing
cir|cu|lar|ly
cir|cu|late
cir|cu|lates
cir|cu|lated
cir|cu|lat|ing
cir|cu|la|tion +s
cir|cu|la|tive
cir|cu|la|tor +s
cir|cu|la|tory
cir|cum|am|bi|
ence
cir|cum|am|bi|
ency
cir|cum|am|bi|ent
cir|cum|am|bu|
late
cir|cum|am|bu|
lates
cir|cum|am|bu|
lated
cir|cum|am|bu|
lat|ing
cir|cum|am|bu|
la|tion +s
cir|cum|am|bu|
la|tory
cir|cum|circle +s
cir|cum|cise
cir|cum|cises
cir|cum|cised
cir|cum|cis|ing
cir|cum|ci|sion +s
cir|cum|fer|ence
+s
cir|cum|fer|en|tial
cir|cum|fer|en|
tial|ly
cir|cum|flex
cir|cum|flexes
cir|cum|flu|ence
cir|cum|flu|ent
cir|cum|fuse
cir|cum|fuses
cir|cum|fused
cir|cum|fus|ing
cir|cum|ja|cent
cir|cum|lit|toral
cir|cum|lo|cu|tion
+s
cir|cum|lo|cu|
tion|al
cir|cum|lo|cu|
tion|ary
cir|cum|lo|cu|tion|
ist +s
cir|cum|lo|cu|tory
cir|cum|lunar

cir|cum|navi|gate
cir|cum|navi|
gates
cir|cum|navi|
gated
cir|cum|navi|
gat|ing
cir|cum|navi|
ga|tion +s
cir|cum|navi|
ga|tor +s
cir|cum|po|lar
cir|cum|scrib|able
cir|cum|scribe
cir|cum|scribes
cir|cum|scribed
cir|cum|scrib|ing
cir|cum|scriber +s
cir|cum|scrip|tion
+s
cir|cum|solar
cir|cum|spect
cir|cum|spec|tion
cir|cum|spect|ly
cir|cum|stance +s
cir|cum|stanced
cir|cum|stan|tial
+s
cir|cum|stan|ti|al|
ity
cir|cum|
stan|ti|al|ly
cir|cum|ter|res|
trial
cir|cum|val|late
cir|cum|val|lates
cir|cum|val|lated
cir|cum|
val|lat|ing
cir|cum|vent +s
+ed +ing
cir|cum|ven|tion
+s
cir|cum|vo|lu|tion
+s
cir|cus
cir|cuses
(travelling show;
junction in town;
Roman arena; etc.
△ cercus)
ciré
Ciren|ces|ter
(town, England)
cire per| due
cirque +s (hollow.
△ circs)
cir|rho|sis
cir|rho|ses
(of liver.
△ sorosis)
cir|rhot|ic

cirri
cirri|ped +s
cirro|cumu|lus
cir|rose
cirro|stra|tus
cir|rous (of cirrus.
△ scirrhous)
cir|rus
cirri
(cloud. △ scirrhus)
cis|alpine
cis|at|lan|tic
cisco
cis|coes
Cis|kei (former
homeland, South
Africa)
cis|lu|nar
Cis|neros,
Fran|cisco de
(Spanish
statesman)
cis|pad|ane
cis|pont|ine
cissy (use sissy)
cis|sies
cist +s (coffin;
burial chamber;
box for sacred
vessels. △ cyst)
Cis|ter|cian +s
cis|tern +s
cis|tus
plural cis|tus
cit|able
cita|del +s
cit|ation +s
cite
cites
cited
cit|ing
(quote. △ sight,
site)
CITES (Convention
on International
Trade in
Endangered
Species)
cit|ies
citi|fied
cit|ify
citi|fies
citi|fied
citi|fy|ing
citi|zen +s
citi|zen|hood +s
citi|zen|ly
citi|zen|ry
Citi|zens' Ad|vice
Bur|eau
Citi|zens' Ad|vice
Bur|eaux

citi|zen's ar|rest
+s
citi|zens' band
Citi|zen's Char|ter
citi|zen|ship +s
Cit|lal|té|petl
(mountain,
Mexico)
cit|ole +s
cit|rate +s
cit|ric
cit|rin (substance in
fruit)
cit|rine +s (stone)
cit|ron +s
cit|ron|ella
cit|rous *adjective*
cit|rus
cit|ruses
noun
cit|tern +s
City, the (in
London)
city
cit|ies
city cen|ter *Am.* +s
city centre *Br.* +s
city dwell|er +s
city|fied (use
citified)
city|scape +s
city slick|er +s
city state +s
city|ward
city|wards
Ciu|dad Bolí|var
(city, Venezuela)
Ciu|dad Tru|jillo
(former name of
Santo Domingo)
Ciu|dad Vic|toria
(city, Mexico)
civet +s
civet-cat +s
civic
civ|ic|al|ly
civ|ics
civil
ci|vil|ian +s
ci|vil|ian|isa|tion
Br. (use
civilianization)
ci|vil|ian|ise *Br.*
(use civilianize)
ci|vil|ian|ises
ci|vil|ian|ised
ci|vil|ian|is|ing
ci|vil|ian|iza|tion
ci|vil|ian|ize
ci|vil|ian|izes
ci|vil|ian|ized
ci|vil|ian|iz|ing

civ|il|is|able *Br.*
(use civilizable)
civ|il|isa|tion *Br.*
+s (use
civilization)
civ|il|ise *Br.* (use
civilize)
civ|il|ises
civ|il|ised
civ|il|is|ing
civ|il|iser *Br.* +s
(use civilizer)
ci|vil|ity
ci|vil|ities
civ|il|iz|able
civ|il|iza|tion +s
civ|il|ize
civ|il|izes
civ|il|ized
civ|il|iz|ing
civ|il|izer +s
Civil List
civ|il|ly
civvy
civ|vies
Civvy Street
clack +s +ed +ing
(sound; chatter.
⚠ claque)
clack|er +s
Clac|ton|ian
clad
clads
clad|ded *or* clad
clad|ding
clad|ding +s
clade +s
clad|ism
cla|dis|tic
cla|dis|tics
clad|ode +s
clado|gram +s
claim +s +ed +ing
claim|able
claim|ant +s
(person making a
claim. ⚠ clamant)
claim|er +s
Clair *also* Claire,
Clare
Clair, René
(French film
director)
Claire *also* Clair,
Clare
clair|voy|ance
clair|voy|ant +s
clair|voy|ant|ly
clam
clams

clam (*cont.*)
clammed
clam|ming
cla|mant (insistent.
⚠ claimant)
cla|mant|ly
clam|ber +s +ed
+ing
clam|mily
clam|mi|ness
clammy
clam|mier
clam|mi|est
clamor *Am.* +s +ed
+ing (*Br.*
clamour)
clam|or|ous
clam|or|ous|ly
clam|or|ous|ness
clam|our *Br.* +s
+ed +ing (*Am.*
clamor)
clamp +s +ed +ing
clamp|down +s
clam|shell +s
clan +s
clan|des|tine
clan|des|tine|ly
clan|des|tin|ity
clang +s +ed +ing
clang|er +s
(mistake.
⚠ clangor,
clangour)
clangor *Am.* (*Br.*
clangour.
clanging; uproar.
⚠ clanger)
clang|or|ous
clang|or|ous|ly
clang|our *Br.* (*Am.*
clangor. clanging;
uproar. ⚠ clanger)
clank +s +ed +ing
clank|ing|ly
clan|nish
clan|nish|ly
clan|nish|ness
clan|ship +s
clans|man
clans|men
(member of clan.
⚠ Klansman)
clans|woman
clans|women
clap
claps
clapped
clap|ping
clap|board
clapped out
adjective

clapped-out
attributive
clap|per +s
clap|per|board +s
Clap|ton, Eric
(English guitarist)
clap|trap
claque +s (hired
applauders.
⚠ clack)
cla|queur +s
Clara
clara|bella +s
Clare, John
(English poet)
Clare *also* Clair,
Claire
(name)
Clare (county,
Republic of
Ireland)
Clar|ence (name)
clar|ence +s
(carriage)
Clar|en|ceux
Heraldry
Clar|en|don, Earl
of (English
statesman and
historian)
Clare of As|sisi
(Italian saint)
claret +s
Clar|ice
clari|fi|ca|tion +s
clari|fi|ca|tory
clari|fier +s
clar|ify
clari|fies
clari|fied
clari|fy|ing
clari|net +s
clari|net|tist +s
clar|ion +s
clar|ion call +s
Clar|issa
clar|ity
clar|ities
Clark
Clark, Wil|liam
(American army
officer)
Clarke, Ar|thur C.
(English writer of
science fiction)
Clarke, Mar|cus
(Anglo-Australian
writer)
clar|kia +s
Clar|rie
clary
clar|ies

clash
  clashes
  clashed
  clash|ing
clash|er +s
clasp +s +ed +ing
clasp|er +s
clasp-knife
  clasp-knives
class
  classes
  classed
  class|ing
class|able
class-conscious
class-
  conscious|ness
clas|sic +s
clas|sic|al
clas|sic|al|ism
clas|sic|al|ist +s
clas|sic|al|ity
clas|sic|al|ly
clas|si|cise Br. (use classicize)
  clas|si|cises
  clas|si|cised
  clas|si|cis|ing
clas|si|cism +s
clas|si|cist +s
clas|si|cize
  clas|si|cizes
  clas|si|cized
  clas|si|ciz|ing
clas|si|cus (in 'locus classicus')
clas|si|fi|able
clas|si|fi|ca|tion +s
clas|si|fi|ca|tory
clas|si|fied +s
clas|si|fier +s
clas|sify
  clas|si|fies
  clas|si|fied
  clas|si|fy|ing
class|ily
classi|ness
class|ism
class|ist +s
class|less
class|less|ness
class-list +s
class|mate +s
class|room +s
classy
  class|ier
  classi|est
clas|tic
clath|rate +s
clat|ter +s +ed +ing
Claud also Claude

Claude also Claud
Claude Lor|rain (French painter)
Claud|ette
Clau|dia
clau|di|ca|tion
Claud|ine
Claud|ius (Roman emperor)
claus|al
claus|al|ly
clause +s
Clause|witz, Karl von (Prussian soldier)
Claus|ius, Ru|dolf (German physicist)
claus|tral
claus|tro|phobe +s
claus|tro|pho|bia
claus|tro|pho|bic +s
claus|tro|pho|bic|al|ly
cla|vate
clave +s
clavi|cem|balo +s
clavi|chord +s
clav|icle +s
cla|vicu|lar
cla|vier +s
clavi|form
claw +s +ed +ing
claw|back +s
claw|er +s
claw ham|mer +s
claw|less
claw-mark +s
Clay, Cas|sius (real name of Muhammad Ali)
clay +s
clayey
clay|ish
clay|like
clay|more +s
clay-pan +s
clay pi|geon +s
Clay|ton's (illusory)
clean +s +ed +ing +er +est
clean|able
clean-cut
clean|er +s
clean|ish
clean|lily
clean|li|ness
clean-living

clean|ly
clean|lier
clean|li|est
clean|ness
clean-out +s noun
cleanse
  cleanses
  cleansed
  cleans|ing
cleans|er +s
clean-shaven
clean|skin +s
clean-up +s noun
clear +s +ed +ing +er +est
clear|able
clear|ance +s
clear|cole
  clear|coles
  clear|coled
  clear|col|ing
clear-cut
clear|er +s
clear-headed
clear|ing +s
clear|ing bank +s
clear|ing house +s
clear|ly
clear|ness
clear-out +s noun
clear-sighted
clear|story Am.
  clear|stor|ies (Br. clerestory)
clear-thinking
clear-up +s noun and attributive
clear|way +s
clear|wing +s
cleat +s
cleav|able
cleav|age +s
cleave
  cleaves
  clove or cleft or cleaved
  cleav|ing
  clo|ven or cleft (split)
cleave
  cleaves
  cleaved or clave
  cleav|ing (adhere)
cleav|er +s (chopper)
cleav|ers (plant)
Cleese, John (English actor)
clef +s
cleft +s (split. ⚠ klepht)

cleg +s
Cleis|the|nes (Athenian statesman)
cleis|to|gam|ic
cleis|to|gam|ic|al|ly
Clem
cle|ma|tis
  plural cle|ma|tis
Clem|ence
Cle|men|ceau, Georges (French statesman)
Clem|ency (name)
clem|ency (mercy)
Clem|ens, Sam|uel (real name of Mark Twain)
Clem|ent (name)
clem|ent (mild)
Clem|en|tine (name)
clem|en|tine +s (fruit)
Clem|ent of Alex|an|dria (Greek saint)
Clem|ent of Rome (pope and saint)
Clem|mie
clench
  clenches
  clenched
  clench|ing
Cleo also Clio
Cleo|patra (Egyptian queen)
clep|sydra +s
clere|story Br.
  clere|stor|ies (Am. clearstory)
clergy
  cler|gies
cler|gy|man
  cler|gy|men
clergy|woman
  clergy|women
cler|ic +s
cler|ic|al +s
cler|ic|al|ism
cler|ic|al|ist +s
cler|ic|al|ity
cler|ic|al|ly
cleri|hew +s
cler|isy
  cleri|sies
clerk +s +ed +ing
clerk|dom +s
clerk|ess
  clerk|esses
clerk|ish

clerk¦ly
clerk|ship +s
Clermont-Ferrand
  (city, France)
Cleve|land
  (county, England;
  city, USA)
Cleve|land,
  Grover
  (American
  president)
clever +er +est
clever-clever
clever Dick +s
clev|er¦ly
clev¦er|ness
Cleves, Anne of
  (wife of Henry
  VIII of England)
clevis
  clev|ises
clew +s +ed +ing
  (*Nautical.* △*clou*,
  clue)
cli¦an|thus
  plural cli¦an|thus
cli¦ché +s
cli|ché
cliché-ridden
click +s +ed +ing
  (sound. △clique)
click-clack +s +ed
  +ing
click¦er +s
clickety-click
cli¦ent +s
cli¦en|tele +s
client-server
  adjective
client|ship +s
Clif|den
  non|par¦eil +s
Cliff (name)
cliff +s (rock face)
cliff|hang¦er +s
cliff|hang¦ing
cliffi|ness
cliff|like
Clif|ford
cliff|side +s
cliff|top +s
cliffy
  cliff|ier
  cliffi|est
cli¦mac|ter¦ic +s
cli¦mac¦tic
cli¦mac¦tic|al¦ly
cli|mate +s
cli¦mat¦ic
cli¦mat¦ic|al
cli¦mat¦ic|al¦ly
cli¦ma¦to|logic¦al

cli¦mat|olo¦gist +s
cli¦mat|ology
cli¦max
  cli|maxes
  cli¦maxed
  cli¦max|ing
climb +s +ed +ing
  (mount. △clime)
climb|able
climb|down +s
climb¦er +s
climb|ing frame
  +s
climb|ing iron +s
clime +s (region;
  climate. △climb)
cli¦nal
clinch
  clinches
  clinched
  clinch|ing
clinch¦er +s
clincher-built
cline +s
  (continuum.
  △Klein)
cling
  clings
  clung
  cling|ing
cling¦er +s
cling film +s
clingi|ness
cling¦ing¦ly
cling|stone +s
clingy
  cling|ier
  clingi|est
clin¦ic +s
clin¦ic|al
clin¦ic|al¦ly
clin|ician +s
clink +s +ed +ing
clink¦er +s
clinker-built
clink|stone +s
clin|om¦eter +s
Clint (name)
clint +s *Geology*
Clin|ton, Bill
  (American
  president)
Clio *also* Cleo
  (name)
Clio *Greek and
  Roman Mythology*
clio|met¦rics
clip
  clips
  clipped
  clip|ping
clip|board +s

clip-clop
  clip-clops
  clip-clopped
  clip-clopping
clip joint +s
clip-on +s *adjective
  and noun*
clip|pable
clip|per +s
clip|pie +s
clip|ping +s
clique +s
  (exclusive group.
  △click)
cliquey
  cliqui¦er
  cliqui|est
cliqu|ish
cliqu¦ish|ness
cliqu|ism
cliquy (use
  cliquey)
clit¦ic
cliti|cisa|tion *Br.*
  (use cliticization)
cliti|ciza|tion
clit|or¦al
clit¦ori|dec¦tomy
clit¦ori|
           dec¦tomies
clit|oris
  clit|orises
Clive
Clive, Rob¦ert
  (British general)
cliv¦ers (use
  cleavers)
clo¦aca
  clo¦acae
clo|acal
cloak +s +ed +ing
cloak-and-dagger
cloak|room +s
clob|ber +s +ed
  +ing
cloche +s
clock +s +ed +ing
clock|maker +s
clock|mak¦ing
clock radio +s
clock tower +s
clock-watch
  clock-watches
  clock-watched
  clock-watching
clock-watcher +s
clock|wise
clock|work
clod +s
Clo|dagh
clod|dish
clod|dish¦ly

clod¦dish|ness
cloddy
clod|hop¦per +s
clod|hop|ping
clod|poll +s
clog
  clogs
  clogged
  clog|ging
clog dance +s *noun*
clog-dance
  clog-dances
  clog-danced
  clog-dancing
  verb
cloggy
  clog|gier
  clog¦gi|est
clois|onné
clois|ter +s +ed
  +ing
clois|tral
clomp +s +ed +ing
clo¦nal
clone
  clones
  cloned
  clon¦ing
clon¦ic
clonk +s +ed +ing
Clon|mel (town,
  Republic of
  Ireland)
clo¦nus
clop
  clops
  clopped
  clop|ping
clo¦*qué*
clos¦able
close
  closes
  closed
  clos¦ing
  (shut. △cloze)
close
  closer
  clos¦est
  (near; stuffy; road;
  etc.)
close-coupled
close-cropped
closed-circuit
closed-door
  adjective
closed-end
closed-ended
closed-in
close-down +s
  noun
closed shop
close-fisted

close-fitting
close-grained
close-hauled
close-in *adjective*
close-knit
close¦ly
close-mouthed
close|ness
close-out +s *noun*
close-quarter
  attributive
close quar|ters
  noun
close-range
  adjective
close-run
close sea¦son
close-set
close shave
close-shaven
closet +s +ed +ing
close-up +s
  adjective and noun
close-woven
clos¦ing time +s
clos¦ish
clos¦trid|ial
clos¦ure +s
clot
  clots
  clot|ted
  clot|ting
cloth +s
cloth cap +s
cloth-cap *attributive*
clothe
  clothes
  clothed
  cloth¦ing
cloth-eared
clothes
clothes horse +s
clothes line +s
clothes-moth +s
clothes-peg +s
clothes-pin +s
clo|thier +s
cloth¦ing
Clotho *Greek Mythology*
clot|ted cream
clo|ture +s
clou +s (central point or idea. △ clew, clue)
cloud +s +ed +ing
cloud base
cloud|berry
  cloud|berries
cloud|burst +s
cloud-castle +s
cloud cham|ber +s

cloud cover
cloud-cuckoo-land
cloud-hopping
cloud|ily
cloudi|ness
cloud-land
cloud|less
cloud|less¦ly
cloud|let +s
cloud|scape +s
cloudy
  cloud|ier
  cloudi|est
Clou¦et (Flemish family of painters)
Clough, Ar¦thur Hugh (English poet)
clough +s
clout +s +ed +ing
clove +s
clove hitch
  clove hitches
clo|ven
cloven-footed
cloven-hoofed
Clo|ver (name)
clo|ver +s (plant)
clo|ver|leaf +s
  (shape; intersection)
clo|ver leaf
  clo|ver leaves
    (leaf)
Clo¦vis *Archaeology*
clown +s +ed +ing
clown|ery
clown|ish
clown|ish¦ly
clown|ish|ness
cloy +s +ed +ing
cloy|ing¦ly
cloze +s (test. △ close)
club
  clubs
  clubbed
  club|bing
club|babil¦ity
club|bable
club|bable|ness
club|bably
club|ber +s
clubby
  club|bier
  club¦bi|est
club class
club-foot
  club-feet
club-footed
club|house +s

club|land
club|man
  club|men
club|mate +s
club|moss
  club|mosses
club|root
club sand|wich
  club sand|wiches
cluck +s +ed +ing
cluck|ily
clucki|ness
clucky
  cluck|ier
  clucki|est
clue
  clues
  clued
  clue|ing
  (piece of evidence etc. △ clew, *clou*)
clue|less
clue|less¦ly
clue|less|ness
Cluj–Napoca (city, Romania)
clump +s +ed +ing
clumpy
  clump|ier
  clumpi|est
clum|si¦ly
clum|si|ness
clumsy
  clum|sier
  clum¦si|est
clung
Clu|niac +s
clunk +s +ed +ing
clunk|er +s
clunky
  clunk|ier
  clunki|est
Cluny (town, France)
clus|ter +s +ed +ing
clus|ter bomb +s
clutch
  clutches
  clutched
  clutch|ing
clutch bag +s
Clu|tha (river, New Zealand)
clut|ter +s +ed +ing
Clwyd (county, Wales)
Clyde (river, Scotland; name)
Clydes|dale +s
cly|peal

cly¦pe|ate
clyp|eus
  clypei
clys|ter +s +ed +ing
Cly¦tem|nes¦tra
  Greek Legend
Cnut (Danish king of England)
Co. (= company)
co-accused
  plural co-accused
co|acer|vate +s
co|acer|va|tion
coach
  coaches
  coached
  coach|ing
coach|build¦er +s
coach-built
coach house +s
coach|load +s
coach|man
  coach|men
coach|wood
coach|work
co|ad|ju¦tor +s
co¦agul|able
co¦agu|lant +s
co¦agu|late
  co¦agu|lates
  co¦agu|lated
  co¦agu|lat|ing
co¦agu|la¦tion
co¦agu|la|tive
co¦agu|la|tor
co¦agu|la|tory
co¦agu|lum
  co|ag¦ula
Coa|huila (state, Mexico)
coal +s (rock, fuel. △ cole, kohl)
coal-bed +s
coal black *noun and adjective*
coal-black
  attributive
coal-burning
coal dust
coal¦er +s (ship. △ cola)
co|alesce
  co|alesces
  co|alesced
  co¦ales|cing
co¦ales|cence
co¦ales|cent
coal|face +s
coal|field +s
coal-fired

coal|fish
  plural coal|fish
coal gas
coal-hole +s
coal|house +s
co|ali|tion +s
co|ali|tion|ist +s
coal|man
  coal|men
coal mine +s
coal miner +s
coal min|ing
coal|mouse
  coal|mice
coal oil
Coal|port (town,
  England; china)
coal-sack +s
coal scut|tle +s
coal-seam +s
coal tar
coal tit +s
coaly (like coal.
  △ coley, choli)
coam|ing +s
co|arc|tate
co|arc|ta|tion +s
coarse
  coars|er
  coars|est
  (rough etc.
  △ corse, course)
coarse fish|ing
coarse|ly
coars|en +s +ed
  +ing
coarse|ness
coars|ish
coast +s +ed +ing
coast|al
coast|er +s
coast|guard +s
coast|land +s
coast|line +s
coast-to-coast
coast|wise
coat +s +ed +ing
  (garment; layer; to
  cover. △ cote)
coat dress
  coat dresses
coatee +s
coat-hanger +s
coat hook +s
coati +s
co|ati|mundi +s
coat|ing +s
coat|less
coat of arms
  coats of arms
coat|room +s

Coats Land
  (region,
  Antarctica)
coat-stand +s
coat-tail +s
co-author +s +ed
  +ing
coax
  coaxes
  coaxed
  coax|ing
coax|er +s
co|axial
co|axial|ly
coax|ing|ly
cob +s (lump of
  coal etc.; loaf;
  corn cob;
  hazelnut; horse;
  swan. △ kob)
co|balt +s
co|balt blue +s
  noun and adjective
cobalt-blue
  attributive
co|balt|ic
co|balt|ous
cob|ber +s
Cob|bett, Wil|liam
  (English political
  reformer)
cob|ble
  cob|bles
  cob|bled
  cob|bling
cob|bler +s
cobble|stone +s
Cob|den, Rich|ard
  (British political
  reformer)
Cob|den|ism
COBE (satellite)
co-belliger|ence
co-belliger|ency
co-belliger|ent +s
coble +s
cob|nut +s
COBOL *Computing*
cobra +s
cob|web +s
cob|webbed
cob|webby
coca +s (plant.
  △ coker)
Coca-Cola +s
  Propr.
co|caine
co|cain|ism
coc|cal
coc|ci|di|osis
  coc|ci|di|oses
coc|coid

coc|cus
  cocci
coc|cy|geal
coc|cyx
  coc|cy|ges *or*
  coc|cyxes
Cocha|bamba
  (city, Bolivia)
co-chairman
  co-chairmen
Co|chin (port,
  India)
co|chin +s (fowl)
Cochin-China
  (former name of
  part of Vietnam)
cochin-china +s
  (= cochin)
coch|in|eal
coch|lea
  coch|leae
coch|lear
Coch|ran, Charles
  (American
  theatrical
  producer)
Coch|ran,
  Jacque|line
  (American
  aviator)
cock +s +ed +ing
cocka|bully
  cocka|bul|lies
cock|ade +s
cock|aded
cock-a-doodle-
  doo +s
cock-a-hoop
cock-a-leekie
cocka|lorum
cock and bull
  adjective and noun
cocka|tiel +s
cocka|too +s
cocka|trice +s
cock|boat +s
cock|chafer +s
Cock|croft, John
  (English physicist)
cock|crow
cock|er +s
  (spaniel)
cock|erel +s
Cock|er|ell,
  Chris|to|pher
  (English engineer,
  inventor of the
  hovercraft)
cock|er spaniel +s
cock-eyed
cock|fight +s
cock|fight|ing

cock-horse +s
cock|ily
cocki|ness
cockle
  cockles
  cockled
  cock|ling
cockle|bur +s
cockle|shell +s
cock loft +s
cock|ney +s
cock|ney|ism
cock-of-the-rock
  +s
cock-of-the-walk
  cocks-of-the-
  walk
cock-of-the-wood
  +s
cock|pit +s
cock|roach
  cock|roaches
cocks|comb +s
cocks|foot
cock|shy
cock spar|row +s
cock|sure
cock|sure|ly
cock|sure|ness
cock|tail +s
cock-up +s *noun*
cocky
  cock|ies
  cock|ier
  cocki|est
cocky-leeky (use
  cock-a-leekie)
coco +s (palm tree
  bearing coconuts)
cocoa +s (powder
  or drink from
  cacao beans)
co|coa|nut +s (use
  coconut)
coco-de-mer
  plural coco-de-
  mer palms *or*
  coco-de-mer
  trees
Cocom
  (= Coordinating
  Committee on
  Multilateral Export
  Controls)
co-conspira|tor +s
co|co|nut +s
co|coon +s +ed
  +ing
co|coon|ery
Cocos Is|lands (in
  Indian Ocean)
co|cotte +s

Coc|teau, Jean
(French dramatist)
cod
plural cod
(fish)
cod
cods
cod|ded
cod|ding
(hoax)
coda +s
(concluding part.
△ coder)
cod|dle
cod|dles
cod|dled
cod|dling
cod|dler +s
code
codes
coded
cod|ing
code book +s
code-breaker +s
code-breaking
co-defend|ant +s
co|deine
code name +s
code-named
code num|ber +s
co|depend|ency
co|depend|ent +s
coder +s (encoder.
△ coda)
co-determin|ation
code word +s
codex
co|di|ces *or*
codexes
cod|fish
plural cod|fish
cod|ger +s
co|di|ces
co|di|cil +s
co|di|cil|lary
co|di|co|logic|al
co|di|co|logic|al|ly
co|di|col|ogy
co|difi|ca|tion +s
co|di|fier +s
co|dify
co|di|fies
co|di|fied
co|di|fy|ing
co-director +s
cod|ling +s
codlings-and-
cream
cod liver oil
co|do|main
codon +s
cod|piece +s

co-driver +s
cods|wal|lop
Cody, Wil|liam
(Buffalo Bill)
Coe, Se|bas|tian
(English runner)
coe|cil|ian +s (use
caecilian)
coed +s
co-editor +s
co-education
co-education|al
co-education|al|ly
co|ef|fi|cient +s
coela|canth +s
coel|en|ter|ate +s
coel|iac Br. (*Am.*
celiac)
coelom Br.
coel|oms *or*
coel|omata
(*Am.* celom)
coel|om|ate Br.
(*Am.* celomate)
coelo|stat +s
coeno|bite Br. +s
(*Am.* cenobite)
coeno|bit|ic Br.
(*Am.* cenobitic)
coeno|bit|ic|al Br.
(*Am.* cenobitical)
co|en|zyme +s
co-equal +s
co-equality
co-equally
co|erce
co|erces
co|erced
co|er|cing
co|ercer +s
co|er|cible
co|er|cion +s
co|er|cive
co|er|cive|ly
co|er|cive|ness
co|er|civ|ity
co|essen|tial
co|eter|nal
co|eter|nal|ly
Coet|zee, J. M.
(South African
novelist)
Coeur de Lion,
Rich|ard (English
king)
co|eval
co|ev|al|ity
co|ev|al|ly
co|ex|ist
co|ex|ist|ence
co|ex|ist|ent
co|ex|ten|sive

cof|fee +s
cof|fee bar +s
cof|fee bean +s
cof|fee break +s
cof|fee cup +s
cof|fee es|sence
cof|fee grind|er +s
cof|fee house +s
coffee-maker +s
cof|fee mill +s
cof|fee morn|ing
+s
cof|fee pot +s
cof|fee shop +s
cof|fee spoon +s
cof|fee table +s
noun
coffee-table
adjective
cof|fer +s (box.
△ cougher)
coffer-dam +s
cof|fered
cof|fin +s +ed +ing
coffin-bone +s
cof|fin cor|ner +s
coffin-joint +s
coffin-nail +s
cof|fle +s
co-founder +s
cog +s
co|gency
co|gent
co|gent|ly
cogged
cogit|able
cogi|tate
cogi|tates
cogi|tated
cogi|tat|ing
cogi|ta|tion +s
cogi|ta|tive
cogi|ta|tor +s
co|gito
Co|gnac (town,
France)
co|gnac +s
(brandy)
cog|nate +s
cog|nate|ly
cog|nate|ness
cog|nat|ic
cog|nis|able Br.
(use cognizable)
cog|nis|ably Br.
(use cognizably)
cog|ni|sance Br.
(use cognizance)
cog|ni|sant Br. (use
cognizant)
cog|nise Br. (use
cognize)

cog|nise (*cont.*)
cog|nises
cog|nised
cog|nis|ing
cog|ni|tion +s
cog|ni|tion|al
cog|ni|tive
cog|ni|tive|ly
cog|ni|tiv|ism
cog|ni|tiv|ist +s
cog|niz|able
cog|niz|ably
cog|ni|zance
cog|ni|zant
cog|nize
cog|nizes
cog|nized
cog|niz|ing
cog|no|men +s
co|gnos|cente
co|gnos|centi
cog|wheel +s
co|habit +s +ed
+ing
co|hab|it|ant +s
co|hab|it|ation
Am.
co|hab|it|ee +s
co|hab|it|er +s
Cohen, Leon|ard
(Canadian singer
and writer)
co|here
co|heres
co|hered
co|her|ing
co|her|ence +s
co|her|ency
co|her|ent
co|her|ent|ly
co|herer +s
co|he|sion +s
co|he|sive
co|he|sive|ly
co|he|sive|ness
Cohn, Fer|di|nand
(German botanist)
coho +s
cohoe +s (use
coho)
co|hort +s
COHSE
(= Confederation
of Health Service
Employees)
coif +s
coif|feur +s *male*
coif|feuse +s
female
coif|fure
coif|fures

coif|fure (cont.)
  coif|fured
  coif|fur|ing
coign +s
  (favourable
  position. △ coin,
  quoin)
coil +s +ed +ing
Co|im|ba|tore (city,
  India)
Co|im|bra (city,
  Portugal)
coin +s +ed +ing
  (money. △ coign,
  quoin)
coin|age
coin box
  coin boxes
co|in|cide
  co|in|cides
  co|in|cided
  co|in|cid|ing
co|in|ci|dence +s
co|in|ci|dent
co|in|ci|den|tal
co|in|ci|den|tal|ly
co|in|ci|dent|ly
coin|er +s
coin-op +s
Coin|treau
  +s Propr.
coir
co|it|al
co|ition
co|itus
co|itus
  inter|rup|tus
Coke +s (drink)
  Propr.
coke
  cokes
  coked
  cok|ing
  (form of coal;
  cocaine)
coker +s (person
  who cokes coal.
  △ coca)
col +s
cola +s (tree; drink.
  △ coaler)
col|an|der +s
co-latitude +s
Col|bert,
  Claud|ette
  (French actress)
Col|bert, Jean
  (French
  statesman)
col|can|non (Irish
  dish)

Col|ches|ter (town,
  England)
col|chi|cine +s
col|chi|cum (plant)
Col|chis (ancient
  region, SW Asia)
cold +s +er +est
cold-blooded
cold-blooded|ly
cold-blooded|ness
cold call +s +ed
  +ing
cold cream +s
cold-eyed
cold frame +s
cold-hearted
cold-hearted|ly
cold-hearted|ness
cold|ish
Cold|itz (town and
  prison, Germany)
cold|ly
cold|ness
cold room +s
cold-short
cold shoul|der
  noun
cold-shoulder +s
  +ed +ing verb
cold sore +s
cold store +s
cold war
cold-work
  cold-works
  cold-worked
  cold-working
  verb
Cole (name)
cole +s (cabbage.
  △ coal, kohl)
co-leader +s
cole|mouse (use
  coalmouse)
  cole|mice
Cole|op|tera
cole|op|teran +s
cole|op|ter|ist +s
cole|op|ter|ous
cole|op|tile +s
Cole|raine (town,
  Northern Ireland)
Cole|ridge,
  Sam|uel Tay|lor
  (English poet and
  critic)
cole|seed
cole|slaw
cole tit +s (use
  coal tit)
Col|ette (French
  novelist)

Col|ette also
  Col|lette
co|leus
  plural co|leus or
  co|leuses
coley +s (fish.
  △ coaly, choli)
colic +s
col|icky
Col|ima (state and
  city, Mexico)
Colin
coli|seum +s
  (stadium. △ the
  Colosseum)
col|itis
Coll (Scottish
  island)
col|lab|or|ate
  col|lab|or|ates
  col|lab|or|ated
  col|lab|or|at|ing
col|lab|or|ation +s
col|lab|ora|tion|ist
  +s
col|lab|ora|tive
col|lab|ora|tive|ly
col|lab|or|ator +s
col|lage +s
col|la|gen +s
col|lagist +s
col|lap|sar +s
col|lapse
  col|lapses
  col|lapsed
  col|laps|ing
col|laps|ibil|ity
col|laps|ible
col|lar +s +ed +ing
  (on garment;
  accost. △ choler)
collar-beam +s
col|lar|bone +s
col|lard +s
  (cabbage.
  △ collared)
col|lar|ette +s
col|lar|less
col|late
  col|lates
  col|lated
  col|lat|ing
col|lat|eral +s
col|lat|eral|ise Br.
  (use collateralize)
  col|lat|eral|ises
  col|lat|eral|ised
  col|lat|eral|is|ing
col|lat|eral|ity
col|lat|eral|ize
  col|lat|eral|izes

col|lat|eral|ize
  (cont.)
  col|lat|eral|ized
  col|lat|eral|iz|ing
col|lat|eral|ly
col|la|tion +s
col|la|tor +s
col|league +s
col|lect +s +ed
  +ing
col|lect|abil|ity
col|lect|able +s
col|lec|ta|nea
col|lect|ed|ly
col|lect|ible +s
  (use collectable)
col|lec|tion +s
col|lect|ive +s
col|lect|ive|ly
col|lect|ive|ness
col|lect|iv|isa|tion
  Br. (use
  collectivization)
col|lect|iv|ise Br.
  (use collectivize)
  col|lect|iv|ises
  col|lect|iv|ised
  col|lect|iv|is|ing
col|lect|iv|ism
col|lect|iv|ist +s
col|lect|iv|is|tic
col|lect|iv|ity
  col|lect|iv|ities
col|lect|iv|iza|tion
col|lect|iv|ize
  col|lect|iv|izes
  col|lect|iv|ized
  col|lect|iv|iz|ing
col|lect|or +s
col|lect|or's item
  +s
Col|leen (name)
col|leen +s (Irish
  girl)
col|lege +s
col|leger +s
col|le|gial
col|le|gi|al|ity
col|le|gian +s
col|le|gi|ate +s
col|le|gi|ate|ly
col|len|chyma
Colles' frac|ture
  +s
col|let +s
Col|lette also
  Col|ette
col|lide
  col|lides
  col|lided
  col|lid|ing
col|lider +s

col¦lie +s
col¦lier +s
col¦liery
  col¦lier¦ies
col¦li¦gate
  col¦li¦gates
  col¦li¦gated
  col¦li¦gat¦ing
col¦li¦ga¦tion +s
col¦li¦mate
  col¦li¦mates
  col¦li¦mated
  col¦li¦mat¦ing
col¦li¦ma¦tion +s
col¦li¦ma¦tor +s
col¦lin¦ear
col¦lin¦ear¦ity
col¦lin¦ear¦ly
Col¦lins
  Col¦linses
  (drink; in 'Tom
  Collins')
Col¦lins, Joan
  (English actress)
Col¦lins, Mi¦chael
  (Irish
  revolutionary)
Col¦lins, Wil¦kie
  (English novelist)
col¦li¦sion +s
col¦li¦sion¦al
col¦lo¦cate
  col¦lo¦cates
  col¦lo¦cated
  col¦lo¦cat¦ing
col¦lo¦ca¦tion +s
col¦locu¦tor +s
col¦lo¦dion +s
col¦lo¦graph +s
col¦logue
  col¦logues
  col¦logued
  col¦loguing
col¦loid +s
col¦loid¦al
col¦lop +s
col¦lo¦quial
col¦lo¦qui¦al¦ism
  +s
col¦lo¦qui¦al¦ly
col¦lo¦quium
  col¦lo¦qui¦ums or
  col¦lo¦quia
col¦lo¦quy
  col¦lo¦quies
col¦lo¦type +s
col¦lude
  col¦ludes
  col¦luded
  col¦lud¦ing
col¦luder +s
col¦lu¦sion +s

col¦lu¦sive
col¦lu¦sive¦ly
col¦lyrium
  col¦lyria
colly¦wob¦bles
colo¦bus
  colo¦buses
colo¦cynth +s
Col¦logne (city,
  Germany)
co¦logne +s
Co¦lom¦bia
Co¦lom¦bian +s
Col¦ombo (capital
  of Sri Lanka)
Colón (port,
  Panama)
colon +s
  (punctuation;
  intestine)
colón
  co¦lo¦nes
  (Costa Rican and
  Salvadorean
  currency)
col¦onel +s (officer.
  ⚠ kernel)
Col¦onel Blimp +s
col¦on¦el¦cy
  col¦on¦el¦cies
co¦lo¦nial +s
co¦lo¦ni¦al¦ism
co¦lo¦ni¦al¦ist +s
co¦lo¦ni¦al¦ly
co¦lon¦ic
col¦on¦isa¦tion Br.
  (use colonization)
col¦on¦ise Br. (use
  colonize)
  col¦on¦ises
  col¦on¦ised
  col¦on¦is¦ing
col¦on¦iser Br. +s
  (use colonizer)
col¦on¦ist +s
col¦on¦iza¦tion
col¦on¦ize
  col¦on¦izes
  col¦on¦ized
  col¦on¦iz¦ing
col¦on¦izer +s
col¦on¦nade +s
col¦on¦naded
col¦ony
  col¦onies
colo¦phon +s
col¦oph¦ony
colo¦quin¦tida +s
  (use colocynth)
color Am. +s +ed
  +ing (Br. colour)

col¦or¦able Am. (Br.
  colourable)
col¦or¦ably Am. (Br.
  colourably)
Col¦or¦ado (state
  and river, USA;
  beetle)
col¦or¦ant Am. +s
  (Br. colourant)
col¦or¦ation +s
col¦ora¦tura +s
color-blind Am.
  (Br. colour-blind)
color-blindness
  Am. (Br. colour-
  blindness)
color code Am. +s
  (noun. Br. colour
  code)
color-code Am.
  color-codes
  color-coded
  color-coding
  (verb. Br. colour-
  code)
Col¦ored Am. +s
  (often offensive
  person. Br.
  Coloured)
col¦ored Am. +s
  (having colour;
  clothes. Br.
  coloured)
color fast Am. (Br.
  colour fast)
color fast¦ness Am.
  (Br. colour
  fastness)
color-field Am.
  attributive (Br.
  colour-field)
col¦or¦ful Am. (Br.
  colourful)
col¦or¦ful¦ly Am.
  (Br. colourfully)
col¦or¦ful¦ness Am.
  (Br.
  colourfulness)
col¦or¦if¦ic
col¦or¦im¦eter +s
  (for measuring
  colour intensity.
  ⚠ calorimeter)
col¦ori¦met¦ric
col¦or¦im¦etry
col¦or¦ing Am. +s
  (Br. colouring)
col¦or¦ist Am. +s
  (Br. colourist)
col¦or¦ize Am.
  col¦or¦izes
  col¦or¦ized

col¦or¦ize (cont.)
  col¦or¦iz¦ing
  (Br. colourise)
col¦or¦less Am. (Br.
  colourless)
col¦or¦less¦ly Am.
  (Br. colourlessly)
color scheme Am.
  +s (Br. colour
  scheme)
color wash Am.
  color washes
  (noun. Br. colour
  wash)
color-wash Am.
  color-washes
  color-washed
  color-washing
  (verb. Br. colour-
  wash)
col¦or¦way Am. +s
  (Br. colourway)
col¦ory Am. (Br.
  coloury)
col¦os¦sal
col¦os¦sal¦ly
Col¦os¦seum, the
  (in Rome)
col¦os¦seum +s
  (other stadium.
  use coliseum)
Col¦os¦sians Bible
col¦os¦sus
  col¦ossi or
  col¦os¦suses
Col¦os¦sus of
  Rhodes (statue)
col¦os¦tomy
  col¦os¦tomies
col¦os¦trum
col¦ot¦omy
  col¦ot¦omies
col¦our Br. +s +ed
  +ing (Am. color)
col¦our¦able Br.
  (Am. colorable)
col¦our¦ably Br.
  (Am. colorably)
col¦our¦ant Br. +s
  (Am. colorant)
col¦our¦ation +s
  (use coloration)
colour-blind Br.
  (Am. color-blind)
colour-blindness
  Br. (Am. color-
  blindness)
col¦our code Br. +s
  (noun. Am. color
  code)
colour-code Br.
  colour-codes

colour-code (*cont.*)
 colour-coded
 colour-coding
 (*Am.* color-code)
Colloured *Br.* +s
 (*often offensive*
 person. *Am.*
 Colored)
colloured *Br.* +s
 (having colour;
 clothes. *Am.*
 colored)
colour fast *Br.*
 (*Am.* color fast)
colour fastness
 Br. (*Am.* color
 fastness)
colour-field *Br.*
 attributive (*Am.*
 color-field)
colourful *Br.* (*Am.*
 colorful)
colourfully *Br.*
 (*Am.* colorfully)
colourfulness *Br.*
 (*Am.*
 colorfulness)
colouring *Br.* +s
 (*Am.* coloring)
colourise *Br.* (use
 colourize)
 colourises
 colourised
 colourising
 (*Am.* colorize)
colourist *Br.* +s
 (*Am.* colorist)
colourless *Br.*
 (*Am.* colorless)
colourlessly *Br.*
 (*Am.* colorlessly)
colour scheme *Br.*
 +s (*Am.* color
 scheme)
colour-sergeant
 Br. +s
colour wash *Br.*
 colour washes
 (*noun. Am.* color
 wash)
colour-wash *Br.*
 colour-washes
 colour-washed
 colour-washing
 (*verb. Am.* color-
 wash)
colourway *Br.* +s
 (*Am.* colorway)
colloury *Br.* (*Am.*
 colory)
colporteur +s
colposcope +s

colposcopy
colposcopies
colpotomy
 colpotomies
Colt +s (gun) *Propr.*
colt +s (young male
 horse)
colter *Am.* +s (*Br.*
 coulter)
colthood +s
coltish
coltishly
coltishness
Coltrane, John
 (American jazz
 musician)
coltsfoot +s
colubrid +s
colubrine
colugo +s
Columba (Irish
 saint)
columbarium
 columbaria *or*
 columbariums
Columbia (river,
 city, and
 university, USA)
Columbia,
 District of (in
 USA)
Columbine
 (pantomime
 character)
columbine +s
columbite
columbium
Columbus (city,
 USA)
Columbus,
 Christopher
 (Italian explorer)
column +s
columnar
columnated
columned
column-inch
 column-inches
columnist +s
colure +s
colza
coma
 comae
 (gas round
 comet's tail; tuft
 on seed)
coma +s
 (unconsciousness)
Coma Berenices
 (constellation)

Comanche
 plural Comanche
 or Comanches
Comaneci, Nadia
 (Romanian
 gymnast)
comaltose
comb +s +ed +ing
combat
 combats
 combated *or*
 combatted
 combating *or*
 combatting
combatant +s
combative
combatively
combativeness
combe +s (use
 coomb. valley.
 △ cwm, khoum)
comber +s
combi +s
combinable
combination +s
combinational
combinative
combinatorial
combinatory
combine
 combines
 combined
 combining
combine
 harvester +s
combings
comb-jelly
 comb-jellies
combo +s
combs
 (= combinations)
combust +s +ed
 +ing
combustibility
combustible +s
combustibly
combustion
combustive
come
 comes
 came
 come
 coming
 (move towards
 speaker etc.
 △ cum)
come-at-able
comeback +s *noun*
Comecon
 (= Council for
 Mutual Economic
 Assistance)

comedian +s
comedic
Comédie
 Française
 (French national
 theatre)
comedienne +s
comedist +s
comedo
 comedones
comedown +s
 noun
comedy
 comedies
come-hither
 adjective
comeliness
comely
 comelier
 comeliest
come-on +s *noun*
comer +s
comestible +s
comet +s
cometary
come-uppance
comfily
comfiness
comfit +s (sweet)
comfort +s +ed
 +ing (ease;
 console)
comfortable
comfortableness
comfortably
comforter +s
comfortingly
comfortless
comfrey +s
comfy
 comfier
 comfiest
comic +s
comical
comicality
comically
comic book +s
comic strip +s
coming +s
Comino (island,
 Malta)
COMINT
 (= communica
 tions intelligence)
Comintern
 (communist
 organization)
comitadji +s
comity
 comities
comma +s

com|mand +s +ed
+ing
com¦mand|ant +s
Commandant-in-
Chief
Commandants-in-
Chief
com¦mand¦ant|
ship +s
com¦man¦deer +s
+ed +ing
com¦mand¦er +s
commander-in-
chief
commanders-in-
chief
com¦mand¦er|ship
+s
com¦mand¦ing¦ly
com¦mand¦ment
+s
com¦mando +s
comme ci, comme
ça
*com¦media
dell'arte*
comme il faut
com¦mem¦or|ate
com¦mem¦or|ates
com¦mem¦or|ated
com¦mem¦or|
at¦ing
com¦mem¦or|ation
+s
com¦mem¦ora|tive
com¦mem¦or|ator
+s
com¦mence
com¦mences
com¦menced
com¦men¦cing
com¦mence|ment
+s
com¦mend +s +ed
+ing
com¦mend|able
com¦mend|ably
com¦men¦da¦tion
+s
com¦men¦da¦tory
com¦mens¦al +s
com¦mens¦al|ism
com¦mens¦al|ity
com¦men¦sur|
abil¦ity
com¦men¦sur|able
com¦men¦sur|ably
com¦men¦sur|ate
com¦men¦sur|
ate¦ly
com¦ment +s +ed
+ing

com¦men|tary
com¦men|tar¦ies
com¦men|tate
com¦men|tates
com¦men|tated
com¦men|tat¦ing
com¦men|ta¦tor +s
com¦ment¦er +s
com¦merce
com¦mer¦cial +s
com¦mer¦cial|
isa¦tion *Br.* (use
commercializa-
tion)
com¦mer¦cial|ise
Br. (use
commercialize)
com¦mer¦cial|ises
com¦mer¦cial|ised
com¦mer¦cial|
is¦ing
com¦mer¦cial|ism
com¦mer¦ci¦al|ity
com¦mer¦cial|
iza¦tion
com¦mer¦cial|ize
com¦mer¦cial|izes
com¦mer¦cial|ized
com¦mer¦cial|
iz¦ing
com¦mer¦cial¦ly
com¦mère +s
Com¦mie +s
(= Communist.
△ commis)
com¦min|ation +s
com¦min¦atory
com¦min¦gle
com¦min¦gles
com¦min¦gled
com¦min¦gling
com¦min¦ute
com¦min¦utes
com¦min¦uted
com¦min¦ut¦ing
com¦minu¦tion +s
com¦mis
plural com¦mis
(waiter; chef.
△ Commie)
com¦mis¦er|ate
com¦mis¦er|ates
com¦mis¦er|ated
com¦mis¦er|at¦ing
com¦mis¦er|ation
+s
com¦mis¦era|tive
com¦mis¦er|ator
+s
com¦mis¦sar +s
com¦mis¦sar¦ial
com¦mis¦sar¦iat +s

com¦mis|sary
com¦mis|sar¦ies
com¦mis|sary|ship
+s
com¦mis|sion +s
com¦mis|sion
agent +s
com¦mis|sion|aire
+s
com¦mis|sion¦er
+s
com¦mis|sural
com¦mis|sure +s
com¦mit
com¦mits
com¦mit|ted
com¦mit|ting
com¦mit|ment +s
com¦mit|table
com¦mit|tal +s
com¦mit|tee +s
com¦mit|tee man
com¦mit|tee men
com¦mit|tee
woman
com¦mit|tee
women
com¦mit|ter +s
com¦mix
com¦mixes
com¦mixed
com¦mix|ing
com¦mix|ture +s
Commo +s
com¦mode +s
com¦modi|fi
ca¦tion
com¦mod|ify
com¦modi|fies
com¦modi|fied
com¦modi|fy|ing
com¦modi|ous
com¦modi|ous|ly
com¦modi|ous|
ness
com¦mod|ity
com¦mod|ities
com¦mo|dore +s
Commodore-in-
Chief
Commodores-in-
Chief
com¦mon
com¦mons
com¦mon¦er
com¦mon|est
com¦mon|able
com¦mon|age
com¦mon|al|ity
com¦mon|al¦ities
com¦mon|alty
com¦mon|al¦ties

com¦mon|er +s
com¦mon|hold
com¦mon|hold¦er
+s
com¦mon law *noun*
common-law
attributive
com¦mon¦ly
com¦mon|ness
com¦mon|place +s
com¦mon|place
book +s
com¦mon|place|
ness
com¦mon room +s
Com¦mons, the
(House of
Commons)
com¦mons (daily
fare; in 'short
commons')
com¦mon sense
com¦mon|
sen¦sic¦al
com¦mon weal
com¦mon|wealth
+s
com¦mo|tion +s
com¦mu¦nal
com¦mu¦nal|
isa¦tion *Br.* (use
communal-
ization)
com¦mu¦nal|ise *Br.*
(use
communalize)
com¦mu¦nal|ises
com¦mu¦nal|ised
com¦mu¦nal|
is¦ing
com¦mu¦nal|ism
com¦mu¦nal|ist +s
com¦mu¦nal|is¦tic
com¦mu¦nal|is¦tic|
al¦ly
com¦mu¦nal|ity
com¦mu¦nal|ities
com¦mu¦nal|
iza¦tion
com¦mu¦nal|ize
com¦mu¦nal|izes
com¦mu¦nal|ized
com¦mu¦nal|
iz¦ing
com¦mu¦nal¦ly
com¦mu¦nard +s
com¦mune
com¦munes
com¦muned
com¦mun¦ing
com¦mu¦nic|
abil¦ity

com|mu'nic|able
com|mu'nic|ably
com|mu'ni|cant+s
com|mu'ni|cate
com|mu'ni|cates
com|mu'ni|cated
com|mu'ni|
    cat'ing
com|mu'ni|ca'tion
  +s
com|mu'ni|
    ca'tion|al
com|mu'ni|ca'tion
  sat'el|lite+s
com|mu'ni|ca'tive
com|mu'ni|
    ca'tive'ly
com|mu'ni|ca'tor
  +s
com|mu'ni|ca'tory
Com|mu'nion
  (Eucharist)
com|mu'nion+s
  (sharing)
com|mu'ni|qué+s
com|mun'isa|tion
  Br. (use
  communization)
com|mun'ise Br.
  (use communize)
com|mun'ises
com|mun'ised
com|mun'is'ing
Com|mun'ism
  (system; society)
com|mun'ism
  (political theory)
Com|mun'ism
  Peak (mountain,
  Tadjikistan)
Com|mun'ist+s
  (member of party)
com|mun'ist+s
  (supporter of
  social system)
com|mun'is'tic
com|mun'is'tic|
  al'ly
com|mu'ni|tar'ian
  +s
com|mu'nity
com|mu'nities
com|mun'iza'tion
com|mun'ize
com|mun'izes
com|mun'ized
com|mun'iz'ing
com'mut|abil'ity
com'mut|able
com'mu|tate
com'mu|tates

com'mu|tate
  (cont.)
com'mu|tated
com'mu|tat'ing
com'mu|ta'tion+s
com'mu|ta'tive
com'mu|ta'tor+s
com|mute
com|mutes
com|muted
com|mut'ing
com|muter+s
Como, Lake (in
  Italy)
Como|doro
  Riva|davia (port,
  Argentina)
Com|orin, Cape (in
  India)
Com|oros (islands,
  Indian Ocean)
co|mose
comp+s +ed +ing
com|pact+s +ed
  +ing
com|pact disc+s
com|pact disk+s
  (use compact
  disc)
com|pac'tion
com|pact'ly
com|pact|ness
com|pact'or+s
com|padre+s
com|pa'ges
  plural com|pa'ges
com|pand+s +ed
  +ing
com|pand'er+s
com|pand'or+s
  (use compander)
com|pan'ion+s
com|pan'ion|able
com|pan'ion|able|
    ness
com|pan'ion|ably
com|pan'ion|ate
com|pan'ion hatch
com|pan'ion
  hatches
com|pan'ion
  hatch|way+s
companion-in-
  arms
companions-in-
  arms
com|pan'ion|ship
com|pan'ion|way
  +s
com|pany
com|panies
com|par|abil'ity

com'par|able
com'par|able|ness
com'par|ably
com|para|tist+s
com|para|tive+s
com|para|tive'ly
com|para|tor+s
com|pare
com|pares
com|pared
com|par'ing
  (liken. △ compère)
com|pari'son+s
com'part|ment+s
  +ed +ing
com'part|men'tal
com'part|men'tal|
  isa'tion Br. (use
  compartmental-
  ization)
com'part|men'tal|
  ise Br. (use
  compartmental-
  ize)
com'part|men'tal|
    ises
com'part|men'tal|
    ised
com'part|men'tal|
    is'ing
com'part|men'tal|
    iza'tion
com'part|men'tal|
    ize
com'part|men'tal|
    izes
com'part|men'tal|
    ized
com'part|men'tal|
    iz'ing
com'part|
    men'tal'ly
com'part|men|
    ta'tion
com|pass
com|passes
com|passed
com|pass'ing
com|pass|able
com|pas'sion
com|pas'sion|ate
com|pas'sion|
    ate'ly
com|pati|bil'ity
com|pati|bil'ities
com|pat'ible+s
com|pat'ibly
com|pat'riot+s
com|pat'ri|ot'ic
com|peer+s
com|pel
com|pels

com|pel (cont.)
com|pelled
com|pel'ling
com|pel'lable
com|pel'ling'ly
com|pen'di|ous
com|pen'di|ous'ly
com|pen'dium
com|pen'diums or
com|pen'dia
com|pen|sate
com|pen|sates
com|pen|sated
com|pen|sat'ing
com|pen|sa'tion
  +s
com|pen|sa'tion|al
com|pen|sa'tive
com|pen|sa'tor+s
com|pen|sa'tory
com|père
com|pères
com|pèred
com|pèr'ing
  (MC. △ compare)
com|pete
com|petes
com|peted
com|pet'ing
com|pe'tence+s
com|pe'tency
com|pe'ten'cies
com|pe'tent
com|pe'tent'ly
com|pe|ti'tion+s
com|peti'tive
com|peti'tive'ly
com|peti'tive|ness
com|peti'tor+s
com|pil|ation+s
com|pile
com|piles
com|piled
com|pil'ing
com|piler+s
com|pla'cence (self-
  satisfaction.
  △ complaisance)
com|pla'cency
com|pla'cent (self-
  satisfied.
  △ complaisant)
com|pla'cent'ly
com|plain+s +ed
  +ing
com|plain|ant+s
com|plain'er+s
com|plain'ing'ly
com|plaint+s
com|plai'sance
  (acquiescence.
  △ complacence)

com|plai|sant
(acquiescent.
⚠ complacen)
com|pleat(*archaic*
= complete)
com|ple|ment+s
+ed +ing
(something that
completes; full
number of people;
Grammar;
Biochemistry;
Mathematics;
Geometry; go well
with.
⚠ compliment)
com|ple|men|tal
com|ple|
men|tar|ily(in a
complementary
way. ⚠ com-
plimentarily)
com|ple|men|tari|
         ness
com|ple|
     men|tar|ity
com|ple|
     men|tar|ities
com|ple|men|tary
(that
complements;
Geometry. ⚠ com-
plimentary)
com|plete
com|pletes
com|pleted
com|plet|ing
com|plete|ly
com|plete|ness
com|ple|tion+s
com|plet|ist+s
com|plex
com|plexes
com|plex|ation
com|plex|ion+s
com|plex|ioned
com|plex|ion|less
com|plex|ity
com|plex|ities
com|plex|ly
com|pli|ance
com|pli|ancy
com|pli|ant
com|pli|ant|ly
com|pli|cacy
com|pli|cacies
com|pli|cate
com|pli|cates
com|pli|cated
com|pli|cat|ing
com|pli|cated|ly
com|pli|cated|ness

com|pli|ca|tion+s
com|pli|cit
com|pli|city
com|pli|ment+s
+ed +ing (praise;
greetings.
⚠ complement)
com|pli|
men|tar|ily(in a
complimentary
way. ⚠ com-
plementarily)
com|pli|men|tary
com|pli|
      men|tar|ies
(expressing praise;
free. ⚠ com-
plementary)
com|pli|ments slip
+s
com|pline+s
com|ply
com|plies
com|plied
com|ply|ing
compo+s
com|pon|ent+s
com|pon|en|tial
com|port+s +ed
+ing
com|port|ment
com|pos
com|pose
com|poses
com|posed
com|pos|ing
com|posed|ly
com|poser+s
com|pos|ite
com|pos|ites
com|pos|ited
com|pos|it|ing
com|pos|ite|ly
com|pos|ite|ness
com|pos|ition+s
com|pos|ition|al
com|pos|ition|
         al|ly
com|posi|tor+s
com|pos men|tis
com|pos|sible
com|post+s +ed
+ing
com|pos|ure
com|pote+s
com|pound+s +ed
+ing
com|pound|able
com|pound|er+s
com|pra|dor+s
com|pra|dore+s
(use comprador)

com|pre|hend+s
+ed +ing
com|pre|hen|
       si|bil|ity
com|pre|hen|sible
com|pre|hen|sibly
com|pre|hen|sion
+s
com|pre|hen|sive
+s
com|pre|hen|
       sive|ly
com|pre|hen|sive|
         ness
com|press
com|presses
com|pressed
com|press|ing
com|press|ibil|ity
com|pres|sible
com|pres|sion+s
com|pres|sive
com|pres|sor+s
com|pris|able
com|prise
com|prises
com|prised
com|pris|ing
com|prom|ise
com|prom|ises
com|prom|ised
com|prom|is|ing
com|prom|iser+s
com|prom|
      is|ing|ly
compte rendu
comptes rendus
Comp|tom|eter+s
Propr.
Comp|ton, Ar|thur
Holly(American
physicist)
Compton-Burnett,
Ivy(English
novelist)
comp|trol|ler+s
com|pul|sion+s
com|pul|sive
com|pul|sive|ly
com|pul|sive|ness
com|pul|sor|ily
com|pul|sori|ness
com|pul|sory
com|punc|tion+s
com|punc|tious
com|punc|tious|ly
com|pur|ga|tion
+s
com|pur|ga|tor+s
com|pur|ga|tory
com|put|abil|ity
com|put|able
com|put|ably

com|pu|ta|tion+s
com|pu|ta|tion|al
com|pu|ta|tion|
         al|ly
com|pute
com|putes
com|puted
com|put|ing
com|puter+s
computer-aided
computer-
    assist|ed
com|puter|ate
computer-based
computer-
    controlled
computer-
    generated
com|pu|ter|
    isa|tion*Br.* (use
    computerization)
com|pu|ter|ise*Br.*
   (use
    computerize)
com|pu|ter|ises
com|pu|ter|ised
com|pu|ter|is|ing
com|pu|ter|
      iza|tion
com|pu|ter|ize
com|pu|ter|izes
com|pu|ter|ized
com|pu|ter|iz|ing
computer-literate
com|rade+s
comrade-in-arms
   comrades-in-
   arms
com|rade|ly
com|rade|ship
Com|sat+s
Comte, Au|guste
(French
philosopher)
Comt|ism
Comt|ist+s
con
   cons
   conned
   con|ning
   (trick; against; a
   convict; to study)
con *Br.*
   cons
   conned
   con|ning
   (steer ship. *Am.*
   conn)
con|acre
Con|akry (capital
   of Guinea)
con amore

Conan
Conan Doyle,
  Ar¦thur (Scottish
  novelist)
con|ation +s
cona|tive
con brio
con|cat¦en|ate
  con|cat¦en|ates
  con|cat¦en|ated
  con|cat¦en|at¦ing
con|cat¦en|ation
  +s
con|cave
con|cave¦ly
con|cav|ity
  con|cav|ities
con|ceal +s +ed
  +ing
con|ceal¦er +s
con|ceal|ment +s
con|cede
  con|cedes
  con|ceded
  con|ced¦ing
con|ceder +s
con|ceit +s
con|ceit¦ed
con|ceit¦ed¦ly
con|ceit¦ed|ness
con|ceiv|abil¦ity
con|ceiv¦able
con|ceiv¦ably
con|ceive
  con|ceives
  con|ceived
  con|ceiv¦ing
con|cele¦brant +s
con|cele¦brate
  con|cele¦brates
  con|cele¦brated
  con|cele¦brat¦ing
con|cele¦bra¦tion
  +s
con|cen¦ter Am. +s
  +ed +ing (Br.
  concentre)
con|cen|trate
  con|cen|trates
  con|cen|trated
  con|cen|trat¦ing
con|cen|trated¦ly
con|cen|tra¦tion +s
con|cen|tra¦tion
  camp +s
con|cen|tra¦tive
con|cen|tra¦tor +s
con|centre Br.
  con|centres
  con|centred
  con|cen¦tring
  (Am. concenter)

con|cen¦tric
con|cen¦tric|al¦ly
con|cen¦tri¦city
Con|cep¦ción (city,
  Chile)
con|cept +s
con|cep¦tion +s
con|cep¦tion|al
con|cep¦tion|al¦ly
con|cep¦tive
con|cep¦tual
con|cep¦tu¦al¦
  isa¦tion Br. +s
  (use conceptual-
  ization)
con|cep¦tu¦al¦ise
  Br. (use
  conceptualize)
  con|cep¦tu¦al¦ises
  con|cep¦tu¦al¦ised
  con|cep¦tu¦al¦
  is¦ing
con|cep¦tu¦al¦ism
con|cep¦tu¦al¦ist
  +s
con|cep¦tu¦al¦
  iza¦tion +s
con|cep¦tu¦al¦ize
  con|cep¦tu¦al¦izes
  con|cep¦tu¦al¦ized
  con|cep¦tu¦al¦
  iz¦ing
con|cep¦tu|al¦ly
con|cep¦tus
  con|cep¦tuses
con|cern +s +ed
  +ing
con|cern|ed¦ly
con|cern|ed|ness
con|cern|ing
con|cern|ment +s
con|cert +s +ed
  +ing
con|cer¦tante
  con|cer¦tanti
concert-goer +s
concert hall +s
con|cer¦tina
  con|cer¦tinas
  con|cer¦tinaed
  con|cer¦tina|ing
con|cer¦tino +s
con|cert mas¦ter
  +s
con|certo
  con|cer¦tos or
  con|certi
con|certo grosso
  con|certi grossi
con|ces¦sion +s
con|ces¦sion|aire
  +s

con|ces¦sion|ary
con|ces¦sive +s
conch
  conchs or
  conches
  (shell; domed
  roof. △ conk)
con¦cha
  conchae
  (hollow of ear.
  △ conker,
  conquer)
con|chie +s
con¦choid|al
con¦cho|logic¦al
con¦cho|logic|al¦ly
conch|olo¦gist +s
conch|ology
con¦chy (use
  conchie)
con|chies
con|ci¦erge +s
con|cili¦ar
con|cili¦ate
  con|cili¦ates
  con|cili¦ated
  con|cili¦at¦ing
con|cili¦ation +s
con|cilia¦tive
con|cili¦ator +s
con|cili¦atori|ness
con|cili¦atory
con|cin¦nity
con|cin¦nous
con|cise
con|cise¦ly
con|cise|ness
con|ci¦sion +s
con|clave +s
con|clude
  con|cludes
  con|cluded
  con|clud¦ing
con|clu¦sion +s
con|clu¦sive
con|clu¦sive¦ly
con|clu¦sive|ness
con|coct +s +ed
  +ing
con|coct¦er +s
con|coc¦tion +s
con|coct¦or +s
  (use concocter)
con|comi¦tance
con|comi¦tancy
con|comi¦tant +s
con|comi¦tant¦ly
Con|cord (towns,
  USA.
  △ Concorde)
con|cord +s
  (agreement)

con¦cord|ance
con¦cord|ances
con¦cord|anced
con¦cord|an¦cing
con¦cord|ant +s
con¦cord|ant¦ly
con¦cordat +s
Con|corde +s
  (aircraft.
  △ Concord)
con|course +s
con|cres¦cence
con|cres¦cent
con|crete
  con|cretes
  con|creted
  con|cret¦ing
con|crete¦ly
con|crete mixer
  +s
con|crete|ness
con|cre¦tion +s
con|cre¦tion|ary
con|cre¦tisa¦tion
  Br. +s (use
  concretization)
con¦cret¦ise Br.
  (use concretize)
  con¦cret|ises
  con¦cret|ised
  con¦cret|is¦ing
con|cre¦tiza¦tion
  +s
concret|ize
  con¦cret|izes
  con¦cret|ized
  con¦cret|iz¦ing
con|cu¦bin|age
con|cu¦bin|ary
con|cu¦bine +s
con|cu¦pis|cence
con|cu¦pis|cent
con|cur
  con|curs
  con|curred
  con|cur|ring
con|cur¦rence +s
con|cur¦rent
con|cur¦rent¦ly
con|cuss
  con|cusses
  con|cussed
  con|cuss|ing
con|cus|sion +s
con|demn +s +ed
  +ing
con|dem|nable
con|dem|na¦tion
  +s
con|dem|na¦tory
con|dens|able
con¦den|sate +s

con¦den¦sa¦tion +s
con¦den¦sa¦tion
  trail
con¦dense
  con¦denses
  con¦densed
  con¦dens¦ing
con¦dens¦er +s
con¦dens¦ery
  con¦dens¦er¦ies
con¦des¦cend +s
  +ed +ing
con¦des¦cend¦
              ing¦ly
con¦des¦cen¦sion
  +s
con¦dign
con¦dign¦ly
con¦di¦ment +s
con¦di¦tion +s +ed
  +ing
con¦di¦tion¦al +s
con¦di¦tion¦al¦ism
con¦di¦tion¦al¦ly
con¦di¦tion¦er +s
condo +s
con¦do¦la¦tory
con¦dole
  con¦doles
  con¦doled
  con¦dol¦ing
con¦dol¦ence +s
con¦dom +s
con¦do¦min¦ium +s
con¦don¦ation
con¦done
  con¦dones
  con¦doned
  con¦don¦ing
con¦doner +s
con¦dor +s
con¦dot¦tiere
  con¦dot¦tieri
con¦duce
  con¦duces
  con¦duced
  con¦du¦cing
con¦du¦cive
con¦du¦cive¦ness
con¦duct +s +ed
  +ing
con¦duct¦ance +s
con¦ducti¦bil¦ity
con¦duct¦ible
con¦duc¦tion
con¦duct¦ive¦ly
con¦duct¦iv¦ity
  con¦duct¦iv¦ities
con¦duct¦or +s
con¦duct¦or¦ship
  +s

con¦duc¦tress
  con¦duc¦tresses
con¦duc¦tus
  con¦ducti
con¦duit +s
con¦dylar
con¦dyle +s
con¦dyl¦oid
cone
  cones
  coned
  con¦ing
cone-shell +s
coney +s (rabbit;
  use cony)
Coney Is¦land
  (resort, USA)
con¦fab
  con¦fabs
  con¦fabbed
  con¦fab¦bing
con¦fabu¦late
  con¦fabu¦lates
  con¦fabu¦lated
  con¦fabu¦lat¦ing
con¦fabu¦la¦tion +s
con¦fabu¦la¦tory
con¦fect +s +ed
  +ing
con¦fec¦tion +s
con¦fec¦tion¦ary
  (*adjective.*
  △ confectionery)
con¦fec¦tion¦er +s
con¦fec¦tion¦er's
  cus¦tard
con¦fec¦tion¦er's
  sugar
con¦fec¦tion¦ery
  con¦fec¦tion¦er¦ies
  (*noun.*
  △ confectionary)
Con¦fed¦er¦acy,
  the *US History*
con¦fed¦er¦acy
  con¦fed¦er¦acies
Con¦fed¦er¦ate +s
  US History
con¦fed¦er¦ate
  con¦fed¦er¦ates
  con¦fed¦er¦ated
  con¦fed¦er¦at¦ing
con¦fed¦er¦ation
  +s
con¦fer
  con¦fers
  con¦ferred
  con¦fer¦ring
con¦fer¦ee +s
con¦fer¦ence +s
con¦fer¦en¦cing
con¦fer¦en¦tial

con¦fer¦ment +s
con¦fer¦rable
con¦fer¦ral +s
con¦fess
  con¦fesses
  con¦fessed
  con¦fess¦ing
con¦fes¦sant +s
con¦fess¦ed¦ly
con¦fes¦sion +s
con¦fes¦sion¦al +s
con¦fes¦sion¦ary
con¦fes¦sor +s
con¦fetti
con¦fi¦dant +s *male*
  (trusted person.
  △ confident)
con¦fi¦dante +s
  female (trusted
  person.
  △ confident)
con¦fide
  con¦fides
  con¦fided
  con¦fid¦ing
con¦fi¦dence +s
con¦fi¦dent (self-
  assured.
  △ confidant,
  confidante)
con¦fi¦den¦tial
con¦fi¦den¦ti¦al¦ity
  con¦fi¦den¦ti¦al¦
                  ities
con¦fi¦den¦tial¦ly
con¦fi¦dent¦ly
con¦fid¦ing¦ly
con¦fig¦ur¦ation +s
con¦fig¦ur¦ation¦al
con¦fig¦ure
  con¦fig¦ures
  con¦fig¦ured
  con¦fig¦ur¦ing
con¦fine
  con¦fines
  con¦fined
  con¦fin¦ing
con¦fine¦ment +s
con¦firm +s +ed
  +ing
con¦firm¦and +s
con¦firm¦ation +s
  (verification;
  religious rite.
  △ conformation)
con¦firma¦tive
con¦firma¦tory
con¦fis¦cable
con¦fis¦cate
  con¦fis¦cates
  con¦fis¦cated
  con¦fis¦cat¦ing

con¦fis¦ca¦tion +s
con¦fis¦ca¦tor +s
con¦fis¦ca¦tory
con¦flag¦ra¦tion +s
con¦flate
  con¦flates
  con¦flated
  con¦flat¦ing
con¦fla¦tion +s
con¦flict +s +ed
  +ing
con¦flic¦tion
con¦flict¦ual
con¦flu¦ence +s
con¦flu¦ent
con¦flux
  con¦fluxes
con¦form +s +ed
  +ing
con¦form¦abil¦ity
con¦form¦able
con¦form¦ably
con¦form¦al
con¦form¦al¦ly
con¦form¦ance
con¦form¦ation +s
  (shape;
  adjustment.
  △ confirmation)
con¦form¦er +s
con¦form¦ism
con¦form¦ist +s
con¦form¦ity
con¦found +s +ed
  +ing
con¦found¦ed¦ly
con¦fra¦tern¦ity
  con¦fra¦tern¦ities
con¦frère +s
con¦front +s +ed
  +ing
con¦fron¦ta¦tion +s
con¦fron¦ta¦tion¦al
Con¦fu¦cian +s
Con¦fu¦cian¦ism
Con¦fu¦cian¦ist +s
Con¦fu¦cius
  (Chinese
  philosopher)
con¦fus¦abil¦ity
con¦fus¦able +s
con¦fuse
  con¦fuses
  con¦fused
  con¦fus¦ing
con¦fused¦ly
con¦fus¦ing¦ly
con¦fu¦sion +s
con¦fut¦ation +s
con¦fute
  con¦futes

con|fute (*cont.*)
  con|futed
  con|fut|ing
conga +s +ed +ing
  (dance. △conger)
congé +*s*
con|geal +s +ed
  +ing
con|geal|able
con|geal|ment
con|gel|ation +s
con|gener +s
con|gen|eric
con|gen|er|ous
con|gen|ial
con|geni|al|ity
con|geni|al|ly
con|geni|tal
con|geni|tal|ly
con|ger +s (eel.
  △conga)
con|ger|ies
  plural con|ger|ies
con|gest +s +ed
  +ing
con|ges|tion +s
con|gest|ive
con|glom|er|ate
  con|glom|er|ates
  con|glom|er|ated
  con|glom|er|
      at|ing
con|glom|er|ation
  +s
Congo (river and
  country, Africa.
  △Kongo)
Con|go|lese
  plural Con|go|lese
con|gou
con|grats (= con
  gratulations)
con|gratu|lant +s
con|gratu|late
  con|gratu|lates
  con|gratu|lated
  con|gratu|lat|ing
con|gratu|la|tion
  +s
con|gratu|la|tive
con|gratu|la|tor +s
con|gratu|la|tory
con|gre|gant +s
con|gre|gate
  con|gre|gates
  con|gre|gated
  con|gre|gat|ing
con|gre|ga|tion +s
Con|gre|ga|tion|al
  (of Congregational
  ism)

con|gre|ga|tion|al
  (generally)
Con|gre|ga|tion|al|
  ise *Br.* (use
  Congregational-
  ize)
  Con|gre|ga|tion|al|
      ises
  Con|gre|ga|tion|al|
      ised
  Con|gre|ga|tion|al|
      is|ing
Con|gre|ga|tion|al|
  ism
Con|gre|ga|tion|al|
  ist +s
Con|gre|ga|tion|al|
  ize
  Con|gre|ga|tion|al|
      izes
  Con|gre|ga|tion|al|
      ized
  Con|gre|ga|tion|al|
      iz|ing
Con|gress
  (legislative body)
con|gress
  con|gresses
  (meeting)
con|gres|sion|al
con|gress|man
con|gress|men
con|gress|woman
  con|gress|women
Con|greve,
  Wil|liam (English
  dramatist)
con|gru|ence +s
con|gru|ency
  con|gru|en|cies
con|gru|ent
con|gru|ent|ly
con|gru|ity
  con|gru|ities
con|gru|ous
con|gru|ous|ly
conic +s
con|ic|al
con|ic|al|ly
con|ics
co|nid|ium
  co|nidia
con|ifer +s
con|ifer|ous
coni|form
coni|ine
con|jec|tur|able
con|jec|tur|ably
con|jec|tural
con|jec|tur|al|ly
con|jec|ture
  con|jec|tures

con|jec|ture (*cont.*)
  con|jec|tured
  con|jec|tur|ing
con|join +s +ed
  +ing
con|joint
con|joint|ly
con|ju|gal +s
con|ju|gal|ity
con|ju|gal|ly
con|ju|gate
  con|ju|gates
  con|ju|gated
  con|ju|gat|ing
con|ju|gate|ly
con|ju|ga|tion +s
con|ju|ga|tion|al
con|junct +s
con|junc|tion +s
con|junc|tion|al
con|junc|tion|al|ly
con|junc|tiva +s
con|junc|tival
con|junct|ive +s
con|junct|ive|ly
con|junc|tiv|itis
con|junc|ture +s
con|jur|ation +s
con|jure
  con|jures
  con|jured
  con|jur|ing
con|juror +s
conk +s +ed +ing
  (nose; head;
  punch; in 'conk
  out'. △conch)
conk|er +s (fruit of
  horse chestnut.
  △concha,
  conquer)
con|man
  con|men
con moto
conn *Am.*
  conns
  conned
  con|ning
  (*Br.* con. steer
  ship. △con)
Con|nacht
  (province,
  Republic of
  Ireland)
con|nate
con|nat|ural
con|nat|ur|al|ly
Con|naught (use
  Connacht)
con|nect +s +ed
  +ing
con|nect|able

con|nect|ed|ly
con|nect|ed|ness
con|nect|er +s
  (person.
  △connector)
con|nect|ible (use
  connectable)
Con|necti|cut
  (state, USA)
con|nect|ing rod
  +s
con|nec|tion +s
con|nec|tion|al
con|nec|tion|ism
con|nec|tion|ist +s
con|nect|ive +s
con|nect|iv|ity
con|nect|or +s
  (device; thing that
  connects.
  △connecter)
Con|ne|mara
  (region, Republic
  of Ireland)
Con|nery, Sean
  (Scottish actor)
con|nex|ion *Br.* +s
  (use connection)
Con|nie
con|ning tower +s
con|niv|ance
con|nive
  con|nives
  con|nived
  con|niv|ing
con|niver +s
con|nois|seur +s
con|nois|seur|ship
Con|nolly,
  Maur|een ('Little
  Mo', American
  tennis player)
Con|nors, Jimmy
  (American tennis
  player)
con|no|ta|tion +s
con|no|ta|tive
con|note
  con|notes
  con|noted
  con|not|ing
con|nu|bial +s
con|nu|bi|al|ity
con|nu|bi|al|ly
con|oid +s
con|oid|al
con|quer +s +ed
  +ing (defeat,
  overcome.
  △concha,
  conker)
con|quer|able

con|queror +s
con|quest +s
con|quis|ta|dor
  con|quis|ta|dores
  or
  con|quis|ta|dors
Con|rad (name)
Con|rad, Jo|seph
  (Polish-born
  British novelist)
Con|ran, Ter|ence
  (English designer
  and businessman)
con-rod +s
con|san|guin|eous
con|san|guin|ity
con|science +s
con|science|less
conscience-
  stricken
conscience-struck
con|scien|tious
con|scien|tious|ly
con|scien|tious|
        ness
con|scious
con|scious|ly
con|scious|ness
consciousness-
  raising
con|scribe
  con|scribes
  con|scribed
  con|scrib|ing
con|script +s +ed
  +ing
con|scrip|tion
con|se|crate
  con|se|crates
  con|se|crated
  con|se|crat|ing
con|se|cra|tion +s
con|se|cra|tor +s
con|se|cra|tory
con|se|cu|tion +s
con|secu|tive
con|secu|tive|ly
con|secu|tive|ness
con|sen|sual
con|sen|su|al|ly
con|sen|sus
con|sent +s +ed
  +ing
con|sent|an|eous
con|sen|tient
con|se|quence +s
con|se|quent +s
con|se|quen|tial
con|se|quen|tial|
        ism
con|se|quen|tial|
        ist +s

con|se|quen|ti|al|
        ity
con|se|quen|tial|ly
con|se|quent|ly
con|ser|vancy
con|ser|van|cies
con|ser|va|tion +s
con|ser|va|tion|al
con|ser|va|tion|ist
  +s
Con|ser|va|tism
  Politics
con|ser|va|tism
Con|ser|va|tive +s
  Politics
con|ser|va|tive +s
con|ser|va|tive|ly
con|ser|va|tive|
        ness
con|ser|va|toire +s
con|ser|va|tor +s
con|ser|va|tor|ium
  +s
con|ser|va|tory
con|ser|va|tor|ies
con|serve
  con|serves
  con|served
  con|serv|ing
con|sider +s +ed
  +ing
con|sid|er|able
con|sid|er|ably
con|sid|er|ate
con|sid|er|ate|ly
con|sid|er|ation +s
con|sign +s +ed
  +ing
con|sign|ee +s
con|sign|ment +s
con|signor +s
con|sist +s +ed
  +ing
con|sist|ence +s
con|sist|ency
  con|sist|en|cies
con|sist|ent
con|sist|ent|ly
con|sis|tor|ial
con|sis|tory
  con|sis|tor|ies
con|so|ci|ate
  con|so|ci|ates
  con|so|ci|ated
  con|so|ci|at|ing
con|so|ci|ation +s
con|sol|able
con|sola|tion +s
con|sola|tory
con|sole
  con|soles
  con|soled

con|sole (*cont.*)
  con|sol|ing
  (comfort;
  instrument panel;
  dresser)
con|soler +s
con|soli|date
  con|soli|dates
  con|soli|dated
  con|soli|dat|ing
con|soli|da|tion +s
con|soli|da|tor +s
con|soli|da|tory
con|sol|ing|ly
con|sols
con|sommé +s
con|son|ance
con|son|ant +s
con|son|ant|al
con|son|ant|ly
con sor|dino
con|sort +s +ed
  +ing
con|sor|tium
  con|sor|tia *or*
  con|sor|tiums
con|spe|cif|ic
con|spec|tus
  con|spec|tuses
con|spicu|ous
con|spicu|ous|ly
con|spicu|ous|
        ness
con|spir|acy
  con|spir|acies
con|spir|ator +s
con|spira|tor|ial
con|spira|tori|al|ly
con|spire
  con|spires
  con|spired
  con|spir|ing
Con|stable, John
  (English painter)
con|stable +s
con|stabu|lary
  con|stabu|lar|ies
Con|stance (name)
Con|stance, Lake
  (in SE Germany)
con|stancy
  con|stan|cies
Con|stant (name)
con|stant +s
  (unchanging; thing
  that never varies)
Con|stanța (port,
  Romania)
con|stantan
Con|stan|tine
  (Roman emperor)

Con|stan|tine (city,
  Algeria)
Con|stan|tin|ople
  (former name of
  Istanbul)
con|stant|ly
Con|stanza (use
  Constanța)
con|sta|ta|tion +s
con|stel|late
  con|stel|lates
  con|stel|lated
  con|stel|lat|ing
con|stel|la|tion +s
con|ster|nate
  con|ster|nates
  con|ster|nated
  con|ster|nat|ing
con|ster|na|tion
con|sti|pate
  con|sti|pates
  con|sti|pated
  con|sti|pat|ing
con|sti|pa|tion
con|stitu|ency
  con|stitu|en|cies
con|stitu|ent +s
con|sti|tute
  con|sti|tutes
  con|sti|tuted
  con|sti|tut|ing
con|sti|tu|tion +s
con|sti|tu|tion|al
  +s
con|sti|tu|tion|al|
  ise *Br.* (use
  constitutionalize)
con|sti|tu|tion|al|
        ises
con|sti|tu|tion|al|
        ised
con|sti|tu|tion|al|
        is|ing
con|sti|tu|tion|al|
        ism
con|sti|tu|tion|al|
        ist +s
con|sti|tu|tion|
        al|ity
con|sti|tu|tion|al|
        ize
con|sti|tu|tion|al|
        izes
con|sti|tu|tion|al|
        ized
con|sti|tu|tion|al|
        iz|ing
con|sti|tu|tion|
        al|ly
con|sti|tu|tive
con|sti|tu|tive|ly
con|sti|tu|tor +s

con|strain +s +ed +ing
con|strain|ed¦ly
con|straint +s
con|strict +s +ed +ing
con|stric'tion +s
con|strict|ive
con|strict¦or +s
con|stru|able
con|stru|al +s
con|struct +s +ed +ing
con|struc'tion +s
con|struc'tion|al
con|struc'tion| al¦ly
con|struc'tion|ism
con|struc'tion|ist +s
con|struct|ive
con|struct¦ive¦ly
con|struct¦ive| ness
con|struct¦iv|ism
con|struct¦iv|ist +s
con|struct¦or +s
con|strue
  con|strues
  con|strued
  con|stru¦ing
con|sub'stan|tial
con|sub'stan'ti¦al| ity
con|sub'stan|ti|ate
  con|sub'stan'ti| ates
  con|sub'stan'ti| ated
  con|sub'stan'ti| at¦ing
con|sub'stan'ti| ation
con|sue'tude
con|sue'tud|in|ary
con|sul +s
con|su'lar
con|sul'ate +s
con|sul|ship +s
con|sult +s +ed +ing
con|sult|ancy
  con|sult|an|cies
con|sult|ant +s
con|sult|ation +s
con|sulta|tive
con|sult|ee +s
con|sult|ing room +s
con|sum|able +s
con|sume
  con|sumes

con|sume (*cont.*)
  con|sumed
  con|sum¦ing
con|sumer +s
con|sumer dur|able +s
con|sumer|ism
con|sumer|ist +s
con|sum|ing¦ly
con|sum|mate
  con'sum|mates
  con'sum|mated
  con'sum|mat¦ing
con'sum|mate¦ly
con'sum|ma'tion +s
con'sum|ma'tive
con'sum|ma'tor +s
con|sump'tion +s
con|sump'tive +s
con|sump'tive¦ly
con|tact +s +ed +ing
con|tact|able
con|tact lens
  con|tact lenses
con|ta'gion +s
con|ta'gious
con|ta'gious¦ly
con|ta'gious|ness
con|tain +s +ed +ing
con|tain|able
con|tain|er +s
container-grown
con|tain|er|
  isa'tion *Br.* (use
  containerization)
con|tain'er|ise *Br.*
  (use containerize)
  con|tain'er|ises
  con|tain'er|ised
  con|tain'er|is¦ing
con|tain'er|
  iza'tion
con|tain'er|ize
  con|tain'er|izes
  con|tain'er|ized
  con|tain'er|iz¦ing
con|tain|ment
con|tam'in|ant +s
con|tam'in|ate
  con|tam'in|ates
  con|tam'in|ated
  con|tam'in|at¦ing
con|tam'in|ation +s
con|tam'in|ator +s
con|tango +s
Conté (pencil etc.)
conte +s (story)

con|temn +s +ed +ing
con|tem'ner +s
con|tem|plate
  con|tem|plates
  con|tem|plated
  con|tem|plat¦ing
con|tem|pla'tion +s
con|tem|pla'tive +s
con|tem| pla'tive¦ly
con|tem|pla'tor +s
con|tem|por| an¦eity
con|tem|por| an¦eous
con|tem|por| an¦eous¦ly
con|tem|por| an¦eous|ness
con|tem|por|ar¦ily
con|tem|por|ari| ness
con|tem|por|ary
  con| tem'por|ar¦ies
con|tem|por|ise *Br.*
  (use contemporize)
  con|tem'por|ises
  con|tem'por|ised
  con|tem'por| is¦ing
con|tem'por|ize
  con|tem'por|izes
  con|tem'por|ized
  con|tem'por| iz¦ing
con|tempt +s
con|tempt|ibil|ity
con|tempt|ible
con|tempt|ibly
con|temp'tu|ous
con|temp'tu| ous¦ly
con|temp'tu|ous| ness
con|tend +s +ed +ing
con|tend'er +s
con|tent +s +ed +ing
con|tent|ed¦ly
con|tent'ed|ness
con|ten'tion +s
con|ten|tious
con|ten|tious¦ly
con|ten|tious|ness
con'tent|ment
con|ter'min|ous

con|ter'min|ous¦ly
con|tessa +s
con|test +s +ed +ing
con|test|able
con|test|ant +s
con|test|ation
con|test|er +s
con|text +s
context- depend|ent
context-specif'ic
con|text|ual
con|text|ual| isa'tion *Br.* +s
  (use contextual- ization)
con|text¦ual|ise *Br.*
  (use contextualize)
  con|text|ual|ises
  con|text|ual|ised
  con|text|ual| is¦ing
con|text|ual|ism
con|text|ual|ist +s
con|text|ual|ity
con|text|ual| iza'tion +s
con|text|ual|ize
  con|text|ual|izes
  con|text|ual|ized
  con|text|ual| iz¦ing
con|text|ual¦ly
con|tigu'ity
con|tigu|ous
con|tigu|ous¦ly
con|tigu|ous|ness
con|tin|ence
Con'tin|ent (European mainland)
con|tin|ent +s
Con'tin|en'tal +s (European)
con|tin|en'tal
con|tin|en'tal¦ly
con|tin|ent¦ly
con|tin|gency
  con|tin|gen'cies
con|tin|gent +s
con|tin|gent¦ly
con|tinu|able
con|tin|ual
con|tinu|al¦ly
con|tinu|ance +s
con|tinu|ant +s
con|tinu|ation +s
con|tinu|ative
con|tinu|ator +s

con|tinue
con|tinues
con|tinued
con|tinu|ing
con|tinu|er +s
con|tinu|ity
con|tinu|ities
con|tinuo +s
con|tinu|ous
con|tinu|ous|ly
con|tinu|ous|ness
con|tinuum
con|tinua
con|tort +s +ed
+ing
con|tor|tion +s
con|tor|tion|ist +s
con|tour +s +ed
+ing
con|tra +s
(revolutionary)
con¦tra preposition
con|tra|band
con|tra|band|ist
+s
con|tra|bass
con|tra|basses
con|tra|bas|soon
+s
con|tra|cep|tion
con|tra|cep|tive +s
con|tract +s +ed
+ing
con|tract|able (of a
disease, able to be
contracted.
△ contractible)
contracted-out
adjective
con|tract|ible (able
to be shrunk etc.
△ contractable)
con|tract|ile
con|tract|il|ity
con|trac|tion +s
con|tract|ive
con|tract|or +s
con|tract|ual
con|trac|tu|al|ly
con|tra|dict +s
+ed +ing
con|tra|dict|able
con|tra|dic|tion +s
con|tra|dic|tious
con|tra|dict|or +s
con|tra|dic|tor|ily
con|tra|dict|ori|
ness
con|tra|dict|ory
con|tra|
dis|tinc|tion +s

con|tra|dis|tin|
guish
con|tra|dis|tin|
guishes
con|tra|dis|tin|
guished
con|tra|
dis|tin|guish|ing
con|tra|flow +s
con|trail +s
con|tra|indi|cate
con|tra|indi|cates
con|tra|indi|cated
con|tra|indi|
cat|ing
con|tra|indi|
ca|tion +s
con|tralto +s
con|tra|pos|ition
+s
con|tra|posi|tive
+s
con|trap|tion +s
con|tra|pun|tal
con|tra|pun|tal|ly
con|tra|pun|tist +s
con|trar|iety
con|trar|ieties
con|trar|ily
con|trari|ness
con|trari|wise
con|trary
con|trar|ies
con|trast +s +ed
+ing
con|trast|ing|ly
con|trast|ive +s
con|trasty
contra-
suggest|ible
con|trate
con|tra|vene
con|tra|venes
con|tra|vened
con|tra|ven|ing
con|tra|vener +s
con|tra|ven|tion
+s
con|tre|temps
plural
con|tre|temps
con|trib|ute
con|trib|utes
con|trib|uted
con|trib|ut|ing
con|tri|bu|tion +s
con|tribu|tive
con|tribu|tor +s
con|tribu|tory
con-trick +s
con|trite
con|trite|ly

con|tri|tion
con|triv|able
con|triv|ance +s
con|trive
con|trives
con|trived
con|triv|ing
con|triver +s
con|trol
con|trols
con|trolled
con|trol|ling
con|trol|labil|ity
con|trol|lable
con|trol|lably
con|trol|ler +s
con|trol|ler|ship
+s
con|tro|ver|sial
con|tro|ver|sial|
ism
con|tro|ver|sial|ist
+s
con|tro|ver|sial|ly
con|tro|versy
con|tro|ver|sies
con|tro|vert +s
+ed +ing
con|tro|vert|ible
con|tu|ma|cious
con|tu|ma|cious|ly
con|tu|macy
con|tu|me|li|ous
con|tu|me|li|ous|ly
con|tumely
con|tuse
con|tuses
con|tused
con|tus|ing
con|tu|sion +s
con|un|drum +s
con|ur|ba|tion +s
con|ure +s
con|va|lesce
con|va|lesces
con|va|lesced
con|va|les|cing
con|va|les|cence
+s
con|va|les|cent +s
con|vec|tion +s
con|vec|tion|al
con|vect|ive
con|vect|or +s
con|ven|able
con¦ven¦ance +s
con|vene
con|venes
con|vened
con|ven|ing
con|vener +s
con|veni|ence +s

con|veni|ent
con|veni|ent|ly
con|venor +s (use
convener)
con|vent +s
con|ven|ticle +s
con|ven|tion +s
con|ven|tion|al
con|ven|tion|al|ise
Br. (use
conventionalize)
con|ven|tion|al|
ises
con|ven|tion|al|
ised
con|ven|tion|al|
is|ing
con|ven|tion|al|
ism
con|ven|tion|al|ist
+s
con|ven|tion|al|ity
con|ven|tion|
al|ities
con|ven|tion|al|ize
con|ven|tion|al|
izes
con|ven|tion|al|
ized
con|ven|tion|al|
iz|ing
con|ven|tion|al|ly
con|ven|tion|eer
+s
con|ven|tual +s
con|verge
con|verges
con|verged
con|ver|ging
con|ver|gence +s
con|ver|gency
con|ver|gent
con|ver|sance
con|ver|sancy
con|ver|sant
con|ver|sa|tion +s
con|ver|sa|tion|al
con|ver|sa|tion|al|
ist +s
con|ver|sa|tion|
al|ly
con|ver|sa|tion|ist
+s
conversation-
stopper +s
con¦ver¦saz¦ione
con¦ver¦saz¦ioni or
con¦ver¦saz¦iones
con|verse
con|verses
con|versed
con|vers|ing

con|verse|ly
con|ver|ser +s
con|ver|sion +s
con|vert +s +ed +ing
con|vert|er +s
con|vert|ibil|ity
con|vert|ible +s
con|vert|ibly
con|ver|tor +s (use converter)
con|vex
con|vex|ity
  con|vex|ities
con|vex|ly
con|vey +s +ed +ing
con|vey|able
con|vey|ance +s
con|vey|an|cer +s
con|vey|an|cing
con|vey|er +s (use conveyor)
con|vey|or +s
con|vey|or belt +s
con|vict +s +ed +ing
con|vic|tion +s
con|vict|ive
con|vince
  con|vinces
  con|vinced
  con|vin|cing
con|vince|ment
con|vin|cer +s
con|vin|cible
con|vin|cibly
con|vin|cing|ly
con|viv|ial
con|vivi|al|ity
con|vivi|al|ly
con|vo|ca|tion +s
con|vo|ca|tion|al
con|voke
  con|vokes
  con|voked
  con|vok|ing
con|vo|luted
con|vo|luted|ly
con|vo|lu|tion +s
con|vo|lu|tion|al
con|volve
  con|volves
  con|volved
  con|volv|ing
con|vol|vu|lus
  con|vol|vu|luses
  or con|vol|vuli
con|voy +s +ed +ing
con|vul|sant +s

con|vulse
  con|vulses
  con|vulsed
  con|vuls|ing
con|vul|sion +s
con|vul|sion|ary
con|vul|sive
con|vul|sive|ly
cony
  conies
coo +s +ed +ing (sound of dove. △ coup)
co-occur
  co-occurs
  co-occurred
  co-occurring
co-occurrence +s
Cooder, Ry (American musician and composer)
cooee
  coo|ees
  coo|eed
  cooee|ing
coo|ing|ly
Cook, James (English explorer)
Cook, Thomas (English tourist agent)
Cook, Mount (in New Zealand)
cook +s +ed +ing
cook|abil|ity
cook|able
cook|book +s
cook-chill
Cooke, Wil|liam Fother|gill (English inventor)
cook|er +s
cook|ery
  cook|er|ies
cook|ery book +s
cook|house +s
cookie +s
cook|ing pot +s
Cook Is|lands (in SW Pacific)
cook|out +s
cook|shop +s
Cook|son, Cath|er|ine (English novelist)
Cook Strait (off New Zealand)
cook|ware
cool +s +ed +ing
coola|bah +s
cool|ant +s

cool bag +s
cool box
  cool boxes
cool|er +s
Cool|gar|die safe +s
cool-headed
cool-headed|ness
coo|li|bah +s (use coolabah)
Cool|idge, Cal|vin (American president)
coolie +s (labourer. △ coolly)
cooling-off noun and attributive
cool|ish
cool|ly (coldly. △ coolie)
cool|ness
coolth
cooly (use coolie)
coomb +s (valley. △ cwm, khoum)
coon +s (offensive when used of a person)
coon-can
coon|skin +s
coop +s +ed +ing (cage. △ coupe)
co-op +s (cooperative enterprise)
Coop|er, Gary (American actor. △ Cowper)
Coop|er, James Feni|more (American novelist. △ Cowper)
coop|er +s +ed +ing
coop|er|age
co|oper|ant
co|oper|ate
  co|oper|ates
  co|oper|ated
  co|oper|at|ing
co|oper|ation
co|opera|tive +s
co|opera|tive|ly
co|opera|tive|ness
co|oper|ator +s
co-opt +s +ed +ing
co-optation +s
co-option +s
co-optive
co|ord|in|ate
  co|ord|in|ates

co|ord|in|ate (cont.)
  co|ord|in|ated
  co|ord|in|at|ing
co|ord|in|ate|ly
co|ord|in|ation +s
co|ord|ina|tive
co|ord|in|ator +s
coot +s
cootie +s
co-own +s +ed +ing
co-owner +s
co-ownership
cop
  cops
  copped
  cop|ping
  (police officer; catch; receive; spindle of thread; also in phrases. △ Kop, kop)
Copa|ca|bana Beach (resort, Brazil)
copa|cet|ic
co|paiba
copal
Copán (ancient Mayan city)
co-partner +s
co-partner|ship
cope
  copes
  coped
  cop|ing
co|peck +s
Cop|en|hagen (capital of Denmark)
co|pe|pod +s
coper +s
Co|per|ni|can +s
Co|per|ni|cus, Nico|laus (Polish astronomer)
cope|stone +s
copi|able
copier +s
co-pilot +s
cop|ing +s
cop|ing saw +s
cop|ing stone +s
co|pi|ous
co|pi|ous|ly
co|pi|ous|ness
co|pita +s
co|pla|nar
co|pla|nar|ity

Cop|land, Aaron
(American
composer)
Cop|ley, John
Single|ton
(American
painter)
co|poly¦mer +s
co|poly¦mer|
isa¦tion *Br.* (use
copolymeriza-
tion)
co|poly¦mer|ise *Br.*
(use
copolymerize)
co|poly¦mer|ises
co|poly¦mer|ised
co|poly¦mer|is¦ing
co|poly¦mer|
iza¦tion
co|poly¦mer|ize
co|poly¦mer|izes
co|poly¦mer|ized
co|poly¦mer|
iz¦ing
cop-out +s *noun*
cop¦per +s
Cop¦per Age
cop¦peras
Cop¦per|belt
(province,
Zambia)
cop¦per belt (area
of central Africa)
copper-bit +s
copper-bottomed
cop¦per|head +s
cop¦per|plate +s
cop¦per|smith +s
cop¦pery
cop¦pice
cop|pices
cop|piced
cop|picing
Cop|pola, Fran|cis
Ford (American
film director and
writer)
copra
co-precipi¦ta¦tion
co-present +s +ed
+ing
co-present¦er +s
co|pro¦ces¦sor +s
co-produce
co-produces
co-produced
co-producing
co-producer +s
co-produc¦tion +s
cop¦ro|lite
cop¦rol¦ogy

cop|ropha|gous
copro|philia
copro|phil¦iac +s
cop|rosma +s
copse
copses
copsed
cops|ing
copse|wood
cop shop +s
copsy
Copt +s
Cop¦tic +s
cop¦ula +s *noun*
copu|lar *adjective*
copu|late
copu|lates
copu|lated
copu|lat¦ing
copu|la¦tion +s
copu¦la|tive +s
copu|la|tive¦ly
copu|la¦tory
copy
cop|ies
cop¦ied
copy|ing
(imitate; imitation;
single specimen;
matter for
printing; etc.
△ kopi, koppie)
copy|book +s
copy|cat +s
copy|desk +s
copy-edit +s +ed
+ing
copy ed¦itor +s
copy|hold +s
copy|hold¦er +s
copy|ist +s
copy|read
copy|reads
copy|read
copy|read|ing
copy|read¦er +s
copy|right +s +ed
+ing (legal right.
△ copywriting)
copy-typist +s
copy|writer +s
copy|writ¦ing
(writing.
△ copyrighting)
coq au vin
co¦quet¦ry
co¦quet|ries
co|quette
co|quettes
co¦quet|ted
co¦quet|ting
co¦quet|tish

co¦quet|tish¦ly
co¦quet|tish|ness
co|quina
co|quito +s
cor (*interjection.*
△ caw, core,
corps)
Cora
cor|acle +s
cor¦ac|oid +s
Coral (name)
coral +s (in sea)
Cora|lie
cor¦al|line +s
cor¦al|lite +s
cor¦al|loid +s
coral-root +s
(plant)
Coral Sea (part of
SW Pacific)
coral snake +s
coram pop¦ulo
cor an|glais
cors an|glais
cor¦bel
cor|bels
cor|belled *Br.*
cor|beled *Am.*
cor¦bel|ling *Br.*
cor¦bel|ing *Am.*
corbel-table +s
cor¦bie +s
corbie-step +s
Corby (town,
England)
Cor¦co|vado
(mountain, Brazil)
Cor|cyra (former
name of Corfu)
cord +s +ed +ing
(twine etc.; vocal
membrane.
△ chord)
cord|age
cord|ate (heart-
shaped.
△ caudate,
chordate)
Cor¦day,
Char|lotte
(French
revolutionary)
Cor|delia (name)
Cor¦del|ier +s
(Franciscan
monk)
cor|dial +s (polite;
drink)
cor|di¦ale (in
'entente cordiale')
cor|di|al¦ity
cor¦di|al¦ly

cor|dil¦lera +s
cord|ite
cord|less
cord|like
Cor|doba (cities,
Argentina and
Spain)
cor|doba +s
(Nicaraguan
currency)
cor¦don +s +ed
+ing
cor¦don bleu
cor|dons bleus
cor¦don sani|taire
cor|dons
sani|taires
Cor|dova
(= Cordoba)
cor|do¦van +s
cor|du¦roy +s
cord|wain¦er +s
cord|wood +s
CORE (= Congress
of Racial Equality)
core
cores
cored
cor¦ing
(centre. △ caw,
cor, corps)
co-referen¦tial
co|rela¦tion +s (use
correlation)
co-religion¦ist +s
cor|ella +s
Cor|elli,
Arc|angelo
(Italian composer)
Cor|elli, Marie
(English writer)
core|op¦sis
core|op¦ses
corer +s
co-respond¦ent +s
(in divorce.
△ correspondent)
corf
corves
Corfu (Greek
island)
corgi +s
cori|aceous
cori|an¦der
Corin (man's name)
Cor|inna
Cor|inne (woman's
name)
Cor|inth (city,
Greece)
Cor|inth, Gulf of
(off Greece)

Cor¦inth¦ian +s
Corio¦lanus
  (Roman general)
Cori¦olis ef¦fect
cor¦ium
Cork (city and
  county, Republic
  of Ireland)
cork +s +ed +ing
  (bark; stopper.
  △ calk, caulk)
cork¦age
cork¦er +s
  (excellent person
  or thing.△ calker,
  caulker)
cork¦like
cork oak +s
cork¦screw +s +ed
  +ing
cork-tipped
cork¦wood +s
corky
  cork¦ier
  corki¦est
corm +s
Cor¦mac
cor¦mor¦ant +s
corn +s
corn¦brash
corn¦bread
corn chand¦ler +s
corn cob +s
corn-cob pipe +s
corn¦cockle +s
corn¦crake +s
corn dolly
  corn dol¦lies
cor¦nea +s
cor¦neal
corned beef
Cor¦neille, Pierre
  (French dramatist)
cor¦nel +s
Cor¦ne¦lia
cor¦ne¦lian +s
Cor¦ne¦lius
corn¦eous (horny)
cor¦ner +s +ed
  +ing
cor¦ner¦back +s
cor¦ner shop +s
cor¦ner¦stone +s
cor¦ner¦ways
cor¦ner¦wise
cor¦net +s (brass
  instrument; wafer;
  cavalry officer.
  △ cornett)
cor¦net¦cy
  cor¦net¦cies

cor¦net¦ist +s (use
  cornettist)
cor¦nett +s
  (cornetto)
cor¦net¦tist +s
cor¦netto
  cor¦netti
  (wind instrument)
corn-factor +s
corn-fed
corn¦field +s
corn¦flake +s
corn¦flour (maize
  flour)
corn¦flower +s
  (plant)
cor¦nice
  cor¦nices
  cor¦niced
  cor¦nicing
cor¦niche +s
corn¦ily
corni¦ness
Corn¦ish
Cor¦nish¦man
  Cor¦nish¦men
Cor¦nish¦woman
  Cor¦nish¦women
corn on the cob
corn¦rows
corn salad
corn¦starch
corn¦stone
cor¦nu¦co¦pia +s
cor¦nu¦co¦pian
Corn¦wall (county,
  England)
corny
  corn¦ier
  corni¦est
cor¦olla +s
cor¦ol¦lary
  cor¦ol¦lar¦ies
Coro¦man¦del
  Coast (in India)
cor¦ona +s (cigar)
cor¦ona
  co¦ro¦nae
  (halo)
Cor¦ona Bor¦ealis
coro¦nach +s
cor¦ona¦graph +s
cor¦onal +s
cor¦on¦ary
  cor¦on¦ar¦ies
cor¦on¦ation +s
cor¦on¦er +s
cor¦on¦er¦ship +s
cor¦onet +s
cor¦on¦et¦ed

Corot, Jean-
  Baptiste
  Cam¦ille (French
  painter)
cor¦ozo +s
corozo-nut +s
Corp. (= Corporal)
cor¦pora
cor¦poral +s
cor¦por¦al¦ity
  cor¦por¦al¦ities
cor¦por¦al¦ly
cor¦por¦ate +s
cor¦por¦ate¦ly
cor¦por¦at¦ic
cor¦por¦ation +s
cor¦por¦at¦ism
cor¦por¦at¦ist
cor¦pora¦tive
cor¦pora¦tiv¦ism
cor¦pora¦tiv¦ist
cor¦por¦eal
cor¦por¦eal¦ity
cor¦por¦eal¦ly
cor¦por¦eity
cor¦po¦sant +s
corps
  plural **corps**
  (body of troops
  etc. △ caw, cor,
  core)
corps de bal¦let
  plural **corps de**
  bal¦let
corps d'élite
  plural **corps d'élite**
corps
  dip¦lo¦ma¦tique +s
corpse +s (dead
  body)
corpse-candle +s
cor¦pu¦lence
cor¦pu¦lency
cor¦pu¦lent
cor¦pus
  cor¦pora *or*
  cor¦puses
  (collection of
  texts; anatomical
  structure)
cor¦pus cal¦lo¦sum
  cor¦pora cal¦losa
Cor¦pus Christi
  (Christian festival;
  city, USA)
cor¦puscle +s
cor¦pus¦cu¦lar
cor¦pus de¦licti
cor¦pus lu¦teum
  cor¦pora lutea
cor¦ral
  cor¦rals

cor¦ral (*cont.*)
  cor¦ralled
  cor¦ral¦ling
  (animal pen.
  △ chorale)
cor¦ra¦sion
cor¦rect +s +ed
  +ing
cor¦rec¦tion +s
cor¦rec¦tion¦al
cor¦rec¦ti¦tude
cor¦rect¦ive +s
cor¦rect¦ive¦ly
cor¦rect¦ly
cor¦rect¦ness
cor¦rect¦or +s
Cor¦reg¦gio,
  An¦tonio Al¦legri
  da (Italian
  painter)
cor¦rel¦ate
  cor¦rel¦ates
  cor¦rel¦ated
  cor¦rel¦at¦ing
cor¦rel¦ation +s
cor¦rel¦ation¦al
cor¦rela¦tive +s
cor¦rela¦tive¦ly
cor¦rela¦tiv¦ity
cor¦res¦pond +s
  +ed +ing
cor¦res¦pond¦ence
  +s
cor¦res¦pond¦ent
  +s (letter-writer.
  △ co-respondent)
cor¦res¦pond¦
  ent¦ly
cor¦res¦pond¦
  ing¦ly
cor¦rida +s
cor¦ri¦dor +s
cor¦rie +s
cor¦ri¦gen¦dum
  cor¦ri¦genda
cor¦ri¦gible
cor¦ri¦gibly
cor¦rob¦or¦ate
  cor¦rob¦or¦ates
  cor¦rob¦or¦ated
  cor¦rob¦or¦at¦ing
cor¦rob¦or¦ation +s
cor¦rob¦ora¦tive
cor¦rob¦or¦ator +s
cor¦rob¦ora¦tory
cor¦rob¦oree +s
cor¦rode
  cor¦rodes
  cor¦roded
  cor¦rod¦ing
cor¦rod¦ible
cor¦ro¦sion

cor¦ro|sive +s
cor¦ro|sive¦ly
cor¦ro¦sive|ness
cor¦ru|gate
  cor¦ru|gates
  cor¦ru|gated
  cor¦ru|gat¦ing
cor¦ru|ga¦tion +s
cor¦ru|ga¦tor +s
cor|rupt +s +ed
  +ing
cor¦rupt|er +s
cor¦rupt|ibil¦ity
cor¦rupt|ible
cor¦rup|tion +s
cor¦rup|tive
cor¦rupt¦ly
cor¦rupt|ness
cor¦sac +s
cor¦sage +s
cor¦sair +s
cor¦sak +s (use
  corsac)
corse +s (*archaic*
  corpse. ⚠ coarse,
  course)
corse|let +s (use
  corselette,
  corslet)
corse|lette +s
  (woman's
  foundation
  garment.
  ⚠ corslet)
cor¦set +s +ed
  +ing
cor¦set|ière +s
cor¦set¦ry
Cor|sica (island,
  Mediterranean)
Cor|sican +s
cors|let +s (close-
  fitting garment;
  armour.
  ⚠ corselette)
Cort, Henry
  (English
  ironmaster)
cor|tège +s
Cor¦tes (Spanish
  legislative
  assembly)
Cor¦tés,
  Her|nando
  (Spanish
  conqueror of
  Mexico)
cor¦tex
  cor|ti¦ces
Cor¦tez,
  Her|nando (use
  Cortés)

Corti (organ of)
cor|tical
cor¦ti|cate
cor¦ti|cated
cor¦ti¦co|ster¦oid
  +s
cor¦ti¦co|troph¦ic
cor¦ti¦co|troph¦in
cor¦ti¦co|trop¦ic
cor¦ti¦co|trop¦in
cor¦ti|sol
cor¦ti|sone +s
cor¦un|dum +s
Cor¦unna (port,
  Spain)
cor¦us|cate
  cor¦us|cates
  cor¦us|cated
  cor¦us|cat¦ing
cor¦us|ca¦tion +s
cor¦vée
corves
cor¦vette +s
cor¦vid +s
cor|vine
cory|ban¦tic
cor¦ymb +s
cor¦ymb|ose
cory|phaeus
cory|phaei
cory|phée +s
cor¦yza
Cos (Greek island,
  Aegean Sea)
cos
  plural cos
  (lettuce)
cos (= cosine;
  because)
'cos (= because;
  use cos)
Cosa Nos¦tra
  (criminal
  organization)
cosec (= cosecant)
co|se¦cant +s
co|seis¦mal +s
coset +s
cosh
  coshes
  coshed
  cosh|ing
cosh|er +s
co-signatory
  co-signator¦ies
cosi¦ly
Cos¦ima
Cos¦imo de'
  Med¦ici
  (Florentine
  statesman and
  banker)

co¦sine +s
cosi|ness
cos¦met¦ic +s
cos¦met¦ic|al¦ly
cos¦met|ician +s
cos¦met|ology
cos¦mic
cos¦mic¦al
cos¦mic¦al¦ly
Cosmo
cosmo|gon¦ic
cosmo|gon¦ic¦al
cos¦mog|on¦ist +s
cos¦mog|ony
cos¦mog|raph¦er
  +s
cosmo|graph¦ic
cosmo|graph¦ic¦al
cos¦mog|raphy
cosmo|logic¦al
cos¦molo¦gist +s
cos¦mol¦ogy
cosmo|naut +s
cosmop|olis
cosmo|pol¦itan +s
cosmo|pol¦it¦an|
  ise *Br.* (use
  cosmopolitanize)
cosmo|pol¦it¦an|
  ises
cosmo|pol¦it¦an|
  ised
cosmo|pol¦it¦an|
  is¦ing
cosmo|pol¦it¦an|
  ism
cosmo|pol¦it¦an|
  ize
cosmo|pol¦it¦an|
  izes
cosmo|pol¦it¦an|
  ized
cosmo|pol¦it¦an|
  iz¦ing
cos|mopo|lite +s
cos¦mos (universe;
  system of ideas;
  experience.)
cos¦mos
  plural cos¦mos
  (plant)
COSPAR
  (= Committee on
  Space Research)
co-sponsor +s +ed
  +ing
Cos¦sack +s
cos¦set +s +ed
  +ing
cos¦sie +s

Cos¦syra (Roman
  name for
  Pantelleria)
cost
  costs
  cost
  cost|ing
  (have as a price)
cost +s +ed +ing
  (estimate price of)
Costa, Lúcio
  (Brazilian
  architect)
Costa Blanca
  (region, Spain)
Costa Brava
  (region, Spain)
cost ac¦count|ing
Costa del Sol
  (region, Spain)
Costa-Gavras,
  Con¦stan|tin
  (Greek film
  director)
cos¦tal
co-star
  co-stars
  co-starred
  co-starring
cos¦tard +s
Costa Rica
Costa Rican +s
cos¦tate
cost-benefit +s
cost-conscious
cost-cutting
cost-effective
cost-effect¦ive¦ly
cost-
  effect¦ive¦ness
cost-efficient
coster +s
cos¦ter|mon¦ger +s
cost|ing +s
cos¦tive
cos¦tive¦ly
cos¦tive|ness
cost¦li|ness
cost¦ly
  cost¦lier
  cost¦li¦est
cost|mary
Cost|ner, Kevin
  (American actor)
cost of liv¦ing
cost-plus
cos¦tume
  cos¦tumes
  cos¦tumed
  cos¦tum¦ing
cos¦tu¦mier +s

cosy *Br.*
cosies
cosied
cosy|ing
cosi¦er
cosi|est
(*Am.* cozy)
cot
cots
cot¦ted
cot|ting
co|tan|gent +s
cot-case +s
cot death +s
cote +s (shelter.
△ coat)
Côte d'Azur
(region, France)
co|terie +s
co|ter¦min|ous
co|ter¦min|ous¦ly
coth (= hyperbolic
cotangent)
co-tidal
co|til|lion +s
co|tinga +s
Cot¦man, John
Sell (English
artist)
co¦to|neas¦ter +s
Coto|nou (city,
Benin)
Coto|paxi
(volcano,
Ecuador)
co-trustee +s
Cots|wold Hills (in
England)
Cots|wolds
(= Cotswold
Hills)
cotta +s (surplice.
△ cottar, cotter)
cot|tage +s
cot|tager +s
cot|tagey
cot|ta¦ging
cot¦tar +s (farm
labourer. △ cotta,
cotter)
Cott|bus (city,
Germany)
cot¦ter +s (bolt;
pin. △ cotta,
cottar)
cot|tier +s
cot¦ton +s +ed
+ing
cot¦ton cake
cot¦ton candy
cot¦ton gin +s
cot¦ton grass

cotton-picking
cot¦ton|tail +s
cot¦ton waste
cot¦ton|wood +s
cot¦ton wool
cot|tony
coty|le¦don +s
coty|le¦don|ary
coty|le¦don|ous
cou¦cal +s
couch
couches
couched
couch|ing
couch|ant
couch|ette +s
couch grass
couch po¦tato
couch po¦ta|toes
coudé +s
Coué, Emile
(French
psychologist)
Coué|ism
cou¦gar +s
cough +s +ed +ing
cough¦er +s
(person who
coughs. △ coffer)
could
couldn't (= could
not)
cou¦lée +s
cou¦lis
plural cou¦lis
cou|lisse +s
coul|oir +s
Cou||lomb, Charles-
Augustin de
(French physicist
and engineer)
cou||lomb +s (unit)
cou¦lo|met¦ric
cou|lom|etry
coul|ter *Br.* +s (*Am.*
colter)
cou|ma¦rin
cou|ma¦rone
coun|cil +s
(assembly.
△ counsel)
coun|cil cham|ber
+s
coun|cil house +s
coun¦cil||lor *Br.* +s
(member of
council.
△ counsellor)
coun¦cil¦lor|ship
+s
coun¦cil|man
coun¦cil|men

coun|cil of war
coun|cils of war
coun|cil¦or *Am.* +s
(member of
council.
△ counselor)
coun|cil|woman
coun|cil|women
coun|sel
coun|sels
coun|selled *Br.*
coun|seled *Am.*
coun|sel|ling *Br.*
coun|sel|ing *Am.*
(advice; barrister;
advise. △ council)
coun|sel|lor *Br.* +s
(adviser; in 'Privy
Counsellor'.
△ councillor)
Coun|sel|lor of
State
Coun|sel|lors of
State
coun|sel|or *Am.* +s
(adviser.
△ councilor)
count +s +ed +ing
count|able
count|back
count|down +s
noun
coun|ten|ance
coun|ten|ances
coun|ten|anced
coun|ten|an¦cing
coun|ter +s +ed
+ing
coun¦ter|act +s
+ed +ing
coun¦ter|action +s
coun¦ter|active
counter-attack +s
+ed +ing
counter-
attrac¦tion +s
coun¦ter|bal¦ance
coun¦ter|
bal¦ances
coun¦ter|
bal¦anced
coun¦ter|
bal¦an¦cing
coun¦ter|blast +s
coun¦ter|change
coun¦ter|changes
coun¦ter|changed
coun¦ter|
chan¦ging
coun¦ter|charge
coun¦ter|charges
coun¦ter|charged

coun¦ter|charge
(*cont.*)
coun¦ter|
char¦ging
coun¦ter|check +s
+ed +ing
counter-claim +s
+ed +ing
counter-clockwise
counter-cultural
counter-culture +s
counter-
demonstra¦tion
+s
counter-
demonstra¦tor
+s
counter-
espion¦age
counter-example
+s
coun¦ter|feit +s
+ed +ing
coun¦ter|feit¦er +s
coun¦ter|foil +s
counter-
inflation¦ary
counter-
insurgency
attributive
counter-
intelli¦gence
counter-intuitive
coun¦ter|ir¦ri|tant
+s
coun¦ter|ir¦ri|
ta¦tion
coun¦ter|mand +s
+ed +ing
coun¦ter|march
coun¦ter|marches
coun¦ter|marched
coun¦ter|march|
ing
coun¦ter|meas¦ure
+s
coun¦ter|mine
coun¦ter|mines
coun¦ter|mined
coun¦ter|min¦ing
coun¦ter|move
coun¦ter|moves
coun¦ter|moved
coun¦ter|mov¦ing
counter|move|
ment +s
counter-offensive
+s
coun¦ter|pane +s
coun¦ter|part +s
coun¦ter|plot
coun¦ter|plots

coun|ter|plot
(*cont.*)
coun|ter|plot|ted
coun|ter|plot|ting
coun|ter|point +s
+ed +ing
coun|ter|poise
coun|ter|poises
coun|ter|poised
coun|ter|pois|ing
counter-
product|ive
counter-proposal
+s
coun|ter|punch
coun|ter|punches
coun|ter|punched
coun|ter|punch|
ing
coun|ter|punch|er
+s
Counter-
Reform|ation
History
counter-
reform|ation +s
counter-
revolu|tion +s
counter-
revolu|tion|ary
counter-
revolu|tion|ar|ies
coun|ter|scarp +s
coun|ter|shaft +s
coun|ter|sign +s
+ed +ing
counter-signature
+s
coun|ter|sink
coun|ter|sinks
coun|ter|sunk
coun|ter|sink|ing
coun|ter|stroke +s
counter-tenor +s
counter-
transfer|ence
coun|ter|vail
coun|ter|vails
coun|ter|vailed
coun|ter|vail|ing
coun|ter|value +s
coun|ter|weight +s
count|ess
count|esses
count|ing house
+s
count|less
Count Pala|tine
Counts Pala|tine
coun|tri|fied
coun|try
coun|tries

coun|try and
west|ern
coun|try club +s
coun|try|fied (use
countrified)
coun|try house +s
coun|try|man
coun|try|men
coun|try music
coun|try|side
country-wide
coun|try|woman
coun|try|women
count|ship +s
county
coun|ties
County Pala|tine
Coun|ties
Pala|tine
county-wide
coup +s (notable
move. △ coo)
coup de foudre
coups de foudre
coup de grâce
coups de grâce
coup de main
coups de main
coup d'état
coups d'état
coup d'œil
coups d'œil
coupe +s (dish.
△ coop)
coupe *Am.* +s (car.
△ coop)
coupé *Br.* +s (car)
Coupe|rin,
Fran|çois (French
composer)
couple
couples
coupled
coup|ling
coup|ler +s
coup|let +s
coup|ling +s
cou|pon +s
cour|age
cour|age|ous
cour|age|ous|ly
cour|age|ous|ness
cour|ante +s
Cour|bet,
Gus|tave (French
painter)
cour|gette +s
cour|ier +s
cour|lan +s
Cour|règes, André
(French couturier)

course
courses
coursed
cours|ing
(direction etc.;
flow; hunt.
△ coarse, corse)
course|book +s
cour|ser +s (person
or animal that
hunts; fast-running
horse or bird.
△ coarser)
course|work
court +s +ed +ing
(court of law;
enclosed space;
tennis court etc.
△ caught)
Cour|tauld,
Sam|uel (English
industrialist)
court bouil|lon
court card +s
cour|te|ous
cour|te|ous|ly
cour|te|ous|ness
cour|tesan +s
cour|tesy
cour|tesies
court|house +s
court|ier +s
court|li|ness
court|ly
court|lier
court|li|est
court mar|tial
courts mar|tial
noun
court-martial
court-martials
court-martialled
Br.
court-martialed
Am.
court-martial|ling
Br.
court-martial|ing
Am.
verb
Court|ney
Court of St
James's (British
royal court)
Cour|trai (French
name for Kortrijk)
court|room +s
court|ship +s
court|yard +s
cous|cous
(semolina dish.

cous|cous (*cont.*)
△ cuscus, khus-
khus)
cousin +s (relation.
△ cozen)
cousin ger|man
cousins ger|man
cous|in|hood
cous|in|ly
cous|in|ship
Cous|teau,
Jacques-Yves
(French
oceanographer)
couth
cou|ture
cou|tur|ier +s *male*
cou|turi|ère +s
female
cou|vade
cou|vert +s
cou|ver|ture +s
co|va|lence
co|va|lency
co|va|lent +s
co|va|lent|ly
cove
coves
coved
cov|ing
coven +s
cov|en|ant +s +ed
+ing
cov|en|ant|al
Cov|en|ant|er +s
Scottish history
cov|en|ant|er +s
(person who
covenants; use
covenantor)
cov|en|ant|or +s
(person who
covenants)
Cov|ent Gar|den
(district, London)
Cov|en|try (city,
England)
cover +s +ed +ing
cov|er|able
cov|er|age +s
cov|er|all +s
Cov|er|dale, Miles
(translator of the
Bible into English)
cover drive +s
cov|er|er +s
cov|er|ing +s
cov|er|let +s
cover point +s
cov|ert +s
cov|ert|ly
cov|ert|ness

cov¦er¦ture +s
cover-up +s *noun*
covet
  covets
  cov¦eted
  cov¦et¦ing
cov¦et¦able
cov¦et¦ous
cov¦et¦ous¦ly
cov¦et¦ous¦ness
covey +s
covin +s
cov¦ing +s
cow +s +ed +ing
cowa¦bunga
cow¦age
Cow¦ard, Noël
  (English writer,
  actor, and
  composer)
cow¦ard +s
cow¦ard¦ice
cow¦ard¦li¦ness
cow¦ard¦ly
cow¦ardy
cow¦bane
cow¦bell +s
cow¦berry
  cow¦berries
cow¦bird +s
cow¦boy +s
cow¦catch¦er +s
cower +s +ed +ing
Cowes (town,
  England)
cow¦fish
  plural cow¦fish
cow¦girl +s
cow¦hage (use
  cowage)
cow¦hand +s
cow-heel +s
cow¦herd +s
cow¦hide +s
cow-house +s
cowl +s
cowled
cow-lick +s
cowl¦ing
cowl¦man
  cowl¦men
co-worker +s
cow-parsley
cow-pat +s
cow¦pea +s
Cow¦per, Wil¦liam
  (English poet.
  △ Cooper)
cow¦poke +s
cow¦pox
cow¦punch¦er +s

cow¦rie +s (shell.
  △ kauri)
co-write
  co-writes
  co-wrote
  co-writing
  co-written
co-writer +s
cow¦shed +s
cow¦slip +s
cow-tree +s
cow-wheat +s
Cox
  Coxes
  (apple)
cox
  coxes
  coxed
  cox¦ing
  (coxswain)
coxa
  coxae
coxal
cox¦comb +s
  (dandy.
  △ cockscomb)
cox¦comb¦ry
  cox¦comb¦ries
cox¦less
Cox's Bazar (port,
  Bangladesh)
Cox's or¦ange
  pip¦pin +s
cox¦swain +s
cox¦swain¦ship
coy +er +est
coyly
coy¦ness
coy¦ote +s
coypu +s
coz (*archaic* cousin)
cozen +s +ed +ing
  (cheat. △ cousin)
coz¦en¦age
Cozu¦mel (island,
  Caribbean)
cozy *Am.*
  cozies
  cozied
  cozy¦ing
  cozi¦er
  cozi¦est
  (*Br.* cosy)
coz¦zie +s
Crab, the
  (constellation;
  sign of zodiac)
crab
  crabs
  crabbed
  crab¦bing
crab apple +s

Crabbe, George
  (English poet)
crab¦bed¦ly
crab¦bed¦ness
crab¦bily
crab¦bi¦ness
crabby
crab¦bier
crab¦bi¦est
crab¦grass
  crab¦grasses
crab¦like
crab¦meat
Crab Neb¦ula
crab pot +s
crab¦wise
crack +s +ed +ing
crack-brained
crack¦down +s
crack¦er +s
cracker-barrel
  adjective
crack¦er¦jack +s
crack¦ers
cracki¦ness
crack¦ing
crack-jaw
crackle
  crackles
  crackled
  crack¦ling
crack¦ly
crack¦nel +s
crack¦pot +s
cracks¦man
  cracks¦men
crack-up +s *noun*
crack-willow
cracky
Cra¦cow (city,
  Poland)
cra¦dle
  cra¦dles
  cra¦dled
  crad¦ling
cradle-snatcher
  +s
cradle-song +s
craft +s +ed +ing
  (skill; trade;
  vessel; to make.
  △ kraft)
craft-brother
  craft-brothers *or*
  craft-brethren
craft guild +s
craft¦ily
crafti¦ness
crafts¦man
  crafts¦men
crafts¦man¦ship

crafts¦person
crafts¦people
crafts¦woman
  crafts¦women
craft¦work
craft¦work¦er +s
crafty
  craft¦ier
  crafti¦est
crag +s
crag¦gily
crag¦gi¦ness
craggy
  crag¦gier
  crag¦gi¦est
crags¦man
  crags¦men
crags¦woman
  crags¦women
Craig
Cra¦iova (city,
  Romania)
crake +s
cram
  crams
  crammed
  cram¦ming
crambo
cram-full
cram¦mer +s
cramp +s +ed +ing
cramp-iron +s
cram¦pon +s
cran +s
Cra¦nach, Lucas
  (German painter)
cran¦age
cran¦berry
  cran¦berries
Crane, Ste¦phen
  (American writer)
crane
  cranes
  craned
  cran¦ing
crane-fly
  crane-flies
cranes¦bill +s
  (plant)
crane's-bill +s (use
  cranesbill)
cra¦nial
cra¦ni¦ate +s
cra¦nio¦logic¦al
cra¦nio¦olo¦gist +s
cra¦ni¦ology
cra¦nio¦met¦ric
cra¦ni¦om¦etry
cra¦ni¦ot¦omy
  cra¦ni¦oto¦mies

cra|nium
cra¦ni|ums *or*
cra¦nia
crank +s +ed +ing
crank|case +s
crank|ily
cranki|ness
crank|pin +s
crank|shaft +s
cranky
crank|ier
cranki|est
Cran|mer,
Thomas (English
archbishop)
cran|nied
cran|nog +s
cranny
cran¦nies
crap
craps
crapped
crap|ping
(*coarse slang*)
crape +s (black
crêpe fabric.
△ crêpe)
crape fern +s
crape hair
crappy
crap|pier
crap¦pi|est
(*coarse slang*)
craps (gambling
game)
crapu|lence
crapu|lent
crapu|lous
crapy (like crape.
△ crêpey)
craque|lure
crash
crashes
crashed
crash|ing
crash bar|rier +s
crash-dive
crash-dives
crash-dived
crash-diving
crash-halt +s
crash hel|met +s
crash-land +s +ed
+ing *verb*
crash land|ing +s
noun
crash pad +s
crash-stop +s
crash-tackle +s
cra¦sis
cra¦ses
crass +er +est

cras|si|tude
crass|ly
crass|ness
Cras|sus, Mar¦cus
Li¦cin|ius (Roman
politician)
cratch
cratches
crate
crates
crated
crat|ing
crate|ful +s
crater +s +ed +ing
cra¦ter|ous
cra¦ton +s
cra¦vat +s
cra¦vat|ted
crave
craves
craved
crav¦ing
cra¦ven
cra¦ven¦ly
cra¦ven|ness
craver +s
crav¦ing +s
craw +s (*Zoology.*
△ crore)
craw|fish
plural craw|fish
Craw|ford, Joan
(American
actress)
Craw|ford, Os¦bert
(British
archaeologist)
crawl +s +ed +ing
crawl¦er +s
crawl|ing¦ly
crawl space +s
crawly
cray +s
cray|fish
plural cray|fish
crayon +s +ed
+ing
craze
crazes
crazed
craz|ing
crazi¦ly
cra¦zi|ness
crazy
cra|zier
crazi|est
Crazy Horse
(Sioux chief)
crazy pav¦ing
creak +s +ed +ing
(noise. △ creek)
creak|ily

creaki|ness
creak|ing¦ly
creaky
creak|ier
creaki|est
cream +s +ed +ing
cream-colored *Am.*
cream-coloured
Br.
cream¦er +s
cream|ery
cream|er¦ies
cream|ily
creami|ness
cream-laid
cream|ware
creamy
cream|ier
creami|est
crease
creases
creased
creas|ing
(fold; line. △ kris)
cre|at¦able
cre|ate
cre¦ates
cre¦ated
cre|at¦ing
cre|at|ine
cre|ation +s
cre|ation|ism
cre|ation|ist +s
cre|ative
cre|ative|ly
cre|ative|ness
cre|ativ|ity
cre|ator +s
cre|atrix
cre|at¦ri|ces
crea|ture +s
crea|ture¦ly
crèche +s
Crécy (battle,
France)
cred
cre¦dal
cre|dence +s
cre¦den|tial +s
cre|denza +s
cred|ibil|ity
cred|ible
cred|ibly
credit +s +ed +ing
cred|it|abil|ity
cred|it|able
cred|it|ably
cred|it|or +s
credit|worthi|ness
credit|worthy
Credo +s (Apostles'
or Nicene Creed)

credo +s
cre¦du|lity
credu|lous
credu|lous¦ly
credu|lous|ness
Cree
plural Cree *or*
Crees
creed +s
creed¦al (use
credal)
Creek
plural Creek
(American Indian)
creek +s (river.
△ creak)
creel +s
creep
creeps
crept
creep|ing
creep¦er +s
creep|ily
creepi|ness
creep|ing Jenny
creep|ing
Jen¦nies
creepy
creep|ier
creepi|est
creepy-crawly
creepy-crawlies
creese +s (dagger;
use kris)
cre|mate
cre|mates
cre|mated
cre|mat¦ing
cre|ma|tion +s
cre|ma|tor +s
crema|tor¦ium
crema|toria *or*
crema|tor¦iums
crema|tory
crema|tor¦ies
crème brû¦lée
crèmes brû|lées
crème cara|mel
crèmes cara|mels
crème de cas¦sis
crème de la crème
crème de menthe
crème fraiche
Cre|mona (city,
Italy)
cren|ate
cren|ated
cren|ation +s
crena|ture
crenel +s
cren¦el|late
cren¦el|lates

cren|el|late (*cont.*)
　cren|el|lated
　cren|el|lat|ing
cren|el|lation +s
cren|elle +s
Cre|ole +s
cre|ol|isa|tion *Br.*
　(use creolization)
cre|ol|ise *Br.* (use
　creolize)
　cre|ol|ises
　cre|ol|ised
　cre|ol|is|ing
cre|ol|iza|tion
cre|ol|ize
　cre|ol|izes
　cre|ol|ized
　cre|ol|iz|ing
creo|sote
　creo|sotes
　creo|soted
　creo|sot|ing
crêpe +s (fabric;
　pancake; rubber;
　paper. △ crape)
crêpe de Chine
crêpe Su|zette
　crêpes Su|zette
crêpey (like crêpe.
　△ crapy)
crepi|tant
crepi|tate
　crepi|tates
　crepi|tated
　crepi|tat|ing
crepi|ta|tion +s
crepi|tus
crept
cre|pus|cu|lar
crêpy (use crêpey.
　like crêpe.
　△ crapy)
cres|cendo +s
Cres|cent, the
　(Islamic world)
cres|cent +s
　(shape)
cres|cent|ic
cre|sol +s
cress
　cresses
cres|set +s
Cres|sida
　(legendary Greek
　woman)
Cres|sida
crest +s +ed +ing
Cresta Run (in
　Switzerland)
crest|fall|en
crest|less
cre|syl

Cret|aceous
　(period)
cret|aceous
　(chalky)
Cre|tan +s
Crete (Greek
　island)
cre|tic +s
cre|tin +s
cret|in|ise *Br.* (use
　cretinize)
　cret|in|ises
　cret|in|ised
　cret|in|is|ing
cret|in|ism
cret|in|ize
　cret|in|izes
　cret|in|ized
　cret|in|iz|ing
cret|in|ous
cre|tonne +s
Creutzfeldt–Jakob
　dis|ease
cre|vasse +s
crev|ice +s
crew +s +ed +ing
　(ship's company
　etc.; past tense of
　crow. △ *cru*)
crew-cut +s
Crewe (town,
　England)
crewel +s (yarn.
　△ cruel)
crewel work
crew|man
　crew|men
crew neck +s
crib
　cribs
　cribbed
　crib|bing
crib|bage
crib|bage board
　+s
crib|ber +s
crib-biting
crib death +s
cribo +s
crib|ri|form
crib|work
Crichton, James
　('the Admirable',
　Scottish
　adventurer)
Crick, Fran|cis
　(British
　biophysicist)
crick +s +ed +ing
cricket +s +ed
　+ing
cricket bag +s

Cricket bat +s
crick|et|er +s
cri|coid +s
cri de cœur
　cris de cœur
cried
crier +s
cri|key
crim +s
crime
　crimes
　crimed
　crim|ing
Cri|mea (peninsula,
　Ukraine)
Cri|mean +s
crime fight|er +s
crime-fighting
crime pas|sion|nel
　crimes
　pas|sion|nels
crime sheet +s
crime wave +s
crime writer +s
crim|inal +s
crim|in|al|isa|tion
　Br. (use
　criminalization)
crim|in|al|ise *Br.*
　(use criminalize)
　crim|in|al|ises
　crim|in|al|ised
　crim|in|al|is|ing
crim|in|al|is|tic
crim|in|al|is|tics
crim|in|al|ity
crim|in|al|iza|tion
crim|in|al|ize
　crim|in|al|izes
　crim|in|al|ized
　crim|in|al|iz|ing
crim|in|al|ly
crim|in|ate
　crim|in|ates
　crim|in|ated
　crim|in|at|ing
crim|in|ation +s
crim|ina|tive
crim|in|atory
crim|ino|logic|al
crim|in|olo|gist +s
crim|in|ology
crimp +s +ed +ing
crimp|er +s
crimp|ily
crimpi|ness
crimp|lene *Propr.*
crimpy
crim|son +s +ed
　+ing
cringe
　cringes

cringe (*cont.*)
　cringed
　crin|ging
crin|ger +s
crin|gle +s
crin|kle
　crin|kles
　crin|kled
　crink|ling
crinkle-cut
crin|kly
crink|lier
crink|li|est
crin|oid +s
crin|oid|al
crin|ol|ine +s
cri|ollo +s
cripes
Crip|pen, Doc|tor
　(American-born
　British murderer)
crip|ple
　crip|ples
　crip|pled
　crip|pling
cripple|dom
cripple|hood
crip|pler +s
crip|pling|ly
cris
　crises
　(use kris. dagger.
　△ crease)
cri|sis
　cri|ses
cri|sis
　man|age|ment
crisp +s +ed +ing
　+er +est
crisp|ate
crisp|bread +s
crisp|er +s
Cris|pian
Cris|pin
crispi|ness
crisp|ly
crisp|ness
crispy
　crisp|ier
　crispi|est
criss-cross
　criss-crosses
　criss-crossed
　criss-crossing
crista
　cris|tae
cris|tate
cris|to|bal|ite
crit +s
cri|ter|ial
cri|ter|ion
　cri|teria

crit|ic +s
crit|ic|al
crit|ic|al|ity
  crit|ic|al|ities
crit|ic|al|ly
crit|ic|al|ness
criti|cas|ter +s
criti|cis|able *Br.*
  (use criticizable)
criti|cise *Br.* (use
  criticize)
  criti|cises
  criti|cised
  criti|cis|ing
criti|ciser *Br.* +s
  (use criticizer)
criti|cism +s
criti|ciz|able
criti|cize
  criti|cizes
  criti|cized
  criti|ciz|ing
criti|cizer +s
cri|tique
  cri|tiques
  cri|tiqued
  cri|tiquing
crit|ter +s
croak +s +ed +ing
croak|er +s
croak|ily
croaki|ness
croaky
  croak|ier
  croaki|est
Croat +s
Cro|atia
Cro|atian +s
croc +s (crocodile.
  △ crock)
Croce, Bene|detto
  (Italian
  philosopher)
cro|ce|ate
cro|chet +s +ed
  +ing
cro|chet|er +s
croci (plural of
  crocus)
cro|cido|lite
crock +s +ed +ing
  (pot; worn-out
  person or thing;
  collapse. △ croc)
crock|ery
crocket +s
  Architecture
Crock|ett, Davy
  (American
  frontiersman)
Crock|ford (clerical
  directory)

croco|dile +s
croco|dil|ian +s
cro|cus
  cro|cuses *or* croci
Croe|sus (Lydian
  king)
croft +s +ed +ing
croft|er +s
Crohn's dis|ease
  (△ crone)
crois|sant +s
Cro-Magnon
Crom|arty
  (shipping area off
  Scotland; in 'Ross
  and Cromarty')
Crom|arty Firth
  (inlet, Scotland)
crom|bec +s
Crome, John
  (English artist)
crom|lech +s
Cromp|ton,
  Rich|mal (English
  writer)
Cromp|ton,
  Sam|uel (English
  inventor)
Crom|well, Oli|ver
  (English general
  and statesman)
Crom|well,
  Thomas (English
  statesman)
crone +s (old
  woman.
  △ Crohn's
  disease)
Cro|nen|berg,
  David (Canadian
  film director)
Cro|nin, A. J.
  (Scottish writer)
cronk
Cro|nus *Greek
  Mythology*
crony
  cro|nies
cro|ny|ism
crook +s +ed +ing
  (hooked staff; to
  bend; criminal;
  unwell; etc.)
crook|back +s
crook-backed
crooked +er +est
  (slanting;
  deformed;
  dishonest)
crook|ed|ly
crook|ed|ness
crook|ery

Crookes, Wil|liam
  (English physicist
  and chemist)
croon +s +ed +ing
  (hum or sing.
  △ kroon)
croon|er +s
crop
  crops
  cropped
  crop|ping
crop dust|ing
crop-eared
crop-full
crop-over
crop|per +s
cro|quet +s +ed
  +ing (game)
cro|quette +s (roll
  or ball of food
  etc.)
crore +s (ten
  million. △ craw)
Crosby, Bing
  (American singer
  and actor)
cro|sier +s
cross
  crosses
  crossed
  cross|ing
  cross|er
  cross|est
  (two intersecting
  lines; traverse;
  angry; etc.
  △ crosse)
cross|bar +s
cross-beam +s
cross-bedding
cross-bench
  cross-benches
cross-bencher +s
cross|bill +s
cross|bones
cross-border
  adjective
cross|bow +s
cross|bow|man
  cross|bow|men
cross-breed
  cross-breeds
  cross-bred
  cross-breeding
cross-Channel
cross-check +s
  +ed +ing
cross-country
  cross-countries
cross-cultural
cross-current +s
cross-curricu|lar

cross-cut
  cross-cuts
  cross-cut
  cross-cutting
cross-dating
cross-dress
  cross-dresses
  cross-dressed
  cross-dressing
cross-dresser +s
crosse +s (lacrosse
  stick. △ cross)
cross-
  examin|ation +s
cross-examine
  cross-examines
  cross-examined
  cross-examin|ing
cross-examiner +s
cross-eyed
cross-fade
  cross-fades
  cross-faded
  cross-fading
cross-
  fertil|isa|tion *Br.*
  (use cross-
  fertilization)
cross-fertilise *Br.*
  (use cross-
  fertilize)
  cross-fertilises
  cross-fertilised
  cross-fertilising
cross-
  fertil|iza|tion
cross-fertilize
  cross-fertilizes
  cross-fertilized
  cross-fertilizing
cross|field
cross|fire
cross-grain +s
cross-grained
cross-hair +s
cross-hatch
  cross-hatches
  cross-hatched
  cross-hatching
cross-head +s
cross-heading +s
cross-holding +s
cross|ing +s
cross|ing point +s
cross-keys
cross-legged
cross-link +s +ed
  +ing
cross-linkage +s
cross|ly
cross|match
  cross|matches

cross|match (*cont.*)
  cross|matched
  cross|match|ing
cross|ness
cross|over +s *noun*
cross|patch
  cross|patches
cross|piece +s
cross-ply
cross-pollin|ate
  cross-pollin|ates
  cross-pollin|ated
  cross-pollin|at|ing
cross-pollin|ation
cross purposes
cross-question +s
  +ed +ing
cross-refer
  cross-refers
  cross-referred
  cross-referring
cross-reference
  cross-references
  cross-referenced
  cross-referen|cing
cross-rhythm +s
cross|road +s
cross-ruff +s +ed
  +ing
cross-section +s
  +ed +ing
cross-section|al
cross-spar +s
cross-species
  adjective
cross stitch *noun*
cross-stitch
  cross-stitches
  cross-stitched
  cross-stitch|ing
  verb
cross-subsidise *Br.*
  (use cross-
  subsidize)
  cross-subsidises
  cross-subsidised
  cross-subsidis|ing
cross-subsidize
  cross-subsidizes
  cross-subsidized
  cross-subsidiz|ing
cross-subsidy
  cross-subsidies
cross-tabula|tion
  +s
cross|talk
cross|trees
cross-voting
cross|walk +s

cross|ways
cross|wind +s
cross-wire
  cross-wires
  cross-wired
  cross-wiring
cross|wise
cross|word +s
cros|tini
crotch
  crotches
crot|chet +s
crot|cheti|ness
crot|chety
cro|ton +s
crouch
  crouches
  crouched
  crouch|ing
croup
croup|ier +s
croupy
crou|ton +s
crow
  crows
  crowed *or* crew
  crow|ing
crow|bar +s
crow|berry
  crow|berries
crow-bill +s
crowd +s +ed +ing
crowd|ed|ness
crowd-pleaser +s
crowd-pleasing
crowd-puller +s
crowd-pulling
crow|foot +s
  (plant. △ crow's-
  foot)
Crown (the)
  (the monarch)
crown +s +ed +ing
  (for head; top;
  etc.)
Crown prince +s
Crown prin|cess
  Crown prin|cesses
crown roast +s
crow's-foot
  crow's-feet
  (wrinkle.
  △ crowfoot)
crow's-nest +s
crow step +s
crow-stepped
crow-toe +s
Cro|zet Is|lands (in
  Indian Ocean)
croz|ier +s (use
  crosier)

cru +*s* (vineyard;
  wine. △ crew)
cru|ces (plural of
  crux)
cru|cial
cru|ci|al|ity
cru|cial|ly
cru|cian +s
cru|ci|ate
cru|cible +s
cru|ci|fer +s
cru|cif|er|ous
cru|ci|fier +s
cru|ci|fix
  cru|ci|fixes
cru|ci|fix|ion +s
cru|ci|form
cru|cify
  cru|ci|fies
  cru|ci|fied
  cru|ci|fy|ing
cruck +s
crud
cruddy
  crud|dier
  crud|di|est
crude
  cruder
  cru|dest
crude|ly
crude|ness
cru|di|tés
cru|dity
  cru|dities
  (crude remarks or
  actions)
cruel
  cruel|ler
  cruel|lest
  (causing pain.
  △ crewel)
cruel|ly
cruel|ness
cruelty
  cruel|ties
cruelty-free
cruet +s
cruet-stand +s
Crufts (dog show)
Cruik|shank,
  George (English
  artist)
cruise
  cruises
  cruised
  cruis|ing
  (sea journey;
  travel at moderate
  speed. △ cruse)
cruise con|trol
cruise mis|sile +s

cruiser +s
cruis|er|weight +s
cruise|way +s
crul|ler +s
crumb +s +ed +ing
crum|ble
  crum|bles
  crum|bled
  crum|bling
crum|bli|ness
crum|bly
  crum|blier
  crum|bli|est
crumby
  crumb|ier
  crumbi|est
  (like crumbs.
  △ crummy)
crum|horn +s
crum|mily
crum|mi|ness
crummy
  crum|mier
  crum|mi|est
  (inferior.
  △ crumby)
crump +s +ed
  +ing
crum|pet +s
crum|ple
  crum|ples
  crum|pled
  crum|pling
crum|ply
  crum|plier
  crum|pli|est
crunch
  crunches
  crunched
  crunch|ing
crunch|er +s
crunch|ily
crunchi|ness
crunchy
  crunch|ier
  crunchi|est
crup|per +s
crural
cru|sade
  cru|sades
  cru|saded
  cru|sad|ing
cru|sader +s
cruse +s (jar.
  △ cruise)
crush
  crushes
  crushed
  crush|ing
crush|able
crush bar|rier +s

crush¦er +s
crush¦ing¦ly
crust +s +ed +ing
Crust|acea
crust|acean +s
crust¦ace|ology
crust|aceous
crust¦al
crust¦ily
crusti|ness
crust|ose
crusty
  crust|ies
  crust|ier
  crusti|est
crutch
  crutches
Crutched Friars
crux
  cruxes or cru¦ces
Crux (Aus|tralis)
  (constellation)
Cruyff, Johan
  (Dutch footballer)
cru|zado +s
cru|zeiro +s
cry
  cries
  cried
  cry¦ing
  (shout; weep.
  △ krai)
cry-baby
  cry-babies
cryer +s (use crier)
cryo|bio|logic|al
cryo|biolo¦gist +s
cryo|biol¦ogy
cryo|gen +s
cryo|gen¦ic
cryo|gen¦ics
cryo|lite
cryo|on¦ic
cryo|on¦ics
cryo|pro¦tect|ant
  +s
cryo|pump +s
cryo|stat +s
cryo|sur¦gery
crypt +s
crypt|analy¦sis
crypt|ana¦lyst +s
crypt|ana¦lyt¦ic
crypt|ana¦lyt¦ic¦al
cryp¦tic +s
cryp¦tic|al¦ly
crypto +s
crypto|crys¦tal|
      line
crypto-fascist +s
crypto|gam +s
crypto|gam¦ic

crypt|og¦am|ous
crypto|gram +s
crypt|og¦raph|er
  +s
crypto|graph¦ic
crypto|graph¦ic|
     al¦ly
crypt|og¦raphy
crypt|olo¦gist +s
crypt|ology
crypto|meria +s
crypto|
     spor¦idi¦osis
crypto|
     spor¦id¦ium
crypto|spor¦idia
crypto|zoic
crypto|zo¦ology
Crys|tal also
  Chrys|tal
  (name)
crys|tal +s
  (mineral)
crys|tal ball +s
crys|tal clear
crystal-clear
  attributive
crystal-gazing
crys|tal|line
crys|tal|lin¦ity
crys|tal|lis|able Br.
  (use
  crystallizable)
crys|tal|lisa¦tion
  Br. (use
  crystallization)
crys|tal|lise Br.
  (use crystallize)
  crys|tal|lises
  crys|tal|lised
  crys|tal|lis¦ing
crys|tal|lite +s
crys|tal|liz|able
crys|tal|liza¦tion
crys|tal|lize
  crys|tal|lizes
  crys|tal|lized
  crys|tal|liz¦ing
crys|tal|
     log¦raph¦er +s
crys|tal|lo|
      graph¦ic
crys|tal|log¦raphy
crys|tal|loid +s
Crys|tal Pal¦ace
  (in London)
csar|das
  plural csar|das
cten|oid
cteno|phore +s
Ctesi|phon
  (ancient city, Iraq)

cub
  cubs
  cubbed
  cub|bing
Cuba
Cuban +s
Cu¦bango
  (= Okavango)
cubby
  cub¦bies
cub¦by|hole +s
cube
  cubes
  cubed
  cu¦bing
cubeb +s
cuber +s
cube root +s
cub|hood
cubic
cu¦bic¦al (cube-
  shaped)
cu¦bic|al¦ly
cu¦bicle +s (small
  room)
cu¦bi|form
cu¦bism
cu¦bist +s
cubit +s
cu¦bit¦al
cu¦boid +s
cu¦boid¦al
Cub Scout +s
cucking-stool +s
cuck|old +s +ed
  +ing
cuck|old¦ry
cuckoo +s
cuckoo clock +s
cuckoo flower +s
cuckoo pint +s
cuckoo spit
cu¦cum|ber +s
cu¦cur|bit +s
cu¦cur|bit|aceous
cud
  cuds
  cud¦ded
  cud¦ding
cud|bear
cud¦dle
  cud¦dles
  cud¦dled
  cud¦dling
cuddle|some
cud¦dly
  cud¦dlier
  cud¦dli|est
cuddy
  cud¦dies
cudgel
  cudgels

cudgel (cont.)
  cudg¦elled Br.
  cudg¦eled Am.
  cudgel|ling Br.
  cudgel|ing Am.
Cud|lipp, Hugh
  (British journalist)
cud|weed +s
cue
  cues
  cued
  cue¦ing or cuing
  (signal; hint; in
  billiards etc.
  △ queue)
cue ball +s
cue-bid +s
cue¦ist +s
Cuenca (city,
  Ecuador)
Cuer¦na|vaca
  (town, Mexico)
cuesta +s
cuff +s +ed +ing
cuff link +s
Cufic (use Kufic)
Cui¦abá (city and
  port, Brazil)
cui bono?
Cuil|lin Hills
  (mountain range,
  Skye)
Cuil|lins (= Cuillin
  Hills)
cuir|ass
  cuir|asses
cuir¦ass|ier +s
cuish
  cuishes
cuis|ine +s
cuisse +s
Cukor, George
  (American film
  director)
Cul¦bert|son, Ely
  (American bridge
  player)
cul|chie +s
Cul|dee +s
cul-de-sac
  culs-de-sac or cul-
  de-sacs
Culi|acán Ros|ales
  (city, Mexico)
cu¦lin|ar¦ily
cu¦lin|ary
cull +s +ed +ing
cull¦er +s
cul¦let
Cul|loden
  (battlefield,
  Scotland)

culm +s
cul¦mif¦er¦ous
cul¦min¦ant
cul¦min¦ate
  cul¦min¦ates
  cul¦min¦ated
  cul¦min¦at¦ing
cul¦min¦ation +s
cu¦lotte *attributive*
cu¦lottes
culpa
culp|abil¦ity
culp|able
culp|ably
Cul|peper,
  Nich|olas
  (English herbalist)
cul|prit +s
cul|shie +s
cult +s
cult¦ic
cult|ism
cult|ist +s
cul¦tiv|able
cul¦ti|var +s
cul¦ti|vat¦able
cul¦ti|vate
  cul¦ti|vates
  cul¦ti|vated
  cul¦ti|vat¦ing
cul¦ti|va¦tion +s
cul¦ti|va¦tor +s
cul|tural
cul¦tur|al|ism
cul¦tur|al|ist +s
cul¦tur|al¦ly
cul|ture
  cul|tures
  cul|tured
  cul¦tur|ing
culture-bound
cul¦tus
  plural cul¦tus
cul|verin +s
cul|vert +s
cum (combined
  with. △ come)
cum¦ber +s +ed
  +ing
Cum¦ber|land
  (former county,
  England; sauce,
  sausage)
Cum¦ber|land,
  Duke of (English
  prince)
Cum¦ber|nauld
  (town, Scotland)
cum¦ber|some
cum¦ber|some¦ly
cum¦ber|some|
        ness

Cum¦bia +s
Cum|bria (county,
  England)
Cum|brian +s
cum|brous
cum|brous¦ly
cum|brous|ness
cum grano salis
cumin
cum¦mer|bund +s
cum¦min (use
  cumin)
cum|mings, e. e.
  (American writer)
cum|quat +s (use
  kumquat)
cu¦mu|late
  cu¦mu|lates
  cu¦mu|lated
  cu¦mu|lat¦ing
cu¦mu|la¦tion +s
cu¦mu|la¦tive
cu¦mu|la¦tive¦ly
cu¦mu|la¦tive|ness
cu¦mu|lo|nim¦bus
  plural
  cu¦mu¦lo|
  nim¦buses *or*
  cu¦mu¦lo|nimbi
cu¦mu|lous
  adjective
cu¦mu|lus
  cu¦muli
  noun
Cu¦nard, Sam¦uel
  (British-Canadian
  shipowner)
cu|ne|ate
cu|nei|form
Cu¦nene (river,
  Angola)
cun|je|voi +s
cun¦ni|lin¦gus
cun|ning
Cun¦ning|ham,
  Merce (American
  dancer and
  choreographer)
cun|ning¦ly
cun|ning|ness
Cu¦no|be¦li¦nus
  (Latin name for
  Cymbeline)
cunt +s (*coarse
  slang*)
cup
  cups
  cupped
  cup|ping
Cupar (town,
  Scotland)
cup|bear¦er +s

cup|board +s
cup|cake +s
cupel
  cu¦pels
  cu¦pelled *Br.*
  cu¦peled *Am.*
  cu¦pel|ling *Br.*
  cu¦pel|ing *Am.*
cu¦pel|la¦tion
Cup Final +s
cup¦ful +s
Cupid *Roman
  Mythology*
cu¦pid|ity
Cupid's bow +s
cu¦pola +s
cu¦po|laed
cupola-furnace +s
cuppa +s
cup¦per +s (use
  cuppa)
cu¦pram|mo¦nium
cu|preous
cu¦pric
cu¦prif¦er¦ous
cu|prite
cupro-nickel
cu|prous
cup-tie +s
cu¦pule +s
cur +s
cur|abil¦ity
cur¦able
Cura|çao (island,
  Netherlands
  Antilles)
cura|çao +s (drink.
  △ curassow)
cura|çoa +s (use
  curaçao)
cur|acy
  cur|acies
cur|are +s
cur|ar|ine
cur|ar|ise *Br.* (use
  curarize)
  cur|ar|ises
  cur|ar|ised
  cur|ar|is|ing
cur|ar|ize
  cur|ar|izes
  cur|ar|ized
  cur|ar|iz|ing
cur|as|sow +s
  (bird. △ curaçao)
cur|ate
  cur|ates
  cur|ated
  cur|at|ing
curate-in-charge
  curates-in-charge
cur|ate's egg

cur|ation
cura|tive
cur|ator +s
cura|tor¦ial
cur|ator|ship +s
curb +s +ed +ing
  (restrain. △ kerb)
curb roof +s
cur|cuma +s
curd +s
cur¦dle
  cur¦dles
  cur¦dled
  curd|ling
curd|ler +s
curdy
cure
  cures
  cured
  cur¦ing
  (remedy;
  preserve)
curé +s (priest)
cure-all +s
curer
cur¦et|tage
cur|ette
  cur|ettes
  cur|et¦ted
  cur|et¦ting
cur¦few +s
Curia (papal court)
Cur¦ial
Curie, Marie and
  Pierre (physicists)
curie +s (unit)
curio +s
curi|osa
curi|os|ity
  curi|os¦ities
curi|ous +er
curi|ous¦ly
curi|ous|ness
Curi¦tiba (city,
  Brazil)
cur¦ium
curl +s +ed +ing
curl¦er +s
cur¦lew
  plural cur¦lew *or*
  cur¦lews
cur¦li|cue +s
curli|ness
curl|ing iron +s
curl|ing pins
curl|ing tongs
curly
  curl|ier
  curli|est
cur|mudg¦eon +s
cur|mudg¦eon¦ly

cur|rach +s
(coracle)
Cur|ragh, the
(plain, Republic of
Ireland)
cur|ragh +s (use
currach)
cur|ra|jong +s (use
kurrajong)
cur|rant +s (dried
fruit. △ current)
cur|ra|wong +s
cur|rency
cur|ren|cies
cur|rent +s
(present; tide;
electricity.
△ currant)
cur|rent ac|count
+s
cur|rent|ly
cur|rent|ness
cur|ricle +s
cur|ricu|lar
adjective
cur|ricu|lum
cur|ric|ula or
cur|ricu|lums
noun
cur|ricu|lum vitae
cur|ric|ula vitae
cur|rier +s
cur|rish
cur|rish|ly
cur|rish|ness
curry
cur|ries
cur|ried
curry|ing
curry-comb +s
+ed +ing
curry pow|der +s
curse
curses
cursed
or curst archaic
curs|ing
curs|ed|ly
curs|ed|ness
curser +s (person
who curses.
△ cursor)
cur|sillo +s
cur|sive
cur|sive|ly
cur|sor +s
(Computing;
Mathematics.
△ curser)
cur|sor|ial
cur|sor|ily
cur|sori|ness

curs|ory
curst (archaic
= cursed)
Curt (name)
curt +er +est
(brusque; short)
cur|tail +s +ed
+ing
cur|tail|ment +s
cur|tain +s +ed
+ing
cur|tain call +s
cur|tain fire +s
curtain-raiser +s
cur|tain wall +s
cur|tana +s
cur|til|age +s
Cur|tin, John
(Australian prime
minister)
Cur|tis, Tony
(American actor)
Cur|tiss, Glenn
Ham|mond
(American
aviation pioneer)
curt|ly
curt|ness
curt|sey (use
curtsy) +s +ed
+ing
curtsy
curt|sies
curt|sied
curt|sy|ing
cur|ule
curv|aceous
curva|ture +s
curve
curves
curved
curv|ing
cur|vet
cur|vets
cur|vet|ted
cur|vet|ting
curvi|fo|li|ate
curvi|form
curvi|lin|ear
curvi|lin|ear|ly
curvi|ness
curvi|ros|tral
curvy
cur|vier
cur|vi|est
cus|cus
cus|cuses
(animal.
△ couscous, khus-
khus)
cusec +s
Cush Bible

Cush (part of
ancient Nubia.
△ Hindu Kush)
cush
cushes
(= cushion)
cushat +s
cush-cush
cush-cushes
cushi|ness
Cush|ing, Har|vey
Wil|liams
(American
surgeon)
Cush|ing's
dis|ease
Cush|ing's
syn|drome
cush|ion +s +ed
+ing
cush|iony
Cush|it|ic
cushy
cush|ier
cushi|est
cusp +s
cus|pate
cusped
cus|pid +s
cus|pid|al
cus|pid|ate
cus|pi|dor +s
cuss
cusses
cussed
cuss|ing
cuss|ed|ly
cuss|ed|ness
cuss word +s
cus|tard +s
cus|tard apple +s
cus|tard pie +s
cus|tardy (like
custard.
△ custody)
Cus|ter, George
Arm|strong
(American cavalry
general)
cus|to|dial
cus|to|dian +s
cus|to|dian|ship
cus|tody
(imprisonment
etc. △ custardy)
cus|tom +s
cus|tom|ar|ily
cus|tom|ari|ness
cus|tom|ary
cus|tom|ar|ies
custom-built
custom-designed

cus|tom|er +s
cus|tom house +s
cus|tom|ise Br.
(use customize)
cus|tom|ises
cus|tom|ised
cus|tom|is|ing
cus|tom|ize
cus|tom|izes
cus|tom|ized
cus|tom|iz|ing
custom-made
Cus|toms
(Government
department)
cus|toms house +s
cut
cuts
cut
cut|ting
cut-and-come-
again adjective
cut and dried
cut-and-dried
attributive
cut-and-paste
cut and thrust
noun
cut-and-thrust
attributive
cu|ta|ne|ous
cut|away +s noun
and adjective
cut|back +s noun
cut-down adjective
cute
cuter
cutest
cute|ly
cute|ness
cutesy
cut glass noun
cut-glass adjective
Cuth|bert (English
saint; name)
cut|icle +s
cu|ticu|lar
cutie +s
cut-in +s noun
cutis
cut|lass
cut|lasses
cut|ler +s
cut|lery
cut|let +s
cut-line +s
cut-off +s adjective
and noun
cut-out +s adjective
and noun
cut-price
cut|purse +s

cut-rate
cut¦ter +s
cut-throat +s
cut¦ting +s
cut¦ting edge +s
cut¦ting¦ly
cut¦tle +s
cuttle-bone +s
cuttle¦fish
    plural cuttle¦fish
cutty
    cut¦ties
Cutty Sark (tea
    clipper)
cutty-stool +s
cut-up +s *adjective
    and noun*
cut¦water +s
cut¦worm +s
cuvée +s
cu¦vette +s
Cu¦vier, Georges
    (French naturalist)
Cuzco (city, Peru)
cwm +s (valley.
    △coomb,
    khoum)
Cwm¦bran (town,
    Wales)
Cy
cyan
cy¦ana¦mide +s
cy¦an¦ate +s
cy¦an¦ic
cy¦an¦ide
cy¦ano¦bac¦terium
    cy¦ano¦bac¦teria
cy¦ano¦co¦bal¦
                amin +s
cy¦ano¦gen +s
cy¦ano¦gen¦ic
cy¦an¦osis
    cy¦an¦oses
cy¦an¦ot¦ic
Cy¦bele *Mythology*
cy¦ber¦nate
    cy¦ber¦nates
    cy¦ber¦nated
    cy¦ber¦nat¦ing
cy¦ber¦na¦tion
cy¦ber¦net¦ic
cy¦ber¦net¦ician +s
cy¦ber¦neti¦cist +s
cy¦ber¦net¦ics
cy¦ber¦punk +s
cyber¦space
cy¦borg +s
cycad +s
Cyc¦la¦des (islands,
    Aegean)
Cyc¦lad¦ic
cyc¦la¦mate +s

cyc¦la¦men +s
cycle
    cycles
    cycled
    cyc¦ling
cycle track +s
cycle-way +s
cyc¦lic
cyc¦lic¦al
cyc¦lic¦al¦ly
cyc¦list +s
cyclo¦alk¦ane +s
cyclo-cross
cyclo¦dex¦trin +s
cyclo¦graph +s
cyclo¦hex¦ane +s
cyclo¦hexyl
cyc¦loid +s
cyc¦loid¦al
cyc¦lom¦eter +s
cyc¦lone +s
cyc¦lon¦ic
cyc¦lon¦ic¦al¦ly
cyclo¦pae¦dia +s
    (use cyclopedia)
cyclo¦pae¦dic (use
    cyclopedic)
cyclo¦paraf¦fin +s
Cyc¦lo¦pean
cyclo¦pedia +s
cyclo¦pedic
cyclo¦pro¦pane
cyclo¦propyl
Cyc¦lops
    plural Cyc¦lops *or*
    Cyc¦lopses *or*
    Cyc¦lo¦pes
    (one-eyed giant)
cyc¦lops
    plural cyc¦lops *or*
    cyc¦lo¦pes
    (crustacean)
cyclo¦rama +s
cyclo¦ram¦ic
cyclo¦sporin
cyclo¦stome +s
cyclo¦style
    cyclo¦styl¦ing
cyclo¦thy¦mia
cyclo¦thy¦mic
cyclo¦tron +s
cyder +s (use
    cider)
cyg¦net +s (young
    swan. △signet)
Cyg¦nus
    (constellation)
cy¦lin¦der +s
cy¦lin¦dric¦al
cy¦lin¦dric¦al¦ly
cyma +s

cym¦bal +s
    (percussion
    instrument.
    △symbol)
cym¦bal¦ist +s
    (cymbal player.
    △symbolist)
cym¦balo +s
Cym¦bel¦ine
    (ancient British
    king)
cym¦bid¦ium +s
cym¦bi¦form
cyme +s
cym¦ose
Cym¦ric
Cymru (Welsh
    name for Wales)
Cyne¦wulf (Anglo-
    Saxon poet)
cyn¦ghan¦edd
Cynic +s (member
    of Greek sect)
cynic +s (doubter)
cyn¦ic¦al
cyn¦ic¦al¦ly
cyni¦cism
cyno¦ceph¦alus
    cyno¦ceph¦ali
cyno¦sure +s
Cyn¦thia
cy¦pher +s (use
    cipher)
cy pres *Law*
cy¦press
    cy¦presses
    (tree)
Cyp¦rian +s (of
    Cyprus)
Cyp¦rian
    (Carthaginian
    saint)
cyp¦rin¦oid +s (like
    carp)
Cyp¦riot +s
cyp¦ri¦pe¦dium +s
Cy¦prus (island,
    Mediterranean)
cyp¦sela
    cyp¦selae
Cyr¦ano de
    Ber¦gerac
    (French soldier
    and writer)
Cyre¦na¦ic +s
Cyre¦na¦ica
    (region, Libya)
Cyr¦ene (region,
    Libya)
Cyril (Greek saint;
    name)
Cyr¦il¦lic +s

Cyril of
    Alex¦an¦dria
    (saint)
Cyrus (name)
Cyrus the Great
    (Persian king)
Cyrus the
    Young¦er
    (Persian
    commander)
cyst +s (*Medicine.*
    △cist)
cyst¦eine
cys¦tic
cyst¦ine +s
    (*Biochemistry.*
    △Sistine)
cyst¦itis
cysto¦scope +s
cysto¦scop¦ic
cyst¦os¦copy
    cyst¦os¦copies
cyst¦ot¦omy
    cyst¦oto¦mies
cyti¦dine
cyto¦chrome +s
cyto¦gen¦et¦ic
cyto¦gen¦et¦ic¦al
cyto¦gen¦et¦ic¦al¦ly
cyto¦gen¦eti¦cist
                +s
cyto¦gen¦et¦ics
cyto¦logic¦al
cyto¦logic¦al¦ly
cy¦tolo¦gist +s
cy¦tology
cyto¦megalo¦virus
    cyto¦megalo¦
                viruses
cyto¦plasm
cyto¦plas¦mic
cyto¦sine
cyto¦skel¦eton +s
cyto¦toxic
czar +s (use tsar)
czar¦das (use
    csardas)
czar¦evich (use
    tsarevich)
    czar¦eviches
czar¦evna +s (use
    tsarevna)
czar¦ina +s (use
    tsarina)
czar¦ism (use
    tsarism)
czar¦ist +s (use
    tsarist)
Czech +s
Czecho¦slo¦vak +s
Czecho¦slo¦vakia

Czecho|slo|vak|
   ian
Czerny, Karl
  (Austrian
  composer and
  musician)
Częs|to|chowa
  (city, Poland)

Dd

....

'd (= had; would)
dab
  dabs
  dabbed
  dab|bing
dab|ber +s
dab|ble
  dab|bles
  dab|bled
  dab|bling
dab|bler +s
dab|bling +s
dab|chick +s
dab hand +s
da capo
Dacca (use Dhaka)
dace
  plural dace
  (fish. △ dais)
dacha +s
Dachau
  (concentration
  camp, Germany)
dachs|hund +s
Dacia (ancient E.
  European country)
Da|cian +s
da|cite +s
dac|oit +s
dac|tyl +s
dac|tyl|ic +s
dad +s
Dada
Dada|ism
Dada|ist +s
Dada|is|tic
daddy
  dad|dies
daddy-long-legs
  plural daddy-long-
  legs
dado +s
Dadra and Nagar
  Ha|veli (territory,
  India)
Dae|da|lian +s
Dae|da|lus *Greek
  Mythology*
dae|mon +s (use
  demon)
dae|mon|ic (use
  demonic)
dae|mono|logic|al
  (use
  demonological)
daff +s
daf|fily
daf|fi|ness

daf|fo|dil +s
daffy
  daf|fier
  daf|fi|est
daft +er +est
daft|ly
daft|ness
Daf|ydd
dag
  dags
  dagged
  dag|ging
da Gama, Vasco
  (Portuguese
  explorer)
Dag|estan
  (republic, Russia)
dagga +s (plant;
  hemp)
dag|ger +s
  (weapon)
dagger|board +s
daggy
  dag|gier
  dag|gi|est
Dag|mar
dago +s (*offensive*)
Dagon *Bible*
Da|guerre, Louis
  (French inventor)
da|guerre|otype
  +s
dah +s
Dahl, Roald
  (British writer)
Dah|lia (name)
dah|lia +s (flower)
Da|ho|mey (former
  name of Benin)
Dai (man's name.
  △ Di)
Dáil (Éire|ann)
  (Irish parliament)
daily
  dai|lies
Daim|ler,
  Gott|lieb
  (German
  engineer)
dai|mon +s (use
  demon)
dai|mon|ic (use
  demonic)
dain|tily
dain|ti|ness
dainty
  dain|ties
  dain|tier
  dain|ti|est
dai|quiri +s
Dai|ren (former
  name of Dalian)

dairy
  dair|ies
dairy-free
dairy|ing
dairy|maid +s
dairy|man
  dairy|men
dais
  daises
  (platform. △ dace)
Daisy (name)
daisy
  dai|sies
  (flower)
daisy chain +s
daisy-cutter +s
daisy wheel +s
Dakar (capital of
  Senegal)
Dak|ota, North
  and South (states,
  USA)
dal +s (use dhal)
Dalai Lama
da|lasi
  plural da|lasi *or*
  da|lasis
Dal|croze (see
  Jacques-
  Dalcroze)
Dale, Henry
  Hal|lett (English
  physiologist and
  pharmacologist)
Dale (name)
dale +s (valley)
dalek +s
dales|folk
dales|man
  dales|men
dales|woman
  dales|women
Daley (name)
Dal|housie,
  Mar|quis of
  (British colonial
  administrator)
Dali, Sal|va|dor
  (Spanish painter)
Da|lian (port,
  China)
Dalit +s
Dal|la|pic|cola,
  Luigi (Italian
  composer)
Dal|las (city, USA)
dal|li|ance +s
dal|lier +s
dally
  dal|lies
  dal|lied
  dally|ing

Dal|ma¦tia (region, Croatia)
Dal|ma¦tian +s
dal|mat¦ic
Dal|ri¦ada (ancient kingdom, Scotland)
dal segno
Dal¦ton, John (English chemist)
dal¦ton +s (unit)
Dal¦ton|ise Br. (use Daltonize)
　Dal¦ton|ises
　Dal¦ton|ised
　Dal¦ton|is¦ing
dal¦ton|ism
Dal¦ton|ize
　Dal¦ton|izes
　Dal¦ton|ized
　Dal¦ton|iz¦ing
dam
　dams
　dammed
　dam|ming
(barrier; mother; block up; etc.
⚠ damn)
dam¦age
　dam|ages
　dam|aged
　dam|aging
dam¦age|able
dam¦aging¦ly
Daman and Diu (territory, India)
Da¦mara
　plural Da¦mara or Da¦ma|ras
Dam¦ara|land (region, Namibia)
Dam|aris
dam¦as|cene
　dam¦as|cenes
　dam¦as|cened
　dam¦as|cen¦ing
Da¦mas|cus (capital of Syria)
dam¦ask +s +ed +ing
Dama|vand (mountain, Iran)
Dam|buster +s
Dame (title)
dame +s (woman)
dame school +s
dam|fool +s (noun; use damn fool)
dam|fool
(attributive; use damn-fool)
Da¦mian

Dami|etta (E. Nile delta and port, Egypt)
dam¦mar +s
dam¦mit
damn +s +ed +ing
(condemn.
⚠ dam)
dam|nable
dam|nably
dam|na¦tion +s
dam|na¦tory
damned +est
damn fool +s noun
damn-fool adjective
dam¦ni¦fi¦ca¦tion
dam|nify
　dam¦ni|fies
　dam¦ni|fied
　dam¦ni¦fy|ing
damn|ing¦ly
dam|num
　damna
Damo|cles
(legendary figure; in 'sword of Damocles')
Damon (legendary Syracusan; name)
damp +s +ed +ing +er +est
damp course +s
damp¦en +s +ed +ing
damp|en¦er +s
damp¦er +s
Damp|ier,
Wil|liam (English explorer)
damping-off noun and adjective
damp|ish
damp¦ly
damp|ness
damp-proof +s +ed +ing
dam¦sel +s
dam¦sel|fish
　plural dam¦sel|fish
dam¦sel|fly
　dam¦sel|flies
dam¦son +s
Dan (Bible; name)
dan +s (in judo; buoy)
Dana, James Dwight (American mineralogist)
Dana, Rich|ard Henry (American writer)

Danae Greek Mythology
Dan¦aids Greek Mythology
Dana|kil
　plural Dana|kil or Dana|kils
Dana|kil De|pres¦sion (region, NE Africa)
Da Nang (city, Vietnam)
dance
　dances
　danced
　dan¦cing
dance|able
dance band +s
dance floor +s
dance hall +s
dan¦cer +s
dance|wear
dan¦cing girl +s
dan|delion +s
dan¦der +s
dan|dify
　dan¦di|fies
　dan¦di|fied
　dan¦di¦fy|ing
dan¦dle
　dan¦dles
　dan¦dled
　dand|ling
Dan|dong (port, China)
dan|druff
dandy
　dan|dies
dan|dier
　dan¦di|est
dandy brush
　dandy brushes
dandy|ish
dandy|ism
Dane +s
Dane|geld
Dane|law
dane|weed
dane|wort
dan¦ger +s
dan¦ger man
　dan¦ger men
dan¦ger|ous
dan¦ger|ous¦ly
dan¦ger|ous|ness
dan¦gle
　dan¦gles
　dan¦gled
　dan|gling
dan|gler +s
dan¦gly

Dan¦iel (Bible; man's name)
Dan¦iela
Dan¦iell cell +s
Dan¦ielle (woman's name)
Dan¦ish
　Dan¦ishes
dank +er +est
dank¦ly
dank|ness
Dank|worth, John (British jazz musician)
d'An¦nun|zio, Gab¦ri|ele (Italian poet)
Danny
Dano-Norwegian
danse ma|cabre
　danses ma|cabres
dan|seur +s male
dan|seuse +s female
Dante (Ali|ghieri) (Italian poet)
Dan|te¦an
Dant|esque
dan|tho¦nia
Dan¦ton, Georges Jacques (French revolutionary)
Dan¦ube (river, Europe)
Dan¦ub|ian +s
Dan¦zig (German name for Gdańsk)
Dão (river and region, Portugal)
dap
　daps
　dapped
　dap|ping
Daphne (Greek Mythology; name)
daphne +s (shrub)
daph|nia
　plural daph|nia
Daph|nis Greek Mythology
Da Ponte, Lor|enzo (Italian librettist and poet)
dap¦per
dap¦per¦ly
dap¦per|ness
dap¦ple
　dap¦ples
　dap¦pled
　dap|pling
dap¦ple gray Am. +s

dap¦ple grey *Br.* +s
Dap¦sang
  (alternative name
  for K2)
dap¦sone
Da¦qing (city,
  China)
dar¦bies (handcuffs)
Darby (name.
  △ Derby)
Darby and Joan
Darby and Joan
  Club +s
Darcy
Dard +s
Dar¦da¦nelles, the
  (strait between
  Europe and
  Asiatic Turkey)
Dard¦ic
dare
  dares
  dared
  dar¦ing
dare¦devil +s
dare¦devil¦ry
Dar¦ell *also*
  Dar|rell, Dar¦ryl,
  Daryl
Daren *also* Dar¦ren
daren't (= dare
  not)
darer +s
dare say (in 'I dare
  say')
Dar es Sa¦laam
  (city, Tanzania)
Dar¦fur (region,
  Sudan)
darg +s
Dari
Dar¦ien (province,
  Panama)
Dar¦ien, Gulf of
  (part of
  Caribbean)
dar¦ing
daring-do (use
  derring-do)
dar¦ing¦ly
dari¦ole +s
Dar¦ius (Persian
  king; name)
Dar¦jee¦ling (town,
  India; tea)
dark +s +er +est
dark¦en +s +ed
  +ing
dark¦en¦er +s
dark-eyed
dark-haired

Dar¦khan (city,
  Mongolia)
darkie +s (*offensive*)
dark¦ish
dark¦ling
dark¦ly
dark¦ness
  dark¦nesses
dark¦room +s
dark-skinned
dark¦some
darky (use darkie)
  dark¦ies
  (*offensive*)
Dar¦lene
Dar¦ling, Grace
  (English heroine)
dar¦ling +s
Dar¦ling River (in
  Australia)
Dar¦ling¦ton (town,
  England)
Darm¦stadt (town,
  Germany)
darn +s +ed +ing
darned¦est
dar¦nel +s
darn¦er +s
darn¦ing nee¦dle
  +s
darn¦ing wool
Darn¦ley, Lord
  (husband of Mary
  Queen of Scots)
Dar¦rell *also*
  Dar¦ell, Dar¦ryl,
  Daryl
Dar¦ren *also* Daren
Dar¦ryl *also* Dar¦ell,
  Dar|rell, Daryl
Dart, Ray|mond
  Ar¦thur
  (Australian-born
  South African
  anthropologist)
dart +s +ed +ing
dart¦board +s
dart¦er +s
Dart¦moor (region,
  England)
Dart¦mouth (port
  and naval college,
  England)
Dar¦win (city,
  Australia)
Dar¦win, Charles
  (English
  naturalist)
Dar¦win¦ian +s
Dar¦win¦ism
Dar¦win¦ist +s
Dar¦win's finches

Daryl *also* Dar¦ell,
  Dar|rell, Dar¦ryl
dash
  dashes
  dashed
  dash¦ing
dash¦board +s
dash¦iki +s
dash¦ing¦ly
dash¦ing¦ness
dash¦pot +s
das¦sie +s
das¦tard +s
das¦tard¦li¦ness
das¦tard¦ly
dasy¦ure +s
data
data bank +s
data¦base +s
dat¦able
DataGlove +s
data pro¦cess¦ing
data pro¦ces¦sor
  +s
date
  dates
  dated
  dat¦ing
date¦less
Date Line
  (on world)
date line +s
  (in newspapers)
date palm +s
date rape
date-stamp +s +ed
  +ing
dat¦ival
dat¦ival¦ly
dat¦ive +s
Da¦tong (city,
  China)
datum
  data
da¦tura +s
daub +s +ed +ing
  (smear)
daube +s (stew)
daub¦er +s
Dau¦bigny,
  Charles-
  François (French
  painter)
daub¦ster +s
dauby
Dau¦det,
  Al¦phonse
  (French novelist)
daugh¦ter +s
daugh¦ter¦hood
daughter-in-law
  daughters-in-law
daugh¦ter¦ly

Dau¦mier, Hon¦oré
  (French artist)
daunt +s +ed +ing
daunt¦ing¦ly
daunt¦less
daunt¦less¦ly
daunt¦less¦ness
dau¦phin +s
Dau¦phiné (former
  province, France)
Davao (port,
  Philippines)
Dave
Daven¦port +s
Davey *also* Davie,
  Davy
David *Bible*
David (Scottish
  kings)
David (patron saint
  of Wales)
David, Eliza¦beth
  (English cookery
  writer)
David, Jacques-
  Louis (French
  painter)
Davie *also* Davey,
  Davy
Davies, Peter
  Max¦well
  (English
  composer)
Davies,
  Rob¦ert¦son
  (Canadian writer)
Davies, W. H.
  (English poet)
da Vinci,
  Leo¦nardo
  (Italian painter
  and designer)
Davis (breathing
  apparatus)
Davis, Bette
  (American
  actress)
Davis, Joe and
  Fred (English
  snooker players)
Davis, Miles
  (American jazz
  musician)
Davis, Steve
  (English snooker
  player)
Davis Cup
Davis¦son,
  Clin¦ton Jo¦seph
  (American
  physicist)

Davis Strait
(between
Greenland and
Baffin Island)
davit +s
Davos (resort,
Switzerland)
Davy also Davey,
Davie
(name)
Davy
Davies
(lamp)
Davy, Hum|phry
(English chemist)
Davy Jones's
locker
daw +s (jackdaw.
△ dor, door)
daw|dle
daw|dles
daw|dled
dawd|ling
dawd|ler +s
Daw|kins,
Rich|ard (English
biologist)
Dawn (name)
dawn +s +ed +ing
(daybreak)
dawn|ing +s
Day, Doris
(American
actress)
day +s
Dayak +s (use
Dyak)
Dayan, Moshe
(Israeli politician
and general)
day|bed +s
day|book +s
day-boy +s
day|break
day-by-day
adjective
day care
day centre +s
day|dream +s +ed
+ing
day|dream|er +s
day-girl +s
Day-Glo Propr.
day|less
Day-Lewis, Cecil
(English writer)
Day-Lewis,
Dan|iel (English
actor)
day|light +s
day lily
day lil|ies

day-long
day nur|sery
day nur|ser|ies
day-old attributive
day-owl +s
day|pack +s
day re|lease
day re|turn +s
day room +s
day|sack +s
day school +s
day|side
day|time +s
day-to-day
adjective
Day|ton (city, USA)
day trip +s
day trip|per +s
day|work
daze
dazes
dazed
daz|ing
dazed|ly
daz|zle
daz|zles
daz|zled
daz|zling
dazzle|ment +s
daz|zler +s
daz|zling|ly
D-Day
de|ac|ces|sion +s
+ed +ing
dea|con +s
dea|con|ate +s
dea|con|ess
dea|con|esses
dea|con|ship +s
de|acti|vate
de|acti|vates
de|acti|vated
de|acti|vat|ing
de|acti|va|tion
de|acti|va|tor +s
dead +er +est
dead-and-alive
dead-ball adjective
dead|beat +s
dead|bolt +s
dead|en +s +ed
+ing
dead end +s noun
dead-end adjective
dead|en|er +s
dead|eye +s
dead|fall +s
dead-head +s +ed
+ing noun and
verb
dead heat +s noun

dead-heat +s +ed
+ing verb
dead let|ter +s
dead|light +s
dead|line +s
dead|li|ness
dead|lock +s +ed
+ing
dead|ly
dead|lier
dead|li|est
dead march
dead marches
dead|ness
dead-nettle +s
dead on
dead|pan
dead|pans
dead|panned
dead|pan|ning
dead reck|on|ing
Dead Sea (in Near
East)
dead|stock
dead weight +s
de-aerate
de-aerates
de-aerated
de-aerating
de-aeration
deaf +er +est
(unable to hear.
△ def)
deaf aid +s
deaf-blind adjective
deaf|en +s +ed
+ing
deaf|en|ing|ly
deaf|ly
deaf mute +s
deaf|ness
deal
deals
dealt
deal|ing
deal|er +s
deal|er|ship +s
deal|ing +s
dealt
de|am|bu|la|tion
de|am|bu|la|tory
de|am|bu|
la|tor|ies
Dean (name)
Dean,
Chris|to|pher
(English ice-
skater)
Dean, James
(American actor)

dean +s (head of
faculty; doyen.
△ dene)
dean|ery
dean|er|ies
(dean's house;
group of parishes.
△ denary)
De|anna
dear +s +er +est
(beloved;
expensive.
△ deer)
dearie +s
Dear John
attributive
dear|ly
dear|ness
dearth +s
deasil (clockwise.
△ diesel)
death +s
death|bed +s
death blow +s
death camp +s
death-defying
death knell
death|less
death|less|ness
death|like
death|li|ness
death|ly
death|lier
death|li|est
death mask +s
death rate +s
death rat|tle +s
death roll +s
death row +s
death toll +s
death trap +s
Death Val|ley
(desert basin,
USA)
death war|rant +s
death-watch
bee|tle +s
death wish
death wishes
de|at|trib|ute
de|at|trib|utes
de|at|trib|uted
de|at|trib|ut|ing
de|at|tri|bu|tion +s
deb +s
de|bacle +s
debag
de|bags
de|bagged
de|bag|ging
debar
de|bars

debar (*cont.*)
de|barred
de|bar|ring
de¦bark +s +ed
+ing
de¦bark|ation
de¦bar|ment +s
de¦base
de|bases
de|based
de|bas¦ing
de¦base|ment +s
de|baser +s
de|bat¦able
de|bat¦ably
de¦bate
de|bates
de|bated
de|bat¦ing
de|bater +s
de|bauch
de|bauches
de|bauched
de|bauch|ing
de|bauch¦ee +s
de|bauch¦er +s
de|bauch|ery
Deb¦bie
de¦beak +s +ed
+ing
de Beau|voir,
Sim¦one (French
writer)
de¦ben|ture +s
de¦bili|tate
de¦bili|tates
de¦bili|tated
de¦bili|tat|ing
de¦bili|tat¦ing¦ly
de¦bili|ta|tion
de¦bili|ta|tive
de¦bil|ity
de¦bil|ities
debit +s +ed +ing
deb¦on|air
deb¦on|air¦ly
Deb¦orah (*Bible*;
name)
de|bouch
de|bouches
de|bouched
de|bouch|ing
de|bouch|ment
Deb¦re|cen (city,
Hungary)
De|brett (peerage
book)
de¦bride|ment
de¦brief +s +ed
+ing
de¦brief|ing +s

deb¦ris
de Brog¦lie, Louis
(French physicist;
wavelength)
debt +s
debt¦or +s
debug
de¦bugs
de|bugged
de|bug|ging
de¦bug|ger +s
de¦bunk +s +ed
+ing
de|bunk¦er +s
debus
de|busses
de|bussed
de|bus|sing
De|bussy, Claude
(French
composer)
debut +s +ed +ing
debu|tant +s *male*
debu|tante +s
female
Debye, Peter
(Dutch-born
American
chemical
physicist)
dec¦adal
dec¦ade +s
deca|dence
deca|dent +s
deca|dent|ism
deca|dent¦ly
de|cad¦ic
decaf *Propr.*
de|caf¦fein|ate
de|caf¦fein|ates
de|caf¦fein|ated
de|caf¦fein|at¦ing
deca|gon +s
dec|agon¦al
dec|agyn¦ous
deca|he¦dral
deca|he¦dron
deca|he¦dra *or*
deca|he¦drons
decal +s
de|cal¦ci¦fi|ca|tion
de|cal¦ci|fier +s
de|cal¦cify
de|cal¦ci|fies
de|cal¦ci|fied
de|cal¦ci|fy|ing
de|cal¦co|mania
+s
deca|liter *Am.* +s
deca|litre *Br.* +s
Deca|logue
De|cam|eron

deca|meter *Am.* +s
deca|metre *Br.* +s
de¦camp +s +ed
+ing
de¦camp|ment
de¦can|al
de¦can|drous
de¦cani
de¦cant +s +ed
+ing
de|cant¦er +s
de|capi¦tate
de|capi|tates
de|capi|tated
de|capi|tat¦ing
de|capi|ta¦tion +s
de|capi|ta¦tor +s
deca|pod +s
deca|pod¦an
de|car¦bon|isa|tion
Br. (use
decarbonization)
de|car¦bon|ise *Br.*
(use decarbonize)
de|car¦bon|ises
de|car¦bon|ised
de|car¦bon|is¦ing
de|car¦bon|iza|tion
de|car|bon|ize
de|car¦bon|izes
de|car¦bon|ized
de|car¦bon|iz¦ing
deca|style +s
de|casu¦al|isa¦tion
Br. (use
decasualization)
de|casu¦al|ise *Br.*
(use decasualize)
de|casu¦al|ises
de|casu¦al|ised
de|casu¦al|is¦ing
de|casu¦al|iza|tion
de|casu¦al|ize
de|casu¦al|izes
de|casu¦al|ized
de|casu¦al|iz¦ing
deca|syl¦lab¦ic
deca|syl|lable +s
dec|ath¦lete +s
dec|ath¦lon +s
decay +s +ed +ing
decay|able
Dec¦can (plateau,
India)
de|cease
de|ceases
de|ceased
de|ceas|ing
de|ce¦dent +s
de¦ceit +s
de¦ceit|ful
de¦ceit|ful¦ly

de¦ceit|ful|ness
de¦ceiv|able
de|ceive
de|ceives
de|ceived
de|ceiv¦ing
de|ceiver +s
de|cel¦er|ate
de|cel¦er|ates
de|cel¦er|ated
de|cel¦er|at¦ing
de|cel¦er|ation +s
de|cel¦er|ator +s
de|cel¦er|om¦eter
+s
De¦cem|ber +s
De¦cem|brist +s
de|cency
de|cen|cies
de|cen|nial
de|cen|ni|al¦ly
de|cen|nium
de|cen|nia
de¦cent
de|cen|ter *Am.* +s
+ed +ing (*Br.*
decentre)
de|cent|ly
de|cen|tral
isa|tion *Br.* (use
decentralization)
de|cen|tral|ise *Br.*
(use decentralize)
de|cen|tral|ises
de|cen|tral|ised
de|cen|tral|is|ing
de|cent¦ral|ist +s
de|cen|tral|
iza|tion
de|cen|tral|ize
de|cen|tral|izes
de|cen|tral|ized
de|cen|tral|iz|ing
de|centre *Br.*
de|centres
de|centred
de|cen|tring
(*Am.* decenter)
de¦cep|tion +s
de¦cep|tive
de¦cep|tive|ly
de¦cep|tive|ness
de|cere|brate
de|chlor¦in|ate
de|chlor¦in|ates
de|chlor¦in|ated
de|chlor¦in|at¦ing
de|chlor¦in|ation
+s
De|cian
deci|bel +s
de|cid¦able

de¦cide
  de¦cides
  de¦cided
  de¦cid¦ing
de¦cided¦ly
de¦cided|ness
de¦cider +s
de¦cidu|ous
de¦cidu|ous|ness
deci|gram +s
deci|gramme Br.
  +s
decile +s
deci|liter Am. +s
deci|litre Br. +s
deci|mal +s
deci|mal|isa|tion
  Br. (use
  decimalization)
deci|mal|ise Br.
  (use decimalize)
  deci|mal|ises
  deci|mal|ised
  deci|mal|is|ing
deci|mal|iza|tion
deci|mal|ize
  deci|mal|izes
  deci|mal|ized
  deci|mal|iz|ing
deci|mal¦ly
deci|mate
  deci|mates
  deci|mated
  deci|mat¦ing
deci|ma¦tion
deci|ma¦tor +s
deci|meter Am. +s
deci|metre Br. +s
de¦cipher +s +ed
  +ing
de¦cipher|able
de¦cipher|ment
de¦ci¦sion +s
de¦ci¦sion maker
  +s
decision-making
de¦cisive
de¦cisive¦ly
de¦cisive|ness
Dec¦ius, Gaius
  Mes¦sius
  Quin¦tus (Roman
  emperor)
deck +s +ed +ing
deck|chair +s
deck|hand +s
deckle +s
deckled
deckle edge +s
deckle-edged
de¦claim +s +ed
  +ing

de¦claim¦er +s
dec¦lam¦ation +s
de¦clama|tory
Dec¦lan
de¦clar|able
de¦clar|ant +s
dec¦lar|ation +s
de¦clara|tive +s
de¦clara|tive¦ly
de¦clara|tive|ness
de¦clara|tory
de¦clare
  de¦clares
  de¦clared
  de¦clar¦ing
de¦clared¦ly
de¦clarer +s
de¦class
  de¦classes
  de¦classed
  de¦class|ing
dé¦classé male
dé¦clas¦sée female
de¦clas¦si¦fi¦ca¦tion
  +s
de¦clas|sify
  de¦clas¦si|fies
  de¦clas¦si|fied
  de¦clas¦si|fy|ing
de-claw +s +ed
  +ing
de¦clen|sion +s
de¦clen|sion|al
de¦clin|able
dec¦lin|ation +s
dec¦lin|ation|al
de¦cline
  de¦clines
  de¦clined
  de¦clin¦ing
de¦cliner +s
dec¦lin|om¦eter +s
de¦cliv|itous
de¦cliv|ity
  de¦cliv|ities
de¦clutch
  de¦clutches
  de¦clutched
  de¦clutch|ing
deco (= art deco.
  △ dekko)
de¦coct +s +ed
  +ing
de¦coc¦tion +s
de¦cod¦able
de¦code
  de¦codes
  de¦coded
  de¦cod¦ing
de¦coder +s
de¦coke
  de¦cokes

de¦coke (cont.)
  de¦coked
  de¦cok¦ing
de¦col¦late
  de¦col¦lates
  de¦col¦lated
  de¦col¦lat¦ing
de¦col¦la¦tion +s
dé¦col¦le¦tage +s
dé¦col¦leté
dé¦col¦letée (use
  décolleté)
de¦col¦on¦isa¦tion
  Br. (use
  decolonization)
de¦col¦on|ise Br.
  (use decolonize)
  de¦col¦on|ises
  de¦col¦on|ised
  de¦col¦on|is|ing
de¦col¦on|iza|tion
de¦col¦on|ize
  de¦col¦on|izes
  de¦col¦on|ized
  de¦col¦on|iz|ing
de¦col¦or|isa|tion
  Br. (use
  decolorization)
de¦col¦or|ise Br.
  (use decolorize)
  de¦col¦or|ises
  de¦col¦or|ised
  de¦col¦or|is|ing
de¦col¦or|iza|tion
de¦col¦or|ize
  de¦col¦or|izes
  de¦col¦or|ized
  de¦col¦or|iz|ing
de¦com¦mis|sion
  +s +ed +ing
de¦com¦mun¦isa|
  tion Br. (use
  decommuniza-
  tion)
de¦com¦mun¦ise
  Br. (use
  decommunize)
  de¦com¦mun¦ises
  de¦com¦mun¦ised
  de¦com¦
    mun¦is¦ing
de¦com¦mun¦iza|
       tion
de¦com¦mun¦ize
  de¦com¦mun¦izes
  de¦com¦mun¦ized
  de¦com¦
    mun¦iz¦ing
de¦com¦pos¦able
de¦com¦pose
  de¦com¦poses

de¦com¦pose
  (cont.)
  de¦com¦posed
  de¦com¦pos¦ing
de¦com¦poser +s
de¦com¦pos¦ition
  +s
de¦com¦pound +s
  +ed +ing
de¦com¦press
  de¦com¦presses
  de¦com¦pressed
  de¦com¦press|ing
de¦com¦pres¦sion
de¦com¦pres¦sor
  +s
de¦con¦gest|ant +s
de¦con¦se¦crate
  de¦con¦se¦crates
  de¦con¦se¦crated
  de¦con¦se¦crat¦ing
de¦con¦se¦cra¦tion
  +s
de¦con¦struct +s
  +ed +ing
de¦con¦struc¦tion
  +s
de¦con¦struc¦tion|
       ism
de¦con¦struc¦tion|
       ist +s
de¦con¦struct|ive
de¦con¦tam¦in|ate
  de¦con¦tam¦in|
       ates
  de¦con¦tam¦in|
       ated
  de¦con¦tam¦in|
       at¦ing
de¦con¦tam¦in|
       ation
de¦con¦text¦ual|ise
  Br. (use
  decontextualize)
  de¦con¦text¦ual|
       ises
  de¦con¦text¦ual|
       ised
  de¦con¦text¦ual|
       is¦ing
de¦con¦text¦ual|ize
  de¦con¦text¦ual|
       izes
  de¦con¦text¦ual|
       ized
  de¦con¦text¦ual|
       iz¦ing
de¦con¦trol
  de¦con¦trols
  de¦con¦trolled
  de¦con¦trol|ling
decor +s

dec¦or¦ate
  dec¦or¦ates
  dec¦or¦ated
  dec¦or¦at¦ing
dec¦or¦ation +s
dec¦ora¦tive
dec¦ora¦tive¦ly
dec¦ora¦tive¦ness
dec¦or¦ator +s
dec¦or¦ous
dec¦or¦ous¦ly
dec¦or¦ous¦ness
de¦cor¦ti¦cate
  de¦cor¦ti¦cates
  de¦cor¦ti¦cated
  de¦cor¦ti¦cat¦ing
de¦cor¦ti¦ca¦tion +s
de¦corum
dé¦coup¦age
de¦couple
  de¦couples
  de¦coupled
  de¦coup¦ling
decoy +s +ed +ing
de¦crease
  de¦creases
  de¦creased
  de¦creas¦ing
de¦creas¦ing¦ly
de¦cree
  de¦crees
  de¦creed
  de¦cree¦ing
de¦cree ab¦so¦lute
  de¦crees
  ab¦so¦lute
de¦cree nisi
  de¦crees nisi
dec¦re¦ment +s
de¦crepit
de¦crepi¦tate
  de¦crepi¦tates
  de¦crepi¦tated
  de¦crepi¦tat¦ing
de¦crepi¦ta¦tion
de¦crepi¦tude
de¦cres¦cendo +s
de¦cres¦cent
de¦cretal +s
de¦crial +s
de¦crier +s
de¦crim¦in¦al
  isa¦tion *Br.* (use
  decriminaliza-
  tion)
de¦crim¦in¦al¦ise
  Br. (use
  decriminalize)
  de¦crim¦in¦al¦ises
  de¦crim¦in¦al¦ised
  de¦crim¦in¦al
    is¦ing

de¦crim¦in¦al
  iza¦tion
de¦crim¦in¦al¦ize
  de¦crim¦in¦al¦izes
  de¦crim¦in¦al¦ized
  de¦crim¦in¦al
    iz¦ing
decry
  de¦cries
  de¦cried
  de¦cry¦ing
de¦crypt +s +ed
  +ing
de¦cryp¦tion
de¦cum¦bent
dec¦uple
  dec¦uples
  dec¦upled
  decu¦pling
decu¦plet +s
de¦cur¦va¦ture +s
de¦curve
  de¦curves
  de¦curved
  de¦curv¦ing
de¦cus¦sate
  de¦cus¦sates
  de¦cus¦sated
  de¦cus¦sat¦ing
de¦cus¦sa¦tion
de¦dans
  plural de¦dans
Dede¦kind,
  Rich¦ard
  (German
  mathematician)
dedi¦cate
  dedi¦cates
  dedi¦cated
  dedi¦cat¦ing
dedi¦cated¦ly
dedi¦catee +s
dedi¦ca¦tion +s
dedi¦ca¦tive
dedi¦ca¦tor +s
dedi¦ca¦tory
de¦duce
  de¦duces
  de¦duced
  de¦du¦cing
de¦du¦cible
de¦duct +s +ed
  +ing
de¦duct¦ibil¦ity
de¦duct¦ible +s
de¦duc¦tion +s
de¦duct¦ive
de¦duct¦ive¦ly
de Duve,
  Chris¦tian René
  (Belgian
  biochemist)

Dee (river,
  Scotland; river,
  Wales and
  England)
dee +s
deed +s
deed-box
  deed-boxes
deed poll
dee¦jay +s
deem +s +ed +ing
  (judge. △ deme)
de-emphasise *Br.*
  (use de-
  emphasize)
  de-emphasises
  de-emphasised
  de-emphasis¦ing
de-emphasize
  de-emphasizes
  de-emphasized
  de-emphasiz¦ing
deem¦ster +s
deep +s +er +est
deep-down
  attributive
deep-drawn
deep¦en +s +ed
  +ing
deep fat *attributive*
deep-freeze
  deep-freezes
  deep-froze
  deep-freezing
  deep-frozen
deep-fry
  deep-fries
  deep-fried
  deep-frying
deep¦ing +s
deep-laid
deep¦ly
deep-mined
deep-mouthed
deep¦ness
deep-rooted
deep-sea *attributive*
deep-seated
deep-throat¦ed
deep-water
  attributive
deer
  plural deer
  (animal. △ dear)
deer for¦est +s
deer¦hound +s
deer-lick +s
deer mouse
  deer mice
deer¦skin +s
deer¦stalk¦er +s
deer stalk¦ing

de-escalate
  de-escalates
  de-escalated
  de-escalat¦ing
de-escalation +s
Dee¦side (regions,
  Scotland and
  Wales)
def (excellent.
  △ deaf)
de¦face
  de¦faces
  de¦faced
  de¦facing
de¦face¦able
de¦face¦ment +s
de¦facer +s
de facto
de¦fal¦cate
  de¦fal¦cates
  de¦fal¦cated
  de¦fal¦cat¦ing
de¦fal¦ca¦tion +s
de¦fal¦ca¦tor +s
de Falla, Ma¦nuel
  (Spanish
  composer)
def¦am¦ation +s
de¦fama¦tory
de¦fame
  de¦fames
  de¦famed
  de¦fam¦ing
de¦famer +s
defat
  de¦fats
  de¦fat¦ted
  de¦fat¦ting
de¦fault +s +ed
  +ing
de¦fault¦er +s
de¦feas¦ance
de¦feas¦ibil¦ity
de¦feas¦ible
de¦feas¦ibly
de¦feat +s +ed
  +ing
de¦feat¦ism
de¦feat¦ist +s
defe¦cate
  defe¦cates
  defe¦cated
  defe¦cat¦ing
defe¦ca¦tion
defe¦ca¦tor +s
de¦fect +s +ed
  +ing
de¦fec¦tion +s
de¦fect¦ive +s
de¦fect¦ive¦ly
de¦fect¦ive¦ness
de¦fect¦or +s

de|fence *Br.* +s
(*Am.* defense)
de|fence|less *Br.*
(*Am.* defenseless)
de|fence|less|ly *Br.*
(*Am.*
defenselessly)
de|fence|less|ness
Br. (*Am.*
defenselessness)
de|fence|man
de|fence|men
(*Am.*
defenseman)
de|fend +s +ed
+ing
de|fend|able
de|fend|ant +s
de|fend|er +s
de|fen|es|trate
de|fen|es|trates
de|fen|es|trated
de|fen|es|trat|ing
de|fen|es|tra|tion
+s
de|fense *Am.* +s
(*Br.* defence)
de|fense|less *Am.*
(*Br.* defenceless)
de|fense|less|ly
Am. (*Br.*
defencelessly)
de|fense|less|ness
Am. (*Br.*
defencelessness)
de|fense|man *Am.*
de|fense|men
(*Br.* defenceman)
de|fens|ibil|ity
de|fens|ible
de|fens|ibly
de|fen|sive
de|fen|sive|ly
de|fen|sive|ness
defer
de|fers
de|ferred
de|fer|ring
def|er|ence
def|er|ens (in
'vas deferens')
def|er|en|tial
def|er|en|tial|ly
de|fer|ment +s
de|fer|rable
de|fer|ral +s
de|fer|rer +s
de|fi|ance
de|fi|ant
de|fi|ant|ly
de|fib|ril|la|tion
de|fib|ril|la|tor +s

de|fi|ciency
de|fi|cien|cies
de|fi|cient
de|fi|cient|ly
def|icit +s
de|fier +s
def|il|ade
def|il|ades
def|il|aded
def|il|ad|ing
de|file
de|files
de|filed
de|fil|ing
de|file|ment
de|filer +s
de|fin|able
de|fin|ably
de|fine
de|fines
de|fined
de|fin|ing
de|finer +s
def|in|ite +s
def|in|ite|ly
def|in|ite|ness
def|in|ition +s
def|in|ition|al
def|in|ition|al|ly
de|fini|tive +s
de|fini|tive|ly
def|la|grate
def|la|grates
def|la|grated
def|la|grat|ing
def|la|gra|tion
def|la|gra|tor +s
de|flate
de|flates
de|flated
de|flat|ing
de|fla|tion +s
de|fla|tion|ary
de|fla|tion|ist +s
de|fla|tor +s
de|flect +s +ed
+ing
de|flec|tion +s
de|flec|tor +s
de|flex|ion +s (use
deflection)
de|flor|ation
de|flower +s +ed
+ing
de|fo|cus
de|fo|cuses *or*
de|fo|cus|ses
de|focused *or*
de|fo|cussed
de|fo|cus|ing *or*
de|fo|cus|sing

Defoe, Dan|iel
(English writer)
de|foli|ant +s
de|foli|ate
de|foli|ates
de|foli|ated
de|foli|at|ing
de|foli|ation
de|foli|ator +s
De For|est, Lee
(American
physicist)
de|for|est +s +ed
+ing
de|for|est|ation
de|form +s +ed
+ing
de|form|able
de|form|ation +s
de|form|ation|al
de|form|ity
de|form|ities
de|fraud +s +ed
+ing
de|fraud|er +s
de|fray +s +ed
+ing
de|fray|able
de|fray|al
de|fray|ment
de|frock +s +ed
+ing
de|frost +s +ed
+ing
de|frost|er +s
deft +er +est
deft|ly
deft|ness
de|funct
de|funct|ness
de|fuse
de|fuses
de|fused
de|fus|ing
defy
de|fies
de|fied
defy|ing
dé|gagé *male*
dé|gagée *female*
Degas, Edgar
(French artist)
degas
de|gasses
de|gassed
de|gas|sing
de Gaulle, Charles
(French
statesman)
de|gauss
de|gausses

de|gauss (*cont.*)
de|gaussed
de|gauss|ing
de|gauss|er +s
de|gen|er|acy
de|gen|er|ate
de|gen|er|ates
de|gen|er|ated
de|gen|er|at|ing
de|gen|er|ate|ly
de|gen|er|ation
de|gen|era|tive
de|grad|abil|ity
de|grad|able
deg|rad|ation +s
de|grada|tive
de|grade
de|grades
de|graded
de|grad|ing
de|grader +s
de|grad|ing|ly
de|granu|late
de|granu|lates
de|granu|lated
de|granu|lat|ing
de|granu|la|tion
de|grease
de|greases
de|greased
de|greas|ing
de|greaser +s
de|gree +s
de|gree|less
de|gres|sive
de haut en bas
de Hav|il|land,
Geof|frey
(English aircraft
designer)
de|hire
de|hires
de|hired
de|hir|ing
de|hisce
de|hisces
de|hisced
de|his|cing
de|his|cence
de|his|cent
de|his|tori|cise *Br.*
(use
dehistoricize)
de|his|tori|cises
de|his|tori|cised
de|his|tori|cis|ing
de|his|tori|cize
de|his|tori|cizes
de|his|tori|cized
de|his|tori|ciz|ing
de Hooch, Pieter
(Dutch painter)

de Hoogh, Pieter
(use de Hooch)
de¦horn +s +ed
+ing
de¦hu¦man¦isa¦tion
Br. (use
dehumanization)
de¦hu¦man¦ise Br.
(use dehumanize)
de¦hu¦man¦ises
de¦hu¦man¦ised
de¦hu¦man¦is¦ing
de¦hu¦man¦
iza¦tion
de¦hu¦man¦ize
de¦hu¦man¦izes
de¦hu¦man¦ized
de¦hu¦man¦iz¦ing
de¦hu¦midi¦fi¦
ca¦tion
de¦hu¦midi¦fier +s
de¦hu¦mid¦ify
de¦hu¦midi¦fies
de¦hu¦midi¦fied
de¦hu¦midi¦fy¦ing
de¦hy¦drate
de¦hy¦drates
de¦hy¦drated
de¦hy¦drat¦ing
de¦hy¦dra¦tion
de¦hy¦dra¦tor +s
de¦hydro¦gen¦ate
de¦hydro¦gen¦
ates
de¦hydro¦gen¦
ated
de¦hydro¦gen¦
at¦ing
de¦hydro¦gen¦
ation
Deia¦nira Greek
Mythology
de-ice
de-ices
de-iced
de-icing
de-icer +s
dei¦cide
deic¦tic +s
dei¦fi¦ca¦tion
dei¦form
deify
dei¦fies
dei¦fied
dei¦fy¦ing
Deigh¦ton, Len
(English writer)
deign +s +ed +ing
Dei gra¦tia
Dei¦mos (Greek
Mythology; moon
of Mars)

de-industrial¦isa¦
tion Br. (use de-
industrialization)
de-industrial¦iza¦
tion
dei¦nony|chus
dei¦nony|chuses
dei¦no|there +s
de¦insti|tu¦tion¦al|
isa|tion Br. (use
deinstitutionaliza-
tion)
de¦insti|tu¦tion¦al|
ise Br. (use
deinstitutional-
ize)
de¦insti|tu¦tion¦al|
ises
de¦insti|tu¦tion¦al|
ised
de¦insti|tu¦tion¦al|
is¦ing
de¦insti|tu¦tion¦al|
iza|tion
de¦insti|tu¦tion¦al|
ize
de¦insti|tu¦tion¦al|
izes
de¦insti|tu¦tion¦al|
ized
de¦insti|tu¦tion¦al|
iz¦ing
de¦ion|isa¦tion Br.
(use deionization)
de¦ion|ise Br. (use
deionize)
de¦ion|ises
de¦ion|ised
de¦ion|is¦ing
de¦ion|iser Br. +s
(use deionizer)
de¦ion|iza¦tion
de¦ion|ize
de¦ion|izes
de¦ion|ized
de¦ion|iz¦ing
de¦ion|izer +s
deip¦noso¦phist +s
Deir¦dre (Irish
Mythology; name)
deism
deist +s
de¦is¦tic
de¦is¦tic¦al
deity
de¦ities
déjà vu
de¦ject +s +ed
+ing
de¦ject|ed¦ly
de¦jec¦tion
de jure

Dek¦ker, Thomas
(English
dramatist)
dekko +s (look.
△deco)
de Klerk, F. W.
(South African
statesman)
de Koon|ing,
Wil¦lem (Dutch-
born American
painter)
de la Beche,
Henry (English
geologist)
De¦la|croix,
Eu¦gène (French
painter)
de¦laine
de la Mare,
Wal¦ter (English
writer)
De¦la|roche, Paul
(French painter)
de¦late
de¦lates
de¦lated
de¦lat¦ing
de¦la¦tion
de¦la¦tor +s
De¦lau|nay,
Rob¦ert (French
painter)
Delaunay-Terk,
Sonia (Russian-
born painter and
textile designer)
Dela|ware (state,
USA)
Dela|ware
plural Dela|ware
or Dela|wares
(American Indian)
delay +s +ed +ing
delayed-action
attributive
de¦lay¦er +s
del cre¦dere
dele
deles
deled
dele|ing
de¦lect|abil¦ity
de¦lect|able
de¦lect|ably
de¦lect|ation
del¦eg|able
dele|gacy
dele|ga¦cies
dele|gate
dele|gates

dele|gate (cont.)
dele|gated
dele|gat¦ing
dele|ga¦tion +s
dele|ga¦tor +s
de Len|clos,
Ninon (French
courtesan)
de¦lete
de¦letes
de¦leted
de¦let¦ing
dele|teri¦ous
dele|teri¦ous¦ly
de¦le¦tion +s
Del|font, Ber|nard
(Lord Delfont,
Russian-born
British impresario)
Delft (city, the
Netherlands)
delft (china)
delft|ware
Delhi (capital of
India)
deli +s
(= delicatessen)
Delia
Delian +s
de¦lib|er¦ate
de¦lib|er¦ates
de¦lib|er¦ated
de¦lib|er¦at¦ing
de¦lib|er¦ate¦ly
de¦lib|er¦ate|ness
de¦lib|er¦ation +s
de¦lib|era¦tive
de¦lib|era¦tive¦ly
de¦lib|era¦tive|
ness
de¦lib|era¦tor +s
De¦libes, Léo
(French
composer)
deli|cacy
deli|ca¦cies
deli|cate
deli|cate¦ly
deli|cate|ness
deli|ca¦tes¦sen +s
de¦li¦cious
de¦li¦cious¦ly
de¦li¦cious|ness
de¦lict +s
de¦light +s +ed
+ing
de¦light|ed¦ly
de¦light|ful
de¦light|ful¦ly
de¦light|ful|ness
De¦li¦lah Bible

de|limit +s +ed
+ing
de|limi|tate
de|limi|tates
de|limi|tated
de|limi|tat|ing
de|limi|ta|tion +s
de|lim|it|er +s
de|lin|eate
de|lin|eates
de|lin|eated
de|lin|eat|ing
de|lin|ea|tion +s
de|lin|ea|tor +s
de|lin|quency
de|lin|quen|cies
de|lin|quent +s
de|lin|quent|ly
deli|quesce
deli|quesces
deli|quesced
deli|ques|cing
deli|ques|cence
deli|ques|cent
de|li|ri|ous
de|li|ri|ous|ly
de|lir|ium +s
de|lir|ium
tre|mens
De|lius, Fred|erick
(English
composer)
de|liver +s +ed
+ing
de|liver|able +s
de|liv|er|ance +s
de|liv|er|er +s
de|liv|ery
de|liv|er|ies
dell +s
Della
Della Crus|can +s
della Fran|cesca,
Piero (Italian
painter)
della Quer|cia,
Ja|copo (Italian
sculptor)
della Rob|bia,
Luca (Florentine
sculptor)
de|lo|cal|isa|tion
Br. (use
delocalization)
de|lo|cal|ise Br.
(use delocalize)
de|lo|cal|ises
de|lo|cal|ised
de|lo|cal|is|ing
de|lo|cal|iza|tion
de|lo|cal|ize
de|lo|cal|izes

de|lo|cal|ize (cont.)
de|lo|cal|ized
de|lo|cal|iz|ing
De|lores also
Do|lores
De|lors, Jacques
(French
statesman)
Delos (Greek
island)
de|louse
de|louses
de|loused
de|lous|ing
Del|phi (city and
site, ancient
Greece)
Del|phian +s
Del|phic
Del|phine
del|phin|ium +s
del|phin|oid +s
del Sarto, An|drea
(Italian painter)
delta +s
del|ta|ic
del|ti|olo|gist +s
del|ti|ology
del|toid +s
de|lude
de|ludes
de|luded
de|lud|ing
de|luder +s
del|uge
del|uges
del|uged
del|uging
de|lu|sion +s
de|lu|sion|al
de|lu|sive
de|lu|sive|ly
de|lu|sive|ness
de|lu|sory
de|lus|ter Am. +s
+ed +ing
de|lustre Br.
de|lustres
de|lustred
de|lus|tring
de luxe
delve
delves
delved
delv|ing
delver +s
delv|ing +s
de|mag|net|
isa|tion Br. (use
demagnetization)
de|mag|net|ise Br.
(use

de|mag|net|ise
(cont.)
demagnetize)
de|mag|net|ises
de|mag|net|ised
de|mag|net|is|ing
de|mag|net|iser Br.
+s (use
demagnetizer)
de|mag|net|
iza|tion
de|mag|net|ize
de|mag|net|izes
de|mag|net|ized
de|mag|net|iz|ing
de|mag|net|izer +s
dema|gog|ic
dema|gogue +s
dema|goguery
dema|gogy
de|mand +s +ed
+ing
de|mand|able
de|mand|ant +s
de|mand|er +s
de|mand|ing|ly
demand-led
adjective
de|mant|oid +s
de|mar|cate
de|mar|cates
de|mar|cated
de|mar|cat|ing
de|mar|ca|tion +s
de|mar|ca|tor +s
dé|marche +s
de|materi|al|
isa|tion Br. (use
dematerializa-
tion)
de|materi|al|ise Br.
(use
dematerialize)
de|materi|al|ises
de|materi|al|ised
de|materi|al|
is|ing
de|materi|al|
iza|tion
de|materi|al|ize
de|materi|al|izes
de|materi|al|ized
de|materi|al|
iz|ing
de Mau|pas|sant,
Guy (French
writer)
Dema|vend (use
Damavand)
deme +s (political
division, Greece;
Biology. △ deem)

de|mean +s +ed
+ing
de|meanor Am. +s
de|mean|our Br. +s
de' Med|ici
(Florentine family)
de' Med|ici,
Cath|er|ine
(French queen)
de' Med|ici,
Cos|imo
(Florentine
statesman and
banker)
de' Med|ici,
Gio|vanni (Pope
Leo X)
de' Med|ici,
Lor|enzo
(Florentine
statesman and
scholar)
de' Med|ici, Maria
(Italian name for
Marie de
Médicis)
de Mé|di|cis,
Marie (French
queen)
De|melza
de|ment +s
de|men|ted
de|men|ted|ly
de|men|ted|ness
dé|menti +s
de|men|tia
de|men|tia
prae|cox
Dem|er|ara (river,
Guyana)
dem|er|ara (sugar)
de|merge
de|merges
de|merged
de|mer|ging
de|mer|ger +s
de|merit +s
de|meri|tori|ous
de|mer|sal
de|mesne +s
Dem|eter Greek
Mythology
demi|god +s
demi|god|dess
demi|god|desses
demi|john +s
de|mili|tar|isa|tion
Br. (use
demilitarization)
de|mili|tar|ise Br.
(use demilitarize)
de|mili|tar|ises

de|mili|tar|ise
(*cont.*)
  de|mili|tar|ised
  de|mili|tar|is|ing
de|mili|tar|iza|tion
de|mili|tar|ize
  de|mili|tar|izes
  de|mili|tar|ized
  de|mili|tar|iz|ing
de Mille, Cecil B.
(American film
producer and
director)
demi-mondaine +s
demi-monde
de|min|er|al|
  isa|tion *Br.* (use
  demineralization)
de|min|er|al|ise *Br.*
  (use
  demineralize)
  de|min|er|al|ises
  de|min|er|al|ised
  de|min|er|al|
    is|ing
de|min|er|al|
  iza|tion
de|min|er|al|ize
  de|min|er|al|izes
  de|min|er|al|ized
  de|min|er|al|
    iz|ing
demi-pension
demi|rep +s
de|mise
  de|mises
  de|mised
  de|mis|ing
demi|semi|quaver
  +s
de|mis|sion
de|mist +s +ed
  +ing
de|mist|er +s
demit
  de|mits
  de|mit|ted
  de|mit|ting
demi|tasse +s
demi|urge +s
demi|ur|gic
demi-vierge +s
Demme,
  Jona|than
  (American film
  director)
demo +s
demob
  de|mobs
  de|mobbed
  de|mob|bing

de|mo|bil|isa|tion
  Br. (use
  demobilization)
de|mo|bil|ise *Br.*
  (use demobilize)
  de|mo|bil|ises
  de|mo|bil|ised
  de|mo|bil|is|ing
de|mo|bil|iza|tion
de|mo|bil|ize
  de|mo|bil|izes
  de|mo|bil|ized
  de|mo|bil|iz|ing
dem|oc|racy
  dem|oc|ra|cies
Demo|crat +s
  (supporter of US
  Democratic Party)
demo|crat +s
Demo|crat|ic (of
  US political party)
demo|crat|ic
demo|crat|ic|al|ly
dem|oc|ra|tisa|
  tion *Br.* (use
  democratization)
dem|oc|ra|tise *Br.*
  (use democratize)
  dem|oc|ra|tises
  dem|oc|ra|tised
  dem|oc|ra|tis|ing
dem|oc|ra|tism
dem|oc|ra|
  tiza|tion
dem|oc|ra|tize
  dem|oc|ra|tizes
  dem|oc|ra|tized
  dem|oc|ra|tiz|ing
Dem|oc|ri|tus
  (Greek
  philosopher)
démodé
de|modu|late
  de|modu|lates
  de|modu|lated
  de|modu|lat|ing
de|modu|la|tion
de|modu|la|tor +s
dem|og|raph|er +s
demo|graph|ic
demo|graph|ical
demo|graph|ic|
  al|ly
demo|graph|ics
dem|og|raphy
de|mois|elle +s
de|mol|ish
  de|mol|ishes
  de|mol|ished
  de|mol|ish|ing
de|mol|ish|er +s
demo|li|tion +s

demo|li|tion|ist +s
demon +s
de|mon|et|isa|tion
  Br. (use
  demonetization)
de|mon|et|ise *Br.*
  (use demonetize)
  de|mon|et|ises
  de|mon|et|ised
  de|mon|et|is|ing
de|mon|et|iza|tion
de|mon|et|ize
  de|mon|et|izes
  de|mon|et|ized
  de|mon|et|iz|ing
de|mon|iac
de|mon|iac|al
de|mon|iac|al|ly
de|mon|ic
de|mon|isa|tion *Br.*
  (use
  demonization)
de|mon|ise *Br.* (use
  demonize)
  de|mon|ises
  de|mon|ised
  de|mon|is|ing
de|mon|ism
de|mon|iza|tion
de|mon|ize
  de|mon|izes
  de|mon|ized
  de|mon|iz|ing
de|mon|olatry
de|mono|logic|al
de|mon|olo|gist +s
de|mon|ology
de|mon|op|ol|ise
  Br. (use
  demonopolize)
  de|mon|op|ol|ises
  de|mon|op|ol|
    ised
de|mon|op|ol|
    is|ing
de|mon|op|ol|ize
  de|mon|op|ol|izes
  de|mon|op|ol|
    ized
de|mon|op|ol|
    iz|ing
dem|on|stra|bil|ity
dem|on|strable
dem|on|strably
dem|on|strate
  dem|on|strates
  dem|on|strated
  dem|on|strat|ing
dem|on|stra|tion
  +s
de|mon|
    stra|tion|al

de|mon|stra|tive
de|mon|
    stra|tive|ly
de|mon|stra|tive|
    ness
dem|on|stra|tor +s
de Mont|fort,
  Simon (English
  soldier)
de|mor|al|isa|tion
  Br. (use
  demoralization)
de|mor|al|ise *Br.*
  (use demoralize)
  de|mor|al|ises
  de|mor|al|ised
  de|mor|al|is|ing
de|moral|is|ing|ly
  Br. (use
  demoralizingly)
de|mor|al|iza|tion
de|mor|al|ize
  de|mor|al|izes
  de|mor|al|ized
  de|mor|al|iz|ing
de|moral|iz|ing|ly
De|mos|thenes
  (Athenian orator)
de|mote
  de|motes
  de|moted
  de|mot|ing
dem|ot|ic
de|mo|tion +s
de|mo|tiv|ate
  de|mo|tiv|ates
  de|mo|tiv|ated
  de|mo|tiv|at|ing
de|mo|tiv|ation
de|mount +s +ed
  +ing
de|mount|able
Demp|sey, Jack
  (American boxer)
de|mul|cent +s
demur
  de|murs
  de|murred
  de|mur|ring
de|mure
  de|murer
  de|mur|est
de|mure|ly
de|mure|ness
de|mur|rable
de|mur|rage +s
de|mur|ral +s
de|mur|rer +s
demy (paper size)
de|mys|ti|fi|ca|tion
de|mys|tify
  de|mys|ti|fies

de|mys|tify (cont.)
  de|mys|ti|fied
  de|mys|ti|fy|ing
de|myth|olo|gise
  Br. (use
  demythologize)
de|myth|olo|gises
de|myth|
      olo|gised
de|myth|
      olo|gis|ing
de|myth|olo|gize
de|myth|olo|gizes
de|myth|
      olo|gized
de|myth|
      olo|giz|ing
den +s
den|ar|ius
den|arii
den|ary (decimal.
  ⚠ deanery)
de|nation|al|
  isa|tion Br. (use
  denationalization)
de|nation|al|ise Br.
  (use
  denationalize)
de|nation|al|ises
de|nation|al|ised
de|nation|al|
      is|ing
de|nation|al|
      iza|tion
de|nation|al|ize
de|nation|al|izes
de|nation|al|ized
de|nation|al|
      iz|ing
de|natur|al|
  isa|tion Br. (use
  denaturalization)
de|natur|al|ise Br.
  (use
  denaturalize)
de|natur|al|ises
de|natur|al|ised
de|natur|al|is|ing
de|natur|al|
      iza|tion
de|natur|al|ize
de|natur|al|izes
de|natur|al|ized
de|natur|al|iz|ing
de|natur|ant +s
de|natur|ation
de|nature
de|natures
de|natured
de|natur|ing
de|nazi|fi|ca|tion

de|nazify
de|nazi|fies
de|nazi|fied
de|nazi|fy|ing
Den|bigh|shire
  (former county,
  Wales)
Dench, Judi
  (English actress)
den|drite +s
den|drit|ic
den|drit|ic|al|ly
den|dro|
    chrono|logic|al
den|dro|
    chron|olo|gist +s
den|dro|
    chron|ology
den|dro|gram +s
den|droid
den|dro|logic|al
den|drolo|gist +s
den|drol|ogy
dene +s (sandhill;
  vale. ⚠ dean)
Deneb (star)
dene-hole +s
de|nest +s +ed
  +ing
de-net
  de-nets
  de-netted
  de-netting
De|neuve,
  Cath|érine
  (French actress)
dengue
Deng Xiao|ping
  (Chinese
  statesman)
Den Haag
  (Dutch name for
  The Hague)
deni|abil|ity
deni|able
de|nial +s
de|nier +s (person
  who denies)
den|ier
  plural den|ier
  (unit)
deni|grate
deni|grates
deni|grated
deni|grat|ing
deni|gra|tion
deni|gra|tor +s
deni|gra|tory
denim +s
De Niro, Rob|ert
  (American actor)

Denis, Maur|ice
  (French painter)
Denis also Den|nis,
  Denys
Denis (Italian-born
  patron saint of
  France)
Den|ise
de|nitri|fi|ca|tion
de|nitrify
  de|nitri|fies
  de|nitri|fied
  de|nitri|fy|ing
deni|zen +s
deni|zen|ship
Den|mark
Den|mark Strait
  (shipping area, N.
  Atlantic)
Den|nis also Denis,
  Denys
de|nom|in|ate
  de|nom|in|ates
  de|nom|in|ated
  de|nom|in|at|ing
de|nom|in|ation
  +s
de|nom|in|ation|al
de|nom|in|ation|al|
    ism
de|nom|in|ation|al|
    ist +s
de|nom|ina|tive
de|nom|in|ator +s
de nos jours
de|nota|tion +s
de|nota|tive
de|note
  de|notes
  de|noted
  de|not|ing
de|noue|ment +s
de|nounce
  de|nounces
  de|nounced
  de|noun|cing
de|nounce|ment
  +s
de|noun|cer +s
de nou|veau
de novo
Den|pa|sar (city,
  Bali)
dense
  dens|er
  dens|est
dense|ly
dense|ness
densi|tom|eter +s
dens|ity
  dens|ities
dent +s +ed +ing

den|tal
den|tal|ise Br. (use
  dentalize)
den|tal|ises
den|tal|ised
den|tal|is|ing
den|ta|lium
den|ta|lia
den|tal|ize
den|tal|izes
den|tal|ized
den|tal|iz|ing
den|tate
den|ticle +s
den|ticu|late
den|ti|frice +s
den|til +s
  Architecture
denti|lin|gual
den|tinal
den|tine +s
den|tist +s
den|tis|try
den|ti|tion
den|ture +s
den|tur|ist +s
de|nuclear|isa|tion
  Br. (use
  denuclearization)
de|nuclear|ise Br.
  (use
  denuclearize)
de|nuclear|ises
de|nuclear|ised
de|nuclear|is|ing
de|nuclear|
    iza|tion
de|nuclear|ize
de|nuclear|izes
de|nuclear|ized
de|nuclear|iz|ing
de|nuda|tion
de|nuda|tive
de|nude
  de|nudes
  de|nuded
  de|nud|ing
de|numer|abil|ity
de|numer|able
de|numer|ably
de|nun|ci|ate
  de|nun|ci|ates
  de|nun|ci|ated
  de|nun|ci|at|ing
de|nun|ci|ation +s
de|nun|cia|tive
de|nun|ci|ator +s
de|nun|ci|atory
Den|ver (city, USA)
deny
  de|nies

deny (*cont.*)
 de¦nied
 deny¦ing
Denys (saint; use
 Denis)
Denys *also* Denis,
 Den¦nis
 (name)
Den¦zil
deoch an doris
deo¦dar +s
de|odor|ant +s
de|odor|isa|tion
 Br. (use
 deodorization)
de|odor|ise *Br.* (use
 deodorize)
 de|odor|ises
 de|odor|ised
 de|odor|is¦ing
de|odor|iser *Br.* +s
 (use deodorizer)
de|odor|iza|tion
de|odor|ize
 de|odor|izes
 de|odor|ized
 de|odor|iz¦ing
de|odor|izer +s
Deo gra¦tias
de¦ontic
de¦onto|logic¦al
de¦ontolo|gist +s
de¦ontol|ogy
Deo vol¦ente
de|oxy¦gen|ate
 de|oxy¦gen|ates
 de|oxy¦gen|ated
 de|oxy¦gen|at¦ing
de|oxy¦gen|ation
de|oxy|ribo|
 nucle¦ic
de|oxy|ri¦bose
De¦par|dieu,
 Gér¦ard (French
 actor)
de¦part +s +ed
 +ing
de¦part|ment +s
de¦part|men¦tal
de¦part|men¦tal
 isa¦tion *Br.* (use
 departmentaliza-
 tion)
de¦part|men¦tal|
 ise *Br.* (use
 departmentalize)
de¦part|men¦tal|
 ises
de¦part|men¦tal|
 ised
de¦part|men¦tal|
 is¦ing

de¦part|men¦tal|
 ism
de¦part|men¦tal|
 iza¦tion
de¦part|men¦tal|
 ize
de¦part|men¦tal|
 izes
de¦part|men¦tal|
 ized
de¦part|men¦tal|ly
de¦part|ure +s
de¦pas¦tur|age
de¦pas¦ture
 de¦pas¦tures
 de¦pas¦tured
 de¦pas¦tur|ing
dé|paysé male
dé¦pay|sée female
de¦pend +s +ed
 +ing
de¦pend|abil¦ity
de¦pend|able
de¦pend|able|ness
de¦pend|ably
de¦pend|ant *Br.* +s
 noun (*Am.*
 dependent)
de¦pend|ence
de¦pend|ency
 de¦pend|en¦cies
de¦pend|ent
 adjective
de¦pend|ent *Am.*
 +s *noun* (*Br.*
 dependant)
de¦pend|ent¦ly
de¦pend|ing
de¦per¦son|al|
 isa¦tion *Br.* (use
 depersonaliza-
 tion)
de¦per¦son|al|ise
 Br. (use
 depersonalize)
de¦per¦son|al|ises
de¦per¦son|al|ised
de¦per¦son|al|
 is¦ing
de¦per¦son|al|
 iza¦tion
de¦per¦son|al|ize
 de¦per¦son|al|izes
 de¦per¦son|al|ized
 de¦per¦son|al|
 iz¦ing
de¦pict +s +ed
 +ing
de¦pict¦er +s
de¦pic¦tion +s

de¦pict|ive
de¦pict|or +s (use
 depicter)
dep¦il|ate
 dep¦il|ates
 dep¦il|ated
 dep¦il|at¦ing
dep¦il|ation +s
de|pila|tory
 de|pila|tor¦ies
de Pisan,
 Chris|tine (Italian-
 born writer)
de Pizan,
 Chris|tine (use de
 Pisan)
de|plane
 de|planes
 de|planed
 de|plan¦ing
de|plete
 de|pletes
 de|pleted
 de|plet¦ing
de|ple¦tion +s
de|plor|able
de|plor|ably
de|plore
 de|plores
 de|plored
 de|plor¦ing
de|plor|ing¦ly
de|ploy +s +ed
 +ing
de¦ploy|ment +s
de|plume
 de|plumes
 de|plumed
 de|plum¦ing
de|polar|isa¦tion
 Br. (use
 depolarization)
de|polar|ise *Br.*
 (use depolarize)
 de|polar|ises
 de|polar|ised
 de|polar|is¦ing
de|polar|iza¦tion
de|polar|ize
 de|polar|izes
 de|polar|ized
 de|polar|iz¦ing
de|pol¦iti|cisa¦tion
 Br. (use
 depoliticization)
de|pol¦iti|cise *Br.*
 (use depoliticize)
 de|pol¦iti|cises
 de|pol¦iti|cised
 de|pol¦iti|cis¦ing
de|pol¦iti|ciza|tion
de|pol¦iti|cize
 de|pol¦iti|cizes

de|pol¦iti|cize
 (*cont.*)
 de|pol¦iti|cized
 de|pol¦iti|ciz¦ing
de|poly¦mer|
 isa¦tion *Br.* (use
 depolymeriza-
 tion)
de|poly¦mer|ise *Br.*
 (use
 depolymerize)
 de|poly¦mer|ises
 de|poly¦mer|ised
 de|poly¦mer|is¦ing
de|poly¦mer|
 iza¦tion
de|poly¦mer|ize
 de|poly¦mer|izes
 de|poly¦mer|ized
 de|poly¦mer|
 iz¦ing
de|pon¦ent +s
de|popu¦late
 de|popu¦lates
 de|popu¦lated
 de|popu¦lat¦ing
de|popu¦la¦tion
de¦port +s +ed
 +ing
de¦port|able
de¦port|ation +s
de¦port|ee +s
de¦port|ment +s
de¦pose
 de¦poses
 de¦posed
 de¦pos¦ing
de¦posit +s +ed
 +ing
de¦pos|it¦ary
 de¦pos|it¦ar¦ies
 (person.
 △ depository)
de¦pos|ition +s
de¦pos|ition|al
de¦pos|it¦or +s
de¦posi|tory
 de¦posi|tor¦ies
 (storehouse.
 △ depositary)
depot +s
dep¦rav|ation +s
 (perversion,
 corruption.
 △ deprivation)
de¦prave
 de¦praves
 de¦praved
 de¦prav¦ing
de¦prav|ity
 de¦prav|ities

dep|re|cate
  dep|re|cates
  dep|re|cated
  dep|re|cat|ing
  (disapprove of)
dep|re|cat|ing|ly
dep|re|ca|tion +s
dep|re|ca|tive
dep|re|ca|tor +s
dep|re|ca|tory
de|pre|ci|ate
  de|pre|ci|ates
  de|pre|ci|ated
  de|pre|ci|at|ing
  (lower in value;
  belittle)
de|pre|ci|at|ing|ly
de|pre|ci|ation +s
de|pre|ci|atory
dep|re|da|tion +s
dep|re|da|tor +s
dep|re|da|tory
de|press
  de|presses
  de|pressed
  de|press|ing
de|pres|sant +s
de|press|ible
de|press|ing|ly
de|pres|sion +s
de|pres|sive +s
de|pres|sor +s
  (muscle)
de|pres|sur|isa|
  tion Br. (use
  depressurization)
de|pres|sur|ise Br.
  (use
  depressurize)
de|pres|sur|ises
de|pres|sur|ised
de|pres|sur|is|ing
de|pres|sur|iza|
    tion
de|pres|sur|ize
de|pres|sur|izes
de|pres|sur|ized
de|pres|sur|iz|ing
De|prez, Jos|quin
  (use des Prez)
de|priv|able
de|prival
de|priv|ation +s
  (hardship, loss.
  ⚠ depravation)
de|prive
  de|prives
  de|prived
  de|priv|ing
de pro|fun|dis
depth +s
depth bomb +s

depth charge +s
depth|less
dep|ur|ate
  dep|ur|ates
  dep|ur|ated
  dep|ur|at|ing
dep|ur|ation
de|pura|tive +s
de|pura|tor +s
depu|ta|tion +s
de|pute
  de|putes
  de|puted
  de|put|ing
depu|tise Br. (use
  deputize)
depu|tises
depu|tised
depu|tis|ing
depu|tize
  depu|tizes
  depu|tized
  depu|tiz|ing
dep|uty
  dep|uties
dep|uty|ship +s
De Quin|cey,
  Thomas (English
  writer)
de|racin|ate
  de|racin|ates
  de|racin|ated
  de|racin|at|ing
de|racin|ation
de|rail +s +ed +ing
de|rail|leur +s
de|rail|ment +s
De|rain, André
  (French artist)
de|range
  de|ranges
  de|ranged
  de|ran|ging
de|range|ment +s
de|rate
  de|rates
  de|rated
  de|rat|ing
de|ration +s +ed
  +ing
Der|bent (city,
  Dagestan)
Derby
  Der|bies
  (city, England;
  horse race.
  ⚠ Darby)
derby
  der|bies
  (shoe. ⚠ darbies)
Derby Day

Derby|shire
  (county, England)
de|rec|og|nise Br.
  (use derecognize)
de|rec|og|nises
de|rec|og|nised
de|rec|og|nis|ing
de|rec|og|ni|tion
de|rec|og|nize
  de|rec|og|nizes
  de|rec|og|nized
  de|rec|og|niz|ing
de|regis|ter +s +ed
  +ing
de|regis|tra|tion
  +s
de règle
de|regu|late
  de|regu|lates
  de|regu|lated
  de|regu|lat|ing
de|regu|la|tion
Derek also Der|rick
dere|lict +s
dere|lic|tion
de|re|qui|si|tion
de|res|trict +s +ed
  +ing
de|res|tric|tion +s
de|ride
  de|rides
  de|rided
  de|rid|ing
de|rider +s
de|rid|ing|ly
de-rig
  de-rigs
  de-rigged
  de-rigging
de ri|gueur
de|ris|ible
de|ri|sion
de|ri|sive
de|ri|sive|ly
de|ri|sive|ness
de|ri|sory
de|riv|able
der|iv|ation +s
der|iv|ation|al
de|riva|tive +s
de|riva|tive|ly
de|rive
  de|rives
  de|rived
  de|riv|ing
derm
derma
der|mal
derma|titis
der|ma|to|glyph|ic
der|ma|to|glyph|ic|
    al|ly

der|ma|to|
    glyph|ics
der|ma|to|logic|al
der|ma|to|logic|
    al|ly
derma|tolo|gist +s
derma|tol|ogy
der|mic
der|mis
Der|mot
der|nier cri
dero|gates
dero|gated
dero|gat|ing
dero|ga|tion
de|roga|tive
de|roga|tor|ily
de|roga|tory
Der|rick also Derek
  (name)
der|rick +s (crane)
Der|rida, Jacques
  (French
  philospher and
  critic)
Der|rid|ean
der|rière +s
derring-do
der|rin|ger +s
der|ris
  plural der|ris
Derry
  (= Londonderry,
  town; name)
derry (in 'have a
  derry on
  someone')
derv (fuel oil)
der|vish
  der|vishes
de|sal|in|ate
  de|sal|in|ates
  de|sal|in|ated
  de|sal|in|at|ing
de|sal|in|ation
de|sal|in|isa|tion
  Br. (use
  desalinization)
de|sal|in|ise Br.
  (use desalinize)
de|sal|in|ises
de|sal|in|ised
de|sal|in|is|ing
de|sal|in|iza|tion
de|sal|in|ize
  de|sal|in|izes
  de|sal|in|ized
  de|sal|in|iz|ing
de|salt +s +ed
  +ing
des|apare|cido +s

de|scale
  de|scales
  de|scaled
  de|scal|ing
des|cant +s +ed
  +ing
Des|cartes, René
  (French
  philosopher and
  mathematician)
des|cend +s +ed
  +ing
des|cend|ant +s
  noun
des|cend|ent
  adjective
des|cend|er +s
des|cend|ible
des|cent +s (act of
  descending.
  △ dissent)
de|scram|ble
  de|scram|bles
  de|scram|bled
  de|scram|bling
de|scram|bler +s
de|scrib|able
de|scribe
  de|scribes
  de|scribed
  de|scrib|ing
de|scriber +s
de|scrip|tion +s
de|scrip|tive
de|scrip|tive|ly
de|scrip|tive|ness
de|scrip|tor +s
des|cry
  des|cries
  des|cried
  des|cry|ing
Des|de|mona
dese|crate
  dese|crates
  dese|crated
  dese|crat|ing
dese|cra|tion +s
dese|cra|tor +s
de|seed +s +ed
  +ing
de|seed|er +s
de|seg|re|gate
  de|seg|re|gates
  de|seg|re|gated
  de|seg|re|gat|ing
de|seg|re|ga|tion
de|select +s +ed
  +ing
de|selec|tion
de|sen|si|tisa|tion
  Br. (use
  desensitization)

de|sen|si|tise *Br.*
  (use desensitize)
  de|sen|si|tises
  de|sen|si|tised
  de|sen|si|tis|ing
de|sen|si|tiser *Br.*
  +s (use
  desensitizer)
de|sen|si|tiza|tion
de|sen|si|tize
  de|sen|si|tizes
  de|sen|si|tized
  de|sen|si|tiz|ing
de|sen|si|tizer +s
des|ert +s +ed
  +ing (barren
  region; abandon;
  recompense.
  △ dessert)
de|sert|er +s
desert|ifi|ca|tion
de|ser|tion +s
desert rat +s
de|serve
  de|serves
  de|served
  de|serv|ing
de|served|ly
de|served|ness
de|serv|er +s
de|serv|ing|ly
de|serv|ing|ness
desex
  de|sexes
  de|sexed
  de|sex|ing
de|sexu|al|isa|tion
  Br. (use
  desexualization)
de|sexu|al|ise *Br.*
  (use desexualize)
  de|sexu|al|ises
  de|sexu|al|ised
  de|sexu|al|is|ing
de|sexu|al|iza|tion
de|sexu|al|ize
  de|sexu|al|izes
  de|sexu|al|ized
  de|sexu|al|iz|ing
dés|ha|billé
De Sica, Vit|torio
  (Italian film
  director and actor)
des|ic|cant +s
des|ic|cate
  des|ic|cates
  des|ic|cated
  des|ic|cat|ing
des|ic|ca|tion
des|ic|ca|tive
des|ic|ca|tor +s

de|sid|er|ate
  de|sid|er|ates
  de|sid|er|ated
  de|sid|er|at|ing
de|sid|era|tive
de|sid|er|atum
  de|sid|er|ata
de|sign +s +ed
  +ing
des|ig|nate
  des|ig|nates
  des|ig|nated
  des|ig|nat|ing
des|ig|na|tion +s
des|ig|na|tor +s
de|sign|ed|ly
de|sign|er +s
de|sign|ing|ly
de|sir|abil|ity
de|sir|able +s
de|sir|able|ness
de|sir|ably
de|sire
  de|sires
  de|sired
  de|sir|ing
De|sir|ée
de|sir|ous
de|sist +s +ed +ing
desk +s
desk-bound
de|skill +s +ed
  +ing
desk|top +s
des|man +s
des|mid +s
Des Moines (city,
  USA)
Des|mond
deso|late
  deso|lates
  deso|lated
  deso|lat|ing
deso|late|ly
deso|late|ness
deso|la|tion +s
deso|la|tor +s
de|sorb +s +ed
  +ing
de|sorb|ent +s
de|sorp|tion +s
des|pair +s +ed
  +ing
des|pair|ing|ly
des|patch (use
  dispatch)
  des|patches
  des|patched
  des|patch|ing
des|patch box
  des|patch boxes

des|patch box
  (*cont.*)
  (use dispatch
  box)
des|patch|er +s
  (use dispatcher)
des|patch rider
  des|patch riders
  (use dispatch
  rider)
des|per|ado
  des|per|adoes
des|per|ate
des|per|ate|ly
des|per|ate|ness
des|per|ation
de|spic|able
de|spic|ably
de Spin|oza,
  Bar|uch (Dutch
  philosopher)
des|pise
  des|pises
  des|pised
  des|pis|ing
des|piser +s
des|pite
des|pite|ful
de|spoil +s +ed
  +ing
de|spoil|er
de|spoil|ment
de|spoli|ation
des|pond
des|pond|ence
des|pond|ency
des|pond|ent
des|pond|ent|ly
des|pot +s
des|pot|ic
des|pot|ic|al|ly
des|pot|ism
des Prés, Jos|quin
  (use des Prez)
des Prez, Jos|quin
  (Flemish
  composer)
des|quam|ate
  des|quam|ates
  des|quam|ated
  des|quam|at|ing
des|quam|ation
des|quam|a|tive
des|quama|tory
des res
  plural des res
Des|sau (city,
  Germany)
des|sert +s (sweet
  course. △ desert)
des|sert|spoon +s

des|sert|spoon|ful
+s
de|sta|bil|isa|tion
Br. (use
destabilization)
de|sta|bil|ise Br.
(use destabilize)
de|sta|bil|ises
de|sta|bil|ised
de|sta|bil|is|ing
de|sta|bil|iza|tion
de|sta|bil|ize
de|sta|bil|izes
de|sta|bil|ized
de|sta|bil|iz|ing
de-stalin|isa|tion
Br. (use de-
stalinization)
de-stalin|iza|tion
De Stijl (Dutch art
movement)
des|tin|ation +s
des|tine
des|tines
des|tined
des|tin|ing
des|tiny
des|tinies
des|ti|tute +s
des|ti|tu|tion
de|stock +s +ed
+ing
dest|rier +s
des|troy +s +ed
+ing
des|troy|able
des|troy|er +s
de|struct +s +ed
+ing
de|struct|ibil|ity
de|struct|ible
de|struc|tion +s
de|struc|tive
de|struc|tive|ly
de|struc|tive|ness
de|struc|tor +s
de|sue|tude
de|sul|fur|iza|tion
Am.
de|sul|fur|ize Am.
de|sul|fur|izes
de|sul|fur|ized
de|sul|fur|iz|ing
de|sul|phur|
isa|tion Br. (use
desulphurization)
de|sul|phur|ise Br.
(use
desulphurize)
de|sul|phur|ises
de|sul|phur|ised
de|sul|phur|is|ing

de|sul|phur|
iza|tion Br.
de|sul|phur|ize Br.
de|sul|phur|izes
de|sul|phur|ized
de|sul|phur|iz|ing
des|ul|tor|ily
des|ul|tori|ness
des|ul|tory
de|tach
de|taches
de|tached
de|tach|ing
de|tach|able
de|tach|ed|ly
de|tach|ment
de|tail +s +ed +ing
de|tain +s +ed
+ing
de|tain|ee +s
de|tain|er +s
de|tain|ment
de|tect +s +ed
+ing
de|tect|able
de|tect|ably
de|tec|tion +s
de|tect|ive +s
de|tect|or +s
de|tent +s
(mechanical
catch)
dé|tente +s
de|ten|tion +s
deter
de|ters
de|terred
de|ter|ring
de|ter|gent +s
de|teri|or|ate
de|teri|or|ates
de|teri|or|ated
de|teri|or|at|ing
de|teri|or|ation +s
de|teri|ora|tive
de|ter|ment
de|ter|min|able
de|ter|min|acy
de|ter|min|ant +s
de|ter|min|ate
de|ter|min|ate|ly
de|ter|min|ate|
ness
de|ter|min|ation
+s
de|ter|mina|tive
de|ter|mina|tive|ly
de|ter|mine
de|ter|mines
de|ter|mined
de|ter|min|ing
de|ter|mined|ly

de|ter|mined|ness
de|ter|miner +s
de|ter|min|ism
de|ter|min|ist +s
de|ter|min|is|tic
de|ter|min|is|tic|
al|ly
de|ter|rence
de|ter|rent +s
de|test +s +ed
+ing
de|test|able
de|test|ably
de|test|ation
de|test|er +s
de|throne
de|thrones
de|throned
de|thron|ing
de|throne|ment
det|on|ate
det|on|ates
det|on|ated
det|on|at|ing
det|on|ation +s
det|ona|tive
det|on|ator +s
de|tour +s +ed
+ing
detox
de|toxes
de|toxed
de|tox|ing
de|toxi|cate
de|toxi|cates
de|toxi|cated
de|toxi|cat|ing
de|toxi|ca|tion
de|toxi|fi|ca|tion
de|tox|ify
de|toxi|fies
de|toxi|fied
de|toxi|fy|ing
de|tract +s +ed
+ing
de|trac|tion +s
de|tract|ive
de|tract|or +s
de|train +s +ed
+ing
de|train|ment
de|trib|al|isa|tion
Br. (use
detribalization)
de|trib|al|ise Br.
(use detribalize)
de|trib|al|ises
de|trib|al|ised
de|trib|al|is|ing
de|trib|al|iza|tion
de|trib|al|ize
de|trib|al|izes

de|trib|al|ize
(cont.)
de|trib|al|ized
de|trib|al|iz|ing
det|ri|ment
det|ri|men|tal
det|ri|men|tal|ly
de|trital
de|trited
de|tri|tion
de|tritus
De|troit (city, USA)
de trop
de Troyes,
Chré|tien (French
poet)
Det|tol Propr.
de|tumes|cence
de|tune
de|tunes
de|tuned
de|tun|ing
Deu|cal|ion Greek
Mythology
deuce +s
deuced
deuced|ly
deus ex mach|ina
deu|ter|ag|on|ist
+s
deu|ter|ate
deu|ter|ates
deu|ter|ated
deu|ter|at|ing
deu|ter|ation
deu|ter|ium
deu|tero|
canon|ic|al
Deutero-Isaiah
(Old Testament
author)
deu|teron +s
Deu|tero|nom|ic
Deu|tero|nom|ical
Deu|ter|on|om|ist
+s
Deu|ter|on|omy
Deutsch|mark +s
deut|zia +s
Dev, Kapil (Indian
cricketer)
deva +s (divine
being)
de Val|era, Eamon
(Irish statesman)
de Val|ois,
Nin|ette (Irish
dancer and
choreographer)
de|valu|ation +s
de|value
de|values

de|value (*cont.*)
  de|valued
  de|valu|ing
Deva|nag|ari
dev|as|tate
  dev|as|tates
  dev|as|tated
  dev|as|tat|ing
dev|as|tat|ing|ly
dev|as|ta|tion +s
dev|as|ta|tor +s
de|vein +s +ed
  +ing
de|velop +s +ed
  +ing
de|vel|op|able
de|vel|op|er +s
de|vel|op|ment +s
de|vel|op|men|tal
de|vel|op|
    men|tal|ly
Devi *Hinduism*
de|vi|ance
de|vi|ancy
  de|vi|an|cies
de|vi|ant +s
de|vi|ate
  de|vi|ates
  de|vi|ated
  de|vi|at|ing
de|vi|ation +s
de|vi|ation|al
de|vi|ation|ism
de|vi|ation|ist +s
de|vi|ator +s
de|vi|atory
de|vice +s
devil
  dev|ils
  dev|illed *Br.*
  dev|iled *Am.*
  dev|il|ling *Br.*
  dev|il|ing *Am.*
devil|dom
devil|fish
  plural devil|fish *or*
  devil|fishes
devil|ish
devil|ish|ly
devil|ish|ness
devil|ism
devil-may-care
devil|ment +s
dev|il|ry
  dev|il|ries
devil's ad|vo|cate
  +s
devil's bit +s
devil's coach-
  horse +s
devil's darn|ing
  nee|dle +s

devil's dozen +s
Devil's Island (off
  coast of French
  Guiana)
devils-on-
  horseback
de|vi|ous
de|vi|ous|ly
de|vi|ous|ness
de|vis|able
  (able to be devised.
  △ divisible)
de|vise
  de|vises
  de|vised
  de|vis|ing
de|visee +s
de|viser +s
  (inventor.
  △ devisor,
  divisor)
de|visor +s (person
  leaving property
  to another.
  △ deviser,
  divisor)
de|vi|tal|isa|tion
  Br. (use
  devitalization)
de|vi|tal|ise *Br.*
  (use devitalize)
  de|vi|tal|ises
  de|vi|tal|ised
  de|vi|tal|is|ing
de|vi|tal|iza|tion
de|vi|tal|ize
  de|vi|tal|izes
  de|vi|tal|ized
  de|vi|tal|iz|ing
de|vit|ri|fi|ca|tion
de|vit|ri|fy
  de|vit|ri|fies
  de|vit|ri|fied
  de|vit|ri|fy|ing
de|void
de|voir +s
de|vo|lute
  de|vo|lutes
  de|vo|luted
  de|vo|lut|ing
de|vo|lu|tion +s
de|vo|lu|tion|ary
de|vo|lu|tion|ist +s
de|volve
  de|volves
  de|volved
  de|volv|ing
de|volve|ment +s
Devon (county,
  England)
Dev|on|ian +s
Dev|on|shire
  (= Devon)

dévot +s *male*
de|vote
  de|votes
  de|voted
  de|vot|ing
dé|vote +s *female*
de|voted|ly
de|voted|ness
de|votee +s
de|vote|ment
de|vo|tion +s
de|vo|tion|al
de|vour +s +ed
  +ing
de|vour|er +s
de|vour|ing|ly
de|vout
de|vout|ly
de|vout|ness
Devoy, Susan
  (New Zealand
  squash player)
de Vries, Hugo
  (Dutch plant
  physiologist)
dew +s +ed +ing
  (moisture. △ due)
dewan +s
Dewar, James
  (Scottish physicist
  and chemist)
dewar +s (flask)
de|water +s +ed
  +ing
dew|berry
  dew|berries
dew|claw +s
dew|drop +s
Dewey (library
  system)
Dewey, John
  (American
  philosopher)
Dewey, Maur|ice
  (American
  librarian)
dew|fall +s
Dewi (name; for
  Welsh saint, use
  David)
dew|ily
dewi|ness
dew|lap +s
de|worm +s +ed
  +ing
dew point +s
dew-pond +s
Dews|bury (town,
  England)
dewy
dewy-eyed
Dexe|drine *Propr.*
Dex|ter (name)

dex|ter +s
  (*Heraldry* on the
  right; cattle)
dex|ter|ity
dex|ter|ous
dex|ter|ous|ly
dex|ter|ous|ness
dex|tral
dex|tral|ity
dex|tral|ly
dex|tran +s
dex|trin
dex|tro|rota|tion
dex|tro|rota|tory
dex|trorse
dex|trose
dex|trous (use
  dexterous)
dex|trous|ly (use
  dexterously)
dex|trous|ness
  (use
  dexterousness)
Dhaka (capital of
  Bangladesh)
dhal +s
Dhan|bad (city,
  India)
dharma
Dharuk
Dhau|la|giri
  (mountain,
  Himalayas)
dhobi +s (washer-
  man. △ dobe)
dhobi itch
dhobi's itch
Dho|far (province,
  Oman)
dhole
  plural dhole *or*
  dholes
  (dog. △ dole)
dhoti +s
dhow +s
dhurra +s (use
  durra)
Di (woman's name)
dia|base +s
dia|betes
dia|bet|ic +s
diab|lerie
dia|bol|ic
dia|bol|ical
dia|bol|ic|al|ly
di|ab|ol|ise *Br.* (use
  diabolize)
  di|ab|ol|ises
  di|ab|ol|ised
  di|ab|ol|is|ing
di|ab|ol|ism
di|ab|ol|ist +s

di¦ab¦ol¦ize
  di¦ab¦ol¦izes
  di¦ab¦ol¦ized
  di¦ab¦ol¦iz¦ing
di¦ab¦olo+s
dia¦chron¦ic
dia¦chron¦ic¦al¦ly
di¦achron¦ism
di¦achron¦is¦tic
di¦achron¦ous
di¦achrony
di¦ac¦onal
di¦ac¦on¦ate+s
dia¦crit¦ic+s
dia¦crit¦ic¦al
di¦adel¦phous
dia¦dem+s
dia¦demed
Dia¦dochi
  (Macedonian
  generals)
di¦aer¦esis Br.
  di¦aer¦eses
  (Am. dieresis)
dia¦gen¦esis
Di¦ag¦hi¦lev,
  Ser¦gei
  Pav¦lo¦vich
  (Russian ballet
  impresario)
diag¦nos¦able
diag¦nose
  diag¦noses
  diag¦nosed
  diag¦nos¦ing
diag¦no¦sis
  diag¦no¦ses
diag¦nos¦tic+s
diag¦nos¦tic¦al¦ly
diag¦nos¦ti¦cian+s
diag¦nos¦tics
di¦ag¦onal+s
di¦ag¦onal¦ly
dia¦gram
  dia¦grams
  dia¦grammed Br.
  dia¦gramed Am.
  dia¦gram¦ming Br.
  dia¦gram¦ing Am.
dia¦gram¦mat¦ic
dia¦gram¦mat¦ic¦
      al¦ly
dia¦gram¦ma¦tise
  Br. (use
  diagrammatize)
  dia¦gram¦ma¦tises
  dia¦gram¦
      ma¦tised
  dia¦gram¦
      ma¦tis¦ing
dia¦gram¦ma¦tize
  dia¦gram¦ma¦tizes

dia¦gram¦ma¦tize
  (cont.)
  dia¦gram¦
      ma¦tized
  dia¦gram¦
      ma¦tiz¦ing
dia¦grid+s
dia¦kin¦esis
dial
  dials
  dialled Br.
  dialed Am.
  dial¦ling Br.
  dial¦ing Am.
dia¦lect+s
dia¦lect¦al
dia¦lect¦ic+s
dia¦lect¦ic¦al
dia¦lect¦ic¦al¦ly
dia¦lect¦ician+s
dia¦lect¦ics
dia¦lect¦olo¦gist+s
dia¦lect¦ology
dial¦er Am. +s
dial¦ler Br. +s
dia¦log Am. +s
dia¦logic
dialo¦gist+s
dia¦logue Br. +s
dia¦lyse Br.
  dia¦lyses
  dia¦lysed
  dia¦lys¦ing
dia¦ly¦sis
  dia¦ly¦ses
dia¦lyt¦ic
dia¦lyze Am.
  dia¦lyzes
  dia¦lyzed
  dia¦lyz¦ing
dia¦mag¦net¦ic+s
dia¦mag¦net¦ic¦
      al¦ly
dia¦mag¦net¦ism
dia¦manté
dia¦man¦tifer¦ous
dia¦mant¦ine
diam¦eter+s
diam¦etral
dia¦met¦ric
dia¦met¦ric¦al
dia¦met¦ric¦al¦ly
dia¦mond+s
dia¦mond¦back+s
diamond-bird+s
dia¦mond¦ifer¦ous
Diana (Roman
  Mythology;
  Princess of Wales)
di¦an¦drous
Diane also Di¦anne
Dia¦net¦ics

di¦an¦thus
  plural di¦an¦thus
  or di¦an¦thuses
dia¦pa¦son+s
dia¦pause+s
di¦aper+s +ed
  +ing (nappy;
  pattern)
di¦aph¦an¦ous
di¦aph¦an¦ous¦ly
dia¦phor¦esis
dia¦phor¦et¦ic+s
dia¦phragm+s
dia¦phrag¦mat¦ic
dia¦pir+s Geology
dia¦posi¦tive+s
di¦arch¦al
di¦arch¦ic
di¦archy
  di¦arch¦ies
diar¦ise Br. (use
  diarize)
  diar¦ises
  diar¦ised
  diar¦is¦ing
diar¦ist+s
diar¦is¦tic
diar¦ize
  diar¦izes
  diar¦ized
  diar¦iz¦ing
diar¦rhea Am.
diar¦rhe¦al Am.
diar¦rhe¦ic Am.
diar¦rhoea Br.
diar¦rhoe¦al Br.
diar¦rhoe¦ic Br.
diary
  diar¦ies
Dias,
  Bar¦tolo¦meu
  (Portuguese
  explorer)
dia¦scope+s
Dias¦pora (of Jews)
dias¦pora+s
  (generally)
dia¦stase+s
dia¦stasic
dia¦stat¦ic
dia¦stema+s
dia¦stole+s
dia¦stol¦ic
dia¦ther¦mancy
dia¦ther¦man¦ous
dia¦ther¦mic
dia¦ther¦mous
dia¦thermy
di¦ath¦esis
  di¦ath¦eses
dia¦tom+s
dia¦tom¦aceous

di¦atom¦ic
di¦atom¦ite
dia¦ton¦ic+s
dia¦tribe+s
Diaz,
  Bar¦tolo¦meu
  (use Dias)
Díaz, Por¦firio
  (Mexican
  president)
di¦aze¦pam+s
diazo
di¦azo¦type+s
dib
  dibs
  dibbed
  dib¦bing
di¦basic
dib¦ber+s
dib¦ble
  dib¦bles
  dib¦bled
  dib¦bling
  dibs
dice
  plural dice
  (noun; also plural
  of die)
dice
  dices
  diced
di¦cing
  verb
dicer+s
dicey
dici¦er
dici¦est
di¦cho¦tom¦ic
di¦chot¦om¦ise Br.
  (use dichotomize)
  di¦chot¦om¦ises
  di¦chot¦om¦ised
  di¦chot¦om¦is¦ing
di¦chot¦om¦ize
  di¦chot¦om¦izes
  di¦chot¦om¦ized
  di¦chot¦om¦iz¦ing
di¦chot¦om¦ous
di¦chot¦omy
  di¦choto¦mies
di¦chro¦ic
di¦chro¦ism
di¦chro¦mat¦ic
di¦chro¦ma¦tism
Dick (name)
dick+s (detective
  etc.)
dicken
Dick¦ens, Charles
  (English writer)
dick¦ens (in 'what
  the dickens?' etc.)

Dick¦ens¦ian +s
Dick¦ens¦ian¦ly
dicker +s +ed +ing
dick¦er¦er +s
dick¦head +s
   (*coarse slang*)
Dickie *also* Dicky
Dick¦in¦son, Emily
   (American poet)
Dicky *also* Dickie
   (name)
dicky
   dick¦ies
   dick¦ier
   dicki¦est
   (shirt-front; seat;
   unsound)
dicky bird +s
dicot +s
di¦coty¦ledon +s
di¦coty¦ledon¦ous
di¦crot¦ic
dicta
Dic¦ta¦phone *Propr.*
dic¦tate
   dic¦tates
   dic¦tated
   dic¦tat¦ing
dic¦ta¦tion +s
dic¦ta¦tor +s
dic¦ta¦tor¦ial
dic¦ta¦tori¦al¦ly
dic¦ta¦tori¦ship +s
dic¦tion +s
dic¦tion¦ary
   dic¦tion¦ar¦ies
Dicto¦graph *Propr.*
dic¦tum
   dicta *or* dic¦tums
dicty
did
di¦dac¦tic
di¦dac¦tic¦al¦ly
di¦dac¦ti¦cism
dida¦kai +s (use
   didicoi)
did¦di¦coy +s (use
   didicoi)
did¦dle
   did¦dles
   did¦dled
   did¦dling
did¦dler +s
diddly-squat
did¦dums
Di¦derot, Denis
   (French
   philosopher)
didg¦eri¦doo +s
didi¦coi +s
didn't

Dido (queen of
   Carthage)
dido
   didos *or* di¦does
   (antic)
didst
Did¦yma
   (sanctuary of
   Apollo)
di¦dym¦ium
die
   dice
   (numbered cube.
   △ dye)
die
   dies
   died
   dying
   (cease living.
   △ dye)
die-away *adjective*
die-back *noun*
die-cast
die-casting
di¦ecious *Am.* (*Br.*
   dioecious)
dief¦fen¦bachia +s
Diego Gar¦cia
   (island, Indian
   Ocean)
die¦hard +s
Die¦kirch (town,
   Luxembourg)
diel¦drin
di¦elec¦tric
di¦elec¦tric¦al¦ly
Dien Bien Phu
   (siege, Vietnam)
diene +s (organic
   compound)
Dieppe (port,
   France)
di¦er¦esis *Am.*
   di¦er¦eses
   (*Br.* diaeresis)
diesel +s (fuel.
   △ deasil)
diesel-electric
diesel¦ise *Br.* (use
   dieselize)
   diesel¦ises
   diesel¦ised
   diesel¦is¦ing
diesel¦ize
   diesel¦izes
   diesel¦ized
   diesel¦iz¦ing
diesel-powered
die-sinker +s
Dies irae
dies non
die-stamping

di¦es¦trus *Am.* (*Br.*
   dioestrus)
diet +s +ed +ing
diet¦ary
   diet¦ar¦ies
diet¦er +s
diet¦et¦ic
diet¦et¦ic¦al¦ly
diet¦et¦ics
di¦ethyl
di¦ethyl¦amide
diet¦ician +s (use
   dietitian)
diet¦itian +s
Diet¦rich,
   Mar¦lene
   (German-born
   American actress
   and singer)
dif¦fer +s +ed +ing
dif¦fer¦ence +s
dif¦fer¦ent
dif¦fer¦en¦tia
   dif¦fer¦en¦tiae
dif¦fer¦en¦tial +s
dif¦fer¦en¦tial¦ly
dif¦fer¦en¦ti¦ate
   dif¦fer¦en¦ti¦ates
   dif¦fer¦en¦ti¦ated
   dif¦fer¦en¦ti¦at¦ing
dif¦fer¦en¦ti¦ation
   +s
dif¦fer¦en¦ti¦ator
   +s
dif¦fer¦ent¦ly
dif¦fer¦ent¦ly
   abled
dif¦fer¦ent¦ness
dif¦fi¦cult
dif¦fi¦cult¦ly
dif¦fi¦cult¦ness
dif¦fi¦culty
   dif¦fi¦cul¦ties
dif¦fi¦dence
dif¦fi¦dent
dif¦fi¦dent¦ly
dif¦fract +s +ed
   +ing
dif¦frac¦tion +s
dif¦fract¦ive
dif¦fract¦ive¦ly
dif¦fract¦om¦eter
   +s
dif¦fuse
   dif¦fuses
   dif¦fused
   dif¦fus¦ing
dif¦fuse¦ly
dif¦fuse¦ness
dif¦fuser +s
dif¦fus¦ible
dif¦fu¦sion +s

dif¦fu¦sion¦ist +s
dif¦fu¦sive
dig
   digs
   dug
   dig¦ging
Di¦gam¦bara +s
dig¦am¦ist +s
di¦gamma +s
dig¦am¦ous
dig¦amy
di¦gas¦tric
di¦gest +s +ed
   +ing
di¦gest¦er +s
di¦gest¦ibil¦ity
di¦gest¦ible
di¦ges¦tion +s
di¦gest¦ive +s
di¦gest¦ive¦ly
Dig¦ger +s (English
   dissenter)
dig¦ger +s (person
   who digs;
   machine;
   Australian; New
   Zealander)
dig¦ging +s
dight
digit +s
digit¦al +s
digi¦talin
digi¦talis
digit¦al¦ise *Br.* (use
   digitalize)
   digit¦al¦ises
   digit¦al¦ised
   digit¦al¦is¦ing
digit¦al¦ize
   digit¦al¦izes
   digit¦al¦ized
   digit¦al¦iz¦ing
digit¦al¦ly
digi¦tate
digi¦tate¦ly
digi¦ta¦tion
digi¦ti¦grade +s
digit¦isa¦tion *Br.*
   (use digitization)
digit¦ise *Br.* (use
   digitize)
   digit¦ises
   digit¦ised
   digit¦is¦ing
digit¦iza¦tion
digit¦ize
   digit¦izes
   digit¦ized
   digit¦iz¦ing
dig¦ni¦fied¦ly
dig¦nify
   dig¦ni¦fies

dig|nify (cont.)
  dig|ni|fied
  dig|ni|fy|ing
dig|ni|tary
  dig|ni|tar|ies
dig|nity
  dig|nities
di|graph +s
di|graph|ic
di|gress
  di|gresses
  di|gressed
  di|gress|ing
di|gress|er +s
di|gres|sion +s
di|gres|sive
di|gres|sive|ly
di|gres|sive|ness
di|he|dral +s
di|hy|brid +s
di|hy|dric
Dijon (city, France; mustard)
dik-dik +s
dike +s (use dyke)
dik|tat +s
di|lapi|date
  di|lapi|dates
  di|lapi|dated
  di|lapi|dat|ing
di|lapi|da|tion +s
di|lat|able
dila|ta|tion
di|late
  di|lates
  di|lated
  di|lat|ing
dila|tion
di|la|tor +s
dila|tor|ily
dila|tori|ness
dila|tory
dildo +s
di|lemma +s
dil|et|tante
  dil|et|tanti or
  dil|et|tan|tes
dil|et|tant|ish
dil|et|tant|ism
Dili (seaport, Timor)
dili|gence +s
dili|gent
dili|gent|ly
dill +s
dill pickle +s
dill-water
dilly
  dil|lies
dilly|bag +s
dilly-dally
  dilly-dallies

dilly-dally (cont.)
  dilly-dallied
  dilly-dallying
di|lo|pho|saur +s
di|lopho|saurus
di|lopho|
    saur|uses
di|lu|ent +s
di|lute
  di|lutes
  di|luted
  di|lut|ing
di|lutee +s
di|luter +s
di|lu|tion +s
di|lu|vial
di|lu|vi|al|ist +s
di|lu|vium
di|lu|via
Dilys
dim
  dims
  dimmed
  dim|ming
  dim|mer
  dim|mest
Di|Maggio, Joe (American baseball player)
Dim|bleby, Rich|ard, David, and Jona|than (English broadcasters)
dime +s
di|men|sion +s
di|men|sion|al
di|men|sion|al|ity
di|men|sion|al|ly
di|men|sion|less
dimer +s
di|mer|ic
di|mer|isa|tion Br. (use dimerization)
di|mer|ise Br. (use dimerize)
  di|mer|ises
  di|mer|ised
  di|mer|is|ing
di|mer|iza|tion
di|mer|ize
  di|mer|izes
  di|mer|ized
  di|mer|iz|ing
di|mer|ous
dim|eter +s
di|methyl|
    sulf|ox|ide Am.
di|methyl|
    sulph|ox|ide Br.
di|met|ro|don +s

di|midi|ate
di|min|ish
  di|min|ishes
  di|min|ished
  di|min|ish|ing
di|min|ish|able
di|minu|endo +s
dim|in|ution
di|minu|tival
di|minu|tive +s
di|minu|tive|ly
di|minu|tive|ness
di|mis|sory
dim|ity
  dim|ities
dimly
dim|mer +s
dim|mish
dim|ness
di|morph|ic
di|morph|ism
di|morph|ous
dimple
  dimples
  dimpled
  dim|pling
dim|ply
dim|plier
dim|pli|est
dim sum
  plural dim sum
dil|wit +s
dim-witted
DIN (technical standard)
din
  dins
  dinned
  din|ning
  (noise; instill)
Dinah
dinar +s
Din|aric Alps (in S. Europe)
din-din
din-dins
dine
  dines
  dined
  din|ing
  (eat dinner. △ dyne)
diner +s
din|ero +s
diner-out
  diners-out
din|ette +s
ding +s +ed +ing
Ding an sich
ding|bat +s
ding-dong +s
dinge
  dinges

dinge (cont.)
  dinged
  dinge|ing
dinghy
  din|ghies
  (small boat. △ dingy)
din|gily
din|gi|ness
din|gle +s
dingo
  din|goes or
  din|gos
Ding|wall (town, Scotland)
dingy
  din|gier
  din|gi|est
  (dull. △ dinghy)
din|ing car +s
din|ing chair +s
din|ing hall +s
din|ing room +s
din|ing table +s
dink +s +ed +ing
Dinka
  plural Dinka or Din|kas
din|kum
dinky
  dink|ier
  dinki|est
din|ner +s
din|ner dance +s
din|ner jacket +s
din|ner party
  din|ner par|ties
din|ner ser|vice +s
din|ner table +s
din|ner time
dino|fla|gel|late +s
dino|saur +s
dino|saur|ian
dino|there +s (use deinothere)
dint +s +ed +ing
di|nucleo|tide +s
dio|cesan +s
dio|cese +s
Dio|cle|tian (Roman emperor)
diode +s
di|oe|cious Br. (Am. diecious)
di|oes|trus Br. (Am. diestrus)
Dioge|nes (Greek philosopher)
diol +s Chemistry
Dione (Greek Mythology; moon of Saturn)

Dio¦nys¦iac
Dio¦nys¦ian
Dio¦nys¦ius (I and II, Syracusan rulers)
Dio¦nys¦ius Ex¦ig¦uus (Scythian monk and chronologer)
Dio¦nys¦ius of Hali¦car¦nas¦sus (Greek historian and writer)
Dio¦nys¦ius the Are¦opa¦gite (Greek saint)
Dio|nysus *Greek Mythology*
Dio|phan¦tine
Dio|phan¦tus (Greek mathematician)
di|opter *Am.* +s
di|optre *Br.* +s
di|op¦tric
di|op¦trics
Dior, Chris¦tian (French couturier)
dio|rama +s
dio|ram¦ic
di¦or|ite +s
di¦or|it¦ic
Dio|scuri (*Greek and Roman Mythology*, = Castor and Pollux)
di¦oxan
di¦oxane
di¦ox¦ide +s
di¦oxin +s
DIP (*Computing* = dual in-line package)
dip
  dips
  dipped
  dip|ping
  (plunge etc.)
Dip. Ed. (= Diploma in Education)
di|pep¦tide +s
di|phos¦phate +s
diph|theria
diph|ther¦ial
diph|ther¦ic
diph|ther¦it¦ic
diph|ther¦oid
diph|thong +s
diph|thong¦al

diph¦thong|
    isa¦tion *Br.* (use diphthongiza-tion)
diph¦thong|ise *Br.* (use diphthongize)
diph¦thong|ises
diph¦thong|ised
diph¦thong|is¦ing
diph¦thong|
    iza¦tion
diph¦thong|ize
diph¦thong|izes
diph¦thong|ized
diph¦thong|iz¦ing
diplo|coc¦cus
diplo|cocci
dip¦lod|ocus
  dip¦lod|ocuses
dip|loid +s
dip|loidy
dip|loma +s
dip|lo¦macy
dip|lo¦maed
dip|lo¦mat +s (official; tactful person)
dip¦lo|mate +s (holder of diploma)
dip¦lo|mat¦ic|al¦ly
dip¦lo|ma¦tise *Br.* (use diplomatize)
  dip¦lo|ma¦tises
  dip¦lo|ma¦tised
  dip¦lo|ma¦tis¦ing
dip¦lo|ma¦tist +s
dip¦lo|ma¦tize
  dip¦lo|ma¦tizes
  dip¦lo|ma¦tized
  dip¦lo|ma¦tiz¦ing
dip|lont +s
dip|lo¦pia
dip¦lo|tene +s
di|polar
di¦pole +s
dip¦per +s
dippy
  dip|pier
  dip|pi¦est
dip|shit +s (*coarse slang*)
dipso +s
dipso|mania
dipso|maniac +s
dip|stick +s
dip switch
  dip switches
Dip|tera
dip|teral

dip|teran +s
dip|ter|ist +s
dip|ter|ous
dip|tych +s
Dirac, Paul (English physicist)
dire
  direr
  dir¦est
dir¦ect +s +ed +ing
dir¦ect dial (telephone)
dir¦ect dial¦ing *Am.*
dir¦ect dial¦ling *Br.*
direct-grant *attributive*
dir¦ec¦tion +s
dir¦ec¦tion|al
dir¦ec¦tion|al¦ity
dir¦ec¦tion|al¦ly
direction-finder +s
direction-finding
dir¦ec¦tion|less
dir¦ect|ive +s
dir¦ect¦ly
dir¦ect mail
dir¦ect mail¦ing
dir¦ect|ness
Dir¦ect¦oire
dir¦ect|or +s
dir¦ect|or¦ate +s
director-general +s
dir¦ect|or¦ial
dir¦ect|or¦ship +s
Dir|ec¦tory *History*
dir|ec¦tory
  dir|ec¦tor¦ies
dir|ec¦tress
  dir|ec¦tresses
dir|ec¦trix
  dir|ec¦tri¦ces
dire|ful
dire|ful¦ly
dire|ly
dire|ness
dirge +s
dirge|ful
dir¦ham +s
diri|gible +s
diri|gisme
diri|giste
diri|ment
dirk +s
dirndl +s
dirt
dirt cheap
dirt|ily
dirti|ness

dirt track +s
dirt-tracker +s
dirty
  dirt|ies
  dirt|ied
  dirty|ing
  dirt|ier
  dirti|est
dis
  disses
  dissed
  dis|sing
dis|abil¦ity
  dis|abil¦ities
dis|able
  dis|ables
  dis|abled
  dis|ab¦ling
dis|able|ment
dis|ablist
dis|abuse
  dis|abuses
  dis|abused
  dis|abus¦ing
di|sac¦char|ide +s
dis|ac¦cord +s +ed +ing
dis|ad¦van|tage
  dis|ad¦van|tages
  dis|ad¦van|taged
  dis|ad¦van|ta¦ging
dis|ad¦van|
    ta¦geous
dis|ad¦van|
    ta¦geous¦ly
dis|af¦fect¦ed
dis|af¦fect¦ed¦ly
dis|af¦fec¦tion
dis|af¦fili|ate
  dis|af¦fili|ates
  dis|af¦fili|ated
  dis|af¦fili|at¦ing
dis|af¦fili|ation
dis|af¦firm +s +ed +ing
dis|af¦firm|ation
dis|af¦for|est +s +ed +ing
dis|af¦for|est|ation
dis|ag¦gre|gate
  dis|ag¦gre|gates
  dis|ag¦gre|gated
  dis|ag¦gre|gat¦ing
dis|ag¦gre|ga¦tion
dis|agree
  dis|agrees
  dis|agreed
  dis|agree|ing
dis|agree|able
dis|agree|able|
    ness

dis|agree|ably
dis|agree|ment +s
dis|allow +s +ed
  +ing
dis|allow|ance +s
dis|am|bigu|ate
dis|am|bigu|ates
dis|am|bigu|ated
dis|am|bigu|
      at|ing
dis|am|bigu|ation
  +s
dis|amen|ity
dis|amen|ities
dis|annul
dis|annuls
dis|annulled
dis|annul|ling
dis|annul|ment
dis|ap|pear +s +ed
  +ing
dis|ap|pear|ance
  +s
dis|ap|point +s
  +ed +ing
dis|ap|point|ed|ly
dis|ap|point|ing|ly
dis|ap|point|ment
  +s
dis|ap|pro|ba|tion
dis|ap|proba|tive
dis|ap|pro|ba|tory
dis|ap|proval +s
dis|ap|prove
dis|ap|proves
dis|ap|proved
dis|ap|prov|ing
dis|ap|prover +s
dis|ap|prov|ing|ly
dis|arm +s +ed
  +ing
dis|arma|ment
dis|arm|er +s
dis|arm|ing
dis|arm|ing|ly
dis|ar|range
dis|ar|ranges
dis|ar|ranged
dis|ar|ran|ging
dis|ar|range|ment
dis|array
dis|ar|ticu|late
dis|ar|ticu|lates
dis|ar|ticu|lated
dis|ar|ticu|lat|ing
dis|ar|ticu|la|tion
dis|as|sem|ble
dis|as|sem|bles
dis|as|sem|bled
dis|as|sem|bling
dis|as|sem|bler +s
dis|as|sem|bly

dis|as|so|ci|ate
dis|as|so|ci|ates
dis|as|so|ci|ated
dis|as|so|ci|at|ing
dis|as|so|ci|ation
dis|as|ter +s
dis|as|trous
dis|as|trous|ly
dis|avow +s +ed
  +ing
dis|avowal +s
dis|band +s +ed
  +ing
dis|band|ment
dis|bar
dis|bars
dis|barred
dis|bar|ring
dis|bar|ment
dis|be|lief
dis|be|lieve
dis|be|lieves
dis|be|lieved
dis|be|liev|ing
dis|be|liever +s
dis|be|liev|ing|ly
dis|bene|fit +s
dis|bound
dis|bud
dis|buds
dis|bud|ded
dis|bud|ding
dis|bur|den +s +ed
  +ing
dis|bur|sal
dis|burse
dis|burses
dis|bursed
dis|burs|ing
dis|burse|ment +s
dis|bur|ser +s
disc *Br.* +s (*Am.*
  disk. senses other
  than *Computing.*
  ⚠ disk)
dis|calced
dis|card +s +ed
  +ing
dis|card|able
dis|car|nate
dis|cern +s +ed
  +ing
dis|cern|er +s
dis|cern|ible
dis|cern|ibly
dis|cern|ing|ly
dis|cern|ment +s
dis|cerp|ti|bil|ity
dis|cerp|tible
dis|cerp|tion +s
dis|charge
dis|charges

dis|charge (*cont.*)
  dis|charged
  dis|char|ging
dis|charge|able
dis|char|ger +s
dis|ciple +s
dis|ciple|ship +s
dis|cip|lin|able
dis|cip|linal
dis|cip|lin|ar|ian +s
dis|cip|lin|ary
dis|cip|line
  dis|cip|lines
  dis|cip|lined
  dis|cip|lin|ing
dis|cipu|lar
disc jockey +s
dis|claim +s +ed
  +ing
dis|claim|er +s
dis|close
  dis|closes
  dis|closed
  dis|clos|ing
dis|closer +s
dis|clos|ure +s
disco +s *noun*
disco
  dis|coes
  dis|coed
  dis|co|ing
  verb
disc|ob|olus
  disc|ob|oli
disc|og|raph|er +s
disc|og|raphy
  disc|og|raph|ies
dis|coid
dis|color *Am.* +s
  +ed +ing
dis|col|or|ation
dis|col|our *Br.* +s
  +ed +ing
dis|com|bobu|late
  dis|com|bobu|
      lates
  dis|com|bobu|
      lated
  dis|com|bobu|
      lat|ing
dis|comfit +s +ed
  +ing (baffle;
  thwart.
  ⚠ discomfort)
dis|com|fit|ure
dis|com|fort +s
  +ed +ing (unease;
  make uneasy.
  ⚠ discomfit)
dis|com|mode
  dis|com|modes
  dis|com|moded
  dis|com|mod|ing

dis|com|mo|di|ous
dis|com|pose
  dis|com|poses
  dis|com|posed
  dis|com|pos|ing
dis|com|pos|ure
dis|con|cert +s
  +ed +ing
dis|con|cert|ed|ly
dis|con|cert|ing
dis|con|cert|ing|ly
dis|con|cer|tion
dis|con|cert|ment
dis|con|firm +s
  +ed +ing
dis|con|firm|ation
dis|con|form|ity
  dis|con|form|ities
dis|con|nect +s
  +ed +ing
dis|con|nect|ed|ly
dis|con|nect|ed|
        ness
dis|con|nec|tion
  +s
dis|con|so|late
dis|con|so|late|
        ness
dis|con|sol|ation
dis|con|tent +s
  +ed +ing
dis|con|tent|ly
dis|con|tent|ment
  +s
dis|con|tent|ness
dis|con|tinu|ance
dis|con|tinu|ation
dis|con|tinue
  dis|con|tinues
  dis|con|tinued
  dis|con|tinu|ing
dis|con|tinu|ity
  dis|con|tinu|ities
dis|con|tinu|ous
dis|con|tinu|ous|ly
dis|cord +s +ed
  +ing
dis|cord|ance
dis|cord|ancy
  dis|cord|an|cies
dis|cord|ant
dis|cord|ant|ly
disco|theque +s
dis|count +s +ed
  +ing
dis|count|able
dis|coun|ten|ance
  dis|coun|ten|
        ances
  dis|coun|ten|
        anced

dis|coun|ten|ance
(*cont.*)
  dis|coun|te|nan|
    cing
dis|counter +s
dis|cour|age
  dis|cour|ages
  dis|cour|aged
  dis|cour|aging
dis|cour|age|ment
  +s
dis|cour|aging|ly
dis|course
  dis|courses
  dis|coursed
  dis|cours|ing
dis|cour|teous
dis|cour|teous|ly
dis|cour|teous|
    ness
dis|cour|tesy
  dis|cour|tesies
dis|cover +s +ed
  +ing
dis|cov|er|able
dis|cov|er|er +s
dis|cov|ery
  dis|cov|er|ies
dis|cred|it|able
dis|cred|it|ably
dis|creet
  (circumspect;
  tactful.
  △ discrete)
dis|creet|ly
dis|creet|ness
dis|crep|ancy
  dis|crep|an|cies
dis|crep|ant
dis|crete (separate.
  △ discreet)
dis|crete|ly
dis|crete|ness
dis|cre|tion
dis|cre|tion|ary
dis|crim|in|ant
dis|crim|in|ate
  dis|crim|in|ates
  dis|crim|in|ated
  dis|crim|in|at|ing
dis|crim|in|ate|ly
dis|crim|in|
    at|ing|ly
dis|crim|in|ation
  +s
dis|crim|ina|tive
dis|crim|in|ator +s
dis|crim|in|atory
dis|cur|sive
dis|cur|sive|ly

dis|cur|sive|ness
dis|cus
  dis|cuses
  (disc)
dis|cuss
  dis|cusses
  dis|cussed
  dis|cuss|ing
  (debate)
dis|cuss|able
dis|cuss|ant +s
dis|cuss|er +s
dis|cuss|ible
dis|cus|sion +s
dis|dain +s +ed
  +ing
dis|dain|ful
dis|dain|ful|ly
dis|dain|ful|ness
dis|ease +s
dis|eased
dis|econ|omy
dis|em|bark +s
  +ed +ing
dis|em|bark|ation
dis|em|bar|rass
  dis|em|bar|rasses
  dis|em|bar|rassed
  dis|em|bar|rass|
    ing
dis|em|bar|rass|
    ment
dis|em|bodi|ment
dis|embody
  dis|em|bod|ies
  dis|em|bod|ied
  dis|em|body|ing
dis|em|bogue
  dis|em|bogues
  dis|em|bogued
  dis|em|boguing
dis|em|bowel
  dis|em|bowels
  dis|em|bow|elled
    Br.
  dis|em|bow|eled
    Am.
  dis|em|bowel|ling
    Br.
  dis|em|bowel|ing
    Am.
dis|em|bowel|
    ment
dis|em|broil +s
  +ed +ing
dis|em|power +s
  +ed +ing
dis|en|chant +s
  +ed +ing
dis|en|chant|ing|ly
dis|en|chant|ment
  +s

dis|en|cum|ber +s
  +ed +ing
dis|en|dow +s +ed
  +ing
dis|en|dow|ment
dis|en|fran|chise
  dis|en|fran|chises
  dis|en|fran|chised
  dis|
    en|fran|chis|ing
dis|en|fran|chise|
    ment
dis|en|gage
  dis|en|gages
  dis|en|gaged
  dis|en|gaging
dis|en|gage|ment
dis|en|tail +s +ed
  +ing
dis|en|tan|gle
  dis|en|tan|gles
  dis|en|tan|gled
  dis|en|tan|gling
dis|en|tangle|ment
dis|en|thral *Br.*
  dis|en|thrals
  dis|en|thralled
  dis|en|thral|ling
dis|en|thrall *Am.* +s
  +ed +ing
dis|en|thrall|ment
  Am.
dis|en|thral|ment
  Br.
dis|en|title
  dis|en|titles
  dis|en|titled
  dis|en|tit|ling
dis|en|title|ment
dis|en|tomb +s
  +ed +ing
dis|en|tomb|ment
dis|equi|lib|rium
dis|es|tab|lish
  dis|es|tab|lishes
  dis|es|tab|lished
  dis|es|tab|lish|ing
  dis|es|tab|lish|
    ment
dis|es|teem +s +ed
  +ing
dis|eur +*s male*
dis|euse +*s female*
dis|favor *Am.* +s
  +ed +ing
dis|favour *Br.* +s
  +ed +ing
dis|fig|ure
  dis|fig|ures
  dis|fig|ured
  dis|fig|ur|ing
dis|fig|ure|ment +s

dis|for|est +s +ed
  +ing
dis|for|est|ation
dis|fran|chise
  dis|fran|chises
  dis|fran|chised
  dis|fran|chis|ing
dis|fran|chise|
    ment +s
dis|frock +s +ed
  +ing
dis|gorge
  dis|gorges
  dis|gorged
  dis|gor|ging
dis|gorge|ment +s
dis|grace
  dis|graces
  dis|graced
  dis|gra|cing
dis|grace|ful
dis|grace|ful|ly
dis|grun|tled
dis|gruntle|ment
dis|guise
  dis|guises
  dis|guised
  dis|guis|ing
dis|guise|ment
dis|gust +s +ed
  +ing
dis|gust|ed|ly
dis|gust|ful
dis|gust|ing|ly
dis|gust|ing|ness
dish
  dishes
  dished
  dish|ing
dis|ha|bille
dis|habitu|ation
dis|har|mo|ni|ous
dis|har|mo|ni|
    ous|ly
dis|har|mon|ise *Br.*
  (use
  disharmonize)
  dis|har|mon|ises
  dis|har|mon|ised
  dis|har|mon|is|ing
dis|har|mon|ize
  dis|har|mon|izes
  dis|har|mon|ized
  dis|har|mon|
    iz|ing
dis|har|mony
  dis|har|monies
dish|cloth +s
dis|heart|en +s
  +ed +ing
dis|heart|en|ing|ly
dis|heart|en|ment

dish|evel
  dish|evels
  dish|ev|elled *Br.*
  dish|ev|eled *Am.*
  dish|ev|el|ling *Br.*
  dish|ev|el|ing *Am.*
dish|ev|el|ment
dish|ful +s
dish|like
dis|hon|est
dis|hon|est|ly
dis|hon|esty
  dis|hon|est|ies
dis|honor *Am.* +s
  +ed +ing
dis|hon|or|able
Am.
dis|hon|or|able|
           ness *Am.*
dis|hon|or|ably
Am.
dis|hon|our *Br.* +s
  +ed +ing
dis|hon|our|able
Br.
dis|hon|our|able|
          ness *Br.*
dis|hon|our|ably
Br.
dish|rag +s
dish|wash|er +s
dish|water
dishy
  dish|ier
  dishi|est
dis|il|lu|sion +s
  +ed +ing
dis|il|lu|sion|ise
Br. (use
  disillusionize)
  dis|il|lu|sion|ises
  dis|il|lu|sion|ised
  dis|il|lu|sion|
          is|ing
dis|il|lu|sion|ize
  dis|il|lu|sion|izes
  dis|il|lu|sion|ized
  dis|il|lu|sion|
          iz|ing
dis|il|lu|sion|ment
  +s
dis|in|cen|tive +s
dis|in|clin|ation
dis|in|cline
  dis|in|clines
  dis|in|clined
  dis|in|clin|ing
dis|in|cor|por|ate
  dis|in|cor|por|
          ates
  dis|in|cor|por|
          ated

dis|in|cor|por|ate
  (*cont.*)
  dis|in|cor|por|
          at|ing
dis|in|fect +s +ed
  +ing
dis|in|fect|ant +s
dis|in|fec|tion
dis|in|fest +s +ed
  +ing
dis|in|fest|ation
dis|in|fla|tion
dis|in|fla|tion|ary
dis|in|for|ma|tion
dis|in|genu|ous
dis|in|genu|ous|ly
dis|in|genu|ous|
          ness
dis|in|herit +s +ed
  +ing
dis|in|herit|ance
dis|in|te|grate
  dis|in|te|grates
  dis|in|te|grated
  dis|in|te|grat|ing
dis|in|te|gra|tion
dis|in|te|gra|tive
dis|in|te|gra|tor +s
dis|in|ter
  dis|in|ters
  dis|in|terred
  dis|in|ter|ring
dis|in|ter|est
dis|in|ter|est|ed
dis|in|ter|est|ed|ly
dis|in|ter|est|ed|
          ness
dis|in|ter|ment +s
dis|in|vest +s +ed
  +ing
dis|in|vest|ment
dis|jecta mem|bra
dis|join +s +ed
  +ing
dis|joint +s +ed
  +ing
dis|joint|ed|ly
dis|joint|ed|ness
dis|junct +s
dis|junc|tion +s
dis|junct|ive
dis|junct|ive|ly
dis|junc|ture +s
disk *Am.* +s (*Br.*
  disc)
disk +s *Computing*
disk drive
disk|ette +s
disk|less
Disko (island,
  Greenland)
dis|lik|able

dis|like
  dis|likes
  dis|liked
  dis|lik|ing
dis|like|able (use
  dislikable)
dis|locate
  dis|locates
  dis|located
  dis|locat|ing
dis|loca|tion +s
dis|lodge
  dis|lodges
  dis|lodged
  dis|lodg|ing
dis|lodge|ment
dis|loyal
dis|loy|al|ist +s
dis|loy|al|ly
dis|loy|alty
  dis|loy|al|ties
dis|mal
dis|mal|ly
dis|mal|ness
dis|man|tle
  dis|man|tles
  dis|man|tled
  dis|mant|ling
dis|mantle|ment
dis|mant|ler +s
dis|mast +s +ed
  +ing
dis|may +s +ed
  +ing
dis|mem|ber +s
  +ed +ing
dis|mem|ber|ment
  +s
dis|miss
  dis|misses
  dis|missed
  dis|miss|ing
dis|miss|able (use
  dismissible)
dis|missal +s
dis|miss|ible
dis|mis|sion
dis|mis|sive
dis|mis|sive|ly
dis|mis|sive|ness
dis|mount +s +ed
  +ing
Dis|ney, Walt
  (cartoon
  producer)
Dis|ney|esque
dis|obedi|ence
dis|obedi|ent
dis|obedi|ent|ly
dis|obey +s +ed
  +ing
dis|obey|er +s

dis|oblige
  dis|obliges
  dis|obliged
  dis|obli|ging
dis|order +s +ed
  +ing
dis|or|der|li|ness
dis|or|der|ly
dis|or|gan|isa|tion
  Br. (use
  disorganization)
dis|or|gan|ise *Br.*
  (use disorganize)
  dis|or|gan|ises
  dis|or|gan|ised
  dis|or|gan|is|ing
dis|or|gan|iza|tion
dis|or|gan|ize
  dis|or|gan|izes
  dis|or|gan|ized
  dis|or|gan|iz|ing
dis|orient +s +ed
  +ing
dis|orien|tate
  dis|orien|tates
  dis|orien|tated
  dis|orien|tat|ised
dis|orien|ta|tion
dis|own +s +ed
  +ing
dis|own|er +s
dis|par|age
  dis|par|ages
  dis|par|aged
  dis|para|ging
dis|par|age|ment
  +s
dis|para|ging|ly
dis|par|ate
dis|par|ate|ly
dis|par|ate|ness
dis|par|ity
  dis|par|ities
dis|pas|sion|ate
dis|pas|sion|ate|ly
dis|pas|sion|ate|
          ness
dis|patch
  dis|patches
  dis|patched
  dis|patch|ing
dis|patch box
  dis|patch boxes
dis|patch|er +s
dis|patch rider +s
dis|pel
  dis|pels
  dis|pelled
  dis|pel|ling
dis|pel|ler +s
dis|pens|abil|ity
dis|pens|able

dis¦pens|ary
  dis¦pens|ar¦ies
dis¦pen|sa¦tion +s
dis¦pen|sa¦tion|al
dis¦pen|sa¦tory
dis¦pense
  dis¦penses
  dis¦pensed
  dis¦pens|ing
dis¦pen¦ser +s
dis¦pers|able (use
  dispersible)
dis¦per¦sal +s
dis¦pers|ant +s
dis¦perse
  dis¦perses
  dis¦persed
  dis¦per|sing
dis¦perser +s
dis¦pers|ible
dis¦per|sion +s
dis¦per|sive
dis¦pirit +s +ed
  +ing
dis¦pir¦it|ed¦ly
dis¦pir¦it|ed|ness
dis¦pir¦it|ing
dis¦pir¦it|ing¦ly
dis¦place
  dis¦places
  dis¦placed
  dis¦placing
dis¦place|ment +s
dis¦play +s +ed
  +ing
dis¦play¦er +s
dis¦please
  dis¦pleases
  dis¦pleased
  dis¦pleas¦ing
dis¦pleas¦ing¦ly
dis¦pleas¦ure
  dis¦pleas¦ures
  dis¦pleas¦ured
  dis¦pleas¦ur¦ing
dis¦port +s +ed
  +ing
dis¦pos|abil¦ity
dis¦pos|able +s
dis¦posal +s
dis¦pose
  dis¦poses
  dis¦posed
  dis¦pos¦ing
dis¦poser +s
dis¦pos¦ition +s
dis¦pos¦sess
  dis¦pos¦sesses
  dis¦pos¦sessed
  dis¦pos¦sess|ing
dis¦pos¦ses|sion +s

dis¦praise
  dis¦praises
  dis¦praised
  dis¦prais¦ing
dis¦proof +s
dis¦pro¦por|tion +s
dis¦pro¦por|tion|al
dis¦pro¦por|tion|
      al¦ly
dis¦pro¦por|tion|
      ate
dis¦pro¦por|tion|
      ate¦ly
dis¦pro¦por|tion|
      ate|ness
dis¦prov|able
dis¦prove
  dis¦proves
  dis¦proved
  dis¦prov¦ing
Dis¦pur (city, India)
dis¦put|able
dis¦put|ably
dis¦pu|tant +s
dis¦pu|ta¦tion +s
dis¦pu|ta¦tious
dis¦pu|ta¦tious|ly
dis¦pu|ta¦tious|
      ness
dis¦pute
  dis¦putes
  dis¦puted
  dis¦put|ing
dis¦puter +s
dis¦quali|fi¦ca¦tion
  +s
dis¦qual|ify
  dis¦quali|fies
  dis¦quali|fied
  dis¦quali|fy¦ing
dis¦quiet +s +ed
  +ing
dis¦quiet¦ing|ly
dis¦quiet|ude
dis¦quisi|tion +s
dis¦quisi|tion|al
Dis¦raeli,
  Ben¦ja¦min
  (British prime
  minister)
dis¦rate
  dis¦rates
  dis¦rated
  dis¦rat¦ing
dis¦re¦gard +s +ed
  +ing
dis¦re¦gard|ful
dis¦re¦gard|ful¦ly
dis¦rel¦ish
  dis¦rel¦ishes
  dis¦rel¦ished
  dis¦rel¦ish|ing

dis¦re¦mem|ber +s
  +ed +ing
dis¦re¦pair
dis¦rep¦ut|able
dis¦rep¦ut|able|
      ness
dis¦rep¦ut|ably
dis¦re¦pute
dis¦res¦pect
dis¦res¦pect|ful
dis¦res¦pect|ful¦ly
dis¦robe
  dis¦robes
  dis¦robed
  dis¦rob¦ing
dis¦rupt +s +ed
  +ing
dis¦rupt¦er +s
dis¦rup|tion +s
dis¦rup|tive
dis¦rup|tive¦ly
dis¦rup|tive|ness
diss (use dis)
  disses
  dissed
  diss|ing
dis¦sat¦is|fac¦tion
  +s
dis¦sat¦is|fac¦tory
dis¦sat¦is|fied¦ly
dis¦sat¦isfy
  dis¦sat¦is|fies
  dis¦sat¦is|fied
  dis¦sat¦is|fy|ing
dis¦sect +s +ed
  +ing
dis¦sec|tion +s
dis¦sect|or +s
dis¦sem|blance
dis¦sem|ble
  dis¦sem|bles
  dis¦sem|bled
  dis¦sem|bling
dis¦sem|bler +s
dis¦sem|bling|ly
dis¦sem|in|ate
  dis¦sem|in|ates
  dis¦sem|in|ated
  dis¦sem|in|at¦ing
dis¦sem|in|ation
dis¦sem|in|ator +s
dis¦sen|sion +s
dis¦sent +s +ed
  +ing (disagree;
  disagreement.
  ⚠ descent)
Dis¦sent¦er +s
  (Nonconformist)
dis¦sent¦er +s
  (generally)
dis¦sen|tient +s
dis¦sent¦ing¦ly

dis¦ser|ta¦tion +s
dis¦ser|ta¦tion|al
dis¦serve
  dis¦serves
  dis¦served
  dis¦serv¦ing
dis¦ser¦vice +s
dis¦sever +s +ed
  +ing
dis¦sev¦er|ance
dis¦sev¦er|ment
dis¦si|dence
dis¦si|dent +s
dis¦simi¦lar
dis¦simi|lar|ity
dis¦simi|lar|ities
dis¦simi|lar¦ly
dis¦simi|late
  dis¦simi|lates
  dis¦simi|lated
  dis¦simi|lat¦ing
dis¦simi|la¦tion +s
dis¦simi|la¦tory
dis¦sim¦ili|tude
dis¦simu|late
  dis¦simu|lates
  dis¦simu|lated
  dis¦simu|lat¦ing
dis¦simu|la¦tion
dis¦simu|la¦tor +s
dis¦si|pate
  dis¦si|pates
  dis¦si|pated
  dis¦si|pat¦ing
dis¦si|pater +s
  (use dissipator)
dis¦si|pa¦tion +s
dis¦si|pa¦tive
dis¦si|pa¦tor +s
dis¦so¦ci|ate
  dis¦so¦ci|ates
  dis¦so¦ci|ated
  dis¦so¦ci|at¦ing
dis¦so¦ci|ation +s
dis¦so¦cia|tive
dis¦solu|bil¦ity
dis¦sol¦uble
dis¦sol¦ubly
dis¦sol¦ute
dis¦sol¦ute|ly
dis¦sol¦ute|ness
dis¦sol¦ution +s
dis¦sol¦ution|ary
dis¦solv|able
dis¦solve
  dis¦solves
  dis¦solved
  dis¦solv¦ing
dis¦solv|ent +s
dis¦son¦ance +s
dis¦son¦ant
dis¦son¦ant¦ly

dis|suade
  dis|suades
  dis|suaded
  dis|suad'ing
dis|suader +s
dis|sua'sion
dis|sua'sive
dis|syl'lable +s
  (use disyllable)
dis|sym'met'rical
dis|sym'metry
  dis|sym|metries
dis'taff +s
dis'tal
dis'tal'ly
dis'tance
  dis|tances
  dis|tanced
  dis|tan'cing
dis'tance learn|ing
dis'tance post +s
dis'tant
dis'tant'ly
dis'taste
dis'taste|ful
dis'taste|ful'ly
dis'taste|ful|ness
dis'tem'per +s +ed
  +ing
dis'tend +s +ed
  +ing
dis'ten'si|bil'ity
dis'ten|sible
dis'ten|sion +s
dis'tich +s
dis'tich|ous
dis'til Br.
  dis|tils
  dis|tilled
  dis|til|ling
dis'till Am. +s +ed
  +ing
dis'til|late +s
dis'til|la'tion +s
dis'til|la'tory
dis'til|ler +s
dis'til|lery
  dis|til|ler|ies
dis'tinct
dis'tinc'tion +s
dis'tinct|ive
dis'tinct|ive'ly
dis'tinct|ive|ness
dis'tinct'ly
dis'tinct|ness
dis|tin'gué male
dis|tin'guée female
dis|tin'guish
  dis|tin'guishes
  dis|tin'guished
  dis|tin'guish|ing
  dis|tin'guish|able

dis|tin'guish|ably
dis|tort +s +ed
  +ing
dis'tort|ed|ly
dis'tort|ed|ness
dis'tort|er +s
dis'tor'tion +s
dis'tor'tion|al
dis'tor'tion|less
dis'tract +s +ed
  +ing
dis'tract|ed|ly
dis'trac'tion +s
dis'tract'or +s
dis'train +s +ed
  +ing
dis'train|ee +s
dis'train|er +s
dis'train|ment
dis'train|or +s
  (use distrainer)
dis'traint
dis'trait *male*
dis'traite *female*
dis'traught
dis'tress
  dis|tresses
  dis|tressed
  dis'tress|ing
dis'tress|ful
dis'tress|ful'ly
dis'tress|ing'ly
dis'trib'ut|able
dis'tribu|tary
  dis'tribu|tar'ies
dis'trib'ute
  dis'trib|utes
  dis'trib|uted
  dis'trib'ut|ing
dis'tri|bu'tion +s
dis'tri|bu'tion|al
dis'tribu|tive
dis'tribu|tive'ly
dis'tribu|tor +s
dis'trict +s
dis'trust +s +ed
  +ing
dis'trust|er +s
dis'trust|ful
dis'trust|ful'ly
dis'turb +s +ed
  +ing
dis'turb|ance +s
dis'turb|er +s
dis'turb|ing'ly
di|sul'fide Am. +s
di|sul'phide Br. +s
dis|union
dis|unite
  dis|unites
  dis|united
  dis|unit'ing

dis|unity
  dis|unities
dis'use
  dis|uses
  dis|used
  dis|us'ing
dis|util'ity
di|syl'lab'ic
di|syl'lable +s
dit +s
ditch
  ditches
  ditched
  ditch|ing
ditch'er +s
ditch|water
di|theism
di|theist +s
dither +s +ed +ing
dith|er'er +s
dith|ery
dithy|ramb +s
dithy|ramb'ic
ditsy (use ditzy)
  dit|sier
  ditsi|est
dit'tany
  dit|tanies
ditto +s *noun*
ditto
  dit'toes
  dit'toed
  ditto|ing
  verb
dit'to|graph'ic
dit'tog'raphy
  dit'tog'raph'ies
ditto marks
ditty
  dit|ties
ditty-bag +s
ditty-box
  ditty-boxes
ditzy
  ditz|ier
  ditzi|est
Diu (island, India)
di|ur'esis
  di|ur'eses
di|ur'et'ic +s
di|ur'nal
di|ur'nal'ly
diva +s
di'va|gate
  di'va|gates
  di'va|gated
  di'va|gat'ing
di'va|ga'tion +s
di'va'lency
di'va'lent
divan +s

di|vari|cate
  di|vari|cates
  di|vari|cated
  di|vari|cat'ing
  di|vari|ca'tion
dive
  dives
  dived
  dove *Am.*
  div'ing
dive-bomb +s +ed
  +ing
dive-bomber +s
diver +s
di|verge
  di|verges
  di|verged
  di|ver'ging
di|ver'gence +s
di|ver'gency
  di|ver'gen'cies
di|ver'gent
di|ver'gent'ly
divers (sundry)
di|verse
di|verse'ly
di|ver'si|fi'able
di|ver'si|fi'ca'tion
  +s
di|ver'sify
  di|ver'si|fies
  di|ver'si|fied
  di|ver'si|fy'ing
di|ver'sion +s
di|ver'sion|al
di|ver'sion|ary
di|ver'sion|ist +s
di|ver'sity
  di|ver'sities
di|vert +s +ed
  +ing
di|ver'ticu|lar
di|ver'ticu|litis
di|ver'ticu|losis
di|ver'ticu|lum
  di|ver'tic|ula
di|ver'ti|mento
  di|ver'ti|menti *or*
  di|ver'ti|men'tos
di|vert|ing'ly
di|ver'tisse|ment
  +s
Dives (rich man)
di|vest +s +ed
  +ing
di|vesti|ture
di|vest|ment +s
di|vest|ure
divi +s (use divvy)
div|ide
  div|ides

div¦ide (*cont.*)
  div¦ided
  div¦id¦ing
divi¦dend +s
dividend-
  stripping
div¦ider +s
divi-divi +s
div¦in¦ation +s
div¦in¦atory
div¦ine
  div¦ines
  div¦ined
  div¦in¦ing
  div¦iner
  div¦inest
div¦ine¦ly
div¦ine¦ness
div¦iner +s
div¦ing bell +s
div¦ing board +s
div¦ing suit +s
div¦in¦ing rod +s
div¦in¦ise *Br.* (use
  divinize)
  div¦in¦ises
  div¦in¦ised
  div¦in¦is¦ing
div¦in¦ity
  div¦in¦ities
div¦in¦ize
  div¦in¦izes
  div¦in¦ized
  div¦in¦iz¦ing
div¦isi¦bil¦ity
div¦is¦ible (capable
  of being divided.
  △ devisable)
div¦ision +s
div¦ision¦al
div¦ision¦al¦
  isa¦tion (use
  divisionalization)
div¦ision¦al¦ise
  (use
  divisionalize)
  div¦ision¦al¦ises
  div¦ision¦al¦ised
  div¦ision¦al¦is¦ing
div¦ision¦al¦
    iza¦tion
div¦ision¦al¦ize
  div¦ision¦al¦izes
  div¦ision¦al¦ized
  div¦ision¦al¦iz¦ing
div¦ision¦al¦ly
div¦ision¦ary
div¦ision¦ism
div¦isive
div¦isive¦ly
div¦isive¦ness

div¦isor +s
  (number.
  △ deviser,
  devisor)
di¦vorce
  di¦vorces
  di¦vorced
  di¦vor¦cing
di¦vorcé *Am.* +s
  male
di¦vor¦cee *Br.* +s
di¦vorcée *Am.* +s
  female
di¦vorce¦ment
divot +s
di¦vul¦ga¦tion
di¦vulge
  di¦vulges
  di¦vulged
  di¦vul¦ging
di¦vulge¦ment
di¦vul¦gence
divvy
  div¦vies
  div¦vied
  divvy¦ing
Di¦wali
Dixie (southern
  states of USA)
dixie +s (cooking
  pot)
Dixie¦land
Di¦yar¦ba¦kir (city
  and province,
  Turkey)
diz¦zily
diz¦zi¦ness
dizzy
  diz¦zies
  diz¦zied
  dizzy¦ing
  diz¦zier
  diz¦zi¦est
Dja¦karta (capital
  of Indonesia)
djel¦laba +s
djel¦la¦bah +s (use
  djellaba)
Djerba (island,
  Tunisia)
djibba +s
  (Muslim's coat;
  use jibba.
  △ gibber, jibber)
djib¦bah +s
  (Muslim's coat;
  use jibba.
  △ gibber, jibber)
Dji¦bouti
Dji¦bou¦tian +s
djinn
  plural djinn *or*

djinn (*cont.*)
  djinns
  (= jinnee. △ gin)
D-layer
D.Litt. (= Doctor of
  Literature)
D.Mus. (= Doctor
  of Music)
DNase
Dnie¦per (river,
  Russia, Belarus,
  and Ukraine)
Dnies¦ter (river,
  Ukraine and
  Moldova)
Dni¦pro¦
  dzer¦zhinsk (city,
  Ukraine)
Dni¦pro¦petrovsk
  (city, Ukraine)
D-notice +s
do
  does
  did
  doing
  done
  verb
do
  dos *or* do's
  noun
do (*Music*; use doh.
  △ doe, dough)
do¦able
dob
  dobs
  dobbed
  dob¦bing
dob¦bin +s
dobe (adobe.
  △ dhobi)
Do¦bell, Wil¦liam
  (Australian
  painter)
Do¦ber¦man
  (pin¦scher) *Am.* +s
Do¦ber¦mann
  (pin¦scher) *Br.* +s
Do¦brich (city,
  Bulgaria)
Do¦bruja (region,
  Romania and
  Bulgaria)
dob¦son¦fly
  dob¦son¦flies
doc +s (doctor.
  △ dock)
Do¦cetae
Do¦cet¦ism
Do¦cet¦ist +s
doch an dorris
  (use deoch an
  doris)
do¦cile
do¦cile¦ly

do¦cil¦ity
dock +s +ed +ing
  (for ships etc.; join
  spacecraft; in law
  court; weed; cut
  short. △ doc)
dock¦age
dock¦er +s
docket +s +ed
  +ing
dock-glass
  dock-glasses
dock¦land +s
dock leaf
  dock leaves
dock¦side +s
dock-tailed
dock work¦er +s
dock¦yard +s
Doc Mar¦ten
  adjective Propr.
Doc Mar¦tens
  (= Dr Martens)
doc¦tor +s +ed
  +ing
doc¦tor¦al
doc¦tor¦ate +s
doctor-blade +s
doc¦tor¦hood
doc¦tor¦ial
doc¦tor¦ly
Doc¦tor Mar¦tens
  (use Dr Martens)
doctor-patient
  attributive
doc¦tor¦ship +s
doc¦trin¦aire +s
doc¦trin¦air¦ism
doc¦tri¦nal
doc¦tri¦nal¦ly
doc¦trin¦ar¦ian +s
doc¦trine +s
doc¦trin¦ism
doc¦trin¦ist +s
docu¦drama +s
docu¦ment +s +ed
  +ing
docu¦men¦tal
docu¦men¦tal¦ist
  +s
docu¦men¦tar¦ian
  +s
docu¦men¦tar¦ily
docu¦men¦tar¦ist
  +s
docu¦men¦tary
  docu¦men¦tar¦ies
docu¦men¦ta¦tion
dod¦der +s +ed
  +ing
dod¦der¦er +s
dodder-grass
dod¦deri¦ness

dod¦dery
dod¦dle +s
do¦deca|gon +s
do¦deca|he¦dral
do¦deca|he¦dron
  do¦deca|he¦dra or
  do¦deca|he¦drons
Do¦decan|ese
  (Greek islands)
do¦deca|phon¦ic
dodge
  dodges
  dodged
  dodg¦ing
Dodge City (city,
  USA)
dodgem +s
dodger +s
Dodg¦son, Charles
  ('Lewis Carroll',
  English writer)
dodgy
  dodgi¦er
  dodgi¦est
dodo +s
Do¦doma (capital
  of Tanzania)
doe +s (deer.
  △ doh, dough)
doe-eyed
doek +s
doer +s
does (plural of doe;
  in 'he does' etc.)
doe|skin +s
doesn't (= does
  not)
doest
doeth
doff +s +ed +ing
dog
  dogs
  dogged
  dog|ging
dog|berry
  dog|berries
dog bis|cuit +s
dog box
  dog boxes
dog cart +s
dog-clutch
  dog-clutches
dog col¦lar +s
dog daisy
  dog dai¦sies
dog days
doge +s
dog-eared
dog-eat-dog
dog-end +s
dog|face +s
dog-fall +s

dog|fight +s
dog|fight¦er +s
dog|fight¦ing
dog|fish
  plural dog|fish or
  dog|fishes
dog food
dog|ged
dog|ged¦ly
dog|ged|ness
Dog¦ger (shipping
  area, North Sea)
dog¦ger +s (boat;
  Geology)
Dog¦ger Bank (in
  North Sea)
dog|gerel
Dog¦gett's Coat
  and Badge
dog¦gie +s (use
  doggy)
dog¦gi|ness
dog|gish
dog|gish¦ly
dog|gish|ness
doggo
dog|gone
doggy
  dog|gies
doggy bag +s
doggy-paddle
  doggy-paddles
  doggy-paddled
  doggy-paddling
dog hand|ler +s
dog-handling
dog|house +s
dogie +s
dog-leg
  dog-legs
  dog-legged
  dog-legging
dog|like
dogma +s
dog¦man
  dog¦men
dog|mat¦ic
dog|mat¦ic|al¦ly
dog|mat¦ics
dog|ma|tise Br.
  (use dogmatize)
  dog|ma|tises
  dog|ma|tised
  dog|ma|tis¦ing
dog|ma|tism
dog|ma|tist +s
dog|ma|tize
  dog|ma|tizes
  dog|ma|tized
  dog|ma|tiz¦ing
do-good +s noun
  and adjective
do-gooder +s

do-goodery
do-goodism
dog-paddle
  dog-paddles
  dog-paddled
  dog-paddling
dog ra¦cing
dog rose +s
dogs|body
  dogs|bodies
dog|shore +s
dog|skin
dog sled +s
dog's meat
dog's mer¦cury
  (plant)
dog's-tail +s
dog-star
dog's tooth
dog tag
dog-tail +s
dog-tired
dog-tooth
dog trials
dog|trot
dog-violet +s
dog|watch
dog|wood +s
doh (Music. △ doe,
  dough)
Doha (capital of
  Qatar)
doily
  doi|lies
doing +s
Dois|neau,
  Rob¦ert (French
  photographer)
doit +s
do-it-yourself
dojo +s
Dolby Propr.
dolce far ni¦¦ente
Dolce|latte
dolce vita
dol|drums
dole
  doles
  doled
  dol|ing
  (benefit; woe.
  △ dhole)
dole-bludger +s
dole|ful
dole|ful¦ly
dole|ful|ness
doler|ite
doli¦cho|ceph¦al¦ic
doli¦cho|
      ceph¦al¦ous
doli¦cho|ceph¦aly
Dolin, Anton
  (British dancer

Dolin (cont.)
  and
  choreographer)
do¦lina +s
do¦line +s
Doll, Rich|ard
  (English
  physician)
doll +s +ed +ing
dol|lar +s
dol|lar|isa|tion
  (use
  dollarization)
dol|lar|iza|tion
Doll|fuss,
  Engel|bert
  (Austrian
  statesman)
doll|house +s
dol|lop +s +ed
  +ing
doll's house +s
Dolly (name)
dolly
  dol|lies
  dol|lied
  dolly|ing
  (doll; dress up
  smartly)
dolly-bird +s
dolly mix|ture +s
Dolly Var¦den +s
dolma
  dol¦mas or
  dol¦ma|des
dol¦man +s
  (sleeve)
dol¦men +s (tomb)
dolo|mite (mineral
  or rock)
Dolo|mite
  Moun|tains (in
  Italy)
Dolo|mites
  (= Dolomite
  Mountains)
dolo|mit¦ic
dolor Am.
Dol|ores also
  Del|ores
dol¦or|ous
dol¦or|ous¦ly
dol¦our Br.
dol|phin +s
dol|phin|arium
  dol¦phin|ariums
  or dol¦phin|aria
dolt +s
dolt|ish
dolt|ish¦ly
dolt|ish|ness
Dom (title)

do¦main +s (realm)
do¦maine +s
(vineyard)
do¦man¦ial
dome
domes
domed
dom¦ing
dome¦like
Domes¦day (Book)
(1086 English
record.
△ doomsday)
do¦mes¦tic +s
do¦mes¦tic¦able
do¦mes¦tic¦al¦ly
do¦mes¦ti¦cate
do¦mes¦ti¦cates
do¦mes¦ti¦cated
do¦mes¦ti¦cat¦ing
do¦mes¦ti¦ca¦tion
do¦mes¦ti¦city
do¦mes¦ti¦ci¦ties
domi¦cile
domi¦ciles
domi¦ciled
domi¦cil¦ing
domi¦cil¦iary
dom¦in¦ance
dom¦in¦ant +s
dom¦in¦ant¦ly
dom¦in¦ate
dom¦in¦ates
dom¦in¦ated
dom¦in¦at¦ing
dom¦in¦ation +s
dom¦in¦ator +s
dom¦in¦atrix
dom¦in¦atrixes or
dom¦in¦atri¦ces
female
dom¦in¦eer +s +ed
+ing
dom¦in¦eer¦ing¦ly
Dom¦ingo,
Pla¦cido (Spanish
tenor)
Dom¦inic (Spanish
saint; name)
Do¦min¦ica (island,
West Indies)
do¦min¦ical
Do¦min¦ic¦an +s
dom¦inie +s
do¦min¦ion +s
Dom¦in¦ique
Dom¦ino, Fats
(American
musician)
dom¦ino
dom¦inoes

Dom¦itian (Roman
emperor)
Don (rivers, Russia,
Scotland, and
Yorkshire; name)
Don +s (Spanish
male title)
don
dons
donned
don¦ning
(university
teacher; put on)
dona +s (woman.
△ doner, donor)
donah +s (woman;
use dona
△ doner, donor)
Don¦ald
Don¦ald Duck
(cartoon
character)
do¦nate
do¦nates
do¦nated
do¦nat¦ing
Dona¦tello
(Florentine
sculptor)
do¦na¦tion +s
Donat¦ism
Donat¦ist +s
do¦na¦tive +s
do¦na¦tor +s
Do¦na¦tus (Roman
grammarian)
Don¦bas (Ukranian
name for the
Donets Basin)
Don¦bass (Russian
name for the
Donets Basin)
Don¦cas¦ter (town,
England)
done (past
participle of do.
△ dun)
donee +s
(recipient)
Don¦egal (county,
Republic of
Ireland)
doner (kebab.
△ dona, donna,
donor)
Don¦ets (river, E.
Europe)
Don¦ets Basin
(region, Ukraine)
Don¦etsk (city,
Ukraine)
dong +s +ed +ing

donga +s
don¦gle +s
Doni¦zetti,
Gae¦tano (Italian
composer)
don¦jon +s (castle
keep. △ dungeon)
Don Juan
(legendary
Spanish libertine)
don¦key +s
don¦key work
don¦key cart +s
don¦key jacket +s
don¦key's years
don¦key work
Don¦kin, Bryan
(English engineer)
Donna (name;
Italian, Spanish, or
Portuguese female
title)
donna +s (Italian,
Spanish, or
Portuguese lady;
in 'prima donna'.
△ doner)
Donne, John
(English poet and
divine. △ Dunne)
donné +s (use
donnée)
don¦née +s
don¦nish
don¦nish¦ly
don¦nish¦ness
Donny¦brook +s
donor +s (giver.
△ dona, doner)
Dono¦van
Don Quix¦ote
(fictional hero)
don't +s (= do not)
donut +s (use
doughnut)
doo¦dad +s
doo¦dah +s
doo¦dle
doo¦dles
doo¦dled
dood¦ling
doodle¦bug +s
dood¦ler +s
dood¦ling +s
doodly-squat
doo¦hickey +s
doo¦jig¦ger +s
Doo¦lit¦tle, Hilda
(American poet)
doom +s +ed +ing
(fate. △ doum)
doom-laden
doom¦say¦er +s

dooms¦day (Last
Judgement.
△ Domesday)
doom¦ster +s
doom¦watch
doom¦watch¦er +s
Doona +s
door +s (of house
etc. △ daw, dor)
door¦bell +s
door¦case +s
do-or-die *attributive*
doored
door frame +s
door handle +s
door head +s
door jamb +s
door¦keeper +s
door¦knob +s
door¦knock +s
door knock¦er +s
door¦man
door¦men
door¦mat +s
door¦nail +s
Door¦nik (Flemish
name for
Tournai)
door plate +s
door¦post +s
Doors, the
(American rock
group)
door¦step
door¦steps
door¦stepped
door¦step¦ping
door¦stop +s
door-to-door
door¦way +s
door¦yard +s
doozy
doo¦zies
dop +s
dopa (amino acid.
△ doper)
dopa¦mine
dop¦ant +s
dope
dopes
doped
dop¦ing
doper +s (person
who gives or takes
drugs. △ dopa)
dopey
dopi¦er
dopi¦est
dop¦ily
dopi¦ness
dop¦pel¦gän¦ger +s
Dop¦per +s

Dop|pler (effect)
dopy (use dopey)
  dopi|er
  dopi|est
dor +s (beetle.
  ⚠ daw, door)
Dora
Dor|ado
  (constellation)
dor|ado +s (fish)
Dor|cas
Dor|ches|ter (town,
  England)
Dor|dogne
  (department,
  France)
Dor|drecht (city,
  the Netherlands)
Doré, Gus|tave
  (French
  illustrator)
Dor|een
Dor|ian +s (ancient
  Hellenic people;
  name)
Dor|ian mode
Doric +s
Dor|inda
Doris
dork +s
dorm +s
dor|mancy
dor|mant
dormer +s
dor|mi|tion
dor|mi|tory
  dor|mi|tor|ies
Dor|mo|bile +s
  Propr.
dor|mouse
  dor|mice
dormy
do|ron|icum +s
Doro|thea
Doro|thy
dorp +s
dor|sal
dor|sal|ly
Dor|set (county,
  England)
dor|sum
  dorsa
Dort (alternative
  name for
  Dordrecht)
Dort|mund (city,
  Germany)
dory
  dor|ies
dory|phore +s
DOS *Computing*
dos-à-dos

dos|age +s
dose
  doses
  dosed
  dos|ing
do-se-do +s
dosh
do-si-do +s (use do-
  se-do)
dos|im|eter +s
dosi|met|ric
dos|im|etry
Dos Passos, John
  (American writer)
doss
  dosses
  dossed
  doss|ing
dos|sal
doss|er +s
doss-house +s
dos|sier +s
dost (in 'thou dost'.
  ⚠ dust)
Dos|to|ev|sky,
  Fyodor (Russian
  novelist)
dot
  dots
  dot|ted
  dot|ting
dot|age
dot|ard +s
dote
  dotes
  doted
  dot|ing
doter +s
doth
  dot|ing|ly
dot mat|rix
dot mat|rix
  print|er +s
dot|ter +s
dot|terel
dot|tily
dot|ti|ness
dot|tle +s
dotty
  dot|tier
  dot|ti|est
Dou|ala (city,
  Cameroon)
dou|ane +s
Douay Bible
double
  doubles
  doubled
  doub|ling
double act +s
double-acting
double-banking

double-barreled
  Am.
double-barrelled
  Br.
double bass
  double basses
double bill +s
double-blind
double bluff +s
double-book +s
  +ed +ing
double-breast|ed
double-check +s
  +ed +ing
double-chinned
double-cross
  double-crosses
  double-crossed
  double-crossing
double-crosser +s
double-dealer +s
double-dealing
double-decker +s
double-declutch
  double-
    declutches
  double-
    declutched
  double-
    declutch|ing
double Dutch
double-dyed
double-edged
double en|ten|dre
  +s
double-faced
double fault +s
  noun
double-fault +s
  +ed +ing *verb*
double-fronted
double-ganger +s
double-glazed
double glaz|ing
double
  Glouces|ter
double-headed
double head|er +s
double-jointed
double knit|ting
double-length
  adjective
double-lock +s
  +ed +ing
double-minded
double|ness
double-park +s
  +ed +ing
double quick
doub|ler +s
double-sided
double|speak

double stop +s
double-stopping
doub|let +s
double take +s
double-talk
double-thick
double|think
double time
double-tonguing
double whammy
  double
    wham|mies
doub|loon +s
doub|lure +s
doubly
doubt +s +ed +ing
doubt|able
doubt|er +s
doubt|ful
doubt|ful|ly
doubt|ful|ness
doubt|ing|ly
doubt|less
doubt|less|ly
douce
dou|ceur +s
douche
  douches
  douched
  douch|ing
Doug
dough +s (mixture
  for bread etc.
  ⚠ doe, doh)
dough|boy +s
doughi|ness
dough|nut +s
dough|nut|ting
dought|ily
doughti|ness
doughty
  dought|ier
  doughti|est
doughy
  dough|ier
  doughi|est
Doug|las (capital of
  the Isle of Man;
  name)
Doug|las, Kirk and
  Mi|chael
  (American actors)
Doug|las fir +s
Douglas-Home,
  Alec (Lord Home,
  British prime
  minister)
doum +s (palm.
  ⚠ doom)
doum-palm +s
dour
dour|ly

dour|ness
Douro (river, Spain and Portugal)
dou|rou|couli +s
douse
  douses
  doused
  dous|ing
  (drench; extinguish, △ dowse)
dove +s (bird)
dove (Am. past tense of dive)
dove|cote +s
dove gray Am. +s
  noun and adjective
dove-gray Am.
  attributive
dove grey Br. +s
  noun and adjective
dove-grey Br.
  attributive
dove|kie +s
dove|like
Dover (port, England; city, USA; shipping area)
dove's-foot +s
dove|tail +s +ed +ing
dove tree +s
dow|ager +s
dow|dily
dow|di|ness
dowdy
  dow|dier
  dow|di|est
dowel
  dowels
  dow|elled Br.
  dow|eled Am.
  dowel|ling Br.
  dowel|ling Am.
dower +s +ed +ing
dower|less
dow|itcher +s
Dow–Jones index
Down (county, Northern Ireland)
down +s +ed +ing
down and out
  adjective
down-and-out +s
  noun and attributive
down at heel
  adjective
down-at-heel
  attributive
down|beat +s
down|cast

down|comer +s
down draft Am. +s
down draught Br. +s
down|er +s
down|fall +s
down|field
down|fold +s
down|grade
  down|grades
  down|graded
  down|grad|ing
down|haul +s
down|heart|ed
down|heart|ed|ly
down|heart|ed| ness
down|hill +s
down|hill|er +s
down-home
down|ily
downi|ness
Down|ing Street (in London)
down in the mouth
down|land +s
down|light|er +s
down|load +s +ed +ing
down|mar|ket
down|most
down pay|ment +s
down|pipe +s
down|play +s +ed +ing
down|pour +s
down|rate
  down|rates
  down|rated
  down|rat|ing
down|right
down|right|ness
down|river
Downs, the (hill region, England)
down|scale
  down|scales
  down|scaled
  down|scal|ing
down|shaft +s +ed +ing
down|shift +s +ed +ing
down|side +s
down|size
  down|sizes
  down|sized
  down|siz|ing
Down|son, Er|nest (English poet)
down|spout +s

Down's
  syn|drome
down|stage
down|stairs
down|state
down|stream
down|stroke +s
down|swing +s
down|throw
  down|throws
  down|threw
  down|throw|ing
  down|thrown
down time
down-to-earth
down|town +s
down|trod|den
down|turn +s +ed +ing
down under
down|ward
down|ward|ly
down|wards
down|warp +s
down|wind
downy
  down|ier
  downi|est
dowry
  dow|ries
dowse
  dowses
  dowsed
  dows|ing
  (search for water. △ douse)
dowser +s
Dow|sing (light vessel, North Sea)
dows|ing rod +s
doxo|logic|al
dox|ology
  dox|ologies
doxy
  doxies
doyen +s male
doy|enne +s female
Doyle, Ar|thur Conan (Scottish novelist)
doy|ley +s (use doily)
D'Oyly Carte, Rich|ard (English impresario)
doze
  dozes
  dozed
  doz|ing
dozen +s
doz|enth
dozer +s
dozi|ly

dozi|ness
dozy
  dozi|er
  dozi|est
D.Phil. (= Doctor of Philosophy)
drab
  drab|ber
  drab|best
Drab|ble, Mar|ga|ret (English novelist)
drab|ble
  drab|bles
  drab|bled
  drab|bling
drab|ly
drab|ness
dra|caena +s
drachm +s (unit. △ DRAM, dram)
drachma +s
drack
Draco (Athenian legislator; constellation)
drac|one +s
dra|co|nian
dra|con|ic
Drac|ula, Count (vampire)
draff
draft +s +ed +ing (preliminary writing or drawing; money order; Military. △ draught)
draft Am. +s (current of air; act of drinking; drawing in; depth of water. Br. draught)
draft dodger +s
draft dodg|ing
draft|ee +s
draft|er +s
draft horse Am. +s (Br. draught horse)
draft|ily Am. (Br. draughtily)
drafti|ness Am. (Br. draughtiness)
draft-proof Am. +s +ed +ing (Br. draught-proof)
drafts|man Am.
  drafts|men (Br. draughtsman)

drafts¦man¦ship
Am. (Br. draughts-
manship)
drafts¦woman Am.
  drafts|women
(Br.
draughtswoman)
drafty Am.
  draft|ier
  drafti|est
(Br. draughty)
drag
  drags
  dragged
  drag|ging
drag-anchor +s
dra¦gée +s
drag¦gle
  drag¦gles
  drag¦gled
  drag¦gling
draggle-tailed
draggy
  drag¦gier
  drag¦gi¦est
drag-hound +s
drag|line +s
drag|net +s
drago|man
  drago|mans or
  drago|men
dragon +s
drag|onet +s
dragon|fish
  plural dragon|fish
  or dragon|fishes
dragon|fly
  dragon|flies
dragon|ish
drag¦on|nade
  drag¦on|nades
  drag¦on|naded
  drag¦on|nad¦ing
dragon's blood
dragon's teeth
dragon tree +s
drag|oon +s +ed
  +ing
drag|ster +s
drail +s
drain +s +ed +ing
drain|age +s
drain|board +s
drain|cock +s
drain¦er +s
drain|ing board +s
drain|pipe +s
Drake, Fran|cis
  (English explorer)
drake +s

Drak¦ens|berg
  Moun|tains (in
  southern Africa)
Drake Pas|sage
  (off S. America)
Dra¦lon Propr.
DRAM (= dynamic
  random access
  memory.
  ⚠ drachm)
dram +s (drink.
  ⚠ drachm)
drama +s
drama|doc +s
drama-
  documen¦tary
  drama-
  documen¦tar¦ies
dra|mat¦ic
dra¦mat¦ic|al¦ly
dra¦mat¦ics
drama|tisa|tion Br.
  +s (use
  dramatization)
drama|tise Br. (use
  dramatize)
  drama|tises
  drama|tised
  drama|tis¦ing
drama|tis
  per|sonae
drama|tist +s
drama|tiza|tion +s
drama|tize
  drama|tizes
  drama|tized
  drama|tiz¦ing
drama|turge +s
drama|tur¦gic
drama|tur¦gic|al
drama|turgy
  drama|tur¦gies
Dram|buie Propr.
Dram|men (port,
  Norway)
drank
drape
  drapes
  draped
  drap¦ing
draper +s
dra¦pery
  dra¦per¦ies
dras|tic
dras¦tic|al¦ly
drat
drat|ted
draught Br. +s +ed
  +ing (current of
  air; act of
  drinking; drawing
  in; depth of water.

draught (cont.)
  In other senses
  use draft. Am.
  draft)
draught|board +s
draught horse Br.
  +s (Am. draft
  horse)
draught¦ily Br.
  (Am. draftily)
draughti|ness Br.
  (Am. draftiness)
draught-proof Br.
  +s +ed +ing
  (Am. draft-proof)
draughts (game)
draughts|man Br.
  draughts|men
  (Am. draftsman)
draughts¦man|
  ship Br. (Am.
  draftsmanship)
draughts|woman
  Br.
  draughts|women
  (Am.
  draftswoman)
draughty Br.
  draught|ier
  draughti|est
  (Am. drafty)
Dra¦vid|ian +s
draw
  draws
  drew
  draw|ing
  drawn
draw|back +s
draw|bridge +s
draw|cord +s
draw|down +s
draw¦ee +s
drawer +s
drawer|ful +s
draw|ing +s
draw|ing board +s
draw|ing paper
draw|ing pin +s
draw|ing room +s
drawl +s +ed +ing
drawl¦er +s
drawn
drawn-out
  attributive
drawn work
draw-sheet +s
draw|string +s
draw-well +s
dray +s (cart.
  ⚠ drey)
dray horse +s
dray|man
  dray|men

dread +s +ed +ing
dread|ful
dread|ful¦ly
dread|ful|ness
dread|locked
dread|locks
dread|nought +s
dream
  dreams
  dreamed or
  dreamt
  dream|ing
dream|boat +s
dream¦er +s
dream|ful
dream|ily
dreami|ness
dream|land +s
dream|less
dream|like
dream|scape +s
dream|time
dream-world +s
dreamy
  dream|ier
  dreami|est
drear +er +est
drear|ily
dreari|ness
dreary
  drear|ier
  dreari|est
dreck
dredge
  dredges
  dredged
  dredg¦ing
dredger +s
dree
  drees
  dreed
  dree|ing
dreg +s
dreggy
Drei|ser,
  Theo|dore
  (American
  novelist)
drench
  drenches
  drenched
  drench¦ing
Drenthe (province,
  the Netherlands)
Dres|den (city,
  Germany)
dress
  dresses
  dressed
  dress|ing
dress|age
dress circle +s

dress'er +s
dressi|ness
dress|ing +s
dress|ing case +s
dress|ing down
　noun
dress|ing gown +s
dress|ing room +s
dress|ing sta|tion
　+s
dress|ing table +s
dress|ing up *noun*
dress|maker +s
dress|mak'ing
dress shield +s
dress shirt +s
dressy
　dress|ier
　dressi|est
Drew (name)
drew (past tense of
　draw)
drey +s (squirrel's
　nest. △ dray)
Drey|fus, Al'fred
　(French army
　officer)
drib'ble
　drib'bles
　drib'bled
　drib|bling
drib|bler +s
drib|bly
drib|let +s
dribs and drabs
dried
dried-out *adjective*
dried-up *adjective*
drier (comparative
　of dry. △ dryer)
dri'est
drift +s +ed +ing
drift|age
drift'er +s
drift-ice
drift-net +s
drift-netter +s
drift-netting
drift|wood
drill +s +ed +ing
drill'er +s
drill ser|geant +s
drily
drink
　drinks
　drank
　drink|ing
　drunk
drink|able
drink-drive
　attributive
drink-driver +s

drink-driving
drink'er +s
drinking-song +s
drinking-up time
drink|ing water
drip
　drips
　dripped
　drip|ping
drip-dry
　drip-dries
　drip-dried
　drip-drying
drip-feed
　drip-feeds
　drip-fed
　drip-feeding
drip-mat +s
drip-moulding
drip|pily
drip'pi|ness
drippy
drip|pier
drip'pi|est
drip|stone +s
driv'able
drive
　drives
　drove
　driv'ing
　driven
drive|able (use
　drivable)
drive-by *adjective*
drive-in +s
　adjective and noun
drivel
　driv'els
　driv|elled *Br.*
　driv|eled *Am.*
　driv'el|ling *Br.*
　driv'el|ling *Am.*
　driv'el|er *Am.* +s
　driv'el|ler *Br.* +s
　driven
drive-on *adjective*
drive-on/drive-off
　adjective
driver +s
driver|less
driver's li|cense
　Am. +s (*Br.*
　driving licence)
drive|shaft +s
drive-through +s
　adjective and noun
drive-thru *Am.* +s
　adjective and noun
　(*Br.* drive-
　through)
drive-time
drive|way +s

driv'ing licence *Br.*
　+s (*Am.* driver's
　license)
driv'ing range +s
driv'ing test +s
driv'ing wheel +s
driz'zle
　driz'zles
　driz'zled
　driz|zling
driz|zly
Dr Mar|tens *Propr.*
Dro|gheda (port,
　Republic of
　Ireland)
drogue +s
droit +s
droit de sei|gneur
droll +er +est
droll|ery
　droll|er'ies
droll|ness
drolly
drome +s
drom|ed'ary
　drom|ed|ar'ies
drom|ond +s
drone
　drones
　droned
　dron'ing
drongo +s
droob +s
drool +s +ed +ing
droop +s +ed +ing
　(sag. △ drupe)
droop|ily
droopi|ness
droop-snoot +s
droopy
　droop|ier
　droopi|est
drop
　drops
　dropped
　drop|ping
drop cur|tain +s
drop-dead *adjective*
drop-forge
　drop-forges
　drop-forged
　drop-forging
drop goal +s
drop ham'mer +s
drop|head +s
drop-in +s *noun*
　and adjective
drop kick +s
drop-leaf
　drop-leaves
drop|let +s
drop-off +s

drop-out +s *noun*
drop|per +s
drop|ping +s
drop scene +s
drop scone +s
drop shot +s
drop|si'cal
dropsy
　drop|sies
drop test +s *noun*
drop-test +s +ed
　+ing *verb*
drop|wort +s
droshky
　drosh|kies
Dros|oph'ila
　(genus)
dros|oph'ila +s
　(fly)
dross
drossy
　dros|sier
　drossi|est
Drott'ning|holm
　(town, Sweden)
drought +s
droughty
drouth
Drouzhba (resort,
　Bulgaria)
drove
　droves
　droved
　drov'ing
drover +s
drove road +s
drown +s +ed
　+ing
drown|ing +s
drowse
　drowses
　drowsed
　drows|ing
drows|ily
drow'si|ness
drowsy
　drows|ier
　drowsi|est
drub
　drubs
　drubbed
　drub|bing
drudge
　drudges
　drudged
　drudg|ing
drudg'ery
　drudg|er|ies
drug
　drugs
　drugged
　drug|ging

drug-crazed
drug deal¦er +s
drug deal¦ing
drug|get +s
drug|gie +s (use
   druggy)
drug|gist +s
druggy
   drug|gies
drug ped|dler +s
drug push¦er +s
drug smug|gler +s
drug smug|gling
drug|store +s
drug traf|fick¦er
   +s
drug traf¦fick|ing
Druid +s
Druid|ess
   Druid|esses
Dru|id¦ic
Dru¦id|ic¦al
Dru¦id|ism
drum
   drums
   drummed
   drum|ming
drum|beat +s
drum|fire
drum fish
   plural drum fish or
   drum fishes
drum|head +s
drum kit +s
drum|lin +s
drum|lin|oid
drum|mer +s
drum|stick +s
drunk +s +er +est
drunk|ard +s
drunk¦en adjective
drunk¦en¦ly
drunk¦en|ness
drup|aceous
drupe +s (fruit.
   △ droop)
drupel +s
drupe|let +s
Drury Lane (in
   London)
Druse +s (Muslim;
   use Druze)
druse +s (cavity)
Dru|silla
druther +s
Druzba (use
   Drouzhba)
Druze +s (Muslim.
   △ druse)
dry
   dries
   dried

dry (cont.)
   dry¦ing
   drier
   dri¦est
dryad +s
dry cell +s
dry-clean +s +ed
   +ing
dry-cleaner +s
dry cure
   dry cures
   dry cured
   dry cur¦ing
Dry¦den, John
   (English writer)
dry dock +s
dryer +s (device.
   △ drier)
dry-eyed
dry fly
   dry flies
   noun
dry-fly
   dry-flies
   dry-flied
   dry-flying
   verb and attributive
dry¦ish
dry|land +s (land
   with low rainfall)
dry land (not sea)
dryly (use drily)
dry|ness
dry-nurse +s
dryo|pith¦ecine
Dryo|pith¦ecus
dry plate +s
dry-point +s
dry-salt +s +ed
   +ing
dry-salter +s
Drys|dale, Rus|sell
   (Australian
   painter)
dry-shod
dry|stone
dry|suit +s
dry|wall
dual
   duals
   dualled Br.
   dualed Am.
   dual|ling Br.
   dual|ing Am.
   (double. △ duel)
dual|ise Br. (use
   dualize)
dual|ises
dual|ised
dual|is¦ing
dual|ism +s
dual|ist +s

dual|is¦tic
dual|is¦tic|al¦ly
dual|ity
   dual|ities
dual|ize
   dual|izes
   dual|ized
   dual|iz¦ing
dual¦ly
dual-purpose
Duane also Dwane
dub
   dubs
   dubbed
   dub|bing
Dubai (state and
   city, UAE)
dub¦bin +s +ed
   +ing
Dub¦ček,
   Alex|an¦der
   (Czech statesman)
du¦bi|ety
du¦bi|ous
du¦bi|ous¦ly
du¦bi|ous|ness
du¦bi|ta¦tion
du¦bi|ta|tive
du¦bi|ta|tive¦ly
Dub|lin (capital and
   county of the
   Republic of
   Ireland)
Dub¦lin Bay
   prawn +s
Dub|lin¦er +s
Du Bois, W. E. B.
   (American writer
   and political
   activist)
Du|bon¦net Propr.
Du¦brov|nik (port,
   Croatia)
ducal
ducat +s
Duc¦cio di
   Buon|in¦segna
   (Sienese painter)
Duce, Il (Mussolini)
Du|champ,
   Mar¦cel (French
   artist)
Du|chenne
   (muscular
   dystrophy)
duch|ess
   duch|esses
   (noblewoman)
du|chesse +s
   (furniture; lace;
   potatoes)
duchy
   duch¦ies

duck +s +ed +ing
duck|bill +s
duck-billed
   platy|pus
duck-billed
   platy|puses
duck|board +s
duck¦er +s
duck-hawk +s
duckie +s (use
   ducky)
ducking-stool +s
duck|ling +s
duck's arse Br.
duck's ass Am.
duck|weed +s
ducky
   duck|ies
duct +s +ed +ing
duc|tile
duc¦til|ity
duct|less
dud +s
dude +s
dudgeon
dudish
Dud¦ley (name)
Dud¦ley, Rob¦ert
   (Earl of Leicester,
   courtier of
   Elizabeth I)
due +s (owed.
   △ dew)
duel
   duels
   duelled Br.
   dueled Am.
   duel|ling Br.
   duel|ing Am.
   (fight. △ dual)
duel¦er Am. +s
duel|ist Am. +s
duel|ler Br. +s
duel|list Br. +s
du|ende +s
du|enna +s
Duero (Spanish
   name for the
   Douro)
duet
   duets
   duet|ted
   duet|ting
duet|tist +s
Dufay, Guil|laume
   (Franco-Flemish
   composer and
   singer)
duff
   duffs
   duffed
   duff|ling

duf'fel
duf'fel bag +s
duf'fel coat +s
duf'fer +s
duf'fle (use duffel)
Dufy, Raoul
  (French artist)
dug +s
du'gong
  plural du'gong *or*
  du'gongs
dug'out +s
duiker +s
Duis|burg (city,
  Germany)
Dukas, Paul
  (French
  composer)
duke +s
duke|dom +s
Du'kho|bor +s
dul'cet
Dul'cie
dul'ci|fi|ca'tion
dul'cify
  dul'ci|fies
  dul'ci|fied
  dul'ci|fy|ing
dul'ci|mer +s
dul'ci|tone
dulia
dull +s +ed +ing
  +er +est
dull|ard +s
Dulles, John
  Foster (American
  statesman)
dull|ish
dull|ness
dull-witted
dully
dulse
duly
duma +s (Russian
  council)
Dumas,
  Alex|andre (père
  and fils, French
  writers)
Du Maur|ier,
  Daphne (English
  writer)
Du Maur|ier,
  George (French-
  born illustrator
  and writer)
dumb +er +est
Dum|bar'ton
  (town, Scotland)
dumb-bell +s
dumb|found +s
  +ed +ing

dumb|head +s
dumb-iron +s
dumb'ly
dumb|ness
dumbo +s
dumb|show +s
dumb|struck
dum'dum +s
dum|found +s +ed
  +ing (use
  dumbfound)
Dum|fries (town,
  Scotland)
Dum|fries and
  Gallo|way
  (region, Scotland)
Dum'fries|shire
  (former county,
  Scotland)
dummy
  dum|mies
  dum|mied
  dummy|ing
dump +s +ed +ing
dump'er +s
dump'er truck +s
dump|ily
dumpi|ness
dump|ling +s
dump truck +s
dumpy
  dump|ier
  dumpi|est
dun
  duns
  dunned
  dun|ning
  (colour; creditor;
  pester; etc.
  ⚠done)
Dun'bar, Wil|liam
  (Scottish poet)
Dun'bar'ton|shire
  (former county,
  Scotland)
dun-bird +s
Dun'can (name)
Dun'can, Isa|dora
  (American dancer)
dunce +s
dunce's cap +s
Dun|dalk (town,
  Republic of
  Ireland)
Dun'dee (city,
  Scotland)
dun'der|head +s
dun'der|head'ed
dun-diver +s
dune +s
Dun|edin (city,
  New Zealand)

Dun|ferm|line
  (city, Scotland)
dung +s +ed +ing
dun|garee +s
Dun|gar'van
  (town, Republic of
  Ireland)
dung-beetle +s
dun|geon +s
  (underground
  prison. ⚠donjon)
dung-fly
  dung-flies
dung|hill +s
dung-worm +s
dunk +s +ed +ing
Dun|kirk (port,
  France)
Dun Lao'ghaire
  (port, Republic of
  Ireland)
dun'lin +s
Dun'lop, John
  Boyd (Scottish
  inventor)
Dun'mow flitch
dun'nage
Dunne, John
  Wil|liam (English
  philosopher.
  ⚠Donne)
Dun'net Head (in
  Scotland)
dunno +s (= don't
  know)
dun|nock +s
dunny
  dun|nies
Duns Scotus,
  John (Scottish
  theologian)
Dun|stable, John
  (English
  composer)
Dun|stan (Anglo-
  Saxon saint;
  name)
duo +s
duo|deci'mal
duo|deci'mal'ly
duo|decimo +s
duo|denal
duo|de'nary
duo'den|itis
duo|de'num +s
duo'log *Am.* +s
duo|logue +s
duomo +s
du|op'oly
  du|op'olies
duo|tone +s
dup'able

dupe
  dupes
  duped
  dup'ing
duper +s
dupery
du'pion +s
duple
du'plet +s
du'plex
  du|plexes
du'plic|able
du'pli|cate
  du'pli|cates
  du'pli|cated
  du'pli|cat'ing
du'pli|ca'tion +s
du'pli|ca'tor +s
du'pli'ci'tous
du'pli'ci'city
  du|pli'ci'ties
duppy
  dup|pies
du Pré,
  Jacque|line
  (English cellist)
dura +s (use durra)
dur|abil'ity
dur'able +s
dur'able|ness
dur'ably
Dur|alu'min (alloy)
  Propr.
dura mater +s
dur|amen
dur|ance
Dur|ango (state
  and city, Mexico)
Duras,
  Mar|guer'ite
  (French writer)
dur|ation +s
dur|ation'al
dura|tive
Dur'ban (city,
  South Africa)
dur'bar +s
*durch|kom|pon|
  iert*
Dürer, Al|brecht
  (German artist)
dur'ess
Durex
  plural **Durex**
  Propr.
Durey, Louis
  (French
  composer)
Durga *Hinduism*
Dur'ham (city,
  England)
dur'ian +s

duri|crust +s
dur|ing
Durk|heim, Émile
  (French
  philosopher)
Durk|heim|ian
dur|mast +s
durn
durned
durra +s
Dur|rell,
  Law|rence
  (English writer)
Dur|rës (port,
  Albania)
durst
durum
durzi +s
Du|shanbe (capital
  of Tadjikistan)
dusk +s
dusk|ily
duski|ness
dusk-to-dawn
dusky
  dusk|ies
  dusk|ier
  duski|est
Düs|sel|dorf (city,
  Germany)
dust +s +ed +ing
  (particles. △ dost)
dust bag +s
dust-bath +s
dust|bin +s
dust bowl +s
dust|cart +s
dust cover +s
dust devil +s
dust|er +s
dust|ily
Dus|tin
dusti|ness
dust|ing pow|der
dust jacket +s
dust|less
dust|man
  dust|men
dust|pan +s
dust sheet +s
dust-shot
dust storm +s
dust-trap +s
dust-up +s noun
dust-wrapper +s
dusty
  dust|ier
  dusti|est
Dutch (of the
  Netherlands etc.;
  in 'go Dutch')

dutch
  dutches
  (= duchess)
Dutch|man
  Dutch|men
Dutch|man's
  breeches
Dutch|man's pipe
Dutch|woman
  Dutch|women
du|teous
du|teous|ly
du|teous|ness
duti|able
duti|ful
duti|ful|ly
duti|ful|ness
duty
  du|ties
duty-bound
duty-free +s
duty of|ficer +s
duty-paid
du|um|vir +s
du|um|vir|ate
Du|val|ier, Papa
  Doc (Haitian
  statesman)
duvet +s
Du Vig|neaud,
  Vin|cent
  (American
  biochemist)
dux
  duxes
duyker +s (use
  duiker)
Dvořák, An|tonin
  (Czech composer)
dwale
Dwane also Duane
dwarf
  dwarfs or
  dwarves
  noun
dwarf +s +ed +ing
  verb
dwarf|ish
dwarf|ism
dweeb +s
dwell
  dwells
  dwelled or dwelt
  dwell|ing
dwell|er +s
dwell|ing +s
dwell|ing house
  +s
dwell|ing place +s
Dwight
dwin|dle
  dwin|dles

dwin|dle (cont.)
  dwin|dled
  dwin|dling
dyad +s
dyad|ic
Dyak +s
dy|archy (use
  diarchy)
dy|arch|ies
dyb|buk
  dyb|buk|im or
  dyb|buks
dye
  dyes
  dyed
  dye|ing
  (colour, stain.
  △ die)
dye|able
dyed-in-the-wool
dye-line +s
dyer +s
dyer's broom
dyer's green|weed
dyer's oak +s
  (tree)
dye|stuff +s
Dyfed (county,
  Wales)
dying (present
  participle of die.
  △ dyeing)
dyke
  dykes
  dyked
  dyk|ing
Dylan (name)
Dylan, Bob
  (American singer
  and songwriter)
Dymphna
dy|nam|ic
dy|nam|ic|al
dy|nam|ic|al|ly
dy|nami|cist
dy|nam|ics
dyna|misa|tion Br.
  (use
  dynamization)
dyna|mise Br. (use
  dynamize)
dyna|mises
dyna|mised
dyna|mis|ing
dyna|mism
dyna|mist +s
dyna|mite
  dyna|mites
  dyna|mited
  dyna|mit|ing
dyna|miter +s
dyna|miza|tion

dyna|mize
  dyna|mizes
  dyna|mized
  dyna|miz|ing
dy|namo +s
dyna|mom|eter +s
dyn|ast +s
dyn|as|tic
dyn|as|tic|al|ly
dyn|asty
  dyn|as|ties
dyna|tron +s
dyne +s (unit.
  △ dine)
dys|en|ter|ic
dys|en|tery
dys|func|tion +s
  +ed +ing
dys|func|tion|al
dys|gen|ic
dys|graphia
dys|graph|ic
dys|lec|tic +s
dys|lexia
dys|lex|ic +s
dys|lo|gis|tic
dys|lo|gis|tic|al|ly
dys|men|or|rhea
  Am.
dys|men|or|rhoea
  Br.
dys|pep|sia
dys|pep|tic
dys|pha|sia
dys|phasic
dys|phem|ism +s
dys|phoria
dys|phoric
dys|pla|sia
dys|plas|tic
dys|pnea Am.
dys|pneic Am.
dys|pnoea Br.
dys|pnoeic Br.
dys|pro|sium
dys|to|cia
dys|to|pia +s
dys|to|pian +s
dys|troph|ic
dys|trophy
dys|uria
Dzaou|dzi (town,
  Mayotte)
Dzau|dzhi|kau
  (former name of
  Vladikavkaz)
Dzer|zhinsk (city,
  Russia)
Dzer|zhin|sky,
  Fe|liks
  Ed|mund|ovich
  (Russian leader)

dzho (use dzo)
  plural **dzho** *or*
  dzhos
dzo
  plural **dzo** *or* **dzos**
Dzong|kha

Ee

....

each
Ead|wig (English
  king)
eager (keen.
  ⚠ eagre)
eager|ly
eagerly-awaited
eager|ness
eagle
  eagles
  eagled
  eag|ling
eagle eye +s
eagle-eyed
eag|let +s
eagre +s (wave.
  ⚠ eager)
Ea|kins, Thomas
  (American artist)
Eal|ing (borough,
  London; film
  studios)
Eamon *also*
  Ea|monn
Ea|monn *also*
  Eamon
ear +s
ear|ache +s
ear|bash
  ear|bashes
  ear|bashed
  ear|bash|ing
ear|bash|er +s
ear drops
ear|drum +s
eared
ear|ful +s
Ear|hart, Am|elia
  (American
  aviator)
ear|hole +s
ear|ing +s (rope.
  ⚠ earring)
earl +s
earl|dom +s
ear|less
Earl Grey (tea)
earli|ness
Earl Mar|shal
ear lobe +s
Earl Pal|at|ine
  Earls Pal|at|ine
early
  earl|ies
  earl|ier
  earli|est
**ear|mark +s +ed
  +ing**

ear|muff +s
earn +s +ed +ing
  (gain. ⚠ ern, erne,
  urn)
earn|er +s
earn|est
earn|est|ly
earn|est|ness
earn|ings
earnings-related
EAROM
  (= electrically
  alterable read-only
  memory)
Earp, Wyatt
  (American
  frontiersman)
ear|phone +s
ear|piece +s
ear-piercing
ear|plug +s
ear|ring +s
  (jewellery.
  ⚠ earing)
ear|shot
ear-splitting
ear-stopple +s
earth +s +ed +ing
earth|bound
earth closet +s
earth|en
earth|en|ware
earth-hog +s
earth|ily
earthi|ness
earth|li|ness
earth|ling +s
earth|ly
earth mother +s
earth mover +s
earth-moving
earth-nut +s
earth-pig +s
earth|quake +s
earth-shaking
earth-shatter|ing
**earth-
  shatter|ing|ly**
earth|shine
earth|star +s
earth|ward
earth|wards
earth|work +s
earth|worm +s
earthy
  earth|ier
  earthi|est
ear-trumpet +s
ear-tuft +s
ear|wax
ear|wig
  ear|wigs

ear|wig (*cont.*)
  ear|wigged
  ear|wig|ging
ease
  eases
  eased
  eas|ing
ease|ful
easel +s
ease|ment +s
easer +s
eas|ily
easi|ness
East, the (part of
  country etc.; E.
  Europe; E. Asia)
east +s (point;
  direction)
east|about
East An|glia
  (region, England)
east|bound
East|bourne (town,
  England)
East Ender +s
Easter +s
Easter Is|land (in
  SE Pacific)
east|er|ly
  east|er|lies
east|ern
east|ern|er +s
east|ern|most
East|er|tide
East India|man +s
east|ing +s
East|man, George
  (American
  inventor)
east-north-east
east-south-east
east|ward
east|ward|ly
east|wards
East-West
  attributive
East|wood, Clint
  (American actor
  and director)
easy
  eas|ier
  easi|est
easy chair +s
easy|going
easy-peasy
easy-to-follow
  attributive
easy-to-use
  attributive
eat
  eats
  ate

eat (cont.)
  eat¦ing
  eaten
eat|able +s
eater +s (person or
  animal that eats.
  ⚠ eta)
eat¦ery
  eat|er¦ies
eat¦ing apple +s
eat¦ing house +s
eat¦ing place +s
eau de Co|logne
  +s
eau-de-Nil
eau de toi¦lette +s
eau-de-vie +s
eau su¦crée
eave +s (under
  roof. ⚠ eve)
eaves|drop
  eaves|drops
  eaves|dropped
  eaves|drop|ping
eaves|drop|per +s
ebb +s +ed +ing
Eben|ezer
Ebla (city, ancient
  Syria)
E-boat +s
eb¦on|ite
ebony
Ebor|acum (Roman
  name for York)
Ebro (river, Spain)
ebul¦li¦ence
ebul¦li¦ency
ebul¦li¦ent
ebul¦li¦ent¦ly
ebul|li¦tion
ecad +s
écarté
Ecce Homo
ec¦cen|tric +s
ec¦cen|tric|al¦ly
ec¦cen|tri¦city
  ec¦cen|tri¦ci¦ties
ec¦chym|osis
  ec¦chym|oses
Ec¦cles, John
  (Australian
  physiologist)
Ec¦cles cake +s
ec¦cle¦sial
Ec¦cle¦si|as¦tes
  Bible
ec¦cle¦si|as¦tic +s
ec¦cle¦si|as¦tic|al
ec¦cle¦si|as¦tic|
      al¦ly
ec¦cle¦si|as¦ti|cism

Ec|cle¦si|as¦ti|cus
  Bible
ec|cle¦sio|logic¦al
ec|cle¦si|olo¦gist
  +s
ec|cle¦si|ology
ec|crine
ec¦dy¦sis
  ec¦dy¦ses
ech|elon +s
eche|veria +s
ech|idna +s
ech¦in|ite +s
ech¦ino|derm +s
ech¦in|oid +s
ech|inus
  ech|inuses
Echo *Greek*
  Mythology
echo
  echoes
  echoed
  echo|ing
echo|car¦dio|gram
  +s
echo|car¦dio|graph
  +s
echo|car¦di|
    og|raph¦er +s
echo|car¦di|
    og¦raphy
echo cham|ber +s
echo|en¦ceph|alo|
    gram +s
echo|en¦ceph|al|
    og¦raphy
echo¦er +s
echoey
echo|gram +s
echo|graph +s
echo¦ic
echo¦ic|al¦ly
echo¦ism
echo¦la¦lia
echo|less
echo|locate
  echo|locates
  echo|located
  echo|locat¦ing
echo|loca¦tion
echo sound¦er +s
echo-sounding
echo|virus
echt
éclair +s
éclair|cisse|ment
eclamp|sia
eclamp|tic
éclat
eclec|tic +s
eclec¦tic|al¦ly

eclec¦ti|cism
eclipse
  eclipses
  eclipsed
  eclips|ing
eclip¦ser +s
eclip|tic +s
eclip¦tic|al¦ly
ec|logue +s
eclo|sion
  eclo|sions
Eco, Um|berto
  (Italian novelist)
eco|cide
eco|cli¦mate +s
eco-friend¦ly
eco-label +s
eco-labeling *Am.*
eco-labelling *Br.*
eco|logic¦al
eco|logic|al¦ly
ecolo|gist +s
ecol|ogy
  ecol|ogies
econo|met¦ric
econo|met¦ric|al
econo|met¦ric|
    al¦ly
econo|met¦ri¦cian
  +s
econo|met¦rics
econo|met¦rist +s
eco|nom¦ic
eco|nom¦ic|al
eco|nom¦ic|al¦ly
eco|nom¦ics
econo|misa¦tion
  Br. (use
  economization)
econo|mise *Br.*
  (use economize)
  econo|mises
  econo|mised
  econo|mis¦ing
econo|miser *Br.* +s
  (use economizer)
econo|mist +s
econo|miza¦tion
econo|mize
  econo|mizes
  econo|mized
  econo|miz¦ing
econo|mizer +s
econ|omy
  econ|omies
econ|omy class
eco|sphere +s
écos|saise +s
eco|sys¦tem +s
eco-terror¦ism
eco-terror¦ist +s

eco|tour¦ism
eco|tour¦ist +s
eco|type +s
ecru +s
ec|sta¦sise *Br.* (use
  ecstasize)
  ec|sta¦sises
  ec|sta¦sised
  ec|sta¦sis¦ing
ec|sta¦size
  ec|sta¦sizes
  ec|sta¦sized
  ec|sta¦siz¦ing
ec|stasy
  ec|sta¦sies
ec|stat¦ic
ec|stat¦ic|al¦ly
ecto|blast +s
ecto|blast¦ic
ecto|derm +s
ecto|der¦mal
ecto|gen¦esis
ecto|gen¦et¦ic
ecto|gen¦et¦ic|al¦ly
ecto|gen¦ic
ecto|gen¦ic|al¦ly
ecto|morph +s
ecto|morph¦ic
ecto|morphy
ecto|para¦site +s
ec|top¦ic
ecto|plasm
ecto|plas¦mic
ecto|zoon
ecu
  plural ecu *or* ecus
  (= European
  currency unit)
écu +s (French
  coin)
Ecua|dor
Ecua¦dor|ean +s
ecu|men¦ic¦al +s
ecu|men¦ic|al|ism
ecu|men¦ic|al¦ly
ecu|meni¦cism
ecu|men|icity
ecu|men|ism
ec|zema (inflamma-
  tion. ⚠ excimer)
ec|zema|tous
Ed (name)
eda¦cious
eda¦city
Edam (town, the
  Netherlands;
  cheese)
ed|aph¦ic
Edda
Eddie
Ed¦ding|ton,
  Ar¦thur Stan|ley

Ed¦ding¦ton (*cont.*)
(English
astronomer and
physicist)
eddo
ed¦does
Eddy, Mary Baker
(American
founder of the
Christian Science
movement)
eddy
ed¦dies
ed¦died
eddy¦ing
Eddy¦stone Rocks
(in English
Channel)
edel¦weiss
plural edel¦weiss
edema *Am.*
ede¦mas *or*
ede¦mata
(*Br.* oedema)
edema¦tous *Am.*
(*Br.* oedematous)
Eden, An¦thony
(British prime
minister)
Eden, Gar¦den of
Bible
edent¦ate +s
Edgar (English
king; name)
edge
edges
edged
edging
Edge¦hill
(battlefield,
England)
edge¦less
edger +s
edge-tool +s
edge¦ways
edge¦wise
Edge¦worth,
Maria (Anglo-
Irish novelist)
edgi¦ly
edgi¦ness
edging +s
edg¦ing shears
edgy
edgi¦er
edgi¦est
edh +s
edi¦bil¦ity
ed¦ible +s
edict +s
edict¦al
Edie

edi¦fi¦ca¦tion
edi¦fice +s
edify
edi¦fies
edi¦fied
edify¦ing
edify¦ing¦ly
Ed¦in¦burgh
(capital of
Scotland)
Edi¦son, Thomas
(American
inventor)
edit +s +ed +ing
Edith
edi¦tion +s (version
of book etc.
△ addition)
edi¦tio prin¦ceps
edi¦ti¦ones
prin¦cipes
edi¦tor +s
edi¦tor¦ial +s
edi¦tori¦al¦ise *Br.*
(use editorialize)
edi¦tori¦al¦ises
edi¦tori¦al¦ised
edi¦tori¦al¦is¦ing
edi¦tori¦al¦ist +s
edi¦tori¦al¦ize
edi¦tori¦al¦izes
edi¦tori¦al¦ized
edi¦tori¦al¦iz¦ing
edi¦tori¦al¦ly
editor-in-chief
editors-in-chief
edit¦or¦ship +s
edit¦ress
edit¦resses
Ed¦mond *also*
Ed¦mund
Ed¦mon¦ton (city,
Canada)
Ed¦mund *also*
Ed¦mond
(name)
Ed¦mund (English
kings and saint)
Ed¦mund Iron¦side
(English king)
Ed¦mund the
Mar¦tyr (East
Anglian king and
saint)
Edna
Edom (ancient
region, Middle
East)
Edom¦ite +s
educ¦abil¦ity
educ¦able
edu¦cat¦able

edu¦cate
edu¦cates
edu¦cated
edu¦cat¦ing
edu¦ca¦tion +s
edu¦ca¦tion¦al
edu¦ca¦tion¦al¦ist
+s
edu¦ca¦tion¦al¦ly
edu¦ca¦tion¦ist +s
edu¦ca¦tive
edu¦ca¦tor +s
educe
educes
educed
edu¦cing
edu¦cible
educ¦tion
educ¦tive
edul¦cor¦ate
edul¦cor¦ates
edul¦cor¦ated
edul¦cor¦at¦ing
edul¦cor¦ation
edu¦tain¦ment
Ed¦ward (English
and British kings;
Prince; name)
Ed¦ward, Lake (in
E. Africa)
Ed¦ward¦ian +s
Ed¦ward¦iana
Ed¦wards, Gar¦eth
(Welsh rugby
player)
Ed¦ward the
Con¦fes¦sor
(English king and
saint)
Ed¦ward the
Mar¦tyr (English
king and saint)
Edwin
Ed¦wina
Edwy (English
king)
eegit +s (use eejit)
eejit +s
eel +s
Eelam (proposed
homeland, Sri
Lanka)
eel¦grass
eel¦grasses
eel-like
eel¦pout +s
eel¦worm +s
eely
e'en (= even)
e'er (= ever. △ air,
ere, heir)

eerie
eer¦ier
eeri¦est
(weird. △ eyrie)
eer¦ily
eeri¦ness
eff +s +ed +ing
ef¦face
ef¦faces
ef¦faced
ef¦facing
ef¦face¦able
ef¦face¦ment
ef¦fect +s +ed +ing
(result; bring
about. △ affect)
ef¦fect¦ive (having
an effect; efficient.
△ affective)
ef¦fect¦ive¦ly (in an
effective way.
△ affectively)
ef¦fect¦ive¦ness
ef¦fect¦iv¦ity
(degree of being
effective.
△ affectivity)
ef¦fect¦or +s
ef¦fec¦tual
ef¦fec¦tu¦al¦ity
ef¦fec¦tu¦al¦ly
ef¦fec¦tual¦ness
ef¦fec¦tu¦ate
ef¦fec¦tu¦ates
ef¦fec¦tu¦ated
ef¦fec¦tu¦at¦ing
ef¦fec¦tu¦ation
ef¦fem¦in¦acy
ef¦fem¦in¦ate
ef¦fem¦in¦ate¦ly
ef¦fendi +s
ef¦fer¦ence
ef¦fer¦ent
ef¦fer¦vesce
ef¦fer¦vesces
ef¦fer¦vesced
ef¦fer¦ves¦cing
ef¦fer¦ves¦cence
ef¦fer¦ves¦cency
ef¦fer¦ves¦cent
ef¦fete
ef¦fete¦ness
ef¦fi¦ca¦cious
ef¦fi¦ca¦cious¦ly
ef¦fi¦ca¦cious¦ness
ef¦fi¦cacy
ef¦fi¦ciency
ef¦fi¦cien¦cies
ef¦fi¦cient
ef¦fi¦cient¦ly
ef¦figy
ef¦fi¦gies

ef'fleur|age
  ef'fleur|ages
  ef'fleur|aged
  ef'fleur|aging
ef'flor|esce
  ef'flor|esces
  ef'flor|esced
  ef'flor|es|cing
ef'flor|es|cence +s
ef'flor|es|cent
ef'flu|ence
ef'flu|ent +s
ef'flu|vium
ef'flux
  ef'fluxes
ef'flux|ion +s
ef'fort +s
ef'fort|ful
ef'fort|ful|ly
ef'fort|less
ef'fort|less|ly
ef'fort|less|ness
ef'front|ery
ef'ful|gence
ef'ful|gent
ef'ful|gent|ly
ef'fuse
  ef'fuses
  ef'fused
  ef'fus|ing
ef'fu|sion +s
ef'fu|sive
ef'fu|sive|ly
ef'fu|sive|ness
Efik
  plural Efik
eft +s
Efta (= European
  Free Trade
  Association)
EFTPOS
  (= electronic
  funds transfer at
  point of sale)
egad
egali|tar|ian +s
egali|tar|ian|ism
Egas Moniz,
  An|tonio
  (Portuguese
  neurologist)
Eg'bert (king of
  Wessex)
Eger (town,
  Hungary)
egg +s +ed +ing
eggar +s (use
  egger)
egg-beater +s
egg'cup +s
egg cus|tard

egger +s
egg-flip +s
egg|head +s
eggi|ness
egg-laying
  attributive
egg|less
egg-nog +s
egg|plant +s
egg-shaped
egg|shell +s
egg-spoon +s
egg-timer +s
egg-tooth
  egg-teeth
egg white +s
eggy
  egg'ier
  eggi'est
egg yolk +s
eg|lan|tine +s
Eg'mont, Mount
  (in New Zealand)
ego +s
ego|cen'tric +s
ego|cen'tric|al|ly
ego|cen'tri|city
ego|cen'trism
ego-ideal
ego'ism
ego'ist +s
ego|is'tic
ego|is'tic|al
ego|is'tic|al|ly
ego|mania
ego|maniac +s
ego|mani|ac|al
egot|ise *Br.* (use
  egotize)
  egot|ises
  egot|ised
  egot|is|ing
egot|ism
egot|ist +s
egot|is'tic
egot|is'tic|al
egot|is'tic|al|ly
egot|ize
  egot|izes
  egot|ized
  egot|iz|ing
ego trip +s
egre|gious
egre|gious|ly
egre|gious|ness
egress
  egresses
egres|sion
egret +s
Egypt
Egyp|tian +s

Egyp|tian|isa'tion
  Br. (use
  Egyptianization)
Egyp|tian|ise *Br.*
  (use Egyptianize)
Egyp|tian|ises
Egyp|tian|ised
Egyp|tian|is|ing
Egyp|tian|iza'tion
Egyp|tian|ize
  Egyp|tian|izes
  Egyp|tian|ized
  Egyp|tian|iz|ing
Egypt|olo'gist +s
Egypt|ology
eh (*interjection.*
  △ aye)
Ehr|en|burg, Ilya
  Gri|gori|evich
  (Russian writer)
Ehr|lich, Paul
  (German scientist)
Eich|mann, Karl
  Adolf (German
  Nazi
  administrator)
Eid (Muslim
  festival)
eider +s
ei|der|down +s
  (quilt)
eider-down (down
  of eider)
eider duck +s
ei|det'ic
ei|det'ic|al|ly
ei|do|lon
  ei|do|lons *or*
  ei|dola
Eif'fel, Alex|andre
  Gus|tave (French
  engineer)
Eif'fel Tower (in
  Paris)
eigen|fre'quency
eigen|
  fre'quen|cies
eigen|func'tion +s
eigen|value +s
Eiger (mountain,
  Switzerland)
Eigg (Scottish
  island)
eight +s (number.
  △ ait, ate)
eight|een +s
eight|eenmo +s
eight|eenth +s
eight|fold
eighth +s
eighth'ly
eight|ieth +s

eight-iron +s
eight|some +s
eight-track
  attributive
8vo (= octavo)
eighty
  eight'ies
eighty-first, eighty-
  second, etc.
eighty|fold
eighty-one, eighty-
  two, etc.
Eijk|man,
  Chris|tiaan
  (Dutch physician)
Eilat (town, Israel)
Ei'leen
Eind|hoven (city,
  the Netherlands)
ein|korn
Ein|stein, Al'bert
  (German
  physicist)
ein|stein|ium
Eint|hoven,
  Wil'lem (Dutch
  physiologist)
Eire (former name
  of Republic of
  Ireland)
eir|en'ic (use
  irenic)
eir|en'ic|al (use
  irenical)
eir|eni|con +s
Ei|sen|hower,
  Dwight ('Ike')
  (American
  president)
Ei|sen|stadt (city,
  Austria)
Ei|sen|stein,
  Ser'gei
  Mikh'ail|ovich
  (Russian film
  director)
ei|stedd|fod
  plural
  ei|stedd|fods *or*
  ei|stedd|fodau
ei|stedd|fod'ic
ei'ther
either/or
eius|dem gen|eris
ejacu|late
  ejacu|lates
  ejacu|lated
  ejacu|lat|ing
ejacu|la'tion +s
ejacu|la'tor +s
ejacu|la'tory
eject +s +ed +ing
ejecta (lava etc.
  △ ejector)

ejec|tion +s
eject|ive
eject|ment
eject|or +s (device.
  △ ejecta)
Ekat|er|in|burg
  (use
  Yekaterinburg)
Ekat|er|ino|dar
  (use
  Yekaterinodar;
  former name of
  Krasnodar)
Ekat|er|ino|slav
  (use
  Yekaterinoslav;
  former name of
  Dnipropetrovsk)
eke
  ekes
  eked
  eking
ekka +s
Ekman, Vagn
  Wall|frid (Swedish
  oceanographer)
El Aaiún (Arabic
  name for
  La'youn)
elab|or|ate
  elab|or|ates
  elab|or|ated
  elab|or|at|ing
  elab|or|ate|ly
  elab|or|ate|ness
elab|or|ation +s
elab|ora|tive
elab|or|ator +s
Ela|gab|alus
  (Roman emperor)
Elaine
El Ala|mein
  (battlefield, N.
  Africa)
Elam (ancient
  kingdom, Middle
  East)
Elam|ite +s
élan
eland +s
elapse
  elapses
  elapsed
  elap|sing
elasmo|branch +s
elasmo|saurus
  elasmo|saur|uses
elas|tane
elas|tic +s
elas|tic|al|ly
elas|ti|cated

elas|ti|cise Br. (use
  elasticize)
elas|ti|cises
elas|ti|cised
elas|ti|cis|ing
elas|ti|city
elas|ti|ci|ties
elas|ti|cize
elas|ti|cizes
elas|ti|cized
elas|ti|ciz|ing
elas|tin +s
elasto|mer +s
elasto|mer|ic
Elasto|plast +s
  Propr.
Elat (use Eilat)
elate
  elates
  elated
  elat|ing
  elated|ly
  elated|ness
elater +s
ela|tion +s
E-layer
Elba (Italian island)
El|ba|san (city,
  Romania)
Elbe (river,
  Germany)
El|bert, Mount (in
  USA)
elbow +s +ed +ing
elbow grease
elbow room
El|brus (mountain,
  Russia)
El|burz
  Moun|tains (in
  Iran)
Elche (town, Spain)
El Cid (Spanish
  warrior)
eld
elder +s
elder|berry
  elder|berries
elder brother
elder breth|ren
  (Trinity House)
elder|flower +s
elder|li|ness
eld|er|ly
elder|ship
eld|est
El Djem (town,
  Tunisia)
El Dor|ado
  (fictitious country)

el|dor|ado +s (any
  imaginary rich
  place)
el|dritch
Elea|nor also
  Eli|nor
Elea|nor Cross
  Elea|nor Crosses
Elea|nor of
  Aqui|taine
  (English queen)
Elea|nor of
  Cas|tile (English
  queen)
Ele|at|ic +s
ele|cam|pane +s
elect +s +ed +ing
elect|able
elec|tion +s
elec|tion|eer +s
  +ed +ing
elect|ive +s
elect|ive|ly
Elect|or +s
  (German prince)
elect|or +s (citizen)
elect|or|al
elect|or|al|ly
elect|or|ate +s
elect|or|ship +s
Elec|tra Greek
  Mythology
Elect|ress
  Elect|resses
  (wife of Elector)
elec|tret +s
elec|tric +s
elec|tric|al +s
elec|tric|al|ly
elec|tric blue +s
  noun and adjective
electric-blue
  attributive
elec|tri|cian +s
elec|tri|city
elec|tri|fi|ca|tion
elec|tri|fier +s
elec|trify
  elec|tri|fies
  elec|tri|fied
  elec|tri|fy|ing
elec|tro +s
electro-acoustic
elec|tro|biol|ogy
elec|tro|car|dio|
     gram +s
elec|tro|car|dio|
    graph +s
elec|tro|car|dio|
    graph|ic
elec|tro|car|di|
    og|raphy

elec|tro|chem|ical
elec|tro|
   chem|ical|ly
elec|tro|chem|ist
  +s
elec|tro|
   chem|is|try
elec|tro|
   con|vul|sive
elec|tro|cute
  elec|tro|cutes
  elec|tro|cuted
  elec|tro|cut|ing
elec|tro|cu|tion +s
elec|trode +s
elec|tro|di|aly|sis
elec|tro|dynam|ic
elec|tro|dynam|ics
elec|tro|
   enceph|alo|gram
  +s
elec|tro|
   enceph|alo|
     graph +s
elec|tro|en|ceph|al|
    og|raphy
elec|tro|lumin|
    es|cence
elec|tro|lumin|
    es|cent
elec|tro|lyse Br.
  elec|tro|lyses
  elec|tro|lysed
  elec|tro|lys|ing
elec|tro|lyser Br.
  +s
elec|troly|sis
  elec|troly|ses
elec|tro|lyte +s
elec|tro|lyt|ic
elec|tro|lyt|ic|al
elec|tro|lyt|ic|al|ly
elec|tro|lyze Am.
  elec|tro|lyzes
  elec|tro|lyzed
  elec|tro|lyz|ing
elec|tro|lyzer Am.
  +s
elec|tro|mag|net
  +s
elec|tro|mag|net|ic
elec|tro|mag|net|ic|
    al|ly
elec|tro|mag|net|
    ism
elec|tro|
   mech|an|ic|al
elec|trom|eter +s
elec|tro|met|ric
elec|trom|etry
elec|tro|mo|tive
elec|tron +s

elec¦tro|nega¦tive
elec¦tron¦ic
elec¦tron¦ic|al¦ly
elec¦tron¦ics
elec¦tron|volt+s
elec¦tro|phile+s
elec¦tro|phil¦ic
elec¦tro|phon¦ic
elec¦tro|phor¦esis
elec¦tro|phor¦et¦ic
elec¦troph|orus
elec¦tro|
   physio¦logic¦al
elec¦tro|
   physi¦ology
elec¦tro|plate
  elec¦tro|plates
  elec¦tro|plated
  elec¦tro|plat¦ing
elec¦tro|plater+s
elec¦tro|plexy
elec¦tro|por¦ation
elec¦tro|posi¦tive
elec¦tro|scope+s
elec¦tro|scop¦ic
electro-shock
elec¦tro|stat¦ic
elec¦tro|stat¦ics
elec¦tro|tech¦nic
elec¦tro|tech¦nic¦al
elec¦tro|tech¦nics
elec¦tro|tech|
   nol¦ogy
elec¦tro|thera|
   peut¦ic
elec¦tro|thera|
   peut¦ic¦al
elec¦tro|ther¦ap¦ist
  +s
elec¦tro|ther¦apy
elec¦tro|ther¦mal
elec¦tro|type
  elec¦tro|types
  elec¦tro|typed
  elec¦tro|typ¦ing
elec¦tro|typer+s
elec¦tro|va¦lence
elec¦tro|va¦lency
elec¦tro|va¦lent
elec¦tro|weak
elec|trum
elec¦tu|ary
  elec¦tu|ar¦ies
ele|emo¦syn|ary
ele|gance
ele|gant
ele|gant¦ly
ele|giac
ele|giac|al¦ly
ele|giacs
ele|gise Br. (use
  elegize)

ele|gise (cont.)
ele|gises
ele|gised
ele|gis¦ing
ele|gist+s
ele|gize
ele|gizes
ele|gized
ele|giz¦ing
elegy
  ele|gies
elem|ent+s
elem|en¦tal+s
elem|en¦tal|ism
elem|en¦tar¦ily
elem|en¦tari|ness
elem|en¦tary
  elem|en¦tar¦ies
elemi+s
elen|chus
  elen|chi
elenc|tic
Eleo|nora
ele|phant+s
elephant-bird+s
ele|phant|ia¦sis
ele|phant|ine
ele|phant|oid
Eleu¦sin|ian
ele|vate
  ele|vates
  ele|vated
  ele|vat¦ing
ele|va¦tion+s
ele|va¦tion|al
ele|va¦tor+s
ele|va¦tory
eleven+s
eleven|fold
eleven-plus
elev|enses
elev|enth+s
ele¦von+s
elf
  elves
elfin
elf¦ish
elf-lock+s
Elgar, Ed¦ward
  (English
  composer)
Elgin, Earl of
  (British colonial
  statesman)
Elgin Mar¦bles
El Giza (full name
  of Giza)
Elgon, Mount (in
  E. Africa)
El Greco (Cretan-
  born Spanish
  painter)

Eli (Bible; name)
Elia (pseudonym of
  Charles Lamb)
Elias
elicit+s +ed +ing
  (draw out.
  ⚠ illicit)
elicit|ation+s
elicit¦or+s
elide
  elides
  elided
  elid¦ing
eli¦gi|bil¦ity
eli|gible
eli|gibly
Eli¦jah (Bible;
  name)
elim¦in|able
elim¦in|ate
  elim¦in|ates
  elim¦in|ated
  elim¦in|at¦ing
elim¦in|ation+s
elim¦in|ator+s
elim¦in|atory
ELINT (covert
  electronic
  intelligence-
  gathering)
Eliot also El¦liot,
  El|liott
Eliot, George
  (English novelist)
Eliot, T. S. (Anglo-
  American poet,
  dramatist, and
  critic)
Elisa|beth also
  Eliza|beth
Elisa¦beth|ville
  (former name of
  Lubumbashi)
Eli¦sha Bible
eli|sion+s
El¦ista (city, Russia)
elite+s
elit¦ism
elit¦ist+s
elixir+s
Eliza
Eliza|beth also
  Elisa|beth (name)
Eliza|beth (English
  and British
  queens; Queen
  Mother)
Eliza|bethan+s
Eliza¦vet|pol
  (former name of
  Gäncäa)

elk
  plural elk or elks
elk-hound+s
ell+s
Ella
Ellen
Elles|mere Is¦land
  (in Canadian
  Arctic)
Elles|mere Port
  (port, England)
El¦lice Is¦lands
  (former name of
  Tuvalu ⚠ Ellis
  Island)
Ellie
El¦ling|ton, Duke
  (American jazz
  musician)
El¦liot also Eliot,
  El|liott
El|liott also Eliot,
  El¦liot
el|lipse+s
el¦lip|sis
  el¦lip|ses
el¦lips|oid+s
el¦lips|oid¦al
el¦lip|tic
el¦lip|tic¦al
el¦lip¦tic|al¦ly
el¦lip|ti¦city
Ellis Is¦land (in
  New York Bay,
  USA. ⚠ Ellice
  Islands)
Ells|worth,
  Lin|coln
  (American
  explorer)
Ells|worth Land
  (region,
  Antarctica)
elm+s
Elmer
elm|wood
elmy
El Niño+s (ocean
  current; climatic
  changes)
elo|cu¦tion
elo|cu¦tion|ary
elo|cu¦tion|ist+s
Elo¦him Bible
Elo|hist+s
elong|ate
  elong|ates
  elong|ated
  elong|at¦ing
elonga|tion+s
elope
  elopes

elope (*cont.*)
  eloped
  elop¦ing
elope|ment +s
eloper +s
elo|quence
elo|quent
elo|quent¦ly
El Paso (city, USA)
Elsa
El Sal¦va¦dor
Elsan +s *Propr.*
else
else|where
Elsie
El¦si¦nore (port,
  Denmark)
El|speth
Elton
elu¦ant +s (use
  eluent)
Élu¦ard, Paul
  (French poet)
elu¦ate +s
elu¦ci|date
  elu¦ci|dates
  elu¦ci|dated
  elu¦ci|dat¦ing
elu¦ci|da¦tion +s
elu¦ci|da¦tive
elu¦ci|da¦tor +s
elu¦ci|da¦tory
elude
  eludes
  eluded
  elud¦ing
  (avoid; escape.
  △allude, illude)
elu¦ent +s
Elul (Jewish month)
elu|sive (difficult to
  catch; avoiding
  the point.
  △allusive,
  illusive)
elu|sive¦ly (in an
  elusive way.
  △allusively,
  illusively)
elu|sive|ness
  (elusive nature.
  △allusiveness,
  illusiveness)
elu|sory (evasive.
  △illusory)
elute
  elutes
  eluted
  elut¦ing
elu|tion
elu¦tri|ate
  elu¦tri|ates

elu¦tri|ate (*cont.*)
  elu¦tri|ated
  elu¦tri|at¦ing
elu¦tri|ation
elver +s
elves
El¦vira
Elvis
elv¦ish
Ely (city, England)
Ely, Isle of (former
  county, England)
Ely¦sée Pal¦ace (in
  Paris)
Elys|ian
Elys|ium *Greek*
  Mythology
ely|tron
  ely¦tra
El¦ze|vir (family of
  Dutch printers)
em +s (printing
  measure)
'em (= them)
ema¦ci|ate
  ema¦ci|ates
  ema¦ci|ated
  ema¦ci|at¦ing
ema¦ci|ation
e-mail +s +ed +ing
ema|lan¦geni
  (plural of
  lilangeni)
em¦an|ate
  em¦an|ates
  em¦an|ated
  em¦an|at¦ing
em¦an|ation +s
em¦ana|tive
eman¦ci|pate
  eman¦ci|pates
  eman¦ci|pated
  eman¦ci|pat¦ing
eman¦ci|pa¦tion
eman¦ci|pa¦tion|ist
  +s
eman¦ci|pa¦tor +s
eman¦ci|pa¦tory
Eman|uel *also*
  Em¦man|uel
emas¦cu|late
  emas¦cu|lates
  emas¦cu|lated
  emas¦cu|lat¦ing
emas¦cu|la¦tion
emas¦cu|la¦tor +s
emas¦cu|la¦tory
em¦balm +s +ed
  +ing
em¦balm¦er +s
em¦balm|ment

em¦bank +s +ed
  +ing
em¦bank|ment +s
em|bargo
  em¦bar¦goes
  em¦bar¦goed
  em|bargo|ing
em¦bark +s +ed
  +ing
em¦bark|ation +s
em¦bar|ras de
  choix
em¦bar|ras de
  ri|chesse
em¦bar|ras de
  ri|chesses (use
  embarras de
  richesse)
em¦bar|rass
  em¦bar|rasses
  em¦bar|rassed
  em¦bar|rass|ing
  em¦bar|rassed¦ly
  em¦bar|rass|ing¦ly
  em¦bar|rass|ment
  +s
em|bassy
  em|bassies
em¦bat¦tle
  em¦bat¦tles
  em¦bat¦tled
  em¦bat¦tling
embay +s +ed
  +ing
em¦bay|ment +s
embed
  em¦beds
  em¦bed|ded
  em¦bed|ding
em¦bed|ment +s
em¦bel¦lish
  em|bel¦lishes
  em|bel¦lished
  em|bel¦lish|ing
em¦bel|lish¦er +s
em¦bel|lish|ment
  +s
ember +s
Ember days
ember-goose
  ember-geese
em¦bez¦zle
  em¦bez¦zles
  em¦bez¦zled
  em¦bez¦zling
em¦bezzle|ment
  +s
em¦bez¦zler +s
em¦bit¦ter +s +ed
  +ing
em¦bit¦ter|ment

em¦bla¦zon +s +ed
  +ing
em¦bla¦zon|ment
  +s
em¦bla¦zon¦ry
em¦blem +s
em¦blem|at¦ic
em¦blem|at¦ic|al
em¦blem|at¦ic|
    al¦ly
em¦blem|at¦ise *Br.*
  (use
  emblematize)
  em¦blem|at¦ises
  em¦blem|at¦ised
  em¦blem|at¦is¦ing
em¦blem|at¦ize
  em¦blem|at¦izes
  em¦blem|at¦ized
  em¦blem|at¦iz¦ing
em|ble¦ments
em¦bodi|ment +s
em¦body
  em|bodies
  em|bodied
  em|body¦ing
em¦bold¦en +s +ed
  +ing
em¦bol|ism +s
em¦bol|is|mic
em|bolus
  em¦boli
em¦bon|point
em¦bosom +s +ed
  +ing
em¦boss
  em|bosses
  em|bossed
  em|boss|ing
em¦boss¦er +s
em¦boss|ment +s
em¦bouch|ure +s
em¦bowel
  em|bowels
  em¦bow¦elled *Br.*
  em¦bow¦eled *Am.*
  em¦bowel|ling *Br.*
  em¦bowel|ing *Am.*
em¦bower +s +ed
  +ing
em¦brace
  em|braces
  em|braced
  em|bra¦cing
em¦brace|able
em¦brace|ment +s
em¦bracer +s
em¦branch|ment
  +s
em¦bran¦gle
  em|bran¦gles

em|bran|gle (*cont.*)
  em|bran|gled
  em|bran|gling
em|brangle|ment
em|bras|ure +s
em|bras|ured
em|brit|tle
  em|brit|tles
  em|brit|tled
  em|brit|tling
em|brittle|ment
em|bro|ca|tion +s
em|broi|der +s
  +ed +ing
em|broi|der|er +s
em|broi|dery
  em|broi|der|ies
em|broil +s +ed
  +ing
em|broil|ment +s
em|brown +s +ed
  +ing
em|bryo +s
em|bryo|gen|esis
em|bryo|oid
em|bryo|logic
em|bryo|logic|al
em|bryo|logic|
        al|ly
em|bry|olo|gist +s
em|bry|ology
em|bry|on|al
em|bry|on|ic
em|bry|on|ic|al|ly
embus
  em|bus|ses *or*
  em|buses
  em|bussed *or*
  em|bused
  em|buss|ing *or*
  em|bus|ing
emcee
  em|cees
  em|ceed
  em|cee|ing
em dash
  em dashes
emend +s +ed
  +ing (remove
  errors. △ amend)
emend|ation +s
emend|ator +s
emen|da|tory
em|er|ald +s
em|er|ald|ine
emerge
  emerges
  emerged
  emer|ging
emer|gence
emer|gency
  emer|gen|cies

emer|gent
emeri|tus
emerse
emersed
emer|sion
Emer|son, Ralph
  Waldo (American
  writer and
  philosopher)
emery
emery board +s
emery cloth
emery paper
emery wheel +s
Emesa (ancient
  city, Syria)
emet|ic +s
emi|grant +s
emi|grate
  emi|grates
  emi|grated
  emi|grat|ing
emi|gra|tion +s
emi|gra|tory
émi|gré +s
Emi Koussi
  (mountain, Chad)
Emilia-Romagna
  (region, Italy)
Emily
emi|nence +s
émi|nence grise
  émi|nences grises
emi|nent
emi|nent|ly
emir +s (title of
  some Muslim
  rulers; Arab
  prince,
  commander, etc.
  △ amir)
emir|ate +s
  (position or
  territory of an
  emir. △ amirate)
emis|sary
  emis|sar|ies
emis|sion +s
emis|sive
emis|siv|ity
emit
  emits
  emit|ted
  emit|ting
  (give off. △ omit)
emit|ter +s
Emlyn
Emma (name)
Em|man|uel *also*
  Eman|uel
Em|me|line

Em|men|tal (Swiss
  valley; cheese)
Em|men|thal (use
  Emmental)
emmer (wheat)
emmet +s
Emmy
  Em|mies
  (television award;
  name)
emol|li|ence
emol|li|ent +s
emolu|ment +s
Emona (Roman
  name for
  Ljubljana)
emote
  emotes
  emoted
  emot|ing
emoter +s
emoti|con +s
emo|tion +s
emo|tion|al
emo|tion|al|ise *Br.*
  (use
  emotionalize)
  emo|tion|al|ises
  emo|tion|al|ised
  emo|tion|al|is|ing
emo|tion|al|ism
emo|tion|al|ist +s
emo|tion|al|ity
emo|tion|al|ize
  emo|tion|al|izes
  emo|tion|al|ized
  emo|tion|al|iz|ing
emo|tion|al|ly
emo|tion|less
emo|tive
emo|tive|ly
emo|tive|ness
emo|tiv|ity
em|panel
  em|panels
  em|pan|elled *Br.*
  em|pan|eled *Am.*
  em|pan|el|ling *Br.*
  em|pan|el|ing *Am.*
em|panel|ment
em|path|et|ic
em|path|et|ic|al|ly
em|path|ic
em|path|ic|al|ly
em|pa|thise *Br.*
  (use empathize)
  em|pa|thises
  em|pa|thised
  em|pa|this|ing
em|pa|thist +s
em|pa|thize
  em|pa|thizes

em|pa|thize (*cont.*)
  em|pa|thized
  em|pa|thiz|ing
em|pathy
  em|pathies
Em|pedo|cles
  (Greek
  philosopher)
em|pen|nage +s
em|peror +s
em|per|or|ship +s
em|phasis
  em|phases
em|pha|sise *Br.*
  (use emphasize)
  em|pha|sises
  em|pha|sised
  em|pha|sis|ing
em|pha|size
  em|pha|sizes
  em|pha|sized
  em|pha|siz|ing
em|phat|ic
em|phat|ic|al|ly
em|phy|se|ma
Em|pire (style)
em|pire +s
em|pire build|er
  +s
em|pire build|ing
em|pir|ic
em|pir|ic|al
em|pir|ic|al|ly
em|piri|cism
em|piri|cist +s
em|place|ment +s
em|plane
  em|planes
  em|planed
  em|plan|ing
em|ploy +s +ed
  +ing
em|ploy|abil|ity
em|ploy|able
em|ploy|ee +s
em|ploy|er +s
em|ploy|ment +s
em|pol|der +s +ed
  +ing (use
  impolder)
em|por|ium
  em|poria *or*
  em|por|iums
em|power +s +ed
  +ing
em|power|ment
emp|ress
  emp|resses
Emp|son, Wil|liam
  (English poet and
  critic)
emp|ti|ly

emp¦ti¦ness
empty
  emp¦ties
  emp¦tied
  empty¦ing
  emp¦tier
  emp¦ti¦est
empty-handed
empty-headed
empty-nester +s
em¦pur¦ple
  em¦pur¦ples
  em¦pur¦pled
  em¦purp¦ling
em¦py¦ema
em¦pyr¦eal
em¦pyr¦ean +s
em rule +s
Emrys
emu +s (bird)
emu¦late
  emu¦lates
  emu¦lated
  emu¦lat¦ing
emu¦la¦tion +s
emu¦la¦tive
emu¦la¦tor +s
emu¦lous
emu¦lous¦ly
emul¦si¦fi¦able
emul¦si¦fi¦ca¦tion
emul¦si¦fier +s
emul¦sify
  emul¦si¦fies
  emul¦si¦fied
  emul¦si¦fy¦ing
emul¦sion +s +ed
  +ing
emul¦sion¦ise *Br.*
  (use emulsionize)
  emul¦sion¦ises
  emul¦sion¦ised
  emul¦sion¦is¦ing
emul¦sion¦ize
  emul¦sion¦izes
  emul¦sion¦ized
  emul¦sion¦iz¦ing
emul¦sive
en +s (printing
  measure)
Ena
en¦able
  en¦ables
  en¦abled
  en¦ab¦ling
en¦able¦ment
en¦abler +s
enact +s +ed +ing
en¦act¦able
en¦action
en¦act¦ive
en¦act¦ment +s

en¦act¦or +s
en¦act¦ory
en¦amel
  en¦amels
  en¦am¦elled *Br.*
  en¦am¦eled *Am.*
  en¦am¦el¦ling *Br.*
  en¦am¦el¦ing *Am.*
en¦amel¦ler +s
en¦amel¦ling
en¦amel¦ware
en¦amel¦work
en¦amor *Am.* +s
  +ed +ing
en¦am¦our *Br.* +s
  +ed +ing
en¦an¦thema
  en¦an¦the¦mas or
  en¦an¦the¦mata
en¦an¦tio¦mer +s
en¦an¦tio¦mer¦ic
en¦an¦tio¦morph
  +s
en¦an¦tio¦morph¦ic
en¦an¦tio¦morph¦
  ism
en¦an¦tio¦morph¦
  ous
en¦arth¦ro¦sis
  en¦arth¦ro¦ses
en bloc
en brosse
en cabo¦chon
en¦cae¦nia +s
en¦cage
  en¦cages
  en¦caged
  en¦caging
en¦camp +s +ed
  +ing
en¦camp¦ment +s
en¦cap¦su¦late
  en¦cap¦su¦lates
  en¦cap¦su¦lated
  en¦cap¦su¦lat¦ing
en¦cap¦su¦la¦tion
  +s
en¦case
  en¦cases
  en¦cased
  en¦cas¦ing
en¦case¦ment +s
en¦cash
  en¦cashes
  en¦cashed
  en¦cash¦ing
en¦cash¦able
en¦cash¦ment +s
en¦caus¦tic +s
en¦ceinte +s

En¦cela¦dus (*Greek
  Mythology*; moon
  of Saturn)
en¦ceph¦al¦ic
en¦ceph¦alin +s
  (use enkephalin)
en¦ceph¦al¦it¦ic
en¦ceph¦al¦itis
en¦ceph¦al¦itis
  leth¦ar¦gica
en¦ceph¦alo¦gram
  +s
en¦ceph¦alo¦graph
  +s
en¦ceph¦alo¦
  my¦eli¦tis
en¦cepha¦lon
en¦ceph¦al¦
  op¦athy
en¦chain +s +ed
  +ing
en¦chain¦ment
en¦chant +s +ed
  +ing
en¦chant¦ed¦ly
en¦chant¦er +s
en¦chant¦ing¦ly
en¦chant¦ment +s
en¦chant¦ress
  en¦chant¦resses
en¦chase
  en¦chases
  en¦chased
  en¦chas¦ing
en¦chil¦ada +s
en¦chir¦id¦ion
  en¦chir¦id¦ions or
  en¦chir¦idia
en¦cipher +s +ed
  +ing
en¦cipher¦ment
en¦cir¦cle
  en¦cir¦cles
  en¦cir¦cled
  en¦circ¦ling
en¦circle¦ment
en clair
en¦clasp +s +ed
  +ing
en¦clave +s
en¦clit¦ic +s
en¦clit¦ic¦al¦ly
en¦close
  en¦closes
  en¦closed
  en¦clos¦ing
en¦clos¦ure +s
en¦code
  en¦codes
  en¦coded
  en¦cod¦ing
en¦coder +s

en¦comi¦ast +s
en¦comi¦as¦tic
en¦co¦mium
  en¦co¦miums or
  en¦co¦mia
en¦com¦pass
  en¦com¦passes
  en¦com¦passed
  en¦com¦pass¦ing
en¦com¦pass¦ment
en¦core
  en¦cores
  en¦cored
  en¦cor¦ing
en¦coun¦ter +s +ed
  +ing
en¦cour¦age
  en¦cour¦ages
  en¦cour¦aged
  en¦cour¦aging
en¦cour¦age¦ment
  +s
en¦cour¦ager +s
en¦cour¦aging¦ly
en¦crin¦ite +s
en¦croach
  en¦croaches
  en¦croached
  en¦croach¦ing
en¦croach¦er +s
en¦croach¦ment +s
en¦crust +s +ed
  +ing
en¦crust¦ation +s
  (use incrustation)
en¦crust¦ment
en¦crypt +s +ed
  +ing
en¦cryp¦tion
en¦cum¦ber +s +ed
  +ing
en¦cum¦ber¦ment
en¦cum¦brance +s
en¦cyc¦lic
en¦cyc¦lic¦al +s
en¦cyclo¦pae¦dia
  Br. +s (*Am.*
  encyclopedia)
en¦cyclo¦pae¦dic
  Br. (*Am.*
  encyclopedic)
en¦cyclo¦pae¦dism
  Br. (*Am.*
  encyclopedism)
en¦cyclo¦pae¦dist
  Br. +s (*Am.*
  encyclopedist)
en¦cyc¦lo¦pe¦dia +s
  (*Br.*
  encyclopaedia)

en|cyclo|pe|dic
(Br.
encyclopaedic)
en|cyclo|ped|ism
(Br.
encyclopaedism)
en|cyclo|ped|ist
+s (Br.
encyclopaedist)
en|cyst+s +ed
+ing
en|cyst|ation
en|cyst|ment
end+s +ed +ing
en|dan|ger+s +ed
+ing
en|dan|ger|ment
end-around+s
en dash
en dashes
en|dear+s +ed
+ing
en|dear|ing|ly
en|dear|ment+s
en|deavor Am. +s
+ed +ing
en|deav|our Br. +s
+ed +ing
en|dem|ic
en|dem|ic|al|ly
en|dem|icity
en|dem|ism
ender+s
End|erby Land
(region,
Antarctica)
en|der|mic
en|der|mic|al|ly
En|ders, John
Frank|lin
(American
virologist)
end|game+s
end|ing+s
en|dive+s
end|less
end|less|ly
end|less|ness
end|most
end|note+s
endo|card|it|ic
endo|card|itis
endo|car|dium
endo|carp+s
endo|carp|ic
endo|crine
endo|crino|logic|al
endo|crin|olo|gist
+s
endo|crin|ology
endo|derm+s
endo|der|mal

endo|der|mic
end-of-season
attributive
end-of-term
attributive
end-of-year
attributive
en|dog|am|ous
en|dog|amy
endo|gen+s
endo|gen|esis
en|dogen|ous
en|dogeny
endo|lymph
endo|met|rial
endo|met|ri|osis
endo|met|ri|tis
endo|met|rium
endo|morph+s
endo|morph|ic
endo|morphy
endo|para|site+s
endo|plasm
endo|plas|mic
re|ticu|lum
en|dor|phin+s
en|dors|able
en|dorse
en|dorses
en|dorsed
en|dors|ing
en|dor|see+s
en|dorse|ment+s
en|dor|ser+s
endo|scope+s
endo|scop|ic
endo|scop|ic|al|ly
en|dos|co|pist+s
endo|scopy
endo|skel|eton+s
endo|sperm
endo|spore+s
endo|the|lial
endo|the|lium
endo|the|lia
endo|ther|mic
endo|thermy
endo|toxin+s
endow+s +ed
+ing
en|dow|er+s
en|dow|ment+s
end|paper+s
end-play+s
end point+s
end prod|uct+s
end re|sult+s
end-stopped
endue
en|dues
en|dued
en|du|ing

en|dur|abil|ity
en|dur|able
en|dur|ance
en|dure
en|dures
en|dured
en|dur|ing
en|dur|ing|ly
en|duro+s
end-user+s
end|ways
end|wise
En|dym|ion Greek
Mythology
enema+s
enemy
en|emies
en|er|get|ic
en|er|get|ic|al|ly
en|er|get|ics
ener|gise Br. (use
energize)
ener|gises
ener|gised
ener|gis|ing
en|er|giser Br. +s
(use energizer)
ener|gize
ener|gizes
ener|gized
ener|giz|ing
en|er|gizer+s
en|er|gu|men+s
en|ergy
en|er|gies
energy-efficiency
energy-efficient
ener|vate
ener|vates
ener|vated
ener|vat|ing
en|er|va|tion
En|ewe|tak (use
Eniwetok)
en fam|ille
en'fant gâté
en'fants gâtés
en'fant ter|rible
en'fants ter|ribles
en|fee|ble
en|fee|bles
en|fee|bled
en|feeb|ling
en|feeble|ment
en|feoff+s +ed
+ing
en|feoff|ment
en fête
en|fet|ter+s +ed
+ing
en|fil|ade
en|fil|ades

en|fil|ade(cont.)
en|fil|aded
en|fil|ad|ing
en|fold+s +ed
+ing (envelop.
△ infold)
en|force
en|forces
en|forced
en|for|cing
en|force|abil|ity
en|force|able
en|force|ably
en|forced|ly
en|force|ment
en|for|cer+s
en|fran|chise
en|fran|chises
en|fran|chised
en|fran|chis|ing
en|fran|chise|ment
en|gage
en|gages
en|gaged
en|gaging
en|gagé
en|gage|ment+s
en|gager+s
en|ga|ging|ly
en|ga|ging|ness
en|gar|land+s +ed
+ing
En|gels, Fried|rich
(German political
philosopher)
en|gen|der+s +ed
+ing
en|gine
en|gines
en|gined
en|gin|ing
en|gine driver+s
en|gin|eer+s +ed
+ing
en|gin|eer|ing
en|gin|eer|ship
en|gine house+s
en|gine|less
en|gine room+s
en|gin|ery
en|gird+s +ed
+ing
en|gir|dle
en|gir|dles
en|gir|dled
en|gird|ling
Eng|land
Eng|lish
Eng|lishes
Eng|lish|man
Eng|lish|men
Eng|lish|ness

Eng|lish|woman
Eng|lish|women
en|gorge
  en|gorges
  en|gorged
  en|gor|ging
en|gorge|ment
en|graft +s +ed
  +ing
en|graft|ment
en|grail +s +ed
  +ing
en|grain +s +ed
  +ing (use ingrain)
en|gram +s
en|gram|mat|ic
en|grave
  en|graves
  en|graved
  en|grav|ing
en|graver +s
en|grav|ing +s
en|gross
  en|grosses
  en|grossed
  en|gross|ing
en|gross|ment
en|gulf +s +ed
  +ing
en|gulf|ment
en|hance
  en|hances
  en|hanced
  en|han|cing
en|hance|ment +s
en|hancer +s
en|har|mon|ic
en|har|mon|ic|
        al|ly
Enid
en|igma +s
en|ig|mat|ic
en|ig|mat|ic|al
en|ig|mat|ic|al|ly
en|igma|tise Br.
  (use enigmatize)
  en|igma|tises
  en|igma|tised
  en|igma|tis|ing
en|igma|tize
  en|igma|tizes
  en|igma|tized
  en|igma|tiz|ing
En|iwe|tok (island,
  N. Pacific)
en|jamb|ment +s
en|join +s +ed
  +ing
en|join|ment
enjoy +s +ed +ing
en|joy|abil|ity
en|joy|able

en|joy|able|ness
en|joy|ably
en|joy|er +s
en|joy|ment +s
en|keph|alin +s
en|kin|dle
  en|kin|dles
  en|kin|dled
  en|kind|ling
en|lace
  en|laces
  en|laced
  en|lacing
en|lace|ment
en|large
  en|larges
  en|larged
  en|lar|ging
en|large|able
en|large|ment +s
en|lar|ger +s
en|light|en +s +ed
  +ing
en|light|en|er +s
en|light|en|ment
  +s
en|list +s +ed +ing
en|list|er +s
en|list|ment
en|liven +s +ed
  +ing
en|liven|er +s
en|liven|ment
en masse
en|mesh
  en|meshes
  en|meshed
  en|mesh|ing
en|mesh|ment
en|mity
  en|mities
en|nead +s
Ennis (town,
  Republic of
  Ireland)
En|nis|kil|len
  (town, Northern
  Ireland)
En|nius, Quin|tus
  (Roman writer)
en|noble
  en|nobles
  en|nobled
  en|nob|ling
en|noble|ment
ennui +s
Enoch (Bible;
  name)
eno|logic|al Am.
  (Br. oenological)
en|olo|gist Am. +s
  (Br. oenologist)

en|ol|ogy Am. (Br.
  oenology)
eno|phile Am. +s
  (Br. oenophile)
en|oph|il|ist Am.
  +s (Br.
  oenophilist)
enor|mity
  enor|mities
enor|mous
enor|mous|ly
enor|mous|ness
eno|sis
enough
enounce
  enounces
  enounced
  enoun|cing
enounce|ment
en pas|sant
en pen|sion
en|plane
  en|planes
  en|planed
  en|plan|ing
en|print +s
en|quire Br.
  en|quires
  en|quired
  en|quir|ing
  (ask. △inquire.
  Am. inquire)
en|quir|er Br. +s
  (person asking for
  information.
  △inquirer. Am.
  inquirer)
en|quir|ing|ly Br.
  (Am. inquiringly)
en|quiry Br.
  en|quir|ies
  (request for
  information.
  △inquiry. Am.
  inquiry)
en|rage
  en|rages
  en|raged
  en|raging
en|rage|ment
en rap|port
en|rap|ture
  en|rap|tures
  en|rap|tured
  en|rap|tur|ing
en|rich
  en|riches
  en|riched
  en|rich|ing
en|rich|ment +s
en|robe
  en|robes

en|robe (cont.)
  en|robed
  en|rob|ing
enrol Br.
  en|rols
  en|rolled
  en|rol|ling
en|roll Am. +s +ed
  +ing
en|roll|ee +s
en|rol|ler +s
en|roll|ment Am.
  +s
en|rol|ment Br. +s
en route
en rule +s
ENSA
  (= Entertainments
  National Service
  Association)
En|schede (city, the
  Netherlands)
en|sconce
  en|sconces
  en|sconced
  en|scon|cing
en|sem|ble +s
en|shrine
  en|shrines
  en|shrined
  en|shrin|ing
en|shrine|ment
en|shroud +s +ed
  +ing
en|si|form
en|sign +s
en|signcy
en|sil|age
  en|sil|ages
  en|sil|aged
  en|sil|aging
en|sile
  en|siles
  en|siled
  en|sil|ing
en|slave
  en|slaves
  en|slaved
  en|slav|ing
en|slave|ment
en|slaver +s
en|snare
  en|snares
  en|snared
  en|snar|ing
en|snare|ment
Ensor, James
  (Belgian artist)
ensue
  en|sues
  en|sued
  en|su|ing

en suite
en|sure
  en|sures
  en|sured
  en|sur|ing
  (make sure.
  ⚠ insure)
en|surer +s (person
  who makes sure.
  ⚠ insurer)
en|swathe
  en|swathes
  en|swathed
  en|swath|ing
en|swathe|ment
en|tab|la|ture +s
en|table|ment
en|tail +s +ed +ing
en|tail|ment +s
en|tan|gle
  en|tan|gles
  en|tan|gled
  en|tan|gling
en|tangle|ment +s
en|tasis
  en|tases
En|tebbe (town,
  Uganda)
en|tel|echy
en|tel|lus
  en|tel|luses
en|tendre +s (in
  'double entendre'
  etc.)
en|tente +s
en|tente cor|di|ale
enter +s +ed +ing
en|ter|able
en|ter|er +s
en|ter|ic
en|ter|itis
en|ter|os|tomy
  en|ter|os|tomies
en|ter|ot|omy
  en|ter|oto|mies
en|tero|virus
  en|tero|viruses
en|ter|prise +s
en|ter|priser +s
en|ter|pris|ing
en|ter|pris|ing|ly
en|ter|tain +s +ed
  +ing
en|ter|tain|er +s
en|ter|tain|ing|ly
en|ter|tain|ment
  +s
en|thalpy
en|thral *Br.*
  en|thrals
  en|thralled
  en|thral|ling

en|thrall *Am.* +s
  +ed +ing
en|thrall|ment *Am.*
en|thral|ment *Br.*
en|throne
  en|thrones
  en|throned
  en|thron|ing
en|throne|ment
en|thuse
  en|thuses
  en|thused
  en|thus|ing
en|thu|si|asm +s
en|thu|si|ast +s
en|thu|si|as|tic
en|thu|si|as|tic|
          al|ly
en|thy|meme +s
en|tice
  en|tices
  en|ticed
  en|ticing
en|tice|ment +s
en|ticer +s
en|ticing|ly
en|tire
en|tire|ly
en|tir|ety
  en|tir|eties
en|ti|ta|tive
en|title
  en|titles
  en|titled
  en|tit|ling
en|title|ment +s
en|tity
  en|tities
en|tomb +s +ed
  +ing
en|tomb|ment +s
en|tom|ic
en|to|mo|logic|al
en|to|molo|gist +s
en|to|mol|ogy
en|to|mopha|gous
en|to|moph|il|ous
en|to|para|site +s
en|to|phyte +s
en|tou|rage +s
en|tr'acte +s
en|trails
en|train +s +ed
  +ing (put on a
  train; carry along)
en|train
  (enthusiasm)
en|train|ment
en|tram|mel
  en|tram|mels
  en|tram|melled *Br.*
  en|tram|meled *Am.*

en|tram|mel (*cont.*)
  en|tram|mel|ling *Br.*
  en|tram|mel|ing
  Am.
en|trance
  en|trances
  en|tranced
  en|tran|cing
en|trance hall +s
en|trance|ment
en|tran|cing|ly
en|trant +s
en|trap
  en|traps
  en|trapped
  en|trap|ping
en|trap|ment +s
en|trap|per +s
en|treat +s +ed
  +ing
en|treat|ing|ly
en|treaty
  en|treaties
entre|chat +s
en|tre|côte +s
en|trée +s
entre|mets
  plural *entre|mets*
en|trench
  en|trenches
  en|trenched
  en|trench|ing
en|trench|ment +s
entre nous
entre|pôt +s
entre|pre|neur +s
entre|pre|neur|ial
entre|pre|neur|ial|
          ism
entre|pre|neur|
          ial|ly
entre|pre|neur|
          ship
entre|sol +s
en|trism
en|trist +s
en|trop|ic
en|trop|ic|al|ly
en|tropy
en|trust +s +ed
  +ing
en|trust|ment
entry
  en|tries
entry|ism
entry|ist +s
entry|phone +s
  Propr.
en|twine
  en|twines

en|twine (*cont.*)
  en|twined
  en|twin|ing
en|twine|ment
enu|cle|ate
  enu|cle|ates
  enu|cle|ated
  enu|cle|at|ing
enu|cle|ation
E-number +s
enu|mer|able
  (countable.
  ⚠ innumerable)
enu|mer|ate
  enu|mer|ates
  enu|mer|ated
  enu|mer|at|ing
  (mention; count.
  ⚠ innumerate)
enu|mer|ation +s
enu|mera|tive
enu|mer|ator +s
enun|ci|ate
  enun|ci|ates
  enun|ci|ated
  enun|ci|at|ing
enun|ci|ation
enun|cia|tive
enun|ci|ator +s
enure
  en|ures
  en|ured
  en|ur|ing
  (*Law* take effect.
  ⚠ inure)
en|ur|esis
en|ur|et|ic +s
en|velop +s +ed
  +ing
en|vel|ope +s
en|velop|ment +s
en|venom +s +ed
  +ing
Enver Pasha
  (Turkish leader)
en|vi|able
en|vi|ably
en|vi|er +s
en|vi|ous
en|vi|ous|ly
en|viron +s +ed
  +ing
en|vir|on|ment +s
en|vir|on|men|tal
en|vir|on|men|tal|
          ism
en|vir|on|men|tal|
          ist +s
en|vir|on|
          men|tal|ly

en|vir|on|
  men|tal|ly
  friend|ly
environment-
  friend|ly
en|vir|ons
en|vis|age
  en|vis|ages
  en|vis|aged
  en|vis|aging
en|vis|age|ment
en|vi|sion +s +ed
  +ing
envoi +s
  (concluding stanza
  or passage)
envoy +s
  (messenger,
  representative)
en|voy|ship +s
envy
  en|vies
  en|vied
  envy|ing
en|weave (use
  inweave)
  en|weaves
  en|wove
  en|weav|ing
  en|woven
en|wind
  en|winds
  en|wound
  en|wind|ing
en|wrap
  en|wraps
  en|wrapped
  en|wrap|ping
en|wreathe
  en|wreathes
  en|wreathed
  en|wreath|ing
Enzed
  Enzeds
En|zed|der +s
en|zo|ot|ic
en|zym|at|ic
en|zyme +s
en|zym|ic
en|zym|ology
Eo|cene
EOKA (Greek-
  Cypriot
  organization)
eo|lian *Am.* (*Br.*
  aeolian)
Eolic *Am.* (*Br.*
  Aeolic)
eo|lith +s
eo|lith|ic
eon +s (use aeon)

Eos (Greek
  goddess. △ Ios)
eosin
eo|sino|phil +s
epact +s
ep|arch +s
ep|archy
  ep|arch|ies
ep|aulet *Am.* +s
ep|aul|lette *Br.* +s
épée +s
épée|ist +s
epeiro|gen|esis
epeiro|gen|ic
epeir|ogeny
epen|thesis
  epen|theses
epen|thet|ic
ep|ergne +s
ep|exe|gesis
  ep|exe|geses
ep|exe|get|ic
ep|exe|get|ic|al
ep|exe|get|ic|al|ly
eph|ebe +s
eph|ebic
eph|edra +s
ephe|drine
ephem|era
  ephem|eras *or*
  ephem|erae
  (insect; also plural
  of ephemeron)
ephem|eral +s
ephem|eral|ity
ephem|eral|ly
ephem|eral|ness
ephem|eris
  ephem|er|ides
ephem|er|ist +s
ephem|eron
  ephem|era
  (printed item;
  short-lived thing)
ephem|eron +s
  (insect)
Ephe|sian +s
Eph|esus (city,
  ancient Greece)
ephod +s
ephor
  eph|ors *or* eph|ori
eph|or|ate +s
eph|or|ship +s
Eph|raim
epi|blast +s
epic +s
epic|al
ep|ic|al|ly
epi|carp +s
epi|ce|dian
epi|ce|dium
  epi|ce|dia

epi|cene +s
epi|cen|ter *Am.* +s
epi|cen|tral
epi|centre *Br.* +s
epi|clesis
  epi|cleses
epi|con|tin|en|tal
epi|cotyl +s
Epic|te|tus (Greek
  philosopher)
epi|cure +s
Epi|cur|ean +s (of
  Epicurus)
epi|cur|ean +s
  (devoted to
  enjoyment)
Epi|cur|ean|ism
epi|cur|ism
Epi|curus (Greek
  philosopher)
epi|cycle +s
epi|cyc|lic
epi|cyc|loid +s
epi|cyc|loid|al
Epi|daurus (city,
  ancient Greece)
epi|deic|tic
epi|dem|ic +s
epi|dem|ic|al
epi|dem|ic|al|ly
epi|demi|ologic|al
epi|demi|olo|gist
  +s
epi|demi|ology
epi|der|mal
epi|der|mic
epi|der|mis
epi|derm|oid
epi|dia|scope +s
epi|didy|mis
  epi|didy|mides
epi|dural +s
epi|fauna
epi|faun|al
epi|gas|tric
epi|gas|trium
  epi|gas|tria
epi|geal
epi|gene
epi|gen|esis
epi|gen|et|ic
epi|glot|tal
epi|glot|tic
epi|glot|tis
  epi|glot|tises
epi|gone
  epi|gones *or*
  epi|goni
epi|gram +s
epi|gram|mat|ic
epi|gram|mat|ic|
    al|ly

epi|gram|ma|tise
  Br. (use
  epigrammatize)
epi|gram|ma|tises
epi|gram|
    ma|tised
epi|gram|
    ma|tis|ing
epi|gram|ma|tist
  +s
epi|gram|ma|tize
epi|gram|ma|tizes
epi|gram|
    ma|tized
epi|gram|
    ma|tiz|ing
epi|graph +s
epi|graph|ic
epi|graph|ic|al
epi|graph|ic|al|ly
epig|raph|ist +s
epig|raphy
epil|ate
  epil|ates
  epil|ated
  epil|at|ing
epil|ation
epi|lepsy
epi|lep|tic +s
epi|lim|nion
  epi|lim|nia
epi|log +s (use
  epilogue)
epi|log|ist +s
epi|logue +s
epi|mer +s
epi|mer|ic
epi|mer|ise *Br.* (use
  epimerize)
epi|mer|ises
epi|mer|ised
epi|mer|is|ing
epi|mer|ism
epi|mer|ize
epi|mer|izes
epi|mer|ized
epi|mer|iz|ing
epi|nasty
epi|neph|rine
epi|phan|ic
Epiph|any
  Christianity
epiph|any
  epiph|anies
  (generally)
epi|phe|nom|en|al
epi|phe|nom|enon
  epi|phe|nom|ena
epiphy|sis
  epiphy|ses
epi|phyt|al
epi|phyte +s

epi|phyt|ic
Epi|rus (coastal region, NW Greece)
epis|cop|acy
epis|cop|acies
Epis|cop|al (Church)
epis|cop|al (of a bishop)
Epis|co|pa|lian +s (of the Episcopal Church)
epis|co|pa|lian +s (advocating church government by bishops)
epis|co|pa|lian|ism
epis|co|pal|ism
epis|co|pal|ly
epis|co|pate +s
epi|scope +s
epi|sem|at|ic
episi|ot|omy
episi|oto|mies
epi|sode +s
epi|sod|ic
epi|sod|ic|al|ly
epi|staxis
epi|staxes
epi|stem|ic
epi|stem|ic|al|ly
epi|stemo|logic|al
epi|stemo|log|ic|al|ly
epis|te|molo|gist +s
epis|te|mol|ogy
epis|te|mol|ogies
epis|tle +s
epis|tol|ary
epis|tol|er +s
epis|trophe +s
epi|style +s
epi|taph +s
epi|tax|ial
epi|taxy
epi|tha|la|mial
epi|tha|lam|ic
epi|tha|la|mium
epi|tha|la|miums
or epi|tha|la|mia
epi|the|lial
epi|the|lium
epi|the|lia
epi|thet +s
epi|thet|ic
epi|thet|ic|al
epi|thet|ic|al|ly
epit|ome +s

epit|om|isa|tion
Br. (use epitomization)
epit|om|ise Br. (use epitomize)
epit|om|ises
epit|om|ised
epit|om|is|ing
epit|om|ist +s
epit|om|iza|tion
epit|om|ize
epit|om|izes
epit|om|ized
epit|om|iz|ing
epi|zoon
epi|zoa
epi|zo|ot|ic
epoch +s
epoch|al
epoch-making
epode +s
ep|onym +s
eponym|ous
EPOS (= electronic point-of-sale)
ep|ox|ide +s
epoxy
epox|ies
EPROM (= erasable programmable read-only memory)
ep|si|lon +s
Epsom (town, England; salts)
Ep|stein, Jacob (American-born British sculptor)
Epstein–Barr (virus)
epyl|lion
epyl|lia
equa|bil|ity
equ|able
equ|ably
equal
equals
equalled Br.
equaled Am.
equal|ling Br.
equal|ing Am.
equal|isa|tion Br. (use equalization)
equal|ise Br. (use equalize)
equal|ises
equal|ised
equal|is|ing
equal|iser Br. +s (use equalizer)
equali|tar|ian +s
equali|tar|ian|ism

equal|ity
equal|ities
equal|iza|tion
equal|ize
equal|izes
equal|ized
equal|iz|ing
equal|izer +s
equal|ly
equa|nim|ity
equani|mous
equat|able
equat|ably
equate
equates
equated
equat|ing
equa|tion +s
equa|tion|al
equa|tor +s
equa|tor|ial
equa|tori|al|ly
equerry
equer|ries
eques|trian +s
eques|tri|an|ism
eques|tri|enne +s
female
equi|angu|lar
equi|dis|tant
equi|dis|tant|ly
equi|lat|eral
equili|brate
equili|brates
equili|brated
equili|brat|ing
equili|bra|tion
equili|bra|tor +s
equili|brist +s
equi|lib|rium
equi|lib|ria or
equi|lib|riums
equine
equi|noc|tial +s
equi|nox
equi|noxes
equip
equips
equipped
equip|ping
equip|age +s
equi|par|ti|tion
equip|ment +s
equi|poise
equi|poises
equi|poised
equi|pois|ing
equi|pol|lence
equi|pol|lency
equi|pol|lent +s
equi|pon|der|ant

equi|pon|der|ate
equi|pon|der|ates
equi|pon|der|ated
equi|pon|der|
at|ing
equi|poten|tial
equip|per +s
equi|prob|abil|ity
equi|prob|able
equi|setum
equi|seta or
equi|setums
equit|able
equit|able|ness
equit|ably
equi|ta|tion
equity
equi|ties
equiva|lence +s
equiva|lency
equiva|len|cies
equiva|lent +s
equiva|lent|ly
equivo|cacy
equivo|cal
equivo|cal|ity
equivo|cal|ly
equivo|cal|ness
equivo|cate
equivo|cates
equivo|cated
equivo|cat|ing
equivo|ca|tion +s
equivo|ca|tor +s
equivo|ca|tory
equi|voke +s (use equivoque)
equi|voque +s
Equu|leus (constellation)
er +s (hesitation. ⚠ err)
era +s
erad|ic|able
eradi|cate
eradi|cates
eradi|cated
eradi|cat|ing
eradi|ca|tion
eradi|ca|tor +s
eras|able
erase
erases
erased
eras|ing
eraser +s
Eras|mus, Desi|der|ius (Dutch humanist)
Eras|tian +s
Eras|tian|ism

Eras¦tus, Thomas
(Swiss physician
and writer)
eras¦ure +s
Erato *Greek and*
Roman Mythology
Era¦tos¦thenes
(Hellenistic
scholar)
er¦bium
ere (before. △ air,
e'er, heir)
Ere¦bus *Greek*
Mythology
Ere¦bus, Mount
(volcano,
Antarctica)
Erech (biblical
name for Uruk)
Erech¦theum (in
Athens)
erect +s +ed +ing
erect¦able
erect¦ile
erec¦tion +s
erect¦ly
erect¦ness
erect¦or +s
E-region +s
er¦em¦ite +s
er¦em¦it¦ic
er¦em¦it¦ic¦al
er¦em¦it¦ism
ereth¦ism
Er¦furt (city,
Germany)
erg +s (unit of
energy)
erg
   areg
   (sand dunes)
erga¦tive +s
ergo
ergo¦cal¦cif¦erol +s
ergo¦nom¦ic
ergo¦nom¦ic¦al¦ly
ergo¦nom¦ics
er¦gono¦mist +s
er¦gos¦terol +s
ergot +s
er¦got¦ism
Eric
Erica (name)
erica +s (heather)
eri¦ca¦ceous
Eric¦son, Leif (use
Ericsson)
Erics¦son, John
(Swedish
engineer)
Erics¦son, Leif
(Norse explorer)

Eric the Red
(Norse explorer)
Eri¦danus
(constellation)
Erie, Lake (in N.
America)
erig¦eron +s
Eriks¦son, Leif
(use Ericsson)
Erin (= Ireland;
name)
Erinys
   Erinyes
   Greek Mythology
eris¦tic +s
eris¦tic¦al¦ly
Eri¦trea (province,
Ethiopia)
Eri¦trean +s
erk +s (naval
rating;
aircraftman;
disliked person.
△ irk)
Er¦lang, Agner
   Krarup (Danish
   mathematician)
Er¦langer, Jo¦seph
(American
physiologist)
erl-king +s
er¦mine
   plural **er¦mine** *or*
   er¦mines
er¦mined
Er¦min¦trude
ern *Am.* **+s** (*Br.*
erne. eagle.
△ earn, urn)
erne *Br.* **+s** (*Am.*
ern. eagle. △ earn,
urn)
Er¦nest
Er¦nest¦ine
Ernie (= electronic
random number
indicating
equipment)
Ernst, Max
(German-born
artist)
erode
   erodes
   eroded
   erod¦ing
erod¦ible
er¦ogen¦ous
Eros (*Greek*
Mythology;
asteroid; statue,
London)
ero¦sion +s

ero¦sion¦al
ero¦sive
erot¦ic
erot¦ica
erot¦ic¦al¦ly
eroti¦cise *Br.* (use
eroticize)
eroti¦cises
eroti¦cised
eroti¦cis¦ing
eroti¦cism
eroti¦cize
eroti¦cizes
eroti¦cized
eroti¦ciz¦ing
erot¦ism
eroto¦gen¦ic
erot¦ogen¦ous
erot¦ology
eroto¦mania
eroto¦maniac +s
err +s +ed +ing (be
mistaken. △ er)
er¦rancy
er¦rand +s
er¦rand boy +s
er¦rand girl +s
er¦rant
er¦rant¦ry
   er¦rant¦ries
er¦rat¦ic +s
er¦rat¦ic¦al¦ly
er¦rati¦cism
er¦ratum
   er¦rata
Er Rif (= Rif
Mountains)
Errol *also* **Er¦roll**
er¦ro¦ne¦ous
er¦ro¦ne¦ous¦ly
er¦ro¦ne¦ous¦ness
error +s
error¦less
er¦satz
Erse
erst
erst¦while
Erté (Russian-born
designer)
Erte¦bølle
   Archaeology
eru¦bes¦cent
eruc¦ta¦tion +s
eru¦dite
eru¦dite¦ly
eru¦di¦tion
erupt +s +ed +ing
(break out
suddenly; eject
lava. △ irrupt)
erup¦tion +s
(breakout;

erup¦tion (*cont.*)
ejection of lava.
△ irruption)
erup¦tive
erup¦tiv¦ity
eryngo +s
ery¦sip¦elas
ery¦thema
ery¦themal
ery¦them¦at¦ic
eryth¦rism
eryth¦ro¦blast +s
eryth¦ro¦cyte +s
eryth¦ro¦cyt¦ic
eryth¦roid
Erz¦ge¦birge
(mountains,
Central Europe)
Erzu¦rum (city,
Turkey)
Esaki, Leo
(Japanese
physicist)
Esau *Bible*
Es¦bjerg (port,
Denmark)
es¦ca¦drille +s
es¦cal¦ade +s
es¦cal¦ate
   es¦cal¦ates
   es¦cal¦ated
   es¦cal¦at¦ing
es¦cal¦ation +s
es¦cal¦ator +s
es¦cal¦lo¦nia +s
es¦cal¦lop +s
   Heraldry
es¦cal¦ope +s
(meat)
es¦cap¦able
es¦cap¦ade +s
es¦cape
   es¦capes
   es¦caped
   es¦cap¦ing
es¦capee +s
es¦cape hatch
   es¦cape hatches
es¦cape¦ment +s
escape-proof
es¦caper +s
es¦cap¦ism
es¦cap¦ist +s
es¦cap¦olo¦gist +s
es¦cap¦ology
es¦car¦got +s
es¦carp +s
es¦carp¦ment +s
eschato¦logic¦al
eschat¦olo¦gist +s
eschat¦ology
   eschat¦ol¦ogies

es|cheat +s +ed
+ing
es|chew +s +ed
+ing
es|chew|al
esch|scholt|zia +s
Es|cof|fier,
Georges-
Auguste (French
chef)
Es|cor|ial, El (in
Madrid)
es|cort +s +ed
+ing
es|cribe
es|cribes
es|cribed
es|crib|ing
es|cri|toire +s
es|crow +s +ed
+ing
es|cudo +s
es|cul|lent
es|cut|cheon +s
es|cut|cheoned
Es|dras
Es|fa|han (use
Isfahan)
eskar +s (use
esker)
esker +s
Es|kimo +s (may
cause offence;
prefer Inuit)
Esky
Eskies
Es|mer|alda
Es|mond
ESOL (= English for
speakers of other
languages)
esopha|geal Am.
(Br. oesophageal)
esopha|gus Am.
esoph|agi
(Br. oesophagus)
eso|ter|ic
eso|ter|ic|al
eso|ter|ic|al|ly
eso|teri|cism
eso|teri|cist +s
es|pa|drille +s
es|pal|ier +s
es|parto +s
es|pe|cial
es|pe|cial|ly
Es|per|ant|ist +s
Es|per|anto
es|pial +s
es|pi|on|age
Es|pir|ito Santo
(state, Brazil)

es|plan|ade +s
es|pousal
es|pouse
es|pouses
es|poused
es|pous|ing
es|pouser +s
es|pres|sivo
es|presso +s
es|prit
es|prit de corps
es|prit de
l'es|cal|ier
espy
espies
espied
espy|ing
Es|qui|mau (use
Eskimo, but may
cause offence;
prefer Inuit)
Es|qui|maux
Es|qui|pu|las (town,
Guatemala)
es|quire +s
essay +s +ed +ing
es|say|ist +s
Essen (city,
Germany)
es|sence +s
Es|sene +s
es|sen|tial +s
es|sen|tial|ism
es|sen|tial|ist +s
es|sen|ti|al|ity
es|sen|tial|ly
es|sen|tial|ness
Esse|quibo (river,
Guyana)
Essex (county,
England)
es|tab|lish
es|tab|lishes
es|tab|lished
es|tab|lish|ing
es|tab|lish|er +s
es|tab|lish|ment
+s
es|tab|lish|ment|
arian +s
es|tab|lish|ment|
arian|ism
es|tam|inet +s
es|tate +s
es|tate agent +s
es|tate car +s
es|teem +s +ed
+ing
Es|telle
ester +s (chemical
compound)

es|ter|ify
es|teri|fies
es|teri|fied
es|teri|fy|ing
Es|ther (Bible;
name)
es|thete Am. +s (Br.
aesthete)
es|thet|ic Am. (Br.
aesthetic)
es|thet|ic|al|ly Am.
(Br. aesthetically)
es|thet|ician Am.
+s (Br.
aesthetician)
es|theti|cism Am.
(Br. aestheticism)
es|thet|ics Am. (Br.
aesthetics)
es|tim|able
es|tim|ably
es|ti|mate
es|ti|mates
es|ti|mated
es|ti|mat|ing
es|ti|ma|tion +s
es|tima|tive
es|ti|ma|tor +s
es|tival Am. (Br.
aestival)
es|tiv|ate Am.
es|tiv|ates
es|tiv|ated
es|tiv|at|ing
(Br. aestivate)
es|tiv|ation Am.
(Br. aestivation)
Es|tonia
Es|to|nian +s
estop
es|tops
es|topped
es|top|ping
es|top|page
es|top|pel
Esto|ril (resort,
Portugal)
est|overs
es|trade +s
es|tral Am. (Br.
oestral)
es|trange
es|tranges
es|tranged
es|tran|ging
es|trange|ment +s
es|treat +s +ed
+ing
Es|tre|ma|dura
(region, Portugal)
es|tro|gen Am. +s
(Br. oestrogen)

es|tro|gen|ic Am.
(Br. oestrogenic)
es|trous Am.
adjective (Br.
oestrous)
es|trum Am. (Br.
oestrum)
es|trus Am. noun
(Br. oestrus)
es|tu|ar|ine
es|tu|ary
es|tu|ar|ies
esuri|ence
esuri|ency
esuri|ent
esuri|ent|ly
Esz|ter|gom (town,
Hungary)
ETA (Basque
separatist
movement)
eta +s (Greek letter.
⚠ eater)
et|aerio +s
eta|lon +s
et cet|era
et|cet|eras
etch
etches
etched
etch|ing
etch|ant +s
etch|er +s
etch|ing +s
eter|nal
eter|nal|ise Br. (use
eternalize)
eter|nal|ises
eter|nal|ised
eter|nal|is|ing
eter|nal|ity
eter|nal|ize
eter|nal|izes
eter|nal|ized
eter|nal|iz|ing
eter|nal|ly
eter|nal|ness
eter|nise Br. (use
eternize)
eter|nises
eter|nised
eter|nis|ing
eter|nity
eter|nities
eter|nize
eter|nizes
eter|nized
eter|niz|ing
Et|es|ian
eth +s
Ethan
etha|nal

eth¦ane
eth¦ane|diol
eth¦ano|ate +s
eth¦an|oic
etha|nol
Ethel
Ethel|red the
  Un|ready
  (English king)
eth¦ene
ether +s
ether|eal
ethere|al|ity
ether|eal¦ly
ether|ial (use
  ethereal)
etheri|al¦ity (use
  ethereality)
eth¦eri|al¦ly (use
  ethereally)
eth¦er¦ic
eth¦er¦isa|tion *Br.*
  (use etherization)
eth¦er¦ise *Br.* (use
  etherize)
eth¦er|ises
eth¦er|ised
eth¦er|is¦ing
eth¦er|iza¦tion
eth¦er|ize
eth¦er|izes
eth¦er|ized
eth¦er|iz¦ing
Ether|net
ethic +s
eth¦ic|al
eth¦ic|al|ity
eth¦ic|al¦ly
ethi|cise *Br.* (use
  ethicize)
ethi|cises
ethi|cised
ethi|cis¦ing
ethi|cist +s
ethi|cize
ethi|cizes
ethi|cized
ethi|ciz¦ing
eth¦ics
Ethi|opia
Ethi|op|ian +s
Ethi|op¦ic +s
eth|moid
eth|moid¦al
Ethna
eth|narch +s
eth|narchy
  eth|narch¦ies
eth¦nic +s
eth¦nic|al
eth¦nic|al¦ly
eth¦ni¦city

ethno|archaeo|
  logic¦al *Br.*
ethno|archae|
  olo¦gist *Br.* +s
ethno|archae|
  ology *Br.*
ethno|archeo|
  logic¦al *Am.*
ethno|arche|
  olo¦gist *Am.* +s
ethno|arche|ology
  Am.
ethno|bot|any
ethno|cen¦tric
ethno|cen¦tric|
  al¦ly
ethno|cen¦tri|city
ethno|cen¦trism
eth|nog|raph¦er +s
ethno|graph¦ic
ethno|graph¦ic|al
ethno|graph¦ic|
  al¦ly
eth|nog|raphy
  eth|nog|raph¦ies
ethno|logic
ethno|logic¦al
ethno|logic|al¦ly
eth|nolo|gist +s
eth|nol|ogy
ethno|meth¦odo|
  logic¦al
ethno|meth¦od|
  olo¦gist +s
ethno|method|
  ology
ethno|music|
  olo¦gist +s
ethno|music|ology
etho|gram +s
etho|logic¦al
etho|logic|al¦ly
eth|olo|gist +s
eth¦ol|ogy
ethos
eth¦oxy|ethane
ethyl
ethyl|ene
ethyl|en¦ic
eth¦yne
eti¦ol|ate
  eti¦ol|ates
  eti¦ol|ated
  eti¦ol|at¦ing
eti¦ola|tion
etio|logic *Am.* (*Br.*
  aetiologic)
etio|logic¦al *Am.*
  (*Br.* aetiological)
etio|logic|al¦ly *Am.*
  (*Br.*
  aetiologically)

eti|ology *Am.* (*Br.*
  aetiology)
eti¦quette +s
Etna (volcano,
  Sicily)
Eton (college,
  England; collar;
  fives; jacket; wall
  game)
Eton|ian +s
Etosha Pan
  (depression,
  Namibia)
étrier +s
Etru¦ria (ancient
  state, Italy)
Etrus|can +s
Etrus|col|ogy
étude +s
étui +s
etymo|logic
etymo|logic¦al
etymo|logic|al¦ly
ety¦molo|gise *Br.*
  (use etymologize)
ety¦molo|gises
ety¦molo|gised
ety¦molo|gis¦ing
ety¦molo|gist +s
ety¦molo|gize
ety¦molo|gizes
ety¦molo|gized
ety¦molo|giz¦ing
ety¦mol|ogy
ety¦molo|gies
ety¦mon
etyma *or*
  ety¦mons
Euan *also* Ewan
Eu¦boea (Greek
  island)
eu¦ca|lypt +s
eu¦ca|lyp¦tus
  eu¦ca|lyp¦tuses *or*
  eu¦ca|lypti
eu¦cary|ote (use
  eukaryote)
eu¦cary|ot¦ic (use
  eukaryotic)
eu|charis
  plural eu|charis
Eu¦char|ist +s
Eu¦char|is¦tic
Eu¦char|is¦tic|al
eu¦chre
  eu¦chres
  eu¦chred
  eu¦chring
Eu¦clid (Greek
  mathematician)
Eu¦clid|ean

eu|dae¦mon¦ic (use
  eudemonic)
eu|dae¦mon|ism
  (use
  eudemonism)
eu|dae¦mon|ist +s
  (use eudemonist)
eu|dae¦mon|is¦tic
  (use
  eudemonistic)
eu|de¦mon¦ic
eu|de¦mon|ism
eu|de¦mon|ist +s
eu|de¦mon|is¦tic
eudi|om¦eter +s
eudio|met¦ric
eudio|met¦ric|al
eudi|om¦etry
Eu¦dora
Eu¦gene
Eu|genia
eu|gen¦ic
eu|gen¦ic|al¦ly
eu|geni|cist +s
eu|gen¦ics
Eugé|nie (French
  empress)
eu|gen|ist +s
eu|glena
eu|hem¦er|ism
eu|kary|ote +s
eu|kary|ot¦ic
Euler, Leon|hard
  (Swiss-born
  mathematician)
Euler, Ulf Svante
  von (Swedish
  physiologist)
Euler-Chelpin,
  Hans van
  (German-born
  Swedish
  biochemist)
eu¦lo|gise *Br.* (use
  eulogize)
  eu¦lo|gises
  eu¦lo|gised
  eu¦lo|gis¦ing
eu¦lo|gist +s
eu¦lo|gis¦tic
eu¦lo|gis¦tic|al¦ly
eu¦lo|gium +s
eu¦lo|gize
  eu¦lo|gizes
  eu¦lo|gized
  eu¦lo|giz¦ing
eu¦logy
  eu|logies
Eu|men|ides *Greek*
  Mythology
Eu¦nice
eu¦nuch +s

eu|nuch|oid
eu|ony|mus
  plural eu|ony|mus
eu|pep|tic
Eu|phe|mia
eu|phem|ise *Br.*
  (use euphemize)
    eu|phem|ises
    eu|phem|ised
    eu|phem|is|ing
eu|phem|ism +s
eu|phem|ist +s
eu|phem|is|tic
eu|phem|is|tic|
                al|ly
eu|phem|ize
    eu|phem|izes
    eu|phem|ized
    eu|phem|iz|ing
eu|phon|ic
eu|pho|ni|ous
eu|pho|ni|ous|ly
eu|phon|ise *Br.*
  (use euphonize)
    eu|phon|ises
    eu|phon|ised
    eu|phon|is|ing
eu|pho|nium +s
eu|phon|ize
    eu|phon|izes
    eu|phon|ized
    eu|phon|iz|ing
eu|phony
    eu|phonies
eu|phor|bia +s
eu|phoria
eu|phori|ant +s
eu|phor|ic
eu|phor|ic|al|ly
eu|phrasy
    eu|phrasies
Eu|phra|tes (river,
  SW Asia)
eu|phu|ism
eu|phu|ist +s
eu|phu|is|tic
eu|phu|is|tic|al|ly
Eur|asian +s
Eur|atom
eur|eka
eu|rhyth|mic *Br.*
  (*Am.* eurythmic)
eu|rhyth|mics *Br.*
  (*Am.* eurythmics)
eu|rhythmy *Br.*
  (*Am.* eurythmy)
Eu|ripi|des (Greek
  dramatist)
Euro +s (European;
  Eurodollar)
euro +s (animal)
Euro|bond +s

Euro|cen|tric
Euro|cen|trism
Euro|cheque *Br.* +s
Euro|
    com|mun|ism
Euro|com|mun|ist
  +s
Euro|crat +s
Euro-currency
Euro|dol|lar +s
Euro-election +s
Euro|mar|ket +s
Euro-MP +s
Eur|opa (*Greek
  Mythology*; moon
  of Jupiter)
Euro|par|lia|ment
Euro|par|lia|men|
              tar|ian +s
Euro|par|lia|men|
                    tary
Eur|ope
Euro|pean +s
Euro|pean|isa|tion
  Br. (use
  Europeanization)
Euro|pean|ise *Br.*
  (use
  Europeanize)
    Euro|pean|ises
    Euro|pean|ised
    Euro|pean|is|ing
Euro|pean|ism
Euro|pean|iza|tion
Euro|pean|ize
    Euro|pean|izes
    Euro|pean|ized
    Euro|pean|iz|ing
Euro|phile +s
euro|pium
Euro|poort (port,
  the Netherlands)
Euro-rebel +s
Euro-sceptic +s
Euro-sceptic|al
Euro|tun|nel
Euro|vision
Eury|dice *Greek
  Mythology*
eu|ryth|mic *Am.*
  (*Br.* eurhythmic)
eu|ryth|mics *Am.*
  (*Br.* eurhythmics)
eu|rythmy *Am.* (*Br.*
  eurhythmy)
Euse|bius (early
  bishop)
Eus|tace
Eus|ta|chian (tube)
eu|stasy
eu|stat|ic

Eus|ton (railway
  station, London)
eu|tec|tic +s
Eu|terpe *Greek and
  Roman Mythology*
eu|tha|nasia
eu|ther|ian +s
eu|troph|ic
eu|trophi|cate
    eu|trophi|cates
    eu|trophi|cated
    eu|trophi|cat|ing
eu|trophi|ca|tion
eu|trophy
Eva
evacu|ant +s
evacu|ate
    evacu|ates
    evacu|ated
    evacu|at|ing
evacu|ation +s
evacu|ative
evacu|ator +s
evac|uee +s
evad|able
evade
    evades
    evaded
    evad|ing
evader +s
Evadne
eva|gin|ate
    eva|gin|ates
    eva|gin|ated
    eva|gin|at|ing
eva|gin|ation
evalu|ate
    evalu|ates
    evalu|ated
    evalu|at|ing
evalu|ation +s
evalu|ative
evalu|ator +s
Evan
evan|esce
    evan|esces
    evan|esced
    evan|es|cing
evan|es|cence
evan|es|cent
evan|es|cent|ly
evan|gel +s
evan|gel|ic
evan|gel|ic|al +s
evan|gel|ic|al|ism
evan|gel|ic|al|ly
Evan|gel|ine
evan|gel|isa|tion
  Br. (use
  evangelization)
evan|gel|ise *Br.*
  (use evangelize)

evan|gel|ise (*cont.*)
    evan|gel|ises
    evan|gel|ised
    evan|gel|is|ing
evan|gel|iser *Br.*
  +s (use
  evangelizer)
evan|gel|ism
evan|gel|ist +s
evan|gel|is|tic
evan|gel|iza|tion
evan|gel|ize
    evan|gel|izes
    evan|gel|ized
    evan|gel|iz|ing
evan|gel|izer +s
Evans, Ar|thur
  (British
  archaeologist)
Evans, Edith
  (English actress)
Evans-Pritch|ard,
  Ed|ward (English
  anthropologist)
evap|or|able
evap|or|ate
    evap|or|ates
    evap|or|ated
    evap|or|at|ing
evap|or|ation
evap|ora|tive
evap|or|ator +s
evap|or|ite +s
eva|sion +s
eva|sive
eva|sive|ly
eva|sive|ness
Eve (*Bible*; name)
eve +s (time before
  something)
evec|tion
Eve|lyn (name)
Eve|lyn, John
  (English writer)
even +s +ed +ing
  +er +est
even-handed
even-handed|ly
even-handed|ness
even|ing +s *noun*
even|ing dress
    even|ing dresses
    (single garment;
    formal outfit)
even|ly
even-money
  attributive
even|ness
even|song +s
even Ste|phen
even Ste|phens

even Ste¦ven (use
  even Stephen)
even Ste¦vens (use
  even Stephens)
event +s +ed +ing
even-tempered
event¦er +s
event¦ful
event¦ful¦ly
event¦ful¦ness
even¦tide
event¦less
event¦less¦ly
even¦tual
even¦tu¦al¦ity
  even¦tu¦al¦ities
even¦tu¦al¦ly
even¦tu¦ate
  even¦tu¦ates
  even¦tu¦ated
  even¦tu¦at¦ing
even¦tu¦ation
ever
ever-changing
Ever¦est, Mount
  (in Himalayas)
Ever¦glades, the
  (area, USA)
ever¦green +s
ever¦last¦ing
ever¦last¦ing¦ly
ever¦last¦ing¦ness
ever¦more
ever-present
ever¦sion
Evert, Chris
  (American tennis
  player)
evert +s +ed +ing
  (turn inside out)
every
every¦body
every¦day
  (ordinary)
every day (each
  day)
Every¦man
every¦one (every
  person,
  everybody)
every one (each
  one)
every¦thing
every way
every¦where
Every¦woman
Ev¦ette *also* Yv¦ette
evict +s +ed +ing
evic¦tion +s
evict¦or +s
evi¦dence
  evi¦dences

evi¦dence (*cont.*)
  evi¦denced
  evi¦den¦cing
evi¦dent
evi¦den¦tial
evi¦den¦tial¦ly
evi¦den¦tiary
evi¦dent¦ly
evil +s
evil¦doer +s
evil¦doing
evil¦ly
evil-minded
evil¦ness
evince
  evinces
  evinced
  evin¦cing
evin¦cible
evin¦cive
evis¦cer¦ate
  evis¦cer¦ates
  evis¦cer¦ated
  evis¦cer¦at¦ing
evis¦cer¦ation
evo¦ca¦tion +s
evoca¦tive
evoca¦tive¦ly
evoca¦tive¦ness
evoca¦tory
evoke
  evokes
  evoked
  evok¦ing
evoker +s
evo¦lute
  evo¦lutes
  evo¦luted
  evo¦lut¦ing
evo¦lu¦tion +s
evo¦lu¦tion¦al
evo¦lu¦tion¦al¦ly
evo¦lu¦tion¦ar¦ily
evo¦lu¦tion¦ary
evo¦lu¦tion¦ism
evo¦lu¦tion¦ist +s
evo¦lu¦tion¦is¦tic
evo¦lu¦tive
evolv¦able
evolve
  evolves
  evolved
  evolv¦ing
evolve¦ment
Evonne *also*
  Yvonne
evul¦sion
ev¦zone +s
Ewan *also* Euan
Ewart
ewe +s (sheep.
  △ yew, you)

ewe-necked
ewer +s
ex
  exes
ex|acer|bate
  ex|acer|bates
  ex|acer|bated
  ex|acer|bat|ing
ex|acer|ba¦tion
exact +s +ed +ing
exact¦able
exact¦ing¦ly
exact¦ing¦ness
exac¦tion +s
exac¦ti¦tude
exact¦ly
exact¦ness
exact¦or +s
ex¦ag¦ger¦ate
  ex¦ag¦ger¦ates
  ex¦ag¦ger¦ated
  ex¦ag¦ger¦at¦ing
ex¦ag¦ger¦ated¦ly
ex¦ag¦ger¦at¦ing¦ly
ex¦ag¦ger¦ation +s
ex¦ag¦gera¦tive
ex¦ag¦ger¦ator +s
exalt +s +ed +ing
exalt¦ation +s
ex¦alt¦ed¦ly
exalt¦ed¦ness
ex¦alt¦er +s
exam +s
exa¦meter *Am.* +s
exa¦metre *Br.* +s
exam¦in¦able
exam¦in¦ation +s
exam¦in¦ation¦al
exam¦ine
  exam¦ines
  exam¦ined
  exam¦in¦ing
exam¦inee +s
exam¦in¦er +s
ex¦ample +s
ex¦ani¦mate
ex ante
exan¦thema
  exan¦the¦mas *or*
  exan¦the¦mata
ex¦arch +s
ex¦arch¦ate +s
ex¦as¦per¦ate
  ex¦as¦per¦ates
  ex¦as¦per¦ated
  ex¦as¦per¦at¦ing
  ex¦as¦per¦ated¦ly
  ex¦as¦per¦at¦ing¦ly
  ex¦as¦per¦ation
Ex¦cali¦bur
ex cath|edra

ex¦cav¦ate
  ex¦cav¦ates
  ex¦cav¦ated
  ex¦cav¦at¦ing
ex¦cav¦ation +s
ex¦cav¦ator +s
ex¦ceed +s +ed
  +ing (go beyond;
  be greater than.
  △ accede)
ex¦ceed¦ing¦ly
excel
  ex¦cels
  ex¦celled
  ex¦cel¦ling
ex¦cel¦lence +s
Ex¦cel¦lency
  Ex¦cel¦len¦cies
  (in titles)
ex¦cel¦lency
  ex¦cel¦len¦cies
ex¦cel¦lent
ex¦cel¦lent¦ly
ex¦cel¦sior
ex¦cen¦tric (use
  eccentric)
ex¦cept +s +ed
  +ing (leave out;
  not including.
  △ accept)
ex¦cep¦tion +s
ex¦cep¦tion¦able
ex¦cep¦tion¦ably
ex¦cep¦tion¦al
ex¦cep¦tion¦al¦ity
ex¦cep¦tion¦al¦ly
ex¦cerpt +s +ed
  +ing
ex¦cerpt¦ible
ex¦cerp¦tion
ex¦cess
  ex¦cesses
ex¦ces¦sive
ex¦ces¦sive¦ly
ex¦ces¦sive¦ness
ex¦change
  ex¦changes
  ex¦changed
  ex¦chan¦ging
ex¦change¦abil¦ity
ex¦change¦able
ex¦chan¦ger +s
ex¦change rate +s
exchange-rate
  mech¦an¦ism +s
ex¦chequer +s
ex¦cimer +s
  (chemical
  compound.
  △ eczema)
ex¦cis¦able

ex|cise
  ex|cises
  ex|cised
  ex|cis|ing
ex'cise|man
  ex'cise|men
ex|ci|sion +s
ex|cit|abil|ity
ex|cit|able
ex|cit|ably
ex|cit|ant +s
ex|ci|ta|tion +s
ex|ci|ta|tive
ex|ci|ta|tory
ex|cite
  ex|cites
  ex|cited
  ex|cit|ing
ex|cited|ly
ex|cited|ness
ex|cite|ment +s
ex|citer +s
ex|cit|ing|ly
ex|cit|ing|ness
ex|citon +s
ex|claim +s +ed
  +ing
ex|clam|ation +s
ex|clama|tory
ex|clave +s
ex|clos|ure +s
ex|clud|able
ex|clude
  ex|cludes
  ex|cluded
  ex|clud|ing
ex|cluder +s
ex|clu|sion +s
ex|clu|sion|ary
ex|clu|sion|ist +s
ex|clu|sive +s
ex|clu|sive|ly
ex|clu|sive|ness
ex|clu|siv|ity
ex|cogit|able
ex|cogi|tate
  ex|cogi|tates
  ex|cogi|tated
  ex|cogi|tat|ing
ex|cogi|ta|tion
ex|cogi|ta|tive
ex|com|mu'ni|cate
  ex|com'mu'ni|
    cates
  ex|com'mu'ni|
    cated
  ex|com'mu'ni|
    cat|ing
ex|com'mu'ni|
    ca'tion +s
ex|com'mu'ni|
    ca'tive

ex|com'mu'ni|
    ca'tor +s
ex|com'mu'ni|
    ca'tory
ex-con +s
ex|cori|ate
  ex|cori|ates
  ex|cori|ated
  ex|cori|at|ing
ex|cori|ation +s
ex|cre|ment +s
ex|cre|men|tal
ex|cres|cence
ex|cres|cent
ex|cres'cen|tial
ex|creta (body
  waste.
  ⚠ excreter)
ex|crete
  ex|cretes
  ex|creted
  ex|cret|ing
ex|creter +s
  (person or thing
  that excretes.
  ⚠ excreta)
ex|cre|tion +s
ex|cre|tive
ex|cre|tory
ex|cru|ci|ate
  ex|cru|ci|ates
  ex|cru|ci|ated
  ex|cru|ci|at|ing
ex|cru|ci|at|ing|ly
ex|cru|ci|ation
ex|cul|pate
  ex|cul|pates
  ex|cul|pated
  ex|cul|pat|ing
ex|cul|pa'tion +s
ex|cul|pa|tory
ex|cur|sion +s
ex|cur|sion|al
ex|cur|sion|ary
ex|cur|sion|ist
ex|cur|sive
ex|cur|sive|ly
ex|cur|sive|ness
ex|cur'sus
  plural ex|cur'sus
  or ex|cur'suses
ex|cus|able
ex|cus|ably
ex|cusa|tory
ex|cuse
  ex|cuses
  ex|cused
  ex|cus|ing
ex|cuse me
  (apology)
excuse-me +s
  (dance)

ex-directory
ex div. (= ex
  dividend)
ex divi|dend
Exe (river, England)
exeat +s
exec +s
exe|crable
exe|crably
exe|crate
  exe|crates
  exe|crated
  exe|crat|ing
exe|cra'tion +s
exe|cra'tive
exe|cra'tory
exe|cut|able
ex'ecu|tant +s
exe|cute
  exe|cutes
  exe|cuted
  exe|cut|ing
exe|cu|tion +s
exe|cu|tion|ary
exe|cu|tion|er +s
ex'ecu|tive +s
ex'ecu|tive|ly
ex'ecu|tor +s (of a
  will)
exe|cu|tor +s (of a
  plan etc.)
ex'ecu|tor'ial
ex'ecu|tor|ship +s
ex'ecu|tory
ex'ecu|trix
  ex'ecu|tri'ces
  female
exe|gesis
  exe|geses
exe|gete +s
exe|get'ic
exe|get'ic|al
exe|ge'tist +s
ex'em|plar +s
ex'em|plar|ily
ex'em|plari|ness
ex'em|plary
ex'em|pli'fi'ca'tion
  +s
ex'em|plify
  ex'em|pli|fies
  ex'em|pli|fied
  ex'em|pli|fy|ing
ex'em|plum
  ex'em|pla
ex'empt +s +ed
  +ing
ex'emp|tion +s
exe|qua'tur +s
exe|quies
ex'er|cis|able

ex'er|cise
  ex'er|cises
  ex'er|cised
  ex'er|cis|ing
  (mental or
  physical activity;
  engage in this.
  ⚠ exorcize)
ex'er|cise book +s
ex'er|ciser +s
ex|ergual
ex|ergue +s
exert +s +ed +ing
  (exercise.
  ⚠ exsert)
ex'er|tion +s
Exe'ter (city,
  England)
exe|unt
ex|fil|trate
  ex|fil|trates
  ex|fil|trated
  ex|fil|trat|ing
ex|fil|tra|tion
ex|foli|ate
  ex|foli|ates
  ex|foli|ated
  ex|foli|at|ing
ex|foli|ation
ex|folia|tive
ex gra|tia
ex|hal|able
ex|hal|ation +s
ex|hale
  ex|hales
  ex|haled
  ex|hal|ing
ex|haust +s +ed
  +ing
ex|haust'er +s
ex|haust|ibil|ity
ex|haust|ible
ex|haust|ibly
ex|haus|tion
ex|haust|ive
ex|haust|ive|ly
ex|haust|ive|ness
ex|haust pipe +s
ex|hibit +s +ed
  +ing
ex|hib|ition +s
ex|hib|ition'er +s
ex|hib|ition|ism
ex|hib|ition|ist +s
ex|hib|ition|is'tic
ex|hib|ition|is'tic|
    al'ly
ex|hib|it|or +s
ex|hibi|tory
ex|hil'ar|ant +s
ex|hil'ar|ate
  ex|hil'ar|ates

ex|hil|ar|ate (*cont.*)
  ex|hil|ar|ated
  ex|hil|ar|at|ing
ex|hil|ar|at|ing|ly
ex|hil|ar|ation +s
ex|hil|ara|tive
ex|hort +s +ed
  +ing
ex|hort|ation +s
ex|hor|ta|tive
ex|hor|ta|tory
ex|hort|er +s
ex|hum|ation +s
ex|hume
  ex|humes
  ex|humed
  ex|hum|ing
ex hy|poth|esi
exi|gence
exi|gency
  exi|gen|cies
exi|gent
exi|gible
exi|gu|ity
ex|igu|ous
ex|igu|ous|ly
ex|igu|ous|ness
exile
  exiles
  exiled
  ex|il|ing
exil|ic
exist +s +ed +ing
ex|ist|ence +s
ex|ist|ent
ex|ist|en|tial
ex|ist|en|tial|ism
ex|ist|en|tial|ist +s
ex|ist|en|tial|ly
exit +s +ed +ing
ex-libris
  plural ex-libris
  (label)
Ex|moor (area,
  England)
ex ni|hilo
exo|bio|lo|gist +s
exo|biol|ogy
Exo|cet +s
exo|crine
exo|derm +s
Exo|dus *Bible*
exo|dus
  exo|duses
  (departure)
ex of|fi|cio
ex|og|am|ous
ex|og|amy
exo|gen +s
ex|ogen|ous
ex|ogen|ous|ly

exon +s
  (commander of
  Yeomen of the
  Guard)
ex|on|er|ate
  ex|on|er|ates
  ex|on|er|ated
  ex|on|er|at|ing
ex|on|er|ation
ex|on|era|tive
ex|oph|thal|mia
ex|oph|thal|mic
ex|oph|thal|mos
ex|oph|thal|mus
  (use
  exophthalmos)
exo|plasm
ex|or|bi|tance
ex|or|bi|tant
ex|or|bi|tant|ly
ex|or|cisa|tion *Br.*
  (use exorcization)
ex|or|cise *Br.* (use
  exorcize)
  ex|or|cises
  ex|or|cised
  ex|or|cis|ing
  (drive away evil
  spirits.
  ⚠ exercise)
ex|or|cism +s
ex|or|cist +s
ex|or|ciza|tion
ex|or|cize
  ex|or|cizes
  ex|or|cized
  ex|or|ciz|ing
  (drive away evil
  spirit. ⚠ exercise)
ex|or|dial
ex|or|di|al|ly
ex|or|dium
  ex|or|dia *or*
  ex|or|diums
exo|skel|etal
exo|skel|eton +s
exo|sphere +s
exo|ter|ic
exo|ter|ic|al
exo|ter|ic|al|ly
exo|teri|cism
exo|ther|mal
exo|ther|mal|ly
exo|ther|mic
exo|ther|mic|al|ly
exot|ic +s
exot|ica
exot|ic|al|ly
exoti|cism
exo|toxin +s
ex|pand +s +ed
  +ing

ex|pand|able
ex|pand|er +s
ex|panse +s
ex|pan|si|bil|ity
ex|pan|sible
ex|pan|sile
ex|pan|sion +s
ex|pan|sion|ary
ex|pan|sion|ism
ex|pan|sion|ist +s
ex|pan|sion|is|tic
ex|pan|sive
ex|pan|sive|ly
ex|pan|sive|ness
ex|pan|siv|ity
ex parte
expat +s
ex|pati|ate
  ex|pati|ates
  ex|pati|ated
  ex|pati|at|ing
ex|pati|ation +s
ex|pati|atory
ex|patri|ate
  ex|patri|ates
  ex|patri|ated
  ex|patri|at|ing
ex|patri|ation
ex|pect +s +ed
  +ing
ex|pect|able
ex|pect|ancy
  ex|pect|an|cies
ex|pect|ant
ex|pect|ant|ly
ex|pect|ation +s
ex|pec|tor|ant +s
ex|pec|tor|ate
  ex|pec|tor|ates
  ex|pec|tor|ated
  ex|pec|tor|at|ing
ex|pec|tor|ation
ex|pec|tor|ator +s
ex|pe|di|ence
ex|pe|di|ency
ex|pe|di|ent +s
ex|pe|di|ent|ly
ex|ped|ite
  ex|ped|ites
  ex|ped|ited
  ex|ped|it|ing
ex|ped|iter +s
ex|ped|ition +s
ex|ped|ition|ary
ex|ped|ition|ist +s
ex|ped|itious
ex|ped|itious|ly
ex|ped|itious|ness
expel
  ex|pels
  ex|pelled
  ex|pel|ling

ex|pel|lable
ex|pel|lee +s
ex|pel|lent +s
ex|pel|ler +s
ex|pend +s +ed
  +ing
ex|pend|abil|ity
ex|pend|able
ex|pend|ably
ex|pend|iture +s
ex|pense +s
ex|pen|sive
ex|pen|sive|ly
ex|pen|sive|ness
ex|peri|ence
  ex|peri|ences
  ex|peri|enced
  ex|peri|en|cing
ex|peri|ence|able
ex|peri|en|tial
ex|peri|en|tial|ism
ex|peri|en|tial|ist
  +s
ex|peri|en|tial|ly
ex|peri|ment +s
  +ed +ing
ex|peri|men|tal
ex|peri|men|tal|ise
  Br. (use
  experimentalize)
ex|peri|men|tal|
       ises
ex|peri|men|tal|
       ised
ex|peri|men|tal|
       is|ing
ex|peri|men|tal|
       ism
ex|peri|men|tal|ist
  +s
ex|peri|men|tal|
       ize
ex|peri|men|tal|
       izes
ex|peri|men|tal|
       ized
ex|peri|men|tal|
       iz|ing
ex|peri|men|tal|ly
ex|peri|men|
       ta|tion
ex|peri|ment|er +s
ex|pert +s
ex|pert|ise *noun*
ex|pert|ise *Br.* (use
  expertize)
  ex|pert|ises
  ex|pert|ised
  ex|pert|is|ing
  verb
ex|pert|ize
  ex|pert|izes

ex¦pert|ize (*cont.*)
  ex¦pert|ized
  ex¦pert|iz¦ing
  verb
ex¦pert¦ly
ex¦pert|ness
ex¦pi|able
ex¦pi|ate
  ex¦pi|ates
  ex¦pi|ated
  ex¦pi|at¦ing
ex¦pi|ation
ex¦pi|ator +s
ex¦pi|atory
ex¦pir|ation +s
ex¦pira|tory
ex¦pire
  ex|pires
  ex|pired
  ex¦pir¦ing
ex¦piry
ex|plain +s +ed
  +ing
ex|plain|able
ex|plain|er +s
ex|plan|ation +s
ex|plana|tor¦ily
ex|plana|tory
ex|plant +s +ed
  +ing
ex|plant|ation
ex|ple¦tive +s
ex|plic|able
ex|pli|cate
  ex|pli|cates
  ex|pli|cated
  ex¦pli|cat¦ing
ex|pli|ca¦tion +s
ex|pli|ca|tive
ex|pli|ca¦tor +s
ex|pli|ca¦tory
ex|pli¦cit
ex|pli¦cit¦ly
ex|pli¦cit|ness
ex|plode
  ex|plodes
  ex|ploded
  ex|plod¦ing
ex|ploder +s
ex|ploit +s +ed
  +ing
ex|ploit|able
ex|ploit|ation +s
ex|ploit|ative
ex|ploit|er +s
ex|ploit|ive
ex|plor|ation +s
ex|plor|ation¦al
ex|plora|tive
ex|plora|tory
ex|plore
  ex|plores

ex|plore (*cont.*)
  ex|plored
  ex|plor¦ing
ex|plorer +s
ex|plo|sion +s
ex|plo|sive +s
ex|plo|sive¦ly
ex|plo|sive|ness
Expo +s
ex|po¦nent +s
ex|po¦nen|tial
ex|po¦nen|tial¦ly
ex¦port +s +ed
  +ing
ex¦port|abil¦ity
ex¦port|able
ex¦port|ation
ex¦port|er +s
ex|pose
  ex|poses
  ex|posed
  ex|pos¦ing
ex¦posé +s
ex|poser +s
ex|pos|ition +s
ex|pos|ition|al
ex|posi|tive
ex|posi|tor +s
ex|posi|tory
ex post
ex post facto
ex|pos¦tu|late
  ex|pos¦tu|lates
  ex|pos¦tu|lated
  ex|pos¦tu|lat¦ing
ex|pos¦tu|la¦tion
  +s
ex|pos¦tu|la¦tory
ex|pos¦ure +s
ex|pound +s +ed
  +ing
ex|pound¦er +s
ex|press
  ex|presses
  ex|pressed
  ex¦press|ing
ex¦press¦er +s
ex¦press|ible
ex¦pres|sion +s
ex¦pres|sion|al
ex¦pres|sion|ism
ex¦pres|sion|ist +s
ex¦pres|sion|is¦tic
ex¦pres|sion|is¦tic|
    al¦ly
ex|pres¦sion|less
ex|pres¦sion|
    less¦ly
ex|pres¦sion|less|
    ness
expression-mark
  +s

ex¦pres|sive
ex¦pres|sive¦ly
ex¦pres|sive|ness
ex¦pres|siv|ity
ex¦press¦ly
ex¦presso +s
ex¦press|way +s
ex|pro¦pri|ate
  ex|pro¦pri|ates
  ex|pro¦pri|ated
  ex|pro¦pri|at¦ing
ex|pro¦pri|ation +s
ex|pro¦pri|ator +s
ex|pul|sion +s
ex|pul|sive
ex|punc¦tion
ex|punge
  ex|punges
  ex|punged
  ex|pun¦ging
ex|punger +s
ex|pur|gate
  ex|pur|gates
  ex|pur|gated
  ex|pur|gat¦ing
ex|pur|ga¦tion
ex|pur|ga¦tor +s
ex|pur|ga|tor¦ial
ex|pur|ga|tory
ex¦quis|ite
ex¦quis|ite¦ly
ex¦quis|ite|ness
ex|san|guin|ate
  ex|san¦guin|ates
  ex|san¦guin|ated
  ex|san¦guin|at¦ing
ex|san¦guin|ation
ex|scind +s +ed
  +ing
ex¦sert +s +ed
  +ing (*Biology* put
  forth. ⚠ exert)
ex-service
ex-serviceman
  ex-servicemen
ex-servicewoman
  ex-servicewomen
ex|sic|cate
  ex|sic|cates
  ex|sic|cated
  ex|sic|cat¦ing
ex si¦len|tio
ex¦tant
ex|tem¦por|an|eous
ex|tem¦por|
    an¦eous¦ly
ex|tem¦por|an|eous|
    ness
ex|tem¦por|ar¦ily
ex|tem¦por|ari|
    ness
ex|tem¦por|ary

ex|tem¦pore
ex|tem¦por|isa|
  tion *Br.* +s (use
  extemporization)
ex|tem¦por|ise *Br.*
  (use
  extemporize)
ex|tem¦por|ises
ex|tem¦por|ised
ex|tem¦por|is¦ing
ex|tem¦por|iza|
    tion +s
ex|tem¦por|ize
ex|tem¦por|izes
ex|tem¦por|ized
ex|tem¦por|iz¦ing
ex¦tend +s +ed
  +ing
ex|tend|abil¦ity
ex|tend|able
extended-play
  attributive
ex|tend¦er +s
ex|tend|ibil¦ity
  (use
  extendability)
ex|tend|ible (use
  extendable)
ex¦ten|si|bil¦ity
ex¦ten|sible
ex¦ten|sile
ex¦ten|sion +s
ex¦ten|sion¦al
ex¦ten|sive
ex¦ten|sive¦ly
ex¦ten|sive|ness
ex¦tens|om¦eter +s
ex¦ten|sor +s
ex¦tent +s
ex|tenu|ate
  ex|tenu|ates
  ex|tenu|ated
  ex|tenu|at¦ing
ex|tenu|at¦ing¦ly
ex|tenu|ation +s
ex|tenu|atory
ex¦ter|ior +s
ex¦ter|ior|ise *Br.*
  (use exteriorize)
ex¦ter|ior|ises
ex¦ter|ior|ised
ex¦ter|ior|is¦ing
ex¦ter|ior|ity
ex¦ter|ior|ize
  ex¦ter|ior|izes
  ex¦ter|ior|ized
  ex¦ter|ior|iz¦ing
ex¦ter|ior¦ly
ex¦ter|min|ate
  ex|ter¦min|ates
  ex|ter¦min|ated
  ex|ter¦min|at¦ing

ex|ter|min|ation
  +s
ex|ter|min|ator +s
ex|ter|min|atory
ex|ter|nal +s
ex|ter|nal|isa|tion
  Br. (use
  externalization)
ex|ter|nal|ise *Br.*
  (use externalize)
  ex|ter|nal|ises
  ex|ter|nal|ised
  ex|ter|nal|is|ing
ex|ter|nal|ity
  ex|ter|nal|ities
ex|ter|nal|iza|tion
ex|ter|nal|ize
  ex|ter|nal|izes
  ex|ter|nal|ized
  ex|ter|nal|iz|ing
ex|ter|nal|ly
ex|tero|cep|tive
ex|ter|ri|tor|ial
ex|ter|ri|tori|al|ity
ex|tinct
ex|tinc|tion +s
ex|tinct|ive
ex|tin|guish
  ex|tin|guishes
  ex|tin|guished
  ex|tin|guish|ing
ex|tin|guish|able
ex|tin|guish|er +s
ex|tin|guish|ment
ex|tir|pate
  ex|tir|pates
  ex|tir|pated
  ex|tir|pat|ing
ex|tir|pa|tion
ex|tir|pa|tor +s
extol
  ex|tols
  ex|tolled
  ex|tol|ling
ex|tol|ler +s
ex|tol|ment
ex|tort +s +ed
  +ing
ex|tort|er +s
ex|tor|tion +s
ex|tor|tion|ate
ex|tor|tion|ate|ly
ex|tor|tion|er +s
ex|tor|tion|ist +s
ex|tort|ive
extra +s
extra|cel|lu|lar
extra|cra|nial
ex|tract +s +ed
  +ing
ex|tract|abil|ity
ex|tract|able

ex|trac|tion +s
ex|tract|ive
ex|tract|or +s
extra-curricu|lar
extra|dit|able
extra|dite
  extra|dites
  extra|dited
  extra|dit|ing
extra|di|tion +s
ex|tra|dos
  ex|tra|doses
extra|gal|ac|tic
extra|judi|cial
extra|judi|cial|ly
extra|lin|guis|tic
extra|mar|it|al
extra|mar|it|al|ly
extra|mun|dane
extra|mural
extra|mural|ly
ex|tra|ne|ous
ex|tra|ne|ous|ly
ex|tra|ne|ous|ness
extra|or|din|ar|ily
extra|or|din|ari|
     ness
extra|or|din|ary
  extra|or|din|ar|ies
extra|phys|ic|al
ex|trapo|late
  ex|trapo|lates
  ex|trapo|lated
  ex|trapo|lat|ing
ex|trapo|la|tion +s
ex|trapo|la|tive
ex|trapo|la|tor +s
extra|sens|ory
extra|ter|res|trial
  +s
extra|ter|ri|tor|ial
extra|ter|ri|tori|
    al|ity
ex|trava|gance +s
ex|trava|gancy
  ex|trava|gan|cies
ex|trava|gant
ex|trava|gant|ly
ex|trava|ganza +s
ex|trava|sate
  ex|trava|sates
  ex|trava|sated
  ex|trava|sat|ing
ex|trava|sa|tion
extra|vehicu|lar
extra|ver|sion (use
  extroversion)
extra|vert +s (use
  extrovert)
extra|vert|ed (use
  extroverted)

ex|trema (plural of
  extremum)
Ex|tre|ma|dura
  (region, Spain)
ex|tremal
ex|treme
  ex|tremes
  ex|trem|est
ex|treme|ly
ex|treme|ness
ex|tremis (in *'in*
  extremis')
ex|trem|ism
ex|trem|ist +s
ex|trem|ity
  ex|trem|ities
ex|tremum
  ex|trem|ums *or*
  ex|trema
ex|tric|able
ex|tri|cate
  ex|tri|cates
  ex|tri|cated
  ex|tri|cat|ing
ex|tri|ca|tion +s
ex|trin|sic
ex|trin|sic|al|ly
ex|tro|ver|sion
ex|tro|vert +s
ex|tro|vert|ed
ex|trude
  ex|trudes
  ex|truded
  ex|trud|ing
ex|tru|sile
ex|tru|sion +s
ex|tru|sive
ex|uber|ance
ex|uber|ant
ex|uber|ant|ly
ex|uber|ate
  ex|uber|ates
  ex|uber|ated
  ex|uber|at|ing
ex|ud|ate +s
ex|ud|ation +s
ex|uda|tive
exude
  ex|udes
  ex|uded
  ex|ud|ing
exult +s +ed +ing
ex|ult|ancy
ex|ult|ant
ex|ult|ant|ly
ex|ult|ation +s
ex|ult|ing|ly
Exuma Cays
  (island group,
  Bahamas)
exurb +s
ex|urban

ex|ur|ban|ite +s
ex|ur|bia
ex|uviae
ex|uvial
ex|uvi|ate
  ex|uvi|ates
  ex|uvi|ated
  ex|uvi|at|ing
ex|uvi|ation
ex-voto +s
eyas
  eyases
eye
  eyes
  eyed
  eye|ing *or* eying
  (organ of sight.
  △ aye, I)
eye|ball +s +ed
  +ing
eye|bath +s
eye|black
eye bolt +s
eye|bright
eye|brow +s
eye-catching
eye con|tact
eye|ful +s
eye|glass
  eye|glasses
eye|hole +s
eye|lash
  eye|lashes
eye|less
eye|let +s
eye level
eye-level *attributive*
eye|lid +s
eye|liner +s
eye-opener +s
eye-opening
eye|patch
  eye|patches
eye|piece +s
eye-rhyme +s
eye-shade +s
eye|shadow +s
eye|shot
eye|sight
eye socket +s
eye|sore +s
eye-spot +s
eye-stalk +s
eye strain
Eye|tie +s
  (*offensive*)
eye-tooth
  eye-teeth
eye|wash
eye|wit|ness
  eye|wit|nesses
eye-worm +s

eyot +s (use ait.
⚠ ate, eight)
eyra +s
Eyre, Ed¦ward
John (Australian
explorer and
statesman)
Eyre, Lake (in
Australia)
eyrie +s (nest.
⚠ eerie)
Ey|senck, Hans
(German-born
British
psychologist)
Eze|kiel (*Bible*;
name)
Ezra (*Bible*; name)

Ff

....

fa (*Music*; use fah.
⚠ far)
fab
Fab|ergé, Peter
Carl (Russian
jeweller)
Fabia
Fa¦bian +s
(member of
Fabian Society;
name)
Fa¦bian|ism
Fa¦bian|ist +s
Fa¦bius (Roman
general and
statesman)
fable
  fables
  fabled
  fab¦ling
fa¦bler +s
fab|liau
  fab¦li|aux
Fab¦lon *Propr.*
Fab¦ri|ano,
Gen|tile da
(Italian painter)
fab¦ric +s
fab¦ri|cate
  fab¦ri|cates
  fab¦ri|cated
  fab¦ri|cat¦ing
fab¦ri|ca¦tion +s
fab¦ri|ca¦tor +s
Fab¦ri|cius, bursa
of
fabu|list +s
fabu|los¦ity
fabu|lous
fabu|lous¦ly
fabu|lous|ness
fa¦çade +s
face
  faces
  faced
  fa¦cing
face-ache +s
face card +s
face|cloth +s
face cream +s
face flannel +s
face|less
face|less¦ly
face|less|ness
face|lift +s
face|lift¦ed
face mask +s
face-off +s *noun*

face pack +s
face paint
face-painter +s
face-painting
face|plate +s
face pow¦der +s
facer +s
face-saver +s
face-saving
facet +s
fa¦cet¦ed
fa|cetiae
fa|cetious
fa|cetious¦ly
fa|cetious|ness
face to face
  adverbial
face-to-face +s
  attributive and
  noun
fa¦cet¦ted (use
  faceted)
face value
face|work¦er +s
facia +s (use
  fascia)
fa¦cial +s (of a face.
  ⚠ fascial)
fa¦cial¦ly
fa¦cies
  plural fa¦cies
fa¦cile
fa¦cile¦ly
fa¦cile|ness
fa¦cili|tate
  fa¦cili|tates
  fa¦cili|tated
  fa¦cili|tat¦ing
fa¦cili|ta¦tion
fa¦cili|ta¦tive
fa¦cili|ta¦tor +s
fa¦cil|ity
  fa¦cil|ities
fa¦cing +s
fac|sim¦ile +s
fact +s
fact-finding
fac|tice
fac|tion +s
fac|tion|al
fac|tion¦al|ise *Br.*
  (use factionalize)
  fac|tion¦al|ises
  fac|tion¦al|ised
  fac|tion¦al|is¦ing
fac|tion¦al|ism
fac|tion¦al|ize
  fac|tion¦al|izes
  fac|tion¦al|ized
  fac|tion¦al|iz¦ing
fac¦tion|al¦ly
fac|tious

fac|tious¦ly
fac|tious|ness
fac|ti¦tious
fac|ti¦tious¦ly
fac|ti¦tious|ness
fac¦ti|tive +s
facto (in 'de facto')
fac|toid +s
fac¦tor +s +ed +ing
fac¦tor|able
fac¦tor|age +s
fac¦tor eight (use
  factor VIII)
fac¦tor VIII (blood
  protein)
fac¦tor|ial +s
fac¦tori|al¦ly
fac¦tori|isa¦tion *Br.*
  (use
  factorization)
fac¦tor|ise *Br.* (use
  factorize)
  fac¦tor|ises
  fac¦tor|ised
  fac¦tor|is¦ing
fac¦tor|iza¦tion
fac¦tor|ize
  fac¦tor|izes
  fac¦tor|ized
  fac¦tor|iz¦ing
fac¦tory
  fac¦tor¦ies
fac|tory farm +s
fac|tory farm|ing
factory-made
fac|to¦tum +s
fact sheet +s
fac|tual
fact|ual|ism
fact|ual|ist +s
factu|al¦ity
fact|ual¦ly
fact|ual|ness
fac¦tum
  fac|tums *or* facta
fac|ture
fac¦ula
  facu|lae
  noun
facu|lar *adjective*
facu|lous
fac¦ul|ta¦tive
fac¦ul|ta¦tive¦ly
fac¦ulty
  fac¦ul|ties
FA Cup (football)
fad +s
fad¦dily
fad¦di|ness
fad|dish
fad|dish¦ly
fad|dish|ness

fad|dism
fad|dist+s
faddy
fad|dier
fad¦di|est
fade
fades
faded
fad¦ing
fade-in+s *noun*
fade|less
fade-out+s *noun*
fader+s
fadge+s
fado+s
fae¦cal *Br. (Am.* fecal)
fae¦ces *Br. (Am.* feces)
Fa¦enza (town, Italy)
fae¦rie (*archaic* Fairyland; visionary. △ fairy)
Faeroe Is¦lands (in N. Atlantic)
Faer|oes (shipping area, N. Atlantic; also = Faeroe Islands)
Faero|ese *plural* Faero|ese
faery (*archaic*; use faerie)
faff+s +ed +ing
fag
fags
fagged
fag|ging
Faga|togo (city, Samoa)
fag end+s
fag¦got+s (*offensive* homosexual; food)
fag¦got *Br.* +s +ed +ing (bundle; embroider. *Am.* fagot)
fag|goty
Fagin (character in Dickens)
fagot *Am.* +s +ed +ing (bundle; embroider. *Br.* faggot. △ faggot)
fah (*Music.* △ far)
Fahr¦en|heit, Gab|riel Dan¦iel (German physicist)

Fahr¦en|heit (temperature scale)
fai|ence
fail+s +ed +ing
fail|ing+s
fail-safe
fail|ure+s
fain (gladly. △ fane, feign)
fai|né¦ancy
fai|né¦ant+s
faint+s +ed +ing +er +est (lose consciousness; pale, dim. △ feint)
faint-hearted
faint-hearted¦ly
faint-hearted¦ness
faint|ing fit+s
faint¦ly
faint|ness
fair+s +er +est (just; light-coloured. △ fare, fayre)
Fair|banks, Doug|las (Senior and Junior, American actors)
Fair|fax, Thomas (Lord Fairfax, English Parliamentary general)
fair|ground+s
fair-haired
fair|ing+s (streamlining. △ faring)
fair|ish
Fair Isle (in North Sea; knitwear; shipping area, NE Atlantic)
fair|lead+s
fair¦ly
fair-minded
fair-minded¦ly
fair-minded¦ness
fair|ness
fair-spoken
fair|water
fair|way+s
fair-weather friend+s
fairy
fair¦ies (imaginary being; *offensive* homosexual. △ faerie, faery)

fairy cake+s
fairy cycle+s
fairy god|mother +s
fairy|land
fairy lights
fairy-like
fairy ring+s
fairy story
fairy stor|ies
fairy tale+s *noun*
fairy-tale *attributive*
Fai¦sal (Iraqi kings)
Fai¦sal|abad (city, Pakistan)
fait ac¦com|pli faits ac¦com|plis
Faith (name)
faith+s (belief; trust)
faith|ful
faith|ful¦ly
faith|ful|ness
faith heal¦er+s
faith heal|ing
faith|less
faith|less¦ly
faith|less|ness
fa|jita+s
fake
fakes
faked
fak¦ing
faker+s (person who fakes)
fak¦ery
fak¦er|ies
fakir+s (holy man)
fala|fel+s (use felafel)
Fa¦lange (Spanish political group. △ Phalange)
Fa¦lan|gism
Fa¦lan|gist+s
Fa¦lasha *plural* Fa¦lasha
fal|bala
fal|cate
fal|chion+s
fal|ci|form
fal¦con+s
fal|con¦er+s
fal|con¦et+s
fal|con¦ry
fal|deral+s
Faldo, Nick (British golfer)
fald|stool+s
Fa¦ler|nian
Falk|land Is¦lands (in S. Atlantic)

Falk|lands (= Falkland Islands)
fall
falls
fell
fall|ing
fall¦en
Falla, Ma¦nuel de (Spanish composer)
fal|la¦cious
fal|la¦cious|ly
fal|la¦cious|ness
fal|lacy
fal|la¦cies
fall-back+s *noun and adjective*
fall¦en
fall¦en|ness
fall¦er+s
fall|fish *plural* fall|fish
fall guy+s
fal|li|bil¦ity
fall|ible
fall|ibly
falling-out fallings-out
fall-off+s *noun*
Fal¦lo|pian
fall|out+s
fal¦low
fal¦low|ness
fall-pipe+s
false
false|hood+s
false¦ly
false|ness
false posi|tive+s
fal|setto+s
false|work
fal¦sies
fal|si|fi|abil¦ity
fal|si|fi|able
fal|si|fi|ca¦tion+s
fals|ify
fal¦si|fies
fal¦si|fied
fal¦si¦fy|ing
fall|sity
fall|sities
Fal|staff (in Shakespeare)
Fal|staff|ian
Fal|ster (Danish island)
fal|ter+s +ed +ing (waver. △ faulter)
fal|ter|er+s
fal|ter|ing¦ly

Fama|gusta (port,
  Cyprus)
fame
famed
fa|mil|ial
fa|mil|iar +s
fa|mil|iar|isa|tion
  Br. (use
  familiarization)
fa|mil|iar|ise *Br.*
  (use familiarize)
  fa|mil|iar|ises
  fa|mil|iar|ised
  fa|mil|iar|is|ing
fa|mil|iar|ity
  fa|mil|iar|ities
fa|mil|iar|iza|tion
fa|mil|iar|ize
  fa|mil|iar|izes
  fa|mil|iar|ized
  fa|mil|iar|iz|ing
fa|mil|iar|ly
fa|mille (in 'en
  famille')
fa|mille jaune
fa|mille noire
fa|mille rose
fa|mille verte
fam|ily
  fam|ilies
family-owned
  attributive
fam|ily plan|ning
family-run
  attributive
fam|ily tree +s
fam|ine +s
fam|ish
  fam|ishes
  fam|ished
  fam|ish|ing
fam|ous
fam|ous|ly
fam|ous|ness
famu|lus
  fam|uli
Fan
  plural **Fan** *or* **Fans**
  (people; language)
fan
  fans
  fanned
  fan|ning
  (make air
  circulate; device
  for doing this etc.)
fan|at|ic +s
fan|at|ic|al
fan|at|ic|al|ly
fan|at|icise *Br.* (use
  fanaticize)
  fan|ati|cises

fan|ati|cise (*cont.*)
  fan|ati|cised
  fan|ati|cis|ing
fan|ati|cism
fan|ati|cize
  fan|ati|cizes
  fan|ati|cized
  fan|ati|ciz|ing
fan belt +s
fan|ci|able
fan|cier +s
fan|ci|ful
fan|ci|ful|ly
fan|ci|ful|ness
fan|cily
fan|ci|ness
fan club +s
fancy
  fan|cies
  fan|cied
  fancy|ing
  fan|cier
  fan|ci|est
fancy dress
fancy-free
fancy-work
fan|dan|gle +s
fan|dango
  fan|dan|goes
fan|dom
fane +s (temple.
  △ fain, feign)
fan|fare +s
fan|faro|nade +s
Fang (use Fan)
fang +s
fanged
Fan|gio, Juan
  Ma|nuel
  (Argentinian
  racing driver)
fang|less
fan-jet +s
fan|light +s
fan|like
fan mail
fan|ner +s
fanny
  fan|nies
  (*coarse slang*)
Fanny Adams
fanny pack +s
fan|tail +s
fan|tailed
fan-tan
fan|ta|sia +s
fan|ta|sise *Br.* (use
  fantasize)
  fan|ta|sises
  fan|ta|sised
  fan|ta|sis|ing
fan|ta|sist +s

fan|ta|size
  fan|ta|sizes
  fan|ta|sized
  fan|ta|siz|ing
fan|tas|mat|ic
fan|tast +s
fan|tas|tic
fan|tas|tic|al
fan|tas|tic|al|ity
fan|tas|tic|al|ly
fan|tas|ti|cate
  fan|tas|ti|cates
  fan|tas|ti|cated
  fan|tas|ti|cat|ing
  fan|tas|ti|ca|tion
fan|tas|ti|cism
fan|tasy
  fan|ta|sies
  fan|ta|sied
  fan|tasy|ing
Fante (use Fanti)
  plural **Fante** *or*
  Fantes
Fanti
  plural **Fanti** *or*
  Fantis
fan|tod +s
fan|zine +s
fa|quir +s (use
  fakir)
far
  fur|ther *or* far|ther
  fur|thest *or*
  far|thest
  (distant. △ fa, fah)
farad +s
fara|daic
Fara|day,
  Mi|chael (English
  scientist)
fara|day +s (unit)
fa|rad|ic
far|an|dole +s
far|away *adjective*
farce +s
far|ceur +s
far|ci|cal
far|ci|cal|ity
far|ci|cal|ly
farcy (illness.
  △ Farsi)
fard|ed
fare
  fares
  fared
  far|ing
  (get on; payment
  for travel; food.
  △ fair, fayre)
Far East|ern
fare stage +s

Fare|well, Cape (in
  Greenland and
  New Zealand)
fare|well +s
far-fetched
far-fetched|ness
far-flung
far gone
Fa|rida|bad (city,
  India)
far|ina +s
far|in|aceous
farl +s
farm +s +ed +ing
farm|able
farm|er +s
farm|hand +s
farm|house +s
farm|land +s
farm|stead +s
farm work
farm|work|er +s
farm|yard +s
Farn|borough
  (town, England)
Farne Is|lands (off
  NE England)
Far|nese (Italian
  ducal family)
far|ness
Faro (port,
  Portugal)
faro (game)
Faro|ese (use
  Faeroese)
  plural **Faro|ese**
far-off *attributive*
fa|rouche
Far|ouk (Egyptian
  king)
far-out *attributive*
Far|quhar, George
  (Irish writer)
far|ra|gin|ous
far|rago +s
far-reaching
Far|rell, J. G.
  (English novelist)
Far|rell, James T.
  (American
  novelist)
far|rier +s
far|ri|ery
far|row +s +ed
  +ing
far|ruca +s
far-seeing
Farsi (language.
  △ farcy)
far-sighted
far-sighted|ly
far-sighted|ness

fart +s +ed +ing
 (*coarse slang*)
far|ther
 (comparative of
 far. ⚠ father)
far|thest
far|thing +s
far|thin|gale +s
fart|lek
Far|vel, Kap
 (Danish name for
 Cape Farewell in
 Greenland)
fas|ces
fa|scia +s
fa|scial (of a fascia.
 ⚠ facial)
fa|sci|ate
fa|sci|ated
fa|scia|tion
fas|cicle +s
fas|cicled
fas|ci|cu|lar
fas|ci|cu|late
fas|ci|cu|la|tion
fas|ci|cule +s
fas|cic|ulus
 fas|cic|uli
fas|ci|itis
fas|cin|ate
 fas|cin|ates
 fas|cin|ated
 fas|cin|at|ing
fas|cin|at|ing|ly
fas|cin|ation +s
fas|cin|ator +s
fas|cine +s
Fas|cism
Fas|cist +s
Fas|cis|tic
fash|ion +s +ed
 +ing
fash|ion|abil|ity
fash|ion|able
fash|ion|able|ness
fash|ion|ably
fash|ion|er +s
Fass|bin|der,
 Rai|ner Wer|ner
 (German film
 director)
fast +s +ed +ing
 +er +est
fast|back +s
fast breed|er +s
fas|ten +s +ed
 +ing
fas|ten|er +s
fas|ten|ing +s
fast|er +s
fast food
fast-growing

fas|tidi|ous
fas|tidi|ous|ly
fas|tidi|ous|ness
fas|tigi|ate
fast|ing +s
fast-moving
fast|ness
 fast|nesses
Fast|net (island, N.
 Atlantic; shipping
 area, Celtic Sea)
fast-talk +s +ed
 +ing
fast-wind
fast-winds
fast-wound
fast-winding
fat
 fats
 fat|ted
 fat|ting
 fat|ter
 fat|test
Fatah, Al
 (Palestinian
 organization)
fatal +s
fa|tal|ism
fa|tal|ist +s
fa|tal|is|tic
fa|tal|is|tic|al|ly
fa|tal|ity
 fa|tal|ities
fa|tal|ly
fa|tal|ness
Fata Morgana
fate
 fates
 fated
 fat|ing
 (doom; destiny.
 ⚠ fête)
fate|ful
fate|ful|ly
fate|ful|ness
Fates, the *Greek
 Mythology*
fat-free
fat-head
fat-headed
fat-headed|ness
father +s +ed +ing
 (male parent.
 ⚠ farther)
Father Christ|mas
 Father
 Christ|mases
father fig|ure +s
father|hood
father-in-law
 fathers-in-law
father|land +s

father|less
father|less|ness
father|like
father|li|ness
father|ly
Father's Day
father|ship
fathom +s +ed
 +ing
fathom|able
Fath|om|eter +s
fathom|less
fa|tidi|cal
fa|tigu|abil|ity
fa|tigu|able
fa|tigue
 fa|tigues
 fa|tigued
 fa|tiguing
fa|tigue|less
Fat|iha
Fat|ihah (use
 Fatiha)
Fat|ima (daughter
 of Muhammad)
Fát|ima (village,
 Portugal)
Fati|mid +s
Fati|mite +s
fat|ism (use
 fattism)
fat|ist +s (use
 fattist)
fat|less
fat|ling +s
fatly
fat|ness
fatso
 fat|soes
 (*offensive*)
fat|stock
fat|ten +s +ed
 +ing
fat|tily
fat|ti|ness
fat|tish
fat|tism
fat|tist +s
fatty
 fat|ties
 fat|tier
 fat|ti|est
fa|tu|ity
fatu|ous
fatu|ous|ly
fatu|ous|ness
fatwa +s
fau|bourg +s
fau|ces
fau|cet +s
fau|cial
Faulk|ner,
 Wil|liam

Faulk|ner (*cont.*)
 (American
 novelist)
fault +s +ed +ing
fault|er +s
 (accuser. ⚠ falter)
fault-finder +s
fault-finding
fault|ily
faulti|ness
fault|less
fault|less|ly
fault|less|ness
faulty
 fault|ier
 faulti|est
faun +s (deity.
 ⚠ fawn)
fauna
 fau|nas *or* fau|nae
 (animals. ⚠ fawner)
fau|nal
faun|ist +s
faun|is|tic
faun|is|tic|al
Faunt|leroy,
 (Lit|tle) Lord
 (boy hero of
 novel)
Fau|nus *Roman
 Mythology*
Fauré, Gab|riel
 (French
 composer)
Faust (astronomer
 and necromancer)
Faust|ian
faute de mieux
fau|teuil +s
fauve +s
fauv|ism
fauv|ist +s
faux (false. ⚠ foe)
faux pas
 plural faux pas
fave +s
fa|vela +s
favor *Am.* +s +ed
 +ing (*Br.* favour)
fa|vor|able *Am.* (*Br.*
 favourable)
fa|vor|able|ness
 Am. (*Br.*
 favourableness)
fa|vor|ably *Am.* (*Br.*
 favourably)
fa|vor|er *Am.* +s
 (*Br.* favourer)
fa|vor|ite *Am.* +s
 (*Br.* favourite)
fa|vor|it|ism *Am.*
 (*Br.* favouritism)

fa¦vour *Br.* +s +ed
+ing (*Am.* favor)
fa¦vour|able *Br.*
(*Am.* favorable)
fa¦vour|able|ness
Br. (*Am.*
favorableness)
fa¦vour|ably *Br.*
(*Am.* favorably)
fa¦vour|er *Br.* +s
(*Am.* favorer)
fa¦vour|ite *Br.* +s
(*Am.* favorite)
fa¦vour|it|ism *Br.*
(*Am.* favoritism)
Fawkes, Guy
(English arsonist)
fawn +s +ed +ing
(deer; brown;
behave servilely.
△ faun)
fawn¦er +s
(person who fawns.
△ fauna)
fawn|ing¦ly
fax
    faxes
    faxed
    fax¦ing
Fay *also* Faye
(name)
fay +s (*literary* fairy.
△ fey)
Faye *also* Fay
(name)
fayre +s (*pseudo-
archaic* fête, sale;
food. △ fair, fare)
faze
    fazes
    fazed
    faz¦ing
(disconcert.
△ phase)
fealty
    feal|ties
fear +s +ed +ing
fear|ful
fear|ful¦ly
fear|ful|ness
fear|less
fear|less¦ly
fear|less|ness
fear|some
fear|some¦ly
fear|some|ness
feasi|bil¦ity
feas|ible
feas|ibly
feast +s +ed +ing
feast day +s
feast¦er +s

feat +s
(achievement.
△ feet)
fea¦ther +s +ed
+ing
fea¦ther bed +s
noun
feather-bed
    feather-beds
    feather-bedded
    feather-bedding
verb
feather-brain +s
feather-brained
fea¦ther edge +s
feather-edged
fea¦ther|head +s
fea¦theri|ness
fea¦theri|less
feather-light
fea¦ther stitch
noun
fea¦ther|weight +s
fea¦thery
fea|ture
    fea|tures
    fea|tured
    fea¦tur|ing
feature-length
adjective
fea¦ture|less
feb¦ri|fugal
feb¦ri|fuge +s
fe|brile
fe|bril|ity
Feb¦ru|ary
    Feb¦ru|ar¦ies
fecal *Am.* (*Br.*
faecal)
feces *Am.* (*Br.*
faeces)
Fech|ner, Gus¦tav
Theo|dor
(German poet,
physicist, and
psychologist)
feck|less
feck|less¦ly
feck|less|ness
fecu|lence
fecu|lent
fec¦und
fe¦cund|abil¦ity
fe¦cund|ate
    fe¦cund|ates
    fe¦cund|ated
    fe¦cund|at¦ing
fe¦cund|ation
fe¦cund|ity
Fed (Federal
Reserve Board)

fed +s (past tense
and past participle
of feed; FBI
agent)
fed¦ay|een
fed|eral +s
fed¦er|al|isa¦tion
Br. (use
federalization)
fed|er|al|ise *Br.*
(use federalize)
    fed|er|al|ises
    fed|er|al|ised
    fed|er|al|is¦ing
fed|er|al|ism
fed¦er|al|ist +s
fed¦er|al|iza¦tion
fed|er|al|ize
    fed|er|al|izes
    fed|er|al|ized
    fed|er|al|iz¦ing
fed¦er|al¦ly
fed¦er|ate
    fed¦er|ates
    fed¦er|ated
    fed¦er|at¦ing
fed¦er|ation +s
fed¦er|ation|ist +s
fed¦er|ative
fe|dora +s
fed up
fed-up *attributive*
fed-upness
fee
    fees
    fee'd
    fee¦ing
fee¦ble
    fee¦bler
    feeb¦lest
feeble-minded
feeble-minded¦ly
feeble-
    minded¦ness
feeble|ness
fee|blish
feebly
feed
    feeds
    fed
    feed|ing
feed|able
feed-and-
    expansion tank
    +s
feed|back *noun*
feed¦er +s
feed|ing bot¦tle +s
feed|stock
feed|stuff +s
feel
    feels

feel (*cont.*)
    felt
    feel|ing
feel¦er +s
feel-good *adjective*
feel|ing +s
feel|ing|less
feel|ing¦ly
fee-paying
feet (plural of foot.
△ feat)
feign +s +ed +ing
(pretend. △ fain,
fane)
fei¦joa +s
feint +s +ed +ing
(sham attack;
pretend; of ruled
lines. △ faint)
feis
    feis|eanna
feist|ily
feisti|ness
feisty
    feist|ier
    feisti|est
fela|fel +s
felch|ing
feld|spar +s
feld|spath¦ic
feld|spath¦oid +s
feli|cif¦ic
fe|lici|tate
    fe|lici|tates
    fe|lici|tated
    fe|lici|tat¦ing
fe|lici|ta¦tion +s
fe|lici|tous
fe|lici|tous¦ly
fe|lici|tous|ness
Fe|li¦city (name)
fe|li¦city
    fe|li¦ci¦ties
    (happiness)
fe|line +s
fe|lin|ity
Felix
Felix|stowe (port,
England)
fell +s +ed +ing
fel|lah
    fel|la¦hin
    (Egyptian peasant.
    △ feller)
fel¦lah +s (= fellow.
    △ feller)
fel|late
    fel|lates
    fel|lated
    fel|lat¦ing
fel|la¦tio
fel|la¦tor +s

fell¦er +s (person
  who fells; also
  = fellow. △ fellah)
Fel¦lini, Fe¦de¦rico
  (Italian film
  director)
fell¦mon¦ger +s
fel¦loe +s (wheel
  rim)
fel¦low +s (man;
  person)
fel¦low
  country¦man
  fel¦low
  country¦men
fel¦low feel¦ing
fel¦low¦ship +s
fellow-travel¦er
  Am. +s
fellow-travel¦ler
  Br. +s
fell walk¦er +s
fell walk¦ing
felly
  fel¦lies
felon +s
fe¦loni¦ous
fe¦loni¦ous¦ly
fel¦on¦ry
fel¦ony
  fel¦on¦ies
fel¦spar +s (use
  feldspar)
fel¦spath¦ic (use
  feldspathic)
fel¦spath¦oid +s
  (use feldspathoid)
felt +s +ed +ing
felt tip +s
felt-tipped
felty
fel¦lucca +s
fel¦wort +s
fe¦male +s
fe¦male¦ness
feme +s
feme co¦vert
  femes co¦vert
feme sole
  femes sole
fem¦inal
femi¦nal¦ity
femi¦neity
femi¦nine
femi¦nine¦ly
femi¦nine¦ness
femi¦nin¦ity
  femi¦nin¦ities
femi¦nisa¦tion Br.
  (use
  feminization)

femi¦nise Br. (use
  feminize)
femi¦nises
femi¦nised
femi¦nis¦ing
femi¦nism
femi¦nist +s
fe¦min¦ity
femi¦niza¦tion
femi¦nize
  femi¦nizes
  femi¦nized
  femi¦niz¦ing
femme +s
femme fa¦tale
  femmes fa¦tales
fem¦oral
femto¦meter Am.
  +s
femto¦metre Br. +s
femur
  fem¦ora or
  fe¦murs
fen +s (marsh)
fen
  plural fen
  (Chinese currency)
fen-berry
  fen-berries
fence
  fences
  fenced
  fen¦cing
fence¦less
fence post +s
fen¦cer +s
fen¦cible
fen¦cing +s
fend +s +ed +ing
Fen¦der, Leo
  (American guitar-
  maker)
fend¦er +s
Fen¦ella
fen¦es¦tella +s
fen¦es¦tra
  fen¦es¦trae
fen¦es¦trate
fen¦es¦trated
fen¦es¦tra¦tion
fen-fire
feng shui
Fe¦nian +s
Fe¦nian¦ism
fen¦land +s
fen¦man
  fen¦men
fen¦nec +s
fen¦nel (plant.
  △ phenyl)
Fenno¦scan¦dia
  (NW Europe)

fenny
fenu¦greek
feof¦fee +s
feoff¦ment +s
feof¦for +s
feral
fer de lance
  fers de lance
Fer¦di¦nand
  (Spanish king)
Fer¦gal
Fer¦gus
fer¦ial
Fer¦man¦agh
  (county, Northern
  Ireland)
Fer¦mat, Pierre de
  (French
  mathematician)
fer¦mata +s
fer¦ment +s +ed
  +ing
fer¦ment¦able
fer¦men¦ta¦tion +s
fer¦men¦ta¦tive
fer¦ment¦er +s
Fermi, En¦rico
  (Italian-born
  physicist)
fermi +s (unit)
fer¦mion +s
fer¦mium
fern
  plural fern or ferns
Fer¦nando Póo
  (former name of
  Bioko)
fern¦ery
  fern¦er¦ies
fern¦less
ferny
fer¦ocious
fer¦ocious¦ly
fer¦ocious¦ness
fer¦ocity
Fer¦ranti,
  Se¦bas¦tian Ziani
  de (English
  electrical
  engineer)
Fer¦rara (city and
  province, Italy)
Fer¦rari, Enzo
  (Italian racing-car
  designer and
  manufacturer)
fer¦rate +s
fer¦rel +s (use
  ferrule)
fer¦ret +s +ed +ing
fer¦ret¦er +s
fer¦rety

fer¦ri¦age +s
fer¦ric
Fer¦rier, Kath¦leen
  (English contralto)
ferri¦mag¦net¦ic
ferri¦mag¦net¦ism
Fer¦ris wheel +s
fer¦rite +s
fer¦rit¦ic
ferro¦con¦crete
ferro¦elec¦tric
ferro¦elec¦tri¦city
ferro¦mag¦net¦ic
ferro¦mag¦net¦ism
fer¦rous
fer¦ru¦gin¦ous
fer¦rule +s (metal
  cap. △ ferule)
ferry
  fer¦ries
  fer¦ried
  ferry¦ing
ferry boat +s
ferry¦man
  ferry¦men
fer¦tile
fer¦til¦is¦able Br.
  (use fertilizable)
fer¦til¦isa¦tion Br.
  +s (use
  fertilization)
fer¦til¦ise Br. (use
  fertilize)
  fer¦til¦ises
  fer¦til¦ised
  fer¦til¦is¦ing
fer¦til¦iser Br. +s
  (use fertilizer)
fer¦til¦ity
fer¦til¦iz¦able
fer¦til¦iza¦tion +s
fer¦til¦ize
  fer¦til¦izes
  fer¦til¦ized
  fer¦til¦iz¦ing
fer¦til¦izer +s
fer¦ula +s
fer¦ule
  fer¦ules
  fer¦uled
  fer¦ul¦ing
  (cane. △ ferrule)
fer¦vency
fer¦vent
fer¦vent¦ly
fer¦vid
fer¦vid¦ly
fer¦vor Am.
fer¦vour Br.
Fès (use Fez)
Fes¦cen¦nine
fes¦cue +s

fess
  fesses
fesse +s (use fess)
Fes|sen|den,
  Regi|nald
  Aub|rey
  (Canadian-born
  American
  physicist)
fes|tal
fes|tal|ly
fes|ter +s +ed +ing
fes|ti|val +s
fes|tive
fes|tive|ly
fes|tive|ness
fes|tiv|ity
  fes|tiv|ities
fes|toon +s +ed
  +ing
fes|toon|ery
Fest|schrift
  Fest|schrift|en or
  Fest|schrifts
feta (cheese. △ fetter)
fetal Am. (Br.
  foetal)
fetch
  fetches
  fetched
  fetch|ing
fetch|er +s
fetch|ing|ly
fête
  fêtes
  fêted
  fêt|ing
  (fair; festival;
  honour or
  entertain lavishly.
  △ fate)
fête cham|pêtre
  fêtes cham|pêtres
fête gal|ante
  fêtes gal|antes
feti|cidal Am. (Br.
  foeticidal)
feti|cide Am. (Br.
  foeticide)
fetid
fetid|ly
fetid|ness
fet|ish
  fet|ishes
fet|ish|ise Br. (use
  fetishize)
  fet|ish|ises
  fet|ish|ised
  fet|ish|is|ing
fet|ish|ism
fet|ish|ist +s
fet|ish|is|tic

fet|ish|ize
  fet|ish|izes
  fet|ish|ized
  fet|ish|iz|ing
fet|lock +s
fetor
fetta (cheese; use feta)
fet|ter +s +ed +ing
  (shackle)
fet|ter|lock +s
fet|tle
  fet|tles
  fet|tled
  fet|tling
fet|tler +s
fet|tuc|cine
fet|tu|cine (use
  fettuccine)
fetus Am.
  fetuses
  (Br. foetus)
feu +s +ed +ing
feud +s +ed +ing
feu|dal
feu|dal|isa|tion Br.
  (use
  feudalization)
feu|dal|ise Br. (use
  feudalize)
  feu|dal|ises
  feu|dal|ised
  feu|dal|is|ing
feu|dal|ism
feu|dal|ist +s
feu|dal|is|tic
feu|dal|ity
feu|dal|iza|tion
feu|dal|ize
  feu|dal|izes
  feu|dal|ized
  feu|dal|iz|ing
feu|dal|ly
feud|atory
  feud|ator|ies
feu de joie
  feux de joie
feud|ist +s
feuille|ton +s
fever +s +ed +ing
fever|few
fe|ver|ish
fe|ver|ish|ly
fe|ver|ish|ness
fe|ver|ous
few +er +est (not
  many. △ phew)
few|ness
fey (strange etc.
  △ fay)
Fey|deau, Georges
  (French
  playwright)

feyly
fey|ness
Feyn|man,
  Rich|ard
  (American
  physicist)
Feyn|man
  dia|gram +s
Fez (city, Morocco)
fez
  fezzes
  (hat)
fezzed
Ffes|tin|iog
  Rail|way (in
  Wales)
fi|acre +s
fi|ancé +s *male*
fi|an|cée +s *female*
fian|chetto
  fian|chet|toes
  fian|chet|toed
  fian|chetto|ing
Fianna Fáil (Irish
  political party)
fi|asco +s
fiat +s
fib
  fibs
  fibbed
  fib|bing
fib|ber +s
fiber Am. +s (Br.
  fibre)
fiber|board Am. +s
  (Br. fibreboard)
fibered Am. (Br.
  fibred)
fiber|fill Am. (Br.
  fibrefill)
fiber|glass Am. (Br.
  fibreglass)
fiber|less Am. (Br.
  fibreless)
fiber-optic Am.
  adjective (Br. fibre-
  optic)
fiber op|tics Am.
  noun (Br. fibre
  optics)
Fi|bo|nacci,
  Leo|nardo
  (Italian
  mathematician)
fibre Br. +s (Am.
  fiber)
fibre|board Br. +s
  (Am. fiberboard)
fibred Br. (Am.
  fibered)
fibre|fill Br. (Am.
  fiberfill)

fibre|glass Br. (Am.
  fiberglass)
fibre|less Br. (Am.
  fiberless)
fibre-optic Br.
  adjective (Am.
  fiber-optic)
fibre op|tics Br.
  noun (Am. fiber
  optics)
fib|ri|form
fi|bril +s
fi|bril|lar
fi|bril|lary
fib|ril|late
  fib|ril|lates
  fib|ril|lated
  fib|ril|lat|ing
fib|ril|la|tion +s
fi|brin
fi|brino|gen
fi|brin|oid
fibro +s
fibro|blast +s
fibro-cement
fi|broid +s
fi|broin
fi|broma
  fi|bro|mas or
  fi|bro|mata
fi|bro|sis
  fi|bro|ses
fi|bro|sit|ic
fi|bro|si|tis
fi|brot|ic
fi|brous
fi|brous|ly
fi|brous|ness
fib|ula
  fibu|lae or fibu|las
  noun
fibu|lar
  adjective
fiche
  plural fiche or
  fiches
Fichte, Jo|hann
  Gott|lieb
  (German
  philosopher)
fichu +s
fickle
fickle|ness
fickly
fic|tile
fic|tion +s
fic|tion|al
fic|tion|al|isa|tion
  Br. +s (use
  fictionalization)
fic|tion|al|ise Br.
  (use fictionalize)
  fic|tion|al|ises

fic|tion|al|ise
   (*cont.*)
fic|tion|al|ised
fic|tion|al|is|ing
fic|tion|al|ity
fic|tion|al|iza|tion
   +s
fic|tion|al|ize
   fic|tion|al|izes
   fic|tion|al|ized
   fic|tion|al|iz|ing
fic|tion|al|ly
fic|tion|ist +s
fic|ti|tious
fic|ti|tious|ly
fic|ti|tious|ness
fic|tive
fic|tive|ly
fic|tive|ness
ficus
   plural ficus *or*
   fi|cuses
fid +s
fid|dle
   fid|dles
   fid|dled
   fid|dling
fiddle-back +s
fiddle-de-dee
fiddle-faddle
   fiddle-faddles
   fiddle-faddled
   fiddle-faddling
fiddle-head +s
fid|dler +s
Fid|dler's Green
   (sailor's Elysium)
fiddle|stick +s
fid|dly
   fid|dlier
   fid|dli|est
Fidei De|fen|sor
fide|ism
fide|ist +s
fide|is|tic
fi|del|ity
   fi|del|ities
fidget +s +ed +ing
fidgeti|ness
fidgety
Fido (fog dispersal
   device; dog's
   name)
fi|du|cial
fi|du|ci|al|ly
fi|du|ciary
   fi|du|ciar|ies
fidus Acha|tes
fie (*interjection.*
   △ phi)
fief +s
fief|dom +s

Field, John (Irish
   composer and
   pianist)
field +s +ed +ing
field-book +s
field-cornet
field day +s
field-effect
   tran|sis|tor +s
field|er +s
field|fare +s
field glasses
Field|ing, Henry
   (English writer)
field mar|shal +s
field mouse
   field mice
field note +s
Fields, Gracie
   (English singer)
Fields, W. C.
   (American
   comedian)
fields|man
   fields|men
field|stone +s
field|work
field|worker +s
fiend +s
fiend|ish
fiend|ish|ly
fiend|ish|ness
fiend|like
fierce
   fier|cer
   fier|cest
fierce|ly
fierce|ness
fieri fa|cias
fieri|ly
fieri|ness
fiery
   fier|ier
   fieri|est
fi|esta +s
FIFA ('International
   Football
   Federation')
Fife (region,
   Scotland)
fife (musical
   instrument)
   fifes
   fifed
   fif'ing
fifer +s
fife-rail +s
FIFO (= first in, first
   out)
fif|teen +s
fif|teenth +s
fifth +s

fifth col|umn
fifth col|umn|ist
   +s
fifth-genera|tion
fifth|ly
Fifth-monarchy-
   man
   Fifth-monarchy-
   men
fif|ti|eth +s
fifty
   fif|ties
fifty-fifty
fifty-first, fifty-
   second, etc.
fifty|fold
fifty-one, fifty-
   two, etc.
fig
   figs
   figged
   fig|ging
fight
   fights
   fought
   fight|ing
fight|back +s *noun*
fight|er +s
fighter-bomber +s
fighting-top +s
fig leaf
   fig leaves
fig|ment +s
fig tree +s
fi|gura +s
fig|ural
fig|ur|ant +s male
fig|ur|ante +s
   (French, *female*)
fig|ur|ante
   fig|ur|anti
   (Italian, *male and*
   female)
fig|ur|ation +s
fig|ura|tive
fig|ura|tive|ly
fig|ura|tive|ness
fig|ure
   fig|ures
   fig|ured
   fig|ur|ing
fig|ure|head +s
fig|ure|less
fig|ure of eight
   fig|ures of eight
   noun
figure-of-eight
   attributive
fig|ure skat|er +s
fig|ure skat|ing
fig|ur|ine +s
fig|wort +s

Fiji
Fiji|an +s
fila|gree +s (use
   filigree)
fila|greed (use
   filigreed)
fila|ment +s
fila|men|tary
fila|ment|ed
fila|ment|ous
fil|aria
   fil|ariae
fil|ar|ial
fil|ar|ia|sis
fila|ture +s
fil|bert +s
filch
   filches
   filched
   filch|ing
filch|er +s
file
   files
   filed
   fil|ing
   (folder; line; tool.
   △ phial)
file|fish
   plural file|fish
filer +s (person or
   thing that files.
   △ phyla)
file serv|er +s
filet +s (net.
   △ fillet)
filet mi|gnon +s
fil|ial
fili|al|ly
fili|ation +s
fili|beg +s
fili|bus|ter +s +ed
   +ing
fili|bus|ter|er +s
fili|gree +s
fili|greed
fil|ing +s
fil|ing cabi|net +s
Filio|que
Fi|li|pina +s *female*
Fi|li|pino +s *male*
fill +s +ed +ing
fille de joie
   filles de joie
fill|er +s
fill|let +s +ed +ing
   (meat; strip; band.
   △ filet)
fill|let|er +s
fill|ing +s
fill|ing sta|tion +s
fil|lip +s +ed +ing
fil|lis

fil|lis|ter +s
Fill|more, Mil|lard
  (American
  president)
fill-up +s *noun*
filly
  fil|lies
film +s +ed +ing
film-goer +s
film-going
film|ic
film|ily
filmi|ness
film-maker +s
film-making
film noir
  films noirs
film|og|raphy
film|set
  film|sets
  film|set
  film|set|ting
  Printing
film set +s *Film-
  making*
film|set|ter +s
film star +s
film|strip +s
filmy
  film|ier
  filmi|est
filo
Filo|fax
  Filo|faxes
  Propr.
filo|plume +s
fi|lo|selle
fils
fil|ter +s +ed +ing
  (remove
  impurities; device
  for doing this.
  ⚠ philter, philtre)
fil|ter|able
filter-bed +s
filter-feeder +s
filter-feeding
filter-paper +s
fil|ter tip +s
filter-tipped
filth
filth|ily
filthi|ness
filthy
  filth|ier
  filthi|est
fil|trable
fil|trate
  fil|trates
  fil|trated
  fil|trat|ing
fil|tra|tion
fim|bri|ate

fim|bri|ated
fin
  fins
  finned
  fin|ning
  (part of fish etc.
  ⚠ Finn)
fin|able
fin|agle
  fin|agles
  fin|agled
  fin|agl|ing
fin|agler +s
final +s
fi|nale +s
fi|nal|isa|tion *Br.*
  (use finalization)
fi|nal|ise *Br.* (use
  finalize)
  fi|nal|ises
  fi|nal|ised
  fi|nal|is|ing
fi|nal|ism
fi|nal|ist +s
fi|nal|is|tic
fi|nal|ity
  fi|nal|ities
fi|nal|iza|tion
fi|nal|ize
  fi|nal|izes
  fi|nal|ized
  fi|nal|iz|ing
fi|nal|ly
fi|nance
  fi|nances
  fi|nanced
  fi|nan|cing
fi|nan|cial +s
fi|nan|cial|ly
fi|nan|cier +s
fin-back +s
Fin|bar
finch
  finches
find
  finds
  found
  find|ing
  (discover.
  ⚠ fined)
find|able
find|er +s
fin de siècle
Find|horn
  (community,
  Scotland)
find|ing +s
find-spot +s
fine
  fines
  fined
  fin|ing

fine (*cont.*)
  finer
  fin|est
fine arts
fine-draw
  fine-draws
  fine-drew
  fine-drawing
  fine-drawn
Fine Gael (Irish
  political party)
fine-grained
fine|ly
fine|ness
fine print
fin|ery
  fin|eries
fines herbes
fine-spun
fi|nesse
  fi|nesses
  fi|nessed
  fi|ness|ing
fine-tooth comb
  +s
fine-tune
  fine-tunes
  fine-tuned
  fine-tuning
Fingal (character in
  poem)
Fingal's Cave (in
  Hebrides)
fin|ger +s +ed +ing
fin|ger|board +s
fin|ger bone +s
fin|ger bowl +s
finger-dry
  finger-dries
  finger-dried
  finger-drying
fin|ger|ing +s
fin|ger|less
finger-licking
fin|ger|ling
fin|ger|mark +s
fin|ger|nail +s
finger-paint +s
  +ed +ing
fin|ger|pick +s +ed
  +ing
finger-plate +s
finger-post +s
fin|ger|print +s
  +ed +ing
finger-stall +s
fin|ger|tip +s
fin|ial +s
fini|cal
fini|cal|ity
fini|cal|ly
fini|cal|ness

fin|icki|ness
fin|ick|ing
fin|icky
finis
fin|ish
  fin|ishes
  fin|ished
  fin|ish|ing
  (end. ⚠ Finnish)
fin|ish|er +s
fin|ish|ing school
  +s
Fin|is|terre
  (shipping area off
  Spain)
Fin|is|terre, Cape
  (in Spain)
fi|nite
fi|nite|ly
fi|nite|ness
fi|nit|ism
fi|nit|ist +s
fini|tude
fink +s +ed +ing
Fin|land
Fin|land|isa|tion
  Br. (use
  Finlandization)
Fin|land|ise *Br.*
  (use Finlandize)
  Fin|land|ises
  Fin|land|ised
  Fin|land|is|ing
Fin|land|iza|tion
Fin|land|ize
  Fin|land|izes
  Fin|land|ized
  Fin|land|iz|ing
fin|less
Finn +s (person
  from Finland;
  name. ⚠ fin)
fin|nan had|dock
  plural fin|nan
  had|dock
finned
Fin|ne|gans Wake
  (novel)
fin|ner +s
fin|nesko
  plural fin|nesko
Finn|ic
Finn|ish (of
  Finland. ⚠ finish)
Finn Mac|Cool
  Irish Mythology
Finno-Ugrian
Finno-Ugric
finny
fino +s
Fiona
fiord +s (use fjord)

fi¦ori|tura
  fi¦ori|ture
fip¦ple +s
fip¦ple flute +s
fir +s (tree. △ fur)
fir cone +s
fire
  fires
  fired
  fir¦ing
fire alarm +s
fire|arm +s
fire|back +s
fire|ball +s
fire-balloon +s
fire-bird +s
fire blight
fire|bomb +s +ed
  +ing
fire|box
  fire|boxes
fire|brand +s
fire|break +s
fire-breath¦ing
fire|brick +s
fire bri|gade +s
fire|bug +s
fire|clay
fire-control
fire|crack¦er +s
fire|crest +s
fire|damp
fire|dog +s
fire-drake +s
fire drill +s
fire-eater +s
fire en¦gine +s
fire es¦cape +s
fire ex¦tin|guish|er
  +s
fire|fight +s
fire|fight¦er +s
fire-fighting
fire|fly
  fire|flies
fire|guard +s
fire hose +s
fire|house +s
fire-irons
fire|less
fire|light
fire|light¦er +s
fire|lock +s
fire|man
  fire|men
fire-office +s
fire-opal +s
fire|place +s
fire|plug +s
fire|power
fire prac|tice +s
fire|proof

firer +s
fire-raiser +s
fire-raising
fire-resist¦ant
fire screen +s
fire|ship +s
fire|side +s
fire-step +s
fire-stone
fire|storm +s
fire|thorn +s
fire-tongs
fire trap +s
fire-walker +s
fire-walking
fire-watcher +s
fire-watching
fire|water
fire|weed +s
fire|woman
  fire|women
fire|wood
fire|work +s
fir¦ing +s
fir¦ing line +s
fir¦ing party
  fir¦ing par¦ties
fir¦ing squad +s
firing-step +s
fir¦kin +s
firm +s +ed +ing
  +er +est
firma|ment +s
firma|men¦tal
fir¦man +s
firm¦ly
firm|ness
firm|ware
firry (of fir trees.
  △ furry)
first +s
first aid *noun*
first-aid *attributive*
first aider +s
first-born +s
first-class *adjective*
  and adverb
first-day cover +s
first-degree
  adjective
first-foot +s +ed
  +ing
first-fruit +s
first-hand *adjective*
  and adverb
first|ling +s
first¦ly
first name +s
first-nighter +s
first-past-the-post
  attributive
first-rate *adjective*

first-strike
  attributive
first-time *attributive*
firth +s
Firth of Forth
  (estuary,
  Scotland)
Firth of Tay
  (estuary,
  Scotland)
fir tree +s
fisc +s (in ancient
  Rome. △ fisk)
fis¦cal +s
fis¦cal|ity
fis¦cal¦ly
Fisch¦er, Bobby
  (American chess
  player)
Fisch¦er, Emil
  Her|mann
  (German chemist)
Fisch¦er, Hans
  (German chemist)
Fischer-Dieskau,
  Diet|rich
  (German baritone)
Fish, the *also* **the**
  Fishes
  (constellation;
  sign of zodiac)
fish
  plural **fish** *or*
  fishes
  noun
fish
  fishes
  fished
  fish|ing
  verb
fish|able
fish and chips
fish-bolt +s
fish|bowl +s
fish cake +s
Fish|er (shipping
  area, North Sea)
Fish|er, Geof|frey
  (English
  archbishop, died
  1972)
Fish|er, Ron|ald
  Ayl|mer (English
  statistician)
Fish|er, St John
  (English
  churchman, died
  1535)
fish|er +s (person
  who fishes.
  △ fissure)
fish|er|folk

fish¦er|man
  fish¦er|men
fish¦er|woman
  fish¦er|women
fish|ery
  fish|er¦ies
fish-eye +s (lens)
fish farm +s
fish fin¦ger +s
fish-glue
fish-hawk +s
fish-hook +s
fish|ily
fishi|ness
fish|ing boat +s
fishing-fly
  fishing-flies
fish|ing ground +s
fish|ing line +s
fish|ing net +s
fish|ing rod +s
fish|ing tackle
fish|ing ves|sel +s
fish ket¦tle +s
fish-knife
  fish-knives
fish|like
fish|meal
fish|mon|ger +s
fish|net +s
fish-plate +s
fish pond +s
fish|pot +s
fish slice +s
fish|tail +s +ed
  +ing
fish|wife
  fish|wives
fishy
  fish|ier
  fishi|est
fisk +s (in
  Scotland. △ fisc)
fis|sile
fis|sil|ity
fis|sion +s +ed
  +ing
fis|sion|able
fis|si|par|ity
fis|sip|ar|ous
fis|sip|ar|ous¦ly
fis|sip|ar|ous|ness
fis|sure
  fis|sures
  fis|sured
  fis|sur|ing
  (crack. △ fisher)
fist +s +ed +ing
fist fight +s
fist|ful +s
fist¦ic
fist|ic¦al
fisti|cuffs

fis|tula +s
fis|tu|lar
fis|tu|lous
fit
  fits
  fit|ted
  fit|ting
  fit|ter
  fit|test
fitch
  fitches
fit|chew +s
fit|ful
fit|ful|ly
fit|ful|ness
fitly
fit|ment +s
fit|ness
  fit|nesses
fit|ter +s
fit|ting +s
fit|ting|ly
fit|ting|ness
fit|ting shop +s
Fit|ti|paldi,
  Emer|son
  (Brazilian racing
  driver)
fit-up +s *noun*
Fitz|Gerald,
  George Fran|cis
  (Irish physicist)
Fitz|ger|ald,
  Ed|ward (English
  scholar and poet)
Fitz|ger|ald, Ella
  (American jazz
  singer)
Fitz|ger|ald, Scott
  and Zelda
  (American
  writers)
Fitz|Gerald
  con|trac|tion
FitzGerald–Lorentz
  con|trac|tion
Fitz|wil|liam
  Mu|seum (in
  Cambridge,
  England)
Fiume (Italian
  name for Rijeka)
five +s
five-a-side +s
five-corner +s
five-eighth +s
five-finger
  exer|cise +s
five|fold
five-iron +s
five o'clock
  shadow +s

five|pence +s
five|penny
  five|pen|nies
fiver +s
five-star *attributive*
five|stones
five-year plan +s
fix
  fixes
  fixed
  fix|ing
fix|able
fix|ate
  fix|ates
  fix|ated
  fix|at|ing
fix|ation +s
fixa|tive +s
fixed-doh
fix|ed|ly
fix|ed|ness
fixer +s
fix|ing +s
fix|ity
  fix|ities
fix|ture +s
fiz|gig +s
fizz
  fizzes
  fizzed
  fizz|ing
  (effervesce; hiss.
  △ phiz)
fizz|er +s
fizz|ily
fizzi|ness
fiz|zle
  fiz|zles
  fiz|zled
  fiz|zling
fizzy
  fizz|ier
  fizzi|est
fjord +s
flab
flab|ber|gast +s
  +ed +ing
flab|bi|ly
flab|bi|ness
flabby
  flab|bier
  flab|bi|est
flac|cid
flac|cid|ity
flac|cid|ly
flack +s (publicity
  agent. △ flak)
flag
  flags
  flagged
  flag|ging
flag-boat +s

flag-captain +s
Flag Day (14 June
  in USA)
flag day +s (money-
  raising day)
fla|gel|lant +s
fla|gel|lar
fla|gel|late
  fla|gel|lates
  fla|gel|lated
  fla|gel|lat|ing
fla|gel|la|tion +s
fla|gel|la|tor +s
fla|gel|la|tory
fla|gel|li|form
fla|gel|lum
  fla|gella
fla|geo|let +s
flag-feather +s
flag|ger +s
fla|gi|tious
fla|gi|tious|ly
fla|gi|tious|ness
flag-lieuten|ant +s
flag-list +s
flag|man
  flag|men
flag-officer +s
flagon +s
flag|pole +s
fla|grancy
flag-rank +s
fla|grant
fla|grante (in 'in
  flagrante delicto')
fla|grant|ly
flag|ship +s
flag|staff +s
flag-station +s
flag|stone +s
flag|stoned
flag-wagging
flag-waver +s
flag-waving
flail +s +ed +ing
flair +s (instinct;
  talent. △ flare)
flak (anti-aircraft
  fire; criticism.
  △ flack)
flake
  flakes
  flaked
  flak|ing
flaki|ly
flaki|ness
flak jacket +s
flaky
  flaki|er
  flaki|est
flambé +s +ed
  +ing

flam|beau
  flam|beaus *or*
  flam|beaux
Flam|bor|ough
  Head
  (promontory,
  England)
flam|boy|ance
flam|boy|ancy
flam|boy|ant
flam|boy|ant|ly
flame
  flames
  flamed
  flam|ing
flame gun +s
flame|less
flame|like
fla|men
  fla|mens *or*
  fla|mi|nes
fla|menco +s
flame|out +s
flame|proof
flame-thrower +s
flame tree +s
fla|mingo +s
flam|ma|bil|ity
flam|mable
Flam|steed, John
  (English
  astronomer)
flamy
flami|er
flami|est
flan +s
flanch
  flanches
  flanched
  flanch|ing
Flan|ders (former
  principality, NW
  Europe)
flân|erie
flân|eur +s
flange
  flanges
  flanged
  flan|ging
flange|less
flank +s +ed +ing
flank|er +s
flan|nel
  flan|nels
  flan|nelled *Br.*
  flan|neled *Am.*
  flan|nel|ling *Br.*
  flan|nel|ling *Am.*
flan|nel|board +s
flan|nel|ette
flan|nel|graph +s
flan|nel|ly

flannel-mouth +s
flap
  flaps
  flapped
  flap|ping
flap|doo|dle
flap|jack +s
flap|per +s
flappy
  flap|pier
  flap|pi|est
flare
  flares
  flared
  flar|ing
  (widen; widening;
  flame. △ flair)
flare-path +s
flare-up +s *noun*
flash
  flashes
  flashed
  flash|ing
flash|back +s
flash-board +s
flash|bulb +s
flash burn +s
flash|card +s
flash-cube +s
flash|er +s
flash flood +s
flash|gun +s
flash|ily
flashi|ness
flash|ing +s
flash|ing point +s
flash lamp +s
flash|light +s
flash-over +s *noun*
flash|point +s
flashy
  flash|ier
  flashi|est
flask +s
flat
  flats
  flat|ted
  flat|ting
  flat|ter
  flat|test
flat-bottomed
flat|car +s
flat-chested
flat|fish
  plural flat|fish
flat|foot
  flat|feet
flat-footed
flat-footed|ly
flat-footed|ness
flat-four
flat-head +s

flat iron +s
flat|let +s
flat|ly
flat|mate +s
flat|ness
flat out
flat-pack +s +ed
  +ing
flat race +s
flat ra|cing
flat rate +s
flat|ten +s +ed
  +ing
flat|ten|er +s
flat|ter +s +ed
  +ing
flat|ter|er +s
flat|ter|ing|ly
flat|tery
  flat|ter|ies
flat|tie +s
flat|tish
flat-top +s
flatu|lence
flatu|lency
flatu|lent
flatu|lent|ly
fla|tus
flat|ware
flat|worm +s
Flau|bert,
  Gus|tave (French
  novelist)
flaunch
  flaunches
  flaunched
  flaunch|ing
flaunt +s +ed +ing
flaunt|er +s
flaunty
flaut|ist +s
fla|ves|cent
Fla|via
Fla|vian +s
fla|vin (yellow dye)
fla|vine (antiseptic)
fla|vone +s
flavo|pro|tein +s
fla|vor *Am.* +s +ed
  +ing (*Br.* flavour)
fla|vor|ful *Am.* (*Br.*
  flavourful)
fla|vor|ing *Am.* +s
  (*Br.* flavouring)
fla|vor|less *Am.*
  (*Br.* flavourless)
fla|vor|ous
fla|vor|some *Am.*
  (*Br.* flavoursome)
fla|vour *Br.* +s +ed
  +ing (*Am.* flavor)

fla|vour|ful *Br.*
  (*Am.* flavorful)
fla|vour|ing *Br.* +s
  (*Am.* flavoring)
fla|vour|less *Br.*
  (*Am.* flavorless)
fla|vour|some *Br.*
  (*Am.* flavorsome)
flaw +s +ed +ing
  (imperfection;
  squall. △ floor)
flaw|less
flaw|less|ly
flaw|less|ness
flax
  flaxes
flax|en
flax-lily
  flax-lilies
Flax|man, John
  (English sculptor)
flax|seed
flay +s +ed +ing
F-layer
flay|er +s
flea +s (insect.
  △ flee)
flea|bag +s
flea|bane
flea bite +s
flea-bitten
flea-bug +s
flea-circus
  flea-circuses
flea col|lar +s
flea mar|ket +s
flea|pit +s
flea|wort
flèche +*s*
fleck +s +ed +ing
Fleck|er, James
  Elroy (English
  poet)
flec|tion +s (use
  flexion)
flec|tion|al (use
  flexional)
flec|tion|less (use
  flexionless)
fled
fledge
  fledges
  fledged
  fledg|ing
fledge|ling +s (use
  fledgling)
fledg|ling +s
flee
  flees
  fled
  flee|ing
  (run away. △ flea)

fleece
  fleeces
  fleeced
  flee|cing
fleece|able
fleece-picker +s
flee|cily
fleeci|ness
fleecy
  flee|cier
  flee|ci|est
fleer +s +ed +ing
fleet +s +ed +ing
  +er +est
fleet-footed
fleet|ing
fleet|ing|ly
fleet|ly
fleet|ness
Fleet Street (in
  London)
Flem|ing +s
  (member of
  Flemish-speaking
  people)
Flem|ing,
  Alex|an|der
  (Scottish doctor
  and scientist)
Flem|ing, Ian
  (English writer)
Flem|ing, John
  Am|brose
  (English engineer)
Flem|ish
flense
  flenses
  flensed
  flen|sing
flesh
  fleshes
  fleshed
  flesh|ing
flesh color *Am.*
flesh-colored *Am.*
flesh col|our *Br.*
flesh-coloured *Br.*
flesh|er +s
flesh-fly
  flesh-flies
fleshi|ness
flesh|ings
flesh|less
flesh|li|ness
flesh|ly
flesh|pots
flesh wound +s
fleshy
  flesh|ier
  fleshi|est

Fletch¦er, John
(English
dramatist)
fletch¦er +s
Fleur
fleur-de-lis
plural **fleur-de-lis**
fleur-de-lys (use
fleur-de-lis)
plural **fleur-de-lys**
fleuret +s
fleuron +s
fleury
Flevo¦land
(province, the
Netherlands)
flew (past tense of
fly. △ flu, flue)
flews (lips of
bloodhound)
flex
  flexes
  flexed
  flex¦ing
flexi¦bil¦ity
flex¦ible
flex¦ibly
flex¦ile
flex¦il¦ity
flex¦ion +s
flex¦ion¦al
flex¦ion¦less
flexi¦time
flexo¦graph¦ic
flex¦og¦raphy
flex¦or +s
flexu¦os¦ity
flexu¦ous
flexu¦ous¦ly
flex¦ural
flex¦ure +s
flib¦ber¦ti¦gib¦bet
  +s
flick +s +ed +ing
flicker +s +ed +ing
flick¦er¦ing +s
flick knife
  flick knives
flier +s (use flyer)
flight +s +ed +ing
(act or manner of
flying; retreat;
shoot wildfowl etc.
△ flyting)
flight bag +s
flight con¦trol
flight deck +s
flight fea¦ther +s
flight¦ily
flighti¦ness
flight¦less

flight lieu¦ten¦ant
  +s
flight of¦ficer +s
flight path +s
flight plan +s
flight re¦cord¦er +s
flight ser¦geant +s
flight-test +s +ed
  +ing
flighty
  flight¦ier
  flighti¦est
flim¦flam
  flim¦flams
  flim¦flammed
  flim¦flam¦ming
flim¦flam¦mer +s
flim¦flam¦mery
flim¦sily
flim¦si¦ness
flimsy
  flim¦sies
  flim¦sier
  flim¦si¦est
flinch
  flinches
  flinched
  flinch¦ing
flinch¦er +s
flinch¦ing¦ly
Flin¦ders,
  Mat¦thew
(English explorer)
flin¦ders
Flin¦ders Is¦land
(off Australia)
fling
  flings
  flung
  fling¦ing
fling¦er +s
flint +s
flint¦ily
flinti¦ness
flint¦lock +s
Flint¦shire (former
county, Wales)
flinty
  flint¦ier
  flinti¦est
flip
  flips
  flipped
  flip¦ping
flip chart +s
flip-flop
  flip-flops
  flip-flopped
  flip-flopping
flip¦pancy
flip¦pant
flip¦pant¦ly

flip¦per +s
flip side +s
flirt +s +ed +ing
flir¦ta¦tion +s
flir¦ta¦tious
flir¦ta¦tious¦ly
flir¦ta¦tious¦ness
flirty
  flirt¦ier
  flirti¦est
flit
  flits
  flit¦ted
  flit¦ting
flitch
  flitches
flitch beam +s
flit¦ter +s +ed +ing
flitter-mouse
  flitter-mice
fliv¦ver +s
flix¦weed
Flo (name)
float +s +ed +ing
float¦abil¦ity
float¦able
float¦age
float¦ation +s (use
flotation)
float-board +s
floatel +s
float¦er +s
float¦ing¦ly
float¦plane +s
float-stone
floaty
floc +s (mass of
fine particles.
△ flock)
floc¦cu¦late
  floc¦cu¦lates
  floc¦cu¦lated
  floc¦cu¦lat¦ing
floc¦cu¦la¦tion
floc¦cule +s
floc¦cu¦lence
floc¦cu¦lent
floc¦cu¦lus
  floc¦culi
floc¦cus
  flocci
flock +s +ed +ing
(group of birds or
animals; go in a
crowd; wallpaper.
△ floc)
flock paper +s
flocky
  flock¦ier
  flocki¦est

Flod¦den (Field)
(battle site,
England)
floe +s (mass of ice.
△ flow)
Flo¦ella
flog
  flogs
  flogged
  flog¦ging
flog¦ger +s
flong
Flood, the *Bible*
flood +s +ed +ing
flood¦gate +s
flood¦ing +s
flood¦light
  flood¦lights
  flood¦lit
  flood¦light¦ing
flood plain +s
flood tide +s
flood water +s
floor +s +ed +ing
(of room; storey;
knock down.
△ flaw)
floor¦board +s
floor¦cloth +s
floor cover¦ing +s
floor¦ing +s
floor lamp +s
floor lead¦er +s
floor-length
floor¦less
floor man¦ager +s
floor plan +s
floor pol¦ish
  floor pol¦ishes
floor show +s
floor¦walk¦er +s
floo¦zie +s
floozy (use floozie)
  floo¦zies
flop
  flops
  flopped
  flop¦ping
flop¦house +s
flop¦pily
flop¦pi¦ness
floppy
  flop¦pies
  flop¦pier
  flop¦pi¦est
flop¦tic¦al *Propr.*
Flora (*Roman
Mythology*; name)
flora
  floras *or* **florae**
floral
flor¦al¦ly

flor¦eat
Flor¦ence (city,
   Italy; name)
Flor¦en¦tine +s
Flores (island,
   Indonesia)
flor¦es¦cence
floret +s
Florey, How¦ard
   Wal¦ter
   (Australian
   pathologist)
Flor¦ian¦ópo¦lis
   (city, Brazil)
flori¦ate
   flori¦ates
   flori¦ated
   flori¦at¦ing
flori¦bunda +s
flori¦cul¦tural
flori¦cul¦ture
flori¦cul¦tur¦ist +s
florid
Flor¦ida (state,
   USA)
Flor¦id¦ian +s
flor¦id¦ity
flor¦id¦ly
flor¦id¦ness
flor¦ifer¦ous
flori¦le¦gium
   flori¦legia
florin +s
Florio, John
   (English scholar)
flor¦ist +s
flor¦is¦tic
flor¦is¦tic¦al¦ly
flor¦is¦tics
flor¦is¦try
flor¦uit
flory
flos¦cu¦lar
flos¦cu¦lous
floss
   flosses
   flossed
   floss¦ing
flossy
   floss¦ier
   flossi¦est
flo¦ta¦tion +s
flo¦tilla +s
flot¦sam
flounce
   flounces
   flounced
   floun¦cing
floun¦der +s +ed
   +ing
floun¦der¦er +s

flour +s +ed +ing
   (grain meal.
   △ flower)
flouri¦ness (state of
   being floury.
   △ floweriness)
flour¦ish
   flour¦ishes
   flour¦ished
   flour¦ish¦ing
flour¦ish¦er +s
flour¦ishy
floury
   flour¦ier
   flouri¦est
   (like flour.
   △ flowery)
flout +s +ed +ing
flow +s +ed +ing
   (move along etc.
   △ floe)
flow chart +s
flower +s +ed +ing
   (plant. △ flour)
flower bed +s
flower¦er +s
flow¦eret +s
flower girl +s
flower head +s
flow¦eri¦ness (state
   of being flowery.
   △ flouriness)
flower¦ing +s
flower¦less
flower¦like
flower¦pot +s
flower show +s
flowery
   flower¦ier
   floweri¦est
   (having flowers;
   ornate. △ floury)
flow¦ing¦ly
flow¦meter +s
flown
flow-on +s noun
flow¦sheet +s
flow¦stone +s
Floyd
flu +s (illness.
   △ flew, flue)
flub
   flubs
   flubbed
   flub¦bing
fluc¦tu¦ate
   fluc¦tu¦ates
   fluc¦tu¦ated
   fluc¦tu¦at¦ing
fluc¦tu¦ation +s
flue +s (smoke
   duct. △ flew, flu)

flue-cure
   flue-cures
   flue-cured
   flue-curing
flu¦ence
flu¦ency
flu¦ent
flu¦ent¦ly
flue pipe +s
fluff +s +ed +ing
fluf¦fily
fluf¦fi¦ness
fluffy
   fluff¦ier
   fluffi¦est
flu¦gel¦horn +s
fluid +s
fluid drachm Br.
   +s (Am. fluidram)
flu¦id¦ic
flu¦id¦ics
flu¦id¦ify
   flu¦idi¦fies
   flu¦idi¦fied
   flu¦id¦ify¦ing
flu¦id¦isa¦tion Br.
   (use fluidization)
flu¦id¦ise Br. (use
   fluidize)
   flu¦id¦ises
   flu¦id¦ised
   flu¦id¦is¦ing
flu¦id¦ity
flu¦id¦iza¦tion
flu¦id¦ize
   flu¦id¦izes
   flu¦id¦ized
   flu¦id¦iz¦ing
flu¦id¦ly
flu¦id¦ness
flu¦id¦ounce Am.
   +s
fluid ounce Br. +s
flui¦dram Am. +s
   (Br. fluid drachm)
fluke
   flukes
   fluked
   fluk¦ing
fluki¦ly
fluki¦ness
fluky
   fluki¦er
   fluki¦est
flume
   flumes
   flumed
   flum¦ing
flum¦mery
   flum¦mer¦ies
flum¦mox
   flum¦moxes

flum¦mox (cont.)
   flum¦moxed
   flum¦mox¦ing
flump +s +ed +ing
flung
flunk +s +ed +ing
flun¦key +s
flun¦key¦ism
flunky (use
   flunkey)
   flun¦kies
fluor¦esce
   fluor¦esces
   fluor¦esced
   fluor¦es¦cing
fluor¦es¦cein
fluor¦es¦cence
fluor¦es¦cent
fluorid¦ate
   fluorid¦ates
   fluorid¦ated
   fluorid¦at¦ing
fluorid¦ation
fluor¦ide +s
fluor¦id¦isa¦tion Br.
   (use
   fluoridization)
fluor¦id¦iza¦tion
fluorin¦ate
   fluorin¦ates
   fluorin¦ated
   fluorin¦at¦ing
fluorin¦ation
fluor¦ine
fluor¦ite +s
fluoro¦car¦bon +s
fluoro¦scope +s
fluor¦osis
fluor¦spar +s
flurry
   flur¦ries
   flur¦ried
   flurry¦ing
flush
   flushes
   flushed
   flush¦ing
flush¦er +s
Flush¦ing (English
   name for
   Vlissingen)
flush¦ness
flus¦ter +s +ed
   +ing
flute
   flutes
   fluted
   flut¦ing
flute¦like
flut¦ist +s
flut¦ter +s +ed
   +ing

flut|ter|er +s
flut|tery
fluty
  fluti|er
  fluti|est
flu|vial
flu|via|tile
flu|vio|gla|cial
flu|vi|om|eter +s
flux
  fluxes
  fluxed
  flux|ing
flux|ion +s
flux|ion|al
flux|ion|ary
fly
  flies
  flew
  fly|ing
  flown
  (insect; move
  through air; flap;
  scenery; part of
  clockwork)
fly
  flys *or* flies
  (carriage)
fly +er +est
  (clever)
fly|able
fly|away *attributive*
fly-blow
fly|blown
fly but|ton +s
fly-by +s *noun*
fly-by-night +s
fly-by-wire
fly|catch|er +s
fly-drive
flyer +s
fly-fish
  fly-fishes
  fly-fished
  fly-fishing
fly-half
  fly-halves
fly|ing boat +s
fly|ing fish
  plural fly|ing fish
fly|leaf
  fly|leaves
fly|ness
Flynn, Errol
  (American actor)
fly|over +s *noun*
fly-paper +s
fly-past +s *noun*
fly-pitcher +s
fly-pitching
fly-post +s +ed
  +ing

fly|sheet +s
flyt|ing +s
  (contention.
  △ flighting)
fly-tip
  fly-tips
  fly-tipped
  fly-tipping
fly-tipper +s
fly|trap +s
fly|way +s
fly|weight +s
fly|wheel +s
f-number +s
Fo, Dario (Italian
  playwright)
foal +s +ed +ing
foam +s +ed +ing
foam|less
foam rub|ber
foamy
  foam|ier
  foami|est
fob
  fobs
  fobbed
  fob|bing
fo|cac|cia
focal
fo|cal|isa|tion *Br.*
  (use focalization)
fo|cal|ise *Br.* (use
  focalize)
  fo|cal|ises
  fo|cal|ised
  fo|cal|is|ing
fo|cal|iza|tion
fo|cal|ize
  fo|cal|izes
  fo|cal|ized
  fo|cal|iz|ing
Foch, Fer|di|nand
  (French general)
fo'c'sle +s
  (= forecastle)
focus
  fo|cuses *or* foci
  noun
focus
  fo|cuses *or*
  fo|cusses
  fo|cused *or*
  fo|cussed
  fo|cus|ing *or*
  fo|cus|sing
  verb
fo|cus|er +s
fod|der +s +ed
  +ing
foe +s (enemy.
  △ faux)
foehn +s (use föhn)

foe|man
  foe|men
foe|tal *Br.* (*Am.*
  fetal)
foeti|cidal *Br.* (*Am.*
  feticidal)
foeti|cide *Br.* (*Am.*
  feticide)
foe|tid (use fetid)
foe|tus *Br.*
  foe|tuses
  (*Am.* fetus)
fog
  fogs
  fogged
  fog|ging
fog bank +s
fog|bound
fog-bow +s
fogey +s
fogey|dom
fogey|ish
Fo|ggia (town,
  Italy)
fog|gily
fog|gi|ness
foggy
  fog|gier
  fog|gi|est
fog|horn +s
fog lamp +s
fog|light +s
fog sig|nal +s
fogy (use fogey)
  fo|gies
fogy|dom (use
  fogeydom)
fogy|ish (use
  fogeyish)
föhn +s
foi|ble +s
foie gras
foil +s +ed +ing
foil|ist +s
foist +s +ed +ing
Fo|kine, Mi|chel
  (Russian-born
  choreographer)
Fok|ker, An|thony
  Her|man Ger|ard
  (Dutch-born
  American aircraft
  designer)
fola|cin
fold +s +ed +ing
fold|able
fold|away *adjective*
fold|back +s
  attributive and
  noun
fold|boat +s
fold|er +s

fol|de|rol +s
fold-out *adjective*
fold-up *adjective*
fo|li|aceous
fo|li|age
fo|liar
fo|li|ate
  fo|li|ates
  fo|li|ated
  fo|li|at|ing
fo|li|ation
folic
Folies-Bergère
folio +s
fo|li|ole +s
fo|li|ose
fo|liot +s
folk
  plural folk *or* folks
folk dance +s
folk dan|cer +s
folk dan|cing
Folke|stone (port,
  England)
folk hero
  folk heroes
folkie +s (person.
  △ folky)
folki|ness
folk|ish
folk|lore
folk|lor|ic
folk|lor|ist +s
folk|lor|is|tic
folk music
folk rock
folk|si|ness
folk sing|er +s
folk song +s
folksy
  folks|ier
  folksi|est
folk tale +s
folk|ways
folk|weave
folk wis|dom
folky
  folk|ier
  folki|est
  (*adjective.*
  △ folkie)
fol|licle +s
fol|licu|lar
fol|licu|late
fol|licu|lated
fol|low +s +ed
  +ing
fol|low|er +s
fol|low|ing +s
follow-on +s *noun*
follow-through
  noun

follow-up +s *noun*
folly
  fol|lies
Fol|som
  (archaeological
  site, USA)
Fom|al|haut (star)
fo|ment +s +ed
  +ing
fo|men|ta|tion
fo|ment|er +s
Fon
  plural Fon *or* Fons
fond +er +est
Fonda, Henry,
  Jane, Peter, and
  Bridget
  (American actors)
fon|dant +s
fon|dle
  fon|dles
  fon|dled
  fond|ling
fond|ler +s
fond|ly
fond|ness
fon|due +s
font +s
Fon|taine|bleau
  (town and palace,
  France)
fon|tal
fon|ta|nel *Am.* +s
fon|ta|nelle *Br.* +s
Fon|teyn, Mar|got
  (British ballet
  dancer)
Foo|chow
  (= Fuzhou)
food +s
food chain +s
foodie +s
food poi|son|ing
food pro|ces|sor
  +s
food|stuff +s
fool +s +ed +ing
fool|ery
  fool|er|ies
fool|har|dily
fool|hardi|ness
fool|hardy
fool|ish
fool|ish|ly
fool|ish|ness
fool|proof
fools|cap
fool's er|rand +s
fool's gold
fool's mate
fool's para|dise
fool's pars|ley

foot
  feet
  noun
foot +s +ed +ing
  verb
foot|age
foot-and-mouth
  (disease)
foot|ball +s +ed
  +ing
foot|ball|er +s
foot|bath +s
foot|bed +s
foot|board +s
foot|brake +s
foot|bridge +s
foot|er +s
foot|fall +s
foot-fault +s +ed
  +ing
foot|hill +s
foot|hold +s
footie (use footy)
foot|ing +s
foo|tle
  foo|tles
  foo|tled
  foot|ling
foot|less
foot|lights
foot|loose
foot|man
  foot|men
foot|mark +s
foot|note +s
foot|pad +s
foot|path +s
foot pedal +s
foot|plate +s
foot-pound +s
foot-pound-
  second
foot|print +s
foot|rest +s
foot-rot
foot-rule +s
Foot|sie *Stock*
  Exchange
foot|sie (amorous
  play with feet)
footsie-footsie
foot|slog
  foot|slogs
  foot|slogged
  foot|slog|ging
foot|slog|ger +s
foot sol|dier +s
foot|sore
foot|stalk +s
foot|step +s
foot|stool +s
foot|strap +s

foot|sure
foot-tapping
foot|way +s
foot|wear
foot|well +s
foot|work
footy
foo yong +s
fop +s
fop|pery
  fop|per|ies
fop|pish
fop|pish|ly
fop|pish|ness
for (*preposition and*
  conjunction.
  ⚠ fore, four)
for|age
  for|ages
  for|aged
  for|aging
for|age cap +s
for|ager +s
fora|men
  for|am|ina
for|am|in|ate
  for|am|in|ates
  for|am|in|ated
  for|am|in|at|ing
fora|mini|fer +s
for|am|in|if|er|an
  +s
for|am|in|ifer|ous
for|as|much
foray +s +ed +ing
for|bade
for|bear
  for|bears
  for|bore
  for|bear|ing
  for|borne
  (refrain; abstain.
  ⚠ forebear)
for|bear|ance
for|bear|ing|ly
for|bid
  for|bids
  for|bade
  for|bid|ding
  for|bid|den
  for|bid|dance
  for|bid|ding|ly
for|bore
for|borne
for|bye
force
  forces
  forced
  for|cing
force|able
  (able to be forced.
  ⚠ forcible)

force-feed
  force-feeds
  force-fed
  force-feeding
force field +s
force|ful
force|ful|ly
force|ful|ness
force-land +s +ed
  +ing
force ma|jeure
force|meat
for|ceps
  plural for|ceps
force-pump +s
for|cer +s
for|cible
  (involving force.
  ⚠ forceable)
for|cible|ness
for|cibly
Ford, Ford Madox
  (English writer)
Ford, Ger|ald
  (American
  president)
Ford, Har|ri|son
  (American actor)
Ford, Henry
  (American car
  maker)
Ford, John
  (American film
  director)
ford +s +ed +ing
ford|able
fore +s (front etc.
  ⚠ for, four)
fore-and-aft
  attributive
fore|arm +s +ed
  +ing
fore|bear +s
  (ancestor.
  ⚠ forbear)
fore|bode
  fore|bodes
  fore|boded
  fore|bod|ing
fore|bod|ing +s
fore|bod|ing|ly
fore|brain +s
fore|cast
  fore|casts
  fore|cast *or*
  fore|cast|ed
  fore|cast|ing
fore|cast|er +s
fore|castle +s
fore|close
  fore|closes
  fore|closed
  fore|clos|ing

fore|clos|ure +s
fore|con|scious
fore|court +s
fore|deck +s
for|edge +s (use
   fore-edge)
fore|doom +s +ed
   +ing
fore-edge +s
fore-end +s
fore|father +s
fore|feel
   fore|feels
   fore|felt
   fore|feel|ing
fore|fin|ger +s
fore|foot
   fore|feet
fore|front
fore|gather +s +ed
   +ing
fore|go
   fore|goes
   fore|went
   fore|going
   fore|gone
   (precede; in 'the
   foregoing' and
   'foregone
   conclusion'.
   ⚠ forgo)
fore|go|er +s
fore|ground +s
   +ed +ing
fore|hand +s
fore|head +s
fore|hock +s
fore|hold +s
for|eign
for|eign|er +s
for|eign|ness
fore|judge
   fore|judges
   fore|judged
   fore|judg|ing
fore|know
   fore|knows
   fore|knew
   fore|know|ing
   fore|known
fore|know|ledge
fore|lady
   fore|ladies
fore|land +s
fore|leg +s
fore|limb +s
fore|lock +s
fore|man
   fore|men
fore|mast +s
fore|most
fore|mother +s

fore|name +s
fore|noon +s
fo|ren|sic
fo|ren|sic|al|ly
fo|ren|sics
fore|or|dain +s
   +ed +ing
fore|or|din|ation
fore|part +s
fore|paw +s
fore|peak +s
fore|play
fore|quar|ter +s
fore|run
   fore|runs
   fore|ran
   fore|run|ning
   fore|run
fore|run|ner +s
fore|sail +s
fore|see
   fore|sees
   fore|saw
   fore|see|ing
   fore|seen
fore|see|abil|ity
fore|see|able
fore|see|ably
fore|seer +s
fore|shadow +s
   +ed +ing
fore|sheets
fore|shock +s
fore|shore +s
fore|short|en +s
   +ed +ing
fore|show
   fore|shows
   fore|showed
   fore|show|ing
   fore|shown
fore|sight
fore|sight|ed
fore|sight|ed|ly
fore|sight|ed|ness
fore|skin +s
for|est +s +ed +ing
fore|stall +s +ed
   +ing
fore|stall|er +s
fore|stal|ment
for|est|ation
fore|stay +s
for|est dwell|er +s
forest-dwelling
   attributive
For|est|er, C. S.
   (English novelist)
for|est|er +s
for|est land +s
for|est|ry
for|est tree +s

fore|taste
   fore|tastes
   fore|tas|ted
   fore|tast|ing
fore|tell
   fore|tells
   fore|told
   fore|tell|ing
fore|tell|er +s
fore|thought
fore|to|ken +s +ed
   +ing
fore|told
fore|top +s
fore-topgal|lant
   +s
fore-topgal|lant-
   mast +s
fore-topgal|lant-
   sail +s
fore-topmast +s
fore-topsail +s
for|ever
   (continually)
for ever (for
   always)
for|ever|more *Am.*
for ever|more *Br.*
fore|warn +s +ed
   +ing
fore|warn|er +s
fore|went
fore|wing +s
fore|woman
   fore|women
fore|word +s
fore|yard +s
For|far (town,
   Scotland)
For|far|shire
   (former name of
   Angus, Scotland)
for|feit +s +ed
   +ing
for|feit|able
for|feit|er +s
for|feit|ure
for|fend +s +ed
   +ing
for|gather +s +ed
   +ing (use
   foregather)
for|gave
forge
   forges
   forged
   for|ging
forge|able
for|ger +s
for|gery
   for|ger|ies

for|get
   for|gets
   for|got
   for|get|ting
   for|got|ten
for|get|ful
for|get|ful|ly
for|get|ful|ness
forget-me-not +s
for|get|table
for|get|ter +s
for|giv|able
for|giv|ably
for|give
   for|gives
   for|gave
   for|giv|ing
   for|given
for|give|ness
for|giver +s
for|giv|ing|ly
forgo
   for|goes
   for|went
   for|go|ing
   for|gone
   (go without.
   ⚠ forego)
for|got
for|got|ten
for|int +s
fork +s +ed +ing
Fork|beard,
   Sweyn (king of
   Denmark and
   England)
fork-lift +s
for|lorn
for|lorn|ly
for|lorn|ness
form +s +ed +ing
   (all senses except
   Br. Printing.
   ⚠ forme)
for|mal +s
for|mal|de|hyde
for|ma|lin
for|mal|isa|tion *Br.*
   (use
   formalization)
for|mal|ise *Br.* (use
   formalize)
   for|mal|ises
   for|mal|ised
   for|mal|is|ing
for|mal|ism +s
for|mal|ist +s
for|mal|is|tic
for|mal|ity
   for|mal|ities
for|mal|iza|tion

for|mal|ize
  for|mal|izes
  for|mal|ized
  for|mal|iz|ing
for|mal|ly
  (officially.
  △ formerly)
for|mal|ness
form|ant +s
for|mat
  for|mats
  for|mat|ted
  for|mat|ting
for|mate
for|ma|tion +s
for|ma|tion|al
for|ma|tive
for|ma|tive|ly
Formby, George
  (English
  comedian)
forme Br. +s (Am.
  form. Printing.
  △ form.)
For|men|tera
  (Spanish island)
for|mer +s
for|mer|ly
  (previously.
  △ formally)
for|mic
For|mica Propr.
for|mi|ca|tion
for|mid|able
for|mid|able|ness
for|mid|ably
form|less
form|less|ly
form|less|ness
For|mosa (former
  name of Taiwan)
for|mula
  for|mu|las or
  for|mu|lae
for|mu|la|ic
for|mu|lar|ise Br.
  (use formularize)
  for|mu|lar|ises
  for|mu|lar|ised
  for|mu|lar|is|ing
for|mu|lar|ize
  for|mu|lar|izes
  for|mu|lar|ized
  for|mu|lar|iz|ing
for|mu|lary
  for|mu|lar|ies
for|mu|late
  for|mu|lates
  for|mu|lated
  for|mu|lat|ing
for|mu|la|tion +s
for|mu|la|tor +s

for|mu|lise Br.
  (use formulize)
  for|mu|lises
  for|mu|lised
  for|mu|lis|ing
for|mu|lism
for|mu|list +s
for|mu|lis|tic
for|mu|lize
  for|mu|lizes
  for|mu|lized
  for|mu|liz|ing
form|work
for|ni|cate
  for|ni|cates
  for|ni|cated
  for|ni|cat|ing
for|ni|ca|tion +s
for|ni|ca|tor +s
for|rad|er
  (= forwarder)
For|rest, John
  (Australian
  statesman)
for|sake
  for|sakes
  for|sook
  for|sak|ing
  for|saken
for|saken|ness
for|saker +s
for|sooth
For|ster, E. M.
  (English novelist.
  △ Vorster)
for|swear
  for|swears
  for|swore
  for|swear|ing
  for|sworn
For|syth,
  Fred|erick
  (English writer)
for|sythia +s
fort +s (fortified
  building.
  △ fought)
For|ta|leza (port,
  Brazil)
Fort-de-France
  (capital of
  Martinique)
forte +s (strong
  point; Music loudly)
forte|piano +s
  (musical
  instrument)
forte piano (Music
  loud then soft)
Forth (river,
  Scotland; shipping
  area off Scotland)

forth (forward.
  △ fourth)
forth|com|ing
forth|com|ing|ness
forth|right
forth|right|ly
forth|right|ness
forth|with
For|ties (part of
  North Sea
  between Scotland
  and S. Norway;
  shipping area off
  Scotland)
for|ti|eth +s
for|ti|fi|able
for|ti|fi|ca|tion +s
for|ti|fier +s
for|tify
  for|ti|fies
  for|ti|fied
  for|ti|fy|ing
for|tis|simo
  for|tis|simos or
  for|tis|simi
for|ti|tude
Fort Knox (gold
  depository, USA)
Fort Lamy (former
  name of
  N'Djamena)
fort|night +s
fort|night|ly
  fort|night|lies
For|tran
fort|ress
  fort|resses
for|tuit|ism
for|tuit|ist +s
for|tuit|ous
for|tuit|ous|ly
for|tuit|ous|ness
for|tu|ity
  for|tu|ities
for|tu|nate +s
for|tu|nate|ly
for|tune +s
for|tune cookie +s
for|tune hunt|er
  +s
fortune-teller +s
fortune-telling
Fort Wil|liam
  (town, Scotland)
Fort Worth (city,
  USA)
forty
  for|ties
forty-first, forty-
  second, etc.
Forty-five, the
  (1745 rebellion)

forty-five +s
  (gramophone
  record)
forty|fold
forty-niner +s
forty-one, forty-
  two, etc.
forum
  forums or fora
for|ward +s +ed
  +ing
for|ward|er +s
forward-looking
for|ward|ly
for|ward|ness
for|wards
for|went
Fos|bury, Dick
  (American high-
  jumper)
fossa
  fos|sae
fosse +s
Fosse Way
  (ancient road,
  England)
fos|sick +s +ed
  +ing
fos|sick|er +s
fos|sil +s
fos|sil fuel
fos|sil|ifer|ous
fos|sil|isa|tion Br.
  (use fossilization)
fos|sil|ise Br. (use
  fossilize)
  fos|sil|ises
  fos|sil|ised
  fos|sil|is|ing
fos|sil|iza|tion
fos|sil|ize
  fos|sil|izes
  fos|sil|ized
  fos|sil|iz|ing
fos|sor|ial
Fos|ter, Jodie
  (American
  actress)
Fos|ter, Ste|phen
  (American
  composer)
fos|ter +s +ed +ing
fos|ter|age
foster-brother +s
foster-child
  foster-children
foster-daughter +s
fos|ter|er +s
foster-father +s
fos|ter|ling +s
foster-mother +s
foster-parent +s

foster-sister +s
foster-son +s
Fou|cault, Jean
   Ber|nard Léon
   (French physicist)
Fou|cault, Mi¦chel
   (French
   philosopher)
fou|etté +s
fought (past tense
   and past participle
   of fight △ fort)
Fou-hsin (= Fuxin)
foul +s +ed +ing
   +er +est (dirty;
   unpleasant;
   tangle; etc.
   △ fowl)
fou|lard +s
foul¦ly
foul-mouthed
foul|ness
foul-up +s noun
fou|mart +s
found +s +ed +ing
foun|da¦tion +s
foun|da¦tion|al
foun|da¦tion|er +s
foun|da¦tion stone
   +s
found¦er +s
   (person who
   founds)
foun|der +s +ed
   +ing (sink; fail;
   horse disorder)
found¦er mem|ber
   +s
found¦er|ship
found|ling +s
found|ress
   found|resses
foun|dry
   foun|dries
fount +s
foun|tain +s
foun|tained
foun¦tain|head +s
foun|tain pen +s
four +s (number.
   △ for, fore)
four|chette +s
four-eyes
   plural four-eyes
four-flush
   four-flushes
   four-flushed
   four-flushing
four-flusher +s
four|fold
Four|ier, Jean
   Bap|tiste

Four|ier (cont.)
   Jo¦seph (French
   mathematician)
Four|ier an¦aly|sis
Four|ier|ism
Four|ier ser|ies
four-in-hand +s
four-iron +s
four-leaf clo¦ver
   +s
four-leaved
   clo¦ver +s
four-letter word
   +s
four o'clock +s
   (plant)
four|pence +s
four|penny
   four|pen¦nies
four-poster +s
four|score
four|some +s
four-square
four-stroke +s
four|teen +s
four|teenth +s
fourth +s (in
   number. △ forth)
fourth¦ly
4to (= quarto)
four-wheel drive
fovea
   fo¦veae
fo¦veal
fo|ve¦ate
fo|ve¦ola
   fo|ve¦olae
fo|ve¦ol|ate
fowl
   plural fowl or
   fowls
   (bird. △ foul)
Fowl¦er, H. W.
   (English
   lexicographer)
fowl¦er +s
Fowles, John
   (English novelist)
fowl|ing
fowl pest
fowl-run +s
Fox, George
   (English preacher
   and founder of
   Quakers)
fox
   foxes
   foxed
   fox¦ing
Foxe, John
   (English author of

Foxe (cont.)
   The Book of
   Martyrs)
fox|glove +s
fox|hole +s
fox|hound +s
fox hunt +s noun
fox-hunt +s +ed
   +ing verb
Fox|hunt|er
   (horse)
fox-hunter +s
fox¦ily
foxi|ness
fox|like
fox|tail +s
Fox Tal¦bot,
   Wil|liam Henry
   (English
   photography
   pioneer)
fox ter|rier +s
fox|trot
   fox|trots
   fox|trot|ted
   fox|trot|ting
foxy
   fox¦ier
   foxi|est
foyer +s
Fra (Italian monk;
   see also under
   name)
frab|jous
frab|jous¦ly
fra¦cas
   plural fra¦cas
frac|tal +s
frac|tion +s
frac|tion¦al
frac|tion|al¦ise Br.
   (use
   fractionalize)
frac|tion¦al|ises
   frac|tion¦al|ised
   frac|tion¦al|is¦ing
frac|tion¦al|ize
   frac|tion¦al|izes
   frac|tion¦al|ized
   frac|tion¦al|iz¦ing
frac|tion|al¦ly
frac|tion|ary
frac|tion|ate
   frac|tion|ates
   frac|tion|ated
   frac|tion|at¦ing
frac|tion|ation
frac|tion|ise Br.
   (use fractionize)
   frac|tion|ises
   frac|tion|ised
   frac|tion|is¦ing

frac|tion|ize
   frac|tion|izes
   frac|tion|ized
   frac|tion|iz¦ing
frac|tious
frac|tious¦ly
frac|tious|ness
frac|ture
   frac|tures
   frac|tured
   frac¦tur|ing
frae¦nu|lum Br.
   frae|nula
   (Am. frenulum)
frae|num Br.
   fraena
   (Am. frenum)
fra|gile
   fra|gile¦ly
   fra|gil|ity
frag|ment +s +ed
   +ing
frag|men¦tal
frag|men¦tar¦ily
frag|men¦tary
frag|men|ta¦tion
frag|ment|ise Br.
   (use fragmentize)
   frag|ment|ises
   frag|ment|ised
   frag|ment|is¦ing
frag|ment|ize
   frag|ment|izes
   frag|ment|ized
   frag|ment|iz¦ing
Fra|go|nard, Jean-
   Honoré (French
   painter)
fra|grance +s
fra|granced
fra|grancy
fra|grant
fra|grant¦ly
frail +s +er +est
frail¦ly
frail|ness
frailty
   frail|ties
Frak|tur
framable
fram|be¦sia Am.
fram|boe¦sia Br.
frame
   frames
   framed
   fram¦ing
frame house +s
frame|less
framer +s
frame-saw +s
frame-up +s noun
frame|work +s

Fran
franc +s (French,
  Swiss, etc.
  currency. △ frank)
France (country)
France, Ana|tole
  (French writer)
Fran|ces (woman's
  name. △ Francis)
Fran|cesca
Franche-Comté
  (region, France)
fran|chise
  fran|chises
  fran|chised
  fran|chis|ing
fran|chisee +s
fran|chiser +s
Fran|cine
Fran|cis (man's
  name. △ Frances)
Fran|cis, Dick
  (British writer)
Fran|cis|can +s
Fran|cis of As|sisi
  (Italian saint)
Fran|cis of Sales
  (French saint)
Fran|cis Xa|vier
  (Spanish
  missionary)
fran|cium
Franck, César
  (Belgian
  composer)
Franck, James
  (German-born
  American
  physicist)
Franco, Fran|cisco
  (Spanish general
  and statesman)
Franco-German
fran|co|lin +s
Franco|mania
Fran|conia
  (medieval duchy,
  Germany)
Franco|phile +s
Franco|phobe +s
franco|pho|bia
franco|phone +s
Franco-Prussian
fran|gible
fran|gi|pane +s
  (almond paste;
  cake)
fran|gi|pani +s
  (perfume tree)
fran|glais

Frank +s
  (Germanic tribe;
  name)
Frank, Anne
  (German Jewish
  diarist)
frank +s +ed +ing
  +er +est (stamp
  or mark for
  posting. △ franc)
frank|able
Fran|ken|stein, Dr
  (scientist in novel)
frank|er +s
Frank|fort (city,
  USA)
Frank|furt in full
  Frank|furt am
  Main
  (city, western
  Germany)
Frank|furt in full
  Frank|furt an der
  Oder
  (city, eastern
  Germany)
frank|furt|er +s
frank|in|cense
Frank|ish
Frank|lin, Aretha
  (American singer)
Frank|lin,
  Ben|ja|min
  (American
  statesman and
  scientist)
Frank|lin,
  Rosa|lind
  (English scientist)
frank|lin +s
frank|ly
frank|ness
fran|tic
fran|tic|al|ly
fran|tic|ness
Franz Josef
  (emperor of
  Austria and king
  of Hungary)
Franz Josef Land
  (island group,
  Arctic Ocean)
frap
  fraps
  frapped
  frap|ping
frappé +s
Fras|cati (region,
  Italy)
fras|cati +s (wine)
Fra|ser (river,
  Canada)

Fra|ser, Dawn
  (Australian
  swimmer.
  △ Frazer)
frass
frat
  frats
  frat|ted
  frat|ting
fra|ter|nal +s
fra|ter|nal|ism
fra|ter|nal|ly
frat|er|nisa|tion
  Br. (use
  fraternization)
frat|er|nise Br. (use
  fraternize)
  frat|er|nises
  frat|er|nised
  frat|er|nis|ing
fra|ter|nity
  fra|ter|nities
frat|er|niza|tion
frat|er|nize
  frat|er|nizes
  frat|er|nized
  frat|er|niz|ing
frat|ri|cidal
frat|ri|cide +s
Frau
  Frauen
  (German woman.
  △ frow)
fraud +s
fraud|ster +s
fraudu|lence
fraudu|lent
fraudu|lent|ly
fraught
Fräu|lein +s
Fraun|hof|er,
  Jo|seph von
  (German optician;
  lines)
fraxi|nella +s
fray +s +ed +ing
Fray Ben|tos (port,
  Uruguay)
Fra|zer, James
  George (Scottish
  anthropologist.
  △ Fraser)
fra|zil (ice crystals
  in stream)
fraz|zle
  fraz|zles
  fraz|zled
  fraz|zling
  (exhaustion; to
  exhaust)
freak +s +ed +ing
freak|ily

freaki|ness
freak|ish
freak|ish|ly
freak|ish|ness
freak-out +s noun
freak show +s
freaky
  freak|ier
  freaki|est
freckle
  freckles
  freckled
  freck|ling
freckle-faced
freckly
Fred
Fred|die also
  Freddy
Freddy also
  Fred|die
Fred|erick
Fred|erick
  Bar|ba|rossa
  (Frederick I,
  German king and
  Holy Roman
  emperor)
Fred|erick the
  Great (Frederick
  II, Prussian king)
Fred|erick
  Wil|liam (Elector
  of Brandenburg)
Fred|eric|ton (city,
  Canada)
free
  frees
  freed
  free|ing
  freer
  freest
free and easy
free|base
  free|bases
  free|based
  free|bas|ing
free|bie +s
free|board +s
free|boot +s +ed
  +ing
free|boot|er +s
free|born
freed|man
  freed|men
free|dom +s
free|dom fight|er
  +s
free fall noun
free-fall
  free-falls
  free-fell

free-fall (*cont.*)
  free-falling
  attributive and verb
Free|fone *Propr.*
free-for-all +s
free-form *attributive*
free|hand
  (drawing)
free hand (freedom
  to act)
free-handed
free-handed¦ly
free-handed¦ness
free|hold +s
free|hold¦er +s
free-kick +s
free|lance
  free|lances
  free|lanced
  free|lan¦cing
free-liver +s
free-living
free|load +s +ed
  +ing
free|load¦er +s
free¦ly
free|man
  free|men
free mar¦ket +s
  noun
free-market
  attributive
free|mar¦tin +s
Free|mason +s
Free|mason¦ry
  (of Freemasons)
free|mason¦ry
  free|mason|ries
  (generally)
free|ness
Free|phone (use
  Freefone)
Free|post
freer
free-range
free sheet +s
free|sia +s
free-spoken
freest
free-standing
free|stone +s
free|style
free|styler +s
free|think¦er +s
free|think¦ing
Free|town (capital
  of Sierra Leone)
free trade *noun*
free-trade
  attributive
free|ware
free|way +s

free|wheel +s +ed
  +ing (cog
  assembly; coast)
free wheel +s
  (wheel)
freez|able
freeze
  freezes
  froze
  freez|ing
  fro¦zen
  (turn to ice.
  △ frieze)
freeze-dry
  freeze-dries
  freeze-dried
  freeze-drying
freeze-frame +s
freezer +s
freeze-up +s *noun*
freezing-mixture
  +s
freez|ing point +s
Frege, Gott|lob
  (German
  philosopher and
  mathematician)
Frei|burg (city,
  Germany)
freight +s +ed
  +ing
freight|age +s
freight¦er +s
Freight|liner +s
  Propr.
Fre|limo (political
  party,
  Mozambique)
Fre|man¦tle (city,
  Australia)
Fré|mont, John
  Charles
  (American
  explorer and
  statesman)
French
French Can|adian
  +s *noun*
French-Canadian
  adjective
French fried
  (potatoes)
French fries
French horn +s
French¦ifi|ca¦tion
French¦ify
  Frenchi¦fies
  Frenchi¦fied
  Frenchi¦fy|ing
French let¦ter +s
French|man
  French|men

French|ness
French pol|ish
  French pol|ishes
  French pol|ished
  French
  pol¦ish|ing
French-speaking
French toast
French win¦dow
  +s
French|woman
  French|women
Frenchy
  French|ies
fre|net¦ic
fre|net¦ic¦al¦ly
frenu|lum *Am.*
  fren|ula
  (*Br.* fraenulum)
fre|num *Am.*
  frena
  (*Br.* fraenum)
fren|zied¦ly
frenzy
  fren|zies
  fren|zied
  frenzy|ing
freon +s *Propr.*
fre|quency
  fre¦quen|cies
fre|quent +s +ed
  +ing
fre¦quen|ta¦tion
fre¦quen|ta¦tive
fre|quent¦er +s
fre|quent¦ly
fresco
  fres|cos *or*
  fres|coes
fres|coed
fresco secco
fresh +er +est
fresh¦en +s +ed
  +ing
fresh¦er +s
freshet +s
fresh-faced
fresh¦ly
fresh|man
  fresh|men
fresh|ness
fresh|water
  adjective
fresh|woman
  fresh|women
Fres|nel,
  Au|gus|tin Jean
  (French physicist)
fres|nel +s
Fresno (city, USA)

fret
  frets
  fret|ted
  fret|ting
fret|board +s
fret|ful
fret|ful¦ly
fret|ful|ness
fret|less
fret|saw +s
fret|work
Freud, Lu|cian
  (German-born
  British painter)
Freud, Sig|mund
  (Austrian
  psychotherapist)
Freud|ian +s
Freud¦ian|ism
Frey *Scandinavian
  Mythology*
Freya
  (*Scandinavian
  Mythology*; name)
Frey|berg,
  Ber|nard Cyril
  (New Zealand
  general)
Freyr (*Scandinavian
  Mythology*,
  = Frey)
fri|abil|ity
fri|able
fri|able|ness
friar +s (*Religion.*
  △ fryer)
fri|ar¦ly
friar's bal¦sam
fri|ary
  fri¦ar|ies
frib¦ble
  frib¦bles
  frib¦bled
  frib|bling
Fri|bourg (town
  and canton,
  Switzerland)
fri¦can|deau
  fri¦can|deaux
  noun
fri¦can|deau +s
  +ed +ing
  verb
fric¦as|see
  fric¦as|sees
  fric¦as|seed
  fric¦as¦see|ing
frica|tive +s
fric|tion +s
fric|tion¦al
fric|tion ball +s

fric|tion|less
Fri|day +s
fridge +s
fridge-freezer +s
Frie|dan, Betty
  (American
  feminist and
  writer)
Fried|man,
  Mil|ton
  (American
  economist)
Fried|rich,
  Cas|par David
  (German painter)
friend +s +ed +ing
friend|less
friend|lily
friend|li|ness
friend|ly
  friend|lies
  friend|lier
  friend|li|est
Friend|ly Is|lands
  (= Tonga)
Friend|ly So|ci|ety
  Friend|ly
  So|ci|eties
friend|ship +s
frier +s (use fryer.
  ⚠ friar)
Frie|sian +s (cattle.
  ⚠ Frisian)
Fries|land
  (province, the
  Netherlands)
frieze +s
  (decoration; cloth.
  ⚠ freeze)
frig
  frigs
  frigged
  frig|ging
  (*coarse slang*)
frig|ate +s
frig|ate bird +s
Frigga *Scandinavian*
  Mythology
fright +s +ed +ing
fright|en +s +ed
  +ing
fright|en|er +s
fright|en|ing|ly
fright|ful
fright|ful|ly
fright|ful|ness
fri|gid
fri|gid|arium
  fri|gid|ariums *or*
  fri|gid|aria
fri|gid|ity
fri|gid|ly

fri|gid|ness
fri|jo|les
frill +s +ed +ing
frill|ery
  frill|er|ies
fril|li|ness
frill|ing +s
frilly
  frill|ies
  frill|ier
  frilli|est
fringe
  fringes
  fringed
  frin|ging
fringe|less
fringy
Frink, Elisa|beth
  (English sculptor
  and artist)
frip|pery
  frip|per|ies
frip|pet +s
fris|bee +s *Propr.*
Frisch, Karl von
  (Austrian
  zoologist)
Frisch, Max (Swiss
  writer)
Frisch, Otto
  (Austrian-born
  British physicist)
Frisch, Rag|nar
  (Norwegian
  economist)
frisé +s (fabric)
fri|sée +s (lettuce)
Frisia (ancient
  region of NW
  Europe)
Fris|ian +s (of
  Friesland; person;
  language.
  ⚠ Friesian)
Fris|ian Is|lands
  (off NW Europe)
frisk +s +ed +ing
frisk|er +s
fris|ket +s
frisk|ily
friski|ness
frisky
  frisk|ier
  friski|est
fris|son +s
frit
  frits
  frit|ted
  frit|ting
frit-fly
  frit-flies

Frith, Wil|liam
  Pow|ell (British
  painter)
frith +s
fri|til|lary
  fri|til|lar|ies
frit|tata
frit|ter +s +ed
  +ing
fritto misto
fritz (in 'on the
  fritz')
Friuli-Venezia
  Giu|lia (region,
  Italy)
frivol
  friv|ols
  friv|olled *Br.*
  friv|oled *Am.*
  friv|ol|ling *Br.*
  friv|ol|ing *Am.*
fri|vol|ity
  fri|vol|ities
frivo|lous
frivo|lous|ly
frivo|lous|ness
frizz
  frizzes
  frizzed
  friz|zing
friz|zi|ness
friz|zle
  friz|zles
  friz|zled
  friz|zling
friz|zly
frizzy
  frizz|ier
  friz|zi|est
fro (in 'to and fro'.
  ⚠ froe)
Fro|bi|sher,
  Mar|tin (English
  explorer)
frock +s +ed +ing
frock coat +s
froe +s (tool. ⚠ fro)
Froe|bel,
  Fried|rich
  (German
  educationist)
Froe|bel|ian +s
Froe|bel|ism
Frog +s (*offensive*
  French person)
frog +s (animal;
  coat-fastening;
  etc.)
frog|bit +s (plant)
frog|fish
  plural frog|fish *or*
  frog|fishes

frogged
frog|ging +s
Froggy
  Frog|gies
  (*offensive* French
  person)
froggy (like a frog;
  offensive French)
frog|hop|per +s
frog|man
  frog|men
frog|march
frog|marches
frog|marched
frog|march|ing
frog|mouth +s
frog|spawn
froid|eur
fro|ing +s (in 'toing
  and froing')
frolic
  frolics
  frol|icked
  frol|ick|ing
frol|ick|er +s
frol|ic|some
frol|ic|some|ly
frol|ic|some|ness
from
from|age blanc
from|age frais
frond +s
frond|age
Fronde
frond|eur +s
frond|ose
front +s +ed +ing
front|age +s
front|ager +s
front|al
front|al|ly
front bench
  front benches
front|bench|er +s
front door +s
fron|tier +s
fron|tier|less
fron|tiers|man
  fron|tiers|men
fron|tiers|woman
  fron|tiers|women
fron|tis|piece +s
front|less
front|let +s
front line +s *noun*
front-line *attributive*
front|man
  front|men
fronto|gen|esis
fron|to|genet|ic
fron|ton +s
front|ward

front|wards
front-wheel drive
frore
Frost, Rob|ert
  (American poet)
frost +s +ed +ing
frost|bite
frost-bitten
frost-free
frost|ily
frosti|ness
frost|ing +s
frost|less
frost-work
frosty
  frost|ier
  frosti|est
froth +s +ed +ing
froth-blower +s
froth|ily
frothi|ness
frothy
  froth|ier
  frothi|est
frot|tage
frou-frou +s
frow +s
  (Dutchwoman;
  housewife.
  △ Frau)
fro|ward
fro|ward|ly
fro|ward|ness
frown +s +ed +ing
frown|er +s
frown|ing|ly
frowst +s +ed +ing
frowst|er +s
frow|sti|ness
frow|sty
  frow|stier
  frow|sti|est
frow|zi|ness
frowzy
  frow|zier
  frow|zi|est
froze
frozen
fro|zen|ly
fruc|tif|er|ous
fruc|ti|fi|ca|tion +s
fruc|tify
  fruc|ti|fies
  fruc|ti|fied
  fruc|ti|fy|ing
fruc|tose
fruc|tu|ous
fru|gal
fru|gal|ity
fru|gal|ly
fru|gal|ness
fru|giv|or|ous

fruit +s +ed +ing
fruit|age
fruit|ar|ian +s
fruit|bat +s
fruit-body
  fruit-bodies
fruit|cake +s
  (person)
fruit cake +s
  (food)
fruit|er +s
fruit|er|er +s
fruit fly
  fruit flies
fruit|ful
fruit|ful|ly
fruit|ful|ness
fruit|ily
fruiti|ness
fru|ition
fruit juice +s
fruit|less
fruit|less|ly
fruit|less|ness
fruit|let +s
fruit tree +s
fruit|wood +s
fruity
  fruit|ier
  fruiti|est
fru|menty
frump +s
frump|ily
frumpi|ness
frump|ish
frump|ish|ly
frumpy
  frump|ier
  frumpi|est
Frunze (city,
  Kirghizia)
frus|trate
frus|trates
frus|trated
frus|trat|ing
frus|trated|ly
frus|trater +s
frus|trat|ing|ly
frus|tra|tion +s
frust|ule +s
frus|tum
  frusta *or*
  frus|tums
fru|tes|cent
fru|tex
  fru|ti|ces
fru|ti|cose
Fry, Chris|to|pher
  (English writer)
Fry, Eliza|beth
  (English reformer)

fry
  fries
  fried
  fry|ing
Frye, North|rop
  (Canadian literary
  critic)
fryer +s (person
  who fries; device
  for frying. △ friar)
fry|ing pan +s
fry|pan +s
fry-up +s *noun*
Fuad (Egyptian
  kings)
fubsy
  fub|sier
  fub|si|est
Fuchs, Klaus
  (German-born
  British physicist)
fuch|sia +s
fuchs|ine
fuck +s +ed +ing
  (*coarse slang*)
fuck all (*coarse
  slang*)
fuck|er +s (*coarse
  slang*)
fuck-up +s *noun*
  (*coarse slang*)
fu|coid
fucus
  fuci
fud|dle
  fud|dles
  fud|dled
  fud|dling
fuddy-duddy
  fuddy-duddies
fudge
  fudges
  fudged
  fudg|ing
fudge|able
fueh|rer +s (use
  führer)
fuel
  fuels
  fuelled *Br.*
  fueled *Am.*
  fuel|ling *Br.*
  fuel|ing *Am.*
fuel-inject|ed
fuel in|jec|tion
fuel rod +s
Fuen|tes, Car|los
  (Mexican writer)
fug
  fugs
  fugged
  fug|ging

fu|ga|cious
fu|ga|cious|ly
fu|ga|cious|ness
fu|ga|city
fugal
fu|gal|ly
Fu|gard, Athol
  (South African
  playwright)
fuggy
  fug|gier
  fug|gi|est
fu|gi|tive +s
fu|gi|tive|ly
fu|gi|tive|ness
fugle
  fugles
  fugled
  fug|ling
fugle|man
  fugle|men
fugue
  fugues
  fugued
  fu|guing
fu|guist +s
Füh|rer (Hitler)
füh|rer +s (leader)
Fu|jai|rah (state
  and city, UAE)
Fuji, Mount
  (volcano, Japan)
Fu|jian (province,
  China)
Fu|ji|yama
  (Japanese name
  for Mount Fuji)
Fu|kien (= Fujian)
Fu|ku|oka (city,
  Japan)
Fu|lani
  plural Fu|lani *or*
  Fu|la|nis
Ful|bright,
  Wil|liam
  (American
  senator; education
  awards)
ful|crum
  ful|cra *or*
  ful|crums
ful|fil *Br.*
  ful|fils
  ful|filled
  ful|fil|ling
ful|fill *Am.*
  +s +ed +ing
ful|fil|able
ful|fil|er +s
ful|fil|ment *Am.*
  +s
ful|fil|ment *Br.* +s

ful|gent
ful|gur|ation +s
ful|gur|ite
fu|li|gin|ous
full +s +ed +ing
　+er +est
full-back +s
full-blooded
full-blooded|ly
full-blooded|ness
full-blown
full-bodied
full-bottomed
full-color *Am.*
　attributive
full-colour *Br.*
　attributive
full-cream
full dress (formal
　clothes)
full-dress
　(important)
full dress uni|form
Ful|ler,
　Buck|min|ster
　(American
　designer)
Ful|ler, Thomas
　(English cleric and
　historian)
full|er +s
ful|ler|ene +s
full|er's earth
full face *adverbial*
full-face *adjective*
full-fashioned
full-fledged
full-frontal
full-grown
full-hearted
full-hearted|ly
full-hearted|ness
full house
full-length *adjective*
full-mouthed
full|ness
full-page *adjective*
full-scale
full-size *adjective*
full-sized (use full-
　size)
full-time *adjective*
full-timer +s
fully
full-year *attributive*
fully-fashioned
fully-fledged
　attributive
fully grown
ful|mar +s
ful|min|ant

ful|min|ate
ful|min|ates
ful|min|ated
ful|min|at|ing
ful|min|ation +s
ful|min|atory
ful|min|ic
ful|ness (use
　fullness)
ful|some
ful|some|ly
ful|some|ness
Ful|ton, Rob|ert
　(American
　engineer)
ful|ves|cent
ful|vous
fu|ma|role +s
fu|ma|rol|ic
fum|ble
　fum|bles
　fum|bled
　fum|bling
fum|bler +s
fum|bling|ly
fume
　fumes
　fumed
　fum|ing
fume|less
fu|mi|gant +s
fu|mi|gate
　fu|mi|gates
　fu|mi|gated
　fu|mi|gat|ing
fu|mi|ga|tion +s
fu|mi|ga|tor +s
fum|ing|ly
fu|mi|tory
　fu|mi|tor|ies
fumy
　fumi|er
　fumi|est
fun
Fu|na|futi (capital
　of Tuvalu)
fu|nam|bu|list +s
fun|board +s
Fun|chal (capital of
　Madeira)
func|tion +s +ed
　+ing
func|tion|al
func|tion|al|ism
func|tion|al|ist +s
func|tion|al|ity
　func|tion|al|ities
func|tion|al|ly
func|tion|ary
　func|tion|ar|ies
func|tion|less
fund +s +ed +ing

fun|da|ment +s
fun|da|men|tal +s
fun|da|men|tal|
　　ism +s
fun|da|men|tal|ist
　+s
fun|da|men|tal|ity
　fun|da|men|tal|
　　ities
fun|da|men|tal|ly
fund|hold|er +s
fund|hold|ing
fund-raiser +s
fund-raising
fun|dus
　fundi
Fundy, Bay of (on
　E coast of
　Canada)
fu|neb|rial
fu|neral +s
fu|ner|ary
fu|ner|eal
fu|ner|eal|ly
fun|fair +s
fun|gal
fungi
fun|gi|bil|ity
fun|gible
fun|gi|cidal
fun|gi|cide +s
fun|gi|form
fun|gi|stat|ic
fun|gi|stat|ic|al|ly
fun|giv|or|ous
fun|goid
fun|gous *adjective*
fun|gus
　fungi *or* fun|guses
　noun
fu|nicu|lar +s
Funk, Casi|mir
　(Polish-born
　American
　biochemist)
funk +s +ed +ing
fun|kia +s
funk|ily
funki|ness
funky
　funk|ier
　funki|est
fun-lover +s
fun-loving
fun|nel
　fun|nels
　fun|nelled *Br.*
　fun|neled *Am.*
　fun|nel|ling *Br.*
　fun|nel|ing *Am.*
funnel-like
fun|nily

fun|ni|ness
fun|ni|os|ity
　fun|ni|os|ities
funny
　fun|nies
　fun|nier
　fun|ni|est
funny bone +s
funny-face *jocular*
funny-ha-ha
funny man
　funny men
　(clown)
funny-peculiar
fun run +s
fun|ster +s
fur
　furs
　furred
　fur|ring
　(animal hair;
　coating. △ fir)
fur|below +s
fur|bish
　fur|bishes
　fur|bished
　fur|bish|ing
fur|bish|er +s
fur|cate
　fur|cates
　fur|cated
　fur|cat|ing
fur|ca|tion
fur|cula +s
fur|fur|aceous
Fur|ies, the *Greek
　Mythology*
furi|ous
furi|ous|ly
furi|ous|ness
furl +s +ed +ing
furl|able
fur|less
fur|long +s
fur|lough +s
fur|mety
　(= frumenty)
fur|nace
　fur|naces
　fur|naced
　fur|na|cing
Fur|neaux
　Is|lands (off
　Australia)
fur|nish
　fur|nishes
　fur|nished
　fur|nish|ing
fur|nish|er +s
fur|nish|ing +s
fur|ni|ture
furor *Am.*
fur|ore *Br.*

furphy
  fur¦phies
fur¦rier +s (fur-
  dealer; more
  furry)
fur¦riery
fur¦ri¦ness
fur¦row +s +ed
  +ing
fur¦row|less
furrow-slice +s
fur¦rowy
furry
  fur|rier
  fur¦ri|est
  (covered with fur.
  △ firry)
fur seal +s
fur|ther +s +ed
  +ing
fur¦ther|ance
fur¦ther|er +s
fur¦ther|more
fur¦ther|most
fur¦thest
fur¦tive
fur¦tive¦ly
fur¦tive|ness
Furt|wän¦gler,
  Wil|helm
  (German
  conductor)
fur|uncle +s
fu¦run¦cu|lar
fu¦run¦cu|lo¦sis
fu¦run¦cu|lous
Fury
  Fur¦ies
  (Greek
  Mythology)
fury
  fur¦ies
  (anger)
furze
furzy
fus|cous
fuse
  fuses
  fused
  fus¦ing
fuse box
  fuse boxes
fusee Br. +s (Am.
  fuzee)
fusel (oil. △ fusil)
fu¦sel|age +s
fuse|less
Fu¦shun (city,
  China)
fusi|bil|ity
fus¦ible
fu¦si|form

fusil +s (musket.
  △ fusel)
fu¦si|lier +s
fu¦sil|lade
  fu¦sil|lades
  fu¦sil|laded
  fu¦sil|lad¦ing
fu¦silli
fu¦sion +s
fu¦sion|al
fu¦sion|ist +s
fuss
  fusses
  fussed
  fuss|ing
fuss¦er +s
fuss|ily
fussi|ness
fuss|pot +s
fussy
  fuss|ier
  fussi|est
fus¦ta|nella +s
fus|tian
fus|tic
fus¦ti|gate
  fus¦ti|gates
  fus¦ti|gated
  fus¦ti|gat¦ing
fus¦ti|ga¦tion
fus|tily
fusti|ness
fusty
  fus|tier
  fus¦ti|est
fu¦thorc
fu¦tile
fu¦tile|ly
fu¦tili|tar¦ian
fu¦til|ity
  fu¦til|ities
futon +s
fut|tock +s
fu¦ture +s
fu¦ture|less
fu¦tur|ism
fu¦tur|ist +s
fu¦tur|is|tic
fu¦tur|is|tic|al¦ly
fu¦tur|ity
fu¦tur|olo¦gist +s
fu¦tur|ology
Fuxin (city, China)
fuze +s (use fuse)
fuzee Am. +s (Br.
  fusee)
Fu¦zhou (city,
  China)
fuzz
  fuzzes
  fuzzed
  fuzz|ing

fuzz-ball +s
fuzz|box
  fuzz|boxes
fuzz|ily
fuzzi|ness
fuzzy
  fuzz|ies
  fuzz|ier
  fuzzi|est
fuzzy-wuzzy
  fuzzy-wuzzies
  (*offensive*)
F-word +s
fyl¦fot +s
fyrd +s
fytte +s (use fit)

Gg

gab
  gabs
  gabbed
  gab|bing
gab¦ar|dine +s
  (cloth; garment,
  esp. raincoat.
  △ gaberdine)
gab¦ber +s
gab¦ble
  gab¦bles
  gab¦bled
  gab|bling
gab|bler +s
gab¦bro +s
gab¦bro¦ic
gab|broid
gabby
  gab|bier
  gab¦bi|est
gab|elle +s
gab¦er|dine +s
  (former long,
  loose upper
  garment.
  △ gabardine)
Gabès (port,
  Tunisia)
ga¦bion +s
ga¦bion|ade +s
ga¦bion|age
Gable, Clark
  (American actor)
gable +s
gabled
gable end +s
gab¦let +s
Gabo, Naum
  (Russian-born
  American
  sculptor)
Gabon
Gab¦on|ese
  plural Gab¦on|ese
Gabor, Den¦nis
  (Hungarian-born
  British electrical
  engineer)
Gab¦or|one (capital
  of Botswana)
Gab¦riel (*Bible;
  Islam*; man's
  name)
Gab¦ri|elle
  (woman's name)
Gad (Hebrew
  patriarch)

gad
  gads
  gad¦ded
  gad¦ding
  (go about idly etc.;
  in 'by gad')
gad|about +s
Gad|ar¦ene
Gad¦dafi,
  Mu¦am¦mer
  Mu¦ham¦mad al
  (Libyan president)
gad¦fly
  gad|flies
gadget +s
gadget|eer +s
gadget¦ry
gadgety
Gad|hel¦ic
gad|oid +s
gado|lin¦ite
gado|lin¦ium
gad|roon +s
gad|rooned
Gads|den
  Pur|chase (area,
  USA)
gad|wall
  plural gad|wall *or*
  gad|walls
gad|zooks
Gaea (use Gaia)
Gael +s
Gael|dom
Gael¦ic (Celtic.
  ⚠ Gallic)
Gael|tacht +s
Gae¦nor *also*
  Gay¦nor
gaff +s +ed +ing
  (spear; spar; in
  'blow the gaff')
gaffe +s (blunder)
gaf¦fer +s
Gafsa (town,
  Tunisia)
gag
  gags
  gagged
  gag|ging
gaga
Ga|garin, Yuri
  (Russian
  cosmonaut)
gag-bit +s
gage *Am.*
  gages
  gaged
  ga¦ging
  (measure. *Br.*
  gauge)

gage
  gages
  gaged
  ga¦ging
  (pledge;
  greengage;
  position relative to
  wind. ⚠ gauge)
gage|able *Am.* (*Br.*
  gaugeable)
gager *Am.* +s (*Br.*
  gauger)
gag¦gle
  gag¦gles
  gag¦gled
  gag|gling
gag man
  gag men
gag|ster +s
Gaia (*Greek
  Mythology*; theory
  of earth. ⚠ Gaya)
Gaian +s
gai¦ety
  gai|eties
gai|jin
  plural gai|jin
Gail *also* Gale,
  Gayle
gail|lar¦dia +s
gaily
gain +s +ed +ing
gain|able
gain|er +s
gain|ful
gain|ful¦ly
gain|ful|ness
gain|ings
gain|say
  gain|says
  gain|said
  gain|say|ing
gain|say|er +s
Gains|bor|ough,
  Thomas (English
  painter)
'gainst (= against)
gait +s (manner of
  speaking. ⚠ gate)
gai¦ter +s (legging.
  ⚠ geta)
gai¦tered
Gait|skell, Hugh
  (British politician)
gal +s (girl; unit of
  acceleration)
gala +s
gal|ac¦ta|gogue +s
gal|ac¦tic
gal|act|ose
gal¦ago +s
galah +s

Gala|had
  (Arthurian knight)
gal|an¦gal +s
gal|an¦tine +s
gal|anty show +s
Gal|apa¦gos
  Is¦lands (in E.
  Pacific)
Gal|atea *Greek
  Mythology*
Gal|aţi (city,
  Romania)
Gal|atia (ancient
  region, Asia
  Minor)
Gal|atian +s
Gal|axy, the (ours)
gal¦axy
  gal|ax¦ies
Galba (Roman
  emperor)
gal|ba¦num
Gal|braith, John
  Ken|neth
  (Canadian-born
  American
  economist)
Gale *also* Gail,
  Gayle
  (name)
gale +s
galea
  ga¦leae *or* ga¦leas
gal|eate
gal|eated
Galen (Greek
  physician)
ga¦lena
gal|en¦ic
gal¦en|ic¦al
gal|ette +s
galia melon +s
Gal¦ibi
  plural Gal|ibi *or*
  Gal|ibis
Gal|icia
Gal|ician +s
Gali|lean +s
Gali|lee (region,
  ancient Palestine)
Gali|lee, Lake (in
  Israel)
galil|lee +s (church
  porch)
Gali|leo (American
  space probe)
Gali|leo Gali|lei
  (Italian
  astronomer)
gali|ma¦tias
gal¦in|gale +s

gal¦iot +s (use
  galliot)
gali|pot (resin.
  ⚠ gallipot)
gall +s +ed +ing
Galla
  plural **Galla** *or*
  Gallas
gal|lant +s +ed
  +ing
gal|lant¦ly
gal|lant¦ry
  gal¦lant|ries
gall blad|der +s
Galle (port, Sri
  Lanka)
gal|leon +s
gal|le¦ria +s
gal|ler¦ied
gal|lery
  gal|ler¦ies
gal|lery|ite +s
gal¦ley +s
gal|ley proof +s
gal|ley slave +s
gall-fly
  gall-flies
gal|li|am¦bic +s
Gal¦lia
  Nar¦bon|en¦sis
  (province,
  Transalpine Gaul)
gal|li¦ard +s
Gal|lic (Gaulish
  French. ⚠ Gaelic)
gal¦lic (acid)
Gal|lican +s
Gal|lican|ism
gal|lice
Gal|li|cise *Br.* (use
  Gallicize)
Gal|li|cises
Gal|li|cised
Gal|li|cis¦ing
Gal|li|cism +s
Gal|li|cize
Gal|li|cizes
Gal|li|cized
Gal|li|ciz¦ing
Gal|li|formes
gal|li|gas¦kins
gal|li|maufry
  gal|li|mauf¦ries
gal|li|mi¦mus
  plural
  gal|li|mi¦mus *or*
  gal|li|mi¦mus|es
gal|lin|aceous
gall|ing¦ly
gal|li|nule +s
gal|liot +s

Gal|lip|oli
(peninsula,
Turkey)
gal'li|pot +s (small
pot. △ galipot)
gal|lium
gal'li|vant +s +ed
+ing
gal'li|wasp +s
gall|nut +s
Gallo|mania
Gallo|maniac +s
gal'lon +s
gal'lon|age +s
gal|loon +s
gal'lop
  gal|lops
  gal|lopped *Br.*
  gal|loped *Am.*
  gal'lop|ping *Br.*
  gal'lop|ing *Am.*
  (horse's pace.
  △ galop)
gal|lop|er +s
Gallo|phile +s
Gallo|phobe +s
Gallo|pho'bia
Gallo-Roman +s
Gal'lo|way (area,
  Scotland)
gal'lo|way +s
  (cattle)
gal|lows
gall|stone +s
Gal'lup poll +s
gal|lus|es
gall wasp +s
Gal'ois, Éva|riste
  (French
  mathematician;
  theory)
gal'oot +s
galop +s +ed +ing
  (dance. △ gallop)
gal'ore
gal'osh
  gal|oshes
Gals|worthy, John
  (English novelist
  and dramatist)
Gal|tieri,
  Leo|poldo
  For'tu|nato
  (Argentinian
  president)
Gal'ton, Fran|cis
  (English scientist)
gall|umph +s +ed
  +ing
Gal'vani, Luigi
  (Italian anatomist)
gal|van'ic

gal'van|ic|al'ly
gal'van|isa|tion +s
  (use
  galvanization)
gal'van|ise *Br.* (use
  galvanize)
gal|van|ises
gal|van|ised
gal|van|is'ing
gal'van|is'er *Br.* +s
  (use galvanizer)
gal'van|ism
gal'van|ist +s
gal'van|iza|tion +s
gal'van|ize
  gal|van|izes
  gal|van|ized
  gal'van|iz'ing
gal'van|iz'er +s
gal'van|om'eter +s
gal'vano|met'ric
Gal|ves'ton (port,
  USA)
galvo +s
Gal'way (county,
  Republic of
  Ireland)
Gama, Vasco da
  (Portuguese
  explorer)
gamba +s
gam|bade +s
gam|bado
  gam|ba'dos or
  gam|ba'does
Gam'bia (in W.
  Africa. △ Gambier
  Islands)
Gam|bian +s
Gambia River (in
  W. Africa)
gam|bier +s
Gam|bier Is'lands
  (in French
  Polynesia.
  △ Gambia)
gam'bit +s
gam|ble
  gam|bles
  gam|bled
  gam|bling
  (bet. △ gambol)
gam|bler +s
gam|boge
gam|bol
  gam|bols
  gam|bolled *Br.*
  gam|boled *Am.*
  gam'bol|ling *Br.*
  gam|bol|ing *Am.*
  (frolic. △ gamble)
gam|brel +s

game
  games
  gamed
  gam|ing
gamer
gamest
game bird +s
game|book +s
Game Boy +s
  Propr.
game|cock +s
game fish|ing
game|fowl
  plural game|fowl
  or game|fowls
game|keep'er +s
game|keep'ing
gam|elan +s
game'ly
game|ness
game plan +s
gamer +s
game show +s
games|man
  games|men
games'man|ship
game|some
game|some'ly
game|some|ness
games|play'er +s
game|ster +s
gam'et|an'gium
  gam'et|an'gia
gam'ete +s
game the'ory
gam|et'ic
gam'eto|cyte +s
gam'eto|gen'esis
gam'eto|phyte +s
gam'eto|phyt'ic
game-warden +s
gami'ly
gamin +s *male*
gam'ine +s *female*
gami|ness
gaming-house +s
gaming-table +s
gamma +s (Greek
  letter. △ gammer)
gam'ma|dion +s
gam'mer +s (old
  woman.
  △ gamma)
gam'mon +s +ed
  +ing
gammy
  gam|mier
  gam'mi|est
Gamow, George
  (Russian-born
  American
  physicist)

gamp +s
gamut +s
gamy
  gami'er
  gami|est
Ga'na|pati
  Hinduism
Gäncä (city,
  Azerbaijan)
Gance, Abel
  (French film
  director)
Gan'der (town and
  airport, Canada)
gan'der +s +ed
  +ing (male goose;
  look)
Gan'dhi, In'dira
  (Indian prime
  minister)
Gan'dhi,
  Ma'hatma
  (Indian statesman)
Gan'dhi, Rajiv
  (Indian prime
  minister)
Gan'dhi|nagar
  (city, India)
Gan|esha *Hinduism*
gang +s +ed +ing
  (band, group; in
  'gang up'.
  △ gangue)
gang-bang +s +ed
  +ing
gang|board +s
gang'er +s
Gan'ges (river,
  India)
Gan|get'ic
gang|land
gan'gle
  gan'gles
  gan'gled
  gan'gling
gan|gliar
gan'gli|form
gan|glion
gan|glia
gan'gli|on|ated
gan'gli|on'ic
gan|gly
  gan|glier
  gan'gli|est
gang|plank +s
gang rape +s *noun*
gang-rape
  gang-rapes
  gang-raped
  gang-raping
  verb

gan|grene
　gan|grenes
　gan|grened
　gan|gren|ing
gan|gren|ous
gang|sta (music)
gang|ster +s
　(criminal)
gang|ster|ism
Gang|tok (city,
　India)
gangue (earth.
　△ gang)
gang|way +s
gan|is|ter
ganja
gan|net +s
gan|net|ry
　gan|net|ries
gan|oid +s
Gansu (province,
　China)
gant|let *Am.* +s
gan|try
　gan|tries
Gany|mede (*Greek
　Mythology*; moon
　of Jupiter)
gaol *Br.* +s +ed
　+ing (use jail)
gaol|er *Br.* +s (use
　jailer)
gap +s
gape
　gapes
　gaped
　gap|ing
gaper +s
gape|worm +s
gap|ing|ly
gapped
gappy
　gap|pier
　gap|pi|est
gap-toothed
gar +s (fish)
gar|age
　gar|ages
　gar|aged
　gar|aging
garam ma|sala
garb +s +ed +ing
gar|bage
gar|ble
　gar|bles
　gar|bled
　garb|ling
garb|ler +s
Garbo, Greta
　(Swedish actress)
gar|board +s
garb|olo|gist +s

garb|ology
Gar|cía Lorca,
　Fe|de|rico
　(Spanish poet and
　dramatist)
Gar|cía Már|quez,
　Gab|riel
　(Colombian
　novelist)
gar|çon +*s*
Garda
　Gar|dai
　(Irish police)
Garda, Lake (in
　Italy)
Gar|den, the (of
　Epicurus)
gar|den +s +ed
　+ing
gar|den|er +s
gardener-bird +s
gar|den|esque
gar|denia +s
Gard|ner, Erle
　Stan|ley
　(American
　novelist)
Gar|eth
Gar|field, James
　(American
　president)
gar|fish
　plural gar|fish
gar|ganey +s
gar|gan|tuan
gar|get
gar|gle
　gar|gles
　gar|gled
　garg|ling
gar|goyle +s
gar|goyl|ism
Ga|ri|baldi,
　Giu|seppe (Italian
　military leader)
ga|ri|baldi +s
　(blouse; biscuit;
　fish)
gar|ish
gar|ish|ly
gar|ish|ness
Gar|land, Judy
　(American singer
　and actress)
gar|land +s
　(wreath; wreathe)
gar|lic
gar|licky
gar|ment +s
gar|ment|ed
Garmo, Mount
　(former name of

Garmo (*cont.*)
　Communism
　Peak)
gar|ner +s +ed
　+ing
gar|net +s
gar|nish
　gar|nishes
　gar|nished
　gar|nish|ing
gar|nish|ee
　gar|nish|ees
　gar|nish|eed
　gar|nish|ee|ing
gar|nish|ing +s
gar|nish|ment +s
gar|ni|ture +s
Ga|ronne (river,
　France)
gar|otte *Br.* (use
　garrotte)
　gar|ottes
　gar|ot|ted
　gar|ot|ting
　(*Am.* garrote)
Ga|roua (river port,
　Cameroon)
gar|pike
　plural gar|pike *or*
　gar|pikes
Gar|ret (name)
gar|ret +s (attic)
gar|ret|eer +s
Gar|rick, David
　(English actor)
gar|rison +s +ed
　+ing
gar|rotte *Br.*
　gar|rottes
　gar|rott|ed
　gar|rott|ing
　(*Am.* garrote)
gar|rot|ter +s
gar|ru|lity
gar|rul|ous
gar|rul|ous|ly
gar|rul|ous|ness
Garry *also* Gary
gar|rya +s
gar|ter +s +ed +ing
Garth (name)
garth +s (open
　space in cloisters)
Ga|ruda *Hinduism*
Gar|vey, Mar|cus
　(Jamaican
　political activist)
Gary *also* Garry
gas
　gases
　gassed
　gas|sing

gas|bag +s
Gas|con +s (native
　of Gascony)
gas|con +s
　(braggart)
gas|con|ade +s
Gas|cony (former
　region, France)
gas-cooled
gas|eous
gas|eous|ness
gas field +s
gas fire +s
gas-fired
gash
　gashes
　gashed
　gash|ing
gas|hold|er +s
gas|ifi|ca|tion
gas|ify
　gasi|fies
　gasi|fied
　gasi|fy|ing
Gas|kell, Mrs
　Eliza|beth
　(English novelist)
gas|ket +s
gas|kin +s
gas|light +s
gas|lit
gas|man
　gas|men
gas mask +s
gaso|hol
gas|olene +s (use
　gasoline)
gas|oline +s
gas|om|eter +s
gasp +s +ed +ing
gasp|er +s
gas|per|eau
　gas|per|eaus *or*
　gas|per|eaux
gas-permeable
Gas|pra (asteroid)
gas-proof
gas ring +s
Gas|sendi, Pierre
　(French
　astronomer and
　philosopher)
Gas|ser, Her|bert
　Spen|cer
　(American
　physiologist)
gas|ser +s
gas|si|ness
gas sta|tion +s
gassy
　gas|sier
　gas|si|est

Gast|ar|bei|ter
  plural
  Gast|ar|bei|ter *or*
  Gast|ar|bei|ters
gas|tero|pod +s
  (use gastropod)
gast|haus
  gast|häuser
gast|hof
  gast|hofs or
  gast|höfe
gas-tight
gas|trec|tomy
  gas|trec|tomies
gas|tric
gas|tri|tis
gas|tro|en|ter|ic
gas|tro|en|ter|itis
gas|tro|entero|
      logic|al
gas|tro|enter|
      olo|gist +s
gas|tro|enter|
      ology
gas|tro|intest|inal
gas|tro|lith +s
gas|tro|nome +s
gas|tro|nom|ic
gas|tro|nom|ic|al
gas|tro|nom|ic|
      al|ly
gas|tron|omy
gas|tro|pod +s
gas|trop|odous
gas|tro|scope +s
gas|trula
  gas|tru|lae
gas|works
gat +s (gun.
  △ ghat)
gate
  gates
  gated
  gat|ing
  (barrier etc.;
  confine. △ gait)
gat|eau
  gat|eaux *or*
  gat|eaus
gate|crash
  gate|crashes
  gate|crashed
  gate|crash|ing
gate|crash|er +s
gate|fold +s
gate|house +s
gate|keep|er +s
gate|leg +s
gate|legged
gate|man
  gate|men
gate money

gate|post +s
Gates, Bill
  (American
  computer
  entrepreneur)
Gates|head (town,
  England)
gate valve +s
gate|way +s
gather +s +ed +ing
gath|er|er +s
gath|er|ing +s
Gat|ling +s
GATT (= General
  Agreement on
  Tariffs and Trade)
Gat|wick (airport,
  England)
gauche
gauche|ly
gauche|ness
gauch|erie +s
gau|cho +s
gaud +s
Gaudí, An|tonio
  (Spanish architect)
Gaudier-Brzeska,
  Henri (French
  sculptor)
gaud|ily
gaudi|ness
gaudy
  gau|dies
  gaud|ier
  gaud|iest
gauge *Br.*
  gauges
  gauged
  gauging
  (measure. *Am.*
  gage. △ gage)
gauge|able *Br.* (*Am.*
  gageable)
gauger *Br.* +s (*Am.*
  gager)
Gau|guin, Paul
  (French painter)
Gau|hati (city,
  India)
Gaul (ancient
  region, Europe)
gau|leiter +s
Gaul|ish
Gaulle, Charles de
  (French
  statesman)
Gaull|ism
Gaull|ist +s
Gaull|oise +s *Propr.*
gault
gaul|theria +s

Gaunt, John of
  (son of Edward III
  of England)
gaunt +er +est
gaunt|let +s
gaunt|ly
gaunt|ness
gaun|try
  gaun|tries
gaur +s
Gauss, Karl
  Fried|rich
  (German
  mathematician
  and physicist)
gauss
  plural gauss *or*
  gausses
Gauss|ian
Gau|tama (family
  name of Buddha)
gauze +s
gauz|ily
gauzi|ness
gauzy
  gauz|ier
  gauzi|est
Gav|as|kar, Sunil
  (Indian cricketer)
gave
gavel
  gavels
  gav|elled *Br.*
  gav|eled *Am.*
  gav|el|ling *Br.*
  gav|el|ling *Am.*
ga|vial +s
Gavin
ga|votte +s
Ga|wain (Arthurian
  knight)
Gawd (= God in
  exclamations)
gawk +s +ed +ing
gawk|ily
gawki|ness
gawk|ish
gawky
  gawk|ier
  gawki|est
gawp +s +ed +ing
gawp|er +s
Gay, John (English
  poet and
  dramatist)
Gay *also* Gaye
  (name)
gay +s +er +est
  (cheerful;
  homosexual)
Gaya (city, India.
  △ Gaia)

gayal +s
Gaye *also* Gay
gay|ety *Am.* (use
  gaiety)
Gayle *also* Gail
Gay-Lussac,
  Jo|seph Louis
  (French chemist
  and physicist)
gay|ness
Gay|nor *also*
  Gae|nor
gaz|ania +s
Ga|zan|kulu
  (former homeland,
  South Africa)
gazar +s
Gaza Strip (coastal
  territory, SE
  Mediterranean)
gaze
  gazes
  gazed
  gaz|ing
gaz|ebo +s
gaz|elle +s
gazer +s
gaz|ette
  gaz|ettes
  gaz|et|ted
  gaz|et|ting
gaz|et|teer +s
Gazi|an|tep (city,
  Turkey)
gaz|pa|cho +s
gaz|ump +s +ed
  +ing
gaz|ump|er +s
  noun
gaz|un|der +s +ed
  +ing *verb*
Gdańsk (port,
  Poland)
Gdy|nia (port,
  Poland)
Ge (*Greek
  Mythology,*
  = Gaia)
gean +s (cherry)
gear +s +ed +ing
gear|box
  gear|boxes
gear change +s
gear|ing
gear lever +s
gear|stick +s
gear|wheel +s
Geber (Arab
  chemist)
gecko
  geckos *or*
  geckoes

gee
  gees
  geed
  gee¦ing
gee-gee +s
geek +s
Gee|long (port, Australia)
geese
gee-string +s (use G-string)
Ge'ez (language)
gee¦zer +s (person. △ geyser)
Ge|henna (hell)
Geh¦rig, Lou (American baseball player)
Gei¦ger, Hans Wil|helm (German nuclear physicist)
Gei¦ger count¦er +s
Gei¦kie, Archi|bald (Scottish geologist)
gei¦sha
  plural gei¦sha or gei¦shas
Geiss|ler tube +s
Gejiu (city, China)
Geju (use Gejiu)
gel
  gels
  gelled
  gel|ling (semi-solid; form jel. △ jell)
gel¦ada
  plural gel¦ada or gel|adas
gel|atin +s (in technical use)
gel|atine +s (generally)
gel¦at¦in|isa¦tion Br. (use gelatinization)
gel¦at¦in|ise Br. (use gelatinize)
  gel¦at¦in|ises
  gel¦at¦in|ised
  gel¦at¦in|is¦ing
gel¦at¦in|iza¦tion
gel¦at¦in|ize
  gel¦at¦in|izes
  gel¦at¦in|ized
  gel¦at¦in|iz¦ing
gel¦at¦in|ous
gel¦at¦in|ous¦ly

gel|ation
gel¦ato
  gel¦ati or gel¦atis or gel|atos
geld +s +ed +ing
Gel|der|land (province, the Netherlands)
geld|ing +s
gelid
gel¦ig|nite
Gell-Mann, Mur¦ray (American physicist)
gelly (= gelignite. △ jelly)
gel¦se|mium
Gel¦sen|kir¦chen (city, Germany)
gem
  gems
  gemmed
  gem|ming
Gem¦ara Judaism
Gem|ayel, Pierre (Lebanese political leader)
gem|in|al
gem|in|al¦ly
gemin|ate
  gemin|ates
  gemin|ated
  gemin|at¦ing
gemin|ation
Gem¦ini (constellation; sign of zodiac)
Gemi|nian +s
Gem|in|ids (meteor shower)
gem|like
Gemma also Jemma (name)
gemma
  gem¦mae (cellular body)
gem|ma¦tion
gem|mif¦er¦ous
gem|mip|ar¦ous
gem|molo¦gist +s
gem|mol¦ogy
gem|mule +s
gemmy (having gems. △ jemmy)
gems|bok +s
gem|stone +s
ge¦müt|lich
gen
  gens

gen (cont.)
  genned
  gen|ning
genco +s
gen|darme +s
gen|darm|erie +s
gen|der +s
gen|dered
Gene (man's name. △ Jean)
gene +s (Biology. △ jean, jeans)
ge|nea|logic¦al
ge|nea|logic|al¦ly
ge|neal|ogise Br. (use genealogize)
ge|neal|ogises
ge|neal|ogised
ge|neal|ogis¦ing
ge|neal|ogist +s
ge|neal|ogize
  ge|neal|ogizes
  ge|neal|ogized
  ge|neal|ogiz¦ing
ge|neal|ogy
  ge|neal|ogies
gen¦era
gen|er|able
gen|eral +s
gen|er|al|is| abil¦ity Br. (use generalizability)
gen|er|al|is|able Br. (use generalizable)
gen|er|al|isa¦tion Br. +s (use generalization)
gen|er|al|ise Br. (use generalize)
  gen|er|al|ises
  gen|er|al|ised
  gen|er|al|is¦ing
gen|er|al|iser Br. +s (use generalizer)
gen|er|al|is|simo +s
gen|er|al|ist +s
gen|er|al|ity
  gen|er|al|ities
gen|er|al|iz| abil¦ity
gen|er|al|iz|able
gen|er|al|iza¦tion +s
gen|er|al|ize
  gen|er|al|izes
  gen|er|al|ized
  gen|er|al|iz¦ing
gen|er|al|izer Am. +s

gen|er|al¦ly
gen|er|al|ness
general-purpose adjective
gen|eral
  sec|re¦tary
  gen|eral
  sec|re¦tar¦ies
gen|er|al|ship +s
gen|er|ate
  gen|er|ates
  gen|er|ated
  gen|er|at¦ing
gen|er|ation +s
gen|er|ation|al
gen|era¦tive
gen|er|ator +s
gen|er¦ic
gen|er¦ic|al¦ly
gen|er|os¦ity
  gen|er|os¦ities
gen|er¦ous
gen|er¦ous¦ly
gen|er¦ous|ness
Gen|esis Bible
gen|esis
Genet, Jean (French writer)
genet +s (catlike mammal. △ jennet)
gen|et¦ic
gen|et¦ic|al¦ly
gen|eti|cist +s
gen|et|ics
Gen|ette also Jan|ette, Jean|ette, Jean|nette (name)
ge|nette +s (catlike mammal; use genet. △ jennet)
Gen|eva (city, Switzerland)
gen|eva (gin)
gen|ever +s
Gene|vieve
Gen|ghis Khan (founder of Mongol empire)
gen¦ial
geni|al¦ity
geni|al¦ly
genic
genie
  genii or gen¦ies
genii (plural of genie and genius)
gen|ista +s
geni|tal +s
geni|talia

geni|tival
geni|tival|ly
geni|tive +s
genito-urinary
ge|nius
  ge|niuses
  (exceptional
  ability; person
  with this)
ge|nius
  ge|niuses *or* genii
  (spirit; influence)
ge|ni|zah +s
Genoa (port, Italy;
  cake)
genoa +s (sail)
geno|cidal
geno|cide +s
Geno|ese
  plural Geno|ese
gen|ome +s
geno|type +s
geno|typ|ic
genre +s
gens
  gen|tes
Gent (Flemish
  name for Ghent)
gent +s
gen|teel
gen|teel|ism
gen|teel|ly
gen|teel|ness
gen|tes
gen|tian +s
Gen|tile +s (non-
  Jewish; non-Jew)
gen|tile +s
  (indicating
  nationality; such a
  word)
Gen|tile da
  Fab|ri|ano
  (Italian painter)
gen|til|ity
  gen|til|ities
Gen|ting
  High|lands (hill
  resort, Malaysia)
gen|tle
  gen|tles
  gen|tled
  gent|ling
  gent|ler
  gent|lest
gentle|folk
gentle|man
  gentle|men
gentleman-at-
  arms
  gentlemen-at-
  arms

gentle|man
  farm|er +s
gentle|man|li|ness
gentle|man|ly
gentle|man's
  agree|ment +s
gentle|men's
  agree|ment +s
  (use gentleman's
  agreement)
gentle|ness
gentle|woman
  gentle|women
gen|tly
gen|too +s
gen|tri|fi|ca|tion
gen|tri|fier +s
gen|tri|fy
  gen|tri|fies
  gen|tri|fied
  gen|tri|fy|ing
gen|try
Gents, the (men's
  lavatory)
genu|flect +s +ed
  +ing
genu|flec|tion +s
genu|flect|or +s
genu|flect|ory
genu|flex|ion *Br.*
  +s (use
  genuflection)
genu|ine
genu|ine|ly
genu|ine|ness
genus
  gen|era
geo|bot|an|ist +s
geo|bot|any
geo|cen|tric
geo|cen|tric|al|ly
geo|chem|ical
geo|chem|ist +s
geo|chem|is|try
geo|chrono|
          logic|al
geo|chrono|lo|gist
  +s
geo|chron|ology
geode +s
geo|des|ic
geo|des|ist +s
geo|desy
geo|det|ic (use
  geodesic)
geo|dic
Geoff *also* Jeff
Geof|frey *also*
  Jef|frey
Geof|frey of
  Mon|mouth
  (British chronicler)

geog|raph|er +s
geo|graph|ic
geo|graph|ic|al
geo|graph|ic|al|ly
geog|raphy
  geog|raph|ies
geoid +s
geo|logic
geo|logic|al
geo|logic|al|ly
geolo|gise *Br.* (use
  geologize)
  geolo|gises
  geolo|gised
  geolo|gis|ing
geolo|gist +s
geolo|gize
  geolo|gizes
  geolo|gized
  geolo|giz|ing
geol|ogy
geo|mag|net|ic
geo|mag|net|ic|
           al|ly
geo|mag|net|ism
geo|mancy
geo|man|tic
geom|eter +s
geo|met|ric
geo|met|ric|al
geo|met|ric|al|ly
geom|etri|cian +s
geo|met|rid +s
  (moth)
geom|etrise *Br.*
  (use geometrize)
  geom|etrises
  geom|etrised
  geom|etris|ing
geom|etrize
  geom|etrizes
  geom|etrized
  geom|etriz|ing
geom|etry
  geom|etries
geo|mor|pho|
          logic|al
geo|morph|
      olo|gist +s
geo|morph|ology
ge|oph|agy
geo|phone +s
geo|phys|ic|al
geo|phys|ic|al|ly
geo|physi|cist +s
geo|phys|ics
geo|pol|it|ical
geo|pol|it|ic|al|ly
geo|pol|it|ician +s
geo|pol|it|ics
Geor|die +s

George (British
  kings)
George (patron
  saint of England)
George (automatic
  pilot)
George Cross
  George Crosses
George|town
  (capital of
  Guyana)
George Town
  (capital of the
  Cayman Islands)
George Town
  (port, Malaysia)
Geor|gette (name)
geor|gette +s
  (fabric)
Geor|gia (country,
  SE Europe; state,
  USA; name)
Geor|gian +s
Geor|giana
Geor|gie
Geor|gina
geo|science +s
geo|sci|en|tist +s
geo|sphere +s
geo|sta|tion|ary
geo|stroph|ic
geo|syn|chron|ous
geo|tech|nic|al
geo|ther|mal
geo|ther|mal|ly
geo|trop|ic
geo|trop|ism
Gera (city,
  Germany)
Ger|aint
Ger|ald
Ger|ald|ine
Ger|ald|ton (port,
  Australia)
ge|ra|nium +s
Ger|ard *also*
  Ger|rard
ger|bera +s
ger|bil +s
ger|enuk
  plural ger|enuk *or*
  ger|enuks
ger|fal|con +s (use
  gyrfalcon)
geri +s
geri|at|ric +s
geria|tri|cian +s
geri|at|rics
geria|trist +s
Gé|ri|cault,
  Théo|dore
  (French painter)

germ+s
Ger|maine
Ger|man+s (from
  Germany)
ger|man (having
  same parents.
  ⚠ germen,
  germon)
Ger|man Bight
  (shipping area,
  North Sea)
ger|man|der+s
ger|mane
ger|mane|ly
ger|mane|ness
Ger|man|ic (having
  German
  characteristics
  etc.; language)
ger|man|ic
  (*Chemistry* of
  germanium)
Ger|mani|cism+s
Ger|man|isa|tion
  Br. (use
  Germanization)
Ger|man|ise *Br.*
  (use Germanize)
  Ger|man|ises
  Ger|man|ised
  Ger|man|is|ing
Ger|man|iser *Br.*
  +s (use
  Germanizer)
Ger|man|ism+s
Ger|man|ist+s
ger|ma|nium
Ger|man|iza|tion
Ger|man|ize
  Ger|man|izes
  Ger|man|ized
  Ger|man|iz|ing
Ger|man|izer+s
Ger|man mea|sles
ger|man|ous
Ger|man shepherd
  +s
Ger|man sil|ver
Ger|many
  Ger|manies
germ cell+s
ger|men+s
  (*Botany.*
  ⚠ German,
  german, germon)
ger|mi|cidal
ger|mi|cide+s
ger|min|al
ger|min|al|ly
ger|min|ant
ger|min|ate
  ger|min|ates

ger|min|ate (*cont.*)
  ger|min|ated
  ger|min|at|ing
ger|min|ation
ger|mina|tive
ger|min|ator+s
Ger|mis|ton (town,
  South Africa)
ger|mon
  plural ger|mon *or*
  ger|mons
  (fish. ⚠ German,
  german, germen)
germy
  germ|ier
  germi|est
Ger|on|imo
  (Apache chief)
ger|on|toc|racy
  ger|on|toc|ra|cies
ger|on|to|logic|al
ger|on|tolo|gist+s
ger|on|tol|ogy
Ger|rard *also*
  Ger|ard
Gerry *also* Jerry
ger|ry|man|der+s
  +ed +ing
ger|ry|man|der|er
  +s
Gersh|win,
  George
  (American
  composer and
  pianist)
Ger|trude
ger|und+s
ger|und|ial
ger|und|ival
ger|und|ive+s
Ger|vaise *also*
  Ger|vase
Ger|vase *also*
  Ger|vaise
gesso
ges|soes
ges|ta|gen+s
ges|ta|gen|ic
ge|stalt+s
ge|stalt|ism
ge|stalt|ist+s
Ge|stapo (Nazi
  German secret
  police)
ges|tate
  ges|tates
  ges|tated
  ges|tat|ing
ges|ta|tion
ges|ta|tor|ial
ges|ticu|late
  ges|ticu|lates

ges|ticu|late (*cont.*)
  ges|ticu|lated
  ges|ticu|lat|ing
ges|ticu|la|tion+s
ges|ticu|la|tive
ges|ticu|la|tor+s
ges|ticu|la|tory
ges|tural
ges|ture
  ges|tures
  ges|tured
  ges|tur|ing
ges|tur|er+s
ge|sund|heit
get
  gets
  got
  get|ting
  got *or*
  got|ten *Am.*
geta (Japanese
  shoes. ⚠ gaiter)
get-at-able
get|away+s
Geth|sem|ane,
  Gar|den of (in
  Jerusalem)
get-out+s *noun*
  and adjective
get-rich-quick
get|table
get|ter+s
get-together+s
Getty, J. Paul
  (American
  industrialist)
Gettys|burg (town,
  USA)
get-up+s *noun*
get-up-and-go
geum+s
gew|gaw+s
Ge|würz|tram|iner
  +s
gey|ser+s (hot
  spring; water
  heater. ⚠ geezer)
Ghana
Ghan|aian+s
ghar|ial+s
gharry
  ghar|ries
ghast|lily
ghast|li|ness
ghastly
  ghast|lier
  ghast|li|est
ghat+s (flight of
  river-steps etc.
  ⚠ gat)

Ghats, East|ern
  and West|ern
  (mountains, India)
ghaut+s (use ghat)
Ghazi+s
Ghazia|bad (city,
  India)
Ghaz|na|vid+s
ghee
Gheg
  plural Gheg *or*
  Ghegs
Ghent (city,
  Belgium)
ghe|rao+s
gher|kin+s
ghetto+s *noun*
ghetto
  ghet|toes
  ghet|toed
  ghetto|ing
  verb
ghetto blast|er+s
ghetto|ise *Br.* (use
  ghettoize)
  ghetto|ises
  ghetto|ised
  ghetto|is|ing
ghetto|ize
  ghetto|izes
  ghetto|ized
  ghetto|iz|ing
ghi (use ghee)
Ghib|el|line+s
  (Italian history)
Ghib|el|lin|ism
Ghi|berti,
  Lor|enzo
  (Florentine
  sculptor)
ghil|lie+s (use
  gillie)
Ghir|lan|daio
  (Italian painter)
ghost+s +ed +ing
ghost|bust|er+s
ghost|bust|ing
  noun
ghost|like
ghost|li|ness
ghost|ly
  ghost|lier
  ghost|li|est
ghost story
  ghost stor|ies
ghost town+s
ghost word+s
ghost-write
  ghost-writes
  ghost-wrote
  ghost-writing
  ghost-written

ghost-writer +s
ghoul +s
ghoul|ish
ghoul|ish|ly
ghoul|ish|ness
Ghul|ghu|leh
    (ancient city,
    Afghanistan)
ghyll +s (use gill)
Gia|co|metti,
    Al|berto (Swiss
    sculptor and
    painter)
giant +s
giant|ess
    giant|esses
giant|ism
giant-killer +s
giant-killing
giant-like
Giant's
    Cause|way
    (rocks, Northern
    Ireland)
gia|our +s (offensive)
Giap, Vo Ngu|yen
    (Vietnamese
    defence minister)
giar|dia|sis
Gib (= Gibraltar)
gib +s (bolt, wedge,
    etc. △ jib)
gib|ber +s +ed
    +ing (speak
    incoherently;
    boulder. △ jibba,
    jibber)
gib|ber|el|lin
gib|ber|ish
gib|bet +s +ed
    +ing
Gib|bon, Ed|ward
    (English historian)
gib|bon +s
Gib|bons,
    Grin|ling (English
    sculptor)
gib|bos|ity
gib|bous
gib|bous|ly
gib|bous|ness
Gibbs, James
    (Scottish
    architect)
Gibbs, Jo|siah
    Wil|lard
    (American
    physical chemist)
gibe
    gibes
    gibed
    gib|ing

gibe (cont.)
    (taunt. △ jibe,
    gybe)
giber +s
gib|lets
Gib|ral|tar
Gib|ral|tar|ian +s
Gib|son, Al|thea
    (American tennis
    player)
Gib|son Des|ert (in
    Australia)
Gib|son girl +s
gid|di|ly
gid|di|ness
giddy
    gid|dies
    gid|died
    giddy|ing
    gid|dier
    gid|di|est
giddy-up
Gide, André
    (French writer)
Gid|eon (Bible
    Israelite leader;
    name)
Gid|eon bible +s
gie
    gies
    gied
    gie|ing
    gien
Giel|gud, John
    (English actor)
GIFT (= gamete
    intrafallopian
    transfer)
gift +s +ed +ing
gift|ed|ly
gift|ed|ness
gift-horse +s
gift token +s
gift|ware
gift|wrap +s noun
gift-wrap
    gift-wraps
    gift-wrapped
    gift-wrapping
    verb
Gifu (city, Japan)
gig
    gigs
    gigged
    gig|ging
giga|byte +s
giga|flop +s
giga|meter Am. +s
giga|metre Br. +s
gi|gant|esque
gi|gan|tic
gi|gan|tic|al|ly

gi|gant|ism
Gi|gan|to|pith|ecus
giga|watt +s
gig|gle
    gig|gles
    gig|gled
    gig|gling
gig|gler +s
gig|gli|ness
gig|gly
    gig|glier
    gig|gli|est
Gigli, Ben|ia|mino
    (Italian singer)
GIGO (= garbage
    in, garbage out)
gig|olo +s
gigot +s (meat;
    sleeve)
gigue +s
Gijón (port, Spain)
Gila mon|ster +s
Gil|bert,
    Hum|phrey
    (English explorer)
Gil|bert, Wil|liam
    (English scientist)
Gil|bert, W. S.
    (English librettist)
Gil|bert
Gil|bert and
    El|lice Is|lands
    (in Pacific Ocean)
Gil|bert|ian
Gil|bert Is|lands
    (now part of
    Kiribati)
gild +s +ed +ing
    (cover with gold.
    △ guild)
gild|er +s (person
    who gilds.
    △ guilder)
Giles also Gyles
gilet +s
gil|gai +s
Gil|ga|mesh
    (legendary
    Sumerian king)
Gil|git (town and
    district, Pakistani
    Kashmir)
Gill, Eric (English
    sculptor etc.)
Gill also Jill
    (name)
gill +s +s +ed +ing
gil|la|roo
    plural gil|la|roo or
    gil|la|roos
gill cover +s
gilled

Gil|les|pie, Dizzy
    (American jazz
    trumpeter)
Gil|lian also Jil|lian
gil|lie +s
Gil|ling|ham
    (town, England)
gil|lion
    plural gil|lion or
    gil|lions
gill-net +s
Gilly also Jilly
gilly|flower +s
gilt +s (past tense
    and past participle
    of gild; gold layer;
    government
    security. △ guilt)
gilt-edged
gilt|wood
gim|bal
    gim|bals
    gim|balled
    gim|bal|ling
gim|crack +s
gim|crack|ery
gim|cracky
gim|let +s
gim|mick +s
gim|mick|ry
gim|micky
gimp +s (lame
    person or leg.
    △ guimp, gymp)
gin
    gins
    ginned
    gin|ning
Gina
ging +s
gin|ger +s +ed
    +ing
gin|ger|bread +s
gin|ger|li|ness
gin|ger|ly
gin|gery
ging|ham +s
gin|gili
gin|giva
    gin|gi|vae
gin|gival
gin|gi|vitis
gingko (use
    ginkgo)
ging|kos or
    ging|koes
gin|gly|mus
    gin|glymi
gink +s
ginkgo
    gink|gos or
    gink|goes

gin¦ner +s
Ginny
gi¦nor|mous
Gins|berg, Allen
  (American poet)
gin|seng
Gio|conda, La
Gio|litti,
  Gio|vanni (Italian
  statesman)
Gior|gione (Italian
  painter)
Giotto (European
  space probe)
Giotto di
  Bon|done (Italian
  painter)
Gio|vanni de'
  Med¦ici (Pope
  Leo X)
gippy (tummy)
gipsy (use gypsy)
  gip|sies
gir|affe +s
gir|an|dole +s
gira|sol +s
gira|sole +s (use
  girasol)
gird
  girds
  gird¦ed or girt
  gird|ing
  (encircle; fasten)
gird +s +ed +ing
  (jeer)
gird¦er +s
gir¦dle
  gir¦dles
  gir¦dled
  gird|ling
girl +s
girl Fri¦day +s
girl|friend +s
Girl Guide +s
  (former name for a
  Guide)
girl|hood +s
girlie +s (noun;
  also in 'girlie
  magazine')
girl|ish
girl|ish¦ly
girl¦ish|ness
Girl Scout +s
girly (girlish)
girn +s +ed +ing
  (use gurn)
girn¦er +s (use
  gurner)
giro +s (credit
  transfer. △ gyro)
giro
  giroes
  giroed

giro (cont.)
  giro|ing
  (pay by giro.
  △ gyro)
Gir|onde (estuary,
  France)
Gir¦on|din +s
Gir¦ond|ist +s
girt +s +ed +ing
girth +s +ed +ing
Gis|borne (port,
  New Zealand)
Giscard d'Estaing,
  Val|éry (French
  statesman)
Gis|elle
Gish, Lil|lian
  (American
  actress)
gismo +s
Gis|sing, George
  (English writer)
gist +s
git +s
gîte +s
Gi¦tega (town,
  Burundi)
git|tern +s
give
  gives
  gave
  giv|ing
  given
give|able
give-away +s noun
  and adjective
given +s
giver +s
Giza, El (city,
  Egypt)
gizmo +s (use
  gismo)
giz|zard +s
gla|bella
  gla¦bel|lae
gla|bel|lar
glab|rous
glacé
gla|cial
gla¦ci|al¦ly
gla¦ci|ated
gla¦ci|ation +s
gla|cier +s
gla¦cio|logic|al
gla¦ci|olo¦gist +s
gla¦ci|ology
gla|cis
  plural gla¦cis
glad
  glads
  glad|ded
  glad|ding

glad (cont.)
  glad|der
  glad|dest
glad|den +s +ed
  +ing (make glad.
  △ gladdon)
glad|den¦er +s
glad|die +s
glad|don +s
  (flower.
  △ gladden)
glade +s
glad hand noun
glad-hand +s +ed
  +ing verb
glad-hander +s
gladi|ator +s
gladia|tor¦ial
gladi|olus
  gladi|oli or
  gladi|olus¦es
glad¦ly
glad|ness
glad|some
Glad|stone,
  Wil|liam Ewart
  (British prime
  minister)
Glad|stone bag +s
Gladys
Gla¦go|lit¦ic
glair (white of egg.
  △ glare)
glaire (use glair.
  △ glare)
glair|eous
glairy
glaive +s
glam
  glams
  glammed
  glam|ming
glamor Am. (use
  glamour)
Gla|mor¦gan
  (former county,
  Wakes)
glam¦or|isa¦tion
  Br. (use
  glamorization)
glam¦or|ise Br. (use
  glamorize)
glam¦or|ises
glam¦or|ised
glam¦or|is¦ing
glam¦or|iza¦tion
glam¦or|ize
  glam¦or|izes
  glam¦or|ized
  glam¦or|iz¦ing
glam¦or|ous

glam¦or|ous¦ly
glam|our
glam¦our|isa¦tion
  (use
  glamorization)
glam¦our|ise (use
  glamorize)
glam¦our|iza¦tion
  (use
  glamorization)
glam¦our|ize (use
  glamorize)
glam¦our|ous (use
  glamorous)
glam¦our|ous¦ly
  (use glamorously)
glance
  glances
  glanced
  glan¦cing
glan|cing¦ly
gland +s
glan|dered
glan|der|ous
glan|ders
glan|du|lar
gland|ule +s
glans
  glan|des
glare
  glares
  glared
  glar¦ing
  (look angrily or
  fixedly. △ glair,
  glaire)
glar¦ing¦ly
glar¦ing|ness
glary
Glas|gow (city,
  Scotland)
glas|nost
Glass, Philip
  (American
  composer)
glass
  glasses
  glassed
  glass|ing
glass-blower +s
glass-blowing
glass cloth (fabric
  made of glass)
glass-cloth +s (for
  drying glasses;
  abrasive)
glass cut¦ter +s
glass fibre
glass|ful +s
glass-gall
glass|house +s

glassie +s *noun*
  (use glassy)
glass|ily
glass|ine
glassi|ness
glass|less
glass|like
glass|maker +s
glass-making
glass|paper
glass snake +s
  (snakelike lizard.
  ⚠ grass snake)
glass|ware
glass wool
glass|work (glass
  objects)
glass|works
  (factory)
glass|wort +s
glassy
  glass|ies
  glass|ier
  glassi|est
Glas|ton|bury
  (town, England)
Glas|we|gian +s
Glau|ber's salt
Glau|ber's salts
  (use Glauber's
  salt)
glau|coma
glau|comat|ous
glau|cous
glaze
  glazes
  glazed
  glaz|ing
glazer +s
glaz|ier +s
glaz|iery
Glaz|unov,
  Alex|an|der
  (Russian
  composer)
glazy
gleam +s +ed +ing
gleam|ing|ly
gleamy
glean +s +ed +ing
glean|er +s
glean|ings
glebe +s
glee +s
glee|ful
glee|ful|ly
glee|ful|ness
glee|some
gleet
Gleich|schal|tung
Glen *also* **Glenn**
glen +s

Glen|coe (glen,
  Scotland)
Glenda
Glen|dower,
  Owen (Welsh
  prince)
Glen|eagles (valley
  and golf course,
  Scotland)
glen|garry
  glen|gar|ries
Glen More (valley,
  Scotland)
Glenn *also* **Glen**
glen|oid cav|ity
  glen|oid cav|ities
Glen|rothes (town,
  Scotland)
Glenys
gley +s
glia +s
glial
glib
  glib|ber
  glib|best
glib|ly
glib|ness
glide
  glides
  glided
  glid|ing
glider +s
glid|ing|ly
glim +s
glim|mer +s +ed
  +ing
glim|mer|ing +s
glim|mer|ing|ly
glimpse
  glimpses
  glimpsed
  glimps|ing
Glinka, Mikh|ail
  Ivan|ovich
  (Russian
  composer)
glint +s +ed +ing
glis|sade
  glis|sades
  glis|saded
  glis|sad|ing
glis|sando
  glis|sandi *or*
  glis|san|dos
glissé +s
glis|ten +s +ed
  +ing
glis|ter +s +ed
  +ing
glitch
  glitches

glit|ter +s +ed
  +ing
glit|ter|ati
glit|ter|ing|ly
Glit|ter|tind
  (mountain,
  Norway)
glit|tery
glitz
glitz|ily
glitzi|ness
glitzy
  glitz|ier
  glitzi|est
Gli|wice (city,
  Poland)
gloam|ing *noun*
gloat +s +ed +ing
gloat|er +s
gloat|ing|ly
glob +s
global
glob|al|isa|tion *Br.*
  (use
  globalization)
glob|al|ise *Br.* (use
  globalize)
  glob|al|ises
  glob|al|ised
  glob|al|is|ing
glob|al|iza|tion
glob|al|ize
  glob|al|izes
  glob|al|ized
  glob|al|iz|ing
glob|al|ly
globe
  globes
  globed
  glob|ing
globe-fish
  plural **globe-fish**
  or **globe-fishes**
globe|flower +s
globe|like
globe-trotter +s
Globe|trot|ters (in
  'the Harlem
  Globetrotters')
globe-trotting
glo|bi|ger|ina
  glo|bi|ger|inas *or*
  glo|bi|ger|inae
glob|oid +s
glob|ose
globu|lar
globu|lar|ity
globu|lar|ly
glob|ule +s
globu|lin
globu|lous
glock|en|spiel +s

glom
  gloms
  glommed
  glom|ming
glom|er|ate
glom|eru|lar
glom|er|ule +s
glom|eru|lus
glom|eruli
gloom +s +ed +ing
  (darkness; be
  gloomy etc.
  ⚠ glume)
gloom|ily
gloomi|ness
gloomy
  gloom|ier
  gloomi|est
gloop
gloopy
glop +s
Gloria (name;
  doxology)
gloria +s
  (doxology)
Glori|ana
  (Elizabeth I)
glori|fi|ca|tion
glori|fier +s
glor|ify
  glori|fies
  glori|fied
  glori|fy|ing
glori|ole +s
glori|ous
glori|ous|ly
glori|ous|ness
glory
  glor|ies
  glor|ied
  glory|ing
glory-box
  glory-boxes
glory-hole +s
glory-of-the-snow
gloss
  glosses
  glossed
  gloss|ing
glossal
gloss|ar|ial
gloss|ar|ist +s
gloss|ary
  gloss|ar|ies
gloss|ator +s
gloss|eme +s
gloss|er +s
gloss|ily
glossi|ness
gloss|itis
glos|sog|raph|er
  +s

glos¦so|lalia
glosso|
   phar¦yn¦geal
glossy
  gloss|ies
  gloss|ier
  glossi|est
glot¦tal
glot¦tal|isa¦tion *Br.*
  (use
  glottalization)
glot¦tal|ise *Br.* (use
  glottalize)
  glot¦tal|ises
  glot¦tal|ised
  glot¦tal|is¦ing
glot¦tal|iza¦tion
glot¦tal|ize
  glot¦tal|izes
  glot¦tal|ized
  glot¦tal|iz¦ing
glot|tis
  glot|tises
Glouces|ter (city,
  England)
Glouces¦ter|shire
  (county, England)
glove
  gloves
  gloved
  glov¦ing
glove|box
  glove|boxes
glow +s +ed +ing
glow¦er +s
glow-worm +s
glox|inia +s
gloze
  glozes
  glozed
  gloz¦ing
glu¦ca|gon
Gluck, Chris|toph
  Wil¦li|bald von
  (German
  composer)
glu|cose
glu¦co|side
glu¦co|sid¦ic
glue
  glues
  glued
  glu¦ing *or* glue|ing
glue ear
glue-like
glue-pot +s
gluer +s
glue-sniffer +s
glue-sniffing
gluey
  glu¦ier
  glui|est

gluey|ness
glug
  glugs
  glugged
  glug|ging
glüh|wein +*s*
glum
  glum|mer
  glum|mest
glu|ma¦ceous
glume +s (*Botany.*
  △ gloom)
glum¦ly
glum|ness
glu|mose
gluon +s
glut
  gluts
  glut|ted
  glut|ting
glu|tam|ate +s
glu|tam|ic
glu|tam|ine
glu|teal +s
glu|ten +s
glu|teus
  glu¦tei
glu¦tin|ous
glu¦tin|ous¦ly
glu¦tin|ous|ness
glut|ton +s
glut|ton|ise *Br.*
  (use gluttonize)
  glut¦ton|ises
  glut¦ton|ised
  glut¦ton|is¦ing
glut¦ton|ize
  glut¦ton|izes
  glut¦ton|ized
  glut¦ton|iz¦ing
glut|ton|ous
glut|ton|ous¦ly
glut|tony
gly¦cer|ide +s
gly¦cerin *Am.*
gly¦cer|ine *Br.*
gly|cerol
gly|cine
glyco|gen
glyco|gen¦esis
glyco|gen¦ic
gly¦col +s
gly|col|ic
gly¦col|lic (use
  glycolic)
gly|coly¦sis
glyco|pro|tein +s
glyco|side +s
glyco|sid¦ic
glyco|suria
glyco|sur¦ic

Glyn *also* Glynn
Glynde|bourne
  (opera festival,
  England)
Glynis *also*
  Glyn|nis
Glynn *also* Glyn
Glyn|nis *also*
  Glynis
glyph +s
glyph¦ic
glyp|tal +s
glyp|tic
glyp¦to|dont +s
glyp¦tog|raphy
G-man
  G-men
gnamma +s
gnarl +s
gnarled
gnarly
  gnarl¦ier
  gnarli|est
gnash
  gnashes
  gnashed
  gnash|ing
gnash¦er +s
gnat +s
gnath¦ic
gnaw
  gnaws
  gnawed
  gnaw|ing
  gnawed *or* gnawn
  (bite. △ nor)
gnaw|ing¦ly
gneiss
  gneisses
gneiss¦ic
gneiss|oid
gneiss|ose
gnoc|chi
gnome +s
gno¦mic
gnom¦ic|al¦ly
gnom¦ish
gnomon +s
gnom|on¦ic
gno¦sis
  gno¦ses
Gnos|tic +s (early
  Christian heretic)
gnos|tic (of
  knowledge)
gnos¦ti|cise *Br.*
  (use gnosticize)
  gnos¦ti|cises
  gnos¦ti|cised
  gnos¦ti|cis¦ing
Gnos¦ti|cism

gnos¦ti|cize
  gnos¦ti|cizes
  gnos¦ti|cized
  gnos¦ti|ciz¦ing
gnu
  plural gnu *or* gnus
go
  goes
  went
  going
  gone
Goa (state, India)
goa
  plural goa *or* goas
  (gazelle. △ goer)
goad +s +ed +ing
go-ahead *noun and*
  adjective
goak +s
goal +s
goal|ball
goalie +s
goal|keep¦er +s
goal|keep¦ing
goal kick +s
goal-kicker +s
goal-kicking
goal|less
goal line +s
goal|mind¦er +s
goal|mouth +s
goal|post +s
goal|scorer +s
goal|scor¦ing *noun*
  and attributive
goal|tend¦er +s
goal|tend¦ing
Goan +s
Goan|ese
  plural Goan|ese
go¦anna +s
goat +s
goat-antelope +s
goatee +s
goat-god
goat|herd +s
goat|ish
goat|ling +s
goat moth +s
goats|beard *Am.*
  +s
goat's-beard +s
goat|skin +s
goat|suck¦er +s
goaty
  goat|ier
  goati|est
gob
  gobs
  gobbed
  gob|bing
go¦bang

Göb|bels, Jo¦seph
(use Goebbels)
gob¦bet +s
Gobbi, Tito (Italian
   baritone)
gob¦ble
   gob¦bles
   gob¦bled
   gob|bling
gobble¦de|gook
gobble¦dy|gook
   (use
   gobbledegook)
gob|bler +s
gobby
   gob|bies
Gobe|lins (French
   tapestry factory)
gobe|mouche +s
go-between +s
   noun
Gobi Des¦ert
   (Mongolia and
   China)
Gobi|neau,
   Jo¦seph Ar¦thur de
   (French
   anthropologist)
gob¦let +s
gob¦lin +s
gob|smacked
gob|smack¦ing
gob|stop¦per +s
goby
   go¦bies
   (fish)
go-by (noun snub)
go-cart +s (hand-
   cart. △ go-kart)
God (chiefly in
   Christianity and
   Judaism)
god +s (other
   superhuman
   being)
God¦ard, Jean-Luc
   (French film
   director)
Go¦da|vari (river,
   India)
God-awful
god|child
   god|chil¦dren
god¦dam
god|damn (use
   goddam)
god|damned
God¦dard, Rob¦ert
   Hutch|ings
   (American
   physicist)

god-daughter +s
god|dess
   god|desses
Gödel, Kurt
   (Austrian
   mathematician)
godet +s
go|de¦tia +s
go-devil +s
god|father +s
God-fearing
god|for¦saken
God|frey
God-given
God|havn (town,
   Greenland)
god|head +s
god|hood +s
God¦iva, Lady
   (English
   noblewoman)
god|less
god|less|ness
god|like
god¦li|ness
godly
God¦man
god|mother +s
go¦down +s
god|par¦ent +s
god|send +s
god|ship +s
god|son +s
God|speed
Godt|hâb (former
   name of Nuuk)
Godu|nov, Boris
   (Russian tsar)
god|ward
god|wards
God¦win, Wil|liam
   (English
   philosopher)
Godwin-Austen,
   Mount (= K2)
god¦wit +s
God|wot¦tery
Goeb|bels,
   Jo¦seph (German
   Nazi leader)
goer +s
   (person or thing
   that goes. △ goa)
Goer|ing,
   Her|mann
   (German Nazi
   leader)
Goes, Hugo van
   der (Flemish
   painter)
goes (in 'she goes'
   etc.; plural of go)
goest

goeth
Goethe, Jo¦hann
   Wolf|gang von
   (German
   polymath)
Goe¦thean +s
Goe¦thian +s (use
   Goethean)
gofer +s (person
   who runs errands.
   △ gopher)
gof¦fer +s +ed
   +ing (to crimp;
   crimping iron.
   △ gofer, gopher)
Gog and Magog
   Bible
go-getter +s
gog¦gle
   gog¦gles
   gog¦gled
   gog|gling
goggle-box
   goggle-boxes
goggle-dive +s
goggle-eyed
gog¦let +s
go-go
Gogol, Ni¦ko|lai
   (Russian writer)
Goi|ânia (city,
   Brazil)
Goiás (state, Brazil)
Goi¦del +s
Goi¦del¦ic
going +s
going away noun
going-away
   attributive
going on (for)
   (approaching)
going-over
   goings-over
goings-on
goi¦ter Am. +s
goitre Br. +s
goitred
goi¦trous
go-kart +s (racing
   car. △ go-cart)
Go¦khale, Gopal
   Krishna (Indian
   political leader)
Golan Heights (in
   Syria and Israel)
Gol|conda +s
gold +s
gold-beater +s
gold-beater's skin
   +s
gold bloc +s (bloc
   of countries)

gold block|ing
   (stamping with
   gold leaf)
gold|brick +s +ed
   +ing verb
gold brick +s noun
Gold Coast (former
   name of Ghana;
   resort region,
   Australia)
gold|crest +s
gold-digger +s
gold dust
gold¦en
golden-ager +s
golden-eye +s
Gold¦en Hind
   (Francis Drake's
   ship)
Gold¦en Horde (of
   Mongols and
   Tartars)
Gold¦en Horn
   (harbour, Istanbul)
gold|en¦ly
gold|en|ness
gold|en|rod +s
gold|field +s
gold|finch
   gold|finches
gold|fish
   plural gold|fish or
   gold|fishes
goldi|locks
   plural goldi|locks
Gold|ing, Wil|liam
   (English novelist)
gold leaf
Gold|man, Emma
   (Lithuanian-born
   American political
   activist)
Gold|mark, Peter
   Carl (Hungarian-
   born American
   inventor)
gold mine +s
gold plate noun
gold-plate
   gold-plates
   gold-plated
   gold-plating
   verb
gold rush
   gold rushes
Gold|schmidt,
   Vic¦tor Mor¦itz
   (Swiss-born
   Norwegian
   chemist)

Gold|smith,
  Oli|ver (Irish
  writer)
gold|smith +s
Gold|wyn,
  Sam|uel (Polish-
  born American
  film director)
golem +s
golf +s +ed +ing
golf bag +s
golf ball +s
golf cart +s
golf club +s
  (implement;
  premises;
  association)
golf course +s
golf|er +s
golf links
Golgi, Cam|illo
  (Italian histologist;
  body, apparatus)
Gol|gotha (site of
  crucifixion of
  Jesus)
Gol|iath *Bible*
Gol|iath bee|tle +s
Gol|iath frog +s
Gol|lancz, Vic|tor
  (British publisher)
gol|li|wog +s
gol|lop +s +ed
  +ing
golly
  gol|lies
gol|osh (use
  galosh)
  gol|oshes
gom|been
Gomel (Russian
  name for Homel)
Gom|or|rah (town,
  ancient Palestine)
gonad +s
gon|adal
gon|ado|troph|ic
gon|ado|troph|in
  +s
gon|ado|trop|ic
Gon|court,
  Ed|mond de and
  Jules de (French
  writers)
gon|dola +s
gon|do|lier +s
Gon|dwana
  (ancient
  continent)
gone

goner +s (doomed
  person etc.
  △ gonna)
gon|fa|lon +s
gon|fa|lon|ier +s
gong +s +ed +ing
gon|gooz|ler +s
goni|om|eter +s
go|nio|met|ric
go|nio|met|ric|al
goni|om|etry
gonk +s
gonna (*slang*
  = going to.
  △ goner)
gono|coc|cal
gono|coc|cus
  gono|cocci
gon|or|rhea *Am.*
gon|or|rhe|al *Am.*
gon|or|rhoea *Br.*
gon|or|rhoe|al *Br.*
gonzo
goo +s
good
  goods
  bet|ter
  best
good|by +s *Am.*
  (use goodbye)
good|bye +s
good-for-nothing
  +s
good-hearted
good-humored *Am.*
good-humored|ly
  Am.
good-humoured
  Br.
good-
  humoured|ly *Br.*
goodie +s (use
  goody)
good|ish
Good King Henry
  (plant)
good|li|ness
good-looker
good-looking
good luck *noun*
good-luck
  attributive
good|ly
Good|man, Benny
  (American jazz
  musician)
good-natured
good-natured|ly
good|ness

good|night +s
  (parting wish)
goodo (*Australian &
  New Zealand
  good*)
good-oh *interjection*
good-sized
good-tempered
good-tempered|ly
good-time
  attributive
good-timer +s
good|wife
  good|wives
good|will (kindly
  feeling; reputation
  of business)
good will
  (intention and
  hope that good
  will result)
Good|win Sands
  (off England)
Good|wood
  (racecourse,
  England)
goody
  good|ies
goody-goody
  goody-goodies
gooey
  goo|ier
  gooi|est
gooey|ness
goof +s +ed +ing
go-off
goof|ily
goofi|ness
goofy
  goof|ier
  goof|iest
goog +s
googly
  goog|lies
goo|gol
goo|gol|plex
gook +s (*offensive*)
goolie +s
goom|bah +s
goon +s
goop +s
goopi|ness
goopy
  goop|ier
  goop|iest
goos|an|der
  plural goos|an|der
  or goos|an|ders
goose
  geese
  (bird)

goose +s (tailor's
  iron)
goose
  gooses
  goosed
  goos|ing
  verb
goose|berry
  goose|berries
goose bumps
goose egg +s
goose-flesh
goose|foot
  goose|feet
  (thing in shape of
  goose's foot)
goose|foot +s
  (plant)
goose|gog +s
goose|grass
  goose|grasses
goose|herd +s
goose-like
goose-pimpled
goose pim|ples
goose-skin
goose-step
  goose-steps
  goose-stepped
  goose-stepping
Goos|sens,
  Eu|gene, Leon,
  Marie, and
  Sid|onie (English
  musicians)
gopak +s
go|pher +s (tree;
  rodent; tortoise.
  △ gofer, goffer)
go|pher snake +s
go|pher wood
Gor|ak|pur (city,
  India)
goral +s
Gor|ba|chev,
  Mikh|ail (Soviet
  president)
Gor|bals, the
  (district, Glasgow)
gor|bli|mey +s
gor|cock +s
Gor|dian knot +s
Gor|di|mer,
  Nad|ine (South
  African writer)
Gor|dium (ancient
  city, Turkey)
gordo +s
Gor|don (name;
  setter; Riots)

Gor¦don, Charles
George (British
general)
gore
gores
gored
gor¦ing
Gó¦recki, Hen¦ryk
(Polish composer)
Gör¦eme (valley,
Turkey)
Gore-Tex *Propr.*
gorge
gorges
gorged
gor¦ging
gor|geous
gor|geous¦ly
gor|geous|ness
gor¦ger +s
gor¦get +s
Gor¦gio +s
gor¦gon +s
gor¦go¦nia
gor|go¦nias *or*
gor|go¦niae
gor|go¦nian +s
gor¦gon|ise *Br.* (use
gorgonize)
gor|gon|ises
gor|gon|ised
gor|gon|is¦ing
gor¦gon|ize
gor|gon|izes
gor|gon|ized
gor|gon|iz¦ing
Gor¦gon|zola +s
(cheese)
gor|illa +s (ape.
△ guerrilla)
gor¦ily
gori|ness
Gör¦ing, Her|mann
(use Goering)
Gorky (former
name of Nizhni
Novgorod)
Gorky, Ar|shile
(Turkish-born
American painter)
Gorky, Maxim
(Russian writer)
Gor|lovka (city,
Ukraine)
gor¦mand|ise *Br.*
(eat voraciously;
use gormandize.
△ gourmandise)
gor¦mand|ises
gor¦mand|ised
gor¦mand|is¦ing

gor¦mand|iser *Br.*
+s (use
gormandizer)
gor¦mand|ize
gor¦mand|izes
gor¦mand|ized
gor¦mand|iz¦ing
(eat voraciously.
△ gourmandise)
gor¦mand|izer +s
gorm|less
gorm|less¦ly
gorm|less|ness
Gorno-Altai
(republic, Russia)
Gorno-Altaisk
(city, Russia)
gorse +s
Gor|sedd
gorsy
gor|sier
gor|si¦est
gory
gor¦ier
gori|est
gosh
gos|hawk +s
gos|ling +s
go-slow +s *noun*
Gos|pel +s *Bible*
gos|pel +s (Christ's
teaching; truth;
principle; singing)
gos|pel|er *Am.* +s
gos|pel|ler +s
gos|samer +s
gos|sa|mered
gos|sa|mery
gos|sip +s +ed
+ing
gos|sip|er +s
gos|sip|mon|ger
+s
gos|sipy
gos|soon +s
got
Gö|te|borg
(Swedish name for
Gothenburg)
Goth +s (Germanic
tribe)
goth +s (rock
music; performer)
Gotha (city,
Germany)
Gotham (village,
England;
nickname for New
York City)
Goth¦am|ite +s
Goth¦en|burg
(port, Sweden)
Goth¦ic

Goth¦ic|al¦ly
Gothi¦cise *Br.* (use
Gothicize)
Gothi|cises
Gothi|cised
Gothi|cis|ing
Gothi|cism +s
Gothi|cize
Gothi|cizes
Gothi|cized
Gothi|ciz|ing
Got|land (island,
Sweden)
go-to-meeting
gotta (= got to)
got|ten
Göt¦ter|däm|mer|
                    ung
Göt|tingen (town,
Germany)
gou|ache +s
Gouda (town, the
Netherlands; also
the cheese orig.
made there)
gouge
gouges
gouged
gou|ging
gou|ger +s
Gough Is|land (in
S. Atlantic)
gou|jons
gou|lash
gou|lashes
Gould, Glenn
(Canadian pianist)
Gould, Ste|phen
Jay (American
palaeontologist)
Gou|nod, Charles
(French
composer)
gou|rami
plural gou|rami *or*
gou|ramis
gourd +s (plant;
fruit)
gourde +s (Haitian
currency)
gourd|ful +s
gour|mand +s
(glutton)
gour¦mand|ise
(gluttony.
△ gormandize)
gour¦mand|ism
gour|met +s
(connoisseur)
gout +s
gout-fly
gout-flies
gout|ily

gouti|ness
gout|weed +s
gouty
gov¦ern +s +ed
+ing
gov¦ern|abil¦ity
gov¦ern|able
gov¦ern|able|ness
gov¦ern|ance
gov¦ern|ess
gov¦ern|esses
gov¦ern|essy
gov¦ern|ment +s
gov¦ern|men|tal
gov¦ern|men|tal¦ly
gov¦ern|or +s
gov¦er¦nor|ate +s
Governor-General
+s
gov¦er¦nor|ship +s
gowan +s
gowk +s
gown +s +ed +ing
gowns|man
gowns|men
Gowon, Ya¦kubu
(Nigerian
statesman)
goy
goyim *or* goys
(*offensive*)
Goya (Spanish
painter)
goy|isch (use
goyish)
goy¦ish
Gozo (Maltese
island)
Graaf|ian
grab
grabs
grabbed
grab|bing
grab bag +s
grab|ber +s
grab¦ble
grab¦bles
grab¦bled
grab|bling
grabby
grab|bier
grab¦bi|est
gra|ben
plural gra¦ben *or*
gra|bens
grab han¦dle +s
grab rail +s
Grac|chus (Roman
tribune)
Grace, W. G.
(English cricketer)
Grace (name)

grace
  graces
  graced
  gra¦cing
  (attractiveness;
  thanksgiving; add
  grace to)
grace and fa¦vour
  (home etc.)
grace|ful
grace|ful¦ly
grace|ful|ness
grace|less
grace|less¦ly
grace|less|ness
grace note +s
Graces *Greek
  Mythology*
Gra¦cias a Dios,
  Cape (in Central
  America)
Gra¦cie
gra¦cile
gra¦cil|ity
graci|os¦ity
gra|cious
gra|cious¦ly
gra|cious|ness
grackle +s
grad +s
grad|ate
  grad|ates
  grad|ated
  grad|at¦ing
grad|ation +s
grad|ation¦al
grad¦ation|al¦ly
Grade, Lew (Lord
  Grade, Russian-
  born British
  television
  producer)
grade
  grades
  graded
  grad¦ing
grader +s
Grad|grind +s
gra¦di|ent +s
gra¦din +s (use
  gradine)
gra|dine +s
grad¦ing +s
grad|ual +s
grad¦ual|ism
grad¦ual|ist +s
grad¦ual|is¦tic
grad¦ual¦ly
grad¦ual|ness
gradu|and +s
gradu|ate
  gradu|ates

gradu|ate (*cont.*)
  gradu|ated
  gradu|at¦ing
gradu|ation +s
gradu|ator +s
Grae¦cise *Br.* (use
  Graecize)
  Grae¦cises
  Grae¦cised
  Grae|cis¦ing
Grae¦cism +s
Grae¦cize
  Grae¦cizes
  Grae¦cized
  Grae|ciz¦ing
Graeco|mania
Graeco|maniac +s
Graeco|phile +s
Graeco-Roman
Graf, Steffi
  (German tennis
  player)
graf|fi¦tied
graf|fi¦tist +s
graf|fito
  graf|fiti
graft +s +ed +ing
graft¦er +s
graft|ing clay +s
graft|ing wax
  graft|ing waxes
Graf|ton, Duke of
  (British prime
  minister)
Gra¦ham, Billy
  (American
  evangelical
  preacher)
Gra¦ham, Mar¦tha
  (American dancer)
Gra¦ham, Thomas
  (Scottish physical
  chemist)
Gra¦ham
Gra¦hame,
  Ken¦neth
  (Scottish writer)
Gra¦ham Land
  (part of
  Antarctica)
Grail (Holy Grail, in
  medieval legend)
grain +s +ed +ing
grain¦er +s
Grain|ger, Percy
  (Australian-born
  American
  composer)
graini|ness
grain lea¦ther
grain|less
grain-side

grainy
  grain|ier
  graini|est
gral¦la|tor¦ial
gram +s
gram-atom +s
gram-equiva¦lent
  +s
gram-force
  grams-force
gra¦min|aceous
gram¦in|eous
grami|niv¦or|ous
gram¦ma|logue +s
gram|mar +s
gram¦mar|ian +s
gram¦mar|less
gram¦mat|ical
gram¦mat|ical|ity
gram¦mat|ical¦ly
gram¦mat|ical|
      ness
gram¦mati|cise *Br.*
  (use
  grammaticize)
  gram¦mati|cises
  gram¦mati|cised
  gram¦mati|cis¦ing
gram¦mati|cize
  gram¦mati|cizes
  gram¦mati|cized
  gram¦mati|ciz¦ing
gramme +s (use
  gram)
gram-molecule +s
Gram-negative
gramo|phone +s
gramo|phon¦ic
Gram|pian (region,
  Scotland)
Gram|pians
  (mountains,
  Scotland)
Gram-positive
gram|pus
  gram|puses
Gram|sci,
  An|tonio (Italian
  political theorist)
Gram stain
gran +s
Gran|ada (cities,
  Spain and
  Nicaragua)
grana|dilla +s (use
  grenadilla)
gran|ary
  gran|ar¦ies
Gran Can|aria
  (capital of the
  Canary Islands)

Gran Chaco (plain,
  S. America)
grand +s +er +est
  (*adjective*; piano)
grand
  plural grand
  (thousand)
gran|dad +s
gran|dam +s
  archaic
gran|dame +s (use
  grandam *archaic*)
grand-aunt +s
grand|child
  grand|chil¦dren
grand|dad +s (use
  grandad)
grand-daddy
  grand-daddies
grand|daugh¦ter
  +s
Grande Co¦more
  (island off
  Madagascar)
grande dame +s
gran|dee +s
grand|eur
grand|father +s
grand|father¦ly
Grand Gui¦gnol +s
gran|di|flora
grand|ilo|quence
grand|ilo|quent
grand|ilo|quent¦ly
gran|di|ose
gran|di|ose¦ly
gran|di|os¦ity
Gran¦di|son¦ian
grand¦ly
grand|ma +s
grand mal
grand|mama +s
Grand Mas¦ter +s
  (of knighthood,
  Freemasons, etc.)
grand|mas¦ter +s
  Chess
grand|mother +s
grand|mother¦ly
grand-nephew +s
grand|ness
grand-niece +s
grand¦pa +s
grand|papa +s
grand|pappy
  grand|pap¦pies
grand|par¦ent +s
Grand Prix
  Grands Prix
grand siècle
grand|sire +s
grand|son +s

grand|stand +s
grand-uncle +s
grange +s
gran|ifer|ous
grani|form
gran|ita
  gran|ite
  (crushed ice drink)
gran|ite +s (rock)
gran|ite|ware
gran|it|ic
gran|it|oid
grani|vore +s
gran|iv|or|ous
gran|ma +s (use
  grandma)
granny
  gran|nies
Granny Smith +s
grano|di|or|ite
grano|lith|ic
gran|pa +s (use
  grandpa)
Grant (name)
Grant, Cary
  (English-born
  American actor)
Grant, Ulys|ses
  Simp|son
  (American
  president)
grant +s +ed +ing
grant|able
grant aid *noun*
grant-aid +s +ed
  +ing *verb*
grant|ee +s
grant|er +s
  (generally.
  △ grantor)
Gran|tha (Indian
  alphabet)
Granth (Sahib)
  (= Adi Granth)
grant-in-aid
  grants-in-aid
grant-maintained
grant|or +s (*Law*.
  △ granter)
gran tur|ismo +s
granu|lar
granu|lar|ity
granu|lar|ly
granu|late
  granu|lates
  granu|lated
  granu|lat|ing
granu|la|tion +s
granu|la|tor +s
gran|ule +s
gran|ulo|cyte +s
gra|nu|lo|cyt|ic
gra|nu|lo|met|ric

Granville-Barker,
  Har|ley (English
  dramatist)
grape +s
grape|fruit
  plural grape|fruit
gra|pery
  gra|per|ies
grape|seed oil
grape|shot
grape-sugar
grape|vine +s
grapey
  grapi|er
  grapi|est
graph +s +ed +ing
graph|em|at|ic
graph|eme +s
graph|em|ic
graph|em|ic|al|ly
graph|em|ics
graph|ic +s
graphi|cacy
graph|ic|al
graph|ic|al|ly
graph|ic|ness
graph|ics
graph|ite +s
graph|it|ic
graph|it|ise *Br.*
  (use graphitize)
  graph|it|ises
  graph|it|ised
  graph|it|is|ing
graph|it|ize
  graph|it|izes
  graph|it|ized
  graph|it|iz|ing
grapho|logic|al
graph|olo|gist +s
graph|ology
grap|nel +s
grappa +s
Grap|pelli,
  Ste|phane
  (French jazz
  violinist)
grap|ple
  grap|ples
  grap|pled
  grap|pling
grap|pler +s
grap|pling hook
  +s
grap|pling iron +s
grap|to|lite +s
grapy (use grapey)
Gras|mere (village
  and lake, England)
grasp +s +ed +ing
grasp|able
grasp|er +s

grasp|ing|ly
grasp|ing|ness
Grass, Gün|ther
  (German writer)
grass
  grasses
  grassed
  grass|ing
grass box
  grass boxes
grass|cloth +s
Grasse (town,
  France)
grass|hop|per +s
grassi|ness
grass|land +s
grass|less
grass|like
grass of
  Par|nas|sus
grass-root
  attributive
grass roots *noun*
grass-roots
  attributive
grass snake +s
  (non-venomous
  snake. △ glass
  snake)
grass-wrack +s
grassy
  grass|ier
  grassi|est
grate
  grates
  grated
  grat|ing
  (grind etc.; in
  fireplace. △ great)
grate|ful
grate|ful|ly
grate|ful|ness
grater +s (used for
  grating cheese etc.
  △ greater)
grat|ic|ule +s
grat|ifi|ca|tion +s
grati|fier +s
grat|ify
  grati|fies
  grati|fied
  grati|fy|ing
grati|fy|ing|ly
gra|tin +s
*grat|iné +s noun
  and masculine
  adjective*
grat|inéed
*grat| inée feminine
  adjective*
grat|ing +s
grat|ing|ly

gra|tis
grati|tude
gra|tuit|ous
gra|tuit|ous|ly
gra|tuit|ous|ness
gra|tu|ity
  gra|tu|ities
gratu|la|tory
graunch
  graunches
  graunched
  graunch|ing
grav|ad|lax (use
  gravlax)
gra|va|men
  gra|va|mens *or*
  gra|va|mina
grave
  graves
  graved
  grav|ing
  graved *or* gra|ven
  graver
  grav|est
grave-clothes
grave|dig|ger +s
gravel
  gravels
  grav|elled *Br.*
  grav|eled *Am.*
  grav|el|ling *Br.*
  grav|el|ling *Am.*
gravel-blind
grave|less
grav|el|ly (of or
  like gravel; deep
  voiced etc.)
grave|ly (seriously)
graven
grave|ness
graver +s
Graves, Rob|ert
  (English writer)
Graves
  plural Graves
  (wine)
Graves' dis|ease
grave|side
grave|stone +s
Gra|vet|tian
grave|ward
grave|yard +s
gravid
grav|im|eter +s
gravi|met|ric
gravi|metry
grav|itas
gravi|tate
  gravi|tates
  gravi|tated
  gravi|tat|ing
gravi|ta|tion

gravi|ta|tion|al
gravi|ta|tion|al|ly
gravi|ton +s
grav|ity
  grav|ities
gravity-fed
grav|ity feed
grav|lax
grav|ure
gravy
  gra|vies
gravy boat +s
gravy train
Gray, Asa
  (American
  botanist)
Gray, Thomas
  (English poet)
gray *Am.* +s +ed
  +ing +er +est
  (colour. *Br.* grey)
gray +s (unit.
  ⚠ grey)
gray|beard *Am.* +s
  (*Br.* greybeard)
gray|ling
  plural gray|ling *or*
  gray|lings
gray|ly *Am.Br.*
  greyly
gray|ness *Am.* (*Br.*
  greyness)
gray|wacke *Am.* +s
  (*Br.* greywacke)
Graz (city, Austria)
graze
  grazes
  grazed
  graz|ing
grazer +s
gra|zier +s
gra|ziery
  gra|zier|ies
grease
  greases
  greased
  greas|ing
grease gun +s
grease|less
grease|paint +s
grease|proof
greaser +s
grease|wood +s
greas|ily
greasi|ness
greasy
  greas|ier
  greasi|est
great +s +er +est
  (big, important,
  etc.; outstanding

great (*cont.*)
  person or thing.
  ⚠ grate, grater)
great-aunt +s
Great Bar|rier
  Reef (off
  Australian coast)
Great Bear Lake
  (in Canada)
Great Brit|ain
great|coat +s
great-grand|child
  great-
  grand|chil|dren
great-
  grand|daughter
  +s
great-grand|father
  +s
great-
  grand|mother +s
great-
  grand|par|ent +s
great-grand|son
  +s
great-hearted
great-
  hearted|ness
Great Lakes (in N.
  America)
great|ly
great-nephew +s
great|ness
great-niece +s
Greats (classics and
  philosophy at
  Oxford University)
great-uncle +s
greave +s (armour.
  ⚠ grieve)
grebe +s
grebo +s
Gre|cian +s
Gre|cise *Br.* (use
  Graecize)
  Gre|cises
  Gre|cised
  Gre|cis|ing
Gre|cism +s
Gre|cize
  Gre|cizes
  Gre|cized
  Gre|ciz|ing
Greco, El (Cretan-
  born Spanish
  painter)
Greece
greed
greed|ily
greedi|ness

greedy
  greed|ier
  greedi|est
greedy-guts
  plural greedy-guts
gree|gree +s
Greek +s
Greek|ness
green +s +ed +ing
  +er +est
Green|away, Kate
  (English artist)
green|back +s
Green Beret +s
green|bot|tle +s
Greene, Gra|ham
  (English novelist)
green|ery
  green|er|ies
green-eyed
green fee +s
green|feed
green|field
  attributive
green|finch
  green|finches
green-fingered
green fin|gers
green|fly
  plural green|fly *or*
  green|flies
green|gage +s
green|gro|cer +s
green|gro|cery
  green|gro|cer|ies
green|head +s
green|heart +s
green|hide +s
green|horn +s
green|house +s
greenie +s
green|ing +s
green|ish
green|keep|er +s
green|keep|ing
Green|land
Green|land|er +s
green|let +s
green|ly
green|mail
green|mail|er +s
green|ness
Green|ock (port,
  Scotland)
Green|peace
green|sand +s
green|shank
  plural
  green|shank *or*
  green|shanks
green|sick
green|sick|ness

greens|keep|er +s
green-stick
  (fracture)
green|stone +s
green|stuff +s
green|sward +s
green|weed +s
Green|wich
  (borough,
  London)
Green|wich Mean
  Time
Green|wich
  me|rid|ian
Green|wich
  Vil|lage (district,
  New York City)
green|wood +s
greeny
green|yard +s
Greer, Ger|maine
  (Australian writer)
Greer *also* Grier
greet +s +ed +ing
greet|er +s
greet|ing +s
gref|fier +s
Greg
gre|gari|ous
gre|gari|ous|ly
gre|gari|ous|ness
Gregor
Gre|gor|ian
Greg|ory (saint;
  popes; name)
Greg|ory of
  Nazi|an|zus
  (early saint)
Greg|ory of Nyssa
  (early saint)
Greg|ory of Tours
  (early saint)
Greg|ory pow|der
grem|ial +s
grem|lin +s
Gren|ada (in West
  Indies)
gren|ade +s
Gren|adian +s
grena|dier +s
  (soldier; fish)
Grena|dier Guards
  (British regiment)
Grena|diers
  (= Grenadier
  Guards)
grena|dilla +s
grena|dine +s
Grena|dine
  Is|lands (in West
  Indies)
Gren|del

Gre|noble (city,
France)
Gren|ville, George
(British prime
minister)
Grepo +s
Gres|ham,
Thomas (English
financier)
Gres|ham's law
Gres|ley, Nigel
(British railway
engineer)
gres|sor|ial
Greta
Gretel (in 'Hansel
and Gretel')
Gretna Green
(village, Scotland)
Gretzky, Wayne
(Canadian ice-
hockey player)
Greuze, Jean-
Baptiste (French
painter)
grew (past tense of
grow. △ grue)
Grey, Lord (British
prime minister)
Grey, George
(British prime
minister of New
Zealand)
Grey, Lady Jane
(English queen)
grey Br. +s +ed
+ing +er +est
(Am. gray. colour.
△ gray)
grey-back +s
grey|beard Br. +s
(Am. graybeard)
Grey Friar +s
(Franciscan friar)
Grey|friars (in
names of roads,
schools, etc.)
grey|hen +s
grey|hound +s
grey|ish
grey|lag
   plural grey|lag or
   grey|lags
grey|ly Br. (Am.
   grayly)
Grey|mouth (city,
New Zealand)
grey|ness Br. (Am.
grayness)
grey|wacke Br. +s
(Am. graywacke)
grid +s

grid|ded
grid|dle
   grid|dles
   grid|dled
   grid|dling
grid|iron +s
grid|lock
grid|locked
grief +s
grief-stricken
Grieg, Ed|vard
(Norwegian
composer)
Grier also Greer
Grier|son, John
(Scottish film
director)
griev|ance +s
grieve
   grieves
   grieved
   griev|ing
(mourn.
△ greave)
griev|er +s
griev|ous
griev|ous|ly
griev|ous|ness
grif|fin +s (fabulous
creature.
△ griffon)
Grif|fith, Ar|thur
(Irish president)
Grif|fith, D. W.
(American film
director)
Grif|fith
grif|fon +s (vulture;
dog. △ griffin)
grift +s +ed +ing
grift|er +s
grig +s
Gri|gnard re|agent
+s
grike +s
grill +s +ed +ing
(cooking
apparatus; food.
△ grille)
grill|ade +s
grill|age +s
grille +s (grating.
△ grill)
grill|er +s
grill|ing +s
grilse
   plural grilse
grim
   grim|mer
   grim|mest
grim|ace
   grim|aces

grim|ace (cont.)
   grim|aced
   grim|acing
grim|acer +s
Gri|maldi,
   Fran|cesco
   Maria (Italian
   physicist)
Gri|maldi, Jo|seph
   (English clown)
gri|mal|kin +s
grime
   grimes
   grimed
   grim|ing
grim-faced
grimi|ly
grimi|ness
grim|ly
Grimm, Jacob and
   Wil|helm
   (German
   philologists)
Grimm's law
grim|ness
Grim|ond, Jo
   (British Liberal
   politician)
Grimsby (port,
   England)
grimy
   grimi|er
   grimi|est
grin
   grins
   grinned
   grin|ning
grind
   grinds
   ground
   grind|ing
grind|er +s
grind|ing|ly
grind|stone +s
gringo +s
grin|ner +s
grin|ning|ly
grip
   grips
   gripped
   grip|ping
gripe
   gripes
   griped
   grip|ing
griper +s
gripe water Propr.
grip|ing|ly
grippe (influenza)
grip|per +s
grip|ping|ly

grippy
grip|pier
grip|pi|est
Gris, Juan
   (Spanish painter)
gris|aille +s
Gri|selda
griseo|ful|vin
gris|ette +s
gris|kin +s
gris|li|ness
grisly
gris|lier
gris|li|est
(horrible.
   △ gristly, grizzly)
grison +s
Gris|ons (canton,
   Switzerland)
gris|sini
grist
   grits
gris|tle
gris|tly (containing
   gristle. △ grisly,
   grizzly)
grit
   grits
   grit|ted
   grit|ting
grit|stone +s
grit|ter +s
grit|tily
grit|ti|ness
gritty
   grit|tier
   grit|ti|est
Gri|vas, George
   Theo|dorou
   (Greek-Cypriot
   patriot)
griz|zle
   griz|zles
   griz|zled
   griz|zling
griz|zler +s
griz|zly
   griz|zlies
   griz|zlier
   griz|zli|est
(bear; grey;
   complaining.
   △ grisly, gristly)
groan +s +ed +ing
   (moan. △ grown)
groan|er +s
groan|ing|ly
groat +s (coin)
groats (grain)
gro|cer +s
gro|cery
gro|cer|ies
grockle +s

Grodno (city, Belarus)
grog
  grogs
  grogged
  grog|ging
grog|gily
grog|gi|ness
groggy
  grog|gier
  grog|gi|est
grog|ram +s
groin +s +ed +ing
  Anatomy;
  Architecture
groin *Am.* **+s** (on seashore. *Br.* groyne)
grom|met +s
grom|well +s
Gro|myko, An|drei (Soviet president)
Gron|ing|en (city and province, the Netherlands)
groom +s +ed +ing
grooms|man
  grooms|men
groove
  grooves
  grooved
  groov|ing
groov|ily
groovi|ness
groovy
  groov|ier
  groovi|est
grope
  gropes
  groped
  grop|ing
groper +s
grop|ing|ly
Gro|pius, Wal|ter (German-born American architect)
gros|beak +s
gro|schen
  plural gro|schen
  or gro|schens
gros|grain +s
gros point
gross
  grosses
  grossed
  gross|ing
  gross|er
  gross|est
  verb and adjective

gross
  plural **gross**
  (*noun* = 144)
Grosse|teste, Rob|ert (English churchman)
Gross|glock|ner (mountain, Austria)
gross|ly
gross|ness
Grosz, George (German-born American painter)
grot +s
gro|tesque +s
gro|tesque|ly
gro|tesque|ness
gro|tesque|rie +s
Gro|tius, Hugo (Dutch jurist)
grotti|ness
grotto
  grot|toes *or*
  grottos
grotty
  grot|tier
  grot|ti|est
grouch
  grouches
  grouched
  grouch|ing
grouch|ily
grouchi|ness
grouchy
  grouch|ier
  grouchi|est
ground +s +ed +ing
ground|age
ground ash
  ground ashes
ground|bait +s
ground cover
ground crew +s
ground|er +s
ground floor *noun*
ground-floor *attributive*
ground|hog +s
ground|ing +s
ground|less
ground|less|ly
ground|less|ness
ground|ling +s
ground|nut +s
ground plan +s
ground rule +s
ground|sel +s
ground|sheet +s
grounds|keep|er +s

grounds|man
  grounds|men
ground squir|rel +s
ground staff
ground stroke +s
ground|swell
ground|water +s
ground|work +s
group +s +ed +ing
group|age
group cap|tain +s
group|er +s
groupie +s
group|ing +s
group|think
group|ware
group work
grouse
  grouses
  groused
  grous|ing
grouser +s
grout +s +ed +ing
grout|er +s
Grove, George (English musicologist)
grove +s
grovel
  grovels
  grov|elled *Br.*
  grov|eled *Am.*
  grov|el|ling *Br.*
  grov|el|ing *Am.*
  grov|el|er +s *Am.*
  grov|el|ing|ly *Am.*
  grov|el|ler +s *Br.*
  grov|el|ling|ly *Br.*
grovy
grow
  grows
  grew
  grow|ing
  grown
grow|able
grow|bag +s
grow|er +s
grow|ing bag +s
grow|ing pains
growl +s +ed +ing
growl|er +s
growl|ing|ly
Grow|more
grown (past participle of grow. △ groan)
grown-up +s *adjective and noun*
growth +s

growth in|dus|try
growth in|dus|tries
groyne *Br.* **+s** (*Am.* groin. on seashore. △ groin)
Grozny (capital of the Chechen Republic)
grub
  grubs
  grubbed
  grub|bing
grub|ber +s
grub|bily
grubbi|ness
grubby
  grub|bier
  grub|bi|est
grub-screw +s
grub|stake
  grub|stakes
  grub|staked
  grub|stak|ing
grub|staker +s
Grub Street (writers)
grudge
  grudges
  grudged
  grudg|ing
grudger +s
grudg|ing|ly
grudg|ing|ness
grue
  grues
  grued
  gru|ing
  (ice; feel horror. △ grew)
gruel +s
gruel|ling *Am.*
gruel|ling|ly *Am.*
gruel|ling *Br.*
gruel|ling|ly *Br.*
grue|some
grue|some|ly
grue|some|ness
gruff +er +est
gruff|ly
gruff|ness
grum|ble
  grum|bles
  grum|bled
  grum|bling
grum|bler +s
grum|bling +s
grum|bling|ly
grum|bly
grum|met +s (use grommet)
grum|ous

grump +s
grump|ily
grumpi|ness
grump|ish
grump|ish|ly
grumpy
    grump|ier
    grumpi|est
Grundy
    Grun|dies
Grundy|ism
Grüne|wald,
    Mathias (German
    painter)
grunge
grungy
    grun|gier
    grun|gi|est
grun|ion
    plural grun|ion or
    grun|ions
grunt +s +ed +ing
grunt|er +s
Gruy|ère +s
    (district,
    Switzerland;
    cheese)
gryke +s (use
    grike)
gryphon +s (use
    griffin)
grys|bok
    plural grys|bok or
    grys|boks
Gryt|viken
    (settlement, South
    Georgia)
Gstaad (ski resort,
    Switzerland)
G-string +s
G-suit +s
gua|ca|mole
gua|charo +s
Gua|da|la|jara
    (cities, Spain and
    Mexico)
Gua|dal|ca|nal
    (island, Solomon
    Islands)
Gua|dal|qui|vir
    (river, Spain)
Gua|de|loupe
    (group of islands,
    Lesser Antilles)
Gua|de|loup|ian
    +s
Gua|di|ana (river,
    Spain and
    Portugal)
guaiac +s
guai|acum +s

Guam (in Mariana
    Islands)
guan +s
gua|naco +s
Gua|na|juato (state
    and city, Mexico)
Guang|dong
    (province, China)
Guangxi Zhu|ang
    (region, China)
Guang|zhou (city,
    China)
guan|ine
guano +s noun
guano
    gua|noes
    gua|noed
guano|ing
    verb
Guan|tánamo Bay
    (on Cuba)
Guar|ani
    plural Guar|ani or
    Guar|anis
    (S. American
    Indian; language)
guar|ani +s
    (Paraguayan
    currency)
guar|an|tee
    guar|an|tees
    guar|an|teed
    guar|an|tee|ing
guar|an|tor +s
guar|anty
    guar|an|ties
    (undertaking of
    liability)
guard +s +ed +ing
guard|ant Heraldry
guard|ed|ly
guarded|ness
guard|ee +s
guard|er +s
guard|house +s
Guardi,
    Fran|cesco
    (Italian painter)
guard|ian +s
guard|ian angel
    +s
guard|ian|ship +s
guard|less
guard rail +s
guard ring +s
guard|room +s
guards|man
    guards|men
guard's van +s
Guar|neri,
    Giu|seppe (Italian
    violin-maker)

Guar|ner|ius
Gua|te|mala (in
    Central America)
Gua|te|mal|an +s
guava +s
Guaya|quil (city,
    Ecuador)
guay|ule +s
gub|bins
gu|ber|na|tor|ial
gudgeon
    plural gudgeon
    (fish)
gudgeon +s
    (person; pivot,
    pin, etc.)
gudgeon pin +s
Gud|run Norse
    Legend
guel|der rose +s
Guelph +s
Guelph|ic
Guelph|ism
gue|non +s
guer|don +s +ed
    +ing
Gue|ricke, Otto
    von (German
    engineer)
guer|illa +s (use
    guerrilla)
Guer|nica (town,
    Spain)
Guern|sey +s
    (Channel Island;
    cattle)
guern|sey +s
    (garment)
Guer|rero (state,
    Mexico)
guer|rilla +s
    (fighter. △ gorilla)
guess
    guesses
    guessed
    guess|ing
guess|able
guess|er +s
guess-rope +s (use
    guest-rope)
guess|ti|mate
    guess|ti|mates
    guess|ti|mated
    guess|ti|mat|ing
guess|work
guest +s +ed +ing
    (invited person.
    △ guessed)
guest house +s
gues|ti|mate
    gues|ti|mates
    gues|ti|mated

gues|ti|mate (cont.)
    gues|ti|mat|ing
    (use guesstimate)
guest night +s
guest room +s
guest-rope +s
guest|ship
Gue|vara, Che
    (Argentinian
    revolutionary)
guff
guf|faw +s +ed
    +ing
Gug|gen|heim,
    Meyer (Swiss-
    born American
    industrialist)
gug|gle
    gug|gles
    gug|gled
    gug|gling
Gui|ana +s (region,
    S. America; also in
    'French Guiana'
    etc. △ Guyana)
Gui|ana
    High|lands
    (plateau, S.
    America)
guid|able
guid|ance
Guide +s (member
    of Guides
    Association)
guide
    guides
    guided
    guid|ing
    (leader, book, etc.;
    to lead)
guide|book +s
guide dog +s
Guide Guider +s
guide|line +s
guide|post +s
Guider +s (leader
    in Guides)
guide rope +s
guide|way +s
gui|don +s
Gui|enne (use
    Guyenne)
Gui|gnol (puppet
    character)
Gui|gnol|esque
guild +s
    (association.
    △ gild)
guil|der +s (Dutch
    currency.
    △ gilder)

Guild|ford (town, England)
Guild|hall, the (in London)
guild|hall +s
guilds|man
  guilds|men
guilds|woman
  guilds|women
guile +s
guile|ful
guile|ful|ly
guile|ful|ness
guile|less
guile|less|ly
guile|less|ness
Gui|lin (city, China)
guil|le|mot +s
guil|loche +s
guil|lo|tine
  guil|lo|tines
  guil|lo|tined
  guil|lo|tin|ing
guil|lo|tin|er +s
guilt +s
  (culpability.
  △ gilt)
guilt com|plex
  guilt com|plexes
guilt|ily
guilti|ness
guilt|less
guilt|less|ly
guilt|less|ness
guilty
  guilt|ier
  guilti|est
guimp +s (use gimp)
Guinea (in W. Africa)
Guinea, Gulf of (off W. Africa)
guinea +s (money)
Guinea-Bissau (in W. Africa)
guinea fowl
  plural guinea fowl or guinea fowls
guinea hen +s
guinea pig +s
Guinea worm +s
Guin|evere
  Arthurian Legend
Guin|ness, Alec (English actor)
gui|pure
guise +s
gui|tar +s
gui|tar|ist +s
gui|tar play|er +s
guiver

Gui|yang (city, China)
Gui|zhou (province, China)
Gu|ja|rat (state, India)
Gu|ja|rati +s
Gu|je|rat (use Gujarat)
Gu|je|rati +s (use Gujarati)
Guj|ran|wala (city, Pakistan)
Guj|rat (city, Pakistan)
Gulag +s
Gul|barga (city, India)
Gul|ben|kian, Cal|ouste (Turkish-born British oil magnate)
gulch
  gulches
gul|den
  plural gul|den or gul|dens
gules
gulf +s +ed +ing
Gulf Stream
gulf|weed
gull +s +ed +ing
Gul|lah +s
gull|ery
  gull|er|ies
gul|let +s
gul|ley +s +ed +ing (use gully)
gul|li|bil|ity
gul|lible
gul|libly
gull-wing attributive
gully
  gul|lies
  gul|lied
  gully|ing
gully-hole +s
gulp +s +ed +ing
gulp|er +s
gulp|ing|ly
gulpy
gum
  gums
  gummed
  gum|ming
gum arab|ic
gum ben|ja|min
Gumbo (patois)
gumbo +s (okra; soup)
gum|boil +s

gum|boot +s
gum|drop +s
gumma
  gum|mas or gum|mata
gum|ma|tous
gum|mily
gum|mi|ness
gummy
  gum|mies
  gum|mier
  gum|mi|est
gump|tion
gum resin +s
gum|shield +s
gum|shoe +s
gum tree +s
gun
  guns
  gunned
  gun|ning
gun bar|rel +s
gun|boat +s
gun car|riage +s
gun cot|ton
gun crew +s
gun dog +s
gundy
gun|fight +s
gun|fight|er +s
gun|fire
gunge
  gunges
  gunged
  gun|ging
gung-ho
gungy
gunk
gun|less
gun|lock +s
gun|maker +s
gun|man
  gun|men
gun|metal
Gunn, Thom (English poet)
gun|nel +s (fish. △ gunwale)
gun|ner +s
gun|nera +s
gun|nery
gunny
  gun|nies
gun|play
gun|point
gun|pow|der +s
gun|power
gun|room +s
gun-runner +s
gun-running
gun|sel +s
gun|ship +s

gun|shot +s
gun-shy
gun|sight +s
gun-site +s
gun|sling|er +s
gun|sling|ing
gun|smith +s
gun|stock +s
Gun|ter's chain +s
gun-toting
Gun|tur (city, India)
gun|wale +s (of ship. △ gunnel)
gun|yah +s
Guo|min|dang (= Kuomintang)
guppy
  gup|pies
Gupta
Gup|tan
Gur|djieff, George Ivan|ovich (Russian spiritual leader)
gurd|wara +s
gur|gi|ta|tion
gur|gle
  gur|gles
  gur|gled
  gurg|ling
gurg|ler +s
gur|jun +s
Gur|kha +s
gurn +s +ed +ing
gur|nard
  plural gur|nard or gur|nards or gur|net
gurn|er +s
gur|net
  plural gur|net or gur|nets
Gur|ney, Ivor (English poet and composer)
guru +s
Gus (name)
gush
  gushes
  gushed
  gush|ing
gush|er +s
gush|ily
gushi|ness
gush|ing|ly
gushy
gus|set +s
gus|set|ed
gussy
  gus|sies

gussy (cont.)
  gus|sied
  gussy|ing
gust +s +ed +ing
gus|ta|tion
gus|ta|tive
gus|ta|tory
Gus|tavus
  Adol|phus
  (Swedish king)
gust|ily
gusti|ness
gusto
  gus|toes
gusty
  gust|ier
  gusti|est
gut
  guts
  gut|ted
  gut|ting
Guten|berg,
  Jo|han|nes
  (German printer)
Guth|rie, Woody
  (American folk
  singer-songwriter)
Gu|tiér|rez,
  Gus|tavo
  (Peruvian
  theologian)
gut|less
gut|less|ly
gut|less|ness
gut-rot
gut|ser +s (use
  gutzer)
guts|ily
gutsi|ness
gutsy
  guts|ier
  gutsi|est
gutta-percha
gut|tate
gut|ter +s +ed
  +ing
gut|ter press
gut|ter|snipe +s
gut|tle
  gut|tles
  gut|tled
  gut|tling
gut|tur|al +s
gut|tur|al|ise Br.
  (use gutturalize)
  gut|tur|al|ises
  gut|tur|al|ised
  gut|tur|al|is|ing
gut|tur|al|ism
gut|tur|al|ize
  gut|tur|al|izes

gut|tur|al|ize
  (cont.)
  gut|tur|al|ized
  gut|tur|al|iz|ing
gut|tur|al|ly
gut|zer +s
guv
Guy (name)
guy +s +ed +ing
  (man; ridicule)
Guy|ana (country,
  S. America.
  △ Guiana)
Guy|an|ese
  plural Guy|an|ese
Guy|enne (region,
  France)
guz|zle
  guz|zles
  guz|zled
  guz|zling
guz|zler +s
Gwa|lior (city,
  India)
Gwen
Gwenda
Gwen|do|len also
  Gwen|do|line
Gwen|do|line also
  Gwen|do|len
Gwent (county,
  Wales)
Gwen|yth also
  Gwyn|eth
Gwyn|edd (county,
  Wales)
Gwyn|eth also
  Gwen|yth
Gwynn, Nell
  (English comedy
  actress; mistress
  of Charles II)
Gyan|dzhe
  (Russian name for
  Gäncä)
gybe Br.
  gybes
  gybed
  gyb|ing
  (Am. jibe. Sailing.
  △ jibe, gibe)
Gyles also Giles
gym +s
gym|khana +s
gym|na|sial
gym|na|sium
  gym|na|siums or
  gym|na|sia
gym|nast +s
gym|nas|tic
gym|nas|tic|al|ly
gym|nas|tics

gym|noso|phist +s
gym|noso|phy
gym|no|sperm +s
gym|no|sperm|ous
gymp +s (use
  gimp)
gym|slip +s
gym tunic +s
gy|nae|ceum +s
  (women's
  apartments.
  △ gynoecium)
gy|nae|coc|racy
  Br.
gy|nae|coc|ra|cies
  (Am.
  gynecocracy)
gy|nae|co|logic|al
  Br. (Am.
  gynecological)
gy|nae|co|logic|
  al|ly Br. (Am.
  gynecologically)
gy|nae|colo|gist
  Br. +s (Am.
  gynecologist)
gy|nae|col|ogy Br.
  (Am. gynecology)
gy|nae|co|mas|tia
  Br. (Am.
  gynecomastia)
gy|nan|dro|morph
  +s
gy|nan|dro|
    morph|ic
gy|nan|dro|morph|
  ism
gy|nan|drous
gyne|coc|racy Am.
gyne|coc|ra|cies
  (Br.
  gynaecocracy)
gyne|co|logic Am.
  (Br.
  gynaecologic)
gyne|co|logic|al
  Am. (Br.
  gynaecological)
gyne|co|logic|al|ly
  Am. (Br.
  gynaecologically)
gyne|colo|gist Am.
  +s (Br.
  gynaecologist)
gyne|cology Am.
  (Br. gynaecology)
gyne|co|mas|tia
  Am. (Br.
  gynaecomastia)
gyn|oc|racy
  gyn|oc|ra|cies

gy|noe|cium
gy|noe|cia
  (part of flower.
  △ gynaeceum)
gyno|pho|bia
gyp
  gyps
  gypped
  gyp|ping
gyppy (use gippy)
gyp|seous
gyp|sif|er|ous
gypso|phila +s
gyp|sum
gypsy
  gyp|sies
Gypsy|dom
Gypsy|fied
Gypsy|hood
Gypsy|ish
gypsy moth +s
gyr|ate
  gyr|ates
  gyr|ated
  gyr|at|ing
gyr|ation +s
gyr|ator +s
gyr|atory
gyre
  gyres
  gyred
  gyr|ing
gyr|fal|con +s
gyri
gyro +s
  (gyroscope;
  gyrocompass.
  △ giro)
gyro|com|pass
  gyro|com|passes
gyro|graph +s
gyro|mag|net|ic
gyro|pilot +s
gyro|plane +s
gyro|scope +s
gyro|scop|ic
gyro|sta|bil|iser
  Br. +s (use
  gyrostabilizer)
gyro|sta|bil|izer
  +s
gyrus
  gyri
gyt|tja
Gyumri (city,
  Armenia)
gyver (use guiver)

Hh

ha
 ha's
 ha'd
 ha'ing
Haag, Den (Dutch
 name for The
 Hague)
haar +s (fog)
Haar|lem (city, the
 Netherlands.
 ⚠ Harlem)
Hab|ak|kuk *Bible*
haba|nera +s
hab|dabs
hab|eas cor|pus
Haber–Bosch
 pro|cess
hab|er|dash|er +s
hab|er|dash|ery
hab|er|dash|er|ies
hab|er|geon +s
ha|bili|ment +s
ha|bili|tate
 ha|bili|tates
 ha|bili|tated
 ha|bili|tat|ing
ha|bili|ta|tion
habit +s
hab|it|abil|ity
hab|it|able
hab|it|able|ness
hab|it|ably
hab|it|ant +s
habi|tat +s
habi|ta|tion +s
hab|it|ed
habit-forming
ha|bit|ual
ha|bit|ual|ly
ha|bit|ual|ness
ha|bitu|ate
 ha|bitu|ates
 ha|bitu|ated
 ha|bitu|at|ing
ha|bitu|ation
habi|tude +s
ha|bi|tué +s
Habs|burg +s (use
 Hapsburg)
habu|tai
háček +s
hach|ure
 hach|ures
 hach|ured
 hach|ur|ing
ha|ci|enda +s
hack +s +ed +ing

hack|berry
 hack|berries
hack|er +s
hack|ery
hack|er|ies
hack|ette +s
hackle
 hackles
 hackled
 hack|ling
hackly
hack|ma|tack +s
Hack|ney (in
 London)
hack|ney +s
 (carriage)
hack|neyed
hack|saw +s +ed
 +ing
had
had|die +s
had|dock
 plural had|dock
hade
 hades
 haded
 had|ing
 (incline)
Ha|dean
Hades *Greek
 Mythology*
Hadhra|maut
 (coastal region,
 Yemen)
Had|ith
hadj (use haj)
hadji (use haji)
Had|lee, Rich|ard
 (New Zealand
 cricketer)
hadn't (= had not)
Ha|drian (Roman
 emperor)
Ha|drian's Wall (in
 N. England)
had|ron +s
had|ron|ic
had|ro|saur +s
hadst
haec|ce|ity
 haec|ce|ities
Haeckel, Ernst
 Hein|rich
 (German biologist
 and philosopher)
haem *Br.* +s (*Am.*
 heme)
haem|al *Br.* (*Am.*
 hemal)
haem|at|ic *Br.* (*Am.*
 hematic)

haem|atin *Br.* (*Am.*
 hematin)
haem|atite *Br.* (*Am.*
 hematite)
haem|ato|cele *Br.*
 +s (*Am.*
 hematocele)
haem|ato|crit *Br.*
 +s (*Am.*
 hematocrit)
haem|ato|logic *Br.*
 (*Am.*
 hematologic)
haem|ato|logic|al
 Br. (*Am.*
 hematological)
haema|tolo|gist *Br.*
 +s (*Am.*
 hematologist)
haema|tol|ogy *Br.*
 (*Am.* hematology)
haem|atoma *Br.* +s
 (*Am.* hematoma)
haema|topha|gous
 Br. (*Am.*
 hematophagous)
haem|aturia *Br.*
 (*Am.* hematuria)
haemo|coel *Br.* +s
 (*Am.* hemocoel)
haemo|cya|nin *Br.*
 (*Am.*
 hemocyanin)
haemo|di|aly|sis
 Br.
 haemo|di|aly|ses
 (*Am.*
 hemodialysis)
haemo|globin *Br.*
 +s (*Am.*
 hemoglobin)
haemo|lymph *Br.*
 (*Am.* hemolymph)
haem|oly|sis *Br.*
 haem|oly|ses
 (*Am.* hemolysis)
haemo|lyt|ic *Br.*
 (*Am.* hemolytic)
haemo|philia *Br.*
 (*Am.* hemophilia)
haemo|phil|iac *Br.*
 +s (*Am.*
 hemophiliac)
haemo|phil|ic *Br.*
 (*Am.* hemophilic)
haem|or|rhage *Br.*
 haem|or|rhages
 haem|or|rhaged
 haem|or|rha|ging
 (*Am.*
 hemorrhage)

haem|or|rhagic *Br.*
 (*Am.*
 hemorrhagic)
haem|or|rhoid *Br.*
 +s (*Am.*
 hemorrhoid)
haem|or|rhoid|al
 Br. (*Am.*
 hemorrhoidal)
haemo|stasis *Br.*
 haemo|stases
 (*Am.* hemostasis)
haemo|stat|ic *Br.*
 (*Am.* hemostatic)
haere mai
hafiz
haf|nium
haft +s +ed +ing
hag +s
Hagar *Bible*
Hagen (city,
 Germany)
hag|fish
 plural hag|fish *or*
 hag|fishes
Hag|ga|dah
 Hag|ga|doth
Hag|gad|ic
Hag|gai *Bible*
Hag|gard, Rider
 (English writer)
hag|gard +s
hag|gard|ly
hag|gard|ness
hag|gis
 hag|gises
hag|gish
hag|gle
 hag|gles
 hag|gled
 hag|gling
hag|gler +s
Hagia So|phia
 (= St Sophia)
hagi|oc|racy
 hagi|oc|racies
Hagi|og|rapha
 (part of Hebrew
 Bible)
hagi|og|raph|er +s
 (writer)
hagio|graph|ic
hagio|graph|ic|al
hagi|og|raphy
 hagi|og|raph|ies
hagi|ol|ater +s
hagi|ol|atry
hagio|logic|al
hagi|olo|gist +s
hagi|ology
hagio|scop|ic
hag-ridden

Hague, The (city, the Netherlands)
hah interjection (use ha)
ha ha (laughter)
ha-ha +s (ditch)
Hahn, Otto (German chemist)
hahn|ium
haick +s (use haik)
Haida
    plural Haida or Haidas
Haifa (port, Israel)
Haig, Doug|las (Earl Haig, British field marshal)
haik +s (Arab garment. △ hake)
Hai|kou (capital of Hainan)
haiku
    plural haiku
hail +s +ed +ing (frozen rain; greet. △ hale)
hail|er +s
Haile Sel|as|sie (Ethiopian emperor)
Hai|ley also Hay|ley
hail-fellow-well-met
Hail Mary
    Hail Mar|ies
hail|stone +s
hail|storm +s
Hail|wood, Mike (English racing motorcyclist)
haily
Hai|nan (Chinese island)
Hain|aut (province, Belgium)
Hai|phong (port, Vietnam)
hair +s (on head etc. △ hare)
hair|breadth
    attributive
hair|brush
    hair|brushes
hair|care
hair|cloth
hair|cut +s
hair|do +s
hair|dress|er +s
hair|dress|ing
hair|drier +s (use hairdryer)

hair|dryer +s
haired
hair-grass
    hair-grasses
hair|grip +s
hair|ily
hairi|ness
hair|less
hair|less|ness
hair|like
hair|line +s
hair|net +s
hair|piece +s
hair|pin +s
hair-raising
hair's breadth +s
hair shirt +s
hair-shirt attributive
hair|slide +s
hair-splitter +s
hair-splitting
hair|spray +s
hair|spring +s
hair|streak +s
hair|style +s
hair|styl|ing
hair|styl|ist +s
hair-trigger +s
hairy
    hair|ier
    hairi|est
Haiti (in Caribbean)
Hai|tian +s
haj (pilgrimage)
haji +s (pilgrim)
hajj (use haj)
hajji +s (use haji)
haka +s
hake
    plural hake or hakes
    (fish. △ haik)
ha|ken|kreuz
    ha|ken|kreuze
hakim +s
Hakka +s
Hak|luyt, Rich|ard (English geographer and historian)
Hako|date (port, Japan)
Hal
Ha|la|cha
Ha|la|ch|ic
Ha|la|fian
Ha|la|kah (use Halacha)
halal
    halals
hal|alled
halal|ling
hal|ation

hal|berd +s
hal|berd|ier +s
hal|cyon +s
Hal|dane, John Bur|don San|der|son (Scottish biologist)
Hale, George El|lery (American astronomer)
hale
    hales
    haled
    hal|ing
    (healthy; drag. △ hail)
hale|ness
haler
    plural haler or hal|eru (Bohemian, Moravian, and Slovak currency)
Hales|owen (town, England)
Haley, Bill (American rock and roll singer)
half
    halves
half a crown
half a dozen
half a litre
half-and-half
half an hour
half an inch
half-back +s
half-baked
half-beak
    plural half-beak or half-beaks
half-binding
half-blood +s
half-blooded
half-blue +s
half board noun
half-board attributive
half-boot +s
half-bottle +s
half-breed +s (offensive)
half-brother +s
half-caste +s (offensive)
half-century
    half-centur|ies
half-crown +s
half-cut
half-deck +s
half-dozen +s
half-duplex

half-hardy
    half-hardies
half-hearted
half-hearted|ly
half-hearted|ness
half hitch
    half hitches
half holi|day +s
half-hose
half-hour +s
half-hourly
half-hunter +s
half-inch
    half-inches
    half-inched
    half-inching
    (unit; steal)
half-integral
half-landing +s
half-lap
half-length +s
half-life
    half-lives
half-light
half-litre +s
half-marathon +s
half-mast
half meas|ures
half-moon +s
half nel|son +s
half note +s
half pay
half|penny
    half|pen|nies
    or half|pence
half|penny|worth
half-pie
half-plate +s
half-price
half-relief +s
half-seas-over
half share +s
half-sister +s
half-size
half-sole +s
half-sovereign +s
half-starved
half-step +s
half-term +s
half-timbered
half-timber|ing
half-time
half-title +s
half-tone +s
half-track +s
half-truth +s
half-volley +s
half|way
half|wit +s
half-witted
half-witted|ly

half-witted¦ness
half year +s *noun*
half-year *attributive*
half-yearly
hali¦but
  plural hali¦but
Hali¦car¦nas¦sus
  (ancient Greek
  city, Asia Minor)
hal¦ide +s
hali¦eut¦ic
Hali¦fax (city,
  Canada; town,
  England)
hali¦otis
  plural hali¦otis
hal¦ite +s
hali¦tosis
Hall, Charles
  Mar¦tin
  (American
  industrial chemist)
Hall, Rad¦clyffe
  (English writer)
hall +s (room.
  ⚠ haul)
hal¦lal (use halal)
Halle (city,
  Germany)
Hallé, Charles
  (German-born
  conductor)
hal¦le¦lu¦jah +s
Hal¦ler, Al¦brecht
  von (Swiss
  physiologist)
Hal¦ley, Ed¦mond
  (English
  astronomer)
Hal¦ley's Comet
hal¦liard +s (use
  halyard)
hall¦mark +s +ed
  +ing
hallo (use hello)
  hal¦loes
  hal¦loed
  hallo¦ing
hal¦loo +s +ed
  +ing
hal¦low +s +ed
  +ing
Hal¦low¦e'en
Hal¦lowes, Odette
  (French secret
  agent)
hall¦stand +s
Hall¦statt (village,
  Austria;
  Archaeology)
hal¦lu¦ces
hal¦lu¦cin¦ant +s

hal¦lu¦cin¦ate
hal¦lu¦cin¦ates
hal¦lu¦cin¦ated
hal¦lu¦cin¦at¦ing
hal¦lu¦cin¦ation +s
hal¦lu¦cin¦ator +s
hal¦lu¦cin¦atory
hal¦lu¦cino¦gen +s
hal¦lu¦cino¦gen¦ic
hal¦lux
  hal¦lu¦ces
hall¦way +s
halm +s (use
  haulm)
halma
Hal¦ma¦hera
  (island, Moluccas)
halo
  ha¦loes *or* halos
  noun
halo
  ha¦loes
  ha¦loed
  ha¦lo¦ing
  verb
halo¦car¦bon +s
halo¦gen +s
halo¦gen¦ated
halo¦gen¦ation
halo¦gen¦ic
halon +s
halo¦peri¦dol
halo¦phyte +s
halo¦thane
Hals, Frans (Dutch
  painter)
halt +s +ed +ing
hal¦ter +s
halter-break
  halter-breaks
  halter-broke
  halter-breaking
  halter-broken
hal¦tere +s
halter-neck +s
  noun and
  attributive
halt¦ing¦ly
halva +s
halve
  halves
  halved
  halv¦ing
  verb
halves (plural of
  half)
hal¦yard +s
Ham *Bible*
ham
  hams
  hammed
  ham¦ming

ham (*cont.*)
  (meat; actor; radio
  operator)
Hama (city, Syria)
Ham¦ada, Shoji
  (Japanese potter)
hama¦dryad +s
  (nymph; snake)
hama¦dryas
  hama¦dry¦ases
  (baboon)
Hamah (use
  Hama)
Hama¦matsu (city,
  Japan)
hama¦melis
  plural hama¦melis
ha¦mar¦tia
Hamas (Palestinian
  Islamic
  fundamentalist
  movement)
hamba
ham¦bone +s
Ham¦burg (city,
  Germany)
ham¦burg¦er +s
  (food)
Ham¦elin (English
  name for Hameln)
Ham¦eln (town,
  Germany)
hames
ham-fisted
ham-fisted¦ly
ham-fisted¦ness
ham-handed
ham-handed¦ly
ham-handed¦ness
Ham¦hung (city,
  North Korea)
Ham¦il¦car
  (Carthaginian
  general)
Ham¦il¦ton (town,
  Scotland, port,
  Canada; city, New
  Zealand; capital of
  Bermuda)
Ham¦il¦ton,
  Charles (New
  Zealand inventor
  and racing driver)
Ham¦il¦ton, Emma
  (mistress of Lord
  Nelson)
Ham¦il¦ton,
  Wil¦liam Rowan
  (Irish
  mathematician
  and physicist)
Ha¦mish

Ham¦ite +s
Ham¦it¦ic +s
Hamito-Semitic
Ham¦let (Danish
  prince)
ham¦let +s (village)
Hamm (city,
  Germany)
ham¦mer +s +ed
  +ing
ham¦mer and
  tongs (vigorously)
ham¦mer¦beam +s
ham¦mer drill +s
ham¦mer¦er +s
Ham¦mer¦fest
  (port, Norway)
ham¦mer¦head +s
  (shark; bird)
ham¦mer head +s
  (head of hammer)
ham¦mer¦ing +s
ham¦mer¦less
ham¦mer¦lock +s
ham¦mer¦man
  ham¦mer¦men
Ham¦mer¦stein,
  Oscar (American
  librettist)
hammer-toe +s
Ham¦mett,
  Dash¦iell
  (American
  detective-story
  writer)
ham¦mock +s
Ham¦mond, Joan
  (Australian
  soprano)
Ham¦mu¦rabi
  (Babylonian king)
hammy
  ham¦mier
  ham¦miest
Ham¦nett,
  Kath¦ar¦ine
  (English fashion
  designer)
ham¦per +s +ed
  +ing
Hamp¦shire
  (county, England)
Hamp¦stead
  (district, London)
Hamp¦ton (city,
  USA)
Hamp¦ton Court
  (palace, London)
Hamp¦ton Roads
  (estuary, USA)
ham¦sin +s (use
  khamsin)

ham|ster +s
ham|string
  ham|strings
  ham|stringed *or*
  ham|strung
  ham|string|ing
Ham|sun, Knut
  (Norwegian
  novelist)
ham|ulus
  ham|uli
Han (Chinese
  dynasty)
Han|cock, Tony
  (English
  comedian)
hand +s +ed +ing
hand-axe +s
hand|bag
  hand|bags
  hand|bagged
  hand|bag|ging
hand|ball +s
hand|basin +s
hand|bell +s
hand|bill +s
hand|book +s
hand|brake +s
hand-built
hand|cart +s
hand|clap +s
hand|clap|ping
hand|craft +s +ed
  +ing
hand cream +s
hand|cuff +s +ed
  +ing
hand|ed|ness
Han|del, George
  Fred|erick
  (German-born
  composer)
hand-eye
  co|ordin|ation
hand|ful +s
hand|glass
  hand|glasses
hand gren|ade +s
hand|grip +s
hand|gun +s
hand-held +s
hand|hold +s
hand-holding
hand-hot
handi|cap
  handi|caps
  handi|capped
  handi|cap|ping
han|di|cap|per +s
han|di|craft +s
handi|ily
handi|ness

hand in glove
hand in hand
  adverbial
hand-in-hand
  attributive
han|di|work
hand|ker|chief
  hand|ker|chiefs *or*
  hand|ker|chieves
hand-knit +s *noun*
  and attributive
hand-knitted
hand-knitting
han|dle
  han|dles
  han|dled
  hand|ling
handle|abil|ity
handle|able
handle|bar +s
hand|ler +s
hand|less
Hand|ley Page,
  Fred|erick
  (English aircraft
  designer)
hand|line
  hand|lines
  hand|lined
  hand|lin|ing
hand|list +s
hand|made (made
  by hand)
hand|maid +s
  (servant)
hand|maiden +s
hand-me-down +s
hand-off +s *noun*
hand|out +s
hand|over +s
hand-painted
hand-pick +s +ed
  +ing
hand|pump +s
hand|rail +s
hand|saw +s
hand|sel
  hand|sels
  hand|selled *Br.*
  hand|seled *Am.*
  hand|sel|ling *Br.*
  hand|sel|ing *Am.*
hand|set +s
hand|shake +s
hands off
  (warning)
hands-off *adjective*
hand|some
  hand|somer
  hand|som|est
  (good-looking.
  ⚠ hansom)

hand|some|ly
hand|some|ness
hands-on *adjective*
hand|spike +s
hand|spring +s
hand|stand +s
hand-to-hand
hand-to-mouth
  attributive
hand tool +s
hand|work
hand|worked
hand|writ|ing +s
hand|writ|ten
handy
  hand|ier
  handi|est
handy|man
  handy|men
hang
  hangs
  hung
  hang|ing
  (suspend)
hang +s +ed +ing
  (execute)
hangar +s (shed.
  ⚠ hanger)
hang|ar|age
Hang|chow
  (= Hangzhou)
hang|dog
hanger +s (coat-
  hanger etc.; wood
  on side of hill.
  ⚠ hangar)
hanger-on
  hangers-on
hang-glide
  hang-glides
  hang-glided
  hang-gliding
hang-glider +s
hang|ing +s *noun*
hang|man
  hang|men
hang|nail +s
hang-out +s *noun*
hang|over +s
Hang Seng index
hang-up +s *noun*
Hang|zhou (city,
  China)
hank +s
han|ker +s +ed
  +ing
han|ker|er +s
han|kie +s (use
  hanky)
hanky
  han|kies
hanky-panky

Han|nah
Han|ni|bal
  (Carthaginian
  general)
Han|nover
  (German name for
  Hanover)
Hanoi (capital of
  Vietnam)
Han|over (city,
  Germany)
Han|over|ian +s
Hansa (guild;
  Hanseatic league)
Han|sard (British
  parliament)
Hanse (use Hansa)
Han|se|at|ic
Han|sel (and
  Gretel)
han|sel (gift; use
  handsel)
han|sels
  han|selled *Br.*
  han|seled *Am.*
  han|sel|ling *Br.*
  han|sel|ing *Am.*
Han|sen's dis|ease
han|som +s (cab.
  ⚠ handsome)
Hants
  (= Hampshire)
Ha|nuk|kah
  (Jewish festival)
Ha|nu|man (Hindu
  mythological
  creature)
ha|nu|man +s
  (monkey)
Haora (use
  Howrah)
hap
  haps
  happed
  hap|ping
hapax
  leg|om|enon
hapax leg|om|ena
ha'|penny
  ha'|pennies *or*
  ha'|pence
hap|haz|ard
hap|haz|ard|ly
hap|haz|ard|ness
hap|less
hap|less|ly
hap|less|ness
hap|log|raphy
hap|loid +s
hap|lol|ogy
ha'p'|orth (= half-
  pennyworth)

hap|pen +s +ed
+ing
hap|pen|ing +s
hap|pen|stance +s
happi +s (Japanese
coat. △ happy)
happi-coat +s
hap|pily
hap|pi|ness
hap|pi|nesses
happy
hap|pier
hap|pi|est
(feeling pleasure.
△ happi)
happy-go-lucky
Haps|burg +s
(central European
dynasty; member
of this)
hap|tic
hara-kiri
har|angue
har|angues
har|angued
har|anguing
har|anguer +s
Har|appa (ancient
city, Pakistan)
Har|are (capital of
Zimbabwe)
har|ass
har|asses
har|assed
har|ass|ing
har|ass|er +s
har|ass|ing|ly
har|ass|ment +s
Har|bin (city,
China)
har|bin|ger +s +ed
+ing
har|bor Am. +s +ed
+ing
har|bor|age Am.
har|bor|less Am.
har|bor|mas|ter
Am. +s
har|bour Br. +s
+ed +ing
har|bour|age Br.
har|bour|less Br.
har|bour mas|ter
Br. +s
hard +s +er +est
hard and fast
hard|back +s
hard|bake
hard-baked
hard|ball +s +ed
+ing
hard|bit|ten

hard|board +s
hard-boiled
hard|core (rubble;
music)
hard core +s
(nucleus)
hard-core adjective
hard|cover +s
hard disk +s
hard-done-by
hard-earned
hard|en +s +ed
+ing
hard|en|er +s
hard hat +s
hard-headed
hard-headed|ly
hard-headed|ness
hard|heads
plural hard|heads
(plant)
hard-hearted
hard-hearted|ly
hard-hearted|ness
hard hit adjective
hard-hit attributive
hard-hitting
Har|die, Keir
(Scottish
politician.
△ Hardy)
hardi|hood
har|dily
hardi|ness
Hard|ing, War|ren
(American
president)
hard|ish
hard|line attributive
hard line noun
(unyielding
adherence to
policy)
hard|liner +s
hard lines (bad
luck)
hard|ly
hard|ness
hard-nosed
hard of hear|ing
hard-on +s (coarse
slang)
hard|pan
hard-paste
adjective
hard-pressed
hard|shell adjective
hard|ship +s
hard|stand|ing
hard tack
hard-top +s (car;
roof)

hard up adjective
hard-up attributive
Har|dwar (city,
India)
hard|ware
hard-wearing
hard-wired
hard|wood +s
hard-working
Hardy, Oli|ver
(American
comedian.
△ Hardie)
Hardy, Thomas
(English writer.
△ Hardie)
hardy
har|dier
har|di|est
Hare, Wil|liam
(Irish body-
snatcher)
hare
hares
hared
har|ing
(animal. △ hair)
hare|bell +s
hare-brained
Hare|foot, Har|old
(English king)
Hare Krishna +s
(chant; sect;
member of sect)
hare|lip +s
(offensive; to avoid
offence, use cleft
lip)
hare|lipped
(offensive)
harem +s
hare's-ear +s
hare's-foot +s
hare|wood
Har|geisa (city,
Somalia)
Har|geysa (use
Hargeisa)
Har|greaves,
James (English
inventor)
hari|cot +s
Hari|jan +s
hark +s +ed +ing
hark|en +s +ed
+ing (use
hearken)
harl
harle (use harl)
Har|lech (village,
Wales)

Har|lem (district,
New York City;
Globetrotters;
Renaissance.
△ Haarlem)
Har|le|quin (in
pantomine)
har|le|quin (duck
etc.)
har|le|quin|ade +s
Har|ley Street (in
London)
har|lot +s
har|lot|ry
Har|low (town,
England)
harm +s +ed +ing
har|mat|tan
harm|ful
harm|ful|ly
harm|ful|ness
harm|less
harm|less|ly
harm|less|ness
har|mon|ic +s
har|mon|ica +s
har|mon|ic|al|ly
har|mo|ni|ous
har|mo|ni|ous|ly
har|mo|ni|ous|
ness
har|mon|isa|tion
Br. (use
harmonization)
har|mon|ise Br.
(use harmonize)
har|mon|ises
har|mon|ised
har|mon|is|ing
har|mon|ist +s
har|mon|is|tic
har|mo|nium +s
har|mon|iza|tion
har|mon|ize
har|mon|izes
har|mon|ized
har|mon|iz|ing
har|mony
har|monies
Harms|worth,
Al|fred Charles
Wil|liam (Lord
Northcliffe)
har|ness
har|nesses
har|nessed
har|ness|ing
har|ness|er +s
Har|old (English
kings)

Haroun-al-
  Raschid (use
  Harun ar-Rashid)
harp +s +ed +ing
har¦per +s
Har¦pers Ferry
  (town, USA)
harp¦ist +s
Har¦poc¦ra¦tes
  Greek Mythology
har¦poon +s +ed
  +ing
har¦poon¦er +s
har¦poon gun +s
harp seal +s
harp¦si¦chord +s
harp¦si¦chord¦ist
  +s
harpy
  har¦pies
har¦que¦bus
  har¦que¦buses
har¦que¦bus¦ier +s
har¦ri¦dan +s
har¦rier +s
Har¦riet
Har¦ris (Scottish
  island; tweed)
Har¦ris¦burg (town,
  USA)
Har¦ri¦son,
  Ben¦ja¦min
  (American
  president)
Har¦ri¦son, Rex
  (English actor)
Har¦ri¦son,
  Wil¦liam Henry
  (American
  president)
Har¦rod, Charles
  Henry (English
  grocer)
Har¦ro¦vian +s
Har¦row (school,
  England)
har¦row +s +ed
  +ing (tool etc.)
har¦row¦er +s
har¦row¦ing¦ly
har¦rumph +s +ed
  +ing
Harry (name)
harry
  har¦ries
  har¦ried
  harry¦ing
  (ravage; worry)
harsh +er +est
harsh¦en +s +ed
  +ing
harsh¦ly

harsh¦ness
hars¦let +s
hart +s (deer.
  △heart)
har¦tal
Harte, Bret
  (American writer)
har¦te¦beest
  plural har¦te¦beest
  or har¦te¦beests
Hart¦ford (city,
  USA. △Hertford)
Hart¦le¦pool (port,
  England)
Hart¦ley, L. P.
  (English novelist)
Hart¦nell,
  Nor¦man (English
  couturier)
harts¦horn
hart's tongue +s
harum-scarum +s
Harun ar-Rashid
  (caliph of
  Baghdad)
haru¦spex
  haru¦spi¦ces
haru¦spicy
Har¦vard
  (university, USA;
  classification)
har¦vest +s +ed
  +ing
har¦vest¦able
har¦vest¦er +s
har¦vest¦man
  har¦vest¦men
Har¦vey
Har¦vey, Wil¦liam
  (English
  physician)
Har¦wich (port,
  England)
Ha¦ry¦ana (state,
  India)
Harz Moun¦tains
  (in Germany)
has
has-been +s
Has¦dru¦bal (two
  Carthaginian
  generals)
Hašek, Jaro¦slav
  (Czech writer)
hash
  hashes
  hashed
  hash¦ing
Hash¦em¦ite +s
hash¦ish
Hasid
  Has¦id¦im

Ha¦sid¦ic
Has¦id¦ism
has¦let +s
Has¦mon¦ean
hasn't (= has not)
hasp +s +ed +ing
Has¦selt (city,
  Belgium)
has¦sle
  has¦sles
  has¦sled
  has¦sling
has¦sock +s
hast (in 'thou hast')
hast¦ate
haste
  hastes
  hasted
  hast¦ing
  (hurry)
has¦ten +s +ed
  +ing
hasti¦ly
hasti¦ness
Hast¦ings (town
  and battle site,
  England)
Hast¦ings,
  War¦ren
  (governor-general
  of India)
hasty
  hasti¦er
  hasti¦est
hat
  hats
  hat¦ted
  hat¦ting
hat¦able (deserving
  to be hated)
hat¦band +s
hat¦box
  hat¦boxes
hatch
  hatches
  hatched
  hatch¦ing
hatch¦back +s
hatch¦ery
  hatch¦er¦ies
hatchet +s
hatchet-faced
hatchet job +s
hatchet man
  hatchet men
hatch¦ing +s
hatch¦ling +s
hatch¦ment +s
hatch¦way +s
hate
  hates

hate (cont.)
  hated
  hat¦ing
hate¦ful
hate¦ful¦ly
hate¦ful¦ness
hater +s
hat¦ful +s
hath
Hath¦away, Anne
  (wife of
  Shakespeare)
hatha yoga
Hathor Egyptian
  Mythology
hat¦less
hat¦peg +s
hat¦pin +s
hat¦red +s
Hat¦shep¦sut
  (Egyptian queen)
hat¦stand +s
hat¦ter +s
Hat¦tie
hat-trick +s
Hat¦tusa (ancient
  city, Turkey)
hau¦berk +s
haught¦ily
haughti¦ness
haughty
  haught¦ier
  haught¦iest
haul +s +ed +ing
  (pull in. △hall)
haul¦age
haul¦er +s
haul¦ier +s
haulm +s
haunch
  haunches
haunt +s +ed +ing
haunt¦er +s
haunt¦ing¦ly
Haupt¦mann,
  Ger¦hart (German
  dramatist)
Hausa
  plural Hausa or
  Hau¦sas
haus¦frau
  haus¦fraus or
  haus¦frau¦en
haut¦boy +s
haute cou¦ture
haute cuis¦ine
haute école
Haute-Normandie
  (region, France)
haut¦eur
haut monde
haut-relief +s

Hav¦ana +s (capital of Cuba; cigar)

Hav¦ant (town, England)

have

  has

  had

  hav¦ing

have-a-go
  attributive

Havel, Vác¦lav (Czech writer and president)

have|lock +s

haven +s

have-not +s

haven't (= have not)

haver +s +ed +ing

hav¦er|sack +s

hav¦er|sin (abbreviation of haversine)

hav¦er|sine +s

hav¦il|dar +s

havoc

  havocs

  hav|ocked

  hav¦ock|ing

haw +s +ed +ing (hawthorn; eyelid; in 'hum and haw'. ⚠ hoar, whore)

Ha¦waii (state and island, USA)

Ha¦wai|ian +s

haw|finch

  haw|finches

hawk +s +ed +ing

hawk|bit +s

Hawke, Bob (Australian prime minister)

Hawke Bay (bay, New Zealand)

hawk¦er +s

Hawke's Bay (region, New Zealand)

hawk-eyed

Hawk|ing, Ste¦phen (English theoretical physicist)

Haw|kins, Cole|man (American jazz saxophonist)

Haw|kins, John (English sailor)

hawk|ish

hawk¦ish|ness

hawk|like

hawk|moth +s

hawk-nosed

Hawks, How¦ard (American film director)

hawks|bill +s

Hawks|moor, Nich|olas (English architect)

hawk|weed +s

Haw|kyns, John (use Hawkins)

Ha¦worth, Wal¦ter Nor¦man (English organic chemist)

hawse +s

hawse-hole +s

hawse-pipe +s

haw¦ser +s

haw|thorn +s

Haw|thorne, Na¦than|iel (American writer)

hay +s +ed +ing (dried grass; dance. ⚠ heigh, hey)

hay¦box

hay|boxes

hay|cock +s

Haydn, Jo¦seph (Austrian composer)

Hayek, Fried|rich Au¦gust von (Austrian-born economist)

Hayes, Ruth¦er|ford (American president)

hay fever

hay|field +s

hay-fork +s

Hay¦ley *also* Hai¦ley

hay|loft +s

hay|maker +s

hay|mak¦ing

hay¦mow

hay|rick +s

hay|seed +s

hay|stack +s

hay|ward +s

hay|wire

Hay|worth, Rita (American actress)

haz¦ard +s +ed +ing

haz¦ard|ous

haz¦ard|ous|ly

haz¦ard|ous|ness

haze

  hazes

  hazed

  haz¦ing

Hazel (name)

hazel +s (tree)

hazel-grouse
  plural hazel-grouse

hazel|nut +s

haz¦ily

hazi|ness

Haz|litt, Wil|liam (British essayist)

hazy

  hazi¦er

  hazi|est

H-block +s

H-bomb +s

he +s

Head, Edith (American costume designer)

head +s +ed +ing

head|ache +s

head|achy

head|age

head|band +s

head|bang¦er +s

head|bang|ing

head|board +s

head-butt +s +ed +ing

head case +s

head-cloth +s

head|count +s

head|dress

  head|dresses

head¦er +s

head|fast +s

head first

head|gear

head height

head|hunt +s +ed +ing

head|hunt¦er +s

head|ily

headi|ness

head|ing +s

head|lamp +s

head|land +s

head|less

head lice

head|light +s

head|line

  head|lines

  head|lined

  head|lin¦ing

head|liner +s

head|lock +s

head|long

head louse

  head lice

head|man

  head|men

head|mas¦ter +s

head|mas¦ter¦ly

head|mis¦tress

  head|mis¦tresses

head|most

head|note +s

head of state

  heads of state

head-on

head|phone +s

head|piece +s

head|quar¦ter +s +ed +ing

head|rest +s

head|room

head|sail +s

head|scarf

  head|scarves

head|set +s

head|ship +s

head|shrink¦er +s

heads|man

  heads|men

head|spring +s

head|square +s

head|stall +s

head start

head|stock +s

head|stone +s

head|strong

head|strong|ly

head|strong|ness

head teach¦er +s

head-to-head

head-up *adjective*

head voice

head|ward

head|water +s

head|way

head|wind +s

head|word +s

head|work

heady

  head|ier

  head|iest

heal +s +ed +ing (cure. ⚠ heel, hele, he'll)

heal|able

heal-all +s

heald +s

heal¦er +s

health

health|ful

health|ful|ly

health|ful|ness

health|ily

healthi|ness
healthy
  health|ier
  healthi|est
Hea¦ney, Sea¦mus
  (Irish poet)
heap +s +ed +ing
hear
  hears
  heard
  hear|ing
  (listen to. △ here)
hear|able
heard (past tense
  and past participle
  of hear. △ herd)
Heard and
  Mc¦Donald
  Is¦lands (in
  Indian Ocean)
hear¦er +s
hear|ing +s
hear|ing aid +s
hark¦en +s +ed
  +ing
hear|say
hearse +s
Hearst, Wil|liam
  Ran|dolph
  (American
  newspaper
  publisher)
heart +s (body
  organ. △ hart)
heart|ache +s
heart|beat +s
heart|break
heart|break¦er +s
heart|break¦ing
heart|broken
heart|burn
heart¦en +s +ed
  +ing
heart¦en|ing¦ly
heart|felt
hearth +s
hearth|rug +s
hearth|stone +s
heart¦ily
hearti|ness
heart|land +s
heart|less
heart|less¦ly
heart|less|ness
heart-lung
  ma|chine +s
heart-rending
heart-rending¦ly
heart's-blood
heart-searching
hearts|ease
heart|sick

heart|sick|ness
heart|sore
heart|strings
heart-throb +s
heart to heart
  adverb
heart-to-heart +s
  adjective and noun
heart-warming
heart|wood
hearty
  heart|ier
  hearti|est
heat +s +ed +ing
heat¦er +s
heat-exchan¦ger
  +s
Heath, Ed¦ward
  (British prime
  minister)
heath +s
heath-bell +s
hea|then +s
hea¦then|dom
hea¦then|ish
hea¦then|ism
hea|then¦ry
Hea|ther (name)
hea¦ther +s (shrub)
hea¦thery
heath|land +s
heath|less
heath|like
Heath Rob¦in|son
  adjective
Heath Rob¦in|son,
  W. (English
  cartoonist)
Heath|row (airport,
  London)
heathy
heat lamp +s
heat|proof
heat-resist¦ant
heat-seeking
heat|stroke
heat-treat +s +ed
  +ing
heat treat|ment
heat|wave +s
heave
  heaves
  heaved
  or hove *Nautical*
  heav|ing
heave-ho
heaven +s
heav¦en|li|ness
heav|en¦ly
heaven-sent
heav¦en|ward
heav¦en|wards

heaver +s
heavier-than-air
  attributive
heav|ily
heavi|ness
Heavi|side, Oli¦ver
  (English physicist)
Heavi|side layer
heavy
  heav|ies
  heav|ied
  heavy|ing
  heav|ier
  heavi|est
heavy-duty
heavy-footed
heavy-handed
heavy-handed¦ly
heavy-
  handed¦ness
heavy-hearted
heavy|ish
heavy-lidded
heavy-set
heavy|weight +s
heb|dom|adal
Hebe (*Greek
  Mythology*;
  asteroid)
hebe +s (shrub)
Hebei (province,
  China)
hebe|tude
Heb|raic
Heb|ra¦ic|al¦ly
Heb|ra|ise *Br.* (use
  Hebraize)
  Heb|ra|ises
  Heb|ra|ised
  Heb|ra|is¦ing
Heb|ra|ism +s
Heb|ra|ist +s
Heb|ra|is¦tic
Heb|ra|ize
  Heb|ra|izes
  Heb|ra|ized
  Heb|ra|iz¦ing
Heb|rew +s
Heb|ri|dean +s
Heb|ri¦des
  (shipping area off
  Scotland)
Heb|ri¦des, the
  (islands off
  Scotland)
Heb|ron (city, West
  Bank)
Heb|ros (ancient
  Greek name for
  the Maritsa)
Hec¦ate *Greek
  Mythology*

heca|tomb +s
heck
heck¦el|phone +s
heckle
  heckles
  heckled
  heck|ling
heck|ler +s
hec¦tar|age
hec|tare +s
hec¦tic
hec¦tic|al¦ly
hecto|gram +s
hecto|graph +s
hecto|liter *Am.* +s
hecto|litre *Br.* +s
hecto|meter *Am.*
  +s
hecto|metre *Br.* +s
Hec¦tor (*Greek
  Mythology*; name)
hec¦tor +s +ed
  +ing (bully)
hec¦tor|ing¦ly
Hec¦uba *Greek
  Mythology*
he'd (= he had; he
  would. △ heed)
hed¦dle +s
hedge
  hedges
  hedged
  hedg¦ing
hedge|hog +s
hedge|hoggy
hedge-hop
  hedge-hops
  hedge-hopped
  hedge-hopping
hedger +s
hedge|row +s
hedge spar¦row +s
hedge trim|mer +s
he|don¦ic
he|don|ism
he|don|ist +s
he|don|is¦tic
heebie-jeebies,
  the
heed +s +ed +ing
  (take notice of.
  △ he'd)
heed|ful
heed|ful¦ly
heed|ful|ness
heed|less
heed|less¦ly
heed|less|ness
hee-haw +s +ed
  +ing
heel +s +ed +ing
  (part of foot or

heel (*cont.*)
  shoe; kick with
  heel; replace heel
  on shoe. ⚠ heal,
  hele, he'll)
heel|ball
heel|less
heel|tap +s
Hefei (city, China)
heft +s +ed +ing
hefti|ly
hefti|ness
hefty
  heft|ier
  hefti|est
Hegel, Georg
  Wil|helm
  Fried|rich
  (German
  philosopher)
He|gel|ian +s
He|gel|ian|ism
hege|mon|ic
he|gem|ony
  he|gem|onies
Heg|ira
  (Muhammad's
  departure from
  Mecca to Medina)
heg|ira +s
  (generally)
Hei|deg|ger,
  Mar|tin (German
  philosopher)
Hei|del|berg (city,
  Germany)
Heidi
heifer +s
heigh (*interjection*
  expressing
  encouragement or
  enquiry. ⚠ hay,
  hey)
heigh-ho
height +s
  (highness.
  ⚠ hight)
height|en +s +ed
  +ing
Heil|bronn (city,
  Germany)
Hei|long (Chinese
  name for Amur)
Hei|long|jiang
  (province, China)
Hei|lung|kiang
  (= Heilongjiang)
Heine, Hein|rich
  (German poet)
hein|ous
hein|ous|ly
hein|ous|ness

Heinz, Henry
  John (American
  food
  manufacturer)
heir +s (inheritor.
  ⚠ air, e're, ere)
heir ap|par|ent
  heirs ap|par|ent
heir-at-law
  heirs-at-law
heir|dom
heir|ess
  heir|esses
heir|less
  (without an heir.
  ⚠ airless)
heir|loom +s
heir pre|sump|tive
  heirs
  pre|sump|tive
heir|ship (being an
  heir. ⚠ airship)
Hei|sen|berg, Karl
  (German
  physicist;
  uncertainty
  principle)
heist +s +ed +ing
hei-tiki +s
Hejaz (region,
  Saudi Arabia)
Hej|ira (use
  Hegira)
hej|ira +s (use
  hegira)
Hekla (volcano,
  Iceland)
HeLa (cells)
held
Hel|den|tenor +s
hele
  heles
  heled
  hel|ing
  (put plant in
  ground. ⚠ heal,
  heel, he'll)
Helen (daughter of
  Zeus and Leda;
  name. ⚠ Hellen)
Hel|ena (town,
  USA; name)
Hel|ena (Roman
  empress and
  saint)
hel|en|ium +s
Helga
he|li|acal
he|li|an|the|mum
  +s
he|li|an|thus
  plural
he|li|an|thus

hel|ic|al
hel|ic|al|ly
heli|ces
heli|chry|sum +s
he|li|city
heli|coid +s
Heli|con, Mount
  (in Greece)
heli|con +s (tuba)
heli|cop|ter +s +ed
  +ing
Heli|go|land
  (German island)
he|lio|cen|tric
he|lio|cen|tric|
            al|ly
He|lio|ga|balus
  (Roman emperor)
he|lio|gram +s
he|lio|graph +s
  +ed +ing
heli|og|raphy
he|lio|gra|vure
he|lio|lith|ic
he|li|om|eter +s
He|li|opo|lis
  (ancient city,
  Egypt)
Hel|ios *Greek*
  Mythology
he|lio|stat +s
he|lio|stat|ic
he|lio|ther|apy
he|lio|trope +s
he|lio|trop|ic
he|lio|trop|ism
he|lio|type +s
heli|pad +s
heli|port +s
heli-skiing
he|lium
helix
  heli|ces
hell (abode of the
  dead; etc.)
he'll (= he shall; he
  will. ⚠ heel, hill)
hell|acious
hell|acious|ly
Hel|lad|ic +s
hell|bend|er +s
hell-bent
hell-cat +s
hel|le|bore +s
hel|le|bor|ine +s
Hel|len (son or
  brother of
  Deucalion.
  ⚠ Helen)
Hel|lene +s
Hel|len|ic

Hel|len|isa|tion *Br.*
  (use
  Hellenization)
Hel|len|ise *Br.* (use
  Hellenize)
Hel|len|ises
Hel|len|ised
Hel|len|is|ing
Hel|len|ism
Hel|len|ist +s
Hel|len|is|tic
Hel|len|iza|tion
Hel|len|ize
  Hel|len|izes
  Hel|len|ized
  Hel|len|iz|ing
Hel|ler, Jo|seph
  (American
  novelist)
Hel|les|pont, the
  (ancient name for
  the Dardanelles)
hell|fire
hell|gram|mite +s
hell-hole +s
hell-hound +s
hell|ion +s
hell|ish
hell|ish|ly
hell|ish|ness
hell-like
Hell|man, Lil|lian
  (American
  dramatist)
hello +s *noun*
hello
  hell|oes
  hell|oed
  hel|lo|ing
  verb
hell|raiser +s
hell|rais|ing
Hell's Angel +s
Hell's Can|yon (in
  USA)
hell|luva (= 'hell of
  a')
hell|ward
helm +s +ed +ing
Hel|mand (river,
  Afghanistan)
hel|met +s +ed
  +ing
Helm|holtz,
  Her|mann
  Lud|wig
  Fer|di|nand von
  (German
  physiologist and
  physicist)
hel|minth +s
hel|minth|ia|sis

hel|minth|ic
hel|minth|oid
hel|minth|olo|gist +s
hel|minth|ology
Hel|mont, Jo|an|nes Bap|tista van (Belgian chemist)
helms|man
    helms|men
Hélo|ïse (French abbess and lover of Peter Abelard)
Helot (serf in ancient Sparta)
helot (serf generally)
hel|ot|ism
hel|ot|ry
help +s +ed +ing
help|er +s
help|ful
help|ful|ly
help|ful|ness
help|ing +s
help|less
help|less|ly
help|less|ness
help|line +s
Help|mann, Rob|ert (Australian ballet dancer and choreographer)
help|mate +s
help|meet +s
Hel|sing|borg (port, Sweden)
Hel|sing|fors (Swedish name for Helsinki)
Hel|sing|ør (Danish name for Elsinore)
Hel|sinki (capital of Finland)
helter-skelter +s
helve +s
Hel|ve|tian +s
hem
    hems
    hemmed
    hem|ming
hemal Am. (Br. haemal)
he-man
    he-men
hem|at|ic Am. (Br. haematic)
hema|tin Am. (Br. haematin)

hema|tite Am. (Br. haematite)
hema|to|cele Am. +s (Br. haematocele)
hema|to|crit Am. +s (Br. haematocrit)
hema|to|logic Am. (Br. haematologic)
hema|to|logic|al Am. (Br. haematological)
hema|tolo|gist Am. +s (Br. haematologist)
hema|tol|ogy Am. (Br. haematology)
hema|toma Am. +s (Br. haematoma)
hema|topha|gous Am. (Br. haematophagous)
hema|turia Am. (Br. haematuria)
heme Am. +s (Br. haem)
Hemel
    Hemel Hemp|stead (town, England)
hem|ero|cal|lis plural hem|ero|cal|lis
hemi|an|opia (use hemianopsia)
hemi|an|op|sia
hemi|cel|lu|lose +s
hemi|chord|ate +s
hemi|cycle +s
hemi|demi|semi| quaver +s
hemi|he|dral
Hem|ing|way, Er|nest (American novelist)
hemi|ple|gia
hemi|ple|gic +s
hemi|sphere +s
hemi|spher|ic
hemi|spher|ic|al
hemi|stich +s
Hem|kund, Lake (in India)
hem|line +s
hem|lock +s
hemo|coel Am. +s (Br. haemocoel)

hemo|cya|nin Am. (Br. haemocyanin)
hemo|di|aly|sis Am. (Br. haemodialysis)
hemo|globin Am. (Br. haemoglobin)
hemo|lymph Am. (Br. haemolymph)
hem|oly|sis Am. (Br. haemolysis)
hemo|lyt|ic Am. (Br. haemolytic)
hemo|philia Am. (Br. haemophilia)
hemo|phil|iac Am. (Br. haemophiliac)
hemo|phil|ic Am. (Br. haemophilic)
hem|or|rhage Am.
    hem|or|rhages
    hem|or|rhaged
    hem|or|rha|ging (Br. haemorrhage)
hem|or|rhagic Am. (Br. haemorrhagic)
hem|or|rhoid Am. +s (Br. haemorrhoid)
hem|or|rhoid|al Am. (Br. haemorrhoidal)
hemo|stasis Am.
    hemo|stases (Br. haemostasis)
hemo|stat|ic Am. (Br. haemostatic)
hemp +s
hemp|en
hemp-nettle +s
hem|stitch
    hem|stitches
    hem|stitched
    hem|stitch|ing
hen +s
Henan (province, China)
hen and chick|ens plural hen and chick|ens (plant)
hen|bane
hence
hence|forth
hence|for|ward

hench|man
    hench|men
hen-coop +s
hen|deca|gon +s
hen|deca| syl|lab|ic
hen|deca|syl|lable +s
hen|dia|dys
Hen|drix, Jimi (American rock musician)
hen|equen
henge +s
Hen|gist (Jutish leader)
hen har|rier +s
hen house +s
Henley-on-Thames (town, England)
Hen|ley (Royal Re|gatta)
henna
hen|naed
heno|the|ism
hen-party
    hen-parties
hen|peck +s +ed +ing
Henri, Rob|ert (American painter)
Henri|etta
Henri|etta Maria (French queen consort)
hen-roost +s
hen-run +s
Henry (English and French kings)
Henry ('the Fowler', Henry I of the Germans)
Henry ('the Navigator', Portuguese prince)
henry
    hen|ries or henrys (unit)
Henry's law
Henze, Hans Wer|ner (German composer)
he|or|tolo|gist +s
he|or|tol|ogy
hep (fruit; stylish; use hip)
hep|arin
hep|ar|in|ise Br. (use heparinize)

hep¦ar¦in¦ise (*cont.*)
  hep¦ar¦in¦ises
  hep¦ar¦in¦ised
  hep¦ar¦in¦is¦ing
hep¦ar¦in¦ize
  hep¦ar¦in¦izes
  hep¦ar¦in¦ized
  hep¦ar¦in¦iz¦ing
hep¦at¦ic
hep¦at¦ica
hepa¦titis
hep¦ato|meg¦aly
Hep|burn, Aud¦rey
  (British actress)
Hep|burn,
  Kath¦ar¦ine
  (American
  actress)
hep¦cat +s
Heph|aes¦tus *Greek*
  Mythology
Heph|zi¦bah
Hepple|white
hepta|chord +s
hep¦tad +s
hepta|glot +s
hepta|gon +s
hept|agon¦al
hepta|he¦dral
hepta|he¦dron
  hepta|he¦dra *or*
  hepta|he¦drons
hept|am¦eter +s
hept|ane +s
hept|arch¦ic
hept|arch¦ic¦al
hept|archy
  hept|arch¦ies
hepta|syl¦lab¦ic
Hepta|teuch *Bible*
hept|ath¦lete +s
hept|ath¦lon +s
hepta|va¦lent
Hep|worth,
  Bar|bara (English
  sculptor)
her
Hera *Greek*
  Mythology
Hera|cles (Greek
  form of Hercules)
Hera|cli¦tus (Greek
  philosopher)
Hera|klion (capital
  of Crete)
her¦ald +s +ed
  +ing
her¦al¦dic
her¦al¦dic|al¦ly
her¦ald|ist +s
her¦ald¦ry
Her|alds' Col|lege

Herat (city,
  Afghanistan)
herb +s
herb|aceous
herb|age
herb¦al +s
herb¦al|ism
herb¦al|ist +s
herb|arium
  herb|aria
herb ben¦net
herb Chris|to¦pher
Her|bert
Her|bert, A. P.
  (English humorist)
Her|bert, George
  (English poet)
herb Ger¦ard
herbi|cidal
herbi|cide +s
herb|ifer|ous
herbi|vore +s
herb|iv|or|ous
herb|less
herb|like
herb Paris
herb Rob¦ert
herb tea +s
herb to|bacco
herby
  herb|ier
  herbi|est
Her¦ce|gov¦ina
  (use
  Herzegovina)
Her¦ce|gov¦in¦ian
  +s (use
  Herzegovinian)
Her¦cu|la¦neum
  (ancient Roman
  town)
Her¦cu|lean
Her¦cu¦les (*Greek
  and Roman
  Mythology*;
  constellation)
Her¦cu¦les bee¦tle
  +s
Her¦cyn|ian
herd +s +ed +ing
  (group of animals.
  ⚠ heard)
herd book +s
herd¦er +s
herds|man
  herds|men
Herd|wick +s
  (sheep)
here (this place.
  ⚠ hear)
here|about
here|abouts

here|after
here¦at
here¦by
her¦ed¦it|able
her¦ed¦ita|ment +s
her¦edi|tar¦ily
her¦edi|tari|ness
her¦edi|tary
her¦ed|ity
Here¦ford +s (city,
  England; cattle)
Here¦ford|shire
  (former county,
  England)
here¦in
here|in|after
here|in|before
here¦of
Her¦ero
  plural Her¦ero *or*
  Her|eros
her¦esi|arch +s
her¦esi|ology
her¦esy
  her|esies
her¦et¦ic +s
her¦et|ic¦al
her¦et¦ic|al¦ly
here¦to
here|to|fore
here|under
here|unto
here|upon
Here|ward the
  Wake (Anglo-
  Saxon rebel
  leader)
here|with
her¦iot +s
her¦it|abil¦ity
her¦it|able
her¦it|ably
heri|tage +s
heri|tor +s
herl (fibre. ⚠ hurl)
Herm (Channel
  Island)
herm +s (pillar)
Her¦man
herm|aph¦ro|dite
  +s
herm|aph¦ro|dit¦ic
herm|aph¦ro|
        dit¦ic¦al
herm|aph¦ro|dit|
        ism
Herm|aph¦ro|ditus
  Greek Mythology
her¦men|eut¦ic
her¦men|eut¦ic¦al
her¦men|eut¦ic|
        al¦ly

her¦men|eut¦ics
Her¦mes *Greek*
  Mythology
Her¦mes
  Tris¦me|gis¦tus
  Mythology
her¦met¦ic (airtight.
  ⚠ hermitic)
her¦met¦ic|al¦ly
her¦met|ism
Her¦mia
Her¦mione
her¦mit +s
Her¦mit|age, the
  (art museum,
  Russia)
her¦mit|age +s
her¦mit crab +s
Her¦mit|ian
her¦mit¦ic (of a
  hermit.
  ⚠ hermetic)
Hermo|sillo (city,
  Mexico)
her¦nia
  her|nias *or*
  her|niae
her|nial
her¦ni|ary
her¦ni|ated
Her|ning (city,
  Denmark)
Hero *Greek*
  Mythology
hero
  her¦oes
Herod Agrippa
  (two rulers of
  ancient Palestine)
Herod Anti|pas
  (ruler of ancient
  Palestine)
Her¦od|otus (Greek
  historian)
Herod the Great
  (ruler of ancient
  Palestine)
hero¦ic
hero¦ic|al¦ly
heroi-comic
heroi-comical
hero|ics
her¦oin (drug)
hero|ine +s
  (person)
hero|ise *Br.* (use
  heroize)
  hero|ises
  hero|ised
  hero|is¦ing
hero|ism

hero|ize
  hero|izes
  hero|ized
  hero|iz¦ing
heron +s
her|on¦ry
  her|on|ries
hero-worship
  hero-worships
  hero-
    worshipped *Br.*
  hero-
    worshiped *Am.*
  hero-
    worship¦ping *Br.*
  hero-
    worship¦ing *Am.*
her¦pes
her¦pes sim|plex
her¦pes|virus
  her¦pes|viruses
her¦pes zos¦ter
her|pet¦ic
her¦peto|logic|al
her¦pe|tolo|gist +s
her¦pe|tol¦ogy
herp|tile +s
Herr
  Herren
Herren|volk
Her|rick, Rob|ert
  (English poet)
her|ring
  plural her|ring *or*
    her|rings
her|ring|bone
  her¦ring|bones
  her¦ring|boned
  her¦ring|bon¦ing
her|ring gull +s
Her|riot, James
  (English writer
  and veterinary
  surgeon)
Herrn|huter +s
hers
Her|schel, John
  and Wil|liam
  (British
  astronomers)
her|self
Hert|ford (town,
  England.
  ⚠ Hartford)
Hert|ford|shire
  (county, England)
Herts.
  (= Hertfordshire)
Hertz, Hein|rich
  Ru|dolf (German
  physicist)

hertz
  plural hertz
  (unit)
Hertz|ian
Hertzsprung–
  Russel dia|gram
Herut
Her¦ze|gov¦ina
  (region, Bosnia–
  Herzegovina)
Her¦ze|gov¦in¦ian
  +s
Herzl, Theo|dor
  (Hungarian-born
  writer and Zionist
  leader)
he's (= he has; he
  is)
Hesh|van (use
  Hesvan)
Hes¦iod (Greek
  poet)
hesi|tance
hesi|tancy
  hesi|tan¦cies
hesi|tant
hesi|tant¦ly
hesi|tate
  hesi|tates
  hesi|tated
  hesi|tat¦ing
hesi|tat¦er +s
hesi|tat¦ing¦ly
hesi|ta|tion +s
hesi|ta¦tive
Hes¦per|ian
Hes¦peri|des, the
  Greek Mythology
hes¦per|idium
  hes¦per|idia
Hes|perus (planet
  Venus)
Hess, Myra
  (English pianist)
Hess, Vic¦tor
  Franz (Austrian-
  born American
  physicist)
Hess, (Wal|ther
  Rich|ard)
  Ru|dolf (German
  Nazi politician)
Hesse (state,
  Germany)
Hesse, Her|mann
  (German-born
  Swiss novelist)
Hes¦sen (German
  name for Hesse)
Hes|sian +s (of
  Hesse; person;
  boot; fly)

hes|sian +s (coarse
  cloth)
hest
Hes¦ter
Hes¦van (Jewish
  month)
het|aera
  het|aeras *or*
  het|aerae
het¦aer|ism
het|aira
  het|airas *or*
  het|airai
het¦air|ism
het¦ero +s
het¦ero|
    chro¦mat¦ic
het¦ero|clite +s
het¦ero|cyc¦lic
het¦ero|dox
het¦ero|doxy
  het¦ero|dox¦ies
het¦ero|dyne
  het¦ero|dynes
  het¦ero|dyned
  het¦ero|dyn¦ing
heter|og¦am¦ous
heter|og¦amy
het¦ero|gen¦eity
het¦ero|ge¦neous
het¦ero|
    ge¦neous¦ly
het¦ero|ge¦neous|
    ness
het¦ero|gen¦esis
het¦ero|gen¦et¦ic
heter|ogen|ous
  (use
  heterogeneous)
heter|ogen|ous¦ly
  (use
  heterogeneously)
heter|ogeny
heter|og¦on¦ous
heter|og¦ony
het¦ero|graft +s
heter|ol¦ogous
heter|ology
heter|om¦er¦ous
het¦ero|morph¦ic
het¦ero|morph¦ism
heter|on¦om¦ous
heter|on¦omy
het¦ero|path¦ic
het¦er|ophony
  het¦ero|phonies
het¦er|oph¦yl¦lous
het¦ero|phylly
het¦ero|plast¦ic
het¦ero|ploid
het¦ero|polar
het¦ero|sex¦ism

het¦ero|sex¦ist
het¦ero|sex¦ual +s
het¦ero|sexu¦al¦ity
het¦ero|sexu¦al¦ly
heter|osis
  heter|oses
het¦ero|taxy
het¦ero|
    trans¦plant +s
het¦ero|troph¦ic
het¦ero|zy¦gote +s
het¦ero|zy¦got¦ic
het¦ero|zy¦gous
het¦man
  het¦men
het up
heu|chera +s
heur|is¦tic +s
heur|is¦tic|al¦ly
hevea +s
Hev¦esy, George
  Charles de
  (Hungarian-born
  radiochemist)
hew
  hews
  hewed
  hew¦ing
  hewn *or* hewed
  (chop. ⚠ hue)
hewer +s
hex
  hexes
  hexed
  hex¦ing
hexa|chord +s
hexad +s
hexa|deci¦mal
hexa|deci¦mal¦ly
hexa|gon +s
hex|agon¦al
hex|agon|al¦ly
hexa|gram +s
hexa|he¦dral
hexa|he¦dron
  hexa|he¦dra *or*
  hexa|he¦drons
hex|am¦eron
hex|am¦eter +s
hexa|met¦ric
hex|am¦etrist +s
hex¦ane
hex|apla
hex|aple +s
hexa|pod +s
hexa|pody
  hexa|podies
hexa|style +s
hexa|syl¦lab¦ic
Hexa|teuch
hexa|va¦lent
hex¦ode +s

hex¦ose +s
hey (*interjection*
  calling attention or
  expressing
  surprise etc.
  ⚠ hay, heigh)
hey¦day +s
Heyer, Geor¦gette
  (English writer)
Heyer¦dahl, Thor
  (Norwegian
  anthropologist)
Heyhoe-Flint,
  Ra¦chael (English
  cricketer)
hey presto!
Hez¦bol¦lah
  (radical Shiite
  Muslim group)
H-hour
hi (*interjection.*
  ⚠ high)
hia¦tal
hia¦tus
  hia¦tuses
Hia¦watha
  (legendary
  American Indian)
Hib (bacterium)
hi¦ber¦nate
  hi¦ber¦nates
  hi¦ber¦nated
  hi¦ber¦na¦ting
hi¦ber¦na¦tion
hi¦ber¦na¦tor +s
Hi¦ber¦nian +s
Hi¦ber¦ni¦cism +s
hi¦bis¦cus
  plural hi¦bis¦cus *or*
  hi¦bis¦cuses
hic
hic¦cough +s +ed
  +ing (use hiccup)
hic¦coughy (use
  hiccupy)
hic¦cup +s +ed
  +ing
hic¦cupy
hic jacet +s
hick +s
hickey +s
hick¦ory
  hick¦or¦ies
Hicks, John
  Rich¦ard (English
  economist)
hid
Hid¦algo (state,
  Mexico)
hid¦algo +s
  (Spanish
  gentleman)

hid¦den
hid¦den¦ness
hide
  hides
  hid
  hid¦ing
  hid¦den
  (conceal; place)
hide
  hides
  hided
  hid¦ing
  (leather; flog)
hide-and-seek
hide¦away +s
hide¦bound
hid¦eos¦ity
  hid¦eos¦ities
hid¦eous
hid¦eous¦ly
hid¦eous¦ness
hide¦out +s
hider +s
hidey-hole +s
hid¦ing place +s
hid¦rosis
hid¦rot¦ic
hie
  hies
  hied
  hie¦ing *or* hying
hier¦arch +s
hier¦arch¦al
hier¦arch¦ic
hier¦arch¦ic¦al
hier¦arch¦ic¦al¦ly
hier¦arch¦ise *Br.*
  (use hierarchize)
  hier¦arch¦ises
  hier¦arch¦ised
  hier¦arch¦is¦ing
hier¦arch¦ism
hier¦arch¦ize
  hier¦arch¦izes
  hier¦arch¦ized
  hier¦arch¦iz¦ing
hier¦archy
  hier¦arch¦ies
hier¦at¦ic
hier¦at¦ic¦al¦ly
hier¦oc¦racy
  hier¦oc¦ra¦cies
hiero¦glyph +s
hiero¦glyph¦ic +s
hiero¦glyph¦ic¦al
hiero¦glyph¦ic¦
              al¦ly
hiero¦gram +s
hiero¦graph +s
hier¦ol¦atry
hier¦ology
hiero¦phant +s

hiero¦phant¦ic
hi-fi +s
hig¦gle
  hig¦gles
  hig¦gled
  hig¦gling
higgledy-piggledy
high +s +er +est
  (tall etc. ⚠ hi)
high and mighty
high¦ball +s
high¦bind¦er +s
high-born
high¦boy +s
high¦brow +s
high chair +s
High Church *noun*
  and adjective
High Church¦man
  High Church¦men
high-class *adjective*
High¦er +s
  (Scottish exam)
high¦er
  (comparative of
  high. ⚠ hire, hiya)
higher-up +s
high ex¦plo¦sive
  +s
high¦fa¦lu¦tin
high fi¦del¦ity
high-five
  high-fives
  high-fived
  high-fiving
high-flier +s (use
  high-flyer)
high-flown
high-flyer +s
high-flying
high-grade
high-handed
high-handed¦ly
high-handed¦ness
high hat +s *noun*
high-hat
  high-hats
  high-hatted
  high-hatting
  adjective and verb
high-heeled
high jinks
high jump
high-jumper +s
high-key
high-kicking
High¦land (fling,
  games, etc.)
high¦land +s (high
  land)
High¦land¦er +s (in
  Scotland)

high¦land¦er +s
  (generally)
High¦land¦man
  High¦land¦men
High¦lands, the
  (mountains,
  Scotland)
high-level *adjective*
high life
high¦light +s +ed
  +ing
high¦light¦er +s
high-lows (boots)
high¦ly
high¦ly strung
  adjective
highly-strung
  attributive
High Mass
  High Masses
high-minded
high-minded¦ly
high-minded¦ness
high-muck-a-
  muck +s
high¦ness
  high¦nesses
high-octane
high-pitched
hikgh-powered
high-quality
high-ranking
high relief +s
high-rise +s
high-risk
high school +s
high-security
high-sounding
high-speed
  attributive
high-spirit¦ed
  attributive
high-
  spirit¦ed¦ness
high-stepper +s
high-stepping
  adjective
High Stew¦ard +s
high street *noun*
high-street
  attributive
high-strung
hight (called.
  ⚠ height)
high¦tail +s +ed
  +ing
high tech *noun*
high-tech *attributive*
high tech¦nol¦ogy
  noun
high-technol¦ogy
  attributive
high-tensile
high-toned

high-up +s *noun*
high water mark +s
high|way +s
high¦way|man
high¦way|men
high wire +s
hi¦jack +s +ed +ing
hi¦jack¦er +s
Hijaz (use Hejaz)
Hijra (use Hegira)
hijra +s (use hegira)
hike
  hikes
  hiked
  hik¦ing
hiker +s
hila (plural of hilum)
hil¦ari¦ous
hil¦ari¦ous¦ly
hil¦ari¦ous|ness
hil¦ar|ity
Hil¦ary (French saint; term)
Hil¦ary *also* Hil|lary (name)
Hil|bert, David (German mathematician)
Hilda *also* Hylda
Hil¦de|gard of Bin¦gen (German saint)
Hil¦des|heim (city, Germany)
Hill, Benny (English comedian)
Hill, Oc¦ta|via (English housing reformer)
Hill, Row|land (British founder of penny post)
hill +s +ed +ing (raised land. △ heal, hele, he'll)
Hil|lary, Ed¦mund (New Zealand mountaineer)
Hil|lary *also* Hil¦ary
hill-billy
  hill-billies
hill climb +s
hill fort +s
hil¦li|ness

hill|man
  hill|men
hill|lock +s
hill|locky
Hills|bor¦ough (football stadium disaster, England)
hill|side +s
hill sta|tion +s
hill|top +s
hill|walk¦er +s
hill|walk¦ing
hilly
  hill|ier
  hilli|est
hilt +s +ed +ing
hilum
  hila
Hil¦ver|sum (town, the Netherlands)
him (objective case of he. △ hymn)
Hi¦ma|chal Pra|desh (state, India)
Hima|layan +s
Hima|layas, the (mountain range, S. Asia)
hi¦mat|ion
Himm|ler, Hein|rich (German Nazi leader)
Hims (= Homs)
him|self
Hin|ault, Ber|nard (French racing cyclist)
Hi¦na|yana (Buddhism)
hind +s
hind|brain +s
Hin¦de|mith, Paul (German composer)
Hin¦den|burg, Paul von (German president)
Hin¦den|burg (German name for Zabrze)
Hin¦den|burg Line (German fortification in First World War)
hin¦der +s +ed +ing
Hindi
hind leg +s
hind|limb +s

hind|most
Hin¦doo +s (use Hindu)
hind|quar¦ters
hin|drance +s
hind|sight +s
Hindu +s
Hin¦du|ise *Br.* (use Hinduize)
  Hin¦du|ises
  Hin¦du|ised
  Hin¦du|is¦ing
Hin¦du|ism
Hin¦du|ize
  Hin¦du|izes
  Hin¦du|ized
  Hin¦du|iz¦ing
Hindu Kush (mountain range, Pakistan and Afghanistan)
Hin¦du|stan
Hin¦du|stani +s
hind|wing +s
hinge
  hinges
  hinged
  hinge|ing *or* hin|ging
hinge|less
hinge-like
hinge|wise
hinny
  hin|nies
Hin¦shel|wood, Cyril Nor¦man (English physical chemist)
hint +s +ed +ing
hin¦ter|land +s
hip
  hips
  hip¦per
  hip|pest
hip bath +s
hip bone +s
hip flask +s
hip hop
hip joint +s
hip-length
hip|less
hip|ness
Hip|par¦chus (Greek astronomer and geographer)
Hip¦par|cos (space satellite)
hip¦pe|as¦trum +s
hipped
hip¦per +s

hip¦pie +s (person. △ hippy)
hippo +s
hippo|cam¦pus
  hippo|campi
hippo|cen¦taur +s
hip pocket +s
hippo|cras
Hip¦poc|ra¦tes (Greek physician)
Hippo|crat¦ic oath
Hippo|crene (natural spring, Greece)
hippo|drome +s
hippo|griff +s
hippo|gryph +s (use hippogriff)
Hip|poly¦tus *Greek Mythology*
hip|poph¦agy
hippo|phile +s
hippo|pho¦bia
hippo|pot¦amus
  hippo|pot¦amuses *or* hippo|pot¦ami
Hippo Re¦gius (ancient Roman city)
hippy
  hip¦pier
  hip¦pi|est (large-hipped. △ hippie)
hip roof +s
hip|ster +s
hip|ster|ism
hira|gana
Hiram
hir|cine
hire
  hires
  hired
  hir¦ing (borrow for a fee. △ higher, hiya)
hire|able
hire car +s
hire|ling +s
hire pur|chase *noun*
hire-purchase *attributive*
hirer +s
Hiro|hito (Japanese emperor)
H-iron +s
Hiro|shima (city, Japan)
hir|sute

hir¦sute|ness
hir¦sut|ism
hi¦run|dine +s
his
His|pan¦ic +s
His|pani|cise *Br.*
　(use Hispanicize)
His¦pani|cises
His¦pani|cised
His¦pani|cis¦ing
His¦pani|cist +s
His¦pani|cize
　His¦pani|cizes
　His¦pani|cized
　His¦pani|ciz¦ing
His¦pani|ola
　(island, West
　Indies)
His|pan¦ist +s
his¦pid
hiss
　hisses
　hissed
　hiss|ing
hist
his|ta¦mine
his|ta|min¦ic
his|ti¦dine
histo|chem¦ical
histo|chem¦is¦try
histo|gen¦esis
histo|gen¦et¦ic
histo|gen¦ic
hist|ogeny
histo|gram +s
histo|logic¦al
hist|olo¦gist +s
hist|ology
hist|oly¦sis
histo|lyt¦ic
his|tone +s
histo|patho|
　　　　logic¦al
histo|path|olo¦gist
　+s
histo|path¦ology
his¦tor|ian +s
his¦tori|ated
his¦tor¦ic
his¦tor|ic¦al
his¦tor|ic¦al|ly
his¦tori|cism
his¦tori|cist +s
his¦tor|icity
his¦tori|ograph¦er
　+s
his¦torio|graph¦ic
his¦torio|
　　　graph¦ic¦al
his¦tori|og¦raphy
his|tory
　his|tor¦ies

his¦tri|on¦ic
his¦tri|on¦ic|al¦ly
his¦tri|oni¦cism
his¦tri|on¦ics
his¦tri|on¦ism
hit
　hits
　hit
　hit|ting
hit-and-miss
hit-and-run
　attributive
hitch
　hitches
　hitched
　hitch|ing
Hitch|cock,
　Al¦fred (English
　film director)
Hitch|ens, Ivon
　(English painter)
hitch¦er +s
hitch-hike
　hitch-hikes
　hitch-hiked
　hitch-hiking
hitch-hiker +s
hi-tech *noun and
　adjective*
hither
hith|er¦to
hith|er|ward
Hit¦ler, Adolf
　(Austrian-born
　German Nazi
　leader)
Hit¦ler|ism
Hit¦ler|ite +s
hit list +s
hit man
　hit men
hit-or-miss
hit-out *noun*
hit¦ter +s
Hit¦tite +s
hive
　hives
　hived
　hiv¦ing
hiya (greeting.
　△ higher, hire)
Hiz|bol¦lah
　(Lebanese militia)
h'm
hmm (use h'm)
ho (*interjection.*
　△ hoe)
hoar (grey with
　age; hoar-frost;
　hoariness. △ haw,
　whore)

hoard +s +ed +ing
　(store. △ horde)
hoard¦er +s
hoard|ing +s
hoar frost
hoar|hound (use
　horehound)
hoar|ily
hoari|ness
hoarse
　hoars¦er
　hoars¦est
　(of voice.
　△ horse)
hoarse¦ly
hoars¦en +s +ed
　+ing
hoarse|ness
hoar|stone +s
hoary
　hoar|ier
　hoari|est
hoat|zin +s
hoax
　hoaxes
　hoaxed
　hoax|ing
hoax¦er +s
hob +s
Ho¦bart (capital of
　Tasmania)
Hob|bema,
　Mein|dert (Dutch
　painter)
Hobbes, Thomas
　(English
　philosopher)
hob¦bit +s
hob¦bit¦ry
hob¦ble
　hob¦bles
　hob¦bled
　hob¦bling
hobble|de¦hoy +s
hob¦bler +s
Hobbs, Jack
　(English cricketer)
hobby
　hob¦bies
hobby-horse +s
hob¦by|ist +s
hob¦day +s +ed
　+ing
hob|gob¦lin +s
hob|nail +s
hob|nailed
hob¦nob
　hob|nobs
　hob|nobbed
　hob|nob|bing
hobo
　ho¦boes *or* hobos

Hob|son's choice
Ho Chi Minh
　(North
　Vietnamese
　president)
Ho Chi Minh City
　(official name of
　Saigon)
hock +s +ed +ing
　(leg joint; wine;
　pawn. △ hough)
hockey (field game.
　△ oche)
hock¦ey|ist +s
Hock|ney, David
　(English painter)
Hock|tide
hocus
　ho¦cus|ses *or*
　ho¦cuses
　ho¦cussed *or*
　ho¦cused
　ho¦cus|sing *or*
　ho¦cus|ing
hocus-pocus
　hocus-pocusses
　or hocus-pocuses
　hocus-pocussed
　or hocus-pocused
　hocus-pocussing
　or hocus-
　pocusing
hod +s
hod¦den
hod¦die +s
Ho|deida (port,
　Yemen)
Hodge +s
　(farmworker)
hodge|podge +s
　(use hotchpotch)
Hodg|kin,
　Doro|thy (British
　chemist)
Hodg|kin's
　dis|ease
ho|di¦ernal
hod¦man
　hod¦men
hodo|graph +s
hod|om¦eter +s
　(use odometer)
Hoe, Rich|ard
　March (American
　inventor and
　industrialist)
hoe
　hoes
　hoed
　hoe¦ing
　(tool. △ ho)
hoe|cake +s

hoe|down +s
Hoek van
  Hol|land (Dutch
  name for the
  Hook of Holland)
hoer +s
Hofei (= Hefei)
Hoff|man, Dus|tin
  Lee (American
  actor)
Hoff|mann, Ernst
  Theo|dor
  Ama|deus
  (German writer)
Hof|manns|thal,
  Hugo von
  (Austrian
  dramatist)
hog
  hogs
  hogged
  hog|ging
hogan +s
Ho|garth, Wil|liam
  (English artist)
hog|back +s
Hogg, James
  (Scottish poet)
hogg +s (use hog)
Hog|gar
  Moun|tains (in
  Algeria)
hog|ger +s
hog|gery
  hog|ger|ies
hog|get +s
hog|gin
hog|gish
hog|gish|ly
hog|gish|ness
hog|like
hog|ma|nay +s
hog's back +s
hogs|head +s
hog-tie
  hog-ties
  hog-tied
  hog-tying
hog|wash
hog|weed +s
Hohen|stau|fen
  (German dynastic
  family)
Hohen|zol|lern
  (German dynastic
  family)
Hoh|hot (capital of
  Inner Mongolia)
ho-ho
ho-hum
hoick +s +ed +ing
hoi pol|loi

hoist +s +ed +ing
hoist|er +s
hoity-toity
hokey
  hoki|er
  hoki|est
  (melodramatic.
  △ hoki)
hokey-cokey
  (dance)
hokey|ness
hokey-pokey
hoki
  plural hoki
  (fish. △ hokey)
hoki|ly
Hok|kaido (island,
  Japan)
hokku
  plural hokku
hokum
Hoku|sai,
  Kat|su|shika
  (Japanese artist)
hoky
  hoki|er
  hoki|est
  (use hokey.
  melodramatic.
  △ hoki)
Hol|arc|tic
Hol|bein, Hans
  (German painter)
hold
  holds
  held
  hold|ing
hold|able
hold|all +s
hold|back +s noun
hold|er +s
Höl|der|lin,
  Jo|hann
  Chris|toph
  Fried|rich
  (German poet)
hold|fast +s
hold|ing +s
hold|out +s
hold-over +s noun
hold-up +s noun
hole
  holes
  holed
  hol|ing
  (empty space.
  △ whole)
hole-and-corner
hole-in-one
  holes-in-one
hole-proof
holey (full of holes.
  △ holy, wholly)

Holi (Hindu festival.
  △ holy, wholly)
holi|but
  plural holi|but
Holi|day, Bil|lie
  (American jazz
  singer)
holi|day +s +ed
  +ing (vacation)
holi|day|maker +s
holier-than-thou
holi|ly
holi|ness
Hol|in|shed,
  Raph|ael (English
  chronicler)
hol|ism
hol|ist +s
hol|is|tic
hol|is|tic|al|ly
holla
  hol|las
  hol|laed or
  holla'd
  holla|ing
  (interjection calling
  attention; to shout.
  △ holler)
Hol|land (the
  Netherlands;
  region, the
  Netherlands;
  former region,
  England)
hol|land (linen)
hol|land|aise
  sauce
Hol|land|er +s
Hol|lands (gin)
hol|ler +s +ed
  +ing (a shout; to
  shout. △ holla)
Hol|ler|ith,
  Her|man
  (American
  computer
  scientist)
hollo +s (noun
  shout)
hollo
  hol|loes
  hol|loed
  hollo|ing
  (verb shout)
hol|low +s +ed
  +ing (empty)
hollow-cheeked
hollow-eyed
hollow-hearted
hol|low|ly
hol|low|ness
hol|low|ware

Holly, Buddy
  (American rock
  and roll musician)
Holly (name)
holly
  hol|lies
  (shrub)
hol|ly|hock +s
Hol|ly|wood
  (centre of
  American film
  industry, Los
  Angeles)
holm +s (islet; oak
  tree. △ hom,
  home)
holme +s (islet; use
  holm)
Holmes, Ar|thur
  (English geologist)
Holmes, Oli|ver
  Wen|dell
  (American
  physician and
  writer)
Holmes, Sher|lock
  (fictional
  detective)
Holmes|ian
hol|mium
holm-oak +s
Holo|caust, the
  (Nazi mass
  murder of Jews)
holo|caust +s
Holo|cene
holo|en|zyme +s
Holo|fer|nes Bible
holo|gram +s
holo|graph +s
holo|graph|ic
holo|graph|ic|al|ly
hol|og|raphy
holo|he|dral
holo|met|abol|ous
holo|phote +s
holo|phyte +s
holo|phyt|ic
holo|thur|ian +s
holo|type +s
hols (= holidays)
Holst, Gus|tav
  (English
  composer)
Hol|stein (former
  duchy, NW
  Europe)
hol|ster +s
holt +s
holus-bolus
holy
  holies
  holi|er

holy (*cont.*)
  holi|est
  (sacred. ⚠ holey,
  Holi, wholly)
holy day +s
  (religious festival)
Holy|head (port,
  Wales)
holy Joe +s
Holy|oake, Keith
  (New Zealand
  prime minister)
Holy Rood Day
Holy See (the
  papacy)
holy|stone
  holy|stones
  holy|stoned
  holy|ston¦ing
hom (plant; juice.
  ⚠ holm, home)
homa (= hom)
hom¦age +s
hom¦bre +s
Hom|burg +s
Home, Lord *in full*
  Lord Home of the
  Hir¦sel of
  Cold|stream
  (British prime
  minister.
  ⚠ Hume)
home
  homes
  homed
  hom¦ing
  (residence;
  provide with a
  home; be guided.
  ⚠ hom, holm)
home-bird +s
home|body
  home|bodies
home|boy +s
home-brew +s
home-brewed
home|buy¦er +s
home|com¦ing +s
home cook|ing
Home Coun|ties
  (in SE England)
home-felt
home from home
home-grown
home help +s
Homel (city,
  Belarus)
home|land +s
home|less
home|less|ness

home life
  home lives
home|like
home¦li|ness
home loan +s
home¦ly
home-made
home|maker +s
home-making
home movie +s
homeo|box
  homeo|boxes
homeo|path *Am.*
  +s (*Br.*
  homoeopath)
homeo|path¦ic *Am.*
  (*Br.*
  homoeopathic)
homeo|path¦ic|
  al¦ly *Am.* (*Br.*
  homoeopathic-
  ally)
hom|eop¦ath|ist
  Am. +s (*Br.*
  homoeopathist)
hom|eop¦athy *Am.*
  (*Br.*
  homoeopathy)
homeo|stasis *Am.*
  homeo|stases
  (*Br.*
  homoeostasis)
homeo|stat¦ic *Am.*
  (*Br.*
  homoeostatic)
homeo|therm *Am.*
  +s (*Br.*
  homoeotherm)
homeo|ther¦mal
  Am. (*Br.*
  homoeothermal)
homeo|ther¦mic
  Am. (*Br.*
  homoeothermic)
homeo|thermy
  Am. (*Br.*
  homoeothermy)
home|owner +s
home own¦er|ship
Homer (Greek epic
  poet)
homer +s (pigeon;
  home run)
Hom|er¦ic
home run +s
home shop|ping
home|sick
home|sick|ness
home|spun
home|stead +s
home|stead¦er +s
home|stead|ing

home|style
home town +s
home|ward
homeward-bound
home|wards
home|work
home|work¦er +s
homey
  homi¦er
  homi¦est
homey|ness
homi|cidal
homi|cidal¦ly
homi|cide +s
homi|let¦ic
homi|let¦ics
ho¦mil|iary
  ho¦mil|iar¦ies
hom|il¦ist +s
hom¦ily
  hom|ilies
hom|inid +s
hom|in|oid +s
hom¦iny
homo +s
  (homosexual)
Homo (genus)
homo|cen¦tric
hom¦oeo|box (use
  homeobox)
  hom¦oeo|boxes
hom¦oeo|path *Br.*
  +s (*Am.*
  homeopath)
hom¦oeo|path¦ic
  Br. (*Am.*
  homeopathic)
hom¦oeo|path¦ic|
  al¦ly *Br.* (*Am.*
  homeopathically)
hom|oe|op¦ath|ist
  Br. +s (*Am.*
  homeopathist)
hom|oe|op¦athy
  Br. (*Am.*
  homeopathy)
hom¦oeo|stasis *Br.*
  hom¦oeo|stases
  (*Am.*
  homeostasis)
hom¦oeo|stat¦ic *Br.*
  (*Am.*
  homeostatic)
hom¦oeo|therm *Br.*
  +s (*Am.*
  homeotherm)
hom¦oeo|therm¦al
  Br. (*Am.*
  homeothermal)
hom¦oeo|therm¦ic
  Br. (*Am.*
  homeothermic)

hom¦oeo|thermy
  Br. (*Am.*
  homeothermy)
homo|erot¦ic
homo|gam¦et¦ic
hom|og¦am¦ous
hom|og¦amy
hom|ogen|ate +s
homo|gen¦eity
homo|ge¦neous (of
  same kind;
  uniform.
  ⚠ homogenous)
homo|ge¦neous¦ly
homo|ge¦neous|
            ness
homo|gen¦et¦ic
hom|ogen|isa|tion
  Br. (use
  homogenization)
hom|ogen|ise *Br.*
  (use homogenize)
  hom|ogen|ises
  hom|ogen|ised
  hom|ogen|is¦ing
hom|ogen|iser *Br.*
  +s (use
  homogenizer)
hom|ogen|iza|tion
hom|ogen|ize
  hom|ogen|izes
  hom|ogen|ized
  hom|ogen|iz¦ing
hom|ogen|izer
homo|gen¦ous
  (*Biology* having
  common descent.
  ⚠ homogeneous)
hom|ogeny
homo|graft +s
homo|graph +s
hom|oio|therm +s
  (use homeotherm
  Am.,
  homoeotherm
  Br.)
hom|oio|ther¦mal
  (use
  homeothermal
  Am.,
  homoeothermal
  Br.)
hom|oio|ther¦mic
  (use
  homeothermic
  Am.,
  homoeothermic
  Br.)
hom|oio|thermy
  (use
  homeothermy
  Am.,

hom¦oio|thermy
(*cont.*)
  homoeothermy
  Br.)
homoi|ous¦ian +s
homo|log *Am.* +s
  (*Br.* homologue)
hom¦olo|gate
  hom¦olo|gates
  hom¦olo|gated
  hom¦olo|gat¦ing
hom¦olo|ga¦tion
homo|logic¦al
hom¦olo|gise *Br.*
  (use homologize)
  hom¦olo|gises
  hom¦olo|gised
  hom¦olo|gis¦ing
hom¦olo|gize
  hom¦olo|gizes
  hom¦olo|gized
  hom¦olo|giz¦ing
hom¦olo|gous
homo|logue *Br.* +s
  (*Am.* homolog)
hom¦ology
  hom¦olo|gies
homo|morph +s
homo|morph¦ic
homo|morph¦ic|
      al¦ly
homo|morph|ism
  +s
homo|morph|ous
homo|morphy
homo|nym +s
homo|nym¦ic
hom|onym|ous
homo|ous¦ian +s
homo|phobe +s
homo|pho¦bia
homo|pho¦bic
homo|phone +s
homo|phon¦ic
homo|phon¦ic|
      al¦ly
hom¦oph¦onous
hom¦oph¦ony
homo|plas¦tic
homo|polar
Homo sa¦pi¦ens
homo|sex¦ual +s
homo|sexu¦al¦ity
homo|sexu¦al¦ly
homo|trans|plant
  +s
hom|ous¦ian +s
  (use homoousian)
homo|zy¦gote +s
homo|zy¦gous
Homs (city, Syria)
hom¦un|cule +s
  (use homunculus)

hom¦un|cu¦lus
  hom¦un|culi
homy (use homey)
Hon. (= Honorary;
  Honourable)
hon (= honey.
  △ Hun)
Honan (= Henan;
  former name of
  Luoyang)
hon¦cho +s *noun*
hon¦cho
  hon|choes
  hon|choed
  hon¦cho|ing
  verb
Honda, Soi¦chiro
  (Japanese car
  maker)
Hon|duran +s
Hon|duras (in
  Central America)
hone
  hones
  honed
  hon¦ing
Hon|ecker, Erich
  (East German
  head of state)
Hon|eg¦ger,
  Ar¦thur (French
  composer)
hon¦est
hon¦est Injun
hon¦est¦ly
honest-to-God
honest-to-
  goodness
hon|esty
honey +s
honey badger +s
honey bee +s
honey|bun +s
honey|bunch
  honey|bunches
honey buz|zard +s
honey|comb +s
  +ed +ing
honey|creep¦er +s
honey|dew +s
honey|eater +s
hon|eyed
honey-fungus
honey|guide +s
honey|moon +s
  +ed +ing
honey|moon¦er +s
honey pot +s
honey sac +s
honey|suckle +s
honey-sweet
Hong Kong

Ho¦ni|ara (capital
  of the Solomon
  Islands)
hon¦ied (use
  honeyed)
Honi|ton (town,
  England; lace)
honk +s +ed +ing
honky
  hon¦kies
  (*offensive*)
honky-tonk +s
hon|nête homme
  hon|nêtes hommes
Hono|lulu (capital
  of Hawaii)
Honor (name)
honor *Am.* +s +ed
  +ing (glory;
  respect. *Br.*
  honour)
Hon¦or|able *Am.*
  (in titles. *Br.*
  Honourable)
hon¦or|able *Am.*
  (worthy of honour.
  Br. honourable)
hon¦or|able|ness
  Am. (*Br.*
  honourableness)
hon¦or|ably *Am.*
  (*Br.* honourably)
hon¦or|and +s
hon¦or|arium
  hon¦or|ariums *or*
  hon¦or|aria
hon¦or|ary
hon¦or|if¦ic +s
hon¦or|if¦ic|al¦ly
hon|oris causa
hon¦our *Br.* +s +ed
  +ing (*Am.* honor)
Hon¦our|able *Br.*
  (in titles. *Am.*
  Honorable)
hon¦our|able *Br.*
  (worthy of honour.
  Am. honorable)
hon¦our|able|ness
  Br. (*Am.*
  honorableness)
hon¦our|ably *Br.*
  (*Am.* honorably)
honour-trick +s
Hon. Sec.
  (= Honorary
  Secretary)
Hon|shu (island,
  Japan)
Hooch, Pieter de
  (Dutch painter)
hooch

Hood, Thomas
  (English poet)
hood +s +ed +ing
hoodie +s
hood|less
hood|like
hood|lum +s
hood-mould +s
hood-moulding +s
hoo¦doo +s +ed
  +ing
hood|wink +s +ed
  +ing
hooey
hoof
  hooves *or* hoofs
  noun
hoof +s +ed +ing
  verb
hoof¦er +s
Hoogh, Pieter de
  (use Hooch)
Hoo¦ghly (river,
  India)
hoo-ha +s
hoo-hah +s (use
  hoo-ha)
hook +s +ed +ing
hoo¦kah +s
Hooke, Rob¦ert
  (English scientist)
Hook¦er, Jo¦seph
  Dal¦ton (English
  botanist)
hook¦er +s
Hooke's law
hookey
hook|less
hook|let +s
hook|like
hook-nose +s
hook-nosed
Hook of Hol|land
  (port, the
  Netherlands)
hook-up +s *noun*
hook|worm +s
hooky (use
  hookey)
hoo¦li|gan +s
hooli¦gan|ism
hoon +s +ed +ing
hoop +s +ed +ing
  (ring; arch.
  △ whoop)
hoop-iron
hoopla +s
hoo¦poe +s
hoo¦ray +s
Hoo¦ray Henry
  Hoo¦ray Hen¦ries
hoo¦roo +s

hoose|gow +s
Hoo|sier +s
hoot +s +ed +ing
hootch (use hooch)
hoote|nanny
  hoote|nan|nies
hoot|er +s
hoots *interjection*
Hoo|ver, Her|bert
  Clark (American
  president)
Hoo|ver, J. Edgar
  (American FBI
  director)
Hoo|ver +s
  (vacuum cleaner)
  Propr.
hoo|ver +s +ed
  +ing *verb*
Hoo|ver|ville +s
  (shanty town,
  USA)
hooves
hop
  hops
  hopped
  hop|ping
hop-bind +s
hop-bine +s
Hope, Bob (British-
  born American
  comedian)
Hope (name)
hope
  hopes
  hoped
  hop|ing
  (wish)
hope|ful +s
hope|ful|ly
hope|ful|ness
Hopeh (former
  name of Hebei)
hope|less
hope|less|ly
hope|less|ness
hoper +s
hop|head +s
Hopi
  plural Hopi *or*
  Hopis
Hop|kins,
  An|thony (Welsh
  actor)
Hop|kins,
  Fred|er|ick
  (English
  biochemist)
Hop|kins, Ger|ard
  Man|ley (English
  poet)
hop|lite +s

hop-o'-my-thumb
  +s
Hop|per, Ed|ward
  (American
  painter)
hop|per +s
hop|ping mad
hop|ple
  hop|ples
  hop|pled
  hop|pling
hop|sack
hop|scotch
hop, skip, and
  jump
hop, step, and
  jump
Hor|ace (Roman
  poet; name)
hor|ary
Hor|atia
Hor|atian
Hor|atio
horde +s (group;
  gang. △ hoard)
hore|hound +s
hori|zon +s
hori|zon|tal
hori|zon|tal|ity
hori|zon|tal|ly
hori|zon|tal|ness
Hork|heimer, Max
  (German
  philosopher)
hor|mo|nal
hor|mo|nal|ly
hor|mone +s
Hor|muz (island
  and strait, Persian
  Gulf)
Horn, Cape (in S.
  America)
horn +s +ed +ing
horn|beam +s
horn|bill +s
horn|blende +s
horn|book +s
horn|er +s
hor|net +s
horn|fels
horni|ness
horn|ist +s
horn|less
horn|like
Horn of Af|rica
  (peninsula in NE
  Africa)
horn|pipe +s
horn play|er +s
horn-rimmed
horn|stone

horn|swog|gle
  horn|swog|gles
  horn|swog|gled
  horn|swog|gling
Hor|nung, Er|nest
  Wil|liam (English
  novelist)
horn|wort +s
horny
  horn|ier
  horni|est
horo|loge +s
hor|ol|oger +s
horo|logic
horo|logic|al
hor|olo|gist +s
hor|ol|ogy
horo|scope +s
horo|scop|ic
horo|scop|ic|al
hor|os|copy
Horow|henua
  (region, New
  Zealand)
Horo|witz,
  Vlad|imir
  (Russian-born
  pianist)
hor|ren|dous
hor|ren|dous|ly
hor|ren|dous|ness
hor|rent
hor|rible
hor|rible|ness
hor|ribly
hor|rid
hor|rid|ly
hor|rid|ness
hor|rif|ic
hor|rif|ic|al|ly
hor|ri|fi|ca|tion
hor|ri|fied|ly
hor|rify
  hor|ri|fies
  hor|ri|fied
  hor|ri|fy|ing
hor|ri|fy|ing|ly
hor|ri|pi|la|tion
hor|ror +s
horror-stricken
horror-struck
Horsa (Jutish
  leader)
hors con|cours
hors de com|bat
hors d'oeuvre +s
horse
  horses
  horsed
  hors|ing
  (animal.
  △ hoarse)

horse-and-buggy
  attributive
horse|back
horse|bean +s
horse-block +s
horse|box
  horse|boxes
horse brass
  horse brasses
horse|break|er +s
horse breed|er +s
horse chest|nut +s
horse-cloth +s
horse-coper +s
horse-doctor +s
horse-drawn
horse|flesh
horse|fly
  horse|flies
Horse Guards
  (cavalry brigade;
  its headquarters)
horse|hair
Horse|head
  Neb|ula
horse|leech
  horse|leeches
horse|less
horse|like
horse mack|erel
  plural horse
  mack|erel *or*
  horse mack|erels
horse|man
  horse|men
horse|man|ship
horse mush|room
  +s
Hor|sens (port,
  Denmark)
horse opera +s
horse-pistol +s
horse|play
horse-pond +s
horse|power
  plural
  horse|power
horse race +s
horse ra|cing
horse|rad|ish
horse sense
horse|shoe +s
horse|shoe crab
  +s
horse's neck +s
  (drink)
horse-soldier +s
horse|tail +s
horse-trading
horse|whip
  horse|whips

horse|whip (*cont.*)
  horse|whipped
  horse|whip|ping
horse|woman
  horse|women
horsey (use horsy)
hors|ily
horsi|ness
horst +s
Horst Wes|sel
  Song
horsy
  hors|ier
  horsi|est
Horta, Vic|tor
  (Belgian architect)
hor|ta|tion +s
hor|ta|tive
hor|ta|tory
Hor|tense
hor|ten|sia +s
horti|cul|tural
horti|cul|tur|al|ist
  +s
horti|cul|ture
horti|cul|tur|ist +s
hor|tus sic|cus
  horti sicci
Horus *Egyptian*
  Mythology
hos|anna +s
hose
  hoses
  hosed
  hos|ing
Hosea *Bible*
hose|pipe +s
ho|sier +s
ho|siery
hos|pice +s
hos|pit|able
hos|pit|ably
hos|pital +s
hos|pi|tal|er *Am.*
  +s (*Br.*
  hospitaller)
hos|pi|tal|isa|tion
  Br. +s (use
  hospitalization)
hos|pi|tal|ise *Br.*
  (use hospitalize)
hos|pi|tal|ises
hos|pi|tal|ised
hos|pi|tal|is|ing
hos|pi|tal|ism
hos|pi|tal|ity
hos|pi|tal|iza|tion
  +s
hos|pi|tal|ize
hos|pi|tal|izes
hos|pi|tal|ized
hos|pi|tal|iz|ing

hos|pi|tal|ler *Br.* +s
  (*Am.* hospitaler)
hos|pital ship +s
hos|pital train +s
host +s +ed +ing
hosta +s
hos|tage +s
hos|tage|ship
hos|tel +s
hos|tel|er *Am.* +s
  (*Br.* hosteller)
hos|tel|ling *Am.* (*Br.*
  hostelling)
hos|tel|ler *Br.* +s
  (*Am.* hosteler)
hos|tel|ling *Br.*
  (*Am.* hosteling)
hos|tel|ry
  hos|tel|ries
host|ess
  host|esses
hos|tile +s
hos|tile|ly
hos|til|ity
  hos|til|ities
host|ler +s
  (mechanic.
  ⚠ ostler)
hot
  hots
  hot|ted
  hot|ting
  hot|ter
  hot|test
hot-air bal|loon +s
hot|bed +s
hot-blooded
Hotch|kiss gun +s
hotch|pot
hotch|potch
hot cross bun +s
hot-desking
hot|dog
  hot|dogs
  hot|dogged
  hot|dog|ging
  verb
hot dog +s *noun*
hot|dog|ger +s
hotel +s
ho|tel|ier +s
hotel-keeper +s
hot|foot +s +ed
  +ing *adverb, verb,*
  and adjective
hot gos|pel|er *Am.*
  +s
hot gos|pel|ler *Br.*
  +s
hot|head +s
hot-headed
hot-headed|ly
hot-headed|ness

hot|house
  hot|houses
  hot|housed
  hot|hous|ing
hot|line +s
hotly
hot|ness
hot pants
hot|plate +s
hot|pot +s
hot-press
  hot-presses
  hot-pressed
  hot-pressing
hot rod
hot-rodder +s
hot-rodding
hot seat +s
hot shoe +s
  Photography
hot-short
hot|shot +s
hot spot +s
Hot|spur, Harry
  (Sir Henry Percy)
hot|spur +s
hot-tempered
Hot|ten|tot
  plural Hot|ten|tot
  or Hot|ten|tots
hot|ter +s
hot|tie +s
hot|tish
hotty (use hottie)
  hot|ties
hot-water bag +s
hot-water bot|tle
  +s
hot-wire
  hot-wires
  hot-wired
  hot-wiring
Hou|dini, Harry
  (Hungarian-born
  American
  escapologist)
hough +s +ed +ing
  (cut of beef; to
  hamstring.
  ⚠ hock.)
hough|er +s
houm|mos (use
  hummus.
  ⚠ humus)
hound +s +ed +ing
hound|er +s
hound|ish
hound's-tongue
  +s
hounds|tooth +s
hour +s (unit of
  time. ⚠ our)

hour|glass
  hour|glasses
hour hand +s
houri +s
hour-long
hour|ly
house
  houses
  housed
  hous|ing
house agent +s
house ar|rest
house|boat +s
house|bound
house|boy +s
house|break|er +s
house|break|ing
house-broken
house|build|er +s
house|build|ing
house|buy|er +s
house-buying
house|carl +s
house|carle +s
  (use housecarl)
house|coat +s
house|craft
house-dog +s
house-father +s
house-flag +s
house|fly
  house|flies
house|ful +s
house|group +s
house guest +s
house|hold +s
house|hold|er +s
house-hunt +s +ed
  +ing
house-hunter +s
house-husband +s
house|keep
  house|keeps
  house|kept
  house|keep|ing
house|keep|er +s
house|leek +s
house|less
house lights
house|maid +s
house|maid's
  knee
house|man
  house|men
house mar|tin +s
house|mas|ter +s
house|mis|tress
  house|mis|tresses
house-mother +s
house owner +s
house-parent +s

house party
  house par¦ties
house plant +s
house-proud
house|room
house-sit
  house-sits
  house-sat
  house-sitting
house|sit¦ter +s
house spar¦row +s
house style +s
house-to-house
house|top +s
house-train +s
  +ed +ing
house-warming
house|wife
  house|wives
house|wife¦li¦ness
house|wife¦ly
house|wif¦ery
house|work
housey-housey
hous|ing +s
Hous|man, A. E.
  (English poet)
Hous¦ton (city,
  Texas)
hout|ing
  plural **hout|ing**
Hove (seaside
  resort, England)
hove (past tense
  and past participle
  of **heave**)
hovel +s
hover +s +ed +ing
hov¦er|craft
  plural **hov¦er|craft**
hov|er|er +s
hov¦er|fly
  hov¦er|flies
hov¦er|port +s
hov¦er|train +s
how +s
How¦ard (name)
How¦ard,
  Cath|er¦ine (wife
  of Henry VIII of
  England)
How¦ard, John
  (English prison
  reformer)
how|beit
how¦dah +s
how-do-you-do +s
  (awkward
  situation)
howdy
  how|dies

how-d'ye-do +s
  (use **how-do-you-**
  do)
Howe, Elias
  (American
  inventor)
how¦e'er
  (= however)
How¦erd, Fran¦kie
  (English
  comedian)
how|ever
how|itz¦er +s
howl +s +ed +ing
howl¦er +s
How¦rah (city,
  India)
how|so¦e'er
  (= howsoever)
how|so¦ever
how¦zat *Cricket*
Hoxha, Enver
  (Albanian prime
  minister)
hoy +s +ed +ing
hoya +s
hoy¦den +s
hoy¦den|ish
Hoyle, Fred
  (English
  astrophysicist)
Hradec Králové
  (town, Czech
  Republic)
Hrodno (city,
  Belarus)
Hsia-men
  (= Xiamen)
Hsian (= Xian)
Hsi|ning (= Xining)
Hsu-chou
  (= Xuzhou)
Huai|nan (city,
  China)
Hual|laga (river,
  Peru)
Huambo (city,
  Angola)
Huang Hai
  (Chinese name for
  the Yellow Sea)
Huang He
  (= Huang Ho)
Huang Ho (Chinese
  name for the
  Yellow River)
Huas¦ca|rán
  (extinct volcano,
  Peru)
hub +s
Hub¦ble, Edwin
  Pow¦ell

Hub¦ble (*cont.*)
  (American
  astronomer;
  classification;
  telescope)
hubble-bubble +s
Hub¦ble's
  constant
hub¦bub
hubby
  hub|bies
hub¦cap +s
Hubei (province,
  China)
Hu¦bert
Hubli (city, India)
hu¦bris
hu¦bris|tic
hucka|back
huckle +s
huckle-back +s
huckle|berry
  huckle|berries
huck|ster +s +ed
  +ing
huck¦ster|ism
huck|stery
Hud¦ders|field
  (town, England)
hud¦dle
  hud¦dles
  hud¦dled
  hud|dling
Hu¦di|bras¦tic
Hud¦son, Henry
  (English explorer)
Hud¦son Bay
  (inland sea,
  Canada)
Hud¦son River (in
  N. America)
Hud¦son's Bay
  Com|pany
Hué (city, Vietnam)
hue +s (colour.
  ⚠ hew)
hue|less
huff +s +ed +ing
huff|ily
huffi|ness
huff|ish
huffy
  huff|ier
  huffi|est
hug
  hugs
  hugged
  hug|ging
huge
  huger
  hug¦est
huge¦ly

huge|ness
hug|gable
hug¦ger +s
hugger-mugger
Hug|gins,
  Wil|liam (British
  astronomer)
Hugh *also* **Huw**
Hughes, How¦ard
  (American
  industrialist)
Hughes, Ted
  (English poet)
Hughie
Hugli (= Hooghly)
Hugo
Hugo, Vic¦tor
  (French writer)
Hu¦gue|not +s
huh
Huhe|hot
  (= Hohhot)
hula +s
hula hoop +s
hula-hula +s
hula skirt +s
hulk +s
hulk|ing
Hull (official name
  Kingston-upon-
  Hull; city,
  England)
hull +s +ed +ing
hul¦la|ba¦loo +s
hullo (use hello)
  hul|loes
  hul|loed
  hullo|ing
hum
  hums
  hummed
  hum|ming
human +s
hu¦mane
hu¦mane¦ly
hu¦mane|ness
hu¦man|isa|tion
  Br. (use
  humanization)
hu¦man|ise *Br.* (use
  humanize)
  hu¦man|ises
  hu¦man|ised
  hu¦man|is¦ing
hu¦man|ism
hu¦man|ist +s
hu¦man|is¦tic
hu¦man|is¦tic|al¦ly
hu¦mani|tar¦ian +s
hu¦mani|tar¦ian|
        ism

hu¦man¦ity
  hu¦man¦ities
  hu¦man¦iza¦tion
hu¦man¦ize
  hu¦man¦izes
  hu¦man¦ized
  hu¦man¦iz¦ing
hu¦man¦kind
hu¦man¦ly
hu¦man¦ness
hu¦man¦oid +s
Hum¦ber (estuary
  and shipping area,
  England)
Hum¦ber¦side
  (county, England)
hum¦ble
  hum¦bles
  hum¦bled
  hum¦bling
  hum¦bler
  hum¦blest
humble-bee +s
hum¦ble¦ness
hum¦bly
Hum¦boldt,
  Fried¦rich
  (German explorer)
hum¦bug
  hum¦bugs
  hum¦bugged
  hum¦bug¦ging
hum¦bug¦gery
hum¦ding¦er +s
hum¦drum
Hume, David
  (Scottish
  philosopher.
  △ Home)
hu¦mec¦tant +s
hu¦meral
hu¦merus
  hu¦meri
  (bone.
  △ humorous)
humic
humid
hu¦midi¦fi¦ca¦tion
hu¦midi¦fier +s
hu¦midi¦fy
  hu¦midi¦fies
  hu¦midi¦fied
  hu¦midi¦fy¦ing
hu¦mid¦ity
  hu¦mid¦ities
hu¦mid¦ly
hu¦midor +s
hu¦mifi¦ca¦tion
hum¦ify
  humi¦fies
  humi¦fied
  humi¦fy¦ing

hu¦mili¦ate
  hu¦mili¦ates
  hu¦mili¦ated
  hu¦mili¦at¦ing
  hu¦mili¦at¦ing¦ly
  hu¦mili¦ation +s
  hu¦mili¦ator +s
hu¦mil¦ity
  hu¦mil¦ities
hum¦mable
hum¦mer +s
hum¦ming¦bird +s
humming-top +s
hum¦mock +s
hum¦mocky
hum¦mus (chick
  pea spread.
  △ humous,
  humus)
hu¦mon¦gous
humor *Am.* +s +ed
  +ing
hu¦moral
hu¦mor¦esque +s
hu¦mor¦ist +s
hu¦mor¦is¦tic
hu¦mor¦less *Am.*
hu¦mor¦less¦ly *Am.*
hu¦mor¦less¦ness
  Am.
hu¦mor¦ous
  (amusing.
  △ humerus)
hu¦mor¦ous¦ly
hu¦mor¦ous¦ness
hu¦mour *Br.* +s
  +ed +ing
hu¦mour¦less *Br.*
hu¦mour¦less¦ly *Br.*
hu¦mour¦less¦ness
  Br.
hum¦ous (of
  humus.
  △ hummus,
  humus)
hump +s +ed +ing
hump¦back +s
hump¦back bridge
  +s
hump¦backed
hump bridge +s
Hum¦per¦dinck,
  Engel¦bert
  (German
  composer)
humph
Hum¦phrey *also*
  Hum¦phry
Hum¦phries, Barry
  (Australian
  comedian)

Hum¦phry *also*
  Hum¦phrey
hump¦less
humpty
  hump¦ties
Humpty-Dumpty
  (nursery-rhyme
  character)
humpty-dumpty
  humpty-
  dumpties
  (person; thing)
humpy
  hump¦ies
  hump¦ier
  hump¦iest
hu¦mun¦gous (use
  humongous)
humus (soil
  constituent.
  △ hummus,
  humous)
hu¦mus¦ify
  hu¦musi¦fies
  hu¦musi¦fied
  hu¦musi¦fy¦ing
Hun +s (Asiatic
  tribe. △ hon)
Hunan (province,
  China)
hunch
  hunches
  hunched
  hunch¦ing
hunch¦back +s
hunch¦backed
hun¦dred
  plural hun¦dred *or*
  hun¦dreds
hun¦dred¦fold
hun¦dredth +s
hun¦dred¦weight
  plural
  hun¦dred¦weight
  or
  hun¦dred¦weights
hung
Hun¦gar¦ian +s
Hun¦gary
hun¦ger +s +ed
  +ing
hun¦ger march
  hun¦ger marches
hun¦ger march¦er
  +s
hun¦ger strike +s
hun¦ger striker +s
hung-over *adjective*
hun¦grily
hun¦gri¦ness

hun¦gry
  hun¦grier
  hun¦gri¦est
hunk +s
hun¦ker +s +ed
  +ing
hunky
  hun¦kies
hunky-dory
Hun¦nish
Hunt, Wil¦liam
  Hol¦man (English
  painter)
hunt +s +ed +ing
hunt¦away +s
Hunt¦er, John
  (Scottish
  anatomist)
hunt¦er +s
hunter-gather¦er
  +s
hunter-killer
hunt¦er's moon
hunt¦ing crop +s
hunt¦ing dog +s
Hun¦ting¦don
  (town, England)
Hun¦ting¦don,
  Count¦ess of
  (English religious
  leader)
Hun¦ting¦don¦
  shire (former
  English county)
hunt¦ing ground
  +s
hunt¦ing horn +s
hunt¦ing pink
Hun¦ting¦ton (city,
  West Virginia,
  USA)
Hun¦ting¦ton
  Beach (city,
  California, USA)
Hun¦ting¦ton's
  chorea
hunt¦ress
  hunt¦resses
hunts¦man
  hunts¦men
Hunts¦ville (city,
  USA)
Hupeh (= Hubei)
hur¦dle
  hur¦dles
  hur¦dled
  hurd¦ling
hurd¦ler +s
hurdy-gurdy
  hurdy-gurdies
hurl +s +ed +ing
  (throw. △ herl)

Hur¦ler's
  syn¦drome
hur¦ley
hurly-burly
Huron
  plural Huron *or*
  Hurons
  (American Indian)
Huron, Lake (in N.
  America)
hur¦rah +s +ed
  +ing
hur¦ray +s (use
  hooray)
Hurri
  plural Hurri *or*
  Hur¦ris
Hur¦rian
hur¦ri¦cane +s
hurricane-bird +s
hur¦ri¦cane deck
  +s
hur¦ri¦cane lamp
  +s
hur¦ried¦ly
hur¦ried¦ness
hur¦roo +s
hurry
  hur¦ries
  hur¦ried
  hurry¦ing
hurry-scurry
hurst +s
Hur¦ston, Zora
  Neale (American
  novelist)
hurt
  hurts
  hurt
  hurt¦ing
hurt¦ful
hurt¦ful¦ly
hurt¦ful¦ness
hur¦tle
  hur¦tles
  hur¦tled
  hurt¦ling
hurt¦less
Hus¦ain (use
  Hussein)
Husák, Gus¦táv
  (Czechoslovak
  statesman)
hus¦band +s +ed
  +ing
hus¦band¦er +s
hus¦band¦hood
hus¦band¦less
hus¦band¦like
hus¦band¦ly

hus¦band¦man
hus¦band¦men
hus¦band¦ry
hus¦band¦ship
hush
  hushes
  hushed
  hush¦ing
hush¦aby
hush¦abye (use
  hushaby)
hush-hush
husk +s +ed +ing
husk¦ily
huski¦ness
husky
  husk¦ies
  husk¦ier
  huski¦est
Huss, John
  (Bohemian
  religious reformer)
huss
  plural huss
hus¦sar +s
Hus¦sein
  (Jordanian king,
  1953–)
Hus¦sein,
  Ab¦dul¦lah ibn
  (Jordanian king,
  1946–51)
Hus¦sein,
  Sad¦dam (Iraqi
  president)
Hus¦serl, Ed¦mund
  (German
  philosopher)
Huss¦ite +s
Huss¦it¦ism
hussy
  hus¦sies
hust¦ings
hus¦tle
  hus¦tles
  hus¦tled
  hust¦ling
hust¦ler +s
Hus¦ton, John
  (American-born
  film director)
hut
  huts
  hut¦ted
  hut¦ting
hutch
  hutches
hut¦like
hut¦ment +s
Hut¦ter¦ite +s

Hut¦ton, James
  (Scottish
  geologist)
Hut¦ton, Len
  (English cricketer)
Hutu
  plural Hutu *or*
  Ba¦hutu
Huw *also* Hugh
Hux¦ley, Al¦dous
  (English writer)
Hux¦ley, Ju¦lian
  (English biologist)
Hux¦ley, Thomas
  (English biologist)
Huy¦gens,
  Chris¦tiaan
  (Dutch physicist;
  eyepiece)
huzzy
  huz¦zies
Hwange (town,
  Zimbabwe)
hwyl (fervour)
Hya¦cinth (name)
hya¦cinth +s
  (flower)
hya¦cinth¦ine
Hya¦cin¦thus *Greek*
  Mythology
Hya¦des (star
  cluster)
hy¦aena +s (use
  hyena)
hya¦lin *noun*
hya¦line *adjective*
hya¦lite
hya¦loid
hyal¦uron¦ic
hy¦brid +s
hy¦brid¦is¦able *Br.*
  (use hybridizable)
hy¦brid¦isa¦tion *Br.*
  (use
  hybridization)
hy¦brid¦ise *Br.* (use
  hybridize)
  hy¦brid¦ises
  hy¦brid¦ised
  hy¦brid¦is¦ing
hy¦brid¦ism
hy¦brid¦ity
hy¦brid¦iz¦able
hy¦brid¦iza¦tion
hy¦brid¦ize
  hy¦brid¦izes
  hy¦brid¦ized
  hy¦brid¦iz¦ing
hyda¦tid +s
hyda¦tidi¦form
Hyde, Ed¦ward
  (Earl of

Hyde (*cont.*)
  Clarendon,
  English statesman
  and historian)
Hyde (in 'Jekyll and
  Hyde')
Hyde Park (in
  London)
Hy¦dera¦bad
  (cities, India and
  Pakistan; former
  state, India)
Hydra (*Greek*
  Mythology;
  constellation)
hydra +s
hy¦dran¦gea +s
hy¦drant +s
hy¦drat¦able
hy¦drate
  hy¦drates
  hy¦drated
  hy¦drat¦ing
hy¦dra¦tion
hy¦dra¦tor +s
hy¦draul¦ic
hy¦draul¦ic¦al¦ly
hy¦draul¦icity
hy¦draul¦ics
hy¦dra¦zine +s
hy¦dric
hy¦dride +s
hy¦dri¦od¦ic
hydro +s
hydro¦bro¦mic
hydro¦car¦bon +s
hydro¦cele +s
hydro¦ceph¦al¦ic
hydro¦cepha¦lus
hydro¦chlor¦ic
hydro¦chlor¦ide +s
hydro¦cor¦ti¦sone
hydro¦cyan¦ic
hydro¦dynam¦ic
hydro¦dynam¦ic¦al
hydro¦
  dy¦nami¦cist +s
hydro¦dynam¦ics
hydro¦elec¦tric
hydro¦elec¦tri¦city
hydro¦fined
hydro¦fin¦ing
hydro¦fluor¦ic
hydro¦foil +s
hydro¦gel +s
hydro¦gen
hy¦dro¦gen¦ase +s
hy¦dro¦gen¦ate
  hy¦dro¦gen¦ates
  hy¦dro¦gen¦ated
  hy¦dro¦gen¦at¦ing
hy¦dro¦gen¦ation

hydro|gen bond +s
hydrogen-bonded
hy|dro|gen|ous
hydro|geo|logic|al
hydro|geolo|gist +s
hydro|geol|ogy
hy|drog|raph|er +s
hydro|graph|ic
hydro|graph|ic|al
hydro|graph|ic|al|ly
hy|drog|raphy
hy|droid +s
hydro|lase +s
hydro|logic
hydro|logic|al
hydro|logic|al|ly
hy|drolo|gist +s
hy|drol|ogy
hydro|lyse Br.
   hydro|lyses
   hydro|lysed
   hydro|lys|ing
hy|droly|sis
   hy|droly|ses
hydro|lyt|ic
hydro|lyze Am.
   hydro|lyzes
   hydro|lyzed
   hydro|lyz|ing
hydro|mag|net|ic
hydro|mag|net|ics
hydro|mania
hydro|mechan|ics
hydro|mel
hy|drom|eter +s
hydro|met|ric
hy|drom|et|ry
hy|dro|nium ion +s
hydro|path|ic
hy|drop|ath|ist +s
hy|drop|athy
hydro|phane +s
hydro|phil
hydro|phile
hydro|phil|ic
hydro|pho|bia
hydro|pho|bic
hydro|phone +s
hydro|phyte +s
hy|drop|ic
hydro|plane
   hydro|planes
   hydro|planed
   hydro|plan|ing
hydro|pneu|mat|ic
hydro|pon|ic
hydro|pon|ic|al|ly
hydro|pon|ics

hydro|quin|one
hydro|sphere
hydro|stat|ic
hydro|stat|ic|al
hydro|stat|ic|al|ly
hydro|stat|ics
hydro|ther|apic
hydro|ther|apist +s
hydro|ther|apy
hydro|ther|mal
hydro|ther|mal|ly
hydro|thorax
hydro|trop|ism
hy|drous
hy|drox|ide +s
hy|drox|onium ion +s
hy|droxyl +s
hydro|zoan +s
hyena +s
Hy|geia
hy|geian
hy|giene
hy|gien|ic
hy|gien|ic|al|ly
hy|gien|ics
hy|gien|ist +s
hy|grol|ogy
hy|grom|eter +s
hy|grom|etry
hy|grophil|ous
hygro|phyte +s
hygro|phyt|ic
hygro|scope +s
hygro|scop|ic
hygro|scop|ic|al|ly
hying
Hyk|sos
Hylda also Hilda
hylic
hylo|morph|ism
hylo|the|ism
hylo|zo|ism
hylo|zo|ist +s
Hymen (cry used at ancient Greek weddings)
hymen +s (membrane)
hy|men|al (of hymen)
hy|men|eal (of marriage)
hy|men|ium
   hy|menia
Hy|men|op|tera
hy|men|op|teran +s
hy|men|op|ter|ous

hymn +s +ed +ing (song. △ him)
hym|nal +s
hym|nary
   hym|nar|ies
hymn book +s
hym|nic
hym|nist +s
hym|nod|ist +s
hym|nody
   hym|nod|ies
hymn|og|raph|er +s
hymn|og|raphy
hymn|olo|gist +s
hymn|ology
hyoid +s
hyos|cine
hyos|cya|mine
hyp|aes|the|sia Br. (Am. hypoesthesia. abnormally low sensitivity. △ hyper-aesthesia)
hyp|aes|thet|ic Br. (Am. hypoesthetic. having hypaesthesia. △ hyperaesthetic)
hyp|aeth|ral
hyp|al|lage +s
Hyp|atia (Greek philosopher and mathematician)
hype
   hypes
   hyped
   hyp|ing
hyper
hyper|active
hyper|activ|ity
hyper|aemia Br. (Am. hyperemia)
hyper|aem|ic Br. (Am. hyperemic)
hyper|aes|the|sia Br. (Am. hyperesthesia. abnormally high sensitivity. △ hypaesthesia)
hyper|aes|thet|ic Br. (Am. hyperesthetic. having hyperaesthesia. △ hypaesthetic)
hyper|bar|ic
hyper|ba|ton

hyper|bola
   hyper|bolas or
   hyper|bolae (curve)
hyper|bole +s (exaggeration)
hyper|bol|ic (of hyperbola)
hyper|bol|ic|al (of hyperbole)
hyper|bol|ic|al|ly (using hyperbole)
hyper|bol|ism (use of hyperbole)
hyper|bol|ist (user of hyperbole)
hyper|bol|oid +s
hyper|bol|oid|al
Hyper|bor|ean +s Greek Mythology
hyper|bor|ean +s (person; of extreme north)
Hyper|Card Propr.
hyper|cata|lec|tic
hyper|cho|les|ter|ol|aemia Br.
hyper|cho|les|ter|ol|emia Am.
hyper|con|scious
hyper|crit|ic|al (over-critical. △ hypocritical)
hyper|crit|ic|al|ly (over-critically. △ hypocritically)
hyper|criti|cism
hyper|cube +s
hyper|du|lia
hyper|emia Am. (Br. hyperaemia)
hyper|em|ic Am. (Br. hyperaemic)
hyper|es|the|sia Am. (Br. hyperaesthesia. abnormally high sensitivity. △ hypoesthesia)
hyper|es|thet|ic Am. (Br. hyperaesthetic. having hyperesthesia. △ hypoesthetic)
hyper|focal
hyper|gamy
hyper|gly|caemia Br. (excess of

hyper|gly|caemia
(*cont.*)
glucose. ⚠ hypo-
glycaemia)
hyper|gly|caem|ic
Br. (of
hyperglycaemia.
⚠ hypo-
glycaemic)
hyper|gly|cemia
Am. (excess of
glucose.
⚠ hypoglycemia)
hyper|gly|cem|ic
Am. (of
hyperglycemia.
⚠ hypoglycemic)
hy|per|gol|ic
hy|peri|cum +s
hyper|in|fla|tion
Hy|perion (*Greek
Mythology*; moon
of Saturn)
hyper|kin|esia
hyper|kin|esis
hyper|kin|et|ic
hyper|lip|id|aemia
Br.
hyper|lip|id|
aem|ic *Br.*
hyper|lip|id|emia
Am.
hyper|lip|id|em|ic
Am.
hyper|mar|ket +s
hyper|media
hyper|met|ric
hyper|met|ric|al
hyper|me|tro|pia
hyper|me|trop|ic
hyper|nym +s
(more general
term.
⚠ hyponym)
hyp|eron +s
hyper|on|ic
hyper|opia
hyper|op|ic
hyper|phys|ic|al
hyper|phys|ic|al|ly
hyper|pla|sia
hyper|sen|si|tive
hyper|sen|si|tive|
ness
hyper|sen|si|tiv|ity
hyper|son|ic
hyper|son|ic|al|ly
hyper|space
hyper|sthene
hyper|ten|sion
(abnormally high

hyper|ten|sion
(*cont.*)
blood pressure.
⚠ hypotension)
hyper|ten|sive
(having
abnormally high
blood pressure.
⚠ hypotensive)
hyper|text +s
hyper|ther|mia
(abnormally high
temperature.
⚠ hypothermia)
hyper|ther|mic
hyper|thy|roid (of
hyperthyroidism.
⚠ hypothyroid)
hyper|thy|roid|ic
hyper|thy|roid|ism
(excessive thyroid
activity. ⚠ hypo-
thyroidism)
hyper|tonia
hyper|ton|ic
hyper|ton|icity
hyper|troph|ic
hyper|tro|phied
hyper|trophy
hyper|tro|phies
hyper|ven|ti|late
hyper|ven|ti|lates
hyper|ven|ti|lated
hyper|ven|ti|
lat|ing
(breathe
abnormally
rapidly.
⚠ hypoventilate)
hyper|ven|ti|
la|tion
(abnormally rapid
breathing. ⚠ hypo-
ventilation)
hyp|es|the|sia *Am.*
(use
hypoesthesia. *Br.*
hypaesthesia)
hyp|es|thetic *Am.*
(use
hypoesthetic. *Br.*
hypaesthetic)
hyp|eth|ral (use
hypaethral)
hypha
hy|phae
hy|phal
Hy|pha|sis (ancient
Greek name for
the Beas)
hy|phen +s +ed
+ing

hy|phen|ate
hy|phen|ates
hy|phen|ated
hy|phen|at|ing
hy|phen|ation
hypno|gen|esis
hyp|nol|ogist +s
hyp|nol|ogy
hypno|pae|dia *Br.*
hypno|pe|dia *Am.*
Hyp|nos *Greek
Mythology*
hyp|no|sis
hyp|no|ses
hypno|ther|ap|ist
+s
hypno|ther|apy
hyp|not|ic
hyp|not|ic|al|ly
hyp|no|tis|able *Br.*
(use
hypnotizable)
hyp|no|tise *Br.* (use
hypnotize)
hyp|no|tises
hyp|no|tised
hyp|no|tis|ing
hyp|no|tism
hyp|no|tist +s
hyp|no|tiz|able
hyp|no|tize
hyp|no|tizes
hyp|no|tized
hyp|no|tiz|ing
hypo +s
hypo|aes|the|sia
Br. (use
hypaesthesia.
Am.
hypoesthesia.
abnormally high
sensitivity.
⚠ hyper-
aesthesia)
hypo|aes|thet|ic
Br. (use
hypaesthetic. *Am.*
hypoesthetic.
having
hypaesthesia.
⚠ hyperaesthetic)
hypo-allergen|ic
hypo|blast +s
hypo|caust +s
hypo|chlor|ite +s
hypo|chlor|ous
hypo|chon|dria
hypo|chon|driac
+s
hypo|cor|is|tic
hypo|cotyl +s
hyp|oc|risy
hyp|ocri|sies

hypo|crite +s
hypo|crit|ical
(of hypocrisy.
⚠ hypercritical)
hypo|crit|ic|al|ly
(with hypocrisy.
⚠ hypercritically)
hypo|cyc|loid +s
hypo|cyc|loid|al
hypo|derma
hypo|der|mata
hypo|der|mal
hypo|der|mic +s
hypo|der|mic|al|ly
hypo|es|the|sia
Am. (*Br.*
hypaesthesia.
abnormally low
sensitivity.
⚠ hyperesthesia)
hypo|es|thet|ic
Am. (*Br.*
hypaesthetic.
having
hypoesthesia.
⚠ hyperesthetic)
hypo|gas|tric
hypo|gas|trium
hypo|gas|tria
hypo|geal
hypo|gene
hypo|geum
hypo|gea
hypo|gly|caemia
Br. (glucose
deficiency.
⚠ hyper-
glycaemia)
hypo|gly|caem|ic
Br. (of
hypoglycaemia.
⚠ hyper-
glycaemic)
hypo|gly|cemia
Am. (glucose
deficiency.
⚠ hyper-
glycemia)
hypo|gly|cem|ic
Am. (of
hypoglycemia.
⚠ hyperglycemic)
hy|poid +s
hypo|lim|nion
hypo|lim|nia
hypo|mania
hypo|maniac +s
hypo|man|ic +s
hypo|nas|tic
hypo|nasty
hypo|nym +s
(more specific

hypo|nym (*cont.*)
term.
⚠ hypernym)
hyp|onym|ous
hyp|onymy
hypo|phys|eal
hypo|phys|ial (use
hypophyseal)
hyp|ophy|sis
hyp|ophy|ses
hy|pos|tasis
hy|pos|tases
hy|pos|ta|sise *Br.*
(use hypostasize)
hy|pos|ta|sises
hy|pos|ta|sised
hy|pos|ta|sis|ing
hy|pos|ta|size
hy|pos|ta|sizes
hy|pos|ta|sized
hy|pos|ta|siz|ing
hypo|stat|ic
hypo|stat|ic|al (use
hypostatic)
hypo|stat|ic|al|ly
hy|pos|ta|tise *Br.*
(use hypostatize)
hy|pos|ta|tises
hy|pos|ta|tised
hy|pos|ta|tis|ing
hy|pos|ta|tize
hy|pos|ta|tizes
hy|pos|ta|tized
hy|pos|ta|tiz|ing
hypo|style
hypo|sul|fite *Am.*
+s
hypo|sul|phite *Br.*
+s
hypo|tac|tic
hypo|taxis
hypo|ten|sion
(abnormally low
blood pressure.
⚠ hypertension)
hypo|ten|sive
(having
abnormally low
blood pressure.
⚠ hypertensive)
hypot|en|use +s
hypo|thal|am|ic
hypo|thal|amus
hypo|thal|ami
hypo|thec
hy|pothe|cary
hy|pothe|car|ies
hy|pothe|cate
hy|pothe|cates
hy|pothe|cated
hy|pothe|cat|ing
hy|pothe|ca|tion

hy|pothe|ca|tor +s
hypo|ther|mia
(abnormally low
temperature.
⚠ hyperthermia)
hy|poth|esis
hy|poth|eses
hy|pothe|sise *Br.*
(use hypothesize)
hy|pothe|sises
hy|pothe|sised
hy|pothe|sis|ing
hy|pothe|siser *Br.*
+s (use
hypothesizer)
hy|pothe|sist +s
hy|pothe|size
hy|pothe|sizes
hy|pothe|sized
hy|pothe|siz|ing
hy|pothe|sizer +s
hypo|thet|ic|al
hypo|thet|ic|al|ly
hypo|thy|roid (of
hypothyroidism.
⚠ hyperthyroid)
hypo|thy|roid|ic
(suffering from
hypothyroidism.
⚠ hyperthyroid-
ic)
hypo|thy|roid|ism
(subnormal
thyroid activity.
⚠ hyperthyroid-
ism)
hypo|ven|ti|late
hypo|ven|ti|lates
hypo|ven|ti|lated
hypo|ven|ti|
lat|ing
(breathe
abnormally
slowly.
⚠ hyperventilate)
hypo|ven|ti|la|tion
(abnormally slow
breathing.
⚠ hyperventila-
tion)
hyp|ox|aemia *Br.*
hyp|ox|emia *Am.*
hyp|oxia
hyp|ox|ic
hypsi|lopho|don
+s
hypso|graph|ic
hypso|graph|ic|al
hyp|sog|raphy
hyp|som|eter +s
hypso|met|ric

hyrax
hyr|axes *or*
hyr|aces
hyson
hys|sop
hys|ter|ec|tom|ise
Br. (use
hysterectomize)
hys|ter|
ec|tom|ises
hys|ter|
ec|tom|ised
hys|ter|
ec|tom|is|ing
hys|ter|ec|tom|ize
hys|ter|
ec|tom|izes
hys|ter|
ec|tom|ized
hys|ter|
ec|tom|iz|ing
hys|ter|ec|tomy
hys|ter|ec|to|mies
hys|ter|esis
hys|ter|eses
hys|teria +s
hys|ter|ic +s
hys|ter|ic|al
hys|ter|ic|al|ly
hysteron pro|ton

Ii

I (myself. ⚠ aye,
eye)
Iain *also* Ian
iamb +s
iam|bic +s
iam|bus
iam|buses *or*
iambi
Ian *also* Iain
Iap|etus (*Greek
Mythology*; moon
of Saturn)
Iaşi (city, Romania)
IATA
(= International
Air Transport
Association)
iat|ro|gen|ic
Iba|dan (city,
Nigeria)
Iban
plural Iban
Ibá|ñez, Vi|cente
Blasco (Spanish
novelist)
Ibar|ruri Gomez,
Dol|ores ('La
Pasionaria',
Spanish
Communist
politician)
I-beam +s
Iberia (ancient
name for Spain
and Portugal)
Iber|ian
Ibero-American
+s
ibex
ibexes
ibid.
ibis
ibises
Ibiza (Spanish
island and city)
Ibn Ba|tuta (Arab
explorer)
ibn Hus|sein,
Ab|dul|lah
(Jordanian king,
1946–51)
Ibo
plural Ibo *or* Ibos
Ibsen, Hen|rik
(Norwegian
dramatist)
ibu|profen

Ica¦rus *Greek*
  Mythology
ice
  ices
  iced
  icing
ice age +s
ice axe +s
ice-bag +s
ice¦berg +s
ice¦blink +s
ice¦block +s (lolly)
ice block +s (block
  of ice)
ice blue +s *noun*
  and adjective
ice-blue *attributive*
ice-boat +s
ice-bound
ice¦box
  ice¦boxes
ice-breaker +s
ice bucket +s
ice cap +s
ice-cold
ice cream +s
ice cube +s
ice dan¦cing
iced lolly
  iced lol¦lies
ice¦fall +s
ice field +s
ice fish
  plural ice fish *or*
  ice fishes
ice floe +s
ice hockey
ice house +s
Ice¦land
Ice¦land¦er +s
Ice¦land¦ic
Ice¦land spar +s
ice lolly
  ice lol¦lies
ice¦man
  ice¦men
Iceni
ice pack +s
ice pick +s
ice plant +s
ice rink +s
ice sheet +s
ice shelf
  ice shelves
ice-skate
  ice-skates
  ice-skated
  ice-skating
ice-skater +s
ice sta¦tion +s
ice storm +s
ice water

Icha¦bod *Bible*
I Ching
ich¦neu¦mon +s
ich¦nog¦raphy
  ich¦nog¦raph¦ies
ichor +s
ich¦or¦ous
ich¦thy¦og¦raph¦er
  +s
ich¦thy¦og¦raphy
ich¦thy¦oid +s
ich¦thy¦ol¦atry
ich¦thyo¦lite +s
ich¦thyo¦logic¦al
ich¦thy¦olo¦gist +s
ich¦thy¦ol¦ogy
ich¦thy¦opha¦gous
ich¦thy¦oph¦agy
ich¦thyo¦saur +s
ich¦thyo¦saurus
  ich¦thyo¦sauri
ich¦thy¦osis
ich¦thy¦ot¦ic
I-chun (= Yichun)
icicle +s
icily
ici¦ness
icing +s
icing sugar +s
Ick¦nield Way
  (ancient track,
  England)
icky
icon +s
icon¦ic
icon¦icity
icono¦clasm
icono¦clast +s
icono¦clas¦tic
icono¦clas¦tic¦al¦ly
icon¦og¦raph¦er +s
icono¦graph¦ic
icono¦graph¦ic¦al
icono¦graph¦ic¦
  al¦ly
icon¦og¦raphy
  icon¦og¦raph¦ies
icon¦ol¦ater +s
icon¦ol¦atry
icon¦ology
  icon¦olo¦gies
icon¦om¦eter +s
icon¦om¦etry
icon¦osta¦sis
  icon¦osta¦ses
ico¦sa¦he¦dral
ico¦sa¦he¦dron
  ico¦sa¦he¦dra *or*
  ico¦sa¦he¦drons
ico¦si¦do¦deca¦
        he¦dron
ico¦si¦do¦deca¦

ico¦si¦do¦deca¦
    he¦dron (*cont.*)
    he¦dra *or*
ico¦si¦do¦deca¦
      he¦drons
ic¦ter¦ic
ic¦terus
Ic¦ti¦nus (Greek
  architect)
ictus
  plural ictus *or*
  ic¦tuses
icy
  icier
  ici¦est
Id (use Eid)
I'd (= I had; I
  should; I would.
  △ ide)
id +s *Psychology*
Ida (name;
  asteroid)
Ida, Mount (in
  Crete)
Idaho (state, USA)
ID card +s
ide +s (fish. △ ides,
  I'd)
idea +s
ideal +s
ideal¦less
ideal¦isa¦tion *Br.*
  +s (use
  idealization)
ideal¦ise *Br.* (use
  idealize)
  ideal¦ises
  ideal¦ised
  ideal¦is¦ing
ideal¦iser *Br.* +s
  (use idealizer)
ideal¦ism
ideal¦ist +s
ideal¦is¦tic
ideal¦is¦tic¦al¦ly
ideal¦ity
  ideal¦ities
ideal¦iza¦tion +s
ideal¦ize
  ideal¦izes
  ideal¦ized
  ideal¦iz¦ing
ideal¦izer +s
ideal¦ly
ide¦ate
  ide¦ates
  ide¦ated
  ideat¦ing
idea¦tion +s
idea¦tion¦al
idea¦tion¦al¦ly

idée fixe
  idées fixes
idée reçue
  idées reçues
idem
iden¦tic
iden¦ti¦cal
iden¦ti¦cal¦ly
iden¦ti¦cal¦ness
iden¦ti¦fi¦able
iden¦ti¦fi¦ably
iden¦ti¦fi¦ca¦tion +s
iden¦ti¦fier +s
iden¦tify
  iden¦ti¦fies
  iden¦ti¦fied
  iden¦ti¦fy¦ing
iden¦ti¦kit +s *Propr.*
iden¦tity
  iden¦tities
iden¦tity card +s
ideo¦gram +s
ideo¦graph +s
ideo¦graph¦ic
ideo¦graph¦ic¦al
ideo¦logic¦al
ideo¦logic¦al¦ly
ideolo¦gist +s
ideo¦logue +s
ideol¦ogy
  ideolo¦gies
ides
idi¦ocy
  idi¦ocies
idio¦lect +s
idiom +s
idiom¦at¦ic
idiom¦at¦ic¦al¦ly
idio¦path¦ic
idi¦op¦athy
idi¦op¦athies
idio¦syn¦crasy
  idio¦syn¦cra¦sies
idio¦syn¦crat¦ic
idio¦syn¦crat¦ic¦
        al¦ly
idiot +s
idi¦ot¦ic
idi¦ot¦ic¦al¦ly
idiot sav¦ant
  plural
  idiot sav¦ants *or*
  idiots sav¦ants
idle
  idles
  idled
  id¦ling
  (lazy; be inactive.
  △ idol)
idle¦ness
idler +s
idly

Ido (language)
idol +s (object of
worship. ⚠ idle)
idol|ater +s
idol|atress
idol|atresses
idol|atrous
idol|atry
idol|atries
idol|isa|tion Br.
(use idolization)
idol|ise Br. (use
idolize)
idol|ises
idol|ised
idol|is|ing
idol|iser Br. +s (use
idolizer)
idol|iza|tion
idol|ize
idol|izes
idol|ized
idol|iz|ing
idol|izer +s
ido|lum
idola
Idome|neus Greek
Mythology
idyll +s
idyl|lic
idyl|lic|al|ly
idyl|lise Br. (use
idyllize)
idyl|lises
idyl|lised
idyl|lis|ing
idyl|list +s
idyl|lize
idyl|lizes
idyl|lized
idyl|liz|ing
if +s
iff Logic;
Mathematics
iffy
if|fier
if|fi|est
Ifni (former Spanish
province,
Morocco)
Ifor also Ivor
Igbo
plural Igbo or
Igbos
Igle|sias, Julio
(Spanish singer)
igloo +s
Ig|na|tius Loy|ola
(Spanish saint)
ig|ne|ous
ig|nim|brite
ignis fat|uus
ignes fatui

ig|nit|abil|ity
ig|nit|able
ig|nite
ig|nites
ig|nited
ig|nit|ing
ig|niter +s
ig|ni|tion +s
ig|ni|tron +s
ig|no|bil|ity
ig|noble
ig|nobler
ig|nob|lest
ig|nobly
ig|no|mini|ous
ig|no|mini|ous|ly
ig|no|mini|ous|
ness
ig|no|miny
ig|no|minies
ig|nor|amus
ig|nor|amuses
ig|nor|ance
ig|nor|ant
ig|nor|ant|ly
ig|nore
ig|nores
ig|nored
ig|nor|ing
ig|norer +s
ig|no|tum per
ig|no|tius
Iguaçu (river,
Brazil)
igu|ana +s
iguano|don +s
IJs|sel (river, the
Netherlands)
IJs|sel|meer (lake,
the Netherlands)
ike|bana
Ikh|na|ton (use
Akhenaten)
ikky (use icky)
ikon +s (use icon)
ilang-ilang (use
ylang-ylang)
ILEA (= Inner
London Education
Authority)
ilea (plural of
ileum)
ileac (of the ileum.
⚠ iliac)
ileal
Île-de-France
(region, France)
ile|itis
ile|os|tomy
ile|os|tomies
Il|esha (city,
Nigeria)

ileum
ilea
(part of small
intestine. ⚠ ilium)
ileus
ilex
ilexes
ilia (plural of ilium)
iliac (of the lower
body or ilium.
⚠ ileac)
Iliad (Greek epic
poem)
Ilium (ancient
Greek city)
ilium
ilia
(pelvic bone.
⚠ ileum)
ilk +s
I'll (I shall; I will.
⚠ aisle, isle)
ill +s (sick;
sickness)
ill-advised
ill-advised|ly
ill-affect|ed
ill-assort|ed
il|la|tion +s
il|la|tive
il|la|tive|ly
ill-behaved
ill blood
ill-bred
ill breed|ing
ill-conceived
ill-consid|ered
ill-defined
ill-disposed
il|legal
il|legal|ity
il|legal|ities
il|legal|ly
il|legi|bil|ity
il|legible
il|legibly
il|legit|im|acy
il|legit|im|ate
il|legit|im|ates
il|legit|im|ated
il|legit|im|at|ing
il|legit|im|ate|ly
il|legit|im|ation
il|legit|im|ise Br.
(use illegitimize)
il|legit|im|ises
il|legit|im|ised
il|legit|im|is|ing
il|legit|im|ize
il|legit|im|izes
il|legit|im|ized
il|legit|im|iz|ing

ill-equipped
ill-fated
ill-favored Am.
ill-favoured Br.
ill feel|ing
ill-fitting
ill-founded
ill-gotten
ill-humored Am.
ill-humoured Br.
il|lib|eral
il|lib|er|al|ity
il|lib|er|al|ities
il|li|ber|al|ly
Il|lich, Ivan
(Austrian-born
American
educationalist)
il|licit (unlawful.
⚠ elicit)
il|licit|ly
il|licit|ness
il|lim|it|abil|ity
il|lim|it|able
il|lim|it|able|ness
il|lim|it|ably
ill-informed
Il|li|nois (state,
USA)
il|liquid
il|liquid|ity
il|lit|er|acy
il|lit|er|ate +s
il|lit|er|ate|ly
il|lit|er|ate|ness
ill-judged
ill-mannered
ill-matched
ill nature +s
ill-natured
ill-natured|ly
ill|ness
ill|nesses
il|logic|al
il|logic|al|ity
il|logic|al|ities
il|logic|al|ly
ill-omened
ill-prepared
ill-starred
ill-suited
ill tem|per +s
ill-tempered
ill-timed
ill-treat +s +ed
+ing
ill-treatment +s
il|lude
il|ludes
il|luded
il|lud|ing
(deceive.
⚠ allude, elude)

il¦lume
  il¦lumes
  il¦lumed
  il¦lum¦ing
il¦lu¦min¦ance +s
il¦lu¦min¦ant +s
il¦lu¦min¦ate
  il¦lu¦min¦ates
  il¦lu¦min¦ated
  il¦lu¦min¦at¦ing
il¦lu¦min¦ati
il¦lu¦min¦at¦ing¦ly
il¦lu¦min¦ation +s
il¦lu¦mina¦tive
il¦lu¦min¦ator +s
il¦lu¦mine
  il¦lu¦mines
  il¦lu¦mined
  il¦lu¦min¦ing
il¦lu¦min¦ism
il¦lu¦min¦ist +s
ill use *noun*
ill-use
  ill-uses
  ill-used
  ill-using
  verb
il¦lu¦sion +s (false
  perception.
  ⚠ allusion)
il¦lu¦sion¦al
il¦lu¦sion¦ism
il¦lu¦sion¦ist +s
il¦lu¦sion¦is¦tic
il¦lu¦sive
  (deceptive.
  ⚠ allusive,
  elusive)
il¦lu¦sive¦ly (in an
  illusive way.
  ⚠ allusively,
  elusively)
il¦lu¦sive¦ness
  (illusive nature.
  ⚠ allusiveness,
  elusiveness)
il¦lu¦sor¦ily
il¦lu¦sori¦ness
il¦lu¦sory
  (deceptive.
  ⚠ elusory)
il¦lus¦trate
  il¦lus¦trates
  il¦lus¦trated
  il¦lus¦trat¦ing
il¦lus¦tra¦tion +s
il¦lus¦tra¦tion¦al
il¦lus¦tra¦tive
il¦lus¦tra¦tive¦ly
il¦lus¦tra¦tor +s
il¦lus¦tri¦ous
il¦lus¦tri¦ous¦ly

il¦lus¦tri¦ous¦ness
ill will
Il¦lyria (ancient
  region, S. Europe)
Il¦lyr¦ian +s
il¦ly¦whack¦er +s
il¦men¦ite +s
Ilo¦ilo (port,
  Philippines)
Ilona
Ilorin (city, Nigeria)
I'm (= I am)
image
  im¦ages
  im¦aged
  im¦aging
im¦age¦able
im¦age¦less
image-maker +s
im¦agery
  im¦ager¦ies
im¦agin¦able
im¦agin¦ably
im¦agi¦nal
im¦agin¦ar¦ily
im¦agin¦ary
im¦agin¦ation +s
im¦agina¦tive
im¦agina¦tive¦ly
im¦agina¦tive¦ness
im¦agine
  im¦agines
  im¦agined
  im¦agin¦ing
im¦aginer +s
im¦agines (plural of
  imago)
im¦agin¦ing +s
im¦agism
im¦agist +s
im¦agis¦tic
imago
  im¦agos *or*
  im¦agi¦nes
imam +s
imam¦ate +s
IMAX
  Cinematography
im¦bal¦ance +s
im¦be¦cile +s
im¦be¦cile¦ly
im¦be¦cil¦ic
im¦be¦cil¦ity
  im¦be¦cil¦ities
imbed (use embed)
  im¦beds
  im¦bed¦ded
  im¦bed¦ding
im¦bibe
  im¦bibes
  im¦bibed
  im¦bib¦ing

im¦biber +s
im¦bi¦bi¦tion +s
im¦bri¦cate
  im¦bri¦cates
  im¦bri¦cated
  im¦bri¦cat¦ing
im¦bri¦ca¦tion +s
im¦bro¦glio +s
Im¦bros (island,
  Turkey)
im¦brue
  im¦brues
  im¦brued
  im¦bru¦ing
im¦brute
  im¦brutes
  im¦bruted
  im¦brut¦ing
imbue
  im¦bues
  im¦bued
  im¦bu¦ing
Im¦ho¦tep (ancient
  Egyptian architect
  and scholar)
imide +s
imine +s
im¦it¦able
imi¦tate
  imi¦tates
  imi¦tated
  imi¦tat¦ing
imi¦ta¦tion +s
imi¦ta¦tive
imi¦ta¦tive¦ly
imi¦ta¦tive¦ness
imi¦ta¦tor +s
im¦macu¦lacy
im¦macu¦late
im¦macu¦late¦ly
im¦macu¦late¦ness
im¦ma¦nence
  (inherency.
  ⚠ imminence)
im¦ma¦nency
  (inherency.
  ⚠ imminency)
im¦ma¦nent
  (inherent.
  ⚠ imminent)
im¦ma¦nent¦ism
im¦ma¦nent¦ist +s
Im¦man¦uel (*Bible.*
  ⚠ Emanuel,
  Emmanuel)
im¦ma¦ter¦ial
im¦ma¦teri¦al¦ise
  Br. (use
  immaterialize)
  im¦ma¦teri¦al¦ises
  im¦ma¦teri¦al¦ised

im¦ma¦teri¦al¦ise
  (*cont.*)
  im¦ma¦teri¦al|
    is¦ing
im¦ma¦teri¦al¦ism
im¦ma¦teri¦al¦ist
  +s
im¦ma¦teri¦al¦ity
im¦ma¦teri¦al¦ize
  im¦ma¦teri¦al¦izes
  im¦ma¦teri¦al¦ized
  im¦ma¦teri¦al|
    iz¦ing
im¦ma¦teri¦al¦ly
im¦ma¦ture
im¦ma¦ture¦ly
im¦ma¦tur¦ity
im¦meas¦ur|
    abil¦ity
im¦meas¦ur¦able
im¦meas¦ur¦able|
    ness
im¦meas¦ur¦ably
im¦me¦di¦acy
im¦me¦di¦ate
im¦me¦di¦ate¦ly
im¦me¦di¦ate¦ness
im¦med¦ic¦able
im¦med¦ic¦ably
im¦me¦mor¦ial
im¦me¦mori¦al¦ly
im¦mense
im¦mense¦ly
im¦mense¦ness
im¦mens¦ity
  im¦mens¦ities
im¦merse
  im¦merses
  im¦mersed
  im¦mers¦ing
im¦mer¦sion +s
im¦mi¦grant +s
im¦mi¦grate
  im¦mi¦grates
  im¦mi¦grated
  im¦mi¦grat¦ing
im¦mi¦gra¦tion +s
im¦mi¦gra¦tory
im¦mi¦nence
  (impending
  nature.
  ⚠ immanence)
im¦mi¦nency
  (impending
  nature.
  ⚠ immanency)
im¦mi¦nent
  (impending.
  ⚠ immanent)
im¦mi¦nent¦ly
Im¦ming¦ham
  (port, England)

im¦mis¦ci¦bil¦ity
im¦mis¦cible
im¦mis¦cibly
im¦mit¦ig¦able
im¦mit¦ig¦ably
im¦mit¦tance +s
im¦mix¦ture +s
im¦mo¦bile
im¦mo¦bil¦isa¦tion
   Br. +s (use
   immobilization)
im¦mo¦bil¦ise *Br.*
   (use immobilize)
   im¦mo¦bil¦ises
   im¦mo¦bil¦ised
   im¦mo¦bil¦is¦ing
im¦mo¦bil¦iser *Br.*
   +s (use
   immobilizer)
im¦mo¦bil¦ism
im¦mo¦bil¦ity
   im¦mo¦bil¦ities
im¦mo¦bil¦iza¦tion
   +s
im¦mo¦bil¦ize
   im¦mo¦bil¦izes
   im¦mo¦bil¦ized
   im¦mo¦bil¦iz¦ing
im¦mo¦bil¦izer +s
im¦mod¦er¦ate
im¦mod¦er¦ate¦ly
im¦mod¦er¦ate¦
                ness
im¦mod¦er¦ation
im¦mod¦est
im¦mod¦est¦ly
im¦mod¦esty
   im¦mod¦est¦ies
im¦mol¦ate
   im¦mol¦ates
   im¦mol¦ated
   im¦mol¦at¦ing
im¦mol¦ation +s
im¦mol¦ator +s
im¦moral
im¦mor¦al¦ity
   im¦mor¦al¦ities
im¦mor¦al¦ly
im¦mor¦tal +s
im¦mor¦tal¦isa¦tion
   Br. +s (use
   immortalization)
im¦mor¦tal¦ise *Br.*
   (use immortalize)
   im¦mor¦tal¦ises
   im¦mor¦tal¦ised
   im¦mor¦tal¦is¦ing
im¦mor¦tal¦ity
   im¦mor¦tal¦ities
im¦mor¦tal¦
      iza¦tion +s

im¦mor¦tal¦ize
   im¦mor¦tal¦izes
   im¦mor¦tal¦ized
   im¦mor¦tal¦iz¦ing
im¦mor¦tal¦ly
im¦mor¦telle +s
   (flower)
im¦mov¦abil¦ity
im¦mov¦able
im¦mov¦able¦ness
im¦mov¦ably
im¦move¦able (use
   immovable)
im¦move¦able¦ness
   (use
   immovableness)
im¦move¦ably (use
   immovably)
im¦mune
im¦mun¦isa¦tion
   Br. +s (use
   immunization)
im¦mun¦ise *Br.* (use
   immunize)
   im¦mun¦ises
   im¦mun¦ised
   im¦mun¦is¦ing
im¦mun¦iser *Br.* +s
   (use immunizer)
im¦mun¦ity
   im¦mun¦ities
im¦mun¦iza¦tion
   +s
im¦mun¦ize
   im¦mun¦izes
   im¦mun¦ized
   im¦mun¦iz¦ing
im¦mun¦izer +s
im¦muno¦assay +s
im¦muno¦
        chem¦is¦try
im¦muno¦
      com¦pe¦tence
im¦muno¦
      com¦pe¦tent
im¦muno¦
      com¦prom¦ised
im¦muno¦
        defi¦ciency
im¦mu¦no¦
        defi¦cien¦cies
im¦muno¦
        defi¦cient
im¦muno¦
        depressed
im¦muno¦
        depres¦sion
im¦muno¦gen¦ic
im¦muno¦globu¦lin
   +s
im¦muno¦logic
im¦muno¦logic¦al

im¦muno¦logic¦
             al¦ly
im¦mun¦olo¦gist +s
im¦mun¦ology
im¦muno¦sup¦pres¦
             sant +s
im¦muno¦
       sup¦pressed
im¦muno¦
       sup¦pres¦sion
im¦muno¦
       sup¦pres¦sive +s
im¦muno¦ther¦apy
im¦muno¦
        ther¦apies
im¦mure
   im¦mures
   im¦mured
   im¦mur¦ing
im¦mure¦ment +s
im¦mut¦abil¦ity
   im¦mut¦abil¦ities
im¦mut¦able
im¦mut¦ably
Imo¦gen
imp +s +ed +ing
im¦pact +s +ed
   +ing
im¦pac¦tion +s
im¦pair +s +ed
   +ing
im¦pair¦ment +s
im¦pala
   plural im¦pala
im¦pale
   im¦pales
   im¦paled
   im¦pal¦ing
im¦pale¦ment +s
im¦palp¦abil¦ity
im¦palp¦able
im¦palp¦ably
im¦panel (use
   empanel)
   im¦panels
   im¦pan¦elled *Br.*
   im¦pan¦eled *Am.*
   im¦panel¦ling *Br.*
   im¦panel¦ling *Am.*
im¦pari¦syl¦lab¦ic
im¦park +s +ed
   +ing
im¦part +s +ed
   +ing
im¦part¦able
im¦par¦ta¦tion +s
im¦par¦tial
im¦par¦ti¦al¦ity
im¦par¦tial¦ly
im¦part¦ible
im¦part¦ment +s

im¦pass¦abil¦ity (of
   road etc.
   △ impassibility)
im¦pass¦able
   (impossible to
   travel over.
   △ impassible)
im¦pass¦able¦ness
   (of road etc.
   △ impassible-
   ness)
im¦pass¦ably (in an
   impassable way.
   △ impassibly)
im¦passe +s
im¦passi¦bil¦ity
   (impassivity.
   △ impassability)
im¦pass¦ible
   (impassive.
   △ impassable)
im¦pass¦ible¦ness
   (impassivity.
   △ impassable-
   ness)
im¦pass¦ibly
   (impassively.
   △ impassably)
im¦pas¦sion +s
   +ed +ing
im¦pas¦sioned
im¦pas¦sive
im¦pas¦sive¦ly
im¦pas¦sive¦ness
im¦pas¦siv¦ity
im¦pasto +s
im¦pa¦tience (lack
   of patience)
im¦pa¦tiens (plant)
im¦pa¦tient
im¦pa¦tient¦ly
im¦peach
   im¦peaches
   im¦peached
   im¦peach¦ing
im¦peach¦able
im¦peach¦ment +s
im¦pec¦cabil¦ity
im¦pec¦cable
im¦pec¦cably
im¦pec¦cancy
im¦pec¦cant
im¦pe¦cu¦ni¦os¦ity
im¦pe¦cu¦ni¦ous
im¦pe¦cu¦ni¦ous¦
                ness
im¦ped¦ance +s
im¦pede
   im¦pedes
   im¦peded
   im¦ped¦ing
im¦pedi¦ment +s

im¦pedi¦menta
im¦pedi¦men¦tal
impel
  im¦pels
  im¦pelled
  im¦pel¦ling
im¦pel¦lent +s
im¦pel¦ler +s
im¦pend +s +ed
  +ing
im¦pend¦ence
im¦pend¦ency
im¦pend¦ent +s
im¦pene¦tra¦bil¦ity
im¦pene¦trable
im¦pene¦trable¦
                ness
im¦pene¦trably
im¦pene¦trate
  im¦pene¦trates
  im¦pene¦trated
  im¦pene¦trat¦ing
im¦peni¦tence
im¦peni¦tency
im¦peni¦tent
im¦peni¦tent¦ly
im¦pera¦tival
im¦pera¦tive +s
im¦pera¦tive¦ly
im¦pera¦tive¦ness
im¦per¦ator +s
im¦pera¦tor¦ial
im¦per¦cepti¦bil¦ity
im¦per¦cept¦ible
im¦per¦cept¦ibly
im¦per¦cipi¦ence
im¦per¦cipi¦ent
im¦per¦fect +s
im¦per¦fec¦tion +s
im¦per¦fect¦ive +s
im¦per¦fect¦ly
im¦per¦for¦ate
im¦per¦ial +s
im¦peri¦al¦ise *Br.*
  (use imperialize)
  im¦peri¦al¦ises
  im¦peri¦al¦ised
  im¦peri¦al¦is¦ing
im¦peri¦al¦ism
im¦peri¦al¦ist +s
im¦peri¦al¦is¦tic
im¦peri¦al¦is¦tic¦
                al¦ly
im¦peri¦al¦ize
  im¦peri¦al¦izes
  im¦peri¦al¦ized
  im¦peri¦al¦iz¦ing
im¦peri¦al¦ly
im¦peril
  im¦perils
  im¦perilled *Br.*
  im¦periled *Am.*

im¦peril (*cont.*)
  im¦peril¦ling *Br.*
  im¦peril¦ing *Am.*
im¦peri¦ous
im¦peri¦ous¦ly
im¦peri¦ous¦ness
im¦per¦ish¦abil¦ity
im¦per¦ish¦able
im¦per¦ish¦able¦
                ness
im¦per¦ish¦ably
im¦per¦ium
im¦per¦man¦ence
im¦per¦man¦ency
  im¦per¦man¦en¦
                cies
im¦per¦man¦ent
im¦per¦man¦ent¦ly
im¦per¦me¦abil¦ity
im¦per¦me¦able
im¦per¦mis¦si¦
              bil¦ity
im¦per¦mis¦sible
im¦per¦script¦ible
im¦per¦son¦al
im¦per¦son¦al¦ity
im¦per¦son¦al¦ly
im¦per¦son¦ate
  im¦per¦son¦ates
  im¦per¦son¦ated
  im¦per¦son¦at¦ing
im¦per¦son¦ation
              +s
im¦per¦son¦ator +s
im¦per¦tin¦ence +s
im¦per¦tin¦ent
im¦per¦tin¦ent¦ly
im¦per¦turb¦
              abil¦ity
im¦per¦turb¦able
im¦per¦turb¦able¦
                ness
im¦per¦turb¦ably
im¦per¦vi¦ous
im¦per¦vi¦ous¦ly
im¦per¦vi¦ous¦ness
im¦pe¦ti¦gin¦ous
im¦pe¦tigo +s
im¦pe¦trate
  im¦pe¦trates
  im¦pe¦trated
  im¦pe¦trat¦ing
im¦pe¦tra¦tion +s
im¦pe¦tra¦tory
im¦petu¦os¦ity
  im¦petu¦os¦ities
im¦petu¦ous
im¦petu¦ous¦ly
im¦petu¦ous¦ness
im¦petus
  im¦petuses

Im¦phal (city,
  India)
impi +s
im¦pi¦ety
  im¦pi¦eties
im¦pinge
  im¦pinges
  im¦pinged
  im¦pin¦ging
im¦pinge¦ment +s
im¦pin¦ger +s
im¦pious
im¦pious¦ly
im¦pious¦ness
imp¦ish
imp¦ish¦ly
imp¦ish¦ness
im¦plac¦abil¦ity
im¦plac¦able
im¦plac¦ably
im¦plant +s +ed
  +ing
im¦plant¦ation +s
im¦plaus¦ibil¦ity
im¦plaus¦ible
im¦plaus¦ibly
im¦plead +s +ed
  +ing
im¦ple¦ment +s
  +ed +ing
im¦ple¦men¦ta¦tion
  +s
im¦ple¦ment¦er +s
im¦pli¦cate
  im¦pli¦cates
  im¦pli¦cated
  im¦pli¦cat¦ing
im¦pli¦ca¦tion +s
im¦pli¦ca¦tive
im¦pli¦ca¦tive¦ly
im¦pli¦cit
im¦pli¦cit¦ly
im¦pli¦cit¦ness
im¦plied¦ly
im¦plode
  im¦plodes
  im¦ploded
  im¦plod¦ing
im¦plore
  im¦plores
  im¦plored
  im¦plor¦ing
im¦plor¦ing¦ly
im¦plo¦sion +s
im¦plo¦sive +s
imply
  im¦plies
  im¦plied
  im¦ply¦ing
im¦pol¦der +s +ed
  +ing
im¦pol¦icy

im¦pol¦ite
im¦pol¦ite¦ly
im¦pol¦ite¦ness
im¦pol¦it¦ic
im¦pol¦it¦ic¦ly
im¦pon¦der¦abil¦ity
  im¦pon¦der¦
                abil¦ities
im¦pon¦der¦able +s
im¦pon¦der¦ably
im¦pon¦ent +s
im¦port +s +ed
  +ing
im¦port¦able
im¦port¦ance
im¦port¦ant
im¦port¦ant¦ly
im¦port¦ation +s
im¦port¦er +s
im¦por¦tun¦ate
im¦por¦tun¦ate¦ly
im¦por¦tune
  im¦por¦tunes
  im¦por¦tuned
  im¦por¦tun¦ing
im¦por¦tun¦ity
  im¦por¦tun¦ities
im¦pose
  im¦poses
  im¦posed
  im¦pos¦ing
im¦pos¦ing¦ly
im¦pos¦ing¦ness
im¦pos¦ition +s
im¦pos¦si¦bil¦ity
  im¦pos¦si¦bil¦ities
im¦pos¦sible
im¦pos¦sibly
im¦post +s
im¦pos¦ter +s (use
  impostor)
im¦pos¦tor +s
im¦pos¦tor¦ous
im¦pos¦trous
im¦pos¦ture +s
im¦po¦tence
im¦po¦tency
im¦po¦tent
im¦po¦tent¦ly
im¦pound +s +ed
  +ing
im¦pound¦able
im¦pound¦er +s
im¦pound¦ment +s
im¦pov¦er¦ish
  im¦pov¦er¦ishes
  im¦pov¦er¦ished
  im¦pov¦er¦ish¦ing
  im¦pov¦er¦ish¦
                ment +s

im|prac|tic|abil|ity
im|prac|tic|
    abil|ities
im|prac|tic|able
im|prac|tic|able|
    ness
im|prac|tic|ably
im|prac|ti|cal
im|prac|ti|cal|ity
im|prac|ti|
    cal|ities
im|prac|tic|al|ly
im|pre|cate
  im|pre|cates
  im|pre|cated
  im|pre|cat|ing
im|pre|ca|tion +s
im|pre|ca|tory
im|pre|cise
im|pre|cise|ly
im|pre|cise|ness
im|pre|ci|sion +s
im|preg|na|bil|ity
im|preg|nable
im|preg|nably
im|preg|nat|able
im|preg|nate
  im|preg|nates
  im|preg|nated
  im|preg|nat|ing
im|preg|na|tion +s
im|pres|ario +s
im|pre|script|ible
im|press
  im|presses
  im|pressed
  im|press|ing
im|press|ible
im|pres|sion
im|pres|sion|
    abil|ity
im|pres|sion|able
im|pres|sion|ably
im|pres|sion|al
Im|pres|sion|ism
Im|pres|sion|ist +s
(painter etc.)
im|pres|sion|ist +s
(entertainer)
im|pres|sion|is|tic
im|pres|sion|is|tic|
    al|ly
im|pres|sive
im|pres|sive|ly
im|pres|sive|ness
im|press|ment
im|prest +s
im|pri|ma|tur +s
im|pri|ma|tura +s
im|print +s +ed
  +ing

im|prison +s +ed
  +ing
im|pris|on|ment
  +s
impro +s
im|prob|abil|ity
  im|prob|abil|ities
im|prob|able
im|prob|ably
im|prob|ity
  im|prob|ities
im|promptu +s
im|proper
im|prop|er|ly
im|pro|pri|ate
  im|pro|pri|ates
  im|pro|pri|ated
  im|pro|pri|at|ing
im|pro|pri|ation
  +s
im|pro|pri|ator +s
im|pro|pri|ety
  im|pro|pri|eties
im|prov +s
im|prov|abil|ity
  im|prov|abil|ities
im|prov|able
im|prove
  im|proves
  im|proved
  im|prov|ing
im|prove|ment +s
im|prover +s
im|provi|dence +s
im|provi|dent
im|provi|dent|ly
im|pro|visa|tion
  +s
im|pro|visa|tion|al
im|pro|visa|tor|ial
im|pro|visa|tory
im|pro|vise
  im|pro|vises
  im|pro|vised
  im|pro|vis|ing
im|pro|viser +s
im|pru|dence +s
im|pru|dent
im|pru|dent|ly
im|pu|dence +s
im|pu|dent
im|pu|dent|ly
im|pu|di|city
im|pugn +s +ed
  +ing
im|pugn|able
im|pugn|ment +s
im|pu|is|sance
im|pu|is|sant
im|pulse +s
im|pul|sion +s
im|pul|sive

im|pul|sive|ly
im|pul|sive|ness
im|pun|ity
  im|pun|ities
im|pure
im|pure|ly
im|pure|ness
im|pur|ity
  im|pur|ities
im|put|able
im|put|ation +s
im|pu|ta|tive
im|pute
  im|putes
  im|puted
  im|put|ing
Imroz (Turkish
  name for Imbros)
imshi
in (*preposition* inside
  etc. △ inn)
Ina (name)
in|abil|ity
  in|abil|ities
in ab|sen|tia
in|access|ibil|ity
in|access|ible
in|access|ible|ness
in|access|ibly
in|accur|acy
in|ac|cur|acies
in|accur|ate
in|accur|ate|ly
in|action
in|acti|vate
  in|acti|vates
  in|acti|vated
  in|acti|vat|ing
in|acti|va|tion
in|active
in|active|ly
in|activ|ity
in|ad|equacy
  in|ad|equa|cies
in|ad|equate
in|ad|equate|ly
in|ad|mis|si|bil|ity
  in|ad|mis|si|
    bil|ities
in|ad|mis|sible
in|ad|mis|sibly
in|ad|ver|tence
in|ad|ver|tency
in|ad|ver|ten|cies
in|ad|vert|ent
in|ad|vert|ent|ly
in|ad|vis|abil|ity
in|ad|vis|able
in|ali|en|abil|ity
in|ali|en|able
in|ali|en|ably
in|alter|abil|ity

in|alter|able
in|alter|ably
in|am|or|ata +s
  female
in|am|or|ato +s
  male
inane
in|ane|ly
in|ane|ness
in|anga +s
in|ani|mate
in|ani|mate|ly
in|ani|ma|tion
in|an|ition
in|an|ity
  in|an|ities
in|appell|able
in|appe|tence
in|appe|tency
in|appe|tent
in|applic|abil|ity
in|applic|able
in|applic|ably
in|appo|site
in|appo|site|ly
in|appo|site|ness
in|appre|ciable
in|appre|ciably
in|appre|ci|ation
in|appre|cia|tive
in|appre|hen|sible
in|appro|pri|ate
in|appro|pri|ate|ly
in|appro|pri|ate|
    ness
inapt
in|apti|tude +s
in|apt|ly
in|apt|ness
in|arch
  in|arches
  in|arched
  in|arch|ing
in|argu|able
in|argu|ably
in|articu|lacy
in|articu|late
in|articu|late|ly
in|articu|late|ness
in|art|is|tic
in|art|is|tic|al|ly
in|as|much
in|atten|tion
in|atten|tive
in|atten|tive|ly
in|atten|tive|ness
in|audi|bil|ity
in|aud|ible
in|aud|ibly
in|aug|ural
in|aug|ur|ate
  in|aug|ur|ates

in|aug|ur|ate
  (*cont.*)
in|aug|ur|ated
in|aug|ur|at|ing
in|aug|ur|ation +s
in|aug|ur|ator +s
in|aug|ur|atory
in|aus|pi|cious
in|aus|pi|cious|ly
in|aus|pi|cious|
         ness
in|authen|tic
in|authen|ti|city
in-between
  attributive
in|board
in|born
in|breathe
  in|breathes
  in|breathed
  in|breath|ing
in|breed
  in|breeds
  in|bred
  in|breed|ing
in|built
Inc.
  (= Incorporated)
Inca
  plural Inca *or*
  Incas
Inca|ic
in|cal|cul|abil|ity
in|cal|cul|able
in|cal|cul|ably
in cam|era
Incan
in|can|desce
  in|can|desces
  in|can|desced
  in|can|des|cing
in|can|des|cence
in|can|des|cent
in|can|des|cent|ly
in|can|ta|tion +s
in|can|ta|tion|al
in|can|ta|tory
in|cap|abil|ity
  in|cap|abil|ities
in|cap|able
in|cap|ably
in|cap|aci|tant +s
in|cap|aci|tate
  in|cap|aci|tates
  in|cap|aci|tated
  in|cap|aci|tat|ing
in|cap|aci|ta|tion
  +s
in|cap|acity
  in|cap|aci|ties
in-car

in|car|cer|ate
in|car|cer|ates
in|car|cer|ated
in|car|cer|at|ing
in|car|cer|ation +s
in|car|cer|ator +s
in|car|na|dine
  in|car|na|dines
  in|car|na|dined
  in|car|na|din|ing
in|car|nate
  in|car|nates
  in|car|nated
  in|car|nat|ing
in|car|na|tion +s
in|case (use
  encase)
  in|cases
  in|cased
  in|cas|ing
in|cau|tion +s
in|cau|tious
in|cau|tious|ly
in|cau|tious|ness
in|cen|di|ar|ism
in|cen|di|ary
  in|cen|di|ar|ies
in|cen|sa|tion +s
in|cense
  in|censes
  in|censed
  in|cens|ing
in|cens|ory
  in|cens|or|ies
in|cen|tive +s
in|cep|tion +s
in|cep|tive
in|cept|or +s
in|cer|ti|tude +s
in|ces|sancy
in|ces|sant
in|ces|sant|ly
in|ces|sant|ness
in|cest
in|ces|tu|ous
in|ces|tu|ous|ly
in|ces|tu|ous|ness
inch
  inches
  inched
  inch|ing
Inch|cape Rock
  (off E. Scotland)
inch|meal
in|cho|ate
  in|cho|ates
  in|cho|ated
  in|cho|at|ing
  in|cho|ate|ly
  in|cho|ate|ness

in|cho|ation +s
in|cho|ative
In|chon (port,
  Korea)
inch|worm +s
in|ci|dence +s
in|ci|dent +s
in|ci|den|tal +s
in|ci|den|tal|ly
in|cin|er|ate
  in|cin|er|ates
  in|cin|er|ated
  in|cin|er|at|ing
in|cin|er|ation +s
in|cin|er|ator +s
in|cipi|ence
in|cipi|ency
  in|cipi|en|cies
in|cipi|ent
in|cipi|ent|ly
in|cipit +s
in|cise
  in|cises
  in|cised
  in|cis|ing
in|ci|sion +s
in|ci|sive
in|ci|sive|ly
in|ci|sive|ness
in|ci|sor +s
in|cit|ation +s
in|cite
  in|cites
  in|cited
  in|cit|ing
  (stir up. △ insight)
in|cite|ment +s
in|citer +s
in|civil|ity
  in|civil|ities
in|civ|ism
in|clem|ency
  in|clem|en|cies
in|clem|ent
in|clem|ent|ly
in|clin|able
in|clin|ation +s
in|cline
  in|clines
  in|clined
  in|clin|ing
in|cliner +s
in|clin|om|eter +s
in|close (use
  enclose)
  in|closes
  in|closed
  in|clos|ing
in|clos|ure +s (use
  enclosure)
in|clud|able

in|clude
  in|cludes
  in|cluded
  in|clud|ing
in|clud|ible (use
  includable)
in|clu|sion +s
in|clu|sive
in|clu|sive|ly
in|clu|sive|ness
incog (= incognito)
in|cog|ni|sance *Br.*
  (use
  incognizance)
in|cog|ni|sant *Br.*
  (use incognizant)
in|cog|nito +s
in|cog|ni|zance
in|cog|ni|zant
in|co|her|ence
in|co|her|ency
  in|co|her|en|cies
in|co|her|ent
in|co|her|ent|ly
in|com|bust|
         ibil|ity
in|com|bust|ible
in|come +s
in|comer +s
in|come tax
  in|come taxes
in|come tax
  re|turn +s
in|com|ing +s
in|com|men|sur|
         abil|ity
in|com|men|sur|
         able +s
in|com|men|sur|
         ably
in|com|men|sur|
         ate
in|com|men|sur|
         ate|ly
in|com|men|sur|
         ate|ness
in|com|mode
  in|com|modes
  in|com|moded
  in|com|mod|ing
in|com|mo|di|ous
in|com|mo|di|
         ous|ly
in|com|mo|di|ous|
         ness
in|com|mu|nic|
         abil|ity
in|com|mu|nic|
         able
in|com|mu|nic|
         able|ness

in|com|mu|nic|
    ably
in|com|mu|ni|cado
in|com|mu|ni|
    ca|tive
in|com|mu|ni|
    ca|tive|ly
in|com|mu|ni|
    ca|tive|ness
in|com|mut|able
in|com|mut|ably
in|com|par|abil|ity
in|com|par|able
in|com|par|able|
    ness
in|com|par|ably
in|com|pati|bil|ity
in|com|pat|ible
in|com|pat|ible|
    ness
in|com|pat|ibly
in|com|pe|tence
in|com|pe|tency
in|com|pe|tent+s
in|com|pe|tent|ly
in|com|plete
in|com|plete|ly
in|com|plete|ness
in|com|pre|hen|
    si|bil|ity
in|com|pre|
    hen|sible
in|com|pre|
    hen|sible|ness
in|com|pre|
    hen|sibly
in|com|pre|
    hen|sion
in|com|press|
    ibil|ity
in|com|press|ible
in|con|ceiv|abil|ity
in|con|ceiv|able
in|con|ceiv|able|
    ness
in|con|ceiv|ably
in|con|clu|sive
in|con|clu|sive|ly
in|con|clu|sive|
    ness
in|con|dens|able
in|con|dite
in|con|gru|ity
in|con|gru|ities
in|con|gru|ous
in|con|gru|ous|ly
in|con|gru|ous|
    ness
in|con|secu|tive
in|con|secu|tive|ly
in|con|secu|tive|
    ness

in|con|se|quence
in|con|se|quent
in|con|se|quen|tial
in|con|se|
    quen|ti|al|ity
in|con|se|
    quen|ti|al|ities
in|con|se|
    quen|tial|ly
in|con|se|quen|tial|
    ness
in|con|se|quent|ly
in|con|sid|er|able
in|con|sid|er|able|
    ness
in|con|sid|er|ably
in|con|sid|er|ate
in|con|sid|er|ate|ly
in|con|sid|er|ate|
    ness
in|con|sid|er|ation
in|con|sist|ency
in|con|sist|en|cies
in|con|sist|ent
in|con|sist|ent|ly
in|con|sol|abil|ity
in|con|sol|able
in|con|sol|able|
    ness
in|con|sol|ably
in|con|son|ance
in|con|son|ant
in|con|son|ant|ly
in|con|spicu|ous
in|con|spicu|
    ous|ly
in|con|spicu|ous|
    ness
in|con|stancy
in|con|stan|cies
in|con|stant
in|con|stant|ly
in|con|test|abil|ity
in|con|test|able
in|con|test|ably
in|con|tin|ence
in|con|tin|ent
in|con|tin|ent|ly
in|con|tro|vert|
    ibil|ity
in|con|tro|vert|ible
in|con|tro|vert|
    ibly
in|con|veni|ence
in|con|veni|ences
in|con|veni|enced
in|con|veni|
    en|cing
in|con|veni|ent
in|con|veni|ent|ly
in|con|vert|ibil|ity
in|con|vert|ible

in|con|vert|ibly
in|co|ord|in|ation
in|corp|or|ate
in|corp|or|ates
in|corp|or|ated
in|corp|or|at|ing
in|corp|or|ation+s
in|corp|or|ator+s
in|cor|por|eal
in|cor|por|eal|ity
in|cor|por|eal|ly
in|cor|por|eity
in|cor|rect
in|cor|rect|ly
in|cor|rect|ness
in|cor|ri|gi|bil|ity
in|cor|ri|gible
in|cor|ri|gible|ness
in|cor|ri|gibly
in|cor|rupt|ibil|ity
in|cor|rupt|ible
in|cor|rupt|ibly
in|cor|rup|tion
in|crass|ate
in|crass|ates
in|crass|ated
in|crass|at|ing
in|creas|able
in|crease
in|creases
in|creased
in|creas|ing
in|creaser+s
in|creas|ing|ly
in|credi|bil|ity
in|cred|ible
in|cred|ible|ness
in|cred|ibly
in|credu|lity
in|credu|lous
in|credu|lous|ly
in|credu|lous|ness
in|cre|ment+s
in|cre|men|tal
in|cre|men|tal|ly
in|crim|in|ate
in|crim|in|ates
in|crim|in|ated
in|crim|in|at|ing
in|crim|in|at|ing|ly
in|crim|in|ation+s
in|crim|in|atory
in|crust+s +ed
    +ing (use
    encrust)
in|crust|ation+s
in|cu|bate
in|cu|bates
in|cu|bated
in|cu|bat|ing
in|cu|ba|tion +s
in|cu|ba|tion|al

in|cu|ba|tive
in|cu|ba|tor+s
in|cu|ba|tory
in|cu|bus
  in|cu|buses *or*
  in|cubi
in|cu|des
in|cul|cate
in|cul|cates
in|cul|cated
in|cul|cat|ing
in|cul|ca|tion+s
in|cul|ca|tor+s
in|cul|pate
in|cul|pates
in|cul|pated
in|cul|pat|ing
in|cul|pa|tion+s
in|cul|pa|tive
in|cul|pa|tory
in|cum|bency
in|cum|ben|cies
in|cum|bent+s
in|cun|able+s
in|cu|nabu|lum
in|cu|nab|ula
incur
in|curs
in|curred
in|cur|ring
in|cur|abil|ity
in|cur|able +s (not
    curable)
in|cur|able|ness
in|cur|ably
in|curi|os|ity
in|curi|ous
in|curi|ous|ly
in|curi|ous|ness
in|cur|rable (able
    to happen)
in|cur|sion +s
in|cur|sive
in|curv|ation +s
in|curve
in|curves
in|curved
in|curv|ing
incus
in|cu|des
in|cuse
in|cuses
in|cused
in|cus|ing
in|daba +s
In|de|bele (plural of
    Ndebele)
in|debt|ed
in|debt|ed|ness
in|decency
in|decen|cies
in|decent

in|decent|ly
in|de|cipher|able
in|deci|sion +s
in|deci|sive
in|deci|sive|ly
in|deci|sive|ness
in|declin|able
in|dec|or|ous
in|dec|or|ous|ly
in|dec|or|ous|ness
in|decorum
in|deed (*adverb and interjection* really; admittedly; etc.)
in deed (in 'in deed but not in word')
in|defat|ig|abil|ity
in|defat|ig|able
in|defat|ig|ably
in|defeasi|bil|ity
in|defeas|ible
in|defeas|ibly
in|defect|ible
in|defens|ibil|ity
in|defens|ible
in|defens|ibly
in|defin|able
in|defin|ably
in|def|in|ite
in|def|in|ite|ly
in|def|in|ite|ness
in|dehis|cence
in|dehis|cent
in|deli|bil|ity
in|del|ible
in|del|ibly
in|deli|cacy
  in|deli|ca|cies
in|deli|cate
in|deli|cate|ly
in|dem|ni|fi|
    ca|tion +s
in|dem|ni|fier +s
in|dem|nify
  in|dem|ni|fies
  in|dem|ni|fied
  in|dem|ni|fy|ing
in|dem|nity
  in|dem|nities
in|dem|on|strable
in|dene +s
in|dent +s +ed +ing
in|den|ta|tion +s
in|dent|er +s (device)
in|den|tion +s
in|dent|or +s (person)
in|den|ture
  in|den|tures
  in|den|tured
  in|den|tur|ing

in|den|ture|ship +s
in|de|pend|ence
in|de|pend|ency
  in|de|pend|en|cies
in|de|pend|ent +s
in|de|pend|ent|ly
in-depth *attributive*
in|des|crib|abil|ity
in|des|crib|able
in|des|crib|ably
in|des|truct|
    ibil|ity
in|des|truct|ible
in|des|truct|ibly
in|de|ter|min|able
in|de|ter|min|ably
in|de|ter|min|acy
in|de|ter|min|ate
in|de|ter|min|
    ate|ly
in|de|ter|min|ate|
    ness
in|de|ter|min|ation
in|de|ter|min|ism
in|de|ter|min|ist +s
in|de|ter|min|is|tic
index
  in|dexes (list)
index
  in|dices *or*
  in|dexes (number)
index
  in|dexes
  in|dexed
  in|dex|ing *verb*
in|dex|ation +s
in|dex|er +s
in|dex|ible
in|dex|ic|al
in|dex|less
Index Libr|orum
  Pro|hib|it|orum
index-linked
index-linking
India
India|man
  India|men
In|dian +s
In|di|ana (state, USA)
In|dian|apo|lis (city, USA)
In|dian rope-trick +s
India rub|ber +s
Indic

in|di|cate
  in|di|cates
  in|di|cated
  in|di|cat|ing
in|di|ca|tion +s
in|di|ca|tive
in|di|ca|tive|ly
in|di|ca|tor +s
in|di|ca|tory
in|dices (plural of index)
in|di|cia
in|di|cial
in|di|cium
  in|di|cia
in|dict +s +ed +ing (accuse. △ indite)
in|dict|able
in|dict|ee +s
in|dict|er +s
in|dic|tion +s
in|dict|ment +s
indie +s (independent pop group etc. △ Indy)
In|dies (in S. Asia; also in 'East Indies', 'West Indies')
in|dif|fer|ence
in|dif|fer|ent
in|dif|fer|ent|ism
in|dif|fer|ent|ist +s
in|dif|fer|ent|ly
in|di|gence
in|di|gen|isa|tion *Br.* (use indigenization)
in|di|gen|ise *Br.* (use indigenize)
  in|di|gen|ises
  in|di|gen|ised
  in|di|gen|is|ing
in|di|gen|iza|tion
in|di|gen|ize
  in|di|gen|izes
  in|di|gen|ized
  in|di|gen|iz|ing
in|di|gen|ous
in|di|gen|ous|ly
in|di|gen|ous|ness
in|di|gent
in|di|gest|ed
in|di|gest|ibil|ity
in|di|gest|ible
in|di|gest|ibly
in|di|ges|tion
in|di|gest|ive
In|di|girka (river, Siberia)
in|dig|nant
in|dig|nant|ly

in|dig|na|tion
in|dig|nity
  in|dig|nities
in|digo +s
in|di|got|ic
In|dira Gan|dhi Canal (in India)
in|dir|ect
in|dir|ec|tion
in|dir|ect|ly
in|dir|ect|ness
in|dis|cern|ibil|ity
in|dis|cern|ible
in|dis|cern|ibly
in|dis|cip|line
in|dis|creet (not discreet, injudicious. △ indiscrete)
in|dis|creet|ly
in|dis|creet|ness
in|dis|crete (not divided into distinct parts. △ indiscreet)
in|dis|cre|tion +s
in|dis|crim|in|ate
in|dis|crim|in|
    ate|ly
in|dis|crim|in|ate|
    ness
in|dis|crim|in|
    ation
in|dis|crim|
    ina|tive
in|dis|pens|abil|ity
in|dis|pens|able
in|dis|pens|able|
    ness
in|dis|pens|ably
in|dis|pose
  in|dis|poses
  in|dis|posed
  in|dis|pos|ing
in|dis|pos|ition +s
in|dis|put|abil|ity
in|dis|put|able
in|dis|put|able|
    ness
in|dis|put|ably
in|dis|solu|bil|ist +s
in|dis|solu|bil|ity
in|dis|sol|uble
in|dis|sol|ubly
in|dis|tinct
in|dis|tinct|ive
in|dis|tinct|ive|ly
in|dis|tinct|ive|
    ness
in|dis|tinct|ly
in|dis|tinct|ness

in|dis|tin|guish|
 able
in|dis|tin|guish|
 able|ness
in|dis|tin|guish|
 ably
in|dite
 in|dites
 in|dited
 in|dit|ing
 (put into words.
 ⚠ indict)
in|dium
in|divert|ible
in|divert|ibly
in|di|vid|ual +s
in|di|vidu|al|isa|
 tion Br. +s (use
 individualization)
in|di|vidu|al|ise Br.
 (use
 individualize)
 in|di|vidu|al|ises
 in|di|vidu|al|ised
 in|di|vidu|al|is|ing
in|di|vidu|al|ism
 +s
in|di|vidu|al|ist +s
in|di|vidu|al|is|tic
in|di|vidu|al|is|tic|
 al|ly
in|di|vidu|al|ity
 in|di|vidu|al|ities
in|di|vidu|al|
 iza|tion +s
in|di|vidu|al|ize
 in|di|vidu|al|izes
 in|di|vidu|al|ized
 in|di|vidu|al|
  iz|ing
in|di|vidu|al|ly
in|di|vidu|ate
 in|di|vidu|ates
 in|di|vidu|ated
 in|di|vidu|at|ing
in|di|vidu|ation +s
in|di|vis|ibil|ity
in|di|vis|ible
in|di|vis|ibly
Indo-Aryan +s
Indo-China
Indo-Chinese
 plural Indo-Chinese
in|docile
in|docil|ity
in|doc|trin|ate
 in|doc|trin|ates
 in|doc|trin|ated
 in|doc|trin|at|ing
in|doc|trin|ation
 +s
in|doc|trin|ator +s
Indo-European +s

Indo-German|ic
Indo-Iranian
in|dole +s
in|dole|acet|ic
in|do|lence +s
in|do|lent
in|do|lent|ly
Ind|olo|gist +s
Ind|ology
in|dom|it|abil|ity
in|dom|it|able
in|dom|it|able|
 ness
in|dom|it|ably
Indo|nesia
Indo|nes|ian +s
in|door
in|doors
Indo-Pacific
In|dore (city, India)
in|dorse (use
 endorse)
 in|dorses
 in|dorsed
 in|dors|ing
in|dorse|ment +s
 (use
 endorsement)
Indra *Hinduism*
in|draft *Am.* +s
in|draught *Br.* +s
in|drawn
indri +s
in|dub|it|able
in|dub|it|ably
in|duce
 in|duces
 in|duced
 in|du|cing
in|duce|ment +s
in|ducer +s
in|du|cible
in|duct +s +ed
 +ing
in|duct|ance +s
in|duct|ee +s
in|duc|tion +s
in|duct|ive
in|duct|ive|ly
in|duct|ive|ness
in|duct|or +s
indue (use endue)
 in|dues
 in|dued
 in|du|ing
in|dulge
 in|dulges
 in|dulged
 in|dul|ging
in|dul|gence +s
in|dul|genced
in|dul|gent

in|dul|gent|ly
in|dul|ger +s
in|dult +s
in|du|men|tum
 in|du|menta
in|duna +s
in|dur|ate
 in|dur|ates
 in|dur|ated
 in|dur|at|ing
in|dur|ation +s
in|dura|tive
Indus (river, Asia)
in|du|sial
in|du|sium
 in|du|sia
in|dus|trial +s
in|dus|tri|al|isa|
 tion Br. (use
 industrialization)
in|dus|tri|al|ise Br.
 (use industrialize)
 in|dus|tri|al|ises
 in|dus|tri|al|ised
 in|dus|tri|al|is|ing
in|dus|tri|al|ism
in|dus|tri|al|ist +s
in|dus|tri|al|iza|
 tion
in|dus|tri|al|izes
in|dus|tri|al|ized
in|dus|tri|al|iz|ing
in|dus|tri|al|ly
industrial-
 strength *adjective*
in|dus|tri|ous
in|dus|tri|ous|ly
in|dus|tri|ous|ness
in|dus|try
 in|dus|tries
in|dwell
 in|dwells
 in|dwelt
 in|dwelling
in|dwell|er +s
Indy
 (= Indianapolis.
 ⚠ indie)
Indy|car +s
Ine (king of
 Wessex)
in|ebri|ate
 in|ebri|ates
 in|ebri|ated
 in|ebri|at|ing
in|ebri|ation
in|ebri|ety
in|edi|bil|ity
in|ed|ible
in|edit|ed
in|educ|abil|ity

in|educ|able
in|effa|bil|ity
in|effable
in|effably
in|ef|face|abil|ity
in|ef|face|able
in|ef|face|ably
in|ef|fect|ive
in|ef|fect|ive|ly
in|ef|fect|ive|ness
in|ef|fec|tual
in|ef|fec|tu|al|ity
 in|ef|fec|tu|al|
  ities
in|ef|fec|tu|al|ly
in|ef|fec|tu|al|ness
in|ef|fi|ca|cious
in|ef|fi|ca|cious|ly
in|ef|fi|ca|cious|
 ness
in|ef|fi|cacy
 in|ef|fi|ca|cies
in|ef|fi|ciency
 in|ef|fi|cien|cies
in|ef|fi|cient
in|ef|fi|cient|ly
in|egali|tar|ian +s
in|elas|tic
in|elas|tic|al|ly
in|elas|ti|city
in|ele|gance
in|ele|gant
in|ele|gant|ly
in|eli|gi|bil|ity
in|eli|gible
in|eli|gibly
in|eluct|abil|ity
in|eluct|able
in|eluct|ably
inept
in|epti|tude
in|ept|ly
in|ept|ness
in|equable
in|equal|ity
 in|equal|ities
in|equit|able
in|equit|ably
in|equity
 in|equi|ties
in|erad|ic|able
in|erad|ic|ably
in|err|abil|ity
in|err|able
in|err|ably
in|err|ancy
in|err|ant
inert
in|er|tia
in|er|tial
in|er|tia|less
in|er|tia reel +s

in|er|tia sell|ing
in|ert|ly
in|ert|ness
in|escap|abil|ity
in|escap|able
in|escap|ably
in|es|cutch|eon
in|es|sen|tial +s
in|estim|able
in|estim|ably
in|ev|it|abil|ity
  in|ev|it|abil|ities
in|ev|it|able
in|ev|it|able|ness
in|ev|it|ably
in|exact
in|exacti|tude +s
in|exact|ly
in|exact|ness
in|ex|cus|able
in|ex|cus|ably
in|ex|haust|ibil|ity
in|ex|haust|ible
in|ex|haust|ibly
in|ex|or|abil|ity
in|ex|or|able
in|ex|or|ably
in|ex|pedi|ency
in|ex|pedi|ent
in|ex|pen|sive
in|ex|pen|sive|ly
in|ex|pen|sive|
          ness
in|ex|peri|ence
in|ex|peri|enced
in|ex|pert
in|ex|pert|ly
in|ex|pert|ness
in|ex|pi|able
in|ex|pi|ably
in|ex|plic|abil|ity
in|ex|plic|able
in|ex|plic|ably
in|ex|pli|cit
in|ex|pli|cit|ly
in|ex|pli|cit|ness
in|ex|press|ible
in|ex|press|ibly
in|ex|pres|sive
in|ex|pres|sive|ly
in|ex|pres|sive|
          ness
in|ex|pugn|able
in|ex|pun|gible
in ex|tenso
in|ex|tin|guish|
          able
in ex|tre|mis
in|ex|tric|abil|ity
in|ex|tric|able
in|ex|tric|ably
in fact

in|fal|li|bil|ity
in|fal|lible
in|fal|libly
in|fam|ous
in|fam|ous|ly
in|famy
  in|famies
in|fancy
  in|fan|cies
in|fant +s
in|fanta +s *female*
in|fante +s *male*
in|fanti|cidal
in|fanti|cide +s
in|fant|ile
in|fant|il|ism
in|fant|il|ity
  in|fant|il|ities
in|fant|ine
in|fan|try
  in|fan|tries
in|fan|try|man
  in|fan|try|men
in|farct +s
in|farc|tion +s
in|fatu|ate
  in|fatu|ates
  in|fatu|ated
  in|fatu|at|ing
in|fatu|ation +s
in|fauna
in|faun|al
in|feasi|bil|ity
in|feas|ible
in|fect +s +ed +ing
in|fec|tion +s
in|fec|tious
in|fec|tious|ly
in|fec|tious|ness
in|fect|ive
in|fect|ive|ness
in|fect|or +s
in|fe|li|ci|tous
in|fe|li|ci|tous|ly
in|feli|city
  in|feli|ci|ties
infer
  in|fers
  in|ferred
  in|fer|ring
in|fer|able
in|fer|ence +s
in|fer|en|tial
in|fer|en|tial|ly
in|fer|ior +s
in|fer|ior|ity
in|fer|ior|ly
in|fer|nal
in|fer|nal|ly
in|ferno +s
in|fer|tile
in|fer|til|ity

in|fest +s +ed +ing
in|fest|ation +s
in|fibu|late
  in|fibu|lates
  in|fibu|lated
  in|fibu|lat|ing
in|fibu|la|tion +s
in|fi|del +s
in|fi|del|ity
  in|fi|del|ities
in|field +s
in|field|er +s
in|fight|er +s
in|fight|ing
in|fill +s +ed +ing
in|fil|trate
  in|fil|trates
  in|fil|trated
  in|fil|trat|ing
in|fil|tra|tion +s
in|fil|tra|tor +s
in|fin|ite +s
in|fin|ite|ly
in|fin|ite|ness
in|fini|tesi|mal +s
in|fini|tesi|mal|ly
in|fini|tival
in|fini|tival|ly
in|fini|tive +s
in|fini|tude +s
in|fin|ity
  in|fin|ities
in|firm
in|firm|ary
  in|firm|ar|ies
in|firm|ity
  in|firm|ities
in|firm|ly
infix
  in|fixes
  in|fixed
  in|fix|ing
in|fix|ation +s
in fla|grante
  de|licto
in|flame
  in|flames
  in|flamed
  in|flam|ing
in|flamer +s
in|flam|ma|bil|ity
in|flam|mable +s
in|flam|mable|
          ness
in|flam|mably
in|flam|ma|tion +s
in|flam|ma|tory
in|flat|able +s
in|flate
  in|flates
  in|flated
  in|flat|ing

in|flated|ly
in|flated|ness
in|flater +s (use
  inflator)
in|fla|tion +s
in|fla|tion|ary
in|fla|tion|ism
in|fla|tion|ist +s
in|fla|tor +s
in|flect +s +ed
  +ing
in|flec|tion +s
in|flec|tion|al
in|flec|tion|al|ly
in|flec|tion|less
in|flect|ive
in|flex|ibil|ity
  in|flex|ibil|ities
in|flex|ible
in|flex|ibly
in|flex|ion +s (use
  inflection)
in|flex|ion|al (use
  inflectional)
in|flex|ion|al|ly
  (use
  inflectionally)
in|flex|ion|less
  (use
  inflectionless)
in|flict +s +ed +ing
in|flict|able
in|flict|er +s
in|flic|tion +s
in|flict|or +s (use
  inflicter)
in-flight *attributive*
in|flor|es|cence +s
in|flow +s
in|flow|ing +s
in|flu|ence
  in|flu|ences
  in|flu|enced
  in|flu|en|cing
in|flu|ence|able
in|flu|en|cer +s
in|flu|ent +s
in|flu|en|tial
in|flu|en|tial|ly
in|flu|enza +s
in|flu|en|zal
in|flux
  in|fluxes
info (= information)
info|bit +s
in|fold +s +ed +ing
  (fold in. △ enfold)
info|mania
info|mer|cial +s
info|pren|eur +s
in|form +s +ed
  +ing
in|for|mal

in|for|mal|ity
  in|for|mal¦ities
  in|for|mal¦ly
in|form|ant +s
in|form|at¦ics
in|for|ma¦tion +s
in|for|ma¦tion|al
in|for|ma¦tion|
        al¦ly
in|forma|tive
in|forma|tive¦ly
in|forma|tive|ness
in|forma|tory
in|form¦ed¦ly
in|form¦ed|ness
in|form¦er +s
infor|mer¦cial +s
  (use infomercial)
info|sphere +s
info|tain¦ment
info|tech
infra (below)
in|fra|class
  in|fra|classes
in|fract +s +ed
  +ing
in|frac¦tion +s
in|fract¦or +s
in|fra|dian
infra dig
in|fra|lap¦sar|ian
  +s
in|fran¦gi|bil¦ity
in|fran¦gible
in|fran¦gible|ness
in|fran¦gibly
in|fra|red (*Am.* and
  in scientific *Br.*
  use)
infra-red (in
  general *Br.* use)
in|fra|renal
in|fra|son¦ic
in|fra|son¦ic|al¦ly
in|fra|sound
in|fra|struc|tural
in|fra|struc|ture +s
in|fre¦quency
in|fre¦quent
in|fre¦quent¦ly
in|fringe
  in|fringes
  in|fringed
  in|frin¦ging
in|fringe¦ment +s
in|frin¦ger +s
in|fruct|es¦cence
  +s
in|fula
  in|fu|lae
in|fun¦dibu|lar

in|furi|ate
  in|furi|ates
  in|furi|ated
  in|furi|at¦ing
in|furi|at¦ing¦ly
in|furi|ation +s
in|fus|able (able to
  be infused.
  △ infusible)
in|fuse
  in|fuses
  in|fused
  in|fus¦ing
in|fuser +s
in|fus|ibil¦ity
in|fus|ible (not
  fusible or
  meltable.
  △ infusable)
in|fu¦sion +s
in|fu¦sive
in|fus¦oria
in|fus¦or¦ial
in|gather +s +ed
  +ing
in|gem¦in|ate
  in|gem¦in|ates
  in|gem¦in|ated
  in|gem¦in|at¦ing
Ingen|housz, Jan
  (Dutch scientist)
in|geni|ous (clever)
in|geni|ous¦ly
  (cleverly)
in|geni¦ous|ness
  (cleverness)
in|génue +s
in|genu|ity
  (cleverness)
in|genu|ous
  (innocent)
in|genu|ous¦ly
  (innocently)
in|genu¦ous|ness
  (innocence)
in|gest +s +ed
  +ing
in|ges¦tion +s
in|gest|ive
ingle|nook +s
in|glori|ous
in|glori|ous¦ly
in|glori|ous|ness
in-goal area +s
in|going
ingot +s
in|graft +s +ed
  +ing (use engraft)
in|grain +s +ed
  +ing
in|grain|ed¦ly
in|grate +s

in|grati|ate
  in|grati|ates
  in|grati|ated
  in|grati|at¦ing
in|grati|at¦ing¦ly
in|grati|ation +s
in|grati|tude +s
in|grav|es¦cence
  +s
in|grav|es¦cent
in|gre¦di|ent +s
Ingres, Jean
  Au¦guste
  Dom¦in|ique
  (French painter)
in|gress
  in|gresses
in|gres¦sion +s
In¦grid
in-group +s
in|grow|ing
in|grown
in|growth +s
in|guin|al
in|guin|al¦ly
in¦gulf +s +ed +ing
  (use engulf)
in|gur¦gi|tate
  in|gur¦gi|tates
  in|gur¦gi|tated
  in|gur¦gi|tat¦ing
in|gur¦gi|ta¦tion +s
in|habit +s +ed
  +ing
in|hab¦it|abil¦ity
in|hab¦it|able
in|hab¦it|ance +s
in|hab¦it|ancy
  in|hab¦it|an¦cies
in|hab¦it|ant +s
in|hab¦it|ation +s
in|hal¦ant +s
in|hal|ation +s
in|hale
  in|hales
  in|haled
  in|hal¦ing
in|haler +s
in|har¦mon¦ic
in|har¦mo¦ni|ous
in|har¦mo¦ni|
        ous¦ly
in¦here
  in¦heres
  in¦hered
  in¦her¦ing
in|her¦ence +s
in|her¦ent
in|her¦ent¦ly
in|herit +s +ed
  +ing
in|her¦it|abil¦ity

in|her¦it|able
in|her¦it|ance +s
in|heri¦tor +s
in|heri¦tress
  in|heri¦tresses
in|heri¦trix
  in|heri¦trices
  female
in|he¦sion +s
in|hibit +s +ed
  +ing
in|hib|ition +s
in|hibi|tive
in|hibi|tor +s
in|hibi|tory
in|homo|gen¦eity
in|homo|gen¦eous
in|hos¦pit|able
in|hos¦pit|able|
        ness
in|hos¦pit|ably
in|hos¦pi|tal¦ity
in-house
in|human
in|hu|mane
in|hu|mane¦ly
in|human|ity
  in|human|ities
in|human¦ly
in|hum¦ation +s
in|hume
  in|humes
  in|humed
  in|hum¦ing
Inigo
in|imi|cal
in|imi|cal¦ly
in|im¦it|abil¦ity
in|im¦it|able
in|im¦it|able|ness
in|im¦it|ably
ini¦qui|tous
ini¦qui|tous¦ly
ini¦qui|tous|ness
ini|quity
  ini|qui¦ties
ini¦tial
  ini¦tials
  ini¦tialled *Br.*
  ini¦tialed *Am.*
  ini¦tial|ling *Br.*
  ini¦tial|ing *Am.*
ini¦tial|isa¦tion *Br.*
  +s (use
  initialization)
ini¦tial|ise *Br.* (use
  initialize)
  ini¦tial|ises
  ini¦tial|ised
  ini¦tial|is¦ing
ini¦tial|ism +s
ini¦tial|iza¦tion +s

ini¦tial¦ize
  ini¦tial¦izes
  ini¦tial¦ized
  ini¦tial¦iz¦ing
ini¦tial¦ly
ini¦ti¦ate
  ini¦ti¦ates
  ini¦ti¦ated
  ini¦ti¦at¦ing
ini¦ti¦ation +s
ini¦tia¦tive +s
ini¦ti¦ator +s
ini¦ti¦atory
in¦ject +s +ed +ing
inject¦able +s
in¦jec¦tion +s
injection-moulded
in¦jec¦tion
  mould¦ing +s
inject¦or +s
in-joke +s
inju¦di¦cious
inju¦di¦cious¦ly
inju¦di¦cious¦ness
Injun +s *offensive*
in¦junct +s +ed
  +ing
in¦junc¦tion +s
in¦junct¦ive
in¦jure
  in¦jures
  in¦jured
  in¦jur¦ing
in¦jurer +s
in¦juri¦ous
in¦juri¦ous¦ly
in¦juri¦ous¦ness
in¦jury
  in¦jur¦ies
in¦jury time
in¦just¦ice +s
ink +s +ed +ing
In¦ka¦tha (Zulu
  organization)
ink-blot test +s
ink-cap +s
inker +s
ink¦horn +s
inki¦ness
ink-jet print¦er +s
ink¦ling +s
ink-pad +s
ink¦stand +s
ink¦well +s
inky
  ink¦ier
  inki¦est
in¦laid
in¦land
in¦land¦er +s
in¦land¦ish

In¦land Sea (off
  Japan)
in¦land sea +s
  (generally)
in-law +s
inlay
  in¦lays
  in¦laid
  in¦lay¦ing
in¦lay¦er +s
inlet +s
in¦lier +s
in-line
in loco par¦en¦tis
inly
in¦ly¦ing
In¦mar¦sat
in¦mate +s
in med¦ias res
in me¦mor¦iam +s
in¦most
inn +s (pub. ⚠ in)
in¦nards
in¦nate
in¦nate¦ly
in¦nate¦ness
inner +s
inner-city
  attributive
inner-direct¦ed
in¦ner¦ly
in¦ner¦most
in¦ner¦ness
inner-spring
  attributive
in¦nerv¦ate
  in¦nerv¦ates
  in¦nerv¦ated
  in¦nerv¦at¦ing
  (supply with nerves.
  ⚠ innovate)
in¦nerv¦ation +s
  (supply of nerves.
  ⚠ innovation)
in¦ning +s *Baseball*
in¦nings
  plural in¦nings *or*
  in¦ningses
  (*Cricket*; period of
  office etc.)
inn¦keep¦er +s
in¦no¦cence
in¦no¦cency
in¦no¦cent +s
in¦no¦cent¦ly
In¦no¦cents' Day
in¦nocu¦ity
in¦nocu¦ous
in¦nocu¦ous¦ly
in¦nocu¦ous¦ness
in¦nom¦in¦ate

in¦nov¦ate
  in¦nov¦ates
  in¦nov¦ated
  in¦nov¦at¦ing
  (bring in
  something new.
  ⚠ innervate)
in¦nov¦ation +s
  (new thing.
  ⚠ innervation)
in¦nov¦ation¦al
in¦nova¦tive
in¦nova¦tive¦ly
in¦nova¦tive¦ness
in¦nov¦ator +s
in¦nov¦atory
Inns¦bruck (city,
  Austria)
in¦nu¦endo
  in¦nu¦en¦does *or*
  in¦nu¦en¦dos
In¦nuit (use Inuit)
  plural In¦nuit *or*
  In¦nuits
in¦nu¦mer¦abil¦ity
in¦nu¦mer¦able (too
  many to count.
  ⚠ enumerable)
in¦nu¦mer¦ably
in¦nu¦mer¦acy
in¦nu¦mer¦ate (not
  numerate.
  ⚠ enumerate)
in¦nu¦tri¦tion
in¦nu¦tri¦tious
in¦ob¦serv¦ance +s
in¦ocul¦able
in¦ocu¦late
  in¦ocu¦lates
  in¦ocu¦lated
  in¦ocu¦lat¦ing
in¦ocu¦la¦tion +s
in¦ocu¦la¦tive
in¦ocu¦la¦tor +s
in¦ocu¦lum
  in¦oc¦ula
in¦odor¦ous
in-off +s
in¦offen¦sive
in¦offen¦sive¦ly
in¦offen¦sive¦ness
in¦offi¦cious
in¦op¦er¦abil¦ity
in¦op¦er¦able
in¦op¦er¦ably
in¦op¦era¦tive
in¦op¦por¦tune
in¦op¦por¦tune¦ly
in¦op¦por¦tune¦
             ness
in¦or¦din¦ate
in¦or¦din¦ate¦ly

in¦or¦gan¦ic
in¦or¦gan¦ic¦al¦ly
in¦oscu¦late
  in¦oscu¦lates
  in¦oscu¦lated
  in¦oscu¦lat¦ing
in¦oscu¦la¦tion +s
in-patient +s
in pro¦pria
  per¦sona
input
  in¦puts
  input *or*
  in¦put¦ted
  in¦put¦ting
input-output
in¦put¦ter +s
in¦quest +s
in¦qui¦et¦ude
in¦quil¦ine +s
in¦quil¦in¦ous
in¦quire
  in¦quires
  in¦quired
  in¦quir¦ing
  (investigate; (*Am.*
  only) ask; *Br.*
  enquire)
in¦quirer +s
  (investigator; (*Am.*
  only) person
  asking for
  information; *Br.*
  enquirer)
in¦quir¦ing¦ly *Am.*
  (*Br.* enquiringly)
in¦quiry
  in¦quir¦ies
  (investigation;
  (*Am.* only) request
  for information;
  Br. enquiry)
in¦qui¦si¦tion +s
in¦qui¦si¦tion¦al
in¦quisi¦tive
in¦quisi¦tive¦ly
in¦quisi¦tive¦ness
in¦quisi¦tor +s
Inquisitor-General
  +s (head of
  Spanish
  Inquisition)
in¦quisi¦tor¦ial
in¦quisi¦tori¦al¦ly
in¦quor¦ate
in re
in¦road +s
in¦rush
  in¦rushes
in¦rush¦ing +s
in¦salu¦bri¦ous

in|salu|brity
in|sane
in|sane|ly
in|sane|ness
in|sani|tary
in|san|ity
  in|san|ities
in|sati|abil|ity
in|sati|able
in|sati|ably
in|sati|ate
in|scape +s
in|scrib|able
in|scribe
  in|scribes
  in|scribed
  in|scrib|ing
in|scriber +s
in|scrip|tion +s
in|scrip|tion|al
in|scrip|tive
in|scrut|abil|ity
in|scrut|able
in|scrut|able|ness
in|scrut|ably
in|sect +s
in|sect|arium +s
in|sect|ary
  in|sect|ar|ies
in|secti|cidal
in|secti|cide +s
in|sect|ile
In|sect|iv|ora
in|sect|ivore +s
in|sect|iv|or|ous
in|sect|ology
in|se|cure
in|se|cure|ly
in|se|cur|ity
  in|se|cur|ities
in|sel|berg +s
in|sem|in|ate
  in|sem|in|ates
  in|sem|in|ated
  in|sem|in|at|ing
in|sem|in|ation +s
in|sem|in|ator +s
in|sens|ate
in|sens|ate|ly
in|sens|ibil|ity
in|sens|ible
in|sens|ibly
in|sensi|tive
in|sensi|tive|ly
in|sensi|tive|ness
in|sensi|tiv|ity
  in|sensi|tiv|ities
in|sen|tience
in|sen|tient
in|sep|ar|abil|ity
in|sep|ar|able
in|sep|ar|ably

in|sert +s +ed +ing
in|sert|able
in|sert|er +s
in|ser|tion +s
in-service
  attributive
INSET (= in-service
  education and
  training)
inset
  in|sets
  inset *or* in|set|ted
  in|set|ting
  (insert)
in|set|ter +s
in|shal|lah
in|shore
in|side +s
in|side for|ward
  +s
in|side left +s
in|side out
inside-out
  attributive
in|sider +s
in|sider deal|ing
  +s
in|side right +s
in|sider trad|ing
in|sidi|ous
in|sidi|ous|ly
in|sidi|ous|ness
in|sight +s (keen
  understanding.
  ⚠ incite)
in|sight|ful
in|sight|ful|ly
in|sig|nia
in|sig|nifi|cance +s
in|sig|nifi|cancy
in|sig|nifi|cant
in|sig|nifi|cant|ly
in|sin|cere
in|sin|cere|ly
in|sin|cer|ity
  in|sin|cer|ities
in|sinu|ate
  in|sinu|ates
  in|sinu|ated
  in|sinu|at|ing
in|sinu|at|ing|ly
in|sinu|ation +s
in|sinu|ative
in|sinu|ator +s
in|sinu|atory
in|sipid
in|sip|id|ity
  in|sip|id|ities
in|sip|id|ly
in|sip|id|ness
in|sist +s +ed +ing
in|sist|ence +s

in|sist|ency
in|sist|ent
in|sist|ent|ly
in|sist|er +s
in|sist|ing|ly
in situ
in|so|bri|ety
in|so|far
in|so|la|tion
  (exposure to sun.
  ⚠ insulation)
in|sole +s
in|so|lence
in|so|lent
in|so|lent|ly
in|solu|bil|ise *Br.*
  (use insolubilize)
in|solu|bil|ises
in|solu|bil|ised
in|solu|bil|is|ing
in|solu|bil|ity
in|solu|bil|ize
in|solu|bil|izes
in|solu|bil|ized
in|solu|bil|iz|ing
in|sol|uble
in|sol|uble|ness
in|sol|ubly
in|solv|able
in|solv|ency
  in|solv|en|cies
in|solv|ent +s
in|som|nia
in|som|niac +s
in|so|much
in|sou|ci|ance
in|sou|ci|ant
in|sou|ci|ant|ly
in|span
  in|spans
  in|spanned
  in|span|ning
in|spect +s +ed
  +ing
in|spec|tion +s
in|spect|or +s
in|spect|or|ate +s
in|spect|or
  gen|eral +s
in|spect|or|ial
in|spect|or|ship +s
in|spir|ation +s
in|spir|ation|al
in|spir|ation|ism
in|spir|ation|ist +s
in|spira|tor +s
in|spira|tory
in|spire
  in|spires
  in|spired
  in|spir|ing
  in|spired|ly

in|spirer +s
in|spir|ing
in|spir|ing|ly
in|spirit +s +ed
  +ing
in|spir|it|ing|ly
in|spis|sate
  in|spis|sates
  in|spis|sated
  in|spis|sat|ing
in|spis|sa|tion +s
in|spis|sa|tor +s
in spite of
in|stabil|ity
  in|stabil|ities
in|stal (use install)
  in|stals
  in|stalled
  in|stall|ing
in|stall +s +ed
  +ing
in|stall|lant +s
in|stal|la|tion +s
in|stall|er +s
in|stall|ment *Am.*
  +s
in|stal|ment *Br.* +s
in|stance
  in|stances
  in|stanced
  in|stan|cing
in|stancy
in|stant +s
in|stant|an|eity
in|stant|an|eous
in|stant|an|eous|ly
in|stant|an|eous|
    ness
in|stan|ter *adverb*
in|stan|ti|ate
  in|stan|ti|ates
  in|stan|ti|ated
  in|stan|ti|at|ing
in|stan|ti|ation +s
in|stant|ly
in|star +s
in|state
  in|states
  in|stated
  in|stat|ing
in statu pu|pil|lari
in|staur|ation +s
in|staur|ator +s
in|stead
in|step +s
in|sti|gate
  in|sti|gates
  in|sti|gated
  in|sti|gat|ing
in|sti|ga|tion +s
in|sti|ga|tive
in|sti|ga|tor +s

in|stil *Br.*
  in|stils
  in|stilled
  in|still|ling
in|still *Am.* +s +ed
  +ing
in|stil|la|tion +s
in|stil|ler +s
in|still|ment *Am.*
  +s
in|stil|ment *Br.* +s
in|stinct +s
in|stinct|ive
in|stinct|ive|ly
in|stinct|ual
in|stinc|tu|al|ly
in|sti|tute
  in|sti|tutes
  in|sti|tuted
  in|sti|tut|ing
in|sti|tu|tion +s
in|sti|tu|tion|al
in|sti|tu|tion|al|
  isa|tion *Br.* (use
  institutional-
  ization)
in|sti|tu|tion|al|ise
  Br. (use
  institutionalize)
in|sti|tu|tion|al|
    ises
in|sti|tu|tion|al|
    ised
in|sti|tu|tion|al|
    is|ing
in|sti|tu|tion|al|
    ism
in|sti|tu|tion|al|
    iza|tion
in|sti|tu|tion|al|ize
in|sti|tu|tion|al|
    izes
in|sti|tu|tion|al|
    ized
in|sti|tu|tion|al|
    iz|ing
in|sti|tu|tion|al|ly
in-store *attributive*
INSTRAW
  (= International
  Research and
  Training Institute
  for the
  Advancement of
  Women)
in|struct +s +ed
  +ing
in|struc|tion +s
in|struc|tion|al
in|struct|ive
in|struct|ive|ly
in|struct|ive|ness

in|struct|or +s
in|struct|or|ship
  +s
in|struc|tress
  in|struc|tresses
in|stru|ment +s
  +ed +ing
in|stru|men|tal +s
in|stru|men|tal|ist
  +s
in|stru|men|tal|ity
in|stru|men|tal|ly
in|stru|men|ta|tion
  +s
in|sub|or|din|ate
in|sub|or|din|
    ate|ly
in|sub|or|din|ation
  +s
in|sub|stan|tial
in|sub|stan|ti|al|
    ity
in|sub|stan|ti|al|
    ities
in|sub|stan|tial|ly
in|suf|fer|able
in|suf|fer|able|
    ness
in|suf|fer|ably
in|suf|fi|ciency
  in|suf|fi|cien|cies
in|suf|fi|cient
in|suf|fi|cient|ly
in|suf|flate
  in|suf|flates
  in|suf|flated
  in|suf|flat|ing
in|suf|fla|tion +s
in|suf|fla|tor +s
in|su|lar
in|su|lar|ism
in|su|lar|ity
in|su|lar|ly
in|su|late
  in|su|lates
  in|su|lated
  in|su|lat|ing
in|su|lat|ing tape
  +s
in|su|la|tion +s
  (separation.
  ⚠ insolation)
in|su|la|tor +s
in|su|lin +s
in|sult +s +ed +ing
in|sult|er +s
in|sult|ing|ly
in|su|per|abil|ity
  in|su|per|abil|ities
in|su|per|able
in|su|per|ably
in|sup|port|able

in|sup|port|able|
    ness
in|sup|port|ably
in|sur|abil|ity
in|sur|able
in|sur|ance +s
in|sur|ant +s
in|sure
  in|sures
  in|sured
  in|sur|ing
  (secure payment
  against damage,
  theft, etc.
  ⚠ ensure)
in|sured +s
in|surer +s (person
  who insures.
  ⚠ ensurer)
in|sur|gence +s
in|sur|gency
  in|sur|gen|cies
in|sur|gent +s
in|sur|mount|able
in|sur|mount|ably
in|sur|rec|tion +s
in|sur|rec|tion|al
in|sur|rec|tion|ary
in|sur|rec|tion|ism
in|sur|rec|tion|ist
  +s
in|sus|cep|ti|bil|ity
in|sus|cep|tible
in-swinger +s
in|tact
in|tact|ness
in|tagli|ated
in|taglio +s *noun*
in|taglio
  in|taglioes
  in|taglioed
  in|taglio|ing
  verb
in|take +s
in|tan|gi|bil|ity
in|tan|gible +s
in|tan|gibly
in|tar|sia +s
in|te|ger +s
in|te|gra|bil|ity
in|te|grable
in|te|gral +s
in|te|gral|ity
  in|te|gral|ities
in|te|gral|ly
in|te|grand +s
in|te|grant
in|te|grate
  in|te|grates
  in|te|grated
  in|te|grat|ing
in|te|gra|tion +s

in|te|gra|tion|ist
  +s
in|te|gra|tive
in|te|gra|tor +s
in|teg|rity
in|tegu|ment +s
in|tegu|men|tal
in|tegu|ment|ary
in|tel|lect +s
in|tel|lec|tion +s
in|tel|lect|ive
in|tel|lec|tual +s
in|tel|lec|tual|ise
  Br. (use
  intellectualize)
  in|tel|lec|tual|ises
  in|tel|lec|tual|ised
  in|tel|lec|tual|
    is|ing
in|tel|lec|tual|ism
in|tel|lec|tual|ist
  +s
in|tel|lec|tu|al|ity
in|tel|lec|tual|ize
  in|tel|lec|tual|izes
  in|tel|lec|tual|
    ized
  in|tel|lec|tual|
    iz|ing
in|tel|lec|tual|ly
in|tel|li|gence +s
in|tel|li|gent
in|tel|li|gen|tial
in|tel|li|gent|ly
in|tel|li|gent|sia +s
in|tel|li|gi|bil|ity
in|tel|li|gible
in|tel|li|gibly
In|tel|post
In|tel|sat
in|tem|per|ance
in|tem|per|ate
in|tem|per|ate|ly
in|tem|per|ate|
    ness
in|tend +s +ed
  +ing
in|tend|ancy
  in|tend|an|cies
in|tend|ant +s
in|tend|ed +s
in|tend|ed|ly
in|tend|ment +s
in|tense
  in|tenser
  in|tens|est
in|tense|ly
in|tense|ness
in|tensi|fi|ca|tion
  +s
in|ten|si|fier +s

in|ten|sify
  in|ten|si|fies
  in|ten|si|fied
  in|ten|si|fy|ing
in|ten|sion +s
  (intensity; *Logic.*
  ⚠ intention)
in|ten|sion|al
  (*Philosophy.*
  ⚠ intentional)
in|ten|sion|al|ity
  (*Philosophy.*
  ⚠ intentionality)
in|ten|sion|al|ly
  (*Philosophy.*
  ⚠ intentionally)
in|ten|sity
  in|ten|sities
in|ten|sive
in|ten|sive|ly
in|ten|sive|ness
in|tent +s
in|ten|tion +s
  (purpose.
  ⚠ intension)
in|ten|tion|al
  (deliberately.
  ⚠ intensional)
in|ten|tion|al|ity
  (deliberateness.
  ⚠ intensionality)
in|ten|tion|al|ly
  (deliberately.
  ⚠ intensionally)
in|ten|tioned
in|tent|ly
in|tent|ness
inter
  in|ters
  in|terred
  in|ter|ring
inter|act +s +ed
  +ing
inter|act|ant +s
inter|action +s
inter|action|al
inter|active
inter|active|ly
inter alia
inter-allied
inter|ar|ticu|lar
inter|atom|ic
inter|bank
inter|bed
  inter|beds
  inter|bed|ded
  inter|bed|ding
inter|blend +s +ed
  +ing
inter|breed
  inter|breeds

inter|breed (*cont.*)
  inter|bred
  inter|breed|ing
inter|cal|ary
inter|cal|ate
  inter|cal|ates
  inter|cal|ated
  inter|cal|at|ing
inter|call|ation +s
inter|cede
  inter|cedes
  inter|ceded
  inter|ced|ing
inter|ceder +s
inter|cel|lu|lar
inter|cen|sal
inter|cept +s +ed
  +ing
inter|cep|tion +s
inter|cep|tive
inter|cept|or +s
inter|ces|sion +s
inter|ces|sion|al
inter|ces|sor +s
inter|ces|sor|ial
inter|ces|sory
inter|change
  inter|changes
  inter|changed
  inter|chan|ging
inter|change|
      abil|ity
inter|change|able
inter|change|able|
      ness
inter|change|ably
Inter|City
  Propr.
inter|city
  inter|cities
inter-class
inter|col|le|gi|ate
inter|co|lo|nial
inter|com +s
inter|com|mu|ni|
      cate
inter|com|mu|ni|
      cates
inter|com|mu|ni|
      cated
inter|com|mu|ni|
      cat|ing
inter|com|mu|ni|
      ca|tion
inter|com|mu|ni|
      ca|tive
inter|com|mu|nion
inter|com|mu|nity
inter|con|nect +s
  +ed +ing
inter|con|nec|tion
  +s

inter|con|tin|en|tal
inter|con|tin|
      en|tal|ly
inter|con|ver|sion
  +s
inter|con|vert +s
  +ed +ing
inter|con|vert|ible
inter|cool +s +ed
  +ing
inter|cool|er +s
inter|cor|rel|ate
  inter|cor|rel|ates
  inter|cor|rel|ated
  inter|cor|rel|
      at|ing
inter|cor|rel|ation
  +s
inter|cos|tal
inter|cos|tal|ly
inter|county
inter|course
inter|crop
  inter|crops
  inter|cropped
  inter|crop|ping
inter|cross
  inter|crosses
  inter|crossed
  inter|cross|ing
inter|crural
inter|cur|rence
inter|cur|rent
inter|cut
  inter|cuts
  inter|cut
  inter|cut|ting
inter|de|nom|in|
      ation|al
inter|de|nom|in|
      ation|al|ly
inter|de|part|
      men|tal
inter|de|part|
      men|tal|ly
inter|de|pend +s
  +ed +ing
inter|de|pend|ence
inter|
    de|pend|ency
inter|de|pend|en|
      cies
inter|de|pend|ent
inter|dict +s +ed
  +ing
inter|dic|tion +s
inter|dict|ory
inter|digit|al|ly
inter|digi|tate
  inter|digi|tates

inter|digi|tate
  (*cont.*)
  inter|digi|tated
  inter|digi|tat|ing
inter|dis|cip|lin|
      ary
inter|est +s +ed
  +ing
inter|est|ed|ly
inter|est|ed|ness
inter|est|ing|ly
inter|est|ing|ness
inter|face
  inter|faces
  inter|faced
  inter|facing
inter|facial
inter|facial|ly
inter|facing +s
inter|faith
inter|femor|al
inter|fere
  inter|feres
  inter|fered
  inter|fer|ing
inter|fer|ence +s
inter|fer|en|tial
inter|ferer +s
inter|fer|ing|ly
inter|fer|om|eter
  +s
inter|fero|met|ric
inter|fero|met|ric|
      al|ly
inter|fer|om|etry
inter|feron +s
inter|fib|ril|lar
inter|file
  inter|files
  inter|filed
  inter|fil|ing
inter|flow +s +ed
  +ing
inter|flu|ent
inter|fuse
  inter|fuses
  inter|fused
  inter|fus|ing
inter|fusion +s
inter|gal|act|ic
inter|gal|act|ic|
      al|ly
inter|gla|cial +s
inter|gov|ern|
      men|tal
inter|gov|ern|
      men|tal|ly
inter|grad|ation
  +s
inter|grade
  inter|grades

inter|grade (cont.)
  inter|graded
  inter|grad|ing
inter|growth+s
in|terim+s
in|ter|ior+s
in|ter|iorise Br.
  (use interiorize)
  in|ter|iorises
  in|ter|iorised
  in|ter|ior|is|ing
in|ter|ior|ize
  in|ter|ior|izes
  in|ter|ior|ized
  in|ter|ior|iz|ing
in|ter|ior|ly
interior-sprung
inter|ject+s+ed
  +ing
inter|jec|tion+s
inter|jec|tion|al
inter|jec|tion|ary
inter|ject|ory
inter|knit
  inter|knits
  inter|knit|ted or
  inter|knit
  inter|knit|ting
inter|lace
  inter|laces
  inter|laced
  inter|lacing
inter|lace|ment+s
In|ter|laken (town,
  Switzerland)
inter|lan|guage+s
inter|lap
  inter|laps
  inter|lapped
  inter|lap|ping
inter|lard+s+ed
  +ing
inter|leaf
  inter|leaves
inter|leave
  inter|leaves
  inter|leaved
  inter|leav|ing
inter|leu|kin+s
inter|lib|rary
inter|line
  inter|lines
  inter|lined
  inter|lin|ing
inter|lin|ear
inter|lin|ea|tion+s
inter|lin|ing+s
inter|link+s+ed
  +ing
inter|lobu|lar
inter|lock+s+ed
  +ing

inter|lock|er+s
inter|locu|tion+s
inter|locu|tor+s
inter|locu|tory
inter|locu|trix
  inter|locu|trixes
  female
inter|lope
  inter|lopes
  inter|loped
  inter|lop|ing
inter|loper+s
inter|lude+s
inter|mar|riage+s
inter|marry
  inter|mar|ries
  inter|mar|ried
  inter|marry|ing
inter|medi|acy
inter|medi|ary
  inter|medi|ar|ies
inter|medi|ate
  inter|medi|ates
  inter|medi|ated
  inter|medi|at|ing
  inter|medi|ate|ly
inter|medi|ate|
         ness
inter|medi|ation
  +s
inter|medi|ator+s
inter|medium
  inter|media
in|ter|ment+s
inter|mesh
  inter|meshes
  inter|meshed
  inter|mesh|ing
inter|mezzo
  inter|mezzi or
  inter|mezzos
in|ter|min|able
in|ter|min|able|
         ness
in|ter|min|ably
inter|min|gle
  inter|min|gles
  inter|min|gled
  inter|min|gling
inter|mis|sion+s
inter|mit
  inter|mits
  inter|mit|ted
  inter|mit|ting
inter|mit|tence+s
inter|mit|tency
inter|mit|tent
inter|mit|tent|ly
inter|mix
  inter|mixes
  inter|mixed
  inter|mix|ing

inter|mix|able
inter|mix|ture+s
inter|modal
inter|mo|lecu|lar
in|tern+s+ed
  +ing
in|tern|al
internal-
  combus|tion
  attributive
in|tern|al|isa|tion
  Br. (use
  internalization)
in|tern|al|ise Br.
  (use internalize)
  in|tern|al|ises
  in|tern|al|ised
  in|tern|al|is|ing
in|tern|al|ity
in|tern|al|iza|tion
in|tern|al|ize
  in|tern|al|izes
  in|tern|al|ized
  in|tern|al|iz|ing
in|tern|al|ly
inter|nation|al+s
Inter|nation|ale,
  the (song;
  organization)
inter|nation|al|
  isa|tion Br. (use
  international-
  ization)
inter|nation|al|ise
  Br. (use
  internationalize)
  inter|nation|al|
         ises
  inter|nation|al|
         ised
  inter|nation|al|
         is|ing
inter|nation|al|ism
inter|nation|al|ist
  +s
inter|nation|al|ity
inter|nation|al|
         iza|tion
inter|nation|al|ize
  inter|nation|al|
         izes
  inter|nation|al|
         ized
  inter|nation|al|
         iz|ing
inter|nation|al|ly
in|terne+s (use
  intern)
inter|necine
in|tern|ee+s

Inter|net
  (computer
  network)
in|tern|ist+s
in|tern|ment+s
inter|node+s
in|tern|ship+s
inter|nuclear
inter|nun|cial
inter|nun|cio+s
inter|ocean|ic
in|tero|cep|tive
inter|oper|abil|ity
inter|oper|able
inter|oscu|late
  inter|oscu|lates
  inter|oscu|lated
  inter|oscu|lat|ing
inter|osse|ous
inter|page
  inter|pages
  inter|paged
  inter|paging
inter|pari|et|al
inter|pari|et|al|ly
in|ter|pel|late
  in|ter|pel|lates
  in|ter|pel|lated
  in|ter|pel|lat|ing
  (question minister.
  ⚠ interpolate)
in|ter|pel|la|tion
  +s (action of
  interpelating.
  ⚠ interpolation)
in|ter|pel|la|tor+s
  (person who
  interpellates.
  ⚠ interpolator)
inter|pene|trate
  inter|pene|trates
  inter|pene|trated
  inter|
       pene|trat|ing
inter|pene|tra|tion
  +s
inter|pene|tra|tive
inter|per|son|al
inter|per|son|al|ly
inter|phase
inter|plait+s+ed
  +ing
inter|plan|et|ary
inter|play+s
inter|plead+s+ed
  +ing
inter|plead|er+s
Inter|pol
in|ter|pol|ate
  in|ter|pol|ates
  in|ter|pol|ated
  in|ter|pol|at|ing

in|ter|pol|ate
  (*cont.*)
  (insert; interject.
  ⚠ interpellate)
in|ter|pol|ation +s
  (insertion;
  interjection.
  ⚠ interpellation)
in|ter|pola|tive
in|ter|pol|ator +s
  (person who
  interpolates.
  ⚠ interpellator)
inter|posal +s
inter|pose
  inter|poses
  inter|posed
  inter|pos|ing
inter|pos|ition +s
in|ter|pret +s +ed
  +ing
in|ter|pret|abil|ity
in|ter|pret|able
in|ter|pret|ation
  +s
in|ter|pret|ation|al
in|ter|pret|ative
in|ter|pret|er +s
in|ter|pret|ive
in|ter|pret|ive|ly
inter|pro|vin|cial
inter|racial
inter|racial|ly
inter|reg|num
  inter|reg|nums *or*
  inter|regna
inter|relate
  inter|relates
  inter|related
  inter|relat|ing
inter|rela|tion +s
inter|rela|tion|ship
  +s
in|ter|ro|gate
  in|ter|ro|gates
  in|ter|ro|gated
  in|ter|ro|gat|ing
in|ter|ro|ga|tion +s
in|ter|ro|ga|tion|al
inter|roga|tive +s
inter|roga|tive|ly
in|ter|ro|ga|tor +s
inter|roga|tory
inter|rupt +s +ed
  +ing
inter|rupt|er +s
inter|rupt|ible
inter|rup|tion +s
inter|rup|tive
inter|rupt|or +s
inter|rup|tory

inter|sect +s +ed
  +ing
inter|sec|tion +s
inter|sec|tion|al
inter|sep|tal
inter|sex
  inter|sexes
inter|sex|ual
inter|sexu|al|ity
inter|sexu|al|ly
inter|space
  inter|spaces
  inter|spaced
  inter|spacing
inter|spe|cif|ic
inter|sperse
  inter|sperses
  inter|spersed
  inter|spers|ing
inter|sper|sion +s
inter|spinal
inter|spin|ous
inter|sta|dial +s
inter|state +s
inter|stel|lar
in|ter|stice +s
inter|sti|tial
inter|sti|tial|ly
inter|text|ual|ity
  inter|text|ual|ities
inter|tidal
inter|tribal
inter|trigo +s
inter|twine
  inter|twines
  inter|twined
  inter|twin|ing
inter|twine|ment
  +s
inter|twist +s +ed
  +ing
inter|val +s
inter|val|lic
inter|vene
  inter|venes
  inter|vened
  inter|ven|ing
inter|vener +s
inter|ve|ni|ent
inter|venor +s
  (use intervener)
inter|ven|tion +s
inter|ven|tion|ism
inter|ven|tion|ist
  +s
inter|ver|te|bral
inter|view +s +ed
  +ing
inter|view|ee +s
inter|view|er +s
inter vivos
inter-war

inter|weave
  inter|weaves
  inter|wove
  inter|weav|ing
  inter|woven
inter|wind
  inter|winds
  inter|wound
  inter|wind|ing
inter|work +s +ed
  +ing
in|tes|tacy
  in|tes|ta|cies
in|tes|tate +s
in|tes|tinal
in|tes|tine +s
in|thrall *Am.* +s
  +ed +ing (use
  enthrall. *Br.*
  enthral)
inti
  plural inti
in|ti|fada
in|tim|acy
  in|tim|acies
in|tim|ate
  in|tim|ates
  in|tim|ated
  in|tim|at|ing
in|tim|ate|ly
in|tim|ater +s
in|tim|ation +s
in|timi|date
  in|timi|dates
  in|timi|dated
  in|timi|dat|ing
in|timi|dat|ing|ly
in|timi|da|tion +s
in|timi|da|tor +s
in|timi|da|tory
in|tinc|tion +s
in|tit|ule
  in|tit|ules
  in|tit|uled
  in|tit|ul|ing
into
in|toler|able
in|toler|able|ness
in|toler|ably
in|toler|ance
in|toler|ant
in|toler|ant|ly
in|ton|ate
  in|ton|ates
  in|ton|ated
  in|ton|at|ing
in|ton|ation +s
in|ton|ation|al
in|tone
  in|tones
  in|toned
  in|ton|ing

in|toner +s
in toto
in|toxi|cant +s
in|toxi|cate
  in|toxi|cates
  in|toxi|cated
  in|toxi|cat|ing
in|toxi|cat|ing|ly
in|toxi|ca|tion +s
intra|cel|lu|lar
intra|cra|nial
intra|cra|ni|al|ly
in|tract|abil|ity
in|tract|able
in|tract|able|ness
in|tract|ably
in|tra|dos
  in|tra|doses
intra|mo|lecu|lar
intra|mural
intra|mur|al|ly
intra|mus|cu|lar
intra|nation|al
in|transi|gence
in|transi|gency
in|transi|gent +s
in|transi|gent|ly
in|transi|tive +s
in|transi|tive|ly
in|transi|tiv|ity
intra|pre|neur +s
intra|pre|neur|ial
intra|uter|ine
intra|ven|ous
intra|ven|ous|ly
in-tray +s
in|trepid
in|trep|id|ity
in|trep|id|ly
in|tri|cacy
  in|tri|ca|cies
in|tri|cate
in|tri|cate|ly
in|tri|gant +s *male*
in|tri|gante +s
  female
in|trigue
  in|trigues
  in|trigued
  in|tri|guing
in|tri|guer +s
in|tri|guing|ly
in|trin|sic
in|trin|sic|al|ly
intro +s
intro|duce
  intro|duces
  intro|duced
  intro|du|cing
intro|ducer +s
intro|du|cible
intro|duc|tion +s

intro|duc|tory
intro|flex|ion +s
intro|gres|sion +s
in|troit +s
intro|jec|tion +s
intro|mis|sion +s
intro|mit
  intro|mits
  intro|mit|ted
  intro|mit|ting
  intro|mit|tent
intro|spect +s +ed
  +ing
intro|spec|tion +s
intro|spect|ive
intro|spect|ive|ly
intro|spect|ive|
        ness
intro|sus|cep|tion
  +s
intro|ver|sible
intro|ver|sion +s
intro|ver|sive
intro|vert +s +ed
  +ing
intro|vert|ive
in|trude
  in|trudes
  in|truded
  in|trud|ing
in|truder +s
in|trud|ing|ly
in|tru|sion +s
in|tru|sion|ist +s
in|tru|sive
in|tru|sive|ly
in|tru|sive|ness
in|trust +s +ed
  +ing (use entrust)
in|trust|ment (use
  entrustment)
in|tub|ate
  in|tub|ates
  in|tub|ated
  in|tub|at|ing
in|tub|ation +s
in|tuit +s +ed +ing
in|tuit|able
in|tu|ition +s
in|tu|ition|al
in|tu|ition|al|ism
in|tu|ition|al|ist +s
in|tu|ition|ism
in|tu|ition|ist +s
in|tui|tive
in|tui|tive|ly
in|tui|tive|ness
in|tui|tiv|ism
in|tui|tiv|ist +s
in|tu|mesce
  in|tu|mesces

in|tu|mesce (*cont.*)
  in|tu|mesced
  in|tu|mes|cing
in|tu|mes|cence +s
in|tu|mes|cent
in|tus|sus|cep|tion
  +s
in|twine (use
  entwine)
  in|twines
  in|twined
  in|twin|ing
in|twine|ment (use
  entwinement)
Inuit
  plural Inuit *or*
  In|uits
Inuk
  plural Inuk *or*
  Inuks
Inuk|ti|tut
in|unc|tion +s
in|un|date
  in|un|dates
  in|un|dated
  in|un|dat|ing
in|un|da|tion +s
Inu|piaq
  plural Inu|piaq *or*
  Inu|piaqs
Inu|piat (use
  Inupiaq)
  plural Inu|piat *or*
  Inu|piats
Inu|pik (use
  Inupiaq)
  plural Inu|pik *or*
  Inu|piks
inure
  in|ures
  in|ured
  in|ur|ing
  (accustom to
  something
  unpleasant.
  △ enure)
in|ure|ment +s
in utero
in vacuo
in|vade
  in|vades
  in|vaded
  in|vad|ing
in|vader +s
in|va|gin|ate
  in|va|gin|ates
  in|va|gin|ated
  in|va|gin|at|ing
in|va|gin|ation +s
in|valid +s +ed
  +ing

in|vali|date
  in|vali|dates
  in|vali|dated
  in|vali|dat|ing
in|vali|da|tion +s
in|val|id|ism
in|val|id|ity
in|val|id|ities
in|val|id|ly
in|valu|able
in|valu|able|ness
in|valu|ably
Invar *Propr.*
in|vari|abil|ity
  in|vari|abil|ities
in|vari|able
in|vari|able|ness
in|vari|ably
in|vari|ance +s
in|vari|ant +s
in|va|sion +s
in|va|sive
in|vec|tive +s
in|veigh +s +ed
  +ing
in|vei|gle
  in|vei|gles
  in|vei|gled
  in|veig|ling
in|veigle|ment +s
in|vent +s +ed
  +ing
in|vent|able
in|ven|tion +s
in|vent|ive
in|vent|ive|ly
in|vent|ive|ness
in|vent|or +s
in|ven|tory
  in|ven|tor|ies
  in|ven|tor|ied
  in|ven|tory|ing
in|vent|ress
  in|vent|resses
In|ver|car|gill (city,
  New Zealand)
In|ver|ness (city,
  Scotland)
Inverness-shire
  (former county,
  Scotland)
in|verse +s
in|verse|ly
in|verse square
  law
in|ver|sion +s
in|ver|sive
in|vert +s +ed
  +ing
in|vert|ase
in|ver|te|brate +s
in|vert|er +s

in|vert|ibil|ity
in|vert|ible
in|vest +s +ed
  +ing
in|vest|able
in|vest|ible (use
  investable)
in|ves|ti|gate
  in|ves|ti|gates
  in|ves|ti|gated
  in|ves|ti|gat|ing
in|ves|ti|ga|tion +s
in|ves|ti|ga|tion|al
in|ves|ti|ga|tive
in|ves|ti|ga|tor +s
in|ves|ti|ga|tory
in|ves|ti|ture +s
in|vest|ment +s
in|vest|or +s
in|vet|er|acy
  in|vet|er|acies
in|vet|er|ate
in|vet|er|ate|ly
in|vidi|ous
in|vidi|ous|ly
in|vidi|ous|ness
in|vigi|late
  in|vigi|lates
  in|vigi|lated
  in|vigi|lat|ing
in|vigi|la|tion +s
in|vigi|la|tor +s
in|vig|or|ate
  in|vig|or|ates
  in|vig|or|ated
  in|vig|or|at|ing
in|vig|or|at|ing|ly
in|vig|or|ation +s
in|vig|ora|tive
in|vig|or|ator +s
in|vin|ci|bil|ity
in|vin|cible +s
in|vin|cible|ness
in|vin|cibly
in|viol|abil|ity
in|viol|able
in|viol|ably
in|viol|acy
in|viol|ate
in|viol|ate|ly
in|viol|ate|ness
in|visi|bil|ity
in|vis|ible +s
in|vis|ible|ness
in|vis|ibly
in|vi|ta|tion +s
in|vi|ta|tion|al +s
in|vi|ta|tory
in|vite
  in|vites
  in|vited
  in|vit|ing

in|vitee +s
in|viter +s
in|vit|ing|ly
in|vit|ing|ness
in vitro adverbial
    and attributive
in vivo
in|voc|able
in|vo|ca|tion +s
in|vo|ca|tory
in|voice
    in|voices
    in|voiced
    in|voi|cing
in|voke
    in|vokes
    in|voked
    in|vok|ing
in|voker +s
in|vo|luc|ral
in|vo|lucre +s
in|vol|un|tar|ily
in|vol|un|tari|ness
in|vol|un|tary
in|vo|lute +s
in|vo|luted
in|vo|lu|tion +s
in|vo|lu|tion|al
in|volve
    in|volves
    in|volved
    in|volv|ing
in|volve|ment +s
in|vul|ner|abil|ity
in|vul|ner|able
in|vul|ner|ably
in|ward
inward-looking
in|ward|ly
in|ward|ness
in|wards
in|weave
    in|weaves
    in|wove
    in|weav|ing
    in|woven
in|wrap (use
    enwrap)
    in|wraps
    in|wrapped
    in|wrap|ping
in|wreathe (use
    enwreathe)
    in|wreathes
    in|wreathed
    in|wreath|ing
in|wrought
in-your-face
    adjective
Io (*Greek Mythology*;
    moon of Jupiter)
iod|ate +s

iodic
iod|ide +s
iod|in|ate
    iod|in|ates
    iod|in|ated
    iod|in|at|ing
iod|in|ation
iod|ine
iod|in|ise *Br.* (use
    iodinize)
    iod|in|ises
    iod|in|ised
    iod|in|is|ing
iod|in|ize
    iod|in|izes
    iod|in|ized
    iod|in|iz|ing
iod|isa|tion *Br.*
    (use iodization)
iod|ise *Br.* (use
    iodize)
    iod|ises
    iod|ised
    iod|is|ing
iod|ism +s
iod|iza|tion
iod|ize
    iod|izes
    iod|ized
    iod|iz|ing
iodo|form
ion +s (charged
    molecule etc.
    △ iron)
Iona (Scottish
    island; name)
Ion|esco, Eu|gene
    (Romanian-born
    French dramatist)
Ionia (ancient
    region, Asia
    Minor)
Ion|ian +s
Ion|ian Is|lands
    (off W. Greece)
Ion|ian mode
    Music
Ion|ian Sea (part of
    Mediterranean)
Ionic +s
    (architectural
    order; Greek
    dialect)
ionic (of ions)
ion|ic|al|ly
ion|is|able *Br.* (use
    ionizable)
ion|isa|tion *Br.*
    (use ionization)
ion|ise *Br.* (use
    ionize)
    ion|ises

ion|ise (*cont.*)
    ion|ised
    ion|is|ing
ion|iser *Br.* +s (use
    ionizer)
ion|ium
ion|iz|able
ion|iza|tion
ion|ize
    ion|izes
    ion|ized
    ion|iz|ing
ion|izer +s
iono|sphere
iono|spher|ic
Ios (Greek island.
    △ Eos)
iota +s
Iowa (state, USA)
Iowa City (in USA)
Ipati|eff, Vlad|imir
    Ni|ko|lai|ev|ich
    (Russian-born
    American
    chemist)
ipe|cac +s
ipe|cacu|anha +s
Iphi|ge|nia *Greek
    Mythology*
Ipoh (city,
    Malaysia)
ipo|moea +s
ipse dixit
ip|si|lat|eral
ip|sis|sima verba
ipso facto
Ips|wich (town,
    England)
Iqbal,
    Mu|ham|mad
    (Indian poet and
    philosopher)
Iqui|tos (port,
    Peru)
Ira
irade +s
Iran
Iran-Contra
    attributive
Iran|gate (US
    political scandal)
Iran|ian +s
Iraq
Iraqi +s
IRAS (= Infrared
    Astronomical
    Satellite)
iras|ci|bil|ity
iras|cible
iras|cibly
irate
ir|ate|ly

ir|ate|ness
ire (anger. △ ayah)
ire|ful
Ire|land
Ire|naeus (Greek
    saint)
Irene
iren|ic
iren|ic|al
iren|icon +s (use
    eirenicon)
Irgun (Zionist
    organization)
Irian Jaya
    (province,
    Indonesia)
iri|da|ceous
iri|des|cence +s
iri|des|cent
iri|des|cent|ly
irid|ium
iri|dolo|gist +s
iri|dol|ogy
Iris (*Greek
    Mythology*; name)
iris
    irises
    (flower)
Irish
Ir|ish|man
    Ir|ish|men
Ir|ish|ness
Ir|ish|woman
    Ir|ish|women
ir|itis
irk +s +ed +ing
    (irritate. △ erk)
irk|some
irk|some|ly
irk|some|ness
Ir|kutsk (city,
    Siberia)
Irma
iroko +s
iron +s +ed +ing
    (metal; tool;
    laundry
    implement; etc.
    △ ion)
Iron Age
iron|bark +s
iron-bound
iron|clad +s
iron|er +s
iron|ic
iron|ic|al
iron|ic|al|ly
iron|ing board +s
iron|ise *Br.* (use
    ironize)
    iron|ises

iron|ise (*cont.*)
  iron|ised
  iron|is|ing
iron|ist +s
iron|ize
  iron|izes
  iron|ized
  iron|iz|ing
iron|less
iron-like
iron|mas|ter +s
iron-mold *Am.* +s
iron|mon|ger +s
iron|mon|gery
  iron|mon|ger|ies
iron-mould *Br.* +s
iron-on *adjective*
Iron|side (Edmund II)
Iron|sides
  (Cromwell's cavalry)
iron|stone +s
iron|ware
iron|work
iron|works
irony
  iron|ies
  (like iron; expression)
Iro|quoian +s
Iro|quois
  plural Iro|quois
ir|radi|ance +s
ir|radi|ant
ir|radi|ate
  ir|radi|ates
  ir|radi|ated
  ir|radi|at|ing
ir|radi|ation +s
ir|radia|tive
ir|ration|al
ir|ration|al|ise *Br.*
  (use irrationalize)
  ir|ration|al|ises
  ir|ration|al|ised
  ir|ration|al|is|ing
ir|ration|al|ity
  ir|ration|al|ities
ir|ration|al|ize
  ir|ration|al|izes
  ir|ration|al|ized
  ir|ration|al|iz|ing
ir|ration|al|ly
Ir|ra|waddy (river, Burma)
ir|re|claim|able
ir|re|claim|ably
ir|re|con|cil|
  abil|ity
ir|re|con|cil|able

ir|re|con|cil|able|
  ness
ir|re|con|cil|ably
ir|re|cov|er|able
ir|re|cov|er|ably
ir|re|cus|able
ir|re|deem|abil|ity
ir|re|deem|able
ir|re|deem|ably
ir|re|den|tism
Ir|re|den|tist +s
  (Italian nationalist)
ir|re|den|tist +s
  (generally)
ir|re|du|ci|bil|ity
ir|re|du|cible
ir|re|du|cibly
ir|ref|rag|able
ir|ref|rag|ably
ir|re|fran|gible
ir|re|fut|abil|ity
ir|re|fut|able
ir|re|fut|ably
ir|re|gard|less
ir|regu|lar +s
ir|regu|lar|ity
  ir|regu|lar|ities
ir|regu|lar|ly
ir|rela|tive
ir|rela|tive|ly
ir|rele|vance +s
ir|rele|vancy
  ir|rele|van|cies
ir|rele|vant
ir|rele|vant|ly
ir|re|li|gion
ir|re|li|gion|ist +s
ir|re|li|gious
ir|re|li|gious|ly
ir|re|li|gious|ness
ir|re|me|di|able
ir|re|me|di|ably
ir|re|mis|sible
ir|re|mis|sibly
ir|re|mov|abil|ity
ir|re|mov|
  abil|ities
ir|re|mov|able
ir|re|mov|ably
ir|rep|ar|abil|ity
ir|rep|ar|able
ir|rep|ar|able|ness
ir|rep|ar|ably
ir|re|place|able
ir|re|place|ably
ir|re|press|ibil|ity
ir|re|press|ible
ir|re|press|ible|
  ness
ir|re|press|ibly

ir|re|proach|
  abil|ity
ir|re|proach|able
ir|re|proach|able|
  ness
ir|re|proach|ably
ir|re|sist|ibil|ity
ir|re|sist|ible
ir|re|sist|ible|ness
ir|re|sist|ibly
ir|reso|lute
ir|reso|lute|ly
ir|reso|lute|ness
ir|reso|lu|tion +s
ir|re|solv|able
ir|re|spect|ive
ir|re|spect|ive|ly
ir|re|spon|si|bil|ity
ir|re|spon|sible
ir|re|spon|sibly
ir|re|spon|sive
ir|re|spon|sive|ly
ir|re|spon|sive|
  ness
ir|re|ten|tive
ir|re|triev|abil|ity
ir|re|triev|able
ir|re|triev|ably
ir|rev|er|ence
ir|rev|er|ent
ir|rev|er|en|tial
ir|rev|er|ent|ly
ir|re|ver|si|bil|ity
ir|re|vers|ible
ir|re|vers|ibly
ir|rev|oc|abil|ity
ir|rev|oc|able
ir|rev|oc|ably
ir|rig|able
ir|ri|gate
  ir|ri|gates
  ir|ri|gated
  ir|ri|gat|ing
ir|ri|ga|tion +s
ir|ri|ga|tive
ir|ri|ga|tor +s
ir|rit|abil|ity
ir|rit|able
ir|rit|ably
ir|ri|tancy
ir|ri|tant +s
ir|ri|tate
  ir|ri|tates
  ir|ri|tated
  ir|ri|tat|ing
ir|ri|tated|ly
ir|ri|tat|ing|ly
ir|ri|ta|tion +s
ir|ri|ta|tive
ir|ri|ta|tor +s

ir|rupt +s +ed +ing
  (enter forcibly.
  △ erupt)
ir|rup|tion +s
  (forcible entry.
  △ eruption)
Ir|tysh (river, central Asia)
Irv|ing (name)
Irv|ing, Henry
  (English actor-manager)
Irv|ing,
  Wash|ing|ton
  (American writer)
Irv|ing|ite +s
  (member of Catholic Apostolic Church)
is
Isaac (*Bible*; name)
Isa|bel *also*
  Isa|belle, Iso|bel
Isa|bella (Castilian queen; English queen consort)
Isa|belle *also*
  Isa|bel, Iso|bel
isa|bel|line
Isa|dora
isa|gogic
isa|gogics
Isaiah (*Bible*; name)
isa|tin +s
is|chae|mia *Br.*
is|chae|mic *Br.*
is|che|mia *Am.*
is|che|mic *Am.*
Is|chia (Italian island)
is|chi|ad|ic
is|chial
is|chi|at|ic
is|chium
  is|chia
Ise (city, Japan)
is|en|trop|ic
Is|eult (legendary beloved of Tristram)
Is|fa|han (city, Iran)
Ish|er|wood,
  Chris|to|pher
  (English writer)
Ishi|guro, Kazuo
  (Japanese-born British novelist)
Ish|mael *Bible*
Ish|mael|ite +s

Ish|tar *Babylonian and Assyrian Mythology*
Isi|dore (Greek mathematician and engineer; name)
Isi|dore of Sev|ille (Spanish saint)
is|in|glass
Isis *Egyptian Mythology*
Is|ken|de|run (port, Turkey)
Isla
Islam
Is|lama|bad (capital of Pakistan)
Is|lam|ic
Is|lam|isa|tion *Br.* (use Islamization)
Is|lam|ise *Br.* (use Islamize)
  Is|lam|ises
  Is|lam|ised
  Is|lam|is|ing
Is|lam|ism
Is|lam|ist +s
Is|lam|ite +s
Is|lam|it|ic
Is|lam|iza|tion
Is|lam|ize
  Is|lam|izes
  Is|lam|ized
  Is|lam|iz|ing
Is|land (Icelandic name for Iceland)
is|land +s (land surrounded by water; etc.)
is|land|er +s
island-hop
  island-hops
  island-hopped
  island-hopping
Islay (Scottish island)
isle +s (island. △ aisle, I'll)
Isle of Man (in Irish Sea)
Isle of Wight (English island)
islet +s
is|lets of Lang|er|hans
ism +s
Is|maili +s
isn't (= is not)
iso|bar +s
iso|bar|ic

Iso|bel *also* Isa|bel, Isa|belle
iso|cheim +s
iso|chro|mat|ic
isoch|ron|ous
isoch|ron|ous|ly
iso|clinal
iso|clin|ic
isoc|racy
  isoc|ra|cies
Isoc|ra|tes (Athenian orator)
iso|crat|ic
iso|cyan|ate +s
iso|cyan|ic
iso|cyc|lic
iso|dy|nam|ic
iso|elec|tric
iso|en|zyme +s
isog|amy
iso|geo|therm +s
iso|geo|ther|mal
iso|gloss
  iso|glosses
iso|gon|ic
iso|hel +s
iso|hyet +s
iso|kin|et|ic
isol|able
isol|at|able
isol|ate
  isol|ates
  isol|ated
  isol|at|ing
isol|ation +s
isol|ation|ism
isol|ation|ist +s
isola|tive
isol|ator +s
Is|olde
iso|leu|cine +s
iso|mer +s
iso|mer|ic
isom|er|ise *Br.* (use isomerize)
  isom|er|ises
  isom|er|ised
  isom|er|is|ing
isom|er|ism
isom|er|ize
  isom|er|izes
  isom|er|ized
  isom|er|iz|ing
isom|er|ous
iso|met|ric
iso|met|ric|al|ly
iso|met|rics
isom|etry
iso|morph +s
iso|morph|ic
iso|morph|ism
iso|morph|ous

ison|omy
iso|phote +s
iso|pleth +s
iso|pod +s
isos|celes
iso|seis|mal
iso|seis|mic
isos|tasy
iso|stat|ic
iso|there +s
iso|therm +s
iso|ther|mal
iso|ther|mal|ly
iso|ton|ic
iso|ton|ic|al|ly
iso|ton|icity
iso|tope +s
iso|top|ic
iso|top|ic|al|ly
isot|opy
iso|trop|ic
iso|trop|ic|al|ly
isot|ropy
Is|pa|han (use Isfahan)
I-spy
Is|rael
Is|raeli +s
Is|rael|ite +s
Is|ra|fel (Muslim angel)
Issa +s
Is|sa|char *Bible*
Is|si|gonis, Alec (British engineer and car designer)
is|su|able
is|su|ance
is|su|ant *Heraldry*
issue
  issues
  is|sued
  is|su|ing
is|sue|less
is|suer +s
Is|tan|bul (port, Turkey)
Isth|mian (of the Isthmus of Corinth)
isth|mian (of an isthmus)
isth|mus
  isth|muses *or* isthmi
istle +s
Is|tria (peninsula in Adriatic Sea)
Is|trian +s
it
Itaipu (dam, Brazil)
Ital|ian +s

Ital|ian|ate
Ital|ic (of Italy)
ital|ic +s (sloping type)
itali|cisa|tion *Br.* +s (use italicization)
itali|cise *Br.* (use italicize)
  itali|cises
  itali|cised
  itali|cis|ing
itali|ciza|tion +s
itali|cize
  itali|cizes
  itali|cized
  itali|ciz|ing
Ital|iot +s
Italy
Ita|nagar (city, India)
ITAR-Tass (Russian news agency)
itch
  itches
  itched
  itch|ing
itchi|ness
itch|ing pow|der +s
itch-mite +s
itchy
  itch|ier
  itchi|est
it'd (= it had; it would)
item +s
item|isa|tion *Br.* (use itemization)
item|ise *Br.* (use itemize)
  item|ises
  item|ised
  item|is|ing
item|iser *Br.* +s (use itemizer)
item|iza|tion
item|ize
  item|izes
  item|ized
  item|iz|ing
item|izer +s
it|er|ance +s
it|er|ancy
it|er|ate
  it|er|ates
  it|er|ated
  it|er|at|ing
it|er|ation +s
it|era|tive
it|era|tive|ly

Ith¦aca (Greek
  island)
ithy|phal¦lic
it|in¦er|acy
it|in¦er|ancy
it|in¦er|ant +s
it|in¦er|ary
  it|in¦er|ar¦ies
it|in¦er|ate
  it|in¦er|ates
  it|in¦er|ated
  it|in¦er|at¦ing
itin¦er|ation +s
it'll (= it will; it
  shall)
Ito, Prince
  Hiro|bumi
  (Japanese
  statesman)
its (of it)
it's (= it is)
it¦self
itsy-bitsy
itty-bitty
IUPAC
  (= International
  Union of Pure and
  Applied
  Chemistry)
Ivan *also* Ivon
  (name)
Ivan (rulers of
  Russia)
I've (= I have)
Ives, Charles
  (American
  composer)
ivied
Ivon *also* Ivan
Ivor *also* Ifor
ivor|ied
Ivory, James
  (American film
  director)
ivory
  iv¦or|ies
Ivory Coast
  (country, W.
  Africa)
ivory-nut +s
Ivy (name)
ivy
  ivies
  (plant)
Iwo Jima (island,
  NW Pacific)
ixia +s
Ixion *Greek
  Mythology*
Iyyar (Jewish
  month)
izard +s

Izh¦evsk (city,
  Russia)
Izmir (port, W.
  Turkey)
Izmit (city, NW
  Turkey)
Iznik (town,
  Turkey)
Iz¦ves¦tia (Russian
  newspaper)

Jj

jab
  jabs
  jabbed
  jab|bing
Jab|al|pur (city,
  India)
jab¦ber +s +ed
  +ing
jab¦ber|wock +s
jab¦ber|wocky
  jab¦ber|wockies
jab¦iru +s
jabo|randi +s
jabot +s
jaca|mar +s
jac¦ana +s
jaca|randa +s
ja¦cinth +s
Jack (name)
jack +s +ed +ing
  (lifting device;
  card; flag; ball;
  etc.)
jackal +s
jacka|napes
  plural jacka|napes
jack|aroo +s
jack|ass
  jack|asses
jack|boot +s
jack|boot¦ed
Jack-by-the-
  hedge
jack|daw +s
jack|eroo +s (use
  jackaroo)
jacket +s +ed +ing
jack|fish
  plural jack|fish
Jack Frost
jack|fruit
  plural jack|fruit
jack|ham¦mer +s
Jackie *also* Jacqui,
  Jacky
jack-in-office
  jacks-in-office
jack-in-the-box
  jack-in-the-boxes
Jack-in-the-pulpit
jack|knife
  jack|knives
  noun
jack|knife
  jack|knifes
  jack|knifed
  jack|knif¦ing
  verb

jack of all trades
  jacks of all trades
jack-o'-lantern +s
jack plane +s
jack plug +s
jack|pot +s
jack|rab¦bit +s
Jack Rus|sell +s
  (terrier)
jack snipe
  plural jack snipe
jack socket +s
Jack|son, An¦drew
  (American
  president)
Jack|son, Glenda
  (English actress
  and politician)
Jack|son, Jesse
  (American
  politician and
  clergyman)
Jack|son,
  Mi¦chael
  (American singer)
Jack|son,
  Stone|wall
  (American
  general)
Jack|son|ville
  (city, USA)
jack|staff +s
jack|stone +s
jack|straw +s
Jack tar +s
Jack the lad
Jack the Rip¦per
  (English
  murderer)
Jacky *also* Jackie,
  Jacqui
  (name)
Jacky
  Jack|ies
  (*offensive* Australian
  Aborigine)
Jacob (*Bible*; name)
Jaco|bean +s
Ja¦cobi, Karl
  Gus¦tav Jacob
  (German
  mathematician)
Jaco|bin +s
  (extreme radical;
  friar)
jaco|bin +s
  (pigeon)
Jaco|bin¦ic
Jaco|bin|ic¦al
Jaco|bin|ism
Jac¦ob|ite +s
Jaco|bit|ic¦al
Jaco¦bit|ism

Ja¦cobs, W. W.
   (English writer)
Jacob's lad¦der +s
Jacob's staff +s
jaco|net +s
Ja¦copo della
   Quer|cia (Italian
   sculptor)
jac¦quard +s
Jacque|line also
   Jacque|lyn
Jacque|lyn also
   Jacque|line
Jac¦quetta
Jac¦qui also Jackie,
   Jacky
jacti|ta¦tion +s
ja|cuzzi +s Propr.
Jade (name)
jade +s (stone;
   horse; woman)
jaded
jaded¦ly
jaded|ness
jade|ite +s
j'adoube
jae¦ger +s
Jaffa +s (city,
   Israel; orange)
Jaffna (district and
   city, Sri Lanka)
jag
   jags
   jagged
   jag|ging
Jag¦an|na¦tha
   Hinduism
jag|ged¦ly
jag¦ged|ness
Jag¦ger, Mick
   (English singer)
jag¦ger +s (thing
   that jags; ship)
jaggy
   jag|gier
   jag¦gi|est
Jago
jag¦uar +s
jag¦uar|undi +s
Jah¦veh (use
   Yahweh)
jai alai
jail +s +ed +ing
jail|bait
jail|bird +s
jail|break +s
jail¦er +s
jail|house +s
Jain +s (adherent
   of Jainism.
   △ Jane, Jayne)
Jain|ism

Jain|ist +s
Jai¦pur (city, India)
Ja|karta (use
   Djakarta)
Jake (name)
jake (all right)
Ja¦kob|son,
   Roman (Russian-
   born American
   linguist)
Jal|ala|bad (city,
   Afghanistan)
Jalal ad-Din ar-
   Rumi (founder of
   whirling
   dervishes)
Jal|an|dhar (use
   Jullundur)
jalap
Jal¦apa
   (En¦ri|quez) (city,
   Mexico)
jala|peño +s
Jal|isco (state,
   Mexico)
jal¦opy
jal|op¦ies
jal¦ou|sie +s
jam
   jams
   jammed
   jam|ming
   (squeeze; block;
   food; etc. △ jamb)
Ja|maica
Ja|mai¦can +s
jamb +s (part of
   door frame.
   △ jam)
jam¦ba|laya
jam|be¦roo +s
jam|bo¦ree +s
James (Scottish
   and English kings)
James, C. L. R.
   (Trinidadian
   writer)
James, Henry
   (American writer)
James, Jesse
   (American outlaw)
James, P. D.
   (English writer)
James, Wil|liam
   (American
   philosopher)
James Bay (in
   Canada)
Jame|son Raid (in
   South Africa)
James|town
   (former

James|town (cont.)
   settlement, USA;
   capital of St
   Helena)
Jamie
jam jar +s
jam¦mer +s
Jammu (city, India)
Jammu and
   Kash|mir (state,
   India)
jammy
jam|mier
jam¦mi|est
Jam|nagar (city,
   India)
jam-packed
jam pot +s
Jam¦shed|pur
   (city, India)
Jam¦shid
   (legendary Persian
   king)
Jan
Janá|ček, Leoš
   (Czech composer)
Jan¦cis
Jane also Jayne
   (name. △ Jain)
jane +s (woman)
JANET (= Joint
   Academic
   Network)
Janet (name)
Jan|ette also
   Gen|ette,
   Jean|ette,
   Jean|nette
Janey also Janie
jan¦gle
   jan¦gles
   jan¦gled
   jan|gling
Jang|lish (use
   Japlish)
Jan¦ice also Janis
Jan¦ine
Janis also Jan¦ice
jan¦is|sary (use
   janizary)
jan¦is|sar¦ies
jani|tor +s
jani|tor¦ial
jani|zary
jani|zar¦ies
jank|ers
Jan Mayen (island,
   Arctic Ocean)
Jan¦sen,
   Cor|ne¦lius
   (Dutch
   theologian)

Jan¦sen|ism
Jan¦sen|ist +s
Jan|sens,
   Cor|ne¦lius
   (Dutch painter;
   use Johnson)
Janu|ary
   Janu|ar¦ies
Janus (Roman
   Mythology; moon
   of Saturn)
Jap +s offensive
Japan
japan
   ja¦pans
   ja|panned
   ja|pan|ning
Jap|an|ese
   plural Jap¦an|ese
jape
   japes
   japed
   jap¦ing
jap¦ery
   jap¦er|ies
Ja|pheth Bible
Ja|phet¦ic
Jap|lish
ja¦pon|ica +s
Jaques-Dalcroze,
   Émile (Swiss
   music teacher)
jar
   jars
   jarred
   jar|ring
jar¦di|nière +s
jar¦ful +s
jar¦gon +s
   (language; stone)
jar¦gon|elle +s
jar¦gon|ise Br. (use
   jargonize)
jar¦gon|ises
jar¦gon|ised
jar¦gon|is¦ing
jar¦gon|is¦tic
jar¦gon|ize
   jar¦gon|izes
   jar¦gon|ized
   jar¦gon|iz¦ing
jar|goon +s
jarl +s
jar¦rah +s
Jar¦row (town,
   England)
Jarry, Al¦fred
   (French dramatist)
Jaru|zel¦ski,
   Woj|ciech (Polish
   general and
   statesman)

Jas¦min *also*
  Jas|mine
  (name)
jas¦min +s (plant;
  use jasmine)
Jas|mine *also*
  Jas¦min
  (name)
jas|mine +s (plant)
Jason (*Greek
  Mythology*; name)
jaspé
Jas¦per (name)
jas¦per +s (stone)
Jassy (German
  name for Iaşi)
Jat +s
Jat¦aka +s
jato +s (= jet-
  assisted take-off)
jaun|dice
  jaun|dices
  jaun|diced
  jaun|dicing
jaunt +s +ed +ing
jaunt|ily
jaunti|ness
jaunt|ing car +s
jaunty
  jaunt|ier
  jaunti|est
Java (island,
  Indonesia)
Java Man
Javan +s
Ja¦van|ese
  plural Ja¦van|ese
jav|elin +s
Jav|elle water
jaw +s +ed +ing
jaw|bone +s
jaw-breaker +s
jaw-jaw +s +ed
  +ing
jaw|line +s
Jay (name)
jay +s (bird)
Jayne *also* Jane
  (name. △ Jain)
jay|walk +s +ed
  +ing
jay|walk¦er +s
jazz
  jazzes
  jazzed
  jazz|ing
Jazz Age
  (American 1920s)
jazz¦er +s
jazz|ily
jazzi|ness

jazz|man
  jazz|men
jazzy
  jazz|ier
  jazzi|est
J-cloth +s *Propr.*
jeal|ous
jeal|ous¦ly
jeal|ousy
  jeal|ousies
Jean (woman's
  name. △ Gene)
jean (cloth. △ gene)
Jean|ette *also*
  Gen|ette,
  Jan|ette,
  Jean|nette
Jeanie *also*
  Jean|nie
Jean|ne¦ret,
  Charles
  Édou¦ard (= Le
  Corbusier)
Jean|nette *also*
  Gen|ette,
  Jan|ette,
  Jean|ette
Jean|nie *also*
  Jeanie
Jean Paul (German
  novelist)
Jeans, James
  Hop|wood
  (English physicist)
jeans (trousers.
  △ genes)
Jed|burgh (town,
  Scotland)
Jed¦dah (= Jiddah)
jeep +s *Propr.*
jee|pers
jeer +s +ed +ing
jeer|ing¦ly
Jeeves, Regi|nald
  (in P. G.
  Wodehouse
  novels)
Jeez *interjection*
Jeff *also* Geoff
Jef|feries,
  Rich|ard (English
  writer)
Jef¦fer|son,
  Thomas
  (American
  president)
Jef¦fer|son City
  (town, USA)
Jef|frey *also*
  Geof|frey
Jef|freys, George
  (Welsh judge)

jehad (use jihad)
Je¦hosha|phat
Je¦ho|vah
Je¦ho|vah's
  Wit|ness
Je¦ho|vah's
  Wit|nesses
Je¦hov|ist +s
Jehu *Bible*
je|june
je|june¦ly
je|june|ness
je|junum +s
Je¦kyll, Ger|trude
  (British gardener)
Jek¦yll and Hyde
jell +s +ed +ing
  (set as jelly. △ gel)
jel|laba +s (use
  djellaba)
Jel¦li|coe, Earl
  (British admiral)
jel|li¦fi|ca¦tion
jel|lify
  jel¦li|fies
  jel¦li|fied
  jel¦li¦fy|ing
Jell-O +s *Propr.*
jello +s
jelly
  jel|lies
  jel|lied
  jelly|ing
  (confection; set as
  jelly. △ gelly)
jelly baby
  jelly babies
jelly bean +s
jel¦ly|fish
  plural jel¦ly|fish *or*
  jel¦ly|fishes
jelly-like
Jem
Jem¦ima
Jemma *also*
  Gemma
jemmy
  jem|mies
  jem|mied
  jemmy|ing
  (crowbar; force
  open. △ gemmy)
Jena (town,
  Germany)
je ne sais quoi
Jeni|fer *also*
  Jen¦ni|fer
Jen|kins's Ear,
  War of (Anglo-
  Spanish war)
Jenna

Jen¦ner, Ed|ward
  (English
  physician)
jen¦net +s (horse.
  △ genet)
Jen¦ni|fer *also*
  Jeni|fer
Jenny *also* Jen¦nie
  (name)
jenny
  jen|nies
  (spinning-jenny;
  female donkey;
  crane)
jenny-wren +s
jeon
  plural jeon
  (South Korean
  currency)
jeop¦ard|ise *Br.*
  (use jeopardize)
  jeop¦ard|ises
  jeop¦ard|ised
  jeop¦ard|is¦ing
jeop¦ard|ize
  jeop¦ard|izes
  jeop¦ard|ized
  jeop¦ard|iz¦ing
jeop|ardy
Jeph|thah *Bible*
je|quir¦ity
  je|quir|ities
Jerba (use Djerba)
jer¦bil +s (use
  gerbil)
jer¦boa +s
jere|miad +s
Jere|miah +s
  (*Bible*; pessimistic
  person)
Jer¦emy
Jerez (de la
  Fron|tera) (town,
  Spain)
Jeri|cho (town,
  Israel)
jerk +s +ed +ing
jerk¦er +s
jerk|ily
jer¦kin +s
jerki|ness
jerky
  jerk|ier
  jerki|est
jero|boam +s
Je¦rome
Je¦rome
  (Dalmatian-born
  saint)
Je¦rome, Je¦rome
  K. (English writer)

Jerry
  Jer¦ries
  (*offensive* German;
  name)
jerry
  jer¦ries
  (chamber pot)
jerry-builder +s
jerry-building
jerry-built
jer¦ry|can +s
jer¦ry|man|der +s
  +ed +ing (use
  gerrymander)
Jer¦sey +s
  (Channel Island;
  cattle)
jer¦sey +s
  (garment)
Jer¦sey City (in
  USA)
Je¦ru¦sa¦lem
  (capital of Israel;
  artichoke)
Jer¦vis, John (Earl
  St Vincent, British
  admiral)
Jes¦per|sen, Otto
  (Danish
  philologist)
Jess (name)
jess
  jesses
  jessed
  jess|ing
  (strap on a hawk's
  leg)
jes¦sa|min +s
  (= jasmine)
jes¦sa|mine +s
  (= jasmine)
Jesse (*Bible*; name.
  △ Jessie)
Jesse win¦dow +s
Jes|sica
Jes¦sie (name
  △ Jesse)
jest +s +ed +ing
jest¦er +s
jest|ful
Jesu
Jes|uit +s
Jesu¦it|ic|al
Jesu¦it¦ic|al¦ly
Jesus (Christ)
JET (= Joint
  European Torus)
jet
  jets
  jet¦ted
  jet|ting

jet (*cont.*)
  (stream; engine;
  stone)
jet black *noun and*
  adjective
jet-black *attributive*
jeté +s
Jet|foil *Am.* +s
  Propr.
jet|foil *Br.* +s
Jethro
jet lag
jet-lagged
jet-propelled
jet¦sam
jet set
jet-setter +s
jet-setting
jet ski +s *noun*
  Propr.
jet-ski +s +ed +ing
  verb
jet stream +s
jet¦ti|son +s +ed
  +ing
jet¦ton +s
jetty
  jet|ties
jeu d'es¦prit
  jeux d'es¦prit
jeunesse dorée
Jew +s
jewel
  jewels
  jew|elled *Br.*
  jew|eled *Am.*
  jew|el|ling *Br.*
  jew|el|ing *Am.*
jew|el|er *Am.* +s
jewel-fish
  plural **jewel-fish** *or*
  jewel-fishes
jew|el|ler *Br.* +s
jew|el|ler's rouge
jew|el|lery *Br.* (*Am.*
  jewelry)
jewel-like
jew|el|ly
jew|el|ry *Am.* (*Br.*
  jewellery)
Jew¦ess
  Jew|esses
jew|fish
  plural **jew|fish** *or*
  jew|fishes
Jew|ish
Jew|ish|ly
Jew|ish|ness
Jewry (Jews.
  △ jury)
Jew's ear +s
  (fungus)

jew's harp +s
jez¦ail +s
Jez|ebel +s (*Bible*;
  shameless
  woman)
Jhansi (city, India)
Jhe¦lum (river, S.
  Asia)
Jiang Jie Shi (=
  Chiang Kai-shek)
Jiangsu (province,
  China)
Jiangxi (province,
  China)
jib
  jibs
  jibbed
  jib|bing
  (sail; crane arm;
  to baulk. △ gib)
jibba +s (Muslim's
  coat. △ gibber,
  jibber)
jib¦bah +s (use
  jibba)
jib¦ber +s (person
  who jibs.
  △ gibber, jibba)
jib-boom +s
jibe (taunt; use
  gibe. △ gybe)
  jibes
  jibed
  jib¦ing
jibe *Am.*
  jibes
  jibed
  jib¦ing
  (*Sailing. Br.* gybe.
  △ gibe)
jibe
  jibes
  jibed
  jib¦ing
  (agree. △ gibe,
  gybe)
jib sheet +s
Jib¦uti (use
  Djibouti)
JICTAR (= Joint
  Industry
  Committee for
  Television
  Advertising and
  Research)
Jid¦dah (city, Saudi
  Arabia)
jiff +s
jiffy
  jif|fies
Jiffy bag +s *Propr.*

jig
  jigs
  jigged
  jig|ging
jig¦ger +s +ed +ing
jiggery-pokery
jig|gle
  jig|gles
  jig|gled
  jig|gling
jig|gly
jig|saw +s
jig¦saw puz¦zle +s
jihad +s
Jilin (province,
  China)
Jill (name)
jill +s (use gill)
jill|aroo +s
jill|eroo +s (use
  jillaroo)
Jil|lian *also* **Gil|lian**
jilt +s +ed +ing
Jim
Jim Crow +s
  (*offensive when
  used of a person*)
Jim Crow|ism
**Ji¦mé|nez de
  Cis|neros**
  (Spanish
  inquisitor)
jim-jams
Jimmu (legendary
  Japanese
  emperor)
Jimmy (name)
jimmy
  jim|mies
  jim|mied
  jimmy|ing
  (jemmy)
jim¦my|grant +s
Jimmy Wood|ser
  +s
jim¦son
jim¦son weed +s
Jin (Chinese
  dynasty)
Jina +s *Jainism*
Jinan (city, China)
jin¦gle
  jin¦gles
  jin¦gled
  jin|gling
jin¦gly
  jin|glier
  jin|gli|est
jingo
  jin|goes
jin¦go|ism
jin¦go|ist +s

jin|go|is|tic
jink+s +ed +ing
jink|er+s
jinn
  plural jinn *or* jinns
  (= jinnee. ⚠ gin)
Jin|nah,
  Mu|ham|mad Ali
  (Indian, then
  Pakistani,
  statesman)
jin|nee
  plural jin|nee *or*
  jin|nees
jinx
  jinxes
  jinxed
  jinx|ing
ji|pi|japa+s (plant;
  hat)
jit|ter+s +ed +ing
jit|ter|bug
  jit|ter|bugs
  jit|ter|bugged
  jit|ter|bug|ging
jit|teri|ness
jit|tery
jiu-jitsu (use ju-
  jitsu)
jive
  jives
  jived
  jiv|ing
jiver+s
jizz
Jo *also* Joe
  (man's name)
Jo (woman's name)
jo
  joes
  (sweetheart)
Joa|chim (saint;
  father of the Virgin
  Mary)
Joa|chim, Jo|seph
  (Hungarian
  violinist)
Joa|chim
Joan
Joan, Pope
  (legendary female
  pope)
Jo|anna
Jo|anne
Joan of Arc
  (French saint)
João Pes|soa (city,
  Brazil)
Job *Bible*
job
  jobs

job(*cont.*)
  jobbed
  job|bing
job|ber+s
job|bery
job|bie+s
job|centre+s
job-control
  lan|guage+s
job-hunt+s +ed
  +ing
job|less
job|less|ness
job lot+s
Job's com|fort|er
  +s
job-share+s
job-sharer+s
job-sharing
job|sheet+s
Job's tears
jobs|worth+s
Joburg
  (= Johannesburg)
job|work
Jo|casta *Greek*
  Mythology
Joce|lyn *also*
  Josce|line
Jock+s (name;
  Scotsman)
jock+s (jockey)
jockey+s +ed
  +ing
jockey|dom
jockey|ship
jock|strap+s
joc|ose
joc|ose|ly
joc|ose|ness
joc|os|ity
  joc|os|ities
jocu|lar
jocu|lar|ity
jocu|lar|ly
joc|und
joc|und|ity
joc|und|ly
Jodh|pur (city,
  India)
jodh|purs
  (garment)
Jodie *also* Jody
Jod|rell Bank (site
  of radio telescope,
  England)
Jody *also* Jodie
Joe *also* Jo
  (man's name)
Joe Bloggs
Joe Blow
Joel *Bible*

joey+s
Joffre, Jo|seph
  (French marshal)
jog
  jogs
  jogged
  jog|ging
jog|ger+s
jog|gle
  jog|gles
  jog|gled
  jog|gling
Jog|ja|karta (=
  Yogyakarta)
jog-shuttle
  attributive
jog|trot
  jog|trots
  jog|trot|ted
  jog|trot|ting
Jo|hanna
Jo|han|nes|burg
  (city, South
  Africa)
John *also* Jon
  (name)
John (English and
  Portuguese kings)
John (Apostle and
  saint)
John, Aug|us|tus
  (British painter)
John, Barry
  (Welsh rugby
  player)
John, Don
  (Spanish general)
John, Elton
  (English singer
  and songwriter)
John, Gwen
  (British painter)
john+s (lavatory)
Johna|than *also*
  Jona|than,
  Jona|thon
  (name.
  ⚠ Jonathan)
John Bull (typical
  Englishman)
John Chrys|ostom
  (early saint)
John Doe+s
John Dory
  John Dories
John Hop+s
John Lack|land
  (English king)
Johnny (name)
johnny
  john|nies
  (fellow)

johnny-come-
  lately+s
John of Gaunt
  (son of Edward III
  of England)
John o'Groats
  (village, Scotland)
Johns, Jas|per
  (American artist)
John Sob|ieski
  (Polish king)
John|son, Amy
  (English aviator)
John|son,
  An|drew
  (American
  president)
John|son,
  Cor|ne|lius
  (English-born
  Dutch painter)
John|son, Jack
  (American boxer)
John|son, Lyn|don
  Baines (American
  president)
John|son, Sam|uel
  ('Dr Johnson',
  English writer and
  lexicographer)
John|son|ian
Johor (state,
  Malaysia)
Johor Ba|haru
  (city, Malaysia)
Jo|hore (use
  Johor)
joie de vivre
join+s +ed +ing
join|able
join|der
join|er+s
join|ery
joint+s +ed +ing
joint|ed|ly
joint|ed|ness
joint|er+s
joint|less
joint|ly
joint|ress
  joint|resses
joint-stock
  attributive
join|ture
  join|tures
  join|tured
  join|tur|ing
joist +s +ed +ing
jo|joba +s
joke
  jokes

joke (cont.)
  joked
  jok¦ing
joker +s
joke|smith +s
jokey
  joki¦er
  joki¦est
joki¦ly
joki|ness
jok|ing¦ly
joky (use jokey)
  jok¦ier
  jok¦iest
Jo¦lene
jolie laide
  jolies laides
Jol¦iot, Jean-
  Frédéric (French
  nuclear physicist)
jol¦li¦fi¦ca¦tion +s
jol|lify
  jol¦li|fies
  jol¦li|fied
  jol¦li¦fy|ing
jol|lily
jol¦li|ness
jol|lity
  jol|lities
jollo +s
jolly
  jol|lies
  jol|lied
  jolly|ing
  jol|lier
  jol¦li|est
Jolly Roger +s
Jol¦son, Al
  (American singer
  and actor)
jolt +s +ed +ing
jolty
  jolt|ier
  jolti|est
Jo¦lyon
Jomon
Jon *also* John
Jonah +s (*Bible*;
  bringer of bad
  luck)
Jona|than +s
  (*Bible*; apple)
Jona|than *also*
  Johna|than,
  Jona|thon
  (name)
Jona|thon *also*
  Johna|than,
  Jona|than
  (name)

Jones, Dan¦iel
  (British
  phonetician)
Jones, Inigo
  (English architect)
Jones, John Paul
  (American
  admiral)
Jones, Bobby
  (American golfer)
Joneses, the
Jong, Erica
  (American writer)
jon|gleur +s
Jön|kö¦ping (city,
  Sweden)
jon|quil +s
Jon¦son, Ben
  (English
  dramatist)
Jop|lin, Scott
  (American
  musician)
Joppa (biblical
  name for Jaffa)
Jor|daens, Jacob
  (Flemish painter)
Jor¦dan (country;
  river; name)
Jor¦dan|ian +s
jorum +s
Jor¦vik (Viking
  name for York)
Josce|line *also*
  Joce|lyn
Jo¦seph (*Bible*;
  name)
Jo¦seph (husband
  of the Virgin
  Mary; saint)
Jo¦seph|ine
  (French empress;
  name)
Jo¦seph of
  Ari¦ma|thea
Jo|se¦phus,
  Fla¦vius (Jewish
  historian and
  general)
Josh (name)
josh
  joshes
  joshed
  josh|ing
  (joke; tease)
josh¦er +s
Joshua *Bible*
Joshua tree +s
Jos¦iah
Josie

Jos|quin des Prez
  (Flemish
  composer)
joss
  josses
joss¦er +s
joss stick +s
jos¦tle
  jos¦tles
  jos¦tled
  jost|ling
jot
  jots
  jot¦ted
  jot|ting
jot¦ter +s
Jotun
  (Scandinavian
  mythological
  giant)
Jotun|heim
  (mountain range,
  Norway)
Joule, James
  (English physicist)
joule +s (unit)
Joule–Thomson
  ef¦fect
jounce
  jounces
  jounced
  joun|cing
jour|nal +s
jour¦nal|ese
jour¦nal|ise Br.
  (use journalize)
  jour¦nal|ises
  jour¦nal|ised
  jour¦nal|is¦ing
jour¦nal|ism
jour¦nal|ist +s
jour¦nal|is¦tic
jour¦nal|is¦tic|al¦ly
jour¦nal|ize
  jour¦nal|izes
  jour¦nal|ized
  jour¦nal|iz¦ing
jour|ney +s +ed
  +ing
jour|ney¦er +s
jour|ney|man
  jour¦ney|men
journo +s
joust +s +ed +ing
joust¦er +s
Jove (*Roman
  Mythology*; in 'by
  Jove')
jo¦vial
jovi|al¦ity
jo|vial¦ly

Jo¦vian
jowar
jowl +s
jowly
Joy (name)
joy +s +ed +ing
  (great pleasure;
  rejoice)
Joyce (name)
Joyce, James
  (Irish writer)
Joy|cean
joy¦ful
joy|ful¦ly
joy|ful|ness
joy|less
joy|less¦ly
joy¦ous
joy|ous¦ly
joy|ous|ness
joy|ride
  joy|rides
  joy|rode
  joy|rid¦ing
  joy|rid¦den
joy|rider +s
joy|stick +s
Juan Car¦los
  (Spanish king)
Juan Fer¦nan¦dez
  Is¦lands (off
  Chile)
Juá¦rez, Ben¦ito
  Pablo (Mexican
  president)
Juba (city, Sudan)
Jubba (river, E.
  Africa)
jube +s
ju¦bi|lance
ju¦bi|lant
ju¦bi|lant¦ly
ju¦bi|late
  ju¦bi|lates
  ju¦bi|lated
  ju¦bi|lat¦ing
ju|bi|la¦tion
ju¦bi|lee +s
Ju¦daea Br.
  (ancient region, S.
  Palestine. Am.
  Judea)
Ju|daean Br. +s
  (Am. Judean)
Judaeo-Christian
  Br. (Am. Judeo-
  Christian)
Judah (Hebrew
  patriarch; tribe;
  kingdom)
Ju¦da¦ic

Ju|da|ism
Ju|da|ist +s
Ju|da|iza|tion
Ju|da|ize
  Ju|da|izes
  Ju|da|ized
  Ju|da|iz|ing
Judas
  Ju|dases
  (traitor)
judas
  ju|dases
  (peep-hole)
Judas Is|car|iot
  (Apostle)
Judas
  Mac|ca|baeus
  (Jewish leader)
Judas tree +s
jud|der +s +ed
  +ing
Jude (Apostle and
  saint)
Judea *Am.* (ancient
  region, Palestine.
  Br. Judaea)
Ju|dean *Am.* +s
  (*Br.* Judaean)
Judeo-Christian
  Am. (*Br.* Judaeo-
  Christian)
judge
  judges
  judged
  judg|ing
Judge Ad|vo|cate
  Gen|eral +s
judge|like
judge|mat|ic
judge|mat|ic|al
judge|mat|ic|al|ly
judge|ment +s
judge|men|tal
judge|men|tal|ly
judgement-seat +s
judge|ship +s
judge's mar|shal
  +s
Judges' Rules
judg|ment +s (use
  judgement)
judg|men|tal (use
  judgemental)
judg|men|tal|ly
  (use
  judgementally)
judgment-seat +s
  (use judgement-
  seat)
Judi *also* Judy
ju|di|ca|ture +s
ju|di|cial

ju|di|cial|ly
ju|di|ciary
  ju|di|ciar|ies
ju|di|cious
ju|di|cious|ly
ju|di|cious|ness
Ju|dith (*Apocrypha*;
  name)
judo
judo|ist +s
ju|doka
  plural ju|doka *or*
  ju|dokas
Judy *also* Judi
  (name)
Judy
  Ju|dies
  (*slang* woman)
jug
  jugs
  jugged
  jug|ging
Ju|gend|stil
jug|ful +s
Jug|ger|naut +s
  (institution; idea;
  etc.)
jug|ger|naut +s
  (vehicle)
jug|gins
jug|gle
  jug|gles
  jug|gled
  jug|gling
jug|gler +s
jug|glery
  jug|gler|ies
Jugo|slav +s (use
  Yugoslav)
Jugo|slavia (use
  Yugoslavia)
Jugo|slav|ian +s
  (use Yugoslavian)
jugu|lar +s
jugu|late
  jugu|lates
  jugu|lated
  jugu|lat|ing
Ju|gur|tha
  (Numidian ruler)
juice
  juices
  juiced
  juicing
juice|less
juicer +s
juici|ly
juici|ness
juicy
  juici|er
  juici|est
ju-jitsu

ju-ju +s
ju|jube +s
ju-jutsu (use ju-
  jitsu)
juke|box
  juke|boxes
julep +s
Julia
Ju|lian (Roman
  emperor; name)
Ju|lian (of Julius
  Caesar)
Ju|lian Alps
  (mountain range,
  Italy and Slovenia)
Ju|lian cal|en|dar
Ju|lian of
  Nor|wich
  (English mystic)
Julie
ju|li|enne
  ju|li|ennes
  ju|li|enned
  ju|li|en|ning
Ju|liet
Ju|liet cap +s
Ju|lius
Ju|lius Cae|sar
  (Roman
  statesman)
Jul|lun|dur (city,
  India)
July +s
jum|ble
  jum|bles
  jum|bled
  jum|bling
jum|bly
  jum|blier
  jum|bli|est
jumbo +s
jumbo|ise *Br.* (use
  jumboize)
  jumbo|ises
  jumbo|ised
  jumbo|is|ing
jumbo|ize
  jumbo|izes
  jumbo|ized
  jumbo|iz|ing
jum|buck +s
Jumna (river,
  India)
jump +s +ed +ing
jump|able
jumped-up
  adjective
jump|er +s
jump|ily
jumpi|ness
jump|ing jack +s

jumping-off place
  +s
jumping-off point
  +s
jump jet +s
jump lead +s
jump-off +s *noun*
jump rope +s
jump seat +s
jump-start +s +ed
  +ing
jump|suit +s
jumpy
  jump|ier
  jumpi|est
jun
  plural jun
  (North Korean
  currency)
junco
  jun|cos *or*
  jun|coes
junc|tion +s
junc|ture +s
June +s (name;
  month)
Ju|neau (port,
  USA)
June bug +s
Jung, Carl
  Gus|tav (Swiss
  psychologist)
Jung|frau
  (mountain,
  Switzerland)
Jung|ian +s
jun|gle +s
jun|gled
jun|gly
  jun|glier
  jun|gli|est
jun|ior +s
jun|ior|ate +s
jun|ior|ity
ju|ni|per +s
junk +s +ed +ing
junk bond +s
jun|ker +s
jun|ker|dom
jun|ket +s +ed
  +ing
junk food +s
junkie +s
junk mail
junk shop +s
junk|yard +s
Juno (*Roman
  Mythology*;
  asteroid; D-Day
  beach)
Ju|no|esque
junta +s

Ju¦pi¦ter(*Roman Mythology*; planet)
Jura(mountain range, France and Switzerland; Scottish island)
jural
Jur¦as¦sic
jurat+s
jur¦id¦ic¦al
jur¦id¦ic¦al¦ly
juried
jur¦is¦con¦sult+s
jur¦is¦dic¦tion+s
jur¦is¦dic¦tion¦al
jur¦is¦pru¦dence
jur¦is¦pru¦dent
jur¦is¦pru¦den¦tial
jur¦ist+s
jur¦is¦tic
jur¦is¦tic¦al
juror+s
jury
　jur¦ies
　(in court.
　△ Jewry)
jury box
　jury boxes
jury¦man
　jury¦men
jury-mast+s
jury-rigged
jury¦woman
　jury¦women
Jus¦sieu, An¦toine (French botanist)
jus¦sive
just
just¦ice+s
just¦ice¦ship
jus¦ti¦ciable
jus¦ti¦ciar
jus¦ti¦ciary
　jus¦ti¦ciar¦ies
jus¦ti¦fi¦abil¦ity
jus¦ti¦fi¦able
jus¦ti¦fi¦able¦ness
jus¦ti¦fi¦ably
jus¦ti¦fi¦ca¦tion+s
jus¦ti¦fi¦ca¦tory
jus¦ti¦fier+s
jus¦tify
　jus¦ti¦fies
　jus¦ti¦fied
　jus¦ti¦fy¦ing
Jus¦tin *also*
　Jus¦tine
　(name)
Jus¦tin (early saint)
Jus¦tine *also*
　Jus¦tin

Jus¦tin¦ian (Roman emperor)
just-in-time
　attributive
just¦ly
just¦ness
jut
　juts
　jut¦ted
　jut¦ting
Jute+s (German tribe)
jute+s (fibre)
Jut¦ish
Jut¦land
　(peninsula, NW Europe)
Juv¦enal (Roman satirist)
ju¦ven¦es¦cence
ju¦ven¦es¦cent
ju¦ven¦ile+s
ju¦ven¦ile¦ly
ju¦ven¦ilia
ju¦ven¦il¦ity
juxta¦pose
　juxta¦poses
　juxta¦posed
　juxta¦pos¦ing
juxta¦pos¦ition+s
juxta¦pos¦ition¦al
Jy¦väs¦kylä (city, Finland)

Kk

....

ka+s (spirit. △ car, carr)
Kaaba(in Mecca)
ka¦baddi
Kaba¦lega (national park, Uganda)
Kaba¦lega Falls (in Uganda)
Kabarda-Balkar
Kabardino-Balkaria (republic, Russia)
Kab¦bala (*Judaism*; use Kabbalah)
kab¦bala (mystic interpretation; use cabbala)
Kab¦ba¦lah *Judaism*
Kab¦bal¦ism *Judaism*
kab¦bal¦ism (generally; use cabbalism)
Kab¦bal¦ist +s *Judaism*
kab¦bal¦ist +s (generally; use cabbalist)
Kab¦bal¦is¦tic *Judaism*
kab¦bal¦is¦tic (generally; use cabbalistic)
ka¦buki
Kabul (capital of Afghanistan)
Kabwe (town, Zambia)
Ka¦byle +s
ka¦china +s (dancer; doll)
ka¦dai¦tcha +s (use kurdaitcha)
Kádár, János (Hungarian prime minister)
Kad¦dish (Jewish prayer. △ caddish)
kadi +s (use cadi)
Ka¦di¦köy (Turkish name for Chalcedon)
Kaf¦fir +s (people; language; *offensive* black person. △ Kafir)

kaf¦fi¦yeh +s (use keffiyeh)
Kafir +s (native of Nuristan. △ Kaffir)
Kafka, Franz (Czech-born novelist)
Kaf¦ka¦esque
kaf¦tan +s
Kago¦shima (city, Japan)
kai (food)
Kai¦feng (city, China)
kail +s (use kale)
kail¦yard +s (use kaleyard)
kain¦ite
Kair¦ouan (city, Tunisia)
Kai¦ser, Georg (German dramatist)
kai¦ser +s
kai¦ser¦ship +s
Kai¦sers¦lau¦tern (city, Germany)
kai¦zen
kaka +s
ka¦kapo +s
kake¦mono +s
Ka¦laal¦lit Nu¦naat (Inuit name for Greenland)
kala-azar
Kala¦hari (desert, Africa)
kal¦an¦choe +s
Ka¦lash¦ni¦kov +s
kale +s
kal¦eido¦scope +s
kal¦eido¦scop¦ic
kal¦eido¦scop¦ic¦al
kal¦ends (use calends)
Kale¦vala
kale¦yard +s
Kal¦goor¦lie (town, Australia)
Kali *Hinduism*
kali +s (plant)
Kali¦dasa (Indian poet and dramatist)
Kali¦man¦tan (region, Indonesia)
Ka¦li¦nin, Mikh¦ail Ivan¦ovich (Soviet statesman)
Ka¦li¦nin (former name of Tver)

Ka¦li¦nin¦grad
(port, Russia)
Ka¦lisz (city,
Poland)
Kal¦mar (city,
Sweden)
Kal¦mar Sound
(off Sweden)
kal¦mia +s
Kal¦muck
plural Kal¦muck *or*
Kal¦mucks
Kal¦mykia
(republic, Russia)
Kalmykia-Khalmg
Tangch (official
name of
Kalmykia)
ka¦long +s
kalpa *Hinduism;*
Buddhism
Kal¦uga (city,
Russia)
Kal¦yan (city,
India)
Kama (Hindu god.
⚠ calmer, karma)
Kama Sutra
Kam¦chatka
(peninsula,
Russia)
kame +s (glacial
deposit. ⚠ came)
Ka¦men¦skoe
(former name of
Dniprodzer-
zhinsk)
Kamensk-Uralsky
(city, Russia)
Ka¦mer¦lingh
Onnes, Heike
(Dutch physicist)
Kamet (mountain,
Himalayas)
kami¦kaze +s
Kam¦ila¦roi
plural Kam¦ila¦roi
Kam¦pala (capital
of Uganda)
kam¦pong +s
Kam¦pong Cham
(port, Cambodia)
Kam¦pong Som
(port, Cambodia)
Kam¦pu¦chea
(Khmer name for
Cambodia)
Kam¦pu¦chean +s
kana +s
kan¦aka +s
Kan¦ar¦ese
plural Kan¦ar¦ese

Kan¦awa, Kiri Te
(New Zealand
soprano)
kan¦ban
Kan¦chen¦junga
(mountain,
Himalayas)
Kan¦da¦har (city,
Afghanistan)
Kan¦din¦sky,
Was¦sily (Russian
artist)
Kandy (town, Sri
Lanka)
Kan¦dy¦an +s
kanga +s
Kan¦gar (city,
Malaysia)
kan¦ga¦roo +s
kan¦ga¦roo rat +s
Kang¦chen¦junga
(use
Kanchenjunga)
Ka¦Ngwane
(former homeland,
South Africa)
kanji
Kan¦nada
(language.
⚠ Canada)
Kano (city, Nigeria)
kan¦oon +s
Kan¦pur (city,
India)
Kan¦sas (state,
USA)
Kan¦sas City (two
cities, USA)
Kansu (= Gansu)
Kant, Im¦man¦uel
(German
philosopher)
Kant¦ian +s
Kanto (region,
Japan)
KANU (= Kenya
African National
Union)
Kao¦hsiung (port,
Taiwan)
kao¦lin
kao¦lin¦ic
kao¦lin¦ise *Br.* (use
kaolinize)
kao¦lin¦ises
kao¦lin¦ised
kao¦lin¦is¦ing
kao¦lin¦ite
kao¦lin¦ize
kao¦lin¦izes
kao¦lin¦ized
kao¦lin¦iz¦ing

kaon +s
Kapa¦chira Falls
(in Malawi)
ka¦pell¦meis¦ter
plural
ka¦pell¦meis¦ter
Kap Far¦vel
(Danish name for
Cape Farewell)
Kapil Dev (Indian
cricketer)
kapok
Ka¦poor, Raj
(Indian actor and
film-maker)
Ka¦posi's
sar¦coma
kappa +s
kaput
kara¦bin¦er +s
(in mountaineering.
⚠ carabineer)
Karachai-
Cherkess
Karachai-
Cherkes¦sia
(republic, Russia)
Ka¦ra¦chi (city,
Pakistan)
Kara¦džić, Vuk
Stef¦an¦ović
(Serbian writer
and linguist)
Kara¦futo
(Japanese name
for Sakhalin)
Kara¦ganda
(Russian name for
Qaraghandy)
Kara¦ite +s
Karaj (city, Iran)
Kara¦jan, Her¦bert
von (Austrian
conductor)
Kara¦koram
(mountain range,
Himalayas)
Kara¦korum
(ruined city,
Mongolia)
kara¦kul +s (sheep.
⚠ caracal)
Kara Kum (desert,
central Asia)
Kara¦kumy
(Russian name for
the Kara Kum)
kara¦oke
Kara Sea (part of
Arctic Ocean)

karat *Am.* +s (*Br.*
carat measure of
purity of gold.
⚠ carat, caret,
carrot)
kar¦ate
Kar¦bala (city, Iraq)
Ka¦re¦lia (region,
Russia and
Finland)
Ka¦re¦lian +s
Karen *also* Karin
(name)
Karen +s (people;
language)
Karen State (state,
Burma)
kar¦ezza
Ka¦riba (town,
Zimbabwe)
Ka¦riba, Lake (in
Zimbabwe)
Karin *also* Karen
Karl *also* Carl
Karl-Marx-Stadt
(former name of
Chemnitz)
Kar¦loff, Boris
(English-born
American actor)
Kar¦lovy Vary
(town, Czech
Republic)
Karls¦bad (German
name for Karlovy
Vary)
Karls¦ruhe (port,
Germany)
karma +s (Hindu
and Buddhist
doctrine.
⚠ calmer, Kama)
kar¦mic
Kar¦nak (village,
Egypt. ⚠ Carnac)
Kar¦na¦taka (state,
India)
Karoo (plateau,
South Africa)
Kar¦pov, Ana¦toli
(Russian chess
player)
karri +s (tree.
⚠ carry)
Kar¦roo (use
Karoo)
Kars (city, Turkey)
karst +s (*Geology.*
⚠ cast, caste)
kart +s (motor-
racing vehicle.

kart (*cont.*)
△ cart, carte, khat, quart)
kart|ing
karyo|kin|esis
karyo|type +s
kas|bah +s
Kash|mir (region, Indian subcontinent. △ cashmere)
Kash|miri +s
Kas|parov, Gary (Russian chess player)
Kas|sel (city, Germany)
Kas|site +s
Kasur (city, Pakistan)
ka|ta|bat|ic
ka|tab|ol|ism (use catabolism)
kata|kana +s
Kat|anga (former name of Shaba)
kata|ther|
    mom|eter +s
Kate
Kath *also* Cath
kath|ar|evousa
Kath|ar|ine *also* Cath|ar|ine, Cath|er|ine, Cath|ryn, Kath|er|ine, Kath|ryn
Kath|er|ine *also* Cath|ar|ine, Cath|er|ine, Cath|ryn, Kath|ar|ine, Kath|ryn
Kathia|war (peninsula, India)
Kathie *also* Cathie, Cathy, Kathy
Kath|leen *also* Cath|leen
Kath|mandu (capital of Nepal)
kath|ode +s (use cathode)
Kath|ryn *also* Cath|ar|ine, Cath|er|ine, Cath|ryn, Kath|ar|ine, Kath|er|ine
Kathy *also* Cathie, Cathy, Kathie
Katia *also* Katya

Katie *also* Katy
Kat|mandu (use Kathmandu)
Kato|wice (city, Poland)
Kat|te|gat (channel between Sweden and Denmark)
Katy *also* Katie
Katya *also* Katia
ka|ty|did +s
Kauai (island, Hawaii)
Kauff|mann, An|gel|ica (Swiss artist)
Kau|nas (city, Lithuania)
Ka|unda, Ken|neth (Zambian statesman)
kauri +s (tree. △ cowrie)
kava +s (shrub; drink made from it. △ carver, cava)
Ka|válla (port, Greece)
Kav|eri (= Cauvery)
Kawa|bata, Yasu|nari (Japanese novelist)
kawa|kawa +s
Kawa|saki (city, Japan)
Kaw|thoo|lay (former name of Karen State, Burma)
Kaw|thu|lei (former name of Karen State, Burma)
Kay *also* Kaye (name)
kayak +s +ed +ing
Kaye, Danny (American actor and comedian)
Kaye *also* Kay (name)
kayo
  kayoes
  kayoed
  kayo|ing
  verb
kayo +s *noun*
Kay|seri (city, Turkey)
Kaz|akh
Kaz|akhs *or* Kaz|akhi

Kaz|akh|stan
Kazan (capital of Tatarstan, Russia)
Kazan, Elia (Turkish-born American film and stage director)
kazoo +s
kbyte +s (= kilobyte)
kea +s (bird. △ keyer)
Kean, Ed|mund (English actor. △ Keene)
Keat|ing, Paul (Australian prime minister)
Kea|ton, Bus|ter (American actor and director)
Keats, John (English poet)
Keats|ian +s
kebab +s
Keble, John (English churchman)
Keb|ne|kaise (mountain, Sweden)
keck +s +ed +ing
ked +s
Kedah (state, Malaysia)
kedge
  kedges
  kedged
  kedg|ing
kedg|eree +s
keek +s +ed +ing
keel +s +ed +ing
keel|boat +s
Keeley
keel|haul +s +ed +ing
Keel|ing Is|lands (alternative name for the Cocos Islands)
keel|less
keel|son +s
keen +s +ed +ing +er +est
Keene, Charles Sam|uel (English caricaturist. △ Kean)
keen|ly
keen|ness
keep
  keeps

keep (*cont.*)
  kept
  keep|ing
keep|able
keep|er +s
keep-fit *noun and adjective*
keep|net +s
keep|sake +s
kees|hond +s
kef +s
Ke|fal|linia (Greek name for Cephalonia)
kef|fi|yeh +s
Kef|la|vik (port, Iceland)
keg +s
keis|ter +s
Keith
Kek|ulé, Fried|rich Au|gust (German chemist)
Ke|lan|tan (state, Malaysia)
kelim +s (use kilim)
Kel|ler, Helen Adams (American writer and social reformer)
Kel|logg, Will Keith (American food manufacturer)
Kel|logg Pact
Kells, Book of
Kelly, Gene (American dancer and actor)
Kelly, Grace (American actress)
Kelly, Ned (Australian bushranger)
Kelly, Petra (German political leader)
Kelly
ke|loid +s
kelp +s
kel|pie +s
kel|son +s (use keelson)
kelt (fish. △ Celt, celt)
kel|ter
Kel|vin, Wil|liam Thom|son (Lord

Kel¦vin (*cont.*)
  Kelvin, British
  physicist)
Kel¦vin (name)
kel¦vin +s (unit)
Kemal Pasha
  (alternative name
  of Atatürk)
Kem¦ble, Fanny
  (English actress)
Kem¦ble, John
  Philip, Ste¦phen,
  and Charles
  (English actors)
Kem¦er¦ovo (city,
  Russia)
kemp
Kem¦pis, Thomas
  à (German
  theologian)
kempt
kempy
Ken (name)
ken
  kens
  kenned *or* kent
  ken¦ning +s
  (knowledge;
  know)
Ken¦dal (town,
  England)
Ken¦dall, Ed¦ward
  Cal¦vin
  (American
  biochemist)
kendo
Ken¦eally,
  Thomas
  (Australian
  novelist)
Ken¦elm
Ken¦nedy,
  Ed¦ward
  ('Teddy')
  (American
  Democratic
  politician)
Ken¦nedy, John
  Fitz¦ger¦ald
  (American
  President)
Ken¦nedy, Rob¦ert
  ('Bobby')
  (American
  Democratic
  statesman)
ken¦nel
  ken¦nels
  ken¦nelled *Br.*
  ken¦neled *Am.*
  ken¦nel¦ling *Br.*
  ken¦nel¦ing *Am.*

Ken¦nelly, Ar¦thur
  Edwin (American
  electrical
  engineer)
Ken¦neth (Scottish
  kings; name)
ken¦ning +s
ken¦osis
ken¦ot¦ic
keno¦tron
Ken¦sing¦ton (in
  London)
ken¦speckle
Kent (county,
  England)
Kent, Wil¦liam
  (English architect,
  designer and
  painter)
kent (past tense
  and past participle
  of ken)
Kent¦ish
kent¦ledge
Ken¦tucky (state,
  USA)
Kenya
Kenya, Mount
Ken¦yan +s
Ken¦yatta, Jomo
  (Kenyan
  statesman)
kepi +s
Kep¦ler,
  Jo¦han¦nes
  (German
  astronomer and
  mathematician)
Kep¦ler¦ian
kept
Ker¦ala (state,
  India)
Ker¦al¦ite +s
kera¦tin
kera¦tin¦isa¦tion
  Br. (use
  keratinization)
kera¦tin¦ise *Br.* (use
  keratinize)
  kera¦tin¦ises
  kera¦tin¦ised
  kera¦tin¦is¦ing
kera¦tin¦iza¦tion
kera¦tin¦ize
  kera¦tin¦izes
  kera¦tin¦ized
  kera¦tin¦iz¦ing
kera¦titis
kera¦tose
kera¦tot¦omy
kerb +s (pavement
  edge. △ curb)

kerb-crawler +s
kerb-crawling
kerb¦side
kerb¦stone +s
Kerch (city,
  Ukraine)
ker¦chief +s
ker¦chiefed
kerf +s +ed +ing
ker¦fuf¦fle +s
Ker¦gue¦len
  Is¦lands (in
  Indian Ocean)
Kerk¦rade (town,
  the Netherlands)
Ker¦madec
  Is¦lands (in SW
  Pacific)
ker¦mes
  plural ker¦mes
  (oak)
ker¦mes (insects)
ker¦mis (carnival;
  fair)
Kern, Je¦rome
  (American
  composer)
kern +s +ed +ing
  (Irish soldier;
  Printing)
ker¦nel +s (centre
  of nut. △ colonel)
kero (= kerosene)
kero¦sene
kero¦sine (use
  kerosene)
Ker¦ouac, Jack
  (American
  novelist)
Kerry
  Ker¦ries
  (county, Republic
  of Ireland; cattle;
  name)
Kerry blue +s
ker¦sey +s
ker¦sey¦mere +s
ker¦ygma
  ker¦yg¦mata
ker¦yg¦mat¦ic
Kesey, Ken
  (American
  novelist)
kes¦ki¦dee +s (use
  kiskadee)
Kes¦te¦ven (area in
  Lincolnshire,
  England)
kes¦trel +s
Kes¦wick (town,
  England)
keta¦mine

ketch
  ketches
ketchup +s
keto¦acid¦osis
ke¦tone +s
ke¦ton¦ic
ke¦to¦nuria
ke¦to¦sis
ke¦tot¦ic
Ket¦ter¦ing,
  Charles
  Frank¦lin
  (American
  engineer)
ket¦tle +s
kettle¦drum +s
kettle¦drum¦mer
  +s
kettle¦ful +s
Kevin
Kev¦lar *Propr.*
Kew Gar¦dens (in
  London)
kew¦pie +s
key +s +ed +ing
  (for lock. △ quay)
key¦board +s +ed
  +ing
key¦board¦er +s
key¦board¦ist +s
key¦board play¦er
  +s
keyer +s
  (electronic device.
  △ kea)
key¦hold¦er +s
key¦hole +s
Key Largo (island,
  USA)
key¦less
Keynes, John
  May¦nard
  (English
  economist)
Keynes¦ian +s
Keynes¦ian¦ism
key¦note +s
key¦pad +s
key¦punch
  key¦punches
key¦punch¦er +s
key¦ring +s
Keys, House of
  (Isle of Man)
Key¦stone
  (American film
  company)
key¦stone +s
  (stone; principle)
Key¦stone Kops
key¦stroke +s
key¦way +s

Key West (city, USA)
key|word +s
Kezia also Ke|ziah
Ke|ziah also Kezia
Kha|ba|rovsk (city and territory, Russia)
khad|dar +s
Kha|kas|sia (republic, Russia)
khaki +s
kha|lasi +s
Khal|kís (Greek name for Chalcis)
Khama, Ser|etse (Botswanan statesman)
Kham|bat, Gulf of
kham|sin +s
Khan, Imran (Pakistani cricketer)
Khan, Ja|han|gir (Pakistani squash player)
khan +s (ruler; caravanserai)
khan|ate +s
Kharg Is|land (in Persian Gulf)
Khar|kiv (city, Ukraine)
Khar|kov (Russian name for Kharkiv)
Khar|toum (capital of Sudan)
khat +s (shrub. △ cart, carte, kart, quart)
Khay|litsa (township, South Africa)
Khe|dival
Khe|dive +s
Khe|div|ial
Kher|son (port, Ukraine)
Khi|tai (= Cathay)
Khmer +s
Khmer Rouge
Khoi|khoi
  plural Khoi|khoi
Khoi|san
Kho|meini, Aya|tol|lah (Iranian Shiite Muslim leader)
Khon|su Egyptian Mythology
Khor|ram|shahr (port, Iran)

khoum +s (Mauritanian currency.
△ coomb, cwm)
Khrush|chev, Ni|kita (Soviet statesman)
Khufu (Egyptian name for Cheops)
Khulna (city, Bangladesh)
Khun|jerab Pass (in Himalayas)
khus-khus (aromatic root.
△ couscous, cuscus)
Khy|ber Pass (between Pakistan and Afghanistan)
kiang +s
Ki|angsi (= Jiangxi)
Ki|angsu (= Jiangsu)
kib|ble
kib|bles
kib|bled
kib|bling
kib|butz
kib|butz|im
kib|butz|nik +s
kibe +s
kib|itka +s
kib|itz
kib|itzes
kib|itzed
kib|itz|ing
kib|itz|er +s
kib|lah
ki|bosh
ki|boshes
ki|boshed
ki|bosh|ing
kick +s +ed +ing
kick|able
kick-ass adjective (coarse slang)
kick|back +s
kick|ball +s
kick-boxer +s
kick-boxing
kick-down +s noun
kick|er +s
kick-off +s noun
kick-pleat +s
kick|shaw +s
kick|sort|er +s
kick|stand +s
kick-start +s +ed +ing
kick-turn +s

kid
  kids
  kid|ded
  kid|ding
Kidd, Wil|liam (British pirate)
kid|der +s
Kid|der|min|ster (town, England; carpet)
kid|die +s
kid|ding|ly
kid|dle +s
kiddo +s
kiddy
  kid|dies
kid-glove attributive
kid|nap
  kid|naps
  kid|napped Br.
  kid|naped Am.
  kid|nap|ping Br.
  kid|nap|ing Am.
kid|nap|er Am. +s
kid|nap|ing Am. +s
kid|nap|per Br. +s
kid|nap|ping Br. +s
kid|ney +s
kidney-shaped
kid|ology
kid|skin +s
kid|vid +s
kie|kie +s
Kiel (port, Germany)
Kiel Canal (in Germany)
Kielce (city, Poland)
Kiel|der Water (reservoir, England)
kier +s (vat. △ Kir)
Kieran also Kieron
Kier|ke|gaard, Søren (Danish philosopher)
Kieron also Kieran
kies|el|guhr
Kiev (capital of Ukraine)
kif +s
Ki|gali (capital of Rwanda)
kike +s (offensive)
Ki|kongo
Ki|kuyu
  plural Ki|kuyu or Ki|ku|yus
Kila|uea (volcano, Hawaii)

Kil|dare (county, Republic of Ireland)
kil|der|kin +s
kilim +s
Kili|man|jaro (in Tanzania)
Kil|kenny (town and county, Republic of Ireland; cats)
kill +s +ed +ing
Kil|lar|ney (town and county, Republic of Ireland)
kill|deer +s (bird)
kill|er +s
kil|lick +s
kil|li|fish
  plural kil|li|fish or kil|li|fishes
kill|ing +s
kill|ing bot|tle +s
kill|ing|ly
kill|joy +s
Kil|mar|nock (town, Scotland)
kiln +s +ed +ing
kiln-dry
  kiln-dries
  kiln-dried
  kiln-drying
kilo +s
kilo|base +s
kilo|byte +s
kilo|cal|orie +s
kilo|cycle +s
kilo|gram +s
kilo|gramme Br. +s
kilo|hertz
  plural kilo|hertz
kilo|joule +s
kilo|liter Am. +s
kilo|litre Br. +s
kilo|meter Am. +s
kilo|metre Br. +s
kilo|met|ric
kilo|ton +s
kilo|tonne +s (use kiloton)
kilo|volt +s
kilo|watt +s
kilowatt-hour +s
Kil|roy (mythical person)
kilt +s
kilt|ed
kil|ter +s
kil|tie +s
Kim

Kim¦ber|ley (city, South Africa)
Kim¦ber|ley *also* Kim|berly (name)
kim¦ber|lite
Kim|berly *also* Kim¦ber|ley (name)
Kim Il Sung (Korean statesman)
ki¦mono +s
ki¦mo|noed
kin
kina
plural kina (currency of Papua New Guinea. △ keener)
Kina|balu (mountain, Malaysia)
kin¦aes|the¦sia *Br.* (*Am.* kinesthesia)
kin¦aes|thet¦ic *Br.* (*Am.* kinesthetic)
kin¦aes|thet¦ic|al¦ly *Br.* (*Am.* kinesthetically)
Kin¦car¦dine|shire (former county, Scotland)
Kin¦chin|junga (use Kanchenjunga)
kin¦cob
kind +s +er +est
kinda (= kind of. △ kinder)
kin¦der +s (= kindergarten)
kin¦der|gar¦ten +s
Kin¦der Scout (mountain, England)
kind-hearted
kind-hearted¦ly
kind-hearted¦ness
kin¦dle
kin¦dles
kin¦dled
kind|ling
kind|ler +s
kind|lily
kind¦li|ness
kind|ling +s
kind¦ly
kind|lier
kind|liest
kind|ness
kind|nesses

kin|dred
kine
kin¦emat¦ic
kin¦emat¦ic¦al
kin¦emat¦ic¦al¦ly
kin¦emat¦ics
kin¦emato|graph +s
kin|es¦ics
kin¦esi|ology
kin|esis
kin¦es|the¦sia *Am.* (*Br.* kinaesthesia)
kin¦es|thet¦ic *Am.* (*Br.* kinaesthetic)
kin¦es|thet¦ic|al¦ly *Am.* (*Br.* kinaesthetically)
kin¦et¦ic
kin¦et¦ic|al¦ly
kin¦et¦ics
kin|etin +s
kin|folk
King, B. B. (American blues musician)
King, Bil¦lie Jean (American tennis player)
King, Mar¦tin Lu¦ther (American civil rights leader and churchman)
King, Wil|liam Lyon Mac|ken¦zie (Canadian statesman)
king +s +ed +ing
king|bird +s
king|bolt +s
king cobra +s
king crab +s
king|craft
king|cup +s
king|dom +s
king|domed
king|fish
plural king|fish *or* king|fishes
king|fish¦er +s
king|hood +s
King Kong
king|less
king|let +s
king|like
king¦li|ness
king|ling +s
King Log (in Roman fable)

king¦ly
king|maker +s
king|pin +s
king post +s
Kings Can¦yon Na|tion¦al Park (in USA)
Kings Cross (railway station, London)
king|ship +s
king-size
king-sized
Kings|ley, Charles (English writer)
Kings|ton (capital of Jamaica; port, Canada)
Kingston-upon-Hull (city, Humberside, England)
Kingston-upon-Thames (town, Surrey, England)
King Stork (in Roman fable)
Kings|town (capital of St Vincent)
kinin +s
kink +s
kin¦ka|jou +s
Kinki (region, Japan)
kink|ily
kinki|ness
kinky
kink|ier
kinki|est
kin|less
kino +s
Kin|ross (town, Scotland)
Kinross-shire (former county, Scotland)
Kin|sey, Al¦fred Charles (American zoologist and sex researcher)
kins|folk
Kin|shasa (capital of Zaire)
kin|ship +s
kins|man
kins|men
kins|woman
kins|women

Kin|tyre (peninsula, Scotland)
kiosk +s
kip
kips
kipped
kip|ping (sleep; animal hide)
kip
plural kip *or* kips (Laotian currency)
Kip|ling, Rud|yard (English writer)
kip¦per +s +ed +ing
kip¦sie +s
kipsy (use kipsie)
kip|sies
Kir +s (drink. △ kier) *Propr.*
kirby grip +s
Kirch|ner, Ernst Lud¦wig (German painter)
Kir|ghiz (use Kyrgyz)
Kir|ghizia (alternative name for Kyrgyzstan)
Kir¦giz (use Kyrgyz)
Kir|gizia (use Kirghizia)
Kiri|bati (island group, SW Pacific)
Kirin (= Jilin)
Kiri¦ti|mati (atoll, SW Pacific)
Kirk (name)
kirk +s (church)
Kirk|caldy (town, Scotland)
Kirk¦cud|bright (town, Scotland)
Kirk¦cud|bright|shire (former county, Scotland)
kirk|man
kirk|men
Kirk-session +s
Kir¦kuk (city, Iraq)
Kirk|wall (town, Orkneys)
Kirov (former name of Vyatka; Ballet)
Ki¦rova|bad (former name of Gyandzhe)
kirsch
kirsches
kirsch|was¦ser +s
Kir|sten

Kir|stie *also* Kirsty
kir|tle +s
Kir|una (town,
   Sweden)
Kir|undi (language)
Ki|san|gani (city,
   Zaire)
Kishi|nev (Russian
   name for
   Chişinău)
kis|ka|dee +s
Kis|lev (Jewish
   month)
Kis|lew (use
   Kislev)
kis|met
kiss
   kisses
   kissed
   kiss|ing
kiss|able
kiss and tell
kiss-curl +s
kiss|er +s
Kis|sin|ger, Henry
   (American
   diplomat)
kiss|ing gate +s
kiss-me-quick
   attributive
kiss-off +s *noun*
kiss of life
kisso|gram +s
kissy
kist +s (coffin;
   burial chamber;
   use cist)
Ki|swa|hili
Kit (name)
kit
   kits
   kit|ted
   kit|ting
   (equipment etc.)
Kita|kyu|shu (city,
   Japan)
kit|bag +s
kit-cat +s (portrait)
Kit-Cat Club
   (political club)
kit|chen +s
Kit|chener (city,
   Canada)
Kit|chener,
   Ho|ra|tio
   Her|bert (British
   soldier and
   statesman; bun)
kit|chen|ette +s
kitchen-sink
   attributive
kit|chen|ware

kite
kites
kited
kit|ing
kite-flying
Kite|mark +s
kit-fox
   kit-foxes
kith
kith and kin
kitsch
kitschi|ness
kitschy
   kitsch|ier
   kitschi|est
kit|ten +s +ed
   +ing
kit|ten|ish
kit|ten|ish|ly
kit|ten|ish|ness
kit|ti|wake +s
kit|tle
Kitty (name)
kitty
   kit|ties
   (common fund;
   cat)
kitty-cornered
Kitty Hawk (town,
   USA)
Kitwe (city,
   Zambia)
Kitz|bühel (winter-
   sports resort,
   Austria)
Kitz|inger, Sheila
   (English childbirth
   educator)
Kivu, Lake (in
   central Africa)
Kiwi +s (New
   Zealander)
kiwi +s (bird)
kiwi fruit
   plural kiwi fruit *or*
   kiwi fruits
Kla|gen|furt (city,
   Austria)
Klai|peda (port,
   Lithuania)
Klans|man
Klans|men
   (= Ku Klux
   Klansman.
   ⚠ clansman)
Klap|roth, Mar|tin
   Hein|rich
   (German chemist)
Klaus|en|burg
   (German name for
   Cluj–Napoca)
klaxon +s *Propr.*

Klee, Paul (Swiss
   painter)
Klee|nex
   plural Klee|nex *or*
   Klee|nexes
   Propr.
Klein (bottle.
   ⚠ cline)
Klein, Cal|vin
   (American
   couturier)
Klein, Mel|anie
   (Austrian-born
   psychoanalyst)
Klem|perer, Otto
   (German-born
   conductor and
   composer)
klepht +s (in Greek
   history. ⚠ cleft)
klep|to|mania
klep|to|maniac +s
Klerk, F. W. de
   (South African
   statesman)
Klerks|dorp (city,
   South Africa)
klieg +s
Klimt, Gus|tav
   (Austrian painter)
klip|spring|er +s
Klon|dike (river
   and district,
   Canada)
klong +s
kloof +s
Klos|ters (ski
   resort,
   Switzerland)
kludge +s
klutz
   klutzes
klutzy
   klutz|ier
   klutzi|est
klys|tron +s
K-meson +s
knack +s
knacker +s +ed
   +ing
knack|ery
   knack|er|ies
knag +s (knot in
   wood. ⚠ nag)
knaggy
knag|gier
knag|gi|est
knap
   knaps
   knapped
   knap|ping

knap (*cont.*)
   (break stones.
   ⚠ nap, nappe)
knap|per +s (stone
   breaker. ⚠ nappa,
   napper)
knap|sack +s
knap|weed +s
knar +s
knave +s (rogue.
   ⚠ nave)
knav|ery
   knav|er|ies
knav|ish
knav|ish|ly
knav|ish|ness
kna|wel +s
knead +s +ed +ing
   (work dough.
   ⚠ need)
knead|able
knead|er +s
knee
   knees
   kneed
   knee|ing
knee-bend +s
knee-breeches
knee|cap
   knee|caps
   knee|capped
   knee|cap|ping
knee|cap|ping +s
knee-deep
knee-high
knee|hole +s
knee-jerk +s
knee joint +s
kneel
   kneels
   kneeled *or* knelt
   kneel|ing
knee-length
kneel|er +s
knee-pad +s
knee-pan +s
knees-up +s
knee-trembler +s
knell +s +ed +ing
Knel|ler, God|frey
   (German-born
   painter)
knelt
Knes|set (Israeli
   parliament)
knew (past tense of
   know. ⚠ new, nu)
knicker *attributive*
   (of knickers.
   ⚠ nicker)
Knick|er|bocker
   +s (New Yorker)

Knick¦er¦bocker
  Glory
Knick¦er¦bocker
  Glor¦ies
knick¦er¦bock¦ers
  (breeches)
knick¦ers
knick-knack +s
knick-knackery
knick-knackish
knife
  knives
  noun
knife
  knifes
  knifed
  knif¦ing
  verb
knife blade +s
knife-board +s
knife-edge +s
knife-grinder +s
knife han¦dle +s
knife¦like
knife ma¦chine +s
knife-pleat +s
knife¦point
knifer +s
knife rest +s
knife-throwing
knight +s +ed +ing
  (person. △ night,
  nite)
knight¦age +s
knight¦hood +s
Knight
  Hos¦pit¦al¦ler
  Knights
  Hos¦pit¦al¦lers
knight¦like
knight¦li¦ness
knight¦ly (of a
  knight. △ nightly)
Knights¦bridge
  (district, London)
knight-service
Knight Temp¦lar
  Knights
  Temp¦lars
kni¦pho¦fia +s
knish
  knishes
knit
  knits
  knit¦ted
  knit¦ting
  (make with yarn
  and needles.
  △ nit)
knit¦ter +s
knit¦ting ma¦chine
  +s

knit¦ting nee¦dle
  +s
knit¦wear
knives
knob
  knobs
  knobbed
  knob¦bing
  (rounded
  protuberance etc.
  △ nob)
knob¦bi¦ness
knob¦ble +s (small
  knob. △ nobble)
knob¦bly
knob¦blier
knob¦bli¦est
knobby
knob¦bier
knob¦bi¦est
knob¦ker¦rie +s
knob¦like
knob¦stick +s
knock +s +ed +ing
  (strike, rap.
  △ nock)
knock¦about +s
knock-back +s
  noun
knock-down +s
  noun and adjective
knock¦er +s
knocker-up
  knockers-up
knock¦ing shop +s
knock-kneed
knock knees
knock-off +s
knock-on +s
  adjective and noun
knock¦out +s
knock-up +s *noun*
  and adjective
knoll +s +ed +ing
knop +s
knop¦kierie +s
  (*South African*
  = knobkerrie)
Knos¦sos (ancient
  city, Crete)
knot
  knots
  knot¦ted
  knot¦ting
  (bow, reef knot,
  etc.; unit of speed;
  in timber; tangle;
  tie; bird. △ not)
knot-garden +s
knot¦grass
  knot¦grasses
knot-hole +s

knot¦less
knot¦ter +s
knot¦tily
knot¦ti¦ness
knot¦ting +s
knotty
  knot¦tier
  knot¦ti¦est
knot¦weed +s
knot¦work
knout +s +ed +ing
  (scourge. △ nowt)
know
  knows
  knew
  know¦ing
  known
  (be aware of.
  △ no, Noh)
know¦able
know-all +s
know¦er +s
know-how
  (expertise.
  △ nohow)
know¦ing¦ly
know¦ing¦ness
know-it-all +s
know¦ledg¦abil¦ity
  (use knowledge-
  ability)
know¦ledg¦able
  (use knowledge-
  able)
know¦ledg¦able¦
  ness (use
  knowledgeable-
  ness)
know¦ledg¦ably
  (use
  knowledgeably)
know¦ledge +s
know¦ledge¦
    abil¦ity
know¦ledge¦able
know¦ledge¦able¦
    ness
know¦ledge¦ably
known (past
  participle of
  know. △ none)
know-nothing +s
Knox, John
  (Scottish
  Protestant
  reformer)
Knox, Ron¦ald
  (English
  theologian)
Knox¦ville (city,
  USA)

knuckle
knuckles
knuckled
knuck¦ling
knuckle-bone +s
knuckle¦dust¦er +s
knuckle¦head +s
knuckly
knur +s
knurl +s
knurled
knurr +s (use knur)
Knut (use Cnut)
koa +s
koala +s
koan +s
kob
  plural kob
  (antelope. △ cob)
Kobe (port, Japan)
ko¦bold *Germanic*
  Mythology
Koch, Rob¦ert
  (German
  bacteriologist)
Kö¦chel (number)
KO'd (= knocked
  out)
Ko¦dály, Zol¦tán
  (Hungarian
  composer)
Ko¦diak +s
koel +s
Koest¦ler, Ar¦thur
  (Hungarian-born
  writer)
kofta +s
Ko¦hima (city,
  India)
Koh-i-noor
  (diamond)
Kohl, Hel¦mut
  (German
  statesman)
kohl (powder.
  △ coal, cole)
kohl¦rabi
  kohl¦rabies
koi
  plural koi
Koil (former city,
  India)
koine +s
Ko¦koschka,
  Oskar (Austrian
  artist)
kola +s (use cola)
Kola Pen¦in¦sula
  (Russia)
Kol¦ha¦pur (city,
  India)

kol¦in¦sky
kol¦in¦skies
Kol¦khis (Greek
name for Colchis)
kol¦khoz
plural kol¦khozy
Ko¦lyma (river,
Siberia)
Komi (republic,
Russia)
komi¦tadji +s (use
comitadji)
Ko¦modo (island,
Indonesia;
dragon)
Kom¦pong Cham
(port, Cambodia)
Kom¦pong Som
(port, Cambodia)
Kom¦somol +s
Kom¦so¦molsk
(city, Russia)
Kongo
plural Kongo *or*
Kon¦gos
(people; language.
△ Congo)
Kö¦nig¦grätz
(German name for
Hradec Králové)
Kö¦nigs¦berg
(German name for
Kaliningrad)
Kon-Tiki
Konya (city,
Turkey)
koo¦doo +s (use
kudu)
kook +s
kooka¦burra +s
kook¦ily
kooki¦ness
kooky
kook¦ier
kooki¦est
Koon¦ing, Wil¦lem
de (Dutch-born
American painter)
Kop +s (*Football*.
△ cop)
kop +s (hill. △ cop)
kopek +s (use
copeck)
kopi (gypsum.
△ copy)
kopje +s (use
koppie. △ copy)
kop¦pie +s (small
hill. △ copy)
kor¦adji +s
Koran +s
Kor¦an¦ic
Kor¦but, Olga
(Soviet gymnast)

Korda,
Alex¦an¦der
(Hungarian-born
film producer and
director)
Kor¦do¦fan (region,
Sudan)
Korea
Kor¦ean +s
korf¦ball
korma +s
Kort¦rijk (city,
Belgium)
kor¦una +s
(Bohemian,
Moravian, or
Slovak currency)
Korup (national
park, Cameroon)
Kos (Greek name
for Cos)
Kos¦ciusko,
Thad¦deus
(Polish soldier)
Kos¦ciusko,
Mount (in
Australia)
ko¦sher
Ko¦šice (city,
Slovakia)
Kos¦ovo (province,
Serbia)
Kos¦suth, Lajos
(Hungarian
statesman and
patriot)
Kost¦roma (city,
Russia)
Ko¦sy¦gin, Alex¦sei
(Soviet statesman)
Kota (city, India)
Kota Ba¦haru (city,
Kelantan)
Kota Kina¦balu
(city, Borneo)
Kotka (port,
Finland)
koto +s
kotow +s +ed +ing
Kotze¦bue,
Au¦gust von
(German
dramatist)
kou¦miss
kou¦prey +s
kour¦bash
kour¦bashes
Kou¦rou (town,
French Guiana)
kow¦hai +s

Kow¦loon
(peninsula, Hong
Kong)
kow¦tow +s +ed
+ing
Kra, Isth¦mus of
(in Thailand)
kraal +s
Krafft-Ebing,
Rich¦ard von
(German
physician and
psychologist)
kraft (paper.
△ craft)
Kra¦gu¦jevac (city,
Serbia)
krai +s (Russian
administrative
territory. △ cry)
krait +s
Kraka¦toa
(volcanic island,
Indonesia)
kra¦ken +s
Kra¦ków (Polish
name for Cracow)
krans
kranses
Kras¦no¦dar
(territory, Russia;
its capital)
Kras¦no¦yarsk
(territory, Russia;
its capital)
Kraut +s (*offensive*)
Krebs, Hans Adolf
(German-born
British biochemist;
cycle)
Kre¦feld (town,
Germany)
Kreis¦ler, Fritz
(Austrian-born
violinist and
composer)
Krem¦en¦chuk
(city, Ukraine)
Krem¦lin (Russian
government)
krem¦lin +s
(Russian citadel)
Krem¦lin¦olo¦gist
+s
Krem¦lin¦ology
krieg¦spiel +s
Kriem¦hild
*Germanic
Mythology*
krill
plural krill
krim¦mer +s

Kow¦loon
Kra
kris
krises
Krishna *Hinduism*
Krishna¦ism
Krish¦na¦murti,
Jiddu (Indian
spiritual leader)
Krishna River (in
India)
Krista *also* Christa
Kris¦tall¦nacht
Kris¦ti¦ania (former
name of Oslo)
Kris¦tian¦sand
(port, Norway)
Kri¦voy Rog
(Russian name for
Kryvy Rih)
krom¦esky
krom¦eskies
krona
kro¦nor
(Swedish
currency)
krona
kro¦nur
(Icelandic
currency)
krone
kro¦ner
(Danish or
Norwegian
currency)
Kro¦nos (use
Cronus)
Kron¦stadt
(German name for
Braşov)
Kroo (use Kru)
plural Kroo
kroon +s (Estonian
currency.
△ croon)
Kro¦pot¦kin, Peter
(Russian
anarchist)
Kru
plural Kru
(people; language)
Kru Coast (in
Liberia)
Kru¦ger, Paul
(South African
soldier and
statesman)
Kru¦ger Na¦tion¦al
Park (in South
Africa)
kru¦ger¦rand +s
krumm¦horn +s

Krupp, Al¦fred
(German arms
manufacturer)
kryp¦ton
Kryvy Rih (city,
Ukraine)
Kshat¦riya +s
K/T bound¦ary
K2 (mountain,
Himalayas)
Kuala Lum¦pur
(capital of
Malaysia)
Kuala
Ter¦eng¦ganu
(use Kuala
Trengganu)
Kuala Treng¦ganu
(town, Malaysia)
Kuan¦tan (city,
Malaysia)
Kuan Yin *Chinese
Buddhism*
Kub¦lai Khan
(Mongol emperor)
Ku¦brick, Stan¦ley
(American film
director)
Ku¦ching (city,
Sarawak)
kudos
kudu
   plural kudus *or*
   kudu
kudzu +s
Kufic
Kui¦by¦shev
(former name of
Samara)
Ku Klux Klan
Ku Klux
   Klans¦man
Ku Klux
   Klans¦men
kukri +s
kulak +s
kulan +s
Kul¦tur
Kul¦tur¦kampf
Kum (use Qom)
Kuma¦moto (city,
Japan)
ku¦mara +s
Ku¦masi (city,
Ghana)
Ku¦mayri (Russian
name for Gyumri)
kumis (use
koumiss)
ku¦miss (use
koumiss)
küm¦mel +s

kum¦quat +s
Kun¦dera, Milan
(Czech novelist)
Kung
   plural Kung
kung fu
Kung Fu-tzu
(Chinese name of
Confucius)
Kun¦lun Shan
(mountains,
China)
Kun¦ming (city,
China)
Kuo¦min¦tang
Kuo¦pio (province,
Finland)
kur¦bash (use
kourbash)
kur¦bashes
kur¦cha¦tov¦ium
   Chemistry
Kurd +s
kur¦dai¦tcha +s
Kurd¦ish
Kur¦di¦stan (region,
E. Europe and W.
Asia)
Kure (city, Japan)
Kur¦gan (city,
Russia)
Kuria Muria
Is¦lands (in
Arabian Sea)
Kur¦ile Is¦lands (in
NW Pacific)
Kuro¦sawa, Akira
(Japanese film
director)
kur¦ra¦jong +s
kur¦saal +s
Kursk (city, Russia)
kurta +s
kur¦tha +s (use
kurta)
kur¦tosis
kuru
Kuşa¦dasi (town,
Turkey)
Kuta¦isi (city,
Georgia)
Kutch, Gulf of
(inlet, India)
Kutch, Rann of
(salt marsh, India
and Pakistan)
Ku¦wait
Ku¦wait City
(capital of Kuwait)
Ku¦waiti +s
Kuz¦bass
(alternative name

Kuz¦bass (*cont.*)
for the Kuznets
Basin)
Kuz¦nets Basin
(region, Russia)
kvass
kvetch
   kvetches
   kvetched
   kvetch¦ing
kvetch¦er +s
Kwa
   plural Kwa
KWAC (= keyword
and context)
kwa¦cha +s
Kwa¦Nde¦bele
(former homeland,
South Africa)
Kwang¦chow
(= Guangzhou)
Kwangju (city,
South Korea)
Kwangsi Chuang
(= Guangxi
Zhuang)
Kwang¦tung
(= Guangdong)
kwanza
   plural kwanza *or*
   kwan¦zas
kwashi¦or¦kor
Kwa¦Zulu (former
homeland, South
Africa)
Kwa¦Zulu/Natal
(province, South
Africa)
Kwei¦chow
(= Guizhou)
Kwei¦lin (= Guilin)
Kwei¦yang
(= Guiyang)
Kwesui (former
name of Hohhot)
KWIC (= keyword
in context)
KWOC (= keyword
out of context)
kyan¦ise *Br.* (use
kyanize)
kyan¦ises
kyan¦ised
kyan¦is¦ing
kyan¦ite
kyan¦it¦ic
kyan¦ize *Am.*
kyan¦izes
kyan¦ized
kyan¦iz¦ing

kyat
   plural kyat *or*
   kyats
ky¦bosh (use
kibosh)
Kyd, Thomas
(English
dramatist)
kyle +s
Kylie (name)
kylie +s
(boomerang)
kylin +s
kyloe +s
kymo¦graph +s
kymo¦graph¦ic
Kyoto (city, Japan)
ky¦phosis
ky¦phoses
ky¦phot¦ic
Kyp¦ri¦anou,
Spy¦ros (Cypriot
statesman)
Kyr¦enia (port,
Cyprus)
Kyr¦gyz
   plural Kyr¦gyz
Kyr¦gyz¦stan
(country, central
Asia)
Kyrie +s
Kyu¦shu (island,
Japan)
Kyzyl (city, Russia)
Kyzyl Kum (desert,
central Asia)

Ll

la (*Music*; use lah)
laa¦ger +s +ed
+ing
(encampment.
△ lager)
Laa¦youne (use
La'youn)
lab +s
(= laboratory)
Laban, Ru¦dolf
von (Hungarian
dance
theoretician)
la¦ba¦rum +s
lab¦da¦num
labe¦fac¦tion +s
label
la¦bels
la¦belled *Br.*
la¦beled *Am.*
la¦bel¦ling *Br.*
la¦bel¦ing *Am.*
la¦bel¦ler +s
la¦bel¦lum
la¦bella
labia
la¦bial
la¦bial¦ise *Br.* (use
labialize)
la¦bial¦ises
la¦bial¦ised
la¦bial¦is¦ing
la¦bial¦ism +s
la¦bial¦ize
la¦bial¦izes
la¦bial¦ized
la¦bial¦iz¦ing
la¦bi¦al¦ly
labia ma¦jora
labia mi¦nora
la¦bi¦ate +s
la¦bile
la¦bil¦ity
la¦bio¦den¦tal
la¦bio¦velar
la¦bium
labia
labor *Am.* +s +ed
+ing
la¦bora¦tory
la¦bora¦tor¦ies
la¦bor¦er *Am.* +s
labor-intensive
Am.
la¦bori¦ous
la¦bori¦ous¦ly
la¦bori¦ous¦ness
La¦bor¦ite *Am.* +s

Labor Party *Am.*,
Austral.
Labor Par¦ties
labor-saving *Am.*
la¦bour *Br.* +s +ed
+ing
la¦bour¦er *Br.* +s
labour-intensive
Br.
la¦bour¦ism *Br.*
La¦bour¦ite *Br.* +s
La¦bour Party *Br.*
La¦bour Par¦ties
labour-saving *Br.*
labra
Lab¦ra¦dor +s
(region, Canada,
dog)
lab¦ra¦dor¦ite
lab¦ret +s
lab¦rum
labra
La Bru¦yère, Jean
de (French
moralist)
La¦buan (island,
Malaysia)
la¦bur¦num +s
laby¦rinth +s
laby¦rin¦thian
laby¦rin¦thine
lac +s (resin; insect.
△ lack, lakh)
Lacan, Jacques
(French
psychoanalyst and
philosopher)
La¦can¦ian +s
Lac¦ca¦dive
Is¦lands (now
part of the
Lakshadweep
Islands)
lac¦co¦lith +s
lace
laces
laced
la¦cing
lace-glass
lace-glasses
La Ceiba (port,
Honduras)
lace¦maker +s
lace¦mak¦ing
lace-pillow +s
la¦cer¦able
la¦cer¦ate
la¦cer¦ates
la¦cer¦ated
la¦cer¦at¦ing
la¦cer¦ation +s
la¦cer¦tian +s

la¦cer¦til¦ian +s
la¦cer¦tine
lace-up +s *adjective
and noun*
lace¦wing +s
lace¦wood
lace¦work
lacey (use lacy)
la¦ches
La¦che¦sis *Greek
Mythology*
Lach¦lan (river,
Australia; name)
lach¦ryma Christi
lach¦ry¦mal +s (in
Anatomy, use
lacrimal)
lach¦ry¦ma¦tion (in
Medicine, use
lacrimation)
lach¦ry¦ma¦tor +s
lach¦ry¦ma¦tory
lach¦ry¦ma¦tor¦ies
lach¦ry¦mose
lach¦ry¦mose¦ly
laci¦ly
laci¦ness
la¦cing +s
la¦cini¦ate
la¦cini¦ated
la¦cini¦ation +s
lack +s +ed +ing
(want. △ lac,
lakh)
lacka¦dai¦si¦cal
lacka¦dai¦si¦cal¦ly
lacka¦dai¦si¦cal¦
ness
lacker +s +ed +ing
(use lacquer)
lackey +s
Lack¦land (King
John of England)
lack¦land +s
lack¦lus¦ter *Am.*
lack¦lustre *Br.*
La¦clos, Pierre
Cho¦der¦los de
(French novelist)
La¦co¦nia
(department,
Greece)
La¦co¦nian +s
la¦con¦ic
la¦con¦ic¦al¦ly
la¦coni¦cism +s
lac¦on¦ism
La Co¦ruña (port,
Spain)
lac¦quer +s +ed
+ing
lac¦quer¦er +s

lac¦quer tree +s
lac¦quer¦ware
lac¦quey +s (use
lackey)
lac¦ri¦mal +s
(*Anatomy*;
generally, use
lachrymal)
lac¦ri¦ma¦tion
(*Medicine*;
generally, use
lachrymation)
lac¦ri¦ma¦tor +s
(use lachrymator)
la¦crosse
lac¦ry¦mal +s (use
lachrymal or, in
Anatomy,
lacrimal)
lac¦ry¦ma¦tion (use
lachrymation or,
in *Medicine*,
lacrimation)
lac¦tase +s
lac¦tate
lac¦tates
lac¦tated
lac¦tat¦ing
lac¦ta¦tion
lac¦teal +s
lac¦tes¦cence +s
lac¦tes¦cent
lac¦tic
lac¦tif¦er¦ous
lacto¦ba¦cil¦lus
lacto¦ba¦cilli
lac¦tom¦eter +s
lac¦tone +s
lacto¦pro¦tein +s
lac¦tose
la¦cuna
la¦cu¦nae *or*
la¦cu¦nas
la¦cu¦nal
la¦cu¦nar
la¦cu¦nary
la¦cu¦nose
la¦cus¦trine
lacy
laci¦er
laci¦est
lad +s
La¦dakh (in India)
lada¦num (plant
resin.
△ laudanum)
lad¦der +s +ed
+ing
ladder-back +s
lad¦der stitch
lad¦der stitches
lad¦die +s

lad|dish
lad¦dish|ness
lade
  lades
  laded
  lad¦ing
  (load. △ laid)
la-di-da +s
la¦dies
la¦dies' chain +s
la¦dies' fin|gers
  (okra.
  △ ladyfinger,
  lady's finger)
La¦dies' Gal|lery
  (in the House of
  Commons)
la¦dies' man
  la¦dies' men
la¦dies' night +s
la¦dies' room +s
la¦dify (use ladyfy)
  la¦di|fies
  la¦di|fied
  la¦di¦fy|ing
Ladin
lad¦ing +s
La¦dino +s (dialect;
  person)
la¦dino +s (plant)
La¦dis|laus
  (Hungarian king
  and saint)
ladle
  ladles
  ladled
  lad¦ling
ladle|ful +s
ladler +s
La¦doga, Lake (in
  Russia)
lady
  la¦dies
lady|bird +s
lady|bug +s
Lady chapel +s
Lady Day +s
lady-fern +s
lady|fin¦ger *Am.*
  (cake. △ ladies'
  fingers, lady's
  finger)
lady¦fy
  lady|fies
  lady|fied
  lady¦fy|ing
lady|hood
lady-in-waiting
  ladies-in-waiting
lady|kill¦er +s
lady|like
lady-love +s

lady's bed|straw
lady's
  com|pan¦ion +s
lady's fin¦ger +s
  (vetch. △ ladies'
  fingers,
  ladyfinger)
lady|ship +s
lady's maid +s
lady's man (use
  ladies' man)
lady's man¦tle +s
Lady|smith (town,
  Natal)
lady-smock +s
  (use lady's
  smock)
lady's slip|per +s
lady's smock +s
lady's tresses
Lae (port, Papua
  New Guinea)
Lae|ti¦tia *also*
  Le|ti¦tia
laevo|dopa
laevo|rota¦tory
laevo|tar¦tar¦ic
lae¦vu|lose
La|fay¦ette,
  Mar|quis de
  (French soldier
  and statesman)
La Fon|taine, Jean
  de (French poet)
lag
  lags
  lagged
  lag|ging
lagan +s
lager +s (beer.
  △ laager)
La|ger|kvist, Pär
  (Swedish novelist
  and dramatist)
La|ger|löf, Selma
  (Swedish writer)
lager lout +s
la¦ger|phone +s
lag|gard +s
lag|gard¦ly
lag|gard|ness
lag¦ger +s
lag|ging +s
lago|morph +s
la¦goon +s
la¦goon¦al
Lagos (city,
  Nigeria)
La|grange,
  Jo¦seph Louis,
  Comte de

La|grange (*cont.*)
  (French
  mathematician)
La|gran|gian point
  +s
lah *Music*
lahar +s
La¦hore (city,
  Pakistan)
laic +s
la¦ical
la¦ic|al¦ly
lai|cisa|tion *Br.*
  (use laicization)
lai|cise *Br.* (use
  laicize)
  lai|cises
  lai|cised
  lai|cis¦ing
lai|city
lai|ciza|tion
lai|cize
  lai|cizes
  lai|cized
  lai|ciz¦ing
laid (past tense and
  past participle of
  lay; paper.
  △ lade)
laid-back
lain (past participle
  of lie. △ lane)
Laing, R. D.
  (Scottish
  psychoanalyst)
lair +s +ed +ing
  (animal's den.
  △ layer)
lair|age +s
laird +s
laird|ship +s
lairy
laissez-aller
laissez-faire
laissez-passer
laity
la|ities
Laius *Greek*
  Mythology
lake +s
Lake Dis|trict (in
  England)
lake-dweller +s
lake-dwelling +s
Lake|land (= Lake
  District etc.)
lake|less
lake|let +s
lake|side +s
lakh +s (hundred
  thousand. △ lac,
  lack)

La|ko|nia (use
  Laconia)
Lak|shad|weep
Is¦lands (in India)
Lak¦shmi *Hinduism*
La¦lage
Lal¦lan
Lal|lans
Lalla Rookh
lal|la¦tion
lally|gag
  lally|gags
  lally|gagged
  lally|gag|ging
Lalo, Édouard
  (French
  composer)
La Lou|vière (city,
  Belgium)
lam
  lams
  lammed
  lam|ming
  (thrust. △ lamb)
lama +s (monk.
  △ llama)
Lama|ism
Lama|ist
La|marck, Jean
  Bap|tiste de
  (French botanist
  and zoologist)
La|marck|ian +s
La|marck|ism
La|mar|tine,
  Al|phonse de
  (French poet)
la|ma|sery
  la|ma|ser¦ies
Lamb, Charles
  (English essayist
  and critic)
lamb +s +ed +ing
  (young sheep.
  △ lam)
lam|bada +s
lam|bast +s +ed
  +ing
  (use lambaste)
lam|baste
  lam|bastes
  lam|basted
  lam|bast¦ing
lambda +s
lam|bency
lam|bent
lam|bent¦ly
lamb|er +s
Lam|bert,
  Con|stant
  (English
  composer)

lam|bert +s
Lam|beth
(borough,
London)
Lam|beth Pal|ace
lamb|hood
lamb|kin +s
lamb|like
lam|bre|quin +s
lamb's ears (plant)
lamb|skin +s
lamb's let|tuce
lamb's-tails
lambs|wool +s
lame
  lames
  lamed
  lam|ing
  lamer
  lam|est
lamê
lame|brain +s
la|mella
  la|mel|lae
la|mel|lar
la|mel|late
la|mel|li|branch +s
la|mel|li|corn +s
la|mel|li|form
la|mel|lose
lame|ly
lame|ness
lam|ent +s +ed
  +ing
lam|ent|able
lam|ent|ably
lam|en|ta|tion +s
Lam|en|ta|tions
  Bible
lam|ent|er +s
lam|ent|ing|ly
lam|ina
  lam|inae
lam|inar
lamin|ate
  lamin|ates
  lamin|ated
  lamin|at|ing
lamin|ation +s
lamin|ator +s
lam|ing|ton +s
lamin|itis
lamin|ose
lam|ish
Lam|mas
lam|mer|geier +s
lam|mer|geyer +s
  (use
  lammergeier)
lamp +s +ed +ing

lamp|black
lamp-chimney +s
lam|pern +s
lamp hold|er +s
lamp|less
lamp|light
lamp|light|er +s
lamp|lit
lam|poon +s +ed
  +ing
lam|poon|er +s
lam|poon|ery
lam|poon|ist +s
lamp-post +s
lam|prey +s
lamp|shade +s
LAN (= local area
  network)
Lana
Lan|ark|shire
  (former county,
  Scotland)
Lan|ca|shire
Lan|cas|ter (city,
  England)
Lan|cas|trian +s
Lance (name)
lance
  lances
  lanced
  lan|cing
  (weapon; pipe;
  pierce; cut open.
  ⚠ launce)
lance
  bom|bard|ier +s
lance cor|poral +s
lance-jack +s
lance|let +s
Lance|lot
  (Arthurian knight;
  name)
lan|ceo|late
lan|cer +s
lance-sergeant +s
lance-snake +s
lan|cet +s
lan|cet|ed
lance|wood +s
Lan|chow
  (= Lanzhou)
lan|cin|ate
  lan|cin|ates
  lan|cin|ated
  lan|cin|at|ing
Lancs.
  (= Lancashire)
land +s +ed +ing
  (solid part of
  earth; come to
  shore etc.)

Land
Län|der
  (province)
land agency
  land agen|cies
land agent +s
Lan|dau, Lev
  (Russian physicist)
lan|dau +s
  (carriage)
lan|dau|let +s
land bank +s
land-based
land bridge +s
land crab +s
land|er +s (person
  or thing that
  lands)
Län|der (plural of
  Land)
Landes
  (department,
  France)
land|fall +s
land|fill +s
land force +s
land|form +s
land girl +s
land-grabber +s
land|grave +s *male*
land|gravi|ate +s
land|gra|vine +s
  female
land|hold|er +s
land|hold|ing +s
land|ing +s
land|ing craft
  plural land|ing
  craft
land|ing gear +s
land|ing net +s
land|ing place +s
land|ing stage +s
land|ing strip +s
land|lady
  land|ladies
land-law +s
länd|ler +s
land|less
land|line +s
land|locked
land|loper +s
land|lord +s
land|lub|ber +s
land|mark +s
land mass
  land masses
land|mine +s
land|oc|ra|cy
  land|oc|ra|cies
lando|crat +s

land-office
  busi|ness
Lan|dor, Wal|ter
  Sav|age (English
  writer)
land|owner +s
land|owner|ship
land|owning
land|rail +s
Land|sat
land|scape
  land|scapes
  land|scaped
  land|scap|ing
land|scape
  gar|den|er +s
land|scape
  gar|den|ing
landscape-marble
land|scape
  paint|er +s
land|scap|ist +s
Land|seer, Edwin
  (English painter)
Land's End (in
  England)
Lands|hut (city,
  Germany)
land|side
land|slide +s
land|slip +s
Lands|mål
lands|man
  lands|men
Land|steiner, Karl
  (Austrian
  physician)
land tax
  land taxes
land-tie +s
land|ward
land|wards
land-wind +s
lane +s (track etc.
  ⚠ lain)
Lang, Fritz
  (Austrian-born
  film director)
Lang|land,
  Wil|liam (English
  poet)
lang|lauf
lang|lauf|er +s
Lang|ley, Sam|uel
  Pier|point
  (American
  astronomer and
  aviation pioneer)
Lang|muir, Ir|ving
  (American
  chemist)

Lango
  plural Lango
lan|gouste +s
lan|gous|tine +s
lang syne
Lang|ton,
  Ste|phen (English
  churchman)
Lang|try, Lil|lie
  (British actress)
lan|guage +s
langue
langue de chat
  langues de chat
Langue|doc
  (former province,
  France)
langue d'oc
Languedoc-
  Roussil|lon
  (region, France)
langue d'oïl
lan|guid
lan|guid|ly
lan|guid|ness
lan|guish
  lan|guishes
  lan|guished
  lan|guish|ing
lan|guish|er +s
lan|guish|ing|ly
lan|guish|ment
lan|guor (idleness.
  △ langur)
lan|guor|ous
lan|guor|ous|ly
lan|gur +s
  (monkey.
  △ languor)
lani|ary
  lani|ar|ies
lan|ifer|ous
lan|iger|ous
lank
lank|ily
lanki|ness
lank|ly
lank|ness
lanky
  lank|ier
  lank|iest
lan|ner +s
lan|neret +s
lano|lin
Lan|sing (city,
  USA)
lans|que|net +s
lan|tana +s
Lan|tau (island,
  Hong Kong)
lan|tern +s

lantern-fish
  plural lantern-fish
  or lantern-fishes
lantern-fly
  lantern-flies
lantern-jawed
lan|tern jaws
lan|tern slide +s
lantern-wheel +s
lan|tha|nide +s
lan|tha|num
la|nugo
lan|yard +s
Lan|zar|ote (one of
  the Canary
  Islands)
Lan|zhou (city,
  China)
Laoc|oon *Greek*
  Mythology
Lao|di|cean +s
Laoighis (use
  Laois)
Laois (county,
  Republic of
  Ireland)
Laos (in SE Asia)
Lao|tian +s
Lao-tzu (legendary
  founder of
  Taoism)
Laoze (use Lao-
  tzu)
lap
  laps
  lapped
  lap|ping
La Palma (one of
  the Canary
  Islands. △ Las
  Palmas, Palma)
lap|aro|scope +s
lap|aros|copy
  lapar|os|cop|ies
lapar|ot|omy
  lapar|oto|mies
La Paz (capital of
  Bolivia)
lap|dog +s
lapel +s
la|pelled
lap|ful +s
lapi|cide +s
lapi|dary
  lapi|dar|ies
lapi|date
  lapi|dat|ing
lapi|da|tion
la|pilli
lapis laz|uli
La|pita

Lap|ith +s *Greek*
  Mythology
lap joint +s
La|place, Mar|quis
  de (French
  mathematician
  and physicist)
Lap|land (region,
  N. Europe)
Lap|land|er +s
Lapp +s
lap|pet +s
lap|pet|ed
Lapp|ish
lap|sang
  sou|chong
lapse
  lapses
  lapsed
  laps|ing
lapser +s
lap|stone +s
lap-strake +s
lap|sus ca|lami
lap|sus lin|guae
Lap|tev Sea (part
  of Arctic Ocean)
lap|top +s
La|pu|tan +s
lap-weld +s +ed
  +ing
lap|wing +s
Lara (first name)
Lara, Brian (West
  Indian cricketer)
Lara|mie (city,
  USA)
lar|board +s
lar|cen|er +s
lar|cen|ist +s
lar|cen|ous
lar|ceny
  lar|cenies
larch
  larches
larch-lap
larch|wood +s
lard +s +ed +ing
lar|der +s
larding-needle +s
larding-pin +s
lar|don +s
lar|doon +s
lardy
lardy-cake +s
lardy-dardy
lares
large
  larger
  larg|est
large|ly
large-minded

lar|gen +s +ed
  +ing
large|ness
large-scale
lar|gess (use
  largesse)
lar|gesse
lar|ghet|to +s
lar|gish
largo +s
lari
  plural lari *or* laris
lar|iat +s
La|ris|sa (city,
  Greece)
lark +s +ed +ing
Lar|kin, Philip
  (English poet and
  novelist)
lar|ki|ness
lark|spur +s
larky
larn +s +ed +ing
La
  Roche|fou|cauld,
  Fran|çois de
  Mar|sil|lac, Duc
  de (French
  moralist)
La Ro|chelle (port,
  France)
La|rousse, Pierre
  (French
  lexicographer and
  encyclopedist)
lar|ri|kin +s
lar|rup +s +ed
  +ing
Larry
larva
  lar|vae
  (form of insect.
  △ lava)
lar|val
lar|vi|cide +s
la|ryn|geal
la|ryn|ges
la|ryn|gic
laryn|git|ic
laryn|gi|tis
laryn|gol|ogy
la|ryn|go|scope +s
laryn|got|omy
  laryn|goto|mies
lar|ynx
  la|ryn|ges
la|sagne +s
La Salle, Rob|ert
  Ca|va|lier
  (French explorer)
La Scala (opera
  house, Italy)

Las¦car +s
Las¦caux (in
  France)
  Archaeology
las¦civi¦ous
las¦civi¦ous¦ly
las¦civi¦ous¦ness
lase
  lases
  lased
  las¦ing
laser +s
laser|disc +s
Laser|Vision *Propr.*
lash
  lashes
  lashed
  lash|ing
lash¦er +s
lash|ing +s
lash|ing¦ly
lash|kar +s
lash|less
lash-up +s *adjective
  and noun*
Las Pal¦mas
  (capital of the
  Canary Islands.
  △ La Palma)
La Spe¦zia (port,
  Italy)
lass
  lasses
Lassa fever
las¦sie +s
las¦si¦tude
lasso
  las¦sos *or* las¦soes
  noun
lasso
  las¦soes
  las¦soed
  lasso|ing
  verb
las¦so¦er +s
Las¦sus, Or¦lande
  de (Flemish
  composer)
last +s +ed +ing
last-ditch *attributive*
last|ing¦ly
last|ing|ness
last¦ly
last-minute
  adjective
Las Vegas (city,
  USA)
lat. (= latitude)
La¦ta¦kia (port,
  Syria)
latch
  latches

latch (*cont.*)
  latched
  latch|ing
latchet +s
latch|key +s
late
  later
  lat¦est
late|comer +s
la¦teen +s
late|ish (use latish)
late la|ment¦ed
late¦ly
laten +s +ed +ing
la¦tency
  la¦ten|cies
La Tène
late|ness
la¦tent
la¦tent¦ly
lat|eral +s
lat|eral¦ly
Lat|eran (in Rome;
  Council; Palace;
  Treaty)
lat¦ere (in 'legate a
  latere')
lat|er¦ite +s
lat|er¦it¦ic
latex
  la¦texes *or*
  la¦ti|ces
lath +s +ed +ing
  (thin strip)
lathe +s (machine)
la¦ther +s +ed
  +ing
la¦thery
lathi +s
lathy
la¦ti|ces
la¦ti|fun¦dium
  la¦ti|fun¦dia
Lati|mer, Hugh
  (English martyr)
Latin +s
La¦tina +s
Lat¦in|ate
Lat|in|isa¦tion *Br.*
  (use Latinization)
Lat|in|ise *Br.* (use
  Latinize)
  Lat¦in|ises
  Lat¦in|ised
  Lat¦in|is¦ing
Lat|in|iser *Br.* +s
  (use Latinizer)
Lat|in|ism +s
Lat|in|ist +s
Lat|in|iza¦tion
Lat|in|ize
  Lat¦in|izes

Lat¦in|ize (*cont.*)
  Lat¦in|ized
  Lat¦in|iz¦ing
Lat¦in|izer +s
La¦tino +s
lat¦ish
lati|tude +s
lati|tu¦din¦al
lati|tu¦din¦al¦ly
lati|tu¦din|ar¦ian
  +s
lati|tu¦din|ar¦ian|
                ism
La¦tium (ancient
  region, Italy)
La¦tona *Roman
  Mythology*
la¦tria +s
la¦trine +s
lat¦ten +s
lat¦ter
latter-day
Latter-day Saints
lat|ter¦ly
lat|tice +s
lat|ticed
lattice-work
lat|ticing
Lat¦via
Lat|vian +s
Laud, Wil|liam
  (English
  churchman)
laud +s +ed +ing
  (praise. △ lord)
Lauda, Niki
  (Austrian motor-
  racing driver)
laud|abil¦ity
laud|able
laud|ably
laud|anum (drug.
  △ ladanum)
laud|ation +s
laud|ative
laud|atory
lauds (prayers.
  △ lords)
laugh +s +ed +ing
laugh|able
laugh|ably
laugh¦er +s
laugh|ing gas
laugh|ing¦ly
laugh|ing stock +s
laugh|ter
Laugh|ton,
  Charles (English-
  born American
  actor)
launce +s (fish.
  △ lance)

Launce|lot
  (Arthurian knight;
  use Lancelot)
Laun¦ces|ton (city,
  Tasmania; town,
  Cornwall)
launch
  launches
  launched
  launch|ing
launch¦er +s
launch pad +s
laun|der +s +ed
  +ing
laun|der¦er +s
laun|der|ette +s
laun|dress
  laun|dresses
laun|drette +s (use
  launderette)
laun|dro|mat +s
laun¦dry
  laun|dries
laun¦dry|man
  laun¦dry|men
Laura
Laur|asia (ancient
  continent)
laure|ate +s
laure¦ate|ship +s
Laurel (name)
laurel
  laurels
  laur|elled *Br.*
  laur|eled *Am.*
  laurel|ling *Br.*
  laurel|ing *Am.*
  (plant)
Laurel and Hardy
  in full Stan Laurel
  and Oli¦ver Hardy
  (American
  comedians)
Lau¦ren
Laur|ence *also*
  Law|rence
Laur¦en|tian
  Plat|eau (in
  Canada)
Lau¦rie
Laur|ier, Wil|frid
  (Canadian prime
  minister)
lau¦rus|ti¦nus
  lau¦rus|ti¦nuses
Lau|sanne (town,
  Switzerland)
LAUTRO (= Life
  Assurance and
  Unit Trust
  Regulatory
  Organization)

lav (= lavatory)
lava +s (volcanic material. △larva, laver)
la|vabo +s
lav|age
lav|ation
lava|tor|ial
lav|atory
lav|ator|ies
lave
　laves
　laved
　lav|ing
Lav|en|der (name)
lav|en|der +s (plant)
lavender-water +s
Laver, Rod (Australian tennis player)
laver +s (seaweed; bread; washing-vessel. △lava, larva)
lav|er|ock +s
Lav|in|ia
lav|ish
　lav|ishes
　lav|ished
　lav|ish|ing
lav|ish|ly
lav|ish|ness
La|vois|ier, An|toine Laur|ent (French scientist)
lavvy
　lav|vies (= lavatory)
Law, Bonar (Canadian-born British prime minister)
law +s (rule. △lore)
law-abiding
law-abiding|ness
law|break|er +s
law|break|ing
law court +s
law|ful
law|ful|ly
law|ful|ness
law|giv|er +s
lawks
law|less
law|less|ly
law|less|ness
law|maker +s
law-making

law|man
　law|men
lawn +s +ed +ing (grass. △lorn)
lawn|mow|er +s
lawn ten|nis
lawny
Law|rence also Laur|ence
Law|rence (Roman saint)
Law|rence, D. H. (English writer and painter)
Law|rence, Er|nest Or|lando (American physicist)
Law|rence, Thomas (English painter)
Law|rence, T. E. (English soldier and writer)
law|ren|cium
law|suit +s
law term +s
law|yer +s
law|yer|ly
lax +er +est
laxa|tive +s
lax|ity
　lax|ities
laxly
lax|ness
lay
　lays
　laid
　lay|ing (place; produce egg; not ordained; not professional; poem; song; past tense of lie. △lei, ley)
lay|about +s
Laya|mon (English poet and priest)
lay-by +s noun
layer +s (person or thing that lays. △lair)
layer +s +ed +ing (thickness; arrange in layers. △lair)
layer-out
　layers-out
lay|ette +s
laying-out noun and adjective

lay|man
　lay|men
lay-off +s noun
La'youn (capital of Western Sahara)
lay|out +s
lay|over +s
lay|per|son +s
lay|shaft +s
lay|stall +s
lay|woman
　lay|women
lazar +s
laza|ret +s
laza|retto +s
Laz|ar|ist +s
laze
　lazes
　lazed
　laz|ing
lazi|ly
lazi|ness
Lazio (region, Italy)
laz|uli
lazy
　lazi|er
　lazi|est
lazy|bones
　plural lazy|bones
l-dopa (= levodopa)
L-driver +s
lea (meadow. △lee, ley)
Leach, Ber|nard (British potter)
leach
　leaches
　leached
　leach|ing (percolate. △leech)
leach|er +s
Lea|cock, Ste|phen (Canadian humorist and economist)
lead +s +ed +ing (metal. △led)
lead
　leads
　led
　lead|ing (guide. △lied, lead = metal)
lead|able
lead|en
lead|en|ly
lead|en|ness
lead|er +s
lead|er board +s

lead|er|ene +s
lead|er|less
lead|er|ship +s
lead-free
lead-in +s noun
lead|ing +s
leading-rein +s
lead|less
lead-off +s noun
lead poi|son|ing
lead time +s
lead|work
lead|wort +s
leaf
　leaves (on tree; paper; etc. △lief)
leaf +s +ed +ing verb
leaf|age
leaf-beetle +s
leaf|cut|ter +s
leaf green +s noun and adjective
leaf-green attributive
leaf|hop|per +s
leafi|ness
leaf|less
leaf|less|ness
leaf|let +s +ed +ing
leaf|like
leaf miner +s
leaf mon|key +s
leaf mould +s
leaf-stalk +s
leafy
　leaf|ier
　leafi|est
league
　leagues
　leagued
　lea|guing
lea|guer +s
Leah
leak +s +ed +ing (escape of liquid etc. △leek)
leak|age +s
leak|er +s
Lea|key, Louis (British archaeologist and anthropologist)
leaki|ness
leak|proof
leaky
　leak|ier
　leaki|est
leal

Leam¦ing¦ton Spa
  official name **Royal**
  Leam¦ing¦ton Spa
  (town, England)
Lean, David
  (English film
  director)
lean
  leans
  leaned *or* leant
  lean¦ing
lean-burn
Le¦an¦der *Greek*
  Mythology
lean¦ing +s
lean¦ly
Le¦anne
lean¦ness
leant (past tense
  and past participle
  of lean. ⚠ lent)
lean-to +s
leap
  leaps
  leaped *or* leapt
  leap¦ing
leap¦er +s
leap¦frog
  leap¦frogs
  leap¦frogged
  leap¦frog¦ging
leap year +s
Lear, Ed¦ward
  (English artist and
  poet)
Lear
  (Shakespearean
  character)
learn
  learns
  learned *or* learnt
  learn¦ing
learn¦abil¦ity
learn¦able
learn¦ed
  (knowledgeable)
learn¦ed¦ly
learn¦ed¦ness
learn¦er +s
leas¦able
lease
  leases
  leased
  leas¦ing
lease¦back +s
lease¦hold +s
lease¦hold¦er +s
Lease-Lend
leas¦er +s
leash
  leashes

leash (*cont.*)
  leashed
  leash¦ing
least
least¦ways
least¦wise
leat +s
  (watercourse.
  ⚠ leet, lied)
lea¦ther +s +ed
  +ing
lea¦ther¦back +s
leather-bound
lea¦ther¦cloth +s
lea¦ther¦ette
lea¦theri¦ness
lea¦ther¦jacket +s
lea¦thern
lea¦ther¦neck +s
lea¦ther¦oid
lea¦ther¦wear
lea¦thery
leave
  leaves
  left
  leav¦ing
leaved
leaven +s +ed
  +ing
leav¦er +s
leave-taking +s
leav¦ings
Lea¦vis, F. R.
  (English literary
  critic)
Leba¦nese
  plural Leba¦nese
Leba¦non
Leba¦non
  Moun¦tains
Le¦bens¦raum
Le¦blanc, Nico¦las
  (French surgeon
  and chemist)
Le¦bowa (former
  homeland, South
  Africa)
Le¦brun, Charles
  (French painter,
  designer, and
  decorator)
Le Carré, John
  (English novelist)
lech
  leches
  leched
  lech¦ing
lech¦er +s
lech¦er¦ous
lech¦er¦ous¦ly
lech¦er¦ous¦ness
lech¦ery

leci¦thin
Le¦clan¦ché,
  Georges (French
  chemist; cell)
Le¦conte de Lisle
  Charles-Marie-
  René (French
  poet)
Le Cor¦bu¦sier
  (French architect)
lec¦tern +s
lec¦tin +s
lec¦tion +s
lec¦tion¦ary
  lec¦tion¦ar¦ies
lec¦tor +s (in
  'lecturer' sense,
  male)
lec¦trice +s *female*
lec¦ture
  lec¦tures
  lec¦tured
  lec¦tur¦ing
lec¦tur¦er +s
lec¦tur¦er¦ship +s
lec¦ture¦ship +s
lecy¦thus
lecy¦thi
led (past tense and
  past participle of
  lead = guide.
  ⚠ lead = metal)
Leda *Greek*
  Mythology
leder¦hosen
ledge +s
ledged
ledger +s
ledger line +s (use
  leger line)
ledger-tackle
ledgy
Led Zep¦pe¦lin
  (British rock
  group)
Lee (name)
Lee, Bruce
  (American actor)
Lee, Gypsy Rose
  (American
  striptease artist)
Lee, Rob¦ert
  Ed¦ward
  (American soldier)
lee (shelter. ⚠ lea,
  ley)
lee-board +s
leech
  leeches
  (worm; healer; on
  sail. ⚠ leach)
leech¦craft

Leeds (city,
  England)
leek +s (vegetable.
  ⚠ leak)
leer +s +ed +ing
  (look slyly. ⚠ lehr)
leeri¦ness
leer¦ing¦ly
leery
  leer¦ier
  leeri¦est
lees
lee shore +s
lee side +s
leet +s (court.
  ⚠ leat, lied)
Leeu¦war¦den
  (town, the
  Netherlands)
Leeu¦wen¦hoek,
  An¦toni van
  (Dutch naturalist)
lee¦ward +s
Lee¦ward Is¦lands
  (in the Caribbean)
lee¦ward¦ly
lee¦way
Le Fanu, Jo¦seph
  Sheri¦dan (Irish
  novelist)
Left *Politics*
left +s (opposite of
  'right'; past tense
  and past participle
  of leave)
left-back +s
Left Bank (district,
  Paris)
left bank +s
left-footed
left hand +s
left-hand *attributive*
left-handed
left-handed¦ly
left-handed¦ness
left-hander +s
leftie +s (use lefty)
left¦ish
left¦ism
left¦ist +s
left lug¦gage
left¦most
left¦over +s
left¦ward
left¦wards
left wing +s *noun*
left-wing *adjective*
left-winger +s
lefty
  left¦ies
leg
  legs

leg (*cont.*)
  legged
  leg|ging
leg|acy
  leg|acies
legacy-hunter +s
legal
legal aid
le|gal|ese
le|gal|isa|tion *Br.*
  (use legalization)
le|gal|ise *Br.* (use
  legalize)
  le|gal|ises
  le|gal|ised
  le|gal|is|ing
le|gal|ism +s
le|gal|ist +s
le|gal|is|tic
le|gal|is|tic|al|ly
le|gal|ity
  le|gal|ities
le|gal|iza|tion
le|gal|ize
  le|gal|izes
  le|gal|ized
  le|gal|iz|ing
le|gal|ly
leg|ate +s
leg|ate a lat|ere
  leg|ates a lat|ere
lega|tee +s
leg|ate|ship +s
lega|tine
le|ga|tion +s
le|gato +s
lega|tor +s
leg-break +s
leg-bye +s
leg-cutter +s
le|gend +s
le|gend|ar|ily
le|gend|ary
  (remarkable; of or
  connected with
  legends)
le|gend|ry (legends
  collectively)
Léger, Fer|nand
  (French painter)
leger +s
le|ger|de|main
leger line +s
leg|ger +s
leg|gi|ness
leg|ging +s
leg-guard +s
leggy
  leg|gier
  leg|gi|est

Leg|hari, Far|ooq
  Ahmed (Pakistani
  president)
Leg|horn +s
  (English name for
  Livorno; domestic
  fowl)
leg|horn +s (straw;
  hat)
le|gi|bil|ity
le|gible
le|gibly
le|gion +s
le|gion|aire +s (use
  legionnaire)
le|gion|ary
  le|gion|ar|ies
le|gioned
le|gion|ella
le|gion|naire +s
le|gion|naires'
  dis|ease
leg-iron +s
le|gis|late
  le|gis|lates
  le|gis|lated
  le|gis|lat|ing
le|gis|la|tion
le|gis|la|tive
le|gis|la|tive|ly
le|gis|la|tor +s
le|gis|la|ture +s
legit +s
  (= legitimate)
le|git|im|acy
le|git|im|ate
  le|git|im|ates
  le|git|im|ated
  le|git|im|at|ing
le|git|im|ate|ly
le|git|im|ation
le|git|ima|tisa|tion
  Br. (use
  legitimatization)
le|git|ima|tise *Br.*
  (use legitimatize)
  le|git|ima|tises
  le|git|ima|tised
  le|git|ima|tis|ing
le|git|ima|tiza|tion
le|git|ima|tize
  le|git|ima|tizes
  le|git|ima|tized
  le|git|ima|tiz|ing
le|git|im|isa|tion
  Br. (use
  legitimization)
le|git|im|ise *Br.*
  (use legitimize)
  le|git|im|ises

le|git|im|ise (*cont.*)
  le|git|im|ised
  le|git|im|is|ing
le|git|im|ism
le|git|im|ist +s
le|git|im|iza|tion
le|git|im|ize
  le|git|im|izes
  le|git|im|ized
  le|git|im|iz|ing
leg|less
leg|man
  leg|men
Lego *Propr.*
leg-of-mutton
  attributive
leg-pull +s
leg-pulling
leg-rest +s
leg|room
leg-show +s
leg slip +s
leg spin +s
leg-spinner +s
leg stump +s
leg the|ory
leg trap +s
leg|ume +s
leg|um|in|ous
leg-up
leg warm|er +s
leg|work
Leh (town, India)
Lehár, Franz
  (Hungarian
  composer)
Le Havre (port,
  France)
lehr +s (furnace.
  △ leer)
lei +s (garland;
  wine-vessel.
  △ lay, ley)
lei (plural of leu.
  △ lay, ley)
Leib|niz,
  Gott|fried
  Wil|helm
  (German
  philosopher)
Leib|niz|ian +s
Leices|ter (city,
  England; cheese)
Leices|ter|shire
  (county, England)
Leich|hardt,
  Fried|rich
  Wil|helm
  Lud|wig (German-
  born explorer)
Lei|den (city, the
  Netherlands)

Leif Erics|son
  (Norse explorer)
Leigh, Viv|ien
  (British actress)
Leigh|ton,
  Fred|eric (English
  painter and
  sculptor)
Leila
Lein|ster (province,
  Republic of
  Ireland)
Leip|zig (city,
  Germany)
leish|man|ia|sis
leis|ter +s +ed
  +ing
leis|ure
leis|ured
leis|ure|less
leis|ure|li|ness
leis|ure|ly
leis|ure|wear
leit|motif +s
leit|motiv +s
Lei|trim (county,
  Republic of
  Ireland)
Leix (use Laois)
lek +s
Lely, Peter (Dutch-
  born painter)
LEM (= lunar
  excursion module)
leman +s (lover.
  △ lemon)
Le Mans (town,
  France)
lemma
  lem|mas *or*
  lem|mata
lemme
lem|ming +s
Lem|mon, Jack
  (American actor)
Lem|nos (island,
  Greece)
lemon +s (fruit.
  △ leman)
lem|on|ade +s
lemon-squeezer
  +s
lem|ony
lem|pira +s
lemur +s
lem|ur|ine
lem|ur|oid
Len
Lena (river, Siberia;
  name)

Len|clos, Ninon
de(French wit
and beauty)
lend
lends
lent
lend|ing
lend|able
lend|er+s
lend|ing lib|rary
lend|ing
lib|rar|ies
Lendl, Ivan(Czech-
born American
tennis player)
Lend-Lease
length+s
length|en+s +ed
+ing
length|en|er+s
length|ily
lengthi|ness
length|man
length|men
length|ways
length|wise
lengthy
length|ier
lengthi|est
le|ni|ence
le|ni|ency
le|ni|ent
le|ni|ent|ly
Lenin, Vlad|imir
Ilich(Soviet
statesman)
Len|in|akan(city,
Armenia)
Len|in|grad
(former name of
St Petersburg)
Len|in|ism
Len|in|ist+s
Len|in|ite+s
len|ition+s
leni|tive+s
len|ity
len|ities
Len|non, John
(English rock
musician)
Len|nox
Lenny
leno+s
Le|nora
Le Nôtre, André
(French landscape
gardener)
lens
lenses
lensed
lens|less

lens|man
lens|men
Lent(period before
Easter)
lent(past tense and
past participle of
lend △ leant)
Lent|en(of or to do
with Lent)
len|ti|cel+s
len|ticu|lar
len|tigo
len|ti|gi|nes
len|til+s
len|tisk+s
lento
len|toid
Leo(constellation;
sign of zodiac;
popes and
Byzantine
emperors)
León(cities, Spain,
Mexico and
Nicaragua)
Leona
Leon|ard
Leo|nardo da
Vinci(Italian
painter and
designer)
leone+s
Leo|nids(meteor
shower)
Léo|nie
Leo|nine(of Pope
Leo)
leo|nine(of lions)
Leo|nine City
(Vatican, Italy)
Leo|nora
leop|ard+s
leop|ard|ess
leop|ard|esses
leop|ard's bane
Leo|pold(Belgian
king; name)
Léo|pold|ville
(former name of
Kinshasa)
leo|tard+s
Le|pan|to(naval
battle off Greece)
Le|pan|to, Gulf of
(alternative name
for the Gulf of
Corinth)
leper+s
Le|pi|dop|tera
le|pi|dop|teran+s
le|pi|dop|ter|ist+s
le|pi|dop|ter|ous

Lepi|dus, Mar|cus
Aem|il|ius
(Roman statesman
and triumvir)
lep|or|ine
lep|re|chaun+s
lep|ro|sarium
lep|ro|saria
lep|rosy
lep|rous
lepta
Lep|tis Magna
(ancient port,
Libya)
lepto|ceph|al|ic
lepto|ceph|al|ous
lepto|dac|tyl+s
lep|ton
lepta
(coin)
lep|ton+s
(particle)
lep|ton|ic
lepto|spir|osis
lepto|tene+s
Lepus
(constellation)
Ler|mon|tov,
Mikh|ail(Russian
novelist and poet)
Leroy
Ler|wick(capital of
the Shetland
Islands)
Les(name)
Le|sage, Alain-
René(French
novelist and
playwright)
Les|bian+s (of
Lesbos)
les|bian+s
(homosexual
woman)
les|bian|ism
Les|bos(island,
Greece)
lèse-majesté
lese-majesty
le|sion+s
Les|ley(chiefly
woman's name)
Les|lie(chiefly
man's name)
Le|so|tho(in
southern Africa)
less
les|see+s
les|see|ship+s
less|en+s +ed
+ing (diminish.
△ lesson)

Les|seps,
Fer|di|nand
Marie, Vi|comte
de(French
diplomat)
less|er(not so
great. △ lessor)
lesser-known
Les|sing, Doris
(English novelist
and short-story
writer)
Les|sing,
Gott|hold
Eph|raim
(German
dramatist and
critic)
Les Six(French
composers)
les|son+s (period
of tuition;
assignment etc.
△ lessen)
les|sor+s (person
who lets property
by lease. △ lessor)
lest
Les|ter
let
lets
let
let|ting
letch(use lech)
letches
letched
letch|ing
let-down+s *noun
and adjective*
le|thal
le|thal|ity
le|thal|ly
leth|ar|gic
leth|ar|gic|al|ly
leth|argy
leth|ar|gies
Lethe *Greek
Mythology*
Le|the|an
Le|ti|cia(port,
Colombia)
Le|ti|tia *also*
Lae|ti|tia
Leto *Greek
Mythology*
let-off+s *noun*
let-out+s *noun and
adjective*
let's (= let us)
Lett+s (*archaic*
= Latvian)
let|ter+s +ed +ing

let¦ter bomb +s
let¦ter box
   let¦ter boxes
letter-card +s
letter-carrier +s
   +ing (abscond)
let¦ter¦er +s
let¦ter¦head +s
letter-heading +s
let¦ter¦ing
let¦ter¦less
letter-perfect
let¦ter¦press
   let¦ter¦presses
letter-quality
letter-writer +s
Let¦tic
Let¦tice (name)
let¦ting +s
Lett¦ish (*archaic*
   = Latvian)
let¦tuce +s
let-up +s *noun*
Letze¦burg¦esch
   (= Luxemburg-
   ish)
leu
   lei
   (Romanian
   currency)
leu¦cine +s
leuco¦blast *Br.* +s
   (*Am.* leukoblast)
leuco¦cyte *Br.* +s
   (*Am.* leukocyte)
leuco¦cyt¦ic *Br.*
   (*Am.* leukocytic)
leu¦coma +s
leu¦cor¦rhea *Am.*
leu¦cor¦rhoea *Br.*
leuco¦tome +s
leu¦cot¦omy
   leu¦coto¦mies
leu¦kae¦mia *Br.* +s
leu¦kaem¦ic *Br.*
leu¦ke¦mia *Am.* +s
leu¦kem¦ic *Am.*
leuko¦blast *Am.* +s
   (*Br.* leucoblast)
leuko¦cyte *Am.* +s
   (*Br.* leucocyte)
leuko¦cytic *Am.*
   (*Br.* leucocytic)
Leu¦ven (town,
   Belgium)
lev
   plural **lev** or **levs**
leva
   plural **leva** or
   levas
   (Bulgarian
   currency; = lev)
Le¦val¦lois

Le¦val¦lois¦ean +s
Le¦vant (E.
   Mediterranean)
le¦vant +s +ed
   +ing (abscond)
Le¦vant¦er +s
   (native or
   inhabitant of the
   Levant)
le¦vant¦er +s
   (breeze; person
   who levants)
Lev¦an¦tine +s (of
   the Levant)
le¦vator +s
levee +s
   (reception;
   embankment.
   △levy)
level
   levels
   lev¦elled *Br.*
   lev¦eled *Am.*
   lev¦el¦ling *Br.*
   lev¦el¦ing *Am.*
level cros¦sing +s
lev¦el¦er *Am.* +s
level-headed
level-headed¦ly
level-headed¦ness
Lev¦el¦ler +s
   (dissenter)
lev¦el¦ler *Br.* +s
levelling-screw +s
lev¦el¦ly
lev¦el¦ness
lever +s +ed +ing
le¦ver¦age
   le¦ver¦ages
   le¦ver¦aged
   le¦ver¦aging
lev¦eret +s
Le¦ver¦hulme,
   Lord (William
   Lever, English
   industrialist)
Le¦ver¦ku¦sen (city,
   Germany)
Le Ver¦rier,
   Ur¦bain (French
   mathematician)
Levi *Bible*
Levi, Peter
   (English poet,
   scholar, and
   writer)
Levi, Primo (Italian
   writer and
   chemist)
levi¦able
le¦via¦than +s

levi¦gate
   levi¦gates
   levi¦gated
   levi¦gat¦ing
levi¦ga¦tion +s
levin +s
lev¦ir¦ate
le¦vir¦at¦ic
le¦vir¦at¦ic¦al
Levis (jeans) *Propr.*
Lévi-Strauss,
   Claude (French
   social
   anthropologist)
levi¦tate
   levi¦tates
   levi¦tated
   levi¦tat¦ing
levi¦ta¦tion +s
levi¦ta¦tor +s
Le¦vite +s
Le¦vit¦ic¦al
Le¦vit¦icus *Bible*
lev¦ity
levo¦dopa
levo¦rota¦tory *Am.*
le¦vu¦lose *Am.*
levy
   lev¦ies
   lev¦ied
   levy¦ing
   (tax; impose.
   △levee)
lewd +er +est
lewd¦ly
lewd¦ness
Lewes (town,
   England)
Lewis (island,
   Scotland; name)
Lewis, Carl
   (American athlete)
Lewis, C. S.
   (English scholar
   and writer)
Lewis,
   Meri¦wether
   (American
   explorer)
Lewis, Percy
   Wynd¦ham
   (British novelist
   and painter)
Lewis, Sin¦clair
   (American
   novelist)
lewis
   lewises
   (lifting device)
Lewis gun +s
Lew¦isham (suburb
   of London)

lew¦is¦ite
lex do¦mi¦ci¦lii
lex¦eme +s
lex fori
lex¦ic¦al
lex¦ic¦al¦ly
lexi¦cog¦raph¦er +s
lex¦ico|graph¦ic
lex¦ico|graph¦ic¦al
lex¦ico|graph¦ic|
   al¦ly
lexi¦cog¦raphy
lex¦ico|logic¦al
lex¦ico|logic¦al¦ly
lexi¦colo|gist +s
lexi¦col¦ogy
lexi¦con +s
lex¦ig¦raphy
Lex¦ing|ton (town,
   USA)
lexis
lex loci
lex tali¦onis
ley +s (field
   temporarily under
   grass; line of
   ancient track.
   △lay, lea, lei, lee)
Ley¦den (town; use
   Leiden)
Ley¦den, Lucas
   van (Dutch
   painter)
Ley¦den jar +s
ley farm¦ing
ley line +s
Leyte (island,
   Philippines)
Lhasa (capital of
   Tibet)
li¦abil¦ity
   li¦abil¦ities
li¦able
li¦aise
   li¦aises
   li¦aised
   li¦ais¦ing
li¦aison +s
Liam
liana +s
Liane (name)
liane +s (plant)
Liao
Liao|dong
   Pen¦in¦sula (in
   China)
Liao|ning (in
   China)
liar +s (person who
   tells a lie. △lyre)
Lias (Jurassic
   strata)

lias (blue
  limestone)
li¦as¦sic
lib (= liberation)
li¦ba¦tion +s
lib¦ber +s
Libby
Lib Dem +s
  (= Liberal
  Democrat)
libel
  li¦bels
  li¦belled *Br.*
  li¦beled *Am.*
  li¦bel¦ling *Br.*
  li¦bel¦ing *Am.*
li¦bel¦ant *Am.* +s
li¦bel¦ee *Am.* +s
li¦bel¦er *Am.* +s
li¦bel¦ist *Am.* +s
li¦bel¦lant *Br.* +s
li¦bel¦lee *Br.* +s
li¦bel¦ler *Br.* +s
li¦bel¦list *Br.* +s
li¦bel¦lous *Br.*
li¦bel¦lous¦ly *Br.*
li¦bel¦ous *Am.*
li¦bel¦ous¦ly *Am.*
liber +s
Li¦ber¦ace
  (American pianist
  and entertainer)
Lib¦eral +s *Politics*
lib¦eral +s
Lib¦eral
  Demo¦crat +s
  Politics
lib¦er¦al¦isa¦tion
  Br. (use
  liberalization)
lib¦er¦al¦ise *Br.* (use
  liberalize)
  lib¦er¦al¦ises
  lib¦er¦al¦ised
  lib¦er¦al¦is¦ing
lib¦er¦al¦iser *Br.* +s
  (use liberalizer)
lib¦er¦al¦ism
lib¦er¦al¦ist +s
lib¦er¦al¦is¦tic
lib¦er¦al¦ity
lib¦er¦al¦ities
lib¦er¦al¦iza¦tion
lib¦er¦al¦ize
  lib¦er¦al¦izes
  lib¦er¦al¦ized
  lib¦er¦al¦iz¦ing
lib¦er¦al¦izer +s
lib¦er¦al¦ly
lib¦er¦al¦ness
lib¦er¦ate
  lib¦er¦ates

lib¦er¦ate (*cont.*)
  lib¦er¦ated
  lib¦er¦at¦ing
lib¦er¦ation +s
lib¦er¦ation¦ist +s
lib¦er¦ator +s
Li¦beria (in W.
  Africa)
Li¦ber¦ian +s
li¦bero +s
lib¦er¦tar¦ian +s
lib¦er¦tar¦ian¦ism
lib¦er¦tin¦age
lib¦er¦tine +s
lib¦er¦tin¦ism
lib¦erty
  lib¦er¦ties
Lib¦erty Bell
lib¦erty bod¦ice +s
lib¦erty hall
li¦bid¦in¦al
li¦bid¦in¦al¦ly
li¦bid¦in¦ous
li¦bid¦in¦ous¦ly
li¦bid¦in¦ous¦ness
li¦bido +s
lib¦itum (in '*ad
  libitum*')
Lib-Lab (= Liberal
  and Labour)
Li Bo (alternative
  name for Li Po)
LIBOR (= London
  Inter-Bank Offered
  Rate)
Libra
  (constellation;
  sign of zodiac)
Libran +s
li¦brar¦ian +s
li¦brar¦ian¦ship +s
li¦brary
  li¦brar¦ies
li¦brary edi¦tion +s
li¦brate
  li¦brates
  li¦brated
  li¦brat¦ing
li¦bra¦tion +s
li¦bra¦tory
li¦bret¦tist +s
li¦bretto
  li¦bretti *or*
  li¦bret¦tos
Libre¦ville (capital
  of Gabon)
Lib¦rium *Propr.*
Libya (in Africa)
Libyan +s
lice
li¦cence *Br.* +s *noun*

li¦cence (*verb*; use
  license)
li¦cences
li¦cenced
li¦cen¦cing
li¦cens¦able
li¦cense
li¦censes
li¦censed
li¦cens¦ing
  verb
li¦cense *Am.* +s
  noun
li¦cen¦see +s
li¦cen¦ser +s
  (use licensor)
li¦cen¦sor +s
li¦cen¦ti¦ate +s
li¦cen¦tious
li¦cen¦tious¦ly
li¦cen¦tious¦ness
li¦chee +s (use
  lychee)
li¦chen +s
li¦chened
li¦chen¦ology
li¦chen¦ous
Lich¦field (town,
  England)
lich-gate +s
Lich¦ten¦stein,
  Roy (American
  painter and
  sculptor)
licit
licit¦ly
lick +s +ed +ing
lick¦er +s
lick¦er¦ish
  (lecherous.
  △ liquorish)
lickety-split
lick¦ing +s
lick¦spit¦tle +s
lic¦orice +s
lic¦tor +s
lid +s
lid¦ded
Lid¦dell, Eric
  (British athlete)
Lid¦dell Hart,
  Basil Henry
  (British military
  historian)
Li¦dingö (island,
  Baltic Sea)
lid¦less
lido +s
lido¦caine
Lido (di
  Mala¦mocco)
  (island off Venice)

Lie, Tryg¦ve
  Halv¦dan
  (Norwegian
  politician)
lie
  lies
  lay
  lying
  lain
  (be horizontal.
  △ lye)
lie
  lies
  lied
  lying
  (tell untruths.
  △ lye)
Lieb¦frau¦milch +s
Lie¦big, Jus¦tus
  von (German
  chemist)
Liech¦ten¦stein
Liech¦ten¦stein¦er
  +s
lied
  lieder
  (German song.
  △ lead, leader,
  leat, leet)
lie de¦tect¦or +s
lie-down +s
lief (gladly. △ leaf)
Liège (city and
  province,
  Belgium)
liege +s
liege¦man
  liege¦men
lie-in +s *noun*
lien +s
li¦erne +s
lieu +s (in 'in lieu
  (of)'. △ loo)
lieu¦ten¦ancy
  lieu¦ten¦an¦cies
lieu¦ten¦ant +s
lieu¦ten¦ant
  col¦onel +s
lieu¦ten¦ant
  com¦mand¦er +s
lieu¦ten¦ant
  gen¦eral +s
lieutenant-
  governor +s
life
  lives
life-and-death
  attributive
life¦belt +s
life¦blood +s
life¦boat +s

life|boat|man
  life|boat|men
life|buoy+s
life cycle+s
life ex|pect|ancy
life
  ex|pect|an|cies
life-force+s
life form+s
life-giving
life|guard+s (on
  beach etc.)
Life Guards
  (British regiment)
life his|tory
  life his|tor|ies
life jacket+s
life|less
life|less|ly
life|less|ness
life|like
life|like|ness
life|line+s
life|long
life-preserver+s
lifer+s
life-raft+s
life-saver+s
life size *noun*
life-size *adjective*
life-sized
life|span+s
life|style+s
life-support
  attributive
life's work
life-threaten|ing
life|time+s
life-work
Liffe (= London
  International
  Financial Futures
  Exchange)
Lif|fey (river,
  Republic of
  Ireland)
Lif|ford (town,
  Republic of
  Ireland)
LIFO (= last in, first
  out)
lift+s +ed +ing
lift|able
lift|er+s
lift-off+s *noun*
lig
  ligs
  ligged
  lig|ging
liga|ment+s
liga|men|tal
liga|men|tary

liga|ment|ous
lig|and+s
li|gate
  li|gates
  li|gated
  li|gat|ing
li|ga|tion+s
liga|ture
  liga|tures
  liga|tured
  liga|tur|ing
liger+s
Lig|eti, György
  (Hungarian
  composer)
lig|ger+s
light
  lights
  lit *or* light|ed
  light|ing
  light|er
  light|est
  (visible radiation;
  illuminate; bright;
  not heavy; (*lights*)
  lungs. ⚠ lite)
light bulb+s
light-emitting
light|en+s +ed
  +ing
light|en|ing+s (in
  pregnancy.
  ⚠ lightning)
light|er+s
light|er|age
light|er|man
  light|er|men
lighter-than-air
  attributive
light|fast
light-fingered
light|foot+s
light-footed
light-footed|ly
light-gun+s
light-headed
light-headed|ly
light-headed|ness
light-hearted
light-hearted|ly
light-hearted|ness
light|house+s
light|ing+s
lighting-up time
  +s
light|ish
light|less
light|ly
light meter+s
light|ness

light|ning (electric
  discharge.
  ⚠ lightening)
light|ning
  con|duct|or+s
light|ning strike
  +s
light-o'-love
light-pen+s
light|proof
lights (lungs)
light|ship+s
light show+s
light|some
light|some|ly
light|some|ness
light|ves|sel+s
light|weight+s
light|wood+s
light year+s
lign-aloe+s
lig|neous
lig|nif|er|ous
ligni|form
lig|nify
  lig|ni|fies
  lig|ni|fied
  lig|ni|fy|ing
lig|nin
lig|nite+s
lig|nit|ic
lig|no|caine
lig|num vitae
lig|roin
ligu|late
lig|ule+s
Li|guria (region,
  Italy)
Li|gur|ian+s
Li|gur|ian Sea (in
  Mediterranean)
li|gus|trum+s
lik|abil|ity (use
  likeability)
lik|able (use
  likeable)
lik|able|ness (use
  likeableness)
lik|ably (use
  likeably)
like
  likes
  liked
  lik|ing
like|abil|ity
like|able
like|able|ness
like|ably
like|li|hood+s
like|li|ness

like|ly
  like|lier
  like|li|est
like-minded
like-minded|ly
like-minded|ness
liken+s +ed +ing
like|ness
  like|nesses
like|wise
lik|ing+s
Likud (Israeli
  political coalition)
li|kuta
  ma|kuta
lilac+s
li|lan|geni
  ema|lan|geni
lili|aceous
Lil|ian *also* Lil|lian
lil|ied
Li|lien|thal, Otto
  (German aviator)
Lil|ith (*Jewish
  Mythology*; name)
Lille (city, France)
Lil|lee, Den|nis
  (Australian
  cricketer)
Lil|lian *also* Lil|ian
Lil|li|bur|lero
lil|li|pu|tian+s
Lilo+s *Propr.*
Li|longwe (capital
  of Malawi)
lilt+s +ed +ing
Lily (name)
lily
  lil|ies
  (flower)
lily-livered
lily of the val|ley
  lil|ies of the
  val|ley
lily pad+s
lily-trotter+s
lily white+s *noun
  and adjective*
lily-white
  attributive
Lima (capital of
  Peru)
lima bean+s
Lim|as|sol (port,
  Cyprus)
limb+s (arm, leg,
  etc.; *Astronomy;
  Botany*. ⚠ limn)
limbed
lim|ber+s +ed
  +ing
lim|ber|ness

lim|bic
limb||less
limbo +s
Lim|burg
   (province,
   Belgium and the
   Netherlands)
Lim|burg|er +s
lime
   limes
   limed
   lim|ing
lime|ade +s
lime green +s *noun and adjective*
lime-green *attributive*
lime|kiln +s
lime|less
lime|light
limen +s
lime|pit +s
Lim|er|ick (county and town, Republic of Ireland)
lim|er|ick +s (verse)
lime|stone +s
lime tree +s
lime|wash
   lime|washes
lime-wort +s
Limey +s (*offensive* Briton. △ limy)
limey *Br.*
   limi|er
   limi|est
   (containing lime. *Am.* limy)
limi|nal
limi|nal|ity
limit +s +ed +ing
limit|able
limit|ary
limi|ta|tion +s
limi|ta|tive
limit|ed|ly
limit|ed|ness
limit|er +s
limit|less
limit|less|ly
limit|less|ness
limn +s +ed +ing
   (paint. △ limb)
lim|ner +s
lim|no|logic|al
lim|nolo|gist +s
lim|nol|ogy
Lim|nos (Greek name for Lemnos)
limo +s

Li|moges (city, France)
Limón (port, Costa Rica)
Li|mou|sin (region, France)
lim|ou|sine +s
limp +s +ed +ing +er +est
lim|pet +s
lim|pid
lim|pid|ity
lim|pid|ly
lim|pid|ness
limp|ing|ly
limp|kin +s
limp|ly
limp|ness
Lim|popo (river, Africa)
limp|wort +s
limp-wristed
lim|ulus
lim|uli
limy *Am.*
   limi|er
   limi|est
   (*Br.* limey. containing lime. △ Limey)
Lin|acre, Thomas (English physician and scholar)
lin|age +s (number of lines. △ lineage)
Lin Biao (Chinese statesman)
linch|pin +s
Lin|coln (cities, Canada and England)
Lin|coln, Abra|ham (American president)
Lin|coln|shire (in England)
Lin|coln's Inn
Lin|crusta *Propr.*
Lincs. (= Lincolnshire)
linc|tus
   linc|tuses
Lind, James (Scottish physician)
Lind, Jenny (Swedish soprano)
Linda *also* Lynda
lin|dane

Lind|bergh, Charles Au|gus|tus (American aviator)
Linde|mann, Fred|erick Alex|an|der (Lord Cherwell, German-born British physicist)
lin|den (name)
lin|den +s (tree)
Lin|dis|farne (island, England)
Lind|say, Lio|nel and Nor|man (Australian artists)
Lind|say *also* Lind|sey, Lyn|sey
Lind|sey *also* Lind|say, Lyn|sey
Lin|dum Col|onia (Roman name for Lincoln, England)
Lindy
line
   lines
   lined
   lin|ing
lin|eage +s (ancestry. △ linage)
lin|eal
lin|eal|ly
lin|ea|ment +s
lin|ear
Lin|ear A
Lin|ear B
lin|ear|ise *Br.* (use linearize)
   lin|ear|ises
   lin|ear|ised
   lin|ear|is|ing
lin|ear|ity
lin|ear|ize
   lin|ear|izes
   lin|ear|ized
   lin|ear|iz|ing
lin|ear|ly
lin|ea|tion +s
line|back|er +s
line draw|ing +s
line|feed
Line Is|lands (in SW Pacific)
line|man
   line|men
linen +s
linen bas|ket +s
lin|en|fold
line-out +s *noun*

line print|er +s
liner +s
line|side
lines|man
   lines|men
line-up +s *noun*
Lin|ford
ling +s
linga +s (phallus. △ linger)
Lin|gala
lin|gam +s
lin|ger +s +ed +ing (be slow to leave. △ linga)
lin|ger|er +s
lin|ge|rie
lin|ger|ing|ly
lingo
   lin|gos *or* lin|goes
lin|gua franca +s
lin|gual
lin|gual|ise *Br.* (use lingualize)
   lin|gual|ises
   lin|gual|ised
   lin|gual|is|ing
lin|gual|ize
   lin|gual|izes
   lin|gual|ized
   lin|gual|iz|ing
lin|gual|ly
lin|gui|form
lin|guine
lin|guist +s
lin|guis|tic
lin|guis|tic|al|ly
lin|guis|ti|cian +s
lin|guis|tics
lin|guo|den|tal
lingy
`lini|ment +s
lin|ing +s
link +s +ed +ing
link|age +s
link|man
   link|men
Lin|köp|ing (town, Sweden)
links (golf course. △ lynx)
link up
   links up
   linked up
   link|ing up
link-up +s *noun*
Lin|lith|gow (town, Scotland)
linn +s
Lin|naean +s
Lin|naeus, Caro|lus

Lin|naeus (*cont.*)
  (Swedish
  naturalist)
lin|net +s
lino +s
lino|cut +s
lino|cut|ting +s
lino|leic
lino|len|ic
li|no|leum +s
li|no|leumed
Lino|type *Propr.*
Lin Piao (= Lin
  Biao)
lin|sang +s
lin|seed +s
linsey-woolsey +s
lin|stock +s
lint +s
lin|tel +s
lin|teled *Am.*
lin|telled *Br.*
lint|er +s
lint-free
linty
Linus
liny
  lini|er
  lini|est
Linz (city, Austria)
Lion, the
  (constellation;
  sign of zodiac)
lion +s
Lio|nel
lion|ess
  lion|esses
Lion-Heart,
  Rich|ard the
  (English king)
lion-heart +s
lion-hearted
lion|hood
lion|isa|tion *Br.*
  (use lionization)
lion|ise *Br.* (use
  lionize)
  lion|ises
  lion|ised
  lion|is|ing
lion|iser *Br.* +s (use
  lionizer)
lion|iza|tion
lion|ize
  lion|izes
  lion|ized
  lion|iz|ing
lion|izer +s
lion-like
Lions (British
  Rugby Union
  team)

lion-tamer +s
lip
  lips
  lipped
  lip|ping
Li|pari Is|lands (off
  Italy)
lip|ase +s
Lip|etsk (city,
  Russia)
lipid +s
lip|id|osis
lip|id|oses
Lip|iz|za|ner +s
lip|less
lip|like
Li Po (Chinese
  poet)
lip|og|raphy
lip|oid
lipo|pro|tein +s
lipo|some +s
lipo|suc|tion
Lippi, Fil|ip|pino
  and Fra Fi|lippo
  (Italian painters)
Lip|pi|za|ner +s
  (use Lipizzaner)
Lipp|mann,
  Gab|riel Jonas
  (French physicist)
lippy
  lip|pier
  lip|pi|est
lip-read
  lip-reads
  lip-read
  lip-reading
lip-reader +s
lip|salve +s
lip-service
lip|stick +s
lip-sync +s +ed
  +ing
lip-syncer +s
lip-synch +s +ed
  +ing (use lip-
  sync)
lip-syncher +s (use
  lip-syncer)
li|quate
  li|quates
  li|quated
  li|quat|ing
li|qua|tion
li|que|fa|cient
li|que|fac|tion
li|que|fac|tive
li|que|fi|able
li|que|fier +s
li|quefy
  li|que|fies

li|quefy (*cont.*)
  li|que|fied
  li|que|fy|ing
li|ques|cent
li|queur +s
li|quid +s
li|quid|am|bar +s
li|quid|ate
  li|quid|ates
  li|quid|ated
  li|quid|at|ing
li|quid|ation +s
li|quid|ator +s
li|quid crys|tal +s
li|quid crys|tal
  dis|play +s
li|quid|ise *Br.* (use
  liquidize)
  li|quid|ises
  li|quid|ised
  li|quid|is|ing
li|quid|iser *Br.* +s
  (use liquidizer)
li|quid|ity
  li|quid|ities
li|quid|ize
  li|quid|izes
  li|quid|ized
  li|quid|iz|ing
li|quid|izer +s
li|quid|ly
li|quid|ness
li|qui|dus
  li|qui|duses
li|quify (use
  liquefy)
  li|qui|fies
  li|qui|fied
  li|qui|fy|ing
li|quor +s
li|quor|ice +s
li|quor|ish (fond of
  liquor.
  △ lickerish)
li|quor|ish|ly
li|quor|ish|ness
lira
  lire
Lisa *also* Liza
Lis|bon (capital of
  Portugal)
Lis|burn (town,
  Northern Ireland)
Lis|doon|varna
  (town, Republic of
  Ireland)
li|sente (plural of
  sente)
lisle +s
lisp +s +ed +ing
lisp|er +s
lisp|ing|ly

lis|som
lis|some (use
  lissom)
lis|som|ly
lis|som|ness
list +s +ed +ing
list|able
lis|ten +s +ed +ing
lis|ten|abil|ity
lis|ten|able
lis|ten|er +s
lis|ten|ing post +s
Lis|ter, Jo|seph
  (English surgeon)
list|er +s
lis|teria +s
lis|teri|osis
list|ing +s
list|less
list|less|ly
list|less|ness
list price +s
Liszt, Franz
  (Hungarian
  composer and
  pianist)
lit
Li T'ai Po
  (alternative name
  for Li Po)
lit|any
  lit|anies
lit|chi +s (use
  lychee)
lit crit (= literary
  criticism)
lite (low-calorie;
  over-simplified.
  △ light)
liter *Am.* +s
lit|er|acy
lit|erae
  hu|ma|ni|ores
lit|eral +s (to the
  letter; misprint.
  △ littoral)
lit|er|al|ise *Br.* (use
  literalize)
lit|er|al|ises
lit|er|al|ised
lit|er|al|is|ing
lit|er|al|ism
lit|er|al|ist +s
lit|er|al|is|tic
lit|er|al|ity
lit|er|al|ize
lit|er|al|izes
lit|er|al|ized
lit|er|al|iz|ing
lit|er|al|ly
literal-minded
lit|er|al|ness

lit¦er¦ar¦ily
lit¦er¦ari¦ness
lit¦er¦ary
lit¦er¦ate +s
lit¦er¦ate¦ly
lit¦er¦ati
lit¦er¦atim
lit¦er¦ation
lit¦er¦ator +s
lit¦era¦ture +s
lith|arge
lithe
lithe¦ly
lithe|ness
lithe|some
lithia
lith¦ic
lith¦ium
litho +s +ed +ing
litho|graph +s +ed +ing
lith|og¦raph¦er +s
lith|og¦raph¦ic
lith|og¦raph¦ic¦al¦ly
lith|og¦raphy
litho|logic¦al
lith|olo¦gist +s
lith|ology
litho|phyte +s
litho|pone
litho|sphere
litho|spher¦ic
lith|ot¦om¦ist +s
lith|ot¦om¦ize
  lith|ot¦om|izes
  lith|ot¦om|ized
  lith|ot¦om|iz¦ing
lith|ot¦omy
  lith|oto¦mies
litho|tripsy
litho|trip¦ter +s
litho|trip¦tic
lith|ot¦rity
  lith|ot¦rities
Lithu|ania
Lithu|anian +s
lit¦ig|able
liti|gant +s
liti|gate
  liti|gates
  liti|gated
  liti|gat¦ing
liti|ga¦tion
liti|ga¦tor +s
li¦ti|gious
li¦ti|gious¦ly
li¦ti|gious|ness
lit¦mus
lit¦mus test +s
li¦to¦tes
litre +s
litre|age +s

Litt.D. (= Doctor of Letters)
lit¦ter +s +ed +ing
lit¦tér|ateur +s
lit¦ter|bug +s
lit¦ter lout +s
lit¦tery
lit¦tle
  lit¦tler
  lit¦tlest
Lit¦tle Big|horn (battle site, USA)
Lit¦tle Eng|land¦er +s
lit¦tle known
little-known *attributive*
little|ness
Lit¦tle Rus¦sian +s (= Ukrainian)
Little|wood, Joan (English theatre director)
lit|toral +s (shore. △ literal)
Littré, Émile (French philosopher and lexicographer)
li¦tur|gic¦al
li¦tur|gic¦al¦ly
li¦tur|gics
li¦tur|gi|ology
lit¦ur¦gist +s
lit|urgy
  lit¦ur|gies
Liu|chow (= Liuzhou)
Liu|zhou (city, China)
liv|abil¦ity (use liveability)
liv|able (use liveable)
liv¦able|ness (use liveableness)
live
  lives
  lived
  liv¦ing *verb*
live *adjective*
live|abil¦ity
live|able
live|able|ness
lived-in *adjective*
live-in +s *adjective and noun*
live¦li|hood +s
live¦li|ly
live¦li|ness
live|long +s

live¦ly
  live|lier
  live¦li|est
liven +s +ed +ing
liver +s
liver color *Am.*
liver col¦our *Br.*
liv|er¦ied
liv|er¦ish
liv|er¦ish¦ly
liv|er¦ish|ness
liv|er¦less
Liv¦er|pool (city, England)
Liv¦er|pud¦lian +s
liv¦er|wort +s
liv¦ery
  liv|er¦ies
liv¦ery|man
  liv¦ery|men
lives (plural of life)
live|stock
live|ware
live wire +s
Livia
livid
liv¦id¦ity
liv¦id¦ly
liv¦id|ness
liv¦ing +s
liv¦ing room +s
Liv¦ing|stone (former name of Maramba)
Liv¦ing|stone, David (Scottish missionary and explorer)
Li|vo¦nia
Li|vorno (port, Italy)
Livy (Roman historian)
lix¦ivi|ate
  lix¦ivi|ates
  lix¦ivi|ated
  lix¦ivi|at¦ing
lix¦ivi|ation
Liz
Liza *also* Lisa
liz¦ard +s
Liz¦zie *also* Lizzy
Lizzy *also* Liz¦zie
Ljub|ljana (capital of Slovenia)
llama +s (animal. △ lama)
Llan|drin¦dod Wells (town, Wales)
Llan|dudno (town, Wales)

lla|nero +s
Llan|gollen (town, Wales)
llano +s
Lle|we|lyn (Welsh prince)
Llosa, Mario Var¦gas (Peruvian writer)
Lloyd, Marie (English music-hall singer)
Lloyd George, David (British prime minister)
Lloyd's *Insurance*
Lloyd's List
Lloyd's Regis¦ter
Lloyd Web¦ber, An¦drew (English composer)
Llu|llai|llaco (mountain, Argentina; volcano, Chile)
lo (*interjection.* △ low)
loa *plural* loa *or* loas (voodoo god. △ lower)
loach
  loaches
load +s +ed +ing (burden; to carry. △ lode)
load-bearing
load-draught +s
load¦er +s
load|ing +s
load line +s
load|star +s (use lodestar)
load|stone +s (use lodestone)
loaf +s +ed +ing (to idle)
loaf loaves (bread)
loaf¦er +s (idler)
loaf¦er +s (shoe) *Propr.*
loam +s
loami|ness
loamy
  loam|ier
  loami|est
loan +s +ed +ing (lend; something lent. △ lone)
loan|able

loan|ee +s
loan|er +s (lender.
△ loner)
loan|hold|er +s
loan shark +s
loan-transla|tion +s
loan|word +s
loath (reluctant)
loathe
loathes
loathed
loath|ing (despise)
loath|er +s
loath|some
loath|some|ly
loath|some|ness
loaves
lob
lobs
lobbed
lob|bing
Lo|ba|chev|ski, Ni|ko|lai Ivan|ovich (Russian mathematician)
lobar
lo|bate
lob|ation
lobby
lob|bies
lob|bied
lobby|ing
lob|by|er +s
lobby|ism
lobby|ist +s
lobe +s
lob|ec|tomy
lob|ec|to|mies
lobed
lobe|less
lo|belia +s
Lo|bito (port, Angola)
lob|lolly
lob|lol|lies
lob|ot|om|ise Br. (use lobotomize)
lob|ot|om|ises
lob|ot|om|ised
lob|ot|om|is|ing
lob|ot|om|ize
lob|ot|om|izes
lob|ot|om|ized
lob|ot|om|iz|ing
lob|ot|omy
lo|boto|mies
lob|scouse
lob|ster +s +ed +ing

lob|ster pot +s
lob|ster
ther|mi|dor Cookery
lobu|lar
lobu|late
lob|ule +s
lob|worm +s
local +s
lo|cale +s
lo|cal|is|able Br. (use localizable)
lo|cal|isa|tion Br. (use localization)
lo|cal|ise Br. (use localize)
lo|cal|ises
lo|cal|ised
lo|cal|is|ing
lo|cal|ism
lo|cal|ity
lo|cal|ities
lo|cal|iz|able
lo|cal|iza|tion
lo|cal|ize
lo|cal|izes
lo|cal|ized
lo|cal|iz|ing
lo|cal|ly
lo|cal|ness
Lo|carno (town, Switzerland)
lo|cat|able
lo|cate
lo|cates
lo|cated
lo|cat|ing
lo|ca|tion +s
lo|ca|tion|al
loca|tive +s
lo|ca|tor +s
loc. cit. (= loco citato)
loch +s (Scottish lake. △ lough)
lochan +s
Loch|gilp|head (town, Scotland)
lo|chia +s
lo|chial
Loch Lo|mond (lake, Scotland)
Loch Maree (lake, Scotland)
Loch Ness (lake, Scotland)
loch|side
loci
loci clas|sici
lock +s +ed +ing
lock|able
lock|age +s

Locke, John (English philosopher)
Locke, Jo|seph (English railway designer)
lock|er +s
Lock|er|bie (town, Scotland)
lock|er room +s
locket +s
lock|fast
lock|jaw
lock-keeper +s
lock-knit
lock|less
lock|nut +s
lock|out +s
locks|man
locks|men
lock|smith +s
lock-up +s adjective and noun
Lock|yer, Jo|seph Nor|man (English astronomer)
loco +s
loco|mo|tion
loco|mo|tive +s
loco|motor
loco|mo|tory
loco-weed +s
locu|lar
locu|lus
loc|uli
locum +s
locum ten|ency
locum ten|en|cies
locum ten|ens
locum ten|en|tes
locus
loci
locus clas|si|cus
loci clas|sici
locus standi Law
lo|cust +s
locust-bird +s
locust-eater +s
lo|cu|tion +s
locu|tory
locu|tor|ies
lode +s (vein of metal ore. △ load)
loden +s
lode|star +s
lode|stone +s
Lodge, Oli|ver Jo|seph (English physicist)
lodge
lodges

lodge (cont.)
lodged
lodg|ing
lodge|ment +s
lodg|er +s
lodg|ing +s
lodg|ing house +s
lo|di|cule +s
Łódź (city, Poland)
loess
loes|sial
Loewi, Otto (German-born American physiologist)
Lo|fo|ten Is|lands (in Norwegian Sea)
loft +s +ed +ing
loft|er +s
loft|ily
lofti|ness
lofty
loft|ier
lofti|est
log
logs
logged
log|ging
Logan, Mount (in Canada)
logan +s
lo|gan|berry
lo|gan|berries
logan-stone +s
loga|oed|ic
loga|rithm +s
loga|rith|mic
loga|rith|mic|al|ly
log|book +s
loge +s
log₌ (= natural logarithm)
log|ger +s
log|ger|head +s
log|gia +s (open-sided gallery. △ logia)
logia (plural of logion. △ loggia)
logic +s
lo|gic|al
logic|al|ity
logic|al|ly
lo|gi|cian +s
log|ion
logia
lo|gis|tic
lo|gis|tic|al
lo|gis|tic|al|ly
lo|gis|tics

log|jam +s
log-line +s
logo +s
logo|gram +s
logo|graph|ic
log|om|achy
  log|om|achies
log|or|rhea *Am.*
log|or|rhe|ic *Am.*
log|or|rhoea *Br.*
log|or|rhoe|ic *Br.*
Logos (word of
  God)
logo|type +s
log|roll +s +ed
  +ing
log|roll|er +s
Lo|groño (town,
  Spain)
log|wood
Lo|hen|grin
  (legendary figure)
loin +s
loin|cloth +s
Loire (river,
  France)
Lois
loi|ter +s +ed +ing
loi|ter|er +s
Loki *Scandinavian
  Mythology*
Lola
Lola Mon|tez
  (mistress of
  Ludwig I of
  Bavaria)
Lo|lita
loll +s +ed +ing
Lol|land (island,
  Baltic Sea)
lol|la|pa|looza +s
Lol|lard +s
Lol|lard|ism
Lol|lardy
loll|er +s
lol|li|pop +s
lol|lop +s +ed +ing
lolly
  lol|lies
Lom|bard +s
Lom|bard|ic
Lom|bard Street
  (in London)
Lom|bardy (region,
  Italy)
Lom|bok (island,
  Indonesia)
Lomé (capital of
  Togo;
  Convention)
lo|ment +s
lo|ment|aceous

lo|men|tum
  lo|menta
Lo|mond, Loch
  (lake, Scotland)
Lon|don (capital of
  the United
  Kingdom; city,
  Canada)
Lon|don, Jack
  (American
  novelist)
Lon|don|derry
  (city, Northern
  Ireland)
Lon|don|er +s
lone (solitary.
  △loan)
lone|li|ness
lone|ly
  lone|lier
  lone|li|est
loner +s (solitary
  person. △loaner)
lone|some
lone|some|ly
lone|some|ness
long +s +ed +ing
  +er +est (not
  short; have a
  longing)
long. (= longitude)
long-ago *adjective*
long-awaited
Long Beach (city,
  USA)
long|board +s
long|boat +s
long|bow +s
long-case (clock)
long-chain
  attributive
long-dated
long-day *adjective*
long-dead
  attributive
long-delayed
long-distance
  adjective
long-drawn
long-drawn-out
longe
  longes
  longed
  longe|ing
lon|geron +s
long-established
  attributive
lon|gev|ity
long-faced
Long|fel|low,
  Henry

Long|fel|low
  (*cont.*)
  Wads|worth
  (American poet)
Long|ford (county,
  Republic of
  Ireland)
long|hair +s
long|hand +s
long-haul *adjective*
long-headed
long-headed|ness
long hop +s
long|horn +s
long|house +s
lon|gi|corn +s
long|ing +s
long|ing|ly
Lon|gi|nus (Greek
  writer)
long|ish
Long Is|land (in
  USA)
lon|gi|tude +s
lon|gi|tu|din|al
lon|gi|tu|din|al|ly
long johns
long jump
long-jumper +s
long-lasting
long-legged
long-life *adjective*
long-lived
long-lost
long off *Cricket*
long on *Cricket*
Long Par|lia|ment
  (1640–1653,
  England)
long-player +s
long-playing
long-range
  adjective
long-running
Long|shan (ancient
  Chinese
  civilization)
long|ship +s
long|shore
long|shore|man
  long|shore|men
long shot +s
long-sighted
long-sighted|ly
long-sighted|ness
long-sleeved
long|spur +s
long-standing
  adjective
long-stay *adjective*
long|stop
long-suffer|ing

long-suffering|ly
long-term *adjective*
long-time *adjective*
lon|gueur +s
long|ways
long-winded
long-winded|ly
long-winded|ness
long|wise
lo|ni|cera +s
Lons|dale (belt)
loo +s (lavatory;
  card game. △lieu)
loof +s +ed +ing
loo|fah +s
look +s +ed +ing
look|alike +s
look|er +s
looker-on
  lookers-on
look-in +s *noun*
looking-glass
  looking-glasses
look|out +s
look-see +s *noun*
loom +s +ed +ing
loon +s
loo|ni|ness
loony
  loon|ies
  loon|ier
  looni|est
loony-bin +s
  (*offensive*)
loop +s +ed +ing
loop|er +s
loop|hole
  loop|holes
  loop|holed
  loop|hol|ing
loopi|ness
loop line +s
loop-the-loop +s
  noun
loopy
  loop|ier
  loopi|est
loose
  looses
  loosed
  loos|ing
  loos|er
  loos|est
  (release; untie; not
  tight. △lose, luce)
loose box
  loose boxes
loose-leaf *adjective*
loose-limbed
loose|ly
loose|ly twist|ed
loose|ly woven

loos¦en +s +ed
+ing
loos¦en¦er +s
loose|ness
loose|strife +s
(plant)
loos¦ish
loot +s +ed +ing
(booty. △ lute)
loot¦er +s
lop
  lops
  lopped
  lop|ping
lope
  lopes
  loped
  lop¦ing
lop-eared
lop-ears
lopho|branch +s
lopho|dont +s
lopho|phore +s
Lop Nor (area,
China)
lopo|lith +s
lop¦per +s
loppy
  lop|pier
  lop|pi¦est
lop|sided
lop|sided¦ly
lop|sided|ness
lo|qua¦cious
lo|qua¦cious¦ly
lo|qua¦cious|ness
lo|qua¦city
lo|quat +s
lo¦qui|tur
lor *interjection*
loran +s
Lorca, Fe¦de|rico
  Gar¦cia (Spanish
  poet and
  dramatist)
lorch
  lorches
lor¦cha +s
Lord (God)
lord +s +ed +ing
(noble; in 'lord it'.
△ laud, lauds)
lord|less
lord|like
lord|li|ness
lord|ling +s
lord¦ly
  lord|lier
  lord¦li|est
lor¦do¦sis
  lor¦do¦ses

lor|do¦tic
Lord's (cricket
  ground, London)
Lord's Day
lord|ship +s
Lord's Prayer
Lord's Sup¦per
Lordy *interjection*
lore +s (traditions;
  Zoology. △ law)
Lore|lei +s
Loren, So¦phia
  (Italian actress)
Lor|entz, Hen|drik
  An¦toon (Dutch
  physicist)
Lor¦enz, Kon¦rad
  (Austrian
  zoologist)
Lor|enzo de'
  Med¦ici
  (Florentine
  statesman and
  scholar)
Lor¦eto (town,
  Italy; name)
Lor|etta
lor¦gnette +s
lor¦gnon +s
lori|cate +s
Lori¦ent (port,
  France)
lori|keet +s
loris
  plural loris
lorn (abandoned.
  △ lawn)
Lorna
Lor|rain, Claude
  (French painter)
Lor|raine (name)
Lor|raine (region,
  France)
lorry
  lor|ries
lorry|load +s
lory
  lor¦ies
los¦able
Los Ala¦mos (town,
  USA)
Los Angel|eno +s
Los An|geles (city,
  USA)
lose
  loses
  lost
  los|ing
  (cease to have.
  △ loose)
loser +s

loss
  losses
loss ad|just¦er +s
loss-leader +s
loss-maker +s
loss-making
lost
Lot *Bible*
Lot (river, France)
lot
  lots
  lot¦ted
  lot|ting
loth (use loath)
Lo|thario +s
Lo|thian (region,
  Scotland)
Lo|thians, the
  (former counties,
  Scotland)
Loti, Pierre
  (French novelist)
loti
  ma¦loti
  (Lesotho
  currency)
lo|tion +s
lotsa (= lots of)
lotta (= lot of)
lot|tery
  lot|ter¦ies
Lot|tie
Lotto, Lor|enzo
  (Italian painter)
lotto (game)
lotus
  lo|tuses
lotus-eater +s
lotus-land +s
Lotus Sutra
  Buddhism
Lou
Lou|ang|
  phra¦bang
  (alternative name
  for Luang
  Prabang)
louche
loud +er +est
loud¦en +s +ed
  +ing
loud hail¦er +s
loud|ish
loud¦ly
loud|mouth +s
loud-mouthed
loud|ness
loud|speak¦er +s
Lou|ella
Lou Geh¦rig's
  disease

lough +s (Irish lake.
  △ loch)
Lough|bor|ough
  (town, England)
Louie
Louis (French and
  Hungarian kings;
  name)
Louis, Joe
  (American boxer)
louis
  plural louis
  (= louis d'or)
Lou¦isa
louis d'or
  plural louis d'or
  (coin)
Lou¦ise
Lou¦isi|ana (state,
  USA)
Louis-Napoleon
  (Napoleon III of
  France)
Louis Phil|ippe
  (French king)
Louis|ville (city,
  USA)
lounge
  lounges
  lounged
  loun¦ging
loun¦ger +s
loupe +s
louping-ill
lour +s +ed +ing
Lourdes (town,
  France)
Lou|renço
  Mar|ques (former
  name of Maputo)
lour|ing|ly
loury
louse
  louses
  loused
  lous|ing
  verb
louse
  lice
  noun
louse|wort +s
lous|ily
lousi|ness
lousy
  lous|ier
  lousi|est
lout +s
Louth (county,
  Republic of
  Ireland; town,
  Lincolnshire)
lout|ish

lout|ish|ly
lout|ish|ness
Lou|vain (French
name for Leuven)
lou¦ver +s (use
louvre)
Louvre (in Paris)
louvre +s
louvre-board +s
louvred
lov|abil|ity
lov¦able
lov¦able|ness
lov¦ably
lov¦age +s
lovat +s
love
  loves
  loved
  lov¦ing
love|able
love af¦fair +s
love-apple +s
love|bird +s
love|bite +s
love child
  love chil|dren
love feast +s
love game +s Sport
love-in-a-mist
Love|lace,
  Count|ess of
  (English
  mathematician)
Love|lace,
  Rich|ard (English
  poet)
love|less
love|less¦ly
love|less|ness
love let¦ter +s
love-lies-bleeding
  (plant)
love life
  love lives
love|lily
love|li|ness
Lov¦ell, Ber|nard
  (English physicist
  and astronomer)
Love|lock, James
  (British scientist)
love|lock +s
love|lorn
love|ly
  love|lies
  love|lier
  love|li|est
love|mak¦ing
love match
  love matches
love nest +s

lover +s
lover|less
lover|like
love seat +s
love|sick
love|sick|ness
love|some
love song +s
love story
  love stor|ies
love|worthy
lovey +s
  (sweetheart.
  △ luvvy)
lovey-dovey
lov¦ing cup +s
lov¦ing kind|ness
lov¦ing|ly
lov¦ing|ness
low +s +ed +ing
  +er +est (not
  high; moo. △ lo)
low-born
low¦boy +s
low-bred
low|brow
low|browed
low-calorie
Low Church noun
  and adjective
low-class adjective
Low Coun|tries
  (= The
  Netherlands,
  Belgium, and
  Luxembourg)
low-cut
low-density
  adjective
low-down +s noun
  and attributive
Low¦ell, Amy
  Law|rence
  (American poet)
Low¦ell, James
  Rus|sell
  (American poet
  and critic)
Low¦ell, Per¦ci|val
  (American
  astronomer)
Low¦ell, Rob|ert
  Traill Spence
  (American poet)
lower +s +ed +ing
  (comparative of
  low; let down;
  make lower.
  △ loa, lour)
lower case noun
lower-case
  attributive

lower-class
  adjective
Lower Hutt (city,
  New Zealand)
lower-middle-
  class adjective
lower|most
Low¦es|toft (port,
  England)
low-fat
low-flying
low gear +s
low-grade
low-growing
low-income
low¦ish
low-key
low|land +s
low|land¦er +s
low-level adjective
low|life
  plural low|lifes or
  low|lives
  (member of the
  underworld)
low life
  (degenerate living;
  criminal
  existence)
low-life (to do with
  low life)
low|light +s (dull
  feature; dark tint)
low light (dim
  light)
low-light (in or
  needing little light)
low|lily
low¦li|ness
low-loader +s
lowly
  low|lier
  low|li|est
low-lying
low-minded
low-minded¦ness
low|ness
low-paid
low-pitched
low-price adjective
low-priced
low-profile
  adjective
low-rise adjective
Lowry, Law|rence
  Ste¦phen (English
  artist)
Lowry, Mal|colm
  (English novelist)
low-spirit¦ed
low-spirit¦ed|ness
low spi¦rits

low water mark
  +s
lox (liquid oxygen;
  smoked salmon)
loxo|drome +s
loxo|drom¦ic
loyal
loyal|ism
loyal|ist +s
loy|al¦ly
loy|alty
  loy|al|ties
Loy|alty Is¦lands
  (in SW Pacific)
loz|enge +s
loz|enged
loz|engy
L-plate +s
Lua|laba (river,
  Zaire)
Lu¦anda (capital of
  Angola)
Luang Pra|bang
  (town, Laos)
lub¦ber +s
lub¦ber|like
lub¦ber line +s
lub¦ber¦ly
Lub|bock (city,
  USA)
Lü|beck (port,
  Germany)
Lu|bianka (use
  Lubyanka)
Lub¦lin (city,
  Poland)
lubra +s (may cause
  offence)
lu¦bri|cant +s
lu¦bri|cate
  lu¦bri|cates
  lu¦bri|cated
  lu¦bri|cat¦ing
lu¦bri|ca¦tion +s
lu¦bri|ca¦tive
lu¦bri|ca¦tor +s
lu¦bri|cious
lu¦bri|city
lu¦bri|cous
Lu|bum|bashi
  (city, Zaire)
Lu|byanka, the
  (KGB
  headquarters etc.,
  Moscow)
Lucan (of St Luke)
Lucan (Roman
  poet)
Lu|ca|nia (ancient
  region, Italy)
lu|carne +s

Lucas, George (American film director)

Lucas van Ley¦den (Dutch painter)

Lucca (city, Italy)

luce

plural luce (fish. △ loose)

lu¦cency

lu¦cent

lu¦cent¦ly

Lu¦cerne (town, Switzerland)

Lu¦cerne, Lake (in Switzerland)

lu¦cerne +s (plant)

Lucia

Lu¦cian (Greek writer)

lucid

lu¦cid¦ity

lu¦cid¦ly

lu¦cid¦ness

Lu¦ci¦fer (Satan)

lu¦ci¦fer +s (match)

Lu¦cille

Lu¦cinda

luck +s +ed +ing

luck¦ily

lucki¦ness

luck¦less

luck¦less¦ly

luck¦less¦ness

Luck¦now (city, India)

lucky

luck¦ier

lucki¦est

lu¦cra¦tive

lu¦cra¦tive¦ly

lu¦cra¦tive¦ness

lucre

Lu¦cre¦tia *Roman Legend*

Lu¦cre¦tius (Roman poet)

lucu¦brate

lucu¦brates

lucu¦brated

lucu¦brat¦ing

lucu¦bra¦tion

lucu¦bra¦tor +s

Lu¦cul¦lan

Lucy

lud (in 'm'lud')

Luda (city, China)

Lud¦dism

Lud¦dite +s

Lud¦dit¦ism

Lu¦den¦dorff, Erich (German general)

Lud¦hiana (city, India)

ludi¦crous

ludi¦crous¦ly

ludi¦crous¦ness

Ludo (= Ludovic)

ludo (game)

Lu¦do¦vic

Lud¦wig (Bavarian kings)

Lud¦wigs¦hafen (city, Germany)

lues (ven¦erea)

lu¦et¦ic

luff +s +ed +ing

luffa +s

Luft¦waffe

lug

lugs

lugged

lug¦ging

Lu¦gano (town, Italy)

Lu¦gansk (Russian name for Luhansk)

Lug¦du¦num (Roman name for Lyons)

luge

luges

luged

lu¦ging

Luger +s (gun)

lug¦gable +s

lug¦gage

lug¦gage van +s

lug¦ger +s

lug¦hole +s

Lu¦gosi, Bela (Hungarian-born American actor)

lug¦sail +s

lu¦gu¦bri¦ous

lu¦gu¦bri¦ous¦ly

lu¦gu¦bri¦ous¦ness

lug¦worm +s

Lu¦hansk (city, Ukraine)

Lu¦kács, György (Hungarian Marxist philosopher)

Luke (evangelist and saint)

luke¦warm

luke¦warm¦ly

luke¦warm¦ness

lull +s +ed +ing

lul¦laby

lul¦la¦bies

lul¦la¦bied

lul¦la¦by¦ing

Lully, Jean-Baptiste (Italian-born French composer)

lulu +s

lum¦bago

lum¦bar (relating to the lower back)

lum¦ber +s +ed +ing (useless objects; timber; move awkwardly; encumber)

lum¦ber¦er +s

lum¦ber¦jack +s

lumber-jacket +s

lum¦ber¦man

lum¦ber¦men

lumber-room +s

lum¦ber¦some

lum¦bri¦cal (muscle)

lumen

plural lumen *Physics*

lumen

lu¦mina *Anatomy*

Lu¦mière, Au¦guste and Louis (French inventors and pioneers of cinema)

lu¦min¦aire +s

Lu¦min¦al (drug) *Propr.*

lu¦min¦al (of a lumen)

lu¦mi¦nance +s

lu¦mi¦nary

lu¦mi¦nar¦ies

lu¦mi¦nes¦cence

lu¦mi¦nes¦cent

lu¦mi¦nif¦er¦ous

lu¦mi¦nos¦ity

lu¦mi¦nos¦ities

lu¦mi¦nous

lu¦mi¦nous¦ly

lu¦mi¦nous¦ness

lumme *interjection*

lum¦mox

lum¦moxes

lump +s +ed +ing

lump¦ec¦tomy

lump¦ec¦to¦mies

lump¦en

lump¦en¦pro¦le¦tar¦iat

lump¦er +s

lump¦fish

plural lump¦fish *or* lump¦fishes

lump¦ily

lumpi¦ness

lump¦ish

lump¦ish¦ly

lump¦ish¦ness

lump¦suck¦er +s

lump sum +s *noun*

lump-sum *attributive*

lumpy

lump¦ier

lumpi¦est

Luna (Soviet moon probes)

lu¦nacy

lu¦na¦cies

luna moth +s

lunar

lun¦ate

lu¦na¦tic +s

lun¦ation +s

lunch

lunches

lunched

lunch¦ing

lunch box

lunch boxes

lunch break +s

lunch¦eon +s

lunch¦eon¦ette +s

lunch¦er +s

lunch hour +s

lunch¦time +s

Lund (city, Sweden)

Lundy (island or shipping area off SW England)

lune +s

lu¦nette +s

lung +s

lunge

lunges

lunged

lun¦ging (thrust etc.)

lunge

lunges

lunged

lunge¦ing (horse's rein)

lung¦fish

plural lung¦fish *or* lung¦fishes

lung¦ful +s

lungi +s

lung|less
lung-power
lung|worm +s
lung|wort +s
luni|solar
lun|ula
  lunu|lae
Luo
  plural Luo *or* Luos
Luo|yang (city,
  China)
Lu|per|calia
lupi|form
lupin +s (flower)
lu|pine +s (flower;
  use lupin)
lu|pine (like a wolf)
lu|poid
lu|pous *adjective*
lupus (**vul**|garis)
  noun
lur +s
lurch
  lurches
  lurched
  lurch|ing
lurch|er +s
lure
  lures
  lured
  lur|ing
  (entice;
  enticement)
lure +s (trumpet;
  use lur)
lurex *Propr.*
lurgy
  lur|gies
lurid
lur|id|ly
lur|id|ness
lur|ing|ly
lurk +s +ed +ing
lurk|er +s
Lu|saka (capital of
  Zambia)
lus|cious
lus|cious|ly
lus|cious|ness
lush
  lushes
  lushed
  lush|ing
  lush|er
  lush|est
lush|ly
lush|ness
Lu|shun (port,
  China)
Lu|si|ta|nia
  (ancient province,
  SW Europe)

Lu|si|ta|nia
  (Cunard liner)
lust +s +ed +ing
lust|er *Am.* +s +ed
  +ing (*Br.* lustre)
lust|er|less *Am.*
  (*Br.* lustreless)
lust|er|ware *Am.*
  (*Br.* lustreware)
lust|ful
lust|ful|ly
lust|ful|ness
lust|ily
lusti|ness
lus|tra
lus|tral
lus|trate
  lus|trates
  lus|trated
  lus|trat|ing
lus|tra|tion +s
lustre *Br.*
  lustres
  lustred
  lus|tring
  (*Am.* luster)
lustre|less *Br.* (*Am.*
  lusterless)
lustre|ware *Br.*
  (*Am.* lusterware)
lus|trous
lus|trous|ly
lus|trous|ness
lus|trum
  lus|tra *or*
  lus|trums
lusty
  lust|ier
  lusti|est
lusus
lu|tan|ist +s (use
  lutenist)
lute
  lutes
  luted
  lut|ing
  (musical
  instrument;
  sealant. △ loot)
lut|ecium (use
  lutetium)
lu|tein +s
lu|tein|iz|ing
  (hormone)
lu|ten|ist +s
luteo|ful|vous
lu|teous
lute|string +s
Lu|te|tia (Roman
  name for Paris)
lu|te|tium
Lu|ther (name)

Lu|ther, Mar|tin
  (German
  Protestant
  theologian)
Lu|ther|an +s
Lu|ther|an Church
Lu|ther|an|ise *Br.*
  (use Lutheranize)
Lu|ther|an|ises
Lu|ther|an|ised
Lu|ther|an|is|ing
Lu|ther|an|ism
Lu|ther|an|ize
Lu|ther|an|izes
Lu|ther|an|ized
Lu|ther|an|iz|ing
lu|thier +s
Lu|thuli, Al|bert
  John (South
  African political
  leader)
Lu|tine Bell
lut|ing +s
Luton (town,
  England)
Lu|to|sław|ski,
  Wi|told (Polish
  composer)
Lu|tuli, Al|bert
  John (use
  Luthuli)
Lut|yens, Edwin
  (English architect)
Lut|yens,
  Eliza|beth
  (English
  composer)
lutz
  lutzes
luv|vie +s (use
  luvvy)
luvvy
  luv|vies
  (effusive actor or
  actress. △ lovey)
lux
  plural lux
  (unit of
  illumination)
lux|ate
  lux|ates
  lux|ated
  lux|at|ing
lux|ation +s
luxe +s (luxury; in
  'de luxe')
Lux|em|bourg
Lux|em|bourg|er
  +s
Lux|em|burg,
  Rosa (Polish-born
  German

Lux|em|burg
  (*cont.*)
  revolutionary
  leader)
Lux|em|burg|ish
Luxor (city, Egypt)
lux|uri|ance
lux|uri|ant
lux|uri|ant|ly
lux|uri|ate
  lux|uri|ates
  lux|uri|ated
  lux|uri|at|ing
lux|uri|ous
lux|uri|ous|ly
lux|uri|ous|ness
lux|ury
  lux|ur|ies
Luzon (island,
  Philippines)
Lviv (city, Ukraine)
Lvov (Russian
  name for Lviv)
lwei +s
Ly|all|pur (former
  name of
  Faisalabad)
ly|can|thrope +s
ly|can|thropy
lycée +s
Ly|ceum *Philosophy*
ly|ceum +s (lecture
  hall etc.)
ly|chee +s
lych-gate +s
lych|nis
  lych|nises
Lycia (ancient
  region, Asia
  Minor)
Ly|cian +s
ly|co|pod +s
ly|co|po|dium
Lycra *Propr.*
Ly|cur|gus (reputed
  founder of Sparta)
Lyd|gate, John
  (English poet)
Lydia (ancient
  name for part of
  Asia Minor; name)
Lyd|ian +s
lye +s (alkaline
  liquid. △ lie)
Lyell, Charles
  (Scottish
  geologist)
lying
lying-in-state *noun*
ly|ing|ly
lyke wake +s

Lyly, John (English
poet and
dramatist)
Lyme dis|ease
lyme-grass
  lyme-grasses
Lyme Regis (town,
England)
lymph
lymph|aden|
     op|athy
lymph|at|ic
lympho|cyte +s
lympho|cyt|ic
lymph|oid
lymph|oma
  lymph|omas or
  lymph|omata
lymph|ous
Lyn also Lynn,
  Lynne
lyn|cean
lynch
  lynches
  lynched
  lynch|ing
lynch|er +s
lynchet +s
lynch|ing +s
lynch|pin +s (use
  linchpin)
Lynda also Linda
Lyn|ette
Lynn also Lyn,
  Lynne
  (name)
Lynn, Vera
  (English singer)
Lynne also Lyn,
  Lynn
  (name)
Lyn|sey also
  Lind|say,
  Lind|sey
lynx
  lynxes
  (animal. △ links)
lynx-eyed
lynx|like
Lyon (French name
  for Lyons)
Ly|on|nais (of
  Lyons)
Lyons (city,
  France)
lyo|phil|ic
ly|oph|il|ise Br.
  (use lyophilize)
  ly|oph|il|ises
  ly|oph|il|ised
  ly|oph|il|is|ing

ly|oph|il|ize
  ly|oph|il|izes
  ly|oph|il|ized
  ly|oph|il|iz|ing
lyo|pho|bic
Lyra (constellation)
lyr|ate
lyre +s (musical
  instrument. △ liar)
lyre-bird +s
lyre-flower +s
lyric +s
lyr|ic|al
lyr|ic|al|ly
lyri|cism
lyri|cist +s
lyr|ist +s
Ly|san|der
  (Spartan general
  and statesman)
lyse
  lyses
  lysed
  lys|ing
Ly|senko, Trofim
  Den|iso|vich
  (Soviet biologist
  and geneticist)
lys|er|gic
lysin +s (blood
  protein)
ly|sine (amino acid)
Ly|sip|pus (Greek
  sculptor)
lysis
  lyses
Lysol Propr.
lyso|some +s
lyso|zyme +s
lytic
lytta
lyt|tae
Lyt|ton, Lord (title
  of Edward
  Bulwer-Lytton)

Mm

m' (= my)
ma (= mother.
  △ mar)
ma'am (= madam.
  △ marm)
Maas (Flemish and
  Dutch name for
  the Meuse)
Maas|tricht (city,
  the Netherlands)
Maat Egyptian
  Mythology
Mabel
Mabi|no|gion Celtic
  Mythology
Ma|buse, Jan
  (Flemish painter)
Mac +s (Scotsman;
  form of address)
mac +s
  (= mackintosh)
ma|cabre
ma|caco +s
mac|adam +s
maca|da|mia +s
mac|ad|am|ise Br.
  (use
  macadamize)
  mac|ad|am|ises
  mac|ad|am|ised
  mac|ad|am|is|ing
mac|ad|am|ize
  mac|ad|am|izes
  mac|ad|am|ized
  mac|ad|am|iz|ing
Mac|Alpin,
  Ken|neth
  (Scottish king)
Maca|nese
  plural Maca|nese
Macao (Portuguese
  dependency,
  China)
Ma|capá (town,
  Brazil)
ma|caque +s
Maca|ro|nesia
  (region of island
  groups, NE
  Atlantic)
Maca|ro|nes|ian
maca|roni +s
  (pasta; penguin)
maca|roni
  maca|ro|nies
  (dandy)
maca|ron|ic +s
maca|roon +s

Mac|Arthur,
  Doug|las
  (American
  general)
Ma|cas|sar (former
  name of Ujung
  Padang)
Ma|cas|sar|ese
  (use Makasarese)
  plural
  Ma|cas|sar|ese
Ma|cas|sar oil +s
Macau (Portuguese
  name for Macao)
Mac|aulay, Rose
  (English writer)
Mac|aulay,
  Thomas
  Bab|ing|ton
  (Lord Macaulay,
  English historian)
macaw +s
Mac|beth (Scottish
  king)
Mac|ca|baeus,
  Judas (Jewish
  leader)
Mac|ca|bean
Mac|ca|bee +s
Mac|Diarmid,
  Hugh (Scottish
  poet)
Mac|Donald,
  Flora (Scottish
  Jacobite heroine)
Mac|Donald,
  Ram|say (British
  prime minister)
Mac|don|ald,
  John (Scottish-
  born Canadian
  prime minister)
Mac|Donnell
  Ranges
  (mountains,
  Australia)
Mace (chemical)
mace +s (club;
  spice)
mace-bearer +s
ma|cé|doine +s
Ma|ce|don
  (= Macedonia)
Ma|ce|do|nia
  (ancient country,
  SE Europe)
Ma|ce|do|nian +s
Ma|ceió (port,
  Brazil)
macer +s
ma|cer|ate
  ma|cer|ates

ma¦cer¦ate (*cont.*)
　ma¦cer¦ated
　ma¦cer¦at¦ing
ma¦cer¦ation +s
ma¦cer¦ator +s
Mac¦gil¦li¦cuddy's
　Reeks (hills,
　Republic of
　Ireland)
Mach, Ernst
　(Austrian
　physicist)
Mach 1 etc.
ma¦chete +s
Ma¦chia¦velli,
　Nic¦colò di
　Ber¦nardo dei
　(Florentine
　statesman)
ma¦chia¦vel¦lian
ma¦chia¦vel¦lian¦
　　ism
ma¦chico¦late
　ma¦chico¦lates
　ma¦chico¦lated
　ma¦chico¦lat¦ing
ma¦chico¦la¦tion
　+s
ma¦chin¦abil¦ity
ma¦chin¦able
ma¦chin¦ate
　ma¦chin¦ates
　ma¦chin¦ated
　ma¦chin¦at¦ing
ma¦chin¦ation +s
ma¦chin¦ator +s
ma¦chine
　ma¦chines
　ma¦chined
　ma¦chin¦ing
machine-gun
　machine-guns
　machine-gunned
　machine-gunning
machine-gunner
　+s
machine-minder
　+s
ma¦chine pis¦tol
　+s
machine-readable
ma¦chin¦ery
ma¦chin¦er¦ies
ma¦chine tool +s
machine-tooled
machine-
　washable
ma¦chin¦ist +s
mach¦ismo
Mach¦meter +s
Mach num¦ber +s
macho +s

Mach's prin¦ciple
Macht¦poli¦tik
Machu Pic¦chu
　(Inca town, Peru)
Ma¦cias Nguema
　(former name of
　Bioko)
mac¦in¦tosh (use
　mackintosh)
mac¦in¦toshes
mack +s (use mac)
Mac¦kay (port,
　Australia)
Mac¦ken¦zie,
　Alex¦an¦der
　(Scottish explorer)
Mac¦ken¦zie,
　Comp¦ton
　(English writer)
Mac¦ken¦zie,
　Wil¦liam Lyon
　(Canadian
　revolutionary)
Mac¦ken¦zie River
　(in Canada)
mack¦erel
　plural mack¦erel
　or mack¦erels
mack¦erel shark
　+s
mack¦erel sky
　mack¦erel skies
Mack¦in¦tosh,
　Charles Ren¦nie
　(Scottish architect
　and designer)
mack¦in¦tosh
　mack¦in¦toshes
mackle +s (printing
　blemish)
macle +s (twin
　crystal; spot in a
　mineral)
Mac¦lean, Ali¦stair
　(Scottish writer)
Mac¦lean, Don¦ald
　(British Soviet
　spy)
Mac¦leod, John
　James Rick¦ard
　(Scottish
　physiologist)
Mac¦mil¦lan,
　Har¦old (British
　prime minister)
Mac¦Neice, Louis
　(British poet)
Mâcon +s (city,
　France; wine)
Mac¦qua¦rie,
　Lach¦lan
　(Scottish-born

Mac¦qua¦rie (*cont.*)
　Australian colonial
　administrator)
Mac¦quarie River
　(in Australia)
mac¦ramé
macro +s
macro¦bi¦ot¦ic
macro¦bi¦ot¦ics
macro¦carpa +s
macro¦ceph¦alic
macro¦ceph¦al¦ous
macro¦ceph¦aly
macro¦cosm +s
macro¦cos¦mic
macro¦cos¦mic¦
　　al¦ly
macro¦eco¦nom¦ic
macro¦
　　eco¦nom¦ics
macro¦evo¦lu¦tion
macro¦evo¦lu¦tion¦
　　ary
macro-instruction
　+s
macro¦lepi¦
　　dop¦tera
macro¦mol¦ecu¦lar
macro¦mol¦ecule
　+s
mac¦ron +s
macro¦nu¦tri¦ent
　+s
macro¦phage +s
macro¦
　　photog¦raphy
macro¦pod +s
macro¦scop¦ic
macro¦scop¦ic¦
　　al¦ly
mac¦ula
macu¦lae
mac¦ula lutea
macu¦lae lu¦teae
macu¦lar
macu¦la¦tion +s
mad
　mads
mad¦ded
mad¦ding
mad¦der
mad¦dest
Mada¦gas¦can +s
Mada¦gas¦car
　(island, Indian
　Ocean)
madam +s (English
　form of address;
　conceited girl;
　brothel-keeper)
Ma¦dame
　Mes¦dames

Ma¦dame (*cont.*)
　(French-speaking
　woman)
mad¦cap +s
mad cow dis¦ease
mad¦den +s +ed
　　+ing
mad¦den¦ing¦ly
mad¦der +s
Mad¦die *also*
　Maddy
Maddy *also*
　Mad¦die
made (past tense
　and past participle
　of make. △ maid)
Ma¦deira (island,
　Atlantic Ocean)
Ma¦deira (river,
　Brazil)
Ma¦deira +s (wine)
Ma¦deir¦an +s
Mad¦elaine *also*
　Mad¦eleine,
　Mad¦eline
Mad¦eleine *also*
　Mad¦elaine,
　Mad¦eline
　(name)
mad¦eleine +s
　(cake)
Mad¦eline *also*
　Mad¦elaine,
　Mad¦eleine
Ma¦de¦mois¦elle
　Mes¦de¦mois¦elles
made-to-measure
　attributive
made-up *attributive*
mad¦house +s
Madhya Pra¦desh
　(state, India)
Madi¦son (city,
　USA)
Madi¦son, James
　(American
　president)
madly
mad¦man
mad¦men
mad¦ness
mad¦nesses
Ma¦donna, the
　(Virgin Mary)
Ma¦donna
　(American singer)
ma¦donna +s
　(picture; statue;
　etc.)
ma¦donna lily
　ma¦donna lil¦ies

Ma¦dras (port, India)

ma¦dras (striped cotton)

mad¦re¦pore +s

mad¦re¦por¦ic

Ma¦drid (capital of Spain)

mad¦ri¦gal +s

mad¦ri¦gal¦esque

mad¦ri¦gal¦ian

mad¦ri¦gal¦ist +s

ma¦drona +s

ma¦droño +s

Ma¦dura (island, Indonesia)

Madu¦rai (city, India)

Madur¦ese

plural Madur¦ese

mad¦woman

mad¦women

Mae *also* May

Mae¦an¦der (ancient name for the Menderes)

Mae¦ce¦nas, Gaius (Roman writer)

mael¦strom +s

mae¦nad +s

mae¦nad¦ic

maes¦toso +s *Music*

maes¦tro

maes¦tri *or*

maes¦tros

Mae¦ter¦linck, Maur¦ice (Belgian writer)

Maeve

Mae West +s (American actress; life jacket)

Mafe¦king (town, South Africa)

MAFF (= Ministry of Agriculture, Fisheries, and Food)

maf¦fick +s +ed +ing

Mafia (in Sicily, USA, etc.)

mafia +s (similar group)

Mafi¦keng (use Mafeking)

Mafi¦oso

Mafi¦osi (member of Mafia)

mafi¦oso

mafi¦osi (member of Mafia)

---

mag +s (= magazine)

Mag¦adha (ancient kingdom, India)

Mag¦adi, Lake (in Kenya)

Mag¦ahi

maga¦logue +s

maga¦zine +s

mag¦da¦len +s

Mag¦da¦lena (river, Colombia; name)

Magd¦alen Col¦lege (at Oxford University)

Mag¦da¦lene (in 'Mary Magdalene')

Magd¦alene Col¦lege (at Cambridge University)

Mag¦da¦len¦ian

Mag¦de¦burg (city, Germany)

mage +s

Ma¦gel¦lan, Fer¦di¦nand (Portuguese explorer)

Ma¦gel¦lan, Strait of (off S. America)

Mag¦el¦lan¦ic clouds (galaxies)

ma¦genta +s

Mag¦gie

Mag¦giore, Lake (Italy and Switzerland)

mag¦got +s

mag¦goty

Magh¦rib (region, Africa)

Magi (the 'wise men')

magi (plural of magus)

ma¦gian

ma¦gian¦ism

magic

magics

ma¦gicked

ma¦gick¦ing

magic¦al

magic¦al¦ly

ma¦gi¦cian +s

ma¦gilp (use megilp)

Magi¦not Line (French fortification)

magis¦ter¦ial

---

magis¦teri¦al¦ly

magis¦ter¦ium

magis¦tracy

magis¦tra¦cies

magis¦tral

magis¦trate +s

magis¦trate¦ship +s

magis¦tra¦ture +s

Mag¦le¦mo¦sian

mag¦lev +s

magma

magmas *or* **mag¦mata**

mag¦mat¦ic

Magna Carta (political charter)

Magna Grae¦cia (group of ancient Greek cities, Italy)

mag¦na¦nim¦ity

mag¦nani¦mous

mag¦nani¦mous¦ly

mag¦nate +s

mag¦ne¦sia +s

mag¦nes¦ian

mag¦ne¦site +s

mag¦ne¦sium

mag¦net +s

mag¦net¦ic

mag¦net¦ic¦al¦ly

mag¦net¦ics

mag¦net¦is¦able *Br.* (use magnetizable)

mag¦net¦isa¦tion *Br.* +s (use magnetization)

mag¦net¦ise *Br.* (use magnetize)

mag¦net¦ises

mag¦net¦ised

mag¦net¦is¦ing

mag¦net¦iser *Br.* +s (use magnetizer)

mag¦net¦ism

mag¦net¦ite

mag¦net¦iz¦able

mag¦net¦iza¦tion +s

mag¦net¦ize

mag¦net¦izes

mag¦net¦ized

mag¦net¦iz¦ing

mag¦net¦izer +s

mag¦neto +s

magneto-electric

magneto-electri¦city

mag¦neto¦graph +s

---

mag¦neto¦hydro¦ dynam¦ic

mag¦neto¦hydro¦ dynam¦ics

mag¦net¦om¦eter +s

mag¦net¦om¦etry

mag¦neto¦mo¦tive

mag¦ne¦ton +s

mag¦neto¦sphere +s

mag¦neto¦ stric¦tion +s

mag¦ne¦tron +s

mag¦ni¦fi¦able

Mag¦nifi¦cat (canticle)

mag¦nifi¦cat +s (song of praise)

mag¦ni¦fi¦ca¦tion +s

mag¦nifi¦cence

mag¦nifi¦cent

mag¦nifi¦cent¦ly

mag¦nif¦ico

mag¦nif¦icoes

mag¦ni¦fier +s

mag¦nify

mag¦ni¦fies

mag¦ni¦fied

mag¦ni¦fy¦ing

mag¦ni¦fy¦ing glass

mag¦ni¦fy¦ing glasses

mag¦nilo¦quence

mag¦nilo¦quent

mag¦nilo¦quent¦ly

Mag¦nito¦gorsk (city, Russia)

mag¦ni¦tude +s

mag¦no¦lia +s

mag¦nox

mag¦noxes

mag¦num +s

mag¦num opus

mag¦num opuses *or* **magna opera**

Mag¦nus

Magog (in 'Gog and Magog')

mag¦pie +s

Ma¦gritte, René (Belgian painter)

mags¦man

mags¦men

ma¦guey +s

magus

magi

Mag¦yar +s

Maha¦bad (city, Iran)

Maha|bhar|ata (Hindu Sanskrit epic poem)
maha|leb +s
maha|raja +s *male*
maha|ra|jah +s (use maharaja)
maha|ra|nee +s *female*
maha|rani +s (use maharanee)
Maha|rash|tra (state, India)
Maha|rash|trian +s
maha|rishi +s
ma|hatma +s
Maha|weli (river, Sri Lanka)
Maha|yana *Buddhism*
Mahdi +s *Islam*
Mahd|ism
Mahd|ist +s
Mah|fouz, Na|guib (Egyptian writer)
Ma|hi|lyow (city, Belarus)
mah-jong
Mah|ler, Gus|tav (Austrian composer)
mahl|stick +s
ma|hog|any
ma|hog|anies
Mahón (capital of Minorca)
ma|ho|nia +s
Ma|hore (alternative name for Mayotte)
ma|hout +s
Mah|ratta +s (use Maratha)
Mah|ratti (use Marathi)
mah|seer +s
Maia *Greek and Roman Mythology*
maid +s (servant; girl. △ made)
mai|dan +s (open space)
maid|en +s (girl)
maid|en|hair
Maid|en|head (town, England)
maid|en|head +s (virginity)
maid|en|hood +s
maid|en|ish
maid|en|like

maid|en|ly
maid|en name +s
maid|en over +s
maid|ish
maid|ser|vant +s
Maid|stone (town, England)
mai|eu|tic
maigre
Mai|gret (fictional detective)
Mai|kop (city, Russia)
mail +s +ed +ing (post. △ male)
mail|able
mail|bag +s
mail|boat +s
mail|box
mail|boxes
mail car|rier +s
mail coach
mail coaches
mail drop +s
Mail|er, Nor|man (American writer)
mail|er +s
mail|ing +s
mail|ing list +s
mail|lot +s
mail|man
mail|men
mail order +s *noun*
mail-order *attributive*
mail|shot +s
mail train +s
maim +s +ed +ing
Mai|moni|des (Spanish-born Jewish philosopher)
Main (river, Germany)
main +s (principal; pipe; cable; ocean. △ mane)
main brace +s
main-course *attributive*
main|crop *attributive*
Maine (state, USA)
main|frame +s
Main|land (islands, Orkney and Shetland)
main|land +s
main|land|er +s
main|line
main|lines
main|lined

main|line (*cont.*)
main|lin|ing (inject drugs intravenously)
main line +s (railway line; principal vein)
main|liner +s
main|ly
main|mast +s
main|plane +s
main|sail +s
main|sheet +s
main|spring +s
main|stay +s
main|stream +s
main street +s
main|tain +s +ed +ing
main|tain|abil|ity
main|tain|able
main|tain|er +s (generally)
main|tain|or +s *Law*
main|ten|ance +s
Main|te|non, Mar|quise de (wife of Louis XIV of France)
main|top +s
main|top|mast +s
main yard +s
Mainz (city, Germany)
mai|ol|ica (use majolica)
Mai|sie
mai|son|ette +s
Mai|thili
maître d'hôtel
maîtres d'hôtel
maize +s (cereal. △ maze)
ma|jes|tic
ma|jes|tic|al|ly
maj|esty
maj|es|ties
Maj|lis
ma|jol|ica +s
Major, John (British prime minister)
major +s +ed +ing
major axis
major axes
Ma|jorca (Spanish island)
Ma|jor|can +s
major-domo +s
ma|jor|ette +s
major gen|eral +s

Ma|jor|ism
ma|jor|ity
ma|jor|ities
ma|jor|ship +s
maj|us|cu|lar
maj|us|cule +s
mak|able
Ma|ka|rios III (Greek Cypriot archbishop and president)
Ma|ka|sa|rese *plural*
Ma|ka|sa|rese
Ma|kas|sar (former name of Ujung Padang)
Ma|kas|sar Strait (between Borneo and Sulawesi)
make
makes
made
mak|ing
make-belief
make-believe
make-over +s
maker +s
make-ready
make|shift +s
make-up +s *noun*
make|weight +s
Mak|ga|dik|gadi Pans (region, Botswana)
Makh|ach|kala (port, Russia)
mak|ing +s
mako +s
Mak|su|tov (telescope)
ma|kuta (plural of likuta)
Mala|bar Chris|tians
Mala|bar Coast (region, India)
Ma|labo (capital of Equatorial Guinea)
mal|ab|sorp|tion +s
Ma|lacca (former name of Melaka)
Ma|lacca, Strait of (between Malaysia and Sumatra)
ma|lacca (cane)
Mal|achi *Bible*
mal|ach|ite +s
mala|col|ogy
mala|con

mala|cos|tra|can +s

mal|adap|ta|tion +s

mal|adap|tive

mal|adjust|ed

mal|adjust|ment +s

mal|admin|is|ter +s +ed +ing

mal|admin|is| tra|tion +s

mal|adroit

mal|adroit|ly

mal|adroit|ness

mal|ady
  mal|ad|ies

mala fide

Mal|aga (port, Spain; wine)

Mala|gasy
  Mala|gas|ies

mala|gueña +s

mal|aise +s

Mala|mud, Ber|nard (American writer)

mala|mute +s

mal|an|ders (use mallenders)

mala|pert +s

mala|prop +s

mala|prop|ism +s

mal|apro|pos

malar +s

Mäla|ren (lake, Sweden)

mal|aria +s

mal|ar|ial

mal|ar|ian

mal|ari|ous

ma|lar|key

mala|thion

Ma|lawi

Ma|la|wian +s

Malay +s

Ma|laya (former country, SE Asia)

Ma|lay|alam

Ma|lay|an +s

Malayo-Chinese
  plural Malayo-Chinese

Malayo-Polynes|ian +s

Ma|lay|sia

Ma|lay|sian +s

Mal|colm (Scottish kings; name)

Mal|colm X (American political activist)

mal|con|tent +s

mal de mer

mal|dis|trib|uted

mal|dis|tri|bu|tion

Mal|dives (islands, Indian Ocean)

Mal|div|ian +s

Male (capital of the Maldives)

male +s (masculine. △ mail)

mal|edic|tion +s

mal|edic|tive

mal|edic|tory

mal|efac|tion +s

mal|efac|tor +s

ma|lef|ic

ma|lefi|cence

ma|lefi|cent

Male|gaon (city, India)

ma|leic

mal|emute +s (use malamute)

male|ness

ma|levo|lence

ma|levo|lent

ma|levo|lent|ly

mal|fea|sance

mal|fea|sant +s

mal|for|ma|tion +s

mal|formed

mal|func|tion +s +ed +ing

Mal|herbe, Fran|çois de (French poet)

Mali (country)

mali +s (gardener)

Mali|an +s

Mal|ibu (resort, USA)

malic

mal|ice

ma|li|cious

ma|li|cious|ly

ma|li|cious|ness

ma|lign +s +ed +ing (malignant; slander. △ moline)

ma|lig|nancy
  ma|lig|nan|cies

ma|lig|nant

ma|lig|nant|ly

ma|lign|er +s

ma|lig|nity
  ma|lig|nities

ma|lign|ly

Malin (shipping area off Ireland)

Ma|lines (French name for Mechelen)

ma|lin|ger +s +ed +ing

ma|lin|ger|er +s

Malin Head (on Irish coast; weather station off Ireland)

Ma|li|now|ski, Bron|isław Kas|par (Polish anthropologist)

mal|ism

mall +s (walk; shopping centre. △ maul)

mal|lard
  plural mal|lard *or* mal|lards

Mal|lar|mé, Sté|phane (French poet)

mal|le|abil|ity

mal|le|able

mal|le|ably

mal|lee +s

mal|lee bird +s

mal|lee fowl
  plural mal|lee fowl

mal|lee hen +s

mal|lei (plural of malleus)

mal|le|muck +s

mal|len|ders

mal|le|olus
  mal|le|oli

mal|let +s

mal|leus
  mal|lei

Mal|lorca (Spanish name for Majorca)

Mal|lor|can +s (use Majorcan)

mal|low +s

malm +s (rock, brick. △ ma'am)

Malmö (port, Sweden)

malm|sey +s

mal|nour|ished

mal|nour|ish|ment

mal|nu|tri|tion

mal|occlu|sion

mal|odor|ous

Mal|ory, Thomas (English writer)

ma|loti (plural of loti)

Mal|pi|ghi, Mar|cello (Italian microscopist)

Mal|pig|hian

Mal|pla|quet (battle site, France)

mal|prac|tice +s

malt +s +ed +ing

Malta

Mal|tese
  plural Mal|tese

mal|tha +s

malt|house +s

Mal|thus, Thomas Rob|ert (English economist)

Mal|thu|sian +s

malti|ness

malt|ing +s

mal|tose

mal|treat +s +ed +ing

mal|treat|er +s

mal|treat|ment +s

malt|ster +s

malty
  malt|ier
  malti|est

Ma|luku (Indonesian name for the Moluccas)

mal|va|ceous

Mal|vern Hills (in W. England)

Mal|verns (= Malvern Hills)

mal|ver|sa|tion

Mal|vi|nas, Islas (Argentinian name for the Falkland Islands)

mal|voisie +s

mam +s

mama +s

mamba +s

mambo +s

mam|elon +s

Mam|eluke +s

Mamet, David (American dramatist)

Mamie

ma|milla *Br.*
  ma|mil|las *or*
  ma|mil|lae
  (*Am.* mammilla)

mam|il|lary (use mammillary)

mam|il|late (use mammillate)

mamma
  mam¦mae
  (breast)
mamma +s
  (mother)
mam¦mal +s
Mam¦ma¦lia
mam¦ma¦lian +s
mam¦mal¦ifer¦ous
mam¦mal¦ogy
mam¦mary
  mam¦mar¦ies
  mam¦mary gland
  +s
mam¦mee +s (tree.
  ⚠ mammy)
mam¦mi¦form
mam¦milla Am.
  mam¦mil¦las or
  mam¦mil¦lae
  (Br. mamilla)
mam¦mil¦lary
mam¦mil¦late
mam¦mo¦gram +s
mam¦mog¦raphy
Mam¦mon
Mam¦mon¦ish
Mam¦mon¦ism
Mam¦mon¦ist +s
Mam¦mon¦ite +s
mam¦moth +s
mammy
  mam¦mies
  (mother.
  ⚠ mammee)
Ma¦mou¦tzu
  (capital of
  Mayotte)
Man, Isle of (in
  Irish Sea)
man
  men
  noun
man
  mans
  manned
  man¦ning
  verb
mana
man¦acle
  man¦acles
  man¦acled
  man¦ac¦ling
man¦age
  man¦ages
  man¦aged
  man¦aging
man¦age¦abil¦ity
man¦age¦able
man¦age¦able¦ness
man¦age¦ably
man¦age¦ment +s

man¦ager +s
man¦ager¦ess
  man¦ager¦esses
man¦ager¦ial
man¦ageri¦al¦ly
man¦ager¦ship +s
Ma¦na¦gua (capital
  of Nicaragua)
man¦akin +s (bird.
  ⚠ manikin,
  mannequin,
  mannikin)
Ma¦nama (capital
  of Bahrain)
ma¦ñana +s
Mana Pools
  (national park,
  Zimbabwe)
Ma¦nas¦seh Bible
Ma¦nas¦ses,
  Prayer of
man-at-arms
  men-at-arms
mana¦tee +s
Ma¦naus (city,
  Brazil)
Mana¦watu (river,
  New Zealand)
Man¦ches¦ter (city,
  England)
man¦chi¦neel +s
Man¦chu +s
Man¦chu¦ria
  (region, China)
Man¦chu¦rian +s
man¦ciple +s
Man¦cu¦nian +s
Man¦dae¦an +s
man¦dala +s
Man¦da¦lay (port,
  Burma)
Man¦da¦mus
Man¦da¦rin
  (language)
man¦da¦rin +s
  (official; orange)
man¦da¦rin¦ate +s
man¦da¦rine +s
  (use mandarin)
man¦da¦tary
  man¦da¦tar¦ies
  (person who
  receives a
  mandate.
  ⚠ mandatory)
man¦date
  man¦dates
  man¦dated
  man¦dat¦ing
man¦da¦tor +s
man¦da¦tor¦ily

man¦da¦tory
  man¦da¦tor¦ies
  (compulsory.
  ⚠ mandatary)
man-day +s
Mande
  plural Mande or
  Mandes
Man¦dela, Nel¦son
  (South African
  president)
Man¦del¦brot
  Mathematics
Man¦del¦stam,
  Osip (Russian
  poet)
Man¦de¦ville,
  John (English
  nobleman)
man¦dible +s
man¦dibu¦lar
man¦dibu¦late
man¦dola +s (large
  mandolin.
  ⚠ mandorla)
man¦do¦lin +s
  (musical
  instrument)
man¦do¦line +s
  (vegetable-slicer)
man¦do¦lin¦ist +s
man¦dorla +s
  (almond-shape.
  ⚠ mandola)
man¦drag¦ora +s
man¦drake +s
man¦drel +s (shaft;
  rod)
man¦drill +s
  (baboon)
man¦du¦cate
  man¦du¦cates
  man¦du¦cated
  man¦du¦cat¦ing
man¦du¦ca¦tion
man¦du¦ca¦tory
mane +s (hair on
  horse, lion, etc.
  ⚠ main)
man-eater +s
man-eating
maned
ma¦nège +s
mane¦less
Manes (Persian
  founder of
  Manichaeism)
manes (deified
  souls; ghost)
Manet, Édouard
  (French painter)

Ma¦netho
  (Egyptian priest)
man¦eu¦ver Am. +s
  +ed +ing (Br.
  manoeuvre)
man¦eu¦ver¦
  abil¦ity Am. (Br.
  manoeuvrability)
man¦eu¦ver¦able
  Am. (Br.
  manoeuvrable)
man¦eu¦ver¦er Am.
  +s (Br.
  manoeuvrer)
man¦eu¦ver¦ing
  Am. +s (Br.
  manoeuvring)
Man¦fred
man¦ful
man¦ful¦ly
man¦ful¦ness
man¦ga¦bey +s
man¦ga¦nate +s
man¦ga¦nese
man¦gan¦ic
man¦gan¦ous
mange +s
man¦gel +s (beet.
  ⚠ mangle)
mangel-wurzel +s
man¦ger +s
mange¦tout
  plural mange¦tout
  or mange¦touts
man¦gily
man¦gi¦ness
man¦gle
  man¦gles
  man¦gled
  man¦gling
  (laundry machine;
  mutilate.
  ⚠ mangel)
man¦gler +s
mango
  man¦goes
man¦gold +s
mangold-wurzel
  +s
man¦gonel +s
man¦go¦steen +s
man¦grove +s
mangy
  man¦gier
  man¦gi¦est
man¦handle
  man¦han¦dles
  man¦han¦dled
  man¦hand¦ling
Man¦hat¦tan
  (island, New York
  City)

man|hat|tan +s (cocktail)
man|hole +s
man|hood +s
man-hour +s
man|hunt +s
mania +s
ma|niac +s
ma|ni|acal
ma|ni|ac|al|ly
manic +s
Ma|nica|land (province, Zimbabwe)
man|ic|al|ly
manic de|pres|sion
manic-depres|sive +s
Mani|chae|an +s
Mani|chae|ism
Mani|che|an +s (use Manichaean)
Mani|chee +s
Mani|che|ism (use Manichaeism)
mani|cure
  mani|cures
  mani|cured
  mani|cur|ing
mani|cur|ist +s
mani|fest +s +ed +ing
mani|fest|ation +s
mani|fest|ative
mani|fest|ly
mani|festo +s
mani|fold +s (various; branching pipe. △ manyfold)
mani|fold|ly
mani|fold|ness
mani|kin +s (little man. △ manakin, mannequin)
Ma|nila (capital of the Philippines)
ma|nila +s (fibre; paper. △ manilla)
ma|nilla +s (bracelet. △ manila)
ma|nille +s
man|ioc +s
man|iple +s
ma|nipu|la|bil|ity
ma|nipu|lable
ma|nipu|lat|able
ma|nipu|late
  ma|nipu|lates

ma|nipu|late (cont.)
  ma|nipu|lated
  ma|nipu|lat|ing
ma|nipu|la|tion +s
ma|nipu|la|tive
ma|nipu|la|tive|ly
ma|nipu|la|tive|ness
ma|nipu|la|tor +s
ma|nipu|la|tory
Mani|pur (state, India)
Mani|puri +s
Mani|toba (province, Canada)
mani|tou +s
man|kind
manky
  mank|ier
  manki|est
man|less
Man|ley, Mi|chael Nor|man (Jamaican prime minister)
man|like
man|li|ness
manly
  man|lier
  man|li|est
man-made
Mann, Thomas (German writer)
manna (food. △ manner)
manna-ash
  manna-ashes (tree)
Man|nar (island and town, Sri Lanka)
Man|nar, Gulf of (between India and Sri Lanka)
manned
man|ne|quin +s (dressmaker's model. △ manakin, manikin)
man|ner +s (way; behaviour. △ manna)
man|nered
man|ner|ism +s
man|ner|ist +s
man|ner|is|tic
man|ner|is|tic|al
man|ner|is|tic| al|ly

man|ner|less
man|ner|li|ness
man|ner|ly
Mann|heim (city, Germany)
man|ni|kin +s (little man; use manikin. △ manakin, mannequin)
man|nish
man|nish|ly
man|nish|ness
Mano (river, W. Africa)
man|oeuv|ra| bil|ity Br. (Am. maneuverability)
man|oeuv|rable Br. (Am. maneuverable)
man|oeuvre Br.
  man|oeuvres
  man|oeuvred
  man|oeuv|ring (Am. maneuver)
man|oeuv|rer Br. +s (Am. maneuverer)
man|oeuv|ring Br. +s (Am. maneuvering)
man-of-war
  men-of-war
man|om|eter +s
mano|met|ric
ma non troppo
manor +s
manor house +s
man|orial
man|power
man|què
Man Ray (American photographer)
Mans, Le (town, France; its motor-racing circuit)
man|sard +s
Man|sart, Fran|çois (French architect)
manse +s
Man|sell, Nigel (English motor-racing driver)
man|ser|vant
  men|ser|vants or man|ser|vants
Mans|field, Kath|er|ine (New Zealand writer)

man|sion +s
Man|sion House (official residence of Lord Mayor, London)
man|sion house +s (house of lord mayor or landed proprietor)
man-size
man-sized
man|slaugh|ter +s +ed +ing
Man|son, Pat|rick (Scottish physician)
man|sue|tude
manta +s
Man|tegna, An|drea (Italian painter)
man|tel +s (mantelpiece. △ mantle)
man|tel|et +s
man|tel|piece +s
man|tel|shelf
  man|tel|shelves
man|tic
man|tid +s
man|tilla +s
man|tis
  plural man|tis or man|tises
man|tissa +s
man|tle
  man|tles
  man|tled
mant|ling (cloak. △ mantel)
mant|let +s
mant|ling +s Heraldry
man|tra +s
man|trap +s
man|tua +s
Manu Hindu Mythology
man|ual +s
manu|al|ly
manu|fac|tory
manu|fac|tor|ies
manu|fac|tur| abil|ity
manu|fac|tur|able
manu|fac|ture
  manu|fac|tures
  manu|fac|tured
  manu|fac|tur|ing
manu|fac|tur|er +s
ma|nuka +s

manu¦mis¦sion +s
manu¦mit
  manu¦mits
  manu¦mit¦ted
  manu¦mit¦ting
ma¦nure
  ma¦nures
  ma¦nured
  ma¦nur¦ing
ma¦nur¦ial
manu¦script +s
Manu¦tius, Aldus
  (Italian printer)
Manx
Manx¦man
  Manx¦men
Manx¦woman
  Manx¦women
many
many¦fold (by
  many times.
  △ manifold)
many¦plies
  plural many¦plies
many-sided
many-sidedness
many-splendored
  Am.
many-
  splendoured *Br.*
man¦za¦nilla +s
man¦za¦nita +s
Man¦zoni,
  Ales¦san¦dro
  (Italian writer)
Mao¦ism
Mao¦ist +s
Maori
  plural Maori *or*
  Maoris
  (New Zealand
  people and
  language. △ Mari)
Maori¦land
Mao Tse-tung (=
  Mao Zedong)
Mao Ze¦dong
  (Chinese head of
  state)
map
  maps
  mapped
  map¦ping
maple +s
map¦less
map-maker +s
map-making
map¦pable
Mappa Mundi
map¦per +s
map-read
  map-reads

map-read *(cont.)*
  map-read
  map-reading
map-reader +s
Ma¦puto (capital of
  Mozambique)
ma¦quette +s
ma¦quil¦lage
Ma¦quis (French
  resistance
  movement)
mar
  mars
  marred
  mar¦ring
  (spoil. △ ma)
mara¦bou +s
  (stork; feather)
mara¦bout +s
  (Muslim hermit or
  monk; shrine)
ma¦raca +s
Mara¦caibo (city
  and port,
  Venezuela)
Mara¦caibo, Lake
  (in Venezuela)
Mara¦dona, Diego
  (Argentinian
  footballer)
Ma¦ramba (city,
  Zambia)
Mara¦nhão (state,
  Brazil)
Mara¦ñón (river,
  Peru)
mar¦as¦chino +s
mar¦as¦mic
mar¦as¦mus
Marat, Jean Paul
  (French
  revolutionary)
Ma¦ra¦tha +s
Ma¦ra¦thi
  (language)
mara¦thon +s
mara¦thon¦er +s
ma¦raud +s +ed
  +ing
ma¦raud¦er +s
mara¦vedi +s
Mar¦bella (resort,
  Spain)
mar¦ble
  mar¦bles
  mar¦bled
  marb¦ling
marb¦ling +s
marbly
Mar¦burg (city,
  Germany; German

Mar¦burg *(cont.)*
  name for
  Maribor)
Marc *also* Mark
  (name)
marc +s (brandy.
  △ mark, marque)
Marc¦an (of or
  relating to St.
  Mark)
mar¦cas¦ite +s
mar¦cato (Music)
Mar¦ceau, Mar¦cel
  (French mime
  artist)
Mar¦cel (name)
mar¦cel
  mar¦cels
  mar¦celled
  marcel¦ling
  (wave in hair)
Mar¦cella
mar¦ces¦cence +s
mar¦ces¦cent
March
  Marches
  (month)
march
  marches
  marched
  march¦ing
Marche (region,
  Italy)
march¦er +s
Marches, the
  (English name for
  Marche; region,
  English-Welsh
  border)
March hare +s
march¦ing order
  +s
mar¦chion¦ess
  mar¦chion¦esses
march¦pane
march past *noun*
Mar¦cia
Mar¦ci¦ano, Rocky
  (American boxer)
Mar¦coni,
  Gugli¦elmo
  (Italian electrical
  engineer)
Marco Polo (Italian
  traveller)
Mar¦cus
Mar¦cus Aur¦elius
  (Roman emperor)
Mar¦cuse,
  Her¦bert (German-
  born American
  philosopher)

Mar del Plata
  (town, Argentina)
Mardi Gras
Mar¦duk
  Babylonian
  Mythology
mardy
Mare, Wal¦ter de
  la (English writer)
mare +s (female
  horse. △ mayor)
mare
  maria *or* mares
  (sea; flat area on
  the moon or Mars)
ma¦remma
  ma¦remme
Ma¦rengo (battle
  site, Italy)
mare's nest +s
mare's tail +s
Mar¦ga¦ret
  (Scottish queen
  and saint; British
  princess)
mar¦gar¦ine +s
Mar¦ga¦rita (port,
  Venezuela)
mar¦gay +s
marge +s (margin;
  edge; margarine)
Mar¦gery *also*
  Mar¦jorie
mar¦gin +s +ed
  +ing
mar¦gin¦al +s
mar¦gi¦na¦lia
mar¦gin¦al¦isa¦tion
  Br. +s (use
  marginalization)
mar¦gin¦al¦ise *Br.*
  (use marginalize)
  mar¦gin¦al¦ises
  mar¦gin¦al¦ised
  mar¦gin¦al¦is¦ing
mar¦gin¦al¦ity
mar¦gin¦al¦ities
mar¦gin¦al¦iza¦tion
  +s
mar¦gin¦al¦ize
  mar¦gin¦al¦izes
  mar¦gin¦al¦ized
  mar¦gin¦al¦iz¦ing
mar¦gin¦al¦ly
mar¦gin¦ate
  mar¦gin¦ates
  mar¦gin¦ated
  mar¦gin¦at¦ing
mar¦gin¦ation +s
Margo *also* Mar¦got
Mar¦got *also* Margo
mar¦grav¦ate +s

mar|grave +s *male*
mar|grav|ine +s
  female
Mar|guer|ite
  (name)
mar|guer|ite +s
  (flower)
Mari (ancient city,
  Syria)
Mari (language of
  European Russia.
  △Maori)
Maria (name)
maria (plural of
  mare)
Maria de' Med|ici
  (Italian name of
  Marie de
  Médicis)
*mari|age de
con|ve|nance*
*mari|ages de
con|ve|nance*
Mar|ian (of the
  Virgin Mary)
Mar|ian *also*
  Mar|ion
  (name)
Mari|ana Is|lands
  (in W. Pacific)
Mari|anas
  (= Mariana
  Islands)
Mari|ana Trench
  (in W. Pacific)
Mari|anne
Maria Ther|esa
  (Habsburg queen)
Mari|bor (city,
  Slovenia)
Marie
Marie An|toin|ette
  (French queen)
Marie Byrd Land
  (region,
  Antarctica)
Marie de Mé|di|cis
  (French queen)
Mari El (republic,
  Russia)
Mari|gold (name)
mari|gold +s
  (flower)
ma|ri|huana (use
  marijuana)
ma|ri|juana
Mari|lyn
ma|rimba +s
Mar|ina (name)
mar|ina +s
  (harbour for

mar|ina (*cont.*)
  pleasure boats
  etc.)
mar|in|ade
  mar|in|ades
  mar|in|aded
  mar|in|ad|ing
marin|ate
  marin|ates
  marin|ated
  marin|at|ing
marin|ation +s
mar|ine +s
Mari|ner
  (American space
  probes)
mari|ner +s
Mari|netti,
  Fi|lippo (Italian
  writer)
Mari|ol|atry
Mari|ology
Mar|ion *also*
  Mar|ian
mar|io|nette +s
Mar|isa
Mar|ist +s
mari|tal
mari|tal|ly
mari|time
Mari|times
  (= Maritime
  Provinces)
Ma|ritsa (river,
  Bulgaria and
  Greece)
Ma|riu|pol (port,
  Russia)
Mar|ius, Gaius
  (Roman general)
mar|joram +s
Mar|jorie *also*
  Mar|gery
Mark *also* **Marc**
  (name)
Mark (Apostle and
  saint)
mark +s +ed +ing
  (sign etc. △marc,
  marque)
Mark An|tony
  (Roman general)
mark|down +s
mark|ed|ly
mark|ed|ness
mark|er +s
mar|ket +s +ed
  +ing
mar|ket|abil|ity
mar|ket|able
mar|ket|eer +s
mar|ket|er +s

mar|ket|ing +s
mar|ket maker +s
mar|ket place +s
mark|hor +s
mark|ing +s
mark|ing ink +s
markka +s
Mar|kova, Ali|cia
  (English dancer)
Marks, Simon
  (Lord Marks,
  English
  businessman)
marks|man
marks|man|ship
marks|woman
marks|women
mark-up +s *noun*
marl +s +ed +ing
Marl|bor|ough
  (town and school,
  England; region,
  New Zealand)
Marl|bor|ough,
  Duke of (British
  general)
Marl|bur|ian +s
Mar|lene
Mar|ley, Bob
  (Jamaican
  musician)
mar|lin +s (fish)
mar|line +s (thin
  rope)
marline-spike +s
  (use marlinspike)
mar|lin|spike +s
mar|lite +s
Mar|lon
Mar|lowe,
  Chris|to|pher
  (English
  dramatist)
marly
Mar|ma|duke
mar|ma|lade +s
Mar|mara, Sea of
  (off Turkey)
Mar|mite (yeast
  extract) *Propr.*
mar|mite +s
  (cooking pot)
mar|mo|lite +s
mar|mor|eal
mar|mor|eal|ly
mar|mo|set +s
mar|mot +s
Marne (river,
  France)
maro|cain +s
Maro|nite +s

ma|roon +s +ed
  +ing
mar|plot +s
marque +s (make
  of car; licence.
  △marc, mark)
mar|quee +s
Mar|que|sas
  Is|lands (in S.
  Pacific)
mar|quess
  mar|quesses
  (British nobleman.
  △marquis)
mar|quess|ate +s
mar|quet|ry
Mar|quette,
  Jacques (French
  missionary)
Már|quez,
  Gab|riel Gar|cía
  (Colombian
  novelist)
mar|quis
  mar|quises
  (non-British
  nobleman.
  △marquess)
mar|quis|ate +s
mar|quise +s (wife
  or widow of
  marquis; female
  marquis)
mar|qui|sette +s
Mar|ra|kesh (town,
  Morocco)
mar|ram +s
Mar|rano +s
mar|riage +s
mar|riage|abil|ity
mar|riage|able
mar|ried +s
mar|ron glacé
  mar|rons glacés
mar|row +s
mar|row|bone +s
mar|row|fat
marry
  mar|ries
  mar|ried
  marry|ing
Mar|ryat, Cap|tain
  (English novelist)
Mars (*Roman
  Mythology*; planet)
Mar|sala (town,
  Sicily; wine.
  △masala)
Mar|seil|laise
  (French national
  anthem)

Mar|seille (French
name for
Marseilles)
Mar|seilles (port,
France)
Marsh, Ngaio
(New Zealand
writer of detective
fiction)
marsh
marshes
Mar|sha
mar|shal
mar|shals
mar|shalled Br.
mar|shaled Am.
mar|shal|ling Br.
mar|shal|ing Am.
Mar|shall, George
C. (American
general and
statesman)
Mar|shall Is|lands
(in NW Pacific)
Mar|shall Plan
mar|shal|ship +s
marshi|ness
marsh|land +s
marsh|mal|low +s
marshy
marshi|er
marshi|est
Mars|ton Moor
(battle site,
England)
mar|su|pial +s
Mar|syas Greek
Mythology
mart +s
Mar|ta|ban, Gulf
of (on the coast
of Burma)
mar|ta|gon +s
Mar|tel, Charles
(Frankish ruler)
Mar|tello +s
(tower)
mar|ten +s (weasel-
like mammal.
△ martin)
Mar|tens, Doc
(= Dr Martens)
Mar|tens, Dr Propr.
mar|tens|ite
Mar|tha (Bible;
name)
Mar|tha's
Vine|yard (island,
USA)
Mar|tial (Spanish-
born Roman poet)
mar|tial

mar|tial|ise Br.
(use martialize)
mar|tial|ises
mar|tial|ised
mar|tial|is|ing
mar|tial|ize
mar|tial|izes
mar|tial|ized
mar|tial|iz|ing
mar|tial|ly
Mar|tian +s
Mar|tin also
Mar|tyn
(name)
Mar|tin (French
saint)
mar|tin +s (bird.
△ marten)
Mar|tina
Mar|tine
mar|tinet +s
mar|tin|gale +s
Mar|tini
(vermouth) Propr.
Mar|tini +s
(cocktail)
Mar|tini, Sim|one
(Italian painter)
Mar|ti|nique
(island, Lesser
Antilles)
Mar|tin|mas
mart|let +s
mar|tyr +s +ed
+ing
mar|tyr|dom +s
mar|tyr|isa|tion
Br. +s (use
martyrization)
mar|tyr|ise Br. (use
martyrize)
mar|tyr|ises
mar|tyr|ised
mar|tyr|is|ing
mar|tyr|iza|tion
+s
mar|tyr|ize
mar|tyr|izes
mar|tyr|ized
mar|tyr|iz|ing
mar|tyr|olo|gic|al
mar|tyr|olo|gist +s
mar|tyr|ology
mar|tyr|ol|ogies
mar|tyry
mar|tyr|ies
Mar|uts Hinduism
mar|vel
mar|vels
mar|velled Br.
mar|veled Am.

mar|vel (cont.)
mar|vel|ling Br.
mar|vel|ing Am.
mar|vel|er Am. +s
Mar|vell, An|drew
(English poet)
mar|vel|ler Br. +s
mar|vel|lous Br.
mar|vel|lous|ly Br.
mar|vel|lous|ness
Br.
mar|vel|ous Am.
mar|vel|ous|ly Am.
mar|vel|ous|ness
Am.
Mar|vin
Marx, Karl
(German political
philosopher)
Marx Broth|ers,
Chico, Harpo,
Groucho, and
Zeppo (family of
American
comedians)
Marx|ian +s
Marx|ism
Marxism-
Leninism
Marx|ist +s
Marxist-Leninist
+s
Mary (name)
Mary (Blessed
Virgin Mary)
Mary (English
queens)
Mary|bor|ough
(town, Australia)
Mary Ce|leste
(ship)
Mary|land (state,
USA)
Mary Mag|da|lene
Bible
Mary, Queen of
Scots
Mary Rose (ship)
Mary Stu|art
(Mary, Queen of
Scots)
mar|zi|pan
mar|zi|pans
mar|zi|panned
mar|zi|pan|ning
Ma|sac|cio (Italian
painter)
Ma|sada (fortress,
Near East)
Masai
plural Masai or
Mas|ais

ma|sala +s (spice;
dish. △ Marsala)
Mas|aryk, Tomáš
(Czech statesman)
Mas|bate (island,
Philippines)
Mas|cagni, Pietro
(Italian composer)
mas|cara +s
Mas|car|ene
Is|lands (in
Indian Ocean)
Mas|car|enes
(= Mascarene
Islands)
mas|car|pone
mas|cle +s
mas|con +s
mas|cot +s
mas|cu|line +s
mas|cu|line|ly
mas|cu|line|ness
mas|cu|lin|isa|tion
Br. (use
masculinization)
mas|cu|lin|ise Br.
(use masculinize)
mas|cu|lin|ises
mas|cu|lin|ised
mas|cu|lin|is|ing
mas|cu|lin|ist +s
mas|cu|lin|ity
mas|cu|lin|ities
mas|cu|lin|iza|tion
mas|cu|lin|ize
mas|cu|lin|izes
mas|cu|lin|ized
mas|cu|lin|iz|ing
mas|cu|list +s
Mase|field, John
(English poet)
maser +s
(electronic device.
△ mazer)
Mas|eru (capital of
Lesotho)
mash
mashes
mashed
mash|ing
mash|er +s
Mash|had (city,
Iran)
mashie +s
Ma|shona
plural Ma|shona
or Ma|sho|nas
Ma|shona|land
(province,
Rhodesia)

mask +s +ed +ing
(cover.
⚠ masque)
mask|er +s
mask|ing tape +s
mas|kin|onge +s
maso|chism
maso|chist +s
maso|chis|tic
maso|chis|tic|al|ly
Mason +s
(= Freemason)
mason +s +ed
+ing
Mason–Dixon
Line (boundary
line between
Pennsylvania and
Maryland)
Ma|son|ic
Ma|son|ry
(= Freemasonry)
ma|son|ry
Ma|sorah
Mas|or|ete +s
Mas|or|et|ic
masque +s
(dramatic
entertainment.
⚠ mask)
mas|quer +s
mas|quer|ade
  mas|quer|ades
  mas|quer|aded
  mas|quer|ad|ing
mas|quer|ader +s
Mass
  Masses
  (Eucharist)
mass
  masses
  massed
  mass|ing
  (quantity of matter
  etc.)
Mas|sa|chu|setts
(state, USA)
mas|sacre
  mas|sacres
  mas|sacred
  mas|sac|ring
mas|sage
  mas|sages
  mas|saged
  mas|sa|ging
mas|sager +s
mas|sa|sauga +s
Mas|sawa (port,
Ethiopia)
massé +s *Billiards*
mas|seter +s
mas|seur +s *male*

mas|seuse +s
  female
mas|si|cot
mas|sif +s
Mas|sif Cen|tral
  (plateau, France)
Mas|sine,
  Léo|nide (Russian-
  born dancer)
Mas|sin|ger,
  Philip (English
  dramatist)
mas|sive
mas|sive|ly
mas|sive|ness
mass|less
mass mar|ket +s
  noun
mass-market +s
  +ed +ing
  attributive and verb
Mas|son, André
  (French painter)
Mas|so|rah (use
  Masorah)
Mas|sor|ete (use
  Masorete)
mass-produce
  mass-produces
  mass-produced
  mass-producing
mass pro|duc|tion
mast +s +ed +ing
mas|taba +s
mast|ec|tomy
mast|ec|to|mies
mas|ter +s +ed
  +ing
master-at-arms
  masters-at-arms
mas|ter build|er
  +s
mas|ter|class
  mas|ter|classes
mas|ter|dom
mas|ter|ful
mas|ter|ful|ly
mas|ter|ful|ness
mas|ter|hood +s
mas|ter key +s
mas|ter|less
mas|ter|li|ness
mas|ter|ly
mas|ter mari|ner
  +s
mas|ter mason +s
mas|ter|mind +s
  +ed +ing
Mas|ter of the
  Rolls
  Mas|ters of the
  Rolls

mas|ter|piece +s
mas|ter plan +s
mas|ter|ship +s
mas|ter|sing|er +s
mas|ter stroke +s
mas|ter switch
  mas|ter switches
mas|ter|work +s
mas|tery
  mas|ter|ies
mast foot
  mast feet
mast|head +s +ed
  +ing
mas|tic +s
mas|ti|cate
  mas|ti|cates
  mas|ti|cated
  mas|ti|cat|ing
mas|ti|ca|tion
mas|ti|ca|tor +s
mas|ti|ca|tory
mas|tiff +s
mas|titis
mas|to|don +s
mas|to|don|tic
mas|toid +s
mas|toid|itis
mas|tur|bate
  mas|tur|bates
  mas|tur|bated
  mas|tur|bat|ing
mas|tur|ba|tion
mas|tur|ba|tor +s
mas|tur|ba|tory
Ma|suria (region,
  Poland)
Ma|sur|ian Lakes
  (alternative name
  for Masuria)
mat
  mats
  mat|ted
  mat|ting
  (on floor;
  entangle; matrix.
  ⚠ matt, matte)
Mata|bele
  plural Mata|bele
Mata|bele|land
  (province,
  Rhodesia)
mata|dor +s
Mata Hari (Dutch
  spy)
match
  matches
  matched
  match|ing
match|able
match|board +s

match|box
  match|boxes
matchet +s
match|less
match|less|ly
match|lock +s
match|maker +s
match|mak|ing +s
match|play +s
match point +s
match|stick +s
match|wood
mate
  mates
  mated
  mat|ing
maté (herbal tea)
mate|less
mate|lot +s (sailor)
mate|lote (fish
  stew)
mater +s
mater|fami|lias
ma|ter|ial +s
ma|teri|al|isa|tion
  Br. +s (use
  materialization)
ma|teri|al|ise *Br.*
  (use materialize)
  ma|teri|al|ises
  ma|teri|al|ised
  ma|teri|al|is|ing
ma|teri|al|ism
ma|teri|al|ist +s
ma|teri|al|is|tic
ma|teri|al|is|tic|
  al|ly
ma|teri|al|ity
ma|teri|al|iza|tion
  +s
ma|teri|al|ize
  ma|teri|al|izes
  ma|teri|al|ized
  ma|teri|al|iz|ing
ma|teri|al|ly
ma|teria med|ica
ma|tér|iel
ma|ter|nal
ma|ter|nal|ism
ma|ter|nal|is|tic
ma|ter|nal|ly
ma|ter|nity
  ma|ter|nities
mate|ship +s
matey
  mateys
mati|er
mati|est
ma|tey|ness
math
  (= mathematics)

math|emat|ic|al
math|emat|ic|al|ly
math|em|at|ician
 +s
math|emat|ics
Mathew *also*
 Mat|thew
Ma|thias *also*
 Mat|thias
Ma|thilda *also*
 Ma|tilda
maths
 (= mathematics)
ma|tico +s
Ma|tilda *also*
 Ma|thilda
 (name)
Ma|tilda (English
 queen)
Ma|tilda +s
 (bundle)
mati|ly
mat|inée +s
mati|ness (use
 mateyness)
mat|ins
Ma|tisse, Henri
 (French painter)
Mat|lock (town,
 England)
Mat|mata (town,
 Tunisia)
Mato Grosso
 (plateau and state,
 Brazil)
Mato Grosso do
 Sul (state, Brazil)
mat|rass
 mat|rasses
 (glass vessel.
 △ mattress)
ma|tri|arch +s
ma|tri|arch|al
ma|tri|archy
 ma|tri|arch|ies
ma|tric
 (= matriculation)
matri|ces
matri|cidal
matri|cide +s
ma|tric|ulate
 ma|tric|ulates
 ma|tric|ulated
 ma|tric|ulat|ing
ma|tricu|la|tion +s
ma|tricu|la|tory
matri|lin|eal
matri|lin|eal|ly
matri|local
matri|mo|nial
matri|mo|ni|al|ly

matri|mony
 matri|monies
mat|rix
 matri|ces *or*
 mat|rixes
ma|tron +s
ma|tron|al
ma|tron|hood +s
ma|tron|ly
Mat|su|yama (city,
 Japan)
Matt (name)
matt +s +ed +ing
 (dull. △ mat,
 matte)
mat|ta|more +s
matte (smelting
 product; mask.
 △ mat, matt)
mat|ter +s +ed
 +ing
Mat|ter|horn
 (mountain, Swiss-
 Italian border)
matter-of-fact
 adjective
matter-of-factly
matter-of-factness
mat|tery
Mat|thew *also*
 Mathew
 (name)
Mat|thew (Apostle
 and saint)
Mat|thew Paris
 (English
 chronicler)
Mat|thews,
 Stan|ley (English
 footballer)
Mat|thias *also*
 Ma|thias
 (name)
Mat|thias (Apostle
 and saint)
mat|ting +s
mat|tins (use
 matins)
mat|tock +s
mat|toid +s
mat|tress
 mat|tresses
 (on bed.
 △ matrass)
mat|ur|ate
 mat|ur|ates
 mat|ur|ated
 mat|ur|at|ing
mat|ur|ation +s
mat|ur|ation|al
ma|tur|ative

ma|ture
 ma|tures
 ma|tured
 ma|tur|ing
ma|turer
ma|tur|est
ma|ture|ly
ma|ture|ness
ma|tur|ity
 ma|tur|ities
ma|tu|tinal
maty (use matey)
mat|ier
mat|iest
matzo
 matzos *or*
 mat|zoth
Maud *also* Maude
 (name)
maud +s (plaid;
 rug)
Maude *also* Maud
maud|lin
Maugham,
 Som|er|set
 (English writer)
Maui (island,
 Hawaii)
maul +s +ed +ing
 (hammer;
 mutilate. △ mall)
maul|er +s
maul|stick +s
Mau Mau (African
 secret society)
Mauna Kea
 (extinct volcano,
 Hawaii)
Mauna Loa
 (volcano, Hawaii)
maun|der +s +ed
 +ing
maun|der|ing +s
Maundy
Maundy money
Maundy
 Thurs|day +s
Mau|pas|sant,
 Guy de (French
 writer)
Maura
Maur|een
Maure|tania
 (ancient name for
 part of Morocco
 and Algeria.
 △ Mauritania)
Maure|ta|nian +s
Maur|iac,
 Fran|çois (French
 writer)

Maur|ice *also*
 Mor|ris
Maur|ist +s
Mauri|ta|nia
 (modern country,
 W. Africa.
 △ Mauretania)
Mauri|ta|nian +s
Maur|itian +s
Maur|itius (island,
 Indian Ocean)
Maury, Mat|thew
 Fon|taine
 (American
 oceanographer)
Mau|rya
mau|so|leum
 mau|so|leums *or*
 mau|so|lea
mauve +s
mauv|ish
maven +s
mav|er|ick +s
Mavis (name)
mavis
 mavises
 (bird)
maw +s (stomach;
 throat. △ mor,
 moor, more)
mawk|ish
mawk|ish|ly
mawk|ish|ness
Maw|lana
 (alternative name
 for Jalal ad-Din
 ar-Rumi)
Max (name)
max
 maxes
 maxed
 max|ing
maxi +s
max|illa
 max|il|lae
max|il|lary
Maxim, Hiram
 Ste|vens
 (American
 engineer)
maxim +s
 (principle)
max|ima
max|imal
max|imal|ist +s
max|imal|ly
Maxim gun +s
Max|imil|ian
 (emperor of
 Mexico; name)

maxi|misa|tion *Br.*
　+s (use
　maximization)
maxi|mise *Br.* (use
　maximize)
　maxi|mises
　maxi|mised
　maxi|mis|ing
maxi|miser *Br.* +s
　(use maximizer)
maxi|miza|tion +s
maxi|mize
　maxi|mizes
　maxi|mized
　maxi|miz|ing
maxi|mizer +s
max|imum
　plural max|ima *or*
　max|imums
Max|ine
Max|well, James
　Clerk (Scottish
　physicist)
Max|well, Rob|ert
　(Czech-born
　British publisher)
max|well +s (unit)
May +s (name;
　month)
may +s (hawthorn)
Maya
　plural **Maya** *or*
　Mayas
　(Central American
　people; language;
　name)
maya +s *Hinduism;*
　Buddhism
Maya|kov|sky,
　Vlad|imir (Soviet
　poet)
Mayan +s
may-apple +s
maybe +s
　(perhaps)
may be *verb*
May-bug +s
May Day +s (1st
　May)
may|day +s (radio
　distress signal)
Mayer, Louis B.
　(Russian-born
　American film
　executive)
may|est
May|fair +s (fair
　held in May;
　district, London)
may|flower +s
　(flower)

May|flower
　(Pilgrim Fathers'
　ship)
may|fly
　may|flies
may|hap
may|hem +s
may|ing +s
May|nooth (village,
　Republic of
　Ireland)
mayn't (= may not)
Mayo (county,
　Republic of
　Ireland)
may|on|naise +s
mayor +s (council
　official. △mare)
may|or|al
may|or|alty
　may|or|al|ties
may|or|ess
　may|or|esses
may|or|ship +s
May|otte (island,
　Indian Ocean)
may|pole +s
May queen +s
mayst
may|weed +s
maz|ard +s
Mazar-e-Sharif
　(city, Afghanistan)
Maza|rin, Jules
　(Italian-born
　French statesman)
Maza|rin Bible
maza|rine +s
Maz|at|lán (port,
　Mexico)
Maz|da|ism
maze
　mazes
　mazed
　maz|ing
　(labyrinth.
　△maize)
mazer +s (bowl.
　△maser)
mazi|ly
mazi|ness
ma|zuma
ma|zurka +s
mazy
　mazi|er
　mazi|est
maz|zard +s (use
　mazard)
Maz|zini,
　Giu|seppe (Italian
　political leader)

Mba|bane (capital
　of Swaziland)
Mc|Carthy,
　Jo|seph R.
　(American
　politician)
Mc|Carthy, Mary
　(American writer)
Mc|Carthy|ism
Mc|Cartney, Paul
　(English pop and
　rock singer)
McCoy +s
Mc|Enroe, John
　(American tennis
　player)
Mc|Gona|gall,
　Wil|liam
　(Scottish writer)
Mc|Kinley,
　Wil|liam
　(American
　president)
Mc|Kinley, Mount
　(in Alaska)
Mc|Luhan,
　Mar|shall
　(Canadian
　communications
　scholar)
Mc|Naugh|ten
　rules
me (objective case
　of I ; *Music*)
mea culpa
Mead, Mar|ga|ret
　(American
　anthropologist)
mead +s (drink,
　meadow. △meed)
meadow +s
meadow|land
meadow|lark +s
meadow|sweet +s
mead|owy
mea|ger *Am.*
mea|ger|ly *Am.*
mea|ger|ness *Am.*
meagre *Br.*
meagre|ly *Br.*
meagre|ness *Br.*
meal +s
meal-beetle +s
mealie +s (maize.
　△mealy)
meali|ness
meals on wheels
meal|time +s
meal|worm +s
mealy
　meal|ier
　meali|est

mealy (*cont.*)
　(powdery; pale.
　△mielie)
mealy bug +s
mealy-mouthed
mean
　means
　meant
　mean|ing
　mean|er
　mean|est
　(intend; signify;
　not generous;
　unkind; inferior;
　average. △mien ,
　mesne)
Me|ander (river,
　Turkey; use
　Meander)
me|ander +s +ed
　+ing
me|ander|ing +s
me|an|drine
meanie +s
mean|ing +s
mean|ing|ful
mean|ing|ful|ly
mean|ing|ful|ness
mean|ing|less
mean|ing|less|ly
mean|ing|less|ness
mean|ing|ly
mean|ly
mean|ness
mean-spirit|ed
means test +s
　noun
means-test +s +ed
　+ing *verb*
meant
mean|time
　(meanwhile;
　intervening
　period)
mean time +s
　(time based on the
　mean sun; but
　Greenwich Mean
　Time)
mean|while
meany (use
　meanie)
　meanies
mea|sles
measly
　meas|lier
　meas|li|est
meas|ur|abil|ity
meas|ur|able
meas|ur|ably
meas|ure
　meas|ures

meas¦ure (*cont.*)
  meas¦ured
  meas¦ur¦ing
meas¦ured¦ly
meas¦ure¦less
meas¦ure¦less¦ly
meas¦ure¦ment +s
meat +s (flesh.
  △ meet, mete)
meat-axe +s
meat¦ball +s
meat-fly
  meat-flies
Meath (county,
  Republic of
  Ireland)
meat¦ily
meati¦ness
meat¦less
meat loaf
  meat loaves
meat safe +s
me¦atus
  plural me¦atus *or*
  me¦atuses
meaty
  meat¦ier
  meati¦est
Mecca (city, Saudi
  Arabia)
Mec¦cano *Propr.*
mech¦an¦ic +s
mech¦an¦ic¦al +s
mech¦an¦ic¦al¦ism
mech¦an¦ic¦al¦ly
mech¦an¦ic¦al¦ness
mech¦an¦ician +s
mech¦an¦ics
mech¦an¦isa¦tion
  Br. (use
  mechanization)
mech¦an¦ise *Br.*
  (use mechanize)
  mech¦an¦ises
  mech¦an¦ised
  mech¦an¦is¦ing
mech¦an¦iser *Br.*
  +s (use
  mechanizer)
mech¦an¦ism +s
mech¦an¦ist +s
mech¦an¦is¦tic
mech¦an¦is¦tic¦
  al¦ly
mech¦an¦iza¦tion
mech¦an¦ize
  mech¦an¦izes
  mech¦an¦ized
  mech¦an¦iz¦ing
mech¦an¦izer +s
mech¦ano¦
  recep¦tor +s

mecha¦tron¦ics
Me¦che¦len (city,
  Belgium)
Mech¦lin +s
Meck¦len¦burg
  (former state,
  Germany)
Mecklenburg-
  West
  Pom¦er¦ania
  (state, Germany)
meco¦nium +s
mecu +s
Med
  (= Mediterranean)
medal +s (award.
  △ meddle)
med¦aled *Am.*
med¦al¦ist *Am.* +s
med¦alled *Br.*
med¦al¦lic
med¦al¦lion +s
med¦al¦list *Br.* +s
Medan (city,
  Indonesia)
Meda¦war, Peter
  (English
  immunologist)
med¦dle
  med¦dles
  med¦dled
  med¦dling
  (interfere.
  △ medal)
med¦dler +s
  (busybody.
  △ medlar)
meddle¦some
meddle¦some¦ly
meddle¦some¦ness
Mede +s
Medea *Greek*
  Mythology
Me¦de¦llín (city,
  Colombia)
Media (country of
  the Medes)
media
  med¦iae
  Phonetics
media (plural of
  medium;
  newspapers,
  television, etc.)
medi¦aeval (use
  medieval)
med¦ial
medi¦al¦ly
Me¦dian +s (of
  Media)
me¦dian +s
  Anatomy;

me¦dian (*cont.*)
  Geometry;
  Mathematics
me¦dian¦ly
me¦di¦ant +s
me¦di¦as¦tin¦al
me¦di¦as¦tinum
me¦di¦as¦tina
me¦di¦ate
  me¦di¦ates
  me¦di¦ated
  me¦di¦at¦ing
me¦di¦ate¦ly
me¦di¦ation +s
me¦dia¦tisa¦tion
  Br. +s (use
  mediatization)
me¦dia¦tise *Br.* (use
  mediatize)
me¦dia¦tises
me¦dia¦tised
me¦dia¦tis¦ing
me¦dia¦tiza¦tion +s
me¦dia¦tize
  me¦dia¦tizes
  me¦dia¦tized
  me¦dia¦tiz¦ing
me¦di¦ator +s
me¦di¦ator¦ial
me¦di¦atory
me¦di¦atrix
me¦di¦atri¦ces
  female
medic +s (doctor.
  △ medick)
med¦ic¦able
Me¦dic¦aid
med¦ic¦al +s
med¦ic¦al¦ly
med¦ic¦ament +s
Medi¦care
medi¦cate
  medi¦cates
  medi¦cated
  medi¦cat¦ing
medi¦ca¦tion +s
med¦ica¦tive
Me¦di¦cean
Med¦ici *also*
  Médi¦cis
  (Florentine family;
  see also under first
  name)
me¦di¦cin¦al
me¦di¦cin¦al¦ly
medi¦cine +s
Medi¦cine Hat
  (town, Canada)
medi¦cine man
  medi¦cine men
Méd¦icis *also*
  Med¦ici

Méd¦icis (*cont.*)
  (Florentine family;
  see also under first
  name)
med¦ick +s (plant.
  △ medic)
med¦ico +s
medi¦eval
medi¦eval¦ise *Br.*
  (use medievalize)
  medi¦eval¦ises
  medi¦eval¦ised
  medi¦eval¦is¦ing
medi¦eval¦ism
medi¦eval¦ist +s
medi¦eval¦ize
  medi¦eval¦izes
  medi¦eval¦ized
  medi¦eval¦iz¦ing
medi¦eval¦ly
Me¦dina (city,
  Saudi Arabia)
me¦dina +s (district
  of N African town)
me¦di¦ocre
me¦di¦oc¦rity
  me¦di¦oc¦rities
medi¦tate
  medi¦tates
  medi¦tated
  medi¦tat¦ing
medi¦ta¦tion +s
medi¦ta¦tive
medi¦ta¦tive¦ly
medi¦ta¦tive¦ness
medi¦ta¦tor +s
Medi¦ter¦ra¦nean
  +s
me¦dium +s
  (spiritualist)
me¦dium
  media *or*
  me¦diums
  (other senses)
me¦dium¦ism
me¦dium¦is¦tic
medium-range
me¦dium¦ship +s
medium-sized
med¦lar +s (tree.
  △ meddler)
med¦ley +s
Medoc +s (wine)
Médoc (region,
  France)
me¦dulla +s
me¦dul¦lary
Me¦dusa *Greek*
  Mythology
me¦dusa
  me¦du¦sae *or*

me¦dusa(*cont.*)
  me¦dusas
  (jellyfish)
me¦du¦san
meed+s (reward.
  ⚠ mead)
meek+er +est
meek¦ly
meek¦ness
meer¦kat+s
meer¦schaum+s
Mee¦rut(city,
  India)
meet
  meets
  met
  meet¦ing
  (encounter.
  ⚠ meat, mete)
meet¦er+s (person
  who meets.
  ⚠ meter, metre)
meet¦ing+s
meet¦ing house+s
meet¦ly
meet¦ness
Meg
mega
mega¦buck+s
mega¦byte+s
mega¦ceph¦al¦ic
mega¦cycle+s
mega¦death+s
Me¦gaera *Greek*
  Mythology
mega¦flop +s
mega¦hertz
  plural mega¦hertz
mega¦lith+s
mega¦lith¦ic
meg¦alo¦mania+s
meg¦alo¦maniac
  +s
meg¦alo¦
    mani¦ac¦al
meg¦alo¦man¦ic
meg¦alop¦olis
  meg¦alop¦olises
meg¦alo¦pol¦itan
meg¦alo¦saur+s
meg¦alo¦saurus
  meg¦alo¦saur¦uses
Megan
mega¦phone+s
mega¦pod+s (use
  megapode)
mega¦pode+s
meg¦aron+s
mega¦scop¦ic
mega¦spore+s
mega¦star+s
mega¦store+s

mega¦ther¦ium
  mega¦theria
mega¦ton+s
mega¦tonne+s
  (use megaton)
mega¦volt+s
mega¦watt+s
Meg¦ger+s *Propr.*
Meg¦ha¦laya(state,
  India)
Me¦giddo(ancient
  city, Israel)
meg¦ilp+s
meg¦ohm+s
meg¦rim+s
Meiji Tenno
  (Japanese
  emperor)
mei¦osis
mei¦oses
  (cell division;
  litotes. ⚠ miosis)
mei¦ot¦ic(to do
  with meiosis.
  ⚠ miotic)
mei¦otic¦al¦ly
Meir, Golda
  (Israeli prime
  minister)
Meis¦sen(city,
  Germany;
  porcelain
  produced there)
Meis¦ter¦singer
  plural
  Meis¦ter¦singer
Meit¦ner, Lise
  (Austrian-born
  Swiss physicist)
Me¦kele (city,
  Ethiopia)
Mek¦nès (city,
  Morocco)
Me¦kong(river, SE
  Asia)
Mel
Me¦laka(state and
  port, Malaysia)
mela¦mine+s
mel¦an¦cho¦lia+s
mel¦an¦chol¦ic
mel¦an¦chol¦ic¦
    al¦ly
mel¦an¦choly
  mel¦an¦chol¦ies
Mel¦anch¦thon,
  Phil¦ipp (German
  Protestant
  reformer)
Mela¦nesia (island
  group, SW Pacific)
Mela¦nes¦ian+s

mé¦lange+s
Mel¦anie
mel¦anin+s
mel¦an¦ism+s
mela¦noma+s
mela¦nosis
  mela¦noses
mela¦not¦ic
Melba, Nel¦lie
  (Australian
  soprano; sauce;
  toast)
Mel¦bourne(city,
  Australia)
Mel¦bourne, Lord
  (British prime
  minister)
Mel¦chior(one of
  the Magi)
Mel¦chite+s
Mel¦chiz¦edek
  Bible
meld+s +ed +ing
Me¦le¦ager(Greek
  hero; Greek poet)
melee *Am.* +s
mêlée *Br.* +s
melic
Me¦lilla (Spanish
  enclave, Morocco)
meli¦lot+s
Me¦linda
meli¦or¦ate
  meli¦or¦ates
  meli¦or¦ated
  meli¦or¦at¦ing
meli¦or¦ation+s
meli¦ora¦tive
meli¦or¦ism
meli¦or¦ist+s
me¦lisma
me¦lis¦mata *or*
  me¦lis¦mas
mel¦is¦mat¦ic
Me¦lissa
mel¦lif¦er¦ous
mel¦lif¦lu¦ence
mel¦lif¦lu¦ent
mel¦lif¦lu¦ous
mel¦lif¦lu¦ous¦ly
mel¦lif¦lu¦ous¦ness
Mel¦lon, An¦drew
  Wil¦liam
  (American
  financier)
mel¦low+s +ed
  +ing
mel¦low¦ly
mel¦low¦ness
me¦lo¦deon+s
me¦lod¦ic
me¦lod¦ic¦al¦ly

me¦lo¦di¦ous
me¦lo¦di¦ous¦ly
me¦lo¦di¦ous¦ness
melo¦dise*Br.* (use
  melodize)
  melo¦dises
  melo¦dised
  melo¦dis¦ing
melo¦diser*Br.* +s
  (use melodizer)
melo¦dist+s
melo¦dize
  melo¦dizes
  melo¦dized
  melo¦diz¦ing
melo¦dizer+s
melo¦drama+s
melo¦dra¦mat¦ic
melo¦dra¦mat¦ic¦
    al¦ly
melo¦dra¦mat¦ics
melo¦drama¦tise
  Br. (use
  melodramatize)
  melo¦drama¦tises
  melo¦drama¦tised
  melo¦drama¦
      tis¦ing
melo¦drama¦tist
  +s
melo¦drama¦tize
  melo¦drama¦tizes
  melo¦drama¦tized
  melo¦drama¦
      tiz¦ing
Mel¦ody(name)
mel¦ody
  mel¦od¦ies
  (tune)
melon+s
Melos (Greek
  island)
Mel¦pom¦ene *Greek*
  and Roman
  Mythology
melt+s +ed +ing
melt¦able
melt¦down+s
melt¦er+s
melt¦ing¦ly
melt¦ing point+s
melt¦ing pot+s
mel¦ton+s (cloth)
Mel¦ton
  Mow¦bray (town,
  England)
melt water+s
Mel¦ville,
  Her¦man
  (American writer)
Mel¦vin *also*
  Mel¦vyn

mem¦ber +s
mem¦bered
mem¦ber¦less
mem¦ber¦ship +s
mem¦ber state +s
mem¦bran¦aceous
mem¦brane +s
mem¦bran¦eous
mem¦bran¦ous
mem¦brum virile
Memel (German
   name for
   Klaipeda; former
   district, East
   Prussia; lower part
   of River Neman)
me¦mento
   me¦men¦toes *or*
   me¦mentos
me¦mento mori
Mem¦non *Greek
   Mythology*
memo +s
mem¦oir +s
mem¦oir¦ist +s
mem¦ora¦bilia
mem¦or¦abil¦ity
mem¦or¦able
mem¦or¦able¦ness
mem¦or¦ably
memo¦ran¦dum
   memo¦randa *or*
   memo¦ran¦dums
me¦mor¦ial +s
Me¦mor¦ial Day
   Am. +s
me¦mor¦ial¦ise *Br.*
   (use memorialize)
me¦mor¦ial¦ises
me¦mor¦ial¦ised
me¦mor¦ial¦is¦ing
me¦mor¦ial¦ist +s
me¦mor¦ial¦ize
me¦mor¦ial¦izes
me¦mor¦ial¦ized
me¦mor¦ial¦iz¦ing
me¦moria
   tech¦nica +s
mem¦or¦is¦able *Br.*
   (use
   memorizable)
mem¦or¦isa¦tion
   Br. (use
   memorization)
mem¦or¦ise *Br.* (use
   memorize)
mem¦or¦ises
mem¦or¦ised
mem¦or¦is¦ing
mem¦or¦iser *Br.* +s
   (use memorizer)
mem¦or¦iz¦able

mem¦or¦iza¦tion
mem¦or¦ize
   mem¦or¦izes
mem¦or¦ized
mem¦or¦iz¦ing
mem¦or¦izer +s
mem¦ory
   mem¦or¦ies
mem¦ory bank +s
Mem¦phis (ancient
   city, Egypt; port,
   USA)
mem¦sahib +s
men (plural of
   man)
men¦ace
   men¦aces
   men¦aced
   men¦acing
men¦acer +s
men¦acing¦ly
mé¦nage +s
mé¦nage à trois
   mé¦nages à trois
men¦agerie +s
Menai Strait
   (channel between
   Anglesey and
   Wales)
Me¦nan¦der (Greek
   writer)
mena¦quin¦one +s
me¦nar¦che +s
Men¦cius (Chinese
   philosopher)
Men¦cken, Henry
   Louis (American
   journalist)
mend +s +ed +ing
mend¦able
men¦da¦cious
men¦da¦cious¦ly
men¦da¦cious¦ness
men¦da¦city
   men¦da¦ci¦ties
Men¦del, Gre¦gor
   Jo¦hann
   (Moravian monk
   and geneticist)
Men¦de¦leev,
   Dmi¦tri
   Ivan¦ovich
   (Russian chemist)
men¦del¦evium
Men¦del¦ian
Men¦del¦ism
Men¦dels¦sohn,
   Felix (German
   composer)
mend¦er +s
Men¦deres (river,
   Turkey)

men¦di¦cancy
men¦di¦cant +s
men¦di¦city
Men¦dip Hills (in
   England)
Men¦dips
   (= Mendip Hills)
Men¦doza,
   An¦tonio de (1st
   viceroy of Mexico)
Men¦doza (city and
   province,
   Argentina)
Mene¦laus *Greek
   Mythology*
Menes (pharaoh)
men¦folk
Meng-tzu (Chinese
   name of Mencius)
Mengzi (alternative
   Chinese name of
   Mencius)
men¦haden +s
men¦hir +s
me¦nial +s
me¦ni¦al¦ly
men¦in¦geal
men¦in¦git¦ic
men¦in¦gi¦tis
men¦in¦go¦cele +s
men¦in¦go¦coc¦cus
   men¦in¦go¦cocci
men¦inx
   men¦in¦ges
me¦nis¦coid
me¦nis¦cus
me¦nisci
Men¦non¦ite +s
men¦ol¦ogy
   men¦olo¦gies
Men¦om¦ini
   plural Men¦om¦ini
meno¦pausal
meno¦pause +s
me¦norah +s
Men¦orca (Spanish
   name for
   Minorca)
Men¦or¦can +s (use
   Minorcan)
men¦or¦rha¦gia
men¦or¦rhea *Am.*
men¦or¦rhoea *Br.*
Mensa
men¦ses
Men¦she¦vik +s
mens rea
men¦strual
men¦stru¦ate
   men¦stru¦ates
   men¦stru¦ated
   men¦stru¦at¦ing

men¦stru¦ation +s
men¦stru¦ous
men¦struum
   men¦strua
men¦sur¦able
men¦sural
men¦sur¦ation +s
mens¦wear
men¦tal
men¦tal¦ism
men¦tal¦ist +s
men¦tal¦is¦tic
men¦tal¦ity
   men¦tal¦ities
men¦tal¦ly
men¦ta¦tion +s
men¦thol +s
men¦thol¦ated
men¦tion +s +ed
   +ing
men¦tion¦able
men¦tor +s
menu +s
menu-driven
Men¦uhin, Ye¦hudi
   (American-born
   British violinist)
Men¦zies, Rob¦ert
   (Australian prime
   minister)
meow +s +ed +ing
   (use miaow)
mepa¦crine
me¦peri¦dine
Meph¦is¦to¦
      phe¦lean
Meph¦is¦toph¦eles
   (German legend)
Meph¦is¦to¦
   phe¦lian (use
   Mephisto-
   phelean)
meph¦it¦ic
meph¦itis
   meph¦itises
me¦ranti +s
mer¦can¦tile
mer¦can¦til¦ism
mer¦can¦til¦ist +s
mer¦cap¦tan
Mer¦ca¦tor,
   Ger¦ar¦dus
   (Flemish-born
   geographer;
   projection)
Mer¦cedes
mer¦cen¦ari¦ness
mer¦cen¦ary
   mer¦cen¦ar¦ies
mer¦cer +s
mer¦cer¦ise *Br.* (use
   mercerize)

mer|cer|ise (*cont.*)
  mer|cer|ises
  mer|cer|ised
  mer|cer|is|ing
mer|cer|ize
  mer|cer|izes
  mer|cer|ized
  mer|cer|iz|ing
mer|cery
  mer|cer|ies
mer|chan|dis|able
mer|chan|dise
  mer|chan|dises
  mer|chan|dised
  mer|chan|dis|ing
mer|chan|diser +s
Mer|chant, Is|mail
  (Indian film
  producer)
mer|chant +s
mer|chant|able
Mer|chant
  Ad|ven|turers
  (English trading
  guild)
mer|chant|man
  mer|chant|men
Mer|cia (ancient
  kingdom, central
  England)
Mer|cian +s
mer|ci|ful
mer|ci|ful|ly
mer|ci|ful|ness
mer|ci|less
mer|ci|less|ly
mer|ci|less|ness
Merckx, Eddy
  (Belgian racing
  cyclist)
Mer|cur|ial (of the
  planet Mercury)
mer|cur|ial
  (volatile;
  containing
  mercury)
mer|curi|al|ism
mer|curi|al|ity
mer|curi|al|ly
mer|cur|ic
mer|cur|ous
Mer|cury (*Roman
  Mythology*; planet)
mer|cury (metal)
Mercy (name)
mercy
  mer|cies
  (clemency)
mere
  meres
  mer|est

Mere|dith (name)
Mere|dith, George
  (English writer)
mere|ly
mer|en|gue +s
mere|tri|cious
mere|tri|cious|ly
mere|tri|cious|
          ness
mer|gan|ser +s
merge
  merges
  merged
  mer|ging
mer|gence +s
mer|ger +s
Mé|rida (cities,
  Spain and Mexico)
me|rid|ian +s
me|rid|ion|al
Me|riel
mer|ingue +s
me|rino +s
Meri|on|eth|shire
  (former county,
  Wales)
meri|stem +s
meri|stem|at|ic
merit +s +ed +ing
mer|it|oc|racy
  mer|it|oc|ra|cies
mer|ito|crat|ic
meri|tori|ous
meri|tori|ous|ly
meri|tori|ous|ness
Merle (name)
merle +s
  (blackbird)
Mer|lin *Arthurian
  Legend*
Mer|lin *also*
  Mer|lyn
  (name)
mer|lin +s (falcon)
mer|lon +s
  (parapet)
Mer|lot +s
Mer|lyn *also*
  Mer|lin
mer|maid +s
mer|maid's purse
  +s
mer|man
  mer|men
mero|blast +s
Meroe (ancient
  city, Sudan)
mero|he|dral
me|ron|ymy
Mero|vin|gian +s
mer|rily
mer|ri|ment

mer|ri|ness
merry
  mer|rier
  mer|ri|est
merry an|drew +s
merry-go-round
  +s
merry|maker +s
merry|mak|ing
merry thought +s
Mersa Ma|truh
  (town, Egypt)
Mer|sey (river,
  England)
Mer|sey|side
  (metropolitan
  county, England)
Mer|sin (port,
  Turkey)
Mer|thyr Tyd|fil
  (town, Wales)
Mer|vin *also*
  Mer|vyn
Mer|vyn *also*
  Mer|vin
Meryl
mesa +s
més|al|li|ance +s
mes|cal +s
mes|cal but|tons
mes|ca|lin (use
  mescaline)
mes|ca|line
Mes|dames (plural
  of Madame)
Mes|de|moi|selles
  (plural of
  Mademoiselle)
mes|em|bry|
  an|the|mum +s
mes|en|ceph|alon
  +s
mes|en|ter|ic
mes|en|ter|itis
mes|en|tery
  mes|en|ter|ies
mesh
  meshes
  meshed
  mesh|ing
Me|shed
  (alternative name
  for Mashhad)
me|sial
me|si|al|ly
mesic
Mes|mer, Franz
  Anton (Austrian
  physician)
mes|mer|ic
mes|mer|ic|al|ly

mes|mer|isa|tion
  Br. (use
  mesmerization)
mes|mer|ise *Br.*
  (use mesmerize)
  mes|mer|ises
  mes|mer|ised
  mes|mer|is|ing
mes|mer|iser *Br.*
  +s (use
  mesmerizer)
mes|mer|is|ing|ly
  Br. (use
  mesmerizingly)
mes|mer|ism
mes|mer|ist +s
mes|mer|iza|tion
mes|mer|ize
  mes|mer|izes
  mes|mer|ized
  mes|mer|iz|ing
mes|mer|izer +s
mes|mer|iz|ing|ly
mesne +s (*Law*
  intermediate.
  △ mean, mien)
Meso-America
  (Central America)
Meso-American
  +s
meso|blast +s
meso|carp +s
meso|ceph|al|ic
meso|derm +s
meso|gas|ter +s
meso|lith|ic
meso|morph +s
meso|morph|ic
meso|morphy
meson +s
mes|on|ic
meso|pause +s
meso|phyll +s
meso|phyte +s
Meso|po|ta|mia
  (region, Iraq)
Meso|po|ta|mian
  +s
meso|sphere +s
meso|tron +s
Meso|zo|ic
mes|quit +s (use
  mesquite)
mes|quite +s
  (shrub)
mess
  messes
  messed
  mess|ing
mes|sage
  mes|sages

mes|sage(*cont.*)
mes|saged
mes|sa|ging
Mes|sa|lina,
  Val|eria(Roman
  empress)
Mes|sei|gneurs
mes|sen|ger+s
Mes|ser|schmitt,
  Willy(German
  aircraft designer)
Mes|siaen,
  Oli|vier(French
  composer)
Mes|siah+s
Mes|siah|ship+s
Mes|si|an|ic
Mes|si|an|ism
Mes|sieurs
mess|ily
Mes|sina(city,
  Sicily)
messi|ness
mess jack|et+s
mess kit+s
mess|mate+s
Messrs
  (= Messieurs)
mess tin+s
mes|suage+s
messy
  mess|ier
  messi|est
mes|tiza+s *female*
mes|tizo+s *male*
met(past tense and
  past participle of
  meet;
  = meteorological,
  metropolitan)
meta|bi|sul|phite
  +s
meta|bol|ic
meta|bol|ic|al|ly
me|tab|ol|is|able
  Br. (use
  metabolizable)
me|tab|ol|ise*Br.*
  (use metabolize)
  me|tab|ol|ises
  me|tab|ol|ised
  me|tab|ol|is|ing
me|tab|ol|ism+s
me|tab|ol|ite+s
me|tab|ol|iz|able
me|tab|ol|ize
  me|tab|ol|izes
  me|tab|ol|ized
  me|tab|ol|iz|ing
meta|car|pal+s
meta|car|pus
  meta|carpi

meta|cen|ter*Am.*
  +s
meta|centre+s
meta|cen|tric
me|tage+s
meta|gen|esis
meta|gen|eses
meta|ge|net|ic
metal
  metals
met|alled *Br.*
met|aled *Am.*
met|al|ling *Br.*
met|al|ing *Am.*
  (iron; copper; etc.
  △ metol mettle)
meta|lan|guage+s
meta|lin|guis|tic
meta|lin|guis|tics
met|al|lize*Am.* (use
  metallize)
  met|al|lizes
  met|al|lized
  met|al|liz|ing
me|tal|lic
me|tal|lic|al|ly
metal|lif|er|ous
met|al|line
met|al|lisa|tion*Br.*
  (use
  metallization)
met|al|lise*Br.* (use
  metallize)
  met|al|lises
  met|al|lised
  met|al|lis|ing
met|al|liza|tion
met|al|lize
  met|al|lizes
  met|al|lized
  met|al|liz|ing
met|al|lo|graph|ic
met|al|lo|
     graph|ic|al
met|al|lo|graph|ic|
     al|ly
met|al|log|raphy
met|al|loid+s
met|al|lo|phone+s
met|al|lur|gic
met|al|lur|gic|al
met|al|lur|gic|al|ly
met|al|lur|gist+s
me|tal|lurgy
met|al|work
met|al|work|er+s
met|al|work|ing
meta|mer+s
meta|mere+s
meta|mer|ic
me|tam|er|ism
meta|morph|ic

meta|morph|ism
meta|morph|ose
  meta|morph|oses
  meta|morph|osed
  meta|
     morph|os|ing
meta|mor|phosis
  meta|mor|phoses
meta|phase+s
meta|phor+s
meta|phor|ic
meta|phor|ic|al
meta|phor|ic|al|ly
meta|phrase
  meta|phrases
  meta|phrased
  meta|phras|ing
meta|phras|tic
meta|phys|ic+s
meta|phys|ic|al
meta|phys|ic|al|ly
meta|phys|ician
  +s
meta|physi|cise
  Br. (use
  metaphysicize)
  meta|physi|cises
  meta|physi|cised
  meta|physi|
     cis|ing
meta|physi|cize
  meta|physi|cizes
  meta|physi|cized
  meta|physi|
     ciz|ing
meta|phys|ics
meta|pla|sia+s
meta|plasm+s
meta|plas|tic
meta|pol|itics
meta|psy|cho|
     logic|al
meta|psych|ology
meta|sta|bil|ity
meta|sta|ble
me|tas|ta|sis
  me|tas|ta|ses
me|tas|ta|sise*Br.*
  (use metastasize)
  me|tas|ta|sises
  me|tas|ta|sised
  me|tas|ta|sis|ing
me|tas|ta|size
  me|tas|ta|sizes
  me|tas|ta|sized
  me|tas|ta|siz|ing
meta|stat|ic
meta|tar|sal+s
meta|tar|sus
  meta|tarsi
meta|ther|ian+s

me|tath|esis
  me|tath|eses
meta|thet|ic
meta|thet|ic|al
meta|zoan+s
mete
  metes
  meted
  met|ing
  (apportion;
  boundary.
  △ meat meet)
met|em|psy|chosis
met|
    em|psy|choses
met|em|psy|chos|
     ist+s
me|teor+s
Met|eora(region,
  Greece)
me|teor|ic
me|teoric|al|ly
me|teor|ite+s
me|teor|it|ic
me|teoro|graph+s
me|teor|oid+s
me|teor|oid|al
me|teoro|logic|al
me|teoro|logic|
     al|ly
me|teor|olo|gist+s
me|teor|ology
meter+s +ed +ing
  (measuring
  device; to
  measure.
  △ meeter metre)
meter*Am.* +s (unit;
  rhythm. *Br.* metre
  △ meeter)
meter|age*Am.* +s
  (*Br.* metreage)
metha|done
meth|am|pheta|
     mine+s
metha|nal
me|thane
metha|no|ate+s
metha|no|ic
metha|nol
methe|drine*Propr.*
me|thinks
me|thought
me|thio|nine
metho+s
method+s
method act|ing
method actor+s
*mé|thode
  cham|pen|oise*
meth|od|ic
meth|od|ic|al

meth¦od¦ic¦al¦ly
meth¦od¦ise *Br.*
    (use methodize)
    meth¦od¦ises
    meth¦od¦ised
    meth¦od¦is¦ing
meth¦od¦iser *Br.*
    +s (use
    methodizer)
Meth¦od¦ism
Meth¦od¦ist +s
    (religious
    denomination)
meth¦od¦ist +s
    (methodical
    person)
Meth¦od¦is¦tic
Meth¦od¦is¦tic¦al
Me¦tho¦dius (Greek
    saint)
meth¦od¦ize
    meth¦od¦izes
    meth¦od¦ized
    meth¦od¦iz¦ing
meth¦od¦izer +s
meth¦odo¦logic¦al
meth¦odo¦logic¦
        al¦ly
meth¦od¦olo¦gist
    +s
meth¦od¦olo¦gies
me¦thought
meths
    (= methylated
    spirits)
Me¦thu¦selah +s
    (*Bible*; very old
    person or thing)
me¦thu¦selah +s
    (wine bottle)
me¦thyl +s
meth¦yl¦ate
    meth¦yl¦ates
    meth¦yl¦ated
    meth¦yl¦at¦ing
meth¦yl¦a¦tion
meth¦yl¦ene
me¦thyl¦ic
metic +s
meti¦cal +s
me¦ticu¦lous
me¦ticu¦lous¦ly
me¦ticu¦lous¦ness
mé¦tier +s
metif +s
Metis
    plural **Metis**
metol +s
    (photographic
    developer.
    ⚠ metal, mettle)

Me¦ton¦ic
meto|nym +s
meto|nym¦ic
meto|nym¦ic¦al
meto|nym¦ic¦al¦ly
me¦ton|ymy
    me¦ton|ymies
met¦ope +s
metre *Br.* +s
    (metric unit;
    poetic rhythm.
    Am. meter.
    ⚠ meeter, meter)
metre|age *Br.* +s
    (*Am.* meterage)
metre-kilogram-
        second +s
met¦ric +s
met¦ric¦al
met¦ric¦al¦ly
met¦ri|cate
    met¦ri|cates
    met¦ri|cated
    met¦ri|cat¦ing
met¦ri|ca¦tion
met¦ri|cian +s
met¦ri|cise *Br.* (use
    metricize)
    met¦ri|cises
    met¦ri|cised
    met¦ri|cis¦ing
met¦ri|cize
    met¦ri|cizes
    met¦ri|cized
    met¦ri|ciz¦ing
met¦ric ton +s
met¦rist +s
me¦tri¦tis
metro +s
met¦ro|logic
met¦ro|logic¦al
me¦trol|ogy
met¦ro|nome +s
met¦ro|nom¦ic
met¦ro|nym¦ic +s
me¦trop|olis
    plural
    me¦trop|olises *or*
    me¦trop|oles
met¦ro|pol¦itan +s
met¦ro|pol¦it¦an|
        ate +s
met¦ro|pol¦it¦an|
        ism
me¦tror|rha¦gia
Met¦ter|nich,
    Kle¦mens
    (Austrian prince
    and statesman)
met¦tle +s
    (courage, spirit.
    ⚠ metal, metol)

met¦tled
mettle|some
Metz (city, France)
meu +s (plant.
    ⚠ mew, mu)
meu|nière
Meuse (river, NW
    Europe)
mew +s +ed +ing
    (cat's cry; gull;
    cage for hawks.
    ⚠ meu, mu)
mewl +s +ed +ing
    (whimper.
    ⚠ mule)
mews (stabling.
    ⚠ muse)
Mexi|cali (city,
    Mexico)
Mex|ican +s
Mex|ico
Mex|ico City
    (capital of
    Mexico)
Meyer|beer,
    Gia|como
    (German
    composer)
Meyer|hof, Otto
    Fritz (German-
    born American
    biochemist)
me¦zer|eon +s
me¦zu|zah
    me¦zu|zoth
mez|za|nine +s
mezza voce
mezzo +s
mezzo forte
Mez¦zo|giorno (in
    Italy)
mezzo piano
mezzo-relievo +s
mezzo-rilievo +s
    (use mezzo-
    relievo)
mezzo-soprano +s
mezzo|tint +s +ed
        +ing
mezzo|tint¦er +s
mho +s (unit.
    ⚠ mo, mow)
mi (*Music*; use me)
Mia
Miami (city, USA)
miaow +s +ed
        +ing
mi¦asma
    mi¦as|mata *or*
    mi|asmas
mi¦as|mal
mi¦as|mat¦ic

mi¦as|mic
mi¦as|mic¦al¦ly
miaul +s +ed +ing
mica +s (mineral)
mi¦ca|ceous
Micah *Bible*
mica-schist
Mi¦caw¦ber +s
Mi¦caw¦ber|ish
Mi¦caw¦ber|ism
mice
mi|celle +s
Mi¦chael
    (archangel and
    saint; name)
Mi¦chaela
Mich¦ael|mas
    Mich¦ael|mases
Mi¦chel|an¦gelo
    (Buon¦ar|roti)
    (Italian artist)
Mich¦èle *also*
    Mich|elle
Miche|lin, André
    and Édu|ard
    (French tyre
    manufacturers)
Mich|elle *also*
    Mich¦èle
Mi¦chel|ozzo
    (Italian architect)
Mich¦el|son,
    Al¦bert
    Abra|ham
    (American
    physicist)
Mich|igan (state,
    USA)
Mich|igan, Lake
    (in N. America)
Mi¦cho|acán (state,
    Mexico)
mick +s (*offensive*)
mick|erie +s (use
    mickery)
mick|ery
    mick|er|ies
Mickey *also* **Micky**
    (name)
mickey (in 'take the
    mickey')
Mickey Finn +s
Mickey Mouse
    (cartoon
    character)
mickey-taking
mickle +s
Mick the Mil¦ler
    (racing
    greyhound)
Micky *also* **Mickey**
    (name)

micky (in 'take the
micky'; use
mickey)
Mic¦mac
plural **Mic¦mac** or
Mic¦macs
micro +s
micro|analy¦sis
micro|analy¦ses
mi¦crobe +s
mi¦cro¦bial
mi¦cro¦bic
micro|bio|logic¦al
micro|bio|logic|
al¦ly
micro|biolo¦gist +s
micro|biol¦ogy
micro|burst +s
micro|ceph¦al¦ic
micro|ceph¦alous
micro|ceph¦aly
micro|chip +s
micro|cir¦cuit +s
micro|cir¦cuit¦ry
micro|cli¦mate +s
micro|cli¦mat¦ic
micro|cli¦mat¦ic|
al¦ly
micro|cline +s
micro|code +s
micro|com¦puter
+s
micro|copy
micro|copies
micro|copied
micro|copy|ing
micro|cosm +s
micro|cos¦mic
micro|cos¦mic|
al¦ly
micro|crys¦tal|line
micro|dot +s
micro|eco¦nom¦ic
micro|eco¦nom¦ics
micro|elec¦tron¦ics
micro|evo¦lu¦tion
micro|evo¦lu¦tion|
ary
micro|fiche
plural **micro|fiche**
or **micro|fiches**
micro|film +s +ed
+ing
micro|floppy
micro|flop¦pies
micro|form +s
micro|gram +s
micro|graph +s
micro|grav¦ity
micro|groove +s
micro|in¦struc¦tion
+s

micro|
lepi¦dop¦tera
micro|light +s
micro|lith +s
micro|lith¦ic
micro|mesh
micro|meshes
mi¦crom|eter +s
(gauge)
micro|meter *Am.*
+s (unit)
micro|metre *Br.* +s
(unit)
mi¦crom|etry
micro|mini¦atur|
isa|tion *Br.* +s
(use micro-
miniaturization)
micro|mini¦atur|
iza|tion +s
mi¦cron +s
Micro|nesia (area
of W. Pacific;
Federated States
of Micronesia)
Micro|nes¦ian +s
micro|nu¦trient +s
micro-organ¦ism
+s
micro|phone +s
micro|phon¦ic
micro|photo¦graph
+s
micro|phyte +s
micro|pro¦ces¦sor
+s
micro|pro¦gram +s
micro|pyle +s
micro|scope +s
micro|scop¦ic
micro|scop¦ic¦al
micro|scop¦ic|al¦ly
mi¦cro|scop¦ist +s
mi¦cro|scopy
micro|sec¦ond +s
micro|seism +s
Micro|soft *Propr.*
micro|some +s
micro|spore +s
micro|struc¦ture
+s
micro|sur¦gery
micro|sur¦gi¦cal
micro|switch
micro|switches
micro|tech¦nique
+s
micro|tome +s
micro|tone +s
micro|tu¦bule +s
micro|wave
micro|waves

micro|wave (*cont.*)
micro|waved
micro|wav¦ing
micro|wave|able
mic|rurgy
mic|tur¦ition
mid (= amid)
Midas *Greek*
Mythology
mid|brain +s
mid¦day +s
mid¦den +s
mid¦dle
mid¦dles
mid¦dled
mid¦dling
mid¦dle age (time
of life)
middle-aged
Mid¦dle Ages
(period of
European history)
middle-age
spread
middle|brow +s
middle-class
adjective
Mid¦dle East|ern
middle|man
middle|men
middle-of-the-
road *attributive*
Middles|brough
(town, England)
Middle|sex (former
county, England)
middle-sized
Middle|ton,
Thomas (English
dramatist)
middle|weight +s
mid|dling +s
mid|dling¦ly
middy
mid|dies
Mid|east
mid|field +s
mid|field¦er +s
Mid|gard
Scandinavian
Mythology
midge +s
midget +s
Mid Gla|mor¦gan
(county, Wales)
mid¦gut +s
MIDI +s (= musical
instrument digital
interface)
Midi (region,
France)
midi +s (dress etc.)

midi|bus
midi|buses
midi|nette +s
Midi-Pyrénées
(region, France)
mid|iron +s
Mid|land
(*attributive* of the
Midlands)
mid|land +s
mid|land¦er +s
Mid|lands, the
(inland counties of
central England)
mid-life
mid|line +s
Mid|lothian
(former county,
Scotland)
mid|most
mid|night +s
mid|night blue +s
noun and adjective
midnight-blue
attributive
mid-off +s *Cricket*
mid-on +s *Cricket*
Mid|rash
Mid|rash¦im
mid¦rib +s
mid¦riff +s
mid|ship +s
mid¦ship|man
mid¦ship|men
mid|ships *adverb*
midst
mid|stream
mid|sum¦mer +s
Mid|sum¦mer Day
+s
Mid|sum¦mer's
Day +s
mid|town
mid¦way
Mid¦way Is¦lands
(in Pacific Ocean)
mid|week
Mid|west
mid|wicket +s
mid|wife
mid|wives
mid|wif¦ery
mid|win¦ter +s
mie¦lie +s (use
mealie. △ mealy)
mien +s (look;
bearing. △ mean,
mesne)
Mies van der
Rohe, Lud¦wig
(German-born
architect)

mife|pris|tone

miff +s +ed +ing

miffy

might (*auxiliary verb*; strength. ⚠ mite)

might|est

might-have-been +s

might|ily

mighti|ness

mightn't (= might not)

mighty

  might|ier

  mighti|est

mign|on|ette +s

mi|graine +s

mi|grain|ous

mi|grant +s

mi|grate

  mi|grates

  mi|grated

  mi|grat|ing

mi|gra|tion +s

mi|gra|tion|al

mi|gra|tor +s

mi|gra|tory

Mi|hail|ović, Drag|oljub (Draža) (Yugoslav soldier)

mih|rab +s

mi|kado +s

Mike (name)

mike

  mikes

  miked

  mik|ing (microphone; shirk)

Mi|ko|nos (Greek name for Mykonos)

mil

  plural mil *or* mils (thousandth of an inch. ⚠ mill)

mi|lady

  mi|la|dies

mil|age +s (use mileage)

Milan (city, Italy)

Mil|an|ese

  plural Mil|an|ese

milch

milch cow +s

mild +er +est

mild|en +s +ed +ing

mil|dew +s +ed +ing

mil|dewy

mild|ish

mild|ly

mild-mannered

mild|ness

Mil|dred

mild steel +s *noun and attributive*

mile +s (unit. ⚠ myall)

mile|age +s

mile|post +s

miler +s

Miles *also* Myles

Mi|le|sian +s

mile|stone +s

Mi|le|tus (ancient Greek city in Asia Minor)

mil|foil +s

Mil|haud, Da|rius (French composer)

mil|iary

mi|lieu

  mi|lieux *or* mi|lieus

mili|tancy

  mili|tan|cies

Mili|tant (British political organization)

mili|tant +s (combative; person)

mili|tant|ly

mili|taria

mili|tar|ily

mili|tari|ness

mili|tar|isa|tion *Br.* (use militarization)

mili|tar|ise *Br.* (use militarize)

  mili|tar|ises

  mili|tar|ised

  mili|tar|is|ing

mili|tar|ism

mili|tar|ist +s

mili|tar|is|tic

mili|tar|is|tic|al|ly

mili|tar|iza|tion

mili|tar|ize

  mili|tar|izes

  mili|tar|ized

  mili|tar|iz|ing

mili|tary

  mili|tar|ies

mili|tate

  mili|tates

  mili|tated

  mili|tat|ing

mili|tia +s

mili|tia|man

  mili|tia|men

milk +s +ed +ing

milk|er +s

milk float +s

milki|ness

milk-leg +s

milk-loaf

  milk-loaves

milk|maid +s

milk|man

  milk|men

Milk of Mag|nesia *Propr.*

milk shake +s

milk|sop +s

milk tooth

  milk teeth

milk-vetch

  milk-vetches

milk|weed +s

milk white +s *noun and adjective*

milk-white *attributive*

milk|wort +s

milky

  milk|ier

  milki|est

Milky Way *Astronomy*

Mill, John Stu|art (English philosopher)

mill +s +ed +ing (building or apparatus for grinding. ⚠ mil)

mill|able

Mil|lais, John Everett (English painter)

mill|board +s

mill-dam +s

Mille, Cecil B. de (American film producer and director)

mille|feuille +s

mil|len|ar|ian +s

mil|len|ar|ian|ism

mil|len|ar|ian|ist +s

mil|len|ary

  mil|len|ar|ies

mil|len|nial

mil|len|nial|ist +s

mil|len|nium

  mil|len|niums *or* mil|len|nia

mille|pede +s (use millipede)

mille|pore +s

Mil|ler, Ar|thur (American playwright)

Mil|ler, Glenn (American jazz musician)

mill|er +s

mill|er's thumb +s (fish)

mil|lesi|mal

mil|lesi|mal|ly

mil|let +s

millet-grass

  millet-grasses

mill|hand +s

milli|am|meter +s

milli|amp +s

milli|am|pere +s

mil|liard +s

milli|bar +s

Mil|li|cent

Mil|lie

milli|gram +s

milli|gramme +s (use milligram)

Mil|li|kan, Rob|ert An|drews (American physicist)

milli|liter *Am.* +s

milli|litre *Br.* +s

milli|meter *Am.* +s

milli|metre *Br.* +s

mill|iner +s

mill|in|ery

mil|lion +s

mil|lion|aire +s

mil|lion|air|ess

  mil|lion|air|esses

mil|lion|fold

mil|lionth +s

milli|pede +s

milli|sec|ond +s

milli|volt +s

mill owner +s

mill|pond +s

mill-race +s

mill-rind +s

Mills, John (English actor)

Mills bomb +s (grenade)

mill|stone +s

mill|stream +s

mill-wheel +s

mill|work|er +s

mill|wright +s

Milne, A. A. (English writer)

Milo
mil|om|eter +s
mi|lord +s
Milos (island,
    Cyclades)
milt +s
milt|er +s
Mil|ton, John
    (English poet)
Mil|ton|ian +s
Mil|ton|ic
Mil|ton Keynes
    (town, England)
Mil|wau|kee (city,
    USA)
Mimas (*Greek
    Mythology*; moon
    of Saturn)
mim|bar +s
mime
    mimes
    mimed
    mim|ing
mim|eo|graph +s
    +ed +ing
mimer +s
mi|mesis
    mi|meses
mi|met|ic
mi|met|ic|al|ly
Mimi
mimic
    mim|ics
    mim|icked
    mim|ick|ling
mim|ick|er +s
mim|ic|ry
miminy-piminy
mi|mosa +s
mimu|lus
    mimu|luses
Min (Chinese
    dialect)
min +s (= minute)
mina +s (bird; use
    mynah. △ miner,
    minor)
min|acious
min|acity
    min|aci|ties
Min|aean +s
min|aret +s
min|aret|ed
Minas Ge|rais
    (state, Brazil)
min|atory
min|bar +s
mince
    minces
    minced
    min|cing
    (grind up; walk;

mince (*cont.*)
    minced meat.
    △ mints)
    minced meat
    (meat)
mince|meat +s
    (mixture of
    currants, apples,
    etc.)
mince pie +s
min|cer +s
Minch, the
    Minches
    (channel off
    Scotland)
min|cing|ly
mind +s +ed +ing
    (intellect; lood
    after; etc.
    △ mined)
Min|da|nao (island,
    Philippines)
mind-bending
mind-blowing
mind-boggling
mind-boggling|ly
mind|er +s
mind|ful
mind|ful|ly
mind|ful|ness
mind|less
mind|less|ly
mind|less|ness
mind-numbing
Min|doro (island,
    Philippines)
mind-read
    mind-reads
    mind-read
    mind-reading
mind-reader +s
mind|set +s
mine
    mines
    mined
    min|ing
mine-detect|or +s
mine|field +s
mine hunt|er +s
mine|lay|er +s
miner +s
    (mineworker.
    △ minor, myna,
    mynah)
min|eral +s
min|er|al|isa|tion
    Br. (use
    mineralization)
min|er|al|ise *Br.*
    (use mineralize)
min|er|al|ises

min|er|al|ise (*cont.*)
    min|er|al|ised
    min|er|al|is|ing
min|er|al|iza|tion
min|er|al|ize
    min|er|al|izes
    min|er|al|ized
    min|er|al|iz|ing
min|er|al|ogic|al
min|er|al|ogist +s
min|er|al|ogy
Min|erva *Roman
    Mythology*
mine shaft +s
min|es|trone +s
mine|sweeper +s
min|ever +s (use
    miniver)
mine|work|er +s
Ming
min|gily
min|gle
    min|gles
    min|gled
    min|gling
min|gler +s
Min|gus, Charles
    (American jazz
    musician)
mingy
    min|gier
    min|gi|est
Minho (river, Spain
    and Portugal)
Mini +s (car) *Propr.*
mini +s (dress etc.)
mini|ate
    mini|ates
    mini|ated
    mini|at|ing
mini|ature
    mini|atures
    mini|atured
    mini|atur|ing
mini|atur|isa|tion
    Br. +s (use
    miniaturization)
mini|atur|ise *Br.*
    (use miniaturize)
mini|atur|ises
    mini|atur|ised
    mini|atur|is|ing
mini|atur|ist +s
mini|atur|iza|tion
    +s
mini|atur|ize
    mini|atur|izes
    mini|atur|ized
    mini|atur|iz|ing
mini|bar +s
mini|bus
    mini|buses

mini|cab +s
Mini|com +s *Propr.*
mini|com|puter +s
Mini|coy Is|lands
    (now part of
    Lakshadweep
    Islands)
mini|dress
    mini|dresses
min|ify
    mini|fies
    mini|fied
    mini|fy|ing
mini|golf
mini|kin +s
minim +s
mini|ma
min|imal
min|im|al|ism
min|im|al|ist +s
min|im|al|ly
mini|max
mini|misa|tion *Br.*
    +s (use
    minimization)
min|im|ise *Br.* (use
    minimize)
min|im|ises
    min|im|ised
    min|im|is|ing
min|im|iser *Br.* +s
    (use minimizer)
mini|miza|tion +s
min|im|ize
    min|im|izes
    min|im|ized
    min|im|iz|ing
min|im|izer +s
min|imum
    plural min|ima *or*
    min|imums
min|ion +s
mini|pill +s
min|is|cule (use
    minuscule)
mini|ser|ies
    plural mini|ser|ies
mini|skirt +s
min|is|ter +s +ed
    +ing
min|is|ter|ial
min|is|teri|al|ist
    +s
min|is|teri|al|ly
min|is|ter|ship +s
min|is|trable
min|is|trant +s
min|is|tra|tion +s
min|is|tra|tive
min|is|try
    min|is|tries
min|iver +s

mink +s (stoatlike
    animal. △ minx)
minke +s (whale)
Min|kow|ski,
    Her|mann
    (Russian-born
    German
    mathematician)
Minna
Min|ne|ap|olis
    (city, USA)
min|ne|sing|er +s
Min|ne|sota (state,
    USA)
Min|nie
min|now +s
Miño (Spanish
    name for Minho)
Min|oan +s
minor +s +ed +ing
    (below legal age;
    unimportant.
    △ mina, miner,
    myna, mynah)
Min|orca (Spanish
    island)
Min|or|can +s
Mi|nor|ite +s
mi|nor|ity
    mi|nor|ities
Minos (legendary
    Cretan king)
Mi|no|taur +s
Minsk (capital of
    Belarus)
min|ster +s
min|strel +s
min|strelsy
    min|strel|sies
mint +s +ed +ing
    (plant; sweet;
    place where
    money is made.
    △ mince)
mint|age +s
Min|ton (pottery)
minty
    mint|ier
    minti|est
minu|end +s
min|uet +s +ed
    +ing
minus
    mi|nuses
min|us|cu|lar
min|us|cule
mi|nute
    mi|nuter
    minut|est
    (tiny)
min|ute
    min|utes

min|ute (cont.)
    min|uted
    min|ut|ing
    (60 seconds;
    proceedings; to
    record)
minute-gun +s
min|ute hand +s
mi|nute|ly
Min|ute|man
    Min|ute|men
mi|nute|ness
min|ute steak +s
mi|nu|tia
    mi|nu|tiae
minx
    minxes
    (girl. △ minks)
minx|ish
minx|ish|ly
Mio|cene
mi|osis
    mi|oses
    (eye disorder.
    △ meiosis)
mi|otic (to do with
    miosis. △ meiotic)
MIPS (= million
    instructions per
    second)
Mi|que|lon (in 'St.
    Pierre and
    Miquelon')
Mir (Soviet space
    station)
Mira (star)
Mi|ra|beau,
    Hon|oré Gab|riel
    Ri|queti, Comte
    de (French
    revolutionary)
Mira|bel
mi|ra|belle +s
mira|cid|ium
    mira|cidia
mir|acle +s
mi|racu|lous
mi|racu|lous|ly
mi|racu|lous|ness
mira|dor +s
mir|age +s
Mi|randa (moon of
    Saturn; name)
MIRAS
    (= mortgage
    interest relief at
    source)
mire
    mires
    mired
    mir|ing

mire|poix
    plural mire|poix
Mir|iam
mirid +s
miri|ness
mirk (use murk)
mirky (use murky)
Miró, Joan
    (Spanish painter)
mir|ror +s +ed
    +ing
mir|ror image +s
mir|ror writ|ing
mirth
mirth|ful
mirth|ful|ly
mirth|ful|ness
mirth|less
mirth|less|ly
mirth|less|ness
MIRV +s
    (= multiple
    independently-
    targeted re-entry
    vehicle)
miry
mis|ad|dress
    mis|ad|dresses
    mis|ad|dressed
    mis|ad|dress|ing
mis|ad|ven|ture +s
mis|align +s +ed
    +ing
mis|align|ment +s
mis|alli|ance +s
mis|ally
    mis|allies
    mis|allied
    mis|ally|ing
mis|andry
mis|an|thrope +s
mis|an|throp|ic
mis|an|throp|ic|al
mis|an|throp|ic|
    al|ly
mis|an|thro|pise
    Br. (use
    misanthropize)
    mis|an|thro|pises
    mis|an|thro|pised
    mis|an|thro|
        pis|ing
mis|an|thro|pist
    +s
mis|an|thro|pize
    mis|an|thro|pizes
    mis|an|thro|pized
    mis|an|thro|
        piz|ing
mis|an|thropy
mis|ap|pli|ca|tion
    +s

mis|ap|ply
    mis|ap|plies
    mis|ap|plied
    mis|ap|ply|ing
mis|ap|pre|hend
    +s +ed +ing
mis|ap|pre|hen|
        sion +s
mis|ap|pre|hen|sive
mis|ap|pro|pri|ate
    mis|ap|pro|pri|
        ates
    mis|ap|pro|pri|
        ated
    mis|ap|pro|pri|
        at|ing
mis|ap|pro|pri|
        ation +s
mis|be|come
    mis|be|comes
    mis|be|came
    mis|be|com|ing
mis|be|got|ten
mis|be|have
    mis|be|haves
    mis|be|haved
    mis|be|hav|ing
mis|be|haver +s
mis|be|hav|ior Am.
mis|be|hav|iour Br.
mis|be|lief +s
mis|cal|cu|late
    mis|cal|cu|lates
    mis|cal|cu|lated
    mis|cal|cu|lat|ing
mis|cal|cu|la|tion
    +s
mis|call +s +ed
    +ing
mis|car|riage +s
mis|carry
    mis|car|ries
    mis|car|ried
    mis|carry|ing
mis|cast
    mis|casts
    mis|cast
    mis|cast|ing
mis|ce|gen|ation
mis|cel|la|nea
mis|cel|lan|eous
mis|cel|
    lan|eous|ly
mis|cel|lan|eous|
        ness
mis|cel|lan|ist +s
mis|cel|lany
    mis|cel|lanies
mis|chance +s
mis|chief +s
mischief-maker
    +s

mischief-making
mis|chiev|ous
mis|chiev|ous|ly
mis|chiev|ous|
        ness
misch metal +s
mis|ci|bil|ity
mis|cible
mis|con|ceive
  mis|con|ceives
  mis|con|ceived
  mis|con|ceiv|ing
mis|con|ceiver +s
mis|con|cep|tion
  +s
mis|con|duct +s
  +ed +ing
mis|con|struc|tion
  +s
mis|con|strue
  mis|con|strues
  mis|con|strued
  mis|con|stru|ing
mis|copy
  mis|cop|ies
  mis|cop|ied
  mis|copy|ing
mis|count +s +ed
  +ing
mis|cre|ant +s
mis|cue
  mis|cues
  mis|cued
  mis|cue|ing *or*
  mis|cuing
mis|date
  mis|dates
  mis|dated
  mis|dat|ing
mis|deal
  mis|deals
  mis|dealt
  mis|deal|ing
mis|dec|lar|ation
  +s
mis|deed +s
mis|de|mean|ant
  +s
mis|de|meanor
  Am. +s
mis|de|mean|our
  Br. +s
mis|de|scribe
  mis|de|scribes
  mis|de|scribed
  mis|de|scrib|ing
mis|de|scrip|tion
  +s
mis|diag|nose
  mis|diag|noses
  mis|diag|nosed
  mis|diag|nos|ing

mis|diag|nosis
  mis|diag|noses
mis|dial
  mis|dials
  mis|dialled *Br.*
  mis|dialed *Am.*
  mis|dial|ling *Br.*
  mis|dial|ing *Am.*
mis|dir|ect +s +ed
  +ing
mis|dir|ec|tion +s
mis|doing +s
mis|doubt +s +ed
  +ing
mis|edu|cate
  mis|edu|cates
  mis|edu|cated
  mis|edu|cat|ing
mis|edu|ca|tion
mise en scène
  mises en scène
mis|em|ploy +s
  +ed +ing
mis|em|ploy|ment
  +s
miser +s
mis|er|able
mis|er|able|ness
mis|er|ably
mis|ère +s
mis|er|ere +s
mis|eri|cord +s
miser|li|ness
miser|ly
mis|ery
  mis|er|ies
mis|feas|ance +s
mis|field +s +ed
  +ing
mis|fire
  mis|fires
  mis|fired
  mis|fir|ing
mis|fit +s
mis|for|tune +s
mis|give
  mis|gives
  mis|gave
  mis|giv|ing
  mis|given
mis|giv|ing +s
mis|gov|ern +s
  +ed +ing
mis|gov|ern|ment
mis|guid|ance
mis|guide
  mis|guides
  mis|guided
  mis|guid|ing
mis|guided|ly
mis|guided|ness
mis|handle
  mis|handles

mis|handle (*cont.*)
  mis|handled
  mis|hand|ling
mis|hap +s
mis|hear
  mis|hears
  mis|heard
  mis|hear|ing
mis|hit
  mis|hits
  mis|hit
  mis|hit|ting
mish|mash
  mish|mashes
Mish|nah
Mish|na|ic
mis|iden|ti|fi|
     ca|tion +s
mis|iden|tify
  mis|iden|ti|fies
  mis|iden|ti|fied
  mis|iden|ti|fy|ing
mis|in|form +s
  +ed +ing
mis|in|for|ma|tion
mis|in|ter|pret +s
  +ed +ing
mis|in|ter|pret|
     ation +s
mis|in|ter|pret|er
  +s
mis|judge
  mis|judges
  mis|judged
  mis|judg|ing
mis|judge|ment +s
mis|judg|ment +s
  (use
  misjudgement)
mis|key +s +ed
  +ing
mis|kick +s +ed
  +ing
Mis|kito
  plural Mis|kito *or*
  Mis|kitos
Mis|kolc (city,
  Hungary)
mis|lay
  mis|lays
  mis|laid
  mis|lay|ing
mis|lead
  mis|leads
  mis|led
  mis|lead|ing
mis|lead|er +s
mis|lead|ing
mis|lead|ing|ly
mis|lead|ing|ness
mis|like
  mis|likes

mis|like (*cont.*)
  mis|liked
  mis|lik|ing
mis|man|age
  mis|man|ages
  mis|man|aged
  mis|man|aging
mis|man|age|ment
  +s
mis|mar|riage +s
mis|match
  mis|matches
  mis|matched
  mis|match|ing
mis|mated
mis|meas|ure
  mis|meas|ures
  mis|meas|ured
  mis|meas|ur|ing
mis|meas|ure|
       ment
mis|name
  mis|names
  mis|named
  mis|nam|ing
mis|nomer +s
miso
mis|og|am|ist +s
mis|og|amy
mis|ogyn|ist +s
mis|ogyn|is|tic
mis|ogyn|ous
mis|ogyny
mis|olo|gist +s
mis|ol|ogy
miso|ne|ism
miso|ne|ist +s
mis|pickel +s
mis|place
  mis|places
  mis|placed
  mis|placing
mis|place|ment +s
mis|play +s +ed
  +ing
mis|print +s +ed
  +ing
mis|pri|sion +s
mis|prize
  mis|prizes
  mis|prized
  mis|priz|ing
mis|pro|nounce
  mis|pro|nounces
  mis|pro|nounced
  mis|pro|noun|
       cing
mis|pro|nun|ci|
      ation +s
mis|quo|ta|tion +s
mis|quote
  mis|quotes

mis|quote (*cont.*)
  mis|quoted
  mis|quot|ing
mis|read
  mis|reads
  mis|read
  mis|read|ing
mis|re|mem|ber +s
  +ed +ing
mis|re|port +s +ed
  +ing
mis|rep|re|sent +s
  +ed +ing
mis|rep|re|sen|
     ta|tion +s
mis|rep|re|sen|
     ta|tive
mis|rule
  mis|rules
  mis|ruled
  mis|rul|ing
miss
  misses
  missed
  miss|ing
miss|able
mis|sal +s (book)
mis|sel thrush (use
  mistle thrush)
  mis|sel thrushes
mis|shape
  mis|shapes
  mis|shaped
  mis|shap|ing
mis|sha|pen
mis|sha|pen|ly
mis|sha|pen|ness
mis|sile +s
mis|sil|ery
  mis|sil|er|ies
mis|sion +s
mis|sion|ary
  mis|sion|ar|ies
mis|sion|er +s
mis|sis
miss|ish
Mis|sis|sauga
  (town, Canada)
Mis|sis|sippi (river,
  USA)
mis|sive +s
Mis|so|lon|ghi
  (city, Greece)
Mis|souri (river
  and state, USA)
mis|spell
  mis|spells
  mis|spelled *or*
  mis|spelt
  mis|spell|ing
mis|spell|ing +s

mis|spend
  mis|spends
  mis|spent
  mis|spend|ing
mis|state
  mis|stat|ing
mis|state|ment +s
mis|step +s
mis|sus
missy
  mis|sies
mist +s +ed +ing
  (condensed
  vapour etc.
  △ missed)
mis|tak|able
mis|tak|ably
mis|take
  mis|takes
  mis|took
  mis|tak|ing
  mis|taken
mis|taken|ly
mis|taken|ness
mis|teach
  mis|teaches
  mis|taught
  mis|teach|ing
mis|ter +s
mist|ful
mis|ti|gris
mist|ily
mis|time
  mis|times
  mis|timed
  mis|tim|ing
misti|ness
mis|title
  mis|titles
  mis|titled
  mis|tit|ling
mis|tle thrush
  mis|tle thrush|es
mistle|toe +s
mist|like
mis|took
mis|tral +s
mis|trans|late
  mis|trans|lates
  mis|trans|lated
  mis|trans|lat|ing
mis|trans|la|tion
  +s
mis|treat +s +ed
  +ing
mis|treat|ment +s
mis|tress
  mis|tresses
Mis|tress of the
  Robes
mis|trial +s

mis|trust +s +ed
  +ing
mis|trust|ful
mis|trust|ful|ly
mis|trust|ful|ness
misty
  mist|ier
  misti|est
mis|type
  mis|types
  mis|typed
  mis|typ|ing
mis|un|der|stand
  mis|un|der|stands
  mis|un|der|stood
  mis|un|der|stand|
     ing
mis|un|der|stand|
     ing +s
mis|us|age +s
mis|use
  mis|uses
  mis|used
  mis|us|ing
mis|user +s
Mi|tanni
  plural Mi|tanni
Mi|tan|nian +s
Mitch|ell, Joni
  (Canadian singer-
  songwriter)
Mitch|ell,
  Mar|ga|ret
  (American
  novelist)
Mitch|ell,
  Regi|nald
  Jo|seph (English
  aeronautical
  designer)
mite +s (arachnid;
  small amount.
  △ might)
miter *Am.* +s +ed
  +ing (*Br.* mitre)
miter block *Am.* +s
  (*Br.* mitre block)
miter box *Am.*
  miter boxes
  (*Br.* mitre box)
miter joint *Am.* +s
  (*Br.* mitre joint)
miter wheel *Am.*
  +s (*Br.* mitre
  wheel)
Mit|ford, Nancy
  (English writer)
Mith|ra|ic
Mith|ra|ism
Mith|ra|ist +s
Mith|ras *Persian*
  Mythology

Mith|ri|da|tes
  (king of Pontus)
mith|ri|dat|ic
mith|rida|tise *Br.*
  (use mithridatize)
  mith|rida|tises
  mith|rida|tised
  mith|rida|tis|ing
mith|ri|da|tism
mith|rida|tize
  mith|rida|tizes
  mith|rida|tized
  mith|rida|tiz|ing
miti|gable
miti|gate
  miti|gates
  miti|gated
  miti|gat|ing
miti|ga|tion +s
miti|ga|tor +s
miti|ga|tory
Miti|lini (Greek
  name for
  Mytilene)
Mitla (ancient city,
  Mexico)
mi|to|chon|drion
  mi|to|chon|dria
mi|tosis
  mi|toses
mi|tot|ic
mit|rail|leuse +s
mi|tral
mitre *Br.*
  mitres
  mitred
  mitr|ing
  (*Am.* miter)
mitre block *Br.* +s
  (*Am.* miter block)
mitre box *Br.*
  mitre boxes
  (*Am.* miter box)
mitre joint *Br.* +s
  (*Am.* miter joint)
mitre wheel *Br.* +s
  (*Am.* miter wheel)
Mit|siwa
  (= Massawa)
mitt +s
Mit|tel|land Canal
  (in Germany)
mit|ten +s
mit|tened
Mit|ter|rand,
  Fran|çois (French
  president)
mit|ti|mus
  mit|ti|muses
Mitty, Wal|ter
  Wal|ter Mittys

mitz|vah
  mitz|voth
mix
  mixes
  mixed
  mix|ing
mix|able
mixed|ness
mixed-up
  attributive
mixer +s
mixer tap +s
Mix|tec +s
mix|ture +s
mix-up +s *noun*
mizen +s (use
  mizzen)
Mi|zo|ram (state,
  India)
miz|zen +s
mizzen-mast +s
mizzen-sail +s
miz|zen yard +s
miz|zle
  miz|zles
  miz|zled
  miz|zling
miz|zly
M.Litt. (= Master
  of Letters)
Mlle +s
  (= Mademoiselle)
m'lud
Mma|batho (town,
  South Africa)
M'Nagh|ten rules
  (use McNaughten
  rules)
mne|mon|ic +s
mne|mon|ic|al|ly
mne|mon|ics
mne|mon|ist +s
Mne|mos|yne
  Greek Mythology
mo +s (= moment.
  △ mho, mow)
moa +s (bird.
  △ mower)
Moab|ite +s
moan +s +ed +ing
  (plaintive sound;
  make a moan;
  complain.
  △ mown)
moan|er +s
moan|ful
moan|ing|ly
moan|ing min|nie
  +s
moat +s +ed +ing
  (ditch. △ mote)

mob
  mobs
  mobbed
  mob|bing
mob|ber +s
mob|bish
mob cap +s
Mo|bile (city, USA)
mo|bile +s
mo|bil|iary
mo|bil|is|able *Br.*
  (use mobilizable)
mo|bil|isa|tion *Br.*
  +s (use
  mobilization)
mo|bil|ise *Br.* (use
  mobilize)
  mo|bil|ises
  mo|bil|ised
  mo|bil|is|ing
mo|bil|iser *Br.* +s
  (use mobilizer)
mo|bil|ity
mo|bil|iz|able
mo|bil|iza|tion +s
mo|bil|ize
  mo|bil|izes
  mo|bil|ized
  mo|bil|iz|ing
mo|bil|izer +s
Mö|bius strip
mob|oc|racy
  mob|oc|ra|cies
mob|ster +s
Mo|butu Sese
  Seko, Lake (in
  Zaire)
Mo|butu (Sese
  Seko) (president
  of Zaire)
moc|ca|sin +s
Mocha +s (stone;
  butterfly; pottery)
mocha +s (coffee;
  leather. △ mocker)
Mo|chica
  plural Mo|chica
mock +s +ed +ing
mock|able
mock|er +s
  (person who mocks.
  △ mocha)
mock|ery
  mock|er|ies
mock-heroic +s
mock|ing|bird +s
mock|ing|ly
mock-up +s *noun*
mod +s
modal
mo|dal|ity
  mo|dal|ities

mo|dal|ly
mod cons
  (= modern
  conveniences)
mode +s
model
  models
  mod|elled *Br.*
  mod|eled *Am.*
  mod|el|ling *Br.*
  mod|el|ing *Am.*
mod|el|er *Am.* +s
mod|el|ler *Br.* +s
modem +s
Mod|ena (city,
  Italy)
mod|er|ate
  mod|er|ates
  mod|er|ated
  mod|er|at|ing
mod|er|ate|ly
mod|er|ate|ness
mod|er|ation +s
Mod|er|ations
  (examination)
mod|er|at|ism
mod|er|ato +s
mod|er|ator +s
mod|er|ator|ship
  +s
mod|ern +s
mod|ern|isa|tion
  Br. +s (use
  modernization)
mod|ern|ise *Br.*
  (use modernize)
  mod|ern|ises
  mod|ern|ised
  mod|ern|is|ing
mod|ern|iser *Br.*
  +s (use
  modernizer)
mod|ern|ism +s
mod|ern|ist +s
mod|ern|is|tic
mod|ern|is|tic|
  al|ly
mod|ern|ity
  mod|ern|ities
mod|ern|iza|tion
  +s
mod|ern|ize
  mod|ern|izes
  mod|ern|ized
  mod|ern|iz|ing
mod|ern|izer +s
mod|ern|ly
mod|ern|ness
mod|est
mod|est|ly
mod|esty
modi|cum

modi|fi|able
modi|fi|ca|tion +s
modi|fi|ca|tory
modi|fier +s
mod|ify
  modi|fies
  modi|fied
  modi|fy|ing
Modi|gliani,
  Ame|deo (Italian
  painter)
mo|dil|lion +s
mod|ish
mod|ish|ly
mod|ish|ness
mod|iste +s
Mods
  (= Moderations)
modu|lar
modu|lar|ity
modu|late
  modu|lates
  modu|lated
  modu|lat|ing
modu|la|tion +s
modu|la|tor +s
mod|ule +s
mod|ulo
modu|lus
  mod|uli
modus op|er|andi
  modi op|er|andi
modus vi|vendi
  modi vi|vendi
Moe|sia (ancient
  country, modern
  Bulgaria and
  Serbia)
mo|fette +s
mog +s
Moga|di|shu
  (capital of
  Somalia)
Moga|don
  plural Moga|don
  or Moga|dons
  Propr.
mog|gie +s
moggy
  mog|gies
  (use moggie)
Mo|ghul +s (use
  Mogul)
Mo|gi|lev (Russian
  name for
  Mahilyow)
Mogul +s
  (Mongolian
  Muslim)
mogul +s
  (important
  person)

Mo¦hács (river port, Hungary)

mo¦hair +s

Mo¦ham¦med (use Muhammad)

Mo¦ham¦medan +s (prefer Muslim)

Mo¦ham¦med¦an¦ism (prefer Islam)

Mo¦ham¦merah (former name of Khorramshahr)

Mo¦have Des¦ert (use Mojave Desert)

Mo¦hawk +s

Mo¦he¦gan +s (people)

Mohenjo-Daro (ancient city, Pakistan)

Mo¦hi¦can +s (hairstyle; for people, prefer Mohegan)

Moho +s

Moholy-Nagy, László (Hungarian-born American artist)

Moho¦ro¦vi¦čić dis¦con¦tinu¦ity

Mohs' scale

moi¦dore +s

moi¦ety
moi¦eties

moil +s +ed +ing

Moira also Moyra

Moi¦rai (Greek name for the Fates)

moire +s (watered fabric; patterned; pattern)

moiré +s (watered)

Mois¦san, Fer¦di¦nand Fréd¦éric Henri (French chemist)

moist +er +est

mois¦ten +s +ed +ing

moist¦ly

moist¦ness

mois¦ture

mois¦ture¦less

mois¦tur¦ise Br. (use moisturize)
mois¦tur¦ises
mois¦tur¦ised
mois¦tur¦is¦ing

mois¦tur¦iser Br. +s (use moisturizer)

mois¦tur¦ize
mois¦tur¦izes
mois¦tur¦ized
mois¦tur¦iz¦ing

mois¦tur¦izer +s

Mo¦jave Des¦ert (in USA)

moke +s

moko +s

mok¦sha

mol (= mole, chemical unit)

molal

mol¦al¦ity
mol¦al¦ities

molar +s

mo¦lar¦ity
mo¦lar¦ities

mo¦las¦ses

Mold (town, Wales)

mold Am. +s +ed +ing (Br. mould)

mold¦able Am. (Br. mouldable)

Mol¦dau (German name for the Vltava)

Mol¦davia (alternative name for Moldova)

Mol¦davian +s

mold-board Am. +s (Br. mould-board)

mold¦er Am. +s (person who moulds. Br. moulder)

mol¦der Am. +s +ed +ing (rot. Br. moulder)

mol¦di¦ness Am. (Br. mouldiness)

mold¦ing Am. +s (Br. moulding)

Mol¦dova

Mol¦do¦van +s

moldy Am.
mold¦ier
moldi¦est
(Br. mouldy)

mole +s

mo¦lecu¦lar

mo¦lecu¦lar¦ity

mo¦lecu¦lar¦ly

mol¦ecule +s

mole¦hill +s

mole¦skin +s

mo¦lest +s +ed +ing

mo¦lest¦ation +s

mo¦lest¦er +s

Mol¦ière (French dramatist)

mo¦line (Heraldry. △ malign)

Mo¦lise (region, Italy)

moll +s

Mol¦lie also Molly

mol¦li¦fi¦ca¦tion +s

mol¦li¦fier +s

mol¦lify
mol¦li¦fies
mol¦li¦fied
mol¦li¦fy¦ing

mol¦lusc +s

mol¦lus¦can

mol¦lusc¦oid

mol¦lusc¦ous

Molly also Mol¦lie (name)

molly
mol¦lies (fish)

molly¦cod¦dle
molly¦cod¦dles
molly¦cod¦dled
molly¦cod¦dling

mol¦ly¦mawk +s

Mo¦loch (god)

mo¦loch +s (reptile)

mo¦los¦sus
mo¦lossi

Molo¦tov (former name of Perm; cocktail)

Molo¦tov, Vyache¦slav Mikh¦ail¦ovich (Soviet statesman)

molt Am. +s +ed +ing (Br. moult)

mol¦ten

molto

Mo¦lucca Is¦lands (in Indonesia)

Mo¦luc¦cas (= Molucca Islands)

moly
molies

mo¦lyb¦den¦ite

mo¦lyb¦denum

mom +s

Mom¦basa (city, Kenya)

mo¦ment +s

mo¦menta

mo¦ment¦ar¦ily

mo¦ment¦ari¦ness

mo¦ment¦ary

mo¦ment¦ly

mo¦men¦tous

mo¦men¦tous¦ly

mo¦men¦tous¦ness

mo¦men¦tum

mo¦menta

momma +s

Mom¦msen, Theo¦dor (German historian)

mommy
mom¦mies

Momus
Mo¦muses or Momi

Mon
plural Mon or Mons (person; language)

Mona (name)

mon¦acal (monastic; use monachal.
△ monocle)

Mon¦acan +s

mon¦achal (monastic.
△ monocle)

mon¦ach¦ism (monasticism.
△ monarchism)

Mon¦aco

monad +s

mona¦del¦phous

mo¦nad¦ic

mon¦ad¦ism

mon¦ad¦nock +s

Mona¦ghan (county and town, Republic of Ireland)

Mona Lisa

mo¦nan¦drous

mo¦nan¦dry

mon¦arch +s

mo¦nar¦chal

mo¦nar¦chial

mo¦nar¦chic

mo¦nar¦chic¦al

mo¦nar¦chic¦al¦ly

mon¦arch¦ism (government by monarchs.
△ monachism)

mon¦arch¦ist +s

mon¦archy
mon¦arch¦ies

Mon|ash, John
(Australian
general)
mon|as|tery
  mon|as|ter|ies
mo|nas|tic
mo|nas|tic|al|ly
mo|nas|ti|cise *Br.*
  (use monasticize)
mo|nas|ti|cises
mo|nas|ti|cised
mo|nas|ti|cis|ing
mo|nas|ti|cism
mo|nas|ti|cize
mo|nas|ti|cizes
mo|nas|ti|cized
mo|nas|ti|ciz|ing
Mon|as|tir (town,
Tunisia)
mon|atom|ic
mon|aural
mon|aural|ly
mona|zite
Mön|chen|
  glad|bach (city,
  Germany)
Monck, George
(Duke of
Albemarle, English
general)
mon|daine +s *female*
Mon|day +s
mon|dial
Mon|drian, Piet
(Dutch painter)
mon|ecious *Am.*
  (*Br.* monoecious)
Moné|gasque +s
Monel *Propr.*
Monet, Claude
(French painter)
mon|et|ar|ily
mon|et|ar|ism
mon|et|ar|ist +s
mon|et|ary
mon|et|isa|tion *Br.*
  (use
  monetization)
mon|et|ise *Br.* (use
  monetize)
mon|et|ises
mon|et|ised
mon|et|is|ing
mon|et|iza|tion
mon|et|ize
mon|et|izes
mon|et|ized
mon|et|iz|ing
money
  plural moneys *or*
  mon|ies

money bag +s (bag
  for money)
money|bags
  (person)
money box
  money boxes
money chan|ger
  +s
mon|eyed
mon|ey|er +s
money-grubber +s
money-grubbing
money|lend|er +s
money|lend|ing
money|less
money|maker +s
money|mak|ing
money mar|ket +s
money order +s
money spi|der +s
money-spinner +s
money-spinning
money's-worth
money|wort +s
mon|ger +s
mon|ger|ing
mongo
  plural mongo *or*
  mon|gos
Mon|gol +s
  (member of Asian
  people)
mon|gol +s
  (*offensive* person
  with Down's
  syndrome)
Mon|go|lia
Mon|go|lian +s
mon|gol|ism
  (*offensive*)
Mon|gol|oid +s
  (characteristic of
  Mongolians)
mon|gol|oid +s
  (*offensive;* affected
  with Down's
  syndrome)
mon|goose +s
mon|grel +s
mon|grel|isa|tion
  Br. +s (use
  mongrelization)
mon|grel|ise *Br.*
  (use mongrelize)
mon|grel|ises
mon|grel|ised
mon|grel|is|ing
mon|grel|ism
mon|grel|iza|tion
  +s
mon|grel|ize
mon|grel|izes

mon|grel|ize
  (*cont.*)
  mon|grel|ized
  mon|grel|iz|ing
mon|grel|ly
'mongst
  (= amongst)
mo|nial +s
Mon|ica (N. African-
  born saint; actual
  name)
mon|icker +s
  (slang word for
  'name'; use
  moniker)
mon|ies (plural of
  money)
moni|ker +s
mo|nili|form
mon|ism +s
mon|ist +s
mo|nis|tic
moni|tion +s
moni|tor +s +ed
  +ing
moni|tor|ial
moni|tor|ship +s
moni|tory
moni|tor|ies
Monk,
  The|lo|nious
  (American jazz
  musician)
monk +s
monk|ery
mon|key +s +ed
  +ing
mon|key|ish
monkey-jacket +s
monkey-nut +s
monkey-puzzle +s
mon|key|shine +s
mon|key|wrench
  mon|key|
       wrenches
  mon|key|
       wrenched
  mon|key|wrench|
       ing
  verb
mon|key wrench
  mon|key
    wrenches
  noun
monk|fish
  plural monk|fish
Mon-Khmer
  (group of
  languages)
monk|ish
monks|hood +s
  (plant)

Mon|mouth (town,
  Wales)
Mon|mouth|shire
  (former county,
  Wales)
mon|nik|er +s (use
  moniker)
mono +s
mono|acid
mono|basic
mono|car|pic
mono|car|pous
mono|caus|al
mono|ceph|al|ous
mono|chord +s
mono|chro|mat|ic
mono|chro|mat|ic|
  al|ly
mono|
    chro|ma|tism
mono|chrome +s
mono|chro|mic
mon|ocle +s
  (eyeglass.
  ⚠ monachal)
mon|ocled
mono|cli|nal
mono|cline +s
mono|clin|ic
mono|clo|nal
mono|coque +s
mono|cot +s
  (= monocoty-
  ledon)
mono|coty|ledon
  +s
mono|coty|ledon|
       ous
mon|oc|racy
  mon|oc|ra|cies
mono|crat|ic
mono|crot|ic
mon|ocu|lar
mon|ocu|lar|ly
mono|cul|ture +s
mono|cycle +s
mono|cyte +s
mono|dac|tyl|ous
mon|od|ic
mon|od|ist +s
mono|drama +s
mon|ody
  mon|odies
mono|e|cious *Br.*
  (*Am.* monecious)
mono|fila|ment +s
mon|og|amist +s
mon|og|am|ous
mon|og|am|ous|ly
mon|og|amy
mono|gen|esis
mono|genet|ic

mono|geny
mono|glot +s
mono|gram +s
mono|gram|mat|ic
mono|grammed
mono|graph +s
  +ed +ing
mon|og|raph|er +s
mono|graph|ic
mon|og|raph|ist
  +s
mon|ogyn|ous
mon|ogyny
mono|hull +s
mono|hy|brid +s
mono|hyd|ric
mono|kini +s
mon|ol|atry
mono|layer +s
mono|lin|gual
mono|lith +s
mono|lith|ic
mono|logic
mono|logic|al
mon|olo|gise Br.
  (use monologize)
  mon|olo|gises
  mon|olo|gised
  mon|olo|gis|ing
mon|olo|gist +s
mon|olo|gize
  mon|olo|gizes
  mon|olo|gized
  mon|olo|giz|ing
mono|logue +s
mono|mania +s
mono|maniac +s
mono|mani|ac|al
mono|mark +s
mono|mer +s
mono|mer|ic
mono|met|al|lism
mono|mial +s
mono|mo|lecu|lar
mono|morph|ic
mono|morph|ism
  +s
mono|morph|ous
mono|nucle|osis
  mono|nucle|oses
mono|pet|al|ous
mono|phon|ic
mono|phon|ic|
       al|ly
mono|ph|thong +s
mono|ph|thong|al
mono|phy|let|ic
Mono|phy|site +s
mono|plane +s
mono|pod +s
mono|pole +s

mon|op|ol|isa|tion
  Br. +s (use
  monopolization)
mon|op|ol|ise Br.
  (use monopolize)
  mon|op|ol|ises
  mon|op|ol|ised
  mon|op|ol|is|ing
mon|op|ol|iser Br.
  +s (use
  monopolizer)
mon|op|ol|ist +s
mon|op|ol|is|tic
mon|op|ol|iza|tion
  +s
mon|op|ol|ize
  mon|op|ol|izes
  mon|op|ol|ized
  mon|op|ol|iz|ing
mon|op|ol|izer +s
Mon|op|oly (game)
  Propr.
mon|op|oly
  mon|op|olies
  (exclusive
  possession etc.)
mon|op|sony
  mon|op|so|nies
mono|psych|ism
mono|rail +s
mono|rhyme +s
mono|sac|char|ide
  +s
mono|so|dium
  glu|ta|mate
mono|sperm|ous
mo|nos|ti|chous
mono|stroph|ic
mono|syl|lab|ic
mono|syl|lab|ic|
       al|ly
mono|syl|lable +s
mono|the|ism
mono|the|ist +s
mono|the|is|tic
mono|the|is|tic|
       al|ly
Mon|oth|elite +s
mono|tint +s
mono|tone +s
mono|ton|ic
mono|ton|ic|al|ly
mon|ot|on|ise Br.
  (use monotonize)
mon|ot|on|ises
mon|ot|on|ised
mon|ot|on|is|ing
mon|ot|on|ize
  mon|ot|on|izes
  mon|ot|on|ized
  mon|ot|on|iz|ing
mon|ot|on|ous

mon|ot|on|ous|ly
mon|ot|on|ous|
        ness
mon|ot|ony
mono|treme +s
Mono|type
  (machine) Propr.
mono|type +s
  (picture)
mono|typ|ic
mono|un|satu|rate
  +s
mono|un|satu|
       rated
mono|va|lence
mono|va|lency
mono|va|lent
mon|ox|ide +s
Mon|roe, James
  (American
  president;
  doctrine)
Mon|roe, Mari|lyn
  (American
  actress)
Mon|ro|via (capital
  of Liberia)
Mons (town,
  Belgian)
Mon|sei|gneur
  Mes|sei|gneurs
  (title of French
  prince, cardinal,
  etc.)
Mon|sieur
  Mes|sieurs
Mon|si|gnor
  Mon|si|gnori
  (Roman Catholic
  title)
mon|soon +s
mon|soon|al
mons pubis
  mon|tes pubis
mon|ster +s
mon|stera +s
  (plant)
mon|strance +s
mon|stros|ity
  mon|stros|ities
mon|strous
mon|strous|ly
mon|strous|ness
mons Ven|eris
  montes Ven|eris
mont|age +s
Mon|tagna,
  Bar|tolom|meo
  Cin|cani (Italian
  painter)
Mon|ta|gue

Mon|tagu's
  har|rier +s
Mon|taigne,
  Mi|chel Ey|quem
  de (French writer)
Mon|tana (state,
  USA)
Mon|tana, Joe
  (American football
  player)
mon|tane
Mon|tan|ism
Mon|tan|ist +s
Mont Blanc
  (mountain, Alps)
mont|bre|tia +s
Mont|calm,
  Mar|quis de
  (French general)
monte (card game)
Monte Albán
  (ancient city,
  Mexico)
Monte Carlo
  (commune,
  Monaco)
Monte Cas|sino
  (hill and
  monastery site,
  Italy)
Mon|tego Bay
  (port, Jamaica)
Mon|te|neg|rin +s
Mon|te|negro
  (Balkan republic)
Mon|terey (city,
  USA)
Mon|ter|rey (city,
  Mexico)
Mon|te|span,
  Mar|quise de
  (mistress of Louis
  XIV)
Mon|tes|quieu,
  Baron de (French
  political
  philosopher)
Mon|tes|sori,
  Maria (Italian
  educationist)
Mon|te|verdi,
  Clau|dio (Italian
  composer)
Mon|te|video
  (capital of
  Uruguay)
Mon|tez, Lola
  (mistress of
  Ludwig I of
  Bavaria)
Mon|te|zuma
  (Aztec ruler)

Mon|te|zuma's re|venge
Mont|fort, Simon de (French soldier, father of Earl of Leicester)
Mont|fort, Simon de (Earl of Leicester; English soldier)
Mont|gol|fier, Jo|seph and Jacques-Étienne (French balloonists)
Mont|gom|ery (city, USA)
Mont|gom|ery, Ber|nard Law ('Monty') (Viscount Montgomery of Alamein, British field marshal)
Mont|gom|ery, Lucy Maud (Canadian novelist)
Mont|gom|ery|shire (former county, Wales)
month +s
month|ly
month|lies
mon|ti|cule +s
Mont|martre (district of Paris, France)
mont|mor|il|lon|ite +s
Mont|par|nasse (district, Paris)
Mont Pelée (mountain, Martinique)
Mont|pel|ier (city, USA)
Mont|pel|lier (city, France)
Mon|treal (city, Canada)
Mon|treux (town, Switzerland)
Mon|trose, Mar|quis of (Scottish general)
Mont|ser|rat (in West Indies)
Mont St Michel (islet off Normandy coast)
Monty

monu|ment +s
monu|men|tal
monu|men|tal|ise Br. (use monumentalize)
monu|men|tal|ises
monu|men|tal|ised
monu|men|tal|is|ing
monu|men|tal|ism
monu|men|tal|ity
monu|men|tal|ize
monu|men|tal|izes
monu|men|tal|ized
monu|men|tal|iz|ing
monu|men|tal|ly
monu|men|tal
mason +s
moo +s +ed +ing (cattle sound. △ moue)
mooch
mooches
mooched
mooch|ing
mooch|er +s
moo-cow +s
mood +s
mood|ily
moodi|ness
moody
mood|ies
mood|ier
moodi|est
Moog +s
moo|lah +s
mooli +s
moolvi +s
mool|vie +s (use moolvi)
Moon, Sun Myung (Korean religious leader)
moon +s +ed +ing
moon|beam +s
moon boot +s
moon|calf
moon|calves
moon-face +s
moon-faced
moon|fish
plural moon|fish or moon|fishes
moon-flower +s
Moonie +s (offensive)
moon|less

moon|light +s +ed +ing
moon|light|er +s
moon|lit
moon|quake +s
moon|rise +s
moon|scape +s
moon|set +s
moon|shee +s
moon|shine +s
moon|shiner +s
moon|shot +s
moon|stone +s
moon|struck
moony
moon|ier
mooni|est
Moor +s (N. African people)
moor +s +ed +ing (open land; tie up boat. △ maw, mor, more)
moor|age +s
moor|cock +s
Moore, Bobby (English footballer)
Moore, Fran|cis (physician and originator of 'Old Moore's Almanac')
Moore, G. E. (English philosopher)
Moore, George (Irish novelist)
Moore, Henry (English sculptor)
Moore, John (British general)
Moore, Thomas (Irish songwriter)
moor|fowl
plural moor|fowl or moor|fowls
moor|hen +s
moor|ing +s
mooring-mast +s
moor|ing place +s
Moor|ish (of Moors)
moor|ish (resembling moorland. △ moreish)
Moor|ish idol +s (fish)
moor|land +s
Moor|man
Moor|men

moory
moose
plural moose
Moose Jaw (town, Canada)
moot +s +ed +ing
mop
mops
mopped
mop|ping
mope
mopes
moped
mop|ing
moped +s
moper +s
mop|head +s
mopi|ly
mopi|ness
mop|ish
mo|poke +s
mop|pet +s
moppy
Mopti (city, Mali)
mopy
mopi|er
mopi|est
mo|quette +s
mor +s (humus. △ maw, moor, more)
Mora|da|bad (city, India)
Morag
mo|rainal
mo|raine +s
mo|rain|ic
moral +s (concerned with acceptable behaviour; lesson; etc.)
mor|ale +s (mental attitude)
mor|al|isa|tion Br. +s (use moralization)
mor|al|ise Br. (use moralize)
mor|al|ises
mor|al|ised
mor|al|is|ing
mor|al|iser Br. +s (use moralizer)
mor|al|is|ing|ly Br. (use moralizingly)
mor|al|ism
mor|al|ist +s
mor|al|is|tic
mor|al|is|tic|al|ly

mor¦al¦ity
  mor¦al¦ities
mor¦al¦iza¦tion +s
mor¦al¦ize
  mor¦al¦izes
  mor¦al¦ized
  mor¦al¦iz¦ing
mor¦al¦izer +s
mor¦al¦iz¦ing¦ly
mor¦al¦ly
Morar (Loch;
  Scotland)
mor¦ass
  mor¦asses
mora¦tor¦ium
  mora¦tor¦iums *or*
  mora¦toria
Mor¦avia (region,
  Czech Republic)
Mor¦avia, Al¦berto
  (Italian writer)
Mor¦avian +s
Moray (former
  county, Scotland)
moray +s (eel)
Moray Firth (in
  Scotland)
mor¦bid
mor¦bid¦ity
mor¦bid¦ly
mor¦bid¦ness
mor¦bif¦ic
mor¦billi
mor¦da¦cious
mor¦da¦city
mor¦dancy
mor¦dant +s
  (corrosive
  substance)
mor¦dant¦ly
mor¦dent +s
  (musical
  ornament)
Mor¦dred *Arthurian*
  Legend
Mord¦vinia
  (republic, Russia)
Mord¦vin¦ian +s
More, Thomas
  (English
  statesman and
  saint)
more (greater in
  number etc.
  ⚠ maw, mor,
  moor)
More¦cambe
  (town, England)
More¦cambe Bay
  (in England)
mor¦een +s

more¦ish (pleasant
  to eat. ⚠ moorish)
morel +s
Mor¦elia (city,
  Mexico)
mor¦ello +s
Mor¦elos (state,
  Mexico)
more¦over
more¦pork +s
  (owl)
mores (customs)
Mor¦esco (use
  Morisco)
Mor¦es¦cos *or*
  Mor¦es¦coes
Mor¦esque
  (Moorish)
Mor¦gan, J. P.
  (American
  philanthropist)
Mor¦gan, Thomas
  Hunt (American
  zoologist)
mor¦ga¦nat¦ic
mor¦ga¦nat¦ic¦al¦ly
Mor¦gan le Fay
  Arthurian Legend
mor¦gen +s
  (measure of land)
morgue +s
mori¦bund
mori¦bun¦dity
morion +s
Mor¦isco +s
mor¦ish (use
  moreish)
Mori¦sot, Berthe
  (French painter)
Mor¦land, George
  (English painter)
Mor¦ley, Ed¦ward
  Wil¦liams
  (American
  chemist)
Mor¦ley, Thomas
  (English
  composer)
Mor¦mon +s
Mor¦mon¦ism
morn +s
mor¦nay
morn¦ing +s (time
  of day.
  ⚠ mourning)
morning-after pill
  +s
morn¦ing coat +s
morn¦ing dress
morn¦ing glory
  morn¦ing glor¦ies

morn¦ing paper +s
  (newspaper.
  ⚠ mourning-
  paper)
morn¦ing room +s
morn¦ing
  sick¦ness
morn¦ing star +s
morn¦ing watch
  morn¦ing
  watches
Moro +s
Mo¦roc¦can +s
Mo¦rocco
mo¦rocco +s
  (leather)
moron +s
Mor¦oni (city,
  Comoros Islands)
mor¦on¦ic
mo¦ron¦ic¦al¦ly
mor¦on¦ism
mor¦ose
mor¦ose¦ly
mor¦ose¦ness
Mor¦peth (town,
  England)
morph +s
mor¦pheme +s
mor¦phem¦ic
mor¦phem¦ic¦al¦ly
mor¦phem¦ics
Mor¦pheus *Roman*
  Mythology
mor¦phia
mor¦phine
morph¦ing
mor¦phin¦ism
mor¦pho¦gen¦esis
mor¦pho¦genet¦ic
mor¦pho¦gen¦ic
mor¦pho¦logic¦al
mor¦pho¦
  logic¦al¦ly
morph¦olo¦gist +s
morph¦ology
Mor¦ris, Wil¦liam
  (English designer;
  chair)
Mor¦ris, Wil¦liam
  Rich¦ard (Lord
  Nuffield, British
  car maker)
Mor¦ris *also*
  Maur¦ice
mor¦ris dance +s
mor¦ris dan¦cer +s
mor¦ris dan¦cing
Mor¦ri¦son, Toni
  (American
  novelist)

Mor¦ri¦son, Van
  (Northern Irish
  musician)
mor¦row +s
Morse, Sam¦uel
  (American
  inventor)
Morse
  Morses
  Morsed
  Mors¦ing
  (code)
morse +s (walrus;
  clasp)
Morse code
mor¦sel +s
mort +s
mor¦ta¦della
  mor¦ta¦delle
mor¦tal +s
mor¦tal¦ity
  mor¦tal¦ities
mor¦tal¦ly
mor¦tar +s +ed
  +ing
mor¦tar¦board +s
mor¦tar¦less
mor¦tary
mort¦gage
  mort¦gages
  mort¦gaged
  mort¦ga¦ging
mort¦gage¦able
mort¦ga¦gee +s
  (creditor in
  mortgage)
mort¦ga¦ger +s
  (debtor in
  mortgage)
mort¦ga¦gor +s
  (use mortgager)
mor¦tice (use
  mortise)
mor¦tices
mor¦ticed
mor¦ticing
mor¦ti¦cian +s
mor¦ti¦fi¦ca¦tion +s
mor¦tify
  mor¦ti¦fies
  mor¦ti¦fied
  mor¦ti¦fy¦ing
  mor¦ti¦fy¦ing¦ly
Mor¦ti¦mer, Roger
  de (English noble)
Mor¦ti¦mer
mor¦tise
  mor¦tises
  mor¦tised
  mor¦tis¦ing
mor¦tise lock +s

mort|main +s
Mor|ton, Jelly
  Roll (American
  jazz musician)
Mor|ton, John
  (English
  statesman)
Mor|ton's Fork
mor|tu|ary
  mor|tu|ar|ies
mor|ula
  mor|ulae
Mor|wenna
mor|wong +s
Mo|saic (of Moses)
mo|saic
  mo|saics
  mo|saicked
  mo|saick|ing
  (picture; pattern)
mo|sai|cist +s
Mos|an|der, Carl
  Gus|tav (Swedish
  chemist)
mosa|saur +s
mosa|saurus
  mosa|sauri
mos|cha|tel +s
  (plant.
  △ muscatel)
Mos|cow (capital of
  Russia)
Mosel +s (river, W.
  Europe; wine)
Mose|ley, Henry
  (English physicist)
Mo|selle +s
  (French name for
  the Mosel; wine)
Moses *Bible*
Moses, Grandma
  (American
  painter)
Moses bas|ket +s
Moses ben
  Mai|mon
  (Spanish-born
  Jewish
  philosopher)
mosey +s +ed
  +ing
MOSFET +s
  (= metal oxide
  semiconductor
  field-effect
  transistor)
mosh
  moshes
  moshed
  mosh|ing
mo|shav
  mo|shav|im
mosh-pit +s

Mos|lem +s (use
  Muslim)
Mos|ley, Os|wald
  (English Fascist
  leader)
Mo|sotho
  Sotho
mosque +s
Mos|quito (Central
  American people;
  use Miskito)
  plural Mos|quito
  or Mos|qui|tos
mos|quito
  mos|qui|toes
  (insect)
mosquito-boat +s
Mos|quito Coast
  (region, S.
  America)
mos|quito net +s
Moss, Stir|ling
  (English motor-
  racing driver)
moss
  mosses
  mossed
  moss|ing
Mos|sad (Israeli
  intelligence
  service)
Mos|sel Bay (port,
  South Africa)
moss-grown
moss-hag +s
mos|sie +s
  (= mosquito)
mos|si|ness
moss|like
mosso *Music*
moss stitch
moss|troop|er +s
mossy
  moss|ier
  mossi|est
  (covered with
  moss)
most
Mos|tar
  (city, Bosnia–
  Herzegovina)
most|ly
Mosul (city, Iraq)
mot +s
mote +s (speck of
  dust. △ moat)
motel +s
motet +s *Music*
moth +s
moth|ball +s +ed
  +ing
moth-eaten

mother +s +ed
  +ing
mother|board +s
Mother Carey's
  chicken +s
mother coun|try
  mother coun|tries
mother|craft
mother-figure +s
mother|fuck|er +s
  (*coarse slang*)
mother|fuck|ing
  (*coarse slang*)
mother god|dess
mother
  god|desses
mother|hood
Mother|ing
  Sun|day +s
mother-in-law
  mothers-in-law
mother-in-law's
  tongue
mother|land +s
mother|less
mother|less|ness
mother|like
mother|li|ness
mother-lode +s
mother|ly
mother-naked
mother-of-pearl
Mother's Day
mother-to-be
  mothers-to-be
mother tongue +s
moth|proof
mothy
moth|ier
  mothi|est
motif +s
mo|tile
mo|til|ity
mo|tion +s +ed
  +ing
mo|tion|al
mo|tion|less
mo|tion|less|ly
mo|tion pic|ture
  +s
mo|tiv|ate
  mo|tiv|ates
  mo|tiv|ated
  mo|tiv|at|ing
mo|tiv|ation +s
mo|tiv|ation|al
mo|tiv|ation|al|ly
mo|tiv|ator +s
mo|tive
  mo|tives
  mo|tived
  mo|tiv|ing

mo|tive|less
mo|tive|less|ly
mo|tive|less|ness
mo|tiv|ity
mot juste
  mots justes
mot|ley
  mot|leys
mot|lier
  mot|li|est
mot|mot +s
moto|cross
moto per|petuo
  Music
motor +s +ed +ing
motor|able
motor bi|cycle +s
motor|bike +s
motor boat +s
motor|cade +s
motor car +s
motor|cycle +s
motor|cyc|ling
motor|cyc|list +s
motor|home +s
motor|ial
motor|isa|tion *Br.*
  (use
  motorization)
motor|ise *Br.* (use
  motorize)
  motor|ises
  motor|ised
  motor|is|ing
motor|ist +s
motor|iza|tion
motor|ize
  motor|izes
  motor|ized
  motor|iz|ing
motor|man
  motor|men
motor|mouth +s
motor mower +s
motor ra|cing
motor scoot|er +s
motor sport +s
motor ve|hicle +s
motor|way +s
mo|tory
motor yacht +s
Mo|town
  (= Detroit, USA)
motte +s
mot|tle
  mot|tles
  mot|tled
  mot|tling
motto
  mot|toes
moue +s (pout.
  △ moo)

mouf|flon +s (use
  mouflon)
mouf|lon +s
mouillé
mou|jik +s (use
  muzhik)
Mou|lay Id|riss
  (Muslim holy
  town, Morocco)
mould *Br.* +s +ed
  +ing (*Am.* mold)
mould|able *Br.*
  (*Am.* moldable)
mould-board *Br.*
  +s (*Am.* mold-
  board)
mould|er *Br.* +s
  (person who
  moulds. *Am.*
  molder)
moul|der *Br.* +s
  +ed +ing (rot.
  Am. molder)
mouldi|ness *Br.*
  (*Am.* moldiness)
mould|ing *Br.* +s
  (*Am.* molding)
mouldy *Br.*
  mould|ier
  mouldi|est
  (*Am.* moldy)
mou|lin +s
Mou|lin Rouge (in
  Paris, France)
Moul|mein (port,
  Burma)
moult +s +ed +ing
moult|er +s
mound +s +ed
  +ing
mount +s +ed
  +ing
mount|able
moun|tain +s
moun|tain avens
  plural moun|tain
  avens
moun|tain bike +s
moun|tain chain
  +s
moun|tain
  climb|er +s
moun|tain
  climb|ing
moun|tain|eer +s
  +ed +ing
moun|tain|ous
moun|tain range
  +s
moun|tain|side +s
moun|tain top +s
moun|tainy

Mount|bat|ten,
  Louis (Earl
  Mountbatten of
  Burma, British
  admiral)
moun|te|bank +s
moun|te|bank|ery
mount|er +s
Moun|tie +s
  (Canadian police)
mount|ing +s
mount|ing block
  +s
Mount Isa (town,
  Australia)
Mount Ver|non
  (home of George
  Washington)
mourn +s +ed
  +ing
Mourne
  Moun|tains (in
  Northern Ireland)
mourn|er +s
mourn|ful
mourn|ful|ly
mourn|ful|ness
mourning-band +s
mourn|ing dove
  +s
mourning-paper
  (black-edged
  notepaper.
  ⚠ morning
  paper)
mourn|ing ring +s
mou|saka +s (use
  moussaka)
Mou|salla, Mount
  (use Mount
  Musala)
mouse
  mice
  noun
mouse
  mouses
  moused
  mous|ing
  verb
mouse-colored
  Am.
mouse-coloured
  Br.
mouse deer
  plural mouse deer
mouse hare +s
mouse|like
mouser +s
mouse|trap +s
mousey (use
  mousy)
mous|ily

mousi|ness
mous|saka +s
mousse +s
mous|se|line +s
Mous|sorg|sky,
  Mo|dest (use
  Mussorgsky)
mous|tache *Br.* +s
  (*Am.* mustache)
mous|tache cup
  Br. +s (*Am.*
  mustache cup)
mous|tached *Br.*
  (*Am.* mustached)
mous|tachio *Br.* +s
  (*Am.* mustachio)
mous|tachi|oed *Br.*
  (*Am.*
  mustachioed)
Mous|ter|ian +s
mousy
  mous|ier
  mousi|est
mouth +s +ed
  +ing
mouth|brood|er
  +s
mouth|er +s
mouth|ful +s
mouth|less
mouth organ +s
mouth|part +s
mouth|piece +s
mouth-to-mouth
mouth|wash
mouth|washes
mouth-watering
mouthy
  mouth|ier
  mouthi|est
mov|abil|ity
mov|able
movable-doh
mov|able|ness
mov|ably
move
  moves
  moved
  mov|ing
move|able (use
  movable)
move|ment +s
mover +s
movie +s
movie-goer +s
movie house +s
movie-maker +s
movie-making
moving-coil
  attributive
mov|ing|ly

mow
  mows
  mowed
  mow|ing
  mowed *or* mown
  (cut grass etc.
  ⚠ mho, mo)
mow|able
mow|burnt
mower +s
  (grasscutter.
  ⚠ moa)
mow|ing +s
mown (past
  participle of mow.
  ⚠ moan)
moxa +s
moxi|bus|tion
moxie +s
Moya
Moyra *also* Moira
Mo|zam|bi|can +s
Mo|zam|bique (in
  southern Africa)
Moz|arab +s
Moz|arab|ic
Moz|art,
  Wolf|gang
  Ama|deus
  (Austrian
  composer)
Moz|art|ian +s
mozz
moz|za|rella +s
moz|zie +s (use
  mossie)
moz|zle
M.Phil. (= Master
  of Philosophy)
mpingo +s
Mr
  Messrs
  (man's title)
Mrs
  plural Mrs *or*
  Mes|dames
  (title of married
  woman)
Ms (woman's title)
M.Tech. (= Master
  of Technology)
mu +s (Greek letter.
  ⚠ meu, mew)
Mu|ba|rak, Hosni
  (Egyptian
  president)
much
Mucha, Al|phonse
  (Czech artist)
Mu|chinga
  Moun|tains (in
  Zambia)

much¦ly
much|ness
muci|lage +s
muci|lagi¦nous
muck +s +ed +ing
muck¦er +s
muck¦er|ish
mucki|ness
muckle +s
muck|rake
  muck|rakes
  muck|raked
  muck|rak¦ing
muck|raker +s
muck-spread¦er
  +s
muck sweat
muck|worm +s
mucky
  muck|ier
  mucki|est
muco|poly|
  sac¦char|ide +s
mu¦cosa
  mu¦cosae
mu¦cos|ity
mu¦cous *adjective*
mucro
  mu¦cro¦nes
mu¦cron|ate
mucus *noun*
mud +s
mud|bank +s
mud|bath +s
mud|brick +s
mud¦dily
mud¦di|ness
mud¦dle
  mud¦dles
  mud¦dled
  mud|dling
muddle-headed
muddle-
  headed¦ness
mud¦dler +s
mud|dling¦ly
muddy
  mud|dies
  mud|died
  muddy|ing
  mud|dier
  mud¦di|est
Mu|dé¦jar
  Mu|dé¦jares
mud|fish
  plural mud|fish or
  mud|fishes
mud|flap +s
mud|flat +s
mud|flow +s
mud|guard +s
mud|lark +s

mud pack +s
mud pie +s
mud puppy
  mud pup|pies
mud|skip¦per +s
mud-sling¦er +s
mud-slinging
mud|stone +s
mud vol|cano
muesli +s
muez|zin +s
muff +s +ed +ing
muf|fetee +s
muf'fin +s
muf'fin|eer +s
muffin-man
  muffin-men
muff|ish
muf'fle
  muf¦fles
  muf¦fled
  muf|fling
muf|fler +s
mufti +s
mug
  mugs
  mugged
  mug|ging
Mu¦gabe, Rob¦ert
  (president of
  Zimbabwe)
Mu|ganda
  Ba|ganda
mug¦ful +s
mug¦ger +s
mug¦gi|ness
mug|ging +s
mug|gins
  plural mug|gins or
  mug|ginses
muggy
  mug|gier
  mug¦gi|est
Mug¦hal +s
mug|shot +s
mug|wort +s
mug|wump +s
Mu¦ham|mad
  (founder of Islam)
Mu¦ham|mad
  Ahmad
  (Sudanese Mahdi)
Mu¦ham|mad Ali
  (pasha of Egypt)
Mu¦ham|mad Ali
  (American boxer)
Mu¦ham|madan
  +s (prefer
  Muslim)
Mu¦ham|mad¦an|
  ism (prefer Islam)

Muir, Edwin
  (Scottish poet)
mu¦ja|hed¦din (use
  mujahedin)
mu¦ja|he¦deen (use
  mujahedin)
mu¦ja|he¦din
mu¦ja|hi¦deen (use
  mujahedin)
mu¦ja|hi¦din (use
  mujahedin)
Mu¦ji|bur
  Rah¦man
  (Bangladeshi
  president)
Mu¦kalla (port,
  Yemen)
Muk¦den (former
  name of
  Shenyang)
mu|latto
  mu|lattos or
  mu¦lat|toes
mul|berry
  mul|berries
mulch
  mulches
  mulched
  mulch|ing
mulct +s +ed +ing
Mul|doon, Rob¦ert
  (New Zealand
  prime minister)
mule +s (animal;
  slipper. ⚠ mewl)
mule|teer +s
mulga +s
Mul¦ha|cén
  (mountain, Spain)
Mül|heim (city,
  Germany)
Mul|house (city,
  France)
muli +s (use mooli)
muli|eb¦rity
mul|ish
mul|ish¦ly
mul|ish|ness
Mull (Scottish
  island)
mull +s +ed +ing
  (ponder; to warm;
  promontory;
  humus; fabric)
mul¦lah +s
  (Muslim scholar.
  ⚠ muller)
mul|lein +s
Mul¦ler, Her|mann
  Jo¦seph
  (American
  geneticist)

Mül¦ler, Fried|rich
  Max (German
  philologist)
Mül¦ler,
  Jo|han¦nes Peter
  (German biologist)
Mül¦ler, Paul
  Her|mann (Swiss
  chemist)
mul¦ler +s
  (grinding stone.
  ⚠ mullah)
Mül|ler|ian
mul|let +s
mul|li¦ga|tawny +s
mul|li|grubs
Mul|lin¦gar (town,
  Republic of
  Ireland)
mul|lion +s
mul|lioned
mul|lock +s
Mull of Kin|tyre
  (tip of Kintyre
  peninsula,
  Scotland)
mul|lo|way +s
Mul|ro|ney, Brian
  (Canadian prime
  minister)
Mul¦tan (city,
  Pakistan)
mult|angu¦lar
multi-access
multi|axial
multi|cel¦lu|lar
multi|chan¦nel
multi|color *Am.*
multi|col¦ored *Am.*
multi|col¦our *Br.*
multi|col¦oured *Br.*
multi|cul¦tural
multi|cul¦tural|
          ism
multi|cul¦tural|ist
  +s
multi|cul¦tur|al¦ly
multi|di¦men|
          sion|al
multi|di¦men¦sion|
          al|ity
multi|di¦men¦sion|
          al¦ly
multi|dir¦ec¦tion|al
multi-ethnic
multi|fa¦cet¦ed
multi|fari¦ous
multi|fari¦ous¦ly
multi|fari¦ous|ness
multi|fid
multi|foil +s
multi|form

multi|form|ity
multi|func|tion
multi|func|tion|al
multi|grade +s
multi|hull +s
multi|lat|eral
multi|lat|eral|ism
multi|lat|eral|ist +s
multi|lat|eral|ly
multi-layered
multi|level
multi|lin|gual
multi|lin|gual|ism
multi|lin|gual|ly
multi|media
multi|mil|lion +s
multi|mil|lion|aire +s
multi|nation|al +s
multi|nation|al|ly
multi|nomial +s
mul|tip|ar|ous
multi|par|tite
multi-party
multi|phase
mul|tiple +s
multiple-choice
  adjective
multi|plex
  multi|plexes
  multi|plexed
  multi|plex|ing
multi|plex|er +s
multi|plex|or +s
  (use multiplexer)
multi|pli|able
multi|plic|able
multi|pli|cand +s
multi|pli|ca|tion +s
multi|plica|tive
multi|pli|city
  multi|pli|ci|ties
multi|plier +s
multi|ply
  multi|plies
  multi|plied
  multi|ply|ing
multi|polar
multi|pro|cess|ing
multi|pro|ces|sor +s
multi|pro|gram|ming
multi-purpose
multi|racial
multi|racial|ly
multi-role
  attributive
multi-stage
  attributive

multi-storey +s
  noun and attributive
multi|task +s +ed +ing
multi|tude +s
multi|tu|di|nous
multi|tu|di|nous|ly
multi|tu|di|nous|ness
multi-user
  attributive
multi|va|lency
multi|va|lent
multi|valve +s
multi|vari|ate
multi|ver|sity
  multi|ver|sities
multi|vocal
multi-way
mul|ture +s
mum
  mums
  mummed
  mum|ming
mum|ble
  mum|bles
  mum|bled
  mum|bling
mum|bler +s
mum|bling +s
mum|bling|ly
mumbo-jumbo
mu-meson +s
mum|mer +s
mum|mers' play +s
mum|mery
  mum|mer|ies
mum|mi|fi|ca|tion
mum|mify
  mum|mi|fies
  mum|mi|fied
  mum|mi|fy|ing
mummy
  mum|mies
mummy's boy +s
mummy's girl +s
mump|ish
mumps
mumsy
Munch, Ed|vard
  (Norwegian painter)
munch
  munches
  munched
  munch|ing
Munch|ausen, Baron (fictional hero)

Munch|ausen's syn|drome
Mün|chen (German name for Munich)
Munda +s
mun|dane
mun|dane|ly
mun|dane|ness
mun|dan|ity
  mun|dan|ities
mung (beans)
Mungo (name)
mungo +s (fibre)
Mun|ich (city, Germany)
mu|ni|ci|pal
mu|ni|ci|pal|isa|tion *Br.* (use municipalization)
mu|ni|ci|pal|ise *Br.* (use municipalize)
  mu|ni|ci|pal|ises
  mu|ni|ci|pal|ised
  mu|ni|ci|pal|is|ing
mu|ni|ci|pal|ity
  mu|ni|ci|pal|ities
mu|ni|ci|pal|iza|tion
mu|ni|ci|pal|ize
  mu|ni|ci|pal|izes
  mu|ni|ci|pal|ized
  mu|ni|ci|pal|iz|ing
mu|ni|ci|pal|ly
mu|nifi|cence
mu|nifi|cent
mu|nifi|cent|ly
mu|ni|ment +s
mu|ni|tion +s +ed +ing
mu|ni|tion|er +s
mun|nion +s
Munro, Hec|tor Hugh (real name of British writer Saki)
mun|shi +s (use moonshee)
Mun|ster (province, Republic of Ireland)
Mün|ster (city, Germany)
munt +s (*offensive*)
munt|jac +s
munt|jak +s (use muntjac)
Muntz metal
muon +s

muon|ic
Muq|disho (alternative name for Mogadishu)
mur|age +s
mural +s
mural|ist +s
Murat, Joa|chim (French general, king of Naples)
Mur|chi|son Falls (in Malawi)
Mur|cia (city and region, Spain)
mur|der +s +ed +ing
mur|der|er +s
mur|der|ess
  mur|der|esses
mur|der|ous
mur|der|ous|ly
mur|der|ous|ness
Mur|doch, Iris (English writer)
Mur|doch, Ru|pert (Australian-born American publisher)
mure
  mures
  mured
  mur|ing
murex
  muri|ces *or* murexes
muri|ate +s
muri|at|ic
Mur|iel
Mu|rillo, Bar|to|lomé Este|ban (Spanish painter)
mur|ine
murk +s
murk|ily
murki|ness
murky
  murk|ier
  murki|est
Mur|mansk (port, Russia)
mur|mur +s +ed +ing
mur|mur|er +s
mur|mur|ing|ly
mur|mur|ous
mur|phy
  mur|phies
Mur|phy's Law
mur|rain +s
Mur|ray (name)

Mur¦ray, Gil¦bert (British classical scholar)
Mur¦ray, James (Scottish-born lexicographer)
Mur¦ray River (in Australia)
murre +s (bird. ⚠ myrrh)
mur¦re¦let +s
mur¦rey
mur¦rhine +s
Mur¦rum¦bidgee (river, Australia)
mur¦ther +s +ed +ing
Muru¦roa (atoll, French Polynesia)
Mu¦sala, Mount (in Bulgaria)
Mus.B. (= Bachelor of Music)
mus¦ca¦del +s
Mus¦ca¦det +s (wine)
mus¦ca¦dine +s (grape)
mus¦car¦ine +s
Mus¦cat (capital of Oman)
mus¦cat +s (grape; wine)
mus¦ca¦tel +s (grape; wine; raisin. ⚠ moschatel)
muscle
    muscles
    muscled
    muscl¦ing (Anatomy. ⚠ mussel)
muscle-bound
muscle¦less
muscle-man
    muscle-men
muscly
musc¦olo¦gist +s
musc¦ology
mus¦co¦vado +s
Mus¦co¦vite +s (citizen of Moscow)
mus¦co¦vite (mica)
Mus¦covy (former principality, Russia; duck)
mus¦cu¦lar
mus¦cu¦lar¦ity
mus¦cu¦lar¦ly
mus¦cu¦la¦ture +s

mus¦cu¦lo¦skel¦etal
Mus.D. (= Doctor of Music)
Muse +s Greek and Roman Mythology
muse
    muses
    mused
    mus¦ing (ponder; inspiration. ⚠ mews)
mu¦seol¦ogy
mu¦sette +s
mu¦seum +s
mu¦seum piece +s
mush
    mushes
    mushed
    mush¦ing
mush¦ily
mushi¦ness
mush¦room +s +ed +ing
mush¦roomy
mushy
    mush¦ier
    mushi¦est
music +s
mu¦sic¦al +s
musi¦cale +s
mu¦sic¦al¦ise Br. (use musicalize)
    mu¦sic¦al¦ises
    mu¦sic¦al¦ised
    mu¦sic¦al¦is¦ing
mu¦sic¦al¦ity
mu¦sic¦al¦ize
    mu¦sic¦al¦izes
    mu¦sic¦al¦ized
    mu¦sic¦al¦iz¦ing
mu¦sic¦al¦ly
mu¦sic¦al¦ness
music box
    music boxes
music centre +s
music drama +s
music hall +s noun
music-hall attributive
mu¦si¦cian +s
mu¦si¦cian¦ly
mu¦si¦cian¦ship
music lover +s
mu¦sico¦logic¦al
mu¦sic¦olo¦gist +s
mu¦sic¦ology
music paper
music stand +s
music stool +s

Musil, Rob¦ert (Austrian novelist)
mus¦ing +s
mus¦ing¦ly
mu¦sique con¦crète
musk +s
mus¦keg +s
mus¦kel¦lunge +s
mus¦ket +s
mus¦ket¦eer +s
mus¦ket¦oon +s
mus¦ket¦ry
mus¦ket shot +s
muski¦ness
Mus¦ko¦gean +s
musk¦rat +s
musk-rose +s
musk this¦tle +s
musk tree +s
musk¦wood
musky
    musk¦ier
    muski¦est
Mus¦lim +s
mus¦lin +s
mus¦lined
mus¦mon +s
muso +s
mus¦quash
    plural mus¦quash
muss
    musses
    mussed
    muss¦ing
mus¦sel +s (mollusc. ⚠ muscle)
Mus¦so¦lini, Ben¦ito (Italian Fascist prime minister)
Mus¦sorg¦sky, Mo¦dest (Russian composer)
Mus¦sul¦man
    Mus¦sul¦mans or Mus¦sul¦men (prefer Muslim)
mussy
must +s
mus¦tache Am. +s (Br. moustache)
mus¦tache cup Am. +s (Br. moustache cup)
mus¦tached Am. (Br. moustached)
mus¦tachio Am. +s (Br. moustachio)

mus¦tachi¦oed Am. (Br. moustachioed)
mus¦tang +s
mus¦tard +s
mus¦tard gas
    mus¦tard gases
mus¦tard seed +s
mus¦te¦lid +s
mus¦ter +s +ed +ing
muster-book +s
mus¦ter¦er +s
muster-roll +s
musth (use must)
must¦ily
musti¦ness
Mus¦tique (island, Caribbean)
mustn't (= must not)
musty
    must¦ier
    musti¦est
Mut Egyptian Mythology
mut¦abil¦ity
mut¦able
muta¦gen +s
muta¦gen¦esis
muta¦gen¦ic
mu¦tant +s
Mu¦tare (town, Zimbabwe)
mu¦tate
    mu¦tates
    mu¦tated
    mu¦tat¦ing
mu¦ta¦tion +s
mu¦ta¦tion¦al
mu¦ta¦tion¦al¦ly
mu¦ta¦tis mu¦tan¦dis
mutch
    mutches
mute
    mutes
    muted
    mut¦ing
mute¦ly
mute¦ness
mu¦ti¦late
    mu¦ti¦lates
    mu¦ti¦lated
    mu¦ti¦lat¦ing
mu¦ti¦la¦tion +s
mu¦ti¦la¦tive
mu¦ti¦la¦tor +s
mu¦tin¦eer +s
mu¦tin¦ous
mu¦tin¦ous¦ly

mu|tiny
  mu|tin|ies
  mu|tin|ied
  mu|tiny|ing
mut|ism
muton +s
Mut|su|hito
  (original name of
  Meiji Tenno)
mutt +s
mut|ter +s +ed
  +ing
mut|terer +s
mut|ter|ing +s
mut|ter|ing|ly
mut|ton +s
mutton-bird +s
mut|ton chop +s
mutton-head +s
mutton-headed
mut|tony
mu|tual (reciprocal.
  ⚠ mutuel)
mu|tu|al|ism
mu|tu|al|ist +s
mu|tu|al|is|tic
mu|tu|al|is|tic|
           al|ly
mu|tu|al|ity
  mu|tu|al|ities
mu|tu|al|ly
mu|tuel +s
  (totalizator.
  ⚠ mutual)
mut|ule +s
muu-muu +s
Muzaf|fara|bad
  (town, Pakistan)
muzak Propr.
mu|zhik +s
Muz|tag (mountain,
  China)
muz|zily
muz|zi|ness
muz|zle
  muz|zles
  muz|zled
  muz|zling
muzzle-loader +s
muz|zler +s
muzzy
  muz|zier
  muz|zi|est
my
my|al|gia
my|al|gic
my|al|ism
myall +s (tree.
  ⚠ mile)
Myan|mar (official
  name of Burma)

Myan|mar|ese
  plural
Myan|mar|ese
my|as|the|nia
my|ce|lial
my|ce|lium
my|ce|lia
My|ce|nae (city of
  ancient Greece)
My|ce|naean +s
myco|logic|al
myco|logic|al|ly
my|colo|gist +s
my|col|ogy
myco|plasma
myco|plas|mas or
  myco|plas|mata
myco|pro|tein
mycor|rhiza
mycor|rhizae
mycor|rhizal
my|co|sis
  my|co|ses
my|cot|ic
myco|toxin +s
my|cot|ro|phy
my|dria|sis
mye|lin +s
mye|lin|ation
mye|li|tis
mye|loid
mye|loma
  mye|lo|mas or
  mye|lo|mata
My|fanwy
Myko|layiv (city,
  Ukraine)
Myk|onos (Greek
  island)
Myles also Miles
my|lo|don +s
My|men|singh
  (port, Bangladesh)
myna +s (bird; use
  mynah. ⚠ miner,
  minor)
mynah +s (bird.
  ⚠ miner, minor)
myo|car|dial
myo|car|di|tis
myo|car|dium
myo|car|dia
myo|fib|ril +s
myo|gen|ic
myo|glo|bin +s
my|ol|ogy
myope +s
my|opia
my|opic
my|opic|al|ly
my|osin

my|osis (use
  miosis
  ⚠ meiosis)
myo|sote +s
myo|so|tis
  myo|so|tises
myo|tonia
myo|ton|ic
Myra
myr|iad +s
myr|ia|pod +s
myr|me|co|logic|al
myr|me|colo|gist
  +s
myr|me|col|ogy
myr|mi|don +s
Myrna
my|robalan +s
Myron (Greek
  sculptor)
myrrh +s (resin,
  incense. ⚠ murre)
myr|rhic
myr|rhy
myr|ta|ceous
Myr|tle (name)
myr|tle +s (shrub)
my|self
Mysia (ancient
  name for part of
  NW Asia Minor)
Mys|ian +s
My|sore (city,
  India; former
  name of
  Karnataka)
mys|ta|go|gic
mys|ta|go|gic|al
mys|ta|gogue +s
mys|teri|ous
mys|teri|ous|ly
mys|teri|ous|ness
mys|tery
  mys|ter|ies
mys|tic +s
mys|tic|al
mys|tic|al|ly
mys|ti|cism
mys|ti|fi|ca|tion +s
mys|tify
  mys|ti|fies
  mys|ti|fied
  mys|ti|fy|ing
  mys|ti|fy|ing|ly
mys|tique +s
myth +s
mythi
myth|ic
myth|ic|al
myth|ic|al|ly
mythi|cise Br. (use
  mythicize)

mythi|cise (cont.)
  mythi|cises
  mythi|cised
  mythi|cis|ing
mythi|cism
mythi|cist +s
mythi|cize
  mythi|cizes
  mythi|cized
  mythi|ciz|ing
myth-maker +s
myth-making
mytho|gen|esis
myth|og|raph|er
  +s
myth|og|raphy
mytho|olo|ger +s
mytho|logic
mytho|logic|al
mytho|logic|al|ly
myth|olo|gise Br.
  (use mythologize)
  myth|olo|gises
  myth|olo|gised
  myth|olo|gis|ing
myth|ol|ogiser Br.
  +s (use
  mythologizer)
myth|olo|gist +s
myth|olo|gize
  myth|olo|gizes
  myth|olo|gized
  myth|olo|giz|ing
myth|olo|gizer +s
myth|ology
  myth|olo|gies
mytho|mania +s
mytho|maniac +s
mytho|poeia +s
mytho|poeic
my|thos
my|thoi
  (myth; narrative
  theme)
my|thus
mythi
  (myth)
Myti|lene (town,
  Lesbos)
myx|edema Am.
myx|oe|dema Br.
myx|oma
  myx|omas or
  myx|omata
myxo|ma|tosis
myxo|my|cete +s
myxo|virus
  myxo|viruses

Nn

'n (= and)
na (= not)
NAAFI (= Navy,
   Army, and Air
   Force Institutes;
   canteen)
naan +s (use nan)
Naas (town,
   Republic of
   Ireland)
nab
   nabs
   nabbed
   nab|bing
Naba|taean +s
Na¦beul (city,
   Tunisia)
Nabi +s
Nab¦lus (town,
   West Bank)
nabob +s
Nab|okov,
   Vlad|imir
   (Russian writer)
Na¦cala (port,
   Mozambique)
nac|arat
na|celle +s
nacho +s
NACODS
   (= National
   Association of
   Colliery Overmen,
   Deputies, and
   Shotfirers)
nacre (mother-of-
   pearl. △ naker)
nacred
nac|re¦ous
nac|rous
Nader, Ralph
   (American
   campaigner)
Nadia
Na¦dine
nadir +s
naev|oid Br. (Am.
   nevoid)
naevus Br.
   naevi
   (Am. nevus)
naff +s +ed +ing
   +er +est
Naffy
NAFTA (= North
   American Free
   Trade Agreement.
   △ naphtha)

nag
   nags
   nagged
   nag|ging
Naga +s (tribe in
   India and Burma;
   language)
naga +s Hinduism
Naga|land (state,
   India)
na¦gana
Naga|saki (city,
   Japan)
nag¦ger +s
nag|ging¦ly
Nagorno-
   Karabakh
   (region,
   Azerbaijan)
Na¦goya (city,
   Japan)
Nag¦pur (city,
   India)
Nagy, Imre
   (Hungarian
   statesman)
Naha (port, Japan)
Na|huatl +s
Na|huat¦lan
Nahum Bible
naiad
   naiads or
   nai¦ades
naïf +s
nail +s +ed +ing
nail-biting
nail brush
   nail brushes
nail enamel +s
nail¦er +s
nail¦ery
   nail|er¦ies
nail file +s
nail head +s
nail|less
nail pol¦ish
   nail pol¦ishes
nail punch
   nail punches
nail scis|sors
nail set +s
nail var|nish
   nail var|nishes
nain|sook +s
Nai¦paul, V. S.
   (West Indian
   writer)
naira +s
Nairn|shire (former
   county, Scotland)
Nai|robi (capital of
   Kenya)

naive
naive¦ly
naive|ness
naïv|eté +s
   (use naivety)
naiv|ety
   naiv|eties
Najaf (city, Iraq)
naked
naked¦ly
naked|ness
naker +s (drum.
   △ nacre)
Na¦khi¦che¦van
   (Russian name for
   Naxçivan)
Na¦khon Sawan
   (port, Thailand)
Na¦kuru (city,
   Kenya)
Nal|chik (capital of
   Kabardino-
   Balkaria)
NALGO (= National
   and Local
   Government
   Officers'
   Association)
Nam (= Vietnam)
Nama
   plural Nama or
   Namas
Nam|an|gan (city,
   Uzbekistan)
Na¦ma¦qua|land
   (homeland, South
   Africa and
   Namibia)
namby-pamby
   namby-pambies
name
   names
   named
   nam¦ing
name|able
name-calling
name-child
   name-children
name-day +s
name-drop
   name-drops
   name-dropped
   name-dropping
name-dropper +s
name|less
name|less¦ly
name|less|ness
name¦ly
Namen (Flemish
   name for Namur)
name part +s
name|plate +s

name|sake +s
name tag +s
name-tape +s
Namib Des¦ert (in
   SW Africa)
Na|mibia
Na|mib|ian +s
namma +s (use
   gnamma)
Namur (province
   and city, Belgium)
Nan (name)
nan +s
   (grandmother;
   Indian bread)
nana +s
Na|naimo (port,
   Canada)
Nanak, Guru
   (Indian founder of
   Sikhism)
nance +s (offensive)
Nan|chang (city,
   China)
Nancy (city,
   France; name)
nancy
   nan|cies
   (offensive)
Nanda Devi
   (mountain, India)
Nandi Hinduism
Nan|ette
Nanga Par¦bat
   (mountain, India)
Nan|jing (city,
   China)
nan|keen +s
Nan|king
   (= Nanjing)
nanna +s
Nan|ning (city,
   China)
nanny
   nan|nies
   nan|nied
   nanny|ing
nanny-goat +s
nano|gram +s
nano|meter Am. +s
nano|metre Br. +s
nano|sec¦ond +s
nano|tech¦nol¦ogy
Nan¦sen, Fridt|jof
   (Norwegian
   explorer and
   statesman)
Nantes (city,
   France)
Nan|tucket (island,
   USA)
Naomi

naos
  naoi
nap
  naps
  napped
  nap|ping
  (short sleep; pile
  on textiles; card
  game; tip as
  winner. △ knap,
  nappe)
napa +s (leather;
  use nappa.
  △ knapper,
  napper)
na|palm +s +ed
  +ing
nape +s
nap|ery
nap hand +s
Naph|tali *Bible*
naph|tha +s (oil.
  △ NAFTA)
naph|tha|lene +s
naph|thal|ic
naph|thene +s
naph|then|ic
Na|pier (port, New
  Zealand)
Na|pier, John
  (Scottish
  mathematician)
Na|pier|ian
Na|pier's bones
nap|kin +s
Na|ples (city, Italy)
Na|po|leon (three
  rulers of France)
na|po|leon +s
  (coin; game)
Na|po|leon|ic
nappa +s (leather.
  △ knapper,
  napper)
nappe +s (*Geology*.
  △ knap, nap)
nappy
  nap|pies
nappy rash
Nara (city, Japan)
Na|ra|yan, R. K.
  (Indian writer)
Nar|ayan|ganj
  (port, Bangladesh)
Nar|bonne (city,
  France)
narc +s (narcotics
  agent. △ nark)
nar|ceine

nar|cis|sism
nar|cis|sist +s
nar|cis|sis|tic
nar|cis|sis|tic|al|ly
Nar|cis|sus *Greek
  Mythology*
nar|cis|sus
  plural nar|cis|sus
  or nar|cissi *or*
  nar|cis|suses
nar|co|lepsy
nar|co|lep|tic +s
nar|co|sis
nar|co|ses
narco|ter|ror|ism
narco|ter|ror|ist +s
nar|cot|ic +s
nar|cot|ic|al|ly
nar|co|tisa|tion *Br.*
  (use
  narcotization)
nar|co|tise *Br.* (use
  narcotize)
nar|co|tises
nar|co|tised
nar|co|tis|ing
nar|co|tism
nar|co|tiza|tion
nar|co|tize
nar|co|tizes
nar|co|tized
nar|co|tiz|ing
nard +s
nar|doo +s
nares (nostrils)
nar|ghile +s
nark +s +ed +ing
  (informer;
  annoying person;
  annoy. △ narc)
narky
  nark|ier
  nark|iest
Nar|mada (river,
  India)
Nar|nia (fictional
  land)
Narra|gan|sett
  plural
  Narra|gan|sett
nar|rat|able
nar|rate
  nar|rates
  nar|rated
  nar|rat|ing
nar|ra|tion +s
nar|ra|tion|al
nar|ra|tive +s
nar|ra|tive|ly
nar|rato|logic|al
nar|ra|tolo|gist +s
nar|ra|tol|ogy

nar|ra|tor +s
nar|row +s +ed
  +ing +er +est
nar|row boat +s
nar|row|cast
  nar|row|casts
  nar|row|cast
  nar|row|cast|ing
nar|row|cast|er +s
narrow-gauge
  adjective
nar|row|ish
nar|row|ly
narrow-minded
narrow-minded|ly
narrow-
  minded|ness
nar|row|ness
nar|thex
  nar|thexes
Nar|vik (port,
  Norway)
nar|whal +s
nary
NASA (= National
  Aeronautics and
  Space
  Administration)
nasal
na|sal|isa|tion *Br.*
  (use nasalization)
na|sal|ise *Br.* (use
  nasalize)
na|sal|ises
na|sal|ised
na|sal|is|ing
na|sal|ity
na|sal|iza|tion
na|sal|ize
na|sal|izes
na|sal|ized
na|sal|iz|ing
nas|al|ly
nas|cency
nas|cent
nase|berry
  nase|berries
Naseby (battle site,
  England)
Nash, Beau
  (English dandy)
Nash, John
  (English architect)
Nash, Ogden
  (American writer)
Nash, Paul
  (English artist)
Nashe, Thomas
  (English writer)
Nash|ville (city,
  USA)
Nasik (city, India)

Nas|myth, James
  (British engineer)
naso-frontal
naso|gas|tric
Nas|sau (capital of
  the Bahamas)
Nas|ser, Gamal
  Abdel (Egyptian
  statesman)
Nas|tase, Ilie
  (Romanian-born
  tennis player)
nas|tic
nas|tily
nas|ti|ness
na|stur|tium +s
nasty
  nas|tier
  nas|ti|est
Natal (former
  province, South
  Africa; port,
  Brazil)
natal
Nat|alie
na|tal|ity
  na|tal|ities
Na|ta|sha
na|ta|tion
nata|tor|ial
na|ta|tor|ium +s
na|ta|tory
natch (= naturally)
nates (buttocks)
NATFHE
  (= National
  Association of
  Teachers in
  Further and
  Higher Education)
Nath|alie
Na|than
Na|than|iel
nath|less
na|tion +s
na|tion|al +s
na|tion|al|isa|tion
  Br. (use
  nationalization)
na|tion|al|ise *Br.*
  (use nationalize)
  na|tion|al|ises
  na|tion|al|ised
  na|tion|al|is|ing
na|tion|al|iser *Br.*
  +s (use
  nationalizer)
na|tion|al|ism +s
na|tion|al|ist +s
na|tion|al|is|tic
na|tion|al|is|tic|
  al|ly

na¦tion|al¦ity
　na¦tion|al¦ities
na¦tion|al¦iza¦tion
na¦tion|al¦ize
　na¦tion|al¦izes
　na¦tion|al¦ized
　na¦tion|al¦iz¦ing
na¦tion|al¦izer +s
na¦tion|al¦ly
na¦tion|hood +s
na¦tion state +s
na¦tion|wide
na¦tive +s
na¦tive|ly
na¦tive|ness
na¦tive speak¦er +s
na¦tiv|ism
na¦tiv|ist +s
na¦tiv|ity
　na¦tiv|ities
NATO (= North
　Atlantic Treaty
　Organization)
Nat¦ron, Lake (in
　Tanzania)
nat¦ron
NATSOPA (former
　British trade
　union)
nat¦ter +s +ed
　+ing
nat¦ter|er +s
nat¦ter|jack +s
nat|tier blue *noun
　and adjective*
nattier-blue
　attributive
nat|tily
nat¦ti|ness
natty
　nat|tier
　nat|ti|est
Na¦tu|fian +s
nat|ural +s
natural-born
nat¦ur|al|isa¦tion
　Br. (use
　naturalization)
nat¦ur|al|ise *Br.*
　(use naturalize)
　nat¦ur|al|ises
　nat¦ur|al|ised
　nat¦ur|al|is¦ing
nat¦ur|al|ism
nat¦ur|al|ist +s
nat¦ur|al|is|tic
nat¦ur|al|is|tic|
　　　al¦ly
nat¦ur|al|iza¦tion
nat¦ur|al|ize
　nat¦ur|al|izes

nat¦ur|al|ize (*cont.*)
　nat¦ur|al|ized
　nat¦ur|al|iz¦ing
nat¦ur|al|ly
nat¦ur|al|ness
na¦ture +s
na¦tured
na¦ture lover +s
nature-loving
na¦ture print|ing
na¦tur|ism
na¦tur|ist +s
na¦turo|path +s
na¦turo|path|ic
na¦tur|op|athy
naught (nothing.
　△ nought)
naugh|tily
naugh|ti|ness
　naugh|ti|nesses
naughty
　naugh|tier
　naugh|ti|est
nau|plius
　nau|plii
Nauru (in SW
　Pacific)
Nau|ru|an +s
nau|sea +s
nau|se|ate
　nau|se|ates
　nau|se|ated
　nau|se|at|ing
nau|se|at|ing|ly
nau|se|ous
nau|se|ous|ly
nau|se|ous|ness
nautch
　nautches
nautch girl +s
naut|ical
naut|ical|ly
Naut|ilus
　(submarine)
naut|ilus
　naut|iluses *or*
　naut|ili
Nav¦aho (use
　Navajo)
　plural Nav¦aho *or*
　Nav¦ahos
Nav¦ajo
　plural Nav¦ajo *or*
　Nav¦ajos
naval (of navies.
　△ navel)
na|val|ly
Navan (town,
　Republic of
　Ireland)

Nava|nagar
　(former state,
　India)
nav|arin +s
Nava|rino (battle)
Na|varre (in Spain)
nave +s (part of
　church or wheel.
　△ knave)
navel +s (*Anatomy.*
　△ naval)
navel-gazing
navel or¦ange +s
na|vel|wort +s
na|vicu|lar +s
nav¦ig|abil|ity
nav¦ig|able
navi|gate
　navi|gates
　navi|gated
　navi|gat|ing
navi|ga¦tion +s
navi|ga|tion|al
navi|ga|tor +s
Nav¦ra|ti|lova,
　Mar|tina (Czech-
　born American
　tennis player)
navvy
　nav|vies
　nav|vied
　navvy|ing
navy
　na|vies
navy blue +s *noun
　and adjective*
navy-blue
　attributive
navy yard +s
nawab +s
Nax¦çi|van
　(republic, S. Asia;
　its capital)
Naxos (island,
　Greece)
nay +s (no. △ né,
　née, neigh)
Naya|rit (state,
　Mexico)
nay|say
　nay|says
　nay|said
　nay|say|ing
nay|say|er +s
Naz¦ar|ene +s
Naz¦ar|eth (town,
　Israel)
Naz¦ar|ite +s
Nazca Lines
Nazi +s
Nazi|dom
Nazi¦fi|ca¦tion

Nazify
　Nazi|fies
　Nazi|fied
　Nazi|fy|ing
Nazi|ism
Naz¦ir|ite (use
　Nazarite)
Nazism
Nde|bele
　plural Nde|bele *or*
　In|de|bele *or*
　Nde|beles
N'Dja|mena
　(capital of Chad)
Ndola (city,
　Zambia)
né (before man's
　previous name.
　△ nay, née,
　neigh)
Neagh, Lough (in
　Northern Ireland)
Neal *also* Neil
Ne|an|der|thal +s
neap +s +ed +ing
　(tide. △ neep)
Nea|pol|itan +s
neap tide +s
near +s +ed +ing
　+er +est
near|by
near-certain
Ne|arc|tic
near-death
　(experience)
Near East|ern
near|ish
near|ly
near miss
　near misses
near-monopoly
　near-monopolies
near|ness
near-perfect
near|side +s
near sight
near-sighted
near-sighted|ly
near-sighted|ness
neat
　plural neat *or*
　neats
　neat|er
　neat|est
neat|en +s +ed
　+ing
Neath (town,
　Wales)
neath (beneath)
neat|ly
neat|ness
neat's-foot oil

neb|bish
  neb|bishes
Neb|lina, Pico da
  (mountain, Brazil)
Neb|raska (state,
  USA)
Ne|bu|chad|
  nez¦zar (king of
  Babylon)
ne|bu|chad|
  nez¦zar +s (wine
  bottle)
neb¦ula
  nebu|lae *or*
  nebu|las
  noun
nebu|lar
  adjective
nebu|lise *Br.* (use
  nebulize)
  nebu|lises
  nebu|lised
  nebu|lis¦ing
nebu|liser *Br.* +s
  (use nebulizer)
nebu|lize
  nebu|lizes
  nebu|lized
  nebu|liz¦ing
nebu|lizer +s
nebu|los¦ity
nebu|lous
nebu|lous|ly
nebu¦lous|ness
neb¦uly *Heraldry*
ne|ces|sar|ian +s
ne|ces|sar¦ian|ism
ne|ces|sar|ily
ne¦ces|sary
  ne¦ces|sar¦ies
ne¦ces|si|tar¦ian +s
ne¦ces|si|tar¦ian|
    ism
ne¦ces|si|tate
  ne¦ces|si|tates
  ne¦ces|si|tated
  ne¦ces|si|tat¦ing
ne¦ces|si|tous
ne¦ces|sity
  ne¦ces|sities
Nech¦tans|mere
  (battlefield)
neck +s +ed +ing
  (part of body,
  clothing, violin,
  etc.; impudence;
  kiss. △ nek)
Neckar (river,
  Germany)
neck|band +s
neck|cloth +s

Necker, Jacques
  (Swiss banker)
neck¦er|chief +s
neck|lace
  neck|laces
  neck|laced
  neck|lacing
neck|let +s
neck|line +s
neck|tie +s
neck|wear
necro|bi¦osis
  necro|bi¦oses
necro|bi¦ot¦ic
necro|gen¦ic
ne|crol|atry
necro|logic|al
ne¦crol|ogy
  ne¦crolo|gies
necro|man¦cer +s
necro|mancy
  necro|man¦cies
necro|man¦tic +s
ne|cropha|gous
necro|phil +s
necro|phile +s
necro|philia
necro|phil¦iac +s
necro|phil¦ic
ne|croph|il|ism
ne|croph|il|ist +s
ne¦croph|ily
necro|phobe
necro|pho¦bia
necro|pho¦bic
ne|crop|olis
  ne¦crop|olises
nec|ropsy
necro|scop¦ic
nec|rosc¦opy
  nec|rosc¦op¦ies
ne|cro|sis
  ne¦cro|ses
nec|rot¦ic
nec¦ro|tise *Br.* (use
  necrotize)
  nec¦ro|tises
  nec¦ro|tised
  nec¦ro|tis¦ing
nec¦ro|tize
  nec¦ro|tizes
  nec¦ro|tized
  nec¦ro|tiz¦ing
nec|tar +s
nec¦tar|ean
nec¦tar|eous
nec¦tar|if¦er¦ous
nec¦tar|ine +s
nec¦tar|ous

nec|tary
  nec¦tar|ies
Ned
NEDC (= National
  Economic
  Development
  Council)
Neddy (National
  Economic
  Development
  Council)
neddy
  ned|dies
  (= donkey)
née *Br.* (before
  woman's maiden
  name. △ nay, né,
  neigh. *Am.* nee)
need +s +ed +ing
  (require. △ knead)
need|ful
need|ful|ly
need|ful|ness
needi|ness
nee¦dle
  nee¦dles
  nee¦dled
  need|ling
needle|cord
needle|craft
needle|fish
  plural needle|fish
  or needle|fishes
needle|ful +s
needle|point +s
Nee¦dles (rocks,
  England)
need|less
need|less|ly
need|less|ness
needle|woman
  needle|women
needle|work
needn't
needy
  need|ier
  needi|est
neem +s
neep +s (turnip.
  △ neap)
ne'er
ne'er-do-well +s
ne¦fari|ous
ne¦fari|ous|ly
ne¦fari|ous|ness
Nef¦er|titi
  (Egyptian queen)
neg +s (= negative)
neg¦ate
  neg|ates
  neg|ated
  neg|at¦ing

neg|ation +s
neg|ation|ist +s
nega|tive +s
nega|tive|ly
nega|tive|ness
nega|tiv|ism
nega|tiv|ist +s
nega|tiv|is¦tic
nega|tiv|ity
neg|ator +s
neg|atory
Negev (desert,
  Israel)
neg|lect +s +ed
  +ing
neg|lect|ful
neg|lect|ful¦ly
neg|lect|ful|ness
nég|ligé +s (use
  negligee)
neg|li¦gee +s
neg|li¦gence
neg|li¦gent
neg|li¦gent|ly
neg|ligi|bil|ity
neg|li¦gible
neg|li¦gibly
Ne|gombo (port,
  Sri Lanka)
ne|go¦ti|abil¦ity
ne|go¦ti|able
ne|go¦ti|ant +s
ne|go¦ti|ate
  ne|go¦ti|ates
  ne|go¦ti|ated
  ne|go¦ti|at¦ing
ne|go¦ti|ation +s
ne|go¦ti|ator +s
Ne|gress
  Ne|gresses
  (*may cause offence*;
  prefer black)
Neg|rillo +s (tribe,
  Africa)
Negri Sem|bilan
  (state, Malaysia)
Neg|rito +s
Neg¦ri|tude
Negro
  Ne|groes
  (*may cause offence*;
  prefer black)
Negro, Rio (river,
  S. America)
Ne|groid +s
Ne|gro|ism
Ne|gro|pho¦bia
Ne|gro|pho¦bic
Neg¦ros (island,
  Philippines)
Negus (title of ruler
  of Ethiopia)

negus
  ne¦guses
  (drink)
Ne¦he¦miah *Bible*
Nehru, Pan¦dit
  Jawa¦har¦lal
  (Indian statesman)
neigh+s +ed +ing
  (of a horse. ⚠ nay,
  né, née)
neigh¦bor *Am.* +s
  +ed +ing
neigh¦bor¦hood
  Am. +s
neigh¦bor¦li¦ness
  Am.
neigh¦bor¦ly *Am.*
neigh¦bour *Br.* +s
  +ed +ing
neigh¦bour¦hood
  Br. +s
neigh¦bour¦li¦ness
  Br.
neigh¦bour¦ly *Br.*
Neil *also* Neal
Neill, Alex¦an¦der
  (Scottish-born
  educationist)
Nei¦sse (rivers,
  German-Polish
  border and S.
  Poland)
nei¦ther
Nejd (region, Saudi
  Arabia)
nek+s (mountain
  col. ⚠ neck)
nek¦ton +s
Nell
Nell¦lore (city,
  India)
nelly
  nel¦lies
Nel¦son (port, New
  Zealand)
Nel¦son, Ho¦ra¦tio
  (British admiral)
nel¦son +s
Nell¦spruit (town,
  South Africa)
ne¦lumbo +s
Neman (river, E.
  Europe)
nem¦at¦ic +s
nem¦ato¦cyst +s
nema¦tode +s
Nem¦butal *Propr.*
nem. con.
  (= nemine
  contradicente,
  without
  dissension)

nem¦er¦tean
nem¦er¦tine
nem¦esia
Nem¦esis *Greek*
  Mythology
nem¦esis
  nem¦eses
Nemu¦nas
  (alternative name
  for the Neman)
nene+s
Nen¦nius (Welsh
  writer)
nenu¦phar+s
neo-Cambrian
neo¦clas¦sic
neo¦clas¦sic¦al
neo¦clas¦si¦cism
neo¦clas¦si¦cist+s
neo¦co¦lo¦nial¦ism
neo¦co¦lo¦nial¦ist
  +s
Neo-Darwin¦ian
  +s
neo¦dym¦ium
neo-fascism
neo-fascist+s
neo-Georgian
neo-Gothic
neo-Hellen¦ism
neo-
  impres¦sion¦ism
neo-
  impres¦sion¦ist
  +s
neo¦lith¦ic
  Archaeology
neo¦lo¦gian +s
neo¦lo¦gise *Br.* (use
  neologize)
  neolo¦gises
  neolo¦gised
  neolo¦gis¦ing
neolo¦gism +s
neolo¦gist +s
neolo¦gize
  neolo¦gizes
  neolo¦gized
  neolo¦giz¦ing
neol¦ogy
  neolo¦gies
neo-Marxist
neo¦my¦cin +s
neon +s
neo¦natal
neo¦nate +s
neo-Nazi +s
neo-Nazism
neon¦tolo¦gist +s
neon¦tol¦ogy
neo¦pen¦tane
neo¦pho¦bia

neo¦pho¦bic
neo¦phron +s
neo¦phyte +s
neo¦plasm +s
neo¦plas¦tic
neo-plasti¦cism *Art*
Neo¦pla¦ton¦ic
Neo¦pla¦ton¦ism
Neo¦pla¦ton¦ist+s
neo¦prene+s
Neop¦tole¦mus
  Greek Mythology
neo-realism
neo-realist+s
neo¦ten¦ic
neot¦enous
neot¦eny
  neot¦enies
neo¦ter¦ic
neo¦trop¦ic¦al
Neo¦zo¦ic *Geology*
Nepal
Nep¦al¦ese
  plural Nep¦al¦ese
Nep¦ali
  plural Nep¦ali *or*
  Nep¦alis
ne¦pen¦the
ne¦pen¦thes
  plural ne¦pen¦thes
neph¦el¦om¦eter
  +s
neph¦elo¦met¦ric
neph¦el¦om¦etry
nephew+s
neph¦ol¦ogy
neph¦rec¦tomy
  neph¦rec¦to¦mies
neph¦rite +s
neph¦rit¦ic
neph¦ritis
neph¦rol¦ogy
neph¦rop¦athy
neph¦rot¦omy
  neph¦roto¦mies
Nepia, George
  (New Zealand
  rugby player)
ne plus ultra
nepo¦tism
nepo¦tist +s
nepo¦tis¦tic
Nep¦tune (*Roman
  Mythology*; planet)
Nep¦tun¦ian
  Geology
Nep¦tun¦ist +s
nep¦tun¦ium
nerd +s
nerdy
  nerd¦ier
  nerdi¦est

Ner¦eid (moon of
  Neptune)
ner¦eid+s *Greek
  Mythology*
Ner¦eus *Greek
  Mythology*
ner¦ine+s
Ner¦issa
nerka+s
Nernst, Her¦mann
  Wal¦ther
  (German chemist)
Nero (Clau¦dius
  Cae¦sar) (Roman
  emperor)
ner¦oli
Nero¦nian
Ne¦ruda, Pablo
  (Chilean poet and
  diplomat)
Nerva, Mar¦cus
  Coc¦ceius
  (Roman emperor)
ner¦vate
nerv¦ation +s
nerve
  nerves
  nerved
  nerv¦ing
nerve-cell +s
nerve cen¦ter *Am.*
  +s
nerve cen¦tre *Br.*
  +s
nerve gas
  nerve gases
nerve¦less
nerve¦less¦ly
nerve¦less¦ness
nerve-racking
Nervi, Pier Luigi
  (Italian engineer)
ner¦vily
ner¦vine +s
nervi¦ness
ner¦vous
ner¦vous¦ly
ner¦vous¦ness
nerv¦ure +s
nervy
  ner¦vier
  ner¦vi¦est
Nerys
Nes¦bit, Edith
  (English writer)
nes¦ci¦ence
nes¦ci¦ent
ness
  nesses
Nessa
nest +s +ed +ing
Nesta

nest box
  nest boxes
nest egg +s
nest|ful +s
nes|tle
  nes|tles
  nes|tled
  nest|ling
nest|like
nest|ling +s
Nes|tor *Greek Mythology*
Nes|tor|ian
Nes|tor|ian|ism
net
  nets
  net|ted
  net|ting
net|ball +s
net|ful +s
nether
Neth|er|land|er +s
Neth|er|land|ish
Neth|er|lands, the
Neth|er|lands
  An|til|les
neth|er|most
net|suke
  plural net|suke *or*
  net|sukes
nett (use net)
net|tle
  net|tles
  net|tled
  net|tling
nettle-rash
nettle|some
net|work +s +ed
  +ing
net|work|er +s
Neu|châ|tel, Lake
  (in Switzerland)
neum +s (use
  neume)
Neu|mann, John
  von (Hungarian-
  born
  mathematician)
neume +s
neur|al
neur|al|gia
neur|al|gic
neur|al|ly
neur|as|the|nia
neur|as|the|nic
neur|it|ic
neur|itis
neuro|ana|tom|
       ic|al
neuro|anat|omy
neuro|bio|logic|al
neuro|biol|ogy

neuro|gen|esis
neuro|gen|eses
neuro|gen|ic
neur|oglia
neuro|hor|mone
  +s
neuro|lin|guis|tic
neuro|lin|guis|tics
neuro|logic|al
neuro|logic|al|ly
neurolo|gist +s
neurol|ogy
neur|oma
  neur|omas *or*
  neur|omata
neuro|mus|cu|lar
neuron +s
neuron|al
neur|one +s
neuron|ic
neuro|path +s
neuro|path|ic
neuro|
  path|olo|gist +s
neuro|path|ol|ogy
neur|opathy
neuro|physio|
      logic|al
neuro|
  physi|olo|gist +s
neuro|physi|ology
neuro|
  psycho|logic|al
neuro|psycho|logy
neur|op|teran +s
neur|op|ter|ous
neuro|sci|ence +s
neuro|sci|en|tist
  +s
neur|osis
  neur|oses
neuro|sur|geon +s
neuro|sur|gery
neuro|sur|gi|cal
neur|ot|ic +s
neur|ot|ic|al|ly
neur|oti|cism
neur|ot|omy
  neur|oto|mies
neuro|toxin +s
neuro|trans|mit|
      ter +s
Neu|sied|ler See
  (lake, Austria and
  Hungary)
neu|ter +s +ed
  +ing
neu|tral +s
neu|tral|isa|tion
  Br. +s (use
  neutralization)

neu|tral|ise *Br.*
  (use neutralize)
neu|tral|ises
neu|tral|ised
neu|tral|is|ing
neu|tral|iser *Br.* +s
  (use neutralizer)
neu|tra|lism
neu|tra|list +s
neu|tral|ity
neu|tral|iza|tion
  +s
neu|tral|ize
  neu|tral|izes
  neu|tral|ized
  neu|tral|iz|ing
neu|tral|izer +s
neu|tral|ly
neu|trino +s
neu|tron +s
neu|tro|phil +s
Neva (river, Russia)
Nev|ada (state,
  USA)
névé +s
never
never-ending
never|more
Never-Never
  (Australian
  outback)
never-never (hire
  purchase)
Never-Never
  Coun|try
  (alternative name
  for Never-Never
  Land)
Never-Never Land
  (region, N.
  Australia)
never-never land
  (imaginary
  utopian place)
Ne|vers (city,
  France)
never|the|less
Nev|ille
Nev|ille, Rich|ard
  (Earl of Warwick,
  English
  statesman)
Nevis (island, West
  Indies)
Nevis, Ben
  (mountain,
  Scotland)
nev|oid *Am.* (*Br.*
  naevoid)
Nev|sky,
  Alex|an|der
  (Russian hero)

nevus *Am.*
  nevi
  (*Br.* naevus)
new +er +est
  (recent; unused.
  △ knew, nu)
New|ark (city,
  USA; town,
  England)
new|born +s
New Cale|donia
  (island, S. Pacific)
New|cas|tle (port,
  Australia)
Newcastle-under-
  Lyme (town,
  England)
Newcastle-upon-
  Tyne (city,
  England)
New|comen,
  Thomas (English
  metal-worker)
new|comer +s
newel +s
new|fan|gled
New|found|land
  (island, Canada)
New|found|
  land|er +s
New|gate (former
  prison, London)
Ne Win (Burmese
  statesman)
new|ish
new-laid
New|lands, John
  (English industrial
  chemist)
new-look *attributive*
newly
newly-appoint|ed
newly-elected
newly-formed
newly-wed +s
New|man, Bar|nett
  (American
  painter)
New|man, John
  Henry (English
  churchman)
New|man, Paul
  (American actor)
New|mar|ket
  (town, England)
new|ness
New Or|leans
  (port, USA)
New|port (port,
  Wales; etc.)
New|port News
  (city, USA)

Newry (port,
Northern Ireland)
news
news agency
  news agen|cies
news|agent +s
news|boy +s
news|brief +s
news|cast +s
news|cast|er +s
news|deal|er +s
news|flash
  news|flashes
news-gather|er +s
news-gather|ing
news|girl +s
news hound +s
news|less
news|let|ter +s
news|man
  news|men
news|mon|ger +s
news|paper +s
news|paper|man
  news|paper|men
New|speak
news|print
news|read|er +s
news|reel +s
news|room +s
news-sheet +s
news-stand +s
new-style
  attributive
news-vendor +s
news|worthi|ness
news|worthy
newsy
  news|ier
  news|iest
newt +s
New Testa|ment
  Bible noun and
  attributive
New|ton, Isaac
  (English
  mathematician
  and physicist)
new|ton +s (unit)
New|ton Abbot
  (town, England)
New|ton|ian
New|town|abbey
  (town, Northern
  Ireland)
New World (*noun*
  and attributive the
  Americas)
New Zea|land
New Zea|land|er
  +s
next

next-best
next door
  adverbial, adjective,
  and noun
next-door
  attributive
nexus
  nexuses
Ney, Mi|chel
  (French soldier)
ngaio +s
Ngali|ema, Mount
  (Zairean name for
  Mount Stanley)
Ngami|land
  (region,
  Botswana)
Ngata, Api|rana
  Tar|upa (Maori
  leader and
  politician)
Ng|bandi
Ngoro|ngoro
  (crater, Tanzania)
Nguni
  plural Nguni
Nhu|lun|buy
  (town, Australia)
nia|cin
Ni|ag|ara (river and
  Falls, Canada)
Niall
Nia|mey (capital of
  Niger)
nib
  nibs
  nibbed
  nib|bing
nib|ble
  nib|bles
  nib|bled
  nib|bling
nib|bler +s
Nibel|ung
  Nibel|ungs *or*
  Nibel|ungen
  Germanic
  Mythology
Nibel|ung|en|lied
  (poem)
nib|let +s
nib|lick +s
nicad +s
Ni|caea (ancient
  city, Asia Minor)
Nicam *Propr.*
Nic|ar|agua (in
  Central America)
Nic|ar|agua, Lake
  (in Nicaragua)
Nic|ar|aguan +s
Nice (city, France)

nice
  nicer
  nicest
  (pleasant)
nice|ish (use
  nicish)
nice|ly
Ni|cene
nice|ness
ni|cety
  ni|ceties
niche
  niches
  niched
  nich|ing *or*
  niche|ing
Nich|iren
Nich|olas *also*
  Nico|las
Nich|olas (patron
  saint of children)
Nich|ol|son, Ben
  (English artist)
Nich|ol|son, Jack
  (American actor)
Ni|chrome *Propr.*
nicish
Nick (name)
nick +s +ed +ing
  (notch; prison;
  steal; etc.)
nickel
  nickels
  nick|elled *Br.*
  nick|eled *Am.*
  nickel|ling *Br.*
  nickel|ing *Am.*
  (element. ⚠ nicol)
nickel brass
nick|el|ic
nick|el|odeon +s
nick|el|ous
nickel-plated
nickel-plating
nick|er +s (tool;
  person who nicks.
  ⚠ knicker,
  knickers)
nicker
  plural nicker
  (pound in money.
  ⚠ knicker)
Nick|laus, Jack
  (American golfer)
nick-nack +s (use
  knick-knack)
nick|name
  nick|names
  nick|named
  nick|nam|ing
Nicky

Nico|bar Is|lands
  (off India)
nicol +s (prism.
  ⚠ nickel)
Nic|ola
Ni|cole
Ni|col|lette
Nico|sia (capital of
  Cyprus)
ni|coti|ana
  plural ni|coti|ana
nico|tina|mide
nico|tine
nico|tin|ic
nico|tin|ise *Br.* (use
  nicotinize)
nico|tin|ises
nico|tin|ised
nico|tin|is|ing
nico|tin|ism
nico|tin|ize
nico|tin|izes
nico|tin|ized
nico|tin|iz|ing
nic|ti|tate
nic|ti|tates
nic|ti|tated
nic|ti|tat|ing
nic|ti|ta|tion
ni|da|men|tal
nide +s
nid|ifi|cate
nid|ifi|cates
nid|ifi|cated
nid|ifi|cat|ing
nidi|fi|ca|tion
nid|ify
nid|ifies
nid|ified
nid|ify|ing
nidus
  nidi *or* nid|uses
niece +s
ni|ello
ni|elli *or* ni|ellos
ni|el|loed
niels|bohr|ium
Niel|sen, Carl
  (Danish
  composer)
Nie|meyer, Oscar
  (Brazilian
  architect)
Nie|möller,
  Mar|tin (German
  Lutheran pastor)
Ni|er|steiner
  (German wine)
Nietz|sche,
  Fried|rich
  Wil|helm

Nietz|sche (*cont.*)
(German
philosopher)
Nietz|sche|an
niff +s +ed +ing
niffy
  niff|ier
  nif|fi|est
Nifl|heim
  Scandinavian
  Mythology
nif|tily
nif|ti|ness
nifty
  nif|tier
  nif|ti|est
Nigel
Ni|gella (name)
ni|gella +s (plant)
Niger (river and
  country, Africa)
Niger-Congo
  (group of
  languages)
Ni|geria
Ni|ger|ian +s (of
  Nigeria)
Ni|ger|ien +s (of
  Niger)
nig|gard +s
nig|gard|li|ness
nig|gard|ly
nig|ger +s
  (*offensive*)
nig|gle
  nig|gles
  nig|gled
  nig|gling
nig|gling|ly
nig|gly
  nig|glier
  nig|gli|est
nigh (near. △ nye)
night +s (period of
  darkness.
  △ knight)
night|bird +s
night-blindness
night|cap +s
night|clothes
night|club +s
night|dress
  night|dresses
night|fall
night fight|er +s
night fly|ing
night|gown +s
night|hawk +s
nightie +s
Night|in|gale,
  Flor|ence
  (English nurse)

night|in|gale +s
night|jar +s
night|life
night light +s
night-long
night|ly (in the
  night; every night.
  △ knightly)
night|mare +s
night|mar|ish
night|mar|ish|ly
night nurse +s
night-owl +s
night safe +s
night school +s
night|shade +s
night shift +s
night|shirt +s
night-soil +s
night|spot +s
night|stick +s
night-time +s
night|watch|man
  night|watch|men
night|wear
night work
night work|er +s
nig|res|cence +s
nig|res|cent
nig|ri|tude
ni|hil|ism
ni|hil|ist +s
ni|hil|is|tic
ni|hil|ity
ni|hil|ities
ni|hilo (in '*ex nihilo*')
nihil ob|stat
Nii|gata (port,
  Japan)
Ni|jin|sky, Vas|lav
  Fom|ich (Russian
  ballet dancer)
Nij|megen (town,
  the Netherlands)
Nike *Greek*
  Mythology
Nik|kei index
Niko|laev (Russian
  name for
  Mykolayiv)
nil
nil
  des|per|an|dum
Nile (river, Africa)
Nile blue +s *noun*
  and adjective
Nile-blue *attributive*
Nile green +s *noun*
  and adjective

Nile-green
  attributive
nil|gai +s
Nil|giri Hills (in
  India)
Nil|giris (= Nilgiri
  Hills)
Nil|ot|ic
Nils|son, Bir|git
  (Swedish soprano)
nim
nim|ble
  nim|bler
  nim|blest
nim|ble|ness
nim|bly
nimbo|stratus
  nimbo|strati
nim|bus *or*
  nimbi *or*
  nim|buses
nim|bused
Nimby +s
Nîmes (city,
  France)
niminy-piminy
Nim|rod *Bible*
Nim|rud (ancient
  Mesopotamian
  city)
Nina
nin|com|poop +s
nine +s
nine days'
  won|der
nine|fold
nine-iron +s
nine|pence +s
nine|penny
  nine|pen|nies
nine|pin +s
nine|teen +s
nine|teenth +s
nine|ti|eth +s
nine-to-five
ninety
  nine|ties
ninety-first,
  ninety-second,
  etc.
ninety|fold
ninety-one, ninety-
  two, etc.
Nin|eveh (city,
  Assyria)
Ning|sia
  (= Ningxia)
Ning|xia (region,
  China)
Nin|ian (Scottish
  saint)
ninja +s

nin|jutsu +s
ninny
  nin|nies
ninon +s
ninth +s
ninth|ly
Niobe *Greek*
  Mythology
nio|bic
nio|bium
nio|bous
Nip +s (*offensive*
  Japanese)
nip
  nips
  nipped
  nip|ping
  (pinch; drink; etc.)
nipa +s (tree)
nip|per +s (tool;
  claw; child)
nip|pily
nip|ple +s
nipple|wort +s
Nip|pon|ese
  plural Nip|pon|ese
nippy
  nip|pier
  nip|pi|est
NIREX (= Nuclear
  Industry
  Radioactive Waste
  Executive)
Niro, Rob|ert De
  (American actor)
nir|vana +s
Niš (town, Serbia)
Nisan (Jewish
  month)
nisei +s
Nish (use Niš)
nisi
Nis|sen, Peter
  (British engineer)
Nis|sen hut +s
nit +s (louse; stupid
  person. △ knit)
nite +s (in
  commercial
  language = night)
niter *Am.* (*Br.* nitre)
Ni|te|rói (port,
  Brazil)
nitid
nit|inol
nit-pick +s +ed
  +ing
nit-picker +s
ni|trate
  ni|trates
  ni|trated
  ni|trat|ing

ni¦tra¦tion +s
nitre *Br.* (*Am.* niter)
ni¦tric
ni¦tride +s
ni¦tri¦fi¦able
ni¦tri¦fi¦ca¦tion +s
ni¦trify
  ni¦tri¦fies
  ni¦tri¦fied
  ni¦tri¦fy¦ing
ni¦trile +s
ni¦trite +s
nitro|ben¦zene
nitro|cel¦lu¦lose
ni¦tro|gen
ni¦tro|gen¦ous
nitro|gly¦cerin (use
  nitroglycerine)
nitro|gly¦cer¦ine
ni¦tro¦sa|mine +s
ni¦trous
nitty-gritty
nit¦wit +s
nit¦wit¦ted
nit¦wit¦ted|ness
nit¦wit¦tery
Niue (island, S.
  Pacific)
Ni¦ver|nais (former
  province, France)
nix
  nixes
  nixed
  nix¦ing
Nixon, Rich|ard
  Mil¦hous
  (American
  president)
Niz¦ari +s
Nizhni Nov|go¦rod
  (former name of
  Gorky)
Nizhni Tagil (city,
  Russia)
Nkomo, Joshua
  (Zimbabwean
  statesman)
Nkru|mah,
  Kwame
  (Ghanaian
  statesman)
No (Japanese
  drama; use Noh.
  ⚠ know, no)
no
  noes
  (negative.
  ⚠ know, Noh)
no-account +s
  adjective and noun
Noah *Bible*
Noah's ark

nob +s (upper-class
  person; head.
  ⚠ knob)
no-ball +s +ed
  +ing
nob¦ble
  nob¦bles
  nob¦bled
  nob¦bling
  (tamper with.
  ⚠ knobble)
nob|bler +s
Nobel, Al¦fred
  (Swedish chemist
  and engineer)
No¦bel|ist +s
no¦bel|ium
no¦bil|iary
no¦bil|iar¦ies
no¦bil|ity
no¦bil|ities
noble +s
  no¦bler
  nob¦lest
noble|man
noble|men
noble|ness
no|blesse
no|blesse ob¦lige
noble|woman
  noble|women
nobly
no¦body
  no|bodies
nock +s +ed +ing
  (notch. ⚠ knock)
no-claim *attributive*
no-claims
  attributive
no-confidence
  attributive
noc¦tam|bu¦lism
noc¦tam|bu¦list +s
noc¦tiv|agant
noc¦tiv|agous
noc|tuid +s
noc|tule +s
noc|turn +s (part of
  matins.
  ⚠ nocturne)
noc|tur¦nal
noc|tur¦nal¦ly
noc|turne +s (piece
  of music; painting.
  ⚠ nocturn)
nocu|ous
nod
  nods
  nod¦ded
  nod¦ding
nodal

nod¦dle
  nod¦dles
  nod¦dled
  nod¦dling
Noddy (children's
  character)
noddy
  nod¦dies
  (simpleton; bird)
node +s
nodi (plural of
  nodus)
nod¦ic¦al
nod¦ose
nod¦os¦ity
nodu|lar
nodu|lated
nodu|la¦tion
nod¦ule +s
nodu|lose
nodu|lous
nodus
  nodi
Noel (Christmas;
  name. ⚠ Nowell)
Noelle
Noe¦ther, Emmy
  (German
  mathematician)
no¦etic
no-fault *attributive*
no-fly zone +s
Nof¦re|tete
  (alternative name
  for Nefertiti)
no-frills *attributive*
nog
  nogs
  nogged
  nog|ging
nog|gin +s
nog|ging +s
no-go area +s
no-good +s *noun*
  and attributive
Noh (Japanese
  drama. ⚠ know,
  no)
no-hitter +s
no-hoper +s
nohow (in no way.
  ⚠ know-how)
noil +s
noise
  noises
  noised
  nois|ing
noise|less
noise|less¦ly
noise|less|ness
noise-maker +s
nois|ette +s

nois|ily
noisi|ness
noi|some
noi|some|ness
noisy
  nois|ier
  noisi|est
Nok (ancient
  Nigerian
  civilization)
Nolan, Sid¦ney
  (Australian
  painter)
no¦lens vo¦lens
nolle pro|sequi
nomad +s
no|mad¦ic
no|mad¦ic|al¦ly
no|mad¦ise *Br.* (use
  nomadize)
  no¦mad|ises
  no¦mad|ised
  no¦mad|is¦ing
no¦mad|ism
no¦mad|ize
  no¦mad|izes
  no¦mad|ized
  no¦mad|iz¦ing
no man's land
nom|bril +s
nom de guerre
  noms de guerre
nom de plume
  noms de plume
nomen
nom¦ina
no|men|cla¦tive
no|men|cla¦tural
no|men|clat¦ure
  +s
nom¦ina
nom|in¦al
nom|in¦al|isa¦tion
  Br. +s (use
  nominalization)
nom|in¦al|ise *Br.*
  (use nominalize)
  nom|in¦al|ises
  nom|in¦al|ised
  nom|in¦al|is¦ing
nom|in¦al|ism
nom|in¦al|ist +s
nom|in¦al|is¦tic
nom|in¦al|iza¦tion
  +s
nom|in¦al|ize
  nom|in¦al|izes
  nom|in¦al|ized
  nom|in¦al|iz¦ing
nom|in¦al¦ly
nom|in¦ate
  nom|in¦ates

nom|in|ate (*cont.*)
nom|in|ated
nom|in|at|ing
nom|in|ation +s
nom|ina|tival
nom|ina|tive +s
nom|in|ator +s
nom|inee +s
nomo|gram +s
nomo|graph +s
nomo|graph|ic
nomo|graph|ic|al|ly
nom|og|raphy
nomo|thet|ic
non-abstain|er +s
non-academ|ic
non-accept|ance
non-access
non-addict|ive
non|age +s
nona|gen|ar|ian +s
non-aggres|sion
non-aggres|sive
non|agon +s
non-alcohol|ic
non-aligned
non-alignment
non-allergic
non-ambigu|ous
non-appear|ance
non-art
non|ary
  non|ar|ies
non-Aryan +s
non-attached
non-attend|ance
non-attrib|ut|able
non-attrib|ut|ably
non-availabil|ity
non-believer +s
non-belliger|ency
non-belliger|ent
non-biologic|al
non-black +s
non-breakable
non-breeding
  attributive
non-capital
non-Cathol|ic +s
nonce +s
nonce-word +s
non|cha|lance
non|cha|lant
non|cha|lant|ly
non-Christian +s
non-citizen +s
non-classi|fied
non-cleric|al
non-collegi|ate
non-com +s

non-combat|ant
  +s
non-commer|cial
non-commis|sioned
non-commit|tal
non-commit|tal|ly
non-communi|cant
  +s
non-communi|cat|ing
non-Commun|ist
  +s (not a
  Communist Party
  member)
non-commun|ist
  +s (not practising
  communism)
non-competi|tive
non-compli|ance
non com|pos
  (men|tis)
non-conduct|ing
non-conduct|or +s
non-confiden|tial
non-confiden|tial|ly
Non|con|form|ism
  Religion
non|con|form|ism
  (general)
Non|con|form|ist
  +s *Religion*
non|con|form|ist
  +s (general)
non|con|form|ity
non-consen|sual
non-contagious
non-content +s
non-conten|tious
non-contribu|tory
non-contro|ver|sial
non-cooper|ation
non-custodial
nonda +s
non-delivery
non-denomin|ation|al
non|de|script +s
non|de|script|ly
non|de|script|ness
non-destruc|tive
non-domestic
non-drinker +s
non-driver +s
none (not any.
  ⚠ nun)
none +s (canonical
  hour of prayer.
  ⚠ known)

non-earning
non-econom|ic
non-effect|ive
non-ego +s
non-emergency
  attributive
non-English
non|en|tity
  non|en|tities
nones
  plural nones
  (Roman calendar)
none-so-pretty
  (plant)
non-essential +s
none|such (use
  nonsuch)
none|suches
nonet +s
none|the|less
non-Euclid|ean
non-European +s
non-event +s
non-executive
non-existence
non-existent
non-explosive +s
non-fatal
non-fatten|ing
non|feas|ance +s
non-ferrous
non-fiction
non-fiction|al
non-financial
non-flam (= non-
  flammable)
non-flammable
non-fulfil|ment
non-function|al
nong +s
non-govern|men|tal
non-human +s
non-infectious
non-inflationary
non-inflect|ed
non-interfer|ence
non-interven|tion
non-interven|tion|ist
  +s
non-intoxi|cat|ing
non-invasive
non-iron
non-Jewish
non|join|der +s
non|jur|ing
non|juror +s
non-jury
non-league *Soccer*
non-linear
non-linguis|tic

non-literary
non-living
  attributive
non-logical
non-logical|ly
non-magnet|ic
non-manual
non-material
non-medical
non-member +s
non-member|ship
non-metal
non-metallic
non-militant
non-military
non-minister|ial
non-moral
non-morally
non-Muslim +s
non-native +s
non-natural
non-negoti|able
non-net
non-nuclear
no-no
  no-noes
non-object|ive
non-observance
non-oil (*attributive*
  of trade)
no-nonsense
  attributive
non-operation|al
non-organic
non|par|eil +s
non-partici|pat|ing
non-partisan
non-party
  non-parties
non-payer +s
non-payment +s
non-penetra|tive
non-perform|ing
non-person +s
non-person|al
non-physic|al
non-physical|ly
non placet +s
non-playing
non|plus
  non|plusses
  non|plussed
  non|plus|sing
non-poison|ous
non-political
non-porous
non poss|umus
non-product|ive
non-product|ive|ly
non-profes|sion|al

non-profit
non-profit-making
non-prolifer¦ation
  attributive
non-qualify¦ing
  attributive
non-racial
non-reader +s
non-refund¦able
non-religious
non-renewable
non-reproduc¦tive
non-residence
non-resident +s
non-residen¦tial
non-resistance
non-return
  attributive
non-return¦able
non-rigid
non-scientif¦ic
non-scientist +s
non-sectar¦ian
non-select¦ive
non|sense +s
non¦sens|ical
non¦sens|ical¦ity
  non¦sens|
      ical¦ities
non¦sens|ical¦ly
non sequi|tur +s
non-sexist
  attributive
non-sexual
non-sexual¦ly
non-skid
non-slip
non-smoker +s
non-smoking
non-soluble
non-special|ist +s
non-specif¦ic
non-standard
non-starter +s
non-statutory
non-stick
non-stop
non-subscriber +s
non|such
  non|suches
non|suit +s
non-surgical
non-swimmer +s
non-taxable
non-taxpay¦er +s
non-teaching
  attributive
non-technical
non-threaten¦ing
non-toxic
non-tradition¦al
non-transfer¦able

non-U
non-uniform
non-union
non-urgent
non-usage
non-use
non-user +s
non-verbal
non-verbal¦ly
non-vintage
non-violence
non-violent
non-volatile
non-voter +s
non-voting
non-Western
non-white +s
non-word +s
non-working
noo¦dle +s
nook +s
nookie (use nooky)
nooky
noon +s
noon|day +s
no one
noon|tide +s
noon|time
Noord|hinder
  (light vessel,
  North Sea)
noose
  nooses
  noosed
  noos¦ing
Nootka
  plural Nootka *or*
  Noot|kas
noo|trop¦ic +s
nopal +s
nope
nor
nor' (= north)
Nora *also* Norah
nor¦adren|alin
nor¦adren|aline
  (use
  noradrenalin)
Norah *also* Nora
Nor¦bert
Nor¦dic +s
Nord|kapp
  (Norwegian name
  for North Cape)
Nord¦kyn
  (promontory,
  Norway)
Nord-Pas-de-
  Calais (region,
  France)
Nor¦een
nor¦epin|eph¦rine

Nor|folk (county,
  England)
Nor|folk Broads,
  the (region,
  England)
Nor|folk Is¦land (in
  SW Pacific)
Nori¦ega, Ma¦nuel
  (Panamanian
  general and
  statesman)
nork +s
nor¦land +s
norm +s
Norma
nor¦mal +s
nor¦malcy
  nor¦mal¦cies
nor¦mal|isa¦tion
  Br. +s (use
  normalization)
nor¦mal|ise *Br.*
  (use normalize)
  nor¦mal|ises
  nor¦mal|ised
  nor¦mal|is¦ing
nor¦mal|iser *Br.* +s
  (use normalizer)
nor¦mal|ity
  nor¦mal|ities
nor¦mal|iza¦tion
  +s
nor¦mal|ize
  nor¦mal|izes
  nor¦mal|ized
  nor¦mal|iz¦ing
nor¦mal|izer *Am.*
  +s
nor¦mal¦ly
Nor¦man +s (of
  Normandy; name)
Nor¦man, Greg
  (Australian golfer)
Nor¦man, Jes¦sye
  (American
  soprano)
Nor|mandy
  (region, France)
Nor|man|esque
  Architecture
Nor¦man|ise *Br.*
  (use Normanize)
Nor¦man|ised
Nor¦man|is¦ing
Nor¦man|ism +s
Nor¦man|ize
  Nor¦man|izes
  Nor¦man|ized
  Nor¦man|iz¦ing
nor¦ma¦tive
nor¦ma¦tive|ly

nor¦ma¦tive|ness
Norn +s
  Scandinavian
  Mythology
Nor¦ris
Norr¦kö¦ping (port,
  Sweden)
Nor¦roy *Heraldry*
Norse
Norse|man
  Norse|men
North, the (part of
  country etc.;
  Arctic)
north +s (point;
  direction)
North|al¦ler¦ton
  (town, England)
North|amp|ton
  (town, England)
North|amp|ton|
  shire (county,
  England)
North¦ants
  (= Northampton-
  shire)
north|bound
North|cliffe, Lord
  (British newspaper
  proprietor)
North Coun|try
  (region, England)
north-
  country¦man
north-
  country¦men
North-East, the
  (part of country
  etc.)
north-east (point;
  direction)
north|east¦er +s
north-easter¦ly
  north-easter¦lies
north-eastern
north-east
  pas|sage (seaway
  north of Europe
  and Asia)
north-eastward
north-eastwards
norther +s
north|er¦ly
  north|er|lies
north|ern
North|ern Cir¦cars
  (former region,
  India)
North|ern Cross
  (constellation;
  = Cygnus)
north|ern|er +s

north|ern|most
north|ing +s
North|land
North|man
North|men
north-north-east
north-north-west
North Rhine-
  Westphalia
  (state, Germany)
north-south
  attributive
North|um|ber|land
  (county, England)
North|um|bria
  (region, England)
North|um|brian +s
north|ward
north|wards
North-West, the
  (part of country
  etc.)
north-west (point;
  direction)
north|wester +s
north-wester|ly
north-wester|lies
north-western
North-West
  Front|ier
  Pro|vince (in NW
  Pakistan)
north-west
  pas|sage (seaway
  north of America)
North-West
  Prov|ince (in
  South Africa)
North|west
  Ter|ri|tor|ies (in
  Canada)
North|west
  Ter|ri|tory
  (region, USA)
north-westward
north-westwards
Nor|way
Nor|we|gian +s
nor'|wester +s
Nor|wich (city,
  England)
no-score draw +s
nose
  noses
  nosed
  nos|ing
nose|bag +s
nose|band +s
nose|bleed +s
nose cap +s
nose-cone +s

nose|dive
nose|dives
nose|dived
nose|div|ing
no-see-em +s
no-see-um +s (use
  no-see-em)
nose flute +s
nose|gay +s
nose|less
nose-piece +s
nose|pipe +s
nose-rag +s
nose|ring +s
nose-to-tail
nose wheel +s
nosey (use nosy)
nosi|er
nosi|est
nosh
  noshes
  noshed
  nosh|ing
nosh|ery
  nosh|er|ies
no-show +s
nosh-up +s
nosi|ly
nosi|ness
nos|ing +s
nos|og|raphy
noso|logic|al
nos|ology
nos|tal|gia +s
nos|tal|gic
nos|tal|gic|al|ly
nos|toc +s
Nos|tra|da|mus
  (Provençal
  astrologer)
no-strike *attributive*
nos|tril +s
nos|triled *Am.*
nos|trilled *Br.*
nos|trum
  nos|trums *or*
  nos|tra
nosy
  nosi|er
  nosi|est
Nosy Par|ker +s
not (negative word.
  △ knot)
nota bene
not|abil|ity
  not|abil|ities
not|able +s
not|able|ness
not|ably
Notam +s
no|tar|ial
no|tari|al|ly

no|tar|ise *Br.* (use
  notarize)
no|tar|ises
no|tar|ised
no|tar|is|ing
no|tar|ize
no|tar|izes
no|tar|ized
no|tar|iz|ing
no|tary
  no|tar|ies
no|tate
  no|tates
  no|tated
  no|tat|ing
no|ta|tion +s
nota|tion|al
notch
  notches
  notched
  notch|ing
notcher +s
notchy
  notch|ier
  notchi|est
note
  notes
  noted
  not|ing
note|book +s
note|case +s
note|less
note|let +s
note|pad +s
note|paper +s
note-row +s
note-taking
note|worthi|ness
note|worthy
noth|ing +s
noth|ing|ness
no|tice
  no|tices
  no|ticed
  no|ticing
no|tice|able
no|tice|ably
no|tice|board +s
no|ti|fi|able
no|ti|fi|ca|tion +s
no|tify
  no|ti|fies
  no|ti|fied
  no|ti|fy|ing
no|tion +s
no|tion|al
no|tion|al|ist +s
no|tion|al|ly
no|to|chord +s
no|tori|ety
no|tori|ous
no|tori|ous|ly

no|tor|nis
Notre Dame
  (university, USA)
Notre-Dame
  (cathedral, Paris)
no-trumper +s
no trumps
Not|ting|ham (city,
  England)
Not|ting|ham|
  shire (county,
  England)
Not|ting Hill
  (district, London)
Notts.
  (= Nottingham-
  shire)
not|with|stand|ing
Nou|ad|hi|bou
  (port, Mauritania)
Nou|ak|chott
  (capital of
  Mauritania)
nou|gat +s
nought +s (the
  digit 0; zero.
  △ naught)
noughts and
  crosses
Nouméa (capital of
  New Caledonia)
nou|menal
nou|men|al|ly
nou|menon
  nou|mena
noun +s
noun|al
nour|ish
  nour|ishes
  nour|ished
  nour|ish|ing
nour|ish|er +s
nour|ish|ing|ly
nour|ish|ment +s
nous (common
  sense)
nouse (use nous)
nou|veau riche
  nou|veaux riches
nou|veau roman
  nou|veaux romans
Nou|velle
  Calé|do|nie
  (French name for
  New Caledonia)
nou|velle cuis|ine
  nou|velles
  cuis|ines
nou|velle vague
  nou|velles vagues
nova
  novae *or* novas

Nova Lis|boa
(former name of
Huambo)
Nova Sco|tia
(province,
Canada)
Nova Sco|tian +s
Nov|aya Zemlya
(islands, Arctic
Ocean)
novel +s
nov|el|ese
nov|el|esque
nov|el|ette +s
nov|el|et|tish
nov|el|isa|tion Br.
+s (use
novelization)
nov|el|ise Br. (use
novelize)
nov|el|ises
nov|el|ised
nov|el|is|ing
nov|el|ist +s
nov|el|is|tic
nov|el|iza|tion +s
nov|el|ize
nov|el|izes
nov|el|ized
nov|el|iz|ing
nov|ella +s
Nov|ello, Ivor
(Welsh actor,
composer, and
playwright)
nov|elty
nov|el|ties
No|vem|ber +s
nov|ena +s
No|verre, Jean-
Georges (French
choreographer
and dancer)
Nov|go|rod (city,
Russia)
nov|ice +s
novi|ci|ate +s
Novi Sad (city,
Serbia)
Novo|caine Propr.
No|vo|kuz|netsk
(city, Siberia)
Novo|si|birsk (city,
Russia)
no-vote +s
No|votný,
Anto|nin
(Czechoslovak
Communist
statesman)
now
now|aday

now|adays
noway
Nowel +s
(interjection; use
Nowell
Christmas; use
Noel)
No|well +s
(interjection.
△ Noel)
no|where
no-win
no|wise
nowt (nothing.
△ knout)
nox|ious
nox|ious|ly
nox|ious|ness
noyau
noy|aux
noz|zle +s
nth
nu +s (Greek letter.
△ knew, new)
Nuala
nu|ance
nu|ances
nu|anced
nu|an|cing
nub +s
nub|ble +s
nub|bly
nub|blier
nub|bli|est
nubby
nub|bier
nub|bi|est
Nubia (region of
Egypt and Sudan)
Nu|bian +s
nu|bile
nu|bil|ity
nu|chal
nucif|er|ous
nuciv|or|ous
nu|clear
nuclear-free
nuclear-powered
nu|cle|ase +s
nu|cle|ate
nu|cle|ates
nu|cle|ated
nu|cle|at|ing
nu|cle|ation +s
nu|clei
nu|cle|ic
nu|cle|olar
nu|cle|olus
nu|cle|oli
nu|cleon +s
nu|cle|on|ic

nu|cle|on|ics
nu|cleo|pro|tein +s
nu|cleo|side +s
nu|cleo|syn|thesis
nu|cle|ot|ide +s
nu|cleus
nu|clei
nu|clide +s
nu|clid|ic
nuddy
nude +s
nudge
nudges
nudged
nudg|ing
nudger +s
nudi|branch +s
nud|ism
nud|ist +s
nud|ity
nud|ities
nuée ar|dente
nuées ar|dentes
Nuer
plural Nuer
(people; language)
Nuevo León (state,
Mexico)
Nuf|field, Lord
(British car maker)
nu|ga|tory
nug|get +s
nuis|ance +s
nuke
nukes
nuked
nuk|ing
Nu|ku'alofa
(capital of Tonga)
null +s
nulla +s (= nulla-
nulla)
nul|lah +s (dry
river bed)
nulla-nulla +s
(Australian
Aboriginal club)
Null|ar|bor Plain
(plain, Australia)
nul|li|fi|ca|tion +s
nul|li|fid|ian +s
nul|li|fier +s
nul|lify
nul|li|fies
nul|li|fied
nul|li|fy|ing
nul|lipara +s
nul|lipar|ous
nul|li|pore +s
null|ity
null|ities

Numa Pom|pil|ius
(legendary Roman
king)
numb
num|bat +s
num|ber +s +ed
+ing
num|ber crunch|er
+s
num|ber
crunch|ing
num|ber|less
num|ber plate +s
Num|ber Ten
(Downing Street,
London)
numb-fish
plural numb-fish
or numb-fishes
numb|ing|ly
num|bles
numb|ly
numb|ness
numb|skull +s (use
numskull)
num|dah +s
numen
nu|mina
nu|mer|able
nu|mer|ably
nu|mer|acy
nu|meral +s
nu|mer|ate
nu|mer|ates
nu|mer|ated
nu|mer|at|ing
nu|mer|ation
nu|mer|ator +s
nu|mer|ic
nu|mer|ic|al
nu|mer|ic|al|ly
nu|mero|logic|al
nu|mer|olo|gist +s
nu|mer|ology
nu|mer|ous
nu|mer|ous|ly
nu|mer|ous|ness
Nu|midia (ancient
kingdom, Africa)
Nu|mid|ian +s
nu|mina
nu|min|ous
nu|mis|mat|ic
nu|mis|mat|ic|
al|ly
nu|mis|mat|ics
nu|mis|ma|tist +s
nu|mis|mat|ology
num|mu|lite +s
num|nah +s
num|skull +s

nun+s (member of religious community. △ none)
nun|atak+s
nun-buoy+s
Nunc Di|mit|tis
nun|ci|ature+s
nun|cio+s
nun|cu|pate
  nun|cu|pates
  nun|cu|pated
  nun|cu|pat|ing
nun|cu|pa|tion+s
nun|cu|pa|tive
Nun|eaton (town, England)
nun|hood+s
nun|like
nun|nery
  nun|ner|ies
nun|nish
NUPE (= National Union of Public Employees)
nup|tial+s
nurd+s (use nerd)
Nur|em|berg (city, Germany)
Nur|eyev, Ru|dolf (Russian ballet dancer)
Nuri|stan (region, Afghanistan)
nurse
  nurses
  nursed
  nurs|ing
nurse|ling+s (use nursling)
nurse|maid+s +ed +ing
nur|sery
  nur|ser|ies
nur|sery|man
  nur|sery|men
nurs|ling+s
nur|ture
  nur|tures
  nur|tured
  nur|tur|ing
nur|turer+s
Nut *Egyptian Mythology*
nut
  nuts
  nut|ted
  nut|ting
nu|tant
nu|ta|tion+s
nut brown+s *noun and adjective*

nut-brown *attributive*
nut-butter+s
nut|case+s
nut|crack|er+s
nut|gall+s
nut|hatch
  nut|hatches
nut|house+s
nut|let+s
nut|like
nut-meat+s
nut|meg+s
nutmeg-apple+s
nut oil+s
nu|tria+s
nu|tri|ent+s
nu|tri|ment+s
nu|tri|men|tal
nu|tri|tion
nu|tri|tion|al
nu|tri|tion|al|ly
nu|tri|tion|ist+s
nu|tri|tious
nu|tri|tious|ly
nu|tri|tious|ness
nu|tri|tive
nut|shell+s
nut|ter+s
nut|ti|ness
nut tree+s
nutty
  nut|tier
  nut|ti|est
Nuu-chah-nulth
  plural Nuu-chah-nulth
  (= Nootka)
Nuuk (capital of Greenland)
nux vom|ica+s
nuz|zle
  nuz|zles
  nuz|zled
  nuz|zling
nyala
  plural nyala or nyalas
Nyanja
  plural Nyanja or Nyan|jas
Nyasa, Lake (in Africa)
Ny|asa|land (former name of Malawi)
nyc|tal|opia
nyc|ti|trop|ic
nye+s (*archaic* = nide. △ nigh)

Nye|rere, Ju|lius (African statesman)
nyl|ghau+s
nylon+s
nymph+s
nym|phae
nymph|al
nym|phalid+s
nymph|ean
nymph|et+s
nymph|like
nym|pho+s
nym|pho|lepsy
  nym|pho|lep|sies
nym|pho|lept+s
nym|pho|lep|tic
nym|pho|mania
nym|pho|maniac+s
Ny|norsk
Nys|lott (Swedish name for Savonlinna)
nys|tag|mic
nys|tag|mus
ny|sta|tin
Nyun|gar
Nyx *Greek Mythology*

Oo

O (used before a name, as in 'O God'. △ oh, owe)
O' (prefix of Irish surnames)
o' (= of; on)
oaf+s
oaf|ish
oaf|ish|ly
oaf|ish|ness
Oahu (island, Hawaii)
oak+s
oak-apple+s
oaken
oak-gall+s
Oak|ham (town, England)
Oak|land (city, USA)
Oak|ley, Annie (American markswoman)
oakum
OAPEC (= Organization of Arab Petroleum Exporting Countries)
oar+s (for rowing. △ or, ore)
oared
oar|fish
  plural oar|fish or oar|fishes
oar|less
oar|lock+s
oars|man
  oars|men
oars|man|ship
oars|woman
  oars|women
oar|weed
oasis
  oases
oast+s
oast house+s
oat+s
oat|cake+s
oaten
Oates, Titus (Protestant clergyman)
oat-grass
  oat-grasses
oath+s
oat|meal
oaty

Oax|aca (state and
city, Mexico)
Ob (river, Siberia)
Oba|diah *Bible*
Oban (port,
Scotland)
ob|bli|gato
  ob|bli|gatos *or*
  ob|bli|gati
ob|con|ic
ob|con|ic|al
ob|cor|date
ob|dur|acy
ob|dur|ate
ob|dur|ate|ly
ob|dur|ate|ness
obeah
ob|eche +s
obedi|ence +s
obedi|ent
obedi|ent|ly
obei|sance +s
obei|sant
obei|sant|ly
obeli
ob|el|ise *Br.* (use
  obelize)
  ob|el|ises
  ob|el|ised
  ob|el|is|ing
ob|el|isk +s
ob|el|ize
  ob|el|izes
  ob|el|ized
  ob|el|iz|ing
ob|elus
  obeli
Ober|am|mer|gau
  (village, Germany)
Ober|hau|sen (city,
  Germany)
Ob|eron (character
  in Shakespeare;
  moon of Uranus)
obese
obese|ness
obes|ity
obey +s +ed +ing
obey|er +s
ob|fus|cate
  ob|fus|cates
  ob|fus|cated
  ob|fus|cat|ing
ob|fus|ca|tion +s
ob|fus|ca|tory
obi +s
obit +s
ob|iter dic|tum
  ob|iter dicta
ob|itu|ar|ial
ob|itu|ar|ist +s

ob|itu|ary
ob|itu|ar|ies
ob|ject +s +ed
  +ing
object-ball +s
object-glass
  object-glasses
ob|ject|ifi|ca|tion
  +s
ob|ject|ify
  ob|jecti|fies
  ob|jecti|fied
  ob|jecti|fy|ing
ob|jec|tion +s
ob|jec|tion|able
ob|jec|tion|able|
                ness
ob|jec|tion|ably
ob|ject|ival
ob|ject|ive +s
ob|ject|ive|ly
ob|ject|ive|ness
ob|ject|iv|isa|tion
  Br. (use
  objectivization)
ob|jec|tiv|ise *Br.*
  (use objectivize)
  ob|jec|tiv|ises
  ob|jec|tiv|ised
  ob|jec|tiv|is|ing
ob|ject|iv|ism
ob|ject|iv|ist +s
ob|ject|iv|is|tic
ob|ject|iv|ity
ob|ject|iv|iza|tion
ob|ject|iv|ize
  ob|ject|iv|izes
  ob|ject|iv|ized
  ob|ject|iv|iz|ing
ob|ject|less
ob|ject lesson +s
ob|ject|or +s
object-orient|ed
objet d'art
  ob|jets d'art
ob|jur|gate
  ob|jur|gates
  ob|jur|gated
  ob|jur|gat|ing
ob|jur|ga|tion +s
ob|jur|ga|tory
ob|lan|ceo|late
ob|last +s
ob|late +s
ob|la|tion +s
ob|la|tion|al
ob|la|tory
ob|li|gate
  ob|li|gates
  ob|li|gated
  ob|li|gat|ing
ob|li|ga|tion +s

ob|li|ga|tor +s
ob|liga|tor|ily
ob|liga|tory
ob|lige
  ob|liges
  ob|liged
ob|li|ging
ob|li|gee +s
ob|li|ger +s
  (generally)
ob|li|ging|ly
ob|li|ging|ness
ob|li|gor +s *Law*
ob|lique
  ob|liques
  ob|liqued
ob|li|quing
ob|lique|ly
ob|lique|ness
ob|li|quity
ob|li|qui|ties
ob|lit|er|ate
  ob|lit|er|ates
  ob|lit|er|ated
  ob|lit|er|at|ing
ob|lit|er|ation +s
ob|lit|era|tive
ob|lit|er|ator +s
ob|liv|ion +s
ob|livi|ous
ob|livi|ous|ly
ob|livi|ous|ness
ob|long +s
ob|lo|quy
  ob|lo|quies
ob|nox|ious
ob|nox|ious|ly
ob|nox|ious|ness
oboe +s
oboe d'amore
  oboes d'amore
obo|ist +s
obol +s
Obote, Mil|ton
  (Ugandan
  statesman)
ob|ov|ate
O'Brien, Edna
  (Irish writer)
O'Brien, Flann
  (Irish writer)
ob|scene
ob|scene|ly
ob|scene|ness
ob|scen|ity
  ob|scen|ities
ob|scur|ant +s
ob|scur|ant|ism
ob|scur|ant|ist +s
ob|scur|ation +s
ob|scure
  ob|scures

ob|scure (*cont.*)
  ob|scured
  ob|scur|ing
ob|scure|ly
ob|scur|ity
  ob|scur|ities
ob|se|cra|tion +s
ob|se|quial
ob|se|quies
ob|se|qui|ous
ob|se|qui|ous|ly
ob|se|qui|ous|ness
ob|serv|able +s
ob|serv|ably
ob|ser|vance +s
ob|ser|vant
ob|ser|vant|ly
ob|ser|va|tion +s
ob|ser|va|tion|al
ob|ser|va|tion|
              al|ly
ob|ser|va|tory
  ob|ser|va|tor|ies
ob|serve
  ob|serves
  ob|served
  ob|serv|ing
ob|ser|ver +s
ob|sess
  ob|sesses
  ob|sessed
  ob|sess|ing
ob|ses|sion +s
ob|ses|sion|al
ob|ses|sion|al|ism
ob|ses|sion|al|ly
ob|ses|sive +s
ob|ses|sive|ly
ob|ses|sive|ness
ob|sid|ian +s
ob|so|les|cence
ob|so|les|cent
ob|so|lete
ob|so|lete|ly
ob|so|lete|ness
ob|so|let|ism
obs|tacle +s
obs|tacle race +s
ob|stat (in '*nihil
  obstat*')
ob|stet|ric
ob|stet|ric|al
ob|stet|ric|al|ly
ob|stet|ri|cian +s
ob|stet|rics
ob|stin|acy
ob|stin|ate
ob|stin|ate|ly
ob|strep|er|ous
ob|strep|er|ous|ly
ob|strep|er|ous|
                ness

ob|struct +s +ed
+ing
ob|struc'tion +s
ob|struc'tion|ism
ob|struc'tion|ist
+s
ob'struct|ive
ob'struct|ive|ly
ob'struct|ive|ness
ob'struct|or +s
ob'stu'pe|fac'tion
ob|stu'pefy
ob|stu'pe|fies
ob|stu'pe|fied
ob|stu'pe|fy|ing
ob'tain +s +ed
+ing
ob'tain|abil'ity
ob'tain|able
ob'tain|er +s
ob'tain|ment +s
ob'ten'tion +s
ob'trude
ob|trudes
ob|truded
ob|trud'ing
ob|truder +s
ob'tru'sion +s
ob'tru'sive
ob'tru'sive|ly
ob'tru'sive|ness
ob'tund +s +ed
+ing
ob'tur'ate
ob|tur'ates
ob|tur'ated
ob|tur'at'ing
ob'tur'ation
ob'tur'ator +s
ob'tuse
ob'tuse'ly
ob'tuse|ness
ob'tus|ity
ob'verse
ob'verse'ly
ob'ver'sion +s
ob'vert +s +ed
+ing
ob'vi|ate
ob'vi|ates
ob'vi|ated
ob'vi|at'ing
ob'vi|ation
ob'vi|ous
ob'vi|ous'ly
ob'vi|ous|ness
oca|rina +s
O'Casey, Sean
(Irish playwright)
Occam, Wil'liam
of (English
philosopher)

Occam's razor
oc'ca|sion +s +ed
+ing
oc|ca'sion|al
oc|ca'sion|al|ism
oc|ca'sion|al|ist +s
oc|ca'sion|al'ity
oc|ca'sion|al'ly
Oc'ci|dent, the
Oc'ci|den'tal +s
(person)
oc'ci|den'tal
adjective (western)
oc'ci|den'tal|ise
Br. (use
occidentalize)
oc'ci|den'tal|ises
oc'ci|den'tal|ised
oc'ci|den'tal|
is'ing
oc'ci|den'tal|ism
oc'ci|den'tal|ist +s
oc'ci|den'tal|ize
oc'ci|den'tal|izes
oc'ci|den'tal|ized
oc'ci|den'tal|
iz'ing
oc'ci|den'tal'ly
oc'cipi'tal +s
oc'ci'put +s
Oc'ci|tan
Oc'ci|tan'ian +s
oc|clude
oc|cludes
oc|cluded
oc|clud'ing
oc'clu'sion +s
oc'clu'sive
oc'cult +s +ed
+ing
oc'cult|ation
oc'cult|ism
oc'cult|ist +s
oc'cult'ly
oc'cult|ness
oc'cu|pancy
oc'cu|pan'cies
oc'cu|pant +s
oc'cu|pa'tion +s
oc'cu|pa'tion|al
oc'cu|pa'tion|al'ly
oc'cu|pier +s
oc'cupy
oc'cu|pies
oc'cu|pied
oc'cu|py'ing
occur
oc|curs
oc|curred
oc'cur|rence +s
oc'cur|rent

ocean +s
ocean|arium
ocean|ariums *or*
ocean|aria
ocean-going
Ocea'nia (Pacific
and nearby
islands)
Ocean|ian +s
Ocean'ic (of
Oceania)
ocean'ic (of the
ocean)
Ocean|id
Oce'an|ids *or*
Oce'ani|des
ocean|og'raph|er
+s
oceano|graph'ic
oceano|graph'ic|al
ocean|og'raphy
Ocea'nus *Greek
Mythology*
ocean|ward
ocel|lar
ocel|late
ocel|lated
ocel|lus
ocelli
oce'lot +s
och *interjection*
oche +s (in darts)
ocher *Am.* +s (*Br.*
ochre)
och|loc'racy
och|loc'ra'cies
och'lo|crat +s
och'lo|crat'ic
och'one
ochre *Br.* +s (*Am.*
ocher)
ochre|ish
ochre|ous
och'rous
ochry
ocker +s
Ock'ham,
Wil'liam of (use
Occam)
Ock'ham's razor
(use Occam's
razor)
o'clock
O'Con|nell,
Dan'iel (Irish
nationalist and
social reformer)
oco|tillo +s
octa|chord +s
octad +s
octa|gon +s
oc'tag|on'al

oc'tag|on'al'ly
octa|he'dral
octa|he'dron
octa|he'dra *or*
octa|he'drons
octal +s
oc'tam'er|ous
oc'tam'eter +s
oc'tane +s
oc'tant +s
oc'tarchy
oc'tarch'ies
octa|roon +s (use
octoroon)
octa|style +s
Octa|teuch
octa|va'lent
oct'ave +s
Oc'ta'via
Oc'ta'vian (Roman
emperor)
oc'tavo +s
oc'ten'nial
octet +s
oc'tette +s
(use octet)
Oc'to|ber +s
Oc'to|brist +s
octo|cen'ten|ary
octo|cen'ten|
ar'ies
octo|decimo +s
octo|gen'ar'ian +s
octo|nar'ian +s
octo|nar'ius
octo|narii
octo|nary
octo|nar'ies
octo|pod +s
octo|pus
octo|puses
octo|roon +s
octo|syl'lab'ic
octo|syl'lable +s
oc'troi +s
OCTU (= Officer
Cadets Training
Unit)
oc'tu|ple
oc'tu|ples
oc'tu|pled
oc'tu|pling
ocu'lar +s
ocu'lar|ist +s
ocu'lar'ly
ocu|late
ocu|list +s
ocu|lis'tic
oculo|nasal
OD
OD's

OD (*cont.*)
  OD'd
  OD'ing
  (= overdose)
od (hypothetical
  force; also = God.
  ⚠ odd)
odal +s
odal|isque +s
odd +s +er +est
  (strange; not
  even; etc. ⚠ od)
odd|ball +s
Odd|fel|low +s
odd|ish
odd|ity
  odd|ities
odd job +s
odd job|ber +s
odd-job man
  odd-job men
oddly
odd|ment +s
odd|ness
odds-on
ode +s
Odense (port,
  Denmark)
Oder (river, central
  Europe)
Odessa (city and
  port, Ukraine)
Odets, Clif|ford
  (American
  dramatist)
Odette
odeum
  odeums *or* odea
  (theatre.
  ⚠ odium)
Odile
Odin *Scandinavian*
  Mythology
odi|ous
odi|ous|ly
odi|ous|ness
odium (dislike.
  ⚠ odeum)
odom|eter +s
odom|etry
Odon|ata
odon|ate +s
odon|to|glos|sum
  +s
odont|oid
odon|to|logic|al
odon|to|lo|gist +s
odon|tol|ogy
odon|to|rhynch|
        ous
odor *Am.* +s (*Br.*
  odour)

odor|ifer|ous
odor|ifer|ous|ly
odor|less *Am.* (*Br.*
  odourless)
odor|ous
odor|ous|ly
odour *Br.* +s (*Am.*
  odor)
odour|less *Br.* (*Am.*
  odorless)
Odys|sean (of
  Odysseus)
Odys|seus *Greek*
  Mythology
Odys|sey (epic
  poem)
odys|sey +s
  (journey)
Oea (ancient name
  for Tripoli, Libya)
oe|cist +s
oe|dema *Br.*
  oe|de|mata *or*
  oe|de|mas
  (*Am.* edema)
oe|dema|tous *Br.*
  (*Am.* edematous)
Oedi|pal
Oedi|pus *Greek*
  Mythology
oeno|logic|al *Br.*
  (*Am.* enological)
oen|olo|gist *Br.* +s
  (*Am.* enologist)
oen|ology *Br.* (*Am.*
  enology)
Oe|none *Greek*
  Mythology
oeno|phile *Br.* +s
  (*Am.* enophile)
oen|oph|il|ist *Br.*
  +s (*Am.*
  enophilist)
o'er (= over)
Oer|sted, Hans
  Chris|tian
  (Danish physicist)
oer|sted +s (unit)
oe|sopha|geal *Br.*
  (*Am.* esophageal)
oe|sopha|gus *Br.*
  oe|soph|agi *or*
  oe|sopha|guses
  (*Am.* esophagus)
oes|tra|diol
oes|tral *Br.* (*Am.*
  estral)
oes|tro|gen *Br.* +s
  (*Am.* estrogen)
oes|tro|gen|ic *Br.*
  (*Am.* estrogenic)

oes|tro|gen|ic|al|ly
  Br. (*Am.*
  estrogenically)
oes|trous *Br.*
  adjective (*Am.*
  estrous)
oes|trum *Br.* (*Am.*
  estrum)
oes|trus *Br. noun*
  (*Am.* estrus)
oeuvre +s
of (belonging to
  etc.)
ofay +s (*offensive*
  white person.
  ⚠ au fait)
off +s +ed +ing
  (away; not on;
  gone bad; etc.)
Offa (king of
  Mercia)
off-air *attributive*
offal +s
Of|faly (county,
  Republic of
  Ireland)
Offa's Dyke
  (earthworks,
  England and
  Wales)
off bal|ance
off|beat +s *noun*
  and adjective
off-break +s
off-center *Am.*
off-centre *Br.*
off chance
off-color *Am.*
off-colour *Br.*
off|cut +s
off day +s
off-drive
  off-drives
  off-drove
  off-driving
  off-driven
off duty
off-duty *attributive*
Of|fen|bach,
  Jacques (German-
  born French
  composer)
of|fence *Br.* +s
  (*Am.* offense)
of|fence|less *Br.*
  (*Am.* offenseless)
of|fend +s +ed
  +ing
of|fend|ed|ly
of|fend|er +s
of|fense *Am.* +s
  (*Br.* offence)

of|fense|less *Am.*
  (*Br.* offenceless)
of|fen|sive +s
of|fen|sive|ly
of|fen|sive|ness
OFFER (= Office of
  Electricity
  Regulation)
offer +s +ed +ing
of|fer|er +s
  (generally)
of|fer|ing +s
of|fer|or +s *Law*
  and Finance
of|fer|tory
off guard
off|hand
off|hand|ed
off|hand|ed|ly
off|hand|ed|ness
of|fice +s
office-bearer +s
of|fi|cer +s
of|fi|cial +s
of|fi|cial|dom
of|fi|cial|ese
of|fi|cial|ism
of|fi|cial|ly
of|fi|ci|ant +s
of|fi|ci|ate
  of|fi|ci|ates
  of|fi|ci|ated
  of|fi|ci|at|ing
of|fi|ci|ation
of|fi|ci|ator +s
of|fi|cin|al
of|fi|cin|al|ly
of|fi|cious
of|fi|cious|ly
of|fi|cious|ness
off|ing
off|ish
off|ish|ly
off|ish|ness
off-key
off-licence *Br.* +s
off-limits
off-line
off|load +s +ed
  +ing
off-peak
off-piste
off-price
off|print +s
off-putting
off-putting|ly
off-road *attributive*
off-roader +s
off-roading
off-screen
off-season +s
off|set
  off|sets

off¦set (*cont.*)
  off¦set
  off¦set¦ting
off¦shoot +s
off¦shore
off¦side +s
  (*Football etc.*; of
  vehicle)
off side *Cricket*
off¦sider +s
off¦spring
  plural off¦spring
off-stage *attributive*
off-street *attributive*
off-the-cuff
  attributive
off-the-shelf
  attributive
off-the-shoulder
  attributive
off-the-wall
  attributive
off-time +s (slack
  period. △ oft-
  times)
off-white +s
Ofgas (= Office of
  Gas Supply)
OFSTED (= Office
  for Standards in
  Education)
oft
Oftel (= Office of
  Telecommuni-
  cations)
often +er +est
often|times
oft-quoted
oft-repeat¦ed
oft-times (often.
  △ off-times)
Ofwat (= Office of
  Water Services)
Oga¦den (region,
  Ethiopia)
ogam +s (use
  ogham)
og¦doad +s
ogee +s
ogee'd
ogham +s
ogival
ogive +s
ogle
  ogles
  ogled
  og¦ling
ogler +s
OGPU (USSR
  counter-
  revolutionary
  organization)

ogre +s
ogre|ish
ogress
  ogresses
ogrish (use
  ogreish)
Ogy|gian
oh (expression of
  surprise, pain, etc.;
  zero. △ O)
O'Hig|gins,
  Ber|nardo
  (Chilean
  revolutionary
  leader)
Ohio (state, USA)
Ohm, Georg
  (German
  physicist)
ohm +s (unit.
  △ om)
ohm¦age
ohmic
ohm|meter +s
Ohm's law
oho
ohone (use
  ochone)
Ohrid, Lake (in SE
  Europe)
oi
oi¦dium
  oidia
oik +s
oil +s +ed +ing
oil-based
oil-bird +s
oil¦cake +s
oil can +s
oil¦cloth +s
oil color *Am.* +s
oil col¦our *Br.* +s
oil drum +s
oiler +s
oil¦field +s
oil-fired
oil gauge +s
oil gland +s
oil¦ily
oili|ness
oil lamp +s
oil¦less
oil¦man
  oil¦men
oil-meal
oil paint +s
oil paint|ing +s
oil-palm +s
oil pan +s
oil-paper
oil plat|form +s

oil-press
  oil-presses
oil-producing
oil rig +s
oil-sand
oil¦seed +s
oil-shale +s
oil¦skin +s
oil slick +s
oil¦stone +s
oil tank¦er +s
oil well +s
oily
  oil¦ier
  oili¦est
oink +s +ed +ing
oint|ment +s
Oire|ach|tas
  (Irish legislature)
Oisin (Irish name
  for Ossian)
Ojibwa
  plural Ojibwa *or*
  Ojib¦was
OK +s *noun*
OK
  OK's
  OK'd
  OK'ing
  verb
okapi
  plural okapi *or*
  oka¦pis
Okara (city, India)
Oka|vango (river,
  Africa)
okay +s +ed +ing
  (use OK)
Oka|yama (city,
  Japan)
Okee|cho¦bee,
  Lake (in USA)
O'Keeffe, Geor|gia
  (American
  painter)
Oke¦fe|no¦kee
  Swamp (in USA)
okey-doke
okey-dokey
Ok¦hotsk, Sea of
  (inlet, NW Pacific)
Oki|nawa (region
  and island, Japan)
Okla|homa (state,
  USA)
Okla|homa City
  (city, USA)
okra +s
okta
  plural okta *or*
  oktas

Olaf (Norwegian
  kings)
Öland (island,
  Baltic Sea)
Ol¦bers' para|dox
old +er +est
old age *noun*
old-age *attributive*
Old Bailey (law
  court, London)
olden
olde worlde (old
  and quaint.
  △ old-world)
old-fashioned
Old¦ham (town,
  England)
oldie +s
old¦ish
old-maidish
old|ness
Old Sarum (hill
  and former town,
  England)
old|ster +s
Old Style (dates)
old-style (*attributive*
  in a former style)
Old Testa|ment
  noun and
  attributive
old-time *attributive*
old-timer +s
Ol¦du|vai Gorge
  (in Tanzania)
Old Vic (theatre,
  London)
old-womanish
Old World (*noun*
  and attributive
  Europe, Asia, and
  Africa)
old-world (of old
  times. △ olde
  worlde)
ole|aceous
ole|agin|ous
ole|an|der +s
ole|as|ter +s
ole|ate +s
olec¦ra|non +s
ole|fin +s
ole|fine +s (use
  olefin)
oleic
ole¦if¦er|ous
oleo|graph +s
oleo|mar¦gar¦ine
  +s
ole¦om|eter +s
oleo|resin +s
oleum

O level +s
ol|fac|tion
ol|fac|tive
ol|fac|tory
Olga
olib|anum
oli|garch +s
oli|garch|ic
oli|garch|ic|al
oli|garch|ic|al|ly
oli|garchy
    oli|garch|ies
oligo|carp|ous
Oligo|cene *Geology*
oligo|chaete +s
oligo|dendro|cyte +s
oligo|mer +s
oli|gop|ol|ist +s
oli|gop|ol|is|tic
oli|gop|oly
    oli|gop|olies
oligo|sac|char|ide +s
oligo|troph|ic
oli|got|rophy
olio +s
oliv|aceous
oliv|ary
Olive (name)
olive +s (tree; fruit)
olive drab +s *noun and adjective*
olive-drab *attributive*
olive green +s *noun and adjective*
olive-green *attributive*
Oli|ver (in the *Chanson de Roland*; name)
Olives, Mount of (in Israel)
Olivia
Oliv|ier, Laur|ence (Lord Olivier, English actor and director)
oliv|ine +s
olla pod|rida +s
Ollie
olm +s
Olmec
    plural Olmec
Olmos (town, Peru)
Olo|mouc (city, Czech Republic)
ol|or|oso +s
Ol|sztyn (city, Poland)
Olwen

Olym|pia (site of pan-Hellenic Olympic Games; city, USA)
Olym|piad +s
Olym|pian +s
Olym|pic
Olym|pus, Mount (in Greece)
om (mantra. ⚠ ohm)
Omagh (town, Northern Ireland)
Omaha
    plural Omaha *or* Oma|has (American Indian)
Omaha (city, USA; D-Day beach)
Oman
Oman, Gulf of (inlet of Arabian Sea)
Omani +s
Omar (Muslim caliph)
Omar Khay|yám (Persian poet, mathematician, and astronomer)
oma|sum
    omasa
Omay|yad +s (use Umayyad)
ombre (card game)
ombré (shaded)
om|brogen|ous
om|brol|ogy
om|brom|eter +s
om|buds|man
    om|buds|men
Om|dur|man (city, Sudan)
omega +s
om|elet +s (use omelette)
om|elette +s
omen +s +ed +ing
omen|tal
omen|tum
    omenta
om|ertà
omi|cron +s
om|in|ous
om|in|ous|ly
om|in|ous|ness
omis|sible
omis|sion +s
omis|sive
omit
    omits

omit (*cont.*)
    omit|ted
    omit|ting
om|ma|tid|ium
    om|ma|tidia
omni|bus
    omni|buses
omni|com|pe|tence
omni|com|pe|tent
omni|dir|ec|tion|al
omni|fari|ous
om|nif|ic
om|nigen|ous
om|nipo|tence
om|nipo|tent
om|nipo|tent|ly
omni|pres|ence
omni|pres|ent
om|nis|ci|ence
om|nis|ci|ent
om|nis|ci|ent|ly
om|nium gath|erum
omni|vore +s
om|niv|or|ous
om|niv|or|ous|ly
om|niv|or|ous|ness
om|pha|los
om|phal|ot|omy
    om|phal|oto|mies
Omsk (city, Russia)
on
on|ager +s
onan|ism
onan|ist +s
onan|is|tic
Onas|sis, Aris|totle (Greek shipping magnate and tycoon)
Onas|sis, Jackie (US First Lady)
on board *adverbial and preposition*
on-board *attributive*
once
once-over +s
oncer +s
on|cho|cer|cia|sis
onco|gene +s
onco|gen|ic
on|cogen|ous
on|colo|gist +s
on|col|ogy
on|com|ing +s
on|cost +s
ondes mar|tenot
    plural ondes mar|tenot
on dit +s

one +s (single; number; a person. ⚠ won)
one-armed
one|fold
Onega, Lake (in Russia)
one-horse *attributive*
On|eida
    plural On|eida *or* On|eidas
O'Neill, Eu|gene (American playwright)
oneir|ic
oneiro|crit|ic +s
oneir|olo|gist +s
oneir|ology
oneiro|man|cer +s
oneiro|mancy
one-iron +s
one-liner +s
one-man *attributive*
one|ness
one-night stand +s
one-off +s
one-piece +s
oner +s (£1; remarkable person or thing)
oner|ous
oner|ous|ly
oner|ous|ness
one|self
one-sided
one-sidedly
one-sidedness
one-step
    one-steps
one-stop *attributive*
one-time *attributive*
one-to-one
one-two +s
one-up *adjective*
one-upmanship
one-way *adjective*
on|flow +s
on|glaze
on|going
on|going|ness
onion +s
onion-skin +s (paper)
on|iony
onkus
on-line
on|look|er +s
on|look|ing
only

only-begotten
on-off *adjective*
ono|mas|tic
ono|mas|tics
ono|mato|poeia
ono|mato|poe|ic
ono|mato|poeic|
   al|ly
ono|mato|po|et|ic
On|on|daga
  plural On|on|daga
  or On|on|da|gas
on|rush
  on|rushes
on-screen
onset +s *noun*
  (beginning)
on-set *adjective and*
  adverb (on a film
  set)
on|shore
on|side *Football etc.*
on side *Cricket*
on-site *attributive*
on|slaught +s
on-stage *attributive*
on-street *attributive*
On|tario (province,
  Canada)
On|tario, Lake (in
  N. America)
on-the-spot
  attributive
onto (use on to
  unless sense is 'to
  a position on' and
  is otherwise
  unclear)
on to
onto|gen|esis
onto|gen|et|ic
onto|gen|et|ic|
  al|ly
onto|gen|ic
onto|gen|ic|al|ly
on|togeny
onto|logic|al
onto|logic|al|ly
on|tolo|gist +s
ontol|ogy
onus
  onuses
on|ward
on|wards
ony|choph|oran
  +s
onym|ous
onyx
  onyxes
oo|cyte +s
oo|dles

oof
oofi|ness
oofy
  oofi|ier
  oofi|est
oog|am|ous
oog|amy
oo|gen|esis
oo|gen|et|ic
ooh +s +ed +ing
oo|lite +s
oo|lith +s
oo|lit|ic
oo|logic|al
oolo|gist +s
ool|ogy
oo|long
oo|miak +s (use
  umiak)
oom|pah +s
oomph
Oona *also* Oo|nagh
oo|phor|ec|tomy
  oo|phor|
    ec|to|mies
oops
oops-a-daisy
Oort, Jan
  Hen|drik (Dutch
  astronomer;
  cloud)
ooze
  oozes
  oozed
  ooz|ing
ooz|ily
oozi|ness
oozy
  oozi|ier
  oozi|est
op (= operation)
op. (= opus;
  operator)
opa|ci|fier +s
opa|cify
  opaci|fies
  opaci|fied
  opaci|fy|ing
opa|city
opah +s
opal +s
opal|esce
  opal|esces
  opal|esced
  opal|es|cing
opal|es|cence
opal|es|cent
opal|ine
opaque
opaque|ly
opaque|ness

op art
op. cit. (= opere
  citato)
OPEC
  (= Organization of
  Petroleum
  Exporting
  Countries)
Opel, Wil|helm
  von (German car
  maker)
open +s +ed +ing
open|able
open air *noun*
open-air *adjective*
open-armed
open|cast
open-door *adjective*
open-ended
open|er +s
open-eyed
open-faced
open-handed
open-handed|ly
open-handed|ness
open-hearted
open-hearted|ness
open-hearth
  pro|cess
open-heart
  sur|gery
open house
open|ing +s
open|ing time +s
open|ly
open-minded
open-minded|ly
open-minded|ness
open-mouthed
open-necked
  attributive
open|ness
open-plan
open pri|son +s
open-reel
open-side
  attributive
open-top
open-topped
open|work
opera +s (dramatic
  musical work)
opera (plural of
  opus)
op|er|abil|ity
op|er|able
opera buffa
  opera buffas *or*
  opere buffe
opéra com|ique
  op|éras com|iques

opera glasses
opera hat +s
opera house +s
op|er|and +s
opera seria
  opera serias *or*
  opere serie
op|er|ate
  op|er|ates
  op|er|ated
  op|er|at|ing
op|er|at|ic
op|er|at|ic|al|ly
op|er|at|ics
op|er|ation +s
op|er|ation|al
op|er|ation|al|ise
  Br. (use
  operationalize)
  op|er|ation|al|ises
  op|er|ation|al|
    ised
  op|er|ation|al|
    is|ing
op|er|ation|al|ize
  op|er|ation|al|izes
  op|er|ation|al|
    ized
  op|er|ation|al|
    iz|ing
op|er|ation|al|ly
op|era|tive +s
op|era|tive|ly
op|era|tive|ness
op|er|ator +s
oper|cu|lar
oper|cu|late
oper|cu|lum
  oper|cula
op|er|etta +s
op|eron +s
Ophe|lia
ophi|cleide +s
ophid|ian +s
ophi|ol|atry
ophi|olo|gist +s
ophi|ology
Ophir (*Bible* region)
oph|ite +s
oph|it|ic
Ophiu|chus
  (constellation)
oph|thal|mia
oph|thal|mic
oph|thal|mitis
oph|thal|mo|
  logic|al
oph|thal|molo|gist
  +s
oph|thal|mol|ogy
oph|thal|mo|scope
  +s

oph¦thal¦mo¦
       scop¦ic
oph¦thal¦mo¦
       scop¦ic¦al¦ly
oph¦thal¦
       mos¦copy
opi¦ate
  opi¦ates
  opi¦ated
  opi¦at¦ing
Opie, John
  (English painter)
opine
  opines
  opined
  opin¦ing
opin¦ion +s
opin¦ion¦ated
opin¦ion¦ated¦ly
opin¦ion¦ated¦ness
opin¦ion¦ative
opi¦oid +s
opi¦som¦eter +s
opis¦tho¦graph +s
opis¦thog¦raphy
opium
opium¦ise Br. (use
  opiumize)
  opium¦ises
  opium¦ised
  opium¦is¦ing
opium¦ize
  opium¦izes
  opium¦ized
  opium¦iz¦ing
opop¦anax
Oporto (city,
  Portugal)
opos¦sum +s
Op¦pen¦heimer,
  Ju¦lius Rob¦ert
  (American
  physicist)
op¦pi¦dan +s
oppo +s
op¦pon¦ency
op¦pon¦ent +s
op¦por¦tune
op¦por¦tune¦ly
op¦por¦tune¦ness
op¦por¦tun¦ism
op¦por¦tun¦ist +s
op¦por¦tun¦is¦tic
op¦por¦tun¦is¦tic¦
        al¦ly
op¦por¦tun¦ity
  op¦por¦tun¦ities
op¦pos¦able
op¦pose
  op¦poses
  op¦posed
  op¦pos¦ing

op¦poser +s
op¦pos¦ite +s
op¦pos¦ite¦ly
op¦pos¦ite¦ness
Op¦pos¦ition
  (party)
op¦pos¦ition +s
op¦pos¦ition¦al
op¦posi¦tive
op¦press
  op¦presses
  op¦pressed
  op¦press¦ing
op¦pres¦sion +s
op¦pres¦sive
op¦pres¦sive¦ly
op¦pres¦sive¦ness
op¦press¦or +s
op¦pro¦bri¦ous
op¦pro¦bri¦ous¦ly
op¦pro¦brium
  op¦pro¦bria
op¦pugn +s +ed
  +ing
op¦pug¦nance
op¦pug¦nancy
op¦pug¦nant
op¦pug¦na¦tion
op¦pugn¦er +s
opsi¦math +s
op¦sim¦athy
op¦son¦ic
op¦so¦nin +s
opt +s +ed +ing
opt¦ant +s
opta¦tive
opta¦tive¦ly
optic +s (measure
  for spirits) Propr.
optic (of the eye)
op¦tic¦al +s
op¦tic¦al¦ly
op¦ti¦cian +s
op¦tics
op¦tima
op¦ti¦mal
op¦ti¦mal¦ly
op¦ti¦misa¦tion Br.
  (use
  optimization)
op¦ti¦mise Br. (use
  optimize)
  op¦ti¦mises
  op¦ti¦mised
  op¦ti¦mis¦ing
op¦ti¦mism
op¦ti¦mist +s
op¦ti¦mis¦tic
op¦ti¦mis¦tic¦al¦ly
op¦ti¦miza¦tion
op¦ti¦mize
  op¦ti¦mizes

op¦ti¦mize (cont.)
  op¦ti¦mized
  op¦ti¦miz¦ing
op¦ti¦mum
  op¦tima or
  op¦ti¦mums
op¦tion +s
op¦tion¦al
op¦tion¦al¦ity
op¦tion¦al¦ly
opto¦elec¦tron¦ics
op¦tom¦eter +s
opto¦met¦ric
op¦tom¦etrist +s
op¦tom¦etry
opto¦phone +s
opt-out +s noun
  and attributive
opu¦lence
opu¦lent
opu¦lent¦ly
opun¦tia +s
opus
  opuses or opera
opus¦cule +s
opus¦cu¦lum
  opus¦cula
Opus Dei
  (organization)
opus dei (worship)
or (conjunction;
  Heraldry gold.
  △ oar, ore)
orach +s (use
  orache)
or¦ache +s
or¦acle +s
or¦acu¦lar
or¦acu¦lar¦ity
or¦acu¦lar¦ly
oracy
Ora¦dea (city,
  Romania)
oral +s (of or
  pertaining to the
  mouth. △ aural)
oral¦ism
oral¦ist +s
oral¦ity
or¦al¦ly
Oran (port, Algeria)
Or¦ange (town,
  France)
Or¦ange (Dutch
  royal house)
or¦ange +s
or¦ange¦ade
Or¦ange Free
  State (province,
  South Africa)
Or¦ange¦ism

Or¦ange¦man
  Or¦ange¦men
Or¦ange Order (in
  Northern Ireland)
Or¦ange River (in
  South Africa)
or¦an¦gery
  or¦an¦ger¦ies
or¦ange stick +s
orange-wood
orang-outang +s
  (use orang-utan)
orang-utan +s
Or¦anje¦stad
  (capital of Aruba)
Ora¦şul Sta¦lin
  (former name of
  Braşov)
orate
  orates
  orated
  orat¦ing
ora¦tion +s
ora¦tor +s
ora¦tor¦ial
ora¦tor¦ian +s
ora¦tor¦ic¦al
ora¦torio +s
ora¦tory
  ora¦tor¦ies
orb +s
or¦bicu¦lar
or¦bicu¦lar¦ity
or¦bicu¦lar¦ly
or¦bicu¦late
Or¦bi¦son, Roy
  (American singer)
orbit +s +ed +ing
or¦bit¦al +s
or¦bit¦er +s
orc +s (monster.
  △ auk)
orca +s
Or¦ca¦dian +s
Or¦cagna (Italian
  painter)
orch¦ard +s
orch¦ard¦ing
orch¦ard¦ist +s
orch¦ard¦man
  orch¦ard¦men
or¦ches¦tic
or¦ches¦tra +s
or¦ches¦tral
or¦ches¦tral¦ly
or¦ches¦trate
  or¦ches¦trates
  or¦ches¦trated
  or¦ches¦trat¦ing
or¦ches¦tra¦tion +s
or¦ches¦tra¦tor +s
or¦ches¦trina +s

or¦chid +s
or¦chid|aceous
or¦chid|ist +s
or¦chid|ology
or¦chil +s
or¦chilla +s
or¦chis
  or|chises
or|chi¦tis
orcin
or|cinol
Orczy, Baron|ess
  (Hungarian-born
  British writer)
or¦dain +s +ed
  +ing
or¦dain¦er +s
or¦dain|ment +s
or¦deal +s
order +s +ed +ing
order book +s
or¦der¦er +s
order form +s
or¦der|ing +s
or¦der¦li|ness
or¦der¦ly
  or¦der|lies
order paper +s
or¦din|aire (in 'vin
  ordinaire')
or¦din¦al +s
or¦din|ance +s
  (decree; rite.
  △ ordnance,
  ordonnance)
or¦din|and +s
or¦din¦ar¦ily
or¦din¦ari|ness
or¦din|ary
  or¦din|ar¦ies
or¦din|ate +s
  Mathematics
or¦din|ation +s
ord|nance (guns.
  △ ordinance,
  ordonnance)
Or¦do|vi¦cian
  Geology
ord¦ure +s
Ord¦zho|ni¦kidze
  (former name of
  Vladikavkaz)
ore +s (mineral.
  △ oar, or)
øre
  plural øre

øre (cont.)
  (Danish or
  Norwegian
  currency)
öre
  plural öre
  (Swedish
  currency)
oread +s
Öre¦bro (city,
  Sweden)
or¦ec|tic
ore|gano
Ore¦gon (state,
  USA)
Orel (city, Russia)
Ore Moun|tains
  (English name for
  the Erzgebirge)
Oren|burg (city,
  Russia)
Oreo +s Propr.
ore|og¦raphy (use
  orography)
Ores|tes Greek
  Mythology
Øre|sund (channel
  between Sweden
  and Zealand)
ore|weed (use
  oarweed)
orfe +s (fish)
Orff, Carl (German
  composer)
organ +s
organ-blower +s
or¦gan|die Br. +s
or¦gandy Am.
  or¦gan|dies
or¦gan|elle +s
organ-grinder +s
or¦gan|ic
or¦gan¦ic|al¦ly
or¦gan¦is|able Br.
  (use organizable)
or¦gan|isa¦tion Br.
  +s (use
  organization)
or¦gan|isa¦tion|al
  Br. (use
  organizational)
or¦gan|isa¦tion|
  al¦ly Br. (use
  organizationally)
or¦gan|ise Br. (use
  organize)
  or¦gan|ises
  or¦gan|ised
  or¦gan|is¦ing
or¦gan|iser Br. +s
  (use organizer)
or¦gan|ism +s

or¦gan|ist +s
or¦gan|iz|able
or¦gan|iza|tion +s
or¦gan|iza|tion|al
or¦gan|iza|tion|
              al¦ly
or¦gan|ize
  or¦gan|izes
  or¦gan|ized
  or¦gan|iz¦ing
or¦gan|izer +s
organ loft +s
or¦gano|chlor¦ine
  +s
or¦gano|lep¦tic
or¦gano|met¦al|lic
or¦ga¦non +s
or¦gano|
  phos¦phate +s
or¦gano|
  phos¦phorus
or¦gano|sul¦fur Am.
or¦gano|sul¦phur Br.
or¦gano|ther¦apy
organ pipe +s
organ-screen +s
organ stop +s
or¦ganum
  or¦gana
or¦ganza +s
or¦gan|zine +s
or¦gasm +s
or¦gas¦mic
or¦gas¦mic|al¦ly
or¦gas|tic
or¦gas¦tic|al¦ly
or¦geat +s
or¦gi|as¦tic
or¦gi|as¦tic|al¦ly
or¦gu|lous
orgy
  or¦gies
oribi
  plural oribi or
  ori¦bis
oriel +s
Ori¦ent, the (the
  East)
ori¦ent +s +ed
  +ing (to place or
  direct)
Orien|tal +s (of the
  East; person)
orien|tal (eastern)
orien¦tal|ise Br.
  (use orientalize)
  orien¦tal|ises
  orien¦tal|ised
  orien¦tal|is¦ing
orien¦tal|ism
orien¦tal|ist +s

orien¦tal|ize
  orien¦tal|izes
  orien¦tal|ized
  orien¦tal|iz¦ing
orien¦tal|ly
orien|tate
  orien|tates
  orien|tated
  orien|tat¦ing
orien|ta¦tion +s
orien|ta¦tion|al
orien|teer +s +ing
ori|fice +s
ori|flamme +s
ori|gami
ori¦gan +s
ori|ganum +s
Ori¦gen (early
  Christian scholar)
ori¦gin +s
ori¦gin¦al +s
ori¦gin|al¦ity
ori¦gin|al¦ly
ori¦gin|ate
  ori¦gin|ates
  ori¦gin|ated
  ori¦gin|at¦ing
ori¦gin|ation +s
ori¦gina|tive
ori¦gin|ator +s
Ori¦mul¦sion Propr.
ori|nasal
O-ring +s
Ori|noco (river, S.
  America)
ori¦ole +s
Orion (Greek
  Mythology;
  constellation)
ori¦son +s
Orissa (state, India)
Oriya
  Ori¦yas
ork +s (monster;
  use orc. △ auk)
Ork¦ney (= Orkney
  Islands)
Ork¦ney Is|lands
  (off Scotland)
Ork|neys
  (= Orkney
  Islands)
Or|lando (city,
  USA)
orle +s (Heraldry
  border. △ all, awl)
Or¦lé¦an|ais
  plural Or¦lé¦an|ais
Or¦lean|ist +s
Or|leans (English
  name for Orléans)

Or|léans (city, France)
Orlon *Propr.*
orlop +s
Or|mazd (alternative name for Ahura Mazda)
ormer +s
or|molu
Ormuz (alternative name for Hormuz)
or|na|ment +s +ed +ing
or|na|men|tal +s
or|na|men|tal|ism
or|na|men|tal|ist +s
or|na|men|tal|ly
or|na|men|ta|tion +s
or|nate
or|nate|ly
or|nate|ness
or|neri|ness
or|nery
or|nith|ic
or|ni|this|chian +s
or|ni|tho|logic|al
or|ni|tho|logic| al|ly
or|ni|tholo|gist +s
or|ni|thol|ogy
or|ni|tho|mancy
or|ni|tho|pod +s
or|ni|tho| rhyn|chus
or|ni|tho| rhyn|chuses
or|ni|thos|copy
oro|gen|esis
oro|gen|et|ic
oro|gen|ic
or|ogeny
oro|graph|ic
oro|graph|ic|al
or|og|raphy
oro|ide +s
oro|logic|al
or|olo|gist +s
or|ol|ogy
Oron|tes (river, Asia)
oro|tund
orphan +s +ed +ing
or|phan|age +s
or|phan|hood
or|phan|ise *Br.* (use orphanize)
or|phan|ises

or|phan|ise (*cont.*)
or|phan|ised
or|phan|is|ing
or|phan|ize
or|phan|izes
or|phan|ized
or|phan|iz|ing
Orph|ean
Orph|eus *Greek Mythology*
Orph|ic
Orph|ism (ancient mystic religion; art movement)
or|phrey +s
or|pi|ment
orpin +s (use orpine)
or|pine +s
orra
or|rery
or|rer|ies
orris
or|rises
orris-powder
orris root
Orsk (city, Russia)
Orson
or|tan|ique +s
Or|tega, Dan|iel (Nicaraguan president)
ortho|ceph|al|ic
ortho|chro|mat|ic
ortho|clase +s
ortho|don|tia
ortho|don|tic
ortho|don|tics
ortho|don|tist +s
ortho|dox
ortho|dox|ly
ortho|doxy
ortho|dox|ies
ortho|ep|ic
ortho|ep|ist +s
ortho|epy
ortho|gen|esis
ortho|gen|et|ic
ortho|gen|et|ic| al|ly
orth|og|nath|ous
orth|og|on|al +s
orth|og|on|al|ly
orth|og|raph|er +s
ortho|graph|ic
ortho|graph|ic|al
ortho|graph|ic| al|ly
orth|og|raphy
ortho-hydrogen
ortho|paed|ic *Br.*
ortho|paed|ics *Br.*

ortho|paed|ist *Br.* +s
ortho|ped|ic *Am.*
ortho|ped|ics *Am.*
ortho|ped|ist *Am.* +s
orth|op|teran +s
orth|op|ter|ous
orth|op|tic
orth|op|tics
orth|op|tist +s
ortho|rhom|bic
ortho|tone +s
or|to|lan +s
Orton, Ar|thur (English butcher, the 'Tichborne claimant')
Orton, Joe (English playwright)
Oruro (city, Bolivia)
Or|vi|eto (town, Italy)
Or|well, George (English writer)
Or|well|ian
oryx
plural oryx
Osage or|ange
Osaka (city, Japan)
Os|bert
Os|borne, John (English dramatist)
Oscan
Oscar +s (film award; name)
os|cil|late
os|cil|lates
os|cil|lated
os|cil|lat|ing
os|cil|la|tion +s
os|cil|la|tor +s
os|cil|la|tory
os|cil|lo|gram +s
os|cil|lo|graph +s
os|cil|lo|graph|ic
os|cil|log|raphy
os|cil|lo|scope +s
os|cil|lo|scop|ic
os|cine
os|cin|ine
os|ci|ta|tion +s
os|cula (plural of osculum)
os|cu|lant
os|cu|lar *adjective*
os|cu|late
os|cu|lates
os|cu|lated
os|cu|lat|ing

os|cu|la|tion +s
os|cu|la|tory
os|cu|lum
os|cula
Osh (city, Kyrgyzstan)
Osh|awa (city, Canada)
osier +s
osier bed +s
Osi|jek (city, Croatia)
Os|iris *Egyptian Mythology*
Osler, Wil|liam (Canadian-born physician and classical scholar)
Oslo (capital of Norway)
Osman (founder of Turkish Ottoman or Osmanli dynasty)
Os|manli +s
osmic
os|mic|al|ly
os|mium
osmo|regu|la|tion
os|mo|sis
os|mo|ses
os|mot|ic
os|mot|ic|al|ly
os|mund +s
os|munda +s
Os|na|brück (city, Germany)
os|prey +s
Ossa, Mount (in Greece or Tasmania)
os|sein
os|se|ous
Os|sete +s
Os|se|tia, North and South (regions, Russia and Georgia)
Os|se|tian +s
ossia
Os|sian (legendary Irish warrior)
Os|si|an|ic
os|sicle +s
Ossie (name)
Ossie +s (Australian; use Aussie)
os|sif|ic
os|si|fi|ca|tion +s
os|si|frage +s

os¦sify
  os¦si¦fies
  os¦si¦fied
  os¦si¦fy¦ing
osso bucco
os¦su¦ary
  os¦su¦ar¦ies
Ost¦ade, Adri¦aen
  van (Dutch
  painter)
os¦te¦itis
Ost¦end (port,
  Belgium)
os¦ten¦sible
os¦ten¦sibly
os¦ten¦sive
os¦ten¦sive¦ly
os¦ten¦sive¦ness
os¦ten¦sory
  os¦ten¦sor¦ies
os¦ten¦ta¦tion
os¦ten¦ta¦tious
os¦ten¦ta¦tious¦ly
osteo¦arth¦rit¦ic
osteo¦arth¦ritis
osteo¦gen¦esis
osteo¦gen¦et¦ic
oste¦ogeny
oste¦og¦raphy
osteo¦logic¦al
osteo¦logic¦al¦ly
oste¦olo¦gist +s
oste¦ology
osteo¦mal¦acia
osteo¦mal¦acic
osteo¦mye¦litis
osteo¦path +s
osteo¦path¦ic
oste¦op¦athy
osteo¦phyte +s
osteo¦por¦osis
Ostia (ancient city,
  Italy)
os¦tin¦ato +s
ost¦ium
  ostia
ost¦ler +s
Ost¦mark +s
  (former East
  German currency)
Ost¦poli¦tik
os¦tra¦cise Br. (use
  ostracize)
  os¦tra¦cises
  os¦tra¦cised
  os¦tra¦cis¦ing
os¦tra¦cism
os¦tra¦cize
  os¦tra¦cizes
  os¦tra¦cized
  os¦tra¦ciz¦ing

os¦tra¦con
  os¦traca
Ost¦rava (city,
  Czech Republic)
os¦trich
  os¦triches
Os¦tro¦goth +s
Os¦tro¦goth¦ic
Ost¦wald,
  Fried¦rich
  Wil¦helm
  (German chemist)
Os¦wald (English
  saint; name)
Os¦wald, Lee
  Har¦vey
  (American alleged
  assassin of John F.
  Kennedy)
Oś¦wię¦cim (Polish
  name for
  Auschwitz)
Otago (region, New
  Zealand)
otary
  otar¦ies
other +s
other-direct¦ed
other¦ness
other¦where
other¦wise
other-worldli¦ness
other-worldly
Oth¦man
  (alternative name
  for Osman)
Otho, Mar¦cus
  Sal¦vius (Roman
  emperor)
otic
oti¦ose
oti¦ose¦ly
oti¦ose¦ness
Otis, Eli¦sha
  Graves
  (American
  inventor)
ot¦itis
oto¦laryn¦go¦
        logic¦al
oto¦laryn¦golo¦gist
  +s
oto¦laryn¦gol¦ogy
oto¦lith +s
oto¦lith¦ic
oto¦logic¦al
ot¦olo¦gist +s
otol¦ogy
Otomi
  plural Otomi
oto¦rhino¦laryn¦
        gol¦ogy

oto¦scope +s
oto¦scop¦ic
Ot¦ranto, Strait of
  (in Mediterranean)
ot¦tava rima
Ot¦tawa (capital of
  Canada)
otter +s
otter-board +s
otter-dog +s
Otto (German king)
Otto, Niko¦laus
  Au¦gust (German
  engineer)
otto (essential oil)
Otto¦line
Ot¦to¦man +s
  (dynasty of
  Osman; Turkish
  person)
ot¦to¦man +s (seat)
Ot¦to¦man Porte,
  the
Otway, Thomas
  (English
  playwright)
oua¦bain
Ouaga¦dou¦gou
  (capital of
  Burkina)
ou¦bli¦ette +s
ouch
Ouden¦arde (town
  and battle site,
  Belgium)
Oudh (region,
  India)
ought (auxiliary
  verb; nought.
  △ aught)
oughtn't (= ought
  not)
ou¦giya +s (use
  ouguiya)
ou¦guiya +s
Ouida (English
  novelist)
Ouija (board) Propr.
Oulu (province,
  Finland)
ounce +s
our (belonging to
  us. △ hour)
ours (the one(s)
  belonging to us.
  △ hours)
our¦self (prefer
  ourselves)
our¦selves
Ouse (rivers,
  England)
ousel +s (use
  ouzel)

oust +s +ed +ing
oust¦er +s
out +s +ed +ing
  (not in etc. △ owt)
out¦act +s +ed
  +ing
out¦age +s
out and out
out-and-outer +s
out¦back +s
out¦back¦er +s
out¦bal¦ance
  out¦bal¦ances
  out¦bal¦anced
  out¦bal¦an¦cing
out¦bid
  out¦bids
  out¦bid
  out¦bid¦ding
out¦bid¦der +s
out¦blaze
  out¦blazes
  out¦blazed
  out¦blaz¦ing
out¦board +s
out¦bound
out¦brave
  out¦braves
  out¦braved
  out¦brav¦ing
out¦break +s
out¦breed
  out¦breeds
  out¦bred
  out¦breed¦ing
out¦build¦ing +s
out¦burst +s
out¦cast +s (person
  cast out)
out¦caste +s
  (Indian without
  caste)
out¦class
  out¦classes
  out¦classed
  out¦class¦ing
out¦come +s
out¦com¦pete
  out¦com¦petes
  out¦com¦peted
  out¦com¦pet¦ing
out¦crop
  out¦crops
  out¦cropped
  out¦crop¦ping
out¦cry
  out¦cries
out¦dance
  out¦dances
  out¦danced
  out¦dan¦cing

out|dare
  out|dares
  out|dared
  out|dar¦ing
out|dated
out|dated|ness
out|dis¦tance
  out|dis¦tances
  out|dis¦tanced
  out|dis¦tan¦cing
outdo
  out|does
  out|did
  out|do¦ing
  out|done
out|door
out|doors
outer +s
outer|most
outer space
outer|wear
out|face
  out|faces
  out|faced
  out|facing
out|fall +s
out|field +s +ed
  +ing
out|field¦er +s
out|fight
  out|fights
  out|fought
  out|fight¦ing
out|fit
  out|fits
  out|fit¦ted
  out|fit|ting
out|fit¦ter +s
out|flank +s +ed
  +ing
out|flow +s
out|flung
out|fly
  out|flies
  out|flew
  out|fly|ing
  out|flown
out|fox
  out|foxes
  out|foxed
  out|fox|ing
out¦gas
  out|gasses
  out|gassed
  out|gas¦sing
out|gen|eral
  out|gen¦er¦als
  out|gen¦er¦alled
  Br.
  out|gen¦er¦aled
  Am.
  out|gen¦er¦al|ling

out|gen¦eral (*cont.*)
  Br.
  out|gen¦er¦al|ing
  Am.
outgo
  out|goes
  out|went
  out|going
  out|gone
out|going +s
out|grow
  out|grows
  out|grew
  out|grow|ing
  out|grown
out|growth +s
out|guess
  out|guesses
  out|guessed
  out|guess|ing
out¦gun
  out|guns
  out|gunned
  out|gun|ning
out|house +s
out|ing +s
out|jockey +s +ed
  +ing
out|jump +s +ed
  +ing
out|land¦er +s
out|land|ish
out|land|ish|ly
out|land|ish|ness
out|last +s +ed
  +ing
out|law +s +ed
  +ing
out|law¦ry
out¦lay +s
out¦let +s
out¦lier +s
out|line
  out|lines
  out|lined
  out|lin¦ing
out|live
  out|lives
  out|lived
  out|liv¦ing
out|look +s
out|ly¦ing
out|man¦euver
  Am. +s +ed +ing
out|man¦oeuvre
  Br.
  out|man¦oeuvres
  out|man¦oeuvred
  out|
    man¦oeuv¦ring
out|match
  out|matches

out|match (*cont.*)
  out|matched
  out|match|ing
out|meas¦ure
  out|meas¦ures
  out|meas¦ured
  out|meas¦ur¦ing
out|moded
out|moded¦ly
out|moded|ness
out|most
out|num¦ber +s
  +ed +ing
out-of-body
  attributive
out of bounds
out-of-court
  attributive
out of date
  adjective
out-of-date
  attributive
out of doors
out-of-pocket
  attributive
out-of-school
  attributive
out-of-season
  attributive
out-of-the-way
  attributive
out-of-town
  attributive
out of work
  adjective
out-of-work
  attributive
out|pace
  out|paces
  out|paced
  out|pacing
out|pa¦tient +s
out|per|form +s
  +ed +ing
out|per¦form|ance
  +s
out|place|ment +s
out|play +s +ed
  +ing
out|point +s +ed
  +ing
out|port +s
out|post +s
out|pour|ing +s
out|psych +s +ed
  +ing
out|put
  out|puts
  out|put *or*
  out|put|ted
  out|put|ting

out|rage
  out|rages
  out|raged
  out|raging
out|ra¦geous
out|ra¦geous¦ly
out|ra¦geous|ness
out|ran
out|range
  out|ranges
  out|ranged
  out|ran¦ging
out|rank +s +ed
  +ing
outré
out|reach
  out|reaches
  out|reached
  out|reach|ing
out-relief
out|ride
  out|rides
  out|rode
  out|rid¦ing
  out|rid¦den
out|rider +s
out|rigged
out|rig¦ger +s
out|right
out|right|ness
out|rival
  out|rivals
  out|rivalled *Br.*
  out|rivaled *Am.*
  out|rival|ling *Br.*
  out|rival|ing *Am.*
outro +s
out|rode
out|run
  out|runs
  out¦ran
  out|run|ning
  out|run
out|rush
  out|rushes
out|sail +s +ed
  +ing
out|sat
out|sell
  out|sells
  out|sold
  out|sell|ing
out¦set +s
out|shine
  out|shines
  out|shone
  out|shin|ing
out|shoot
  out|shoots
  out|shot
  out|shoot|ing
out|side +s

out|sider+s
out|sit
  out|sits
  out|sat
  out|sit|ting
out|size+s
out|size|ness
out|skirts
out|smart+s +ed
  +ing
out|sold
out|source
  out|sources
  out|sourced
  out|sour|cing
out|span
  out|spans
  out|spanned
  out|span|ning
out|spend
  out|spends
  out|spent
  out|spend|ing
out|spoken
out|spoken|ly
out|spoken|ness
out|spread
  out|spreads
  out|spread
  out|spread|ing
out|stand|ing
out|stand|ing|ly
out|stare
  out|stares
  out|stared
  out|star|ing
out|sta|tion+s
out|stay+s +ed
  +ing
out|step
  out|steps
  out|stepped
  out|step|ping
out|stretch
  out|stretches
  out|stretched
  out|stretch|ing
out|strip
  out|strips
  out|stripped
  out|strip|ping
out-swinger+s
out-take+s
out-talk +s +ed
  +ing
out-think
  out-thinks
  out-thought
  out-thinking
out-thrust
  out-thrusts

out-thrust (*cont.*)
  out-thrust
  out-thrust|ing
out-top
  out-tops
  out-topped
  out-topping
out-tray+s
out-turn+s
out|value
  out|values
  out|valued
  out|valu|ing
out|vote
  out|votes
  out|voted
  out|vot|ing
out|walk+s +ed
  +ing
out|ward
outward-looking
out|ward|ly
out|ward|ness
out|wards
out|wash
  out|washes
out|watch
  out|watches
  out|watched
  out|watch|ing
out|wear
  out|wears
  out|wore
  out|wear|ing
  out|worn
out|weigh +s +ed
  +ing
out|went
out|wit
  out|wits
  out|wit|ted
  out|wit|ting
out|with
out|wore
out|work+s
out|work|er+s
out|work|ing
out|worn
ouzel+s
ouzo+s
ova (plural of
  ovum. △ over)
oval+s
oval|ity
oval|ly
oval|ness
Ov|ambo
  plural Ov|ambo or
  Ov|am|bos
Ov|ambo|land
  (homeland,
  Namibia)

ovar|ian
ovari|ec|tomy
  ovari|ec|to|mies
ovari|ot|omy
  ovari|oto|mies
ovar|itis
ovary
  ovar|ies
ovate
ova|tion+s
ova|tion|al
oven+s
oven|bird+s
oven|proof
oven-ready
oven|ware
over+s (across;
  past; above; etc.;
  Cricket. △ ova)
over-abundance
  +s
over-abundant
over-abundant|ly
over|achieve
  over|achieves
  over|achieved
  over|achiev|ing
over|achieve|ment
  +s
over|achiever+s
over|act +s +ed
  +ing
over|active
over|activ|ity
over|age +s
  (surplus)
over-age (*attributive*
  above age limit)
over|all +s
over|alled
over|am|bi|tion
over|am|bi|tious
over|
      am|bi|tious|ly
over-anxiety
over-anxious
over-anxious|ly
over|arch
  over|arches
  over|arched
  over|arch|ing
over|arm
over|ate (past tense
  of overeat.
  △ overrate)
over|awe
  over|awes
  over|awed
  over|aw|ing
over|bal|ance
  over|bal|ances

over|bal|ance
  (*cont.*)
  over|bal|anced
  over|bal|an|cing
over|bear
  over|bears
  over|bore
  over|bear|ing
  over|borne
over|bear|ing|ly
over|bear|ing|ness
over|bid
  over|bids
  over|bid
  over|bid|ding
over|bid|der+s
over|bite
over|blouse+s
over|blow
  over|blows
  over|blew
  over|blow|ing
  over|blown
over|board
over|bold
over|book +s +ed
  +ing
over|boot+s
over|bore
over|borne
over-borrow+s
  +ed +ing
over|bought
over|breed
  over|breeds
  over|bred
  over|breed|ing
over|brim
  over|brims
  over|brimmed
  over|brim|ming
over|build
  over|builds
  over|built
  over|build|ing
over|bur|den+s
  +ed +ing
over|bur|den|
        some
Over|bury,
  Thomas (English
  poet and courtier)
over|busy
over|buy
  over|buys
  over|bought
  over|buy|ing
over|call +s +ed
  +ing
over|came
over|cap|acity

over|cap|it|al|ised
  Br. (use
  overcapitalized)
over|cap|it|al|ized
over|care|ful
over|care|ful|ly
over|cast
  over|casts
  over|cast
  over|cast|ing
over|cau|tion
over|cau|tious
over|cau|tious|ly
over|cau|tious|
      ness
over|charge
  over|charges
  over|charged
  over|char|ging
over|check +s
over|cloud +s +ed
  +ing
over|coat +s
over|come
  over|comes
  over|came
  over|com|ing
  over|come
over|com|mit
  over|com|mits
  over|com|mit|ted
  over|com|mit|
      ting
over|com|pen|sate
  over|com|pen|
      sates
  over|com|pen|
      sated
  over|com|pen|
      sat|ing
over|com|pen|
      sa|tion
over|com|pen|
      sa|tory
over|con|fi|dence
over|con|fi|dent
over|con|fi|dent|ly
over|cook +s +ed
  +ing
over|crit|ic|al
over|crop
  over|crops
  over|cropped
  over|crop|ping
over|crowd +s +ed
  +ing
over-curios|ity
over-curious
over-curious|ly
over-delicacy
over-delicate

over|de|ter|min|
      ation
over|de|ter|mine
over|de|ter|mines
over|de|ter|mined
over|
  de|ter|min|ing
over|de|velop +s
  +ed +ing
over|do
  over|does
  over|did
  over|do|ing
  over|done
over|dos|age +s
over|dose
  over|doses
  over|dosed
  over|dos|ing
over|draft +s
over|drama|tise
  Br. (use
  overdramatize)
  over|drama|tises
  over|drama|tised
  over|drama|
      tis|ing
over|drama|tize
  over|drama|tizes
  over|drama|tized
  over|drama|
      tiz|ing
over|draw
  over|draws
  over|drew
  over|draw|ing
  over|drawn
over|draw|er +s
over|dress
  over|dresses
  over|dressed
  over|dress|ing
over|drink
  over|drinks
  over|drank
  over|drink|ing
  over|drunk
over|drive +s
over|dub
  over|dubs
  over|dubbed
  over|dub|bing
over|due
over|eager
over|eager|ly
over|eager|ness
over|eat
  over|eats
  over|ate
  over|eat|ing
over-elabor|ate
over-elabor|ate|ly

over-elabor|ation
over-emotion|al
over-
  emotion|al|ly
over|empha|sis
over|empha|sise
  Br. (use
  overemphasize)
  over|empha|sises
  over|empha|sised
  over|
      empha|sis|ing
over|empha|size
  over|empha|sizes
  over|empha|sized
  over|
      empha|siz|ing
over|enthu|si|asm
over|enthu|si|
      as|tic
over|enthu|si|
      as|tic|al|ly
over|esti|mate
  over|esti|mates
  over|esti|mated
  over|esti|mat|ing
over|esti|mation
  +s
over|ex|cite
  over|ex|cites
  over|ex|cited
  over|ex|cit|ing
over|ex|cite|ment
over-exercise
  over-exercises
  over-exercised
  over-exercis|ing
over|ex|ert +s +ed
  +ing
over|ex|er|tion +s
over|ex|pose
  over|ex|poses
  over|ex|posed
  over|ex|pos|ing
over|ex|pos|ure +s
over|ex|tend +s
  +ed +ing
over|fall +s
over|fa|mil|iar
over|fa|mil|iar|ity
over|fa|tigue
over|feed
  over|feeds
  over|fed
  over|feed|ing
over|fill +s +ed
  +ing
over|fine
over|fish
  over|fishes
  over|fished
  over|fish|ing

over|flight +s
over|flow +s +ed
  +ing
over|fly
  over|flies
  over|flew
  over|flown
  over|fly|ing
over|fold +s
over|fond
over|fond|ly
over|fond|ness
over|ful|fil *Br.*
  over|ful|fils
  over|ful|filled
  over|ful|fil|ling
over|ful|fill *Am.*
  over|ful|fills
  over|ful|filled
  over|ful|fill|ing
over|ful|fil|ment
  Am.
over|ful|fil|ment
  Br.
over|full
over|gar|ment +s
over|gen|er|al|
  isa|tion *Br.* +s
  (use overgeneral-
  ization)
over|gen|er|al|ise
  Br. (use
  overgeneralize)
  over|gen|er|al|
      ises
  over|gen|er|al|
      ised
  over|gen|er|al|
      is|ing
over|gen|er|al|
      iza|tion +s
over|gen|er|al|ize
  over|gen|er|al|
      izes
  over|gen|er|al|
      ized
  over|gen|er|al|
      iz|ing
over|gen|er|ous
over|gen|er|ous|ly
over|glaze
  over|glazes
  over|glazed
  over|glaz|ing
over|graze
  over|grazes
  over|grazed
  over|graz|ing
over|ground
over|grow
  over|grows
  over|grew

over|grow (*cont.*)
  over|grow|ing
  over|grown
over|growth +s
over|hand
over|hang
  over|hangs
  over|hung
  over|hang|ing
over|haste
over|hasti|ly
over|hasty
over|haul +s +ed
  +ing
over|head +s
over|hear
  over|hears
  over|heard
  over|hear|ing
over|heat +s +ed
  +ing
over|hung
Over|ijs|sel
  (province, the
  Netherlands)
over-indulge
  over-indulges
  over-indulged
  over-indulging
over-indulgence
  +s
over-indulgent
over-inflated
over-insurance
over-insure
  over-insures
  over-insured
  over-insuring
over|issue
  over|issues
  over|issued
  over|issu|ing
over|joyed
over|kill +s +ed
  +ing
over|laden
over|laid
over|lain
over|land
over|land|er +s
over|lap
  over|laps
  over|lapped
  over|lap|ping
over-large
over|lay
  over|lays
  over|laid
  over|lay|ing
over|leaf
over|leap
  over|leaps

over|leap (*cont.*)
  over|leaped *or*
  over|leapt
  over|leap|ing
over|lie
  over|lies
  over|lay
  over|ly|ing
  over|lain
over|load +s +ed
  +ing
over|long
over|look +s +ed
  +ing
over|look|er +s
over|lord +s
over|lord|ship +s
over|ly
  over|ly|ing
over|man
  over|mans
  over|manned
  over|man|ning
over|man|tel +s
over-many
over|mas|ter +s
  +ed +ing
over|mas|tery
over|match
  over|matches
  over|matched
  over|match|ing
over|meas|ure
  over|meas|ures
  over|meas|ured
  over|meas|ur|ing
over-mighty
over|much
over|nice
over|nice|ness
over|nicety
over|night
over|night|er +s
over-optimis|tic
over|paid
over|paint +s +ed
  +ing
over|part|ed
over-particu|lar
over|pass
  over|passes
  over|passed
  over|pass|ing
over|pay
  over|pays
  over|paid
  over|pay|ing
over|pay|ment +s
over|per|suade
  over|per|suades
  over|per|suaded
  over|per|suad|ing

over|pitch
  over|pitches
  over|pitched
  over|pitch|ing
over|play +s +ed
  +ing
over|plus
  over|pluses
over|popu|lated
over|popu|la|tion
over|power +s +ed
  +ing
over|power|ing|ly
over|praise
  over|praises
  over|praised
  over|prais|ing
over-prescribe
  over-prescribes
  over-prescribed
  over-prescrib|ing
over|price
  over|prices
  over|priced
  over|pricing
over|print +s +ed
  +ing
over|pro|duce
  over|pro|duces
  over|pro|duced
  over|pro|du|cing
over|pro|duc|tion
  +s
over|proof
over|pro|tect +s
  +ed +ing
over|pro|tec|tion
over|pro|tect|ive
over|quali|fied
over|ran
over|rate
  over|rates
  over|rated
  over|rat|ing
over|reach
  over|reaches
  over|reached
  over|reach|ing
over|react +s +ed
  +ing
over|reac|tion +s
over-refine
  over-refines
  over-refined
  over-refining
over-refine|ment
  +s
over|ride
  over|rides
  over|rode
  over|rid|ing
  over|rid|den

over|rider +s
over|ripe
over|ruff +s +ed
  +ing
over|rule
  over|rules
  over|ruled
  over|rul|ing
over|run
  over|runs
  over|ran
  over|run
  over|run|ning
over|sail|ing
over|saw
over|scru|pu|lous
over|sea (abroad)
over|seas (abroad)
over|see
  over|sees
  over|saw
  over|seen
  over|see|ing
  (supervise)
over|seer +s
over|sell
  over|sells
  over|sold
  over|sell|ing
over|sen|si|tive
over|sen|si|tive|
         ness
over|sen|si|tiv|ity
over|set
  over|sets
  over|set
  over|set|ting
over|sew +s +ed
  +ing
over|sexed
over|shadow +s
  +ed +ing
over|shoe +s
over|shoot
  over|shoots
  over|shot
  over|shoot|ing
over|side
over|sight +s
over|sim|pli|fi|
         ca|tion
over|sim|plify
  over|sim|pli|fies
  over|sim|pli|fied
  over|sim|pli|fy|
         ing
over|size
over|sized
over|skirt +s
over|slaugh +s
  +ed +ing

over|sleep
over|sleeps
over|slept
over|sleep|ing
over|sleeve +s
over|sold
over|so|lici|tous
over|so|lici|tude
over|soul
over|spe|cial|
  isa|tion *Br.*
  (use overspecial-
  ization)
over|spe|cial|ise
  Br. (use
  overspecialize)
over|spe|cial|ises
over|spe|cial|ised
over|spe|cial|
    is|ing
over|spe|cial|
    iza|tion
over|spe|cial|ize
over|spe|cial|izes
over|spe|cial|ized
over|spe|cial|
    iz|ing
over|spend
over|spends
over|spent
over|spend|ing
over|spill +s
over|spread
over|spreads
over|spread
over|spread|ing
over|staff +s +ed
  +ing
over|state
over|states
over|stated
over|stat|ing
over|state|ment
  +s
over|stay +s +ed
  +ing
over|steer +s +ed
  +ing
over|step
over|steps
over|stepped
over|step|ping
over|stitch
over|stitches
over|stitched
over|stitch|ing
over|stock +s +ed
  +ing
over|strain +s +ed
  +ing
over|stress
over|stresses

over|stress (*cont.*)
over|stressed
over|stress|ing
over|stretch
over|stretches
over|stretched
over|stretch|ing
over|strong
over|strung
over|study
over|studies
over|studied
over|study|ing
over|stuff +s +ed
  +ing
over|sub|scribe
over|sub|scribes
over|sub|scribed
over|
  sub|scrib|ing
over|subtle
over|sup|ply
over|sup|plies
over|sup|plied
over|sup|ply|ing
over|sus|cep|tible
overt
over|take
over|takes
over|took
over|tak|ing
over|taken
over|task +s +ed
  +ing
over|tax
over|taxes
over|taxed
over|tax|ing
over-the-counter
  attributive
over-the-top
  attributive
over|throw
over|throws
over|threw
over|throw|ing
over|thrown
over|thrust +s
over|time
over|tire
over|tires
over|tired
over|tir|ing
overt|ly
overt|ness
over|tone +s
over|took
over|top
over|tops
over|topped
over|top|ping

over|train +s +ed
  +ing
over|trick +s
over|trump +s +ed
  +ing
over|ture +s
over|turn +s +ed
  +ing
over|use
over|uses
over|used
over|us|ing
over|valu|ation +s
over|value
over|values
over|valued
over|valu|ing
over|view +s
over|water +s +ed
  +ing
over|ween|ing
over|ween|ing|ly
over|ween|ing|
    ness
over|weight
over|whelm +s
  +ed +ing
over|whelm|ing|ly
over|whelm|ing|
    ness
over|wind
over|winds
over|wound
over|wind|ing
over|win|ter +s
  +ed +ing
over|work +s +ed
  +ing
over|wound
over|write
over|writes
over|wrote
over|writ|ing
over|writ|ten
over|wrought
over|zeal|ous
ovi|bov|ine +s
ovi|cide
Ovid (Roman poet)
ovi|ducal
ovi|duct +s
ovi|duct|al
Ovi|edo (city,
  Spain)
ovi|form
ovine
ovi|par|ity
ovip|ar|ous
ovip|ar|ous|ly
ovi|posit +s +ed
  +ing
ovi|pos|ition

ovi|posi|tor +s
ovoid
ovolo
ovoli
ovo|tes|tis
ovo|tes|tes
ovo|vivi|par|ity
ovo|vi|vip|ar|ous
ovu|lar
ovu|late
ovu|lates
ovu|lated
ovu|lat|ing
ovu|la|tion +s
ovu|la|tory
ovule +s
ovum
ova
ow *interjection*
owe
owes
owed
owing
  (be in debt etc.
  ⚠ O, oh)
Owen (name)
Owen, David
  (Lord Owen,
  British statesman)
Owen, Rich|ard
  (English
  anatomist)
Owen, Rob|ert
  (British socialist
  and
  philanthropist)
Owen, Wil|fred
  (English poet)
Owens, Jesse
  (American athlete)
owl +s
owl|ery
owl|er|ies
owlet +s
owl|ish
owl|ish|ly
owl|ish|ness
owl-light
owl-like
owl mon|key +s
own +s +ed +ing
own brand +s *noun*
own-brand
  attributive
owner +s
own|er|less
owner-occupied
owner-occupier
  +s
own|er|ship +s
owt (anything.
  ⚠ out)

ox
  oxen
ox|al|ate +s
ox|al|ic
ox|alis
oxbow +s
Ox|bridge (Oxford
  and Cambridge
  universities)
oxen
oxer +s
ox-eye +s
ox-eyed
Oxfam (= Oxford
  Committee for
  Famine Relief)
ox-fence +s
Ox|ford (city,
  England)
Ox|ford|shire
  (county, England)
ox|herd +s
ox|hide +s
oxi|dant +s
oxi|date
  oxi|dates
  oxi|dated
  oxi|dat|ing
oxi|da|tion +s
oxi|da|tion|al
oxi|da|tive
oxide +s
oxi|dis|able Br.
  (use oxidizable)
oxi|disa|tion Br. +s
  (use oxidization)
oxi|dise Br. (use
  oxidize)
  oxi|dises
  oxi|dised
  oxi|dis|ing
oxi|diser Br. +s
  (use oxidizer)
oxi|diz|able
oxi|diza|tion +s
oxi|dize
  oxi|dizes
  oxi|dized
  oxi|diz|ing
oxi|dizer +s
oxlip +s
Oxon
  (= Oxfordshire)
Ox|on|ian +s
ox-pecker +s
ox|tail +s
oxter +s
ox-tongue +s
Oxus (ancient
  name of Amu
  Darya)
oxy|acet|yl|ene

oxy|acid +s
oxy|carp|ous
oxy|gen
oxy|gen|ate
  oxy|gen|ates
  oxy|gen|ated
  oxy|gen|at|ing
oxy|gen|ation
oxy|gen|ator +s
oxy|gen|ise Br.
  (use oxygenize)
  oxy|gen|ises
  oxy|gen|ised
  oxy|gen|is|ing
oxy|gen|ize
  oxy|gen|izes
  oxy|gen|ized
  oxy|gen|iz|ing
oxy|gen|ous
oxy|haemo|glo|bin
oxy-hydrogen
oxy|moron +s
oxy|opia
oxy-salt +s
oxy|tetra|cyc|line
oxy|to|cin +s
oxy|tone +s
oyes (use oyez)
oyez
oys|ter +s
oys|ter bank +s
oys|ter bed +s
oys|ter|catch|er +s
oyster-farm +s
oyster-plant +s
oys|ter white +s
  noun and adjective
oyster-white
  attributive
Oz (= Australia)
Ozark Moun|tains
  (in USA)
Oz|arks (= Ozark
  Mountains)
Ozawa, Seiji
  (Japanese
  conductor)
ozo|cer|ite
ozone
ozone-deplet|ing
  attributive
ozone de|ple|tion
ozone-friend|ly
ozon|ic
ozon|isa|tion Br.
  (use ozonization)
ozon|ise Br. (use
  ozonize)
  ozon|ises
  ozon|ised
  ozon|is|ing
ozon|iza|tion

ozon|ize
  ozon|izes
  ozon|ized
  ozon|iz|ing
Ozzie +s (use
  Aussie)

Pp

pa +s (father.
  △ pah, par)
pa'anga +s
Paarl (town, South
  Africa)
pabu|lum
PAC +s (= political
  action committee)
paca +s (rodent.
  △ packer)
pace
  paces
  paced
  pa|cing
  (step)
pace (with due
  deference to)
pace|maker +s
pace|mak|ing
pace|man
  pace|men
pacer +s
pace-setter +s
pace-setting
pacey (use pacy)
paci|er
paci|est
pacha +s (use
  pasha)
Pach|el|bel,
  Jo|hann (German
  composer)
pa|chinko
pa|chisi
Pa|chuca (de Soto)
  (city, Mexico)
pachy|derm +s
pachy|der|mal
pachy|der|ma|tous
pachy|tene
Pa|cif|ic (Ocean)
pa|cif|ic (peaceful)
pacif|ic|al|ly
paci|fi|ca|tion
paci|fi|ca|tory
paci|fier +s
paci|fism
paci|fist +s
pacify
  paci|fies
  paci|fied
  paci|fy|ing
pack +s +ed +ing
pack|able
pack|age
  pack|ages
  pack|aged
  pack|aging

pack|ager +s
pack ani|mal +s
pack drill
Pack|er, Kerry
  (Australian media
  entrepreneur)
pack|er +s (person
  who packs.
  △ paca)
packet +s +ed
  +ing
packet switch|ing
pack|horse +s
pack ice
pack|ing +s
pack|ing case +s
pack rat +s
pack|sad|dle +s
pack|thread
pact +s
  (agreement.
  △ packed)
pacy
  paci|er
  paci|est
pad
  pads
  pad|ded
  pad|ding
Pa|dang (city,
  Indonesia)
Pad|ding|ton
  (railway station,
  London)
pad|dle
  pad|dles
  pad|dled
  pad|dling
pad|dle boat +s
pad|dler +s
pad|dle steam|er
  +s
pad|dle wheel +s
pad|dock +s +ed
  +ing
Paddy
  Pad|dies
  (offensive
  Irishman; name)
paddy
  pad|dies
  (rage; rice field)
paddy field +s
paddy|whack +s
pade|melon +s
Pade|rew|ski,
  Ig|nacy Jan
  (Polish pianist and
  prime minister)
pad|lock +s +ed
  +ing

Padma (river,
  Bangladesh)
pa|douk +s
padre +s
pad|saw +s
Padua (city, Italy)
Pad|uan +s
paean Br. +s (Am.
  pean. song of
  praise. △ paeon,
  peon)
paed|er|ast Br. +s
  (use pederast)
paed|er|as|tic Br.
  (use pederastic)
paed|er|asty Br.
  (use pederasty)
paedi|at|ric Br.
  (Am. pediatric)
paedi|at|ri|cian Br.
  +s (Am.
  pediatrician)
paedi|at|rics Br.
  (Am. pediatrics)
paedi|at|rist Br. +s
  (Am. pediatrist)
paedo|morph|osis
paedo|phile Br. +s
  (Am. pedophile)
paedo|philia Br.
  (Am. pedophilia)
paedo|phil|iac Br.
  +s (Am.
  pedophiliac)
pa|ella +s
paeon +s (metrical
  foot. △ paean,
  pean, peon)
pae|on|ic
pae|ony (use
  peony)
pae|onies
Pa|galu (former
  name of
  Annobón)
Pagan (town,
  Burma)
pagan +s
Paga|nini,
  Nic|colò (Italian
  violinist)
pa|gan|ise Br. (use
  paganize)
pa|gan|ises
pa|gan|ised
pa|gan|is|ing
pa|gan|ish
pa|gan|ism
pa|gan|ize
pa|gan|izes
pa|gan|ized
pa|gan|iz|ing

Page, Fred|erick
  Hand|ley
  (English aircraft
  designer)
page
  pages
  paged
  pa|ging
pa|geant +s
pa|geant|ry
  pa|geant|ries
pa|ginal
pa|gin|ary
pa|gin|ate
  pa|gin|ates
  pa|gin|ated
  pa|gin|at|ing
pa|gin|ation
pa|goda +s
pa|goda tree +s
pah (interjection.
  △ pa, par)
Pa|hang (state,
  Malaysia)
Pah|lavi (language;
  member of Iranian
  dynasty)
Pah|lavi,
  Mu|ham|mad
  Reza (shah of
  Iran, 1941–79)
Pah|lavi, Reza
  (shah of Iran,
  1925–41)
pa|hoe|hoe
paid
paid-up attributive
Paign|ton (resort,
  England)
pail +s (bucket.
  △ pale)
pail|ful +s
Pai|lin (town,
  Cambodia)
pail|lasse +s (use
  palliasse)
pail|lette +s
pain +s +ed +ing
  (hurt. △ pane)
Paine, Thomas
  (English political
  writer)
Paine Towers
  (peaks, Chile)
pain|ful
pain|ful|ly
pain|ful|ness
pain|kill|er +s
pain|kill|ing
pain|less

pain|less|ly
pain|less|ness
pains|tak|ing
pains|tak|ing|ly
pains|tak|ing|ness
paint +s +ed +ing
paint|able
paint|ball
paint|box
  paint|boxes
paint|brush
  paint|brushes
paint|er +s
paint|er|li|ness
paint|er|ly
paint|ing +s
paint shop +s
paint|stick +s
paint|work
painty
pair +s +ed +ing
  (two. △ pare,
  pear, père)
pair|ing +s
  (forming pair.
  △ paring)
pair|work
paisa
  paise
Pais|ley +s
  (pattern; garment)
Pais|ley (town,
  Scotland)
Pais|ley, Ian
  (Northern Irish
  politician)
Pais|ley|ite +s
Pai|ute
  plural Pai|ute or
  Pai|utes
pa|jama Am.
  attributive (Br.
  pyjama)
pa|ja|mas Am. (Br.
  pyjamas)
paka|poo
pak|apu (use
  pakapoo)
pa|keha +s
Pakh|tun +s
  (= Pathan)
Paki +s (offensive)
Paki|stan
Paki|stani +s
pa|kora +s
Pakse (town, Laos)
pal
  pals
  palled
  pal|ling
pal|ace +s
pal|adin +s

Palae|arc|tic *Br.*
(*Am.* Palearctic)
palaeo|an|thro|po|
logic|al *Br.* (*Am.*
paleoanthropo-
logical)
palaeo|
an|thro|polo|gist
Br. +s (*Am.* paleo-
anthropologist)
palaeo|an|thro|
pol|ogy *Br.* (*Am.*
paleoanthropol-
ogy)
palaeo|bot|any *Br.*
(*Am.*
paleobotany)
Palaeo|cene *Br.*
(*Am.* Paleocene)
palaeo|cli|mat|
ology *Br.* (*Am.*
paleoclimato-
logy)
palaeo|eco|logic|al
Br. (*Am.*
paleoecological)
palaeo|ecolo|gist
Br. +s (*Am.*
paleoecologist)
palaeo|ecol|ogy *Br.*
(*Am.*
paleoecology)
palaeo|
geog|raph|er *Br.*
+s (*Am.*
paleogeographer)
palaeo|geog|raphy
Br. (*Am.*
paleogeography)
palae|og|raph|er
Br. +s (*Am.*
paleographer)
palaeo|graph|ic *Br.*
(*Am.*
paleographic)
palaeo|graph|ic|al
Br. (*Am.*
paleographical)
palaeo|graph|ic|
al|ly *Br.* (*Am.*
paleographically)
palae|og|raphy *Br.*
(*Am.*
paleography)
palaeo|lith|ic *Br.*
(*Am.* paleolithic)
palaeo|mag|net|
ism *Br.* (*Am.*
paleomagnetism)
palae|onto|logic|al
Br. (*Am.*
paleontological)

palae|on|tolo|gist
Br. +s (*Am.*
paleontologist)
palae|on|tology *Br.*
(*Am.*
paleontology)
Palaeo|zo|ic *Br.*
(*Am.* Paleozoic)
pal|aes|tra +s
pal|ais
plural pal|ais
pal|an|keen +s
(use palanquin)
pal|an|quin +s
pal|at|abil|ity
pal|at|able
pal|at|able|ness
pal|at|ably
pal|atal +s
pal|at|al|isa|tion
Br. (use
palatalization)
pal|at|al|ise *Br.*
(use palatalize)
pal|at|al|ises
pal|at|al|ised
pal|at|al|is|ing
pal|at|al|iza|tion
pal|at|al|ize
pal|at|al|izes
pal|at|al|ized
pal|at|al|iz|ing
pal|at|al|ly
pal|ate +s (part of
mouth. △ palette,
pallet)
pa|la|tial
pa|la|tial|ly
pa|lat|in|ate +s
pal|at|ine
Palau (island group,
W. Pacific)
pa|la|ver +s +ed
+ing
Pa|la|wan (island,
Philippines)
pale
pales
paled
pal|ing
paler
pal|est
(lacking colour;
become pale.
△ pail)
palea
pa|leae
Pale|arc|tic *Am.*
(*Br.* Palaearctic)
pale|face +s
pale-faced

pale|ly (in a pale
way. △ paly)
Palem|bang (city,
Indonesia)
pale|ness
Pa|len|que (ancient
city, Mexico)
paleo|an|thro|po|
logic|al *Am.* (*Br.*
palaeoanthropo-
logical)
paleo|an|thro|polo|
gist *Am.* +s (*Br.*
palaeoanthropolo-
gist)
paleo|an|thro|
pol|ogy *Am.* (*Br.*
palaeoanthropol-
ogy)
paleo|bot|any *Am.*
(*Br.*
palaeobotany)
Paleo|cene *Am.* (*Br.*
Palaeocene)
paleo|cli|mat|
ology *Am.* (*Br.*
palaeoclimat-
ology)
paleo|eco|logic|al
Am. (*Br.*
palaeoecological)
paleo|ecolo|gist
Am. +s (*Br.*
palaeoecologist)
paleo|ecol|ogy *Am.*
(*Br.*
palaeoecology)
paleo|
geog|raph|er *Am.*
+s (*Br.* palaeo-
geographer)
paleo|geog|raphy
Am. (*Br.* palaeo-
geography)
pale|og|raph|er
Am. +s (*Br.*
palaeographer)
paleo|graph|ic *Am.*
(*Br.*
palaeographic)
paleo|graph|ic|al
Am. (*Br.*
palaeographical)
paleo|graph|ic|
al|ly *Am.* (*Br.*
palaeographic-
ally)
pale|og|raphy *Am.*
(*Br.*
palaeography)
paleo|lith|ic *Am.*
(*Br.* palaeolithic)

paleo|mag|net|ism
Am. (*Br.* palaeo-
magnetism)
pale|onto|logic|al
Am. (*Br.*
palaeontological)
pale|on|tolo|gist
Am. +s (*Br.*
palaeontologist)
pale|on|tology *Am.*
(*Br.*
palaeontology)
Paleo|zo|ic *Am.*
(*Br.* Palaeozoic)
Pa|lermo (capital of
Sicily)
Pal|es|tine
Pal|es|tin|ian +s
pa|les|tra +s (use
palaestra)
Pal|es|trina,
Gio|vanni
Pier|luigi da
(Italian composer)
pale|tot +s
pal|ette +s (in
painting. △ palate,
pallet)
palette-knife
palette-knives
pal|frey +s
Pali (language.
△ parley)
pali|mony
pal|imp|sest +s
pal|in|drome +s
pal|in|drom|ic
pal|in|drom|ist +s
pal|ing +s
pal|in|gen|esis
pal|in|gen|et|ic
pal|in|ode +s
pal|is|ade
pal|is|ades
pal|is|aded
pal|is|ad|ing
Pal|is|ades, the
(district of New
Jersey, USA)
pal|ish
Pa|lissy, Ber|nard
(French potter)
Palk Strait
(between India
and Sri Lanka)
pall +s +ed +ing
(covering; become
uninteresting.
△ pawl)
Pal|la|dian +s
Pal|la|dian|ism

Pal|ladio, An|drea (Italian architect)
pal|la|dium
pal|la|dia
Pal|las (Greek Mythology; asteroid)
pall-bearer +s
pal|let +s (mattress; platform. △ palate, palette)
pal|let|isa|tion Br. (use palletization)
pal|let|ise Br. (use palletize)
pal|let|ises
pal|let|ised
pal|let|is|ing
pal|let|iza|tion
pal|let|ize
pal|let|izes
pal|let|ized
pal|let|iz|ing
pal|lia (plural of pallium. △ pallier)
pal|lial
pal|li|asse +s
pal|li|ate
pal|li|ates
pal|li|ated
pal|li|at|ing
pal|li|ation
pal|lia|tive +s
pal|lia|tive|ly
pal|li|ator +s
pal|lid
pal|lid|ity
pal|lid|ly
pal|lid|ness
pal|lium
pal|liums or pal|lia
Pall Mall (street, London)
pall-mall (game)
pal|lor
pally
pal|lier
pal|li|est
palm +s +ed +ing
Palma (city, Majorca. △ La Palma, Parma)
pal|ma|ceous
pal|mar +s
Pal|mas (town, Brazil)
pal|mate

Palme, Olof (Swedish prime minister)
Pal|mer, Ar|nold (American golfer)
Pal|mer +s
Pal|mer|ston, Henry (British prime minister)
Pal|mer|ston North (city, New Zealand)
pal|mette +s
pal|metto +s
palm|ful +s
pal|mier +s
palmi|ped +s
palmi|pede +s
palm|ist +s
palm|is|try
palmi|tate +s
palm|it|ic
Palm Springs (desert resort, USA)
Palm Sun|day +s
palm|top +s
palm tree +s
palmy
palm|ier
palmi|est
Pal|myra (ancient city, Syria)
pal|myra +s (tree)
pa|lolo +s
Palo|mar, Mount (California, USA)
palo|mino +s
palo|verde +s
palp +s
palp|abil|ity
palp|able
palp|ably
palp|al
pal|pate
pal|pates
pal|pated
pal|pat|ing
pal|pa|tion
pal|pe|bral
pal|pi|tant
pal|pi|tate
pal|pi|tates
pal|pi|tated
pal|pi|tat|ing
pal|pi|ta|tion +s
pal|pus
palpi
pals|grave +s
pal|stave +s
palsy
pal|sies

palsy (cont.)
pal|sied
palsy|ing
pal|ter +s +ed +ing
pal|ter|er +s
pal|tri|ness
pal|try
pal|trier
pal|tri|est
pal|udal
pal|ud|ism
paly (striped. △ palely)
palyno|logic|al
paly|nolo|gist +s
paly|nol|ogy
Pam
Pam|ela
Pamir Moun|tains (in central Asia)
Pa|mirs (= Pamir Mountains)
pam|pas
pam|pas grass
pam|pas grasses
pam|per +s +ed +ing
pam|per|er +s
pam|pero +s
pamph|let +s +ed +ing
pamph|let|eer
pamph|let|eers
pamph|let|eered
pamph|let|eer|ing
Pam|phylia (ancient region, Turkey)
Pam|phyl|ian +s
Pam|plona (city, Spain)
Pan Greek Mythology
pan
pans
panned
pan|ning (vessel; leaf; swing camera. △ panne)
pana|cea +s
pana|cean
pan|ache +s
pan|ada
pan-African
pan-African|ism
Pan-African|ist Con|gress (of Azania) (South African political movement)

Pa|naji (city, India)
Pan|ama (in Central America)
pan|ama +s (hat)
Pan|ama Canal (in Central America)
Pan|ama City (capital of Panama)
Pana|ma|nian +s
pan-American
pan-Anglican
pana|tella +s
Panay (island, Philippines)
pan|cake
pan|cakes
pan|caked
pan|cak|ing
Pan|cake Day +s
pan|chayat +s
Pan|chen lama +s
pan|chro|mat|ic
pan|cos|mism
pan|creas
pan|creases
pan|cre|at|ic
pan|crea|tin
pan|crea|titis
panda +s (animal. △ pander)
pan|da|nus
plural pan|da|nus
Pan|darus Greek Mythology
pan|dean +s
pan|dect +s
pan|dem|ic
pan|de|mon|ium
pan|der +s +ed +ing (indulge; go-between. △ panda)
Pan|dit, Vi|jaya (Indian politician and diplomat)
pan|dit +s (use pundit)
Pan|dora Greek Mythology
Pan|dora's box
pane +s (in window etc. △ pain)
pan|egyr|ic +s
pan|egyric|al
pan|egyr|ise Br. (use panegyrize)
pan|egyr|ises
pan|egyr|ised
pan|egyr|is|ing
pan|egyr|ist +s

pan¦egyr¦ize
  pan¦egyr¦izes
  pan¦egyr¦ized
  pan¦egyr¦iz¦ing
panel
  panels
  pan¦elled *Br.*
  pan¦eled *Am.*
  pan¦el¦ling *Br.*
  pan¦el¦ing *Am.*
panel beat¦er +s
pan¦el¦ist *Am.* +s
pan¦el¦list *Br.* +s
pan¦et¦tone
  pan¦et¦toni
pan-European
pan¦forte
pan-fry
  pan-fries
  pan-fried
  pan-frying
pan¦ful +s
pang +s
panga +s
Pan¦gaea
  (continent)
pan¦go¦lin +s
pan¦han¦dle
  pan¦han¦dles
  pan¦han¦dled
  pan¦hand¦ling
pan¦hand¦ler +s
pan-Hellen¦ic
pan-Hellen¦ism
panic
  panics
  pan¦icked
  pan¦ick¦ing
pan¦icky
pan¦icle +s
pan¦icled
panic¦mon¦ger +s
panic-stricken
panic-struck
Pa¦nini (Indian
  grammarian)
Pan¦jabi +s (use
  Punjabi)
pan¦jan¦drum +s
Pan¦jim (= Panaji)
Panj¦shir
  (mountain range,
  Afghanistan)
Pank¦hurst,
  Em¦me¦line,
  Chris¦ta¦bel, and
  Syl¦via (English
  suffragettes)
pan¦like
Pan¦mun¦jom
  (village, Korea)
pan¦nage

panne (velvet.
  △ pan)
pan¦ner +s
pan¦nier +s
pan¦ni¦kin +s
Pan¦no¦nia (ancient
  country, SE
  Europe)
pan¦op¦lied
pan¦oply
  pan¦op¦lies
pan¦op¦tic
pan¦or¦ama +s
pan¦or¦am¦ic
pan¦or¦am¦ic¦al¦ly
pan pipes
pansy
  pan¦sies
pant +s +ed +ing
pan¦ta¦lets
pan¦ta¦lettes (use
  pantalets)
Pan¦ta¦loon (Italian
  commedia dell'arte
  character)
pan¦ta¦loons
  (breeches; baggy
  trousers)
Pan¦ta¦nal (swamp
  region, Brazil)
pan¦tech¦nicon +s
Pan¦tel¦le¦ria
  (island,
  Mediterranean)
Pan¦tha¦lassa
  (ocean)
pan¦the¦ism
pan¦the¦ist +s
pan¦the¦is¦tic
pan¦the¦is¦tic¦al
pan¦the¦is¦tic¦al¦ly
Pan¦theon (in
  Rome)
pan¦theon +s
  (generally)
pan¦ther +s
pantie-girdle +s
pan¦ties
panti¦hose (use
  pantyhose)
pan¦tile +s
pan¦tiled
pant¦ing¦ly
panto +s
panto¦graph +s
panto¦graph¦ic
panto¦logic
panto¦tol¦ogy
panto¦mime
  panto¦mimes
  panto¦mimed
  panto¦mim¦ing

panto¦mim¦ic
panto¦mim¦ist
panto¦morph¦ic
panto¦scop¦ic
panto¦then¦ic
pan¦try
  pan¦tries
pan¦try¦man
  pan¦try¦men
pants
pants suit +s
pant suit +s (use
  pants suit)
panty¦hose
panty line +s
panty liner +s
pan¦zer +s
Pao¦lozzi,
  Ed¦uardo
  (Scottish artist)
pap +s
papa +s
papa¦bile
pap¦acy
  pap¦acies
pa¦pain
papal
pap¦al¦ism
pap¦al¦ist +s
pap¦al¦ly
Papal States (in
  central Italy)
Pap¦an¦dreou,
  An¦dreas (Greek
  prime minister)
pap¦ar¦azzo
  pap¦ar¦azzi
pa¦pa¦ver¦aceous
pa¦pa¦ver¦ous
papaw +s (use
  pawpaw)
pa¦paya +s
Pa¦pe¦ete (capital
  of French
  Polynesia)
paper +s +ed +ing
paper¦back +s
paper boy +s
pa¦per¦chase +s
paper clip +s
pa¦per¦er +s
paper girl +s
paper¦hanger +s
paper¦knife
  pa¦per¦knives
paper¦less
paper¦maker +s
paper¦mak¦ing
paper mill +s
paper round +s
paper tape +s
paper-thin

paper¦weight +s
paper¦work
pa¦pery
Paph¦la¦gonia
  (ancient region,
  Asia Minor)
Paph¦la¦gon¦ian +s
pa¦pier mâché
pa¦pil¦ion¦aceous
pa¦pilla
  pa¦pil¦lae
pap¦il¦lary
pap¦il¦late
pap¦il¦loma
  pap¦il¦lo¦mas *or*
  pap¦il¦lo¦mata
pap¦il¦lon +s
pap¦il¦lose
Papi¦neau, Louis
  Jo¦seph (French-
  Canadian
  politician)
pap¦ism
pap¦ist +s
pap¦is¦tic
pap¦is¦tic¦al
pap¦is¦try
pap¦poose +s (child)
pap¦par¦delle
pap¦pose (of a
  pappus)
Pap¦pus (Greek
  mathematician)
pap¦pus
  pappi
  (hairs on thistle
  etc.)
pappy
  pap¦pier
  pap¦pi¦est
pap¦rika +s
pap test +s
Papua (part of
  Papua New
  Guinea)
Pap¦uan +s
pap¦ula
  pap¦ulae *or*
  pap¦ulas
papu¦lar
pap¦ule +s
papu¦lose
papu¦lous
papyr¦aceous
papyro¦logic¦al
pa¦pyr¦olo¦gist
pa¦pyr¦ology
pa¦pyrus
  pa¦pyri
par +s (average;
  equality; *Golf*;
  Stock Exchange;

par (*cont.*)
  paragraph. △pa, pah)
Pará (state, Brazil)
para +s
  (= paratrooper; paragraph)
para|basis
  para|bases
para|bi|osis
  para|bi|oses
para|bi|ot|ic
par|able +s
para|bola +s
para|bol|ic
para|bol|ic|al
para|bol|ic|al|ly
para|bol|oid +s
para|bol|oid|al
Para|cel Is|lands
  (in South China Sea)
Para|cel|sus (Swiss physician)
para|ceta|mol +s
para|chron|ism +s
para|chute
  para|chutes
  para|chuted
  para|chut|ing
para|chut|ist +s
Para|clete
par|ade
  par|ades
  par|aded
  par|ad|ing
par|ade ground +s
par|ader +s
para|di|chloro|ben|zene
para|did|dle +s
para|digm +s
para|dig|mat|ic
para|dig|mat|ic|al|ly
para|disa|ical
para|disal
para|dise +s
para|dis|iacal
para|dis|ical
para|dor +s
para|dos
  para|doses
para|dox
  para|doxes
para|dox|ical
para|dox|ic|al|ly
para|dox|ure +s
par|aes|the|sia *Br.*
  (*Am.* paresthesia)
par|af|fin +s
para|glide

para|glider +s
para|glid|ing
para|goge +s
para|gogic
para|gon +s
  (model of excellence.
    △parergon)
para|graph +s
para|graph|ic
para|graph|ist +s
Para|guay
Para|guay|an +s
para|hy|dro|gen
Para|íba (state, Brazil)
para|keet +s
para|lan|guage
par|al|de|hyde
para|legal +s
para|leip|om|ena
  (use paralipomena)
para|leip|sis (use paralipsis)
  para|leip|ses
para|lin|guis|tic
para|lip|om|ena
para|lip|sis
  para|lip|ses
par|al|lac|tic
par|al|lax
par|al|lel +s +ed +ing
par|al|lel|epi|ped +s
par|al|lel|ism +s
par|al|lelo|gram +s
par|alo|gise *Br.*
  (use paralogize)
  par|alo|gises
  par|alo|gised
  par|alo|gis|ing
par|alo|gism +s
par|alo|gist +s
par|alo|gize
  par|alo|gizes
  par|alo|gized
  par|alo|giz|ing
Para|lym|pic
Para|lym|pics
para|lysa|tion *Br.*
para|lyse *Br.*
  para|lyses
  para|lysed
  para|lys|ing
para|lys|ing|ly *Br.*
par|aly|sis
  par|aly|ses
para|lyt|ic +s
para|lyt|ic|al|ly

para|lyza|tion *Am.*
para|lyze *Am.*
  para|lyzes
  para|lyzed
  para|lyz|ing
para|lyz|ing|ly *Am.*
para|mag|net|ic
para|mag|net|ism
Para|ma|ribo
  (capital of Suriname)
para|matta (use parramatta)
para|me|cium
  para|me|cia *or* para|me|ciums
para|med|ic +s
para|med|ic|al
par|am|eter +s
par|am|et|ric
par|am|et|rise *Br.*
  (use parametrize)
  par|am|et|rises
  par|am|et|rised
  par|am|et|ris|ing
par|am|et|rize
  par|am|et|rizes
  par|am|et|rized
  par|am|et|riz|ing
para|mili|tary
  para|mili|tar|ies
par|am|nesia
par|amo +s
para|moe|cium
  (use paramecium)
  para|moe|cia *or* para|moe|ciums
Para|mount
  (American film company)
para|mount
  (supreme)
para|mount|cy
para|mount|ly
par|amour +s
Par|aná (river, S. America; city, Argentina; state, Brazil)
par|ang +s
para|noia
para|noiac +s
para|noi|ac|al|ly
para|no|ic
para|no|ic|al|ly
para|noid +s
para|nor|mal
para|nor|mal|ly
Par|an|thro|pus
para|pet +s
para|pet|ed

par|aph +s
para|pher|na|lia
para|phrase
  para|phrases
  para|phrased
  para|phras|ing
para|phras|tic
para|ple|gia
para|ple|gic +s
para|psycho|logic|al
para|psych|olo|gist +s
para|psych|ology
para|quat
para|sail +s
para|sail|er +s
para|sail|ing
para|sail|or +s
  (use parasailer)
par|as|cend +s +ed +ing
par|as|cend|er +s
para|se|lene
  para|se|lenes *or* para|se|lenae
para|site +s
para|sit|ic
para|sit|ic|al
para|sit|ic|al|ly
para|siti|cide
para|sit|isa|tion *Br.* (use parasitization)
para|sit|ise *Br.* (use parasitize)
  para|sit|ises
  para|sit|ised
  para|sit|is|ing
para|sit|ism
para|sit|iza|tion
para|sit|ize
  para|sit|izes
  para|sit|ized
  para|sit|iz|ing
para|sit|oid +s
para|sit|olo|gist +s
para|sit|ology
para|sol +s
para|statal +s
para|sui|cide +s
para|sym|pa|thet|ic
para|syn|thesis
  para|syn|theses
para|syn|thet|ic
para|tac|tic
para|tac|tic|al|ly
para|taxis
par|atha +s
para|thion
para|thy|roid +s

para|troop +s
para|troop|er +s
para|ty|phoid
para|vane +s
par avion
par|boil +s +ed
  +ing
par|buckle
  par|buckles
  par|buckled
  par|buck|ling
Par|cae *Roman*
  Mythology
par|cel
  par|cels
  par|celled *Br.*
  par|celed *Am.*
  par|cel|ling *Br.*
  par|cel|ing *Am.*
parch
  parches
  parched
  parch|ing
parch|ment +s
par|close +s
pard +s
par|da|lote +s
pard|ner +s
par|don +s +ed
  +ing
par|don|able
par|don|ably
par|don|er +s
pare
  pares
  pared
  par|ing
  (trim; peel. △ pair,
  pear, *père*)
par|egor|ic +s
par|eira
paren +s
  (= parenthesis)
par|en|chyma
par|en|chy|mal
par|en|chy|mat|
         ous
par|ent +s +ed
  +ing
par|ent|age
par|en|tal
par|en|tal|ly
par|en|teral
par|en|teral|ly
par|en|thesis
  par|en|theses
par|en|the|sise *Br.*
  (use
  parenthesize)
  par|en|the|sises
  par|en|the|sised
  par|en|the|sis|ing

par|en|the|size
  par|en|the|sizes
  par|en|the|sized
  par|en|the|siz|ing
par|en|thet|ic
par|en|thet|ic|al
par|en|thet|ic|al|ly
par|ent|hood
parer +s
par|er|gon
  par|erga
  (subsidiary work.
  △ paragon)
par|esis
  par|eses
par|es|the|sia *Am.*
  (*Br.* paraesthesia)
par|et|ic
par ex|cel|lence
par|fait +s
par|gana +s
par|get +s +ed
  +ing
par|he|li|acal
par|he|lic
par|he|lion
  par|he|lia
par|iah +s
par|iah dog +s
Par|ian +s
par|ietal
pari-mutuel
par|ing +s (piece
  cut off. △ pairing)
pari passu
Paris (capital of
  France; in *Greek*
  Mythology)
Paris, Mat|thew
  (English
  chronicler)
par|ish
  par|ishes
pa|rish|ion|er +s
Paris|ian +s
pari|son +s
pari|syl|lab|ic
par|ity
  par|ities
Park, Mungo
  (Scottish explorer)
park +s +ed +ing
parka +s (jacket.
  △ parker)
park-and-ride +s
Park Chung Hee
  (South Korean
  president)
Par|ker, Char|lie
  (American
  saxophonist)

Par|ker, Doro|thy
  (American
  humorist)
park|er +s (person
  who parks;
  parking light.
  △ parka)
par|kin
park|ing light +s
park|ing lot +s
park|ing meter +s
park|ing ticket +s
Par|kin|son|ism
Par|kin|son's
  dis|ease
Par|kin|son's law
park|land +s
park|way +s
parky
  park|ier
  park|iest
par|lance
par|lay +s +ed
  +ing (bet)
par|ley +s +ed
  +ing (conference.
  △ Pali)
par|lia|ment +s
par|lia|men|tar|ian
  +s
par|lia|men|tary
par|lor *Am.* +s
par|lor|maid *Am.* +s
par|lour *Br.* +s
par|lour|maid *Br.* +s
par|lous
par|lous|ly
par|lous|ness
Parma (province
  and city, Italy;
  ham. △ Palma)
Par|meni|des
  (Greek
  philosopher)
Par|mesan
Par|mi|gian|ino
  (Italian painter)
Par|mi|giano
  (= Parmigianino)
Par|nas|sian +s
Par|nas|sus,
  Mount (in
  Greece)
Par|nell, Charles
  (Irish nationalist)
pa|ro|chial
pa|ro|chial|ism
pa|ro|chi|al|ity
pa|ro|chi|al|ly
par|od|ic
par|od|ist +s

par|ody
  par|odies
  par|odied
  par|ody|ing
parol +s (oral;
  declaration)
par|ole
  par|oles
  par|oled
  par|ol|ing
  (release)
par|ole Linguistics
par|olee +s
par|ono|masia
paro|nym +s
par|onym|ous
Paros (Greek
  island)
par|otid +s
parot|itis
Par|ou|sia *Theology*
par|ox|ysm +s
par|ox|ys|mal
par|oxy|tone +s
par|pen +s
par|quet +s +ed
  +ing
par|quet|ry
Parr, Cath|er|ine
  (wife of Henry
  VIII of England)
parr
  plural parr *or*
  parrs
  (salmon)
parra|matta
parri|cidal
parri|cide +s
par|rot +s +ed
  +ing
parrot-fashion
par|rot|fish
  plural par|rot|fish
  or par|rot|fishes
Parry, Hu|bert
  (English
  composer)
parry
  par|ries
  par|ried
  parry|ing
parse
  parses
  parsed
  pars|ing
par|sec +s
Par|see +s
Par|see|ism
parser +s
Par|si|fal
  (alternative name
  for Perceval)

par¦si¦mo¦ni¦ous
par¦si¦mo¦ni¦ous¦ly
par¦si¦mo¦ni¦ous¦
    ness
par¦si¦mony
pars¦ley
parsley-piert+s
pars¦nip+s
par¦son+s
par¦son¦age+s
par¦son¦ical
Par¦sons, Charles
  (English engineer)
par¦son's nose+s
part+s +ed +ing
  (portion;
  component; role;
  to divide; etc.
  ⚠ pâte)
par¦tak¦able
par¦take
  par¦takes
  par¦took
  par¦tak¦ing
  par¦taken
par¦taker+s
par¦tan+s
par¦terre+s
part ex¦change+s
  noun
part-exchange
  part-exchanges
  part-exchanged
  part-exchan¦ging
  verb
par¦theno¦gen¦esis
par¦theno¦
    gen¦et¦ic
par¦theno¦
    gen¦et¦ic¦al¦ly
Par¦thenon
  (temple, Athens)
Par¦thian+s
par¦tial+s
  par¦ti¦al¦ity
  par¦ti¦al¦ities
par¦tial¦ly
par¦tial¦ness
part¦ible
par¦tici¦pant+s
par¦tici¦pate
  par¦tici¦pates
  par¦tici¦pated
  par¦tici¦pat¦ing
par¦tici¦pa¦tion+s
par¦tici¦pa¦tive
par¦tici¦pa¦tor+s
par¦tici¦pa¦tory
par¦ti¦ci¦pial
par¦ti¦ci¦pi¦al¦ly
par¦ti¦ciple+s
par¦ticle+s

parti¦col¦ored*Am.*
parti¦col¦oured*Br.*
par¦ticu¦lar+s
par¦ticu¦lar¦
  isa¦tion*Br.* (use
  particularization)
par¦ticu¦lar¦ise*Br.*
  (use
  particularize)
  par¦ticu¦lar¦ises
  par¦ticu¦lar¦ised
  par¦ticu¦lar¦is¦ing
par¦ticu¦lar¦ism
par¦ticu¦lar¦ist+s
par¦ticu¦lar¦ity
  par¦ticu¦lar¦ities
par¦ticu¦lar¦
    iza¦tion
par¦ticu¦lar¦ize
  par¦ticu¦lar¦izes
  par¦ticu¦lar¦ized
  par¦ticu¦lar¦iz¦ing
par¦ticu¦lar¦ly
par¦ticu¦late+s
part¦ing+s
parti pris
  partis pris
par¦ti¦san+s
par¦ti¦san¦ship
par¦tita+s
par¦tite
par¦ti¦tion+s +ed
  +ing
par¦ti¦tion¦er+s
par¦ti¦tion¦ist+s
par¦ti¦tive
par¦ti¦tive¦ly
par¦ti¦zan+s (use
  partisan)
part¦ly
part¦ner+s +ed
  +ing
part¦ner¦less
part¦ner¦ship+s
part of speech
  parts of speech
Par¦ton, Dolly
  (American singer)
par¦took
par¦tridge+s
part-song+s
part-time
part-timer+s
par¦turi¦ent
par¦tur¦ition
part-way
part-work
party
  par¦ties
  par¦tied
  party¦ing
party-goer+s

party line+s
party pol¦it¦ical+s
party pol¦it¦ics
party-poop+s
party-pooper+s
party-pooping
party pop¦per+s
party wall+s
par¦ure+s
Par¦vati*Hinduism*
par¦venu+s *male*
par¦venue+s
  female
par¦vis
  par¦vises
par¦vise+s (use
  parvis)
parvo¦virus
  parvo¦viruses
pas
  plural pas
Pasa¦dena(city,
  USA)
Pas¦cal(computer
  language)
Pas¦cal, Blaise
  (French
  mathematician
  and physicist)
pas¦cal+s (unit)
pas¦chal(Easter)
pas de chat
  plural pas de chat
pas de deux
  plural pas de deux
pas glissé+s
pash
  pashes
pasha+s
pash¦al¦ic+s
pashm
Pashto
Pash¦tun+s
  (= Pathan)
Pašić, Ni¦kola
  (Serbian prime
  minister)
Pas¦ion¦aria, La
  (Dolores Ibarruri
  Gomez, Spanish
  Communist
  politician)
Pa¦siphaë *Greek*
  Mythology
pas¦kha
paso doble+s
pasque flower+s
pas¦quin¦ade+s
pass
  passes
  passed
  pass¦ing

pass(*cont.*)
  (move; go past; be
  accepted; etc.;
  passage between
  mountains.
  ⚠ past)
pass¦able
  (adequate;
  unobstructed.
  ⚠ passible)
pass¦able¦ness
pass¦ably
pas¦sa¦caglia+s
pas¦sage
  pas¦sages
  pas¦saged
  pas¦sa¦ging
pas¦sage¦way+s
pas¦sant
pass¦band+s
pass¦book+s
Pas¦schen¦daele
  (battle site,
  Belgium)
passé
passed pawn+s
passe¦ment¦erie
pas¦sen¦ger+s
passenger-mile+s
pas¦sen¦ger
  pi¦geon+s
passe¦par¦tout+s
passe¦pied+s
pass¦er+s
passer-by
  passers-by
pas¦ser¦ine+s
pas seul+s
pass¦ibil¦ity
pass¦ible(capable
  of suffering.
  ⚠ passable)
Pas¦si¦formes
pas¦sim
pass¦ing+s
pass¦ing¦ly
passing-out *noun*
  and attributive
Pas¦sion (of Christ)
pas¦sion+s
pas¦sion¦al+s
pas¦sion¦ate
pas¦sion¦ate¦ly
pas¦sion¦ate¦ness
pas¦sion flower+s
pas¦sion fruit+s
Pas¦sion¦ist+s
pas¦sion¦less
pas¦sion play+s
Pas¦sion Sun¦day
Pas¦sion¦tide
Pas¦sion Week

pas|siv|ate
  pas|siv|ates
  pas|siv|ated
  pas|siv|at|ing
pas|siv|ation
pas|sive +s
pas|sive|ly
pas|sive|ness
pas|siv|ity
pass-key +s
pass-mark +s
Pass|over (Jewish festival)
pass|port +s
pass|word +s
past +s (gone by in time; former time; beyond; so as to pass. △ passed)
pasta +s
paste
  pastes
  pasted
  past|ing
paste|board +s
pas|tel +s (colour. △ pastille)
pas|tel|ist +s Am.
pas|tel|list +s Br.
pas|tern +s
Pas|ter|nak, Boris (Russian writer)
paste-up +s noun
Pas|teur, Louis (French chemist)
pas|teur|isa|tion Br. (use pasteurization)
pas|teur|ise Br. (use pasteurize)
  pas|teur|ises
  pas|teur|ised
  pas|teur|is|ing
pas|teur|iser Br. +s (use pasteurizer)
pas|teur|iza|tion
pas|teur|ize
  pas|teur|izes
  pas|teur|ized
  pas|teur|iz|ing
pas|teur|izer +s
pas|tic|cio +s
pas|tiche +s
pas|tille +s (lozenge. △ pastel)
pastille-burner +s
past|ily
pas|time +s
pasti|ness

pas|tis
  plural pas|tis
past master +s
pas|tor +s +ed +ing
pas|tor|al +s (adjective; poem etc.; letter from bishop)
pas|tor|ale
  pas|tor|ales or pas|tor|ali (music; musical play)
pas|tor|al|ism
pas|tor|al|ist +s
pas|tor|al|ity
pas|tor|al|ly
pas|tor|ate +s
pas|tor|ship +s
past per|fect +s
pas|trami
pas|try
  pas|tries
pastry-cook +s
pas|tur|age
pas|ture
  pas|tures
  pas|tured
  pas|tur|ing
pas|ture|land +s
pasty
  pas|ties
  pasti|er
  pasti|est
Pat +s (name; often offensive Irishman)
pat
  pats
  pat|ted
  pat|ting (strike gently; gentle stroke; glib)
pat-a-cake
pa|ta|gium
  pa|ta|gia
Pata|gonia (region, S. America)
Pata|gon|ian +s
Pa|tali|putra (ancient name of Patna)
Pata|vin|ity
Pa|ta|vium (Latin name for Padua)
pat|ball
patch
  patches
  patched
  patch|ing
patch|board +s
patch cord +s

patch|er +s
patch|ily
patchi|ness
patch|ouli
patch panel +s
patch|work +s
patchy
  patch|ier
  patchi|est
pate +s (head)
pâte +s (paste for making porcelain. △ part)
pâté +s (meat etc. paste. △ pattée)
pâté de foie gras (goose liver paste)
pa|tella
  pa|tel|lae
pa|tel|lar
pa|tel|late
paten +s (shallow dish. △ patten, pattern)
pa|tency
pa|tent +s +ed +ing
pa|tent|able
pa|tent|ee +s
pa|tent|ly
pa|tent|or +s
Pater, Wal|ter (English essayist and critic)
pater +s
pater|famil|ias
pa|ter|nal
pa|ter|nal|ism
pa|ter|nal|ist +s
pa|ter|nal|is|tic
pa|ter|nal|is|tic|al|ly
pa|ter|nal|ly
pa|ter|nity
  pa|ter|nities
pater|nos|ter +s
path +s
Pa|than +s
Pathé, Charles (French film pioneer)
path|et|ic
path|et|ic|al|ly
path|find|er +s
path|less
patho|gen +s
patho|gen|esis
patho|gen|et|ic
patho|gen|ic
path|ogen|ous
path|ogeny

path|og|no|mon|ic +s
path|og|nomy
patho|logic|al
patho|logic|al|ly
path|olo|gist +s
path|ology
  path|olo|gies
pathos
path|way +s
Pa|tience (name)
pa|tience (calm endurance)
pa|tient +s
pa|tient|ly
pat|ina +s
pat|in|ated
pat|in|ation
pat|in|ous
patio +s
pa|tis|serie +s
patly
Pat|more, Cov|en|try (English poet)
Pat|mos (Greek island)
Patna (city, India)
pat|ness
pat|ois
  plural pat|ois
Paton, Alan (South African writer)
Pa|tras (port, Greece)
pat|rial +s
pat|ri|al|ity
patri|arch +s
patri|arch|al
patri|arch|al|ly
patri|arch|ate +s
patri|arch|ism
patri|archy
  patri|arch|ies
Pa|tri|cia
pa|tri|cian +s
pa|trici|ate +s
patri|cidal
patri|cide +s
Pat|rick (patron saint of Ireland; name)
patri|lin|eal
patri|mo|nial
patri|mony
  patri|monies
pat|riot +s
pat|ri|ot|ic
pat|ri|ot|ic|al|ly
pat|ri|ot|ism
pa|tris|tic
pa|tris|tics

Pa¦troc|lus *Greek Mythology*
pa¦trol
  pa|trols
  pa|trolled
  pa|trol|ling
pa¦trol|ler+s
pa¦trol|man
  pa¦trol|men
patro|logic|al
pa¦trolo|gist+s
pa¦trol|ogy
  pa¦trolo|gies
pat¦ron+s
pat¦ron|age+s
pat¦ron|al
pat¦ron|ess
  pat¦ron|esses
pat¦ron|isa¦tion *Br.* (use patronization)
pat¦ron|ise *Br.* (use patronize)
  pat¦ron|ises
  pat¦ron|ised
  pat¦ron|is¦ing
pat¦ron|iser *Br.* +s (use patronizer)
pat¦ron|is¦ing¦ly *Br.* (use patronizingly)
pat¦ron|iza¦tion
pat¦ron|ize
  pat¦ron|izes
  pat¦ron|ized
  pat¦ron|iz¦ing
pat¦ron|izer+s
pat¦ron|iz¦ing¦ly
patro|nym|ic+s
pa¦troon+s
Patsy (name)
patsy
  pat|sies (person easily ridiculed, blamed etc.)
Pat¦taya (resort, Thailand)
pat¦tée (type of cross. ⚠ pâté)
pat¦ten+s (shoe. ⚠ paten, pattern)
pat¦ter+s +ed +ing
pat¦tern+s +ed +ing (design; model. ⚠ paten, patten)
pat¦tern|ing+s
Patty (name)

patty
  pat|ties (pie; cake)
patty|pan+s
patu|lous
patu|lous¦ly
patu|lous|ness
pat¦zer+s
paua+s (shellfish. ⚠ power)
pau|city
  pau¦ci|ties
Paul (saint; name)
Paul, Les (American jazz guitarist)
Paula
Paul|ette
Pauli, Wolf|gang (Austrian-born American physicist)
Paul|ine (of St Paul; name)
Paul|ing, Linus (American chemist)
Paul Jones (dance)
paul|ow|nia+s
Paul Pry (inquisitive person)
paunch
  paunches
  paunched
  paunch|ing
paunchi|ness
paunchy
  paunch|ier
  paunchi|est
pau|per+s
pau¦per|dom
pau¦per|isa¦tion *Br.* (use pauperization)
pau¦per|ise *Br.* (use pauperize)
  pau¦per|ises
  pau¦per|ised
  pau¦per|is¦ing
pau¦per|ism
pau¦per|iza¦tion
pau¦per|ize
  pau¦per|izes
  pau¦per|ized
  pau¦per|iz¦ing
Pau|san¦ias (Greek geographer and historian)
pause
  pauses

pause (*cont.*)
  paused
  paus|ing
pav¦age
pavan+s (use pavane)
pav¦ane+s
Pava|rotti, Lu|ciano (Italian tenor)
pave
  paves
  paved
  pav¦ing
pavé+s
pave|ment+s
paver+s
Pa¦vese, Ce¦sare (Italian writer)
pa¦vil|ion+s +ed +ing
pav¦ing+s
pav¦ing stone+s
pa¦vior+s
pa|viour+s (use pavior)
Pav¦lov, Ivan Pet¦ro|vich (Russian physiologist)
Pav¦lova, Anna (Russian dancer)
pav¦lova+s (cake)
Pav¦lov|ian
pav¦on|ine
paw+s +ed +ing (animal's foot. ⚠ poor, pore, pour)
pawk|ily
pawki|ness
pawky
  pawk|ier
  pawki|est (drily humorous; shrewd. ⚠ porky)
pawl+s (lever etc. ⚠ pall)
pawn+s +ed +ing (chess piece, deposit as security for loan. ⚠ porn)
pawn|broker+s
pawn|brok|ing
pawn|shop+s
paw¦paw+s
pax (peace)
Pax¦ton, Jo¦seph (English gardener and architect)
pay
  pays

pay (*cont.*)
  paid
  pay¦ing
pay|able+s
pay-as-you-earn
pay-as-you-go
pay|back+s
pay-bed+s
pay claim+s
pay day+s
pay dirt
payee+s
pay en¦vel|ope+s
payer+s
pay|load+s
pay|mas¦ter+s
Pay|mas¦ter Gen|eral
  Pay|mas¦ters Gen|eral
pay|ment+s
pay|nim+s
pay-off+s *noun*
pay|ola+s
pay-out+s *noun*
pay packet+s
pay|phone+s
pay|roll+s
pays| age+s
pays|agist+s
Pays de la Loire (region, France)
pay|slip+s
pay sta|tion+s
Paz, Octa|vio (Mexican poet and essayist)
P-Celtic
pea+s (vegetable; plant. ⚠ pee)
pea-brain+s
peace (quiet; freedom from war. ⚠ piece)
peace|able
peace|able|ness
peace|ably
Peace Corps
peace|ful
peace|ful¦ly
peace|ful|ness
peace|keep¦er+s
peace|keep¦ing
peace|maker+s
peace|mak¦ing
peace|nik+s
peace-offering+s
peace pipe+s
peace stud|ies
peace|time
peach
  peaches

peach (*cont.*)
  peached
  peach|ing
peach-bloom
peach-blow
pea-chick +s
peachi|ness
peach Melba +s
peachy
  peach|ier
  peachi|est
Pea|cock, Thomas
  Love (English
  writer)
pea|cock +s
pea|cock blue +s
  noun and adjective
peacock-blue
  attributive
pea|cock|ery
pea|fowl
  plural pea|fowl
pea green +s *noun*
  and adjective
pea-green
  attributive
pea|hen +s
pea-jacket +s
peak +s +ed +ing
  (summit; reach
  highest value.
  △ peek, peke,
  pique)
Peak Dis|trict
  (in N. England)
Peake, Mer|vyn
  (British writer)
peak hour +s *noun*
peak-hour
  attributive
peaki|ness
peak|ish
peak load +s *noun*
peak-load
  attributive
peaky
  peak|ier
  peaki|est
peal +s +ed +ing
  (ring; fish. △ peel)
pean *Am.* +s (song
  of praise. *Br.*
  paean. △ paeon,
  peon)
pean (fur. △ peen)
pea|nut +s
pea|nut but|ter
pear +s (fruit.
  △ pair, pare, *père*)
pear drop +s

Pearl (name)
pearl +s +ed +ing
  (gem. △ purl)
pearl-diver +s
pearl|er +s (pearl-
  fisher. △ purler)
pearl|es|cent
pearl-fisher +s
Pearl Har|bor (in
  Hawaii)
pearli|ness
pearl|ised *Br.* (use
  pearlized)
pearl|ite (use
  perlite)
pearl|ized
pearl-oyster +s
Pearl River (in
  China)
pearl|ware
pearl|wort +s
pearly
  pearl|ies
  pearl|ier
  pearli|est
pear|main +s
Pear|son, Karl
  (English
  mathematician)
Pear|son, Les|ter
  (Canadian prime
  minister)
peart +er +est
  (cheerful. △ pert)
Peary, Rob|ert
  (American
  explorer)
Peary Land
  (region,
  Greenland)
peas|ant +s
peas|ant|ry
peas|anty
pease (*archaic*
  peas)
pease pud|ding
pea-shooter +s
pea-souper +s
pea stick +s
peat +s
peat|bog +s
peat|land +s
peat|moss
  peat|mosses
peaty
  peat|ier
  peati|est
peau-de-soie
peb|ble
  peb|bles
  peb|bled
  peb|bling

pebble-dash
pebble-dashed
pebbly
  peb|blier
  peb|bli|est
pecan +s (nut.
  △ pekan)
pecca|bil|ity
pec|cable
pecca|dillo
  pecca|dil|loes *or*
  pecca|dil|los
pec|cancy
pec|cant
pec|cary
  pec|car|ies
pec|cavi +s
pêche Melba +s
Pech|enga (region,
  Russia)
Pe|chora (river,
  Russia)
Peck, Greg|ory
  (American actor)
peck +s +ed +ing
peck|er +s
peck|ing order +s
peck|ish
peck order +s
pec|or|ino +s
Pécs (city,
  Hungary)
pec|ten
  pec|tens *or*
  pec|tines
  Zoology
pec|tic
pec|tin +s
  Biochemistry
pec|tin|ate
pec|tin|ated
pec|tin|ation
pec|toral +s
pec|tose
pecu|late
  pecu|lates
  pecu|lated
  pecu|lat|ing
pecu|la|tion
pecu|la|tor +s
pe|cu|liar +s
pe|cu|li|ar|ity
  pe|cu|li|ar|ities
pe|cu|li|ar|ly
pe|cu|ni|ar|ily
pe|cu|ni|ary
peda|gogic
peda|gogic|al
peda|gogic|al|ly
peda|gogics
peda|gog|ism
peda|gogue +s

peda|goguism (use
  pedagogism)
peda|gogy
pedal
  pedals
  ped|alled *Br.*
  ped|aled *Am.*
  ped|al|ling *Br.*
  ped|al|ing *Am.*
  (foot lever; to
  rotate a pedal.
  △ peddle)
ped|al|er *Am.* +s
  (person who
  pedals. △ peddler,
  pedlar)
ped|al|ler *Br.* +s
  (person who
  pedals. △ peddler,
  pedlar)
ped|alo
  ped|alos *or*
  ped|aloes
pedal-pusher +s
ped|ant +s
pe|dan|tic
pe|dan|tic|al|ly
ped|ant|ry
  ped|ant|ries
ped|ate
ped|dle
  ped|dles
  ped|dled
  ped|dling
  (sell; promote.
  △ pedal)
ped|dler +s *Am.*
  (hawker. △
  pedlar. △ pedaler,
  pedaller)
ped|dler +s (drug
  pusher. △ pedaler,
  pedaller, pedlar)
ped|er|ast +s
ped|er|as|tic
ped|er|asty
ped|es|tal
  ped|es|tals
  ped|es|talled *Br.*
  ped|es|taled *Am.*
  ped|es|tal|ling *Br.*
  ped|es|tal|ing *Am.*
ped|es|trian +s
ped|es|tri|an|
  isa|tion *Br.* (use
  pedestrian-
  ization)
ped|es|tri|an|ise
  Br. (use
  pedestrianize)
ped|es|tri|an|ises
ped|es|tri|an|ised

ped¦es¦tri¦an¦ise
(cont.)
  ped¦es¦tri¦an¦
       is¦ing
ped¦es¦tri¦an¦
       iza¦tion
ped¦es¦tri¦an¦ize
  ped¦es¦tri¦an¦izes
  ped¦es¦tri¦an¦ized
  ped¦es¦tri¦an¦
       iz¦ing
pedi¦at¦ric Am. (Br.
  paediatric)
pedi¦at¦ri¦cian Am.
  +s (Br.
  paediatrician)
pedi¦at¦rics Am.
  (Br. paediatrics)
pedi¦at¦rist Am. +s
  (Br. paediatrist)
pedi¦cab +s
pedi¦cel +s
pedi¦cel¦late
ped¦icle +s
pe¦dicu¦lar
pe¦dicu¦late
pe¦dicu¦losis
pe¦dicu¦lous
pedi¦cure
  pedi¦cures
  pedi¦cured
  pedi¦cur¦ing
pedi¦gree +s
pedi¦greed
pedi¦ment +s
pedi¦men¦tal
pedi¦ment¦ed
ped¦lar Br. +s (Am.
  peddler. hawker.
  △ pedaler,
  pedaller, peddler)
ped¦lary
pedo¦logic¦al
ped¦olo¦gist +s
ped¦ology
ped¦ometer +s
pedo¦phile Am. +s
  (Br. paedophile)
pedo¦philia Am.
  (Br. paedophilia)
pedo¦phil¦iac Am.
  +s (Br.
  paedophiliac)
ped¦uncle +s
ped¦un¦cu¦lar
ped¦un¦cu¦late
ped¦way +s
pee
  pees
  peed
  pee¦ing

pee (cont.)
  (urine; urinate.
  △ pea)
Peebles¦shire
  (former county,
  Scotland)
peek +s +ed +ing
  (peep. △ peak,
  peke, pique)
peek¦aboo
Peel, Rob¦ert
  (British prime
  minister)
peel +s +ed +ing
  (skin, rind, etc.;
  shovel; tower.
  △ peal)
peel¦er +s
peel¦ing +s
Peel¦ite +s
peen +s +ed +ing
  (part of hammer.
  △ pean)
Peene¦munde
  (rocket site,
  Germany)
peep +s +ed +ing
peep-bo
peep¦er +s
peep¦hole +s
peep¦ing Tom +s
peep-show +s
peep-sight +s
peep-toe
peep-toed
pee¦pul +s (bo tree.
  △ people)
peer +s +ed +ing
  (look; noble;
  equal. △ pier)
peer¦age +s
peer¦ess
  peer¦esses
peer group +s noun
peer¦less
peeve
  peeves
  peeved
  peev¦ing
peev¦ish
peev¦ish¦ly
peev¦ish¦ness
pee¦wee +s
  (lapwing; magpie
  lark. △ pewee)
pee¦wit +s
peg
  pegs
  pegged
  peg¦ging
Pega¦sean
Pega¦sus Greek
  Mythology

peg¦board +s
Peggy
peg-leg +s
peg¦mat¦ite
peg¦top +s
Pegu (city, Burma)
Peh¦levi
  (= Pahlavi)
Pei, I. M.
  (American
  architect)
Pei¦gan
  plural Pei¦gan or
  Pei¦gans
pei¦gnoir +s
Peirce, C. S.
  (American
  philosopher.
  △ Pierce)
Pei¦sis¦tra¦tus (use
  Pisistratus)
pe¦jora¦tive +s
pe¦jora¦tive¦ly
pekan (animal.
  △ pecan)
peke +s (dog.
  △ peak, peek,
  pique)
Pe¦kin¦ese
  plural Pe¦kin¦ese
  (dog)
Pe¦king (= Beijing)
Pe¦king¦ese
  plural Pe¦king¦ese
  (inhabitant of
  Peking)
Pe¦king man
pekoe
pel¦age +s
Pe¦la¦gian +s (of
  Pelagius)
pe¦la¦gian +s (of
  the sea)
Pe¦la¦gian¦ism
pe¦la¦gic
Pe¦la¦gius (British
  or Irish monk)
pel¦ar¦go¦nium +s
Pe¦las¦gian +s
Pe¦las¦gic
Pelé (Brazilian
  footballer)
pele +s (tower; use
  peel. △ peal)
pel¦er¦ine +s
Pel¦eus Greek
  Mythology
pelf
Pel¦ham, Henry
  (British prime
  minister)
pel¦ham +s
peli¦can +s

Pel¦ion (mountain,
  Greece)
pe¦lisse +s
pel¦ite +s
pel¦lagra
pel¦lag¦rous
pel¦let +s +ed +ing
Pel¦le¦tier, Pierre-
  Joseph (French
  chemist)
pel¦let¦ise Br. (use
  pelletize)
  pel¦let¦ises
  pel¦let¦ised
  pel¦let¦is¦ing
pel¦let¦ize
  pel¦let¦izes
  pel¦let¦ized
  pel¦let¦iz¦ing
pel¦licle +s
pel¦licu¦lar
pel¦li¦tory
  pel¦li¦tor¦ies
pell-mell
pel¦lu¦cid
pel¦lu¦cid¦ity
pel¦lu¦cid¦ly
Pel¦man¦ise Br.
  (use Pelmanize)
  Pel¦man¦ises
  Pel¦man¦ised
  Pel¦man¦is¦ing
Pel¦man¦ism
Pel¦man¦ize
  Pel¦man¦izes
  Pel¦man¦ized
  Pel¦man¦iz¦ing
pel¦met +s
Pelo¦pon¦nese
  (peninsula,
  Greece)
Pelo¦pon¦nes¦ian
  +s
Pe¦lops Greek
  Mythology
pe¦lorus
pe¦lota +s
pelt +s +ed +ing
pelta
  pel¦tae
pel¦tate
pelt¦ry
pel¦vic
pel¦vis
  pel¦vises or
  pel¦ves
Pemba (port,
  Mozambique)
Pem¦broke (town,
  Wales)

Pem¦broke¦shire
(former county,
Wales)
pem¦mican
pem¦phig¦oid
pem¦phig¦ous
pem¦phigus
PEN
(= International
Association of
Poets,
Playwrights,
Editors, Essayists,
and Novelists)
pen
  pens
  penned
  pen¦ning
penal
pen¦al¦isa¦tion *Br.*
  (use penalization)
pen¦al¦ise *Br.* (use
  penalize)
  pen¦al¦ises
  pen¦al¦ised
  pen¦al¦is¦ing
pen¦al¦iza¦tion
pen¦al¦ize
  pen¦al¦izes
  pen¦al¦ized
  pen¦al¦iz¦ing
pen¦al¦ly
pen¦alty
  pen¦al¦ties
pen¦ance
  pen¦ances
  pen¦anced
  pen¦an¦cing
pen and ink *noun*
pen-and-ink
  adjective
Pen¦ang (island and
  state, Malaysia)
pen¦an¦nu¦lar
pe¦na¦tes
pence
pen¦chant +s
pen¦cil
  pen¦cils
  pen¦cilled *Br.*
  pen¦ciled *Am.*
  pen¦cil¦ling *Br.*
  pen¦cil¦ing *Am.*
pen¦cil box
  pen¦cil boxes
pen¦cil case +s
pen¦cil¦er *Am.* +s
pen¦cil¦ler *Br.* +s
pencil-pusher +s
pencil-pushing
pen¦cil sharp¦en¦er
  +s

pen¦dant +s *noun*
pen¦dency
pen¦dent *adjective*
pen¦dente lite
pen¦dent¦ive +s
Pen¦de¦recki,
  Krzysz¦tof
  (Polish composer)
pend¦ing
pend¦ing tray +s
pen¦dragon
pen¦du¦late
  pen¦du¦lates
  pen¦du¦lated
  pen¦du¦lat¦ing
pen¦du¦line
pen¦du¦lous
pen¦du¦lous¦ly
pen¦du¦lum +s
Pe¦nel¦ope (*Greek
  Mythology*; name)
pe¦ne¦plain +s
pene¦tra¦bil¦ity
pene¦trable
pene¦tra¦lia
pene¦trant +s
pene¦trate
  pene¦trates
  pene¦trated
  pene¦trat¦ing
pene¦trat¦ing¦ly
pene¦tra¦tion +s
pene¦tra¦tive
pene¦tra¦tor +s
pen-feather +s
pen¦friend +s
pen¦guin +s
pen hold¦er +s
peni¦cil¦late
peni¦cil¦lin +s
pen¦ile
pen¦ill¦ion
pen¦in¦sula +s
  noun
pen¦in¦su¦lar
  adjective
penis
  pen¦ises
peni¦tence +s
peni¦tent +s
peni¦ten¦tial +s
peni¦ten¦tial¦ly
peni¦ten¦tiary
  peni¦ten¦tiar¦ies
peni¦tent¦ly
pen¦knife
  pen¦knives
pen¦light +s
pen¦man
  pen¦men
pen¦man¦ship

Penn, Wil¦liam
  (English Quaker,
  founder of
  Pennsylvania)
pen-name +s
pen¦nant +s
penne (pasta)
penni
  pen¦niä
  (Finnish currency.
  ⚠ penny)
pen¦nies
pen¦ni¦less
pen¦ni¦less¦ly
pen¦ni¦less¦ness
pen¦nill
  pen¦ill¦ion
Pen¦nine Hills (in
  England)
Pen¦nines
  (= Pennine Hills)
pen¦non +s
pen¦noned
penn'orth
Penn¦syl¦va¦nia
  (state, USA)
Penn¦syl¦va¦nian
  +s
Penny (name)
penny
  pen¦nies *or* pence
  (British currency;
  US cent. ⚠ penni)
penny-a-liner +s
penny black +s
penny dread¦ful
  +s
penny-farthing +s
  (bicycle)
penny-in-the-slot
penny-pincher +s
penny-pinching
penny¦royal
penny¦weight +s
penny whis¦tle +s
penny wise
penny¦wort +s
penny¦worth +s
peno¦logic¦al
pen¦olo¦gist +s
pen¦ology
pen pal +s
pen-pusher +s
pen-pushing
pen¦sée +s
pen¦sile
pen¦sion +s +ed
  +ing (payment)
pen¦sion +s
  (boarding house)
pen¦sion¦abil¦ity
pen¦sion¦able

pen¦sion¦ary
  pen¦sion¦ar¦ies
pen¦sion¦er +s
pen¦sion¦less
pen¦sive
pen¦sive¦ly
pen¦sive¦ness
pen¦ste¦mon +s
pen¦stock +s
pent
penta¦chord +s
pent¦acle +s
pen¦tad +s
penta¦dac¦tyl +s
Penta¦gon (US
  defence HQ)
penta¦gon +s (five-
  sided figure)
pen¦tagon¦al
penta¦gram +s
pent¦agyn¦ous
penta¦he¦dral
penta¦he¦dron
  penta¦he¦dra *or*
  penta¦he¦drons
pen¦tam¦er¦ous
pen¦tam¦eter +s
pen¦tan¦drous
pen¦tane +s
pent¦angle +s
penta¦no¦ic
penta¦prism +s
Penta¦teuch
Penta¦teuchal
pent¦ath¦lete +s
pent¦ath¦lon +s
penta¦tonic
penta¦va¦lent
Pente¦cost
Pente¦cos¦tal +s
Pente¦cos¦tal¦ism
Pente¦cos¦tal¦ist
  +s
Pen¦the¦si¦lea
  Greek Mythology
pent¦house +s
penti¦mento
  penti¦menti
Pent¦land Firth
  (off Scotland)
pento¦bar¦bital
pento¦bar¦bit¦one
pen¦tode +s
pen¦tose +s
Pento¦thal
pent roof +s
pent¦ste¦mon +s
  (use penstemon)
pen¦tyl
pen¦ult
pen¦ul¦ti¦mate

pen|um|bra
pen|um|brae
pen|um|bral
pen|uri|ous
pen|uri|ous|ly
pen|uri|ous|ness
pen|ury
Penza (city, Russia)
Pen|zance (town,
  England)
peon +s (labourer.
  △ paean, paeon,
  pean)
pe|on|age
peony
  peon|ies
people
  peoples
  peopled
  peop|ling
  (persons. △ peepul)
people's
  dem|oc|racy
people's
  dem|oc|ra|cies
Pe|oria (city, USA)
PEP (= Personal
  Equity Plan)
pep
  peps
  pepped
  pep|ping
  (vigour; enliven)
pep|er|ino
pep|er|oni +s (use
  pepperoni)
pep|lum +s
pepo +s
pep|per +s +ed
  +ing
pep|per|box
  pep|per|boxes
pep|per|corn +s
pep|peri|ness
pep|per mill +s
pep|per|mint +s
pep|per|minty
pep|per|oni
pep|per pot +s
pep|per|wort +s
pep|pery
pep pill +s
pep|pily
pep|pi|ness
peppy
  pep|pier
  pep|pi|est
Pepsi(-Cola) +s
  Propr.
pep|sin
pep talk +s
pep|tic
pep|tide +s

pep|tone +s
pep|ton|ise Br. (use
  peptonize)
pep|ton|ises
pep|ton|ised
pep|ton|is|ing
pep|ton|ize
pep|ton|izes
pep|ton|ized
pep|ton|iz|ing
Pepys, Sam|uel
  (English diarist)
per
per|ad|ven|ture
Perak (state,
  Malaysia)
per|am|bu|late
  per|am|bu|lates
  per|am|bu|lated
  per|am|bu|lat|ing
per|am|bu|la|tion
per|am|bu|la|tor
  +s
per|am|bu|la|tory
per annum
per|cale
per cap|ita
per caput
per|ceiv|able
per|ceive
  per|ceives
  per|ceived
  per|ceiv|ing
per|ceiver +s
per|cent Am.
per cent Br.
per|cent|age +s
per|cent|ile +s
per|cept +s
per|cep|ti|bil|ity
per|cep|tible
per|cep|tibly
per|cep|tion +s
per|cep|tion|al
per|cep|tive
per|cep|tive|ly
per|cep|tive|ness
per|cep|tiv|ity
per|cep|tual
per|cep|tual|ly
Per|ce|val
  (legendary hero.
  △ Percival)
Per|ce|val,
  Spen|cer (British
  prime minister)
perch
  perches
  perched
  perch|ing
  (branch; measure)
perch
  plural perch *or*

perch (*cont.*)
  perches
  (fish)
per|chance
perch|er +s
per|cheron +s
per|chlor|ate +s
per|chlor|ic
per|chloro|ethyl
           ene
per|cipi|ence
per|cipi|ent +s
per|cipi|ent|ly
Per|ci|val (name.
  △ Perceval)
per|col|late
  per|col|lates
  per|col|lated
  per|col|lat|ing
per|co|la|tion
per|co|la|tor +s
per con|tra
per|cuss
  per|cusses
  per|cussed
  per|cuss|ing
per|cus|sion +s
per|cus|sion|ist +s
per|cus|sive
per|cus|sive|ly
per|cus|sive|ness
per|cu|tan|eous
Percy (name)
Percy, Henry
  ('Harry Hotspur',
  English soldier)
per diem
per|di|tion
per|dur|abil|ity
per|dur|able
per|dur|ably
père +s (father.
  △ pair, pare,
  pear)
Père David's deer
  plural Père
  David's deer
pere|grin|ate
  pere|grin|ates
  pere|grin|ated
  pere|grin|at|ing
pere|grin|ation +s
pere|grin|ator +s
Pere|grine (name)
pere|grine +s
  (falcon)
Perel|man,
  Sid|ney Jo|seph
  (American writer)
per|emp|tor|ily
per|emp|tori|ness
per|emp|tory

per|en|nial +s
per|en|ni|al|ity
per|en|ni|al|ly
Peres, Shi|mon
  (Israeli prime
  minister)
pere|stroika
Pérez de Cuél|lar,
  Ja|vier (Peruvian
  Secretary-General
  of the UN)
per|fect +s +ed
  +ing
per|fecta +s (type
  of bet.
  △ perfecter
  perfector)
per|fect|er +s
  (person or thing
  that perfects.
  △ perfecta
  perfector)
per|fect|ibil|ity
per|fect|ible
per|fec|tion +s
per|fec|tion|ism
per|fec|tion|ist +s
per|fect|ive +s
per|fect|ly
per|fect|ness
per|fecto +s
per|fect|or +s
  (printing machine.
  △ perfecta,
  perfecter)
per|fer|vid
per|fer|vid|ly
per|fer|vid|ness
per|fidi|ous
per|fidi|ous|ly
per|fidy
  per|fid|ies
per|fin +s
per|fo|li|ate
per|for|ate
  per|for|ates
  per|for|ated
  per|for|at|ing
per|for|ation +s
per|fora|tive
per|for|ator +s
per|force
per|forin
per|form +s +ed
  +ing
per|form|abil|ity
per|form|able
per|form|ance +s
per|forma|tive +s
per|forma|tory
  per|forma|tor|ies
per|form|er +s

per|fume
  per|fumes
  per|fumed
  per|fum|ing
per|fumer +s
per|fumery
  per|fumer|ies
per|fumy
per|func|tor|ily
per|func|tori|ness
per|func|tory
per|fuse
  per|fuses
  per|fused
  per|fus|ing
per|fu|sion +s
per|fu|sive
Per|ga|mene +s
Per|ga|mum
  (ancient city)
per|gana +s (use
  pargana)
per|gola +s
per|gun|nah +s
  (use pargana)
per|haps
peri +s
peri|anth +s
peri|apt +s
peri|car|diac
peri|car|dial
peri|card|itis
peri|car|dium
  peri|car|dia
peri|carp +s
peri|chon|drium
  peri|chon|dria
peri|clase
Peri|cles (Athenian
  statesman)
peri|clinal
peri|cope +s
peri|cra|nium +s
peri|dot +s
peri|gean
peri|gee +s
peri|gla|cial
Péri|gord (district,
  France)
per|igyn|ous
peri|he|lion
  peri|he|lia
peril
  perils
  per|illed *Br.*
  per|iled *Am.*
  per|il|ling *Br.*
  per|il|ing *Am.*
peri|il|ous
peri|il|ous|ly
peri|il|ous|ness
peri|lune

peri|lymph
peri|im|eter +s
peri|met|ric
peri|natal
peri|neal
peri|neum +s
period +s
peri|od|ate +s
peri|od|ic
peri|od|ic|al +s
peri|od|ic|al|ly
peri|od|icity
peri|od|isa|tion *Br.*
  (use
  periodization)
peri|od|ise *Br.* (use
  periodize)
  peri|od|ises
  peri|od|ised
  peri|od|is|ing
peri|od|iza|tion
peri|od|ize
  peri|od|izes
  peri|od|ized
  peri|od|iz|ing
peri|odon|tal
peri|odon|tics
peri|odon|tist +s
peri|odon|tol|ogy
peri|opera|tive
peri|os|teal
peri|os|teum
  peri|os|tea
peri|ost|itis
peri|pat|et|ic
peri|pat|et|ic|al|ly
peri|pat|eti|cism
peri|pet|eia
peri|iph|eral +s
peri|iph|er|al|ly
peri|iph|ery
  peri|iph|er|ies
peri|phrasis
  peri|phrases
peri|phras|tic
peri|phras|tic|al|ly
peri|ip|teral
per|ique
peri|scope +s
peri|scop|ic
peri|scop|ic|al|ly
per|ish
  per|ishes
  per|ished
  per|ish|ing
per|ish|abil|ity
per|ish|able +s
per|ish|able|ness
per|ish|er +s
per|ish|ing
per|ish|ing|ly
per|ish|less

peri|sperm +s
peri|isso|dac|tyl +s
peri|ista|lith +s
peri|stal|sis
peri|stal|tic
peri|stal|tic|al|ly
peri|stome +s
peri|style +s
peri|ton|eal
peri|ton|eum
  peri|ton|eums *or*
  peri|tonea
peri|ton|itis
peri|wig +s
peri|wigged
peri|win|kle +s
per|jure
  per|jures
  per|jured
  per|jur|ing
per|jurer +s
per|juri|ous
per|jury
  per|jur|ies
perk +s +ed +ing
perk|ily
Per|kin, Wil|liam
  Henry (English
  chemist)
perki|ness
perky
  perk|ier
  perki|est
Per|lis (state,
  Malaysia)
perl|ite
Perm (city, Russia)
perm +s +ed +ing
perma|cul|ture
perma|frost
perm|al|loy
per|man|ence
per|man|ency
per|man|ent
per|man|ent|ise
  Br. (use
  permanentize)
  per|man|ent|ises
  per|man|ent|ised
  per|man|ent|
        is|ing
per|man|ent|ize
  per|man|ent|izes
  per|man|ent|ized
  per|man|ent|
        iz|ing
per|man|ent|ly
per|man|gan|ate
  +s
per|man|gan|ic
per|mea|bil|ity
  per|mea|bil|ities

per|me|able
per|me|ance
per|me|ant
per|me|ate
  per|me|ates
  per|me|ated
  per|me|ating
per|me|ation +s
per|me|ator +s
per|meth|rin
Per|mian
per mil
per mille
per|mis|si|bil|ity
per|mis|sible
per|mis|sibly
per|mis|sion +s
per|mis|sive
per|mis|sive|ly
per|mis|sive|ness
per|mit
  per|mits
  per|mit|ted
  per|mit|ting
per|mit|tee +s
per|mit|ter +s
per|mit|tiv|ity
per|mu|tate
  per|mu|tates
  per|mu|tated
  per|mu|tat|ing
per|mu|ta|tion +s
per|mu|ta|tion|al
per|mute
  per|mutes
  per|muted
  per|mut|ing
Per|mu|tit *Propr.*
Per|nam|buco
  (state, Brazil;
  former name of
  Recife)
per|ni|cious
per|ni|cious|ly
per|ni|cious|ness
per|nick|ety
per|noc|tate
  per|noc|tates
  per|noc|tated
  per|noc|tat|ing
per|noc|ta|tion
Per|nod +s *Propr.*
Perón, Evita
  (Argentinian
  politician)
Perón, Juan
  Dom|ingo
  (Argentinian
  president)
pero|neal
Peron|ism
Peron|ist +s

per|or|ate
  per|or|ates
  per|or|ated
  per|or|at|ing
per|or|ation +s
per|ox|id|ase +s
per|ox|ide
  per|ox|ides
  per|ox|ided
  per|ox|id|ing
per|pend +s +ed
  +ing
Per|pen|dicu|lar
  Architecture
per|pen|dicu|lar
  +s
per|pen|dicu|lar|
    ity
per|pen|dicu|lar|ly
per|pet|rable
per|pet|rate
  per|pet|rates
  per|pet|rated
  per|pet|rat|ing
per|pet|ra|tion
per|pet|ra|tor +s
per|pet|ual
per|petu|al|ism
per|petu|al|ly
per|petu|ance
per|petu|ate
  per|petu|ates
  per|petu|ated
  per|petu|at|ing
per|petu|ation
per|petu|ator +s
per|petu|ity
  per|petu|ities
per|petuum
  mo|bile +s
Per|pignan (city,
  France)
per|plex
  per|plexes
  per|plexed
  per|plex|ing
per|plex|ed|ly
per|plex|ing|ly
per|plex|ity
  per|plex|ities
per pro.
per|quis|ite +s
Per|rault, Charles
  (French writer)
Per|rier +s *Propr.*
Per|rin, Jean
  Bap|tiste (French
  physical chemist)
per|ron +s
Perry (name)
Perry, Fred
  (English lawn

Perry (*cont.*)
  tennis and table
  tennis player)
perry
  per|ries
  (drink)
per se
per|se|cute
  per|se|cutes
  per|se|cuted
  per|se|cut|ing
per|se|cu|tion +s
per|se|cu|tor +s
per|se|cu|tory
Per|seids (meteor
  shower)
Per|seph|one *Greek
  Mythology*
Per|sep|olis (city,
  ancient Persia)
Per|seus *Greek
  Mythology*
per|se|ver|ance
per|sev|er|ate
  per|sev|er|ates
  per|sev|er|ated
  per|sev|er|at|ing
per|sev|er|ation
per|se|vere
  per|se|veres
  per|se|vered
  per|se|ver|ing
Per|shing (missile)
persh|merga
  plural
  persh|merga *or*
  persh|mer|gas
Per|sia
Per|sian +s
Per|sian Gulf
per|si|ennes
per|si|flage
per|sim|mon +s
per|sist +s +ed
  +ing
per|sist|ence
per|sist|ency
per|sist|ent
per|sist|ent|ly
per|snick|ety
per|son
  plural per|sons *or*
  people
per|sona
  per|so|nae *or*
  per|so|nas
per|son|able
per|son|able|ness
per|son|ably
per|son|age +s
per|sona grata

per|son|al (private.
  ⚠ personnel)
per|son|al|isa|tion
  Br. (use
  personalization)
per|son|al|ise *Br.*
  (use personalize)
per|son|al|ises
per|son|al|ised
per|son|al|is|ing
per|son|al|ity
  per|son|al|ities
per|son|al|iza|tion
per|son|al|ize
  per|son|al|izes
  per|son|al|ized
  per|son|al|iz|ing
per|son|al|ly
per|son|alty
  per|son|al|ties
per|sona non grata
per|son|ate
  per|son|ates
  per|son|ated
  per|son|at|ing
per|son|ation
per|son|ator +s
per|son|hood
per|soni|fi|ca|tion
  +s
per|son|ifier +s
per|son|ify
  per|soni|fies
  per|soni|fied
  per|soni|fy|ing
per|son|nel
  (employees.
  ⚠ personal)
person-to-person
per|spec|tival
per|spec|tive +s
per|spec|tive|ly
per spex *Propr.*
per|spi|ca|cious
per|spi|ca|cious|ly
per|spi|ca|cious|
    ness
per|spi|ca|city
per|spi|cu|ity
per|spicu|ous
per|spicu|ous|ly
per|spicu|ous|ness
per|spir|ation
per|spira|tory
per|spire
  per|spires
  per|spired
  per|spir|ing
per|suad|abil|ity
per|suad|able
per|suade
  per|suades

per|suade (*cont.*)
  per|suaded
  per|suad|ing
per|suader +s
per|sua|sible
per|sua|sion +s
per|sua|sive
per|sua|sive|ly
per|sua|sive|ness
PERT
  (= programme
  evaluation and
  review technique)
pert +er +est
  (impudent.
  ⚠ peart)
per|tain +s +ed
  +ing
Perth (town,
  Scotland; city,
  Australia)
Perthes, Jacques
  Bou|cher de
  (French
  archaeologist)
Perth|shire (former
  county, Scotland)
per|tin|acious
per|tin|acious|ly
per|tin|acious|
    ness
per|tin|acity
per|tin|ence
per|tin|ency
per|tin|ent
per|tin|ent|ly
pert|ly
pert|ness
per|turb +s +ed
  +ing
per|turb|able
per|turb|ation +s
per|turb|ative
per|turb|ing|ly
per|tus|sis
Peru
Peru|gia (city,
  Italy)
per|uke +s
per|usal +s
per|use
  per|uses
  per|used
  per|us|ing
per|user +s
Peru|vian +s
perv +s (use perve)
per|vade
  per|vades
  per|vaded
  per|vad|ing
per|va|sion

per|va|sive
per|va|sive|ly
per|va|sive|ness
perve
  perves
  perved
  perv|ing
per|verse
per|verse|ly
per|verse|ness
per|ver|sion +s
per|vers|ity
  per|vers|ities
per|ver|sive
per|vert +s +ed
  +ing
per|vert|ed|ly
per|vert|er +s
per|vi|ous
per|vi|ous|ness
Pe|sach
pe|seta +s
pe|sewa +s
Pe|sha|war (city,
  Pakistan)
Pe|shitta
pesh|merga
  plural pesh|merga
  or pesh|mer|gas
pesk|ily
peski|ness
pesky
  pesk|ier
  peski|est
peso +s
pes|sary
  pes|sar|ies
pes|sim|ism
pes|sim|ist +s
pes|sim|is|tic
pes|sim|is|tic|al|ly
pest +s
Pesta|lozzi,
  Jo|hann
  Hein|rich (Swiss
  educationalist)
pes|ter +s +ed
  +ing
pes|ter|er +s
pest-house +s
pesti|cidal
pesti|cide +s
pest|ifer|ous
pesti|lence +s
pesti|lent
pesti|len|tial
pesti|len|tial|ly
pesti|lent|ly
pes|tle
  pes|tles
  pes|tled
  pest|ling

pesto
pesto|logic|al
pest|olo|gist +s
pest|ology
pet
  pets
  pet|ted
  pet|ting
  (animal; favourite;
  fondle; temper)
Peta (woman's
  name. △ Peter)
Pé|tain, Henri
  Phil|ippe (French
  general)
petal +s
pet|aled *Am.*
petal|ine
pet|alled *Br.*
petal-like
petal|oid
pet|alon
peta|meter *Am.* +s
peta|metre *Br.* +s
pé|tanque
pe|tard +s
peta|sus
pe|taur|ist +s
Pete
pe|techia
  pe|techiae
pe|tech|ial
Peter (Apostle and
  saint; man's name.
  △ Peta)
peter +s +ed +ing
  (diminish; prison
  cell)
Peter|bor|ough
  (city, England)
peter|man
  peter|men
Peter Pan (boy
  hero of play)
Peter Prin|ciple
peter|sham +s
Peter|son, Oscar
  (Canadian jazz
  musician)
Peter's pence
Peters pro|jec|tion
peth|id|ine
peti|olar
peti|ol|ate
peti|ole +s
Pe|tipa, Mar|ius
  (French
  choreographer)
petit (*Law* minor.
  △ petty)
petit bour|geois
  petits bour|geois

pe|tite *female*
pe|tite
  bour|geoisie
petit four
  petits fours
pe|ti|tion +s +ed
  +ing
pe|ti|tion|able
pe|ti|tion|ary
  pe|ti|tion|ar|ies
pe|ti|tion|er +s
pe|ti tio prin|cipii
petit jury (use
  petty jury)
  petit jur|ies
petit-maître +s
petit mal
petit point
pe|tits pois
pet name +s
Petra (ancient city,
  SW Asia; name)
Pet|rarch (Italian
  poet)
Pet|rarch|an
pet|rel +s (bird.
  △ petrol)
Petri dish
  Petri dishes
Pe|trie, Flin|ders
  (English
  archaeologist)
petri|fac|tion
pet|rify
  petri|fies
  petri|fied
  petri|fy|ing
petro|chem|ical +s
petro|chem|is|try
petro|dol|lar +s
petro|gen|esis
petro|glyph +s
Petro|grad (former
  name of St
  Petersburg)
pet|rog|raph|er +s
petro|graph|ic
petro|graph|ic|al
pet|rog|raphy
pet|rol +s (fuel.
  △ petrel)
pet|rol|atum
pet|rol|eum +s
pet|rol|ic
petro|logic
petro|logic|al
pet|rolo|gist +s
pet|rology
pet|ronel +s
Pe|tro|nius, Gaius
  (Roman writer)

Petro|pav|lovsk *in
  full* Petropavlovsk-
  Kamchat|sky
  (port, Russia)
pet|rous
Petro|za|vodsk
  (city, Russia)
Pet|samo (former
  name of
  Pechenga)
pet|ter +s
petti|coat +s
petti|coat|ed
petti|coat|less
petti|fog
  petti|fogs
  petti|fogged
  petti|fog|ging
petti|fog|ger +s
petti|fog|gery
pet|tily
petti|ness
pet|tish
pet|tish|ly
pet|tish|ness
petti|toe +s
petty
  pet|tier
  pet|ti|est
  (trivial; mean.
  △ petit)
petty bour|geois
  (use petit
  bourgeois)
  plural petty
  bour|geois
petty bour|geoisie
  (use petite
  bourgeoisie)
petty jury
  petty jur|ies
petu|lance
petu|lant
petu|lant|ly
pe|tu|nia +s
pe|tun|tse
Pevs|ner, An|toine
  (Russian-born
  French artist)
pew +s +ed +ing
  (bench. △ *più*)
pew|age
pewee +s
  (flycatcher.
  △ peewee)
pewit +s (use
  peewit)
pew|less
pew|ter +s
pew|ter|er +s
pey|ote +s
pey|ot|ism

pfen|nig +s
Phae|acian +s
Phae|dra *Greek*
  Mythology
Phae|thon *Greek*
  Mythology
phae|ton +s
  (carriage; car)
phage +s
pha|ged|aena
pha|ged|aen|ic
phago|cyte +s
phago|cyt|ic
phago|cyt|ise *Br.*
  (use phagocytize)
phago|cyt|ises
phago|cyt|ised
phago|cyt|is|ing
phago|cyt|ize
phago|cyt|izes
phago|cyt|ized
phago|cyt|iz|ing
phago|cyt|ose
phago|cyt|oses
phago|cyt|osed
phago|cyt|os|ing
phago|cyt|osis
Phai|stos (town,
  Crete)
Phal|ange
  (Lebanese activist
  party. △ Falange)
phal|ange +s
  (bone)
pha|lan|geal
pha|lan|ger +s
Pha|lan|gist +s
phal|an|ster|ian
phal|an|stery
  phal|an|ster|ies
phal|anx
  phal|anxes *or*
  pha|lan|ges
phala|rope +s
phalli
phal|lic
phal|lic|al|ly
phalli|cism
phal|lism
phallo|cen|tric
phal|lo|cen|tri|city
phal|lo|cen|trism
phal|lus
  phalli *or*
  phal|luses
phan|ariot +s
phan|ero|gam +s
phan|ero|gam|ic
phan|er|og|am|ous
phan|ta|sise *Br.*
  (use fantasize)
  phan|ta|sises

phan|ta|sise (*cont.*)
  phan|ta|sised
  phan|ta|sis|ing
phan|ta|size (use
  fantasize)
  phan|ta|sizes
  phan|ta|sized
  phan|ta|siz|ing
phan|tasm +s
phan|tas|ma|goria
  +s
phan|tas|ma|gor|ic
phan|tas|ma|
    gor|ic|al
phan|tas|mal
phan|tas|mic
phan|tast +s (use
  fantast)
phan|tasy (use
  fantasy)
  phan|ta|sies
phantom +s
Phar|aoh +s
Phar|aoh's ant +s
Phar|aoh's
  ser|pent +s
Phar|aon|ic
Phari|sa|ic
Phari|saic|al
Phari|sa|ism
Phari|see +s
pharma|ceut|ical
  +s
pharma|ceut|ic|
    al|ly
pharma|ceut|ics
pharma|cist +s
pharma|cog|nosy
pharma|co|logic|al
pharma|co|logic|
    al|ly
pharma|colo|gist
  +s
pharma|col|ogy
pharma|co|poeia
  +s
pharma|co|poeial
phar|macy
  phar|ma|cies
Pharos (island and
  ancient lighthouse
  off Egypt)
pharos
  phar|oses
  (any lighthouse)
pha|ryn|gal
pha|ryn|geal
pha|ryn|gitis
pha|ryn|go|scope
  +s

pha|ryn|got|omy
pha|ryn|
    goto|mies
phar|ynx
  pha|ryn|ges
phase
  phases
  phased
  phas|ing
  (stage. △ faze)
phas|ic
phat|ic
phea|sant +s
phea|sant|ry
  phea|sant|ries
Phei|dip|pi|des
  (Athenian
  messenger)
phen|acetin
phen|cyc|lid|ine
pheno|bar|bital
pheno|bar|bit|one
pheno|cryst +s
phe|nol +s
phen|ol|ic
pheno|logic|al
phen|olo|gist +s
phen|ology
phe|nol|phthal|ein
phe|nom +s
phe|nom|ena
  (plural of
  phenomenon)
phe|nom|enal
phe|nom|en|al|ise
  Br. (use
  phenomenalize)
  phe|nom|en|al|
    ises
phe|nom|en|al|
    ised
phe|nom|en|al|
    is|ing
phe|nom|en|al|ism
phe|nom|en|al|ist
  +s
phe|nom|en|al|
    is|tic
phe|nom|en|al|ize
  phe|nom|en|al|
    izes
phe|nom|en|al|
    ized
phe|nom|en|al|
    iz|ing
phe|nom|en|al|ly
phe|nom|eno|
    logic|al
phe|nom|eno|logic|
    al|ly
phe|nom|en|
    olo|gist +s

phe|nom|en|ology
phe|nom|enon
  phe|nom|ena
pheno|type +s
pheno|typ|ic
pheno|typ|ic|al
pheno|typ|ic|al|ly
phenyl (chemical
  radical. △ fennel)
phenyl|alan|ine
phenyl|ke|ton|uria
phero|monal
phero|mone +s
phew (*interjection.*
  △ few)
phi +s (Greek letter.
  △ fie)
phial +s (small
  bottle. △ file)
Phi Beta Kappa +s
Phid|ias (Athenian
  sculptor)
Phil
phila|beg +s (use
  filibeg)
Phila|delphia (city,
  USA)
phila|delphus
phil|an|der +s +ed
  +ing
phil|an|der|er +s
phil|an|thrope +s
phil|an|throp|ic
phil|an|throp|ic|
    al|ly
phil|an|thro|pise
  Br. (use
  philanthropize)
  phil|an|thro|pises
  phil|an|thro|pised
  phil|an|thro|
    pis|ing
phil|an|throp|ism
phil|an|throp|ist
  +s
phil|an|thro|pize
  phil|an|thro|pizes
  phil|an|thro|pized
  phil|an|thro|
    piz|ing
phil|an|thropy
phila|tel|ic
phila|tel|ic|al|ly
phil|atel|ist +s
phil|ately
Philby, Kim
  (British Soviet
  spy)
Phi|le|mon *Greek*
  Mythology
phil|har|mon|ic
phil|hel|lene +s

phil|hel|len|ic
phil|hel|len|ism
phil|hel|len|ist +s
Philip (Prince,
    Duke of
    Edinburgh;
    Apostle and saint;
    Macedonian,
    French, and
    Spanish kings)
Philip also Phil|lip
    (name)
Phil|ippa
Phil|ippi (city,
    ancient
    Macedonia)
Phil|ip|pian +s
phil|ip|pic +s
phil|ip|pina +s
Phil|ip|pine
Phil|ip|pines
    (archipelago)
Phil|ip|popo|lis
    (ancient Greek
    name for Plovdiv)
Phil|is|tine +s
    (member of
    ancient people)
phil|is|tine +s
    (uncultured
    person)
phil|is|tin|ism
Phil|lida also
    Phyl|lida
Phil|lip also Philip
    (name)
Phil|lips (screw;
    screwdriver)
    Propr.
Phil|lips curve +s
phil|lu|men|ist +s
phil|lu|meny
Philly
    (= Philadelphia)
philo|den|dron
    philo|den|drons
    or philo|den|dra
phil|ogy|nist +s
Philo Ju|daeus
    (Jewish
    philosopher)
philo|lo|ger +s
philo|lo|gian +s
philo|logic|al
philo|logic|al|ly
phil|olo|gise Br.
    (use philologize)
    phil|olo|gises
    phil|olo|gised
    phil|olo|gis|ing
phil|olo|gist +s

phil|olo|gize
    phil|olo|gizes
    phil|olo|gized
    phil|olo|giz|ing
phil|ology
Philo|mel Greek
    Mythology
Philo|mela
    (= Philomel)
Philo|mena
philo|pro|geni|tive
philo|soph|as|ter
    +s
phil|oso|pher +s
phil|oso|phers'
    stone
philo|soph|ic
philo|soph|ic|al
philo|soph|ic|al|ly
phil|oso|phise Br.
    (use
    philosophize)
    phil|oso|phises
    phil|oso|phised
    phil|oso|phis|ing
phil|oso|phiser Br.
    +s (use
    philosophizer)
phil|oso|phize
    phil|oso|phizes
    phil|oso|phized
    phil|oso|phiz|ing
phil|oso|phizer +s
phil|oso|phy
    phil|oso|phies
phil|ter Am. +s (love
    potion. △ filter)
phil|tre Br. +s (love
    potion. △ filter)
phi|mo|sis
    phi|mo|ses
phi|mot|ic
Phin|eas
phiz (face. △ fizz)
phizog +s
phle|bit|ic
phle|bitis
phle|bot|om|ise Br.
    (use
    phlebotomize)
    phle|bot|om|ises
    phle|bot|om|ised
    phle|bot|om|
        is|ing
phle|bot|om|ist +s
phle|bot|om|ize
    phle|bot|om|izes
    phle|bot|om|ized
    phle|bot|om|
        iz|ing

phle|bot|omy
    phle|boto|mies
phlegm
phleg|mat|ic
phleg|mat|ic|al|ly
phlegmy
phloem
phlo|gis|tic
phlo|gis|ton
phlox
    phloxes
Phnom Penh
    (capital of
    Cambodia)
pho|bia +s
pho|bic +s
Pho|bos (Greek
    Mythology; moon
    of Mars)
Phoebe (Greek
    Mythology; moon
    of Saturn; name)
phoebe +s (bird)
Phoe|bus Greek
    Mythology
Phoe|ni|cia
    (ancient country,
    Near East)
Phoen|ician +s
Phoe|nix (city,
    USA)
phoe|nix
    phoe|nixes
    (mythical bird;
    unique person or
    thing)
Phoe|nix Is|lands
    (in W. Pacific)
pho|las
    pho|lases
phon +s
phon|ate
    phon|ates
    phon|ated
    phon|at|ing
phon|ation
phon|atory
phon|auto|graph
    +s
phone
    phones
    phoned
    phon|ing
phone book +s
phone|card +s
phone-in +s noun
    and adjective
phon|eme +s
phon|em|ic
phon|em|ics
phon|endo|scope
    +s

phon|et|ic
phon|et|ic|al|ly
phon|eti|cian +s
phon|eti|cise Br.
    (use phoneticize)
    phon|eti|cises
    phon|eti|cised
    phon|eti|cis|ing
phon|eti|cism
phon|eti|cist +s
phon|eti|cize
    phon|eti|cizes
    phon|eti|cized
    phon|eti|ciz|ing
phon|et|ics
phon|et|ist +s
pho|ney
    pho|neys
    pho|nier
    pho|ni|est
phon|ic
phon|ic|al|ly
phon|ics
pho|nily
pho|ni|ness
phono attributive
phono|gram +s
phono|graph +s
phono|graph|ic
phon|og|raphy
phono|lite +s
phono|logic|al
phono|lo|gic|al|ly
phon|olo|gist +s
phon|ology
    phon|olo|gies
phon|ometer +s
pho|non +s
phono|scope +s
phony (use
    phoney)
    pho|nies
    pho|nier
    pho|ni|est
phooey
phor|esy
phor|et|ic
phor|mium
phos|gene
phos|phat|ase +s
phos|phate +s
phos|phat|ic
phos|phene
    (sensation in eye.
    △ phosphine)
phos|phide +s
phos|phine (gas.
    △ phosphene)
phos|phin|ic
phos|phite +s
phos|pho|lipid +s
phos|phor +s

phos¦phor¦ate
  phos¦phor¦ates
  phos¦phor¦ated
  phos¦phor¦at¦ing
  phos¦phor¦esce
  phos¦phor¦esces
  phos¦phor¦esced
  phos¦phor¦es¦cing
phos¦phor|
    es¦cence
phos¦phor¦es¦cent
phos¦phor¦ic
phos¦phor¦ite
phos¦phor¦ous
  adjective
phos¦phorus *noun*
phos¦phor¦yl¦ate
  phos¦phor¦yl¦ates
  phos¦phor¦yl¦ated
  phos¦phor¦yl|
    at¦ing
phos¦phor¦yl¦ation
phossy jaw
phot +s
phot¦ic
phot¦ism +s
Pho¦tius (Byzantine
  scholar)
photo +s *noun*
photo
  pho¦toes
  pho¦toed
  photo¦ing
  verb
photo¦biol¦ogy
photo booth +s
photo¦call +s
photo¦cell +s
photo¦chem¦ical
photo¦chem¦is¦try
photo¦chro¦mic
photo¦com|
    pos¦ition
photo|
  con¦duct¦ive
photo¦con¦duct|
    iv¦ity
photo¦con¦duct¦or
  +s
photo¦copi¦able
photo¦copier +s
photo¦copy
  photo¦cop¦ies
  photo¦cop¦ied
  photo¦copy¦ing
photo¦degrad¦able
photo¦diode +s
photo¦elec¦tric
photo¦elec¦tri¦city
photo¦elec¦tron +s
photo¦emis¦sion
photo¦emit¦ter +s

photo¦engrav¦ing
photo fin¦ish
photo¦fit +s
photo¦gen¦ic
photo¦gen¦ic¦al¦ly
photo¦gram +s
photo¦gram|
    met¦rist +s
photo¦gram¦metry
photo¦graph +s
  +ed +ing
photo¦graph¦able
pho¦tog¦raph¦er +s
photo¦graph¦ic
photo¦graph¦ic|
    al¦ly
pho¦tog¦raphy
photo¦grav¦ure
photo¦jour¦nal¦ism
photo¦jour¦nal¦ist
  +s
photo¦lith|
  ·og¦raph¦er +s
photo¦litho|
    graph¦ic
photo¦litho|
    graph¦ic¦al¦ly
photo¦lith|
    og¦raphy
photo¦lyse
  photo¦lyses
  photo¦lysed
  photo¦lys¦ing
pho¦toly¦sis
pho¦lyt¦ic
photo|
  mech¦an¦ical
photo¦mech¦an¦ic|
    al¦ly
pho¦tometer +s
pho¦tomet¦ric
pho¦tom¦etry
photo¦micro¦graph
  +s
photo|
    microg¦raphy
photo¦mon¦tage
  +s
photo¦multi¦plier
  +s
pho¦ton +s
pho¦ton¦ics
photo¦novel +s
photo-offset
photo
  op¦por¦tun¦ity
photo
  op¦por¦tun¦ities
photo¦period +s
photo¦peri¦od¦ic
photo¦period¦ism
photo¦pho¦bia

photo¦pho¦bic
photo¦real¦ism
photo¦recep¦tor +s
photo¦sensi¦tive
photo¦sensi¦tiv¦ity
photo¦set
  photo¦sets
photo¦set
  photo¦set¦ting
photo¦set¦ter +s
photo shoot +s
photo¦sphere +s
photo¦spher¦ic
photo¦stat +s *noun*
  Propr.
photo¦stat
  photo¦stats
  photo¦stat¦ted
  photo¦stat¦ting
  verb
photo¦stat¦ic
photo¦syn¦thesis
photo¦syn¦the¦sise
  Br. (use
  photosynthesize)
photo|
    syn¦the¦sises
photo|
    syn¦the¦sised
photo|
    syn¦the¦sis¦ing
photo¦syn¦the¦size
photo|
    syn¦the¦sizes
photo|
    syn¦the¦sized
photo|
    syn¦the¦siz¦ing
photo¦syn¦thet¦ic
photo¦syn¦thet¦ic|
    al¦ly
photo¦tran¦sis¦tor
  +s
photo¦trop¦ic
photo¦trop¦ism
photo¦type¦set
photo¦type¦set¦ter
  +s
photo¦type¦set|
    ting
photo¦vol¦ta¦ic
phrasal
phrase
  phrases
  phrased
  phras¦ing
phrase book +s
phraseo¦gram +s
phraseo¦logic¦al
phrase¦ology
  phraseo¦olo¦gies
phras¦ing +s

phre¦at¦ic
phren¦et¦ic
  (use frenetic)
phren¦et¦ic¦al¦ly
  (use frenetically)
phren¦ic
phreno¦logic¦al
phren¦olo¦gist +s
phren¦ology
Phry¦gia (ancient
  region, Asia
  Minor)
Phry¦gian +s
phthal¦ate +s
phthal¦ic
phthi¦sic
phthi¦sic¦al
phthi¦sis
Phu¦ket (island and
  port, Thailand)
phut
phyco¦logic¦al
phy¦colo¦gist +s
phy¦cology
phyco¦my¦cete +s
phyla (plural of
  phylum. ⚠ filer)
phyl¦ac¦tery
  phyl¦ac¦ter¦ies
phy¦let¦ic
phy¦let¦ic¦al¦ly
Phyl¦lida *also*
  Phil¦lida
Phyl¦lis
phyllo (use filo)
phyl¦lode +s
phyl¦lopha¦gous
phyl¦lo¦quin¦one
phyl¦lo¦tac¦tic
phyl¦lo¦taxis
phyl¦lo¦taxy
phyl¦lox¦era
phylo¦gen¦esis
phylo¦gen¦et¦ic
phylo¦gen¦et¦ic|
    al¦ly
phylo¦gen¦ic
phyl¦ogeny
  phyl¦ogen¦ies
phy¦lum
  phyla
phy¦salis
physic
  phys¦ics
  phys¦icked
  phys¦ick¦ing
phys¦ic¦al +s
phys¦ic¦al¦ism
phys¦ic¦al¦ist +s
phys¦ic¦al¦is¦tic
phys¦ic¦al¦ity
phys¦ic¦al¦ly

phys|ic|al|ness
phys|ician +s
physi|cist +s
phys|icky
physico-chemical
phys|ics
physio +s
physi|ocracy
  physi|ocra|cies
physio|crat +s
physio|crat|ic
physio|gnom|ic
physio|gnom|ic|al
physio|gnom|ic|
    al|ly
physi|ognom|ist
  +s
physi|ognomy
  physi|ogno|mies
physi|og|raph|er
  +s
physio|graph|ic
physio|graph|ic|al
physio|graph|ic|
    al|ly
physi|og|raphy
physio|logic|al
physio|lo|gic|al|ly
physi|olo|gist +s
physi|ology
  physi|olo|gies
physio|ther|ap|ist
  +s
physio|ther|apy
phys|ique +s
phyto|chem|ical
phyto|chem|ist +s
phyto|chem|is|try
phyto|chrome +s
phyto|gen|esis
phy|togeny
phyto|geog|raphy
phy|tog|raphy
phyto|path|ology
phy|topha|gous
phyto|plank|ton
phyt|ot|omy
phyto|toxic
phyto|toxin +s
pi +s (Greek letter;
  pious. △ pie)

pi *Am.*
  pies
  pied
  piing *or* pie|ing
  (*Br.* pie. muddle.
  △ pie)
pi|acu|lar
Piaf, Edith (French
  singer)
pi|affe
  pi|affes

pi|affe (*cont.*)
  pi|affed
  pi|aff|ing
pi|aff|er
Pia|get, Jean
  (Swiss
  psychologist)
pia mater
piani
pi|an|ism
pi|an|is|simo +s
pi|an|ist +s
pi|an|is|tic
pi|an|is|tic|al|ly
piano +s
  (instrument)
piano
  pi|anos *or* piani
  (soft passage)
piano ac|cor|dion
  +s
pi|ano|forte +s
pi|an|ola +s *Propr.*
piano no|bile
piano organ +s
piano play|er +s
piano-tuner +s
pi|as|sava +s
pi|aster *Am.* +s
pi|astre *Br.* +s
Piat +s (anti-tank
  weapon)
Piauí (state, Brazil)
pi|azza +s
pi|broch +s
PIBS (= permanent
  interest-bearing
  share)
pic +s (picture.
  △ pick)
pica +s (printing
  measure; eating
  non-food. △ pika,
  piker)
pica|dor +s
pica|ninny *Am.*
  (use pickaninny)
pica|nin|nies
Pic|ardy (region,
  France)
pic|ar|esque
pic|ar|oon +s
Pi|casso, Pablo
  (Spanish painter)
pic|ay|une +s
Pic|ca|dilly (street,
  London)
Pic|ca|dilly Cir|cus
  (in London)
pic|ca|lilli +s
pic|ca|ninny *Br.*
  pic|ca|nin|nies

pic|ca|ninny (*cont.*)
  (*often offensive;*
  Am. pickaninny)
pic|colo +s
pich|ici|ago +s
pick +s +ed +ing
  (choose; pluck;
  tool. △ pic)
pick|aback
pick|able
picka|ninny *Am.*
  picka|nin|nies
  (*often offensive; Br.*
  piccaninny)
pickax *Am.*
  pick|axes
  pick|axed
  pick|ax|ing
pick|axe *Br.*
  pick|axes
  pick|axed
  pick|ax|ing
pick|el|haube +s
pick|er +s
pick|erel
  plural pick|erel *or*
  pick|erels
Pick|er|ing,
  Wil|liam
  Hay|ward (New
  Zealand-born
  American rocket
  engineer)
picket +s +ed +ing
  (sentry; person
  supporting strike;
  stake. △ piquet)
pick|et|er +s
picket line +s
Pick|ford, Mary
  (Canadian-born
  American actress)
picki|ness
pick|ing +s
pickle
  pickles
  pickled
  pick|ling
pick|ler +s
pick|lock +s
pick-me-up +s
pick|pocket +s
pick|pock|et|ing
pick-up +s *adjective*
  and noun
Pick|wick|ian +s
picky
  pick|ier
  picki|est
pick-your-own +s
  adjective and noun

pic|nic
pic|nics
pic|nicked
pic|nick|ing
  (meal. △ pyknic)
pic|nick|er +s
pic|nicky
Pico da Neb|lina
  (mountain, Brazil)
Pico de Ori|zaba
  (Spanish name for
  Citlaltépetl)
pico|meter *Am.* +s
pico|metre *Br.* +s
pico|sec|ond +s
picot +s
pi|cotee +s
picquet +s (sentry
  etc.; use picket.
  △ piquet)
pic|rate +s
pic|ric
Pict +s
Pict|ish
picto|gram +s
picto|graph +s
picto|graph|ic
pic|tog|raphy
pic|tor|ial +s
pic|tori|al|ly
pic|ture
  pic|tures
  pic|tured
  pic|tur|ing
pic|ture book +s
pic|ture card +s
pic|ture frame +s
pic|ture gal|lery
  pic|ture
  gal|ler|ies
pic|ture|goer +s
pic|ture hat +s
picture-moulding
  +s
pic|ture pal|ace +s
pic|ture post|card
  +s
pic|tur|esque
pic|tur|esque|ly
pic|tur|esque|ness
pic|ture win|dow
  +s
picture-writing
pid|dle
  pid|dles
  pid|dled
  pid|dling
pid|dler +s
pid|dock +s
pidgin +s
  (language.
  △ pigeon)

pi-dog +s (use pye-dog)

pie +s (food; magpie; former Indian currency. △ pi)

pie *Br.*

pies

pied

pie¦ing (*Am.* pi. muddle. △ pi)

pie¦bald +s

piece

pieces

pieced

piecing (part, coin, etc.; to join. △ peace)

pièce de ré¦sist¦ance

pièces de ré¦sist¦ance

piece-goods

piece|meal

piecer +s

piece-rate +s

piece|work

pie chart +s

pie|crust +s

pied

pied-à-terre

pieds-à-terre

Pied|mont (region, Italy)

pied|mont +s (slope)

pie-dog +s (use pye-dog)

pie-eater +s

pie-eyed

Pie¦gan (use Peigan)

plural Pie¦gan *or* Pie|gans

pie in the sky

pie¦man

pie¦men

pier +s (at seaside; pillar. △ peer)

Pierce, Frank|lin (American president. △ Peirce)

pierce

pierces

pierced

pier|cing

pier|cer +s

pier|cing¦ly

pier glass

pier glasses

Pi¦er|ian

Piero della Fran|cesca (Italian painter)

Pierre (city, USA)

Pier|rette +s *female*

Pier|rot +s *male*

Piers (name)

pietà +s (sculpture etc.)

pietas (respect for an ancestor)

Pieter|maritz|burg (city, South Africa)

Pie¦ters|burg (town, South Africa)

Piet|ism (movement)

piet|ism (sentiment)

piet|ist +s

piet|is¦tic

piet|is¦tic¦al

piety

piet|ies

piezo|elec¦tric

piezo|elec¦tric|al¦ly

piezo|elec¦tri¦city

pi¦ez|ometer +s

pif¦fle

pif¦fles

pif¦fled

pif¦fling

pif|fler +s

pig

pigs

pigged

pig¦ging

pi¦geon +s (bird. △ pidgin)

pigeon-breast +s

pigeon-breast¦ed

pigeon-chest +s

pigeon-chested

pi¦geon fan|cier +s

pigeon-fancying

pigeon-hawk +s

pigeon-hearted

pigeon-hole

pigeon-holes

pigeon-holed

pigeon-holing

pi¦geon pair +s

pi¦geon|ry

pi¦geon|ries

pigeon-toed

pig|gery

pig|ger¦ies

pig|gish

pig|gish¦ly

pig|gish|ness

Pig|gott, Les¦ter (English jockey)

piggy

pig|gies

pig|gier

pig|gi|est

pig¦gy|back +s +ed +ing

piggy bank +s

piggy in the mid¦dle

pig-headed

pig-headed¦ly

pig-headed¦ness

pigh¦tle +s

pig-ignorant

pig in the mid¦dle

pig-iron

Pig Is¦land (New Zealand)

pig-jump +s +ed +ing

pig Latin

pig|let +s

pig|like

pig|ling +s

pig|maean (use pygmaean)

pig|mean (use pygmaean)

pig meat

pig|ment +s +ed +ing

pig|men¦tal

pig|men¦tary

pig|men¦ta¦tion +s

pigmy (use pygmy)

pig|mies

pig|nut +s

pig|pen +s

pig|skin +s

pig-sticker +s

pig|stick¦ing

pig|sty

pig|sties

pig's wash

pig|swill

pig|tail +s

pig|tailed

pig|wash

pig|weed +s

pi jaw +s

pika +s (animal. △ pica, piker)

pike

pikes

piked

pik¦ing (weapon; hilltop; toll; dive)

pike

plural pike *or* pikes (fish)

pike¦let +s

pike|man

pike|men

pike|perch

plural pike|perch

piker +s (person. △ pica, pika)

pike|staff +s

Pik Po¦bedy (mountain, Kyrgyzstan)

pilaf +s

pi¦laff +s (use pilaf)

pi¦las|ter +s

pi¦las|tered

Pi¦late, Pon|tius (Roman procurator of Judaea)

pilau +s

pilaw +s (use pilau)

pilch

pilches

pil|chard +s

pile

piles

piled

pil¦ing

pil|eate

pil|eated

pile|driver +s

pile|driv¦ing

pile-dwelling +s

piles

pile-up +s *noun*

pi|leus

pilei

pile|wort +s

pil|fer +s +ed +ing

pil|fer|age

pil|fer|er +s

pil|grim +s +ed +ing

pil|grim|age

pil|grim|ages

pil|grim|aged

pil|grim|aging

pil|grim|ise *Br.* (use pilgrimize)

pil|grim|ises

pil|grim|ised

pil|grim|is¦ing

pil|grim|ize

pil|grim|izes

pil|grim|ized

pil|grim|iz¦ing

pi¦lif¦er|ous

pi|li|form
pil|ing +s
Pili|pino
pill +s +ed +ing
pil|lage
  pil|lages
  pil|laged
  pil|laging
pil|la|ger +s
pil|lar +s
pil|lar box
  pil|lar boxes
pillar-box red
pil|lared
pil|laret +s
pill|box
  pill|boxes
pil|lion +s
pil|li|winks
pil|lock +s
pil|lory
  pil|lor|ies
  pil|lor|ied
  pil|lory|ing
pil|low +s +ed
  +ing
pil|low|case +s
pillow-fight +s
pil|low lace
pil|low lava
pil|low|slip +s
pil|low talk
pil|lowy
pill-popper +s
pill-pusher +s
pil|lule +s (use
  pilule)
pill|wort +s
pil|ose
pil|os|ity
pilot +s +ed +ing
pi|lot|age
pilot bal|loon +s
pilot-bird +s
pilot chute +s
pilot-cloth +s
pilot fish
  plural pilot fish
pilot house +s
pilot-jacket +s
pi|lot|less
pilot light +s
pil|ous
Pil|sen (city, Czech
  Republic)
Pil|sen|er +s (use
  Pilsner)
Pils|ner +s
Pilt|down man
pilu|lar
pil|ule +s
pilu|lous

pi|mento +s
pi-meson +s
pi|miento
  pi|mien|tos or
  pi|mien|toes
pimp +s +ed +ing
pim|per|nel +s
pim|ple +s
pim|pled
pim|ply
  pim|plier
  pim|pli|est
PIN (= personal
  identification
  number)
pin
  pins
  pinned
  pin|ning
  (for sewing; etc.)
pina co|lada +s
pina|fore +s
Pin|ang (use
  Penang)
pin|as|ter +s
Pina|tubo, Mount
  (in the
  Philippines)
pin|ball
PINC (= property
  income certificate)
pince-nez
  plural pince-nez
pin|cer +s +ed
  +ing
pin|cette +s
pinch
  pinches
  pinched
  pinch|ing
pinch|beck +s
pinch-hit
  pinch-hits
  pinch-hit
  pinch-hitting
pinch-hitter +s
pinch|penny
  pinch|pen|nies
pinch-run
  pinch-runs
  pinch-ran
  pinch-running
pinch-runner +s
pin|cush|ion +s
Pin|dar (Greek lyric
  poet)
Pin|dar|ic
pin-down *noun and*
  attributive
Pin|dus
  Moun|tains (in
  Greece)

pine
  pines
  pined
  pin|ing
pin|eal
pine|apple +s
pine cone +s
pine mar|ten +s
pine nee|dle +s
pine nut +s
Pin|ero, Ar|thur
  Wing (English
  dramatist)
pin|ery
  pin|eries
pine tree +s
pin|etum
  pin|eta
Pine|wood (film
  studios, England)
pine|wood (timber)
pine wood +s
  (forest)
piney
pin-feather +s
pin|fold +s +ed
  +ing
ping +s +ed +ing
ping|er +s
pingo +s
ping-pong
pin|guid
pin|guin +s
pin|head +s
pin|head|ed
pin|head|ed|ness
pin-high
pin|hole +s
pin|ion +s +ed
  +ing
pink +s +ed +ing
  +er +est
pink-collar
  attributive
Pink|er|ton, Allan
  (Scottish-born
  American
  detective)
pink-eye
Pink Floyd
  (English rock
  group)
pinkie +s (little
  finger; wine; white
  person. △ pinky)
pink|ish
pink|ly
pink|ness
pinko
  pinkos or
  pink|oes

Pink|ster
  (Whitsuntide)
pink|ster flower
  +s
pinky
  pink|ier
  pinki|est
  (slightly pink.
  △ pinkie)
pin money
pinna
  pin|nae or pin|nas
pin|nace +s
pin|na|cle
  pin|na|cles
  pin|na|cled
  pin|na|cling
pin|nate
pin|nated
pin|nate|ly
pin|na|tion
pinni|grade
pinni|ped +s
pin|nu|lar
pin|nule +s
PIN num|ber +s
pinny
  pin|nies
Pino|chet,
  Au|gusto
  (Chilean
  president)
pin|ochle
pino|cyt|osis
pin|ole
piñon +s
Pinot Blanc +s
Pinot Noir +s
pin|point +s +ed
  +ing
pin|prick +s
pin|stripe +s
pin|striped
pint +s
pinta +s (= a pint
  of milk)
pin-table +s
pin|tado +s
pin|tail +s
Pin|ter, Har|old
  (English
  dramatist)
pin|tle +s
pinto +s
pint pot +s
pint-sized
pin-tuck +s
pin-tucked
pin-up +s *noun and*
  attributive
pin|wheel +s +ed
  +ing

pin|worm +s
piny
Pin|yin
pin|yon +s (use
  piñon)
pio|let +s
pion +s
Pi|on|eer
  (American space
  probes)
pi|on|eer +s +ed
  +ing
pi|onic
pious
pi|ous|ly
pi|ous|ness
Pip (name)
pip
  pips
  pipped
  pip|ping
  (seed; remove
  pips; high-pitched
  sound; defeat;
  etc.)
pipa +s (toad)
pipal +s (= bo tree;
  use peepul.
  △ people)
pipe
  pipes
  piped
  pip|ing
pipe|clay +s +ed
  +ing
pipe-cleaner +s
pipe dream +s
pipe|fish
  plural pipe|fish
pipe|ful +s
pipe|less
pipe-light +s
pipe|line
  pipe|lines
  pipe|lined
  pipe|lin|ing
pipe major +s
pip emma (= p.m.)
pipe organ +s
Piper, John
  (English painter)
piper +s
pipe-rack +s
Piper Alpha
pi|pera|zine
pi|peri|dine
pipe roll +s
pipe-stem +s
pipe-stone
pip|ette
  pip|ettes

pip|ette (cont.)
  pip|et|ted
  pip|et|ting
pipe|work
pip|ing hot
pipi|strelle +s
pipit +s
pip|kin +s
pip|less
Pippa
pip|pin +s
pippy
pip|squeak +s
pipy
pi|quancy
pi|quant
pi|quant|ly
pique
  piques
  piqued
  piquing
  (resentment;
  irritate; in card
  games. △ peak,
  peek, peke)
piqué +s
pi|quet (game.
  △ picket)
pir|acy
  pir|acies
Pi|raeus (port,
  Greece)
pi|ra|gua +s
Piran|dello, Luigi
  (Italian writer)
Pira|nesi,
  Gio|vanni
  Bat|tista (Italian
  engraver)
pi|ranha +s
pir|ate
  pir|ates
  pir|ated
  pir|at|ing
pir|at|ic
pir|at|ic|al
pir|at|ic|al|ly
pi|raya +s
piri|piri +s
pi|rogue +s
pirou|ette
  pirou|ettes
  pirou|et|ted
  pirou|et|ting
Pisa (city, Italy)
pis aller
Pisan, Chris|tine
  de (Italian-born
  writer)
Pi|sano, An|drea,
  Gio|vanni,

Pi|sano (cont.)
  Ni|cola, and Nino
  (Italian sculptors)
pis|cary
pisca|tor|ial
pisca|tori|al|ly
pisca|tory
Pis|cean +s
Pis|ces
  (constellation;
  sign of zodiac)
pisci|cul|tural
pisci|cul|ture
pisci|cul|tur|ist +s
pis|cina
  pis|ci|nae or
  pis|ci|nas
pis|cine +s
pis|civ|or|ous
pish
Pish|pek (former
  name of Bishkek)
Pi|sidia (ancient
  region, Asia
  Minor)
Pi|sid|ian +s
pisi|form
Pi|sis|tra|tus
  (tyrant of Athens)
pis|mire +s
piss
  pisses
  pissed
  piss|ing
  (coarse slang)
Pis|sarro, Cam|ille
  (French artist)
piss art|ist +s
  (coarse slang)
pis|soir +s
piss|pot +s (coarse
  slang)
piss-take +s
piss-taker +s
  (coarse slang)
piss-taking (coarse
  slang)
piss-up +s noun
  (coarse slang)
pis|ta|chio +s
piste +s
pis|teur +s
pis|til +s (of flower.
  △ pistol)
pis|til|lary
pis|til|late
pis|til|lif|er|ous
pis|til|line
pis|tol
  pis|tols
  pis|tolled Br.
  pis|toled Am.

pis|tol (cont.)
  pis|tol|ling Br.
  pis|tol|ing Am.
  (gun. △ pistil)
pis|tole +s (coin)
pis|tol|eer +s
pis|tol grip +s
pis|tol shot +s
pistol-whip
  pistol-whips
  pistol-whipped
  pistol-whipping
pis|ton +s
piston-engined
  attributive
pit
  pits
  pit|ted
  pit|ting
pita +s (use pitta)
pit-a-pat
pit bull +s
pit bull ter|rier +s
Pit|cairn Is|lands
  (in S. Pacific)
pitch
  pitches
  pitched
  pitch|ing
pitch-and-toss
pitch black noun
  and adjective
pitch-black
  attributive
pitch|blende
pitch|er +s
pitch|er|ful +s
pitcher-plant +s
pitch|fork +s +ed
  +ing
pitch pine
pitch-pipe +s
pitch|stone
pitchy
  pitch|ier
  pitchi|est
pit|eous
pit|eous|ly
pit|eous|ness
pit|fall +s
pith
pit|head +s
Pithe|can|thro|pus
pithe|coid +s
pith hel|met +s
pith|ily
pithi|ness
pith|less
pithos
  pithoi

pithy
  pith|ier
  pithi|est
piti|able
piti|able|ness
piti|ably
piti|ful
piti|ful|ly
piti|ful|ness
piti|less
piti|less|ly
piti|less|ness
Pit|man, Isaac
  (English shorthand
  inventor)
pit|man
  pit|men
  (miner)
pit|man +s
  (connecting rod)
piton +s (spike)
Pi|tons, the (two
  mountains, St
  Lucia)
Pitot tube +s
pit|pan +s
pit pony
  pit po|nies
pit prop +s
pit-saw +s
pit stop +s
Pitt, Wil|liam
  (British prime
  ministers)
pitta +s
pit|tance +s
pitter-patter
Pitti (art gallery and
  museum, Italy)
Pitt Is|land (one of
  the Chatham
  Islands)
pitto|sporum +s
Pitt-Rivers,
  Au|gus|tus
  (English
  archaeologist)
Pitts|burgh (city,
  USA)
pi|tu|it|ary
  pi|tu|it|ar|ies
pit|uri
pity
  pit|ies
  pit|ied
  pity|ing
pity|ing|ly
pityr|ia|sis
  pityr|ia|ses
più (*Music* more.
  △ pew)
Pius (popes)

pivot +s +ed +ing
piv|ot|abil|ity
piv|ot|able
piv|otal
pix (= pictures.
  △ pyx)
pixel +s
pix|el|ate
  pix|el|ates
  pix|el|ated
  pix|el|at|ing
  (display as or
  divide into pixels)
pixie +s (elf.
  △ pyxes)
pix|il|ated (crazy;
  drunk)
pix|il|lated (use
  pixilated)
pixy (use pixie)
  pixies
Pizan, Chris|tine
  de (use Pisan)
Pi|zarro,
  Fran|cisco
  (Spanish
  conquistador)
pi|zazz (use
  pizzazz)
pizza +s
piz|zazz
piz|zeria +s
pizzi|cato
  pizzi|ca|tos or
  pizzi|cati
piz|zle +s
plac|abil|ity
plac|able
plac|ably
plac|ard +s +ed
  +ing
pla|cate
  pla|cates
  pla|cated
  pla|cat|ing
  pla|cat|ing|ly
pla|ca|tion
pla|ca|tory
place
  places
  placed
  pla|cing
  (position.
  △ plaice)
place-bet +s
pla|cebo +s
place brick +s
place card +s
place-kick +s
place-kicker +s
place|less

place|man
  place|men
place mat +s
place|ment +s
place name +s
pla|centa
  pla|cen|tae or
  pla|cen|tas
pla|cen|tal +s
pla|cer +s
place set|ting +s
pla|cet +s (vote)
pla|cid
pla|cid|ity
pla|cid|ly
pla|cid|ness
pla|cing +s
placket +s
  (opening in
  garment.
  △ plaquette)
placky bag +s
plac|oid +s
pla|fond +s
pla|gal
plage +s (beach;
  part of sun)
pla|giar|ise *Br.* (use
  plagiarize)
  pla|giar|ises
  pla|giar|ised
  pla|giar|is|ing
pla|giar|iser *Br.* +s
  (use plagiarizer)
pla|giar|ism +s
pla|giar|ist +s
pla|giar|is|tic
pla|giar|ize
  pla|giar|izes
  pla|giar|ized
  pla|giar|iz|ing
pla|giar|izer +s
plagio|ceph|al|ic
plagio|clase +s
plagio|clas|tic
plagio|stome +s
plague
  plagues
  plagued
  pla|guing
  (disease etc.)
plague|some
pla|guy
plaice
  plural plaice
  (fish. △ place)
plaid +s
Plaid Cymru
  (Welsh Nationalist
  Party)
plaid|ed

plain +s +er +est
  (flat land; simple;
  not milk
  (chocolate); not
  self-raising (flour);
  not a court card;
  not trumps.
  △ plane)
plain|chant +s
plain clothes
plain-clothes
  attributive
plain cook +s
plain|ly
plain|ness
plain sail|ing
  (straightforward;
  uncomplicated.
  △ plane sailing)
Plains In|dian +s
plains|man
  plains|men
Plains of
  Abra|ham (in
  Canada)
plain|song
plain-spoken
plaint +s
plain|tiff +s
plain|tive
plain|tive|ly
plain|tive|ness
plait +s +ed +ing
  (interlace hair etc.
  △ plat)
plan
  plans
  planned
  plan|ning
pla|nar
  (*Mathematics.*
  △ planer)
plan|ar|ian +s
plan|chet +s (coin-
  blank)
plan|chette +s
  (board at seance)
Planck, Max
  (German
  physicist)
plane
  planes
  planed
  plan|ing
  (aircraft; flat
  surface; tool; tree;
  skim; shave.
  △ plain)
plane chart +s
plane|load +s
plane|maker +s
plane|mak|ing

planer +s (tool.
  △ planar)
plane sail|ing
  (position-finding.
  △ plain sailing)
planet +s
plane-table +s
plan¦et|arium +s
plan¦et|ary
plan¦et|esimal +s
plan¦et|oid +s
plan¦et|ology
plane tree +s
plan|gency
plan|gent
plan|gent¦ly
plan|im¦eter +s
plani|met¦ric
plani|met¦ric¦al
plan|im¦etry
plan|ish
  plan|ishes
  plan|ished
  plan|ish|ing
plan|ish¦er +s
plani|sphere +s
plani|spher¦ic
plank +s +ed +ing
plank|ton
plank|ton¦ic
plan|ner +s
plano|con¦cave
plano|con¦vex
plano|graph¦ic
plan|og¦raphy
plan|om¦eter +s
plant +s +ed +ing
plant|able
Plan|tagenet +s
plan|tain +s
plan|tar (of the sole
  of the foot)
plan|ta¦tion +s
plant|er +s
  (person;
  container)
planti|grade +s
Plan|tin,
  Chris|tophe
  (Belgian printer;
  typeface)
plant|ing +s
plant|let +s
plant life
plant|like
plant-louse
  plant-lice
plants|man
  plants|men
plants|woman
  plants|women
plaque +s

pla|quette +s
  (small plaque.
  △ placket)
plash
  plashes
  plashed
  plash|ing
plasm +s
plasma +s
plas|mat¦ic
plas|mic
plas|mid +s
plasmo|desma
  plasmo|des¦mata
plas|mo¦dial
plas|mo¦dium
  plas|modia
plasmo|lyse Br.
  plasmo|lyses
  plasmo|lysed
  plasmo|lys¦ing
plas|moly¦sis
plasmo|lyze Am.
  plasmo|lyzes
  plasmo|lyzed
  plasmo|lyz¦ing
Plas|sey (battle
  site, India)
plas|teel
plas|ter +s +ed
  +ing
plas¦ter|board +s
plas¦ter cast +s
plas¦ter|er +s
plas¦ter of Paris
plas¦ter|work
plas|tery
plas|tic +s
plas|tic|al¦ly
plas¦ti|cine Propr.
plas¦ti|cisa¦tion Br.
  (use
  plasticization)
plas¦ti|cise Br. (use
  plasticize)
  plas¦ti|cises
  plas¦ti|cised
  plas¦ti|cis¦ing
plas¦ti|ciser Br. +s
  (use plasticizer)
plas¦ti|city
plas¦ti|ciza|tion
plas¦ti|cize
  plas¦ti|cizes
  plas¦ti|cized
  plas¦ti|ciz¦ing
plas¦ti|cizer +s
plas|ticky
plas|tid +s
plas|tron +s
plat +s (land.
  △ plait)

Pla|taea (battle site,
  Greece)
platan +s (tree.
  △ platen)
plat du jour
  plats du jour
Plate, River
  (estuary, S.
  America)
plate
  plates
  plated
  plat¦ing
plat|eau
  plat|eaux or
  plat|eaus
plate|ful +s
plate glass noun
plate-glass
  adjective
plate|lay¦er +s
plate|less
plate|let +s
plate|maker +s
plate-mark +s
platen +s (plate;
  roller. △ platan)
plater +s
plate rack +s
plat¦er|esque
plat|form +s
Plath, Syl¦via
  (American poet)
plat¦ing +s
pla|tin¦ic
plat¦in|isa|tion Br.
  (use
  platinization)
plat¦in|ise Br. (use
  platinize)
  plat¦in|ises
  plat¦in|ised
  plat¦in|is¦ing
plat¦in|iza|tion
plat¦in|ize
  plat¦in|izes
  plat¦in|ized
  plat¦in|iz¦ing
plat¦in|oid +s
plat¦ino|type +s
plat|inum
platinum-black
plat|inum blonde
  +s
plati|tude +s
plati|tud¦in|ar¦ian
  +s
plati|tud¦in|ise Br.
  (use
  platitudinize)
plati|tud¦in|ises

plati|tud¦in|ise
  (cont.)
  plati|tud¦in|ised
  plati|tud¦in|is¦ing
plati|tud¦in|ize
  plati|tud¦in|izes
  plati|tud¦in|ized
  plati|tud¦in|iz¦ing
plati|tud¦in|ous
Plato (Greek
  philosopher)
Pla|ton¦ic (of Plato)
pla|ton¦ic (not
  sexual;
  theoretical)
Pla|ton¦ic|al¦ly (in
  a Platonic way)
pla|ton¦ic|al¦ly (in
  a platonic way)
Pla|ton|ism
Pla|ton|ist +s
pla|toon +s
Platt|deutsch
platte|land
platte|land¦er +s
plat|ter +s
platy|hel¦minth +s
platy|pus
  platy|puses
platyr|rhine +s
plau|dit +s
plausi|bil¦ity
  plausi|bil¦ities
plaus|ible
plaus|ibly
Plau|tus, Titus
  Mac|cius (Roman
  dramatist)
play +s +ed +ing
playa +s
play|abil¦ity
play|able
play-act +s +ed
  +ing
play-actor +s
play|back +s
play|bill +s
play|boy +s
Play¦er, Gary
  (South African
  golfer)
play¦er +s
player-manager
  +s
player-piano +s
Play|fair, John
  (Scottish
  mathematician
  and geologist)
play|fel¦low +s
play|ful
play|ful¦ly

play|ful|ness
play|girl +s
play|goer +s
play|ground +s
play|group +s
play|house +s
play|ing card +s
play|ing field +s
play|ing time
play|let +s
play|list +s
play|maker +s
play|mate +s
play-off +s *noun*
play|pen +s
play-reading +s
play|room +s
play|school +s
play|suit +s
play|thing +s
play|time +s
play|wright +s
play|writ|ing
plaza +s
plea +s
plea bar|gain +s
plea bar|gain|ing
pleach
  pleaches
  pleached
  pleach|ing
plead
  pleads
  pleaded
  pled *Am.*
  plead|ing
plead|able
plead|er +s
plead|ing +s
plead|ing|ly
pleas|ance +s
pleas|ant +er +est
pleas|ant|ly
pleas|ant|ness
pleas|ant|ry
  pleas|ant|ries
please
  pleases
  pleased
  pleas|ing
pleas|ing|ly
pleas|ur|able
pleas|ur|able|ness
pleas|ur|ably
pleas|ure
  pleas|ures
  pleas|ured
  pleas|ur|ing
pleat +s +ed +ing
pleb +s
plebby
ple|beian +s

ple|beian|ism
ple|bis|cit|ary
pleb|is|cite +s
plec|trum
  plec|trums *or*
  plec|tra
pled
pledge
  pledges
  pledged
  pledg|ing
pledge|able
pledgee +s
pledger +s
  (generally)
pledget +s
pledgor +s (*Law*)
pleiad +s
Plei|ades (star
  cluster)
plein-air
plein-airist +s
pleio|trop|ic
plei|otrop|ism
plei|otropy
Pleis|to|cene
plen|ary
  plen|ar|ies
pleni|po|ten|tiary
pleni|po|ten|
    tiar|ies
pleni|tude
plent|eous
plent|eous|ly
plent|eous|ness
plen|ti|ful
plen|ti|ful|ly
plen|ti|ful|ness
plenty
ple|num +s
pleo|chro|ic
ple|och|ro|ism
pleo|morph|ic
pleo|morph|ism
ple|on|asm +s
ple|on|as|tic
ple|on|as|tic|al|ly
ple|sio|saur +s
ple|sio|saurus
  ple|sio|sauri
ples|sor +s
pleth|ora
pleth|or|ic
pleth|or|ic|al|ly
pleura
  pleurae
pleural
pleur|isy
pleur|it|ic
pleuro|dynia
pleuron
  pleura

pleuro|
  pneu|mo|nia
Plé|ven (town,
  Bulgaria)
plexi|form
plexi|glas *Propr.*
plexor +s
plexus
  plural plexus *or*
  plex|uses
pli|abil|ity
pli|able
pli|able|ness
pli|ably
pli|ancy
pli|ant
pli|ant|ly
pli|cate
pli|cated
pli|ca|tion +s
plié +s
pli|ers
plight +s +ed +ing
plim|sole +s (use
  plimsoll)
plim|soll +s
Plim|soll line +s
Plim|soll mark +s
plinth +s
Pliny ('the Elder',
  Roman scholar)
Pliny ('the
  Younger', Roman
  writer)
Plio|cene
plio|saur +s
plio|saurus
  plio|saur|uses
plissé
plod
  plods
  plod|ded
  plod|ding
plod|der +s
plod|ding|ly
ploidy
ploi|dies
Ploi|eşti (city,
  Romania)
plonk +s +ed +ing
plonk|er +s
plonko +s
plop
  plops
  plopped
  plop|ping
plo|sion +s
plo|sive +s
plot
  plots
  plot|ted
  plot|ting

Plo|tinus (Roman
  philosopher)
plot|less
plot|less|ness
plot|ter +s
Plough
  (constellation)
plough *Br.* +s +ed
  +ing (*Am.* plow)
plough|able *Br.*
  (*Am.* plowable)
plough|er *Br.* +s
  (*Am.* plower)
plough|land *Br.* +s
  (*Am.* plowland)
plough|man *Br.*
  plough|men
  (*Am.* plowman)
plough|man's
  lunch
  plough|man's
  lunches
plough|man's
  spike|nard
Plough Mon|day
  +s
plough|share *Br.*
  +s (*Am.*
  plowshare)
Plov|div (city,
  Bulgaria)
plover +s
plow *Am.* +s +ed
  +ing (*Br.* plough)
plow|able *Am.* (*Br.*
  ploughable)
plow|er *Am.* +s (*Br.*
  plougher)
plow|land *Am.* +s
  (*Br.* ploughland)
plow|man *Am.*
  plow|men
  (*Br.* ploughman)
plow|share *Am.* +s
  (*Br.* ploughshare)
ploy +s
pluck +s +ed +ing
pluck|er +s
pluck|ily
pluck|iness
pluck|less
plucky
  pluck|ier
  pluck|iest
plug
  plugs
  plugged
  plug|ging
plug|ger +s
plug|hole +s
plug-in *adjective*
plug|ola +s

plug-ugly
  plug-uglies
plum +s (fruit.
  △ plumb)
plum¦age
plum¦aged
plu¦mas¦sier +s
plumb +s +ed +ing
  (measure depth;
  vertical; exactly;
  fit pipes. △ plum)
plum|bagin|ous
plum|bago +s
plum|bate +s
plum|be¦ous
plumb¦er +s
plum|bic
plum|bif¦er|ous
plum|bism
plumb|less
plumb line +s
plum|bous
plumb rule +s
plume
  plumes
  plumed
  plum¦ing
plume|less
plume|like
plu|mery
plum¦met +s +ed
  +ing
plummy
  plum|mier
  plum¦mi|est
plum|ose
plump +s +ed +ing
  +er +est
plump|ish
plump¦ly
plump|ness
plumpy
plumul|aceous
plumu|lar
plum|ule +s
plumy
  plu|mier
  plu¦mi|est
plun|der +s +ed
  +ing
plun|der¦er +s
plun¦der|ing +s
plunge
  plunges
  plunged
  plun|ging
plun|ger +s
plunk +s +ed +ing
plu|per¦fect
plural +s

plur¦al|isa¦tion *Br.*
  (use
  pluralization)
plur¦al|ise *Br.* (use
  pluralize)
  plur¦al|ises
  plur¦al|ised
  plur¦al|is¦ing
plur¦al|ism
plur¦al|ist +s
plur¦al|is¦tic
plur¦al|is¦tic|al¦ly
plur¦al|ity
plur¦al|iza¦tion
plur¦al|ize
  plur¦al|izes
  plur¦al|ized
  plur¦al|iz¦ing
plur¦al|ly
pluri|po¦ten|tial
pluri|pres¦ence
plurry
plus
  pluses
plus ça change
plus fours
plush +er +est
plushi|ness
plush¦ly
plush|ness
plushy
  plush|ier
  plushi|est
Plu|tarch (Greek
  biographer)
plu|tarchy
  plu|tarch¦ies
Pluto (*Greek
  Mythology*; planet;
  = pipeline under
  the ocean)
plu|toc|racy
  plu|toc|ra¦cies
plu|to|crat +s
plu|to|crat¦ic
plu|to|crat¦ic|al¦ly
plu|tol|atry
plu|ton +s
Plu¦to|nian
Plu|ton¦ic (theory;
  infernal)
plu|ton¦ic (rock)
Plu|to|nism
Plu|to|nist +s
plu|to|nium
plu|vial +s
pluvi|om¦eter +s
pluvio|met¦ric
pluvio|met¦ric¦al
pluvio|met¦ric|
          al¦ly
plu¦vi|ous

ply
  plies
  plied
  ply¦ing
Ply|mouth (port,
  England; town,
  USA; capital of
  Montserrat, West
  Indies)
ply|wood +s
pneu|mat¦ic
pneu|mat¦ic|al¦ly
pneuma|ti|city
pneu|mat¦ics
pneum|ato|cyst +s
pneum|ato|logic¦al
pneuma|tol|ogy
pneu¦mato|phore
  +s
pneumo|coc¦cus
  pneumo|cocci
pneumo|coni|osis
pneumo|cystis
  (car|inii
  pneu|mo|nia)
pneumo|gas¦tric
pneu|mon|ec|tomy
  pneu¦mon|
       ec¦to|mies
pneu|mo|nia +s
pneu|mon¦ic
pneu|mon|itis
pneumo|thorax
Po (river, Italy)
po +s (chamber
  pot)
poach
  poaches
  poached
  poach|ing
poach¦er +s
Poca|hon¦tas
  (American Indian
  princess)
po|chard
  plural po|chard *or*
  po|chards
po|chette +s
pock +s +ed +ing
pocket +s +ed
  +ing
pock¦et|able
pocket battle|ship
  +s
pock¦et|book +s
pocket bor|ough
  +s
pock¦et|ful +s
pocket go|pher +s
pocket knife
  pocket knives
pock¦et|less

pocket money
pocket watch
  pocket watches
pock|ety
pock|mark +s
pock-marked
pocky
poco
pod
  pods
  pod¦ded
  pod|ding
pod|agra
pod|ag¦ral
pod|ag¦ric
pod|ag¦rous
poddy
  pod|dies
po|*destà*
podgi|ness
Pod|gorica (capital
  of Montenegro)
podgy
  podgi¦er
  podgi|est
po|dia|trist +s
po|dia|try
po|dium
  po|di|ums *or*
  podia
Pod|olsk (city,
  Russia)
podo|phyl¦lin
pod¦sol +s (use
  podzol)
pod|zol +s
pod|zol|isa¦tion
  Br. (use
  podzolization)
pod|zol|ise *Br.* (use
  podzolize)
  pod¦zol|ises
  pod¦zol|ised
  pod¦zol|is¦ing
pod|zol|iza¦tion
pod|zol|ize
  pod¦zol|izes
  pod¦zol|ized
  pod¦zol|iz¦ing
Poe, Edgar Allan
  (American writer)
poem +s
poesy
poet +s
poet|as¦ter +s
poet|ess
  poet|esses
poet¦ic
poet|ic¦al
poet|ic|al¦ly
poeti|cise *Br.* (use
  poeticize)

poeti|cise (*cont.*)
  poeti|cises
  poeti|cised
  poeti|cis|ing
poeti|cize
  poeti|cizes
  poeti|cized
  poeti|ciz|ing
poet|ics
poet|ise *Br.* (use
  poetize)
  poet|ises
  poet|ised
  poet|is|ing
poet|ize
  poet|izes
  poet|ized
  poet|iz|ing
Poet Laure|ate +s
poet|ry
  poet|ries
Poets' Cor|ner (in
  Westminster
  Abbey)
po-faced
pogo +s *noun*
pogo
  po|goes
  po|goed
  pogo|ing
  verb
pog|rom +s
Po Hai (= Bo Hai)
poign|ance
poign|ancy
poign|ant
poign|ant|ly
poi|kilo|therm +s
poi|kilo|ther|mal
poi|kilo|ther|mia
poi|kilo|ther|mic
poi|kilo|thermy
poilu +s
Poin|caré, Jules-
  Henri (French
  mathematician)
poin|ci|ana +s
poind +s +ed +ing
poin|set|tia +s
point +s +ed +ing
point-blank
point duty
Pointe-à-Pitre
  (port,
  Guadeloupe)
point|ed|ly
point|ed|ness
Pointe-Noire (port,
  the Congo)
point|er +s
Point|ers (two stars
  in the Plough or
  Southern Cross)

poin|til|lism
poin|til|list +s
poin|til|lis|tic
point|less
point|less|ly
point|less|ness
point of sale *noun*
point-of-sale
  attributive
point-scoring
points|man
  points|men
point-to-point +s
point-to-pointer
  +s
point-to-pointing
pointy
  point|ier
  pointi|est
Poirot, Her|cule
  (fictional
  detective)
poise
  poises
  poised
  pois|ing
poi|sha
  plural poi|sha
poi|son +s +ed
  +ing
poi|son|er +s
poi|son|ing +s
poi|son|ous
poi|son|ous|ly
poi|son pen let|ter
  +s
Pois|son, Siméon-
  Denis (French
  mathematical
  physicist;
  distribution)
Poi|tiers (city,
  France)
Poi|tou (former
  province, France)
Poitou-Charentes
  (region, France)
poke
  pokes
  poked
  pok|ing
poker +s
poker dice
poker-face +s
poker-faced
poker play|er +s
poker|work
poke|weed +s
pokey (prison.
  △ poky)
poki|ly

po|ki|ness
poky
  poki|er
  poki|est
  (small. △ pokey)
po|lacca +s (dance.
  △ polacre)
po|lack +s *offensive*
po|lacre +s (sailing
  vessel. △ polacca)
Pol|and
Pol|an|ski, Roman
  (film director of
  Polish descent)
polar
po|lar|im|eter +s
po|lari|met|ric
po|lar|im|etry
Po|laris (North
  Star)
po|lar|is|able *Br.*
  (use polarizable)
po|lar|isa|tion *Br.*
  +s (use
  polarization)
po|lari|scope +s
po|lari|scop|ic
po|lar|ise *Br.* (use
  polarize)
  po|lar|ises
  po|lar|ised
  po|lar|is|ing
po|lar|iser *Br.* +s
  (use polarizer)
po|lar|ity
  po|lar|ities
po|lar|iz|able
po|lar|iza|tion +s
po|lar|ize
  po|lar|izes
  po|lar|ized
  po|lar|iz|ing
po|lar|izer +s
po|lar|ly
po|laro|graph|ic
po|lar|og|raphy
Po|lar|oid +s *Propr.*
pola|touche +s
pol|der +s
Pole +s (Polish
  person)
pole
  poles
  poled
  pol|ing
  (piece of wood.
  △ poll)
pole|ax *Am.*
  pole|axes
  pole|axed
  pole|ax|ing

pole-axe *Br.*
  pole-axes
  pole-axed
  pole-axing
pole|cat +s
po|lem|ic +s
po|lem|ic|al
po|lem|ic|al|ly
po|lemi|cise *Br.*
  (use polemicize)
  po|lemi|cises
  po|lemi|cised
  po|lemi|cis|ing
po|lemi|cist +s
po|lemi|cize
  po|lemi|cizes
  po|lemi|cized
  po|lemi|ciz|ing
po|lem|ics
po|lenta
pole vault +s *noun*
pole-vault +s +ed
  +ing *verb*
pole-vaulter +s
pole|ward
pole|wards
po|lice
  po|lices
  po|liced
  po|licing
po|lice|man
  po|lice|men
po|lice|woman
  po|lice|women
poli|clinic +s (use
  polyclinic)
pol|icy
  pol|icies
pol|icy|hold|er +s
polio
polio|my|el|itis
polis (= police)
Poli|sario
Pol|ish
  plural Pol|ish
  (of Poland;
  person)
pol|ish
  pol|ishes
  pol|ished
  pol|ish|ing
  (make shiny;
  substance)
pol|ish|able
pol|ish|er +s
pol|it|buro +s
po|lite
  po|liter
  po|litest
po|lite|ly
po|lite|ness
  po|lite|nesses

poli|tesse
pol|it|ic
  pol|it|ics
  pol|it|icked
  pol|it|ick|ing
pol|it|ic|al +s
pol|it|ic|al|ly (in a
  political way.
  △ politicly)
pol|it|ician +s
pol|iti|cisa|tion Br.
  (use
  politicization)
pol|iti|cise Br. (use
  politicize)
  pol|iti|cises
  pol|iti|cised
  pol|iti|cis|ing
pol|iti|ciza|tion
pol|iti|cize
  pol|iti|cizes
  pol|iti|cized
  pol|iti|ciz|ing
pol|it|ic|ly
  (judiciously.
  △ politically)
pol|it|ico +s
politico-
  econom|ical
pol|it|ics
pol|ity
  pol|ities
Polk, James Knox
  (American
  president)
polka
  pol|kas
  pol|kaed or
  polka'd
  pol|ka|ing
polka dot +s noun
polka-dot
  attributive
poll +s +ed +ing
  (vote. △ pole)
pol|lack
  plural pol|lack or
  pol|lacks
Pol|lai|uolo,
  An|tonio and
  Piero (Italian
  artists)
pol|lan
  plural pol|lan
  (fish. △ pollen)
pol|lard +s +ed
  +ing
poll|ee +s (person
  questioned in a
  poll)

pol|len +s (grains
  in flower.
  △ pollan)
pol|len|less
pol|lex
  pol|li|ces
pol|li|ci|ta|tion
pol|lie +s (use
  polly)
pol|lin|ate
  pol|lin|ates
  pol|lin|ated
  pol|lin|at|ing
pol|lin|ation
pol|lin|ator +s
poll|ing booth +s
poll|ing day +s
poll|ing sta|tion
  +s
pol|linic
pol|lin|ifer|ous
polli|wog +s
Pol|lock, Jack|son
  (American
  painter)
pol|lock
  plural pol|lock or
  pol|locks
  (use pollack)
poll par|rot +s
poll|ster +s
poll tax
pol|lu|tant +s
pol|lute
  pol|lutes
  pol|luted
  pol|lut|ing
pol|luter +s
pol|lu|tion +s
Pol|lux (Greek
  Mythology; star)
Polly (name)
polly
  pol|lies
  (Apollinaris water;
  politician. △ poly)
Polly|anna +s
Polly|anna|ish
Polly|anna|ism
polly|wog +s (use
  polliwog)
Polo, Marco
  (Italian traveller)
polo +s
polo|crosse
pol|on|aise +s
polo neck +s noun
polo-neck
  attributive
po|lo|nium
Po|lon|na|ruwa
  (town, Sri Lanka)

po|lony
  po|lo|nies
polo play|er+s
polo stick+s
Pol Pot
  (Cambodian prime
  minister)
Pol|tava (city,
  Ukraine)
pol|ter|geist +s
Pol|tor|atsk
  (former name of
  Ashgabat)
pol|troon +s
pol|troon|ery
poly +s
  (= polytechnic.
  △ polly)
poly|adelph|ous
poly|amide +s
poly|an|drous
poly|an|dry
poly|an|thus
  poly|an|thuses
poly|atom|ic
poly|basic
Po|lyb|ius (Greek
  historian)
poly|car|bon|ate
  +s
Poly|carp (Greek
  saint)
poly|chaetan
poly|chaete +s
poly|chaet|ous
poly|chlor|in|ated
poly|chro|mat|ic
poly|chro|ma|tism
poly|chrome +s
poly|chro|mic
poly|chro|mous
poly|chromy
poly|clinic +s
Poly|cli|tus (Greek
  sculptor)
poly|cot|ton +s
poly|crys|tal +s
poly|crys|tal|line
poly|cyc|lic +s
poly|dac|tyl +s
poly|dae|mon|ism
Poly|deu|ces
  (Greek Mythology;
  alternative name
  for Pollux)
poly|es|ter +s
poly|eth|ene +s
  (= polythene)
poly|ethyl|ene
poly|gam|ic
pol|yg|am|ist +s
pol|yg|am|ous

pol|yg|am|ous|ly
pol|yg|amy
poly|gene +s
poly|gen|esis
poly|gen|et|ic
poly|gen|ic
poly|gen|ism
poly|gen|ist +s
poly|geny
poly|glot +s
poly|glot|tal
poly|glot|tic
poly|glot|tism
poly|gon +s
pol|yg|on|al
pol|yg|onum +s
poly|graph +s
pol|ygyn|ous
pol|ygyny
poly|he|dral
poly|he|dric
poly|he|dron
  poly|he|dra or
  poly|he|drons
poly|his|tor +s
Poly|hym|nia
  Greek and Roman
  Mythology
poly|math +s
poly|math|ic
pol|ym|athy
poly|mer +s
poly|mer|ase +s
poly|mer|ic
poly|mer|isa|tion
  Br. (use
  polymerization)
poly|mer|ise Br.
  (use polymerize)
  poly|mer|ises
  poly|mer|ised
  poly|mer|is|ing
poly|mer|ism
poly|mer|iza|tion
poly|mer|ize
  poly|mer|izes
  poly|mer|ized
  poly|mer|iz|ing
poly|mer|ous
poly|morph|ic
poly|morph|ism
poly|morph|ous
Poly|nesia (region,
  Pacific Ocean)
Poly|nes|ian +s
poly|neur|it|ic
poly|neur|itis
poly|no|mial +s
po|lynya +s
poly|opia
polyp +s

polyp|ary
  polyp|ar|ies
poly|pep|tide +s
pol|ypha|gous
poly|phase
Poly|phe|mus
  Greek Mythology
poly|phone +s
poly|phon|ic
poly|phon|ic|al|ly
pol|yph|on|ous
pol|yph|ony
  pol|yph|on|ies
poly|phos|phate
  +s
poly|phyl|et|ic
polypi
poly|ploid +s
poly|ploidy
poly|pod +s
poly|pody
  poly|pod|ies
polyp|oid
polyp|ous
poly|pro|pene +s
poly|pro|pyl|ene
  +s
polyp|tych +s
poly|pus
  polypi
poly|rhythm +s
poly|sac|char|ide
  +s
poly|sem|ic
poly|sem|ous
poly|semy
poly|styr|ene +s
poly|syl|lab|ic
poly|syl|lab|ic|
    al|ly
poly|syl|lable +s
poly|syn|thet|ic
poly|tech|nic +s
poly|tetra|fluoro|
    ethyl|ene
poly|the|ism
poly|the|ist +s
poly|the|is|tic
poly|thene +s
poly|tonal
poly|ton|al|ity
poly|un|sat|ur|ate
  +s
poly|un|sat|ur|
    ated
poly|ur|eth|ane
  poly|ur|eth|anes
  poly|ur|eth|aned
  poly|ur|eth|an|ing
poly|va|lence
poly|va|lent
poly|vi|nyl +s

poly|zoan +s
Pom +s (dog;
  offensive Briton)
pom|ace
po|made
  po|mades
  po|maded
  po|mad|ing
po|man|der +s
po|ma|tum +s +ed
  +ing
pombe
pome +s
pom|egran|ate +s
pom|elo +s
Pom|er|ania
  (region, N.
  Europe)
Pom|er|anian +s
pom|fret +s
pomfret-cake +s
pomi|cul|ture
pom|ifer|ous
pom|mel +s (knob)
pom|mel (use
  pummel)
  pom|mels
  pom|melled *Br.*
  pom|meled *Am.*
  pom|mel|ling *Br.*
  pom|mel|ing *Am.*
pom|mel horse +s
Pom|mie +s (use
  Pommy)
Pommy
  Pom|mies
  (*offensive*)
pomo|logic|al
pom|olo|gist +s
pom|ology
pomp +s
Pom|pa|dour,
  Ma|dame de
  (French
  noblewoman)
pom|pa|dour +s
pom|pano +s
Pom|peii (ancient
  city, Italy)
Pom|pey (Roman
  general;
  = Portsmouth,
  England)
Pom|pi|dou,
  Georges (French
  president)
pom|pom +s
  (use pompon)
pom-pom +s (gun)
pom|pon +s
  (ornament)
pom|pos|ity
pom|pos|ities

pom|pous
pom|pous|ly
pom|pous|ness
'pon (= upon)
ponce
  ponces
  ponced
pon|cing
pon|ceau +s
Ponce de León,
  Juan (Spanish
  explorer)
poncey
pon|cier
pon|ci|est
pon|cho +s
poncy
  pon|cier
  pon|ci|est
  (use poncey)
pond +s +ed +ing
pond|age
pon|der +s +ed
  +ing
pon|der|abil|ity
pon|der|able
pon|der|ation
pon|der|ing +s
pon|der|osa +s
pon|der|os|ity
pon|der|ous
pon|der|ous|ly
pon|der|ous|ness
Pondi|cherry (city
  and territory,
  India)
pond life
pond-skater +s
pond|weed +s
pone +s
pong +s +ed +ing
pon|gal
pon|gee +s
pon|gid +s
pongo +s (*offensive*
  in sense
  'Englishman')
pongy
  pong|ier
  pongi|est
pon|iard +s
pons
  pon|tes
pons as|in|orum
  pon|tes
  as|in|orum
pons Var|olii
  pon|tes Var|olii
pont +s
Ponte, Lor|enzo
  Da (Italian
  librettist and poet)

Pontefract-cake
  +s
pon|tes
Ponti|anak (port,
  Indonesia)
pon|ti|fex
  pon|tifi|ces
pon|tiff +s
pon|tif|ic|al
pon|tifi|calia
pon|tif|ic|al|ly
pon|tifi|cate
  pon|tifi|cates
  pon|tifi|cated
  pon|tifi|cat|ing
pon|tifi|ces
Pon|tine Marshes
  (in Italy)
pon|toon +s +ed
  +ing
Pon|tormo,
  Ja|copo da
  (Italian painter)
Pon|tus (ancient
  region, Asia
  Minor)
pony
  po|nies
pony|tail +s
pony-trekker +s
pony-trekking
poo +s (excrement.
  △ pooh)
pooch
  pooches
poo|dle +s
poof +s (*offensive*
  male homosexual;
  interjection.
  △ pouffe)
poof|ter +s
  (*offensive*)
poofy
  poof|ier
  poofi|est
  (*offensive*)
Pooh, Win|nie the
  (bear)
pooh +s
  (*interjection*.
  △ poo)
Pooh-Bah +s
pooh-pooh +s +ed
  +ing (dismiss.
  △ poo-poo)
pooja +s (use
  puja)
poo|jah +s (use
  puja)
pooka +s

pool +s +ed +ing
(body of water;
common supply;
share etc. △ pul)
Poole (town,
England)
pool hall +s
pool room +s
pool|side
poon +s
Poona (city, India)
poon oil
poop +s +ed +ing
pooper scoop|er
+s
poo-poo +s
(excrement.
△ pooh-pooh)
poop scoop +s
poor +er +est (not
rich. △ paw, pore,
pour)
poor box
poor boxes
Poor Clare +s
(nun)
poor|house +s
poor|ly
poor man's
weather-glass
poor|ness
poor rate +s
poor-spirit|ed
poo|tle
poo|tles
poo|tled
poot|ling
poove +s (offensive)
pop
pops
popped
pop|ping
popa|dam +s (use
poppadom)
popa|dom +s (use
poppadom)
pop|corn
Pope, Alex|an|der
(English poet)
pope +s (head of
Roman Catholic
Church; Orthodox
parish priest)
pope|dom
Pope Joan
(legendary female
pope)
pope|less
Pope|mo|bile +s
popery
pope's eye +s
(gland in sheep)

pop-eyed
pop|gun +s
pop|in|jay +s
pop|ish
pop|ish|ly
Pop|ish Plot
English history
pop|lar +s
pop|lin
pop|lit|eal
Popo|caté|petl
(volcano, Mexico)
poppa +s (father.
△ popper)
pop|pa|dom +s
pop|pa|dum +s
(use poppadom)
Pop|per, Karl
(Austrian-born
British
philosopher)
pop|per +s (press-
stud; person or
thing that pops;
vial. △ poppa)
pop|pet +s
poppet-head +s
poppet-valve +s
pop|pied
pop|ping crease
+s
pop|ple
pop|ples
pop|pled
pop|pling
pop|ply
Poppy (name)
poppy
pop|pies
(flower)
poppy|cock
Poppy Day +s
poppy-head +s
pop-shop +s
Pop|sicle +s Propr.
popsy
pop|sies
popu|lace (the
masses.
△ populous)
popu|lar
popu|lar|isa|tion
Br. (use
popularization)
popu|lar|ise Br.
(use popularize)
popu|lar|ises
popu|lar|ised
popu|lar|is|ing
popu|lar|iser Br.
+s (use
popularizer)

popu|lar|ism
popu|lar|ity
popu|lar|iza|tion
popu|lar|ize
popu|lar|izes
popu|lar|ized
popu|lar|iz|ing
popu|lar|izer +s
popu|lar|ly
popu|late
popu|lates
popu|lated
popu|lat|ing
popu|la|tion +s
popu|lism
popu|list +s
popu|lis|tic
popu|lous (densely
populated.
△ populace)
popu|lous|ly
popu|lous|ness
pop-up *adjective*
por|bea|gle +s
por|cel|ain +s
porcelain-shell +s
por|cel|lan|eous
por|cel|lan|ous
porch
porches
porched
porch|less
por|cine
por|cu|pine +s
por|cu|pine fish
plural por|cu|pine
fish
por|cu|pin|ish
por|cu|piny
pore
pores
pored
por|ing
(tiny opening;
study intently.
△ paw, poor,
pour)
porgy
por|gies
Pori (port, Finland)
pori|fer +s
por|if|er|an +s
por|ism +s
por|is|mat|ic
pork
pork bar|rel *noun*
pork-barrel
attributive
pork butch|er +s
porker +s
pork|ling +s
pork pie +s

pork-pie hat +s
porky
pork|ies
pork|ier
pork|iest
(fat; like pork; a
lie. △ pawky)
porky-pie
porky-pies
porn
(= pornography.
△ pawn)
porno
porn|og|raph|er +s
porno|graph|ic
porno|graph|ic|
al|ly
porn|og|raphy
poro|plas|tic
por|os|ity
por|os|ities
por|ous
por|ous|ly
por|ous|ness
por|phy|ria
por|phy|rin +s
por|phy|rit|ic
por|phyro|gen|ite
+s
Por|phyry (ancient
philosopher)
por|phyry
por|phy|ries
por|poise +s
por|rect +s +ed
+ing
por|ridge
por|ridgy
por|rin|ger +s
Porsche,
Fer|di|nand
(Austrian car
designer)
Por|senna, Lars
(legendary
Etruscan chieftain)
port +s +ed +ing
(harbour; town;
wine; left;
opening)
port|abil|ity
port|able +s
port|able|ness
port|ably
port|age
port|ages
port|aged
port|aging
Porta|kabin +s
Propr.
por|tal +s

por¦ta¦mento
por¦ta¦menti *or*
por¦ta¦men¦tos
porta¦tive
Port-au-Prince
(capital of Haiti)
Port Blair (capital
of the Andaman
and Nicobar
Islands)
Port|cul¦lis
Heraldry
port|cul¦lis
port|cul¦lises
port|cul¦lised
Porte (Ottoman
court at
Constantinople)
porte co¦chère +s
Port Eliza|beth
(port, South
Africa)
por|tend +s +ed
+ing
por|tent +s
por|tent|ous
por|tent|ous|ly
por|tent|ous|ness
Por|ter, Cole
(American
composer and
lyricist)
Por|ter,
Kath|er¦ine Anne
(American writer)
Por|ter, Peter
(Australian poet)
por|ter +s +ed
+ing
por|ter|age
por|ter|house +s
por|ter|house
steak +s
Port Éti|enne
(former name of
Nouadhibou)
port|fire +s
port|folio +s
Port-Gentil (port,
Gabon)
Port Har|court
(port, Algeria)
Port Hed|land
(port, Australia)
port|hole +s
Por¦tia
por|tico
por¦ti|coes *or*
por¦ti|cos
por¦ti|coed
por¦ti|ère +s

por|tion +s +ed
+ing
por|tion|less
Port|land (port,
USA; shipping
area, English
Channel; cement;
stone; vase)
Port|land, Isle of
(peninsula,
England)
Port|laoighise (use
Portlaoise)
Port|laoise (town,
Republic of
Ireland)
port¦li|ness
Port Louis (capital
of Mauritius)
port¦ly
port|lier
port¦li|est
Port Mahon
(alternative name
for Mahón)
port|man¦teau
port|man¦teaus *or*
port|man¦teaux
Port Moresby
(capital of Papua
New Guinea)
Porto (Portuguese
name for Oporto)
Pôrto Alegre (city,
Brazil)
Port-of-Spain
(capital of
Trinidad and
Tobago)
por¦to|lan +s
por¦to|lano +s
Porto Novo
(capital of Benin)
Pôrto Velho (town,
Brazil)
Port Pet|rovsk
(former name of
Makhachkala)
Port Pirie (port,
Australia)
por|trait +s
por|trait|ist +s
por|trait|ure +s
por|tray +s +ed
+ing
por|tray|able
por|tray|al +s
por|tray|er +s
Port Said (port,
Egypt)
Port Salut (cheese)

Ports|mouth (port,
England)
Port Stan|ley (port,
Falkland Islands)
Port Sudan (port,
Sudan)
Por¦tu|gal
Por¦tu|guese
plural
Por¦tu|guese
Port Vila (capital of
Vanuatu)
pose
poses
posed
pos¦ing
Po¦sei|don *Greek
Mythology*
poser +s (problem)
pos¦eur +s (*male
person who poses*)
pos¦euse +s (*female
person who poses*)
posey (pretentious.
△ posy)
posh +er +est
posh¦ly
posh|ness
posit +s +ed +ing
pos|ition +s +ed
+ing
pos|ition|al
pos|ition|al¦ly
pos|ition|er +s
posi|tive +s
posi|tive¦ly
posi|tive|ness
posi|tiv|ism
posi¦tiv|ist +s
posi¦tiv|is¦tic
posi¦tiv|is¦tic|al¦ly
posi|tiv|ity
posi|tron +s
posi|tron|ic
posi|tro¦nium
poso|logic|al
pos|ology
posse +s
posse comi|ta¦tus
pos|sess
pos|sesses
pos|sessed
pos¦sess|ing
pos|ses|sion +s
pos|ses|sion|less
pos|ses|sive +s
pos|ses|sive¦ly
pos|ses|sive|ness
pos|ses|sor +s
pos|ses|sory
pos¦set +s

pos¦si|bil¦ity
pos¦si|bil¦ities
pos|sible +s
pos|sibly
pos¦sum +s
post +s +ed +ing
post|age
pos¦tal +s
pos¦tal code +s
pos|tal¦ly
post|bag +s
post|box
post|boxes
post-boy +s
post|card +s
post-chaise +s
post-classic|al
post|code +s
post-coital
post-coital¦ly
post-colonial
post-date
post-dates
post-dated
post-dating
post|doc¦tor¦al
post-entry
pos¦ter +s
poste rest|ante
pos|ter|ior +s
pos|ter|ior|ity
pos|ter|ior¦ly
pos|ter|ity
pos|tern +s
pos¦ter paint +s
post ex|change +s
post|face +s
post-feminism
post-feminist +s
post|fix
post|fixes
post|fixed
post|fix|ing
post-free
post|gla¦cial
post|grad +s
post|gradu¦ate +s
post-haste
post-horn +s
post|hu¦mous
post|hu¦mous¦ly
pos|tiche +s
pos¦tie +s
pos|til +s
pos|til|ion +s
post-
   Impres¦sion|ism
post-
   Impres¦sion|ist
   +s
post-industrial
post|ing +s

post|lim|iny
post|lude +s
post|man
  post|men
post|man's knock
post|mark +s +ed
  +ing
post|mas|ter +s
post|mas|ter
  gen|eral
  post|mas|ters
  gen|eral
post-mill +s
post-millen|nial
post-
  millen|nial|ism
post-
  millen|nial|ist +s
post|mis|tress
  post|mis|tresses
post|mod|ern
post|mod|ern|ism
post|mod|ern|ist
  +s
post|mod|ern|ity
post-mortem +s
post-natal
post-natally
post-nuptial
post-obit +s
Post Of|fice +s
  (organization)
post of|fice +s
  (individual office)
post of|fice box
  post of|fice boxes
post-operative
post-paid
post-partum
post|pon|able
post|pone
  post|pones
  post|poned
  post|pon|ing
post|pone|ment +s
post|poner +s
post|pos|ition +s
post|pos|ition|al
post|posi|tive +s
post|posi|tive|ly
post|pran|dial
post-produc|tion
post-
  revolu|tion|ary
post room +s
post|script +s
post-
  structur|al|ism
post-
  structur|al|ist +s
post-tax
post town +s

post-traumat|ic
  stress dis|order
pos|tu|lant +s
pos|tu|late
  pos|tu|lates
  pos|tu|lated
  pos|tu|lat|ing
pos|tu|la|tion +s
pos|tu|la|tor +s
pos|tural
pos|ture
  pos|tures
  pos|tured
  pos|tur|ing
pos|turer +s
  pos|tur|ing +s
post-war
post|woman
  post|women
Posy (name)
posy
  po|sies
  (flowers. △ posey)
posy ring +s
pot
  pots
  pot|ted
  pot|ting
pot|abil|ity
pot|able
pot|age
pota|ger +s
pot|am|ic
pot|am|ology
pot|ash
po|tas|sic
po|tas|sium
potassium–argon
  dat|ing
po|ta|tion +s
po|tato
  po|ta|toes
pot|atory
pot-au-feu
pot-bellied
pot-belly
  pot-bellies
pot|boil|er +s
pot-bound
potch
  potches
pot cheese
po|teen +s
Po|tem|kin
  (Russian
  battleship)
po|tence
po|tency
  po|ten|cies
po|tent
po|ten|tate +s
po|ten|tial +s

po|ten|ti|al|ity
  po|ten|ti|al|ities
po|ten|tial|ly
po|ten|tial|ate
po|tenti|ates
po|tenti|ated
po|tenti|at|ing
po|ten|tilla +s
po|tenti|om|eter
  +s
po|tentio|met|ric
po|tenti|om|etry
po|tent|isa|tion Br.
  (use
  potentization)
po|tent|ise Br. (use
  potentize)
  po|tent|ises
  po|tent|ised
  po|tent|is|ing
po|tent|iza|tion
po|tent|ize
  po|tent|izes
  po|tent|ized
  po|tent|iz|ing
po|tent|ly
Po|tenza (town,
  Italy)
pot|ful +s
pot|head +s
po|theen +s (use
  poteen)
pother +s +ed
  +ing
pot-herb +s
pot|hole
  pot|holes
  pot|holed
  pot|hol|ing
pot|holer +s
pot-hook +s
pot-hunter +s
po|tion +s
Poti|phar Bible
pot|latch
  pot|latches
pot|latch|ing
pot|luck
Poto|mac (river,
  USA)
poto|roo +s
Pot|osi (city,
  Bolivia)
pot plant +s
pot-pourri +s
po|trero +s
pot roast +s noun
pot-roast +s +ed
  +ing verb
Pots|dam (city,
  Germany)
pot|sherd +s

pot-shot +s
pot|stone
pot|tage +s
Pot|ter, Bea|trix
  (English writer)
pot|ter +s +ed
  +ing
pot|ter|er +s
Pot|ter|ies, the
  (district, England)
pot|ter's field +s
pot|ter's wheel +s
pot|tery
  pot|ter|ies
pot|ti|ness
pot|tle +s
potto +s
Pott's frac|ture +s
potty
  pot|ties
pot|tier
pot|ti|est
potty-train
  potty-trains
  potty-trained
  potty-training
pot-valiant
pot-valour
pouch
  pouches
  pouched
  pouch|ing
pouchy
  pouch|ier
  pouchi|est
pouf +s (cushion;
  use pouffe.
  △ poof)
pouffe +s (cushion.
  △ poof)
poul|lard +s
Poulenc, Fran|cis
  (French
  composer)
poult +s
poult-de-soie
poult|er|er +s
poult|ice
  poult|ices
  poult|iced
  poult|icing
poult|ry
pounce
  pounces
  pounced
  poun|cing
poun|cer +s
pouncet-box
  pouncet-boxes
Pound, Ezra
  (American poet)
pound +s +ed +ing

pound|age +s
pound|al +s
pound|er +s
pour +s +ed +ing
(flow; rain.
  ⚠ paw, poor,
  pore)
pour|able
pour|boire +s
pour|er +s
pous|sette
  pous|settes
  pous|set|ted
  pous|set|ting
Pous|sin, Nico|las
  (French painter)
pous|sin +s
pout +s +ed +ing
pout|er +s
pout|ing|ly
pouty
  pout|ier
  pouti|est
pov|erty
poverty-stricken
pow
powan
  plural powans *or*
  powan
pow|der +s +ed
  +ing
pow|der blue +s
  noun and adjective
powder-blue
  attributive
pow|der flask +s
pow|der keg +s
pow|der mon|key
  +s
pow|der puff +s
pow|der room +s
pow|dery
Pow|ell, An|thony
  (English novelist)
Pow|ell, Enoch
  (English politician)
power +s +ed +ing
  (energy; ability;
  etc. ⚠ paua)
power-assist|ed
power base +s
power block +s
power|boat +s
power-broker +s
power-broking
power-crazed
power cut +s
power-dive
  power-dives
  power-dived
  power-diving
power|ful

power|ful|ly
power|ful|ness
power|house +s
power-hungry
power|less
power|less|ly
power|less|ness
power line +s
power pack +s
power plant +s
power play +s
power point +s
power pol|it|ics
power-sharing
power sta|tion +s
power sup|ply
power tool +s
power train +s
Powis (Lord; castle,
  Wales)
pow|wow +s +ed
  +ing
Powys (county,
  Wales)
pox
poxy
  pox|ier
  poxi|est
Pozi|driv
  (screwdriver)
  Propr.
Poz|nań (city,
  Poland)
poz|zo|lana
praam +s (use
  pram)
prac|tic|abil|ity
prac|tic|able
prac|tic|able|ness
prac|tic|ably
prac|tic|al +s
prac|ti|cal|ity
prac|ti|cal|ities
prac|tic|al|ly
prac|tic|al|ness
prac|tice +s *noun*
prac|tice *Am.*
  prac|tices
  prac|ticed
  prac|ticing
  (*verb. Br.* practise)
prac|ticer *Am.* +s
  (*Br.* practiser)
prac|ti|cian +s
prac|tise *Br.*
  prac|tises
  prac|tised
  prac|tis|ing
  (*verb. Am.*
  practice)
prac|tiser *Br.* +s
  (*Am.* practicer)

prac|ti|tion|er +s
prad +s
Prado (art gallery,
  Madrid)
prae|cipe +s
prae|co|cial (use
  precocial)
prae|dial (use
  predial)
prae|mu|nire
prae|no|men +s
prae|pos|tor +s
Prae|sepe (cluster
  of stars)
prae|sid|ium +s
  (use presidium)
prae|tor +s
prae|tor|ial
prae|tor|ian +s
prae|tor|ship +s
prag|mat|ic
prag|mat|ic|al
prag|mat|ic|al|ity
prag|mat|ic|al|ly
prag|mat|ics
prag|ma|tise *Br.*
  (use pragmatize)
  prag|ma|tises
  prag|ma|tised
  prag|ma|tis|ing
prag|ma|tism
prag|ma|tist +s
prag|ma|tis|tic
prag|ma|tize
  prag|ma|tizes
  prag|ma|tized
  prag|ma|tiz|ing
Prague (capital of
  the Czech
  Republic)
prahu +s
Praia (port, São
  Tiago, Cape Verde
  Islands)
prairie +s
praise
  praises
  praised
  prais|ing
  (approval.
  ⚠ prase)
praise|ful
praiser +s
praise|wor|thily
praise|worthi|ness
praise|worthy
Prak|rit
pra|line +s
prall|trill|er +s
pram +s
prana

prance
  pran|ces
  pranced
  pran|cing
pran|cer +s
pran|dial
Prandtl, Lud|wig
  (German
  physicist)
prang +s +ed +ing
prank +s
prank|ful
prank|ish
prank|some
prank|ster +s
prase (quartz.
  ⚠ praise)
praseo|dym|ium
prat +s
prate
  prates
  prated
  prat|ing
prater +s
prat|fall +s
pra|tie +s
prat|in|cole +s
prat|ique +s
Prato (city, Italy)
prat|tle
  prat|tles
  prat|tled
  prat|tling
prat|tler +s
prau +s
Pravda (Russian
  newspaper)
prawn +s +ed +ing
praxis
Prax|it|eles
  (Athenian
  sculptor)
pray +s +ed +ing
  (say prayers.
  ⚠ prey)
pray|er +s (request
  etc. to god; person
  who prays.
  ⚠ preyer)
pray|er book +s
pray|er|ful
pray|er|ful|ly
pray|er|ful|ness
pray|er|less
pray|er mat +s
pray|er wheel +s
pray|ing man|tis
preach
  preaches
  preached
  preach|ing
preach|able

preach|er +s
preach|ify
  preachi|fies
  preachi|fied
  preachi|fy|ing
preachi|ness
preach|ing +s
preach|ment +s
preachy
pre-adolescence
pre-adolescent +s
pre|amble +s
pre|ambu|lar
pre|amp +s
  (= preamplifier)
pre|amp|li|fied
pre|amp|li|fier +s
pre-arrange
  pre-arranges
  pre-arranged
  pre-arranging
pre-arrange|ment
pre|atom|ic
preb|end +s
preb|endal
preb|end|ary
  preb|end|ar|ies
preb|end|ary|ship
  +s
pre-book +s +ed
  +ing
pre-bookable
Pre|cam|brian
pre|can|cer|ous
pre|car|ious
pre|car|ious|ly
pre|car|ious|ness
pre-cast
preca|tive +s
preca|tory
pre|cau|tion +s
pre|cau|tion|ary
pre|cede
  pre|cedes
  pre|ceded
  pre|ced|ing
  (go before.
  ⚠ proceed)
pre|ce|dence
pre|ce|dency
  pre|ce|den|cies
pre|ce|dent +s
pre|ce|dented
pre|ce|dent|ly
pre|cent +s +ed
  +ing
pre|cent|or +s
pre|cen|tor|ship +s
pre|cen|trix
  pre|cen|tri|ces
  female
pre|cept +s

pre|cep|tive
pre|cept|or +s
pre|cep|tor|ial
pre|cep|tor|ship +s
pre|cep|tress
  pre|cep|tresses
pre|ces|sion (of the
  equinoxes etc.
  ⚠ procession)
pre|ces|sion|al (of
  precession.
  ⚠ processional)
pre-Christian +s
pre-Christmas
pre|cinct +s
pre|ci|os|ity
pre|cious
pre|cious|ly
pre|cious|ness
preci|pice +s
pre|cipit|abil|ity
pre|cipit|able
pre|cipi|tance
pre|cipi|tancy
pre|cipi|tant +s
pre|cipi|tate
  pre|cipi|tates
  pre|cipi|tated
  pre|cipi|tat|ing
pre|cipi|tate|ly
pre|cipi|tate|ness
pre|cipi|ta|tion
pre|cipi|ta|tor +s
pre|cipit|ous
pre|cipit|ous|ly
pre|cipit|ous|ness
pré|cis
  plural pré|cis
  noun
pré|cis
  pré|cises
  pré|cised
  pré|cis|ing
  verb
pre|cise
pre|cise|ly
pre|cise|ness
pre|ci|sian +s
  (precise person.
  ⚠ precision)
pre|ci|sian|ism
  (the practice of a
  precisian.
  ⚠ precisionism)
pre|ci|sion
  (accuracy.
  ⚠ precisian)
pre|ci|sion|ism
  (the practice of a
  precisionist.
  ⚠ precisianism)
pre|ci|sion|ist +s

pre|clas|sic|al
pre|clin|ic|al
pre|clude
  pre|cludes
  pre|cluded
  pre|clud|ing
pre|clu|sion
pre|clu|sive
pre|co|cial +s
pre|co|cious
pre|co|cious|ly
pre|co|cious|ness
pre|co|city
pre|cog|ni|tion
pre|cog|ni|tive
pre-coital
pre-coital|ly
pre-Columbian
pre|con|ceive
  pre|con|ceives
  pre|con|ceived
  pre|con|ceiv|ing
pre|con|cep|tion
  +s
pre|con|cert +s
  +ed +ing
pre|con|di|tion +s
  +ed +ing
pre|con|isa|tion *Br.*
  (use
  preconization)
pre|con|ise *Br.* (use
  preconize)
  pre|con|ises
  pre|con|ised
  pre|con|is|ing
pre|con|iza|tion
pre|con|ize
  pre|con|izes
  pre|con|ized
  pre|con|iz|ing
pre|con|scious
pre|con|scious|
           ness
pre-cook +s +ed
  +ing
pre-cool +s +ed
  +ing
pre|cor|dial
pre|cos|tal
pre|cur|sive
pre|cur|sor +s
pre|cur|sory
pre-cut
  pre-cuts
  pre-cut
  pre-cutting
pre|da|cious
pre|da|cious|ness
pre|da|city
pre|date
  pre|dates

pre|date (*cont.*)
  pre|dated
  pre|dat|ing
  (prey on)
pre-date
  pre-dates
  pre-dated
  pre-dating
  (be earlier than)
pre|da|tion
preda|tor +s
preda|tor|ily
preda|tori|ness
preda|tory
pre-dawn
pre|de|cease
  pre|de|ceases
  pre|de|ceased
  pre|de|ceas|ing
pre|de|ces|sor +s
pre-decimal
pre|della +s
pre|des|tin|ar|ian
  +s
pre|des|tin|ate
  pre|des|tin|ates
  pre|des|tin|ated
  pre|des|tin|at|ing
pre|des|tin|ation
pre|des|tine
  pre|des|tines
  pre|des|tined
  pre|des|tin|ing
pre|de|ter|min|
           able
pre|de|ter|min|ate
pre|de|ter|min|
           ation
pre|de|ter|mine
  pre|de|ter|mines
  pre|de|ter|mined
  pre|de|ter|min|ing
pre|de|ter|miner
  +s
pre|dial +s (rural;
  slave)
pred|ic|abil|ity
pred|ic|able +s
pre|dica|ment +s
predi|cant +s
predi|cate
  predi|cates
  predi|cated
  predi|cat|ing
predi|ca|tion +s
predi|ca|tive +s
predi|ca|tive|ly
predi|ca|tor +s
predi|ca|tory
pre|dict +s +ed
  +ing

pre|dict|abil|ity
  pre|dict|abil|ities
pre|dict|able
pre|dict|ably
pre|dic'tion +s
pre|dict|ive
pre|dict|ive|ly
pre|dict|or +s
pre|digest +s +ed
  +ing
pre|di|ges'tion
predi|kant +s
pre|di|lec'tion +s
pre|dis'pose
  pre|dis|poses
  pre|dis|posed
  pre|dis|pos'ing
pre|dis|pos|ition
  +s
pred|nis|one
pre|dom|in|ance
pre|dom|in|ant
pre|dom|in|ant|ly
pre|dom|in|ate
  pre|dom|in|ates
  pre|dom|in|ated
  pre|dom|in|at|ing
pre|dom|in|ate|ly
pre|doom +s +ed
  +ing
pre|dor|sal
pre|dyn|as|tic
pre-echo
  pre-echoes
  pre-echoed
  pre-echoing
pre-eclamp|sia
pre-eclamp|tic
pre-elect +s +ed
  +ing
pre-election +s
pre-embryo +s
pre-embryon|ic
pre-eminence
pre-eminent
pre-eminent|ly
pre-empt +s +ed
  +ing
pre-emption
pre-emptive
pre-emptive|ly
pre-emptor +s
pre-emptory
preen +s +ed +ing
preen|er +s
pre-engage
  pre-engages
  pre-engaged
  pre-engaging
pre-engage|ment
pre-establish
  pre-establishes

pre-establish
  (*cont.*)
  pre-established
  pre-establish|ing
pre-exist +s +ed
  +ing
pre-existence
pre-existent
pre|fab +s
  (= prefabricated
  building)
pre|fab|ri|cate
  pre|fab|ri|cates
  pre|fab|ri|cated
  pre|fab|ri|cat|ing
pre|fab|ri|ca'tion
pref|ace
  pref|aces
  pref|aced
  pref|acing
prefa|tor|ial
prefa|tory
pre|fect +s
pre|fect|oral
pre|fect|orial
pre|fec|tural
pre|fec|ture +s
pre|fer
  pre|fers
  pre|ferred
  pre|fer|ring
pref|er|abil|ity
pref|er|able
pref|er|ably
pref|er|ence +s
pref|er|en|tial
pref|er|en|tial|ly
pre|fer|ment
pre|fig|ur|ation
pre|fig|ura|tive
pre|fig|ure
  pre|fig|ures
  pre|fig|ured
  pre|fig|ur|ing
pre|fig|ure|ment
pre|fix
  pre|fixes
  pre|fixed
  pre|fix|ing
pre|fix|ation
pre|fix|ion
pre|fix|ture
pre-flight
pre|form +s +ed
  +ing
pre|form|ation
pre|form|ation|ist
  +s
pre|forma|tive +s
pre-format|ted
pre|front|al
pre|gla|cial

preg|nable
preg|nancy
  preg|nan|cies
preg|nant
preg|nant|ly
pre|heat +s +ed
  +ing
pre|hen|sile
pre|hen|sil|ity
pre|hen|sion
pre|his|tor|ian +s
pre|his|toric
pre|his|tor|ic|al|ly
pre|his|tory
pre-human
pre-ignition
pre-industrial
pre|judge
  pre|judges
  pre|judged
  pre|judg|ing
pre|judge|ment +s
pre|judg|ment +s
  (use
  prejudgement)
preju|dice
  preju|dices
  preju|diced
  preju|dicing
preju|di|cial
preju|di|cial|ly
prel|acy
  prel|acies
pre|lap|sar|ian +s
prel|ate +s
prel|at|ic
prel|at|ic|al
prel|at|ure +s
pre-launch
pre|lect +s +ed
  +ing
pre|lec'tion +s
pre|lec|tor +s
pre|li|ba'tion +s
pre|lim +s
pre|lim|in|ar|ily
pre|lim|in|ary
  pre|lim|in|ar|ies
pre-linguis|tic
pre|lit|er|ate +s
prel|ude
  prel|udes
  prel|uded
  prel|ud|ing
prel|ud|ial
pre|mar|ital
pre|mar|it|al|ly
pre|ma'ture
pre|ma'ture|ly
pre|ma'ture|ness
pre|ma'tur|ity
pre|max|il|lary

pre|med +s
  (premedical
  studies; student)
pre-med +s (pre-
  medication)
pre|med|ical
pre-medica'tion
pre|medi|tate
  pre|medi|tates
  pre|medi|tated
  pre|medi|tat|ing
pre|medi|ta'tion
pre|men|strual
pre|men|stru|al|ly
pre|mia (plural of
  premium)
prem|ier +s (first in
  importance etc.;
  prime minister)
premi|ère
  premi|ères
  premi|èred
  premi|èr|ing
  (first performance)
prem|ier|ship +s
pre|mil'len|nial
pre|mil'len|nial|
           ism
pre|mil'len|nial|ist
  +s
prem|ise +s
  (buildings etc.)
prem|ise
  prem|ises
  prem|ised
  prem|is|ing
  verb
prem|iss
  prem|isses
  (statement)
pre|mium
  pre|miums *or*
  pre|mia
Pre|mium Bond +s
pre|molar +s
pre|mon|ition +s
pre|moni|tor +s
pre|moni|tory
Pre|mon|stra|
      ten|sian +s
pre|morse
pre|mo|tion
  (*Theology.*
  △ promotion)
pre|natal
pre|natal|ly
pren|tice
  pren|tices
  pren|ticed
  pren|ticing
pren|tice|ship +s
pre|nup|tial

pre|occu¦pa¦tion
+s
pre|occupy
pre|occu¦pies
pre|occu¦pied
pre|occu¦py|ing
pre|ocu¦lar
pre|or¦dain +s +ed
+ing
pre-owned
prep
preps
prepped
prep|ping
pre-pack +s +ed
+ing
pre-package
pre-packages
pre-packaged
pre-packaging
prep|ar|ation +s
pre|para|tive
pre|para|tive¦ly
pre|para|tor¦ily
pre|para|tory
pre|pare
pre|pares
pre|pared
pre|par¦ing
pre|pared|ness
pre|parer +s
pre|pay
pre|pays
pre|paid
pre|pay|ing
pre|pay|able
pre|pay|ment +s
pre|pense
pre|pense¦ly
pre-plan
pre-plans
pre-planned
pre-planning
pre|pon¦der|ance
pre|pon¦der|ant
pre|pon¦der|ant¦ly
pre|pon¦der|ate
pre|pon¦der|ates
pre|pon¦der|ated
pre|pon¦der|
at¦ing
pre|pone
pre|pones
pre|poned
pre|pon¦ing
pre|pose
pre|poses
pre|posed
pre|pos¦ing
prep|os¦ition +s
(word)

pre-position +s
+ed +ing (put in
place beforehand)
prep|os¦ition|al
prep|os¦ition|al¦ly
pre|posi¦tive
pre|pos|sess
pre|pos|sesses
pre|pos|sessed
pre|pos|sess|ing
pre|pos¦ses|sion
+s
pre|pos¦ter|ous
pre|pos¦ter|ous|ly
pre|pos¦ter|ous|
ness
pre|pos¦tor +s (use
praepostor)
pre|po¦tence
pre|po¦tency
pre|po¦tent
prep|pie +s (use
preppy)
preppy
prep|pies
prep|pier
prep|pi¦est
pre-prandial
pre-prefer¦ence
pre|print +s noun
pre-print +s +ed
+ing verb
pre-process
pre-processes
pre-processed
pre-process|ing
pre-proces¦sor +s
pre-produc¦tion
pre-program
pre-programs
pre-programmed
pre-
program|ming
(Computing)
pre-pubertal
pre-puberty
pre-pubescence
pre-pubescent +s
pre-publica¦tion
pre|puce +s
pre|pu¦tial
pre-qualifier +s
pre-qualify
pre-qualifies
pre-qualified
pre-qualify|ing
pre|quel +s
Pre-Raphael
Pre-Raphael¦ism
Pre-Raphael¦ite +s
Pre-
Raphael¦it¦ism

pre-record +s +ed
+ing
pre|requis¦ite +s
pre-
revolu¦tion|ary
pre|roga|tive +s
pres|age
pres|ages
pres|aged
pres|aging
pres|ager +s
pres¦by|opia
pres¦by|op¦ic
pres¦by|ter +s
pres¦by|ter|al
pres¦by|ter|ate +s
pres¦by|ter|ial
Pres¦by|ter|ian +s
(Church)
Pres¦by|ter|ian|
ism
pres¦by|ter|ship +s
pres¦by|tery
pres¦by|ter¦ies
pre-school
pre-schooler +s
pres¦ci|ence
pres¦ci|ent
pres¦ci|ent¦ly
pre|scind +s +ed
+ing
pre|scribe
pre|scribes
pre|scribed
pre|scrib¦ing
(advise use of
medicine etc.;
impose.
⚠ proscribe)
pre|scriber +s
pre|script +s
pre|scrip¦tion +s
(prescribing;
doctor's
instruction;
medicine.
⚠ proscription)
pre|scrip¦tive
(prescribing.
⚠ proscriptive)
pre|scrip¦tive¦ly
pre|scrip¦tive|ness
pre|scrip¦tiv|ism
pre|scrip¦tiv|ist +s
pre-season
pre-select +s +ed
+ing
pre-selection +s
pre-select¦ive
pre-select¦or +s
pres|ence +s

pre|sent +s +ed
+ing (introduce
etc.)
pres|ent +s (not
absent; current;
time now passing;
gift)
pre|sent|abil¦ity
pre|sent|able
pre|sent|able|ness
pre|sent|ably
pre|sen¦ta|tion +s
pre|sen¦ta|tion|al
pre|sen¦ta|tion|
al¦ly
pre|sen¦ta|tion|ism
pre|sen¦ta|tion|ist
+s
pre|senta|tive
present-day
attributive
pre|sent¦ee +s
pre|sent¦er +s
pre|sen¦tient
pre|sen¦ti|ment +s
(foreboding)
pres|ent¦ly
pre|sent|ment +s
(presentation;
statement)
pre|serv|able
pre|ser|va|tion
pre|ser|va|tion|ist
+s
pre|ser|va|tive +s
pre|serve
pre|serves
pre|served
pre|serv|ing
pre|server +s
pre-set
pre-sets
pre-set
pre-setting
pre-shrink
pre-shrinks
pre-shrunk
pre-shrink|ing
pre|side
pre|sides
pre|sided
pre|sid¦ing
presi|dency
presi|den|cies
presi|dent +s
president-elect
presidents-elect
presi|den|tial
presi|den|tial|ly
presi|dent|ship +s
pre|sidi|ary
pre|sidio +s

pre|sid|ium +s
Pres|ley, Elvis
  (American pop
  singer)
pre|soc|rat|ic
press
  presses
  pressed
  press|ing
press agent
press box
  press boxes
Press|burg
  (German name for
  Bratislava)
press-button +s
press cut|ting +s
press-gang +s +ed
  +ing
pres|sie +s (use
  prezzie)
press|ing +s
press|ing|ly
press|man
  press|men
press|mark +s
press-on adjective
press stud +s
press-up +s noun
pres|sure
  pres|sures
  pres|sured
  pres|sur|ing
pressure-cook
  pressure-cooks
  pressure-cooked
  pressure-cooking
pres|sure cook|er
  +s
pres|sur|isa|tion
  Br. (use
  pressurization)
pres|sur|ise Br.
  (use pressurize)
  pres|sur|ises
  pres|sur|ised
  pres|sur|is|ing
pres|sur|iza|tion
pres|sur|ize
  pres|sur|izes
  pres|sur|ized
  pres|sur|iz|ing
pressurized-water
  re|ac|tor +s
Pres|tel Propr.
Pres|ter John
  (legendary king)
pres|ti|digi|ta|tion
pres|ti|digi|ta|tor
  +s
pres|tige
pres|tige|ful

pres|ti|gious
pres|ti|gious|ly
pres|ti|gious|ness
pres|tis|simo +s
presto +s (Music; in
  'hey presto!')
Pres|ton (city,
  England)
Pres|ton|pans
  (town and battle
  site, Scotland)
pre|stressed
Prest|wick (airport,
  Scotland)
pre|sum|able
pre|sum|ably
pre|sume
  pre|sumes
  pre|sumed
  pre|sum|ing
pre|sumed|ly
pre|sum|ing|ly
pre|sum|ing|ness
pre|sump|tion +s
pre|sump|tive
pre|sump|tive|ly
pre|sump|tu|ous
pre|sump|tu|
        ous|ly
pre|sump|tu|ous|
              ness
pre|sup|pose
  pre|sup|poses
  pre|sup|posed
  pre|sup|pos|ing
pre|sup|pos|ition
  +s
pre-tax
pre-teen +s
pre|tence Br. +s
  (Am. pretense)
pre|tend +s +ed
  +ing
pre|tend|er +s
pre|tense Am. +s
  (Br. pretence)
pre|ten|sion +s
  (claim)
pre-tension +s
  +ed +ing
  (something
  beforehand)
pre-tension|er +s
pre|ten|tious
pre|ten|tious|ly
pre|ten|tious|ness
pre|ter|hu|man
pret|erit Am. +s
pret|er|ite Br. +s
pret|er|ition +s
pre-term
pre|ter|mis|sion

pre|ter|mit
  pre|ter|mits
  pre|ter|mit|ted
  pre|ter|mit|ting
pre|ter|nat|ural
pre|ter|nat|ur|al|
              ism +s
pre|text +s
pre|tone +s
pre|ton|ic +s
pre|tor +s (use
  praetor)
Pre|toria
  (administrative
  capital of South
  Africa)
pre|tor|ial (use
  praetorial)
pre|tor|ian +s (use
  praetorian)
pre|tor|ship +s
  (use praetorship)
pre|treat +s +ed
  +ing
pre|treat|ment +s
pre-trial
pret|ti|fi|ca|tion +s
pret|ti|fier +s
pret|tify
  pret|ti|fies
  pret|ti|fied
  pret|ti|fy|ing
pret|tily
pret|ti|ness
pretty
  pret|ties
  pret|tied
  pretty|ing
  pret|tier
  pret|ti|est
pret|ty|ish
pret|ty|ism
pretty-pretty
pret|zel +s
pre|vail +s +ed
  +ing
pre|vail|ing|ly
preva|lence
preva|lent
preva|lent|ly
pre|vari|cate
  pre|vari|cates
  pre|vari|cated
  pre|vari|cat|ing
pre|vari|ca|tion +s
pre|vari|ca|tor +s
pre|veni|ent
pre|vent +s +ed
  +ing
pre|vent|abil|ity
pre|vent|able

pre|venta|tive +s
pre|venta|tive|ly
pre|vent|er +s
pre|ven|tion +s
pre|vent|ive +s
pre|vent|ive|ly
pre|view +s +ed
  +ing
Pre|vin, André
  (German-born
  American
  conductor)
pre|vi|ous
pre|vi|ous|ly
pre|vi|ous|ness
pre|vise
  pre|vises
  pre|vised
  pre|vis|ing
pre|vi|sion +s
  (foresight.
  △ provision)
pre|vi|sion|al (of
  foresight.
  △ provisional)
pre-vocation|al
Pré|vost d'Exiles,
  Antoine-
  François (French
  novelist)
pre|vue Am. +s (Br.
  preview)
pre-war
pre-wash
  pre-washes
  pre-washed
  pre-washing
prex
  prexes
prexy
  prex|ies
prey +s +ed +ing
  (food. △ pray)
prey|er +s (feeder.
  △ prayer)
Prez, Jos|quin des
  (Flemish
  composer)
prez|zie +s
Priam Greek
  Mythology
pri|ap|ic
pri|ap|ism
Pria|pus Greek
  Mythology
Pri|bi|lof Is|lands
  (off Alaska)
Price, Vin|cent
  (American actor)
price
  prices

price(cont.)
priced
pri¦cing
price-fixing
price¦less
price¦less¦ly
price list+s
pricer+s
price ring+s
price-sensitive
price tag+s
price war+s
pricey
prici¦er
prici¦est
pri¦ci¦ness
prick+s +ed +ing
prick¦er+s
pricket+s
prickle
prickles
prickled
prick¦ling
prick¦li¦ness
prick¦ly
prick¦lier
prick¦li¦est
pricy
prici¦er
prici¦est
(use pricey)
pride
prides
prided
prid¦ing
pride¦ful
pride¦ful¦ly
pride¦less
Pride's Purge
prie-dieu
prie-dieux
priest+s +ed +ing
priest¦craft
priest¦ess
priest¦esses
priest¦hood
priest-in-charge
priests-in-charge
priest¦less
Priest¦ley, J. B.
(English writer)
Priest¦ley, Jo¦seph
(English chemist)
priest¦like
priest¦li¦ness
priest¦ling+s
priest¦ly
priest¦lier
priest¦li¦est
prig+s
prig¦gery
prig¦gish

prig¦gish¦ly
prig¦gish¦ness
prig¦gism
prim
prims
primmed
prim¦ming
prim¦mer
prim¦mest
prima bal¦ler¦ina
+s
pri¦macy
pri¦ma¦cies
prima donna+s
prima donna-ish
prim¦aeval(use
primeval)
prima facie
prima inter pares
female (male
primus inter pares)
primal
pri¦mal¦ly
pri¦mar¦ily
pri¦mary
pri¦mar¦ies
Pri¦mate+s (title of
archbishop)
pri¦mate+s
(individual animal;
archbishop)
Pri¦mates (order of
mammals)
pri¦ma¦tial
pri¦mat¦olo¦gist+s
pri¦mat¦ology
pri¦ma¦vera+s
prime
primes
primed
prim¦ing
prime¦ness
primer+s
prime time noun
prime-time
attributive
pri¦meval
pri¦mev¦al¦ly
primi¦grav¦ida
primi¦grav¦idae
prim¦ipara
prim¦iparae
prim¦ipar¦ous
primi¦tive+s
primi¦tive¦ly
primi¦tive¦ness
primi¦tiv¦ism
primi¦tiv¦ist+s
prim¦ly
prim¦ness
primo+s

Primo de Ri¦vera,
Mi¦guel(Spanish
general and
statesman)
primo¦geni¦tal
primo¦geni¦tary
primo¦geni¦tor+s
primo¦geni¦ture
prim¦or¦dial
prim¦or¦di¦al¦ity
prim¦or¦di¦al¦ly
prim¦or¦dium
prim¦or¦dia
Pri¦mor¦sky Krai
(territory, Russia)
primp+s +ed +ing
Prim¦rose(name)
prim¦rose+s
(flower)
prim¦ula+s
pri¦mum mo¦bile+s
Pri¦mus
Pri¦muses
(stove) Propr.
pri¦mus
pri¦muses
(bishop)
pri¦mus inter pares
male (female prima
inter pares)
prince+s
prince con¦sort+s
prince¦dom+s
Prince Ed¦ward
Is¦land(province,
Canada)
prince¦like
prince¦li¦ness
prince¦ling+s
prince¦ly
Prince Ru¦pert's
Land(= Rupert's
Land)
prince's fea¦ther
+s (plant)
prince¦ship+s
prince's metal
prin¦cess
prin¦cesses
Prince¦ton
(university, USA)
prin¦ci¦pal+s
(chief.
△ principle)
prin¦ci¦pal¦ity
prin¦ci¦pal¦ities
prin¦ci¦pal¦ly
prin¦ci¦pal¦ship+s
prin¦ci¦pate+s
Prin¦cipe (island,
Gulf of Guinea)

prin¦ciple+s
(fundamental truth
etc. △ principal)
prin¦cipled
prink+s +ed +ing
print+s +ed +ing
print¦abil¦ity
print¦able
print¦er+s
print¦er's devil+s
print¦er's mark+s
print¦er's pie
print¦ery
print¦er¦ies
print¦head+s
print¦ing+s
print¦ing press
print¦ing presses
print¦less
print¦maker+s
print¦mak¦ing
print¦out+s
print¦works
prion+s
prior+s
pri¦or¦ate+s
pri¦or¦ess
pri¦or¦esses
pri¦ori¦tisa¦tion Br.
(use
prioritization)
pri¦ori¦tise Br. (use
prioritize)
pri¦ori¦tises
pri¦ori¦tised
pri¦ori¦tis¦ing
pri¦ori¦tiza¦tion
pri¦ori¦tize
pri¦ori¦tizes
pri¦ori¦tized
pri¦ori¦tiz¦ing
pri¦or¦ity
pri¦or¦ities
prior¦ship+s
pri¦ory
pri¦or¦ies
Pri¦pyat(river, E.
Europe)
Pris¦cian
(Byzantine
grammarian)
Pris¦cilla
prise Br.
prises
prised
pris¦ing
(force. Am. prize)
prism+s
pris¦mal
pris¦mat¦ic
pris¦mat¦ic¦al¦ly
pris¦moid+s

pris|moid|al
prison+s +ed +ing
prison-breaking
prison camp+s
pris|on|er+s
pris|on|er of war
　pris|on|ers of war
prisoner-of-war
　attributive
pris|on|er's base
pris|sily
pris|si|ness
prissy
　pris|sier
　pris|si|est
Priš|tina (city,
　Serbia)
pris|tine
Prit|chett, V. S.
　(English writer)
pri|thee
priv|acy
　priv|acies
pri|vate+s
pri'vat|eer+s
pri'vat|eer|ing
pri'vat|eers|man
　pri'vat|eers|men
pri|vate first class
　pri|vates first
　class
pri|vate|ly
pri|vate
　mem|ber's bill
　+s
pri'va|tion+s
pri'vat|isa|tion *Br.*
　+s (use
　privatization)
pri'vat|ise *Br.* (use
　privatize)
　pri'vat|ises
　pri'vat|ised
　pri'vat|is|ing
pri'vat|iser+s (use
　privatizer)
priv|ative
priv|ative|ly
pri'vat|iza|tion+s
pri'vat|ize
　pri'vat|izes
　pri'vat|ized
　pri'vat|iz|ing
pri'vat|izer+s
privet+s
priv|il|ege
　priv|il|eges
　priv|il|eged
　priv|il|eging
priv|ily
priv|ity
　priv|ities

privy
　priv|ies
Privy Coun|cil
Privy Coun|cil|lor
　+s (use Privy
　Counsellor)
Privy Coun|sel|lor
　+s
privy seal+s
Prix Gon|court
　plural Prix
　Gon|court
prize
　prizes
　prized
　priz|ing
　(award. △ prise)
prize *Am.*
　prizes
　prized
　priz|ing
　(force. *Br.* prise)
prize court+s
prize|fight+s
prize|fight|er+s
prize|fight|ing
prize-giving+s
prize|man
　prize|men
prize-money
prize ring+s
prize|win|ner+s
prize|win|ning
pro+s
proa+s
pro|action
pro|active
pro|active|ly
pro|activ|ity
pro-am+s
prob+s
prob|abil|ism
prob|abil|ist+s
prob|abil|is|tic
prob|abil|ity
　prob|abil|ities
prob|able+s
prob|ably
pro|band+s
pro|bang+s
pro|bate
　pro|bates
　pro|bated
　pro|bat|ing
pro|ba|tion
pro|ba|tion|al
pro|ba|tion|ary
pro|ba|tion|er+s
pro|ba|tion|er|ship
　+s
pro|ba|tive

probe
　probes
　probed
　prob|ing
probe|able
prober+s
prob|ing+s
prob|ing|ly
pro|bit+s
prob|ity
prob|lem+s
prob|lem|at|ic
prob|lem|at|ic|al
prob|lem|at|ic|
　　　　al|ly
prob|lem|atisa|
　tion *Br.* (use
　problematiza-
　tion)
prob|lem|atise *Br.*
　(use
　problematize)
　prob|lem|atises
　prob|lem|atised
　prob|lem|atis|ing
prob|lem|atiza|
　　　　tion
prob|lem|atize
　prob|lem|atizes
　prob|lem|atized
　prob|lem|atiz|ing
problem-solving
pro bono
pro'bos|cid|ean+s
pro'bos|cid|ian+s
　(use
　proboscidean)
pro'bos|cid|ifer|
　　　　ous
pro'bos|cis
　pro'bos|ces *or*
　pro'bos|cides *or*
　pro'bos|cises
pro|cain (use
　procaine)
pro|caine
pro|cary|ote+s
　(use prokaryote)
pro|cary|ot|ic (use
　prokaryotic)
pro|ced|ural
pro|ced|ur|al|ly
pro|ced|ure+s
pro|ceed+s +ed
　+ing (go forward.
　△ precede)
pro|ceed|ing+s
　(action.
　△ preceding)
pro|ceeds (money)

pro|cess
　pro|cesses
　pro|cessed
　pro|cess|ing
pro|cess|able
pro|ces|sion+s
　(movement of
　people or vehicles.
　△ precession)
pro|ces|sion|al+s
　(relating to
　processions; book
　of processional
　hymns.
　△ precessional)
pro|ces|sion|ary
pro|ces|sion|ist+s
pro|ces|sor+s
procès-verbal
　procès-verbaux
pro-choice
pro|chron|ism+s
pro|claim+s +ed
　+ing
pro|claim|er+s
proc|lam|ation+s
pro|clama|tory
pro|clit|ic+s
pro|clit|ic|al|ly
pro|cliv|ity
　pro|cliv|ities
Procne *Greek
　Mythology*
pro|con|sul+s
pro|con|su|lar
pro|con|su|late+s
pro|con|sul|ship
　+s
Pro|co|pius
　(Byzantine
　historian)
pro|cras|tin|ate
　pro|cras|tin|ates
　pro|cras|tin|ated
　pro|cras|tin|at|ing
pro|cras|tin|ation
　+s
pro|cras|tina|tive
pro|cras|tin|ator
　+s
pro|cras|tin|atory
pro|cre|ant+s
pro|cre|ate
　pro|cre|ates
　pro|cre|ated
　pro|cre|at|ing
pro|cre|ation
pro|cre|ative
pro|cre|ator+s
Pro|crus|tean
Pro|crus|tes *Greek
　Mythology*

procto|logic|al
proc|tolo|gist+s
proc|tol|ogy
proc|tor+s
proc|tor|ial
proc|tor|ship+s
procto|scope+s
pro|cum|bent
pro|cur|able
pro|cural
pro|cur|ance
proc|ur|ation+s
proc|ur|ator+s
proc|ur|ator fis|cal
  proc|ur|ators
  fis|cal
proc|ura|tor|ial
proc|ur|ator|ship
  +s
proc|ura|tory
pro|cure
  pro|cures
  pro|cured
  pro|cur|ing
pro|cure|ment+s
pro|curer+s
pro|cur|ess
  pro|cur|esses
Pro|cyon (star)
Prod+s (*offensive*)
prod
  prods
  prod|ded
  prod|ding
prod|der+s
Prod|die+s
  (*offensive*)
Proddy
  Prod|dies
  (*offensive*)
pro-democracy
prod|igal+s
prod|ig|al|ise *Br.*
  (use prodigalize)
  prod|ig|al|ises
  prod|ig|al|ised
  prod|ig|al|is|ing
prod|ig|al|ity
  prod|ig|al|ities
prod|ig|al|ize
  prod|ig|al|izes
  prod|ig|al|ized
  prod|ig|al|iz|ing
prod|ig|al|ly
pro|di|gious
pro|di|gious|ly
pro|di|gious|ness
prod|igy
  prodi|gies
pro|dromal
pro|drome+s
pro|drom|ic

pro|duce
  pro|duces
  pro|duced
  pro|du|cing
pro|du|cer+s
pro|du|ci|bil|ity
pro|du|cible
prod|uct+s
pro|duc|tion+s
pro|duc|tion|al
pro|duct|ive
pro|duct|ive|ly
pro|duct|ive|ness
prod|uct|iv|ity
  prod|uct|iv|ities
proem+s
pro|em|ial
prof+s
prof|an|ation+s
pro|fane
  pro|fanes
  pro|faned
  pro|fan|ing
pro|fane|ly
pro|fane|ness
pro|faner+s
pro|fan|ity
  pro|fan|ities
pro|fess
  pro|fesses
  pro|fessed
  pro|fess|ing
pro|fess|ed|ly
pro|fes|sion+s
pro|fes|sion|al+s
pro|fes|sion|al|
  isa|tion *Br.* (use
  professionaliza-
  tion)
pro|fes|sion|al|ise
  Br. (use
  professionalize)
pro|fes|sion|al|
      ises
pro|fes|sion|al|
      ised
pro|fes|sion|al|
      is|ing
pro|fes|sion|al|ism
pro|fes|sion|al|
     iza|tion
pro|fes|sion|al|ize
pro|fes|sion|al|
     izes
pro|fes|sion|al|
     ized
pro|fes|sion|al|
     iz|ing
pro|fes|sion|al|ly
pro|fes|sion|less
pro|fes|sor+s
pro|fes|sor|ate+s

pro|fes|sor|ial
pro|fes|sori|al|ly
pro|fes|sori|ate+s
pro|fes|sor|ship+s
prof|fer+s +ed
  +ing
pro|fi|ciency
  pro|fi|cien|cies
pro|fi|cient
pro|fi|cient|ly
pro|file
  pro|files
  pro|filed
  pro|fil|ing
pro|filer+s
pro|fil|ist+s
profit+s +ed +ing
  (gain. ⚠ prophet)
prof|it|abil|ity
  prof|it|abil|ities
prof|it|able
prof|it|able|ness
prof|it|ably
prof|it|eer+s +ed
  +ing
pro|fit|er|ole+s
prof|it|less
profit-making
profit-related
profit-sharing
profit-taking
prof|li|gacy
prof|li|gate+s
prof|li|gate|ly
pro forma+s *noun*
pro-forma
  attributive
pro|found+er +est
pro|found|ly
pro|found|ness
Pro|fumo, John
  (British politician)
pro|fund|ity
  pro|fund|ities
pro|fuse
pro|fuse|ly
pro|fuse|ness
pro|fu|sion+s
prog+s
  (= programme)
pro|geni|tive
pro|geni|tor+s
pro|geni|tor|ial
pro|geni|tor|ship
pro|geni|tress
  pro|geni|tresses
pro|geni|trix
pro|geni|tri|ces
  female
pro|geni|ture
pro|geny
  pro|gen|ies

pro|ges|ter|one
pro|ges|to|gen+s
pro|glot|tid+s
pro|glot|tis
  pro|glot|tides
prog|nath|ic
prog|nath|ism
prog|nath|ous
prog|no|sis
  prog|no|ses
prog|nos|tic
prog|nos|tic|able
prog|nos|tic|al|ly
prog|nos|ti|cate
  prog|nos|ti|cates
  prog|nos|ti|cated
  prog|nos|ti|
      cat|ing
prog|nos|ti|ca|tion
  +s
prog|nos|ti|ca|tive
prog|nos|ti|ca|tor
  +s
prog|nos|ti|ca|tory
pro|gram+s (for
  computer.
  ⚠ programme)
  noun
pro|gram *Br.*
  pro|grams
  pro|grammed
  pro|gram|ming
  (in computing.
  ⚠ programme)
  verb
pro|gram *Am.*
  pro|grams
  pro|grammed
  pro|gram|ming
  (*verb. Br.*
  programme)
pro|gram|
     ma|bil|ity
pro|gram|mable
pro|gram|mat|ic
pro|gram|mat|ic|
     al|ly
pro|gramme *Br.*
  pro|grammes
  pro|grammed
  pro|gram|ming
  (*Am.* program. all
  senses except
  computing.
  ⚠ program)
pro|gram|mer+s
pro|gress
  pro|gresses
  pro|gressed
  pro|gress|ing
progress-chaser
  +s

pro|gres|sion +s
pro|gres|sion|al
pro|gres|sion|ist +s
pro|gres|sive +s
pro|gres|sive|ly
pro|gres|sive|ness
pro|gres|siv|ism
pro|gres|siv|ist +s
pro hac vice
pro|hibit +s +ed +ing
pro|hib|it|er +s
pro|hib|ition +s
pro|hib|ition|ary
pro|hib|ition|ist +s
pro|hibi|tive
pro|hibi|tive|ly
pro|hibi|tive|ness
pro|hibi|tor +s
pro|hibi|tory
pro|ject +s +ed +ing
pro|ject|ile +s
pro|jec|tion +s
pro|jec|tion|ist +s
pro|ject|ive
pro|ject|ive|ly
pro|ject|or +s
pro|kary|ote +s
pro|kary|ot|ic
Pro|kof|iev, Ser|gei (Russian composer)
Pro|kop|evsk (city, Russia)
pro|lac|tin
pro|lapse
  pro|lapses
  pro|lapsed
  pro|laps|ing
pro|lap|sus
pro|late
pro|late|ly
pro|la|tive
prole +s
pro|leg +s
pro|leg|om|en|ary
pro|leg|om|enon
  pro|leg|om|ena
pro|leg|om|en|ous
pro|lep|sis
  pro|lep|ses
pro|lep|tic
pro|le|tar|ian +s
pro|le|tar|ian|
  isa|tion *Br.* (use proletarianiza-tion)
pro|le|tar|ian|ise *Br.* (use proletarianize)

pro|le|tar|ian|ise (*cont.*)
  pro|le|tar|ian|ises
  pro|le|tar|ian|ised
  pro|le|tar|ian|
    is|ing
pro|le|tar|ian|ism
pro|le|tar|ian|
    iza|tion
pro|le|tar|ian|ize
  pro|le|tar|ian|izes
  pro|le|tar|ian|ized
  pro|le|tar|ian|
    iz|ing
pro|le|tar|iat +s
pro-life
pro|lif|er|ate
  pro|lif|er|ates
  pro|lif|er|ated
  pro|lif|er|at|ing
pro|lif|er|ation
pro|lif|era|tive
pro|lif|er|ator +s
pro|lif|er|ous
pro|lif|ic
pro|lif|ic|acy
pro|lif|ic|al|ly
pro|li|fi|city
pro|lif|ic|ness
pro|line +s
pro|lix
pro|lix|ity
pro|lix|ly
pro|locu|tor +s
pro|locu|tor|ship +s
Pro|log *Computing*
pro|log|ise *Br.* (use prologize)
  pro|log|ises
  pro|log|ised
  pro|log|is|ing
pro|log|ize
  pro|log|izes
  pro|log|ized
  pro|log|iz|ing
pro|logue
  pro|logues
  pro|logued
  pro|loguing
pro|long +s +ed +ing
pro|longa|tion +s
pro|long|ed|ly
pro|long|er +s
pro|lu|sion +s
pro|lu|sory
prom +s
  (= promenade; promenade concert)

prom|en|ade
  prom|en|ades
  prom|en|aded
  prom|en|ad|ing
prom|en|ader +s
pro|meth|az|ine
Pro|me|thean
Pro|me|theus *Greek Mythology*
pro|me|thium
prom|in|ence +s
prom|in|ency
prom|in|ent +s
prom|in|enti
prom|in|ent|ly
prom|is|cu|ity
  prom|is|cu|ities
pro|mis|cu|ous
pro|mis|cu|ous|ly
pro|mis|cu|ous|
    ness
prom|ise
  prom|ises
  prom|ised
  prom|is|ing
prom|isee +s
prom|iser +s
  (generally.
    △ promisor)
prom|is|ing|ly
prom|isor +s (*Law.*
    △ promiser)
prom|is|sory
prom|mer +s
promo +s
prom|on|tory
  prom|on|tor|ies
pro|mot|abil|ity
pro|mot|able
pro|mote
  pro|motes
  pro|moted
  pro|mot|ing
pro|moter +s
pro|mo|tion +s
  (advancement etc.
    △ premotion)
pro|mo|tion|al
pro|mo|tive
prompt +s +ed +ing
prompt book +s
prompt-box
  prompt-boxes
prompt|er +s
prompt|ing +s
prompti|tude
prompt|ly
prompt|ness
prompt-note +s
prompt side

pro|mul|gate
  pro|mul|gates
  pro|mul|gated
  pro|mul|gat|ing
pro|mul|ga|tion
pro|mul|ga|tor +s
pro|mulge
  pro|mulges
  pro|mulged
  pro|mul|ging
pro|naos
pro|naoi
pro|nate
  pro|nates
  pro|nated
  pro|nat|ing
pro|na|tion
pro|na|tor +s
prone
prone|ly
prone|ness
pron|eur +s
prong +s +ed +ing
prong|horn +s
prong-horned
  ante|lope +s
pro|nom|inal
pro|nom|in|al|ise
  Br. (use pronominalize)
pro|nom|in|al|
    ises
pro|nom|in|al|
    ised
pro|nom|in|al|
    is|ing
pro|nom|in|al|ize
pro|nom|in|al|
    izes
pro|nom|in|al|
    ized
pro|nom|in|al|
    iz|ing
pro|nom|in|al|ly
pro|noun +s
pro|nounce
  pro|nounces
  pro|nounced
  pro|noun|cing
pro|nounce|able
pro|nounced|ly
pro|nounce|ment +s
pro|noun|cer +s
pronto
pro|nun|cia|mento +s
pro|nun|ci|ation +s
pro-nuncio +s
proof +s +ed +ing
proof|less

proof-plane +s
proof-read
  proof-reads
  proof-read
  proof-reading
proof-reader +s
proof-sheet +s
prop
  props
  propped
  prop|ping
pro|pae|deutic +s
pro|pae|deut|ic|al
propa|ganda
propa|gand|ise Br.
  (use
  propagandize)
  propa|gand|ises
  propa|gand|ised
  propa|gand|is|ing
propa|gand|ism
propa|gand|ist +s
propa|gand|is|tic
propa|gand|is|tic|
        al|ly
propa|gand|ize
  propa|gand|izes
  propa|gand|ized
  propa|gand|iz|ing
propa|gate
  propa|gates
  propa|gated
  propa|gat|ing
propa|ga|tion +s
propa|ga|tive
prop|aga|tor +s
pro|pane
pro|pan|oic
pro|pan|one
pro|par|oxy|tone
  +s
pro|pel
  pro|pels
  pro|pelled
  pro|pel|ling
pro|pel|lant +s
  noun
pro|pel|lent
  adjective
pro|pel|ler +s
pro|pene
pro|pen|sity
  pro|pen|sities
proper +s
pro|peri|
      spo|menon
pro|peri|
      spo|mena
prop|er|ly
prop|er|ness
prop|er|tied

Pro|per|tius,
  Sex|tus (Roman
  poet)
prop|erty
  prop|er|ties
pro|phase +s
proph|ecy
  proph|ecies
  noun
proph|esier +s
proph|esy
  proph|es|ies
  proph|es|ied
  proph|esy|ing
Prophet, the
  (Muhammad;
  Joseph Smith)
prophet +s
  (foreteller.
  △ profit)
proph|et|ess
  proph|et|esses
proph|et|hood
proph|et|ic
proph|et|ic|al
proph|et|ic|al|ly
proph|eti|cism +s
proph|et|ism
proph|et|ship
prophy|lac|tic +s
prophy|laxis
  prophy|laxes
pro|pin|quity
  pro|pin|qui|ties
pro|pi|on|ate +s
pro|pi|on|ic
pro|piti|ate
  pro|piti|ates
  pro|piti|ated
  pro|piti|at|ing
pro|piti|ation
pro|piti|ator +s
pro|piti|ator|ily
pro|piti|atory
pro|pi|tious
pro|pi|tious|ly
pro|pi|tious|ness
prop-jet +s
prop|olis
pro|pon|ent +s
Pro|pon|tis
  (ancient name for
  the Sea of
  Marmara)
pro|por|tion +s
  +ed +ing
pro|por|tion|able
pro|por|tion|ably
pro|por|tion|al
pro|por|tion|al|ist
  +s

pro|por|tion|al|ity
pro|por|tion|al|
        ities
pro|por|tion|al|ly
pro|por|tion|ate
pro|por|tion|ate|ly
pro|por|tion|less
pro|por|tion|ment
pro|posal +s
pro|pose
  pro|poses
  pro|posed
  pro|pos|ing
pro|poser +s
prop|os|ition +s
  +ed +ing
prop|os|ition|al
pro|pound +s +ed
  +ing
pro|pound|er +s
pro|prae|tor +s
pro|pri|etary
  pro|pri|etar|ies
pro|pri|etor +s
pro|pri|etor|ial
pro|pri|etori|al|ly
pro|pri|etor|ship
  +s
pro|pri|etress
  pro|pri|et|resses
pro|pri|ety
  pro|pri|eties
pro|prio|cep|tion
pro|prio|cep|tive
pro-proctor +s
prop|tosis
  prop|toses
pro|pul|sion
pro|pul|sive
pro|pul|sor +s
pro|pyl
propy|laeum
  propy|laea
pro|pyl|ene
pro|pylon
  pro|pylons or
  pro|pyla
pro rata
pro|rate
  pro|rates
  pro|rated
  pro|rat|ing
pro|ra|tion
pro|roga|tion +s
pro|rogue
  pro|rogues
  pro|rogued
  pro|roguing
pro|sa|ic
pro|saic|al|ly
pro|saic|ness
pro|sa|ism +s

pro|sa|ist +s
pro|scen|ium
  pro|scen|iums or
  pro|scenia
pro|sciutto +s
pro|scribe
  pro|scribes
  pro|scribed
  pro|scrib|ing
  (banish;
  denounce.
  △ prescribe)
pro|scrip|tion +s
  (banishment;
  denouncement
  etc.
  △ prescription)
pro|scrip|tive
  (proscribing.
  △ prescriptive)
prose
  proses
  prosed
  pros|ing
pro|sec|tor +s
pros|ecut|able
pros|ecute
  pros|ecutes
  pros|ecuted
  pros|ecut|ing
pros|ecu|tion +s
pros|ecu|tor +s
pros|ecu|tor|ial
pros|ecu|trix
  pros|ecu|tri|ces
  female
pros|elyte +s
pros|elyt|ise Br.
  (use proselytize)
  pros|elyt|ises
  pros|elyt|ised
  pros|elyt|is|ing
pros|elyt|iser Br.
  +s (use
  proselytizer)
pros|elyt|ism
pros|elyt|ize
  pros|elyt|izes
  pros|elyt|ized
  pros|elyt|iz|ing
pros|elyt|izer +s
pros|en|ceph|alon
  +s
pros|en|chyma
pros|en|chy|mal
pros|en|chy|ma|
        tous
prose poem +s
prose poet|ry
proser +s
Pro|ser|pina (use
  Proserpine)

Pro¦ser¦pine
  (Roman name for
  Persephone)
pros¦ify
  prosi¦fies
  prosi¦fied
  prosi¦fy¦ing
prosi¦ly
pro¦sim¦ian +s
pro¦si¦ness
pro¦ sit
pros¦od¦ic
pros¦od¦ist +s
pros¦ody
  pros¦od¦ies
pros¦op|og¦raph¦er
  +s
pros¦opo¦graph¦ic
pros¦opo¦
    graph¦ic¦al
pros¦op|og¦raphy
  pros¦op¦
    og¦raph¦ies
pros¦opo¦poeia
pro¦spect +s +ed
  +ing
pro¦spect¦ive
pro¦spect¦ive¦ly
pro¦spect¦ive¦ness
pro¦spect¦less
pro¦spect¦or +s
pro¦spec¦tus
  pro¦spec¦tuses
pros¦per +s +ed
  +ing
pros¦per¦ity
  pros¦per¦ities
pros¦per¦ous
pros¦per¦ous¦ly
pros¦per¦ous¦ness
Prost, Alain
  (French motor-
  racing driver)
prost
pros¦ta¦glandin +s
pro¦state +s
pro¦stat¦ic
pros¦thesis
  pros¦theses
pros¦thet¦ic
pros¦thet¦ic¦al¦ly
pros¦thet¦ics
pros¦ti¦tute
  pros¦ti¦tutes
  pros¦ti¦tuted
  pros¦ti¦tut¦ing
pros¦ti¦tu¦tion
pros¦ti¦tu¦tion¦al
pros¦ti¦tu¦tor +s
pros¦trate
  pros¦trates

pros¦trate (*cont.*)
  pros¦trated
  pros¦trat¦ing
pros¦tra¦tion +s
pro¦style +s
prosy
  prosi¦er
  prosi¦est
prot¦ac¦tin¦ium
prot¦ag¦on¦ist +s
prot¦am¦ine +s
prot¦asis
  prot¦ases
pro¦tat¦ic
pro¦tea +s
pro¦tean
pro¦te¦ase +s
pro¦tect +s +ed
  +ing
pro¦tec¦tion +s
pro¦tec¦tion¦ism
  +s
pro¦tec¦tion¦ist +s
pro¦tect¦ive +s
pro¦tect¦ive¦ly
pro¦tect¦ive¦ness
pro¦tect¦or +s
pro¦tect¦or¦al
pro¦tect¦or¦ate +s
pro¦tect¦or¦ship
pro¦tec¦tress
  pro¦tec¦tresses
pro¦tégé +s *male*
pro¦té¦gée +s
  female
pro¦tei¦form
pro¦tein +s
pro¦tein¦aceous
pro¦tein¦ic
pro¦tein¦ous
pro¦tem
pro tem¦pore
pro¦te¦oly¦sis
  pro¦te¦oly¦ses
pro¦teo¦lyt¦ic
Pro¦tero¦zo¦ic
pro¦test +s +ed
  +ing
Prot¦est¦ant +s
  (Christian)
prot¦est¦ant +s
  (generally)
Prot¦est¦ant¦ise *Br.*
  (use
  Protestantize)
Prot¦est¦ant¦ises
Prot¦est¦ant¦ised
Prot¦est¦ant¦is¦ing
Prot¦est¦ant¦ism
Prot¦est¦ant¦ize
Prot¦est¦ant¦izes
Prot¦est¦ant¦ized

Prot¦est¦ant¦ize
  (*cont.*)
  Prot¦est¦ant¦
    iz¦ing
prot¦est¦ation +s
pro¦test¦er +s
pro¦test¦ing¦ly
pro¦test¦or +s (use
  protester)
Pro¦teus (*Greek
  Mythology*; moon
  of Neptune)
pro¦teus
  pro¦tei *or*
  pro¦teuses
  (bacterium)
pro¦tha¦lam¦ion
  (use
  prothalamium)
pro¦tha¦lamia
pro¦tha¦lam¦ium
  pro¦tha¦lamia
pro¦thal¦lium
  pro¦thal¦lia
pro¦thal¦lus
  pro¦thalli
pro¦thesis
  pro¦theses
pro¦thet¦ic
pro¦tho¦not¦ary
  pro¦tho¦not¦ar¦ies
pro¦tist +s
pro¦tist¦ology
pro¦tium
proto¦col
  proto¦cols
  proto¦colled
  proto¦col¦ling
Proto-Indo-
  European
proto¦mar¦tyr +s
pro¦ton +s
pro¦ton¦ic
proto¦not¦ary
  proto¦not¦ar¦ies
proto¦pec¦tin +s
proto¦phyte +s
proto¦plasm
proto¦plas¦mal
proto¦plas¦mat¦ic
proto¦plas¦mic
proto¦plast +s
proto¦plas¦tic
proto¦theria
proto¦ther¦ian +s
proto¦typal
proto¦type
  proto¦types
  proto¦typed
  proto¦typ¦ing
proto¦typ¦ic
proto¦typ¦ic¦al

proto¦typ¦ic¦al¦ly
proto¦zoal
proto¦zoan +s
proto¦zo¦ic
proto¦zo¦ology
proto¦zoon
  proto¦zoa
pro¦tract +s +ed
  +ing
pro¦tract¦ed¦ly
pro¦tract¦ed¦ness
pro¦tract¦ile
pro¦trac¦tion
pro¦tract¦or +s
pro¦trude
  pro¦trudes
  pro¦truded
  pro¦trud¦ing
pro¦tru¦dent
pro¦tru¦sible
pro¦tru¦sile
pro¦tru¦sion +s
pro¦tru¦sive
pro¦tu¦ber¦ance +s
pro¦tu¦ber¦ant
proud +er +est
proud-hearted
Proud¦hon, Pierre
  Jo¦seph (French
  social
  philosopher)
proud¦ly
proud¦ness
Proust, Jo¦seph
  Louis (French
  analytical chemist)
Proust, Mar¦cel
  (French writer)
Prout, Wil¦liam
  (English chemist
  and biochemist)
prov¦abil¦ity
prov¦able
prov¦ably
prove
  proves
  proved
  prov¦ing
  proved *or* proven
prov¦en¦ance +s
prov¦en¦anced
Pro¦ven¦çal +s
Pro¦vence (former
  province, France)
Provence–Alpes–
  Côte d'Azur
  (region, France)
prov¦en¦der +s
  +ed +ing
pro¦veni¦ence +s
prov¦erb +s +s
pro¦verb¦ial +s

pro|verbi|al|ity
pro|verbi|al|ly
pro|vide
  pro|vides
  pro|vided
  pro|vid|ing
Provi|dence (city, USA; God)
provi|dence (care; foresight)
provi|dent
provi|den|tial
provi|den|tial|ly
provi|dent|ly
pro|vider +s
Pro|vie +s
prov|ince +s
pro|vin|cial +s
pro|vin|cial|ise Br. (use provincialize)
  pro|vin|cial|ises
  pro|vin|cial|ised
  pro|vin|cial|is|ing
pro|vin|cial|ism
pro|vin|ci|al|ity
pro|vin|cial|ize
  pro|vin|cial|izes
  pro|vin|cial|ized
  pro|vin|cial|iz|ing
pro|vin|cial|ly
pro|vi|sion +s +ed +ing (providing; food; etc. △ prevision)
Pro|vi|sion|al +s (of IRA)
pro|vi|sion|al +s (temporary. △ previsional)
pro|vi|sion|al|ity
pro|vi|sion|al|ly
pro|vi|sion|al|ness
pro|vi|sion|er +s
pro|vi|sion|less
pro|vi|sion|ment
pro|viso +s
pro|visor +s
pro|visor|ily
pro|vi|sory
Provo +s
provo|ca|tion +s
pro|voca|tive
pro|voca|tive|ly
pro|voca|tive|ness
pro|vok|able
pro|voke
  pro|vokes
  pro|voked
  pro|vok|ing
pro|voker +s

pro|vok|ing|ly
prov|ost +s
prov|ost|ship +s
prow +s
prow|ess
prowl +s +ed +ing
prowl|er +s
prox. (= proximo)
prox|em|ics
Prox|ima Cen|tauri (star)
prox|imal
prox|im|al|ly
prox|im|ate
prox|im|ate|ly
prox|ime ac|ces|sit
prox|im|ity
  prox|im|ities
prox|imo
proxy
  prox|ies
Pru *also* Prue
prude +s
Pru|dence (name)
pru|dence (care; discretion)
pru|dent
pru|den|tial +s
pru|den|tial|ism
pru|den|tial|ist +s
pru|den|tial|ly
pru|dent|ly
prud|ery
Prud|hoe Bay (on coast of Alaska)
prud|ish
prud|ish|ly
prud|ish|ness
Prue *also* Pru
pru|in|ose
prune
  prunes
  pruned
  prun|ing
Pru|nella (name)
pru|nella +s (plant; fabric)
pruner +s
prun|ing hook +s
pruri|ence
pruri|ency
pruri|ent
pruri|ent|ly
pruri|gin|ous
prur|igo
prur|it|ic
prur|itus
Prus|sia (former German state)
Prus|sian +s
Prus|sian blue +s
  noun and adjective

Prussian-blue
  attributive
prus|sic
Prut (river, SE Europe)
pry
  pries
  pried
  pry|ing
pry|ing|ly
psalm +s +ed +ing
psalm-book +s
psalm|ic
psalm|ist +s
psalm|od|ic
psalm|od|ise Br. (use psalmodize)
  psalm|od|ises
  psalm|od|ised
  psalm|od|is|ing
psalm|od|ist +s
psalm|od|ize
  psalm|od|izes
  psalm|od|ized
  psalm|od|iz|ing
psalm|ody
psal|ter +s
psal|ter|ium +s
psal|tery
  psal|ter|ies
psepho|logic|al
psepho|logic|al|ly
pseph|olo|gist +s
pseph|ology
pseud +s
pseud|epig|rapha
pseud| epig|raph|al
pseud| epi|graph|ic
pseud|epi|graph| ic|al
pseudo +s
pseudo|carp +s
pseudo|graph +s
pseudo|morph +s
pseudo|morph|ic
pseudo|morph| ism
pseudo|morph| ous
pseudo|nym +s
pseudo|nym|ity
pseud|onym|ous
pseud|onym| ous|ly
pseudo|pod +s
pseudo|po|dium
  pseudo|po|dia
pseudo-science
pseudo-scientif|ic
pshaw

psi +s (Greek letter)
psil|an|throp|ic
psil|an|throp|ism
psil|an|throp|ist +s
psilo|cybin +s
psil|osis
psil|oses
psit|ta|cine
psit|ta|cism +s
psit|ta|cosis
  psit|ta|coses
psoas
  plural psoas muscles
psor|ia|sis
psor|ia|ses
psori|at|ic
psst
psych +s +ed +ing
Psy|che *Greek Mythology*
psy|che +s (the soul; the mind)
psy|che|delia
psy|che|del|ic +s
psy|che|del|ic| al|ly
psy|chi|atric
psy|chi|atric|al
psy|chi|atric|al|ly
psych|iatrist +s
psych|iatry
psy|chic +s
psych|ic|al
psych|ic|al|ly
psy|chi|cism
psy|chi|cist +s
psy|cho +s
psy|cho|active
psy|cho|ana|lyse Br.
  psy|cho|ana|lyses
  psy|cho| ana|lysed
  psy|cho| ana|lys|ing
psy|cho|analy|sis
psy|cho|ana|lyst +s
psy|cho|ana|lyt|ic
psy|cho|ana|lyt| ic|al
psy|cho|ana|lyt|ic| al|ly
psy|cho|ana|lyze Am.
  psy|cho|ana|lyzes
  psy|cho| ana|lyzed
  psy|cho| ana|lyz|ing
psy|cho|bab|ble

psy¦cho¦
    bio¦logic¦al
psy¦cho¦biolo¦gist
  +s
psy¦cho¦biol¦ogy
psy¦cho¦drama +s
psy¦cho¦dynam¦ic
psy¦cho¦dynam¦ic¦
    al¦ly
psy¦cho¦
    dynam¦ics
psy¦cho¦gen¦esis
psy¦cho¦graph +s
psy¦cho¦graph¦ic
psy¦cho¦graph¦ics
psy¦cho¦kin¦esis
psy¦cho¦kin¦et¦ic
psy¦cho¦lin¦guist
  +s
psy¦cho¦
    lin¦guis¦tic
psy¦cho¦
    lin¦guis¦tics
psy¦cho¦logic¦al
psy¦cho¦logic¦al¦ly
psych¦olo¦gise Br.
  (use
  psychologize)
psych¦olo¦gises
psych¦olo¦gised
psych¦olo¦gis¦ing
psych¦olo¦gist +s
psych¦olo¦gize
psych¦olo¦gizes
psych¦olo¦gized
psych¦olo¦giz¦ing
psych¦ology
psych¦olo¦gies
psy¦cho¦met¦ric
psy¦cho¦met¦ric¦
    al¦ly
psy¦cho¦met¦rics
psych¦om¦etrist +s
psych¦om¦etry
psy¦cho¦motor
psy¦cho¦neur¦osis
 psy¦cho¦
    neur¦oses
psy¦cho¦neur¦ot¦ic
psy¦cho¦path +s
psy¦cho¦path¦ic
psy¦cho¦path¦ic¦
    al¦ly
psy¦cho¦patho¦
    logic¦al
psy¦cho¦
    path¦ology
psych¦op¦athy
psy¦cho¦phys¦ic¦al
psy¦cho¦phys¦ics
psy¦cho¦
    physio¦logic¦al

psy¦cho¦
    physi¦ology
psy¦cho¦sex¦ual
psy¦cho¦sexu¦al¦ly
psych¦osis
  psych¦oses
  (mental disorder.
  ⚠ sycosis)
psy¦cho¦social
psy¦cho¦social¦ly
psy¦cho¦somat¦ic
psy¦cho¦somat¦ic¦
    al¦ly
psy¦cho¦sur¦gery
psy¦cho¦sur¦gi¦cal
psy¦cho¦
    thera¦peut¦ic
psy¦cho¦ther¦ap¦ist
  +s
psy¦cho¦ther¦apy
psych¦ot¦ic +s
psych¦otic¦al¦ly
psy¦cho¦trop¦ic
psy¦chrom¦eter +s
Ptah Egyptian
  Mythology
ptar¦migan +s
PT boat +s
pter¦ano¦don +s
pter¦ido¦logic¦al
pter¦id¦olo¦gist +s
pter¦id¦ology
pter¦ido¦phyte +s
ptero¦dac¦tyl +s
ptero¦pod +s
ptero¦saur +s
pteroyl¦glut¦am¦ic
pterygoid
pti¦san +s
  (nourishing drink,
  esp. barley water.
  ⚠ tisane)
Ptol¦em¦aic
Ptol¦emy
  Ptol¦emies
  (Egyptian kings)
Ptol¦emy (Greek
  astronomer and
  geographer)
pto¦maine +s
pto¦sis
  pto¦ses
ptot¦ic
ptya¦lin
pub +s
pub crawl +s noun
pub-crawl
  pub-crawls
  pub-crawled
  pub-crawling
  verb
pu¦ber¦tal

pu¦berty
pubes
  plural **pubes**
  (part of abdomen)
pubes (plural of
  pubis)
pu¦bes¦cence
pu¦bes¦cent
pubic
pubis
  pubes
  (bone)
pub¦lic +s
pub¦lican +s
pub¦li¦ca¦tion +s
pub¦lic house +s
pub¦li¦cise Br. (use
  publicize)
  pub¦li¦cises
  pub¦li¦cised
  pub¦li¦cis¦ing
pub¦li¦cism
pub¦li¦cist +s
pub¦li¦cis¦tic
pub¦li¦city
pub¦li¦cize
  pub¦li¦cizes
  pub¦li¦cized
  pub¦li¦ciz¦ing
pub¦lic¦ly
public-spirit¦ed
public-spirit¦ed¦ly
public-
  spirit¦ed¦ness
pub¦lish
  pub¦lishes
  pub¦lished
  pub¦lish¦ing
pub¦lish¦able
pub¦lish¦er +s
Puc¦cini,
  Gia¦como (Italian
  composer)
puc¦coon +s
puce
Puck (mischievous
  sprite, 'Robin
  Goodfellow')
puck +s (sprite
  generally; child;
  disc in ice hockey)
pucka (good;
  genuine; use
  pukka)
puck¦er +s +ed
  +ing (wrinkle.
  ⚠ pukka)
puck¦ery
puck¦ish
puck¦ish¦ly
puck¦ish¦ness
puck¦like

pud +s
pud¦ding +s
pud¦ding basin +s
pud¦ding cloth +s
pud¦ding face +s
pudding-head +s
pudding-stone
pud¦dingy
pud¦dle
  pud¦dles
  pud¦dled
  pud¦dling
pud¦dler +s
pud¦dly
pu¦dency
pu¦den¦dal
pu¦den¦dum
  pu¦denda
pudge +s
pudg¦ily
pudgi¦ness
pudgy
  pudgi¦er
  pudgi¦est
pudic
Pue¦bla (city and
  state, Mexico)
Pue¦blo +s
  (American Indian)
pue¦blo +s (village)
pu¦er¦ile
pu¦er¦ile¦ly
pu¦er¦il¦ity
pu¦er¦peral
Puerto Cor¦tés
  (port, Honduras)
Puerto Limón
  (alternative name
  for Limón)
Puerto Plata
  (resort town,
  Dominican
  Republic)
Puerto Rican +s
Puerto Rico
  (island, West
  Indies)
puff +s +ed +ing
puff-adder +s
puff¦ball +s
puff¦er +s
puff¦er fish
  plural **puff¦er fish**
puff¦ery
puff¦ily
puf¦fin +s
puf¦fi¦ness
puff-puff +s
puffy
  puff¦ier
  puffi¦est

pug
  pugs
  pugged
  pug|ging
pug-dog +s
pug-faced
pug|garee +s
pug|gish
puggy
pu¦gil|ism
pu¦gil|ist +s
pu¦gil|is¦tic
Pugin, Au¦gus|tus
  (English architect)
Pu¦glia (Italian
  name for Apulia)
pug-mill +s
pug|na¦cious
pug|na¦cious|ly
pug|na¦cious|ness
pug|na¦city
pug-nose +s
pug-nosed
puisne (*Law.*
  △ puny)
puis|sance
puis|sant
puis|sant¦ly
puja +s
puke
  pukes
  puked
  puk¦ing
pu¦keko +s
pukey
pukka (good;
  genuine.
  △ pucker)
puk¦kah (use
  pukka)
puku +s
pul
  puls *or* puli
  (Afghan currency.
  △ pool)
pula +s
  (Botswanan
  currency.
  △ puller)
pulao +s (use
  pilau)
Pulau Ser¦ibu
  (Indonesian name
  for the Thousand
  Islands)
pul¦chri|tude
pul¦chri|tud¦in|ous
pule
  pules
  puled
  pul¦ing
  (whimper)

Pul|it¦zer, Jo¦seph
  (Hungarian-born
  American
  newspaper
  proprietor)
Pul|it¦zer prize +s
pull +s +ed +ing
pull-back +s *noun*
pull-down +s
  adjective and noun
pull¦er +s (person
  or thing that pulls.
  △ pula)
pul¦let +s
pul¦ley +s
pull-in +s *noun*
Pull|man +s
pull-off +s *noun*
pull-on +s *adjective
  and noun*
pull-out +s
  adjective and noun
pull|over +s
pul¦lu|lant
pul¦lu|late
  pul¦lu|lates
  pul¦lu|lated
  pul¦lu|lat¦ing
pul¦lu|la¦tion +s
pull-up +s
pul¦mon|ary
pul¦mon|ate
pul¦mon|ic
pulp +s +ed +ing
pulp¦er +s
pulpi|ness
pul¦pit +s
pul¦pit|eer +s +ed
  +ing
pulp|less
pulp|ous
pulp|wood
pulpy
  pulp|ier
  pulp|iest
pul¦que
pul¦sar +s
pul¦sate
  pul|sates
  pul|sated
  pul|sat¦ing
pul¦sa|tile
pul¦sa|tilla +s
pul¦sa|tion +s
pul¦sa|tor +s
pul¦sa|tory
pulse
  pulses
  pulsed
  puls|ing
pulse|less
puls|im¦eter +s

Pulu (alternative
  name for Tiglath-
  pileser III)
pul¦ver|is|able *Br.*
  (use pulverizable)
pul¦ver|isa|tion *Br.*
  (use
  pulverization)
pul¦ver|isa|tor *Br.*
  +s (use
  pulverizator)
pul¦ver|ise *Br.* (use
  pulverize)
  pul¦ver|ises
  pul¦ver|ised
  pul¦ver|is¦ing
pul¦ver|iser *Br.* +s
  (use pulverizer)
pul¦ver|iz|able
pul¦ver|iza|tion
pul¦ver|iza|tor +s
pul¦ver|ize
  pul¦ver|izes
  pul¦ver|ized
  pul¦ver|iz¦ing
pul¦ver|izer +s
pul¦veru|lent
pul¦vin|ate
pul¦vin|ated
puma +s
pum¦ice
  pum|ices
  pum|iced
  pum|icing
pu¦mi|ceous
pum¦ice stone +s
pum¦mel
  pum|mels
  pum|melled *Br.*
  pum|meled *Am.*
  pum|mel|ling *Br.*
  pum|mel|ing *Am.*
  (hit. △ pommel)
pump +s +ed +ing
pump-action
pump-brake +s
pum¦per|nickel
pump-handle
  pump-handles
  pump-handled
  pump-handling
pump|kin +s
pump|kin|seed +s
pump-priming
pump room +s
pun
  puns
  punned
  pun|ning
puna +s (plateau;
  mountain
  sickness)

punch
  punches
  punched
  punch|ing
Punch and Judy
  show +s
punch|bag +s
punch|ball +s
punch|bowl +s
punch|card +s
punch-drunk
pun|cheon +s
punch|er +s
punch|ily
Pun|chin|ello +s
punchi|ness
punch|ing bag +s
punch|line +s
punch-up +s
punchy
  punch|ier
  punchi|est
puncta
punc|tate
punc|ta|tion
punc|tilio +s
punc|tili|ous
punc|tili|ous|ly
punc|tili|ous|ness
punc|tual
punc|tu|al¦ity
punc|tu|al¦ly
punc|tu|ate
  punc|tu|ates
  punc|tu|ated
  punc|tu|at¦ing
punc|tu|ation +s
punc|tum
  puncta
punc|ture
  punc|tures
  punc|tured
  punc|tur|ing
pun|dit +s
pun|dit¦ry
Pune (use Poona)
pun|gency
pun|gent
pun|gent¦ly
Punic
puni¦ly
pu¦ni|ness
pun|ish
  pun|ishes
  pun|ished
  pun|ish|ing
pun|ish|able
pun|ish|er +s
pun|ish|ing|ly
pun|ish|ment +s
pu¦ni|tive
pu¦ni|tive¦ly

pu|ni|tory
Pun|jab
Pun|jabi +s
punk +s
pun|kah +s
punkah-wallah +s
punk|ish
punky
  punk|ier
  punki|est
pun|ner +s
pun|net +s
pun|ning|ly
pun|ster +s
punt +s +ed +ing
Punta Arenas
  (port, Chile)
punt|er +s
puny
  puni|er
  puni|est
  (weak. △ puisne)
pup
  pups
  pupped
  pup|ping
pupa
  pupae
pupal
pu|pate
  pu|pates
  pu|pated
  pu|pat|ing
pu|pa|tion
pupil +s
pu|pil|lage +s (use
  pupillage)
pu|pilar (use
  pupillar)
pu|pil|ar|ity (use
  pupillarity)
pu|pil|ary (use
  pupillary)
pu|pil|lage +s
pu|pil|lar
pu|pil|lar|ity
pu|pil|lary
pu|pip|ar|ous
pup|pet +s
pup|pet|eer +s
pup|pet|eer|ing
pup|pet|ry
pup|pet state +s
puppy
  pup|pies
puppy fat
puppy|hood
puppy|ish
puppy love
Pur|ana +s
Pur|an|ic

Pur|beck, Isle of
  (peninsula,
  England; marble)
pur|blind
pur|blind|ness
Pur|cell, Henry
  (English
  composer)
pur|chas|able
pur|chase
  pur|chases
  pur|chased
  pur|chas|ing
pur|chaser +s
pur|chase tax
  pur|chase taxes
pur|dah +s
pure
  purer
  purest
pure-bred
purée
  pur|ées
  pur|éed
  pur|ée|ing
pure|ly
pure|ness
pur|fle
  pur|fles
  pur|fled
  pur|fling
pur|ga|tion
pur|ga|tive +s
pur|ga|tor|ial
pur|ga|tory
  pur|ga|tor|ies
purge
  purges
  purged
  pur|ging
pur|ger +s
puri|fi|ca|tion +s
puri|fi|ca|tor +s
puri|fi|ca|tory
puri|fier +s
pur|ify
  puri|fies
  puri|fied
  puri|fy|ing
Purim
pur|ine +s
Pur|ism (in 20th-
  century painting)
pur|ism (generally)
pur|ist +s
pur|is|tic
Pur|itan +s
  (English
  Protestant)
pur|itan +s
  (generally)
pur|it|an|ic

pur|it|an|ic|al
pur|it|an|ic|al|ly
Pur|itan|ism (of
  Puritans)
pur|itan|ism
  (generally)
pur|ity
  pur|ities
purl +s +ed +ing
  (stitch; babble.
  △ pearl)
pur|ler +s (fall.
  △ pearler)
pur|lieu +s
pur|lin +s
pur|loin +s +ed
  +ing
pur|loin|er +s
pur|ple
  pur|ples
  pur|pled
  purp|ling
Pur|ple Heart +s
  (medal)
pur|ple heart +s
  (drug)
purple|ness
purp|lish
pur|ply
pur|port +s +ed
  +ing
pur|port|ed|ly
pur|pose
  pur|poses
  pur|posed
  pur|pos|ing
purpose-built
pur|pose|ful
pur|pose|ful|ly
pur|pose|ful|ness
pur|pose|less
pur|pose|less|ly
pur|pose|less|ness
pur|pose|ly
purpose-made
pur|pos|ive
pur|pos|ive|ly
pur|pos|ive|ness
pur|pura
pur|pure
pur|pur|ic
pur|purin
purr +s +ed +ing
purse
  purses
  pursed
  purs|ing
pur|ser +s
pur|ser|ship
purse seine +s
  noun

purse-seine
  attributive
purse-seiner +s
purse strings
pursi|ness
purs|lane +s
pur|su|able
pur|su|ance
pur|su|ant
pur|su|ant|ly
pur|sue
  pur|sues
  pur|sued
  pur|su|ing
pur|suer +s
pur|suit +s
pur|sui|vant +s
pursy
  purs|ier
  pursi|est
puru|lence
puru|lency
puru|lent
puru|lent|ly
pur|vey +s +ed
  +ing
pur|vey|ance
pur|vey|or +s
pur|view +s
pus (matter.
  △ puss)
Pusan (city, South
  Korea)
Pusey, Ed|ward
  Bou|verie
  (English
  theologian)
push
  pushes
  pushed
  push|ing
push-bike +s
push-button +s
push|cart +s
push|chair +s
push|er +s
push|ful
push|ful|ly
push|ily
pushi|ness
push|ing|ly
Push|kin,
  Alek|sandr
  (Russian writer)
push|over +s
push-pull
push|rod +s
push-start +s
Pushtu
push-up +s

pushy
  push¦ier
  pushi¦est
pu¦sil|lan¦im|ity
pu¦sil|lan¦im|ous
pu¦sil|lan¦im|
  ous¦ly
Pus¦kas, Fer¦enc
  (Hungarian
  footballer)
puss
  pusses
  (cat. △ pus)
puss moth +s
pussy
  puss¦ies
pussy|foot +s +ed
  +ing
pussy|foot¦er +s
pussy wil¦low +s
pus¦tu|lar
pus¦tu|late
  pus¦tu|lates
  pus¦tu|lated
  pus¦tu|lat¦ing
pus¦tu|la¦tion
pus¦tule +s
pus¦tu|lous
put
  puts
  put
  put|ting
  (place. △ putt)
pu¦ta|tive
pu¦ta|tive¦ly
put-down +s
put|lock +s
put¦log +s
put-on +s
put-put
  put-puts
  put-putted
  put-putting
pu¦tre|fa¦cient
pu¦tre|fac¦tion
pu¦tre|fac¦tive
pu¦trefy
  pu¦tre|fies
  pu¦tre|fied
  pu¦tre|fy¦ing
pu¦tres|cence
pu¦tres|cent
pu¦tres|cible
pu¦trid
pu¦trid|ity
pu¦trid|ly
pu¦trid|ness
putsch
  putsches

putt +s +ed +ing
  (Golf. △ put)
put¦tee +s (leg-
  cloth)
putt¦er +s +ed
  +ing
putt|ing green +s
putto
  putti
  (cherub)
putty
  put|ties
  put|tied
  putty|ing
  (cement)
put-up attributive
put-upon attributive
put-you-up +s
  noun and
  attributive
puy +s
puz¦zle
  puz¦zles
  puz¦zled
  puz¦zling
puzzle|ment +s
puz¦zler +s
puz¦zling¦ly
puz¦zo|lana
pya +s
py|aemia Br. (Am.
  pyemia)
py|aem¦ic Br. (Am.
  pyemic)
pyc¦nic +s (stocky;
  use pyknic.
  △ picnic)
pye-dog +s
py¦el|itis
py¦elo|gram +s
py¦emia Am. (Br.
  pyaemia)
py¦emic Am. (Br.
  pyaemic)
pyg|maean
Pyg|ma¦lion (kings
  of Tyre and
  Cyprus)
pyg|mean (use
  pygmaean)
pygmy
  pyg|mies
py¦jama Br.
  attributive (Am.
  pajama)
py|ja¦mas Br. (Am.
  pajamas)
pyk¦nic +s (stocky.
  △ picnic)
pylon +s
pyl|or¦ic

pyl|orus
  pyl¦ori
Pyong|yang
  (capital of North
  Korea)
pyor|rhea Am.
pyor|rhoea Br.
pyra|can¦tha +s
pyra|lid +s
pyra|mid +s
pyr¦am|idal
pyr¦am|id|al¦ly
pyra|mid¦ic
pyra|mid|ical¦ly
pyra|mid|wise
Pyra|mus Roman
  Mythology
pyre +s
Pyr¦en|ean
Pyr¦en|ees
  (mountains, SW
  Europe)
pyr¦eth¦rin +s
pyr¦eth¦roid +s
pyr¦eth¦rum +s
pyr¦et¦ic
Pyrex Propr.
pyr¦exia
pyr¦exial
pyr¦ex¦ic
pyr¦exic|al
pyr¦heli|om¦eter
  +s
pyr¦i|dine
pyr¦id|ox¦ine
pyr¦imi|dine +s
pyr¦ite
pyr¦ites
pyr¦it¦ic
pyr¦it|ifer|ous
pyr¦it|ise Br. (use
  pyritize)
  pyr|it¦ises
  pyr|it¦ised
  pyr|it|is¦ing
pyr¦it|ize
  pyr|it¦izes
  pyr|it¦ized
  pyr|it|iz¦ing
pyr¦it|ous
pyro (= pyrogallic
  acid)
pyro|clast +s
pyro|clas¦tic +s
pyro|elec¦tric
pyro|elec¦tri¦city
pyro|gal¦lic
pyro|gal¦lol
pyro|gen¦ic
pyr¦ogen|ous (use
  pyrogenic)
pyr|og|raphy

pyr|ol¦atry
pyro|lig¦neous
pyro|lyse Br.
  pyro|lyses
  pyro|lysed
  pyro|lys¦ing
pyr|oly¦sis
pyro|lyt¦ic
pyro|lyze Am.
  pyro|lyzes
  pyro|lyzed
  pyro|lyz¦ing
pyro|mancy
pyro|mania
pyro|maniac +s
pyr|om¦eter +s
pyro|met¦ric
pyro|met¦ric|al¦ly
pyr|om¦etry
pyr¦ope +s
pyro|phor¦ic
pyr|osis
pyro|tech¦nic
pyro|tech¦nic|al
pyro|tech¦nics
pyro|tech¦nist +s
pyro|techny
pyr¦ox¦ene +s
pyr|oxy|lin
Pyr¦rha Greek
  Mythology
pyr¦rhic +s
Pyr¦rho (Greek
  philosopher)
Pyr¦rho|nian
Pyr¦rhon|ic
Pyr¦rhon|ism
Pyr¦rhon|ist +s
Pyr¦rhus (king of
  Epirus)
pyr¦role
pyr¦roli|dine
pyru|vate +s
pyru|vic
Py|thag|oras
  (Greek
  philosopher)
Py|thag|oras'
  the|orem
Py|thag|or|ean +s
Pythia (Greek
  priestess)
Pyth|ian +s
Pyth|ian games
Pyth|ias (friend of
  Damon)
py|thon +s
Py|thon|esque
py|thon|ess
  py|thon|esses
py|thon¦ic
py¦uria

pyx
  pyxes
  (box. △ pix)
pyx|id|ium
  pyx|idia
pyxis
  pyx|ides
pzazz (use
  pizzazz)

Qq

Qabis (use Gabès)
Qad|dafi,
  Mu'am|mer
  Mu|ham|mad al
  (use Gaddafi)
Qaf|sah (use
  Gafsa)
Qara|ghandy (city,
  Kazakhstan)
Qatar (sheikhdom,
  Middle East)
Qa|tari +s
Qat|tara
  De|pres|sion
  (desert basin,
  Libyan desert)
Q-boat +s
Q fever
qibla (use kiblah)
Qin (Chinese
  dynasty)
Qin|dao (port,
  China)
Qing (Chinese
  dynasty)
Qing|hai (province,
  China)
Qiqi|har (city,
  China)
Qom (city, Iran)
Q-ship +s
Qua
  plural Qua
  (person; language;
  use Kwa)
qua (in the capacity
  of)
quack +s +ed +ing
quack|ery
  quack|eries
quack|ish
quad +s
  (= quadrangle;
  quadruplet;
  Printing;
  quadraphony;
  quadraphonic.
  △ quod)
quadra|gen|ar|ian
  +s
Quadra|ges|ima
  +s
quadra|gesi|mal
quad|ran|gle +s
quad|ran|gu|lar
quad|rant +s
quad|rantal

Quad|ran|tids
  (meteor shower)
quadra|phon|ic
quadra|phon|ic|
  al|ly
quadra|phon|ics
quad|raph|ony
quad|rat +s (area
  of ground)
quad|rate
  quad|rates
  quad|rated
  quad|rat|ing
  (square; bone;
  muscle; make
  square)
quad|rat|ic +s
quad|ra|ture +s
quad|ren|nial
quad|ren|ni|al|ly
quad|ren|nium
  quad|ren|niums
  or quad|ren|nia
quad|ric +s
quad|ri|ceps
  plural
  quad|ri|ceps
quad|ri|fid
quad|riga
  quad|rigae
quad|ri|lat|eral +s
quad|ri|lin|gual
quad|rille +s
quad|ril|lion
  plural
  quad|ril|lion or
  quad|ril|lions
quadri|nomial +s
quadri|par|tite
quadri|ple|gia
quadri|ple|gic +s
quadri|reme +s
quadri|syl|lab|ic
quadri|syl|lable
  +s
quadri|va|lent
quad|riv|ium
  quad|riv|ia
quad|roon +s
quadro|phon|ic
  (use
  quadraphonic)
quadro|phon|ic|
  al|ly (use quadra-
  phonically)
quadro|phon|ics
  (use
  quadraphonics)
quad|ro|ph|ony
  (use
  quadraphony)
quad|ru|man|ous

quad|ru|ped +s
quad|ru|pedal
quad|ru|ple
  quad|ru|ples
  quad|ru|pled
  quad|ru|pling
quad|ru|plet +s
quad|ru|pli|cate
  quad|ru|pli|cates
  quad|ru|pli|cated
  quad|ru|pli|
              cat|ing
quad|ru|pli|ca|tion
  +s
quad|ru|pli|city
quad|ruply
quad|ru|pole +s
quaes|tor +s
quaes|tor|ial
quaes|tor|ship +s
quaff +s +ed +ing
quaff|able
quaff|er +s
quag +s
quagga +s
quaggy
  quag|gier
  quag|gi|est
quag|mire +s
qua|haug Am. +s
qua|hog Br. +s
quaich +s
Quai d'Orsay
  (street, Paris)
quail +s +ed +ing
  (flinch)
quail
  plural quail or
  quails
  (bird)
quail|ery
  quail|eries
quaint +er +est
quaint|ly
quaint|ness
quake
  quakes
  quaked
  quak|ing
Quaker +s
Quaker|ish
Quaker|ism +s
Quaker|ly
quaking-grass
  quaking-grasses
quaky
  quaki|er
  quaki|est
quali|fi|able
quali|fi|ca|tion +s
quali|fi|ca|tory
quali|fier +s

quall|ify
  quali|fies
  quali|fied
  quali|fy|ing
quali|ta|tive
quali|ta|tive|ly
qual|ity
  qual|ities
qualm +s
qualm|ish
quan|dary
  quan|dar|ies
quand même
quango +s
Quant, Mary
  (English fashion
  designer)
quant +s +ed +ing
  (pole)
quanta
quant|al
quant|al|ly
quant|ic +s
quan|ti|fi|abil|ity
quan|ti|fi|able
quan|ti|fi|ca|tion
  +s
quan|ti|fier +s
quan|tify
  quan|ti|fies
  quan|ti|fied
  quan|ti|fy|ing
quant|isa|tion *Br.*
  +s (use
  quantization)
quant|ise *Br.* (use
  quantize)
  quant|ises
  quant|ised
  quant|is|ing
quan|ti|ta|tive
quan|ti|ta|tive|ly
quan|ti|tive
quanti|tive|ly
quan|tity
  quan|tities
quant|iza|tion +s
quant|ize
  quant|izes
  quant|ized
  quant|iz|ing
quan|tum
  quanta
quantum-
  mechan|ic|al
quantum-
  mechan|ic|al|ly
quan|tum
  mech|anics
qua|qua|versal
quar|an|tine
  quar|an|tines

quar|an|tine (*cont.*)
  quar|an|tined
  quar|an|tin|ing
quark +s
quar|rel
  quar|rels
  quar|relled *Br.*
  quar|reled *Am.*
  quar|rel|ling *Br.*
  quar|rel|ing *Am.*
quar|rel|er *Am.* +s
quar|rel|ler +s
quar|rel|some
quar|rel|some|ly
quar|rel|some|
       ness
quar|rian +s
quar|rion +s (use
  quarrian)
quarry
  quar|ries
  quar|ried
  quarry|ing
quar|ry|man
  quar|ry|men
quart +s (liquid
  measure)
quart (*Fencing.*
  △ cart, kart, khat)
quar|tan
quar|ta|tion +s
quarte (*Fencing*;
  use quart. △ cart,
  kart, khat)
quar|ter +s +ed
  +ing
quar|ter|age +s
quar|ter|back +s
quarter-binding
  +s
quar|ter day +s
quar|ter|deck +s
quarter-final +s
quarter-hour +s
quar|ter|ing +s
quarter-light +s
quarter-line +s
quar|ter|ly
  quar|ter|lies
quar|ter|mas|ter
  +s
Quar|ter|mas|ter
  Gen|eral +s
quar|ter|mas|ter
  ser|geant +s
quar|tern +s
quar|ter note +s
quarter-plate +s
quarter-pounder
  +s
quar|ter ses|sions

quar|ter|staff
  quar|ter|staves
quarter-tone +s
quar|tet +s
quar|tic +s
quar|tile +s
quarto +s
quartz
  quartzes
quartz|ite +s
qua|sar +s
quash
  quashes
  quashed
  quash|ing
quasi
Quasi|modo,
  Sal|va|tore
  (Italian poet)
quas|sia +s
quat|er|cen|ten|
       ary
quat|er|cen|ten|
       ar|ies
Qua|ter|nary
  Geology
qua|ter|nary
qua|ter|nar|ies
  (fourth; *Chemistry*)
qua|ter|nion +s
qua|tern|ity
  qua|tern|ities
quat|orz|ain +s
quat|orze +s
quat|rain +s
quatre|foil +s
quat|tro|cent|ist
  +s
quat|tro|cento *Art*
qua|ver +s +ed
  +ing
qua|veri|ness
qua|ver|ing|ly
qua|very
quay +s (landing
  place. △ key)
quay|age +s
quay|side +s
quean +s
  (impudent
  woman. △ queen)
queas|ily
queasi|ness
queasy
  queas|ier
  queasi|est
Que|bec (province
  and city, Canada)
Que|bec|er +s (use
  Quebecker)
Que|beck|er +s

Que|bec|ois
  plural Que|bec|ois
que|bra|cho +s
Que|chua
  plural Que|chua
Que|chuan
Queen, El|lery
  (two American
  writers)
queen +s +ed +ing
  (sovereign etc.
  △ quean)
Queen Anne's
  Bounty
  (charitable fund)
Queen Anne's
  lace (plant)
queen bee +s
queen cake +s
Queen Char|lotte
  Is|lands (off
  Canada)
queen con|sort +s
queen|dom +s
queen dow|ager
  +s
queen|hood +s
Queenie (name)
queenie +s (*slang*
  queen)
queen|less
queen|like
queen|li|ness
queen|ly
Queen Maud Land
  (in Antarctica)
queen mother +s
queen post +s
Queens (borough,
  New York City)
Queens|berry
  Rules
Queen's County
  (former name of
  Laois)
queen|ship +s
queen-size
queen-sized
Queens|land
  (state, Australia)
Queens|land|er +s
queen's-ware
  (ceramics)
queer +s +ed +ing
  +er +est
queer|ish
queer|ly
queer|ness
quell
  quells
  quelled
  quell|ing

quell¦er +s
quench
  quenches
  quenched
  quench¦ing
quench¦able
quench¦er +s
quench¦less
que¦nelle +s
Quen¦tin
Quer¦cia, Ja¦copo
  della (Italian
  sculptor)
Que¦rétaro (city
  and state, Mexico)
quer¦ist +s
quern +s
quern-stone +s
queru¦lous
queru¦lous¦ly
queru¦lous¦ness
query
  quer¦ies
  quer¦ied
  query¦ing
quest +s +ed +ing
quest¦er +s
quest¦ing¦ly
ques¦tion +s +ed
  +ing
ques¦tion¦abil¦ity
ques¦tion¦able
ques¦tion¦able¦
        ness
ques¦tion¦ably
ques¦tion¦ary
  ques¦tion¦ar¦ies
ques¦tion¦er +s
ques¦tion¦ing +s
ques¦tion¦ing¦ly
ques¦tion¦less
ques¦tion mark +s
question-master
  +s
ques¦tion¦naire +s
ques¦tion time +s
quest¦or +s (use
  quester)
Quetta (city,
  Pakistan)
quet¦zal +s
Quet¦zal¦có¦atl
  (Toltec and Aztec
  god)
queue
  queues
  queued
  queu¦ing or
  queue¦ing
  (line of people.
  △ cue)
queue-jump +s
  +ed +ing

Que¦vedo y
  Vil¦le¦gas,
  Fran¦cisco
  Gómez de
  (Spanish writer)
Que¦zon City (city,
  Philippines)
Qufu (town, China)
quib¦ble
  quib¦bles
  quib¦bled
  quib¦bling
quib¦bler +s
quib¦bling¦ly
quiche +s
Qui¦chua
  (= Quechua)
quick +s +er +est
quick-drying
quick¦en +s +ed
  +ing
quick-fire
quick-freeze
  quick-freezes
  quick-froze
  quick-freezing
  quick-frozen
quick-growing
quickie +s
quick¦lime +s
quick¦ly
quick march
quick¦ness
quick¦sand +s
quick¦set +s
quick¦sil¦ver +s
quick¦step
  quick¦steps
  quick¦stepped
  quick¦step¦ping
  (dance)
quick step (march)
quick-tempered
quick-thinking
  attributive
quick¦thorn +s
quick time
quick-witted
quick-witted¦ness
quid
  plural quid or
  quids
quid¦dity
  quid¦dities
quid¦nunc +s
quid pro quo +s
qui¦es¦cence
qui¦es¦cency
qui¦es¦cent
qui¦es¦cent¦ly
quiet +s +ed +ing
  +er +est (silent
  etc.)

quiet¦en +s +ed
  +ing
quiet¦ism
quiet¦ist +s
quiet¦is¦tic
quiet¦ly
quiet¦ness
quiet-spoken
quiet¦ude
qui¦etus
quiff +s
quill +s +ed +ing
quill-coverts
Quiller-Couch,
  Ar¦thur (British
  novelist)
quilt +s +ed +ing
quilt¦er +s
quim +s (*coarse
  slang*)
quin +s
  (= quintuplets)
quina¦crine
quin¦ary
quin¦ate
quince +s
quin¦cen¦ten¦ary
  quin¦cen¦ten¦
        ar¦ies
quin¦cen¦ten¦nial
Quin¦cey, Thomas
  De (English
  writer)
quin¦cun¦cial
quin¦cun¦cial¦ly
quin¦cunx
  quin¦cunxes
Quine, Wil¦lard
  Van Orman
  (American
  philosopher)
quin¦ella +s
quin¦ine
quinol
quin¦oline +s
quin¦one +s
quin¦qua¦
  gen¦ar¦ian +s
quin¦qua¦gen¦ary
quin¦qua¦
  gen¦ar¦ies
Quin¦qua¦ges¦ima
quin¦que¦cen¦ten¦
        nial
quin¦que¦lat¦eral
quin¦quen¦nial
quin¦quen¦ni¦al¦ly
quin¦quen¦nium
  quin¦quen¦niums
  or quin¦quen¦nia
quin¦que¦reme +s
quin¦que¦va¦lent

quin¦sied
quinsy
  quin¦sies
quint +s (five
  cards; quintuplet)
quinta +s
quin¦tain +s
quin¦tal +s
quin¦tan
Quin¦tana Roo
  (state, Mexico)
quinte +s *Fencing*
quint¦es¦sence +s
quint¦es¦sen¦tial
quint¦es¦sen¦
        tial¦ly
quin¦tet +s
Quin¦til¦ian
  (Roman
  rhetorician)
quin¦til¦lion
  plural quin¦til¦lion
  or quin¦til¦lions
quin¦til¦lionth
Quin¦tin
quint major +s
Quin¦ton *also*
  Quen¦tin,
  Quin¦tin
quin¦tu¦ple
  quin¦tu¦ples
  quin¦tu¦pled
  quin¦tu¦pling
quin¦tu¦plet +s
quin¦tu¦pli¦cate
  quin¦tu¦pli¦cates
  quin¦tu¦pli¦cated
  quin¦tu¦pli¦cat¦ing
quin¦tu¦pli¦ca¦tion
  +s
quin¦tuply
quip
  quips
  quipped
  quip¦ping
quip¦ster +s
quipu +s
quire +s (paper.
  △ choir)
quirk +s
quirk¦ily
quirki¦ness
quirk¦ish
quirky
  quirk¦ier
  quirki¦est
quirt +s +ed +ing
quis¦ling +s
quis¦ling¦ite +s
quit
  quits

quit (*cont.*)
  quit|ted *or* quit
  quit|ting
quitch
  quitches
quit|claim +s +ed
  +ing
quite (completely;
  rather; definitely)
Quito (capital of
  Ecuador)
quit|rent +s
quit|tance +s
quit|ter +s
quiver +s +ed +ing
quiver|ful +s
quiver|ing +s
quiver|ing|ly
quivery
qui vive (in 'on the
  qui vive')
Quix|ote, Don
  (fictional hero)
quix|ot|ic
quix|ot|ic|al|ly
quix|ot|ise *Br.* (use
  quixotize)
  quix|ot|ises
  quix|ot|ised
  quix|ot|is|ing
quix|ot|ism
quix|ot|ize
  quix|ot|izes
  quix|ot|ized
  quix|ot|iz|ing
quix|otry
quiz
  quiz|zes
  quizzed
  quiz|zing
quiz|master +s
quiz|zer +s
quiz|zical
quiz|zi|cal|ity
quiz|zi|cal|ly
quiz|zi|cal|ness
Qum (use Qom)
Qum|ran (region,
  Israel)
quod +s (prison.
  △ quad)
quod erat
  dem|on|
      stran|dum
quod|libet +s
quod|libet|arian
  +s
quod|libet|ic|al
quod|libet|ic|al|ly
quod vide
quoin +s +ed +ing
  (angle of building;

quoin (*cont.*)
  cornerstone.
  △ coin, coign)
quoit +s +ed +ing
quokka +s
quon|dam
Quon|set +s *Propr.*
quor|ate
Quorn *Propr.*
quorum +s
quota +s (share.
  △ quoter)
quot|able
quota|tion +s
quota|tion mark
  +s
quota|tive
quote
  quotes
  quoted
  quot|ing
quoter +s (person
  who quotes.
  △ quota)
quoth
quo|tid|ian +s
quo|tient +s
Quran (use Koran)
Qu|ran|ic (use
  Koranic)
Qwa|qwa (former
  homeland, South
  Africa)
qwerty

Rr

Ra *Egyptian
  Mythology*
Rabat (capital of
  Morocco)
Ra|baul (port, New
  Britain, Papua
  New Guinea)
rab|bet +s +ed
  +ing (groove in
  wood. △ rabbit)
rabbi +s
rab|bin
  plural rab|bin *or*
  rab|bins
rab|bin|ate +s
rab|bin|ic
rab|bin|ic|al
rab|bin|ic|al|ly
rab|bin|ism
rab|bin|ist +s
rab|bit +s +ed
  +ing (animal; to
  chatter; in 'Welsh
  rabbit'. △ rabbet)
rab|bity
rab|ble +s
rabble-rouser +s
rabble-rousing
Rabe|lais,
  Fran|çois (French
  satirist)
Rabe|lais|ian
rabi +s
rabid
ra|bid|ity
ra|bid|ly
ra|bid|ness
ra|bies
Rabin, Yit|zhak
  (Israeli prime
  minister)
rac|coon +s (use
  racoon)
race
  races
  raced
  ra|cing
race|card +s
race|course +s
race|goer +s
race|going
race|horse +s
ra|cem|ate +s
  Chemistry
ra|ceme +s
ra|cemic
ra|cem|ise *Br.* (use
  racemize)

ra|cem|ise (*cont.*)
  ra|cem|ises
  ra|cem|ised
  ra|cem|is|ing
ra|cem|ize
  ra|cem|izes
  ra|cem|ized
  ra|cem|iz|ing
ra|cem|ose
racer +s
race|track +s
race|way +s
Ra|chael *also*
  Ra|chel
Ra|chel *also*
  Ra|chael
  (name)
ra|chel +s (colour)
ra|chid|ial
ra|chis
ra|chil|des
rach|it|ic
rach|itis
Rach|man|inov,
  Ser|gei (Russian
  composer)
Rach|man|ism
ra|cial
ra|cial|ism
ra|cial|ist +s
ra|cial|ly
raci|ly
Ra|cine, Jean
  (French dramatist)
raci|ness
ra|cing car +s
ra|cing driver +s
ra|cism
ra|cist +s
rack +s +ed +ing
  (framework;
  instrument of
  torture;
  destruction; joint
  of meat; draw off
  wine or beer;
  clouds; horse's
  gait; to torture;
  put on rack.
  △ wrack)
rack-and-pinion
  attributive
racket +s +ed +ing
rack|et|eer +s
rack|et|eer|ing
rack|ets (game)
racket-tail +s
rack|ety
rack rail|way +s
rack-rent +s +ed
  +ing
rack-renter +s

rack-wheel +s
ra¦clette +s
racon +s
ra¦con¦teur +s *male*
ra¦con¦teuse +s
female
ra¦coon +s
rac¦quet +s (use
racket)
racy
raci¦er
raci¦est
rad +s
RADA (= Royal
Academy of
Dramatic Art)
radar +s
Rad¦cliffe, Mrs
Ann Ward
(English novelist)
rad¦dle
rad¦dles
rad¦dled
rad¦dling
Radha *Hinduism*
Radha¦krish¦nan,
Sar¦ve¦palli
(Indian
philosopher and
president)
ra¦dial +s
ra¦di¦al¦ly
ra¦dian +s
ra¦di¦ance +s
ra¦di¦ancy
ra¦di¦an¦cies
ra¦di¦ant +s
ra¦di¦ant¦ly
ra¦di¦ate
ra¦di¦ates
ra¦di¦ated
ra¦di¦at¦ing
ra¦di¦ate¦ly
ra¦di¦ation +s
ra¦di¦ation¦al
ra¦di¦ation¦al¦ly
ra¦dia¦tive
ra¦di¦ator +s
rad¦ical +s (of the
root;
revolutionary.
⚠ radicle)
rad¦ic¦al¦isa¦tion
Br. (use
radicalization)
rad¦ic¦al¦ise *Br.*
(use radicalize)
rad¦ic¦al¦ises
rad¦ic¦al¦ised
rad¦ic¦al¦is¦ing
rad¦ic¦al¦ism
rad¦ic¦al¦iza¦tion

rad¦ic¦al¦ize
rad¦ic¦al¦izes
rad¦ic¦al¦ized
rad¦ic¦al¦iz¦ing
rad¦ic¦al¦ly
rad¦ic¦al¦ness
rad¦ical sign +s
rad¦icchio +s
rad¦ices
rad¦icle +s (rootlet;
subdivision of
vein. ⚠ radical)
ra¦dicu¦lar
radii
radio +s *noun*
radio
ra¦dioes
ra¦dioed
radio¦ing
verb
radio¦active
radio¦active¦ly
radio¦activ¦ity
radio-assay +s
radio as¦tron¦omy
radio¦bio¦logic¦al
radio¦bio¦logic¦
al¦ly
radio¦biolo¦gist +s
radio¦biol¦ogy
radio-caesium
radio¦car¦bon +s
radio-carpal +s
radio cas¦sette
play¦er +s
radio¦chem¦ical
radio¦chem¦ist +s
radio¦chem¦is¦try
radio-cobalt
radio-controlled
radio-element +s
radio¦gen¦ic
radio¦gen¦ic¦al¦ly
radio-goniom¦eter
+s
radio¦gram +s
radio¦graph +s
+ed +ing
radi¦og¦raph¦er +s
radio¦graph¦ic
radio¦graph¦ic¦
al¦ly
radi¦og¦raphy
radio¦im¦mun¦
ology
radio¦iso¦tope +s
radio¦iso¦top¦ic
radio¦iso¦top¦ic¦
al¦ly
radio¦lar¦ian +s
radio¦loca¦tion +s
radio¦logic

radio¦logic¦al
radi¦olo¦gist +s
radi¦ology
radi¦om¦eter +s
radi¦om¦etric
radi¦om¦etry
radi¦on¦ics
radio¦nuclide +s
radio-opaque (use
radiopaque)
radi¦opa¦city
radi¦opaque
radio¦phon¦ic
radio¦scop¦ic
radi¦os¦copy
radio¦sonde +s
radio-telegram +s
radio-telegraph +s
radio-telegraphy
radio-telephone
+s
radio-telephon¦ic
radio-telepho¦ny
radio tele¦scope
+s
radio¦telex
radio¦telexes
radio¦thera¦peut¦ic
radio¦thera¦pist +s
radio¦ther¦apy
rad¦ish
rad¦ishes
ra¦dium
ra¦dius
radii
ra¦diused
radix
ra¦di¦ces
Rad¦nor¦shire
(former county,
Wales)
Radom (city,
Poland)
ra¦dome +s
radon
rad¦ula
radu¦lae
radu¦lar
Rae¦burn, Henry
(Scottish painter)
RAF (= Royal Air
Force)
Raf¦fer¦ty's rules
raf¦fia +s
raf¦fin¦ate +s
raff¦ish
raff¦ish¦ly
raff¦ish¦ness
raf¦fle
raf¦fles
raf¦fled
raf¦fling

Raf¦fles, Stam¦ford
(British colonial
administrator)
Raf¦san¦jani, Ali
Akbar Hash¦emi
(Iranian president)
raft +s +ed +ing
raft¦er +s (person
who rafts)
raf¦ter +s (beam)
raf¦tered
rafts¦man
rafts¦men
rag
rags
ragged
rag¦ging
raga +s (Indian
musical piece or
pattern)
raga¦muf¦fin +s
rag-and-bone man
rag-and-bone
men
rag¦bag +s
rag bolt +s
rag book +s
Rag¦doll +s (cat)
rag doll +s (doll)
rage
rages
raged
ra¦ging
ragee (cereal)
ragga (style of
popular music)
rag¦ged (torn,
frayed)
rag¦ged¦ly
rag¦ged¦ness
rag¦ged robin +s
rag¦gedy
rag¦gee (use ragee)
raggle-taggle
rag¦lan +s
rag¦man
rag¦men
Rag¦na¦rök
*Scandinavian
Mythology*
ra¦gout +s +ed
+ing
rag paper +s
rag¦pick¦er +s
rag¦stone +s
rags-to-riches
rag¦tag
rag¦tail
rag¦time
rag¦uly *Heraldry*

Ra¦gusa (former
    name of
    Dubrovnik)
rag|weed +s
rag-wheel +s
rag|worm +s
rag|wort +s
rah
Rah¦man, Tunku
    Abdul (Malayan
    and Malaysian
    prime minister)
rah-rah +s
rai (*Music.* △rye,
    wry)
raid +s +ed +ing
raid¦er +s
rail +s +ed +ing
rail|age +s
rail|car +s
rail|card +s
rail¦er +s
rail gun +s
rail|head +s
rail|ing +s
rail|lery
    rail|ler¦ies
rail|less
rail|man
    rail|men
rail|road +s +ed
    +ing
rail|way +s
rail¦way|man
    rail¦way|men
rail|way yard +s
rai|ment +s
rain +s +ed +ing
    (water. △reign,
    rein)
rain|bird +s
rain|bow +s
rain check +s
rain cloud +s
rain|coat +s
rain dance +s
rain|drop +s
rain|fall +s
rain|for¦est +s
rain gauge +s
Rai|nier, Mount
    (volcanic peak,
    USA)
rain|ily
raini|ness
rain|less
rain|maker +s
rain|mak|ing
rain|out +s
rain|proof
rain shadow +s
rain-soaked

rain|storm +s
rain|swept
rain-wash
rain|water
rain|wear
rain-worm +s
rainy
    rain|ier
    raini|est
Rai¦pur (city, India)
rais|able
raise
    raises
    raised
    rais|ing
    (lift. △raze)
rai|sin +s
rai|siny
rai¦son d'être
    rai|sons d'être
raita
Raj
raja +s
rajah +s (use raja)
ra¦jah|ship +s (use
    rajaship)
raja|ship +s
Ra¦jas|than (state,
    India)
Ra¦jas|thani +s
raja yoga
Raj¦kot (city, India)
Raj|neesh,
    Bhag|wan Shree
    (Indian guru)
Raj|poot +s (use
    Rajput)
Raj|put +s
Raj¦pu|tana (in
    India)
Raj|shahi (port,
    Bangladesh)
rake
    rakes
    raked
    rak¦ing
rake-off +s *noun*
raker +s
raki +s
rak¦ish
rak¦ish|ly
rak¦ish|ness
Rá¦kosi, Mát¦yás
    (Hungarian
    Communist prime
    minister)
raku
rale +s
Ra|leigh (city, USA)
Ra|leigh, Wal¦ter
    (English explorer)
rall. (= rallentando)

ral¦len|tando +s
    Music
ralli car +s (horse-
    drawn vehicle.
    △rally car)
ral|lier +s
ral|line
rally
    ral|lies
    ral|lied
    rally|ing
rally car +s (motor
    vehicle. △ralli
    car)
rally|cross
Ralph
RAM +s (= random-
    access memory)
Ram, the
    (constellation;
    sign of zodiac)
ram
    rams
    rammed
    ram|ming
Rama *Hinduism*
Ram|adan *Islam*
Ram|adhan (use
    Ramadan)
Rama|krishna,
    Gad|adhar
    Chat|terji (Indian
    Hindu mystic)
ramal
Raman,
    Chan¦dra|
    sekh¦ara
    Ven|kata (Indian
    physicist)
Raman ef¦fect
    Physics
Ra¦manu|jan,
    Srini|vasa
    Aai¦yan|gar
    (Indian
    mathematician)
Rama|yana
    (Sanskrit epic)
Ram|bert, Marie
    (Polish-born
    British ballet
    dancer)
ram¦ble
    ram¦bles
    ram¦bled
    ram|bling
ram|bler +s
ram|bling +s
ram|bling¦ly
Rambo (fictional
    hero)
rambo +s (apple)

ram|bunc¦tious
ram|bunc¦tious|ly
ram|bunc¦tious|
    ness
ram|bu¦tan +s
Ram¦eau, Jean-
    Philippe (French
    composer)
ram|ekin +s
ramen
Ram|eses
    (= Ramses)
ramie +s
ram|ifi|ca¦tion +s
ram¦ify
    rami|fies
    rami|fied
    rami¦fy|ing
Ram¦il|lies (battle
    site, Belgium)
ramin +s
ram|jet +s
ram¦mer +s
rammy
    ram|mies
Ramón y Cajal,
    San|tiago
    (Spanish
    histologist)
ram¦ose
ramp +s +ed +ing
ram|page
    ram|pages
    ram|paged
    ram|paging
ram|pageous
ram|pager +s
ram|pancy
ram|pant
ram|pant¦ly
ram|part +s +ed
    +ing
ram|pion +s
Ram¦pur (city,
    India)
ram-raid +s +ed
    +ing
ram|rod +s
Ram¦say, Allan
    (Scottish portrait
    painter)
Ram¦say, Wil|liam
    (Scottish chemist)
Ram|ses
    (pharaohs)
ram|shackle
ram's-horn snail
    +s
ram|sons
ran
ranch
    ranches

ranch (*cont.*)
  ranched
  ranch|ing
ranch¦er +s
ranch¦ero +s
Ran¦chi (city, India)
ran¦cid
ran¦cid|ity
ran¦cid|ness
ran¦cor *Am.* +s (*Br.*
  rancour.
  bitterness.
  ⚠ ranker)
ran¦cor|ous
ran¦cor|ous¦ly
ran¦cour *Br.* +s
  (*Am.* rancor.
  bitterness.
  ⚠ ranker)
Rand, the
  (= Witwaters-
  rand)
rand +s (South
  African or
  Namibian
  currency; ridge;
  part of shoe)
ran¦dan +s
Rand|ers (port,
  Denmark)
ran|dily
ran|di|ness
Ran|dolf *also*
  Ran|dolph
Ran|dolph *also*
  Ran|dolf
ran¦dom
random-access
  adjective
ran¦dom error +s
ran¦dom|isa|tion
  Br. (use
  randomization)
ran¦dom|ise *Br.*
  (use randomize)
  ran¦dom|ises
  ran¦dom|ised
  ran¦dom|is|ing
ran¦dom|iza|tion
ran¦dom|ize
  ran¦dom|izes
  ran¦dom|ized
  ran¦dom|iz¦ing
ran¦dom¦ly
ran¦dom|ness
Rand|stad
  (conurbation, the
  Netherlands)
Randy (name)
randy
  ran|dier

randy (*cont.*)
  ran¦di|est
  (lustful)
ranee +s
rang
ran|ga|tira +s
range
  ranges
  ranged
  ran¦ging
  rangé male
  ran¦gée female
range|find¦er +s
Ran¦ger (former
  name for a
  Ranger Guide)
ran¦ger +s (forest
  warden etc.;
  soldier)
Ran¦ger Guide +s
  (senior Guide)
ran¦ger|ship +s
ranging-pole +s
Ran|goon (capital
  of Burma)
rangy
  ran¦gier
  ran¦gi|est
rani +s (use ranee)
Ran¦jit Singh (Sikh
  ruler)
Ran¦jit¦sinhji
  Vi|bhaji (Indian
  cricketer and
  statesman)
Rank, J. Ar¦thur
  (English film
  executive)
rank +s +ed +ing
rank-and-file
  attributive
rank¦er +s (soldier.
  ⚠ rancor,
  rancour)
rank|ing +s
ran¦kle
  ran¦kles
  ran¦kled
  rank|ling
rank¦ly
rank|ness
Rann of Kutch
  (salt marsh, India
  and Pakistan)
ran|sack +s +ed
  +ing
ran|sack¦er +s
ran|som +s +ed
  +ing
Ran|some, Ar¦thur
  (English writer)
ran|somer +s

rant +s +ed +ing
Rant¦er +s
  (member of
  Christian sect)
rant¦er +s (person
  who rants)
rant|ing +s
rant|ing¦ly
ranti|pole
  ranti|poles
  ranti|poled
  ranti|pol¦ing
Ran|ulf
ra|nun|cul|aceous
ra|nun|cu|lus
  ra|nun|cu|luses *or*
  ra|nun|culi
Rao, P. V.
  Nara|simha
  (Indian prime
  minister)
rap
  raps
  rapped
  rap|ping
  (knock. ⚠ rapt,
  wrap)
ra|pa|cious
ra|pa|cious¦ly
ra|pa|cious|ness
rap|acity
rape
  rapes
  raped
  rap¦ing
rape-cake +s
rape-oil +s
raper +s
rape|seed +s
Raph|ael *Bible*
Raph|ael (Italian
  painter)
raphia +s (use
  raffia)
raph|ide +s
rapid +s +er +est
rapid eye-
  movement +s
rapid-fire *attributive*
rap|id|ity
rap|id¦ly
rap|id|ness
ra|pier +s
ra|pine +s
rap|ist +s
rap|paree +s
rap|pee +s
rap|pel
  rap|pels
  rap|pelled *Br.*
  rap|peled *Am.*

rap|pel (*cont.*)
  rap|pel|ling *Br.*
  rap|pel|ing *Am.*
rap|per +s
rap|port +s
rap|por|teur +s
rap|proche|ment
  +s
rap|scal|lion +s
rapt (absorbed.
  ⚠ rapped,
  wrapped)
rapt¦ly
rapt|ness
rap|tor +s
rap|tor|ial
rap|ture +s
rap|tured
rap|tur|ous
rap|tur|ous¦ly
rap|tur|ous|ness
Ra|quel
rara avis
  rarae aves
rare
  rarer
  rar¦est
rare|bit +s (in
  'Welsh rarebit';
  use rabbit)
raree-show +s
rar|efac¦tion +s
rar|efac¦tive
rar|efi|ca|tion +s
rar¦efy
  rar|efies
  rar|efied
  rar|efy|ing
rare¦ly
rare|ness
rar¦ify (use rarefy)
  rari|fies
  rari|fied
  rari¦fy|ing
rar¦ing
rar¦ity
  rar|ities
Raro|tonga (island,
  S. Pacific)
Raro|tongan +s
Ras al Khai|mah
  (state and city,
  UAE)
ras¦cal +s
ras|cal|dom
ras|cal|ism
ras|cal|ity
  ras|cal|ities
ras|cal¦ly
raschel +s
rase (use raze.
  destroy; erase.

rase (*cont.*)
  ⚠ raise)
rases
rased
ras¦ing
rash
rashes
rash¦er
rash¦est
rasher +s *noun*
rash¦ly
rash|ness
rasp +s +ed +ing
rasp|atory
  rasp|ator¦ies
rasp|berry
  rasp|berries
rasp|berry cane +s
rasp¦er +s
rasp|ing¦ly
Ras|pu¦tin,
  Gri|gori
  Efimo|vich
  (Russian monk)
raspy
Rasta
  (= Rastafarian.
  ⚠ raster)
Ras¦ta|fari
  plural Ras¦ta|fari
  or Ras¦ta|faris
Ras¦ta|far¦ian +s
Ras¦ta|far¦ian|ism
ras¦ter +s
  (*Electronics.*
  ⚠ Rasta)
ras¦ter|isa¦tion *Br.*
  (use
  rasterization)
ras¦ter|ise *Br.* (use
  rasterize)
  ras¦ter|ises
  ras¦ter|ised
  ras¦ter|is¦ing
ras¦ter|iser *Br.* +s
  (use rasterizer)
ras¦ter|iza¦tion
ras¦ter|ize
  ras¦ter|izes
  ras¦ter|ized
  ras¦ter|iz¦ing
ras¦ter|izer +s
Ras¦tya|pino
  (former name of
  Dzerzhinsk)
rat
  rats
  rat¦ted
  rat|ting
rata +s
ratabil|ity (use
  rateability)

rat¦able (use
  rateable)
rat¦ably (use
  rateably)
rata|fia +s
ratan +s (use
  rattan)
Ra¦tana,
  Ta¦hu|po|tiki
  Wi¦remu (Maori
  leader)
rata|plan
  rata|plans
  rata|planned
  rata¦plan|ning
rat-arsed
rata|tat +s
rata|touille +s
rat¦bag +s
rat-catcher +s
ratch
  ratches
ratchet +s +ed
  +ing
rate
  rates
  rated
  rat¦ing
rate|abil¦ity
rate|able
rate|ably
rate-capped
rate-capping
ratel +s
rate|pay¦er +s
rat|fink +s
rathe
ra¦ther
rathe-ripe
Rath|lin Is¦land
  (off Ireland)
rat-hole +s
raths|keller +s
rati|fi¦able
rati|fi¦ca¦tion +s
rati|fier +s
rat|ify
  rati|fies
  rati|fied
  rati|fy|ing
rat|ing +s
ratio +s
rati|ocin|ate
  rati|ocin|ates
  rati|ocin|ated
  rati|ocin|at¦ing
rati|ocin|ation +s
rati|ocina|tive
rati|ocin|ator +s
ra¦tion +s +ed
  +ing
ra|tion|al

ra¦tion|ale +s
ra¦tion|al¦isa¦tion
  Br. +s (use
  rationalization)
ra¦tion|al¦ise *Br.*
  (use rationalize)
  ra¦tion|al|ises
  ra¦tion|al|ised
  ra¦tion|al|is¦ing
ra¦tion|al¦iser *Br.*
  +s (use
  rationalizer)
ra¦tion|al¦ism
ra¦tion|al¦ist +s
ra¦tion|al¦is¦tic
ra¦tion|al¦is¦tic|
             al¦ly
ra¦tion|al¦ity
ra¦tion|al¦iza¦tion
  +s
ra¦tion|al¦ize
  ra¦tion|al¦izes
  ra¦tion|al¦ized
  ra¦tion|al¦iz¦ing
ra¦tion|al¦izer +s
ra¦tion|al¦ly
ra¦tion book +s
rat¦ite +s
rat kan|ga¦roo +s
rat|line +s
ra|toon +s +ed
  +ing
rat race +s
rat-run +s
rats|bane +s
rat's tail +s
rat-tail +s (fish;
  horse; spoon)
rat¦tan +s
rat-tat +s
rat¦ter +s
Ratti|gan,
  Ter|ence (English
  dramatist)
rat|tily
rat¦ti|ness
Rat¦tle, Simon
  (English
  conductor)
rat¦tle
  rat¦tles
  rat¦tled
  rat|tling
rattle|box
  rattle|boxes
rat¦tler +s
rattle|snake +s
rattle|trap +s
rat|tling +s
rat¦tly

ratty
rat|tier
rat|ti|est
rau|cous
rau|cous|ly
rau|cous|ness
raunch|ily
raunchi|ness
raunchy
  raunch|ier
  raunchi|est
rav¦age
  rav|ages
  rav|aged
  rav|aging
rav|ager +s
rave
  raves
  raved
  rav¦ing
Ravel, Maur¦ice
  (French
  composer)
ravel
  ravels
  rav|elled *Br.*
  rav|eled *Am.*
  rav|el|ling *Br.*
  rav|el|ing *Am.*
rav|elin +s
raven +s +ed +ing
Rav|enna (city,
  Italy)
rav¦en|ous
rav¦en|ous|ly
rav¦en|ous|ness
raver +s
rave-up +s *noun*
Ravi (river, India
  and Pakistan)
ravin +s
rav¦ine +s
rav|ined
rav|ing +s
rav|ing|ly
ravi|oli
rav¦ish
  rav|ishes
  rav|ished
  rav|ish|ing
rav|ish¦er +s
rav|ish|ing|ly
rav|ish|ment +s
raw
  rawer
  raw¦est
  (uncooked etc.
  ⚠ roar)
Rawal|pindi (city,
  Pakistan)
raw-boned
raw|hide +s

raw|ish
Rawl|plug +s
    Propr.
Rawls, John
    (American
    philosopher)
rawly
raw|ness
Raw|son (city,
    Argentina)
Ray, John (English
    naturalist)
Ray, Man
    (American
    painter)
Ray, Sat|ya|jit
    (Indian film
    director)
ray +s +ed +ing
    (beam of light etc.;
    fish; *Music*)
rayah +s
ray gun +s
Ray|leigh, Lord
    (English physicist;
    scattering)
ray|less
ray|let +s
Ray|mond
rayon +s
raze
    razes
    razed
    raz|ing
    (destroy; erase.
    △ raise)
razoo +s
razor +s +ed +ing
razor|back +s
razor|bill +s
razor blade +s
razor cut
    razor cuts
    razor cut
    razor cut|ting
razor edge +s
razor-edged
razor-fish
    plural razor-fish *or*
    razor-fishes
razor's edge
razor-sharp
razor-shell +s
razor wire
razz
    razzes
    razzed
    razz|ing
raz|za|ma|tazz
    (use razzmatazz)
raz|zia +s
raz|zle +s

razzle-dazzle +s
razz|ma|tazz
Re (*Egyptian
    Mythology*; use
    Ra)
re (concerning)
re (*Music*; use ray)
re|absorb +s +ed
    +ing
re|absorp|tion +s
re|accept +s +ed
    +ing
re|accept|ance +s
re|accus|tom +s
    +ed +ing
reach
    reaches
    reached
    reach|ing
reach|able
reach|er +s
reach-me-down
    +s
re|acquaint +s +ed
    +ing
re|acquaint|ance
    +s
re|acquire
    re|acquires
    re|acquired
    re|acquir|ing
re|acqui|si|tion +s
re-act +s +ed +ing
    (respond to)
re-act +s +ed +ing
    (act again)
react|ance +s
react|ant +s
re|ac|tion +s
re|ac|tion|ary
re|ac|tion|ar|ies
re|ac|tion|ist +s
re|acti|vate
    re|acti|vates
    re|acti|vated
    re|acti|vat|ing
re|acti|va|tion +s
re|act|ive
re|activ|ity
re|act|or +s
read
    reads
    read
    read|ing
    (interpret writing.
    △ reed, red, rede,
    redd)
read|abil|ity
read|able
read|able|ness
read|ably

re|adapt +s +ed
    +ing
re|adap|ta|tion +s
re|address
    re|addresses
    re|addressed
    re|address|ing
Reade, Charles
    (English writer)
read|er +s
read|er|ship +s
read|ily
read-in +s *noun*
readi|ness
Read|ing (town,
    England)
read|ing +s
    (interpreting
    writing.
    △ reeding)
re|adjust +s +ed
    +ing
re|adjust|ment +s
re|admis|sion +s
re|admit
    re|admits
    re|admit|ted
    re|admit|ting
re|admit|tance
read-only
    mem|ory
read-only
    mem|or|ies
re|adopt +s +ed
    +ing
re|adop|tion +s
read-out +s *noun*
re-advertise
    re-advertises
    re-advertised
    re-advertis|ing
re-advertise|ment
    +s
read-write *adjective*
ready
    read|ies
    read|ied
    ready|ing
    read|ier
    readi|est
    (prepared etc.
    △ reddy)
ready-made +s
ready-mix
    ready-mixes
ready-mixed
ready money
ready reck|on|er
    +s
ready-to-wear
re|affirm +s +ed
    +ing

re|affirm|ation +s
re|affor|est +s +ed
    +ing
re|affor|est|ation
    +s
Rea|gan, Ron|ald
    (American
    president)
re|agency
re|agen|cies
re|agent +s
real (genuine.
    △ reel)
real +s (Brazilian
    and former
    Spanish currency)
re|algar
re|align +s +ed
    +ing
re|align|ment +s
real|is|abil|ity *Br.*
    (use realizability)
real|is|abil|ities
real|is|able *Br.* (use
    realizable)
real|isa|tion *Br.* +s
    (use realization)
real|ise *Br.* (use
    realize)
real|ises
real|ised
real|is|ing
real|iser *Br.* +s (use
    realizer)
real|ism
real|ist +s
real|is|tic
real|is|tic|al|ly
real|ity
real|ities
real|iz|abil|ity
real|iz|abil|ities
real|iz|able
real|iza|tion +s
real|ize
    real|izes
    real|ized
    real|iz|ing
real|izer +s
real life
    real lives
    noun (not fiction,
    drama, etc.)
real-life *attributive*
    (not fictional)
real live *attributive*
    (not pretended or
    simulated)
re|allo|cate
    re|allo|cates
    re|allo|cated
    re|allo|cat|ing
re|allo|ca|tion +s

re|allot
  re|allots
  re|allot|ted
  re|allot|ting
re|allot|ment +s
real|ly
realm +s
real|ness
Real|poli|tik
real-time *attributive*
real|tor +s
realty
ream +s +ed +ing
ream|er +s
re|ana|lyse *Br.*
  re|ana|lyses
  re|ana|lysed
  re|ana|lys|ing
re|analy|sis
re|ana|lyze *Am.*
  re|ana|lyzes
  re|ana|lyzed
  re|ana|lyz|ing
re|ani|mate
  re|ani|mates
  re|ani|mated
  re|ani|mat|ing
re|ani|ma|tion +s
reap +s +ed +ing
reap|er +s
re|appear +s +ed
  +ing
re|appear|ance +s
re|appli|ca|tion +s
re|apply
  re|applies
  re|applied
  re|apply|ing
re|appoint +s +ed
  +ing
re|appoint|ment
  +s
re|appor|tion +s
  +ed +ing
re|appor|tion|
  ment +s
re|appraisal +s
re|appraise
  re|appraises
  re|appraised
  re|apprais|ing
rear +s +ed +ing
  (back; raise.
  △ rhea, ria)
rear ad|miral +s
rear-arch
  rear-arches
rear-end +s +ed
  +ing *verb*
rear|er +s
rear-facing
rear|guard +s

rear lamp +s
rear light +s
rearm +s +ed +ing
re|arma|ment +s
rear|most
re|arrange
  re|arranges
  re|arranged
  re|arran|ging
re|arrange|ment
  +s
re|arrest +s +ed
  +ing
rear-view mir|ror
  +s
rear|ward +s
rear-wheel drive
re|ascend +s +ed
  +ing
re|ascen|sion +s
rea|son +s +ed
  +ing
rea|son|able
rea|son|able|ness
rea|son|ably
rea|son|er +s
rea|son|ing +s
rea|son|less
re|assem|ble
  re|assem|bles
  re|assem|bled
  re|assem|bling
re|assem|bly
re|assert +s +ed
  +ing
re|asser|tion +s
re|assess
  re|assesses
  re|assessed
  re|assess|ing
re|assess|ment +s
re|assign +s +ed
  +ing
re|assign|ment +s
re|assume
  re|assumes
  re|assumed
  re|assum|ing
re|assump|tion +s
re|assur|ance +s
re|assure
  re|assures
  re|assured
  re|assur|ing
re|assurer +s
re|assur|ing|ly
re|attach
  re|attaches
  re|attached
  re|attach|ing
re|attach|ment +s

re|attain +s +ed
  +ing
re|attain|ment +s
re|attempt +s +ed
  +ing
Rê|au|mur, René
  An|toine
  Fer|chault de
  (French naturalist;
  temperature scale)
reave
  reaves
  reft
  reav|ing
  (deprive of; carry
  off. △ reeve,
  reive)
re|awaken +s +ed
  +ing
re|badge
  re|badges
  re|badged
  re|badg|ing
re|bal|ance
  re|bal|ances
  re|bal|anced
  re|bal|an|cing
re|bap|tise *Br.* (use
  rebaptize)
  re|bap|tises
  re|bap|tised
  re|bap|tis|ing
re|bap|tize
  re|bap|tizes
  re|bap|tized
  re|bap|tiz|ing
re|bar|ba|tive
re|base
  re|bases
  re|based
  re|bas|ing
re|bat|able
re|bate
  re|bates
  re|bated
  re|bat|ing
re|bater +s
rebec +s
Re|becca (*Bible*;
  name)
re|beck +s (use
  rebec)
rebel +s *noun*
rebel
  re|bels
  re|belled
  re|bel|ling
  verb
re|bel|lion +s
re|bel|li|ous
re|bel|li|ous|ly
re|bel|li|ous|ness

rebid
  re|bids
  rebid
  re|bid|ding
re|bind
  re|binds
  re|bound
  re|bind|ing
re|birth +s +ed
  +ing
re|birth|er +s
re|birth|ing +s
re|boot +s +ed
  +ing
re|bore
  re|bores
  re|bored
  re|bor|ing
re|born
re|bound +s +ed
  +ing
re|bound|er +s
re|broad|cast
  re|broad|casts
  re|broad|cast *or*
  re|broad|cast|ed
  re|broad|cast|ing
re|buff +s +ed
  +ing
re|build
  re|builds
  re|built
  re|build|ing
re|build|er +s
re|build|ing +s
re|buke
  re|bukes
  re|buked
  re|buk|ing
re|buker +s
re|buk|ing|ly
re|burial +s
re|bury
  re|buries
  re|buried
  re|bury|ing
rebus
  re|buses
rebut
  re|buts
  re|but|ted
  re|but|ting
re|but|ment +s
re|but|table
re|but|tal +s
re|but|ter +s
rec +s (= recreation
  ground. △ reck,
  wreck)
re|cal|ci|trance
re|cal|ci|trant +s
re|cal|ci|trant|ly

re|cal|cu|late
  re|cal|cu|lates
  re|cal|cu|lated
  re|cal|cu|lat|ing
re|cal|cu|lation +s
re|cal|esce
  re|cal|esces
  re|cal|esced
  re|cal|es|cing
re|cal|es|cence
re|call +s +ed +ing
re|call|able
re|cant +s +ed
  +ing
re|can|ta|tion +s
re|cant|er +s
recap
  re|caps
  re|capped
  re|cap|ping
re|cap|it|al|
  isa|tion *Br.* (use
  recapitalization)
re|cap|it|al|ise *Br.*
  (use recapitalize)
  re|cap|it|al|ises
  re|cap|it|al|ised
  re|cap|it|al|is|ing
re|cap|it|al|
        iza|tion
re|cap|it|al|ize
  re|cap|it|al|izes
  re|cap|it|al|ized
  re|cap|it|al|iz|ing
re|cap|itu|late
  re|cap|itu|lates
  re|cap|itu|lated
  re|cap|itu|lat|ing
re|cap|itu|la|tion
  +s
re|cap|itu|la|tive
re|cap|itu|la|tory
re|cap|ture
  re|cap|tures
  re|cap|tured
  re|cap|tur|ing
re|cast
  re|casts
  re|cast
  re|cast|ing
recce
  rec|ces
  rec|ced
  recce|ing
re|cede
  re|cedes
  re|ceded
  re|ced|ing
  (go or shrink
  back)
re-cede
  re-cedes

re-cede (*cont.*)
  re-ceded
  re-ceding
  (cede back)
re|ceipt +s +ed
  +ing
re|ceiv|able
re|ceive
  re|ceives
  re|ceived
  re|ceiv|ing
re|ceiver +s
re|ceiv|er|ship +s
re|ceiv|ing order
  +s
re|cency
re|cen|sion +s
re|cent
re|cent|ly
re|cent|ness
recep
  plural recep *or*
  receps
  (= reception
  room)
re|cep|tacle +s
re|cep|tion +s
re|cep|tion|ist +s
re|cep|tive
re|cep|tive|ly
re|cep|tive|ness
re|cep|tiv|ity
re|cep|tor +s
re|cess
  re|cesses
  re|cessed
  re|cess|ing
re|ces|sion +s
re|ces|sion|al
re|ces|sion|ary
re|ces|sive
re|ces|sive|ly
re|ces|sive|ness
Rech|ab|ite +s
re|charge
  re|charges
  re|charged
  re|char|ging
re|charge|able
re|char|ger +s
ré chauffé +s
re|check +s +ed
  +ing
re|cher|ché
re|chris|ten +s +ed
  +ing
re|cid|iv|ism
re|cid|iv|ist +s
re|cid|iv|is|tic
Re|cife (port,
  Brazil)
re|cipe +s

re|cipi|ency
re|cipi|ent +s
re|cip|ro|cal +s
re|cip|ro|cal|ity
  re|cip|ro|cal|ities
  re|cip|ro|cal|ly
re|cip|ro|cate
  re|cip|ro|cates
  re|cip|ro|cated
  re|cip|ro|cat|ing
re|cip|ro|ca|tion +s
re|cip|ro|ca|tor +s
reci|procity
  reci|proci|ties
re|cir|cu|late
  re|cir|cu|lates
  re|cir|cu|lated
  re|cir|cu|lat|ing
re|cir|cu|la|tion +s
re|cital +s
re|cital|ist +s
reci|ta|tion +s
reci|ta|tive +s
re|cite
  re|cites
  re|cited
  re|cit|ing
re|citer +s
reck +s +ed +ing
  (pay heed to.
  ⚠ rec, wreck)
reck|less
reck|less|ly
reck|less|ness
reckon +s +ed
  +ing
reck|on|er +s
reck|on|ing +s
re|claim +s +ed
  +ing
re|claim|able
re|claim|er +s
rec|lam|ation +s
re|clas|si|fi|ca|tion
  +s
re|clas|sify
  re|clas|si|fies
  re|clas|si|fied
  re|clas|si|fy|ing
re|clin|able
rec|lin|ate
re|cline
  re|clines
  re|clined
  re|clin|ing
re|cliner +s
re|clothe
  re|clothes
  re|clothed
  re|cloth|ing
re|cluse +s
re|clu|sion

re|clu|sive
re|clu|sive|ness
re|code
  re|codes
  re|coded
  re|cod|ing
rec|og|nis|abil|ity
  Br. (use
  recognizability)
rec|og|nis|able *Br.*
  (use
  recognizable)
rec|og|nis|ably *Br.*
  (use
  recognizably)
re|cog|ni|sance *Br.*
  +s (use
  recognizance)
re|cog|ni|sant *Br.*
  (use recognizant)
rec|og|nise *Br.* (use
  recognize)
  rec|og|nises
  rec|og|nised
  rec|og|nis|ing
rec|og|niser *Br.* +s
  (use recognizer)
rec|og|ni|tion +s
rec|og|ni|tory
rec|og|niz|abil|ity
rec|og|niz|able
rec|og|niz|ably
re|cog|ni|zance +s
re|cog|ni|zant
rec|og|nize
  rec|og|nizes
  rec|og|nized
  rec|og|nizer +s
re|coil +s +ed +ing
re|coil|less
re|coin +s +ed
  +ing
rec|ol|lect +s +ed
  +ing (remember)
re-collect +s +ed
  +ing (collect
  again)
rec|ol|lec|tion +s
rec|ol|lect|ive
re|col|on|isa|tion
  Br. +s (use
  recolonization)
re|col|on|ise *Br.*
  (use recolonize)
  re|col|on|ises
  re|col|on|ised
  re|col|on|is|ing
re|col|on|iza|tion
  +s
re|col|on|ize
  re|col|on|izes

re|col|on|ize (*cont.*)
  re|col|on|ized
  re|col|on|iz|ing
re|color *Am.* +s
  +ed +ing
re|col|our *Br.* +s
  +ed +ing
re|com|bin|ant +s
re|com|bin|ation
  +s
re|com|bine
  re|com|bines
  re|com|bined
  re|com|bin|ing
re|com|mence
  re|com|mences
  re|com|menced
  re|com|men|cing
re|com|mence|
       ment +s
rec|om|mend +s
  +ed +ing
rec|om|mend|able
rec|om|
    men|da|tion +s
rec|om|
    men|da|tory
re|com|mend|er
  +s
re|com|mis|sion
  +s +ed +ing
re|com|mit
  re|com|mits
  re|com|mit|ted
  re|com|mit|ting
re|com|mit|ment
  +s
re|com|mit|tal +s
rec|om|pense
  rec|om|penses
  rec|om|pensed
  rec|om|pens|ing
re|com|pose
  re|com|poses
  re|com|posed
  re|com|pos|ing
recon (= reconnaiss
  ance)
rec|on|cil|abil|ity
rec|on|cil|able
rec|on|cile
  rec|on|ciles
  rec|on|ciled
  rec|on|cil|ing
rec|on|cile|ment
  +s
rec|on|ciler +s
rec|on|cili|ation +s
rec|on|cili|atory
rec|on|dite
rec|on|dite|ly
rec|on|dite|ness

re|con|di|tion +s
  +ed +ing
re|con|di|tion|er
  +s
re|con|fig|ur|ation
  +s
re|con|fig|ure
  re|con|fig|ures
  re|con|fig|ured
  re|con|fig|ur|ing
re|con|firm +s +ed
  +ing
re|con|firm|ation
  +s
re|con|nais|sance
  +s
re|con|nect +s +ed
  +ing
re|con|nec|tion +s
rec|on|noiter *Am.*
  +s +ed +ing
rec|on|noitre *Br.*
  rec|on|noitres
  rec|on|noitred
  rec|on|noi|tring
re|con|quer +s +ed
  +ing
re|con|quest +s
re|con|se|crate
  re|con|se|crates
  re|con|se|crated
  re|con|se|crat|ing
re|con|se|cra|tion
re|con|sider +s
  +ed +ing
re|con|sid|er|ation
  +s
re|con|sign +s +ed
  +ing
re|con|sign|ment
  +s
re|con|soli|date
  re|con|soli|dates
  re|con|soli|dated
  re|con|soli|
       dat|ing
re|con|soli|da|tion
  +s
re|con|sti|tute
  re|con|sti|tutes
  re|con|sti|tuted
  re|con|sti|tut|ing
re|con|sti|tu|tion
  +s
re|con|struct +s
  +ed +ing
re|con|struct|able
re|con|struc|tion
  +s
re|con|struct|ive
re|con|struct|or +s

re|con|vene
  re|con|venes
  re|con|vened
  re|con|ven|ing
re|con|ver|sion +s
re|con|vert +s +ed
  +ing
re|cord +s +ed
  +ing
re|cord|able
record-breaking
re|cord|er +s
re|cord|er|ship +s
rec|ord hold|er +s
re|cord|ing +s
re|cord|ist +s
rec|ord play|er +s
re|count +s +ed
  +ing (narrate)
re-count +s +ed
  +ing (count again)
re|coup +s +ed
  +ing
re|coup|able
re|coup|ment +s
re|course +s
re|cover +s +ed
  +ing (reclaim; etc.)
re-cover +s +ed
  +ing (cover again)
re|cov|er|abil|ity
re|cov|er|
      abil|ities
re|cov|er|able
re|cov|er|er +s
re|cov|ery
  re|cov|er|ies
rec|re|ancy
rec|re|ant +s
rec|re|ant|ly
rec|re|ate
  rec|re|ates
  rec|re|ated
  rec|re|at|ing
  (create again)
rec|re|ate
  rec|re|ates
  rec|re|ated
  rec|re|at|ing
  (take recreation)
rec|re|ation +s
  (entertainment)
re-creation +s
  (creation of
  something again)
rec|re|ation|al
rec|re|ation|al|ly
rec|re|ation
  ground +s
rec|re|ative
re|crim|in|ate
  re|crim|in|ates

re|crim|in|ate
  (*cont.*)
  re|crim|in|ated
  re|crim|in|at|ing
re|crim|in|ation +s
re|crim|ina|tive
re|crim|in|atory
re|cross
  re|crosses
  re|crossed
  re|cross|ing
re|cru|desce
  re|cru|desces
  re|cru|desced
  re|cru|des|cing
re|cru|des|cence
  +s
re|cru|des|cent
re|cruit +s +ed
  +ing
re|cruit|able
re|cruit|al +s
re|cruit|er +s
re|cruit|ment +s
re|crys|tal|lisa|
    tion *Br.* (use
    recrystallization)
re|crys|tal|lise *Br.*
  (use recrystallize)
  re|crys|tal|lises
  re|crys|tal|lised
  re|crys|tal|lis|ing
re|crys|tal|liza|
    tion +s
re|crys|tal|lize
  re|crys|tal|lizes
  re|crys|tal|lized
  re|crys|tal|liz|ing
recta (plural of
  rectum . △ rector)
rec|tal
rec|tal|ly
rect|angle +s
rect|angu|lar
rect|angu|lar|ity
rect|angu|lar|ly
recti
rec|ti|fi|able
rec|ti|fi|ca|tion +s
rec|ti|fier +s
rect|ify
  rec|ti|fies
  rec|ti|fied
  rec|ti|fy|ing
rec|ti|lin|eal
rec|ti|lin|ear
rec|ti|lin|ear|ity
rec|ti|lin|ear|ly
rec|ti|tude
recto +s
rec|tor +s (priest.
  △ recta)

rec|tor|ate +s
rec|tor|ial
rec|tor|ship +s
rec|tory
   rec|tor|ies
rec|trix
   rec|tri|ces
rec|tum
   rec|tums *or* recta
rec|tus
   recti
re|cum|bency
re|cum|bent
re|cum|bent|ly
re|cu|per|able
re|cu|per|ate
   re|cu|per|ates
   re|cu|per|ated
   re|cu|per|at|ing
re|cu|per|ation +s
re|cu|pera|tive
re|cu|per|ator +s
recur
   re|curs
   re|curred
   re|cur|ring
re|cur|rence +s
re|cur|rent
re|cur|rent|ly
re|cur|sion +s
re|cur|sive
re|cur|sive|ly
re|cur|vate
re|cur|vat|ure +s
re|curve
   re|curves
   re|curved
   re|curv|ing
recu|sance
recu|sancy
recu|sant +s
re|cyc|lable
re|cycle
   re|cycles
   re|cycled
   re|cyc|ling
re|cyc|ler +s
Red +s
   (Communist)
red
   reds
   red|der
   red|dest
   (colour. △ redd,
   read)
re|dact +s +ed
   +ing
re|dac|tion +s
re|dac|tion|al
re|dact|or +s
redan +s
red-back +s

red bark +s (tree)
red-blooded
red-blooded|ness
red|breast +s
red-brick *attributive*
red|bud +s
red|cap +s
red|coat +s
red|cur|rant +s
redd
   redds
   redd
   redd|ing
   (clear up; arrange.
   △ red, read)
red|den +s +ed
   +ing
red|dish
Red|ditch (town,
   England)
red|dle +s
reddy (reddish.
   △ ready)
rede
   redes
   reded
   red|ing
   (advise; advice.
   △ read, reed)
re|dec|or|ate
   re|dec|or|ates
   re|dec|or|ated
   re|dec|or|at|ing
re|dec|or|ation +s
re|dedi|cate
   re|dedi|cates
   re|dedi|cated
   re|dedi|cat|ing
re|dedi|ca|tion
re|deem +s +ed
   +ing
re|deem|able
re|deem|er +s
re|define
   re|defines
   re|defined
   re|defin|ing
re|def|in|ition +s
re|demp|tion +s
re|demp|tive
Re|demp|tor|ist +s
re|deploy +s +ed
   +ing
re|deploy|ment +s
re|des|cend +s +ed
   +ing
re|design +s +ed
   +ing
re|des|ig|nate
   re|des|ig|nates
   re|des|ig|nated
   re|des|ig|nat|ing

re|des|ig|na|tion
re|de|ter|min|ation
   +s
re|de|ter|mine
   re|de|ter|mines
   re|de|ter|mined
   re|de|ter|min|ing
re|develop +s +ed
   +ing
re|devel|oper +s
re|devel|op|ment
   +s
red-eye +s (fish;
   effect in
   photograph)
red-faced
red|fish
   plural red|fish *or*
   red|fishes
Red|ford, Rob|ert
   (American actor)
Red|grave,
   Mi|chael,
   Van|essa, Corin,
   and Lynn (family
   of English actors)
red-handed
red|head +s
red-headed
red-hot
re|dial
   re|dials
   re|dialled *Br.*
   re|dialed *Am.*
   re|dial|ling *Br.*
   re|dial|ing *Am.*
redid
re|dif|fu|sion +s
Red In|dian +s
   (*offensive*)
red|in|gote +s
red|in|te|grate
   red|in|te|grates
   red|in|te|grated
   red|in|te|grat|ing
red|in|te|gra|tion
   +s
red|in|te|gra|tive
re|dir|ect +s +ed
   +ing
re|dir|ec|tion
re|dis|cover +s
   +ed +ing
re|dis|cov|er|er +s
re|dis|cov|ery
re|dis|cov|er|ies
re|dis|so|lu|tion +s
re|dis|solve
   re|dis|solves
   re|dis|solved
   re|dis|solv|ing

re|dis|trib|ute
   re|dis|trib|utes
   re|dis|trib|uted
   re|dis|trib|ut|ing
re|dis|tri|bu|tion
   +s
re|dis|tribu|tive
re|div|ide
   re|div|ides
   re|div|ided
   re|div|id|ing
re|div|ision +s
redi|vivus
red-letter day +s
red-light dis|trict
   +s
redly
Red|mond, John
   Ed|ward (Irish
   statesman)
red|neck +s
red|ness
redo
   re|does
   redid
   re|do|ing
   re|done
redo|lence
redo|lent
redo|lent|ly
Redon, Odi|lon
   (French painter)
re|double
   re|doubles
   re|doubled
   re|doub|ling
re|doubt +s
re|doubt|able
re|doubt|ably
re|dound +s +ed
   +ing
redox
red|poll +s
re|draft +s +ed
   +ing
re|draw
   re|draws
   re|drew
   re|draw|ing
   re|drawn
re|dress
   re|dresses
   re|dressed
   re|dress|ing
   (remedy; readjust)
re-dress
   re-dresses
   re-dressed
   re-dressing
   (dress again)
re|dress|able
re|dress|al +s

re|dress|er +s
re|dress|ment +s
red|shank +s
red shift +s
  Astronomy
red-shifted
red|skin +s
  (*offensive*)
red spi|der +s
  (mite)
red|start +s
re|duce
  re|duces
  re|duced
  re|du|cing
re|ducer +s
re|du|ci|bil|ity
  re|du|ci|bil|ities
re|du|cible
re|du|cing agent
  +s
re|duc|tio ad
  ab|sur|dum
re|duc|tion +s
re|duc|tion|ism
re|duc|tion|ist +s
re|duc|tion|is|tic
re|duc|tive
re|dun|dance
re|dun|dancy
  re|dun|dan|cies
re|dun|dant
re|dun|dant|ly
re|dupli|cate
  re|du|pli|cates
  re|du|pli|cated
  re|du|pli|cat|ing
re|dupli|ca|tion +s
re|dupli|ca|tive
red|water
red|wing +s
red|wood +s
redye
  re|dyes
  re|dyed
  re|dye|ing
ree|bok +s
re-echo
  re-echoes
  re-echoed
  re-echoing
Reed, Carol
  (English film
  director)
Reed, Wal|ter
  (American
  physician)
reed +s +ed +ing
  (grass; thatch with
  reed. △ read,
  rede)
reed-bed +s

reed|buck +s
reed bunt|ing +s
reedi|ness
reed|ing +s
  (architectural
  moulding.
  △ reading)
re-edit +s +ed
  +ing
re-edition +s
reed|ling +s
reed mace
reed-organ +s
reed pipe +s
reed-stop +s
re-educate
  re-educates
  re-educated
  re-educat|ing
re-education
reed warb|ler +s
reedy
  reed|ier
  reedi|est
reef +s +ed +ing
reef|er +s
reefing-jacket +s
reef knot +s
reef|point +s
reek +s +ed +ing
  (smell. △ wreak)
reeky
  reek|ier
  reeki|est
reel +s +ed +ing
  (winding device;
  dance; wind in,
  up, etc.; stagger.
  △ real)
re-elect +s +ed
  +ing
re-election +s
reel|er +s
re-eligible
re-embark +s +ed
  +ing
re-embark|ation
  +s
re-emerge
  re-emerges
  re-emerged
  re-emerging
re-emergence +s
re-emergent
re-emphasis
  re-emphases
re-emphasise *Br.*
  (use re-
  emphasize)
  re-emphasises
  re-emphasised
  re-emphasis|ing

re-emphasize
  re-emphasizes
  re-emphasized
  re-emphasiz|ing
re-employ +s +ed
  +ing
re-employ|ment
re-enact +s +ed
  +ing
re-enactment +s
re-enforce
  re-enforces
  re-enforced
  re-enforcing
  (enforce again.
  △ reinforce)
re-enforce|ment
  (act of re-enforcing.
  △ reinforcement)
re-engineer +s
  +ed +ing
re-enlist +s +ed
  +ing
re-enlist|er +s
re-enter +s +ed
  +ing
re-entrance +s
re-entrant +s
re-entry
  re-entries
re-equip
  re-equips
  re-equipped
  re-equipping
re-erect +s +ed
  +ing
re-erection
re-establish
  re-establishes
  re-established
  re-establish|ing
re-establish|ment
re-evaluate
  re-evaluates
  re-evaluated
  re-evaluat|ing
re-evaluation +s
reeve
  reeves
  rove *or* reeved
  reev|ing
  (magistrate; bird;
  to thread.
  △ reave, reive)
re-examin|ation
  +s
re-examine
  re-examines
  re-examined
  re-examin|ing
re-export +s +ed
  +ing

re-export|ation +s
re-export|er +s
ref
  refs
reffed
ref|fing
  (= referee)
re|face
  re|faces
  re|faced
  re|fa|cing
re|fash|ion +s +ed
  +ing
re|fec|tion +s
re|fec|tory
  re|fec|tor|ies
refer
  re|fers
  re|ferred
  re|fer|ring
re|fer|able
ref|er|ee
  ref|er|ees
  ref|er|eed
  ref|er|ee|ing
ref|er|ence
  ref|er|ences
  ref|er|enced
  ref|er|en|cing
ref|er|en|dum
  ref|er|en|dums *or*
  ref|er|enda
ref|er|ent +s
ref|er|en|tial
ref|er|en|ti|al|ity
ref|er|en|tial|ly
re|fer|ral +s
re|fer|rer +s
re|fill +s +ed +ing
re|fill|able
re|fin|able
re|fi|nance
  re|fi|nances
  re|fi|nanced
  re|fi|nan|cing
re|fine
  re|fines
  re|fined
  re|fin|ing
re|fine|ment +s
re|finer +s
re|finery
  re|finer|ies
re|fin|ish
  re|fin|ishes
  re|fin|ished
  re|fin|ish|ing
refit
  re|fits
  re|fit|ted
  re|fit|ting
re|fit|ment +s

re|flag
  re|flags
  re|flagged
  re|flag|ging
re|flate
  re|flates
  re|flated
  re|flat|ing
re|fla|tion +s
re|fla|tion|ary
re|flect +s +ed
  +ing
re|flect|ance +s
re|flec|tion +s
re|flec|tion|al
re|flect|ive
re|flect|ive|ly
re|flect|ive|ness
re|flect|iv|ity
  re|flect|iv|ities
re|flect|or +s
re|flet +s
re|flex
  re|flexes
re|flexed
re|flex|ibil|ity
re|flex|ible
re|flex|ion +s (use
  reflection)
re|flex|ive +s
re|flex|ive|ly
re|flex|ive|ness
re|flex|iv|ity
re|flex|ly
re|flex|olo|gist +s
re|flex|ology
re|float +s +ed
  +ing
ref|lu|ence +s
ref|lu|ent
re|flux
  re|fluxes
re|focus
  re|focuses *or*
  re|focus|ses
  re|focused *or*
  re|focussed
  re|focus|ing *or*
  re|focus|sing
re|fold +s +ed
  +ing
re|for|est +s +ed
  +ing
re|for|est|ation
re|forge
  re|forges
  re|forged
  re|for|ging
re|form +s +ed
  +ing (correct,
  improve)

re-form +s +ed
  +ing (form again)
re|form|able
re|format
  re|formats
  re|format|ted
  re|format|ting
ref|or|ma|tion +s
re-formation +s
  (act or process of
  forming again)
re|forma|tive
re|forma|tory
  re|forma|tor|ies
re|form|er +s
re|form|ism
re|form|ist +s
re|for|mu|late
  re|for|mu|lates
  re|for|mu|lated
  re|for|mu|lat|ing
re|for|mu|la|tion
  +s
re|fract +s +ed
  +ing
re|frac|tion +s
re|fract|ive
re|fract|om|eter +s
re|fracto|met|ric
re|fract|om|etry
re|frac|tor +s
re|frac|tor|ily
re|frac|tori|ness
re|frac|tory
  re|fract|or|ies
re|frain +s +ed
  +ing
re|frain|ment +s
re|fran|gi|bil|ity
re|fran|gible
re|freeze
  re|freezes
  re|froze
  re|freez|ing
  re|frozen
re|fresh
  re|freshes
  re|freshed
  re|fresh|ing
re|fresh|er +s
re|fresh|er course
  +s
re|fresh|ing|ly
re|fresh|ment +s
re|friger|ant +s
re|friger|ate
  re|friger|ates
  re|friger|ated
  re|friger|at|ing
re|friger|ation
re|frigera|tive
re|friger|ator +s

re|frigera|tory
  re|fri|gera|tor|ies
re|frin|gent
re|froze
re|frozen
reft
re|fuel
  re|fuels
  re|fuelled *Br.*
  re|fueled *Am.*
  re|fuel|ling *Br.*
  re|fuel|ing *Am.*
ref|uge +s
refu|gee +s
re|fu|gium
  re|fu|gia
re|ful|gence
re|ful|gent
re|ful|gent|ly
re|fund +s +ed
  +ing (pay back)
re-fund +s +ed
  +ing (fund again)
re|fund|able
re|fund|er +s
re|fund|ment +s
re|fur|bish
  re|fur|bishes
  re|fur|bished
  re|fur|bish|ing
re|fur|bish|ment
  +s
re|furn|ish
  re|furn|ishes
  re|furn|ished
  re|furn|ish|ing
re|fus|able
re|fusal +s
re|fuse
  re|fuses
  re|fused
  re|fus|ing
  (withhold consent
  etc.)
ref|use (rubbish)
re-fuse
  re-fuses
  re-fused
  re-fusing
  (fuse again)
re|fuse|nik +s
re|fuser +s
re|fut|able
re|futal +s
refu|ta|tion +s
re|fute
  re|futes
  re|futed
  re|fut|ing
re|futer +s
Reg (name)

reg +s
  (= registration
  mark or
  regulation)
re|gain +s +ed
  +ing
regal
re|gale
  re|gales
  re|galed
  re|gal|ing
re|gale|ment +s
re|galia
re|gal|ism
re|gal|ity
  re|gal|ities
re|gal|ly
re|gard +s +ed
  +ing
re|gard|ant
  Heraldry
re|gard|ful
re|gard|less
re|gard|less|ly
re|gard|less|ness
re|gather +s +ed
  +ing
re|gatta +s
re|gel|ate
  re|gel|ates
  re|gel|ated
  re|gel|at|ing
re|gel|ation +s
re|gency
  re|gen|cies
re|gen|er|ate
  re|gen|er|ates
  re|gen|er|ated
  re|gen|er|at|ing
re|gen|er|ation +s
re|gen|era|tive
re|gen|era|tive|ly
re|gen|er|ator +s
re|gen|esis
  re|gen|eses
re|gent +s
regent-bird +s
re|ger|min|ate
  re|ger|min|ates
  re|ger|min|ated
  re|ger|min|at|ing
re|ger|min|ation
  +s
reg|gae +s
Reg|gio di
  Ca|lab|ria (port,
  Italy)
regi|cidal
regi|cide +s
re|gild +s +ed +ing
re|gime +s
regi|men +s

regi|ment +s +ed
+ing
regi|men|tal +s
regi|men|tal|ly
regi|men|ta|tion
Re|gina (city,
Canada; name)
Re|gina (queen)
Regi|nald
Regio|mon|ta|nus,
Jo|han|nes
(German
astronomer and
mathematician)
re|gion +s
re|gion|al +s
re|gion|al|isa|tion
Br. (use
regionalization)
re|gion|al|ise *Br.*
(use regionalize)
re|gion|al|ises
re|gion|al|ised
re|gion|al|is|ing
re|gion|al|ism +s
re|gion|al|ist +s
re|gion|al|iza|tion
re|gion|al|ize
re|gion|al|izes
re|gion|al|ized
re|gion|al|iz|ing
re|gion|al|ly
regis|seur +s
regis|ter +s +ed
+ing
regis|trable
regis|trar +s
Regis|trar
Gen|eral +s
regis|trar|ship +s
regis|trary
regis|trar|ies
regis|tra|tion +s
regis|tra|tion
mark +s
regis|try
regis|tries
Re|gius (professor)
re|glaze
re|glazes
re|glazed
re|glaz|ing
reg|let +s
reg|nal
reg|nant
rego +s
rego|lith +s
re|gorge
re|gorges
re|gorged
re|gor|ging

re|grade
re|grades
re|graded
re|grad|ing
re|grate
re|grates
re|grated
re|grat|ing
re|green +s +ed
+ing
re|gress
re|gresses
re|gressed
re|gress|ing
re|gres|sion +s
re|gres|sive
re|gres|sive|ly
re|gres|sive|ness
re|gret
re|grets
re|gret|ted
re|gret|ting
re|gret|ful
re|gret|ful|ly
re|gret|ful|ness
re|gret|table
re|gret|tably
re|group +s +ed
+ing
re|group|ment +s
re|grow
re|grows
re|grew
re|grow|ing
re|grown
re|growth +s
regu|lable
regu|lar +s
regu|lar|isa|tion
Br. (use
regularization)
regu|lar|ise *Br.* (use
regularize)
regu|lar|ises
regu|lar|ised
regu|lar|is|ing
re|gu|lar|ity
re|gu|lar|ities
regu|lar|iza|tion
regu|lar|ize
regu|lar|izes
regu|lar|ized
regu|lar|iz|ing
regu|lar|ly
regu|late
regu|lates
regu|lated
regu|lat|ing
regu|la|tion +s
regu|la|tive
regu|la|tor +s
regu|la|tory

regu|line
reg|ulo +s
Regu|lus (star)
regu|lus
regu|luses *or*
reg|uli
(metallic
substance)
re|gur|gi|tate
re|gur|gi|tates
re|gur|gi|tated
re|gur|gi|tat|ing
re|gur|gi|ta|tion +s
rehab
(= rehabilitation)
re|habili|tate
re|habili|tates
re|habili|tated
re|habili|tat|ing
re|habili|ta|tion +s
re|habili|ta|tive
re|han|dle
re|han|dles
re|han|dled
re|hand|ling
re|hang
re|hangs
re|hung
re|hang|ing
re|hash
re|hashes
re|hashed
re|hash|ing
re|hear
re|hears
re|heard
re|hear|ing
re|hearsal +s
re|hearse
re|hearses
re|hearsed
re|hears|ing
re|hearser +s
re|heat +s +ed
+ing
re|heat|er +s
re|heel +s +ed
+ing
Re|ho|boam (king
of Israel)
re|ho|boam +s
(wine bottle)
re|home
re|homes
re|homed
re|hom|ing
re|house
re|houses
re|housed
re|hous|ing
re|hung
re|hy|drat|able

re|hy|drate
re|hy|drates
re|hy|drated
re|hy|drat|ing
re|hy|dra|tion
Reich +s (German
state)
Reich, Steve
(American
composer)
Reichs|tag
(German
parliament)
re|ifi|ca|tion +s
re|ifi|ca|tory
reify
re|ifies
re|ified
re|ify|ing
Rei|gate (town,
England)
reign +s +ed +ing
(rule. △ rain, rein)
re|ignite
re|ignites
re|ignited
re|ignit|ing
Reilly (in 'the life of
Reilly'; use Riley)
re|im|burs|able
re|im|burse
re|im|burses
re|im|bursed
re|im|burs|ing
re|im|burse|ment
+s
re|im|burser +s
re|im|port +s +ed
+ing
re|im|port|ation
re|im|pose
re|im|poses
re|im|posed
re|im|pos|ing
re|im|pos|ition
Reims (city,
France)
rein +s +ed +ing
(control-strap;
restrain. △ rain,
reign)
re|incar|nate
re|incar|nates
re|incar|nated
re|incar|nat|ing
re|incar|na|tion +s
re|incor|por|ate
re|incor|por|ates
re|incor|por|ated
re|incor|por|
at|ing
re|incor|por|ation

rein|deer
  plural rein|deer *or*
  rein|deers
re|in|dus|trial|
  isa|tion *Br.* (use
  reindustrializa-
  tion)
re|in|dus|trial|ise
  Br. (use
  reindustrialize)
  re|in|dus|trial|ises
  re|in|dus|trial|
      ised
  re|in|dus|trial|
      is|ing
re|in|dus|trial|
      iza|tion
re|in|dus|trial|ize
  re|in|dus|trial|
      izes
  re|in|dus|trial|
      ized
  re|in|dus|trial|
      iz|ing
re|infect +s +ed
  +ing
re|infec|tion +s
re|inforce
  re|inforces
  re|inforced
  re|infor|cing
  (strengthen. △ re-
  enforce)
re|inforce|ment +s
  (act of reinforcing;
  troops. △ re-
  enforcement)
re|infor|cer +s
Rein|hardt,
  Django (Belgian
  jazz guitarist)
Rein|hardt, Max
  (Austrian theatre
  director)
re|inject +s +ed
  +ing
rein|less
re|insert +s +ed
  +ing
re|inser|tion +s
re|inspect +s +ed
  +ing
re|inspec|tion +s
re|instal (use
  reinstall)
  re|instals
  re|installed
  re|instal|ling
re|install +s +ed
  +ing
re|instate
  re|instates

re|instate (*cont.*)
  re|instated
  re|instat|ing
re|instate|ment +s
re|insti|tute
  re|insti|tutes
  re|insti|tuted
  re|insti|tut|ing
re|insti|tu|tion
re|insur|ance
re|insure
  re|insures
  re|insured
  re|insur|ing
re|insurer +s
re|inte|grate
  re|inte|grates
  re|inte|grated
  re|inte|grat|ing
re|inte|gra|tion
re|inter
  re|inters
  re|interred
  re|inter|ring
re|inter|ment +s
re|inter|pret
  +ed +ing
re|inter|pret|ation
  +s
re|intro|duce
  re|intro|duces
  re|intro|duced
  re|intro|du|cing
re|intro|duc|tion
  +s
re|invent +s +ed
  +ing
re|inven|tion
re|invest +s +ed
  +ing
re|inves|ti|gate
  re|inves|ti|gates
  re|inves|ti|gated
  re|inves|ti|gat|ing
re|inves|ti|ga|tion
  +s
re|invest|ment +s
re|invig|or|ate
  re|invig|or|ates
  re|invig|or|ated
  re|invig|or|at|ing
re|invig|or|ation
re|issue
  re|issues
  re|issued
  re|issu|ing
re|iter|ate
  re|iter|ates
  re|iter|ated
  re|iter|at|ing
re|iter|ation +s
re|itera|tive

Reith, John
  (director-general
  of the BBC)
reive
  reives
  reived
  reiv|ing
  (go plundering.
  △ reave, reeve)
reiver +s
re|ject +s +ed +ing
re|ject|able
re|jec|ta|menta
re|ject|er +s
  (person who
  rejects.
  △ rejector)
re|jec|tion +s
re|jec|tion|ist +s
re|ject|ive
re|ject|or +s
  (electronic circuit.
  △ rejecter)
rejig
  re|jigs
  re|jigged
  re|jig|ging
re|joice
  re|joices
  re|joiced
  re|joi|cing
re|joi|cer +s
re|joi|cing +s
re|joi|cing|ly
re|join +s +ed +ing
re|join|der +s
re|ju|ven|ate
  re|ju|ven|ates
  re|ju|ven|ated
  re|ju|ven|at|ing
re|ju|ven|ation
re|ju|ven|ator +s
re|ju|ven|esce
  re|ju|ven|esces
  re|ju|ven|esced
  re|ju|ven|es|cing
re|ju|ven|es|cence
re|ju|ven|es|cent
rekey +s +ed +ing
re|kin|dle
  re|kin|dles
  re|kin|dled
  re|kind|ling
re|label
  re|labelled *Br.*
  re|labeled *Am.*
  re|label|ling *Br.*
  re|label|ing *Am.*
re|laid (past tense
  and past participle
  of relay.
  △ relayed)

re|lapse
  re|lapses
  re|lapsed
  re|laps|ing
re|lapser +s
re|lat|able
re|late
  re|lates
  re|lated
  re|lat|ing
re|lated|ness
re|later +s (person
  who relates
  something.
  △ relator)
re|la|tion +s
re|la|tion|al
re|la|tion|al|ly
re|la|tion|ism
re|la|tion|ist +s
re|la|tion|ship +s
rela|tival
rela|tive +s
rela|tive|ly
rela|tive|ness
rela|tiv|isa|tion *Br.*
  (use
  relativization)
rela|tiv|ise *Br.* (use
  relativize)
  rela|tiv|ises
  rela|tiv|ised
  rela|tiv|is|ing
rela|tiv|ism
rela|tiv|ist +s
rela|tiv|is|tic
rela|tiv|is|tic|al|ly
rela|tiv|ity
rela|tiv|ities
rela|tiv|iza|tion
rela|tiv|ize
  rela|tiv|izes
  rela|tiv|ized
  rela|tiv|iz|ing
re|la|tor +s (*Law.*
  △ relater)
re|launch
  re|launches
  re|launched
  re|launch|ing
relax
  re|laxes
  re|laxed
  re|lax|ing
re|lax|ant +s
re|lax|ation +s
re|lax|ed|ly
re|lax|ed|ness
re|lax|er +s
relay +s +ed +ing
  (pass on)

relay
　re¦lays
　re¦laid
　re¦lay¦ing
　(lay again)
re¦learn +s +ed
　　+ing
re¦leas¦able
re¦lease
　re¦leases
　re¦leased
　re¦leas¦ing
re¦leasee +s
re¦leaser +s
　(person who
　releases
　something)
re¦leasor +s *Law*
rele¦gable
rele¦gate
　rele¦gates
　rele¦gated
　rele¦gat¦ing
rele¦ga¦tion +s
re¦lent +s +ed +ing
re¦lent¦less
re¦lent¦less¦ly
re¦lent¦less¦ness
relet
　re¦lets
　relet
　re¦let¦ting
rele¦vance
rele¦vancy
　rele¦van¦cies
rele¦vant
rele¦vant¦ly
re¦li¦abil¦ity
re¦li¦able
re¦li¦able¦ness
re¦li¦ably
re¦li¦ance
re¦li¦ant
relic +s
rel¦ict +s
re¦lief +s
re¦liev¦able
re¦lieve
　re¦lieves
　re¦lieved
　re¦liev¦ing
re¦lieved¦ly
re¦liever +s
re¦lievo +s
re¦light +s +ed
　　+ing
re¦li¦gion +s
re¦li¦gion¦er +s
re¦li¦gion¦ism
re¦li¦gion¦ist +s
re¦li¦gion¦less
religio-political

re¦ligi¦ose
re¦ligi¦os¦ity
re¦li¦gious
re¦li¦gious¦ly
re¦li¦gious¦ness
re¦line
　re¦lines
　re¦lined
　re¦lin¦ing
re¦lin¦quish
　re¦lin¦quishes
　re¦lin¦quished
　re¦lin¦quish¦ing
re¦lin¦quish¦ment
　　+s
reli¦quary
　reli¦quar¦ies
re¦liquiae
rel¦ish
　rel¦ishes
　rel¦ished
　rel¦ish¦ing
rel¦ish¦able
re¦live
　re¦lives
　re¦lived
　re¦liv¦ing
re¦load +s +ed
　　+ing
re¦locate
　re¦locates
　re¦located
　re¦locat¦ing
re¦loca¦tion +s
re¦lucent
re¦luc¦tance
re¦luc¦tant
re¦luc¦tant¦ly
rely
　re¦lies
　re¦lied
　rely¦ing
REM (= rapid eye-
　movement)
rem
　plural rem *or* rems
　(unit of radiation)
re¦made
re¦main +s +ed
　　+ing
re¦main¦der +s
　　+ed +ing
re¦mains
re¦make
　re¦makes
　re¦made
　re¦mak¦ing
reman
　re¦mans
　re¦manned
　re¦man¦ning

re¦mand +s +ed
　　+ing
rem¦an¦ence +s
rem¦an¦ent
　(remaining,
　residual.
　△ remnant)
re¦mark +s +ed
　　+ing
re¦mark¦able
re¦mark¦able¦ness
re¦mark¦ably
re¦mar¦riage +s
re¦marry
　re¦mar¦ries
　re¦mar¦ried
　re¦marry¦ing
re¦mas¦ter +s +ed
　　+ing
re¦match
　re¦matches
Rem¦brandt
　(Har¦mensz van
　Rijn) (Dutch
　painter)
REME (= Royal
　Electrical and
　Mechanical
　Engineers)
re¦meas¦ure
　re¦meas¦ures
　re¦meas¦ured
　re¦meas¦ur¦ing
re¦meas¦ure¦ment
　　+s
re¦medi¦able
re¦med¦ial
re¦medi¦al¦ly
rem¦edy
　rem¦ed¦ies
　rem¦ed¦ied
　rem¦edy¦ing
re¦mem¦ber +s
　　+ed +ing
re¦mem¦ber¦able
re¦mem¦ber¦er +s
re¦mem¦brance +s
re¦mem¦bran¦cer
　　+s
remex
　remi¦ges
re¦mind +s +ed
　　+ing
re¦mind¦er +s
re¦mind¦ful
rem¦in¦isce
　rem¦in¦isces
　rem¦in¦isced
　rem¦in¦is¦cing
rem¦in¦is¦cence +s
rem¦in¦is¦cent
rem¦in¦is¦cen¦tial

rem¦in¦is¦cent¦ly
rem¦in¦is¦cer +s
re¦mint +s +ed
　　+ing
re¦mise
　re¦mises
　re¦mised
　re¦mis¦ing
re¦miss
re¦mis¦sible
re¦mis¦sion +s
re¦mis¦sive
re¦miss¦ly
re¦miss¦ness
remit
　re¦mits
　re¦mit¦ted
　re¦mit¦ting
re¦mit¦table
re¦mit¦tal +s
re¦mit¦tance +s
re¦mit¦tee +s
re¦mit¦tent
re¦mit¦ter +s
remix
　re¦mixes
　re¦mixed
　re¦mix¦ing
re¦mix¦er +s
rem¦nant +s (small
　remaining
　quantity.
　△ remanent)
re¦model
　re¦models
　re¦mod¦elled *Br.*
　re¦mod¦eled *Am.*
　re¦mod¦el¦ling *Br.*
　re¦mod¦el¦ing *Am.*
re¦modi¦fi¦ca¦tion
　　+s
re¦mod¦ify
　re¦modi¦fies
　re¦modi¦fied
　re¦modi¦fy¦ing
re¦mold *Am.* +s
　　+ed +ing (*Br.*
　remould)
re¦mon¦et¦isa¦tion
　Br. (use
　remonetization)
re¦mon¦et¦ise *Br.*
　(use remonetize)
re¦mon¦et¦ises
re¦mon¦et¦ised
re¦mon¦et¦is¦ing
re¦mon¦et¦iza¦tion
re¦mon¦et¦ize
re¦mon¦et¦izes
re¦mon¦et¦ized
re¦mon¦et¦iz¦ing
rem¦on¦strance +s

Re|mon|strant +s
(Dutch protestant)
re|mon|strant
(remonstrating)
rem|on|strate
rem|on|strates
rem|on|strated
rem|on|strat|ing
rem|on|stra|tion
+s
rem|on|stra|tive
rem|on|stra|tor +s
re|mon|tant +s
rem|ora +s
re|morse
re|morse|ful
re|morse|ful|ly
re|morse|less
re|morse|less|ly
re|morse|less|ness
re|mort|gage
re|mort|gages
re|mort|gaged
re|mort|ga|ging
re|mote
re|moter
re|mot|est
re|mote con|trol
remote-controlled
re|mote|ly
re|mote|ness
re|mould *Br.* +s
+ed +ing (*Am.*
remold)
re|mount +s +ed
+ing
re|mov|abil|ity
re|mov|able
re|moval +s
re|move
re|moves
re|moved
re|mov|ing
re|move|able (use
removable)
re|mover +s
re|mu|ner|ate
re|mu|ner|ates
re|mu|ner|ated
re|mu|ner|at|ing
re|mu|ner|ation +s
re|mu|nera|tive
re|mu|nera|tory
Remus *Roman
Mythology*
re|nais|sance
renal
re|name
re|names
re|named
re|nam|ing

Re|namo (guerilla
movement,
Mozambique)
Renan, Er|nest
(French historian)
re|nas|cence
re|nas|cent
re|nation|al|
isa|tion *Br.* (use
renationaliza-
tion)
re|nation|al|ise *Br.*
(use
renationalize)
re|nation|al|ises
re|nation|al|ised
re|nation|al|is|ing
re|nation|al|
iza|tion
re|nation|al|ize
re|nation|al|izes
re|nation|al|ized
re|nation|al|iz|ing
Ren|ault, Louis
(French car
maker)
Ren|ault, Mary
(British novelist)
ren|contre +s
ren|coun|ter +s
+ed +ing
rend
rends
rent
rend|ing
Ren|dell, Ruth
(English writer)
ren|der +s +ed
+ing
ren|der|er +s
ren|der|ing +s
render-set
render-sets
render-set
render-setting
ren|dez|vous
ren|dez|vouses
ren|dez|voused
ren|dez|vous|ing
ren|di|tion +s
ren|dzina
Renée
rene|gade
rene|gades
rene|gaded
rene|gad|ing
rene|gado
rene|gadoes
re|nege
re|neges
re|neged
re|neg|ing

re|neg|er +s
re|nego|ti|able
re|nego|ti|ate
re|nego|ti|ates
re|nego|ti|ated
re|nego|ti|at|ing
re|nego|ti|ation +s
re|negue (use
renege)
re|negues
re|negued
re|neguing
re|neguer +s (use
reneger)
renew +s +ed +ing
re|new|abil|ity
re|new|able +s
re|newal +s
re|new|er +s
Ren|frew|shire
(former county,
Scotland)
reni|form
reni|tence
reni|tency
reni|tent
Rennes (city,
France)
ren|net +s
Ren|nie, John
(Scottish civil
engineer)
ren|nin +s
Reno (city, USA)
Ren|oir, Jean
(French film
director)
Ren|oir, Pierre
Au|guste (French
painter)
re|nomin|ate
re|nomin|ates
re|nomin|ated
re|nomin|at|ing
re|nomin|ation +s
re|nounce
re|nounces
re|nounced
re|noun|cing
re|nounce|able
re|nounce|ment +s
re|noun|cer +s
reno|vate
reno|vates
reno|vated
reno|vat|ing
reno|va|tion +s
reno|va|tive
reno|va|tor +s
re|nown
re|nowned
rent +s +ed +ing

rent|abil|ity
rent|able
ren|tal +s
rent boy +s
rent|er +s
rent-free
ren|tier +s
rent roll +s
re|num|ber +s +ed
+ing
re|nun|ci|ant +s
re|nun|ci|ation +s
re|nun|cia|tive
re|nun|ci|atory
ren|voi +s
re|occu|pa|tion
re|occupy
re|occu|pies
re|occu|pied
re|occu|py|ing
re|occur
re|occurs
re|occurred
re|occur|ring
re|occur|rence +s
re|offend +s +ed
+ing
re|open +s +ed
+ing
re|open|ing +s
re|order +s +ed
+ing
re|organ|isa|tion
Br. +s (use
reorganization)
re|organ|ise *Br.*
(use reorganize)
re|organ|ises
re|organ|ised
re|organ|is|ing
re|organ|iser *Br.*
+s (use
reorganizer)
re|organ|iza|tion
+s
re|organ|ize
re|organ|izes
re|organ|ized
re|organ|iz|ing
re|organ|izer +s
re|ori|ent +s +ed
+ing
re|orien|tate
re|orien|tates
re|orien|tated
re|orien|tat|ing
re|orien|ta|tion +s
rep
reps
repped
rep|ping

re¦pack +s +ed
   +ing
re¦pack¦age
   re¦pack¦ages
   re¦pack¦aged
   re¦pack¦aging
re¦pagin¦ate
   re¦pagin¦ates
   re¦pagin¦ated
   re¦pagin¦at¦ing
re¦pagin¦ation +s
re¦paid
re¦paint +s +ed
   +ing
re¦pair +s +ed
   +ing
re¦pair|able
   (capable of being
   repaired.
   △ reparable)
re¦pair|er +s
re¦pair|man
   re¦pair|men
re¦pand
re¦paper +s +ed
   +ing
rep¦ar|abil¦ity
rep¦ar|able (of a
   loss etc., that can
   be made good.
   △ repairable)
rep¦ar|ably
rep¦ar|ation +s
rep¦ara|tive
rep¦ar|tee +s
re¦par|ti¦tion +s
   +ed +ing
re¦pass
   re¦passes
   re¦passed
   re¦pass|ing
re¦past +s
repat +s
   (= repatriate)
re¦pat¦ri|ate
   re¦pat¦ri|ates
   re¦pat¦ri|ated
   re¦pat¦ri|at¦ing
re¦pat¦ri|ation +s
repay
   re¦pays
   re¦paid
   re¦pay|ing
re¦pay|able
re¦pay|ment +s
re¦peal +s +ed
   +ing
re¦peal|able
re¦peat +s +ed
   +ing
re¦peat|abil¦ity
re¦peat|able

re¦peat|ed¦ly
re¦peat¦er +s
re¦pêch|age +s
repel
   re¦pels
   re¦pelled
   re¦pel|ling
re¦pel|lence
re¦pel|lency
re¦pel|lent +s
re¦pel|lent¦ly
re¦pel|ler +s
re¦pent +s +ed
   +ing
re¦pent|ance
re¦pent|ant
re¦pent¦er +s
re¦people
   re¦peoples
   re¦peopled
   re¦peop|ling
re¦per¦cus|sion +s
re¦per¦cus|sive
rep¦er|toire +s
rep¦er|tory
   rep¦er|tor¦ies
rep¦er|tory
   com|pany
   rep¦er|tory
   com|panies
rep¦et|end +s
ré¦péti|teur +s
repe¦ti|tion +s
repe¦ti|tion|al
repe¦ti|tion|ary
repe¦ti|tious
repe¦ti|tious¦ly
repe¦ti|tious|ness
re¦peti|tive
re¦peti|tive¦ly
re¦peti|tive|ness
re¦phrase
   re¦phrases
   re¦phrased
   re¦phras|ing
re¦pine
   re¦pines
   re¦pined
   re¦pin|ing
re¦pique
   re¦piques
   re¦piqued
   re¦piquing
re¦place
   re¦places
   re¦placed
   re¦placing
re¦place|able
re¦place|ment +s
re¦placer +s
re¦plan
   re¦plans

re¦plan (cont.)
   re¦planned
   re¦plan|ning
re¦plant +s +ed
   +ing
re¦play +s +ed
   +ing
re¦plen|ish
   re¦plen|ishes
   re¦plen|ished
   re¦plen|ish|ing
re¦plen|ish¦er +s
re¦plen|ish|ment
   +s
re¦plete
re¦plete|ness
re¦ple|tion +s
re¦plevin +s
re¦plevy
   re¦plev¦ies
   re¦plev¦ied
   re¦plevy|ing
rep|lica +s
rep¦lic|abil¦ity
rep¦lic|able
rep¦li|cate
   rep¦li|cates
   rep¦li|cated
   rep¦li|cat¦ing
rep¦li|ca¦tion +s
rep¦li|ca¦tive
rep¦li|ca¦tor +s
re¦plier +s
reply
   re¦plies
   re¦plied
   re¦ply|ing
reply-paid
repo +s
re¦point +s +ed
   +ing
re¦pol¦ish
   re¦pol¦ishes
   re¦pol¦ished
   re¦pol¦ish|ing
re¦popu|late
   re¦popu|lates
   re¦popu|lated
   re¦popu|lat¦ing
re¦popu|la¦tion
re¦port +s +ed
   +ing
re¦port|able
rep¦or|tage +s
re¦port|ed¦ly
re¦port¦er +s
rep¦or|tor¦ial
re¦por|tori|al¦ly
re¦posal +s
re¦pose
   re¦poses

re¦pose (cont.)
   re¦posed
   re¦pos¦ing
re¦pose|ful
re¦pose|ful¦ly
re¦pose|ful|ness
re¦pos|ition +s +ed
   +ing
re¦posi|tory
   re¦posi|tor¦ies
re¦pos¦sess
   re¦pos¦sesses
   re¦pos¦sessed
   re¦pos¦sess|ing
re¦pos¦ses|sion +s
re¦pos¦ses|sor +s
repot
   re¦pots
   re¦pot|ted
   re¦pot|ting
re¦poussé +s
repp (use rep)
rep¦re|hend +s
   +ed +ing
rep¦re|hen¦si|
                bil¦ity
rep¦re|hen|sible
rep¦re|hen|sibly
rep¦re|hen|sion +s
rep¦re|sent +s +ed
   +ing (stand for)
re-present +s +ed
   +ing (present
   again)
rep¦re|sent|abil¦ity
rep¦re|sent|able
rep¦re|sen¦ta¦tion
   +s (representing
   something)
re-presen¦ta¦tion
   (presenting
   something again)
rep¦re|sen|
                ta¦tion|al
rep¦re|sen|
                ta¦tion|al|ism
rep¦re|sen|
                ta¦tion|al|ist +s
rep¦re|sen|ta¦tion|
                ism
rep¦re|sen|ta¦tion|
                ist +s
rep¦re|sen|ta¦tive
   +s
rep¦re|sen|
                ta¦tive¦ly
rep¦re|sen|ta¦tive|
                ness
re¦press
   re¦presses
   re¦pressed
   re¦press|ing

re|press|er +s (use
  repressor)
re|press|ible
re|pres|sion +s
re|pres|sive
re|pres|sive|ly
re|pres|sive|ness
re|pres|sor +s
re|pres|sur|isa|
  tion Br. (use
  repressurization)
re|pres|sur|ise Br.
  (use repressurize)
re|pres|sur|ises
re|pres|sur|ised
re|pres|sur|is|ing
re|pres|sur|iza|
         tion
re|pres|sur|ize
re|pres|sur|izes
re|pres|sur|ized
re|pres|sur|iz|ing
re|price
re|prices
re|priced
re|pricing
re|prieve
re|prieves
re|prieved
re|priev|ing
rep|ri|mand +s
  +ed +ing
re|print +s +ed
  +ing
re|print|er +s
re|print|ing +s
re|prisal +s
re|prise +s
repro +s
  (= reproduction)
re|proach
re|proaches
re|proached
re|proach|ing
re|proach|able
re|proach|er +s
re|proach|ful
re|proach|ful|ly
re|proach|ful|ness
re|proach|ing|ly
rep|ro|bate
  rep|ro|bates
  rep|ro|bated
  rep|ro|bat|ing
rep|ro|ba|tion
re|pro|cess
  re|pro|cesses
  re|pro|cessed
  re|pro|cess|ing
re|pro|duce
  re|pro|duces

re|pro|duce (cont.)
  re|pro|duced
  re|pro|du|cing
re|pro|du|cer +s
re|pro|du|ci|bil|ity
re|pro|du|cible
re|pro|du|cibly
re|pro|duc|tion +s
re|pro|duct|ive +s
re|pro|duc|tive|ly
re|pro|duc|tive|
         ness
re|pro|gram Br.
re|pro|grams
re|pro|grammed
re|pro|gram|ming
  (in computing)
re|pro|gram Am.
re|pro|grams
re|pro|grammed
re|pro|gram|ming
  (generally)
re|pro|gram|
      ma|bil|ity
re|pro|gram|mable
re|pro|gramme Br.
  re|pro|grammes
  re|pro|grammed
  re|pro|gram|ming
  (generally)
rep|rog|raph|er +s
repro|graph|ic
repro|graph|ic|
      al|ly
repro|graph|ics
rep|rog|raphy
re|proof +s +ed
  +ing
re|prov|able
re|prove
  re|proves
  re|proved
  re|prov|ing
re|prover +s
re|prov|ing|ly
re|pro|vi|sion +s
  +ed +ing
rep|tant
rep|tile +s
Rep|tilia
rep|til|ian +s
Rep|ton,
  Hum|phry
  (English landscape
  gardener)
re|pub|lic +s
Re|pub|lic|an +s
  (of US Republican
  Party)
re|pub|lic|an +s
  (generally)

re|pub|lic|an|ism
re|pub|li|ca|tion
re|pub|lish
  re|pub|lishes
  re|pub|lished
  re|pub|lish|ing
re|pudi|able
re|pudi|ate
  re|pudi|ates
  re|pudi|ated
  re|pudi|at|ing
re|pudi|ation +s
re|pudi|ator +s
re|pug|nance
re|pug|nant
re|pug|nant|ly
re|pulse
  re|pulses
  re|pulsed
  re|puls|ing
re|pul|sion +s
re|pul|sive
re|pul|sive|ly
re|pul|sive|ness
re|pur|chase
  re|pur|chases
  re|pur|chased
  re|pur|chas|ing
re|puri|fi|ca|tion
  +s
re|pur|ify
  re|puri|fies
  re|puri|fied
  re|puri|fy|ing
rep|ut|able
rep|ut|ably
repu|ta|tion +s
re|pute
  re|putes
  re|puted
  re|put|ing
re|puted|ly
re|quest +s +ed
  +ing
re|quest|er +s
re|quick|en +s +ed
  +ing
re|quiem +s
requi|escat +s
re|quire
  re|quires
  re|quired
  re|quir|ing
re|quire|ment +s
re|quirer +s
requis|ite +s
requis|ite|ly
requi|si|tion +s
  +ed +ing
requi|si|tion|er +s
requi|si|tion|ist +s
re|quital +s

re|quite
re|quites
re|quited
re|quit|ing
reran
re|rate
re|rates
re|rated
re|rat|ing
re|read
re|reads
re|read
re|read|ing
re-readable
re-record +s +ed
  +ing
rere|dos
rere|doses
re-release
re-releases
re-released
re-releas|ing
re-roof +s +ed
  +ing
re-route
re-routes
re-routed
re-routing or re-
  routeing
rerun
re|runs
reran
re|run|ning
rerun
re|sal|able (use
  resaleable)
re|sale +s
re|sale|able
resat
re|sched|ule
  re|sched|ules
  re|sched|uled
  re|sched|ul|ing
re|scind +s +ed
  +ing
re|scind|able
re|scind|ment +s
re|scis|sion +s
re|script +s +ed
  +ing
res|cu|able
res|cue
  res|cues
  res|cued
  res|cu|ing
res|cuer +s
re|seal +s +ed
  +ing
re|seal|able
re|search
re|searches

re|search (*cont.*)
  re|searched
  re|search|ing
re|search|able
re|search|er +s
re|seat +s +ed
  +ing
re|sect +s +ed
  +ing
re|sec|tion +s
re|sec|tion|al
re|sec|tion|ist +s
res|eda +s
re|seed +s +ed
  +ing
re|se|lect +s +ed
  +ing
re|se|lec|tion +s
re|sell
  re|sells
  re|sold
  re|sell|ing
re|sell|er +s
re|sem|blance +s
re|sem|blant
re|sem|ble
  re|sem|bles
  re|sem|bled
  re|sem|bling
re|sem|bler +s
re|sent +s +ed
  +ing
re|sent|ful
re|sent|ful|ly
re|sent|ful|ness
re|sent|ment +s
re|ser|pine +s
re|serv|able
res|er|va|tion +s
re|serve
  re|serves
  re|served
  re|serv|ing
  (put aside)
re-serve
  re-serves
  re-served
  re-serving
  (serve again)
re|served|ly
re|serv|ed|ness
re|server +s
re|serv|ist +s
res|er|voir +s
reset
  re|sets
  reset
  re|set|ting
re|set|tabil|ity
re|set|table
re|set|tle
  re|set|tles

re|set|tle (*cont.*)
  re|set|tled
  re|set|tling
re|settle|ment +s
re|shape
  re|shapes
  re|shaped
  re|shap|ing
re|ship
  re|ships
  re|shipped
  re|ship|ping
re|shuf|fle
  re|shuf|fles
  re|shuf|fled
  re|shuf|fling
res|ide
  res|ides
  res|ided
  res|id|ing
resi|dence +s
resi|dency
  resi|den|cies
resi|dent +s
resi|den|tial
resi|den|tial|ly
resi|den|tiary
  resi|den|tiar|ies
resi|dent|ship +s
re|sidua
re|sidual +s
re|sidu|al|ly
re|sidu|ary
resi|due +s
re|siduum
  re|sidua
re|sign +s +ed
  +ing (give up
  employment etc.)
re-sign +s +ed
  +ing (sign again)
re|sig|nal
  re|sig|nals
  re|sig|nalled *Br.*
  re|sig|naled *Am.*
  re|sig|nal|ling *Br.*
  re|sig|nal|ing *Am.*
res|ig|na|tion +s
re|sign|ed|ly
re|sign|ed|ness
re|sign|er +s
re|sile
  re|siles
  re|siled
  re|sil|ing
re|sili|ence
re|sili|ency
re|sili|ent
re|sili|ent|ly
re-silver +s +ed
  +ing
resin +s +ed +ing

res|in|ate
res|in|ates
res|in|ated
res|in|at|ing
  (treat with resin.
  ⚠ resonate)
res|in|ifer|ous
res|ini|fi|ca|tion
res|ini|form
res|in|ify
  res|ini|fies
  res|ini|fied
  res|ini|fy|ing
res|in|oid +s
res|in|ous
re|sist +s +ed +ing
re|sist|ance +s
re|sist|ant
re|sist|er +s
  (person who
  resists. ⚠ resistor)
re|sist|ibil|ity
re|sist|ible
re|sist|ive
re|sist|iv|ity
re|sist|less
re|sist|less|ly
re|sis|tor +s
  (electrical device.
  ⚠ resister)
resit
  re|sits
  resat
  re|sit|ting
re|site
  re|sites
  re|sited
  re|sit|ing
re|size
  re|sizes
  re|sized
  re|siz|ing
re|skill +s +ed
  +ing
Res|nais, Alain
  (French film
  director)
re|sold
re|sole
  re|soles
  re|soled
  re|sol|ing
re|sol|uble (that
  can be resolved)
re-soluble (that
  can be dissolved
  again)
reso|lute
reso|lute|ly
reso|lute|ness
reso|lution +s
reso|lu|tive

re|solv|abil|ity
re|solv|able
re|solve
  re|solves
  re|solved
  re|solv|ing
re|solved|ly
re|solv|ed|ness
re|solv|ent +s
re|solver +s
res|on|ance +s
res|on|ant
res|on|ant|ly
res|on|ate
  res|on|ates
  res|on|ated
  res|on|at|ing
  (produce or show
  resonance.
  ⚠ resinate)
res|on|ator +s
re|sorb +s +ed
  +ing
re|sorb|ence
re|sorb|ent
re|sor|cin
re|sor|cinol
re|sorp|tion +s
re|sorp|tive
re|sort +s +ed
  +ing (seaside
  resort etc.;
  recourse; turn to)
re-sort +s +ed
  +ing (sort again)
re|sort|er +s
re|sound +s +ed
  +ing
re|sound|ing|ly
re|source
  re|sources
  re|sourced
  re|sour|cing
re|source|ful
re|source|ful|ly
re|source|ful|ness
re|source|less
re|source|less|
          ness
re|spect +s +ed
  +ing
re|spect|abil|ity
re|spect|able
re|spect|ably
re|spect|er +s
re|spect|ful
re|spect|ful|ly
re|spect|ful|ness
re|spect|ive
re|spect|ive|ly
re|spell
  re|spells

re|spell (*cont.*)
  re|spelled *or*
  re|spelt
  re|spell|ing
Res|pighi,
  Otto|rino (Italian
  composer)
res¦pir|able
res¦pir|ate
  res¦pir|ates
  res¦pir|ated
  res¦pir|at¦ing
res¦pir|ation +s
res¦pir|ator +s
re|spira|tory
re|spire
  re|spires
  re|spired
  re|spir¦ing
res|pite
  res|pites
  res|pited
  res|pit¦ing
re|splen|dence
re|splen|dency
re|splen|dent
re|splen|dent¦ly
re|spond +s +ed
  +ing
re|spond|ence +s
re|spond|ency
re|spond|ent +s
re|spond¦er +s
re|sponse +s
re|spon¦si|bil¦ity
  re|spon¦si|bil¦ities
re|spon|sible
re|spon|sible|ness
re|spon|sibly
re|spon|sive
re|spon|sive¦ly
re|spon|sive|ness
re|spon|sor¦ial
re|spon|sory
  re|spon¦sor¦ies
re|spray +s +ed
  +ing
rest +s +ed +ing
  (repose;
  remainder.
  △ wrest)
re|stage
  re|stages
  re|staged
  re|staging
re|start +s +ed
  +ing
re|state
  re|states
  re|stated
  re|stat¦ing
re|state|ment +s

res¦taur|ant +s
res¦taur|ant car +s
res|taura|teur +s
rest-balk +s
rest-cure +s
rest day +s
rest|ful
rest|ful¦ly
rest|ful|ness
rest-harrow +s
rest home +s
rest house +s
rest|ing place +s
res¦ti|tu¦tion +s
res|titu|tive
rest|ive
rest|ive¦ly
rest|ive|ness
rest|less
rest|less¦ly
rest|less|ness
rest mass
  rest masses
re|stock +s +ed
  +ing
re|stor¦able
res|tor|ation +s
res|tor|ation|ism
res|tor|ation|ist +s
re|stora|tive +s
res|tora|tive¦ly
re|store
  re|stores
  re|stored
  re|stor¦ing
re|storer +s
re|strain +s +ed
  +ing (control etc.)
re-strain +s +ed
  +ing (strain again)
re¦strain|able
re|strain|ed¦ly
re|strain¦er +s
re|straint +s
re|strict +s +ed
  +ing
re|strict|ed¦ly
re|strict|ed|ness
re|stric|tion +s
re|stric|tion|ist +s
re|strict|ive
re|strict|ive¦ly
re|strict|ive|ness
re|string
  re|strings
  re|strung
  re|string|ing
rest|room +s
re|struc|ture
  re|struc|tures
  re|struc|tured
  re|struc¦tur¦ing

re|struc¦tur|ing +s
re|study
  re|stud¦ies
  re|stud|ied
  re|study|ing
re|style
  re|styles
  re|styled
  re|styl¦ing
re|sub¦mit
  re|sub¦mits
  re|sub¦mit¦ted
  re|sub¦mit¦ting
re|sult +s +ed +ing
re|sult|ant +s
re¦sult|ful
re¦sult|less
re|sum¦able
re|sume
  re|sumes
  re|sumed
  re|sum¦ing
  (begin again; get
  back; etc.)
ré¦sumé +s
  (summary;
  curriculum vitae)
re|sump|tion +s
re|sump|tive
re|su¦pin|ate
re|sup¦ply
  re|sup¦plies
  re|sup¦plied
  re|sup¦ply|ing
re|sur|face
  re|sur¦faces
  re|sur¦faced
  re|sur¦facing
re|sur|gence +s
re|sur|gent
res¦ur|rect +s +ed
  +ing
res¦ur|rec¦tion +s
res¦ur|rec¦tion|al
re|sur|vey +s +ed
  +ing
re|sus¦ci|tate
  re|sus¦ci|tates
  re|sus¦ci|tated
  re|sus¦ci|tat¦ing
re|sus¦ci|ta¦tion +s
re|sus¦ci|ta¦tive
re|sus¦ci|ta¦tor +s
ret
  rets
  ret¦ted
  ret¦ting
re|table +s
re¦tail +s +ed +ing
re|tail¦er +s
re¦tain +s +ed
  +ing

re|tain|abil¦ity
re|tain|able
re|tain¦er +s
re|tain|ment +s
re|take
  re|takes
  re|took
  re|tak¦ing
  re|taken
re|tali|ate
  re|tali|ates
  re|tali|ated
  re|tali|at¦ing
re|tali|ation +s
re|talia|tive
re|tali|ator +s
re|tali|atory
re¦tard +s +ed
  +ing
re¦tard|ant +s
re¦tard|ate +s
re¦tard|ation +s
re|tarda|tive
re|tarda|tory
re¦tard¦er +s
re¦tard|ment +s
retch
  retches
  retched
  retch|ing
  (vomit. △ wretch)
rete
  retia
re|teach
  re|teaches
  re|taught
  re|teach|ing
re|tell
  re|tells
  re|told
  re|tell|ing
re|ten¦tion +s
re|ten¦tive
re|ten¦tive¦ly
re|ten¦tive|ness
re|tex¦ture
  re|tex¦tures
  re|tex¦tured
  re|tex¦tur¦ing
re|think
  re|thinks
  re|thought
  re|think|ing
Rethym|non (port,
  Crete)
retia
reti|ar¦ius
  reti|arii
re|tiary
  re|tiar¦ies
reti|cence
reti|cent

reti|cent|ly
ret|icle +s
re|ticula (plural of reticulum)
re|ticu|lar (of the reticulum)
re|ticu|late
re|ticu|lates
re|ticu|lated
re|ticu|lat|ing
re|ticu|late|ly
re|ticu|la|tion +s
reti|cule +s
re|ticu|lo|cyte +s
re|ticu|lose
re|ticu|lum
  re|tic|ula
retie
  re|ties
  re|tied
  re|tying
reti|form
re-time
  re-times
  re-timed
  re-timing
ret|ina
  ret|inas or
  ret|inae
ret|inal
ret|in|itis
ret|in|itis
  pig|ment|osa
ret|inol
ret|inue +s
re|tir|acy
re|tiral +s
re|tire
  re|tires
  re|tired
  re|tir|ing
re|tired|ness
re|tiree +s
re|tire|ment +s
re|tirer +s
re|tir|ing|ly
re|title
  re|titles
  re|titled
  re|tit|ling
re|told
re|took
re|tool +s +ed
  +ing
re|tort +s +ed +ing
re|tor|tion +s
re|touch
  re|touches
  re|touched
  re|touch|ing
re|touch|er +s

re|trace
  re|traces
  re|traced
  re|tracing
re|tract +s +ed
  +ing
re|tract|able
re|tract|ation +s
  (further treatment
  and corrections.
  ⚠ retraction)
re|tract|ile
re|tract|il|ity
re|trac|tion +s
  (revocation,
  withdrawal.
  ⚠ retractation)
re|trac|tive
re|tract|or +s
re|train +s +ed
  +ing
ret|ral
re|trans|late
  re|trans|lates
  re|trans|lated
  re|trans|lat|ing
re|trans|la|tion +s
re|trans|mis|sion
  +s
re|trans|mit
  re|trans|mits
  re|trans|mit|ted
  re|trans|mit|ting
re|tread
  re|treads
  re|trod
  re|tread|ing
  re|trod|den
  (tread again)
re|tread +s +ed
  +ing (tyre; put
  fresh tread on)
re|treat +s +ed
  +ing
re|trench
  re|trenches
  re|trenched
  re|trench|ing
re|trench|ment +s
re|trial +s
ret|ri|bu|tion +s
re|tribu|tive
re|tribu|tory
re|triev|able
re|trieval +s
re|trieve
  re|trieves
  re|trieved
  re|triev|ing
re|triever +s
re|trim
  re|trims

re|trim (cont.)
  re|trimmed
  re|trim|ming
retro +s
retro|act +s +ed
  +ing
retro|action +s
retro|active
retro|active|ly
retro|activ|ity
retro|cede
  retro|cedes
  retro|ceded
  retro|ced|ing
retro|ced|ence
retro|ced|ent
retro|ces|sion
retro|ces|sive
retro|choir +s
re|trod
re|trod|den
retro|fit
  retro|fits
  retro|fit|ted
  retro|fit|ting
retro|flex
retro|flexed
retro|flex|ion +s
retro|grad|ation
  +s
retro|grade
  retro|grades
  retro|graded
  retro|grad|ing
retro|grade|ly
retro|gress
  retro|gresses
  retro|gressed
  retro|gress|ing
retro|gres|sion
retro|gres|sive
retro|gres|sive|ly
retro|ject +s +ed
  +ing
retro-rocket +s
ret|rorse
ret|rorse|ly
retro|spect +s
retro|spec|tion +s
retro|spect|ive +s
retro|spect|ive|ly
retro|sternal
re|troussé
retro|ver|sion
retro|vert +s +ed
  +ing
retro|virus
  retro|viruses
retry
  re|tries
  re|tried
  re|try|ing

ret|sina +s
ret|tery
  ret|ter|ies
re|tune
  re|tunes
  re|tuned
  re|tun|ing
re|turf +s +ed +ing
re|turn +s +ed
  +ing
re|turn|able
re|turn|ee +s
re|turn|er +s
re|turn|less
re|tuse
re|tying (present
  participle of retie)
re|type
  re|types
  re|typed
  re|typ|ing
Reu|ben Bible
re|uni|fi|ca|tion
re|unify
  re|uni|fies
  re|uni|fied
  re|uni|fy|ing
Ré|union (island,
  Indian Ocean)
re|union +s
re|unite
  re|unites
  re|united
  re|unit|ing
re|uphol|ster +s
  +ed +ing
re|uphol|stery
re|urge
  re|urges
  re|urged
  re|ur|ging
re|usable
reuse
  re|uses
  re|used
  re|us|ing
re|use|able (use
  reusable)
Reu|ter, Paul
  Ju|lius von
  (German founder
  of Reuters)
Reu|ters
  (international
  news agency)
re|util|isa|tion Br.
  (use reutilization)
re|util|ise Br. (use
  reutilize)
  re|util|ises
  re|util|ised
  re|util|is|ing

re|util|iza|tion
re|util|ize
  re|util|izes
  re|util|ized
  re|util|iz|ing
rev
  revs
  revved
  rev|ving
re|vac|cin|ate
  re|vac|cin|ates
  re|vac|cin|ated
  re|vac|cin|at|ing
re|vac|cin|ation +s
re|val|or|isa|tion
  Br. +s (use
  revalorization)
re|val|or|ise *Br.*
  (use revalorize)
  re|val|or|ises
  re|val|or|ised
  re|val|or|is|ing
re|val|or|iza|tion
  +s
re|val|or|ize
  re|val|or|izes
  re|val|or|ized
  re|val|or|iz|ing
re|valu|ation +s
re|value
  re|values
  re|valued
  re|valu|ing
re|vamp +s +ed
  +ing
re|vanch|ism
re|vanch|ist +s
re|var|nish
  re|var|nishes
  re|var|nished
  re|var|nish|ing
re|veal +s +ed
  +ing
re|veal|able
re|veal|er +s
re|veal|ing
re|veal|ing|ly
re|vege|tate
  re|vege|tates
  re|vege|tated
  re|vege|tat|ing
re|vege|ta|tion
re|veille +s
revel
  revels
  rev|elled *Br.*
  rev|eled *Am.*
  rev|el|ling *Br.*
  rev|el|ing *Am.*
reve|la|tion +s
reve|la|tion|al
reve|la|tion|ist +s

rev|ela|tory
rev|el|er *Am.* +s
rev|el|ler *Br.* +s
rev|el|ry
  rev|el|ries
rev|enant +s
re|ven|di|ca|tion
  +s
re|venge
  re|venges
  re|venged
  re|ven|ging
re|venge|ful
re|venge|ful|ly
re|venge|ful|ness
re|ven|ger +s
rev|enue +s
re|verb +s
  (= reverberation)
re|ver|ber|ant
re|ver|ber|ant|ly
re|ver|ber|ate
  re|ver|ber|ates
  re|ver|ber|ated
  re|ver|ber|at|ing
re|ver|ber|ation +s
re|ver|bera|tive
re|ver|ber|ator +s
re|ver|ber|atory
Re|vere, Paul
  (American patriot)
re|vere
  re|veres
  re|vered
  re|ver|ing
  (venerate.
  △ revers)
rev|er|ence
  rev|er|ences
  rev|er|enced
  rev|er|en|cing
rev|er|end +s
  (deserving
  reverence)
rev|er|ent (feeling
  or showing
  reverence)
rev|er|en|tial
rev|er|en|tial|ly
rev|er|ent|ly
rev|erie +s
re|vers
  plural re|vers
  (on garment.
  △ revere)
re|ver|sal +s
re|verse
  re|verses
  re|versed
  re|vers|ing
reverse-charge
  attributive

re|verse|ly
re|verser +s
re|vers|ibil|ity
re|vers|ible
re|vers|ibly
re|ver|sion +s
re|ver|sion|al
re|ver|sion|ary
re|ver|sion|er +s
re|vert +s +ed
  +ing
re|vert|er +s
re|vert|ible
revet
  re|vets
  re|vet|ted
  re|vet|ting
  (face with
  masonry. △ rivet)
re|vet|ment +s
re|victual
  re|victuals
  re|victualled *Br.*
  re|victualed *Am.*
  re|victual|ling *Br.*
  re|victual|ing *Am.*
re|view +s +ed
  +ing (assess; (as
  noun) assessment.
  △ revue)
re|view|able
re|view|al +s
re|view|er +s
re|vile
  re|viles
  re|viled
  re|vil|ing
re|vile|ment +s
re|viler +s
re|vil|ing +s
re|vis|able
re|visal +s
re|vise
  re|vises
  re|vised
  re|vis|ing
re|viser +s
re|vi|sion +s
re|vi|sion|ary
re|vi|sion|ism
re|vi|sion|ist +s
re|visit +s +ed
  +ing
re|vis|ory
re|vit|al|isa|tion
  Br. (use
  revitalization)
re|vit|al|ise *Br.*
  (use revitalize)
  re|vit|al|ises
  re|vit|al|ised
  re|vit|al|is|ing

re|vit|al|iza|tion
re|vit|al|ize
  re|vit|al|izes
  re|vit|al|ized
  re|vit|al|iz|ing
re|viv|able
re|vival +s
re|vival|ism
re|vival|ist +s
re|vival|is|tic
re|vive
  re|vives
  re|vived
  re|viv|ing
re|viver +s
re|vivi|fi|ca|tion
re|viv|ify
  re|vivi|fies
  re|vivi|fied
  re|vivi|fy|ing
re|viv|is|cence
re|viv|is|cent
rev|oc|abil|ity
rev|oc|able
revo|ca|tion +s
revo|ca|tory
re|voke
  re|vokes
  re|voked
  re|vok|ing
re|voker +s
re|volt +s +ed
  +ing
re|volt|ing|ly
revo|lute
revo|lu|tion +s
revo|lu|tion|ary
  revo|lu|tion|ar|ies
revo|lu|tion|ise *Br.*
  (use
  revolutionize)
  revo|lu|tion|ises
  revo|lu|tion|ised
  revo|lu|tion|is|ing
revo|lu|tion|ism
revo|lu|tion|ist +s
revo|lu|tion|ize
  revo|lu|tion|izes
  revo|lu|tion|ized
  revo|lu|tion|iz|ing
re|volv|able
re|volve
  re|volves
  re|volved
  re|volv|ing
re|volver +s
revue +s (theatrical
  entertainment.
  △ review)
re|vul|sion
re|vul|sive

re¦ward +s +ed +ing
re¦ward¦ing¦ly
re¦ward|less
rewa|rewa +s
re¦wash
  re|washes
  re|washed
  re|wash|ing
re¦weigh +s +ed +ing
re¦wind
  re|winds
  re|wound
  re|wind|ing
re¦wind¦er +s
re¦wir¦able
re¦wire
  re|wires
  re|wired
  re|wir¦ing
re¦word +s +ed +ing
re¦work +s +ed +ing
re¦work|ing +s
re¦wound
re¦wrap
  re|wraps
  re|wrapped
  re|wrap|ping
re|write
  re|writes
  re|wrote
  re|writ¦ing
  re|writ¦ten
Rex (name)
Rex (reigning king; in lawsuits)
Rex¦ine *Propr.*
Rey¦kja|vik (capital of Iceland)
Rey|nard +s
Rey|nolds, Joshua (English painter)
Rey|nolds
num¦ber +s
Reza Shah (ruler of Iran)
rhab¦do|mancy
Rhada|man¦thine
Rhada|man¦thus
  Greek Mythology
Rhae|tian +s
Rhae|tic +s
Rhaeto-Romance
Rhaeto-Romanic
Rha¦kine (state, Burma)
rhap|sode +s
rhap|sodic
rhap¦sodic¦al

rhap¦sod|ise *Br.* (use rhapsodize)
rhap¦sod|ises
rhap¦sod|ised
rhap¦sod|is¦ing
rhap¦sod|ist +s
rhap¦sod|ize
rhap¦sod|izes
rhap¦sod|ized
rhap¦sod|iz¦ing
rhap|sody
rhap¦sod|ies
rhat|any
rhat|anies
Rhea (*Greek Mythology*; moon of Saturn)
rhea +s (bird. △ rear, ria)
rhe¦bok +s (use reebok)
Rheims (use Reims)
Rheinland-Pfalz (German name for Rhineland-Palatinate)
Rhem|ish
Rhen|ish
rhe|nium
rheo|logic¦al
rhe|olo¦gist +s
rhe|ology
rheo|stat +s
rheo|stat¦ic
rheo|trop¦ic
rheo|trop|ism
rhe¦sus
rhesus-negative
rhesus-positive
rhe¦tor +s
rhet|oric
rhet|oric¦al
rhet¦oric|al¦ly
rhet¦or|ician +s
rheum +s (watery discharge. △ room)
rheum|at¦ic +s
rheum|atic|al¦ly
rheum|aticky
rheum|atics
rheuma|tism
rheuma|toid
rheum¦ato|logic¦al
rheuma|tolo¦gist +s
rheuma|tol¦ogy
rheumy (full of rheum. △ roomie, roomy)
rhinai

Rhine (river, W. Europe)
Rhine|land (region, Germany)
Rhineland-Palatin¦ate (state, Germany)
rhine|stone +s
rhin|itis
rhino +s (= rhinoceros)
rhi|noceros
  plural rhi|noceros or rhi|nocer¦oses
rhi¦nocer|ot¦ic
rhino|pharyn¦geal
rhino|plas¦tic
rhino|plasty
  rhino|plas¦ties
rhino|scope +s
rhi|zo¦bium
  rhi|zo¦bia
rhizo|carp +s
rhi|zoid
rhi|zome +s
rhizo|pod +s
rho +s (Greek letter. △ roe, row)
Rhoda
rhoda|mine +s
Rhode Is|land (state, USA)
Rhodes (Greek island)
Rhodes, Cecil (British-born South African statesman; scholarship)
Rhodes, Wil¦fred (English cricketer)
Rho|desia (in former names of Zambia and Zimbabwe)
Rho|desian +s
Rho|dian +s
rho|dium
rhodo|chros¦ite
rhodo|den¦dron +s
Rho|dope Moun|tains (in SE Europe)
rhod|op|sin
rho|dora +s
rhomb +s
rhomb|
  en¦ceph|alon +s
rhombi
rhom|bic
rhombo|he¦dral
rhombo|he¦dron
  rhombo|he¦dra or rhombo|he¦drons

rhom|boid +s
rhom|boid|al
rhom¦boid|al¦ly
rhom¦boid|eus
  rhom|boidei
rhom|bus
  rhom|buses or rhombi
Rhona *also* Rona
Rhon|dda (district, Wales)
Rhône (river, W. Europe)
Rhône-Alpes (region, France)
rho¦tic
rhu|barb +s
Rhum (Scottish island)
rhumb +s (on compass. △ rum)
rhumba (use rumba)
rhum|bas
rhum¦baed *or* rhum¦ba'd
rhumba|ing
rhumb-line +s
rhyme
  rhymes
  rhymed
  rhym¦ing
  (in poetry. △ rime)
rhyme|less
rhymer +s
rhyme|ster +s
rhym|ist +s
rhyo|lite +s
Rhys, Jean (British writer)
rhythm +s
rhythm and blues *noun*
rhythm-and-blues *attributive*
rhyth|mic
rhyth|mic¦al
rhyth|mic|al¦ly
rhyth|mi¦city
rhyth|mist +s
rhythm|less
ria +s (narrow inlet. △ rear, rhea)
rial +s (gold coin; Iranian or Omani currency. △ riyal)
Ri¦alto (island, Venice; Bridge)
rib
  ribs

rib (*cont.*)
  ribbed
  rib|bing
rib¦ald +s
rib¦ald¦ry
  rib¦ald¦ries
rib¦and +s
Riba|tejo
  (province,
  Portugal)
Rib¦ben|trop,
  Joa|chim von
  (German Nazi
  politician)
rib¦ber +s
rib¦bing +s
rib¦bon +s
rib¦boned
rib¦bon|fish
  plural rib¦bon|fish
  or rib¦bon|fishes
rib¦bon worm +s
rib¦cage +s
Ri¦bera, José
  (Spanish painter)
rib|less
ribo|fla¦vin
ribo|fla¦vine
ribo|nucle¦ic
rib¦ose +s
ribo|so¦mal
ribo|some +s
rib-tickler +s
rib|wort +s
Ric¦ard|ian +s
rice
  rices
  riced
  ri¦cing
rice-bowl +s (rice-
  producing area)
rice-paper +s
ricer +s
ri¦cer|car +s
ri¦cer|care +s
rich +er +est
Rich|ard (English
  kings)
Rich|ard, Cliff
  (British pop
  singer)
Rich|ards,
  Gor¦don (English
  jockey)
Rich|ards, Viv
  (West Indian
  cricketer)
Rich¦ard|son,
  Sam¦uel (English
  novelist)
Riche|lieu,
  Ar¦mand Jean

Riche|lieu (*cont.*)
  du Ples|sis
  (French cardinal)
rich¦en +s +ed
  +ing
riches
Richie
rich¦ly
Rich|mond (towns,
  England; city,
  USA)
rich|ness
Rich|ter, Jo¦hann
  Fried|rich
  (German novelist)
Rich|ter scale
ricin
Rick (name)
rick +s +ed +ing
  (haystack; sprain)
rick¦eti|ness
rick|ets
rick|ett|sia
  rick¦ett|siae
  rick¦ett|sial
rick|ety
rickey +s
rick|rack (use
  ricrac)
rick|sha +s (use
  rickshaw)
rick|shaw +s
rico|chet
  rico|chets
  rico|cheted *or*
  rico|chet|ted
  rico|chet|ing *or*
  rico¦chet|ting
ri|cotta +s
ric|rac +s
ric¦tal
ric|tus
  ric|tuses
rid
  rids
  rid
  rid|ding
rid¦able (use
  rideable)
rid|dance
rid¦den
rid|dle
  rid|dles
  rid|dled
  rid|dling
rid|dler +s
rid|dling¦ly
ride
  rides
  rode
  rid|ing
  rid¦den

ride|able
ride-off +s *noun*
ride-on +s *adjective
  and noun*
rider +s
rider|less
ridge
  ridges
  ridged
  ridg|ing
ridge piece +s
ridge pole +s
ridge tile +s
ridge tree +s
ridge|way +s
ridgy
  ridgi¦er
  ridgi¦est
ridi|cule
  ridi|cules
  ridi|culed
  ridi|cul¦ing
ri|dicu|lous
ri|dicu|lous¦ly
ri|dicu|lous|ness
rid¦ing +s
rid¦ing light +s
rid¦ing school +s
Rid¦ley, Nich|olas
  (English
  Protestant martyr)
Rief¦en|stahl, Leni
  (German film-
  maker)
Riel, Louis
  (Canadian political
  leader)
Rie|mann,
  Bern¦hard
  (German
  mathematician)
Rie|mann|ian
Ries|ling +s
rife
rife|ness
riff +s +ed +ing
rif¦fle
  rif¦fles
  rif¦fled
  rif¦fling
riff-raff
rifle
  ri¦fles
  ri¦fled
  rif¦ling
rifle bird +s
rifle|man
  rifle|men
rifle range +s
rifle|scope +s
rifle shot +s
rifl¦ing +s

Rif Moun|tains (in
  Morocco)
rift +s +ed +ing
rift|less
rift val¦ley +s
rifty
  rift|ier
  rifti|est
rig
  rigs
  rigged
  rig|ging
Riga (capital of
  Latvia)
riga|doon +s
riga|toni
Rigel (star)
rig¦ger +s (person
  who rigs. △ rigor,
  rigour)
rig|ging +s
Right *Politics*
right +s +ed +ing
  +er +est (just;
  correct; not left;
  entitlement;
  immediately;
  completely;
  restore. △ rite,
  wright, write)
right|able
right angle +s
right-angled
right-back +s *Sport*
right¦en +s +ed
  +ing
right|eous
right|eous¦ly
right|eous|ness
right¦er +s
  (comparative of
  right; in 'animal-
  righter' etc.
  △ writer)
right-footed
right|ful
right|ful¦ly
right|ful|ness
right hand +s *noun*
right-hand
  attributive
right-handed
right-handed¦ly
right-handed¦ness
right-hander +s
right|ish
right|ism
right|ist +s
right|less
right|less|ness
right¦ly
right-minded

right|most
right|ness
righto
right of search
  rights of search
right of visit
  rights of visit
right of way
  rights of way
right|ward
right|wards
right whale +s
right wing +s *noun*
right-wing *adjective*
right-winger +s
rigid
ri¦gid|ify
  ri¦gidi|fies
  ri¦gidi|fied
  ri¦gidi¦fy|ing
ri¦gid|ity
  ri¦gid|ities
ri¦gid|ly
ri¦gid|ness
rig'mar|ole +s
rigor +s (feeling of
  cold; rigidity.
  ⚠ rigger, rigour)
rigor *Am.* +s
  (severity. *Br.*
  rigour. ⚠ rigger)
rig'or|ism
rigor mor'tis
rig'or|ous
rig'or|ous|ly
rig'or|ous|ness
rig'our *Br.* +s (*Am.*
  rigor. severity.
  ⚠ rigger, rigor)
rig-out +s *noun*
Rig-veda *Hinduism*
Rij'eka (port,
  Croatia)
Rijks|mu¦seum (art
  gallery, the
  Netherlands)
Riks|mål
Rila Moun|tains
  (in Bulgaria)
rile
  riles
  riled
  ril¦ing
Riley (in 'the life of
  Riley')
Riley, Brid¦get
  (English painter)
ri|lievo +s (use
  relievo)
Rilke, Rai¦ner
  Maria (German
  poet)

rill +s (small
  stream)
rille +s (valley on
  moon)
rim
  rims
  rimmed
  rim|ming
Rim|baud, Ar¦thur
  (French poet)
rim-brake +s
rime
  rimes
  rimed
  rim¦ing
  (frost; also *archaic*
  = rhyme)
Rim¦ini (resort,
  Italy)
rim|less
Rim¦mon (ancient
  deity)
rim¦ose
rim¦ous
Rimsky-Korsakov,
  Niko|lai (Russian
  composer)
rimu +s
rimy
rimi¦er
rimi|est
rind +s +ed +ing
rin|der|pest
rind|less
ring +s +ed +ing
  (circle etc.
  ⚠ wring)
ring
  rings
  rang
  ring|ing
  rung
  (sound. ⚠ wring)
ring|bark +s +ed
  +ing
ring-binder +s
ring|bolt +s
ring-dove +s
rin|gent
ringer +s
ring|ette
ring-fence
  ring-fences
  ring-fenced
  ring-fencing
ring fin¦ger +s
ring|hals (use
  rinkhals)
  ring|halses
ring|ing|ly
ring|ing tone +s
ring|lead¦er +s

ring|less
ring|let +s
ring|let¦ed *Am.*
ring|let|ted *Br.*
ring|lety
ring|mas¦ter +s
ring-neck +s
ring-necked
ring-pull +s
ring road +s
ring|side +s
ring|sider +s
ring|ster +s
ring|tail +s
ring-tailed
ring-wall +s
ring|worm
rink +s
rink|hals
  rink|halse
rinse
  rinses
  rinsed
  rins|ing
rinser +s
Rio Branco (city,
  Brazil)
Rio de Ja|neiro
  (city, Brazil)
Rio de Oro (region,
  NW Africa)
Rio Grande (river,
  N. America)
Rio Grande do
  Norte (state,
  Brazil)
Rio Grande do Sul
  (state, Brazil)
Rioja, La (region,
  Spain)
Rio Muni (region,
  Equatorial Guinea)
Rio Negro (river, S.
  America)
riot +s +ed +ing
  (disturbance.
  ⚠ ryot)
riot'er +s
riot|less
riot|ous
riot|ous|ly
riot|ous|ness
rip
  rips
  ripped
  rip|ping
ri¦par|ian +s
rip|cord +s
ripe
  riper
  rip'est
ripe¦ly

ripen +s +ed +ing
ripe|ness
ri¦pi|eno
  ri¦pi|enos *or*
  ri¦pi|eni
rip-off +s
ri|poste
  ri|postes
  ri|posted
  ri|post|ing
rip|per +s
rip|ping¦ly
rip|ple
  rip¦ples
  rip¦pled
  rip|pling
rip|plet +s
rip|ply
rip|plier
  rip¦pli|est
rip¦rap
rip-roaring
rip-roaring¦ly
rip¦saw +s
rip|snort¦er +s
rip|snort¦ing
rip|snort|ing¦ly
rip|stop
Ripu|arian +s
Rip Van Win¦kle
  (fictional
  character)
RISC (*Computing.*
  ⚠ risk)
rise
  rises
  rose
  risen
  ris|ing
riser +s
rishi +s
risi|bil¦ity
ris|ible
ris|ibly
ris|ing +s
risk +s +ed +ing
  (chance. ⚠ RISC)
risk-free
risk|ily
riski|ness
risk-taker +s
risk-taking
risky
  risk|ier
  riski|est
Ri¦sor¦gi|mento
ris|otto +s
ris¦qué
ris|sole +s
rit. (= ritardando.
  ⚠ writ)
Rita

rit¦ar¦dando
  rit¦ar¦dandos *or*
  rit¦ar¦dandi
rite +s (ritual.
  ⚠ right, wright,
  write)
rite|less
rit¦en¦uto
  rit¦en¦utos *or*
  rit¦en¦uti
rit¦orn¦ello
  rit¦orn¦el¦los *or*
  rit¦orn¦elli
rit¦ual +s
ritu¦al¦isa¦tion *Br.*
  (use ritualization)
ritu¦al¦ise *Br.* (use
  ritualize)
ritu¦al¦ises
ritu¦al¦ised
ritu¦al¦is¦ing
ritu¦al¦ism
ritu¦al¦ist +s
ritu¦al¦is¦tic
ritu¦al¦is¦tic¦al¦ly
ritu¦al¦iza¦tion
ritu¦al¦ize
  ritu¦al¦izes
  ritu¦al¦ized
  ritu¦al¦iz¦ing
ritu¦al¦ly
ritz|ily
ritzi|ness
ritzy
  ritz|ier
  ritzi|est
rival
  ri¦vals
  ri¦valled *Br.*
  ri¦valed *Am.*
  ri¦val¦ling *Br.*
  ri¦val¦ing *Am.*
ri¦val¦ry
  ri¦val¦ries
rive
  rives
  rived
  riv¦ing
  riven
river +s
Ri¦vera, Diego
  (Mexican painter)
river|ain +s
river bank +s
river bed +s
river|boat +s
riv|ered
river-head +s
river|ine
river|less
River|side (city,
  USA)

river|side +s
rivet +s +ed +ing
  (nail or bolt;
  fasten with rivets.
  ⚠ revet)
riv|et¦er +s
Rivi|era
  (Mediterranean
  coastal region)
rivi|era +s (similar
  region)
rivi|ère +s
  (necklace)
Rivne (city,
  Ukraine)
rivu|let +s
Riy¦adh (capital of
  Saudi Arabia)
riyal +s (Saudi
  Arabian, Qatari, or
  Yemeni currency.
  ⚠ rial)
roach
  plural roach
  (fish)
roach
  roaches
  (cockroach;
  marijuana
  cigarette butt;
  curve on sail)
road +s +ed +ing
  (street; highway;
  track game birds
  by scent. ⚠ rode,
  roed, rowed)
road|bed +s
road|block +s
road fund li¦cence
  +s
road hog +s
road-holding
road|house +s
roadie +s
road|less
road|man
  road|men
road map +s
road metal
road-pricing
road|roll¦er +s
road|run¦ner +s
road|show +s
road|side +s
road sign +s
road|stead +s
road|ster +s
road sweep¦er +s
road tax
  road taxes
road test +s *noun*

road-test +s +ed
  +ing
  verb
Road Town
  (capital of the
  British Virgin
  Islands)
road train +s (lorry
  pulling trailer)
road user +s
road|way +s
road|work +s
road|worthi|ness
road|worthy
roam +s +ed +ing
roam¦er +s
  (wanderer.
  ⚠ romer)
roan +s (colour;
  animal. ⚠ rone)
roar +s +ed +ing
  (sound of lion; etc.
  ⚠ raw)
roar¦er +s
roar|ing +s
roar|ing¦ly
roast +s +ed +ing
roast¦er +s
roast|ing +s
Rob (name)
rob
  robs
  robbed
  rob|bing
  (steal)
Robbe-Grillet,
  Alain (French
  novelist)
Rob¦ben Is¦land
  (off South Africa)
rob¦ber +s
rob¦ber baron +s
rob|bery
  rob|ber|ies
Rob¦bia, Luca
  della (Italian
  sculptor and
  ceramicist)
Rob¦bie
Rob|bins, Je¦rome
  (American
  choreographer)
robe
  robes
  robed
  rob|ing
Rob¦ert (Scottish
  kings; name)
Rob¦erta
Rob¦erts,
  Fred|erick Sleigh
  (Lord Roberts of

Rob|erts (*cont.*)
  Kandahar, British
  field marshal)
Rob¦ert the Bruce
  (Scottish king)
Robe|son, Paul
  (American singer)
Robes|pierre,
  Max¦imil¦ian
  (French
  revolutionary)
Robey, George
  (British comedian)
Robin (name)
robin +s (bird)
Rob¦ina
Robin
  Good|fel¦low
  (another name for
  Puck)
Robin Hood (semi-
  legendary English
  outlaw)
rob|inia +s (tree)
Robin|son,
  Ed¦ward G.
  (Romanian-born
  American actor)
Robin|son, Sugar
  Ray (American
  boxer)
Robin|son Cru¦soe
  (fictional
  character)
ro¦bor¦ant +s
robot +s
ro¦bot¦ic
ro¦bot¦ic¦al¦ly
ro¦bot¦ics
ro¦bot¦isa¦tion *Br.*
  (use robotization)
ro¦bot¦ise *Br.* (use
  robotize)
  ro¦bot¦ises
  ro¦bot¦ised
  ro¦bot¦is¦ing
ro¦bot¦iza¦tion
ro¦bot¦ize
  ro¦bot¦izes
  ro¦bot¦ized
  ro¦bot¦iz¦ing
Rob Roy (Scottish
  outlaw)
Rob|sart, Amy
  (wife of Robert
  Dudley)
Rob|son, Flora
  (English actress)
ro¦bust +er +est
  (sturdy)
ro|busta +s
  (coffee)

ro¦bus¦tious
ro¦bust¦ly
ro¦bust¦ness
roc +s (legendary
    bird. △ rock)
ro¦caille
roc'am¦bole +s
Roch¦dale (town,
    England)
roche
    mou¦ton¦née
roches
    mou¦ton¦nées
    Geology
Ro¦ches¦ter (town,
    England; city,
    USA)
Ro¦ches¦ter, Earl
    of (English poet)
rochet +s
rock +s +ed +ing
    (stone;
    confectionery;
    move to and fro;
    music. △ roc)
rocka¦billy *Music*
Rock¦all (islet and
    shipping area, N.
    Atlantic)
rock and roll
rock and roll¦er +s
rock-bed +s
rock-bottom
rock-bound
rock¦burst +s
rock cake +s
rock candy
rock-climber +s
rock-climbing
rock crys¦tal
rock-dove +s
Rocke¦fel¦ler,
    John Davi¦son
    (American
    industrialist)
rock¦er +s
rock¦ery
    rock¦er¦ies
rocket +s +ed +ing
rock¦et¦eer +s
rocket launch¦er
    +s
rocket-propelled
rock¦et¦ry
rock face +s
rock¦fall +s
rock¦fish
    plural rock¦fish *or*
    rock¦fishes
rock gar¦den +s
Rock¦hamp¦ton
    (town, Australia)

rock¦hop¦per +s
Rock¦ies (= Rocky
    Mountains)
rock¦ily
rocki¦ness
rock¦ing chair +s
rock¦ing horse +s
rocking-stone +s
rock¦less
rock¦let +s
rock¦like
rock¦ling
    plural rock¦ling
rock'n'roll (use
    rock and roll)
rock'n'roll¦er +s
    (use rock and
    roller)
rock-pigeon +s
rock pipit +s
rock plant +s
rock pool +s
rock rab¦bit +s
rock sal¦mon
    plural rock
    sal¦mon
rock salt
rock-shaft +s
rock-solid
rock-steady
rocku¦men¦tary
    rocku¦men¦tar¦ies
rock-wool
rocky
    rock¦ier
    rocki¦est
Rocky Moun¦tains
    (in N. America)
ro¦coco
rod +s
Rod¦den¦berry,
    Gene (American
    television
    producer)
rode
    rodes
    roded
    rod¦ing
    (past tense of
    ride; to fly.
    △ road, roed,
    rowed)
ro¦dent +s
ro¦den¦tial
ro¦den¦ti¦cide +s
rodeo +s
Rod¦er¦ick
Rodger *also* Roger
Rodg¦ers, Rich¦ard
    (American
    composer)
rod¦ham +s

Rodin, Au¦guste
    (French sculptor)
rod¦less
rod¦let +s
rod¦like
Rod¦ney
rodo¦mon¦tade
    rodo¦mon¦tades
    rodo¦mon¦taded
    rodo¦mon¦tad¦ing
roe +s (fish eggs or
    milt. △ ro, row)
roe
    plural roe *or* roes
    (deer. △ rho, row)
roe¦buck +s
roed (having roe.
    △ road, rode,
    rowed)
Roe¦dean (school,
    England)
roe-deer
    plural roe-deer
Roeg, Nich¦olas
    (English film
    director)
roent¦gen +s
roent¦gen¦
        og¦raphy
roent¦gen¦ology
Roese¦lare (town,
    Belgium)
roe-stone +s (rock)
ro¦ga¦tion +s
ro¦ga¦tion¦al
Ro¦ga¦tion¦tide
Roger (name)
roger +s +ed +ing
    (on radio etc.; also
    coarse slang)
Rogers, Gin¦ger
    (American actress
    and dancer)
Rogers, Rich¦ard
    (British architect)
Roget, Peter Mark
    (English scholar)
rogue
    rogues
    rogued
    roguing
roguery
    roguer¦ies
rogues' gal¦lery
    rogues' gal¦ler¦ies
roguish
roguish¦ly
roguish¦ness
roil +s +ed +ing
rois¦ter +s +ed
    +ing
rois¦ter¦er +s

rois¦ter¦ing +s
rois¦ter¦ous
Ro¦land (paladin of
    Charlemagne)
Ro¦land *also*
    Row¦land
    (name)
role +s (part in play
    etc. △ roll)
role-play
role-playing
role re¦ver¦sal +s
roll +s +ed +ing
    (turn over;
    cylinder; list;
    bread. △ role)
roll¦able
Roll¦and, Ro¦main
    (French writer)
roll¦away +s
roll-back +s *noun*
roll bar +s
roll-call +s
roll¦er +s
roll¦er¦ball +s
Roll¦er¦blade +s
    Propr.
roll¦er¦blade
    roll¦er¦blades
    roll¦er¦bladed
    roll¦er¦blad¦ing
roll¦er¦blader +s
roller-coast +s
    +ed +ing
roll¦er coast¦er +s
    noun
roller-coaster +s
    +ed +ing *verb and
    attributive*
roll¦er skate
    roll¦er skates
    roll¦er skated
    roll¦er skat¦ing
roll¦er skater +s
roll¦er towel +s
roll¦lick +s +ed
    +ing
roll¦ing mill +s
roll¦ing pin +s
roll¦ing stock
Roll¦ing Stones,
    the (English rock
    group)
roll¦mop +s
roll-neck +s
roll-on +s *adjective
    and noun*
roll-on roll-off
    adjective
roll-out +s *noun*
roll-over +s *noun
    and attributive*

Rolls, Charles
Stew|art (English
motoring and
aviation pioneer)
Rolls-Royce +s
Propr.
roll-top +s
roll-top desk +s
roll-up +s
roly-poly
  roly-polies
ROM +s (= read-
only memory)
Rom
  Roma
  (male gypsy)
Ro|maic
ro|maine
ro|maji
Roman
roman (typeface)
roman-à-clef
  romans-à-clef
Ro|mance
  (languages)
ro|mance
  ro|man|ces
  ro|manced
  ro|man|cing
  (romantic
  atmosphere; love
  affair; story;
  exaggerate)
ro|man|cer +s
Roman de la rose
Ro|manes (the
  Romany language)
Ro|man|esque
roman-fleuve
  romans-fleuves
Ro|mania
Ro|ma|nian +s
Ro|man|ic
ro|man|isa|tion Br.
  (use
  romanization)
ro|man|ise Br. (use
  romanize)
  ro|man|ises
  ro|man|ised
  ro|man|is|ing
Ro|man|ish
Ro|man|ism
Ro|man|ist +s
ro|man|iza|tion
ro|man|ize
  ro|man|izes
  ro|man|ized
  ro|man|iz|ing
Ro|mano +s
Romano-British

Rom|anov (Russian
  dynasty)
Ro|mansh
  (dialects)
ro|man|tic +s
ro|man|tic|al|ly
ro|man|ti|cisa|tion
  Br. (use
  romanticization)
ro|man|ti|cise Br.
  (use romanticize)
  ro|man|ti|cises
  ro|man|ti|cised
  ro|man|ti|cis|ing
ro|man|ti|cism
ro|man|ti|cist +s
ro|man|ti|ciza|tion
ro|man|ti|cize
  ro|man|ti|cizes
  ro|man|ti|cized
  ro|man|ti|ciz|ing
Rom|any
  Rom|anies
Rom|berg,
  Sig|mund
  (Hungarian-born
  American
  composer)
Rome (capital of
  Italy)
Romeo +s (in
  Romeo and Juliet;
  male lover)
romer +s (map-
  reading device.
  △ roamer)
Rom|ish
Rom|mel, Erwin
  (German field
  marshal)
Rom|ney, George
  (English portrait
  painter)
rom|neya +s
romp +s +ed +ing
romp|er +s
romp|ing|ly
rompy
  romp|ier
  rompi|est
Rom|ulus Roman
  Mythology
Ron
Rona also Rhona
Ron|ald
Ronces|valles also
  Ronces|vaux
  (battle site, Spain)
ron|davel +s
ronde +s (dance)

ron|deau
  ron|deaux
  (poem. △ rondo)
ron|del +s
rondo +s (music.
  △ rondeau)
Ron|dônia (state,
  Brazil)
rone +s (gutter.
  △ roan)
roneo
  ro|neoes
  ro|neoed
  ro|neo|ing
ronin +s
Rönt|gen,
  Wil|helm
  Con|rad (German
  physicist)
rönt|gen +s (use
  roentgen)
rönt|gen|og|raphy
  (use
  roentgenography)
rönt|gen|ology
  (use
  roentgenology)
roo +s (= kangaroo.
  △ roux, rue)
rood +s (crucifix.
  △ rude)
rood-loft +s
rood-screen +s
roof
  roofs (or rooves)
  noun
roof +s +ed +ing
  verb
roof|age +s
roof|er +s
roof gar|den +s
roof|less
roof light +s
roof-rack +s
roof|scape +s
roof space +s
roof tile +s
roof|top +s
roof-tree +s (in
  roof)
rooi|bos
rooi|nek +s
  (offensive)
rook +s +ed +ing
rook|ery
  rook|er|ies
rookie +s
rook|let +s
rook|ling +s
room +s +ed +ing
  (space; enclosed

room (cont.)
  part of building; to
  lodge. △ rheum)
room|er +s
room|ette +s
room|ful +s
roomie +s (room-
  mate. △ rheumy,
  roomy)
room|ily
roomi|ness
room|ing house +s
room|mate Am. +s
room-mate Br. +s
room ser|vice
roomy
  room|ier
  roomi|est
  (spacious.
  △ rheumy,
  roomie)
Roose|velt,
  Elea|nor
  (American
  humanitarian)
Roose|velt,
  Frank|lin D.
  (American
  president)
Roose|velt,
  Theo|dore
  ('Teddy')
  (American
  president)
roost +s +ed +ing
roost|er +s
root +s +ed +ing
  (part of plant;
  basis; grow roots.
  △ route)
root|age +s
root beer +s
root canal +s
root|ed|ness
root|er +s
  (supporter.
  △ router)
roo|tle
  roo|tles
  roo|tled
  root|ling
root|less
root|let +s
root|like
root-mean-square
  +s
root sign +s
root|stock +s
rootsy
  root|sier
  root|si|est

rooty
  root|ier
  rooti|est
rooves (use
  roofs)
rope
  ropes
  roped
  rop|ing
rope|able
rope lad|der +s
rope|man|ship
rope-moulding +s
rope's end +s
rope-walk +s
rope-walker +s
rope-walking
rope|way +s
ropey (use ropy)
rope-yard +s
rope-yarn +s
ropi|ly
ropi|ness
rop|ing +s
ropy
  ropi|er
  ropi|est
roque
Roque|fort
  (cheese) *Propr.*
roque|laure +s
ro|quet +s +ed
  +ing (croquet)
ro|*quette* (= rocket,
  the herb)
Ror|aima (state,
  (Brazil; mountain,
  S. America)
ro-ro (= roll-on roll-
  off)
ror|qual +s
Ror|schach test +s
rort +s (trick.
  ⚠ wrought)
rorty
  rort|ier
  rorti|est
Rory
Ros *also* Roz
Rosa, Sal|va|tor
  (Italian painter)
Rosa
ros|ace +s
ros|aceous
Rosa|leen
Rosa|lie
Rosa|lind
rosa|line +s
Rosa|lyn
Rosa|mond *also*
  Rosa|mund

Rosa|mund *also*
  Rosa|mond
ros|an|il|ine +s
Ros|anna
Ros|anne *also*
  Rose|anne
ros|ar|ian +s
Ros|ario (port,
  Argentina)
ros|ar|ium
ros|ar|iums *or*
  ros|aria
ros|ary
ros|ar|ies
  (devotion; beads.
  ⚠ rosery)
Ros|cian
Ros|cius (Roman
  actor)
ros|coe +s
Ros|com|mon
  (county and town,
  Republic of
  Ireland)
Rose (name)
rose +s (flower;
  past tense of rise)
rosé +s (wine)
Rose|anne *also*
  Ros|anne
rose-apple +s
ros|eate
Ros|eau (capital of
  Dominica, West
  Indies)
rose|bay +s
Rose|bery, Lord
  (British prime
  minister)
rose|bowl +s
rose|bud +s
rose bush
  rose bushes
rose-chafer +s
  (beetle)
rose color *Am.*
rose-colored *Am.*
rose colour *Br.*
rose-coloured *Br.*
rose comb +s
rose-cut
rose dia|mond +s
rose-engine +s
rose-fish
  plural rose-fish *or*
  rose-fishes
rose-hip +s
rose leaf
  rose leaves
rose|less
rose|like
ro|sella +s

rose mad|der
rose|mal|ing
rose-mallow +s
Rose|mary (name)
rose|mary (herb)
rose nail +s
ros|eola (rash;
  disease)
ros|eo|lar
ros|eo|lous
rose pink +s *noun
  and adjective*
rose-pink *attributive*
rose-point +s
rose quartz
rose red +s *noun
  and adjective*
rose-red *attributive*
rose-root +s
  (plant)
ros|ery
ros|er|ies
  (rose garden.
  ⚠ rosary)
rose-tinted
rose tree +s
Ros|etta Stone
ros|ette +s
ros|et|ted
rose-water +s
rose-window +s
rose|wood +s
Rosh Hash|ana
Rosh Hash|anah
  (use Rosh
  Hashana)
Roshi +s
Rosi|cru|cian +s
Rosi|cru|cian|ism
Rosie
rosi|ly
rosin +s +ed +ing
  (resin, esp. the
  type obtained
  from turpentine.
  ⚠ resin)
Ros|in|ante (horse)
rosi|ness
ros|iny
Ros|kilde (port,
  Denmark)
ro|soglio +s (use
  rosolio)
ro|solio +s
RoSPA (= Royal
  Society for the
  Prevention of
  Accidents)
Ross, Diana
  (American pop
  singer)

Ross, James Clark
  (British explorer)
Ross, John (British
  explorer)
Ross, Ron|ald
  (British physician)
Ross and
  Crom|arty
  (former county,
  Scotland)
Ross
  De|pend|ency (in
  Antarctica)
Ros|sel|lini,
  Rob|erto (Italian
  film director)
Ros|setti,
  Chris|tina
  (English poet)
Ros|setti, Dante
  Gab|riel (English
  painter)
Ros|sini,
  Gioacch|ino
  (Italian composer)
Ross|lare (port,
  Republic of
  Ireland)
Ross Sea (off
  Antarctica)
Ross-shire (former
  county, Scotland)
Ros|tand,
  Ed|mond (French
  playwright)
ros|ter +s +ed
  +ing
Ros|tock (port,
  Germany)
Rostov-on-Don
  (city, Russia)
ros|tra
ros|tral
ros|tral|ly
ros|trate
ros|trated
ros|trif|er|ous
ros|tri|form
ros|trum
  ros|trums *or*
  ros|tra
rosy
  rosi|er
  rosi|est
rot
  rots
  rot|ted
  rot|ting
  (decay. ⚠ wrot)
rota +s (list; roster.
  ⚠ rotor)
Ro|tar|ian +s

Ro¦tary (society)
ro¦tary
  ro¦tar¦ies
Ro¦tary club +s
rotary-wing
  adjective
ro¦tat¦able
ro¦tate
  ro¦tates
  ro¦tated
  ro¦tat¦ing
ro¦ta¦tion +s
ro¦ta¦tion¦al
ro¦ta¦tion¦al¦ly
ro¦ta¦tive
ro¦ta¦tor +s
ro¦ta¦tory
ro¦ta¦vate
  ro¦ta¦vates
  ro¦ta¦vated
  ro¦ta¦vat¦ing
Ro¦ta¦va¦tor +s
  Propr.
rote +s (repetition.
  △ wrote)
rote learn¦ing
rote¦none
rot-gut
Roth, Philip
  (American
  novelist)
Rother¦ham (town,
  England)
Rothko, Mark
  (American
  painter)
Roths¦child,
  Meyer Am¦schel
  (German
  financier)
Roths¦child
  (banking-house)
ro¦ti¦fer +s
ro¦tis¦serie +s
ro¦to¦grav¦ure
rotor +s (rotating
  part. △ rota)
Ro¦to¦rua (resort,
  New Zealand)
roto¦till +s +ed
  +ing
Ro¦to¦va¦tor +s
  (alternative
  spelling of
  Rotavator) *Propr.*
rot-proof
rot¦ten
  rot¦tener
  rot¦ten¦est
rot¦ten¦ly
rot¦ten¦ness
rotten-stone

rot¦ter +s
Rot¦ter¦dam (city,
  the Netherlands)
Rott¦weiler +s
ro¦tund
ro¦tunda +s
ro¦tund¦ity
ro¦tund¦ly
Rou¦ault, Georges
  (French painter)
rou¦ble +s
rou¦cou +s
roué +s
Rouen (port,
  France)
rouge
  rouges
  rouged
  rou¦ging
rouge-et-noir
rough +s +ed +ing
  +er +est (coarse;
  treat roughly.
  △ ruff, ruffe)
rough¦age
rough-and-ready
rough-and-tumble
rough¦cast
  rough¦casts
  rough¦cast
  rough¦cast¦ing
rough-dry
  rough-dries
  rough-dried
  rough-drying
rough¦en +s +ed
  +ing
rough-handle
  rough-handles
  rough-handled
  rough-handling
rough-hew
  rough-hews
  rough-hewed
  rough-hewing
  rough-hewed *or*
  rough-hewn
rough hound +s
  (dogfish)
rough-house
  rough-houses
  rough-housed
  rough-housing
roughie +s
  (hooligan;
  outsider in horse
  race; unfair act.
  △ roughy)
rough¦ish
rough¦ly
rough¦neck +s
rough¦ness

rough-rider +s
rough¦shod
roughy
  rough¦ies
  (fish. △ roughie)
roul¦ade +s
roul¦eau
  roul¦eaux
Roul¦ers (French
  name for
  Roeselare)
roul¦ette +s
roul¦et¦ted
Rou¦mania (use
  Romania)
Rou¦ma¦nian (use
  Romanian)
Rou¦melia (use
  Rumelia)
round +s +ed +ing
round¦about +s
round-arm
  adjective
roundel +s
round¦elay +s
round¦er +s
Round¦head +s
round¦house +s
round¦ish
round¦ly
round¦ness
round-shouldered
rounds¦man
  rounds¦men
Round Tabler +s
round-the-clock
round-the-world
round-up +s *noun*
round¦worm +s
roup +s +ed +ing
roupy
rous¦able
rouse
  rouses
  roused
  rous¦ing
rouse¦about +s
rous¦er +s
rous¦ing¦ly
Rousse (use Ruse)
Rous¦seau, Henri
  (French painter)
Rous¦seau, Jean-
  Jacques (French
  philosopher)
Rous¦seau,
  Théo¦dore
  (French landscape
  painter)
Rous¦sil¦lon +s
  (wine; former
  French province)

roust +s +ed +ing
roust¦about +s
rout +s +ed +ing
  (defeat; riot; cut a
  groove)
route
  routes
  routed
  route¦ing
  (way taken.
  △ root)
router +s (tool.
  △ rooter)
rou¦tine
  rou¦tines
  rou¦tined
  rou¦tin¦ing
rou¦tine¦ly
rou¦tin¦isa¦tion *Br.*
  (use
  routinization)
rou¦tin¦ise *Br.* (use
  routinize)
  rou¦tin¦ises
  rou¦tin¦ised
  rou¦tin¦is¦ing
rou¦tin¦ism
rou¦tin¦ist +s
rou¦tin¦iza¦tion
rou¦tin¦ize
  rou¦tin¦izes
  rou¦tin¦ized
  rou¦tin¦iz¦ing
roux
  plural roux
  (sauce. △ roo,
  rue)
Ro¦van¦iemi (town,
  Finnish Lapland)
rove
  roves
  roved
  rov¦ing
rove bee¦tle +s
rover +s
Rovno (Russian
  name for Rivne)
row +s +ed +ing
  (series; propel
  boat; noise;
  quarrel; etc.
  △ rho, roe)
Rowan (name)
rowan +s (tree.
  △ rowen)
rowan-berry
  rowan-berries
row¦boat +s
row¦dily
row¦di¦ness
rowdy
  row¦dies

rowdy (*cont.*)
  row|dier
  row|di|est
rowdy|ism
Rowe, Nich|olas
  (English
  dramatist)
rowel
  rowels
  row|elled *Br.*
  row|eled *Am.*
  row|el|ling *Br.*
  ro|wel|ing *Am.*
rowen +s (second
  growth of grass.
  ⚠ rowan)
Row|ena
rower +s
row house +s
row|ing boat +s
row|ing ma|chine
  +s
Row|land *also*
  Ro|land
Row|land|son,
  Thomas (English
  artist)
row|lock +s
Rown|tree (family
  of English
  entrepreneurs and
  philanthropists)
Row|ton house +s
Rox|burgh|shire
  (former county,
  Scotland)
Roy
royal +s
royal blue +s *noun*
  and adjective
royal-blue
  attributive
roy|al|ism
roy|al|ist +s
roy|al|is|tic
roy|al|ly
roy|alty
  roy|al|ties
Royce, Henry
  (English engine
  designer)
Roy|ston (town,
  England)
Roz *also* Ros
roz|zer +s
rub
  rubs
  rubbed
  rub|bing
rub-a-dub
  rub-a-dubs

rub-a-dub (*cont.*)
  rub-a-dubbed
  rub-a-dubbing
ru|bato
  ru|ba|tos *or*
  ru|bati
Rub'al Khali
  (desert, Arabian
  Peninsula)
rub|ber +s
rub|beri|ness
rub|ber|ise *Br.* (use
  rubberize)
  rub|ber|ises
  rub|ber|ised
  rub|ber|is|ing
rub|ber|ize
  rub|ber|izes
  rub|ber|ized
  rub|ber|iz|ing
rubber-like
rub|ber|neck +s
  +ed +ing
rub|ber plant +s
rub|ber stamp +s
  noun
rubber-stamp +s
  +ed +ing *verb*
rub|ber tree +s
rub|bery
rub|bing +s
rub|bish
  rub|bishes
  rub|bished
  rub|bish|ing
rub|bishy
rub|bity
rubbity-dub
rub|ble
rub|bly
Rub|bra, Ed|mund
  (English
  composer)
rub-down +s *noun*
rube +s
ru|be|fa|cient +s
ru|be|fac|tion
ru|befy
  ru|be|fies
  ru|be|fied
  ru|be|fy|ing
ru|bella (virus;
  German measles.
  ⚠ rubeola)
ru|bel|lite +s
Ru|bens, Peter
  Paul (Flemish
  painter)
ru|beola (measles.
  ⚠ rubella)
Ru|bi|con (stream,
  Italy)

ru|bi|con +s (in
  piquet)
ru|bi|cund
ru|bi|cund|ity
ru|bid|ium
ru|bify (use rubefy)
  ru|bi|fies
  ru|bi|fied
  ru|bi|fy|ing
ru|bigin|ous
Rubik's cube +s
  Propr.
Rub|in|stein,
  Anton (Russian
  composer)
Rub|in|stein,
  Artur (Polish-
  born American
  pianist)
Rub|in|stein,
  Hel|ena
  (American
  beautician)
ruble +s (use
  rouble)
ru|bric +s
ru|bric|al
ru|bri|cate
  ru|bri|cates
  ru|bri|cated
  ru|bri|cat|ing
ru|bri|ca|tion
ru|bri|ca|tor +s
ru|bri|cian +s
ru|bri|cism
ru|bri|cist +s
rub-up +s
Ruby (name)
ruby
  ru|bies
  ru|bied
  ruby|ing
  (precious stone;
  dye ruby-colour)
ruby-tail +s
ruche
  ruches
  ruched
  ruch|ing
ruck +s +ed +ing
ruckle
  ruckles
  ruckled
  ruck|ling
ruck|sack +s
ruckus
  ruck|uses
ruc|tion +s
ru|da|ceous
rud|beckia +s
rudd
  plural rudd

rud|der +s
rud|der|less
rud|dily
rud|di|ness
rud|dle
  rud|dles
  rud|dled
  rud|dling
rud|dock +s
ruddy
  rud|dies
  rud|died
  ruddy|ing
  rud|dier
  rud|di|est
rude
  ruder
  rud|est
rude|ly
rude|ness
ru|deral +s
rudery
  ruder|ies
ru|di|ment +s
ru|di|men|tar|ily
ru|di|men|tari
          ness
ru|di|men|tary
rud|ish
Ru|dolf *also*
  Ru|dolph
Ru|dolf, Lake
  (former name of
  Lake Turkana)
Ru|dolph *also*
  Ru|dolf
Rudra
Rud|ras
rue
  rues
  rued
  rue|ing *or* ruing
  (shrub; regret.
  ⚠ roo, roux)
rue|ful
rue|ful|ly
rue|ful|ness
ruf|es|cence
ruf|es|cent
ruff +s +ed +ing
  (collar; bird;
  trump at cards.
  ⚠ rough, ruffe)
ruffe +s (fish.
  ⚠ rough, ruff)
ruf|fian +s
ruf|fian|ism
ruf|fian|ly
ruf|fle
  ruf|fles
  ruf|fled
  ruf|fling

ruff|like
rufi|yaa
plural rufi|yaa
ruf|ous
Rufus (name)
Rufus, Wil|liam
(William II of
England)
rug +s
Rug|beian +s
Rugby (town and
school, England)
rugby (football)
Rugby League
rugby play|er +s
Rugby Union
Rügen (island,
Baltic Sea)
rug|ged
rug|ged|isa|tion
(use
ruggedization)
rug|ged|ise (use
ruggedize)
rug|ged|ises
rug|ged|ised
rug|ged|is|ing
rug|ged|iza|tion
rug|ged|ize
rug|ged|izes
rug|ged|ized
rug|ged|iz|ing
rug|ged|ly
rug|ged|ness
rug|ger
ru|gosa +s
ru|gose
ru|gose|ly
ru|gos|ity
Ruhr (river and
region, Germany)
ruin +s +ed +ing
ruin|ation
ruin|ous
ruin|ous|ly
ruin|ous|ness
Ruis|dael, Jacob
van (Dutch
painter)
Ruiz de Alar|cón y
Men|doza, Juan
(Spanish
playwright)
rule
rules
ruled
rul|ing
rule book +s
rule-governed
rule|less
ruler +s
ruler|ship +s

rul|ing +s
rum
rums
rum|mer
rum|mest
Ru|mania (use
Romania)
Ru|ma|nian +s
(use Romanian)
Ru|mansh (use
Romansh)
rumba
rum|bas
rum|baed *or*
rumba'd
rumba|ing
rum baba +s
rum|ble
rum|bles
rum|bled
rum|bling
rum|bler +s
rum|bling +s
rum|bus|tious
rum|bus|tious|ly
rum|bus|tious|
ness
Ru|melia (former
region, S.E.
Europe)
rumen
ru|mens *or*
ru|mina
Rumi (Persian
Islamic poet)
ru|min|ant +s
ru|min|ate
ru|min|ates
ru|min|ated
ru|min|at|ing
ru|min|ation +s
ru|mina|tive
ru|mina|tive|ly
ru|min|ator +s
rumly
rum|mage
rum|mages
rum|maged
rum|ma|ging
rum|ma|ger +s
rum|mer +s
rummy
rum|mier
rum|mi|est
rum|ness
rumor *Am.* +s +ed
+ing
ru|mor|mon|ger
Am. +s
ru|mor|mon|ger|
ing *Am.*

ru|mour *Br.* +s +ed
+ing
rumour-monger
Br. +s
rumour-
mongering *Br.*
rump +s
rum|ple
rum|ples
rum|pled
rum|pling
rump|less
rum|ply
rum|pus
rum|puses
rumpy
rum|pies
rumpy-pumpy
run
runs
ran
run|ning
run
run|about +s
run-around +s
noun
run|away +s
run|cible spoon +s
run|cin|ate
Run|corn (town,
England)
run|dale +s
run|down +s *noun*
run-down *adjective*
rune +s
rune-staff +s
rung +s (of ladder;
past participle of
ring. △ wrung)
runged
rung|less
runic
run-in +s *noun*
run|let +s
run|nable
run|nel +s
run|ner +s
runner-up
runners-up
running-board +s
run|ning race +s
run|ning shoe +s
runny
run|nier
run|ni|est
Runny|mede (site
of signing of
Magna Carta,
England)
run-off +s *noun and
attributive*
run-of-the-mill

run-out +s *noun*
runt +s
run-through +s
noun
runty
run-up +s *noun*
run|way +s
Run|yon, Damon
(American writer)
rupee +s
Ru|pert (name)
Ru|pert, Prince
(English Royalist
general)
Ru|pert's Land (in
Canada)
ru|pes|trian
ru|piah +s
rup|tur|able
rup|ture
rup|tures
rup|tured
rup|tur|ing
rural
rur|al|isa|tion *Br.*
(use ruralization)
rur|al|ise *Br.* (use
ruralize)
rur|al|ises
rur|al|ised
rur|al|is|ing
rur|al|ism
rur|al|ist +s
rur|al|ity
rur|al|ities
rur|al|iza|tion
rur|al|ize
rur|al|izes
rur|al|ized
rur|al|iz|ing
rur|al|ly
ruri|decan|al
Rurik +s (Russian
dynasty)
Ruri|ta|nia
Ruri|ta|nian +s
rusa +s
Ruse (city,
Bulgaria)
ruse +s (trick)
rush
rushes
rushed
rush|ing
Rush|die, Sal|man
(Indian-born
British novelist)
rush|er +s
rush hour +s *noun*
rush-hour *adjective*
rush|ing|ly
rush|light

rush|like
Rush|more,
   Mount (in USA)
rushy
   rush|ier
   rushi|est
rusk +s
Rus'kin, John
   (English art and
   social critic)
Russ
Rus|sell (name)
Rus|sell, Ber|trand
   (3rd Earl Russell,
   British
   philosopher)
Rus|sell, George
   Wil|liam (Irish
   poet)
Rus|sell, Henry
   Nor'ris (American
   astronomer)
Rus|sell, John (1st
   Earl Russell,
   British prime
   minister)
rus'set +s
rus'sety
Rus|sia +s
Rus|sian +s
Rus|sian|isa'tion
   Br. (use
   Russianization)
Rus|sian|ise Br.
   (use Russianize)
   Rus|sian|ises
   Rus|sian|ised
   Rus|sian|is'ing
Rus|sian|iza'tion
Rus|sian|ize
   Rus|sian|izes
   Rus|sian|ized
   Rus|sian|iz'ing
Rus|sian|ness
Rus|si'fi|ca'tion
Rus|sify
   Rus|si|fies
   Rus|si|fied
   Rus|si'fy|ing
Russki +s (often
   offensive)
Russo-Japanese
Russo|phile +s
Russo|phobe +s
Russo|pho'bia
rust +s +ed +ing
Rust Belt (region,
   USA)
rust belt
   (generally)
rus'tic +s
rus'tic|al'ly

rus'ti|cate
   rus'ti|cates
   rus'ti|cated
   rus'ti|cat'ing
rus'ti|ca'tion +s
rus'ti|city
rust|ily
rusti|ness
rus'tle
   rus'tles
   rus'tled
   rust|ling
rust|ler +s
rust|less
rust|ling +s
rust|proof +s +ed
   +ing
rustre +s Heraldry
rusty
   rust|ier
   rusti|est
rut
   ruts
   rut'ted
   rut'ting
ru'ta|baga +s
Ruth (Bible; name)
Ruth, Babe
   (American
   baseball player)
Ru|the'nia (region,
   Ukraine)
ru|the'nium
Ruth'er|ford,
   Er'nest (New
   Zealand physicist)
Ruth'er|ford,
   Mar|ga'ret
   (English actress)
ruth'er|ford'ium
ruth|less
ruth|less'ly
ruth|less|ness
ru'tile +s
Rut|land (former
   county, England)
rut|tish
rutty
   rut|tier
   rut'ti|est
Ru'wen|zori
   (national park,
   Uganda)
Ruys|dael, Jacob
   van (use
   Ruisdael)
Rwanda
Rwan|dan +s
Rwan|dese
   plural Rwan|dese
Ryan

Rya'zan (city,
   Russia)
Ry|binsk (city,
   Russia)
Ryder, Sue
   (English
   philanthropist)
Ryder Cup +s (golf
   tournament)
rye +s (grain. △ rai,
   wry)
rye|grass
   rye|grasses
Ryle, Gil|bert
   (English
   philosopher)
Ryle, Mar|tin
   (English
   astronomer)
ry|okan +s
ryot +s (bird.
   △ riot)
Rysy (mountain,
   Poland)
Ryu|kyu Is|lands
   (in W. Pacific)
Ryurik +s (use
   Rurik)

Ss

Saadi (use Sadi)
Saale (river,
   Germany)
Saar (river, France
   and Germany)
Saar|brücken (city,
   Germany)
Saar|land (state,
   Germany)
sab
   sabs
   sabbed
   sab|bing
Saba (island,
   Netherlands
   Antilles)
saba|dilla +s
Sa|baean +s (of
   ancient Yemen.
   △ Sabian)
Sabah (state,
   Malaysia)
Saba|ism
Saba|oth
Sab|ba|tar|ian +s
Sab|ba|tar|ian|ism
sab|bath +s
sab|bat|ic +s
sab|bat|ic|al +s
sab|bat|ic|al|ly
sab|ba|tisa'tion Br.
   (use
   sabbatization)
sab|ba|tise Br. (use
   sabbatize)
   sab|ba|tises
   sab|ba|tised
   sab|ba|tis'ing
sab|ba|tiza'tion
sab|ba|tize
   sab|ba|tizes
   sab|ba|tized
   sab|ba|tiz'ing
Sa|bel|lian +s
saber Am. +s +ed
   +ing (Br. sabre)
saber-bill Am. +s
   (Br. sabre-bill)
saber-cut Am. +s
   (Br. sabre-cut)
saber-rattling Am.
   +s (Br. sabre-
   rattling)
saber|tooth Am. +s
   (Br. sabretooth)
saber-toothed Am.
   (Br. sabre-
   toothed)

Sa¦bian +s (of
ancient religious
sect. △ Sabaean)
sab¦icu +s
Sabin, Al¦bert
Bruce (Russian-
born American
microbiologist;
vaccine)
Sab¦ina
Sab¦ine +s
sable +s
sabled
sably
sabot +s
sabo|tage
sabo|tages
sabo|taged
sabo|ta¦ging
sab|oted
sabo|teur +s
sabra +s
Sab|rata
(= Sabratha)
Sab|ra¦tha (ancient
city, Libya)
sabre Br.
sabres
sabred
sab¦ring
(Am. saber)
sabre-bill Br. +s
(Am. saber-bill)
sabre-cut Br. +s
(Am. saber-cut)
sabre-rattling Br.
+s (Am. saber-
rattling)
sabre|tache +s
sabre|tooth Br. +s
(Am. sabertooth)
sabre-toothed Br.
(Am. saber-
toothed)
sab|reur +s
sabre|wing +s
Sab¦rina
sac +s (baglike
cavity. △ sack)
sac|cade +s
sac|cad¦ic
sac|cate
sac¦char¦ide +s
sac¦char¦im¦eter
+s
sac¦char¦im¦etry
sac¦charin +s noun
sac¦char¦ine
adjective
sac¦charo|gen¦ic
sac¦char¦om¦eter
+s

sac¦char¦om¦etry
sac¦char¦ose
sac¦ci¦form
sac|cu|lar
sac|cu|late
sac|cu|lated
sac|cu|la¦tion +s
sac|cule +s
sacer|dot¦age
sacer|dotal
sacer|dot¦al|ism
sacer|dot¦al|ist +s
sacer|dot¦al|ly
Sacha also Sasha
sa|chem +s
Sach¦er|torte
Sach¦er|tor¦ten
sa|chet +s
Sa|chev¦er|ell
Sachs, Hans
(German poet)
sack +s +ed +ing
(large bag; wine;
dismiss; plunder.
△ sac)
sack|able
sack|but +s
sack|cloth +s
sack¦er +s
sack|ful +s
sack|ing +s
sack|less
sack|like
Sackville-West,
Vita (English
novelist)
sacra
sac|ral
sac|ra|ment +s
sac|ra|men|tal
sac|ra|men|tal|ism
sac|ra|men|tal|ist
+s
sac|ra|men|tal|ity
sac|ra|men|tal¦ly
sac|ra|ment|arian
+s
Sac¦ra|mento (city,
USA)
sac|rar¦ium
sac|raria
sac¦red
sac¦red¦ly
sac¦red|ness
sac¦ri|fice
sac¦ri|fices
sac¦ri|ficed
sac¦ri|ficing
sac¦ri|fi¦cial
sac¦ri|fi¦cial|ly
sac¦ri|lege +s
sac¦ri|le¦gious

sac¦ri|le¦gious|ly
sac¦ring
sac¦rist +s
sac¦ris|tan +s
sac¦risty
sac|ris¦ties
sacro|iliac
sacro|sanct
sacro|sanct|ity
sac¦rum
sacra
sad
sad¦der
sad|dest
Sadat, Anwar al-
(Egyptian
president)
Sad¦dam Hus¦sein
(Iraqi president)
sad¦den +s +ed
+ing
sad|dish
sad|dle
sad|dles
sad|dled
sad|dling
saddle|back +s
saddle|backed
saddle|bag +s
sad¦dle bow +s
saddle-cloth +s
saddle-horse +s
saddle|less
sad|dler +s
sad|dlery
sad¦dler|ies
saddle-sore
sad¦dle stitch noun
sad¦dle tree +s
(saddle frame;
tree)
Sad|du|cean
Sad|du|cee +s
Sad|du|cee|ism
Sade, Mar|quis de
(French writer)
sadhu +s
Sadi (Persian poet)
Sadie (name)
sad-iron +s
sad|ism
sad|ist +s
sad|is¦tic
sad|is¦tic|al|ly
Sad|ler's Wells
(theatre, London)
sadly
sad|ness
sad|nesses
sado|maso¦chism
sado|maso¦chist
+s

sado|maso¦chis¦tic
sae¦ter +s (pasture.
△ setter)
Safa¦qis
(alternative name
for Sfax)
sa|fari +s
Safa|vid +s
safe
safes
safer
saf¦est
safe-blower +s
safe-breaker +s
safe-cracker +s
safe|guard +s +ed
+ing
safe keep|ing
safe|ly
safe|ness
safety
safe|ties
safety belt +s
safety catch
safety catches
safety net +s
safety pin +s
safety valve +s
saf|flower +s
saf|fron +s
saf|froned
saf|frony
saf|ranin +s
saf|ran|ine +s
sag
sags
sagged
sag|ging
saga +s
sa|ga¦cious
sa|ga¦cious|ly
sa|ga¦city
saga|more +s
Sagan, Fran|çoise
(French writer)
sage +s
sage|brush
sage green +s noun
and adjective
sage-green
attributive
sage grouse
plural sage grouse
sage|ly
sage|ness
sage|ship +s
sag|gar +s
sag|ger +s (use
saggar)
saggy
sag|gier
sag|gi|est

sag|itta +s
sag|it|tal
Sag|it|tar|ian +s
Sag|it|tar|ius
  (constellation;
  sign of zodiac)
sag|it|tate
sago +s
sa|guaro +s
Sa|guia el Hamra
  (river and region,
  Western Sahara)
sagy
Saha, Megh|nad
  (Indian physicist)
Sa|hara (desert,
  Africa)
Sa|haran +s
Sahel (savannah
  region, W. Africa)
Sa|hel|ian (of or
  pertaining to this
  region)
sahib +s
sa|huaro +s (use
  saguaro)
Said, Ed|ward W.
  (American critic)
said (past tense and
  past participle of
  say)
Saida (Arabic name
  for Sidon)
saiga +s
Sai|gon (city,
  Vietnam)
sail +s +ed +ing
  (on boat; travel on
  the sea; move
  easily. △ sale)
sail|able
sail-arm +s
sail|bag +s
sail|board +s
sail|board|er +s
sail|board|ing
sail|boat +s
sail|cloth +s
sail|er +s (ship.
  △ sailor)
sail|fish
  plural sail|fish
sail-fluke +s
sail|ing +s
sail|ing boat +s
sail|ing mas|ter +s
sail|ing ship +s
sail|ing yacht +s
sail|less
sail|maker +s
sail|or +s (seaman.
  △ sailer)

sail|or|ing
sail|or|less
sail|or|ly
sailor-man
  sailor-men
sail|plane +s
  (glider)
Sai|maa Canal (in
  Finland)
sain|foin +s
Sains|bury, John
  James (English
  grocer)
saint +s +ed +ing
St Al|bans (city,
  England)
St An|drews (town,
  Scotland)
St An|drew's cross
St An|thony cross
St An|thony's
  cross
St An|thony's fire
St Anton (ski
  resort, Austria)
St Ber|nard +s
  (dog)
St Ber|nard Pass
  ('Great' and
  'Little', in the
  European Alps)
St Chris|to|pher
  and Nevis, The
  Fed|er|ation of
  (official name of
  St Kitts and
  Nevis)
St Croix (island, US
  Virgin Islands)
St David's (city,
  Wales)
Saint-Denis
  (suburb, Paris;
  capital of
  Réunion)
saint|dom +s
Sainte-Beuve,
  Charles
  Au|gus|tin
  (French critic)
St Elmo's fire
St Émil|ion +s
  (wine)
St-Étienne (city,
  France)
St Eu|sta|tius
  (Caribbean island)
St George's
  (capital of
  Grenada, West
  Indies)

St George's
  Chan|nel
  (between Wales
  and Ireland)
St Got|thard Pass
  (in Switzerland)
St Hel|ena (island,
  S. Atlantic)
St Hel|ens (town,
  England)
St Hel|ens, Mount
  (volcano, USA)
St Hel|ier (town,
  Jersey, Channel
  Islands)
saint|hood +s
St James's, Court
  of (British royal
  court)
St James's Pal|ace
  (in London)
St John (island, US
  Virgin Islands)
St John
  Am|bu|lance
  (first-aid
  organization)
St John's (cities,
  Canada and
  Antigua)
St John's wort
St Kilda (group of
  Scottish islands)
St Kitts and Nevis
  (islands, West
  Indies)
Saint Laur|ent,
  Yves (French
  couturier)
St Law|rence
  River (in N.
  America)
St Law|rence
  Sea|way
St Leger (horse
  race)
saint|like
saint|li|ness
saint|ling +s
St Louis (city, USA)
St Lucia (island,
  West Indies)
saint|ly
  saint|lier
  saint|li|est
St Malo (port,
  France)
St Mar|tin (island,
  Caribbean Sea)
St Mor|itz (winter-
  sports resort,
  Switzerland)

St-Nazaire (port,
  France)
Saint Nico|las
  (town, Belgium)
St Pan|cras
  (railway station,
  London)
St Paul (city, USA)
saint|paulia +s
St Peter Port
  (capital of
  Guernsey)
St Peters|burg
  (city, Russia)
St Pierre and
  Mique|lon (island
  group off
  Newfoundland)
St Pöl|ten (city,
  Austria)
Saint-Saëns,
  Cam|ille (French
  composer)
saint|ship +s
Saint-Simon,
  Claude-Henri de
  Rouv|roy, Comte
  de (French social
  reformer)
Saint-Simon,
  Louis de
  Rouv|roy, Duc
  de (French writer)
St So|phia
  (museum,
  Istanbul)
St Ste|phens
  (House of
  Commons)
St Thomas (island,
  US Virgin Islands)
St Trin|ian's
  (fictional school)
St-Tropez (resort,
  France)
St Vin|cent (island,
  West Indies)
St Vin|cent, Cape
  (in Portugal)
St Vitus's dance
Sai|pan (island, W.
  Pacific)
saith (archaic
  = says)
saithe
  plural saithe
  (fish)
Sa|jama (mountain,
  Bolivia)
Sakai (city, Japan)
sake +s (in 'for my
  sake' etc.;

sake (*cont.*)
  Japanese drink.
  ⚠ saki)
saker +s
sa¦keret +s
Sakha, Re¦pub¦lic
  of (official name
  of Yakutia)
Sakh¦alin (island,
  Sea of Okhotsk)
Sakh¦arov,
  An¦drei (Russian
  nuclear physicist)
Saki (British writer)
saki +s (monkey.
  ⚠ sake)
Sakta +s
Sakti
Sakt¦ism
sal +s
sa¦laam +s +ed
  +ing
sal¦able (use
  saleable)
sal¦acious
sal¦acious¦ly
sal¦acious¦ness
sal¦acity
salad +s (food)
salad dress¦ing +s
sal¦ade +s (helmet)
Sala¦din (sultan of
  Egypt and Syria)
Salam, Abdus
  (Pakistani
  physicist)
Sala¦manca (city,
  Spain)
sala¦man¦der +s
sala¦man¦drian
sala¦man¦drine
sala¦man¦droid +s
sa¦lami +s
Sala¦mis (island,
  Saronic Gulf,
  Greece)
sal am¦mo¦niac
sal¦an¦gane
Sa¦lang Pass
  (Afghanistan)
sal¦ar¦iat +s
sal¦ar¦ied
sal¦ary
  sal¦ar¦ies
sal¦ary¦man
  sal¦ary¦men
Sala¦zar, An¦tonio
  de Oli¦veira
  (Portuguese prime
  minister)
sal¦bu¦ta¦mol

sal¦chow +s
sale +s (selling.
  ⚠ sail)
sale¦abil¦ity
sale¦able
Salem (cities, USA
  and India)
salep +s
sal¦er¦atus
sale ring +s
Sal¦erno (port,
  Italy)
sale¦room +s
sales force +s
sales¦girl +s
Sal¦es¦ian +s
sales¦lady
  sales¦ladies
sales¦man
  sales¦men
sales¦man¦ship
sales¦per¦son
  sales¦per¦sons *or*
  sales¦people
sales¦room +s
sales¦woman
  sales¦women
Sal¦ford (city,
  England)
Sa¦lian +s
Salic +s
sali¦cet +s
sali¦cin
sali¦cine
sal¦icional +s
sa¦li¦cyl¦ate +s
sali¦cyl¦ic
sa¦li¦ence
sa¦li¦ency
sa¦li¦ent +s
sa¦li¦en¦tian +s
sa¦li¦ent¦ly
Sali¦eri, An¦tonio
  (Italian composer)
sal¦ifer¦ous
sal¦ina +s
sa¦line +s
Sal¦in¦ger, J. D.
  (American writer)
salin¦isa¦tion *Br.*
  (use salinization)
sal¦in¦ity
salin¦iza¦tion
salin¦om¦eter +s
Salis¦bury (city,
  England; former
  name of Harare)
Salis¦bury, Lord
  (British prime
  minister)
Sa¦lish
  plural Sa¦lish

sal¦iva +s
sal¦iv¦ary
sali¦vate
  sali¦vates
  sali¦vated
  sali¦vat¦ing
sali¦va¦tion
Salk vac¦cine
sal¦lee +s (tree.
  ⚠ sally)
sal¦len¦ders
sal¦let +s
sal¦low +s +ed
  +ing
sal¦low¦ish
sal¦low¦ness
sal¦lowy
Sal¦lust (Roman
  historian)
Sally (name)
sally
  sal¦lies
  sal¦lied
  sally¦ing
  (sortie etc.; part of
  bell-rope)
sally-hole +s
Sally Lunn +s
sally-port +s
sal¦ma¦gundi +s
sal¦ma¦nazar +s
salmi +s
sal¦mon
  plural sal¦mon *or*
  sal¦mons
sal¦mon¦ella
  sal¦mon¦el¦lae
sal¦mon¦el¦losis
sal¦monid +s
salmon-ladder +s
sal¦mon¦oid +s
sal¦mon pink +s
  noun and adjective
salmon-pink
  attributive
sal¦mon trout
  plural sal¦mon
  trout *or* sal¦mon
  trouts
sal¦mony
Sal¦ome *Bible*
Salon, the (French
  art exhibition)
salon +s (room)
Sal¦on¦ica
  (alternative name
  for Thessaloníki)
sal¦oon +s
saloon-keeper +s
Salop (alternative
  name for
  Shropshire)

sal¦op¦ette +s
Sal¦op¦ian +s
sal¦pi¦glos¦sis
sal¦pin¦gec¦tomy
  sal¦pin¦
          gec¦to¦mies
sal¦pin¦gitis
salsa +s
sal¦sify
  sal¦si¦fies
SALT (= Strategic
  Arms Limitation
  Talks)
salt +s +ed +ing
salt-and-pepper
  attributive
sal¦tar¦ello
  sal¦tar¦el¦los *or*
  sal¦tar¦elli
sal¦ta¦tion +s
sal¦ta¦tor¦ial
sal¦ta¦tory
salt¦bush
  salt¦bushes
salt-cat +s
salt cellar +s
salt¦er +s
salt¦ern +s
salt-glaze
  salt-glazes
  salt-glazed
  salt-glazing
salt grass
  salt grasses
sal¦ti¦grade +s
Sal¦tillo (city,
  Mexico)
salti¦ness
salt¦ing +s
sal¦tire +s *Heraldry*
sal¦tire¦wise
salt¦ish
Salt Lake City
  (city, USA)
salt¦less
salt lick +s
salt¦ly
salt marsh
  salt marshes
salt mine +s
salt¦ness
salt pan +s
salt¦peter *Am.*
salt¦petre *Br.*
salt shaker +s
salt spoon +s
sal¦tus
  plural sal¦tus
salt water *noun*
salt-water
  attributive
salt well +s

salt works
  plural salt works
salt|wort +s
salty
  salt|ier
  salti|est
sa¦lu¦bri¦ous
sa¦lu¦bri¦ous¦ly
sa¦lu¦bri¦ous|ness
sa¦lu¦brity
sa¦luki +s
salu|tar¦ily
salu|tary
sa¦lu¦ta¦tion +s
sa¦lu¦ta¦tion|al
sa¦lu¦ta¦tor¦ian +s
sa¦lu¦ta¦tory
sa¦lute
  sa¦lutes
  sa¦luted
  sa¦lut¦ing
sa¦luter +s
sa¦lut¦ing base +s
salv|able
Sal¦va¦dor (port,
  Brazil)
Sal¦va¦dor, El (in
  Central America)
Sal¦va¦dor|ean +s
sal|vage
  sal|vages
  sal|vaged
  sal|va¦ging
sal|vage|able
sal|va¦ger +s
sal|va¦tion
sal|va¦tion|ism
sal|va¦tion|ist +s
salve
  salves
  salved
  salv|ing
  (ointment; soothe)
sal¦ver +s (tray.
  △ salvor)
sal¦via +s
Salvo +s (member
  of Salvation Army)
salvo
  salvos *or* sal|voes
  (gunfire)
salvo +s (saving
  clause; excuse)
sal vola|tile
sal¦vor +s
  (salvager.
  △ salver)
Sal|ween (river, SE
  Asia)
Sal¦yut +s (Soviet
  space stations)

Salz|burg (state
  and city, Austria)
Salz|git¦ter (city,
  Germany)
Salz|kam¦mer|gut
  (area, Austria)
SAM (= surface-to-
  air missile)
Sam (name)
sam|adhi
Sam|an¦tha
Samar (island,
  Philippines)
Sam|ara (city,
  Russia)
sam¦ara +s
  (winged seed)
Sam|aria (ancient
  Hebrew city and
  surrounding
  region)
Sam¦ar|inda (city,
  Indonesia)
Sa¦mar¦itan +s
Sa¦mar¦it¦an|ism
sa¦mar¦ium
Sam¦ar|kand (city,
  central Asia)
Sam|arra (city,
  Iraq)
Sama-veda
  Hinduism
samba
  sam¦bas
  sam¦baed *or*
  samba'd
  samba|ing
  (dance)
sam|bar +s (large
  deer)
sam|bhar +s (use
  sambar)
Sambo
  Sam¦bos *or*
  Sam|boes
  (*offensive*)
Sam Browne +s
sam|bur +s (use
  sambar)
same
samel
same|ness
samey
samey|ness
samfu +s
Sam|hain +s
Sami (Lapps;
  Lappish)
Sa¦mian +s
sami|sen +s
sam¦ite +s
sam¦iz|dat +s

sam|let +s
Sammy
Sam|nite +s
Samoa (group of
  Polynesian
  islands)
Sa¦moan +s
Samos (island,
  Aegean Sea)
sa¦mosa +s
samo|var +s
Sam|oyed +s
Sam|oy|ed|ic
samp
sam¦pan +s
sam¦phire +s
sam¦ple
  sam¦ples
  sam¦pled
  sam¦pling
sam¦pler +s
sam¦pling +s
sam|sara
sam|sar¦ic
sam|skara +s
Sam|son *Bible*
Sam|son post +s
Sam¦son's post +s
  (use Samson
  post)
Sam|uel (*Bible*;
  name)
sam|urai
  plural sam|urai
San
  plural San
  (African aboriginal
  Bushman)
san +s
  (= sanatorium)
Sa¦na'a (capital of
  Yemen)
San An|dreas fault
  (in California)
San An¦drés
  (island, Caribbean
  Sea)
San An¦tonio (city,
  USA)
sana|tive
sana|tor¦ium
  sana|tor¦iums *or*
  sana|toria
sana|tory (healing.
  △ sanitary)
san|ben¦ito +s
San Car¦los de
  Bari|loche (ski
  resort, Argentina)
San¦chi (site of
  Buddhist shrines,
  India)

San¦cho Panza
  (fictional
  character)
sanc¦ti¦fi¦ca¦tion
sanc¦ti¦fier +s
sanc¦tify
  sanc¦ti|fies
  sanc¦ti|fied
  sanc¦ti¦fy|ing
sanc¦ti¦mo¦ni|ous
sanc¦ti¦mo¦ni|
      ous|ly
sanc¦ti¦mo¦ni¦ous|
      ness
sanc¦ti¦mony
sanc|tion +s +ed
  +ing
sanc|tion|able
sanc¦ti|tude
sanc|tity
  sanc|tities
sanc|tu|ary
  sanc|tu|ar¦ies
sanc|tum +s
sanc|tum
  sanc|torum
  sancta
  sanc|torum *or*
  sanc|tum
  sanc|tor¦ums
sanc|tus
Sand, George
  (French novelist)
sand +s +ed +ing
  (grains etc.
  △ sans)
san|dal
  san|dals
  san|dalled *Br.*
  san|daled *Am.*
  san|dal|ling *Br.*
  san|dal|ing *Am.*
san|dal tree +s
san¦dal|wood +s
San|dal|wood
  Is|land
  (alternative name
  for Sumba)
san|darac
san|dar¦ach (use
  sandarac)
sand|bag
  sand|bags
  sand|bagged
  sand|bag|ging
sand|bag|ger +s
sand|bank +s
sand|bar +s
sand-bath +s
sand-bed +s
sand|blast +s +ed
  +ing

sand|blast|er +s
sand|box
  sand|boxes
sand|boy +s
sand|cas|tle +s
sand cloud +s
sand-crack +s
sand dune +s
sand|er +s (person
  or thing that
  sands)
san|der|ling +s
san|ders
  plural san|ders
  (tree)
sand flea +s
sand|fly
  sand|flies
sand-glass
  sand-glasses
  (hourglass)
sand-groper +s
sand|grouse
  plural
  sand|grouse
san|dhi
sand|hill +s
sand|hog +s
sand-hopper +s
Sand|hurst (Royal
  Military Academy,
  England)
San Diego (city,
  USA)
sandi|ness
San|di|nista +s
san|di|ver
sand|like
sand|lot +s
sand|man
  sand|men
sand mar|tin +s
sand|paper +s +ed
  +ing
sand|piper +s
sand|pit +s
San|dra
San|dring|ham
  House (royal
  residence,
  England)
sand-shoe +s
sand-skipper +s
sand|soap +s
sand|stock
sand|stone +s
sand|storm +s
Sand|wich (town,
  England)
sand|wich
  sand|wiches
  sand|wiched

sand|wich (*cont.*)
  sand|wich|ing
  (food)
sandwich-board
  +s
Sand|wich
  Is|lands (former
  name of Hawaii)
sandwich-man
  sandwich-men
Sand|wich tern +s
sand|wort +s
Sandy (name)
sandy
  sand|ier
  sandi|est
  (like or having
  much sand)
sand yacht +s
sandy|ish
sane
  saner
  san|est
  (not mad. △ seine,
  seiner)
sane|ly
sane|ness
San|for|ised (use
  Sanforized)
San|for|ized *Propr.*
San Fran|cisco
  (city, USA)
sang
sanga +s (use
  sangar)
san|gar +s
  (stone breastwork.
  △ sangha)
san|garee +s
sang-de-boeuf
Sang|er,
  Mar|ga|ret
  (American birth-
  control
  campaigner)
sang-froid
sangha +s
  (Buddhist
  monastic order.
  △ sangar)
Sango
san|grail
san|gria +s
san|gui|fi|ca|tion
san|guin|ar|ily
san|guin|ari|ness
san|guin|ary
san|guine +s
san|guine|ly
san|guine|ness
san|guin|eous

San|hed|rim
  (= Sanhedrin)
San|hed|rin
san|icle +s
san|ify
  sani|fies
  sani|fied
  sani|fy|ing
sani|tar|ian +s
sani|tar|ily
sani|tari|ness
sani|tar|ium
  sani|tar|iums *or*
  sani|taria
sani|tary (healthy,
  hygienic.
  △ sanatory)
sani|tate
  sani|tates
  sani|tated
  sani|tat|ing
sani|ta|tion
sani|ta|tion|ist +s
sani|tisa|tion *Br.*
  (use sanitization)
sani|tise *Br.* (use
  sanitize)
  sani|tises
  sani|tised
  sani|tis|ing
sani|tiser *Br.* +s
  (use sanitizer)
sani|tiza|tion
sani|tize
  sani|tizes
  sani|tized
  sani|tiz|ing
sani|tizer +s
san|ity
San Jose (city,
  USA)
San José (capital of
  Costa Rica)
San Juan (capital
  of Puerto Rico)
sank
San Luis Pot|osí
  (state, Mexico)
San Mar|ino
  (republic)
San Mar|tín, José
  de (Argentinian
  soldier)
san|nyasi
  plural san|nyasi *or*
  san|nya|sis
San Pedro Sula
  (city, Honduras)
san|pro (= sanitary
  protection)
sans (without.
  △ sand)

San Sal|va|dor
  (capital of El
  Salvador)
sans-culotte +s
sans-culott|ism
San Se|bas|tián
  (port, Spain)
san|serif (use sans
  serif)
San|skrit
San|skrit|ic
San|skrit|ist +s
San|so|vino,
  Ja|copo Tatti
  (Italian sculptor)
sans serif +s
Santa +s (= Santa
  Claus)
Santa Ana (city, El
  Salvador)
Santa Bar|bara
  (city, USA)
Santa Cata|rina
  (state, Brazil)
Santa Claus
  Santa Clauses
Santa Cruz (city,
  Bolivia)
Santa Fe (cities,
  USA and
  Argentina)
Santa Mon|ica
  (city, USA)
San|tan|der (port,
  Spain)
Santa So|phia
  (= St Sophia)
San|tiago (capital
  of Chile)
San|tiago de
  Com|po|stela
  (city, Spain)
San|tiago de Cuba
  (city, Cuba)
Santo Dom|ingo
  (capital of the
  Dominican
  Republic)
san|to|lina +s
san|ton|ica +s
san|tonin
San|tor|ini
  (alternative name
  for Thera)
San|tos (port,
  Brazil)
san|yasi
  plural san|yasi *or*
  san|ya|sis
  (use sannyasi)
São Fran|cisco
  (river, Brazil)

São Luís (port, Brazil)

Saône (river, France)

São Paulo (city and state, Brazil)

São Tomé (capital of São Tomé and Príncipe)

São Tomé and Prin|cipe (islands, Gulf of Guinea)

sap
  saps
  sapped
  sap|ping

sapa|jou +s

sapan|wood (use sappanwood)

sa|pele +s

sap|ful

sap green +s *noun and adjective*

sap-green *attributive*

sapid

sa|pid|ity

sapi|ence

sapi|ens (in 'Homo sapiens')

sapi|ent

sa|pi|en|tial

sa|pi|ent|ly

Sapir, Ed|ward (German-born American linguistics scholar)

sap|less

sap|ling +s

sapo|dilla +s

sap|on|aceous

sa|poni|fi|able

sa|poni|fi|ca|tion

sa|pon|ify
  sa|poni|fies
  sa|poni|fied
  sa|poni|fy|ing

sap|onin +s

sapor +s

sap|pan|wood

sap|per +s

Sap|phic +s (of Sappho or her poetry; lesbian)

sap|phic +s (verse)

sap|phire +s

sap|phire blue +s *noun and adjective*

sapphire-blue *attributive*

sap|phir|ine

Sap|phism

Sap|pho (Greek lyric poet)

sap|pily

sap|pi|ness

Sap|poro (city, Japan)

sappy
  sap|pier
  sap|pi|est

sapro|gen|ic

sap|ropha|gous

sapro|phile +s

sap|roph|il|ous

sapro|phyte +s

sapro|phyt|ic

sap|suck|er +s

sap|wood

Saq|qara (necropolis, ancient Memphis)

Sara *also* Sarah

sara|band +s

Sara|cen +s

Sara|cen|ic

Sara|gossa (city, Spain)

Sarah *Bible*

Sarah *also* Sara (name)

Sara|jevo (capital of Bosnia–Herzegovina)

sar|angi +s

Sar|ansk (city, Russia)

sar|ape +s (use serape)

Sara|toga (city, USA)

Sara|tov (city, Russia)

Sara|wak (state, Malaysia)

sar|casm +s

sar|cas|tic

sar|cas|tic|al|ly

sar|celle +s

sar|cenet +s (use sarsenet)

sar|coma
  sar|co|mas *or* sar|co|mata

sar|coma|tosis

sar|coma|tous

sar|copha|gus

sar|coph|agi

sarco|plasm

sar|cous

Sard +s (= Sardinian)

sard +s

Sar|da|na|pa|lian

Sar|da|napa|lus (Assyrian king)

sar|dar +s

sar|delle +s

sar|dine +s

Sar|dinia (island, Mediterranean)

Sar|din|ian +s

Sar|dis (ancient city, Asia Minor)

sar|dius

sar|don|ic

sar|don|ic|al|ly

sar|doni|cism +s

sard|onyx

saree +s (use sari)

sar|gasso +s

Sar|gasso Sea (part of W. Atlantic)

sarge (= sergeant)

Sar|gent, John Sing|er (American painter)

Sar|gent, Mal|colm (English conductor)

Sar|godha (city, Pakistan)

Sar|gon (founder of Akkad)

Sar|gon II (Assyrian king)

sari +s

sarin

Sark (Channel Island)

sark +s (garment)

sar|kar +s

sark|ily

sarki|ness

sark|ing

sarky
  sark|ier
  sark|iest

Sar|ma|tia (ancient region, E. Europe)

Sar|ma|tian +s

sar|men|tose

sar|men|tous

sar|nie +s (= sandwich)

sar|ong +s

Sar|on|ic Gulf (on coast of Greece)

saros

Sarre (French name for the Saar)

sar|ruso|phone +s

sar|sa|par|illa +s

sar|sen +s

sar|senet +s

Sarto, An|drea del (Italian painter)

sar|tor|ial

sar|tori|al|ly

sar|tor|ius
  plural sar|tor|ius muscles

Sartre, Jean-Paul (French philosopher)

Sar|trean +s

Sarum (former name of Salisbury, England; in 'Old Sarum')

sash
  sashes

Sasha *also* Sacha

sashay +s +ed +ing

sash cord +s

sashed

sash|imi +s

sash tool +s

sash weight +s

sash win|dow +s

sasin +s (gazelle)

sas|ine +s *Law*

Sas|katch|ewan (province and river, Canada)

Sas|ka|toon (city, Canada)

Sas|kia

Sas|quatch
  Sas|quatches

sass
  sasses
  sassed
  sass|ing

sas|saby
  sas|sa|bies

sas|sa|fras

Sas|sa|nian +s

Sas|sanid +s

Sas|sen|ach +s (*may cause offence*)

sas|si|ly

sas|si|ness

Sas|soon, Sieg|fried (English writer)

Sas|soon, Vidal (English hairstylist)

sassy

sas|sier

sas|si|est

sas|trugi

SAT +s (= standard assessment task)

sat (past tense and past participle of sit)
satai +s (use satay)
Satan
sat|ang
plural sat|ang or sat|angs
sa|tan|ic
sa|tan|ic|al|ly
Sa|tan|ise Br. (use Satanize)
Sa|tan|ises
Sa|tan|ised
Sa|tan|is|ing
Sa|tan|ism
Sa|tan|ist +s
Sa|tan|ize
Sa|tan|izes
Sa|tan|ized
Sa|tan|iz|ing
Sa|tan|ology
satay +s
satchel +s
sate
sates
sated
sat|ing
(gratify; surfeit)
saté +s (food; use satay)
sat|een +s
sate|less
sat|el|lite +s
sat|el|lit|ic
sat|el|lit|ism
Sati (wife of Siva)
sati +s (widow who immolates herself; such self-immolation; use suttee)
sa|tiable
sa|ti|ate
sa|ti|ates
sa|ti|ated
sa|ti|at|ing
sa|ti|ation
Satie, Erik (French composer)
sa|ti|ety
satin +s +ed +ing
sat|inet +s (use satinette)
satin|ette +s
satin|flower +s
satin|ised Br. (use satinized)
satin|ized
satin stitch
satin-stitched

satin white +s
noun and adjective
satin-white
attributive
satin|wood +s
sat|iny
sat|ire +s
sa|tir|ic
sa|tir|ic|al
sa|tir|ic|al|ly
sat|ir|isa|tion Br. (use satirization)
sat|ir|ise Br. (use satirize)
sat|ir|ises
sat|ir|ised
sat|ir|is|ing
sat|ir|ist +s
sat|ir|iza|tion
sat|ir|ize
sat|ir|izes
sat|ir|ized
sat|ir|iz|ing
sat|is|fac|tion +s
sat|is|fac|tor|ily
sat|is|fac|tori|ness
sat|is|fac|tory
sat|is|fi|abil|ity
sat|is|fi|able
sat|is|fied|ly
sat|isfy
sat|is|fies
sat|is|fied
sat|is|fy|ing
sat|is|fy|ing|ly
sat|nav (= satellite navigation)
sa|tori
sat|ranji +s
sat|rap +s
sat|rapy
sat|rap|ies
Sat|suma (former province, Japan; pottery)
sat|suma +s (fruit)
sat|ur|able
sat|ur|ant +s
sat|ur|ate
sat|ur|ates
sat|ur|ated
sat|ur|at|ing
sat|ur|ation +s
sat|ur|ation point +s
Sat|ur|day +s
Sat|urn (Roman Mythology; planet)
Sat|ur|na|lia (Roman festival)
sat|ur|na|lia +s (orgy)

Sat|ur|na|lian (of Saturnalia)
sat|ur|na|lian (orgiastic)
Sat|urn|ian
sat|urn|ic
sat|urn|id +s
sat|ur|nine
sat|ur|nine|ly
sat|urn|ism
sat|ya|graha +s
satyr +s
satyr|ia|sis
sa|tyr|ic
sa|tyrid +s
sauce
sauces
sauced
sau|cing
sauce-boat +s
sauce|box
sauce|boxes
sauce|less
sauce|pan +s
sauce|pan|ful +s
sau|cer +s
sau|cer|ful +s
sau|cer|less
sau|cily
sau|ci|ness
saucy
sau|cier
sau|ci|est
Saudi +s
Saudi Ara|bia
Saudi Ara|bian +s
sauer|kraut +s
sau|ger +s
Saul Bible
Sault Sainte Marie (cities, USA and Canada)
Sau|mur +s (town, France; wine)
sauna +s
saun|ders
saun|ter +s +ed +ing
saun|ter|er +s
saur|ian +s
saur|is|chian +s
sauro|pod +s
saury
saur|ies
saus|age +s
Saus|sure, Fer|di|nand de (Swiss linguistics scholar)
sauté +s +ed +ing
Sau|ternes
plural Sau|ternes

Sau|ternes (cont.) (district, France; wine)
Sauve|ter|rian +s
Sau|vi|gnon +s
sav|able
Sav|age, Mi|chael (New Zealand prime minister)
sav|age
sav|ages
sav|aged
sav|aging
sav|age|dom
sav|age|ly
sav|age|ness
sav|agery
sav|ager|ies
Sav|ai'i (island, Western Samoa)
sa|vanna +s (use savannah)
Sa|van|nah (port and river, USA)
sa|van|nah +s (grassy plain)
Sa|van|na|khet (town, Laos)
sav|ant +s male
sav|ante +s female
sa|vate (form of boxing)
save
saves
saved
sav|ing
save-all +s
sav|eloy +s
saver +s
Sav|ery, Thomas (English engineer)
savin +s
sav|ine +s (use savin)
sav|ing +s
sa|vior Am. +s
sa|viour Br. +s
sav|oir faire
sav|oir vivre
Sav|ona|rola, Gir|ol|amo (Italian preacher)
Sav|on|linna (town, Finland)
Sav|on|nerie +s
savor Am. +s +ed +ing (Br. savour)
sa|vor|ily Am. (Br. savourily)
sa|vori|ness Am. (Br. savouriness)

sa¦vor|less *Am.* (*Br.*
  savourless)
sa¦vory
  sa¦vor|ies
  (herb. △ savoury)
sa¦vory *Am.*
  sa¦vor|ies
  (not sweet; dish.
  △ savoury)
sa¦vour *Br.* +s +ed
  +ing (*Am.* savor)
sa¦vour|ily *Br.* (*Am.*
  savorily)
sa¦vouri|ness *Br.*
  (*Am.* savoriness)
sa¦vour|less *Br.*
  (*Am.* savorless)
sa¦voury *Br.*
  sa¦vour|ies
  (*Am.* savory. not
  sweet; dish.
  △ savory)
Savoy (region,
  France)
savoy +s (cabbage)
Sa¦voy|ard +s
Savu Sea (part of
  Indian Ocean)
savvy
  sav|vies
  sav|vied
  savvy|ing
saw
  saws
  sawed
  saw¦ing
  sawn *or* sawed
  (tool; cut;
  proverb; past
  tense of see.
  △ soar, sore)
saw|bench
  saw|benches
saw|bill +s
saw|bones
  plural saw|bones
saw|buck +s
saw¦cut +s
saw-doctor +s
saw|dust
saw-edged
sawed-off
  attributive
saw|fish
  plural saw|fish *or*
  saw|fishes
saw¦fly
  saw|flies
saw frame +s
saw-gate +s
saw-gin +s

saw|grass
  saw|grasses
saw|horse +s
saw|like
saw|mill +s
sawn
sawn-off *attributive*
saw-pit +s
saw-set +s
saw|tooth
saw|toothed
saw-wort +s
saw¦yer +s
sax
  saxes
  (saxophone; tool.
  △ saxe)
saxa|tile
sax|board +s
saxe +s (colour.
  △ sax)
saxe blue +s *noun*
  and adjective
saxe-blue
  attributive
Saxe-Coburg-
  Gotha (former
  name of royal
  house of Windsor)
sax|horn +s
sax|icol|ine
sax|ico|lous
saxi|frage +s
sax|ist +s
Saxon +s
Saxon blue
Saxon|dom
Saxon|ise *Br.* (use
  Saxonize)
  Saxon|ises
  Saxon|ised
  Saxon|is¦ing
Saxon|ism
Saxon|ist +s
Saxon|ize
  Saxon|izes
  Saxon|ized
  Saxon|iz¦ing
Sax|ony (state,
  Germany)
sax¦ony
  sax¦on|ies
  (wool; cloth)
Saxony-Anhalt
  (state, Germany)
saxo|phone +s
saxo|phon¦ic
sax|opho|nist +s
say
  says
  said

say (*cont.*)
  say¦ing
  (utter. △ sei)
say|able
sayer +s
Say¦ers, Doro¦thy
  L. (English writer)
say¦ing +s
say-so
S-bend +s
scab
  scabs
  scabbed
  scab¦bing
scab¦bard +s
scabbard-fish
  plural scabbard-
  fish *or* scabbard-
  fishes
scab¦bi|ness
scabby
scab|bier
scab¦bi|est
sca|bies
sca¦bi|ous
  plural sca¦bi|ous
scab|like
scab|rous
scab|rous¦ly
scab|rous|ness
scad +s
Sca|fell Pike (peak,
  England)
scaf|fold +s +ed
  +ing
scaf|fold¦er +s
scaf¦fold|ing +s
scag +s (use skag)
scagli|ola
scal|abil¦ity
scal|able
sca|lar +s
  (*Mathematics.*
  △ scaler)
sca|lari|form
scala|wag +s (use
  scallywag)
scald +s +ed +ing
  (burn with liquid
  or steam. △ skald)
scald¦er +s
scald-head +s
scale
  scales
  scaled
  scal¦ing
scale armor *Am.*
scale ar¦mour *Br.*
scale-board +s
scale-bug +s
scale-fern +s

scale-leaf
scale-leaves
scale|less
scale|like
scale-moss
  scale-mosses
sca|lene +s
sca|lenus
  sca|leni
scale-pan +s
scaler +s (person
  or thing that
  scales. △ scalar)
Scales, the
  (constellation;
  sign of zodiac)
scale-winged
scale work
Scali|ger, Jo¦seph
  Justus (French
  scholar of ancient
  chronology)
Scali|ger, Ju¦lius
  Cae¦sar (Italian-
  born French
  classical scholar
  and physician)
scali|ness
scaling-ladder +s
scalla|wag +s (use
  scallywag)
scal|lion +s
scal|lop +s +ed
  +ing
scal|lop¦er +s
scally|wag +s
scalp +s +ed +ing
scal|pel +s
scalp¦er +s
scalp|less
scal¦pri|form
scaly
  scali¦er
  scali|est
scam +s
scam|mony
  scam|monies
scamp +s +ed
  +ing
scam|per +s +ed
  +ing
scampi
scamp|ish
scan
  scans
  scanned
  scan|ning
scan|dal +s
scan|dal|ise *Br.*
  (use scandalize)
  scan¦dal|ises

scan|dal|ise (*cont.*)
  scan|dal|ised
  scan|dal|is|ing
scan|dal|ize
  scan|dal|izes
  scan|dal|ized
  scan|dal|iz|ing
scan|dal|mon|ger +s
scan|dal|ous
scan|dal|ous|ly
scan|dal|ous|ness
Scan|di|navia
  (peninsula, NW
  Europe; or wider
  region)
Scan|di|navian +s
scan|dium
scan|nable
scan|ner +s
scan|sion
scan|sor|ial
scant +s +ed +ing
scant|ies
scant|ily
scanti|ness
scant|ling +s
scant|ly
scant|ness
scanty
  scant|ier
  scanti|est
Scapa Flow (strait
  in the Orkney
  Islands)
scape +s
scape|goat +s +ed
  +ing
scape|goat|er +s
scape|grace +s
scaph|oid +s
scap|ula
  scapu|lae *or*
  scapu|las
  (shoulder blade)
scapu|lar +s (of the
  shoulder; cloak;
  bandage; feather)
scapu|lary
  scapu|lar|ies
scar
  scars
  scarred
  scar|ring
  (mark on skin etc.;
  outcrop. △ ska)
scarab +s
scara|baeid +s
scara|mouch
  scara|mouches
Scar|bor|ough
  (town, England)

scarce
  scar|cer
  scar|cest
scarce|ly
scarce|ness
scar|city
  scar|ci|ties
scare
  scares
  scared
  scar|ing
scare|crow +s
scaredy-cat +s
scare|mon|ger +s
scare|monger|ing
  +s
scarer +s
scarf
  scarves *or* scarfs
  (piece of material
  worn around
  neck)
scarf +s +ed +ing
  (join ends; cut
  whale blubber; eat
  or drink greedily)
scarfed (wearing a
  scarf)
scarf pin +s
scarf ring +s
scarf-skin
scarf-wise
scari|fi|ca|tion +s
scari|fi|ca|tor +s
scari|fier +s
scari|fy
  scari|fies
  scari|fied
  scari|fy|ing
scari|ly
scari|ness
scari|ous
scar|lat|ina (scarlet
  fever)
Scar|latti,
  Do|men|ico
  (Italian composer)
Scar|latti,
  Ales|san|dro
  (Italian composer)
scar|less
scar|let +s (colour)
Scar|lett (name)
scar|oid +s
scarp +s +ed +ing
scar|per +s +ed
  +ing
Scart (*Video.*
  △ skat)
scarus
  scari
scarves

scary
  scari|er
  scari|est
scat
  scats
  scat|ted
  scat|ting
scathe
  scathes
  scathed
  scath|ing
scathe|less
scath|ing|ly
scato|logic|al
scat|ology
scat|opha|gous
scat|ter +s +ed
  +ing
scat|ter|brain +s
scat|ter|brained
scat|ter|er +s
scatter-gun +s
scat|ter|shot
scat|tily
scat|ti|ness
scatty
  scat|tier
  scat|ti|est
scaup +s
scaup|er +s
scaur +s +ed +ing
  (outcrop. △ score)
scav|enge
  scav|enges
  scav|enged
  scav|en|ging
scav|en|ger +s
scav|en|gery
sca|zon +s
scena +s
scen|ario +s
scen|ar|ist +s
scend +s +ed +ing
scene +s (place;
  view; part of play.
  △ seen)
scene-dock +s
scen|ery
scene-shifter +s
scene-shifting
scenic
scen|ic|al|ly
scen|og|raph|er +s
scen|og|raphy
scent +s +ed +ing
  (smell; perfume.
  △ cent, sent)
scent-bag +s
scent gland +s
scent|less
scep|sis *Br.* (*Am.*
  skepsis)

scep|ter *Am.* (*Br.*
  sceptre.
  sovereign's rod.
  △ septa)
scep|tered *Am.* (*Br.*
  sceptred)
scep|tic *Br.* +s (*Am.*
  skeptic)
scep|tic|al *Br.* (*Am.*
  skeptical)
scep|tic|al|ly *Br.*
  (*Am.* skeptically)
scep|ti|cism *Br.* +s
  (*Am.* skepticism)
sceptre *Br.* +s (*Am.*
  scepter.
  sovereign's rod.
  △ septa)
sceptred *Br.* (*Am.*
  sceptered)
schad|en|freude
Schaff|hausen
  (town and canton,
  Switzerland)
schappe +s
sched|ule
  sched|ules
  sched|uled
  sched|ul|ing
sched|uler +s
Scheele, Carl
  Wil|helm
  (Swedish chemist)
scheel|ite +s
Sche|hera|zade (in
  the *Arabian Nights*)
Scheldt (river in
  France, Belgium,
  the Netherlands)
Schel|ling,
  Fried|rich
  Wil|helm
  Jo|seph von
  (German
  philosopher)
schema
  sche|mata *or*
  sche|mas
  (plan etc.
  △ schemer)
sche|mat|ic +s
sche|mat|ic|al|ly
sche|ma|tisa|tion
  Br. (use
  schematization)
sche|ma|tise *Br.*
  (use schematize)
  sche|ma|tises
  sche|ma|tised
  sche|ma|tis|ing
sche|ma|tism +s
sche|ma|tiza|tion

sche|ma|tize
  sche|ma|tizes
  sche|ma|tized
  sche|ma|tiz|ing
scheme
  schemes
  schemed
  schem|ing
schemer +s
schem|ing +s
schem|ing|ly
sche|moz|zle +s
  (use shemozzle)
scherz|ando
  scherz|an|dos or
  scherz|andi
scherzo +s
Schia|pa|relli, Elsa
  (Italian-born
  French fashion
  designer)
Schia|pa|relli,
  Gio|vanni
  Vir|gi|nio (Italian
  astronomer)
Schie|dam (port,
  the Netherlands)
Schiele, Egon
  (Austrian painter)
Schil|ler,
  Fried|rich von
  (German writer)
schil|ling +s
  (Austrian
  currency.
  ⚠ shilling)
Schind|ler, Oskar
  (German rescuer
  of Jews)
schip|perke +s
schism +s
schis|mat|ic +s
schis|mat|ic|al
schis|mat|ic|al|ly
schis|ma|tise Br.
  (use schismatize)
  schis|ma|tises
  schis|ma|tised
  schis|ma|tis|ing
schis|ma|tize
  schis|ma|tizes
  schis|ma|tized
  schis|ma|tiz|ing
schist +s
schis|tose
schis|to|some +s
schis|to|som|ia|sis
schis|to|
      som|ia|ses
schiz|an|thus
  schiz|an|thuses
schizo +s

schizo|carp +s
schizo|car|pic
schizo|car|pous
schiz|oid +s
schizo|my|cete +s
schizo|phre|nia
schizo|phren|ic +s
schizo|thy|mia
schizo|thy|mic
Schle|gel, Au|gust
  Wil|helm von
  (German
  translator of
  Shakespeare)
Schle|gel,
  Fried|rich von
  (German
  philosopher)
schle|miel +s
schlep
  schleps
  schlepped
  schlep|ping
schlepp +s +ed
  +ing (use schlep)
Schles|wig (former
  duchy, N. Europe)
Schleswig-
  Holstein (state,
  Germany)
Schlie|mann,
  Hein|rich
  (German
  archaeologist)
schlier|en +s
schlock
schlump +s
schmaltz
schmaltzy
  schmaltz|ier
  schmaltzi|est
Schmidt
  (telescope;
  camera)
Schmidt–Cassegrain
  (telescope)
schmooze
  schmoozes
  schmoozed
  schmooz|ing
schmuck +s
schnapps
  plural schnapps
schnau|zer +s
Schnei|der,
  Jacques (French
  flying enthusiast)
schnit|zel +s
schnook +s
schnor|kel +s (use
  snorkel)
schnor|rer +s

Schoen|berg,
  Ar|nold (Austrian-
  born American
  composer)
scholar +s
schol|ar|li|ness
schol|ar|ly
schol|ar|ship +s
scho|las|tic +s
scho|las|tic|al|ly
scho|las|ti|cism
scho|li|ast +s
scho|li|as|tic
scho|lium
  scho|lia
school +s +ed
  +ing
school|able
school age noun
school-age
  attributive
school-aged
school book +s
school|boy +s
school|child
  school|chil|dren
school day, the
school|days
school|fel|low +s
school friend +s
school|girl +s
school|house +s
schoolie +s
school in|spect|or
  +s
school|kid +s
school leav|er +s
school-leaving
  age +s
school-ma'm +s
  (use school-
  marm)
school|man
  school|men
school-marm +s
school-marmish
school|mas|ter +s
school|mas|ter|ing
school|mas|ter|ly
school|mate +s
school|mis|tress
  school|
      mis|tresses
school|mis|tressy
school|room +s
school-ship +s
school|teach|er +s
school|teach|ing
school time +s
school work
school|yard +s
schooner +s

Schop|en|hauer,
  Ar|thur (German
  philosopher)
schorl +s (mineral.
  ⚠ shawl)
schot|tische +s
Schottky ef|fect
Schrei|ner, Olive
  (South African
  novelist)
Schröd|inger,
  Erwin (Austrian
  physicist;
  equation)
Schu|bert, Franz
  (Austrian
  composer)
Schu|bert|ian +s
Schulz, Charles
  (American
  cartoonist)
Schu|macher, E.
  F. (German
  economist and
  conservationist)
Schu|mann,
  Rob|ert (German
  composer)
schuss
  schusses
  schussed
  schuss|ing
Schütz, Hein|rich
  (German
  composer)
schwa +s
Schwäb|isch
  Gmünd (city,
  Germany)
Schwann,
  Theo|dor
  (German
  physiologist)
Schwarz|kopf,
  Elisa|beth
  (German soprano)
Schwarz|wald
  (German name for
  the Black Forest)
Schwein|furt (city,
  Germany)
Schweit|zer,
  Al|bert (German
  theologian)
Schwerin (city,
  Germany)
Schwyz (city and
  canton,
  Switzerland)
scia|gram +s
scia|graph +s +ed
  +ing

scia|graph|ic
sci|ag|raphy
sci|am|achy
sci|at|ic
sci|at|ica
sci|at|ic|al|ly
sci|ence +s
sci|en|ter
sci|en|tial +s
sci|en|tif|ic
sci|en|tif|ic|ally
sci|en|tism +s
sci|en|tist +s
sci|en|tis|tic
Sci|en|tolo|gist +s
Sci|en|tol|ogy
    Propr.
sci-fi (= science
    fiction)
scili|cet
scilla +s (plant.
    △ Scylla)
Scil|lies (= Scilly
    Isles)
Scil|lo|nian +s (of
    the Scilly Isles)
Scilly Isles (off
    England)
scimi|tar +s
scin|ti|gram +s
scin|tig|raphy
scin|tilla +s
scin|til|lant
scin|til|late
    scin|til|lates
    scin|til|lated
    scin|til|lat|ing
scin|til|lat|ing|ly
scin|til|la|tion +s
scin|ti|scan +s
sci|ol|ism
sci|ol|ist +s
sci|ol|is|tic
scion +s
Scipio
    Ae|mili|anus
    (Roman general)
Scipio Af|ri|canus
    (Roman general)
scire fa| cias
sci|rocco +s (use
    sirocco)
scir|rhoid
scir|rhos|ity
scir|rhous (of a
    scirrhus. △ cirrous)
scir|rhus
    scir|rhi
    (carcinoma.
    △ cirrus)
scis|sel (metal
    clippings)

scis|sile (able to be
    cut)
scis|sion +s
scis|sor +s +ed
    +ing
scissor-bill +s
scissor-bird +s
scis|sor|wise
sci|ur|ine
sci|ur|oid
sclera +s
scleral
scler|en|chyma
scler|ite +s
scler|itis
sclero|derma
scler|oid
scler|oma
    scler|omata
scler|om|eter +s
sclero|phyll +s
scler|ophyl|lous
sclero|pro|tein +s
scler|osed
scler|osis
    scler|oses
scler|ot|ic +s
sclero|titis
scler|otomy
    scler|oto|mies
scler|ous
scoff +s +ed +ing
scoff|er +s
scoff|ing|ly
scold +s +ed +ing
scold|er +s
scold|ing +s
sco|lex
scol|le|ces
scoli|osis
    scoli|oses
scoli|ot|ic
scol|lop +s (use
    scallop)
scolo|pen|drium
    scolo|pen|dri|ums
    or scolo|pen|dria
scom|ber +s
scom|brid +s
scom|broid +s
sconce
    sconces
    sconced
scon|cing
Scone (village,
    Scotland)
scone +s (cake)
scoop +s +ed +ing
scoop|er +s
scoop|ful +s
scoop neck +s
scoop-net +s

scoot +s +ed +ing
    (run away.
    △ scute)
scoot|er +s +ed
    +ing (vehicle.
    △ scuta)
scoot|er|ist +s
scopa
    sco|pae
scope +s
sco|pol|am|ine +s
scop|ula
    scopu|lae
scor|bu|tic +s
scor|bu|tic|al|ly
scorch
    scorches
    scorched
    scorch|ing
scorch|er +s
scorch|ing|ly
score
    scores
    scored
    scor|ing
    (number of points;
    music; groove.
    △ scaur)
score|board +s
score|book +s
score|card +s
score|less
score|line +s
scorer +s
score sheet +s
scoria
    scor|iae
scori|aceous
scori|fi|ca|tion
scori|fier
scori|fy
    scori|fies
    scori|fied
    scori|fy|ing
scorn +s +ed +ing
scorn|er +s
scorn|ful
scorn|ful|ly
scorn|ful|ness
scorp|er +s
Scor|pian +s
    (pertaining to
    Scorpio or
    Scorpius; person.
    △ scorpion)
Scor|pio (sign of
    zodiac)
scor|pi|oid +s
scor|pion +s
    (arachnid.
    △ Scorpian)
Scor|pius
    (constellation)

Scor|sese, Mar|tin
    (American film
    director)
scor|zon|era +s
Scot +s (person
    from Scotland.
    △ Scott)
scot +s (tax)
Scotch
    Scotches
    (whisky; Scottish)
scotch
    scotches
    scotched
    scotch|ing
    (put an end to)
Scotch|man
    Scotch|men
Scotch|woman
    Scotch|women
sco|ter
    plural sco|ter *or*
    sco|ters
scot-free
sco|tia +s
Scoti|cise *Br.* (use
    Scotticize)
    Scoti|cises
    Scoti|cised
    Scoti|cis|ing
Scoti|cism +s (use
    Scotticism)
Scoti|cize (use
    Scotticize)
    Scoti|cizes
    Scoti|cized
    Scoti|ciz|ing
Scot|ism +s
Scot|ist +s
Scot|land
scot|oma
    scot|omata
Scots (Scottish;
    Scots people)
Scots|man
    Scots|men
Scots|woman
    Scots|women
Scott (name.
    △ Scot)
Scott, Gil|bert
    (English architect)
Scott, Peter
    (English
    naturalist)
Scott, Rob|ert
    (English explorer)
Scott, Wal|ter
    (Scottish writer)
Scot|ti|cise *Br.* (use
    Scotticize)
    Scot|ti|cises

Scot|ti|cise (cont.)
  Scot|ti|cised
  Scot|ti|cis|ing
Scot|ti|cism +s
Scot|ti|cize
  Scot|ti|cizes
  Scot|ti|cized
  Scot|ti|ciz|ing
Scot|tie +s (Scotch
  terrier; a Scot)
Scot|tish
Scot|tish|ness
scoun|drel +s
scoun|drel|dom
scoun|drel|ism
scoun|drel|ly
scour +s +ed +ing
scour|er +s
scourge
  scourges
  scourged
  scour|ging
scour|ger +s
scouring-rush
  scouring-rushes
  (plant)
Scouse +s
  (Liverpudlian)
scouse +s (food)
Scouser +s
Scout +s (member
  of Scout
  Association)
scout +s +ed +ing
Scout
  As|so|ci|ation
Scout|er +s (adult
  member of Scout
  Association)
scout|er +s (person
  who scouts)
Scout|mas|ter +s
scow +s
scowl +s +ed +ing
scowl|er +s
Scrab|ble (game)
  Propr.
scrab|ble
  scrab|bles
  scrab|bled
  scrab|bling
  (scratch; grope)
Scrab|bler +s
scrag
  scrags
  scragged
  scrag|ging
scrag|gily
scrag|gi|ness
scrag|gly

scraggy
scrag|gier
scrag|gi|est
scram
  scrams
  scrammed
  scram|ming
scram|ble
  scram|bles
  scram|bled
  scram|bling
scram|bler +s
scran
Scran|ton (city,
  USA)
scrap
  scraps
  scrapped
  scrap|ping
scrap|book +s
scrape
  scrapes
  scraped
  scrap|ing
scraper +s
scraper|board +s
scrap heap +s
scra|pie
scrap|ing +s
scrap|per +s
scrap|pily
scrap|pi|ness
scrappy
  scrap|pier
  scrap|pi|est
scrap|yard +s
scratch
  scratches
  scratched
  scratch|ing
scratch|board +s
scratch|er +s
scratch|ily
scratchi|ness
scratch|ing +s
scratchy
  scratch|ier
  scratchi|est
scrawl
  scrawls
  scrawled
  scrawl|ing
scrawly
scrawni|ness
scrawny
  scrawn|ier
  scrawni|est
scream +s +ed
  +ing
scream|er +s
scream|ing|ly
scree +s

screech
  screeches
  screeched
  screech|ing
screech|er +s
screech owl +s
screechy
  screech|ier
  screechi|est
screed +s +ed
  +ing
screen +s +ed
  +ing
screen|able
screen|er +s
screen|ing +s
screen|play +s
screen print +s
  noun
screen-print +s
  +ed +ing verb
screen print|er +s
screen print|ing
  noun
screen test +s
screen|writer +s
screen|writ|ing
screw +s +ed +ing
screw|able
screw|ball +s
screw cap +s noun
screw-cap adjective
screw-coupling +s
screw|driver +s
screw|driv|ing
screw|er +s
screw-hole +s
screwi|ness
screw-jack +s
screw-plate +s
screw-tap +s
screw top +s noun
screw-top adjective
screw-up +s
screwy
  screw|ier
  screwi|est
Scria|bin,
  Alek|sandr
  (Russian
  composer)
scribal
scrib|ble
  scrib|bles
  scrib|bled
  scrib|bling
scrib|bler +s
scrib|bling +s
scrib|bly
scribe
  scribes

scribe (cont.)
  scribed
  scrib|ing
scriber +s
scrim +s
scrim|mage
  scrim|mages
  scrim|maged
  scrim|ma|ging
scrim|ma|ger +s
scrimp +s +ed
  +ing
scrimpy
  scrimp|ier
  scrimpi|est
scrim|shander +s
  +ed +ing
scrim|shank +s
  +ed +ing
scrim|shank|er +s
scrim|shaw +s
  +ed +ing
scrip +s
script +s +ed +ing
scrip|tor|ial
scrip|tor|ium
  scrip|tor|iums or
  scrip|toria
script|ory
  script|or|ies
scrip|tural
scrip|tur|al|ism
scrip|tur|al|ist +s
scrip|tur|al|ly
Scrip|ture +s (of a
  particular religion)
scrip|ture +s
  (generally)
script|writer +s
script|writ|ing
scriv|en|er +s
scro|bicu|late
scrod +s
scrof|ula
  scrofu|las or
  scrofu|lae
scrofu|lous
scroll +s +ed +ing
scroll|er +s
scroll-head +s
scroll-lathe +s
scroll saw +s
scroll|work
Scrooge +s
scro|tal
scrot|itis
scro|tum
  scro|tums or
  scrota
scrounge
  scrounges
  scrounged
  scroun|ging

scrounˈger +s
scrub
  scrubs
  scrubbed
  scrub|bing
scrub|ber +s
scrubbing-brush
  scrubbing-
  brushes
scrub-brush
  scrub-brushes
scrubby
  scrub|bier
  scrub|bi|est
scrub|land +s
scruff +s
scruff|ily
scruffi|ness
scruffy
  scruff|ier
  scruffi|est
scrum +s
scrum-half
  scrum-halves
scrum|mage
  scrum|mages
  scrum|maged
  scrum|maˈging
scrum|maˈger +s
scrummy
  scrum|mier
  scrum|miˈest
scrump +s +ed
  +ing
scrum|ple
  scrum|ples
  scrum|pled
  scrump|ling
scrump|tious
scrump|tious|ly
scrump|tious|ness
scrumpy
  scrump|ies
scrunch
  scrunches
  scrunched
  scrunch|ing
scrunch-dry
  scrunch-dries
  scrunch-dried
  scrunch-drying
scrunchie +s (use
  scrunchy)
scrunchy
  scrunch|ies
scruˈple
  scruˈples
  scruˈpled
  scrupˈling
scruˈpuˈlosˈity
scruˈpuˈlous
scruˈpuˈlousˈly

scruˈpuˈlous|ness
scruˈtaˈtor +s
scruˈtinˈeer +s
scruˈtinˈisaˈtion
  Br. (use
  scrutinization)
scruˈtinˈise *Br.* (use
  scrutinize)
  scruˈtinˈises
  scruˈtinˈised
  scruˈtinˈisˈing
scruˈtinˈiser *Br.* +s
  (use scrutinizer)
scruˈtinˈizaˈtion
scruˈtinˈize
  scruˈtinˈizes
  scruˈtinˈized
  scruˈtinˈizˈing
scruˈtinˈizer +s
scruˈtiny
  scruˈtinˈies
scry
  scries
  scried
  scry|ing
scryˈer +s
scuba +s
scuba-dive
  scuba-dives
  scuba-dived
  scuba-diving
  scuba-diver +s
Scud +s (missile)
scud
  scuds
  scud|ded
  scud|ding
  (move fast)
scuff +s +ed +ing
scufˈfle
  scufˈfles
  scufˈfled
  scuf|fling
scul|dugˈgery (use
  skulduggery)
scull +s +ed +ing
  (oar. △ skull)
scullˈer +s
scull|ery
  scullˈerˈies
scul|lion +s
sculp +s +ed +ing
scul|pin +s
sculpt +s +ed +ing
sculp|tor +s
  (person who
  sculpts.
  △ sculpture)
sculp|tress
  sculp|tresses
sculp|tural
sculp|turˈalˈly

sculp|ture
  sculp|tures
  sculp|tured
  sculp|turˈing
  (art form.
  △ sculptor)
sculp|turˈesque
scum
  scums
  scummed
  scum|ming
scum|bag +s
scumˈble
  scum|bles
  scum|bled
  scum|bling
scummy
  scum|mier
  scum|miˈest
scun|cheon +s
scunge +s
scungy
  scun|gier
  scun|giˈest
scun|ner +s +ed
  +ing
Scunˈthorpe (town,
  England)
scup
  scups
  scupped
  scup|ping
scup|per +s +ed
  +ing
scurf
scurfy
  scurf|ier
  scurfi|est
scurˈrilˈity
  scurˈrilˈities
scurˈrilˈous
scurˈriˈlousˈly
scurˈriˈlous|ness
scurry
  scur|ries
  scur|ried
  scurry|ing
scur|vied
scur|vily
scurvy
  scurˈvier
  scurˈviˈest
scut +s
scuta (plural of
  scutum.
  △ scooter)
scutˈage +s
scuˈtal
Scuˈtari (Italian
  name for
  Shkodër)

Scuˈtari (former
  name of Üsküdar)
scuˈtate
scutch
  scutches
  scutched
  scutch|ing
scutch|eon +s
scutch|er +s
scute +s (bony
  plate. △ scoot)
scuˈtelˈlate
scuˈtelˈlaˈtion +s
scuˈtelˈlum
  scuˈtella
scuˈtiˈform
scut|ter +s +ed
  +ing
scut|tle
  scut|tles
  scut|tled
  scut|tling
scuttle|butt +s
  (water-butt)
scuˈtum
  scuta
scuzzy
  scuzz|ier
  scuzˈziˈest
Scylla (*Greek*
  Mythology.
  △ scilla)
scyphi|form
scy|phose
scyˈphoˈzoan +s
scy|phus
  scyˈphi
scythe
  scythes
  scythed
  scyth|ing
Scythia (ancient
  region, SE Europe
  and Asia)
Scyth|ian +s
sea +s (ocean.
  △ see, si)
sea-angel +s
sea|bed +s
sea|bird +s
sea|board +s
sea-boat +s
sea|boot +s
Sea|borg, Glenn
  (American nuclear
  chemist)
sea|borg|ium
sea|borne
sea bot|tom
sea change +s
sea-chest +s
sea coast +s

sea|cock +s
Sea Dyak +s
  (alternative name
  for the Iban)
sea-ear +s
sea|farer +s
sea|far|ing
sea fish
  plural sea fish *or*
  sea fishes
sea floor +s
sea|food +s
sea|front +s
sea-girt
sea|going
sea green +s *noun*
  and adjective
sea-green
  attributive
sea|gull +s
sea horse +s
sea-island cot|ton
  +s
sea|jack +s +ed
  +ing
sea|jack|er +s
sea|kale
seal +s +ed +ing
  (sea mammal;
  fasten; fastening.
  ⚠ ceiling, seel)
seal|able
seal|ant +s
sealed-beam
  attributive
sea legs
seal|er +s
  (something used
  for sealing joints;
  hunter; ship.
  ⚠ selah)
seal|ery
  seal|er|ies
sea level +s
sea-level *attributive*
seal|ing wax
  seal|ing waxes
sea lion +s
seal|point +s
seal|skin +s
seal|stone +s
Sealy|ham +s
seam +s +ed +ing
  (line; join with a
  seam. ⚠ seem)
sea mam|mal +s
sea|man
  sea|men
  (sailor. ⚠ semen)
sea|man|like
sea|man|ly
sea|man|ship

sea|mark +s
seam|er +s
seami|ness
seam|less
seam|less|ly
seam|stress
  seam|stresses
Sea|mus
seamy
  seam|ier
  seami|est
Sean *also* Shaun
Seanad (upper
  House in Irish
  Parliament)
se|ance +s
sea|plane +s
sea|port +s
SEAQ (= Stock
  Exchange
  Automated
  Quotations)
sea|quake +s
sear +s +ed +ing
  (scorch. ⚠ cere,
  seer, sere)
search
  searches
  searched
  search|ing
search|able
search|er +s
search|ing +s
search|ing|ly
search|less
search|light +s
search party
  search par|ties
sear|ing|ly
Sears Tower
  (skyscraper,
  Chicago, USA)
sea|scape +s
sea shanty
  sea shan|ties
sea|shell +s
sea|shore +s
sea|sick
sea|sick|ness
sea|side +s
sea|son +s +ed
  +ing
sea|son|able
sea|son|able|ness
sea|son|ably
sea|son|al
sea|son|al|ity
sea|son|al|ly
sea|son|er +s
sea|son|ing +s
sea|son|less
sea|son ticket +s

seat +s +ed +ing
seat belt +s
-seater +s (in
  'single-seater' etc.)
seat|ing +s
seat|less
SEATO (= South-
  East Asia Treaty
  Organization)
Se|attle (city, USA)
sea ur|chin +s
sea|ward
sea|wards
sea water
sea|way +s
sea|weed +s
sea-wife
  sea-wives
sea-wind +s
sea|worthi|ness
sea|worthy
sea-wrack +s
se|ba|ceous
Se|bas|tian
  (Roman saint;
  name)
Se|bas|to|pol
  (naval base,
  Ukraine)
Sebat (Jewish
  month)
se|bes|ten +s
seb|or|rhea *Am.*
seb|or|rhe|ic *Am.*
seb|or|rhoea *Br.*
seb|or|rhoe|ic *Br.*
sebum
sec (dry)
sec +s (= secant;
  second)
se|cant +s
seca|teurs
secco +s
se|cede
  se|cedes
  se|ceded
  se|ced|ing
se|ceder +s
se|ces|sion +s
se|ces|sion|al
se|ces|sion|ism
se|ces|sion|ist +s
Se|chuana (use
  Setswana)
se|clude
  se|cludes
  se|cluded
  se|clud|ing
se|clu|sion +s
se|clu|sion|ist +s
se|clu|sive

sec|ond +s +ed
  +ing (unit of time;
  next after first;
  support)
se|cond +s +ed
  +ing (transfer.
  ⚠ seconde)
sec|ond|ar|ily
sec|ond|ari|ness
sec|ond|ary
  sec|ond|ar|ies
second-best
second-class
  adjective and
  adverb
second-degree
  adjective
se|conde +s (in
  fencing.
  ⚠ second)
se|cond|ee +s
  (person
  transferred)
sec|ond|er +s
  (person seconding
  a motion)
second-floor
  adjective
second-
  generation
  adjective
second-guess
  second-guesses
  second-guessed
  second-guessing
sec|ond hand (on
  clock; in 'at
  second hand')
second-hand
  adjective and
  adverb
sec|ond|ly
se|cond|ment +s
se|condo
  se|condi
  Music
second-rate
  adjective
second-rater +s
second-sighted
se|crecy
se|cret +s
sec|re|taire +s
sec|re|tar|ial
sec|re|tar|iat +s
sec|re|tary
  sec|re|tar|ies
  (in office.
  ⚠ secretory)
Secretary-General
  +s

Sec|re|tary of
State
  Sec|re|tar|ies of
  State
sec|re|tary|ship +s
se|crete
  se|cretes
  se|creted
  se|cret|ing
se|cre|tion +s
se|cret|ive
se|cret|ive|ly
se|cret|ive|ness
se|cret|ly
se|cre|tor +s
se|cre|tory
  (producing by
  secretion.
  ⚠ secretary)
sect +s (religious
  group. ⚠ Sekt)
sect|ar|ian +s
sect|ar|ian|ise *Br.*
  (use sectarianize)
  sect|ar|ian|ises
  sect|ar|ian|ised
  sect|ar|ian|is|ing
sect|ar|ian|ism
sect|ar|ian|ize
  sect|ar|ian|izes
  sect|ar|ian|ized
  sect|ar|ian|iz|ing
sect|ary
  sect|ar|ies
sec|tion +s +ed
  +ing
sec|tion|al
sec|tion|al|ise *Br.*
  (use sectionalize)
  sec|tion|al|ises
  sec|tion|al|ised
  sec|tion|al|is|ing
sec|tion|al|ism
sec|tion|al|ist +s
sec|tion|al|ize
  sec|tion|al|izes
  sec|tion|al|ized
  sec|tion|al|iz|ing
sec|tion|al|ly
section-mark +s
sec|tor +s
sec|tor|al
sec|tor|ial
secu|lar +s
secu|lar|isa|tion
  Br. (use
  secularization)
secu|lar|ise *Br.* (use
  secularize)
  secu|lar|ises
  secu|lar|ised
  secu|lar|is|ing

secu|lar|ism
secu|lar|ist +s
secu|lar|ity
secu|lar|iza|tion
secu|lar|ize
  secu|lar|izes
  secu|lar|ized
  secu|lar|iz|ing
secu|lar|ly
se|cund
Se|cun|dera|bad
  (town, India)
se|cund|ly
se|cur|able
se|cure
  se|cures
  se|cured
  se|cur|ing
se|cure|ly
se|cure|ment +s
Se|curi|tate
  (former Romanian
  internal security
  force)
se|curi|tisa|tion *Br.*
  (use
  securitization)
se|curi|tise *Br.* (use
  securitize)
  se|curi|tises
  se|curi|tised
  se|curi|tis|ing
se|curi|tiza|tion
se|curi|tize
  se|curi|tizes
  se|curi|tized
  se|curi|tiz|ing
se|cur|ity
  se|cur|ities
Sedan (battle site,
  France)
sedan +s (chair)
sedan chair +s
sed|ate
  sed|ates
  sed|ated
  sed|at|ing
sed|ate|ly
sed|ate|ness
sed|ation
seda|tive +s
sed|en|tar|ily
sed|en|tari|ness
sed|en|tary
Seder +s (Jewish
  ritual)
se|der|unt +s
sedge +s
Sedge|moor (battle
  site, England)
sedge warb|ler +s

Sedg|wick, Adam
  (English geologist)
sedgy
se|dile
  se|dilia
sedi|ment +s +ed
  +ing
sedi|ment|ary
sedi|men|ta|tion
  +s
se|di|tion +s
se|di|tion|ary
  se|di|tion|ar|ies
se|di|tion|ist +s
se|di|tious
se|di|tious|ly
se|duce
  se|duces
  se|duced
  se|du|cing
se|du|cer +s
se|du|cible
se|duc|tion +s
se|duc|tive
se|duc|tive|ly
se|duc|tive|ness
se|duc|tress
  se|duc|tresses
se|du|lity
sedu|lous
sedu|lous|ly
sedu|lous|ness
sedum +s
see
  sees
  saw
  see|ing
  seen
  (discern with the
  eyes; diocese;
  archdiocese.
  ⚠ sea, si)
see|able
seed +s +ed +ing
  (of plant; sow or
  remove seeds; in
  sports
  competition.
  ⚠ cede)
seed|bed +s
seed cake +s
seed-coat +s
seed|corn +s
seed-eater +s
seed|er +s (person
  or thing that
  seeds. ⚠ cedar)
seed-fish
  plural seed-fish
seed-head +s
seed|ily
seedi|ness

seed-leaf
  seed-leaves
seed|less
seed|ling +s
seed-lip +s
seed|pearl +s
seed-plot +s
seed po|tato
  seed po|ta|toes
seeds|man
  seeds|men
seed-time +s
seed ves|sel +s
seedy
  seed|ier
  seedi|est
See|ger, Pete
  (American
  musician)
see|ing +s
seek
  seeks
  sought
  seek|ing
  (look for. ⚠ Sikh)
seek|er +s (person
  who seeks. ⚠ sika,
  caeca)
seel +s +ed +ing
  (close a person's
  eyes. ⚠ seal)
seem +s +ed +ing
  (appear to be.
  ⚠ seam)
seem|ing +s
seem|ing|ly
seem|li|ness
seem|ly
  seem|lier
  seem|li|est
seen (past participle
  of see. ⚠ scene)
seep +s +ed +ing
seep|age +s
seer +s (prophet;
  measure. ⚠ cere,
  sear, sere)
seer|sucker +s
see-saw +s +ed
  +ing
seethe
  seethes
  seethed
  seeth|ing
seeth|ing|ly
see-through +s
  adjective and noun
Se|feris, George
  (Greek poet)
seg|ment +s +ed
  +ing
seg|men|tal

seg¦men¦tal¦
  isa¦tion *Br.* (use
  segmentaliza-
  tion)
seg¦men¦tal¦ise *Br.*
  (use
  segmentalize)
seg¦men¦tal¦ises
seg¦men¦tal¦ised
seg¦men¦tal¦is¦ing
seg¦men¦tal¦
  iza¦tion
seg¦men¦tal¦ize
seg¦men¦tal¦izes
seg¦men¦tal¦ized
seg¦men¦tal¦iz¦ing
seg¦men¦tal¦ly
seg¦men¦tary
seg¦men¦ta¦tion +s
sego +s
Sego|via (city,
  Spain)
Sego|via, An¦drés
  (Spanish guitarist)
seg¦reg¦able
seg¦re|gate
  seg¦re|gates
  seg¦re|gated
  seg¦re|gat¦ing
seg¦re|ga¦tion
seg¦re|ga¦tion|al
seg¦re|ga¦tion|ist
  +s
seg¦re|ga¦tive
segue
  segues
  segued
  segue|ing
segui|dilla +s
Sehn|sucht
sei +s (whale.
  △ say)
sei¦cent|ist +s
sei|cento (artistic
  and literary style)
sei|cento|ist +s
seiche +s
Seid|litz pow|der
  +s
seif +s
sei|gneur +s
sei|gneur|ial
sei|gneury (use
  seigniory)
sei¦gneur|ies
sei|gnior +s (use
  seigneur)
sei|gnior|age +s
sei|gnior|ial (use
  seigneurial)
sei|gniory
  sei¦gnor|ies

sei|gnor|age +s
  (use seigniorage)
Sei|kan Tun¦nel (in
  Japan)
Seine (river,
  France)
seine
  seines
  seined
  sein|ing
  (fishing net; fish or
  catch with a seine.
  △ sane)
seiner +s
  (fisherman; boat.
  △ saner)
seise (use seize)
  seises
  seised
  seis|ing
sei|sin +s
seis|mal
seis|mic
seis|mic|al
seis|mic|al|ly
seis|mi|city
seis|mo|gram +s
seis|mo|graph +s
seis|mo|graph¦er
  +s
seis|mo|graph¦ic
seis|mo|
      graph¦ic|al
seis|mog¦raphy
seis|mo|logic¦al
seis|mo|logic¦al|ly
seis|molo|gist +s
seis|mol¦ogy
seis|mom¦eter +s
seis|mo|met¦ric
seis|mo|met¦ric|al
seis|mom¦etry
seis|mo|scope +s
seis|mo|scop¦ic
sei whale +s
seiz|able
seize
  seizes
  seized
  seiz|ing
seizer +s
sei¦zin +s (use
  seisin)
seiz|ing +s
seiz|ure +s
se|jant
Sekh|met *Egyptian
  Mythology*
Sekt +s (wine.
  △ sect)
se|lach|ian +s
se|la|dang +s

selah (in Psalms.
  △ sealer)
Se|langor (state,
  Malaysia)
Sel|craig,
  Alex|an¦der
  (alternative name
  for Alexander
  Selkirk)
sel¦dom
se|lect +s +ed +ing
se|lect|able
se|lect|ee +s
se|lec|tion +s
se|lec|tion|al
se|lec|tion|al|ly
se|lect|ive
se|lect|ive|ly
se|lect|ive|ness
se|lect|iv¦ity
se|lect|man
  se|lect|men
se|lect|ness
se|lect|or +s
Sel|ena *also* Sel¦ina
sel|en|ate +s
Sel¦ene *Greek
  Mythology*
sel|en¦ic
sel|en|ide +s
sel|eni|ous
sel|en|ite
sel|en|it¦ic
sel|en|ium
sel|eno|cen¦tric
sel|eno|dont +s
sel|en|og¦raph¦er
  +s
sel|eno|graph¦ic
sel|en|og¦raphy
sel|en|olo¦gist +s
sel|en|ology
Se|leu|cid +s
self
  selves
  (individual)
self +s (flower)
self-abandon
self-abandoned
self-
  abandon|ment
self-abasement
self-abhorrence
self-abnegation
self-absorbed
self-absorp¦tion
self-abuse
self-accusa¦tion
self-accusa¦tory
self-acting
self-action
self-activity

self-addressed
self-adhesive
self-adjust|ing
self-adjust|ment
self-admiration
self-advance|ment
self-
  advertise|ment
self-advertiser +s
self-affirm¦ation
self-aggrand¦ise|
  ment *Br.* (use self-
  aggrandizement)
self-aggrand¦is|ing
  Br. (use self-
  aggrandizing)
self-aggrand¦ize|
      ment
self-
  aggrand¦iz|ing
self-analys|ing
self-analysis
self-appoint|ed
self-appreci¦ation
self-approba¦tion
self-approval
self-assembly
self-assert|ing
self-assertion
self-assert|ive
self-
  assert|ive|ness
self-assurance
self-assured
self-assured|ly
self-aware
self-awareness
self-begotten
self-betray|al
self-binder +s
self-born
self-catering
self-censor|ship
self-centred
self-centred|ly
self-centred|ness
self-certifi|ca¦tion
self-certify
  self-certifies
  self-certified
  self-certify|ing
self-cleaning
self-closing
self-cocking
self-collect|ed
self-colored *Am.*
self-coloured *Br.*
self-command
self-commun|ion
self-conceit
self-conceit|ed

self-
condem¦na¦tion
self-condemned
self-confessed
self-confidence
self-confident
self-confident¦ly
self-
congratu¦la¦tion
self-
congratu¦la¦tory
self-conquest
self-conscious
self-conscious¦ly
self-
conscious¦ness
self-consist¦ency
self-consist¦ent
self-constituted
self-contained
self-contain¦ment
self-contempt
self-
contemp¦tu¦ous
self-content
self-content¦ed
self-contra¦dic¦tion
+s
self-
contra¦dict¦ory
self-control
self-controlled
self-convict¦ed
self-correct¦ing
self-created
self-creation
self-critical
self-criticism
self-deceit
self-deceiver +s
self-deceiv¦ing
self-deception +s
self-deceptive
self-defeat¦ing
self-defence
self-defensive
self-delight
self-delusion +s
self-denial
self-denying
self-depend¦ence
self-depend¦ent
self-deprecat¦ing
self-
deprecat¦ing¦ly
self-depreca¦tion
self-depreci¦ation
self-deprecia¦tory
self-despair
self-destroy¦ing
self-destruct +s
+ed +ing

self-destruc¦tion
self-destruc¦tive
self-
destruc¦tive¦ly
self-
determin¦ation
self-determined
self-determin¦ing
self-develop¦ment
self-devotion
self-discip¦line
self-discip¦lined
self-discov¦ery
self-disgust
self-doubt
self¦hood
self-drive
self-educated
self-education
self-efface¦ment
self-effacing
self-effacing¦ly
self-elective
self-employed
self-employ¦ment
self-esteem
self-evidence
self-evident
self-evident¦ly
self-examin¦ation
self-execut¦ing
self-existent
self-explana¦tory
self-expres¦sion
self-expres¦sive
self-faced
self-feeder +s
self-feeding
self-fertile
self-fertil¦isa¦tion
Br. (use self-
fertilization)
self-fertil¦ised Br.
(use self-
fertilized)
self-fertil¦is¦ing Br.
(use self-
fertilizing)
self-fertil¦ity
self-fertil¦iza¦tion
self-fertil¦ized
self-fertil¦iz¦ing
self-finance
self-finances
self-financed
self-financing
self-flagel¦la¦tion
self-flatter¦ing
self-flattery
self-forget¦ful
self-
forget¦ful¦ness
self-fulfil¦ling

self-fulfill¦ment
Am.
self-fulfil¦ment Br.
self-generat¦ing
self-glorifi¦ca¦tion
self-governed
self-govern¦ing
self-govern¦ment
self-gratifi¦ca¦tion
self-gratify¦ing
self-hate
self-hatred
self-heal +s
self-help
self¦hood
self-image +s
self-immolat¦ing
self-immola¦tion
self-import¦ance
self-import¦ant
self-import¦ant¦ly
self-imposed
self-improve¦ment
self-induced
self-induct¦ance
self-induction
self-induct¦ive
self-indulgence +s
self-indulgent
self-indulgent¦ly
self-inflict¦ed
self-interest +s
self-interest¦ed
self-involved
self-involve¦ment
self¦ish
self¦ish¦ly
self¦ish¦ness
self-justifi¦ca¦tion
self-justify¦ing
self-knowledge
self¦less
self¦less¦ly
self¦less¦ness
self-loader +s
self-loading
self-locking
self-love
self-made
self-mastery
self¦mate +s Chess
self-mocking
self-motion
self-motivated
self-motiva¦tion
self-moving
self-murder
self-murder¦er +s
self-mutila¦tion +s
self-neglect
self¦ness
self-obsessed

self-opinion
self-opinion¦ated
self-parody
self-parody¦ing
self-perpetu¦at¦ing
self-perpetu¦ation
self-pity
self-pitying
self-pitying¦ly
self-pollin¦ated
self-pollin¦at¦ing
self-pollin¦ation
self-pollin¦ator +s
self-portrait +s
self-possessed
self-posses¦sion
self-praise
self-preser¦va¦tion
self-proclaimed
self-propagat¦ing
self-propelled
self-propel¦ling
self-protec¦tion
self-protect¦ive
self-raising
self-realisa¦tion
Br. (use self-
realization)
self-realiza¦tion
self-record¦ing
self-referen¦tial
self-regard
self-regard¦ing
self-register¦ing
self-regulat¦ing
self-regula¦tion
self-regula¦tory
self-reliance
self-reliant
self-reliant¦ly
self-renewal
self-renunci¦ation
self-reproach
self-reproach¦ful
self-respect
self-respect¦ing
self-restrained
self-restraint
self-reveal¦ing
self-revela¦tion
Self¦ridge, Harry
Gor¦don
(American-born
British
businessman)
self-righteous
self-righteous¦ly
self-
righteous¦ness
self-righting
self-rising
self-rule
self-sacrifice

self-sacrifi¦cing
self|same
self-satisfac¦tion
self-satisfied
self-satisfied¦ly
self-sealing
self-seed +s +ed
    +ing
self-seeker +s
self-seeking
self-select¦ing
self-selection
self-service
self-serving
self-slaugh¦ter
self-sown
self-starter +s
self-sterile
self-steril¦ity
self-styled
self-sufficiency
self-sufficient
self-sufficient¦ly
self-sufficing
self-sugges¦tion
self-support
self-support¦ing
self-surren¦der
self-sustained
self-sustain¦ing
self-tanning
self-tapping
self-taught
self-torture
self-
    understand¦ing
self-will
self-willed
self-winding
self-worth
Sel¦ima
Sel¦ina *also* Sel¦ena
Sel¦juk +s
Sel¦juk¦ian +s
Sel¦kirk,
    Alex¦an¦der
    (Scottish sailor)
Sel¦kirk|shire
    (former county,
    Scotland)
sell
    sells
    sold
    sell¦ing
    (dispose of for
    money. △ cell)
sell|able
Sel¦la|field (nuclear
    installation,
    England)
sell-by date +s

sell¦er +s (person
    who sells.
    △ cellar)
Sel¦lers, Peter
    (English comic
    actor)
sell¦ing point +s
sell¦ing race +s
sell-off +s *noun*
Sel¦lo|tape *noun*
    Propr.
sel¦lo|tape
    sel¦lo|tapes
    sel¦lo|taped
    sel¦lo|tap¦ing
    verb
sell-out +s *noun*
    and attributive
sell-through *noun*
    and attributive
Selma
Se¦lous, Fred¦erick
    Court¦enay
    (English explorer)
selt|zer +s
selv|age +s (use
    selvedge)
selv|edge +s
selves
Sel¦wyn
Selye, Hans Hugo
    Bruno (Austrian-
    born Canadian
    physician)
Selz|nick, David
    O. (American film
    producer)
se¦man¦teme +s
se¦man¦tic
se¦man¦tic¦al¦ly
se¦man¦ti¦cian +s
se¦man¦ti¦cist +s
se¦man¦tics
sema|phore
    sema|phores
    sema|phored
    sema|phor¦ing
sema|phor¦ic
sema|phor¦ic¦al¦ly
Se¦mar|ang (port,
    Indonesia)
se¦masio|logic¦al
se¦masi|ology
se¦mat¦ic
sem|blable +s
semb|lance +s
semé (*Heraldry.*
    △ semi)
semée (use semé)
Semei (city,
    Kazakhstan)

semei|ology (use
    semiology)
semei|ot¦ics (use
    semiotics)
Sem¦ele *Greek*
    Mythology
sem¦eme +s
semen (sperm.
    △ seaman)
se¦mes¦ter +s
Semey (use Semei)
semi +s (house;
    semi-final; semi-
    trailer. △ semé)
semi-annual
semi-annual¦ly
semi|aquat¦ic
semi|automat¦ic
semi-
    autono¦mous
semi-basement +s
semi-bold
semi|breve +s
semi|circle +s
semi|cir¦cu¦lar
semi-civilised *Br.*
    (use semi-
    civilized)
semi-civilized
semi|colon +s
semi|con¦duct|ing
semi|con¦duct¦or
    +s
semi-conscious
semi|cyl¦in|der +s
semi|cyl¦in¦drical
semi-darkness
semi|demi|semi|
    quaver +s
semi-deponent
semi-derelict
semi-detached +s
semi|diam¦eter +s
semi-
    documen¦tary
semi-
    documen¦tar¦ies
semi-dome +s
semi-double
semi-final +s
semi-finalist +s
semi-finished
semi-fitted
semi-fluid +s
semi-
    independ¦ent
semi-infinite
semi-invalid +s
semi-liquid +s
semi-literacy
semi-literate
Sé¦mil|lon +s

semi-lunar
semi-metal +s
semi-metallic
semi-monthly
sem|inal
sem¦in|al¦ly
sem|inar +s
sem¦in|ar|ian +s
sem¦in|ar|ist +s
sem¦in|ary
    sem¦in|ar|ies
sem¦in|ifer|ous
Sem|in|ole
    plural Sem|in|ole
    or Sem¦in|oles
semi-official
semi-official¦ly
semio|logic¦al
semi|olo¦gist +s
semi|ology
semi-opaque
semi|ot¦ic
semi|ot¦ic¦al
semi|ot¦ic¦al¦ly
semio|ti¦cian +s
semi|ot¦ics
Semi|pa¦la¦tinsk
    (former name of
    Semei)
semi|palm¦ated
semi-perman¦ent
semi-permeable
semi-plume +s
semi-precious
semi-pro +s
semi-
    profes¦sion|al +s
semi|quaver +s
Se¦mira|mis *Greek*
    Mythology
semi-retired
semi-retire¦ment
semi-rigid
semi-skilled
semi-skimmed
semi-smile +s
semi-solid
semi-sweet
semi-synthet¦ic
Sem¦ite +s
Sem¦it¦ic
Sem¦it¦isa|tion *Br.*
    (use
    Semitization)
Sem¦it¦ise *Br.* (use
    Semitize)
    Sem¦it¦ises
    Sem¦it¦ised
    Sem¦it¦is¦ing
Sem¦it¦ism
Sem¦it¦ist +s
Sem¦it¦iza|tion

Sem¦it¦ize
  Sem¦it¦izes
  Sem¦it¦ized
  Sem¦it¦iz¦ing
semi¦tone +s
semi-trailer +s
semi-transpar¦ent
semi-tropic¦al
semi-tropics
semi-uncial +s
semi¦vowel +s
semi-weekly
Sem¦mel¦weis,
  Ignaz Phil¦ipp
  (Austro-Hungarian
  obstetrician)
sem¦mit +s
semo¦lina
sem¦per¦vivum +s
sem¦pi¦ter¦nal
sem¦pi¦ter¦nal¦ly
sem¦pi¦ter¦nity
sem¦plice
sem¦pre
semp¦stress (use
  seamstress)
  semp¦stresses
Sem¦tex *Propr.*
Sena¦nay¦ake,
  Don Ste¦phen
  (Ceylonese prime
  minister)
sen¦ar¦ius
  sen¦arii
sen¦ary
sen¦ate +s
  (legislative body.
  ⚠ sennet, sennit)
sen¦ator +s
sen¦at¦or¦ial
sen¦at¦or¦ship +s
send
  sends
  sent
  send¦ing
send¦able
Sen¦dai (city,
  Japan)
sen¦dal +s
send¦er +s
sending-off
  sendings-off
send-off +s
send-up +s
Sen¦eca
  plural Sen¦eca *or*
  Sen¦ecas
  (American Indian)
Sen¦eca, Lu¦cius
  An¦naeus ('the
  Younger', Roman

Sen¦eca (*cont.*)
  statesman,
  philosopher, and
  dramatist)
Sen¦eca, Mar¦cus
  An¦naeus ('the
  Elder', Roman
  rhetorician)
se¦necio +s
Sene¦gal
Sene¦gal¦ese
  plural
  Sen¦egal¦ese
Sene¦gam¦bia
  (region, W. Africa)
sen¦esce
  sen¦esces
  sen¦esced
  sen¦es¦cing
sen¦es¦cence
sen¦es¦cent
sene¦schal +s
senhor +s
  (Portuguese or
  Brazilian man.
  ⚠ señor)
senhora +s
  (Portuguese
  woman; Brazilian
  married woman.
  ⚠ señora)
senhor¦ita +s
  (Brazilian
  unmarried
  woman.
  ⚠ señorita)
se¦nile +s
sen¦il¦ity
se¦nior +s
se¦ni¦or¦ity
sen¦iti
  plural sen¦iti
Senna, Ayr¦ton
  (Brazilian motor-
  racing driver)
senna +s
Sen¦nach¦erib
  (Assyrian king)
sen¦net +s
  (trumpet call.
  ⚠ senate, sennit)
sen¦night (week)
sen¦nit (plaited
  straw; in sense
  'braided cordage',
  use sinnet.
  ⚠ senate, sennet)
señor
  se¦ñores
  (Spanish-speaking
  man. ⚠ senhor)

se¦ñora +s (Spanish-
  speaking married
  woman.
  ⚠ senhora)
se¦ñor¦ita +s
  (Spanish-speaking
  unmarried
  woman.
  ⚠ senhorita)
sen¦sate
sen¦sa¦tion +s
sen¦sa¦tion¦al
sen¦sa¦tion¦al¦ise
  Br. (use
  sensationalize)
  sen¦sa¦tion¦al¦ises
  sen¦sa¦tion¦al¦
        ised
  sen¦sa¦tion¦al¦
        is¦ing
sen¦sa¦tion¦al¦ism
sen¦sa¦tion¦al¦ist
  +s
sen¦sa¦tion¦al¦
        is¦tic
sen¦sa¦tion¦al¦ize
  sen¦sa¦tion¦al¦izes
  sen¦sa¦tion¦al¦
        ized
  sen¦sa¦tion¦al¦
        iz¦ing
sen¦sa¦tion¦al¦ly
sense
  senses
  sensed
  sens¦ing
sense-datum
  sense-data
sense-experi¦ence
  +s
sense¦less
sense¦less¦ly
sense¦less¦ness
sense-organ +s
sens¦ibil¦ity
  sens¦ibil¦ities
sens¦ible
sens¦ible¦ness
sens¦ibly
sen¦si¦tisa¦tion *Br.*
  (use
  sensitization)
sen¦si¦tise *Br.* (use
  sensitize)
  sen¦si¦tises
  sen¦si¦tised
  sen¦si¦tis¦ing
sen¦si¦tiser *Br.* +s
  (use sensitizer)
sen¦si¦tive
sen¦si¦tive¦ly
sen¦si¦tive¦ness

sen¦si¦tiv¦ity
  sen¦si¦tiv¦ities
sen¦si¦tiza¦tion
sen¦si¦tize
  sen¦si¦tizes
  sen¦si¦tized
  sen¦si¦tiz¦ing
sen¦si¦tizer +s
sen¦si¦tom¦eter +s
sen¦sor +s
  (detecting or
  measuring device.
  ⚠ censer, censor)
sen¦sor¦ial
sen¦sori¦al¦ly
sen¦sor¦ily
sen¦sor¦ium
  sen¦sor¦iums *or*
  sen¦soria
sens¦ory
sens¦ual
sens¦ual¦ise *Br.*
  (use sensualize)
  sens¦ual¦ises
  sens¦ual¦ised
  sens¦ual¦is¦ing
sens¦ual¦ism
sens¦ual¦ist +s
sens¦u¦al¦ity
sens¦ual¦ize
  sens¦ual¦izes
  sens¦ual¦ized
  sens¦ual¦iz¦ing
sens¦u¦al¦ly
sen¦sum
  sensa
sen¦su¦ous
sen¦su¦ous¦ly
sen¦su¦ous¦ness
sensu stricto
sent +s (past tense
  and past participle
  of send; Estonian
  currency. ⚠ cent,
  scent)
sente
  li¦sente
sen¦tence
  sen¦tences
  sen¦tenced
  sen¦ten¦cing
sen¦ten¦tial
sen¦ten¦tious
sen¦ten¦tious¦ly
sen¦ten¦tious¦ness
sen¦tience
sen¦tiency
sen¦tient
sen¦tient¦ly
sen¦ti¦ment +s
sen¦ti¦men¦tal

sen|ti|men|tal|
  isa|tion*Br.* (use
  sentimentaliza-
  tion)
sen|ti|men|tal|ise
Br. (use
  sentimentalize)
sen|ti|men|tal|
           ises
sen|ti|men|tal|
           ised
sen|ti|men|tal|
         is|ing
sen|ti|men|tal|ism
sen|ti|men|tal|ist
 +s
sen|ti|men|tal|ity
sen|ti|men|tal|
      iza|tion
sen|ti|men|tal|ize
sen|ti|men|tal|
          izes
sen|ti|men|tal|
          ized
sen|ti|men|tal|
        iz|ing
sen|ti|men|tal|ly
sen|ti|nel
 sen|ti|nels *Br.*
 sen|ti|nelled *Br.*
 sen|ti|neled *Am.*
 sen|ti|nel|ling *Br.*
 sen|ti|nel|ing *Am.*
sen|try
 sen|tries
 sen|try box
 sen|try boxes
sentry-go
Se|nussi
 plural Se|nussi
Seoul (capital of
 South Korea)
sepal +s
sep|ar|abil|ity
sep|ar|able
sep|ar|able|ness
sep|ar|ably
sep|ar|ate
 sep|ar|ates
 sep|ar|ated
 sep|ar|at|ing
sep|ar|ate|ly
sep|ar|ate|ness
sep|ar|ation +s
sep|ar|at|ism
sep|ar|at|ist +s
sep|ara|tive
sep|ar|ator +s
sep|ar|atory
Seph|ardi
 Seph|ar|dim
 Seph|ar|dic

sepia +s
sepoy +s
sep|puku
sep|sis
 sep|ses
sept +s
 septa (plural of
  septum
  ⚠ scepter,
  sceptre)
sep|tal
sept|ate
sept|ation
septa|va|lent
sept|cen|ten|ary
 sept|cen|ten|
       ar|ies
Sep|tem|ber +s
sep|ten|ar|ius
 sep|ten|arii
sep|ten|ary
 sep|ten|ar|ies
sep|ten|ate
sep|ten|nial
sep|ten|nium
 sep|ten|niums *or*
 sep|ten|nia
sep|tet +s
sept|foil +s
sep|tic
septi|cae|mia *Br.*
septi|caem|ic *Br.*
sep|tic|al|ly
septi|cemia *Am.*
septi|cem|ic *Am.*
sep|ti|city
septi|lat|eral
sep|til|lion
 plural sep|til|lion
sep|timal
sep|time +s
Sep|tim|ius
 Se|verus (Roman
 emperor)
septi|va|lent
sep|tua|gen|ar|ian
 +s
sep|tua|gen|ary
 sep|tua|gen|ar|ies
Sep|tua|ges|ima
Sep|tua|gint
sep|tum
 septa
sep|tu|ple
 sep|tu|ples
 sep|tu|pled
 sep|tu|pling
sep|tu|plet +s
sep|ul|cher *Am.* +s
 +ed +ing
se|pul|chral
se|pul|chral|ly

sep|ul|chre *Br.*
 sep|ul|chres
 sep|ul|chred
 sep|ul|chring
sep|ul|ture +s
se|qua|cious
se|qua|cious|ly
se|qua|city
se|quel +s
se|quela
 se|que|lae
se|quence
 se|quences
 se|quenced
 se|quen|cing
se|quen|cer +s
se|quent
se|quen|tial
se|quen|ti|al|ity
se|quen|tial|ly
se|quent|ly
se|ques|ter +s +ed
 +ing
se|ques|trable
se|ques|tral
se|ques|trate
 se|ques|trates
 se|ques|trated
 se|ques|trat|ing
se|ques|tra|tion
se|ques|tra|tor +s
se|ques|trot|omy
se|ques|
      troto|mies
se|ques|trum
se|ques|tra
se|quin +s
se|quinned *Am.*
se|quinned *Br.*
sequi|tur (in 'non
 sequitur')
se|quoia +s
sera
serac +s
se|ra|glio +s
serai +s
Se|raing (town,
 Belgium)
Seram Sea (use
 Ceram Sea)
se|rang +s
se|rape +s
ser|aph
 ser|aph|im *or*
 ser|aphs
ser|aph|ic
ser|aph|ic|al|ly
Sera|pis *Egyptian
 Mythology*
ser|as|kier +s
Serb +s
Ser|bia

Ser|bian +s
Serbo-Croat +s
Serbo-Croatian +s
SERC (= Science
 and Engineering
 Research Council)
sere +s (of gun;
 sequence of
 animal or plant
 communities.
 ⚠ cere, sear, seer)
se| *rein* (fine rain)
Ser|em|ban (city,
 Malaysia)
Ser|ena
ser|en|ade
 ser|en|ades
 ser|en|aded
 ser|en|ad|ing
ser|en|ader +s
ser|en|ata +s
ser|en|dip|it|ous
ser|en|dip|it|ous|ly
ser|en|dip|ity
se|rene
 se|rener
 se|ren|est
 (calm. ⚠ serine)
se|rene|ly
se|rene|ness
Ser|en|geti (plain,
 Tanzania)
Se|ren|ity
 Se|ren|ities
 (title)
se|ren|ity
 se|ren|ities
 (tranquillity)
serf +s (labourer.
 ⚠ surf)
serf|age
serf|dom +s
serf|hood
serge +s (cloth.
 ⚠ surge)
ser|geancy
 ser|gean|cies
ser|geant +s (army,
 air force, or police
 officer,
 ⚠ serjeant)
Ser|geant Baker
 +s (fish)
sergeant-fish
 plural sergeant-
 fish *or* sergeant-
 fishes
ser|geant major
 +s
ser|geant|ship +s
Ser|gipe (state,
 Brazil)

Ser|gius (Russian saint)
ser|ial +s (story in episodes; forming a series. △cereal)
seri|al|isa|tion Br. +s (use serialization)
seri|al|ise Br. (use serialize)
seri|al|ises
seri|al|ised
seri|al|is|ing
seri|al|ism
seri|al|ist +s
seri|al|ity
seri|al|iza|tion +s
seri|al|ize
seri|al|izes
seri|al|ized
seri|al|iz|ing
ser|ial kill|er +s
seri|al|ly
ser|ial num|ber +s
ser|ial rights
seri|ate
seri|ates
seri|ated
seri|at|ing
seri|atim
seri|ation +s
Seric
se|ri|ceous
seri|cul|tural
seri|cul|ture
seri|cul|tur|ist +s
seri|ema +s
ser|ies
 plural ser|ies
serif +s
ser|iffed
seri|graph +s
ser|ig|raph|er +s
ser|ig|raphy
serin +s
ser|ine (amino acid. △serene)
ser|in|ette +s
ser|inga +s
serio-comic
serio-comical|ly
ser|ious
ser|ious|ly
ser|ious|ness
ser|jeant +s
 (barrister; army sergeant in official lists. △sergeant)
serjeant-at-arms
 serjeants-at-arms
serjeant-at-law
 serjeants-at-law

ser|jeant|ship +s
ser|mon +s
ser|mon|ette +s
ser|mon|ise Br. (use sermonize)
ser|mon|ises
ser|mon|ised
ser|mon|is|ing
ser|mon|iser Br. +s (use sermonizer)
ser|mon|ize
ser|mon|izes
ser|mon|ized
ser|mon|iz|ing
ser|mon|izer +s
sero|logic|al
sero|olo|gist +s
ser|ology
sero|nega|tive
sero|posi|tive
ser|osa +s
ser|os|ity
sero|tine +s
sero|tonin +s
ser|ous
serow +s
Ser|pens (constellation)
ser|pent +s
ser|pen|ti|form
ser|pen|tine
ser|pen|tines
ser|pen|tined
ser|pen|tin|ing
ser|pigin|ous
SERPS (= state earnings-related pension scheme)
ser|pula
ser|pu|lae
serra
ser|rae
ser|ra|dilla +s
ser|ran +s
ser|ranid +s
ser|rate
ser|rates
ser|rated
ser|rat|ing
ser|ra|tion +s
ser|ried
ser|ru|late
ser|ru|la|tion +s
serum
 sera *or* ser|ums
ser|val +s
ser|vant +s
serve
 serves
 served
 serv|ing
ser|ver +s

serv|ery
 serv|er|ies
Ser|vian +s
 (*archaic* variant of Serbian)
Ser|vian (of Servius Tullius, Roman king)
ser|vice
 ser|vices
 ser|viced
 ser|vicing
ser|vice|abil|ity
ser|vice|able
ser|vice|able|ness
ser|vice|ably
service-berry
 service-berries
ser|vice book +s
ser|vice|man
 ser|vice|men
ser|vice|woman
 ser|vice|women
ser|vi|lette +s
ser|vile
ser|vile|ly
ser|vil|ity
serv|ing +s
Ser|vite +s
ser|vi|tor +s
ser|vi|tor|ship +s
ser|vi|tude
servo +s
servo-mechan|ism +s
servo-motor +s
ses|ame +s
ses|am|oid
Se|so|tho
ses|qui|cen|ten|ary
ses|qui|cen|ten|ar|ies
ses|qui|cen|ten|nial +s
ses|qui|ped|alian +s
sess (use cess)
ses|sile
ses|sion +s
 (meeting; bout. △cession)
ses|sion|al
ses|terce +s
ses|ter|tium
 ses|ter|tia
ses|ter|tius
 ses|ter|tii
ses|tet +s
ses|tina +s
Set (= Seth)

set
 sets
 set
 set|ting
 (all senses except badger's burrow and paving block; for these, use sett)
seta
 setae
se|ta|ceous
set-aside +s *noun and attributive*
set|back +s
se-tenant
Seth (*Egyptian Mythology*; name)
SETI (= Search for Extraterrestrial Intelligence)
se|tif|er|ous
se|tiger|ous
set-off +s *noun*
seton +s
se|tose
set piece +s *noun*
set-piece *attributive*
set square +s
Set|swana (language)
sett +s (badger's burrow; paving-block. △set)
set|tee +s
set|ter +s (dog; person or thing that sets. △saeter)
set|ter|wort
set|ting +s
set|tle
 set|tles
 set|tled
 set|tling
settle|able
settle|ment +s
set|tler +s (person who settles in a new place)
set|tlor +s *Law*
set-to +s *noun*
Setú|bal (port, Portugal)
set-up +s *noun*
set|wall +s
Seu|rat, Georges Pierre (French painter)
Se|vas|to|pol (Russian name for Sebastopol)
seven +s

seven|fold
seven-iron +s
seven|teen +s
seven|teenth +s
sev|enth +s
Seventh-Day
Ad¦vent|ist +s
sev|enth¦ly
seven|ti¦eth +s
sev|enty
sev¦en|ties
seventy-first,
    seventy-second,
    etc.
sev|enty|fold
seventy-one,
    seventy-two,
    etc.
sever +s +ed +ing
sev|er|able
sev|eral +s
sev|er|al¦ly
sev|er|al¦ty
    sev¦er|al|ties
sev|er|ance +s
se¦vere
    se|verer
    se|ver¦est
se|vere¦ly
se|ver|ity
    se|ver|ities
Sev|ern (river,
    England and
    Wales)
Se|ver|naya
    Zem¦lya (island
    group, north of
    Russia)
Sev|er¦od|vinsk
    (port, Russia)
Se|verus (Roman
    emperor)
sev|ery
    sev¦er|ies
se|viche
Sev|ille (city, Spain;
    orange)
Sèvres (town,
    France; porcelain)
sew
    sews
    sewed
    sew¦ing
    sewn
    (stitch. △ so, soh,
    sow)
sew¦age
se|wel|lel +s
sewen +s (use
    sewin)
sewer +s
sew¦er|age

sewin +s
sew¦ing ma|chine
    +s
sewn (past
    participle of sew.
    △ sown)
sex
    sexes
    sexed
    sex¦ing
sexa|gen¦ar¦ian +s
sexa|gen¦ary
    sexa|gen¦ar|ies
Sexa|ges¦ima
    (church calendar)
sexa|ges¦imal +s
sexa|ges¦im|al¦ly
sex|angu¦lar
sexa|va¦lent
sex|cen¦ten¦ary
    sex|cen¦ten|ar¦ies
sex|digi¦tate
sex|en¦nial
sexer +s
sex|foil +s
sex¦ily
sexi|ness
sex¦ism
sex¦ist +s
sexi|syl¦lab¦ic
sexi|syl¦lable +s
sexi|va¦lent
sex|less
sex|less¦ly
sex|less|ness
sex-linked
sexo|logic¦al
sex|olo¦gist +s
sex|ology
sex|par¦tite
sex|ploit|ation
sex|pot +s
sex-starved
sext +s
sex|tain +s
sex|tant +s
sex|tet +s
sex|til|lion
    plural sex|til|lion
    or sex¦til|lions
sex|til|lionth +s
sexto +s
sexto|decimo +s
sex|ton +s
sex|tu¦ple
    sex|tu¦ples
    sex|tu¦pled
    sex¦tu¦pling
sex|tu¦plet +s
sex|tu¦ply
sex|ual

sexu¦al|ise Br. (use
    sexualize)
    sexu¦al|ises
    sexu¦al|ised
    sexu¦al|is¦ing
sexu¦al|ist +s
sexu|al¦ity
    sexu|al¦ities
sexu¦al|ize
    sexu¦al|izes
    sexu¦al|ized
    sexu¦al|iz¦ing
sexu|al¦ly
sex|va¦lent
sexy
    sex¦ier
    sexi|est
Sey|chelles
    (islands, Indian
    Ocean)
Sey¦chel|lois
    plural
    Sey¦chel|lois
    male
Sey¦chel|loise +s
    female
Sey|mour, Jane
    (wife of Henry
    VIII of England)
Sey|mour, Lynn
    (Canadian ballet
    dancer)
sez (= says)
Sfax (port, Tunisia)
sforz|ando
sforz¦an¦dos or
    sforz|andi
sforz|ato
sfu|mato
sfu|mati
sgraf|fito
    sgraf|fiti
's-Gravenhage
    (= The Hague, the
    Netherlands)
sh
Shaanxi (province,
    China)
Shaba (region,
    Zaire)
Sha|baka (pharaoh)
shab|bily
shab|bi|ness
shabby
    shab|bier
    shab|bi|est
shab|by|ish
shab|rack +s
shack +s +ed +ing
shackle
    shackles

shackle (cont.)
    shackled
    shack|ling
shackle-bolt +s
Shackle|ton,
    Er¦nest (Irish
    explorer)
shad
    plural shad or
    shads
shad|dock +s
shade
    shades
    shaded
    shad¦ing
shade|less
shadi¦ly
shadi|ness
shad|ing +s
sha|doof +s
shadow +s +ed
    +ing
shadow-boxing
shad|ow¦er +s
shad|ow|graph +s
shad|owi|ness
shad|ow|less
shad|owy
shady
    shadi¦er
    shadi|est
shaft +s +ed +ing
Shaftes|bury, Lord
    (English social
    reformer)
shag
    shags
    shagged
    shag|ging
    (hair etc.; carpet
    pile; tobacco; bird;
    also coarse slang)
shag|ger +s (coarse
    slang)
shag|gily
shag¦gi|ness
shaggy
    shag|gier
    shag¦gi|est
shag pile +s
sha|green +s
shah +s
Shah Alam (city,
    Malaysia)
shah|dom +s
shaikh +s (use
    sheikh. △ shake)
Shaka (Zulu chief)
shake
    shakes
    shook
    shak¦ing

shake (*cont.*)
  shaken
  (agitate. △ sheikh)
shake|able
shake|down +s
shake-out +s *noun*
Shaker +s
  (religious sect
  member)
shaker +s (person
  or thing that
  shakes)
Shaker|ess
  Shaker|esses
Shaker|ism
Shake|speare,
  Wil|liam (English
  dramatist)
Shake|spear|ean
  +s
Shake|speare|ana
Shake|spear|ian
  +s (use
  Shakespearean)
Shake|speari|ana
  (use
  Shakespeareana)
shake-up +s *noun*
Shakhty (city,
  Russia)
shaki|ly
shaki|ness
shako +s
shaku|hachi +s
shaky
  shaki|er
  shaki|est
shale +s
shall
shal|loon +s
shal|lop +s
shal|lot +s (plant.
  △ Shalott)
shal|low +er +est
shal|low|ly
shal|low|ness
Shal|man|eser
  (Assyrian kings)
sha|lom +s
Sha|lott (in *'The
  Lady of Shalott'*.
  △ shallot)
shalt
shal|war
shaly
  shali|er
  shali|est
sham
  shams
  shammed
  sham|ming
shaman +s

sha|man|ic
sham|an|ism
sham|an|ist +s
sham|an|is|tic
shama|teur +s
shama|teur|ism
sham|ble
  sham|bles
  sham|bled
  sham|bling
  (walk or run
  awkwardly)
sham|bles (mess;
  slaughterhouse;
  scene of carnage)
sham|bol|ic
shame
  shames
  shamed
  sham|ing
shame|faced
shame|faced|ly
shame|faced|ness
shame|ful
shame|ful|ly
shame|ful|ness
shame|less
shame|less|ly
shame|less|ness
sham|ing|ly
Sha|mir, Yit|zhak
  (Israeli prime
  minister)
sham|mer +s
shammy
  sham|mies
sham|poo +s +ed
  +ing
sham|rock +s
sha|mus
sha|muses
Shand|ean +s
Shan|dong
  (province, China)
shan|dry|dan +s
shandy
  shan|dies
shandy|gaff +s
Shang (Chinese
  dynasty)
Shan|gaan
  plural Shan|gaan
  or Shan|gaans
Shang|hai (city,
  China)
shang|hai +s +ed
  +ing (trick into
  joining ship's
  crew; shoot with
  catapult)
Shangri-La +s
  (fictional utopia)

shank +s
Shan|kar, Ravi
  (Indian musician)
shanked
shanks's mare
shanks's pony
Shan|non (river
  and airport,
  Republic of
  Ireland; shipping
  area, NE Atlantic)
Shan|non, Claude
  El|wood
  (American
  engineer)
shanny
  shan|nies
Shansi (= Shanxi)
shan't (= shall not)
Shan|tou (port,
  China)
Shan|tung
  (= Shandong)
shan|tung +s (silk)
shanty
  shan|ties
shanty|man
  shanty|men
shanty town +s
Shanxi (province,
  China)
shap|able
SHAPE (= Supreme
  Headquarters
  Allied Powers in
  Europe)
shape
  shapes
  shaped
  shap|ing
shape|able (use
  shapable)
shape|chan|ger +s
shape|chan|ging
shape|less
shape|less|ly
shape|less|ness
shape|li|ness
shape|ly
  shape|lier
  shape|li|est
shaper +s
shap|ing +s
Shap|ley, Har|low
  (American
  astronomer)
shard +s
share
  shares
  shared
  shar|ing
share|able

share|crop
  share|crops
  share|cropped
  share|crop|ping
share|crop|per +s
share-farmer +s
share|hold|er +s
share|hold|ing +s
share-out +s *noun*
sharer +s
share|ware
sha|ria
sha|riah (use
  sharia)
sha|rif +s
Shar|jah (city state,
  UAE)
shark +s
shark|skin +s
Sharma, Shan|kar
  Dayal (Indian
  president)
Sharon (coastal
  plain, Israel)
Sharon *also*
  Shar|ron
  (name)
sharon fruit +s
Sharp, Cecil
  (English collector
  of folk-songs and
  folk dances)
sharp +s +ed +ing
  +er +est
shar-pei +s
sharp|en +s +ed
  +ing
sharp|en|er +s
sharp|en|ing +s
sharp|er +s
Sharpe|ville
  (township, South
  Africa)
sharp-eyed
sharp|ish
sharp|ly
sharp|ness
sharp-set
sharp|shoot|er +s
sharp|shoot|ing
sharp-tongued
sharp-witted
sharp-witted|ly
sharp-witted|ness
Shar|ron *also*
  Sharon
shash|lik +s
Shasta +s (daisy)
Shas|tra
shat (*coarse slang*)
Shatt al-Arab
  (river, Iraq)

shat|ter +s +ed
  +ing
shat|ter|er +s
shat|ter|ing|ly
shatter-proof
Shaun *also* Sean
shave
  shaves
  shaved
  shav|ing
shave|ling +s
shaven
shaven-headed
shaver +s
Sha|vian +s
shav|ing +s
Sha|vuot (use
  Shavuoth)
Sha|vu|oth (Jewish
  Pentecost)
Shaw, George
  Ber|nard (Irish
  playwright)
shaw +s (vegetable
  stalks and leaves.
  △ shore, sure)
shawl +s (garment.
  △ schorl)
shawled
shawlie +s
  (working-class
  woman. △ surely)
shawm +s
Shaw|nee
  plural Shaw|nee *or*
  Shaw|nees
Shcher|ba|kov
  (former name of
  Rybinsk)
shchi +s (soup)
she
s/he (= she or he)
shea +s (tree)
shea-butter +s
shead|ing +s
  (administrative
  division, Isle of
  Man)
sheaf
  sheaves
  noun
sheaf +s +ed +ing
  verb
sheal|ing +s (use
  shieling)
shear
  shears
  sheared
  shear|ing
  sheared *or* shorn
  (cut with shears.
  △ sheer)

shear|bill +s
Shear|er, Moira
  (Scottish ballet
  dancer)
shear|er +s (person
  who shears sheep)
shear|ing +s
shear|ling +s
shear|tail +s
shear|water +s
sheath +s
sheathe
  sheathes
  sheathed
  sheath|ing
sheath|ing +s
sheath|less
sheath-like
sheave
  sheaves
  sheaved
  sheav|ing
sheaves (plural of
  sheaf)
Sheba (ancient
  country)
she|bang +s
She|bat (use Sebat)
she|been +s
She|chi|nah (use
  Shekinah)
shed
  sheds
  shed
  shed|ding
  (building; throw
  off, spill, separate,
  etc.)
shed
  sheds
  shed|ded
  shed|ding
  (keep in shed)
she'd (= she had;
  she would)
shed|der +s
she-devil +s
shed|hand +s
Shee|lagh *also*
  Sheila, She|lagh
Sheela-na-gig +s
sheen +s +ed +ing
Sheena
Sheene, Barry
  (English racing
  motorcyclist)
sheeny
sheen|ier
sheeni|est
sheep
  plural sheep
sheep-dip +s

sheep|dog +s
sheep farm|er +s
sheep farm|ing
sheep|fold +s
sheep|ish
sheep|ish|ly
sheep|ish|ness
sheep|like
sheep|meat
sheep-run +s
sheep's-bit +s
  (plant)
sheep|shank +s
  (knot)
sheep|skin +s
sheep|walk +s
sheep-worrying
sheer +s +ed +ing
  +est (swerve;
  shape of ship;
  mere; unqualified;
  steep; thin.
  △ shear)
sheer|legs
  plural sheer|legs
sheer|ly
Sheer|ness (port,
  England)
sheer|ness
sheet +s +ed +ing
sheet|ing
Shef|field (city,
  England)
sheik +s (use
  sheikh. △ shake)
sheik|dom +s (use
  sheikhdom)
sheikh +s (Arab
  chief; Muslim
  leader. △ shake)
sheikh|dom +s
Sheila *also*
  Shee|lagh,
  She|lagh (name)
sheila +s
  (young woman)
shekel +s
She|ki|nah
She|lagh *also*
  Shee|lagh, Sheila
shel|drake +s
shel|duck +s
shelf
  shelves
  (ledge)
shelf +s +ed +ing
  (inform; informer.
  △ shelve)
shelf|ful +s
shelf-life
  shelf-lives
shelf-like

shelf mark +s
shelf-room
shell +s +ed +ing
  (case of mollusc,
  egg, etc.)
she'll (= she will;
  she shall. △ shill)
shel|lac
  shel|lacs
  shel|lacked
  shel|lack|ing
shell|back +s
shell-bit +s
Shel|ley (name)
Shel|ley, Mary
  Woll|stone|craft
  (English writer)
Shel|ley, Percy
  Bysshe (English
  poet)
shell|fire
shell|fish
  plural shell|fish *or*
  shell|fishes
shell-heap +s
shell-jacket +s
shell-keep +s
shell-less
shell-like
shell-lime
shell-money
shell-out +s *noun*
shell pink +s *noun*
  and attributive
shell-pink
  attributive
shell|proof
shell-shock
shell-shocked
shell suit +s
shell-work
shelly
Shelta (language)
shel|ter +s +ed
  +ing (protection;
  protect)
shel|ter belt +s
shel|ter|er +s
shel|ter|less
shel|tie +s
shelve
  shelves
  shelved
  shelv|ing
shelver +s
shelves (plural of
  shelf)
Shem *Bible*
Shema +s
she|moz|zle +s
Shen|an|doah
  (river and

Shen|an|doah
(*cont.*)
National Park,
USA)
she|nani|gan +s
Shensi (= Shaanxi)
Shen|yang (city,
China)
Shen|zhen (city,
China)
Sheol
shep|herd +s +ed
+ing
shep|herd|ess
shep|herd|esses
shep|herd's purse
+s
Shep|pey, Isle of
(in England)
sher|ard|ise *Br.*
(use sherardize)
she|rard|ises
sher|ard|ised
sher|ard|is|ing
sher|ard|ize
sher|ard|izes
sher|ard|ized
sher|ard|iz|ing
Shera|ton (style of
furniture)
sher|bet +s
sherd +s
she|reef +s (use
sharif)
Sheri|dan,
Rich|ard
Brins|ley (Irish
dramatist)
Sheri|dan
she|rif +s (*Islam*;
use sharif)
sher|iff +s (civil or
law officer)
sher|iff|alty
sher|iff|al|ties
sheriff-depute +s
sher|iff|dom +s
sher|iff|hood +s
sher|iff|ship +s
Sher|lock +s
Sher|man,
Wil|liam
(American
general)
Sherpa
plural Sherpa *or*
Sher|pas
Sher|rill (man's
name. △ Sheryl)
Sher|ring|ton,
Charles Scott

Sher|ring|ton
(*cont.*)
(English
physiologist)
Sherry (name)
sherry
sher|ries
(drink)
sherry glass
sherry glasses
's-Hertogenbosch
(city, the
Netherlands)
Sheryl (woman's
name. △ Sherrill)
she's (= she is; she
has)
Shet|land (region,
Scotland)
Shet|land|er +s
Shet|land Is|lands
(in Scotland)
Shet|lands
(= Shetland
Islands)
sheva +s (use
schwa)
Shev|ard|nadze,
Ed|uard
(Georgian
statesman)
She|vat (use Sebat)
shew
shews
shewed
shew|ing
shewn *or* shewed
(*archaic*; use
show)
shew|bread
Shia +s (branch of
Islam; Shi'ite)
shi|atsu (Japanese
therapy. △ shih-
tzu)
shib|bo|leth +s
shicer +s
shick|er
shick|ered
shield +s +ed +ing
shield bug +s
shield|less
shiel|ding +s
shier (comparative
of shy)
shiest (superlative
of shy)
shift +s +ed +ing
shift|able
shift|er +s
shift|ily
shifti|ness

shift|less
shift|less|ly
shift|less|ness
shift work
shifty
shift|ier
shifti|est
shi|gella +s
shih-tzu +s (dog.
△ shiatsu)
Shi'|ism
shii|take +s
Shi'|ite +s
Shi|jiaz|huang
(city, China)
shi|kar +s
shi|kara +s
shi|kari +s
Shi|koku (island,
Japan)
shiksa +s (*often
offensive*)
shill +s (person
who drums up
business. △ she'll)
shil|le|lagh +s
shil|ling +s
(Kenyan,
Tanzanian,
Ugandan, and
former British
currency.
△ schilling)
shilling-mark +s
shil|lings|worth +s
Shil|long (city,
India)
shilly-shallier +s
(use shilly-
shallyer)
shilly-shally
shilly-shallies
shilly-shallied
shilly-shally|ing
shilly-shally|er +s
shim
shims
shimmed
shim|ming
shim|mer +s +ed
+ing
shim|mer|ing|ly
shim|mery
shimmy
shim|mies
shim|mied
shimmy|ing
shin
shins
shinned
shin|ning
shin bone +s

shin|dig +s
shindy
shin|dies
shine
shines
shined *or* shone
shin|ing
shiner +s
shin|gle
shin|gles
shin|gled
shin|gling
shin|gly
shin-guard +s
shini|ly
shini|ness
shin|ing|ly
Shin|kan|sen
plural
Shin|kan|sen
shinny
shin|nies
shin|nied
shinny|ing
shin-pad +s
Shinto
Shin|to|ism
Shin|to|ist +s
shinty
shin|ties
shiny
shini|er
shini|est
ship
ships
shipped
ship|ping
ship|board
ship-breaker +s
ship-broker +s
ship|build|er +s
ship|build|ing
ship canal +s
ship-fever
ship|lap
ship|laps
ship|lapped
ship|lap|ping
ship|less
ship|load +s
ship|mas|ter +s
ship|mate +s
ship|ment +s
ship money
ship|owner +s
ship|pable
ship|per +s
ship|ping agent +s
shipping-articles
shipping-bill +s
shipping-master
+s

shipping-office +s
ship-rigged
ship|shape
ship-to-shore +s
ship|way +s
ship|worm +s
ship|wreck +s +ed +ing
ship|wright +s
ship|yard +s
shira|lee +s
Shi|raz
　Shi|razes
　(city, Iran; grape;
　wine)
shire +s (county.
　△ shyer)
shire-horse +s
shire-moot +s
shirk +s +ed +ing
shirk|er +s
Shir|ley
shirr +s +ed +ing
shirt +s
shirt-dress
　shirt-dresses
shirt|ed
shirt-front +s
shirt|ily
shirti|ness
shirt|ing +s
shirt|less
shirt|sleeve +s
shirt-sleeved
shirt-tail +s
shirt|waist +s
shirt|waist|er +s
shirty
　shirt|ier
　shirti|est
shish kebab +s
shit
　shits
　shit|ted *or* shit *or*
　shat
　shit|ting
　(*coarse slang*)
shit|bag +s (*coarse
　slang*)
shit creek (*coarse
　slang*)
shite +s (*coarse
　slang*)
shit|house +s
　(*coarse slang*)
shit|less (*coarse
　slang*)
shit-scared (*coarse
　slang*)
shitty
　shit|tier

shitty (*cont.*)
　shit|ti|est
　(*coarse slang*)
Shiva (use Siva)
Shi|vaji (Indian
　raja)
shiva|ree +s
shiver +s +ed +ing
shiv|er|er +s
shiv|er|ing|ly
shiv|ery
shi|voo +s
Shizu|oka (city,
　Japan)
Shko|dër (city,
　Albania)
shoal +s +ed +ing
shoaly
shoat +s
shock +s +ed +ing
shock|abil|ity
shock|able
shock-brigade +s
shock cord +s
shock|er +s
shock|ing|ly
shock|ing|ness
shock|ing pink
Shock|ley,
　Wil|liam
　(American
　physicist)
shock|proof
shock wave +s
shock-worker +s
shod
shod|dily
shod|di|ness
shoddy
　shod|dier
　shod|di|est
shoe
　shoes
　shod
　shoe|ing
　(footwear; on
　horse. △ choux,
　shoo)
shoe|bill +s
shoe|black +s
shoe|box
　shoe|boxes
shoe-buckle +s
shoe|horn +s +ed
　+ing
shoe|lace +s
shoe lea|ther +s
shoe|less
shoe|maker +s
Shoemaker–Levy
　9 (comet)
shoe|mak|ing

shoe|shine
shoe|string +s
shoe-tree +s
sho|far
　shof|roth
　(ram's-horn
　trumpet.
　△ chauffeur)
sho|gun +s
sho|gun|ate +s
Sho|la|pur (city,
　India)
Sholo|khov,
　Mikh|ail (Russian
　writer)
Shona
　plural Shona *or*
　Sho|nas
　(group of Bantu
　peoples; any of
　their languages;
　name)
shone
shonky
　shonk|ier
　shonki|est
shoo +s +ed +ing
shoo-in +s *noun*
shook +s
shoot
　shoots
　shot
　shoot|ing
　(fire gun etc.; act
　of shooting.
　△ chute)
shoot|able
shoot|er +s
shoot|ing +s
shoot|ing box
　shoot|ing boxes
shoot|ing brake +s
shoot|ing coat +s
shoot|ing gal|lery
　shoot|ing
　gal|ler|ies
shoot|ing iron +s
shoot|ing match
shoot|ing range +s
shoot|ing stick +s
shoot-out +s *noun*
shop
　shops
　shopped
　shop|ping
shop|ahol|ic +s
shop-bought
shop boy +s
shop|fit|ter +s
shop|fit|ting
shop floor +s *noun*

shop-floor
　attributive
shop|front +s
shop girl +s
shop|keep|er +s
shop|keep|ing
shop|less
shop|lift +s +ed
　+ing
shop|lift|er +s
shop|man
　shop|men
shop owner +s
shop|per +s
shoppy
shop-soiled
shop talk
shop|walk|er +s
shop win|dow +s
shop|work|er +s
shop|worn
shoran
shore
　shores
　shored
　shor|ing
　(coast; prop.
　△ shaw, sure)
shore-based
shore|bird +s
shore|less
shore|line +s
shore|ward
shore|wards
shore|weed +s
shorn
short +s +ed +ing
　+er +est
short|age +s
short-arm *adjective*
short|bread +s
short|cake +s
short-change
　short-changes
　short-changed
　short-changing
　verb
short-circuit +s
　+ed +ing *verb*
short|com|ing +s
short|crust
short cut +s
short-dated
short-day *adjective*
short-eared owl
　+s
short|en +s +ed
　+ing
short|en|ing +s
short|fall +s
short|hair +s
short-haired

short|hand
short-handed
short-haul
  attributive
short-head +s +ed
  +ing *verb*
short|hold
short|horn +s
shortie +s (use
  shorty)
short|ish
short|list +s +ed
  +ing
short-lived
short|ly
short|ness
short-order
  attributive
short-pitched
short-range
  adjective
short-sighted
short-sighted|ly
short-sighted|ness
short-sleeved
short-staffed
short|stop +s
short-tempered
short-term
  adjective
short-termism
short-winded
shorty
  short|ies
Sho|shone
  plural Sho|shone
  or Sho|shones
Sho|shon|ean
Shosta|ko|vich,
  Dmi|tri (Russian
  composer)
shot +s
shot-blasting +s
shot-firer +s
shot|gun +s
shot|proof
shot-put +s
shot-putter +s
shot|ten
shot-tower +s
should
shoul|der +s +ed
  +ing
shoul|der bag +s
shoulder-belt +s
shoul|der blade +s
shoulder-high
shoul|der hol|ster
  +s
shoulder-knot +s
shoulder-length
shoul|der note +s
shoul|der pad +s

shoul|der strap +s
shouldn't
  (= should not)
shout +s +ed +ing
shout|er +s
shout-up +s *noun*
shove
  shoves
  shoved
  shov|ing
shove-halfpenny
shovel
  shovels
  shov|elled *Br.*
  shov|eled *Am.*
  shov|el|ling *Br.*
  shov|el|ing *Am.*
shovel|board
shov|el|er *Am.* +s
  (*Br.* shoveller)
shovel|ful +s
shovel|head +s
shov|el|ler *Br.* +s
  (*Am.* shoveler)
show
  shows
  showed
  show|ing
  shown *or* showed
show|band +s
show|biz
show|boat +s
show|card +s
show|case
  show|cases
  show|cased
  show|cas|ing
show|down +s
shower +s +ed
  +ing
shower|proof +s
  +ed +ing
show|ery
show flat +s
show|girl +s
show|ground +s
show home +s
show house +s
show|ily
showi|ness
show|ing +s
show|jump +s +ed
  +ing
show|jump|er +s
show|man
  show|men
show|man|ship
shown
show-off +s *noun*
show|piece +s
show|place +s
show|room +s
show-stopper +s

show-stopping
show|time
show-window +s
showy
  show|ier
  showi|est
shoyu
shrank
shrap|nel +s
shred
  shreds
  shred|ded
  shred|ding
shred|der +s
Shreve|port (city,
  USA)
shrew +s
shrewd +er +est
shrewd|ly
shrewd|ness
shrew|ish
shrew|ish|ly
shrew|ish|ness
Shrews|bury
  (town, England)
shriek +s +ed +ing
shriek|er +s
shrieval
shriev|al|ty
  shriev|al|ties
shrift +s
shrike +s
shrill +s +ed +ing
shrill|ness
shrilly
shrimp +s +ed
  +ing
shrimp|er +s
shrine
  shrines
  shrined
  shrin|ing
shrink
  shrinks
  shrank
  shrink|ing
  shrunk
shrink|able
shrink|age +s
shrink|er +s
shrink|ing|ly
shrink-proof
shrink-resist|ant
shrink-wrap
  shrink-wraps
  shrink-wrapped
  shrink-wrapping
shrive
  shrives
  shrove
  shriv|ing
  shriven

shrivel
  shrivels
  shriv|elled *Br.*
  shriv|eled *Am.*
  shriv|el|ling *Br.*
  shriv|el|ing *Am.*
Shrop|shire
  (county, England)
shroud +s +ed
  +ing
shroud-laid
shroud|less
shrove
Shrove|tide +s
Shrove Tues|day
  +s
shrub +s
shrub|bery
  shrub|ber|ies
shrubby
  shrub|bier
  shrub|bi|est
shrug
  shrugs
  shrugged
  shrug|ging
shrunk
shrunk|en
shtick +s
shtook
shu|bun|kin +s
shuck +s +ed +ing
shuck|er +s
shucks
shud|der +s +ed
  +ing
shud|der|ing|ly
shud|dery
shuf|fle
  shuf|fles
  shuf|fled
  shuf|fling
shuffle-board
shuf|fler +s
shuf|fling +s
shufti +s
shul +*s*
Shula
Shula|mit *also*
  Shula|mith
shule +*s* (use *shul*)
Shu|men (city,
  Bulgaria)
shun
  shuns
  shunned
  shun|ning
shunt +s +ed +ing
shunt|er +s
shush
  shushes

shush (*cont.*)
shushed
shush|ing
shut
shuts
shut
shut|ting
shut|down +s
Shute, Nevil
(English novelist)
shut-eye
shut-in +s *adjective
and noun*
shut-off +s *noun
and attributive*
shut|out +s
adjective and noun
shut-out bid +s
shut|ter +s +ed
+ing
shut|ter|less
shut|tle
shut|tles
shut|tled
shut|tling
shuttle|cock +s
shy
shies
shied
shy|ing
shyer
shy|est
shyer +s (horse etc.
that shies.
△ shire)
Shy|lock (character
in Shakespeare)
shyly
shy|ness
shy|ster +s
si (*Music.* △ sea,
see)
Sia|chen Gla|cier
(in India)
sial
siala|gogue +s (use
sialogogue)
Si|al|kot (city,
Pakistan)
sialo|gogue +s
Siam (former name
of Thailand)
Siam, Gulf of
(former name of
the Gulf of
Thailand)
sia|mang +s
Siam|ese
plural Siam|ese
Siân
sib +s

Si|bel|ius, Jean
(Finnish
composer)
Ši|benik (port,
Croatia)
Si|ber|ia
Si|ber|ian +s
sibi|lance
sibi|lancy
sibi|lant +s
sibi|late
sibi|lates
sibi|lated
sibi|lat|ing
sibi|la|tion +s
Sibiu (city,
Romania)
sib|ling +s
sib|ship +s
Sibyl *also* Sybil
(name)
sibyl +s
(prophetess)
sibyl|line (of a
sibyl; prophetic)
Sibyl|line books
(Roman oracles)
sic (correct thus.
△ sick)
sic|ca|tive +s
sice +s (the six on
dice. △ syce)
Si|chuan (province,
China)
Si|cil|ian +s
si|cili|ana +s
si|cili|ano +s
Si|cily
sick +s +ed +ing
+er +est (ill.
△ *sic*)
sick bag +s
sick|bay +s
sick|bed +s
sick bene|fit +s
sick call +s
sick|en +s +ed
+ing
sick|en|er +s
sick|en|ing|ly
Sick|ert, Wal|ter
Rich|ard (British
painter)
sick flag +s
sickie +s
sick|ish
sickle +s
sick leave
sickle-bill +s
sickle-cell +s
sickle-feather +s
sick|li|ness

sick list +s
sick|ly
sick|lier
sick|li|est
sick-making
sick|ness
sick|nesses
sicko +s
sick pay
sick|room +s
si|dal|cea +s
Sid|dhar|tha
Gau|tama
(founder of
Buddhism)
Sid|dons, Sarah
(English actress)
side
sides
sided
sid|ing
side|arm *Baseball*
side arm +s
(weapon)
side band +s
side-bet +s
side|board +s
side-bone +s
side|burn +s
side|car +s
side chapel +s
side dish
side dishes
sided|ness
side door +s
side drum +s
side ef|fect +s
side glance +s
side-handled
side|hill +s
side issue +s
side|kick +s
side|lamp +s
side|less
side|light +s
side|line
side|lines
side|lined
side|lin|ing
side|long
side note +s
side-on *adverb*
si|der|eal
sid|er|ite +s
side road +s
sid|ero|stat +s
side-saddle +s
side-screen +s
side seat +s
side shoot +s
side|show +s

side-slip
side-slips
side-slipped
side-slipping
sides|man
sides|men
side-splitting
side|step
side|steps
side|stepped
side|step|ping
side|step|per +s
side street +s
side|stroke +s
side|swipe
side|wipes
side|swiped
side|swip|ing
side table +s
side|track +s +ed
+ing
side trip +s
side view +s
side|walk +s
side|ward
side|wards
side|ways
side-wheeler +s
side-whiskers
side wind +s
side|wind|er +s
side|wise
Sidi bel Abbès
(town, Algeria)
sid|ing +s
sidle
sidles
sidled
sid|ling
Sid|ney *also*
Syd|ney
(name)
Sid|ney, Philip
(English poet)
Sidon (city,
Lebanon)
Sidra, Gulf of (off
Libya)
Sie|ben|ge|birge
(hills, Germany)
siege +s
siege gun +s
Sieg|fried (hero of
Nibelungenlied)
Sieg|fried Line
(German
defences)
Sie|mens, Ernst
Wer|ner von
(German electrical
engineer)
sie|mens (unit)
plural sie|mens

Siena (city, Italy)
Sien|ese
  plural Sien|ese
Sien|kie|wicz,
  Hen|ryk (Polish
  novelist)
si|enna +s
  (pigment)
si|erra +s
Si|erra Leone (in
  West Africa)
Si|erra Leon|ian
  +s
Si|erra Madre
  (mountain range,
  Mexico)
Si|erra Nev|ada
  (mountain range,
  Spain)
si|esta +s
sieve
  sieves
  sieved
  siev|ing
sieve|like
sie|vert +s
si|faka +s
sif|fleur +s *male*
sif|fleuse +s *female*
sift +s +ed +ing
sift|er +s
sigh +s +ed +ing
sight +s +ed +ing
  (vision; see;
  observe. ⚠ cite,
  site)
sight|er +s
sight-glass
  sight-glasses
sight|ing +s
sight|less
sight|less|ly
sight|less|ness
sight line +s
sight|li|ness
sight|ly
  sight|lier
  sight|li|est
sight-read
  sight-reads
  sight-read
  sight-reading
sight-reader +s
sight-screen +s
sight|see
  sight|sees
  sight|saw
  sight|see|ing
sight|seer +s
sight-sing
  sight-sings

sight-sing (*cont.*)
  sight-sang
  sight-singing
sight|worthy
sigil|late
SIGINT (= signals
  intelligence)
sig|lum
  sigla
sigma +s
sig|mate
sig|moid +s
sign +s +ed +ing
  (signal. ⚠ sine,
  syne)
sign|able
Si|gnac, Paul
  (French painter)
sign|age
sig|nal
  sig|nals
  sig|nalled *Br.*
  sig|naled *Am.*
  sig|nal|ling *Br.*
  sig|nal|ing *Am.*
signal-book +s
sig|nal box
  sig|nal boxes
sig|nal|ise *Br.* (use
  signalize)
  sig|nal|ises
  sig|nal|ised
  sig|nal|is|ing
sig|nal|ize
  sig|nal|izes
  sig|nal|ized
  sig|nal|iz|ing
sig|nal|ler +s
sig|nal|ly
sig|nal|man
  sig|nal|men
sig|nal tower +s
sig|nary
  sig|nar|ies
  (list of signs.
  ⚠ signory)
sig|na|tory
  sig|na|tor|ies
sig|na|ture +s
sign|board +s
sign|ee +s
sign|er +s
sig|net +s (seal
  used as
  authentication.
  ⚠ cygnet)
sig|net ring +s
sig|nifi|cance +s
sig|nifi|cancy
sig|nifi|cant
sig|nifi|cant|ly
sig|ni|fi|ca|tion +s

sig|nifi|ca|tive
sig|ni|fied +s
sig|ni|fier +s
sig|nify
  sig|ni|fies
  sig|ni|fied
  sig|ni|fy|ing
sign|ing +s
sign-off +s *noun*
si|gnor
  si|gnori
  male
si|gnora +s *female*
si|gnor|ina +s
  female
si|gnory (governing
  body. ⚠ signary)
  si|gnor|ies
sign-painter +s
sign-painting
sign|post +s +ed
  +ing
sign|writer +s
sign|writ|ing
Sig|urd *Norse Legend*
Siha|nouk, Prince
  Noro|dom
  (Cambodian ruler)
Siha|nouk|ville
  (former name of
  Kampong Som)
sika +s (deer.
  ⚠ caeca, seeker)
Sikh +s (adherent
  of Sikhism.
  ⚠ seek)
Sikh|ism
Si|king (former
  name of Xian)
Sik|kim (state,
  India)
Sik|kim|ese
  plural Sik|kim|ese
Si|kor|sky, Igor
  (Russian-born
  American aircraft
  designer)
Sik|sika
sil|age
  sil|ages
  sil|aged
  sil|aging
Silas
Sil|bury Hill
  (neolithic site,
  England)
Sil|ches|ter
  (village, England)
sild
  plural sild
si|lence
  si|lences

si|lence (*cont.*)
  si|lenced
  si|len|cing
si|len|cer +s
si|lent
si|lent|ly
Si|lenus (*Greek
  Mythology*; teacher
  of Dionysus)
si|lenus
  si|leni
  (*Greek Mythology*;
  woodland spirit
  generally)
Si|le|sia (region of
  central Europe)
Si|le|sian +s
silex
sil|hou|ette
  sil|hou|ettes
  sil|hou|et|ted
  sil|hou|et|ting
sil|ica (silicon
  dioxide. ⚠ siliqua)
sili|cate +s
si|li|ceous
si|li|cic
sili|cif|er|ous
si|lici|fi|ca|tion
si|licify
  si|lici|fies
  si|lici|fied
  si|lici|fy|ing
sil|icon (element)
sili|cone
  sili|cones
  sili|coned
  sili|con|ing
  (compound; treat
  with silicone)
Sili|con Val|ley
  (industrial region,
  USA)
sili|cosis
  sili|coses
sili|cot|ic
sili|qua
  sili|quae
  (seed pod.
  ⚠ silica)
si|lique +s
sili|quose
sili|quous
silk +s
silk|en
silk-fowl
  plural silk-fowl
silk-gland +s
silk|ily
silki|ness
silk|like

silk-screen +s +ed
+ing
silk|worm +s
silky
  silk|ier
  silki|est
sill +s
sil|la|bub +s (use
  syllabub)
sil|lily
sil|li|man|ite +s
sil|li|ness
Sil|li|toe, Alan
  (English writer)
silly
  sil|lies
  sil|lier
  sil|li|est
silo +s *noun*
silo
  si|loes
  si|loed
  silo|ing
  verb
Si|loam *Bible*
silt +s +ed +ing
silt|ation +s
silt|stone +s
silty
  silt|ier
  silti|est
Si|lur|ian +s
  Geology
silva +s (use sylva.
  △ silver)
sil|van (use
  sylvan)
Sil|vanus *Roman
  Mythology*
sil|ver +s +ed +ing
  (precious metal;
  colour. △ sylva)
sil|ver|back +s
sil|ver|fish
  plural sil|ver|fish
  or sil|ver|fishes
silver-grey +s
sil|veri|ness
sil|ver leaf (thin
  silver)
silver-leaf (disease
  of fruit trees)
sil|ver mine +s
sil|vern (made of
  or coloured like
  silver. △ sylvan)
sil|ver plate *noun*
silver-plate
  silver-plates
  silver-plated
  silver-plating
  verb

silver-point
sil|ver|side +s
sil|ver|smith +s
sil|ver|smith|ing
Sil|ver|stone
  (motor-racing
  circuit, England)
sil|ver|ware
sil|ver|weed +s
sil|very
silvi|cul|tural
silvi|cul|ture
silvi|cul|tur|ist +s
sima
Sim|birsk (city,
  Russia)
Sime|non,
  Georges (Belgian-
  born French
  novelist)
Sim|eon (*Bible*;
  name)
Sim|eon Sty|lites
  (Syrian saint)
Sim|fero|pol (city,
  Russia)
sim|ian +s (ape)
simi|lar +s
simi|lar|ity
  simi|lar|ities
simi|lar|ly
sim|ile +s
si|mili|tude +s
Simla (city, India)
sim|mer +s +ed
+ing
Sim|nel, Lam|bert
  (English claimant
  to the throne)
sim|nel cake +s
Simon (Apostle and
  saint ('the
  Zealot'); name)
Simon, Neil
  (American
  playwright)
Simon, Paul
  (American singer-
  songwriter)
Sim|one
simo|niac +s
si|mo|ni|ac|al
si|mo|ni|ac|al|ly
Si|moni|des (Greek
  lyric poet)
simon-pure
si|mony
si|moom +s
si|moon +s
simp +s
  (= simpleton)

sim|pat|ico
sim|per +s +ed
+ing
sim|per|ing|ly
sim|ple
  sim|pler
  sim|plest
simple-minded
simple-minded|ly
simple-
  minded|ness
simple|ness
simple|ton +s
sim|plex
  sim|plexes
sim|pli|city
  sim|pli|ci|ties
sim|pli|fi|ca|tion
+s
sim|plify
  sim|pli|fies
  sim|pli|fied
  sim|pli|fy|ing
sim|plism
sim|plis|tic
sim|plis|tic|al|ly
Sim|plon (Alpine
  pass, Switzerland)
sim|ply
Simp|son, James
  Young (Scottish
  surgeon)
Simp|son, Wal|lis
  (American wife of
  Edward VIII)
Simp|son Des|ert
  (in Australia)
simu|lac|rum
  simu|lacra
simu|late
  simu|lates
  simu|lated
  simu|lat|ing
simu|la|tion +s
simu|la|tive
simu|la|tor +s
sim|ul|cast +s
sim|ul|tan|eity
sim|ul|tan|eous
sim|ul|tan|eous|ly
sim|ul|tan|eous|
    ness
sim|urg +s
sin
  sins
  sinned
  sin|ning
Sinai (peninsula,
  Egypt)
Sina|it|ic
Sina|iti|cus (in
  'Codex Sinaiticus')

Sina|loa (state,
  Mexico)
Sin|an|thro|pus
sin|ap|ism
Sin|atra, Frank
  (American singer)
Sin|bad the Sailor
  (in the *Arabian
  Nights*)
since
sin|cere
  sin|cerer
  sin|cerest
sin|cere|ly
sin|cere|ness
sin|cer|ity
  sin|cer|ities
sin|cipi|tal
sin|ci|put +s
Sin|clair, Clive
  (English
  electronics
  engineer)
Sind (province,
  Pakistan)
Sind|bad the
  Sailor (use
  Sinbad the
  Sailor)
Sin|de|bele
Sindhi +s
sin|don|ology
Sindy *also* Cindy
sine +s
  (trigonometric
  function. △ sign,
  syne)
Sin|ead
sine|cure +s
sine|cur|ism
sine|cur|ist +s
sine die
sine qua non
sinew +s +ed +ing
sin|ew|less
sinewy
sin|fonia +s
sin|foni|etta +s
sin|ful
sin|ful|ly
sin|ful|ness
sing
  sings
  sang
  sing|ing
  sung
sing|able
sing|along +s
Singa|pore
Singa|por|ean +s
singe
  singes

singe (*cont.*)
  singed
  singe|ing
Sing|er, Isaac
  Bash|evis (Polish-
  born American
  novelist)
Sing|er, Isaac
  Mer|rit
  (American
  inventor)
sing|er +s
singer-songwriter
  +s
Singh (Sikh
  adopted name)
Sing|hal|ese (use
  Sinhalese)
  plural Sing|hal|ese
sing|ing|ly
sin|gle
  sin|gles
  sin|gled
  sin|gling
single-acting
single-breast|ed
single-decker +s
sin|gle file
single-handed
single-handed|ly
single-lens re|flex
  single-lens
  re|flexes
single-line
  attributive
single-minded
single-minded|ly
single-
  minded|ness
single|ness
single-seater +s
sing|let +s
single|ton +s
single|tree +s
sin|gly
Sing Sing (prison,
  USA)
sing-song +s +ed
  +ing
sin|gu|lar +s
sin|gu|lar|isa|tion
  Br. (use
  singularization)
sin|gu|lar|ise *Br.*
  (use singularize)
  sin|gu|lar|ises
  sin|gu|lar|ised
  sin|gu|lar|is|ing
sin|gu|lar|ity
  sin|gu|lar|ities
sin|gu|lar|iza|tion

sin|gu|lar|ize
  sin|gu|lar|izes
  sin|gu|lar|ized
  sin|gu|lar|iz|ing
sin|gu|lar|ly
sinh (= hyperbolic
  sine)
Sin|hala
Sin|hal|ese
  plural Sin|hal|ese
Si|ning (= Xining)
sin|is|ter
sin|is|ter|ly
sin|is|ter|ness
sin|is|tral +s
sin|is|tral|ity
sin|is|tral|ly
sin|is|trorse
sink
  sinks
  sank *or* sunk
  sink|ing
  sunk
  (fall; founder.
  △ cinque)
sink|able
sink|age
sink|er +s
sink-hole +s
Sin|kiang
  (= Xinjiang)
sink|ing +s
sin|less
sin|less|ly
sin|less|ness
sin|ner +s
sin|net
Sinn Fein (Irish
  political
  movement and
  party)
Sinn Fein|er +s
Sino-British
Sino-Japanese
sino|logic|al
sino|olo|gist +s
sino|logue +s
sin|ology
Sino|mania
Sino|phile +s
Sino|phobe +s
Sino|pho|bia
Sino-Soviet
Sino-Tibetan +s
Sino-US
sin|ter +s +ed +ing
Sint-Niklaas
  (town, Belgium)
Sin|tra (town,
  Portugal)
sinu|ate

Sin|uiju (port,
  North Korea)
sinu|os|ity
  sinu|os|ities
sinu|ous
sinu|ous|ly
sinu|ous|ness
sinus
  si|nuses
si|nus|itis
si|nus|oid +s
si|nus|oid|al
si|nus|oid|al|ly
Sio|bhan
Sion (use Zion)
Siouan +s
Sioux
  plural Sioux
sip
  sips
  sipped
  sip|ping
sipe +s
si|phon *Am.* +s +ed
  +ing (pipe for
  transferring liquid;
  cause to flow. *Br.*
  syphon)
si|phon +s (of
  mollusc)
si|phon|age *Am.*
  (*Br.* syphonage)
si|phon|al
si|phon|ic *Am.*
  (pertaining to a
  pipe for siphoning.
  Br. syphonic)
si|phon|ic
  (pertaining to a
  mollusc's siphon)
si|phono|phore +s
siph|uncle +s
sip|per +s
sip|pet +s
sir +s
Sira|cusa (Italian
  name for
  Syracuse, Italy)
si:|dar +s
Sir|daryo (river,
  central Asia)
sire
  sires
  sired
  sir|ing
siren +s
si|ren|ian +s
sir|gang +s
Sir|ius (star)
sir|loin +s
si|rocco +s
sir|rah +s

sir|ree
Sirte, Gulf of
  (= Gulf of Sidra)
sirup *Am.* +s (*Br.*
  syrup)
sis (= sister)
sisal +s
sis|kin +s
Sis|ley, Al|fred
  (French painter)
sis|si|fied
sis|si|ness
sis|soo
sissy
  sis|sies
  sis|sier
  sis|si|est
sissy|ish
sis|ter +s
sis|ter|hood +s
sister-in-law
  sisters-in-law
sis|ter|less
sis|ter|li|ness
sis|ter|ly
Sis|tine (of popes
  called Sixtus, esp.
  Sixtus IV.
  △ cystine)
Sis|tine Chapel (in
  the Vatican.
  △ cystine)
sis|trum
sis|tra
Sisy|phean
Sisy|phus *Greek*
  Mythology
sit
  sits
  sat
  sit|ting
Sita *Hinduism*
sitar +s
sitar|ist +s
sita|tunga
  plural sita|tunga
  or sita|tungas
sit|com +s
  (= situation
  comedy)
sit-down +s
  adjective and noun
site
  sites
  sited
  sit|ing
  (of building etc.;
  locate. △ cite,
  sight)
sit-fast +s
sit-in +s *adjective*
  and noun
Sitka +s

sito|pho¦bia
sit¦rep +s
  (= situation
  report)
sit¦ringee
sits vac
  (= situations
  vacant)
Sit¦tang (river,
  Burma)
sit¦ter +s
sitter-in
  sitters-in
sit|ting +s
Sit|ting Bull (Sioux
  chief)
sit|ting room +s
situ (in 'in situ')
situ|ate
  situ|ates
  situ|ated
  situ|at¦ing
situ|ation +s
situ|ation|al
situ|ation|al¦ly
situ|ation|ism
situ|ation|ist +s
sit-up +s
sit-upon +s noun
Sit|well, Edith
  (English poet)
sitz-bath +s
Siva Hinduism
Siva|ism
Siva|ite +s
Sivaji (use Shivaji)
Sivan (Jewish
  month)
Si|walik Hills (in
  India and Nepal)
six
  sixes
six¦ain +s
Six Day War
sixer +s
six|fold
six-gun +s
six-iron +s
six-pack +s
six|pence +s
six|penny
  six|pen¦nies
six-shooter +s
sixte +s Fencing
six|teen +s (16.
  △ Sixtine)
six|teenmo +s
six|teenth +s
sixth +s
sixth-form
  col|lege +s
sixth-former +s

sixth¦ly
six|ti¦eth +s
Six|tine (= Sistine.
  △ sixteen)
sixty
  six|ties
sixty-first, sixty-
  second, etc.
six|ty|fold
sixty-fourmo +s
sixty-one, sixty-
  two, etc.
siz¦able (use
  sizeable)
sizar +s (college
  grant. △ sizer)
siz¦ar|ship +s
size
  sizes
  sized
  siz¦ing
size|able
size|ably
sizer +s (person
  who assesses size.
  △ sizar)
size-stick +s
Size|well (nuclear
  power station,
  England)
sizy
siz¦zle
  siz¦zles
  siz¦zled
  siz|zling
siz|zler +s
sjam|bok +s +ed
  +ing (whip)
ska (Music. △ scar)
skag +s
Skag¦er¦rak (strait
  linking Baltic and
  North Seas)
skald +s (bard.
  △ scald)
skald¦ic
Skanda Hinduism
Skara Brae
  (neolithic
  settlement,
  Orkney)
skat (card game.
  △ Scart)
skate
  skates
  skated
  skat¦ing
skate|board +s
  +ed +ing
skate|board¦er +s
skate|park +s
skater +s

skat¦ing rink +s
skean +s (dagger)
skean-dhu +s
sked
  skeds
  sked|ded
  sked|ding
ske|dad¦dle
  ske|dad¦dles
  ske|dad¦dled
  ske|dad¦dling
skeet (shooting
  sport)
skeet¦er +s
  (mosquito)
skeg +s
skein +s (bundle of
  yarn; flock of
  geese)
skel|etal
skel|et|al¦ly
skel|eton +s
Skel|eton Coast
  (in Namibia)
skel|et|on|ise Br.
  (use skeletonize)
  skel|et|on|ises
  skel|et|on|ised
  skel|et|on|is¦ing
skel|et|on|ize
  skel|et|on|izes
  skel|et|on|ized
  skel|et|on|iz¦ing
skelf +s
Skel|ton, John
  (English poet)
skep +s
skep¦sis Am. (Br.
  scepsis)
skep|tic Am. (Br.
  sceptic)
skep|tic¦al Am. (Br.
  sceptical)
skep|tic|al¦ly Am.
  (Br. sceptically)
skep|ti|cism Am.
  +s (Br.
  scepticism)
sker|rick +s
skerry
  sker|ries
sketch
  sketches
  sketched
  sketch|ing
sketch|book +s
sketch¦er +s
sketch|ily
sketchi|ness
sketch map +s
sketch pad +s

sketchy
sketch|ier
sketchi|est
skeuo|morph +s
skeuo|morph¦ic
skew +s +ed +ing
skew|back +s
skew|bald +s
skew¦er +s +ed
  +ing (spike.
  △ skua)
skew-eyed
skew|ness
skew-whiff
ski
  skis
  skied
  ski¦ing
ski|able
ski|ag¦raphy
ski|am¦achy
Ski|athos (Greek
  island)
ski-bob
  ski-bobs
  ski-bobbed
  ski-bobbing
ski-bobber +s
skid
  skids
  skid|ded
  skid|ding
skid|doo +s (use
  skidoo)
skid-lid +s
ski¦doo +s (vehicle)
  Propr.
ski¦doo +s +ed
  +ing (ride on
  skidoo; go away)
skid-pan +s
skier +s (person
  who skis. △ skyer)
skiff +s
skif¦fle
ski-jorer +s
ski-joring
ski jump +s
ski jump¦er +s
ski jump¦ing
skil|ful Br. (Am.
  skillful)
skil|ful¦ly
skil|ful|ness
ski lift +s
skill +s
skil|let +s
skill|ful Am. (Br.
  skilful)
skill-less
skilly
  skil|lies

skim
skims
skimmed
skim|ming
skim|mer +s
skim|mia +s
skimp +s +ed +ing
skimp|ily
skimpi|ness
skimpy
skimp|ier
skimpi|est
skin
skins
skinned
skin|ning
skin|care
skin-deep
skin diver +s
skin div|ing
skin-flick +s
skin|flint +s
skin-food +s
skin|ful +s
skin graft +s
skin|head +s
skink +s
skin|less
skin|like
Skin|ner, B. F.
(American
psychologist)
skin|ner +s
skin|ni|ness
skinny
skin|nier
skin|ni|est
skinny-dipping
skint
skin|tight
skip
skips
skipped
skip|ping
skip|jack +s
ski-plane +s
skip|per +s +ed
+ing
skip|pet +s
skip|ping rope +s
skirl +s +ed +ing
skir|mish
skir|mishes
skir|mished
skir|mish|ing
skir|mish|er +s
skirr +s +ed +ing
skir|ret +s
skirt +s +ed +ing
skirt-dance +s
skirt|ing +s
skirt|ing board +s

skirt|less
ski run +s
ski slope +s
skit +s
skite
skites
skited
skit|ing
skit|ter +s +ed
+ing
skit|tery
skit|tish
skit|tish|ly
skit|tish|ness
skit|tle
skit|tles
skit|tled
skit|tling
skive
skives
skived
skiv|ing
skiver +s
skivvy
skiv|vies
skiv|vied
skivvy|ing
ski|wear
skol
Skopje (city,
Macedonia)
Skrya|bin,
Alek|sandr (use
Scriabin)
skua +s (bird.
△ skewer)
skul|dug|gery
skulk +s +ed +ing
skulk|er +s
skull +s +ed +ing
(bone. △ scull)
skull|cap +s
skunk +s +ed +ing
skunk-bear +s
skunk-cabbage +s
sky
skies
skied
sky|ing
sky blue +s noun
and adjective
sky-blue attributive
sky-blue pink
sky-clad
sky|dive
sky|dives
sky|dived
sky|dove Am.
sky|div|ing
sky|diver +s
Skye (Scottish
island; terrier)

skyer +s (Cricket.
△ skier)
skyey
sky-high
sky|jack +s +ed
+ing
sky|jack|er +s
Sky|lab (American
space laboratory)
sky|lark +s +ed
+ing
sky|less
sky|light +s
sky|line +s
sky|rocket +s +ed
+ing
sky|sail +s
sky|scape +s
sky|scraper +s
sky-shouting
sky-sign +s
sky|walk +s
sky|ward
sky|wards
sky|watch
sky|watches
sky|way +s
sky-writing
slab
slabs
slabbed
slab|bing
slack +s +ed +ing
slack|en +s +ed
+ing
slack|er +s
slack|ly
slack|ness
slag
slags
slagged
slag|ging
slaggy
slag|gier
slag|gi|est
slag heap +s
slag-wool +s
slain
slainte
slake
slakes
slaked
slak|ing
sla|lom +s
slam
slams
slammed
slam|ming
slam|bang
slam dunk +s noun
slam-dunk +s +ed
+ing verb

slam|mer +s
slan|der +s +ed
+ing
slan|der|er +s
slan|der|ous
slan|der|ous|ly
slang +s +ed +ing
slang|ily
slangi|ness
slang|ing match
slang|ing
matches
slangy
slang|ier
slangi|est
slant +s +ed +ing
slant-eyed
slant|ways
slant|wise
slap
slaps
slapped
slap|ping
slap bang
slap|dash
slap-happy
slap|head +s
(offensive)
slap|jack +s
slap|per +s
slap|stick +s
slap-up adjective
slash
slashes
slashed
slash|ing
slash-and-burn
slash|er +s
slat
slats
slat|ted
slat|ting
slate
slates
slated
slat|ing
slate blue +s noun
and adjective
slate-blue
attributive
slate color Am.
slate-colored Am.
slate col|our Br.
slate-coloured Br.
slate grey +s noun
and adjective
slate-grey
attributive
slate-pencil +s
slater +s
slather +s +ed
+ing

slat|ing +s
slat|tern +s
slat|tern|li|ness
slat|tern|ly
slaty
  slati|er
  slati|est
slaugh|ter +s +ed +ing
slaugh|ter|er +s
slaugh|ter|house +s
slaugh|ter|ing +s
slaugh|ter|ous
Slav +s
slave
  slaves
  slaved
  slav|ing
slave-bangle +s
slave-born
slave-bracelet +s
slave-drive
  slave-drives
  slave-drove
  slave-driving
  slave-driven
slave-driver +s
slaver +s +ed +ing
slav|ery
Slave State +s (in USA)
slave trade
slave trader +s
slavey
Slav|ic
slav|ish
slav|ish|ly
slav|ish|ness
Slav|ism
Sla|vo|nian +s
Sla|von|ic
Slavo|phile +s
Slavo|phobe +s
slaw +s
slay
  slays
  slew
  slay|ing
  slain
  (kill. △ sleigh, sley)
slay|er +s
slay|ing +s
Slea|ford (town, England)
sleaze
  sleazes
  sleazed
  sleaz|ing
sleaze|bag +s
sleaze|ball +s

sleaz|ily
sleazi|ness
sleaz|oid +s
sleazy
  sleaz|ier
  sleazi|est
sled
  sleds
  sled|ded
  sled|ding
sledge
  sledges
  sledged
  sledg|ing
sledge|ham|mer +s
sleek +s +ed +ing +er +est
sleek|ly
sleek|ness
sleeky
sleep
  sleeps
  slept
  sleep|ing
sleep|er +s
sleep|ily
sleep-in +s *noun and adjective*
sleepi|ness
sleep|ing bag +s
sleep|ing car +s
sleep|ing draught +s
sleep|ing pill +s
sleep|ing suit +s
sleep-learning
sleep|less
sleep|less|ly
sleep|less|ness
sleep-out +s *adjective and noun*
sleep|over +s
sleep|walk +s +ed +ing
sleep|walk|er +s
sleepy
  sleep|ier
  sleepi|est
sleepy|head +s
sleet +s +ed +ing
sleety
  sleet|ier
  sleeti|est
sleeve +s
sleeve board +s
sleeve-coupling +s
sleeved
sleeve|less
sleeve link +s
sleeve note +s
sleeve-nut +s

sleeve-valve +s
sleev|ing +s
sleigh +s +ed +ing
  (sledge; travel on a sledge. △ slay, sley)
sleigh-bell +s
sleight +s
  (dexterity. △ slight)
slen|der +er +est
slen|der|ise *Br.*
  (use slenderize)
slen|der|ises
slen|der|ised
slen|der|is|ing
slen|der|ize
slen|der|izes
slen|der|ized
slen|der|iz|ing
slen|der|ly
slen|der|ness
slept
sleuth +s +ed +ing
sleuth-hound +s
slew +s +ed +ing
sley +s (weaver's reed. △ slay, sleigh)
slice
  slices
  sliced
  sli|cing
slice|able
slice +s
slicer +s
slick +s +ed +ing +er +est
slick|er +s
slick|ly
slick|ness
slid|able
slid|ably
slide
  slides
  slid
  slid|ing
slider +s
slide rule +s
slide-valve +s
slide|way +s
slight +s +ed +ing +er +est
  (inconsiderable; slender; be disrespectful towards; instance of slighting. △ sleight)
slight|ing|ly
slight|ish
slight|ly
slight|ness

Sligo (county and town, Republic of Ireland)
slily (use slyly)
slim
  slims
  slimmed
  slim|ming
  slim|mer
  slim|mest
slime
  slimes
  slimed
  slim|ing
slimi|ly
slimi|ness
slim|line
slim|ly
slim|mer +s
slim|mish
slim|ness
slimy
  slimi|er
  slimi|est
sling
  slings
  slung
  sling|ing
sling-back +s
sling-bag +s
sling|er +s
sling|shot +s
slink
  slinks
  slunk
  slink|ing
  (go stealthily)
slink +s +ed +ing
  (produce young prematurely)
slink|ily
slinki|ness
slink|weed
slinky
  slink|ier
  slinki|est
slip
  slips
  slipped
  slip|ping
slip-carriage +s
slip case +s
slip-coach
  slip-coaches
slip cover +s
slip-hook +s
slip-knot +s
slip-on +s *adjective and noun*
slip|over +s *noun*
slip-over *adjective*
slip|page +s

slip|per +s +ed
+ing
slip|per'ily
slip|peri|ness
slip|per|wort +s
slip|pery
slip|pi|ness
slippy
  slip|pier
  slip|pi|est
slip ring +s
slip road +s
slip-rope +s
slip|shod
slip stitch
  slip stitches
  noun
slip-stitch
  slip-stitches
  slip-stitched
  slip-stitch|ing
  verb
slip|stream +s +ed
+ing
slip-up +s *noun*
slip|ware
slip|way +s
slit
  slits
  slit
  slit|ting
  (see also slitted)
slit-eyed
slither +s +ed +ing
slith|ery
slit pocket +s
slit|ted *adjective*
slit|ter +s
slitty
  slit|tier
  slit|ti|est
Sliven (city,
  Bulgaria)
sliver +s +ed +ing
slivo|vitz (plum
  brandy)
Sloane +s
  (= Sloane Ranger)
Sloane, Hans
  (English
  physician)
Sloaney
slob +s
slob|ber +s +ed
+ing
slob|bery
slob|bish
sloe +s (fruit.
  △slow)
sloe-eyed
sloe gin +s

slog
  slogs
  slogged
  slog|ging
slo|gan +s
slog|ger +s
sloid +s
sloop +s
sloop-rigged
sloosh
  slooshes
  slooshed
  sloosh|ing
sloot +s
slop
  slops
  slopped
  slop|ping
slop basin +s
slope
  slopes
  sloped
  slop|ing
slope|wise
slop pail +s
slop|pily
slop|pi|ness
sloppy
  slop|pier
  slop|pi|est
slosh
  sloshes
  sloshed
  slosh|ing
sloshy
  slosh|ier
  slosh|iest
slot
  slots
  slot|ted
  slot|ting
sloth +s
sloth|ful
sloth|ful|ly
sloth|ful|ness
slot ma|chine +s
slouch
  slouches
  slouched
  slouch|ing
slouchy
  slouch|ier
  slouch|iest
Slough (town,
  England)
slough +s +ed
+ing
sloughy
  slough|ier
  slough|iest
Slo|vak +s
Slo|vakia

Slo|vak|ian +s
sloven +s
Slo|vene +s
Slo|venia
Slo|ven|ian +s
slov|en|li|ness
slov|en|ly
slow +s +ed +ing
  +er +est (not fast;
  reduce speed.
  △sloe)
slow|coach
  slow|coaches
slow|down +s
slow-growing
slow|ish
slow|ly
slow-moving
slow|ness
slow|poke +s
slow-witted
slow-worm +s
slub
  slubs
  slubbed
  slub|bing
sludge +s
sludgy
  sludgi|er
  sludgi|est
slue (use slew)
  slues
  slued
  slu|ing
slug
  slugs
  slugged
  slug|ging
slug|abed +s
slug|gard +s
slug|gard|li|ness
slug|gard|ly
slug|ger +s
slug|gish
slug|gish|ly
slug|gish|ness
sluice
  sluices
  sluiced
  slui|cing
sluice-gate +s
sluit +s (use sloot)
slum
  slums
  slummed
  slum|ming
slum|ber +s +ed
+ing
slum|ber|er +s
slum|ber|ous
slum|ber|wear
slum|brous

slum|gul|lion +s
slum|mi|ness
slummy
  slum|mier
  slum|mi|est
slump +s +ed +ing
slung
slunk
slur
  slurs
  slurred
  slur|ring
slurp +s +ed +ing
slurry
  slur|ries
slush
  slushes
  slushed
  slush|ing
slushi|ness
slushy
  slush|ier
  slushi|est
slut +s
slut|tish
slut|tish|ness
sly
  slyer
  sly|est
sly|boots
slyly
sly|ness
slype +s
smack +s +ed
+ing
smack-dab
smack|er +s
smack|eroo +s
small +s +er +est
smal|lage +s
small-bore
  adjective
small|goods
  (delicatessen
  meats)
small|hold|er +s
small|hold|ing +s
small|ish
small-minded
small-minded|ly
small-
  minded|ness
small|ness
small|pox
small-scale
small-sword +s
  (light tapering
  sword)
small talk
small-time
small-timer +s

small-town
   adjective
small|wares
smalt +s
smarm +s +ed
   +ing
smarm|ily
smarmi|ness
smarmy
   smarm|ier
   smarmi|est
smart +s +ed +ing
   +er +est
smart alec +s
smart aleck +s
   (use smart alec)
smart-alecky
smart alick +s (use
   smart alec)
smart-arse +s
smart card +s
smart|en +s +ed
   +ing
smart|ing|ly
smart|ish
smart|ly
smart|ness
smart|weed
smarty
   smart|ies
smarty-boots
smarty-pants
smash
   smashes
   smashed
   smash|ing
smash-and-grab
   +s
smash|er +s
smash|ing|ly
smash-up +s *noun*
smat|ter +s
smat|ter|er +s
smat|ter|ing +s
smear +s +ed +ing
smear|er +s
smeari|ness
smeary
smec|tic +s
smegma +s
smeg|mat|ic
smell
   smells
   smelled *or* smelt
   smell|ing
smell|able
smell|er +s
smelli|ness
smell|ing bot|tle
   +s
smell|ing salts
smell-less

smelly
   smell|ier
   smelli|est
smelt +s +ed +ing
smelt|er +s
smelt|ery
   smelt|er|ies
Smersh (Russian
   counter-espionage
   organization)
Smet|ana,
   Bed|řich (Czech
   composer)
smew +s
smidgen +s
smidg|eon +s (use
   smidgen)
smidgin +s (use
   smidgen)
smi|lax
smile
   smiles
   smiled
   smil|ing
smile|less
smiler +s
smiley
smil|ing|ly
smirch
   smirches
   smirched
   smirch|ing
smirk +s +ed +ing
smirk|er +s
smirk|ily
smirk|ing|ly
smirky
smit (*archaic*
   smitten)
smite
   smites
   smote
   smit|ing
   smit|ten
smiter +s
Smith, Adam
   (Scottish
   economist)
Smith, Bes|sie
   (American singer)
Smith, Ian
   (Rhodesian prime
   minister)
Smith, Jo|seph
   (American
   founder of the
   Mormon Church)
Smith, Stevie
   (English poet)
Smith, Syd|ney
   (English
   churchman)

Smith, Wil|liam
   (English geologist)
smith +s +ed +ing
smith|er|eens
smith|ers
smith|ery
   smith|er|ies
Smith|field
   (market, London)
Smith|son|ian
   In|sti|tu|tion
   (American
   foundation)
smithy
   smith|ies
smit|ten
smock +s +ed
   +ing
smock-mill +s
smog +s
smoggy
   smog|gier
   smog|gi|est
smok|able
smoke
   smokes
   smoked
   smok|ing
smoke|able (use
   smokable)
smoke-ball +s
smoke bomb +s
smoke box
   smoke boxes
smoke bush
   smoke bushes
smoke-dried
smoke-free
smoke-ho +s
smoke|less
smoke-plant +s
smoker +s
smoke ring +s
smoke-room +s
smoke|screen +s
smoke|stack +s
smoke-stone +s
smoke-tunnel +s
smoki|ly
smoki|ness
smok|ing jacket
   +s
smok|ing room +s
smoko +s
smoky
   smoki|er
   smoki|est
smol|der *Am.* +s
   +ed +ing (*Br.*
   smoulder)

smol|der|ing|ly
   Am. (*Br.*
   smoulderingly)
Smo|lensk (city,
   Russia)
Smol|lett, To|bias
   (Scottish novelist)
smolt +s
smooch
   smooches
   smooched
   smooch|ing
smooch|er +s
smoochy
   smooch|ier
   smoochi|est
smoodge
   smoodges
   smoodged
   smoodg|ing
smooth +s +ed
   +ing +er +est
smooth|able
smooth-bore +s
smoothe (use
   smooth)
   smoothes
   smoothed
   smooth|ing
smoother +s
smooth-faced
smoothie +s
smooth|ing iron
   +s
smooth|ing plane
   +s
smooth|ish
smooth|ly
smooth|ness
smooth-talk +s
   +ed +ing *verb*
smooth-tongued
smor|gas|bord +s
smorz|ando
   smorz|an|dos *or*
   smorz|andi
smote
smother +s +ed
   +ing
smoth|ery
smoul|der *Br.* +s
   +ed +ing (*Am.*
   smolder)
smoul|der|ing|ly
   Br. (*Am.*
   smolderingly)
smriti
smudge
   smudges
   smudged
   smudg|ing
smudge|less

smudge pot +s
smudgi¦ly
smudgi¦ness
smudgy
  smudgi¦er
  smudgi¦est
smug
  smug¦ger
  smug¦gest
smug¦gle
  smug¦gles
  smug¦gled
  smug¦gling
smug¦gler +s
smug¦ly
smug¦ness
smut
  smuts
  smut¦ted
  smut¦ting
smut-ball +s
smut-mill +s
Smuts, Jan
  Chris¦tiaan
  (South African
  prime minister)
smut¦tily
smut¦ti¦ness
smutty
  smut¦tier
  smut¦ti¦est
Smyrna (former
  name of Izmir)
Smyth, Ethel
  (English
  composer)
snack +s +ed +ing
snack bar +s
snaf¦fle
  snaf¦fles
  snaf¦fled
  snaf¦fling
snafu
snag
  snags
  snagged
  snag¦ging
snaggle-tooth
  snaggle-teeth
snaggle-toothed
snaggy
snail +s
snail-like
snail mail
snail's pace
snake
  snakes
  snaked
  snak¦ing
snake|bite +s
snake-charmer +s
snake|like

snake-pit +s
snake|root +s
snake|skin +s
snaki¦ly
snaki¦ness
snaky
  snaki¦er
  snaki¦est
snap
  snaps
  snapped
  snap|ping
snap-bolt +s
snap-brim
snap|dragon +s
snap-fasten¦er +s
snap-hook +s
snap-lock +s
snap|pable
snap|per +s
snap¦pily
snap¦pi|ness
snap¦ping¦ly
snap¦pish
snap¦pish¦ly
snap¦pish|ness
snappy
  snap¦pier
  snap¦pi|est
snap|shot +s
snare
  snares
  snared
  snar¦ing
snarer +s
snark +s
snarl +s +ed +ing
snarl¦er +s
snarl|ing¦ly
snarl-up +s noun
snarly
  snarl|ier
  snarli|est
snatch
  snatches
  snatched
  snatch|ing
snatch¦er +s
snatchy
snavel
  snavels
  snav|elled
  snav¦el|ling
snaz|zily
snaz|zi|ness
snazzy
  snaz|zier
  snaz|zi|est
sneak
  sneaks
  sneaked

sneak (cont.)
  snuck Am.
  sneak|ing
sneak¦er +s
sneak|ily
sneaki|ness
sneak|ing¦ly
sneak-thief
  sneak-thieves
sneaky
  sneak|ier
  sneaki|est
sneck +s +ed +ing
Sneek (town, the
  Netherlands)
sneer +s +ed +ing
sneer¦er +s
sneer|ing¦ly
sneeze
  sneezes
  sneezed
  sneez|ing
sneezer +s
sneeze|wort +s
sneezy
Snell's law
snib
  snibs
  snibbed
  snib|bing
snick +s +ed +ing
snicker +s +ed
  +ing
snick¦er|ing¦ly
snicket +s
snide +s
snide¦ly
snide|ness
sniff +s +ed +ing
sniff|able
sniff¦er +s
sniff¦er dog +s
sniff¦ily
sniffi|ness
sniff|ing¦ly
snif¦fle
  snif¦fles
  snif¦fled
  snif¦fling
snif¦fler +s
sniffly
sniffy
  sniff|ier
  sniffi|est
snif¦ter +s
snifter-valve +s
snig
  snigs
  snigged
  snig|ging
snig|ger +s +ed
  +ing

snig|ger¦er +s
snig|ger|ing¦ly
snig|gery
snig|ging chain +s
snig¦gle
  snig¦gles
  snig¦gled
  snig¦gling
snip
  snips
  snipped
  snip|ping
snipe
  plural snipe or
  snipes
  (bird)
snipe
  snipes
  sniped
  snip¦ing
  (shoot)
snipe fish
  plural snipe fish
sniper +s
snip|pet +s
snip|pety
snip|pily
snip¦pi|ness
snip|ping +s
snippy
  snip|pier
  snip|pi|est
snit +s
snitch
  snitches
  snitched
  snitch|ing
snivel
  snivels
  sniv|elled Br.
  sniv|eled Am.
  sniv¦el|ling Br.
  sniv¦el|ing Am.
sniv|el¦er Am. +s
sniv¦el|ing¦ly Am.
sniv¦el|ler Br. +s
sniv¦el|ling¦ly Br.
snob +s
snob|bery
snob|ber¦ies
snob|bish
snob|bish¦ly
snob|bish|ness
snobby
  snob|bier
  snob|bi|est
SNOBOL
  Computing
snoek +s (fish.
  ⚠ snook)
snog
  snogs

snog (*cont.*)
  snogged
  snog|ging
snood +s
snook +s (gesture.
  ⚠ snoek)
snook|er +s +ed
  +ing
snook|er play|er
  +s
snoop +s +ed +ing
snoop|er +s
snoop|er|scope +s
snoopy
snoot +s
snoot|ily
snooti|ness
snooty
  snoot|ier
  snooti|est
snooze
  snoozes
  snoozed
  snooz|ing
snoozer +s
snoozy
  snooz|ier
  snoozi|est
snore
  snores
  snored
  snor|ing
snorer +s
snor|ing|ly
Snor|kel +s (fire-
fighting platform)
Propr.
snor|kel
  snor|kels
  snor|kelled *Br.*
  snor|keled *Am.*
  snor|kel|ling *Br.*
  snor|kel|ing *Am.*
  (tube for swimmer
  or submarine)
snor|kel|er *Am.* +s
snor|kel|ler *Br.* +s
Snorri Stur|lu|son
  (Icelandic
  historian)
snort +s +ed +ing
snort|er +s
snot +s
snot-rag +s
snot|tily
snot|ti|ness
snotty
  snot|tier
  snot|ti|est
snotty-nosed
snout +s
snout-beetle +s

snout|ed
snout|like
snouty
Snow, C. P.
  (English novelist)
snow +s +ed +ing
snow|ball +s +ed
  +ing
snow|ball tree +s
snow|berry
  snow|berries
snow-blind
snow-blindness
snow-blink
snow|blow|er +s
snow|board +s
snow|board|er +s
snow|board|ing
snow boot +s
snow|bound
snow-broth
snow|cap +s
snow-capped
snow-covered
Snow|don
  (mountain, Wales)
Snow|donia
  (region, Wales)
snow|drift +s
snow|drop +s
snow|fall +s
snow|field +s
snow|flake +s
snow goose
  snow geese
snow-ice
snow|ily
snowi|ness
snow job +s *noun*
snow-job
  snow-jobs
  snow-jobbed
  snow-jobbing
  verb
snow|less
snow|like
snow|line +s
snow|mak|ing
snow|man
  snow|men
snow|mobile +s
snow|plough *Br.* +s
snow|plow *Am.* +s
snow|scape +s
snow|shoe +s
snow|shoer +s
snow ski|ing
snow-slip +s
snow|storm +s
snow white +s
  noun and adjective
snow-white
  attributive

snowy
  snow|ier
  snowi|est
snub
  snubs
  snubbed
  snub|bing
snub|ber +s
snub|bing|ly
snub-nosed
snuck
snuff +s +ed +ing
snuff|box
  snuff|boxes
snuff-colored *Am.*
snuff-coloured *Br.*
snuf|fer +s
snuf|fle
  snuf|fles
  snuf|fled
  snuf|fling
snuff|ler +s
snuffly
snuffy
  snuff|ier
  snuffi|est
snug
  snugs
  snug|ger
  snug|gest
snug|gery
  snug|ger|ies
snug|gle
  snug|gles
  snug|gled
  snug|gling
snug|ly
snug|ness
so (*adverb and
  conjunction.*
  ⚠ sew, soh, sow)
soak +s +ed +ing
  (drench; drink;
  drinker. ⚠ soke)
soak|age
soak|away +s
soak|er +s
  (drinker; heavy
  rain; on roof.
  ⚠ soca)
soak|ing +s
so-and-so +s
Soane, John
  (English architect)
soap +s +ed +ing
soap|bark +s
soap|berry
  soap|berries
soap|box
  soap|boxes
soap|ily
soapi|ness

soap|less
soap|like
soap opera +s
soap|stone +s
soap|suds
soap|wort +s
soapy
  soap|ier
  soapi|est
soar +s +ed +ing
  (rise. ⚠ saw, sore)
soar|er +s (person
  or thing that soars.
  ⚠ sora)
soar|ing|ly
sob
  sobs
  sobbed
  sob|bing
sob|ber +s
sob|bing|ly
sober +s +ed +ing
  +er +est
sober|ing|ly
sober|ly
So|bers, Gar|field
  ('Gary') (West
  Indian cricketer)
Sob|ieski, John
  (Polish king)
so|bri|ety
so|bri|quet +s
sob-stuff
soca (music.
  ⚠ soaker)
soc|age +s
so-called
soc|cer
  (= Association
  Football)
soc|cer play|er +s
Sochi (port, Russia)
so|ci|abil|ity
so|ci|able
so|ci|able|ness
so|ci|ably
so|cial +s
so|cial|isa|tion *Br.*
  (use
  socialization)
so|cial|ise *Br.* (use
  socialize)
  so|cial|ises
  so|cial|ised
  so|cial|is|ing
so|cial|ism
so|cial|ist +s
so|cial|is|tic
so|cial|is|tic|al|ly
so|cial|ite +s
so|ci|al|ity
so|cial|iza|tion

so¦cial¦ize
  so¦cial¦izes
  so¦cial¦ized
  so¦cial¦iz¦ing
so¦cial¦ly
so¦ci¦etal
so¦ci¦et¦al¦ly
so¦ci¦ety
  so¦ci¦eties
So¦ci¦ety Is¦lands
  (in S. Pacific)
So¦cin¦ian +s
socio|bio|logic¦al
socio|bio|logic|
      al¦ly
socio|biolo¦gist +s
socio|biol¦ogy
socio|cul¦tural
socio|cul¦tur|al¦ly
socio-econom¦ic
socio-
  economic¦al¦ly
socio|lin¦guist +s
socio|lin¦guis¦tic
socio|lin¦guis¦tic|
      al¦ly
socio|lin¦guis¦tics
socio|logic¦al
socio|logic¦al¦ly
soci|olo¦gist +s
soci|ology
socio|met¦ric
socio|met¦ric|al¦ly
soci|om¦et|rist +s
soci|om¦etry
socio-politic¦al
sock +s +ed +ing
socket +s +ed
  +ing
sock|eye +s
sock|less
socle +s
So|cotra (island,
  Arabian Sea)
Soc¦ra|tes (Greek
  philosopher)
So|crat¦ic
So|crat¦ic|al¦ly
sod
  sods
  sod¦ded
  sod|ding
  (*coarse slang*
  except in sense of
  'turf, ground')
soda +s
so|dal¦ity
  so|dal¦ities
sod¦den
sod¦den¦ly
sod¦den¦ness

Soddy, Fred|erick
  (English physicist)
sodic
so¦dium
sodium-vapor *Am.*
  attributive
sodium-vapour *Br.*
  attributive
Sodom (town,
  ancient Palestine)
sod¦om|ise *Br.* (use
  sodomize)
  sod¦om|ises
  sod¦om|ised
  sod¦om|is¦ing
sod¦om|ite +s
sod¦om|ize
  sod¦om|izes
  sod¦om|ized
  sod¦om|iz¦ing
sod¦omy
Sodor (medieval
  diocese, Hebrides
  and Isle of Man)
Sod's Law
so¦ever
sofa +s
sofa bed +s
So|fala (province,
  Mozambique)
Sofar (= sound
  fixing and ranging)
sof¦fit +s
Sofia (capital of
  Bulgaria)
soft +er +est (not
  hard; etc.)
softa +s (Muslim
  student of law and
  theology)
soft|ball (game)
soft-boiled
soft-centred
soft¦en +s +ed
  +ing
soft¦en¦er +s
soft-headed
soft-headed¦ness
soft-hearted
soft-hearted¦ness
softie +s
soft|ish
soft-land +s +ed
  +ing
soft¦ly
softly-softly
soft|ness
soft-paste *adjective*
soft-pedal
  soft-pedals
  soft-pedalled *Br.*
  soft-pedaled *Am.*

soft-pedal (*cont.*)
  soft-pedalling *Br.*
  soft-pedaling *Am.*
soft-sell
  soft-sells
  soft-sold
  soft-selling
soft-soap +s +ed
  +ing
soft-spoken
soft-top +s (car;
  roof)
soft|ware
soft|wood +s
softy (use softie)
  soft|ies
SOGAT (= Society
  of Graphical and
  Allied Trades)
sog|gily
sog|gi|ness
soggy
  sog|gier
  sog|gi|est
Sogne Fiord (in
  Norway)
soh (*Music.* △ sew,
  so, sow)
Soho (district,
  London)
soi-disant
soi¦gné male
soi¦gnée female
soil +s +ed +ing
soil-less
soily
soirée +s
soixante-neuf
so|journ +s +ed
  +ing
so|journ¦er +s
Soka Gak¦kai
  (Japanese
  organization)
soke +s (district.
  △ soak)
Sol *Roman
  Mythology*
sol (*Music;* = soh)
sol +s *Chemistry*
sola +s (plant.
  △ solar)
sola *female* (alone;
  male solus.
  △ solar)
sol¦ace
  sol|aces
  sol|aced
  sol|acing
solan +s
so|lan|aceous
sol|an¦der +s

solar +s (of the sun.
  △ sola)
so|lar|isa¦tion *Br.*
  (use solarization)
so|lar|ise *Br.* (use
  solarize)
  so|lar|ises
  so|lar|ised
  so|lar|is|ing
sol|ar|ism
so|lar|ist +s
sol|ar|ium
  sol|ar|iums *or*
  sol|aria
so|lar|iza¦tion
so|lar|ize
  so|lar|izes
  so|lar|ized
  so|lar|iz¦ing
so|la|tium
  so|la|tia
sola topi +s
sold (past tense and
  past participle of
  sell. △ soled)
sol|dan|ella +s
sol¦der +s +ed
  +ing
sol¦der|able
sol|der¦er +s
sol|der¦ing iron +s
sol|dier +s +ed
  +ing
soldier-like
sol|dier¦ly
sol|dier¦ship
sol|diery
  sol¦dier|ies
Sole (shipping area,
  NE Atlantic)
sole
  soles
  soled
  sol¦ing
  (of foot or shoe;
  fish; single.
  △ soul)
sol|ecism +s
sol|ecist +s
sol|ecis¦tic
sole¦ly (only.
  △ soli)
sol¦emn
sol¦em|ness
sol¦em|nisa|tion
  Br. (use
  solemnization)
sol¦em|nise *Br.*
  (use solemnize)
sol¦em|nises
sol¦em|nised
sol¦em|nis¦ing

so¦lem¦nity
  so¦lem¦nities
sol¦em¦niza¦tion
sol¦em¦nize
  sol¦em¦nizes
  sol¦em¦nized
  sol¦em¦niz¦ing
so¦lemn¦ly
Sol¦emn Mass
  Sol¦emn Masses
solen +s
so¦leno¦don +s
so¦len¦oid +s
so¦len¦oid¦al
So¦lent (river,
  England)
sole-plate +s
sol-fa +s +ed +ing
  Music
sol¦fa¦tara +s
sol¦feg¦gio
  sol¦feggi
soli (plural of solo.
  △ solely)
so¦licit +s +ed
  +ing
so¦lici¦ta¦tion +s
so¦lici¦tor +s
solicitor-advocate
  +s
Solicitor-General
  Solicitors-
  General
so¦lici¦tous
so¦lici¦tous¦ly
so¦lici¦tous¦ness
so¦lici¦tude
solid +s +er +est
Soli¦dar¦ity (Polish
  trade-union
  movement)
soli¦dar¦ity
  soli¦dar¦ities
solid-drawn
sol¦idi
so¦lidi¦fi¦ca¦tion
so¦lidi¦fier +s
so¦lid¦ify
  so¦lidi¦fies
  so¦lidi¦fied
  so¦lidi¦fy¦ing
so¦lid¦ity
sol¦id¦ly
sol¦id¦ness
solid-state *adjective*
solid¦un¦gu¦late +s
sol¦idus
  sol¦idi
sol¦ifid¦ian +s
soli¦fluc¦tion
Soli¦hull (town,
  England)

so¦lilo¦quise *Br.*
  (use soliloquize)
  so¦lilo¦quises
  so¦lilo¦quised
  so¦lilo¦quis¦ing
so¦lilo¦quist +s
so¦lilo¦quize
  so¦lilo¦quizes
  so¦lilo¦quized
  so¦lilo¦quiz¦ing
so¦lilo¦quy
  so¦lilo¦quies
Soli¦man
  (= Suleiman)
soli¦ped +s
sol¦ip¦sism
sol¦ip¦sist +s
sol¦ip¦sis¦tic
sol¦ip¦sis¦tic¦al¦ly
soli¦taire +s
soli¦tar¦ily
soli¦tari¦ness
soli¦tary
  soli¦tar¦ies
soli¦tude +s
sol¦miz¦ate
  sol¦miz¦ates
  sol¦miz¦ated
  sol¦miz¦at¦ing
sol¦miza¦tion
solo
  plural **solos** *or* **soli**
  Music; Dancing
solo +s (flight; card
  game; etc.)
solo
  so¦loes
  so¦loed
  solo¦ing
  verb
solo¦ist +s
Solo¦mon (king of
  Israel; name)
Solo¦mon¦ic
Solo¦mon Is¦lands
  (in S. Pacific)
Solo¦mon's seal
  (plant)
Solon (Athenian
  statesman)
So¦lo¦thurn (town
  and canton,
  Switzerland)
sol¦stice +s
sol¦sti¦tial
solu¦bil¦isa¦tion *Br.*
  (use
  solubilization)
solu¦bil¦ise *Br.* (use
  solubilize)
  solu¦bil¦ises

solu¦bil¦ise (*cont.*)
  solu¦bil¦ised
  solu¦bil¦is¦ing
solu¦bil¦iza¦tion
solu¦bil¦ize
  solu¦bil¦izes
  solu¦bil¦ized
  solu¦bil¦iz¦ing
sol¦uble
solus *male* (*female*
  sola)
sol¦ute +s
so¦lu¦tion +s
So¦lu¦trean +s
solv¦able
solv¦ate
  solv¦ates
  solv¦ated
  solv¦at¦ing
solv¦ation +s
Sol¦vay pro¦cess
solve
  solves
  solved
  solv¦ing
solv¦ency
solv¦ent +s
solv¦er +s
Sol¦way Firth
  (inlet, Irish Sea)
Soly¦man
  (= Suleiman)
Sol¦zhen¦it¦syn,
  Alek¦sandr
  (Russian novelist)
soma +s
So¦mali
  plural So¦mali *or*
  So¦malis
So¦ma¦lia (country,
  NE Africa)
So¦ma¦lian +s
So¦ma¦li¦land
  (former
  protectorates, NE
  Africa)
som¦at¦ic
som¦at¦ic¦al¦ly
som¦ato|gen¦ic
soma¦tol¦ogy
som¦ato¦tonic
som¦ato¦troph¦in
  +s
som¦ato¦type +s
som¦ber *Am.*
sombre *Br.*
sombre¦ly
sombre¦ness
som¦brero +s
som¦brous

some (unspecified
  amount or
  number. △ sum)
some|body
  some|bodies
some day *adverbial*
some|how
some|one
some|place
som¦er|sault +s
  +ed +ing
Som¦er|set (county,
  England)
some|thing +s
some|time (at
  some point in
  time)
some time (a
  certain amount of
  time)
some|times
some|what
some|when
some|where
so|mite +s
so|mit¦ic
Somme (river and
  battle site, France)
som|mel¦ier +s
som|nam¦bu|lant
som|nam¦bu|
     lant¦ly
som|nam¦bu|lism
som|nam¦bu|list
  +s
som|nam¦bu|lis¦tic
som|nam¦bu|lis¦tic|
     al¦ly
som|nif¦er¦ous
som|no|lence
som|no|lency
som|no|lent
som|no|lent¦ly
Som|oza,
  Ana|sta¦sio
  (Nicaraguan
  president)
son +s (male child.
  △ sun, sunn)
son|ancy
son|ant +s
sonar +s
son|ata +s
sona|tina +s
sonde +s
Sond|heim,
  Ste|phen
  (American
  composer)
sone +s (unit.
  △ sewn, sown)

son et lu¦mi¦ère
  +*s*
Song (Chinese
  dynasty; = Sung)
song +s
song|bird +s
song|book +s
song|ful
song|ful¦ly
song|less
song|smith
song|ster +s
song|stress
  song|stresses
song|writer +s
song|writ¦ing
Sonia *also* Sonya
sonic
son¦ic|al¦ly
son-in-law
  sons-in-law
son|less
son¦net +s +ed
  +ing
son¦net|eer +s
sonny
  son|nies
  (form of address.
  ⚠ sunny)
sono|buoy +s
son of a bitch
  sons of bitches
son of a gun
  sons of guns
sono|gram +s
son|om¦eter +s
Son¦ora (state,
  Mexico; Desert)
son¦or|ity
  son¦or|ities
son¦or|ous
son¦or¦ous¦ly
son¦or¦ous|ness
son|ship
son¦sie (use sonsy)
  son|sier
  son|si|est
sonsy
  son|sier
  son|si|est
Son¦tag, Susan
  (American critic)
Sonya *also* Sonia
Soo|chow
  (= Suzhou)
sook +s (coward;
  calf. ⚠ souk)
sool +s +ed +ing
sool¦er +s
soon +er +est
soon|ish
soot +s +ed +ing

soot¦er|kin +s
sooth +s (truth)
soothe
  soothes
  soothed
  sooth|ing
  (calm; ease pain)
sooth¦er +s
sooth|ing¦ly
sooth|say
  sooth|says
  sooth|said
  sooth|say|ing
  sooth|say¦er +s
soot¦ily
sooti|ness
sooty
  soot¦ier
  sooti|est
sop
  sops
  sopped
  sop|ping
So|phia (in 'St
  Sophia'; name.
  ⚠ Sofia)
So|phie (name.
  ⚠ Sophy)
soph|ism +s
soph|ist +s
soph|ist¦er +s
so|phis|tic
so|phis|tic|al
so|phis|tic|al¦ly
so|phis|ti|cate
  so|phis|ti|cates
  so|phis|ti|cated
  so|phis|ti|cat|ing
so|phis|ti|cated|ly
so|phis|ti|ca|tion
  +s
soph|is|try
  soph¦is|tries
Sopho|clean
Sopho|cles (Greek
  dramatist)
sopho|more +s
sopho|mor¦ic
Sophy
  So|phies
  (Persian ruler.
  ⚠ Sophie)
sop¦or|ifer|ous
sop¦or|if¦ic
sop¦or|if¦ic|al¦ly
sop|pily
sop|pi|ness
sop|ping
soppy
  sop|pier
  sop|pi|est
sop|ra|nino +s

sop|ran|ist +s
sop|rano +s
Sop|with, Thomas
  (English aircraft
  designer)
sora +s (bird.
  ⚠ soarer)
Sorb +s (person)
sorb +s (tree; fruit)
sor|be|fa¦cient +s
sor¦bet +s
Sorb|ian +s
sorb|itol
Sorbo (rubber)
  Propr.
Sor|bonne
  (University of
  Paris)
sor¦cer¦er +s
sor¦cer|ess
  sor¦cer|esses
sor¦cer|ous
sor¦cery
  sor¦cer|ies
sor|did
sor|did¦ly
sor|did|ness
sor|dino
  sor|dini
sor¦dor +s
sore
  sores
  sorer
  sor¦est
  (painful; vexed;
  painful place.
  ⚠ saw, soar)
sore|head +s
sorel +s (deer.
  ⚠ sorrel)
sore¦ly
sore|ness
sor|ghum +s
sori (plural of
  sorus)
sor|ites
  plural so|rites
sor|iti¦cal
Sor¦op|ti|mist +s
sor¦ori|cidal
sor¦ori|cide +s
sor¦or|ity
  sor¦or|ities
sor|osis
  sor|oses
  (fruit. ⚠ cirrhosis)
sorp|tion
sor¦rel +s (herb;
  colour. ⚠ sorel)
Sor|rento (town,
  Italy)
sor|rily

sor¦ri|ness
sor|row +s +ed
  +ing
sor|row¦er +s
sor|row|ful
sor|row|ful¦ly
sor|row|ful|ness
sorry
  sor|rier
  sor¦ri|est
sort +s +ed +ing
  (class of things;
  piece of printing;
  type; arrange.
  ⚠ sought)
sort|able
sort¦er +s
sor¦tie
  sor|ties
  sor|tied
  sor|tie|ing
sor¦ti|lege +s
sor|ti¦tion +s
sort-out +s *noun*
sorus
  sori
Sos|no|wiec (town,
  Poland)
so-so
sos|ten¦uto +s
sot
  sots
  sot¦ted
  sot|ting
so|terio|logic¦al
so|teri|ology
So|thic
Sotho
  plural Sotho *or*
  So|thos *or*
  Ba|sotho
  (people; language)
sot|tish
sotto voce
sou +s (former
  French coin; very
  small amount of
  money. ⚠ sue, xu)
sou|brette +s
sou|bri|quet +s
  (use sobriquet)
sou|chong +s
souf¦fle +s
  (murmur in body)
souf|flé +s (food)
Sou|frière
  (volcanoes,
  Guadeloupe and
  St Vincent)
sough +s +ed +ing
  (moan; whistle.
  ⚠ sow)

sought (past tense
  and past participle
  of seek. △ sort)
sought after
  adjective
sought-after
  attributive
souk +s (market.
  △ sook)
sou|kous
soul +s (spirit.
  △ sole)
soul-destroy|ing
soul|ful
soul|ful|ly
soul|ful|ness
soul|less
soul|less|ly
soul|less|ness
soul|mate +s
soul-searching +s
sound +s +ed +ing
  +er +est
sound|alike +s
sound|bite +s
sound|board +s
sound|box
  sound|boxes
sound|check +s
sound|er +s
sound|hole +s
sound|ing +s
sounding-balloon
  +s
sound|ing board
  +s
sound|ing line +s
sound|ing rod +s
sound|less
sound|less|ly
sound|less|ness
sound|ly
sound|ness
sound post +s
sound|proof +s
  +ed +ing
sound|track +s
sound wave +s
soup +s +ed +ing
soup|çon +s
souped-up *adjective*
soup|ily
soupi|ness
soup kitchen +s
soup plate +s
soup spoon +s
soupy
  soup|ier
  soupi|est
sour +s +ed +ing
  +er +est

source
  sources
  sourced
  sour|cing
source|book +s
source-criticism
  +s
sour|dough +s
sour|ish
sour|ly
sour|ness
sour|puss
  sour|pusses
sour|sop +s
Sousa, John
  Philip (American
  composer)
sousa|phone +s
sousa|phon|ist +s
souse
  souses
  soused
  sous|ing
sous|lik +s
Sousse (port,
  Tunisia)
sou|tache +s
sou|tane +s
sou|ten|eur +s
souter +s
  (shoemaker.
  △ suiter, suitor)
sou|ter|rain +s
South, the (part of
  country etc.)
south +s +ed +ing
  (point; direction;
  move southwards)
South|amp|ton
  (port, England)
south|bound
South|down +s
  (sheep)
South Downs
  (hills, England)
South-East, the
  (part of country
  etc.)
south-east (point;
  direction)
south|easter +s
south-easter|ly
  south-easter|lies
south-eastern
south-eastern|er
  +s
South-East
  Ice|land (shipping
  area)
south-eastward
south-eastwards

Southend-on-Sea
  (resort, England)
souther +s
south|er|ly
  south|er|lies
south|ern
south|ern|er +s
south|ern|most
south|ern|wood
  +s
Southey, Rob|ert
  (English poet)
south-facing
South Geor|gia
  (island, S.
  Atlantic)
South
  Gla|mor|gan
  (county, Wales)
south|ing +s
South Orkney
  Is|lands (in S.
  Atlantic)
south|paw +s
South|port (town,
  England)
South Sand|wich
  Is|lands (in S.
  Atlantic)
South Shet|land
  Is|lands (in S.
  Atlantic)
south-south-east
south-south-west
south|ward
south|wards
South-West, the
  (part of country
  etc.)
south-west (point;
  direction)
south|wester +s
  (wind.
  △ sou'wester)
south-wester|ly
  south-wester|lies
south-western
south-western|er
  +s
south-westward
south-westwards
Sou|tine, Chaim
  (French painter)
sou|venir +s +ed
  +ing
souv|la|ki
  souv|la|kia *or*
  souv|la|kis
sou'|wester +s
  (hat.
  △ southwester)

sov +s
  (= sovereign)
sov|er|eign +s
sov|er|eign|ly
sov|er|eign|ty
  sov|er|eign|ties
So|viet +s (of the
  Soviet Union;
  citizen)
so|viet +s (council)
So|viet|isa|tion *Br.*
  (use
  Sovietization)
So|viet|ise *Br.* (use
  Sovietize)
  So|viet|ises
  So|viet|ised
  So|viet|is|ing
So|viet|iza|tion
So|viet|ize
  So|viet|izes
  So|viet|ized
  So|viet|iz|ing
so|viet|olo|gist +s
sow
  sows
  sowed
  sow|ing
  sown *or* **sowed**
  (plant seed etc.
  △ sew, so, soh)
sow +s (female pig.
  △ sough)
sow|back +s
sow|bread +s
sower +s (person
  who sows.
  △ sewer)
So|wetan +s
So|weto (township,
  South Africa)
sow|ing +s
  (planting seed etc.
  △ sewing)
sown (past
  participle of sow.
  △ sewn)
sow|this|tle +s
Sox (in name of
  baseball teams)
sox (clothing; use
  socks)
soy (sauce)
soya (plant)
soya bean +s
soy|bean +s
Soy|inka, Wole
  (Nigerian writer)
soy sauce +s
Soyuz (Soviet
  spacecraft)
soz|zled

Spa (town,
  Belgium)
spa +s (spring.
  △ spar)
space
  spaces
  spaced
  spa|cing
space-age
space bar +s
space|craft +s
space|man
  space|men
spa|cer +s
space-saving
space|ship +s
space|suit +s
space-time
space|woman
  space|women
spacey
  spaci|er
  spaci|est
spa|cial (use
  spatial)
spa|cing +s
spa|cious
spa|cious|ly
spa|cious|ness
spacy (use spacey)
  spaci|er
  spaci|est
spade
  spades
  spaded
  spad|ing
spade|ful +s
spade|work
spa|di|ceous
spadi|cose
spa|dille +s
spa|dix
  spa|di|ces
spado +s
spae
  spaes
  spaed
  spae|ing
  (foretell. △ spay)
spae|wife
  spae|wives
spag bol
  (= spaghetti
  Bolognese)
spa|ghetti +s
spahi +s
Spain
spake
spall +s +ed +ing
Spal|lan|zani,
  Laz|zaro (Italian
  biologist)

spal|la|tion +s
spal|peen +s
spam *Propr.*
span
  spans
  spanned
  span|ning
Span|dex *Propr.*
span|drel +s
spang
span|gle
  span|gles
  span|gled
  span|gling
span|gly
  span|glier
  span|gli|est
Span|iard +s
span|iel +s
Span|ish
Spanish-American
  +s
Span|ish|ness
spank +s +ed +ing
spank|er +s
spank|ing +s
span|ner +s
span|sule +s *Propr.*
span-worm +s
spar
  spars
  sparred
  spar|ring
  (fight; dispute;
  pole; mineral.
  △ spa)
spar|able +s (nail)
spa|raxis
  spa|raxes
  (plant)
spar-buoy +s
spar-deck +s
spare
  spares
  spared
  spar|ing
  sparer
  spar|est
spare|ly
spare|ness
sparer +s
spare-rib +s (food)
spare time *noun*
spare-time
  attributive
sparge
  sparges
  sparged
  spar|ging
spar|ger +s
sparid +s
spar|ing|ly

spar|ing|ness
Spark, Mur|iel
  (Scottish novelist)
spark +s +ed +ing
spark-gap +s
spark|ing plug +s
spark|ish
spar|kle
  spar|kles
  spar|kled
  spark|ling
spark|ler +s
spark|less
spark|ling|ly
sparkly
spark plug +s
sparky
  spark|ier
  sparki|est
spar|ling
  plural spar|ling *or*
  spar|lings
spar|oid +s
spar|row +s
sparrow-grass
spar|row|hawk +s
sparry
sparse
sparse|ly
sparse|ness
spars|ity
Sparta (city,
  Greece)
Spar|ta|cist +s
Spar|ta|cus
  (Thracian
  gladiator)
Spar|tan +s
spar|tina +s
spasm +s +ed +ing
spas|mod|ic
spas|mod|ic|al|ly
spas|tic +s
  (*offensive as term of
  abuse*)
spas|tic|al|ly
spas|ti|city
spat
  spats
  spat|ted
  spat|ting
spatch|cock +s
  +ed +ing
spate +s
spa|tha|ceous
spathe +s
spath|ic
spath|ose
spa|tial
spa|tial|ise Br. (use
  spatialize)
  spa|tial|ises

spa|tial|ise (*cont.*)
  spa|tial|ised
  spa|tial|is|ing
spa|ti|al|ity
spa|tial|ize
  spa|tial|izes
  spa|tial|ized
  spa|tial|iz|ing
spa|tial|ly
spatio-temporal
spatio-
  tempor|al|ly
Spät|lese
  Spät|lesen or
  Spät|leses
spat|ter +s +ed
  +ing
spat|ter|dash
  spat|ter|dashes
spat|ula +s
spatu|late
Spätzle
spavin +s
spav|ined
spawn +s +ed
  +ing
spawn|er +s
spawn|ing +s
spay +s +ed +ing
  (sterilize. △ spae)
speak
  speaks
  spoke
  speak|ing
  spoken
speak|able
speak|easy
  speak|easies
speak|er +s
speak|er|phone +s
speak|er|ship +s
speaking-trumpet
  +s
speaking-tube +s
spear +s +ed +ing
spear-carrier +s
spear|gun +s
spear|head +s +ed
  +ing
spear|man
  spear|men
spear|mint +s
spear|wort +s
spec +s
  (= speculation;
  specification;
  (*specs*) spectacles.
  △ speck)
spe|cial +s
spe|cial|isa|tion
  Br. +s (use
  specialization)

spe¦cial¦ise Br. (use
  specialize)
  spe¦cial¦ises
  spe¦cial¦ised
  spe¦cial¦is¦ing
spe¦cial¦ism +s
spe¦cial¦ist +s
spe¦cial¦is¦tic
spe¦ci¦al¦ity
  spe¦ci¦al¦ities
spe¦cial¦iza¦tion
  +s
spe¦cial¦ize
  spe¦cial¦izes
  spe¦cial¦ized
  spe¦cial¦iz¦ing
spe¦cial¦ly
spe¦cial¦ness
spe¦cialty
  spe¦cial¦ties
spe¦cial¦ty
  spe¦cial¦ties
  Law
spe¦ci¦ation +s
spe¦cie (coins)
spe¦cies
  plural spe¦cies
  (category of
  animals or plants)
spe¦cies¦ism
spe¦cies¦ist +s
spe¦ci¦fi¦able
spe¦cif¦ic +s
spe¦cif¦ic¦al¦ly
spe¦ci¦fi¦ca¦tion +s
spe¦ci¦fi¦city
spe¦cif¦ic¦ness
spe¦ci¦fier +s
spe¦cify
  spe¦ci¦fies
  spe¦ci¦fied
  spe¦ci¦fy¦ing
spe¦ci¦men +s
spe¦cio¦logic¦al
spe¦ci¦ology
spe¦ci¦os¦ity
spe¦cious
spe¦cious¦ly
spe¦cious¦ness
speck +s +ed +ing
  (spot. △ spec)
speckle
  speckles
  speckled
  speck¦ling
speck¦less
specs
  (= spectacles)
spec¦tacle +s
spec¦tacled
spec¦tacle frame
  +s

spec¦tacu¦lar +s
spec¦tacu¦lar¦ly
spec¦tate
  spec¦tates
  spec¦tated
  spec¦tat¦ing
spec¦ta¦tor +s
spec¦ta¦tor¦ial
spec¦ter *Am.* +s
  (*Br.* spectre)
Spec¦tor, Phil
  (American record
  producer and
  songwriter)
spec¦tra
spec¦tral
spec¦tral¦ly
spectre *Br.* +s (*Am.*
  specter)
spec¦tro|
     chem¦is¦try
spec¦tro|gram +s
spec¦tro|graph +s
spec¦tro|graph¦ic
spec¦tro|graph¦ic¦
     al¦ly
spec¦trog¦raphy
spec¦tro|helio|
     graph +s
spec¦tro|helio|
     scope +s
spec¦trom¦eter +s
spec¦trom¦etry
spec¦tro|
    pho¦tom¦eter +s
spec¦tro|photo|
      met¦ric
spec¦tro|
    pho¦tom¦etry
spec¦tro|scope +s
spec¦tro|scop¦ic
spec¦tro|scop¦ic¦al
spec¦tros¦co¦pist
  +s
spec¦tros¦copy
spec¦trum
  spec¦tra
spec¦ula (plural of
  speculum)
specu¦lar (of a
  speculum)
specu¦late
  specu¦lates
  specu¦lated
  specu¦lat¦ing
specu¦la¦tion +s
specu¦la¦tive
specu¦la¦tive¦ly
specu¦la¦tive¦ness
specu¦la¦tor +s

specu¦lum
  spec¦ula
speculum-metal
  +s
sped
speech
  speeches
speech¦ful
speech¦ifi¦ca¦tion +s
speechi¦fier +s
speech¦ify
  speechi¦fies
  speechi¦fied
  speechi¦fy¦ing
speech¦less
speech¦less¦ly
speech¦less¦ness
speech-reading
speech-writer +s
speed +s +ed +ing
  (travel at illegal or
  dangerous speed;
  regulate speed of)
speed
  speeds
  sped
  speed|ing
  (other senses)
speed|ball
speed|boat +s
speed¦er +s
speed¦ily
speedi¦ness
speedo +s
speed|om¦eter +s
speed|ster +s
speed-up +s *noun*
speed|way +s
speed|well +s
speedy
  speed¦ier
  speedi¦est
speiss (metallic
  compound.
  △ spice)
Speke, John
  Han¦ning
  (English explorer)
speleo¦logic¦al
spele¦olo¦gist +s
spele¦ology
spell
  spells
  spelt *or* **spelled**
  spell¦ing
spell¦able
spell¦bind
  spell¦binds
  spell¦bound
  spell¦bind¦ing
spell¦bind¦er +s
spell¦bind¦ing¦ly

spell-check +s +ed
  +ing
spell-checker +s
spell¦er +s
spelli¦can +s
spell¦ing +s
spelling-bee +s
spelling-checker
  +s
spelt
spel¦ter
spe¦lunk¦er +s
spe¦lunk¦ing
Spence, Basil
  (British architect)
spence +s
Spen|cer, Her|bert
  (English
  philosopher.
  △ Spenser)
Spen|cer, Stan|ley
  (English painter.
  △ Spenser)
spen¦cer +s
Spen¦cer|ian +s (of
  Herbert Spencer;
  handwriting.
  △ Spenserian)
spend
  spends
  spent
  spend|ing
spend¦able
Spend¦er,
  Ste¦phen (English
  poet)
spend¦er +s
spend¦thrift +s
Spen|gler,
  Os¦wald (German
  philosopher)
Spen|ser,
  Ed¦mund
  (English poet.
  △ Spencer)
Spen¦ser|ian +s (of
  Spenser.
  △ Spencerian)
spent
sperm
  plural sperm *or*
  sperms
sperma¦ceti
sperma¦cet¦ic
sperm¦ary
  sperm¦ar¦ies
sperm¦at¦ic
sperm¦atid +s
sperm¦at¦id¦al
sperm¦ato|blast +s
sperm¦ato|cyte +s

sperm|ato|gen|esis
sperm|ato|
      gen|et|ic
sperm|ato|
      gon|ium
sperm|ato|gonia
sperm|ato|phore
  +s
sperm|ato|phor|ic
sperm|ato|phyte
  +s
sperm|ato|zoal
sperm|ato|zoan
  adjective
sperm|ato|zo|ic
sperm|ato|zoid +s
sperm|ato|zoon
  sperm|ato|zoa
  noun
spermi|cidal
spermi|cide +s
spermo|blast +s
spermo|cyte +s
spermo|gen|esis
spermo|gon|ium
  spermo|gonia
spermo|phore +s
spermo|phyte +s
spermo|zoid +s
spermo|zoon
  spermo|zoa
spew +s +ed +ing
spew|er +s
Spey (river,
  Scotland)
sphag|num
  sphagna
sphal|er|ite +s
sphen|oid +s
sphen|oid|al
spheral
sphere
  spheres
  sphered
  spher|ing
spher|ic
spher|ic|al
spher|ic|al|ly
spher|icity
spher|oid +s
spher|oid|al
spher|oid|icity
spher|om|eter +s
spher|ular
spher|ule +s
spher|ul|ite +s
spher|ul|it|ic
sphinc|ter +s
sphinc|ter|al
sphinc|tered
sphinc|ter|ial
sphinc|ter|ic

sphin|gid +s
sphinx
  sphinxes
sphra|gis|tics
sphyg|mo|gram +s
sphyg|mo|graph
  +s
sphyg|mo|graph|ic
sphyg|mo|graph|ic|
  al|ly
sphyg|mog|raphy
sphyg|mo|logic|al
sphyg|mol|ogy
sphyg|mo|
  man|om|eter +s
sphyg|mo|mano|
    met|ric
spic +s (*offensive*
  Mexican etc.
  ⚠ spick and
  span)
Spica (star)
spica +s (spike;
  bandage)
spi|cate
spi|cated
spi|cato +s
spice
  spices
  spiced
  spi|cing
  (flavouring etc.
  ⚠ speiss)
spice|bush
  spice|bushes
Spice Is|lands
  (former name of
  the Moluccas)
spicery
  spicer|ies
spicey (use spicy)
  spici|er
  spici|est
spici|ly
spici|ness
spick and span
spick|nel +s
spicu|lar
spicu|late
spic|ule +s
spicy
  spici|er
  spici|est
spider +s +ed +ing
spider|ish
spider|man
  spider|men
spider|wort +s
spi|dery
spie|gel|eisen
spiel +s +ed +ing

Spiel|berg,
  Ste|ven
  (American film
  director)
spiel|er +s
spiff +s +ed +ing
spiff|ily
spiffy
  spiff|ier
  spiffi|est
spif|li|cate
  spif|li|cates
  spif|li|cated
  spif|li|cat|ing
spif|li|ca|tion
spig|nel +s
spigot +s
spike
  spikes
  spiked
  spik|ing
spike|let +s
spike|nard +s
spiki|ly
spiki|ness
spiky
  spiki|er
  spiki|est
spile
  spiles
  spiled
  spil|ing
spill
  spills
  spilled *or* spilt
  spill|ing
spill|age +s
spill|er +s
spilli|kin +s
spill|over +s
spill|way +s
spilt
spilth +s
spin
  spins
  spun *or* span
  spin|ning
spina bif|ida
spin|aceous
spin|ach
  spin|aches
spin|achy
spinal
spinal|ly
spin|dle
  spin|dles
  spin|dled
  spind|ling
spindle-berry
  spindle-berries
spindle-shanked
spindle-shanks

spindly
  spind|lier
  spind|li|est
spin doc|tor +s
spin-drier +s (use
  spin-dryer)
spin|drift +s
spin-dry
  spin-dries
  spin-dried
  spin-drying
spin-dryer +s
spine +s
spine-chiller +s
spine-chilling
spined
spi|nel +s
spine|less
spine|less|ly
spine|less|ness
spi|net +s
spine-tingling
spini|fex
  spini|fexes
spini|ness
spin|naker +s
spin|ner +s
spin|neret +s
spin|ney +s
spin|ning *noun*
spin|ning jenny
  spin|ning jen|nies
spin|ning
  ma|chine +s
spin|ning mule +s
spin|ning top +s
spin|ning wheel
  +s
spin-off +s *noun*
  and attributive
spin|ose
spin|ous
Spin|oza, Bar|uch
  de (Dutch
  philosopher)
Spin|oz|ism
Spin|oz|ist +s
Spin|oz|is|tic
spin|ster +s
spin|ster|hood +s
spin|ster|ish
spin|ster|ish|ness
spin|thari|scope
  +s
spin|ule +s
spinu|lose
spinu|lous
spiny
  spini|er
  spini|est
spir|acle +s
spir|acu|lar

spir¦acu¦lum
  spir¦acula
spir¦aea *Br.* +s
  (*Am.* spirea)
spiral
  spir¦als
  spir¦alled *Br.*
  spir¦aled *Am.*
  spiral¦ling *Br.*
  spiral¦ing *Am.*
spiral¦ity
spir¦al¦ly
spir¦ant +s
spire
  spires
  spired
  spir¦ing
spirea *Am.* +s (*Br.*
  spiraea)
spir¦il¦lum
  spir¦illa
spir¦it +s +ed +ing
spir¦it¦ed¦ly
spir¦it¦ed¦ness
spir¦it¦ism
spir¦it¦ist +s
spirit lamp +s
spir¦it¦less
spir¦it¦less¦ly
spir¦it¦less¦ness
spirit level +s
spir¦it¦ous
spir¦it¦ual +s
spir¦itu¦al¦isa¦tion
  Br. (use
  spiritualization)
spir¦itu¦al¦ise *Br.*
  (use spiritualize)
  spir¦itu¦al¦ises
  spir¦itu¦al¦ised
  spir¦itu¦al¦is¦ing
spir¦itu¦al¦ism
spir¦itu¦al¦ist +s
spir¦itu¦al¦is¦tic
spir¦itu¦al¦ity
  spir¦itu¦al¦ities
spir¦itu¦al¦iza¦tion
spir¦itu¦al¦ize
  spir¦itu¦al¦izes
  spir¦itu¦al¦ized
  spir¦itu¦al¦iz¦ing
spir¦itu¦al¦ly
spir¦itu¦al¦ness
spiri¦tuel *male*
spiri¦tu¦elle *female*
spir¦itu¦ous
spir¦itu¦ous¦ness
spir¦ket¦ting
spiro|chaete *Br.* +s
spiro|chete *Am.* +s
spiro|graph +s
spiro|graph¦ic

spiro|graph¦ic|
  al¦ly
spiro|gyra +s
spir|om¦eter +s
spirt +s +ed +ing
  (use spurt)
spiry
spit
  spits
  spat *or* spit
  spit|ting
  (eject saliva etc.;
  spatter; rain
  lightly)
spit
  spits
  spit|ted
  spit|ting
  (skewer; cook on
  spit)
spit
  plural spit *or* spits
  (spade-depth)
spit|ball +s +ed
  +ing
spit|ball|er +s
spitch|cock +s
  +ed +ing
spite
  spites
  spited
  spit|ing
spite|ful
spite|ful|ly
spite|ful|ness
spit|fire +s
Spit|head (channel
  off S. England)
spit-roast +s +ed
  +ing
Spits|ber|gen
  (island, Arctic
  Ocean)
spit|ter +s
spit|tle
spit|tly
spit|toon +s
spitty
Spitz, Mark
  (American
  swimmer)
spitz
  spitzes
spiv +s
spiv|very
spiv|vish
spivvy
splake +s
splanch|nic
splanch|nol¦ogy

splanch|not¦omy
splanch|
      noto¦mies
splash
  splashes
  splashed
  splash|ing
splash|back +s
splash-board +s
splash|down +s
splash|ily
splashy
  splash|ier
  splashi|est
splat
  splats
  splat|ted
  splat|ting
splat|ter +s +ed
  +ing
splay +s +ed +ing
splay-foot
  splay-feet
splay-footed
spleen +s
spleen|ful
spleen|wort +s
spleeny
  spleen|ier
  spleeni|est
splen|dent
splen|did
splen|did|ly
splen|did|ness
splen|dif¦er|ous
splen|dif¦er|ous|ly
splen|dif¦er|ous|
      ness
splen|dor *Am.* +s
splen|dour *Br.* +s
splen|ec¦tomy
  splen|ec¦to|mies
splen|et¦ic
splen|et¦ic|al¦ly
sple|nial
splen|ic
splen|itis
sple|nius
  sple|nii
splen|oid
splen|ology
spleno|meg¦aly
  spleno|meg¦alies
splen|ot¦omy
  splen|oto¦mies
splice
  splices
  spliced
  spli¦cing
spli¦cer +s
splif +s (use spliff)
spliff +s

spline
  splines
  splined
  splin¦ing
splint +s +ed +ing
splint-bone +s
splint-coal +s
splin|ter +s +ed
  +ing
splinter-bar +s
splinter-proof +s
  +ed +ing
splin|tery
Split (port, Croatia)
split
  splits
  split
  split|ting
  (divide; break)
split-level *adjective*
split-screen +s
split-second
  adjective
split|ter +s
splodge
  splodges
  splodged
  splodg|ing
splodgy
  splodgi|er
  splodgi|est
sploosh
  splooshes
  splooshed
  sploosh|ing
splosh
  sploshes
  sploshed
  splosh|ing
splotch
  splotches
  splotched
  splotch|ing
splotchy
  splotch|ier
  splotchi|est
splurge
  splurges
  splurged
  splur|ging
splut|ter +s +ed
  +ing
splut|ter|er +s
splut|ter|ing|ly
splut|tery
Spock, Dr
  Ben|ja|min
  (American
  paediatrician)
Spode (pottery)
spoil
  spoils

spoil (cont.)
  spoilt or spoiled
  spoil|ing
spoil|age +s
spoil|er +s
spoils|man
  spoils|men
spoil|sport +s
spoilt
Spo|kane (city and river, USA)
spoke
  spokes
  spoked
  spok|ing
spoken
spoke|shave +s
spokes|man
  spokes|men
spokes|per|son
  spokes|per|sons
  or spokes|people
spokes|woman
  spokes|women
spoke|wise
Spo|leto (town, Italy)
spoli|ation +s
spoli|ator +s
spoli|atory
spon|da|ic
spon|dee +s
spon|du|licks
spon|dyl|itis
sponge
  sponges
  sponged
  spon|ging or sponge|ing
sponge|able
sponge|like
spon|ger +s
spongi|form
spon|gily
spon|gi|ness
spongy
  spon|gier
  spon|gi|est
spon|sion +s
spon|son +s
spon|sor +s +ed +ing
spon|sor|ial
spon|sor|ship +s
spon|tan|eity
spon|tan|eous
spon|tan|eous|ly
spon|tan|eous|ness
spon|toon +s
spoof +s +ed +ing
spoof|er +s

spoof|ery
spook +s +ed +ing
spook|ily
spooki|ness
spooky
  spook|ier
  spooki|est
spool +s +ed +ing
spoon +s +ed +ing
spoon|beak +s
spoon|bill +s
spoon-bread +s
spoon|er +s
spoon|er|ism +s
spoon-feed
  spoon-feeds
  spoon-fed
  spoon-feeding
spoon|ful +s
spoon|ily
spooni|ness
spoony
  spoon|ies
  spoon|ier
  spooni|est
spoor +s +ed +ing
spoor|er +s
Spora|des (two groups of Greek islands)
spor|ad|ic
spor|ad|ic|al|ly
spor|an|gial
spor|an|gium
  spor|an|gia
spore +s
spore case +s
sporo|cyst +s
sporo|gen|esis
sporo|gen|ous
sporo|gony
sporo|phore +s
sporo|phyll +s
sporo|phyte +s
sporo|phyt|ic
sporo|phyt|ic|al|ly
sporo|zo|ite +s
spor|ran +s
sport +s +ed +ing
sport|er +s
sportif
sport|ily
sporti|ness
sport|ing|ly
sport|ive
sport|ive|ly
sport|ive|ness
sports car +s
sports|cast +s
sports|cast|er +s
sports ground +s

sports|man
sports|men
sports|man|like
sports|man|ly
sports|man|ship
sports|per|son
  sports|people or sports|per|sons
sports|wear
sports|woman
  sports|women
sports writer +s
sporty
  sport|ier
  sporti|est
spor|ular
spor|ule +s
spot
  spots
  spot|ted
  spot|ting
spot check +s noun
spot-check +s +ed +ing verb
spot|lamp +s
spot|less
spot|less|ly
spot|less|ness
spot|light
  spot|lights
  spot|light|ed or spot|lit
  spot|light|ing
spot on
spot|ted|ness
spot|ter +s
spot|tily
spot|ti|ness
spotty
  spot|tier
  spot|ti|est
spot weld +s noun
spot-weld +s +ed +ing verb
spot-welder +s
spou|sal
spouse +s
spout +s +ed +ing
spout|er +s
spout|less
sprad|dle
  sprad|dles
  sprad|dled
  sprad|dling
sprag +s
sprain +s +ed +ing
spraint
  plural spraint
sprang
sprat
  sprats

sprat (cont.)
  sprat|ted
  sprat|ting
Spratly Is|lands (in South China Sea)
sprat|ter +s
sprauncy
  spraun|cier
  spraun|ci|est
sprawl +s +ed +ing
sprawl|er +s
sprawl|ing|ly
spray +s +ed +ing
spray|able
spray-dry
  spray-dries
  spray-dried
  spray-drying
spray|er +s
sprayey
spray-gun +s
spray-paint +s +ed +ing
spread
  spreads
  spread
  spread|ing
spread|able
spread|eagle
  spread|eagles
  spread|eagled
  spread|eag|ling verb
spread eagle +s noun
spread-eagle adjective
spread|er +s
spread|sheet +s
Sprech|ge|sang
Sprech|stimme
spree
  sprees
  spreed
  spree|ing
sprig
  sprigs
  sprigged
  sprig|ging
spriggy
  sprig|gier
  sprig|gi|est
spright|li|ness
spright|ly
  spright|lier
  spright|li|est
spring
  springs
  sprang

spring (*cont.*)
  spring|ing
  sprung
spring|board +s
spring|bok +s
spring-clean +s
  +ed +ing
springe +s
spring|er +s
Spring|field (city, USA)
spring|ily
springi|ness
spring|less
spring|let +s
spring|like
spring-loaded
Spring|steen, Bruce (American rock musician)
spring|tail +s
spring|tide (springtime)
spring tide +s (tide of greatest range)
spring|time +s
springy
  spring|ier
  springi|est
sprin|kle
  sprin|kles
  sprin|kled
  sprink|ling
sprink|ler +s
sprink|ling +s
sprint +s +ed +ing
sprint|er +s
sprit +s
sprite +s
sprite|ly
  sprite|lier
  sprite|li|est
(use sprightly)
sprit|sail +s
spritz
  spritzes
  spritzed
  spritz|ing
spritz|er +s
sprocket +s
sprog +s
sprout +s +ed +ing
spruce
  spruces
  spruced
  spru|cing
spruce|ly
spruce|ness
spru|cer +s
sprue +s

spruik +s +ed +ing
spruik|er +s
spruit +s
sprung
spry +er +est
spry|ly
spry|ness
spud
  spuds
  spud|ded
  spud|ding
spud-bashing
spue (use spew)
  spues
  spued
  spu|ing
spu|mante +s
spume
  spumes
  spumed
  spum|ing
spu|moni +s
spu|mous
spumy
  spumi|er
  spumi|est
spun
spunk
spunk|ily
spunki|ness
spunky
  spunk|ier
  spunki|est
spur
  spurs
  spurred
  spur|ring
spurge +s
spur-gear +s
spuri|ous
spuri|ous|ly
spuri|ous|ness
spur|less
spurn +s +ed +ing
spurn|er +s
spur-of-the-moment *adjective*
spur|rey +s
spur|rier +s
spurry (use spurrey)
  spur|ries
spurt +s +ed +ing
spur-wheel +s
spur|wort +s
sput|nik +s
sput|ter +s +ed +ing
sput|ter|er +s
spu|tum
  sputa

spy
  spies
  spied
  spy|ing
spy|glass
  spy|glasses
spy|hole +s
spy|mas|ter +s
squab +s
squab|ble
  squab|bles
  squab|bled
  squab|bling
squab|bler +s
squabby
squab-chick +s
squacco +s
squad +s
squad|die +s
squad|ron +s
squail +s
squail-board +s
squalid
squal|id|ity
squal|id|ly
squal|id|ness
squall +s +ed +ing
squally
squa|loid +s
squalor +s
squama
  squa|mae
squa|mate
squa|mose
squa|mous
squa|mule +s
squan|der +s +ed +ing
squan|der|er +s
square
  squares
  squared
  squar|ing
squarer
squar|est
square-bashing *noun*
square-built
square-eyed
square|ly
square|ness
squarer +s
square-rigged
square-shouldered
square-toed
squar|ial +s *Propr.*
squar|ish
squar|rose
squash
  squashes
  squashed

squash (*cont.*)
  squash|ing
(crush; game)
squash
  plural squash *or* squashes
(vegetable)
squash court +s
squash|ily
squashi|ness
squash play|er +s
squashy
  squash|ier
  squashi|est
squat
  squats
  squat|ted
  squat|ting
squat|ter
squat|test
squat|ly
squat|ness
squat|ter +s
squaw +s
(*offensive*)
squawk +s +ed +ing
squawk-box
  squawk-boxes
squawk|er +s
squaw-man
  squaw-men
(*offensive*)
squeak +s +ed +ing
squeak|er +s
squeak|ily
squeaki|ness
squeaky
  squeak|ier
  squeaki|est
squeal +s +ed +ing
squeal|er +s
squeam|ish
squeam|ish|ly
squeam|ish|ness
squee|gee
  squee|gees
  squee|geed
  squee|gee|ing
squeez|able
squeeze
  squeezes
  squeezed
  squeez|ing
squeeze-box
  squeeze-boxes
squeezer +s
squeezy
squelch
  squelches

squelch (*cont.*)
  squelched
  squelch|ing
  squelch¦er +s
squelchy
  squelch|ier
  squelchi|est
squib
  squibs
  squibbed
  squib|bing
SQUID +s (= super
  conducting
  quantum
  interference
  device)
squid
  plural squid *or*
  squids
  noun
squid
  squids
  squid|ded
  squid|ding
squidgy
  squidgi¦er
  squidgi|est
squiffed
squiffy
  squif|fier
  squif¦fi|est
squig¦gle
  squig¦gles
  squig¦gled
  squig¦gling
squig¦gly
squill +s
squil|lion +s
squinch
  squinches
squint +s +ed +ing
squint¦er +s
squint-eyed
squinty
squire
  squires
  squired
  squir¦ing
squire|arch +s
squire|arch|ical
squire|archy
  squire|arch¦ies
squire|dom +s
squir¦een +s
squire|hood +s
squire|let +s
squire|ling +s
squire¦ly
squire|ship +s
squirl +s
squirm +s +ed
  +ing

squirm¦er +s
squirmy
squir|rel
  squir|rels
  squir|relled *Br.*
  squir|reled *Am.*
  squir¦rel|ling *Br.*
  squir¦rel|ing *Am.*
squir|rel¦ly
squirrel-monkey
  +s
squirt +s +ed +ing
squirt¦er +s
squirt gun +s
squish
  squishes
  squished
  squish|ing
squishy
  squish|ier
  squishi|est
squit +s
squitch
  squitches
squit|ters
squiz
Sri Lanka
Sri Lankan +s
Sri|nagar (city,
  India)
stab
  stabs
  stabbed
  stab|bing
stab|ber +s
stab|bing +s
sta¦bil|ator +s
sta|bile +s
sta¦bil|isa|tion *Br.*
  (use stabilization)
sta¦bil|ise *Br.* (use
  stabilize)
  sta¦bil|ises
  sta¦bil|ised
  sta¦bil|is¦ing
sta¦bil|iser *Br.* +s
  (use stabilizer)
sta¦bil|ity
sta¦bil|iza|tion
sta¦bil|ize
  sta¦bil|izes
  sta¦bil|ized
  sta¦bil|iz¦ing
sta¦bil|izer +s
stable
  stables
  stabled
  stab|ling
  stabler
  stab¦lest
stable boy +s

stable
  com|pan¦ion +s
stable|ful +s
stable girl +s
stable lad +s
stable|man
  stable|men
stable|mate +s
stable|ness
stab|lish
  stab|lishes
  stab|lished
  stab|lish|ing
sta¦bly
stac|cato +s
Sta¦cey
stack +s +ed +ing
stack|able
stack¦er +s
stack-yard +s
stacte +s
stad¦dle +s
staddle-stone +s
sta|dium
  sta|diums *or*
  sta|dia
stadt|hold¦er +s
stadt|hold¦er|ship
  +s
Staël, Mme de
  (French writer)
staff +s +ed +ing
  (personnel;
  provide with staff)
staff
  staffs *or* staves
  Music
Staffa (Scottish
  island)
staff|age
staff¦er +s
Staf|ford (town,
  England)
Staf¦ford|shire
  (county, England)
staff|room +s
Staffs.
  (= Staffordshire)
stag
  stags
  stagged
  stag|ging
stage
  stages
  staged
  sta|ging
stage|abil¦ity
stage|able
stage|coach
  stage|coaches
stage|craft

stage fright
stage|hand +s
stage-manage
  stage-manages
  stage-managed
  stage-managing
stage
  man|age|ment
stage man|ager +s
stager +s
stage-struck
stagey (use stagy)
  sta¦gier
  stagi|est
stag|fla¦tion
stag|ger +s +ed
  +ing
stag|ger¦er +s
stag|ger|ing¦ly
stag|gers
stag-horn +s
stag|hound +s
stagi¦ly
stagi|ness
sta|ging +s
stag|nancy
stag|nant
stag|nant¦ly
stag|nate
  stag|nates
  stag|nated
  stag|nat¦ing
stag|na¦tion
stag-night +s
stagy
  stagi¦er
  stagi|est
staid +er +est
staid¦ly
staid|ness
stain +s +ed +ing
stain|able
stained glass *noun*
stained-glass
  attributive
Stain¦er, John
  (English
  composer)
stain¦er +s
stain|less
stair +s (in
  building. △ stare)
stair|case +s
stair|head +s
stair|lift +s
stair-rod +s
stair|way +s
stair|well +s
staithe +s
stake
  stakes

stake(*cont.*)
staked
stak¦ing
(stick; bet.
△ steak)
stake-boat+s
stake-body
stake-bodies
stake|build¦ing
stake|hold¦er+s
stake-net+s
stake-out+s *noun*
staker+s
Stakh¦an¦ov|ism
Stakh¦an¦ov|ist+s
Stakh¦an¦ov|ite+s
stal¦ac|tic
stal¦ac|ti|form
stal¦ac|tite+s
stal¦ac|tit¦ic
Stalag+s
stal¦ag|mite+s
stal¦ag|mit¦ic
stale
  stales
  staled
  stal¦ing
  staler
  stal¦est
stale¦ly
stale|mate
  stale|mates
  stale|mated
  stale|mat¦ing
stale|ness
Sta¦lin (former
  name of Donetsk)
Sta¦lin, Jo¦seph
  (Soviet leader)
Sta¦lin|abad
  (former name of
  Dushanbe)
Sta¦lin|grad
  (former name of
  Volgograd)
Sta¦lin|ism
Sta¦lin|ist+s
Sta¦lino (former
  name of Donetsk)
stalk+s +ed +ing
  (stem of plant etc.;
  pursue stealthily.
  △ stork)
stalk¦er+s
stalk-eyed
stalking-horse+s
stalk|less
stalk|let+s
stalk|like
stalky
stall+s +ed +ing
stall|age+s

stall-feed
  stall-feeds
  stall-fed
  stall-feeding
stall|hold¦er+s
stal|lion+s
stal|wart+s
stal|wart¦ly
stal|wart|ness
Stam|boul (former
  name of Istanbul)
sta¦men+s
stam|ina
stam|inal
stam|in|ate
stam|in|ifer|ous
stam|mer+s +ed
  +ing
stam|mer¦er+s
stam|mer|ing¦ly
stamp+s +ed +ing
stamp col¦lect|ing
stamp col|lect¦or
  +s
stamp duty
  stamp duties
stam|pede
  stam|pedes
  stam|peded
  stam|ped¦ing
stam|peder+s
stamp¦er+s
stamp hinge+s
stamp|ing ground
  +s
stamp ma|chine
  +s
stamp-mill+s
stamp of¦fice+s
stamp paper
stance+s
stanch (use
  staunch)
  stanches
  stanched
  stanch|ing
stan|chion+s +ed
  +ing
stand
  stands
  stood
  stand|ing
stand-alone
  adjective
stand|ard+s
standard-bearer
  +s
Stand¦ard|bred +s
stand¦ard|is|able
  Br. (use
  standardizable)

stand¦ard|isa|tion
  Br. +s (use
  standardization)
stand¦ard|ise *Br.*
  (use standardize)
  stand¦ard|ises
  stand¦ard|ised
  stand¦ard|is¦ing
stand¦ard|iser *Br.*
  +s (use
  standardizer)
stand¦ard|iz|able
stand¦ard|iza¦tion
  +s
stand¦ard|ize
  stand¦ard|izes
  stand¦ard|ized
  stand¦ard|iz¦ing
stand¦ard|izer+s
stand¦by+s
stand¦ee+s
stand¦er+s
stand-in+s *noun
  and attributive*
stand|ing+s
stand|ing room
stand-off+s *noun
  and attributive*
stand-offish
stand-offish¦ly
stand-offish|ness
stand|out+s
stand|pipe+s
stand|point+s
stand|still+s
stand-to *noun*
stand-up+s
  adjective and noun
Stan|ford
  (university, USA)
Stan|ford, Charles
  Vil|liers (British
  composer)
Stan|hope, Lady
  Hes¦ter Lucy
  (English traveller)
stan|hope+s
stan|iel+s
Stan|ier, Wil|liam
  (English railway
  engineer)
Stan¦is|laus
  (patron saint of
  Poland)
Stan¦is|lav¦sky,
  Kon¦stan|tin
  (Russian theatre
  director)
stank
Stan|ley, Henry
  Mor¦ton (Welsh
  explorer)

Stan|ley, Mount
  (in central Africa)
Stan|ley, Port
  (town, Falkland
  Islands)
Stan|ley knife
  Stan|ley knives
  Propr.
stan|nary
  stan|nar¦ies
stan|nate
stan|nic
stan|nite+s
stan|nous
Stan|sted (airport,
  England)
stanza+s
stan¦za'd
stan|zaed (use
  stanza'd)
stan|za¦ic
sta|pelia+s
stapes
  plural stapes
staphylo|coc¦cal
staphylo|coc¦cus
  staphylo|cocci
staple
  staples
  stapled
  stapl¦ing
staple gun+s
stapler+s
star
  stars
  starred
  star|ring
star-apple+s
Stara Za¦gora (city,
  Bulgaria)
star|board+s
star|burst+s
starch
  starches
  starched
  starch|ing
starch¦er+s
starch¦ily
starchi|ness
starch-reduced
starchy
  starch|ier
  starchi|est
star-crossed
star|dom
star|dust
stare
  stares
  stared

stare (*cont.*)
  star|ing
  (gaze fixedly.
  ⚠ stair)
starer +s
star|fish
  plural star|fish *or*
  star|fishes
star fruit
  plural star fruit
star|gaze
  star|gazes
  star|gazed
  star|gaz|ing
star|gazer +s
stark +er +est
Stark ef|fect
stark|ers
stark|ly
stark|ness
star|less
star|let +s
star|light
star|like
Star|ling, Er|nest
  Henry (English
  physiologist)
star|ling +s
star|lit
star|rily
star|ri|ness
starry
  star|rier
  star|ri|est
starry-eyed
star|ship +s
star-spangled
star-struck
star-studded
START (= Strategic
  Arms Reduction
  Talks)
start +s +ed +ing
start|er +s
start|ing block +s
start|ing gate +s
starting-handle +s
start|ing point +s
star|tle
  star|tles
  star|tled
  start|ling
start|ler +s
start|ling|ly
start-up +s
  attributive and
  noun
star|va|tion
starve
  starves
  starved
  starv|ing

starve|ling +s
star|wort +s
stash
  stashes
  stashed
  stash|ing
Stasi +s (security
  police of German
  Democratic
  Republic)
sta|sis
  sta|ses
  (inactivity)
stat +s
  (= thermostat;
  (*stats*) statistics)
stat|able
statal
state
  states
  stated
  stat|ing
state|craft
stated|ly
state|hood
state house +s
state|less
state|less|ness
state|let +s
state|li|ness
state|ly
  state|lier
  state|li|est
state|ment +s +ed
  +ing
Staten Is|land (in
  New York)
sta|ter +s (coin.
  ⚠ stator)
state|room +s
state's evi|dence
state|side
states|man
  states|men
states|man|like
states|man|ly
states|man|ship
states|per|son +s
states' rights
states|woman
  states|women
State trial +s
state|wide
static
stat|ic|al
stat|ic|al|ly
stat|ice +s
stat|ics
sta|tion +s +ed
  +ing
sta|tion|ari|ness

sta|tion|ary (not
  moving.
  ⚠ stationery)
station-bill +s
sta|tion|er +s
Sta|tion|ers' Hall
  (in London)
sta|tion|ery (paper
  etc. ⚠ stationary)
station-keeping
sta|tion|mas|ter +s
sta|tion wagon +s
stat|ism
stat|ist +s
stat|is|tic +s
stat|is|tic|al
stat|is|tic|al|ly
stat|is|ti|cian +s
stat|is|tics
Sta|tius, Pub|lius
  Pap|in|ius
  (Roman poet)
sta|tor +s (in
  electric motor etc.
  ⚠ stater)
stato|scope +s
stats (= statistics)
statu|ary
  statu|ar|ies
statue +s
stat|ued
statu|esque
statu|esque|ly
statu|esque|ness
statu|ette +s
stat|ure +s
stat|ured
sta|tus
  sta|tuses
sta|tus quo
sta|tus quo ante
stat|ut|able
stat|ut|ably
stat|ute +s
statute-barred
statute-book +s
statute-roll +s
statu|tor|ily
statu|tory
staunch
  staunches
  staunched
  staunch|ing
  staunch|er
  staunch|est
staunch|ly
staunch|ness
Sta|vanger (port,
  Norway)
stave
  staves

stave (*cont.*)
  staved *or* stove
  stav|ing
staves|acre +s
Stav|ro|pol (city
  and territory,
  Russia)
stay +s +ed +ing
stay-at-home +s
  adjective and noun
stay-bar +s
stay|er +s
stay-in strike +s
stay-rod +s
stay|sail +s
stay-up +s *noun*
stead +s
stead|fast
stead|fast|ly
stead|fast|ness
stead|ier +s
stead|ily
steadi|ness
stead|ing +s
steady
  stead|ies
  stead|ied
  steady|ing
  stead|ier
  steadi|est
steady-going
steak +s (meat.
  ⚠ stake)
steak|house +s
steak knife
  steak knives
steal
  steals
  stole
  steal|ing
  stolen
  (rob; a bargain.
  ⚠ steel, stele)
steal|er +s (thief.
  ⚠ stela, stelar)
stealth
stealth|ily
stealthi|ness
stealthy
  stealth|ier
  stealthi|est
steam +s +ed +ing
steam|boat +s
steam en|gine +s
steam|er +s
steam-heat
steam|ily
steami|ness
steam|ing +s
steam-jacket +s
steam|roll +s +ed
  +ing

steam|roll|er +s
  +ed +ing
steam|ship +s
steam-tight
steamy
  steam|ier
  steami|est
stear|ate +s
ste|aric
stearin +s
stea|tite +s
stea|tit|ic
steato|pygia
stea|topy|gous
steed +s
steel +s +ed +ing
  (metal; make
  resolute. △ steal,
  stele)
steel-clad
Steele, Rich|ard
  (Irish writer)
steel|head +s (fish)
steeli|ness
steel-making
steel|work (steel
  articles)
steel|work|er +s
steel|works
  plural steel|works
  (factory)
steely
  steel|ier
  steeli|est
  (like steel.
  △ stelae, stele)
steel|yard +s
steen|bok
  plural steen|bok
steen|kirk +s
steep +s +ed +ing
  +er +est
steep|en +s +ed
  +ing
steep|ish
steeple +s
steeple|chase +s
steeple|chaser +s
steeple|chas|ing
steeple-crowned
steepled
steeple|jack +s
steep|ly
steep|ness
steer +s +ed +ing
  (guide or direct;
  guidance; animal.
  △ stere)
steer|able
steer|age
steerage-way
steer|er +s

steer|ing col|umn
  +s
steer|ing wheel +s
steers|man
  steers|men
steeve
  steeves
  steeved
  steev|ing
stego|saur +s
stego|saurus
  stego|saur|uses
Stein, Ger|trude
  (American writer)
stein +s
Stein|beck, John
  (American
  novelist)
stein|bock
  plural stein|bock
Steiner, Ru|dolf
  (Austrian founder
  of anthroposophy)
Stein|way, Henry
  (German piano-
  builder)
stela
  ste|lae
  (pillar. △ stealer,
  stelar)
ste|lar (pertaining to
  a stele. △ stealer,
  stela)
stele +s (plant
  tissue. △ steal,
  steel, steely)
Stella (name)
Stella, Frank
  (American
  painter)
stel|lar (of stars)
stel|late
stel|lated
Stel|len|bosch
  (town, South
  Africa)
Stel|ler's sea cow
  +s
stelli|form
stel|lini
stel|lu|lar
stem
  stems
  stemmed
  stem|ming
stem|less
stem|let +s
stem|like
stemma
stem|mata
stem|ple +s
stem turn +s

stem|ware
stem-winder +s
stench
  stenches
sten|cil
  sten|cils
  sten|cilled *Br.*
  sten|ciled *Am.*
  sten|cil|ling *Br.*
  sten|cil|ing *Am.*
Stend|hal (French
  novelist)
Sten gun +s
Steno, Nico|laus
  (Danish geologist)
steno +s
  (= stenographer)
sten|og|raph|er +s
steno|graph|ic
sten|og|raphy
sten|osis
  sten|oses
sten|ot|ic
steno|type +s
steno|typ|ist +s
Sten|tor +s
sten|tor|ian
step
  steps
  stepped
  step|ping
  (pace; stair.
  △ steppe)
Step|ana|kert
  (Russian name for
  Xankändi)
step|brother +s
step|child
  step|chil|dren
step-cut
  step-cuts
  step-cut
  step-cutting
step|dad +s
step|daugh|ter +s
step|fam|ily
  step|fam|ilies
step|father +s
step-grand|child
  step-
  grand|chil|dren
step-
  grand|daugh|ter
  +s
step-grand|father
  +s
step-
  grand|mother +s
step-
  grand|par|ent +s
step-grand|son +s
Steph|anie

steph|an|otis
  steph|an|otises
Ste|phen *also*
  Ste|ven (name)
Ste|phen (English
  king; early saint;
  patron saint of
  Hungary)
Ste|phens (in 'even
  Stephens')
Ste|phen|son,
  George (English
  engineer)
step-in +s *adjective
  and noun*
step|lad|der +s
step|like
step|mother +s
step|mum +s
step-parent +s
steppe +s (grassy
  plain. △ step)
step|ping stone +s
step|sis|ter +s
step|son +s
step-up +s *noun
  and attributive*
step|wise
ster|adian +s
ster|cor|aceous
ster|coral
stere +s (unit.
  △ steer)
stereo +s
stereo|bate +s
stereo|chem|is|try
stereo|graph +s
ster|eog|raphy
stereo|iso|mer +s
stere|om|etry
stereo|phon|ic
stereo|phon|ic|
    al|ly
stere|oph|ony
stere|op|sis
stere|op|tic
stere|op|ticon +s
stereo|scope +s
stereo|scop|ic
stereo|scop|ic|
    al|ly
stere|os|copy
stereo|spe|cif|ic
stereo|spe|cif|ic|
    al|ly
stereo|speci|fi|city
stereo|tac|tic
stereo|taxic
stereo|taxis
stereo|taxy
stereo|type
  stereo|types

stereo|type (*cont.*)
  stereo|typed
  stereo|typ¦ing
stereo|typ¦ic
stereo|typ¦ical
stereo|typ¦ic|al¦ly
stereo|typy
steric
ster|ile
ster|ile¦ly
ster¦il|is|able *Br.*
  (use sterilizable)
ster¦il|isa|tion *Br.*
  +s (use
  sterilization)
ster¦il|ise *Br.* (use
  sterilize)
  ster¦il|ises
  ster¦il|ised
  ster¦il|is¦ing
ster¦il|iser *Br.* +s
  (use sterilizer)
ster¦il|ity
ster¦il|iz|able
ster¦il|iza|tion +s
ster¦il|ize
  ster¦il|izes
  ster¦il|ized
  ster¦il|iz¦ing
ster¦il|izer +s
ster|let +s
ster|ling +s
ster|ling|ness
Ster¦lita|mak (city,
  Russia)
stern +s +er +est
ster¦nal
Stern|berg,
  Jo¦seph von
  (Austrian-born
  American film
  director)
Sterne, Laur¦ence
  (Irish novelist)
Stern Gang
  (Zionist group)
stern¦ly
stern|most
stern|ness
stern|post +s
stern|num
  ster|nums *or*
  sterna
ster¦nu¦ta¦tion +s
ster¦nu¦ta¦tor +s
ster¦nu¦ta¦tory
stern|ward
stern|wards
stern|way +s
stern|wheel¦er +s
ster|oid +s
ster|oid¦al

sterol +s
ster¦tor|ous
ster¦tor|ous¦ly
ster¦tor|ous|ness
stet
  stets
  stet|ted
  stet|ting
stetho|scope +s
stetho|scop¦ic
stetho|scop¦ic|
  al¦ly
steth|os¦co|pist +s
steth|os¦copy
stet|son +s
Stet|tin (German
  name for
  Szczecin)
steve|dore
  steve|dores
  steve|dored
  steve|dor¦ing
Ste¦ven *also*
  Ste¦phen
Ste¦ven|age (town,
  England)
ste¦ven|graph +s
Ste¦vens, Wal¦lace
  (American poet)
Ste¦ven|son,
  Rob¦ert Louis
  (Scottish novelist)
stew +s +ed +ing
stew|ard +s +ed
  +ing
stew¦ard|ess
  stew¦ard|esses
stew¦ard|ship +s
Stew|art *also*
  Stuart
  (name)
Stew|art, Jackie
  (British motor-
  racing driver.
  △ Stuart)
Stew|art, James
  (American actor.
  △ Stuart)
Stew|art Is¦land
  (off New Zealand)
stew|pot +s
sthen¦ic
sticho|mythia
stick
  sticks
  stuck
  stick|ing
stick|abil¦ity
stick¦er +s
stick¦ily
sticki|ness

stick|ing plas|ter
  +s
stick|ing point +s
stick in¦sect +s
stick-in-the-mud
  +s
stick|jaw +s
stickle|back +s
stick|ler +s
stick|less
stick|like
stick|pin +s
stick-up +s
stick|weed +s
sticky
  stick|ier
  sticki|est
sticky|beak +s +ed
  +ing
Stieg|litz, Al¦fred
  (American
  photographer)
stiff +s +er +est
stiff|en +s +ed
  +ing
stiff|en¦er +s
stiff|en|ing +s
stiff|ish
stiff¦ly
stiff-necked
stiff|ness
stiffy
  stiff|ies
stifle
  stifles
  stifled
  stif|ling
stifle-bone
stifler +s
stifl¦ing¦ly
stigma
  stig|mas *or*
  stig|mata
stig|mat|ic +s
stig|mat¦ic|al¦ly
stig¦ma|tisa|tion
  Br. (use
  stigmatization)
stig¦ma|tise *Br.*
  (use stigmatize)
  stig¦ma|tises
  stig¦ma|tised
  stig¦ma|tis¦ing
stig¦ma|tist +s
stig¦ma|tiza|tion
stig¦ma|tize
  stig¦ma|tizes
  stig¦ma|tized
  stig¦ma|tiz¦ing
Stijl, De (Dutch art
  movement)
stilb +s

stil|bene
stil|bes¦trol *Am.*
stil|boes¦trol *Br.*
stile +s (steps over
  fence; part of
  door. △ style)
stil|etto +s
still +s +ed +ing
  +er +est
still|age +s
still|birth +s
still|born
stilli|cide +s
still life +s *noun*
still-life *attributive*
still|ness
  still|nesses
still room +s
Still|son +s
stilly
stilt +s
stilt|ed
stilt|ed¦ly
stilt|ed|ness
stilt|less
Stil|ton +s (village,
  England; cheese)
  Propr.
stimu|lant +s
stimu|late
  stimu|lates
  stimu|lated
  stimu|lat¦ing
stimu¦lat|ing¦ly
stimu¦la¦tion +s
stimu|la¦tive
stimu|la¦tor +s
stimu|la¦tory
stimu|lus
  stim|uli
stimy (use stymie)
  sti¦mies
  sti¦mied
  stimy|ing
sting
  stings
  stung
  sting|ing
sting|aree +s
sting|er +s
stin|gily
stingi|ness
sting|ing¦ly
sting|ing net¦tle
  +s
sting|less
sting|like
sting|ray +s
stingy
  stin|gier
  stin|gi|est

stink
  stinks
  stank *or* stunk
  stink|ing
  stunk
stink|ard +s
stink¦er +s
stink|horn +s
stink|ing¦ly
stinko
stink|pot +s
stink|weed +s
stink|wood +s
stinky
  stink|ier
  stinki|est
stint +s +ed +ing
stint¦er +s
stint|less
stipe +s
sti¦pel +s
sti¦pel|late
sti¦pend +s
sti¦pen|diary
  sti¦pen|diar¦ies
sti¦pes
  stipi|tes
stipi|form
stipi|tate
sti¦piti|form
stip¦ple
  stip¦ples
  stip¦pled
  stip¦pling
stip¦pler +s
stipu|lar
stipu|late
  stipu|lates
  stipu|lated
  stipu|lat¦ing
stipu|la¦tion +s
stipu|la¦tor +s
stip¦ule +s
stir
  stirs
  stirred
  stir|ring
stir-crazy
stir-fry
  stir-fries
  stir-fried
  stir-frying
stirk +s
stir|less
Stir|ling (city, Scotland)
Stir|ling, James (Scottish mathematician)
Stir|ling, Rob¦ert (Scottish engineer)

stir¦pi|cul¦ture
stirps
  stir|pes
stir|rer +s
stir|ring +s
stir|ring¦ly
stir|rup +s
stir|rup cup +s
stir|rup iron +s
stir|rup lea¦ther +s
stir|rup pump +s
stitch
  stitches
  stitched
  stitch|ing
stitch¦er +s
stitch|ery
stitch|less
stitch-up +s
stitch|wort +s
sti¦ver +s
Stoa, the (Stoic school of philosophy)
stoa +s *Architecture*
stoat +s
sto¦chas|tic
sto¦chas|tic|al¦ly
stock +s +ed +ing
stock|ade
  stock|ades
  stock|aded
  stock|ad¦ing
stock-book +s
stock|breed¦er +s
stock|breed|ing
stock|broker +s
stock|broker|age
stock|brok¦ing
stock car +s
stock¦er +s
stock|fish
  plural stock|fish
Stock|hausen, Karl|heinz (German composer)
stock|hold¦er +s
stock|hold¦ing +s
Stock|holm (capital of Sweden)
stock|ily
stocki|ness
stock|inet
stock¦in|ette (use stockinet)
stock|ing +s
stock|inged
stocking-filler +s
stock¦ing|less
stock|ing stitch

stock-in-trade
stock|ist +s
stock|job¦ber +s
stock|job¦bing
stock|less
stock|list +s
stock|man
  stock|men
stock mar¦ket +s
stock|out +s
stock|pile
  stock|piles
  stock|piled
  stock|pil¦ing
stock|piler +s
Stock|port (town, England)
stock|pot +s
stock|room +s
stock-still
stock|take +s
stock|tak¦ing
Stockton-on-Tees (town, England)
stocky
  stock|ier
  stocki|est
stock|yard +s
stodge
  stodges
  stodged
  stodg|ing
stodgi¦ly
stodgi|ness
stodgy
  stodgi¦er
  stodgi|est
stoep +s (veranda.
  ⚠ stoop, stoup)
sto¦gie +s (use stogy)
stogy
  sto¦gies (cigar)
Stoic +s *Philosophy*
stoic +s (stoical person)
sto¦ic|al
sto¦ic|al¦ly
stoi¦chio|met¦ric
stoi¦chi|om¦etry
Sto¦icism (philosophy of the Stoics)
sto¦icism (stoical attitude)
stoke
  stokes
  stoked
  stok¦ing
stoke|hold +s
stoke|hole +s

Stoke-on-Trent (city, England)
Stoker, Bram (Irish novelist)
stoker +s
stokes
  plural stokes
Sto¦kow|ski, Leo|pold (British-born American conductor)
STOL (= short take-off and landing)
stola
  sto¦lae
stole +s
stolen
stolid
stol¦id|ity
stol¦id¦ly
stol¦id|ness
stollen +s
sto¦lon +s
sto¦lon|ate
sto¦lon|ifer|ous
stoma
  stomas *or* sto¦mata
stom|ach +s +ed +ing
stomach-ache +s
stom|ach¦er +s
stom|ach|ful +s
stom|ach¦ic
stom|ach|less
stom|ach pump +s
stom|ach tube +s
sto¦mal
sto¦mata
sto¦ma|tal
sto¦ma|titis
sto¦mato|logic|al
sto¦ma|tolo|gist +s
sto¦ma|tol¦ogy
stomp +s +ed +ing
stomp¦er +s
stone
  stones
  stoned
  ston¦ing
Stone Age (prehistoric period)
stone|chat +s
stone-coal +s
stone-cold
stone-cold sober
stone|crop +s
stone|cut¦ter +s
stone-dead
stone-deaf

stone|fish
  plural stone|fish *or*
  stone|fishes
stone|fly
  stone|flies
stone fruit +s
stone|ground
stone|hatch
  stone|hatches
Stone|henge
  (megalithic
  monument,
  England)
stone|less
stone|mason +s
stone|mason¦ry
stone-pit +s
stoner +s
stone|wall +s +ed
  +ing
stone|wall¦er +s
stone|ware
stone|washed
stone|weed +s
stone|work
stone|work¦er +s
stone|wort +s
stoni¦ly
stoni|ness
stonk¦er +s +ed
  +ing
stonk|ing
stony
  stoni¦er
  stoni¦est
stony-broke
stony-hearted
stood
stooge
  stooges
  stooged
  stoo¦ging
stook +s +ed +ing
stool +s +ed +ing
stool|ball
stoolie +s
stool-pigeon +s
stoop +s +ed +ing
  (bend forward;
  stooping posture;
  swoop onto prey.
  ⚠ stoep, stoup)
stop
  stops
  stopped
  stop|ping
stop|bank +s
stop|cock +s
stop-drill +s
stope +s
Stopes, Marie
  (Scottish birth-

Stopes (*cont.*)
  control
  campaigner)
stop|gap +s
stop-go +s
stop-knob +s
stop|less
stop|off +s
stop|over +s
stop|pable
stop|page +s
Stop|pard, Tom
  (British
  playwright)
stop|per +s +ed
  +ing
stop|ping +s
stop|ping place +s
stop|ple
  stop|ples
  stop|pled
  stop|pling
stop-start *adjective*
stop-volley +s
stop|watch
  stop|watches
stor|able
stor|age
storax
stor|axes
store
  stores
  stored
  stor|ing
store|front +s
store|house +s
store|keep¦er +s
store|man
  store|men
storer +s
store|room +s
storey +s (floor of
  building. ⚠ story)
stor¦eyed (divided
  into storeys, in
  'three-storeyed'
  etc. ⚠ storied)
stori|ated
stori|ation +s
stor|ied (celebrated
  in stories.
  ⚠ storeyed)
stork +s (bird.
  ⚠ stalk)
stork's-bill +s
  (plant)
storm +s +ed +ing
storm-bird +s
storm|bound
storm-cock +s
storm-collar +s
storm cone +s

storm-door +s
storm¦er +s
storm-finch
  storm-finches
storm-glass
  storm-glasses
storm|ily
stormi|ness
storming-party
  storming-parties
storm lan|tern +s
storm|less
Stor|mont (castle,
  Northern Ireland)
storm pet¦rel +s
storm|proof
storm-sail +s
storm-signal +s
storm troop¦er +s
storm troops
stormy
  storm|ier
  stormi|est
Stor|no|way (port,
  Scotland)
story
  stor|ies
  (tale; plot; fib.
  ⚠ storey)
story|board +s
story book +s
story|line +s
story|tell¦er +s
story|tell¦ing
sto|tinka
  sto|tinki
stoup +s (holy-
  water basin;
  flagon. ⚠ stoep,
  stoop)
Stour (rivers,
  England)
stoush
  stoushes
  stoushed
  stoush|ing
stout +er +est
stout-hearted
stout-hearted¦ly
stout-
  hearted¦ness
stout|ish
stout¦ly
stout|ness
stove
  stoves
  stoved
  stov¦ing
stove-enamel
  stove-enamels
  stove-enamelled

stove-enamel
  (*cont.*)
  stove-
    enamel¦ling
stove-pipe +s
stow +s +ed +ing
stow|age +s
stow|away +s
Stowe, Har|riet
  Bee|cher
  (American
  novelist)
Stra|bane (county,
  Northern Ireland)
stra|bis|mal
stra|bis|mic
stra|bis|mus
Strabo (geographer
  of Greek descent)
Stra|chey, Lyt|ton
  (English
  biographer)
Strad +s
  (= Stradivarius)
strad|dle
  strad|dles
  strad|dled
  strad|dling
strad|dler +s
Stradi|vari,
  An|tonio (Italian
  violin maker)
Stradi|var¦ius
strafe
  strafes
  strafed
  straf¦ing
strag|gle
  strag|gles
  strag|gled
  strag|gling
strag|gler +s
strag|gly
  strag|glier
  strag|gli|est
straight +s +er
  +est (not bent
  etc.; straight part;
  heterosexual;
  direct. ⚠ strait)
straight|away
straight-bred
straight-cut
straight-edge +s
straight-eight +s
straight|en +s +ed
  +ing (make or
  become straight.
  ⚠ straiten)
straight|en¦er +s
straight-faced
straight|for¦ward

straight|
  for|ward|ly
straight|for|ward|
  ness
straight|ish
straight|jacket
  (use straitjacket)
  +s +ed +ing
straight-laced (use
  strait-laced)
straight|ly
straight|ness
  (quality of being
  straight.
  ⚠ straitness)
straight-out
straight-up
straight|way
strain +s +ed +ing
strain|able
strain|er +s
strait +s (water
  connecting seas;
  narrow; trouble.
  ⚠ straight)
strait|en +s +ed
  +ing (restrict.
  ⚠ straighten)
strait|jacket +s
  +ed +ing
strait-laced
strait|ly
strait|ness
  (severity;
  hardship.
  ⚠ straightness)
Straits
  Settle|ments
  (former British
  colony, SE Asia)
strake +s
Stral|sund (town,
  Germany)
stra|mo|nium
strand +s +ed
  +ing
strand|ing +s
strange
  stran|ger
  stran|gest
strange|ly
strange|ness
stran|ger +s
stran|gle
  stran|gles
  stran|gled
  stran|gling
strangle|hold +s
stran|gler +s
stran|gling +s
stran|gu|late
  stran|gu|lates

stran|gu|late
  (cont.)
  stran|gu|lated
  stran|gu|lat|ing
stran|gu|la|tion
stran|guri|ous
stran|gury
stran|gur|ies
Stran|raer (port,
  Scotland)
strap
  straps
  strapped
  strap|ping
strap-hang
  strap-hangs
  strap-hung
  strap-hanging
strap|hang|er +s
strap|less
strap|pado +s
strap|per +s
strappy
strap-work
Stras|berg, Lee
  (American actor
  and drama
  teacher)
Stras|bourg (city,
  France)
strata (plural of
  stratum)
strata|gem +s
stratal
stra|tegic
stra|tegic|al
stra|tegic|al|ly
stra|tegics
strat|egist +s
strat|egy
  strat|egies
Stratford-upon-
  Avon (town,
  England)
strath +s
Strath|clyde (in
  Scotland)
strath|spey +s
strati
stra|ticu|late
strati|fi|ca|tion +s
strati|fi|ca|tion|al
strat|ify
  strati|fies
  strati|fied
  strati|fy|ing
strati|graph|ic
strati|graph|ic|al
stra|tig|raphy
strato|cir|rus
stra|toc|racy
  stra|toc|ra|cies

strato|cumu|lus
strato|pause
strato|sphere
strato|spher|ic
stra|tum
  strata
stra|tus
  strati
Strauss, Jo|hann
  (father and son,
  Austrian
  composers)
Strauss, Rich|ard
  (German
  composer)
Stra|vin|sky, Igor
  (Russian-born
  American
  composer)
straw +s
straw|berry
  straw|berries
straw|berry tree
  +s
straw|board +s
straw color Am. +s
straw-colored Am.
straw colour Br.
  +s
straw-coloured Br.
straw-worm +s
strawy
stray +s +ed +ing
stray|er +s
streak +s +ed +ing
streak|er +s
streak|ily
streaki|ness
streaky
  streak|ier
  streaki|est
stream +s +ed
  +ing
stream-anchor +s
stream|er +s
stream|less
stream|let +s
stream|line
  stream|lines
  stream|lined
  stream|lin|ing
Streep, Meryl
  (American
  actress)
street +s
street|car +s
street|ed
street lamp +s
street light +s
street light|ing
street trader +s
street|walk|er +s

street|walk|ing
street|ward
street|wise
Strei|sand,
  Bar|bra
  (American singer)
stre|litzia +s
strength +s
strength|en +s
  +ed +ing
strength|en|er +s
strength|less
strenu|ous
strenu|ous|ly
strenu|ous|ness
strep
  (= streptococcus)
strepto|car|pus
strepto|coc|cal
strepto|coc|cus
  strepto|cocci
strepto|kin|ase
strepto|mycin
Strep|yan
stress
  stresses
  stressed
  stress|ing
stress|ful
stress|ful|ly
stress|ful|ness
stress|less
stretch
  stretches
  stretched
  stretch|ing
stretch|abil|ity
stretch|able
stretch|er +s
stretcher-bearer
  +s
stretchi|ness
stretch mark +s
stretchy
  stretch|ier
  stretchi|est
stretta
  strette or stret|tas
stretto
  stretti or stret|tos
strew
  strews
  strewn or strewed
  strew|ing
strew|er +s
strewth
stria
  striae
stri|ate
  stri|ates
  stri|ated
  stri|at|ing

stri|ation +s
stricken
strickle +s
strict +er +est
strict|ly
strict|ness
stric|ture +s
stric|tured
stride
  strides
  strode
  strid|ing
  strid|den
stri|dency
stri|dent
stri|dent|ly
strider +s
stridu|lant
stridu|late
  stridu|lates
  stridu|lated
  stridu|lat|ing
stridu|la|tion +s
strife +s
stri|gil +s
stri|gose
strik|able
strike
  strikes
  struck *or*
  strick|en
  strik|ing
strike-bound
strike-breaker +s
strike-breaking
strike call +s
strike force +s
strike-measure +s
strike-out +s
striker +s
strike rate +s
strike-slip fault +s
striking-circle +s
strik|ing force +s
strik|ing|ly
strik|ing|ness
strim|mer +s *Propr.*
Strind|berg,
  Au|gust (Swedish
  writer)
Strine
string
  strings
  strung
  string|ing
string|board +s
string-course +s
strin|gency
  strin|gen|cies
strin|gendo
strin|gent

strin|gent|ly
string|er +s
string|halt +s
string|ily
stringi|ness
string|less
string|like
string-piece +s
string play|er +s
stringy
  stringi|er
  stringi|est
stringy-bark +s
strip
  strips
  stripped
  strip|ping
strip|agram +s
stripe
  stripes
  striped
  strip|ing
strip farm|ing
strip light +s
strip|ling +s
strip-mining
strip|pa|gram +s
  (use stripagram)
strip|per +s
strip|per|gram +s
  (use stripagram)
strip-search
  strip-searches
  strip-searched
  strip-search|ing
strip|tease
  strip|teases
  strip|teased
  strip|teas|ing
strip|teaser +s
stripy
  stripi|er
  stripi|est
strive
  strives
  strove *or* strived
  striv|ing
  striven *or* strived
striver +s
strobe
  strobes
  strobed
  strob|ing
stro|bila
stro|bilae
stro|bile +s
stro|bilus
stro|bili
strobo|scope +s
strobo|scop|ic
strobo|scop|ic|al

strobo|scop|ic|
    al|ly
strode
Strog|an|off +s
stroke
  strokes
  stroked
  strok|ing
stroke|play
stroll +s +ed +ing
stroll|er +s
stroma
  stro|mata
stro|mat|ic
stro|mato|lite +s
Strom|boli
  (volcano off Italy)
strong +er +est
strong-arm
  attributive
strong|box
  strong|boxes
strong|hold +s
strong|ish
strong|ly
strong|man
  strong|men
  (forceful leader;
  circus performer)
strong-minded
strong-
  minded|ness
strong|room +s
stron|tia
stron|tium
strontium-90
strop
  strops
  stropped
  strop|ping
stro|phan|thin
strophe +s
stroph|ic
strop|pily
strop|pi|ness
stroppy
  strop|pier
  strop|pi|est
strove
strow
  strows
  strowed
  strow|ing
  strowed *or*
  strown
struck
struc|tural
struc|tur|al|ism
struc|tur|al|ist +s
struc|tur|al|ly

struc|ture
  struc|tures
  struc|tured
  struc|tur|ing
struc|ture|less
stru|del +s
strug|gle
  strug|gles
  strug|gled
  strug|gling
strug|gler +s
strum
  strums
  strummed
  strum|ming
struma
stru|mae
strum|mer +s
stru|mose
stru|mous
strum|pet +s
strung
strut
  struts
  strut|ted
  strut|ting
struth (use
  strewth)
stru|thi|ous
strut|ter +s
strut|ting|ly
Struve, Otto
  (Russian-born
  American
  astronomer)
Struw|wel|peter
  (fictional
  character)
strych|nic
strych|nine
strych|nin|ism
strych|nism
Stu|art *also*
  Stew|art
  (name)
Stu|art +s (royal
  house of Scotland
  and later England)
Stu|art, Charles
  Ed|ward ('Bonnie
  Prince Charlie',
  'Young Pretender'
  to the British
  throne)
Stu|art, James
  ('Old Pretender' to
  the British throne)
Stu|art, John
  McDou|all
  (Scottish explorer.
  △ Stewart)

stub
  stubs
  stubbed
  stub|bing
stub-axle +s
stub|bily
stub|bi|ness
stub|ble
stub|bled
stub|bly
stub|born
stub|born|ly
stub|born|ness
Stubbs, George
  (English painter)
Stubbs, Wil|liam
  (English historian)
stubby
  stub|bier
  stub|bi|est
stucco
  stuc|coes
  stuc|coed
  stucco|ing
stuck
stuck-up *adjective*
stud
  studs
  stud|ded
  stud|ding
stud-book +s
stud|ding +s
studding-sail +s
stu|dent +s
stu|dent|ship +s
stud farm +s
stud-horse +s
stud|ied|ly
stud|ied|ness
stu|dio +s
stu|di|ous
stu|di|ous|ly
stu|di|ous|ness
stud poker
study
  stud|ies
  stud|ied
  study|ing
study-bedroom +s
stuff +s +ed +ing
stuff|er +s
stuff|ily
stuffi|ness
stuff|ing +s
stuff|ing box
  stuff|ing boxes
stuffy
  stuff|ier
  stuffi|est
stul|ti|fi|ca|tion
stul|ti|fier +s

stul|tify
  stul|ti|fies
  stul|ti|fied
  stul|ti|fy|ing
stum
  stums
  stummed
  stum|ming
stum|ble
  stum|bles
  stum|bled
  stum|bling
stumble|bum +s
stum|bler +s
stum|bling block
  +s
stum|bling|ly
stu|mer +s
stump +s +ed +ing
stump|er +s
stump|ily
stumpi|ness
stumpy
  stump|ier
  stumpi|est
stun
  stuns
  stunned
  stun|ning
stung
stun gun +s
stunk
stun|ner +s
stun|ning|ly
stun|sail +s
stunt +s +ed +ing
stunt|ed|ness
stunt|er +s
stunt|man
  stunt|men
stupa +s (shrine.
  △ stupor)
stupe
  stupes
  stuped
  stup|ing
stu|pe|fa|cient +s
stu|pe|fac|tion
stu|pe|fac|tive
stu|pe|fier +s
stu|pefy
  stu|pe|fies
  stu|pe|fied
  stu|pe|fy|ing
stu|pe|fy|ing|ly
stu|pen|dous
stu|pen|dous|ly
stu|pen|dous|ness
stu|pid +er +est
stu|pid|ity
  stu|pid|ities
stu|pid|ly

stu|por +s (dazed
  state. △ stupa)
stu|por|ous
stur|died
stur|dily
stur|di|ness
sturdy
  stur|dier
  stur|di|est
stur|geon +s
Sturm|ab|teil|ung
Sturm und Drang
Sturt, Charles
  (English explorer)
stut|ter +s +ed
  +ing
stut|ter|er +s
stut|ter|ing|ly
Stutt|gart (city,
  Germany)
sty
  sties
  stied
  sty|ing
stye +s (use sty)
Sty|gian
style
  styles
  styled
  styl|ing
  (fashion; writing
  implement; part of
  flower. △ stile)
style|less
style|less|ness
styler +s
sty|let +s
styli
styl|isa|tion *Br.*
  (use stylization)
styl|ise *Br.* (use
  stylize)
  styl|ises
  styl|ised
  styl|is|ing
styl|ish
styl|ish|ly
styl|ish|ness
styl|ist +s
styl|is|tic
styl|is|tic|al|ly
styl|is|tics
styl|ite +s
styl|iza|tion
styl|ize
  styl|izes
  styl|ized
  styl|iz|ing
stylo +s
stylo|bate +s
stylo|graph +s
stylo|graph|ic

styl|oid +s
sty|lus
  styli *or* sty|luses
sty|mie
  sty|mies
  sty|mied
  sty|mie|ing *or*
  sty|mying
styp|tic +s
sty|rax
styr|ene
Styria (state,
  Austria)
styro|foam
Styx (river in
  Hades)
Su *also* Sue
  (name)
su|abil|ity
su|able
sua|sion
sua|sive
suave
suave|ly
suave|ness
suav|ity
  suav|ities
sub
  subs
  subbed
  sub|bing
sub|abdom|inal
sub|acid
sub|acid|ity
sub|acute
sub|adult +s
sub|agency
  sub|agen|cies
sub|agent +s
su|bah|dar +s
sub|alpine
sub|al|tern +s
sub|ant|arc|tic
sub-aqua
sub|aqua|tic
sub|aque|ous
sub|arc|tic
sub|astral
sub|atom|ic
sub|audi|tion
sub|axil|lary
sub-basement +s
sub-branch
  sub-branches
sub-breed +s
sub|cat|egor|isa|
  tion *Br.* +s (use
  subcategoriza-
  tion)
sub|cat|egor|ise
  Br. (use

sub|cat|egor|ise (*cont.*)
  subcategorize)
  sub|cat|egor|ises
  sub|cat|egor|ised
  sub|cat|egor| is|ing
sub|cat|egor|iza| tion +s
sub|cat|egor|ize
  sub|cat|egor|izes
  sub|cat|egor|ized
  sub|cat|egor| iz|ing
sub|cat|egory
  sub|cat|egor|ies
sub|caudal
sub|class
  sub|classes
sub-clause +s
sub|clavian +s
sub|clin|ical
sub|com|mis| sioner +s
sub|com|mit|tee +s
sub|con|ic|al
sub|con|scious
sub|con|scious|ly
sub|con|scious| ness
sub|con|tin|ent +s
sub|con|tin|en|tal
sub|con|tract +s +ed +ing
sub|con|tract|or +s
sub|con|trary
  sub|con|trar|ies
sub|cord|ate
sub|cort|ical
sub|cos|tal
sub|cra|nial
sub|crit|ic|al
sub|cul|tural
sub|cul|ture +s
sub|cuta|ne|ous
sub|cuta|ne|ous|ly
sub|cuticu|lar
sub|deacon +s
sub|dean +s
sub|dean|ery
  sub|dean|er|ies
sub|decan|al
sub|deliri|ous
sub|delir|ium
sub|diac|on|ate +s
sub|div|ide
  sub|div|ides

sub|div|ide (*cont.*)
  sub|div|ided
  sub|div|id|ing
sub|div|ision +s
sub|dom|in|ant +s
sub|du|able
sub|dual +s
sub|duct +s +ed +ing
sub|duc|tion
sub|due
  sub|dues
  sub|dued
  sub|du|ing
sub|dural
sub-edit +s +ed +ing
sub-editor +s
sub-editor|ial
sub|erect
su|ber|eous
su|ber|ic
su|ber|ose
sub|fam|ily
  sub|fam|ilies
sub|floor +s
sub|form +s
sub-frame +s
sub|fusc
sub|gen|er|ic
sub|genus
  sub|gen|era
sub|gla|cial
sub|group +s
  Mathematics
sub-group +s (generally)
sub-head +s
sub-heading +s
sub|human
sub|jacent
sub|ject +s +ed +ing
subject-heading +s
sub|jec|tion +s
sub|ject|ive +s
sub|ject|ive|ly
sub|ject|ive|ness
sub|ject|iv|ism
sub|ject|iv|ist +s
sub|ject|iv|ity
  sub|ject|iv|ities
sub|ject|less
subject mat|ter +s
sub|join +s +ed +ing
sub|joint +s
sub ju|dice
sub|jug|able

sub|ju|gate
  sub|ju|gates
  sub|ju|gated
  sub|ju|gat|ing
sub|ju|ga|tion
sub|ju|ga|tor +s
sub|junct|ive +s
sub|junct|ive|ly
sub|king|dom +s
sub|lap|sar|ian +s
sub-lease
  sub-leases
  sub-leased
  sub-leasing
sub-lessee +s
sub-lessor +s
sub-let
  sub-lets
  sub-let
  sub-letting
sub-licence +s
  noun
sub-license
  sub-licenses
  sub-licensed
  sub-licensing
  verb
sub-licensee +s
sub-licensor +s
sub lieu|ten|ant +s
sub|lim|ate
  sub|lim|ates
  sub|lim|ated
  sub|lim|at|ing
sub|lim|ation +s
sub|lime
  sub|limes
  sub|limed
  sub|lim|ing
  sub|limer
  sub|lim|est
sub|lime|ly
Sub|lime Porte, the
sub|lim|inal
sub|lim|in|al|ly
sub|lim|ity
  sub|lim|ities
sub|lin|gual
sub|lit|toral
sub|lun|ary
sub|lux|ation +s
sub-machine gun +s
sub|man
  sub|men
sub|mar|gin|al
sub|mar|ine +s
sub|mari|ner +s
sub|mas|ter +s
sub|max|il|lary

sub|medi|ant +s
  Music
sub|men|tal
sub|merge
  sub|merges
  sub|merged
  sub|mer|ging
sub|mer|gence
sub|mer|gible
sub|merse
  sub|merses
  sub|mersed
  sub|mers|ing
sub|mers|ible +s
sub|mer|sion +s
sub|micro|scop|ic
sub|mini|ature
sub|mis|sion +s
sub|mis|sive
sub|mis|sive|ly
sub|mis|sive|ness
sub|mit
  sub|mits
  sub|mit|ted
  sub|mit|ting
sub|mit|tal +s
sub|mit|ter +s
sub|mul|tiple +s
sub|nor|mal
sub|nor|mal|ity
sub-nuclear
sub|ocu|lar
sub|opti|mal
sub-orbital
sub|order +s
sub|or|dinal
sub|or|din|ary
  sub|or|din|ar|ies
sub|or|din|ate
  sub|or|din|ates
  sub|or|din|ated
  sub|or|din|at|ing
sub|or|din|ate|ly
sub|or|din|ation
sub|or|dina|tive
sub|orn +s +ed +ing
sub|orn|ation +s
sub|orn|er +s
sub|oxide +s
sub-paragraph +s
sub|phy|lum
  sub|phyla
sub-plot +s
sub|poena
  sub|poenas
  sub|poenaed *or* sub|poena'd
  sub|poena|ing
sub-postmas|ter +s

sub-postmis¦tress
sub-
    postmis¦tresses
sub-post of¦fice +s
sub¦prior +s
sub¦pro¦cess
    sub¦pro¦cesses
sub¦pro¦gram +s
sub¦region +s
sub¦region¦al
sub¦rep¦tion +s
sub¦ro¦gate
    sub¦ro¦gates
    sub¦ro¦gated
    sub¦ro¦gat¦ing
    sub¦ro¦ga¦tion +s
sub rosa
sub¦rou¦tine +s
sub-Saharan
sub¦scribe
    sub¦scribes
    sub¦scribed
    sub¦scrib¦ing
sub¦scriber +s
sub¦script +s
sub¦scrip¦tion +s
sub¦sec¦tion +s
sub-sector +s
sub¦sel¦lium
    sub¦sel¦lia
sub¦se¦quence +s
    (consequence)
sub-sequence +s
    (part of larger
    sequence)
sub¦se¦quent
sub¦se¦quent¦ly
sub¦serve
    sub¦serves
    sub¦served
    sub¦serv¦ing
sub¦ser¦vi¦ence
sub¦ser¦vi¦ency
sub¦ser¦vi¦ent
sub¦ser¦vi¦ent¦ly
sub¦set +s
sub¦shrub +s
sub¦side
    sub¦sides
    sub¦sided
    sub¦sid¦ing
sub¦sid¦ence
sub¦sidi¦ar¦ily
sub¦sidi¦ar¦ity
sub¦sid¦iary
    sub¦sid¦iar¦ies
sub¦sid¦isa¦tion Br.
    (use
    subsidization)
sub¦sid¦ise Br. (use
    subsidize)
    sub¦sid¦ises

sub¦sid¦ise (cont.)
    sub¦sid¦ised
    sub¦sid¦is¦ing
sub¦sid¦iser Br. +s
    (use subsidizer)
sub¦sid¦iza¦tion
sub¦sid¦ize
    sub¦sid¦izes
    sub¦sid¦ized
    sub¦sid¦iz¦ing
sub¦sid¦izer +s
sub¦sidy
    sub¦sid¦ies
sub¦sist +s +ed
    +ing
sub¦sist¦ence
sub¦sist¦ent
sub¦soil +s
sub¦son¦ic
sub¦son¦ic¦al¦ly
sub¦spe¦cies
    plural
    sub¦spe¦cies
sub¦spe¦cif¦ic
sub¦stance +s
sub-standard
sub¦stan¦tial
sub¦stan¦tial¦ise
    Br. (use
    substantialize)
    sub¦stan¦tial¦ises
    sub¦stan¦tial¦ised
    sub¦stan¦tial¦
        is¦ing
sub¦stan¦tial¦ism
sub¦stan¦tial¦ist +s
sub¦stan¦ti¦al¦ity
sub¦stan¦tial¦ize
    sub¦stan¦tial¦izes
    sub¦stan¦tial¦ized
    sub¦stan¦tial¦
        iz¦ing
sub¦stan¦tial¦ly
sub¦stan¦ti¦ate
    sub¦stan¦ti¦ates
    sub¦stan¦ti¦ated
    sub¦stan¦ti¦at¦ing
sub¦stan¦ti¦ation
sub¦stan¦tival
sub¦stan¦tiv¦al¦ly
sub¦stan¦tive +s
sub¦stan¦tive¦ly
sub-station +s
sub¦stitu¦ent +s
sub¦sti¦tut¦abil¦ity
sub¦sti¦tut¦able
sub¦sti¦tute
    sub¦sti¦tutes
    sub¦sti¦tuted
    sub¦sti¦tut¦ing
sub¦sti¦tu¦tion +s
sub¦sti¦tu¦tion¦al

sub¦sti¦tu¦tion¦ary
sub¦sti¦tu¦tive
sub¦strate +s
sub¦stra¦tum
    sub¦strata
sub¦struc¦tural
sub¦struc¦ture +s
sub¦sum¦able
sub¦sume
    sub¦sumes
    sub¦sumed
    sub¦sum¦ing
sub¦sump¦tion +s
sub¦sur¦face +s
sub¦sys¦tem +s
sub¦ten¦ancy
    sub¦ten¦an¦cies
sub¦ten¦ant +s
sub¦tend +s +ed
    +ing
sub¦ter¦fuge +s
sub¦ter¦minal
sub¦ter¦ra¦nean +s
sub¦ter¦ra¦ne¦
        ous¦ly
sub¦text +s
sub¦til¦isa¦tion Br.
    (use subtilization)
sub¦til¦ise Br. (use
    subtilize)
    sub¦til¦ises
    sub¦til¦ised
    sub¦til¦is¦ing
sub¦til¦iza¦tion
sub¦til¦ize
    sub¦til¦izes
    sub¦til¦ized
    sub¦til¦iz¦ing
sub¦title
    sub¦titles
    sub¦titled
    sub¦titling
sub¦tle
    sub¦tler
    sub¦tlest
    (mysterious; faint;
    clever; etc.
    ⚠ sutler)
subtle¦ness
subtle¦ty
    subtle¦ties
subtly
sub¦tonic +s Music
sub¦topia +s
sub¦topian
sub¦total +s
sub¦tract +s +ed
    +ing
sub¦tract¦er +s
    (person or thing
    that subtracts)
sub¦trac¦tion +s

sub¦tract¦ive
sub¦tract¦or +s
    Electronics
sub¦tra¦hend +s
sub¦trop¦ic¦al
sub¦trop¦ics
sub-type +s
subu¦late
sub¦unit +s
sub¦urb +s
sub¦ur¦ban
sub¦ur¦ban¦
    isa¦tion Br. (use
    suburbanization)
sub¦ur¦ban¦ise Br.
    (use suburbanize)
    sub¦ur¦ban¦ises
    sub¦ur¦ban¦ised
    sub¦ur¦ban¦is¦ing
sub¦ur¦ban¦ite +s
sub¦ur¦ban¦
    iza¦tion
sub¦ur¦ban¦ize
    sub¦ur¦ban¦izes
    sub¦ur¦ban¦ized
    sub¦ur¦ban¦iz¦ing
sub¦ur¦bia
sub¦ven¦tion +s
sub¦ver¦sion +s
sub¦ver¦sive +s
sub¦ver¦sive¦ly
sub¦ver¦sive¦ness
sub¦vert +s +ed
    +ing
sub¦vert¦er +s
sub¦way +s
sub¦woof¦er +s
sub-zero
suc¦ced¦an¦eous
suc¦ced¦an¦eum
    suc¦ced¦anea
suc¦ceed +s +ed
    +ing
suc¦ceed¦er +s
suc¦cen¦tor +s
suc¦cen¦tor¦ship
    +s
*suc¦cès de
    scan¦dale*
suc¦cess
    suc¦cesses
suc¦cess¦ful
suc¦cess¦ful¦ly
suc¦cess¦ful¦ness
suc¦ces¦sion +s
suc¦ces¦sion¦al
suc¦ces¦sive
suc¦ces¦sive¦ly
suc¦ces¦sive¦ness
suc¦ces¦sor +s
suc¦cin¦ate +s
suc¦cinct

suc¦cinct¦ly
suc¦cinct¦ness
suc¦cin¦ic
suc¦cor *Am.* +s +ed
+ing (*Br.* succour.
help. △ sucker)
suc¦cor¦less *Am.*
(*Br.* succourless)
suc¦cory
  suc¦cor¦ies
suc¦co¦tash
Suc¦coth (Jewish
festival)
suc¦cour *Br.* +s
+ed +ing (*Am.*
succor. help.
△ sucker)
suc¦cour¦less *Br.*
(*Am.* succorless)
suc¦cuba
  suc¦cu¦bae
suc¦cu¦bus
  suc¦cubi
suc¦cu¦lence
suc¦cu¦lent +s
suc¦cu¦lent¦ly
suc¦cumb +s +ed
+ing
suc¦cur¦sal
suc¦cuss
  suc¦cusses
  suc¦cussed
  suc¦cuss¦ing
suc¦cus¦sion +s
such
such¦like
Su¦chou
(= Suzhou)
Su¦chow
(= Xuzhou)
suck +s +ed +ing
suck¦er +s (person
or thing that
sucks; gullible or
susceptible
person; attaching-
device; plant
shoot. △ succor,
succour)
suck¦ered
sucking-disc +s
sucking-fish
  plural sucking-fish
  or sucking-fishes
suckle
  suckles
  suckled
  suck¦ling
suck¦ler +s
Suck¦ling, John
(English poet)
suck¦ling +s

Sucre (city, Bolivia)
Sucre, An¦tonio
  José de
  (president of
  Bolivia)
su¦crose
suc¦tion
suc¦tion pump +s
suc¦tor¦ial
suc¦tor¦ian +s
Sudan
Su¦dan¦ese
  plural Su¦dan¦ese
su¦dar¦ium
  su¦daria
suda¦tor¦ium
  suda¦toria
suda¦tory
  suda¦tor¦ies
Sud¦bury (city,
Canada)
sudd +s (floating
vegetation.
△ suds)
sud¦den
sud¦den¦ly
sud¦den¦ness
Su¦deten¦land
(region, Czech
Republic)
su¦dor¦ifer¦ous
su¦dor¦if¦ic +s
Sudra +s *Hinduism*
suds
  sudses
  sudsed
  suds¦ing
  (lather. △ sudd)
sudsy
  suds¦ier
  sudsi¦est
Sue *also* Su
  (name)
sue
  sues
  sued
  suing
  (take legal
  proceedings;
  entreat etc. △ sou,
  xu)
suede +s
suer +s (person
who sues.
△ sewer)
suet
Sueto¦nius (Roman
biographer)
suety
Suez (port, Egypt)
Suez, Isth¦mus of
(in Egypt)

Suez Canal (in
  Egypt)
suf¦fer +s +ed +ing
suf¦fer¦able
suf¦fer¦ance
suf¦fer¦er +s
suf¦fer¦ing +s
suf¦fice
  suf¦fices
  suf¦ficed
  suf¦ficing
suf¦fi¦ciency
  suf¦fi¦cien¦cies
suf¦fi¦cient
suf¦fi¦cient¦ly
suf¦fix
  suf¦fixes
suf¦fix¦ation
suf¦fixed
suf¦fo¦cate
  suf¦fo¦cates
  suf¦fo¦cated
  suf¦fo¦cat¦ing
suf¦fo¦cat¦ing¦ly
suf¦fo¦ca¦tion +s
Suf¦folk (county,
England)
suf¦fra¦gan +s
suf¦fra¦gan¦ship +s
suf¦frage +s
suf¦fra¦gette +s
suf¦fra¦gism
suf¦fra¦gist +s
suf¦fuse
  suf¦fuses
  suf¦fused
  suf¦fus¦ing
suf¦fu¦sion +s
Sufi +s
Sufic
Suf¦ism
sugar +s +ed +ing
sugar beet
sugar-candy
  sugar-candies
sugar cane +s
sugar-coated
sugar daddy
  sugar dad¦dies
sugar-gum +s
  (tree)
sug¦ari¦ness
sugar¦less
Sugar Loaf
Moun¦tain (near
Rio de Janeiro,
Brazil)
sugar maple +s
sugar pea +s
sugar¦plum +s
sug¦ary

sug¦gest +s +ed
+ing
sug¦gest¦er +s
sug¦gest¦ibil¦ity
sug¦gest¦ible
sug¦ges¦tion +s
sug¦gest¦ive
sug¦gest¦ive¦ly
sug¦gest¦ive¦ness
Sui (Chinese
dynasty)
sui¦cidal
sui¦cid¦al¦ly
sui¦cide
  sui¦cides
  sui¦cided
  sui¦cid¦ing
sui gen¦eris
sui juris
su¦il¦line
suint
suit +s +ed +ing
suit¦abil¦ity
suit¦able
suit¦able¦ness
suit¦ably
suit¦case +s
suit¦case¦ful +s
suite +s (set of
things. △ sweet)
suit¦er +s (bag.
△ souter, suitor)
suit¦ing +s
suitor +s (wooer;
plaintiff. △ souter,
suiter)
suk +s (market; use
souk. △ sook)
Su¦karno,
Ach¦mad
(Indonesian
president)
sukh +s (market;
use souk. △ sook)
Sukho¦tai (town,
Thailand)
suki¦yaki +s
Suk¦kur (city,
Pakistan)
Su¦lai¦man¦iya (use
Sulaymaniyah)
Sula¦wesi (island,
Indonesia)
Su¦lay¦man¦iyah
in full
  As Su¦lay¦man¦iyah
(town, Iraq)
sul¦cate
sul¦cus
  sulci

Su¦lei¦man I (sultan of Ottoman empire)

sulfa Am. (Br. sulpha. class of drugs. ⚠ sulfur)

sulfa¦dimi¦dine Am. (Br. sulphadimidine)

sulfa¦mate Am. +s (Br. sulphamate)

sul¦fam¦ic Am. (Br. sulphamic)

sulf¦anila¦mide Am. (Br. sulphanilamide)

sul¦fate Am. (Br. sulphate)

sul¦fide Am. +s (Br. sulphide)

sul¦fite Am. +s (Br. sulphite)

sul¦fona¦mide Am. +s (Br. sulphonamide)

sul¦fon¦ate Am.
sul¦fon¦ates
sul¦fon¦ated
sul¦fon¦at¦ing (Br. sulphonate)

sul¦fon¦ation Am. (Br. sulphonation)

sul¦fone Am. +s (Br. sulphone)

sul¦fon¦ic Am. (Br. sulphonic)

sul¦fur Am. +s +ed +ing (Br. sulphur. chemical element. ⚠ sulfa)

sul¦fur¦ate Am.
sul¦fur¦ates
sul¦fur¦ated
sul¦fur¦at¦ing (Br. sulphurate)

sul¦fur¦ation Am. (Br. sulphuration)

sul¦fur¦ator Am. +s (Br. sulphurator)

sul¦fur¦eous Am. (Br. sulphureous)

sul¦fur¦et¦ed Am. (Br. sulphuretted)

sul¦fur¦ic Am. (Br. sulphuric)

sul¦fur¦iza¦tion Am. (Br. sulphurization)

sul¦fur¦ize Am.
sul¦fur¦izes
sul¦fur¦ized

sul¦fur¦ize (cont.)
sul¦fur¦iz¦ing (Br. sulphurize)

sul¦fur¦ous Am. (Br. sulphurous)

sul¦fury Am. (Br. sulphury)

sulk +s +ed +ing

sulk¦er +s

sulk¦ily

sulki¦ness

sulky
sulki¦er
sulki¦est

Sulla (Roman general)

sul¦lage

sul¦len

sul¦len¦ly

sul¦len¦ness

Sulli¦van, Ar¦thur (English composer)

sully
sul¦lies
sul¦lied
sully¦ing

sulpha Br. +s (Am. sulfa. class of drugs. ⚠ sulphur)

sulpha¦dimi¦dine Br. (Am. sulfadimidine)

sulpha¦mate Br. +s (Am. sulfamate)

sul¦pham¦ic Br. (Am. sulfamic)

sulph¦anila¦mide Br. (Am. sulfanilamide)

sul¦phate Br. +s (Am. sulfate)

sul¦phide Br. +s (Am. sulfide)

sul¦phite Br. +s (Am. sulfite)

sul¦phona¦mide Br. +s (Am. sulfonamide)

sul¦phon¦ate Br.
sul¦phon¦ates
sul¦phon¦ated
sul¦phon¦at¦ing (Am. sulfonate)

sul¦phon¦ation Br. (Am. sulfonation)

sul¦phone Br. +s (Am. sulfone)

sul¦phon¦ic Br. (Am. sulfonic)

sul¦phur Br. +s +ed +ing (Am.

sul¦phur (cont.)
sulfur. chemical element. ⚠ sulpha)

sul¦phur¦ate Br.
sul¦phur¦ates
sul¦phur¦ated
sul¦phur¦at¦ing (Am. sulfurate)

sul¦phur¦ation Br. (Am. sulfuration)

sul¦phur¦ator Br. +s (Am. sulfurator)

sul¦phur¦eous Br. (Am. sulfureous)

sul¦phur¦et¦ted Br. (Am. sulfureted)

sul¦phur¦ic Br. (Am. sulfuric)

sul¦phur¦isa¦tion Br. (use sulphurization)

sul¦phur¦ise Br. (use sulphurize)
sul¦phur¦ises
sul¦phur¦ised
sul¦phur¦is¦ing

sul¦phur¦iza¦tion

sul¦phur¦ize
sul¦phur¦izes
sul¦phur¦ized
sul¦phur¦iz¦ing

sul¦phur¦ous Br. (Am. sulfurous)

sul¦phury Br. (Am. sulfury)

sul¦tan +s

sul¦tana +s

sul¦tan¦ate +s

sul¦trily

sul¦tri¦ness

sul¦try
sul¦trier
sul¦tri¦est

Sulu Sea (in SE Asia)

sum
sums
summed
sum¦ming (total; arithmetical problem. ⚠ some)

sumac +s

su¦mach +s (use sumac)

Su¦ma¦tra (island, Indonesia)

Su¦ma¦tran +s

Sumba (island, Indonesia)

Sum¦bawa (island, Indonesia)

Sum¦burgh (weather station off Shetland Islands)

Sum¦burgh Head (Shetland Islands)

Sumer (ancient region, Iraq)

Su¦mer¦ian +s

Sum¦gait (Russian name for Sumqayit)

summa
sum¦mae

summa cum laude

sum¦mar¦ily

sum¦mari¦ness

sum¦mar¦is¦able Br. (use summarizable)

sum¦mar¦isa¦tion Br. (use summarization)

sum¦mar¦ise Br. (use summarize)
sum¦mar¦ises
sum¦mar¦ised
sum¦mar¦is¦ing

sum¦mar¦iser Br. +s (use summarizer)

sum¦mar¦ist +s

sum¦mar¦iz¦able

sum¦mar¦iza¦tion

sum¦mar¦ize
sum¦mar¦izes
sum¦mar¦ized
sum¦mar¦iz¦ing

sum¦mar¦izer +s

sum¦mary
sum¦mar¦ies (brief account; without formalities. ⚠ summery)

sum¦ma¦tion +s

sum¦ma¦tion¦al

sum¦mer +s +ed +ing

sum¦mer house +s

sum¦mer¦less

sum¦mer¦ly

sum¦mer¦sault +s +ed +ing (use somersault)

sum¦mer¦time (period of summer)

sum¦mer time (time advanced

sum¦mer time
  (*cont.*)
  during summer;
  but British
  Summer Time)
summer-weight
  adjective
sum¦mery
  (characteristic of
  summer.
  △summary)
summing-up
  summings-up
  noun
sum¦mit +s
sum¦mit¦eer +s
sum¦mit¦less
sum¦mit¦ry
sum¦mon +s +ed
  +ing
sum¦mon¦able
sum¦mon¦er +s
sum¦mons
  sum¦monses
  sum¦monsed
  sum¦mons¦ing
sum¦mum bonum
sumo +s
sump +s
sump¦ter +s
sump¦tu¦ary
sump¦tu¦os¦ity
sump¦tu¦ous
sump¦tu¦ous¦ly
sump¦tu¦ous¦ness
Sum¦qa¦yit (city,
  Azerbaijan)
Sumy (city,
  Ukraine)
sun
  suns
  sunned
  sun¦ning
  (star. △son,
  sunn)
sun-baked
sun-bath +s
sun¦bathe
  sun¦bathes
  sun¦bathed
  sun¦bath¦ing
sun¦bather +s
sun¦beam +s
sun¦bed +s
sun¦belt +s
sun¦bird +s
sun¦blind +s
sun¦block +s
sun-bonnet +s
sun¦bow +s
sun-bronzed

sun¦burn
  sun¦burns
  sun¦burnt *or*
  sun¦burned
  sun¦burn¦ing
sun¦burst +s
Sun City (resort,
  South Africa)
sun cream +s
sun¦dae +s (ice-
  cream dish.
  △Sunday)
Sunda Is¦lands (in
  Malay
  Archipelago)
sun-dance +s
Sun¦dan¦ese
  plural Sun¦dan¦ese
Sun¦dar¦bans
  (swamp,
  Bangladesh)
Sun¦day +s (day of
  the week.
  △sundae)
sun deck +s
sun¦der +s +ed
  +ing
Sun¦der¦land (city,
  England)
sun¦dew +s
sun¦dial +s
sun-disc +s
sun-dog +s
sun¦down +s
sun¦down¦er +s
sun¦dress
  sun¦dresses
sun-dried
sun¦dries¦man
  sun¦dries¦men
sun¦dry
  sun¦dries
sun¦fast
sun¦fish
  plural sun¦fish *or*
  sun¦fishes
sun¦flower +s
Sung (Chinese
  dynasty)
sung (past
  participle of sing)
sun¦glasses
sun-god +s
sun¦hat +s
sun-helmet +s
sunk
sunk¦en
sun-kissed
sun¦lamp +s
sun¦less
sun¦less¦ness
sun¦light

sun¦like
sun¦lit
sun¦loun¦ger +s
sun-lover +s
sunn (fibre. △son,
  sun)
Sunna (Islamic
  customs and
  practices)
Sunni
  plural Sunni *or*
  Sun¦nis
  (branch of Islam)
sun¦nily
sun¦ni¦ness
Sun¦nite +s
sunny
  sun¦nier
  sun¦ni¦est
  (bright with
  sunlight. △sonny)
sun¦proof
sun¦ray +s
sun¦rise
sun¦roof +s
sun¦room +s
sun¦screen +s
sun¦set +s
sun¦shade +s
sun¦shine
sun¦shiny
sun¦spot +s
sun¦star +s
sun¦stone +s
sun¦stroke
sun¦suit +s
sun¦tan
  sun¦tans
  sun¦tanned
  sun¦tan¦ning
sun¦trap +s
sunup
sun¦ward
sun¦wards
Sun Yat-sen
  (Chinese
  statesman)
sup
  sups
  supped
  sup¦ping
Supa¦driv
  (screwdriver)
  Propr.
super +s
super¦able
super¦abound +s
  +ed +ing
super¦abun¦dance
super¦abun¦dant
super¦
  abun¦dant¦ly

super¦add +s +ed
  +ing
super¦add¦ition +s
super¦altar +s
super¦annu¦able
super¦annu¦ate
  super¦annu¦ates
  super¦annu¦ated
  super¦annu¦at¦ing
super¦annu¦ated
super¦annu¦ation
super¦aqueous
su¦perb
su¦perb¦ly
su¦perb¦ness
Super Bowl +s
  Propr.
super¦cal¦en¦dar
  +s +ed +ing
super¦cargo
  super¦car¦goes
super¦cede (use
  supersede)
  super¦cedes
  super¦ceded
  super¦ced¦ing
super¦celes¦tial
super¦charge
  super¦charges
  super¦charged
  super¦char¦ging
super¦char¦ger +s
super¦cil¦iary
super¦cili¦ous
super¦cili¦ous¦ly
super¦cili¦ous¦ness
super¦class
  super¦classes
super¦co¦lum¦nar
super¦co¦lum¦ni¦
    ation
super¦com¦puter
  +s
super¦com¦put¦ing
super¦con¦duct¦ing
super¦con¦duct¦ive
super¦con¦duct¦
  iv¦ity
super¦con¦duct¦or
  +s
super¦con¦scious
super¦
    con¦scious¦ly
super¦con¦scious¦
    ness
super¦con¦tin¦ent
  +s
super¦cool
super¦crit¦ical
super-duper
super¦ego +s

super|eleva|tion +s
super|emi|nence +s
super|emi|nent
super|emi|nent|ly
super|eroga|tion
super|eroga|tory
super|ex|cel|lence
super|ex|cel|lent
super| ex|cel|lent|ly
super|fam|ily
super|fam|ilies
super|fat|ted
super|fec|und| ation +s
super|feta|tion +s
super|fi|cial
super|fici|al|ity
super|fici|al|ities
super|fi|cial|ly
super|fi|cial|ness
super|fi|cies
plural super|fi|cies
super|fine
super|fluid +s
super|flu|id|ity
super|flu|ity
super|flu|ities
su|per|flu|ous
su|per|flu|ous|ly
su|per|flu|ous|ness
super|giant +s
super|glue
super|glues
super|glued
super|glu|ing or
super|glue|ing
super|grass
super|grasses
super|gun +s
super|heat +s +ed +ing
super|heat|er +s
super|hero
super|heroes
super|het +s
super|het|ero| dyne +s
super|high|way +s
super|human +s
super|human|ly
super|humeral +s
super|im|pose
super|im|poses
super|im|posed
super|im|pos|ing
super|im|pos|ition +s
super|in|cum|bent

super|in|duce
super|in|duces
super|in|duced
super|in|du|cing
super|in|tend +s +ed +ing
super|in|tend|ence
super|in|tend|ency
super|in|tend|ent +s
Su|per|ior, Lake (in N. America)
su|per|ior +s
su|per|ior|ess
su|per|ior|esses
su|per|ior|ity
su|per|ior|ities
su|per|ior|ly
super|jacent
su|per|la|tive +s
su|per|la|tive|ly
su|per|la|tive|ness
super|lumi|nal
super|lun|ary
Super|man (American cartoon character)
super|man
super|men (man of exceptional strength or ability)
super|mar|ket +s
super|mini +s
super|model +s
super|mun|dane
super|nacu|lar
super|nacu|lum
su|per|nal
su|per|nal|ly
super|natant +s
super|nat|ural
super|nat|ur|al|ise Br. (use supernaturalize)
super|nat|ur|al| ises
super|nat|ur|al| ised
super|nat|ur|al| is|ing
super|nat|ur|al| ism
super|nat|ur|al|ist +s
super|nat|ur|al|ize
super|nat|ur|al| izes
super|nat|ur|al| ized
super|nat|ur|al| iz|ing

super|nat|ur|al|ly
super|nat|ur|al| ness
super|nor|mal
super|nor|mal|ity
super|nova
super|novae
super|numer|ary
super|numer| ar|ies
super|order +s
super|ordinal
super|ordin|ate +s
super|phos|phate +s
super|phys|ic|al
super|pose
super|poses
super|posed
super|pos|ing
super|pos|ition +s
super|power +s
super|sat|ur|ate
super|sat|ur|ates
super|sat|ur|ated
super|sat|ur| at|ing
super|sat|ur|ation
super|scribe
super|scribes
super|scribed
super|scrib|ing
super|script +s
super|scrip|tion +s
super|sede
super|sedes
super|seded
super|sed|ing
super|sedence
super|sedure
super|ses|sion
super|sonic
super|son|ic|al|ly
super|son|ics
super|star +s
super|star|dom
super|state +s
super|sti|tion +s
super|sti|tious
super|sti|tious|ly
super|sti|tious| ness
super|store +s
super|stra|tum
super|strata
super|string +s
super|struc|tural
super|struc|ture +s
super|subtle
super|subtle|ty
super|subtle|ties

super|sym|met|ric
super|sym|metry
super|tank|er +s
super|tax
super|taxes
super|tem|poral
super|ter|rene
super|ter|res|trial
super|title +s
super|tonic +s
super|vene
super|venes
super|vened
super|ven|ing
super|ven|ient
super|ven|tion +s
super|vise
super|vises
super|vised
super|vis|ing
super|vi|sion
super|visor +s
super|vis|ory
super|woman
super|women
su|pin|ate
su|pin|ates
su|pin|ated
su|pin|at|ing
su|pin|ation
su|pin|ator +s
su|pine
su|pine|ly
su|pine|ness
sup|per +s
sup|per|less
sup|per|time +s
sup|plant +s +ed +ing
sup|plant|er +s
sup|ple
sup|ples
sup|pled
sup|pling
sup|pler
sup|plest
supple|jack +s
sup|ple|ly (use supply)
sup|ple|ment +s +ed +ing
sup|ple|men|tal
sup|ple|men|tal|ly
sup|ple|men| tar|ily
sup|ple|men|tary
sup|ple|men| tar|ies
sup|ple|men| ta|tion
supple|ness
sup|ple|tion +s
sup|ple|tive

sup|pli|ant +s
sup|pli|ant|ly
sup|pli|cant +s
sup|pli|cate
　sup|pli|cates
　sup|pli|cated
　sup|pli|cat|ing
sup|pli|ca|tion +s
sup|pli|ca|tory
sup|plier +s
sup|ply
　sup|plies
　sup|plied
　sup|ply|ing
supply-side
sup|port +s +ed
　+ing
sup|port|abil|ity
sup|port|able
sup|port|ably
sup|port|er +s
sup|port|ing|ly
sup|port|ive
sup|port|ive|ly
sup|port|ive|ness
sup|port|less
sup|pos|able
sup|pose
　sup|poses
　sup|posed
　sup|pos|ing
sup|posed|ly
sup|pos|ition +s
sup|pos|ition|al
sup|pos|itious
sup|pos|itious|ly
sup|pos|itious|
　　　　ness
sup|posi|ti|tious
sup|posi|ti|tious|ly
sup|posi|ti|tious|
　　　　ness
sup|posi|tory
　sup|posi|tor|ies
sup|press
　sup|presses
　sup|pressed
　sup|press|ing
sup|pres|sant +s
sup|press|ible
sup|pres|sion +s
sup|pres|sive
sup|pres|sor +s
sup|pur|ate
　sup|pur|ates
　sup|pur|ated
　sup|pur|at|ing
sup|pur|ation +s
sup|pura|tive
supra
supra|lap|sar|ian
　+s

supra|max|il|lary
supra|mund|ane
supra|nation|al
supra|nation|al|
　　　　ism
supra|nation|al|ity
supra|orbit|al
supra|renal
supra|seg|men|tal
su|prema|cism
su|prema|cist +s
su|prem|acy
　su|prem|acies
su|prema|tism
su|preme +s
su|prême +s
　Cookery
su|preme|ly
su|preme|ness
Su|premes, the
　(American pop
　group)
su|premo +s
suq +s (market; use
　souk. △ sook)
sura +s (section of
　Koran. △ surah)
Sura|baya (port,
　Indonesia)
surah +s (fabric.
　△ sura)
sural
Surat (port, India)
sur|cease
　sur|ceases
　sur|ceased
　sur|ceas|ing
sur|charge
　sur|charges
　sur|charged
　sur|char|ging
sur|cin|gle +s
sur|coat +s
sur|cu|lose
surd +s
sure
　surer
　sur|est
　(certain. △ shaw,
　shore)
sure-fire
sure-footed
sure-footed|ly
sure-footed|ness
sure|ly (with
　certainty.
　△ shawlie)
sure|ness
surety
　sure|ties
surety|ship

surf +s +ed +ing
　(breaking waves;
　go surfing. △ serf)
sur|face
　sur|faces
　sur|faced
　sur|facing
surface-active
sur|facer +s
surface-to-air
　(missile)
surface-to-surface
　(missile)
sur|fac|tant +s
surf|bird +s
surf|board +s
surf-casting
sur|feit +s +ed
　+ing
surf|er +s
sur|fi|cial
sur|fi|cial|ly
surfie +s (surfer.
　△ surfy)
surf-riding
surfy
　surf|ier
　surfi|est
　(having much surf.
　△ surfie)
surge
　surges
　surged
　sur|ging
　(swell; increase.
　△ serge)
sur|geon +s
sur|geon gen|eral
　sur|geons
　gen|eral
sur|gery
　sur|ger|ies
sur|gi|cal
sur|gi|cal|ly
suri|cate +s
Suri|nam (use
　Suriname)
Suri|name (in S.
　America)
Suri|nam|er +s
Suri|nam|ese
　plural
　Suri|nam|ese
sur|lily
sur|li|ness
surly
　sur|lier
　sur|li|est
sur|mise
　sur|mises
　sur|mised
　sur|mis|ing

sur|mount +s +ed
　+ing
sur|mount|able
sur|mul|let
　plural sur|mul|let
　or sur|mul|lets
sur|name
　sur|names
　sur|named
　sur|nam|ing
sur|pass
　sur|passes
　sur|passed
　sur|pass|ing
　sur|pass|ing|ly
sur|plice +s
　(vestment)
sur|pliced
sur|plus
　sur|pluses
　(amount left over)
sur|plus|age +s
sur|prise
　sur|prises
　sur|prised
　sur|pris|ing
　sur|prised|ly
　sur|pris|ing|ly
　sur|pris|ing|ness
surra
sur|real
sur|real|ism
sur|real|ist +s
sur|real|is|tic
sur|real|is|tic|al|ly
sur|real|ity
sur|real|ly
sur|rebut|ter +s
sur|rejoin|der +s
sur|ren|der +s +ed
　+ing
sur|rep|ti|tious
sur|rep|ti|tious|ly
sur|rep|ti|tious|
　　　　ness
Sur|rey (county,
　England)
sur|rey +s
　(carriage)
sur|ro|gacy
sur|ro|gate +s
sur|ro|gate|ship +s
sur|round +s +ed
　+ing
sur|round|ings
sur|tax
　sur|taxes
Sur|tees, Rob|ert
　Smith (English
　writer)
sur|title +s
sur|tout +s

Surt|sey (island off
  Iceland)
sur|veil|lance
sur|vey +s +ed
  +ing
sur|vey|or +s
sur|vey|or|ship +s
sur|viv|abil|ity
sur|viv|able
sur|vival +s
sur|viv|al|ism
sur|viv|al|ist +s
sur|vive
  sur|vives
  sur|vived
  sur|viv|ing
sur|vivor +s
Surya *Hinduism*
sus (use suss)
  susses
  sussed
  suss|ing
Susa (ancient city,
  SW Asia;
  alternative name
  for Sousse)
Susah (alternative
  name for Sousse)
Susan
Su|sanna *also*
  Su|san|nah,
  Su|zanna
Su|sanna
  Apocrypha
Su|san|nah *also*
  Su|sanna,
  Su|zanna
Su|sanne *also*
  Su|zanne
sus|cep|ti|bil|ity
  sus|cep|ti|bil|ities
sus|cep|tible
sus|cep|tibly
sus|cep|tive
sushi
Susie *also* Suzie,
  Suzy
sus|lik +s (use
  souslik)
sus|pect +s +ed
  +ing
sus|pend +s +ed
  +ing
sus|pend|er +s
sus|pense
sus|pense|ful
sus|pen|sible
sus|pen|sion +s
sus|pen|sive
sus|pen|sive|ly
sus|pen|sive|ness
sus|pen|sory

sus|pi|cion +s
sus|pi|cious
sus|pi|cious|ly
sus|pi|cious|ness
sus|pir|ation +s
sus|pire
  sus|pires
  sus|pired
  sus|pir|ing
Sus|que|hanna
  (river, USA)
suss
  susses
  sussed
  suss|ing
Sus|sex, East and
  West (counties,
  England)
sus|tain +s +ed
  +ing
sus|tain|abil|ity
sus|tain|able
sus|tain|ably
sus|tain|ed|ly
sus|tain|er +s
sus|tain|ment +s
sus|ten|ance
sus|ten|ta|tion
su|sur|ra|tion +s
su|sur|rus
Suth|er|land,
  Gra|ham (English
  painter)
Suth|er|land, Joan
  (Australian
  soprano)
Sut|lej (river, S.
  Asia)
sut|ler +s (army
  provisioner.
  △subtler)
Sutra +s
sut|tee +s
Sut|ton Cold|field
  (town, England)
Sut|ton Hoo
  (archaeological
  site, England)
su|tural
su|ture
  su|tures
  su|tured
  su|tur|ing
Suva (capital of
  Fiji)
Su|wan|nee (river,
  USA. △Swanee)
Su|zanna *also*
  Su|sanna,
  Su|san|nah
Su|zanne *also*
  Su|sanne

su|zer|ain +s
su|zer|ainty
Su|zette (in 'crêpe
  Suzette')
Su|zhou (city,
  China)
Suzie *also* Susie,
  Suzy
Suz|man, Helen
  (South African
  politician)
Sval|bard (island
  group, Arctic
  Ocean)
svelte
Sven (=Sweyn)
Sven|gali +s
Sverd|lovsk
  (former name of
  Yekaterinburg)
Svet|am|bara +s
swab
  swabs
  swabbed
  swab|bing
Swabia (former
  German duchy)
Swab|ian +s
swad|dle
  swad|dles
  swad|dled
  swad|dling
swaddling-clothes
swaddy
  swad|dies
swag
  swags
  swagged
  swag|ging
swage
  swages
  swaged
  swa|ging
swage-block +s
swag|ger +s +ed
  +ing
swag|ger|er +s
swag|ger|ing|ly
swag|gie +s
swag|man
  swag|men
Swa|hili
  plural Swa|hili
swain +s
swal|low +s +ed
  +ing
swal|low|able
swallow-dive
  swallow-dives
  swallow-dived
  swallow-diving
swal|low|er +s

swallow-hole +s
swal|low|tail +s
swallow-tailed
swam
swami +s
Swam|mer|dam,
  Jan (Dutch
  naturalist)
swamp +s +ed
  +ing
swamp|land +s
swampy
  swamp|ier
  swampi|est
Swan, Jo|seph
  Wil|son (English
  scientist)
swan
  swans
  swanned
  swan|ning
swan-dive +s
Swanee (in 'down
  the Swanee'.
  △Suwannee)
swank +s +ed
  +ing
swank|ily
swanki|ness
swank|pot +s
swanky
  swank|ier
  swanki|est
swan|like
swan-neck +s
swan|nery
  swan|ner|ies
swans|down
Swan|sea (city,
  Wales)
Swan|son, Gloria
  (American
  actress)
swan|song +s
swan-upping
swap
  swaps
  swapped
  swap|ping
Swapo (= South
  West Africa
  People's
  Organization)
swap|per +s
Swa|raj
Swa|raj|ist +s
sward +s
sward|ed
sware (*archaic*
  = swore)
swarf

swarm +s +ed
　+ing
swart
swar|thily
swar|thi|ness
swar|thy
　swar|thier
　swar|thi|est
swash
　swashes
　swashed
　swash|ing
swash|buck|ler +s
swash|buck|ling
swash-plate +s
swas|tika +s
swat
　swats
　swat|ted
　swat|ting
　(hit sharply.
　△ swot)
swatch
　swatches
swath +s
swathe
　swathes
　swathed
　swath|ing
Swa|tow (former
　name of Shantou)
swat|ter +s
sway +s +ed +ing
sway-back +s
sway-backed
Swazi
　plural Swazi or
　Swa|zis
Swa|zi|land
swear
　swears
　swore
　swear|ing
　sworn
swear|er +s
swear word +s
sweat +s +ed +ing
sweat|band +s
sweat|er +s
sweat|ily
sweati|ness
sweating-sickness
sweat|pants
sweat|shirt +s
sweat|shop +s
sweat|suit +s
sweaty
　sweat|ier
　sweati|est
Swede +s (Swedish
　person)
swede +s (turnip)

Swe|den
Swe|den|borg,
　Eman|uel
　(Swedish scientist)
Swed|ish
Swee|ney, the
　(flying squad)
sweep
　sweeps
　swept
　sweep|ing
sweep|back +s
sweep|er +s
sweep|ing +s
sweep|ing|ly
sweep|ing|ness
sweep|stake +s
sweet +s +er +est
　(confectionery;
　not bitter. △ suite)
sweet and sour
sweet|bread +s
sweet-brier +s
sweet|corn
sweet|en +s +ed
　+ing
sweet|en|er +s
sweet|en|ing +s
sweet gale
sweet|heart +s
sweetie +s
sweetie-pie +s
sweet|ing +s
sweet|ish
sweet|ly
sweet|meal +s
sweet|meat +s
sweet|ness
sweet|shop +s
sweet-smelling
sweet|sop +s
sweet-talk
　sweet-talks
　sweet-talked
　sweet-talking
sweet-tempered
swell
　swells
　swelled
　swell|ing
　swol|len
swell-box
　swell-boxes
swell|ing +s
swell|ish
swell-organ +s
swel|ter +s +ed
　+ing
swel|ter|ing|ly
swept
swept-back
　adjective

swept-up *adjective*
swept-wing
　adjective
swerve
　swerves
　swerved
　swerv|ing
swerve|less
swerver +s
Sweyn (Danish
　king)
Swift, Jona|than
　(Irish writer)
swift +s +er +est
swiftie +s
swift|let +s
swift|ly
swift|ness
swig
　swigs
　swigged
　swig|ging
swig|ger +s
swill +s +ed +ing
swill|er +s
swim
　swims
　swam
　swim|ming
　swum
swim-bladder +s
swim|mable
swim|mer +s
swim|meret +s
swim|ming bath
　+s
swim|ming
　cos|tume +s
swim|ming|ly
swim|ming pool
　+s
swim|ming trunks
swim|suit +s
swim|suit|ed
swim|wear
Swin|burne,
　Alger|non
　Charles (English
　poet)
swin|dle
　swin|dles
　swin|dled
　swind|ling
swind|ler +s
Swin|don (town,
　England)
swine
　plural swine
swine|herd +s
swin|ery
　swin|eries

swing
　swings
　swung
　swing|ing
swing|bin +s
swing|boat +s
swing-bridge +s
swing-door +s
swinge
　swinges
　swinged
　swinge|ing
swinge|ing|ly
swing|er +s
swing|ing|ly
swin|gle
　swin|gles
　swin|gled
　swin|gling
swingle|tree +s
swing|om|eter +s
swing-wing +s
swingy
　swing|ier
　swingi|est
swin|ish
swin|ish|ly
swin|ish|ness
swipe
　swipes
　swiped
　swip|ing
swiper +s
swip|ple +s
swirl +s +ed +ing
swirly
　swirl|ier
　swirli|est
swish
　swishes
　swished
　swish|ing
swishy
　swish|ier
　swishi|est
Swiss
　plural Swiss
switch
　switches
　switched
　switch|ing
switch|able
switch|back +s
switch|blade +s
switch|board +s
switched-on
　adjective
switch|er +s
switch|gear
switch-over +s
　noun

swither +s +ed
+ing
Swithin (English
saint)
Swithun (use
Swithin)
Switz¦er¦land
swivel
swivels
swiv¦elled Br.
swiv¦eled Am.
swiv¦el¦ling Br.
swiv¦el¦ing Am.
swivet
swiz (use swizz)
swizzes
swizz
swizzes
swiz¦zle
swiz¦zles
swiz¦zled
swiz¦zling
swizzle-stick +s
swob (use swab)
swobs
swobbed
swob¦bing
swol¦len
swoon +s +ed
+ing
swoop +s +ed
+ing
swoosh
swooshes
swooshed
swoosh¦ing
swop (use swap)
swops
swopped
swop¦ping
sword +s
sword-bearer +s
sword¦bill +s
sword¦fish
  plural sword¦fish
  or sword¦fishes
sword¦like
sword¦play
swords¦man
  swords¦men
swords¦man¦ship
sword¦stick +s
sword-swallow¦er
+s
sword¦tail +s
swore
sworn
swot
swots
swot¦ted
swot¦ting

swot (*cont.*)
  (study hard.
  △ swat)
swum
swung
swy +s
syb¦ar¦ite +s
syb¦ar¦it¦ic
syb¦ar¦it¦ic¦al
syb¦ar¦it¦ic¦al¦ly
syb¦ar¦it¦ism
Sybil *also* Sibyl
  (name. △ sibyl)
syca¦mine +s
syca¦more +s
syce +s (groom.
  △ sice)
syco¦more +s (use
  sycamore)
sy¦co¦nium
  sy¦co¦nia
syco¦phancy
syco¦phant +s
syco¦phan¦tic
syco¦phan¦tic¦al¦ly
sy¦cosis
  sy¦coses
  (skin disease.
  △ psychosis)
Syd¦en¦ham,
  Thomas (English
  physician)
Syd¦en¦ham's
  cho¦rea
Syd¦ney (city,
  Australia)
Syd¦ney *also*
  Sid¦ney
  (name)
sy¦en¦ite +s
sy¦en¦it¦ic
Syk¦tyv¦kar (city,
  Russia)
syl¦lab¦ary
  syl¦lab¦ar¦ies
syl¦labi
syl¦lab¦ic
syl¦lab¦ic¦al¦ly
syl¦labi¦ca¦tion
syl¦lab¦icity
syl¦labi¦fi¦ca¦tion
syl¦lab¦ify
  syl¦labi¦fies
  syl¦labi¦fied
  syl¦labi¦fy¦ing
syl¦lab¦ise Br. (use
  syllabize)
  syl¦lab¦ises
  syl¦lab¦ised
  syl¦lab¦is¦ing
syl¦lab¦ize
  syl¦lab¦izes

syl¦lab¦ize (*cont.*)
  syl¦lab¦ized
  syl¦lab¦iz¦ing
syl¦lable
  syl¦lables
  syl¦labled
  syl¦lab¦ling
syl¦la¦bub +s
syl¦la¦bus
  syl¦la¦buses *or*
  syl¦labi
syl¦lep¦sis
  syl¦lep¦ses
syl¦lep¦tic
syl¦lep¦tic¦al¦ly
syl¦lo¦gise Br. (use
  syllogize)
  syl¦lo¦gises
  syl¦lo¦gised
  syl¦lo¦gis¦ing
syl¦lo¦gism +s
syl¦lo¦gis¦tic
syl¦lo¦gis¦tic¦al¦ly
syl¦lo¦gize
  syl¦lo¦gizes
  syl¦lo¦gized
  syl¦lo¦giz¦ing
sylph +s
sylph¦like
sylva
  syl¦vas *or* syl¦vae
  (trees of a region
  etc.; list of such
  trees. △ silver)
syl¦van (of woods;
  wooded.
  △ silvern)
Syl¦via
syl¦vi¦cul¦ture (use
  silviculture)
Syl¦vie
sym¦biont +s
sym¦bi¦osis
  sym¦bi¦oses
sym¦bi¦ot¦ic
sym¦bi¦ot¦ic¦al¦ly
sym¦bol
  sym¦bols
  sym¦bolled Br.
  sym¦boled Am.
  sym¦bol¦ling Br.
  sym¦bol¦ing Am.
  (sign. △ cymbal)
sym¦bol¦ic
sym¦bol¦ic¦al
sym¦bol¦ic¦al¦ly
sym¦bol¦ics
sym¦bol¦isa¦tion
  Br. (use
  symbolization)
sym¦bol¦ise Br.
  (use symbolize)

sym¦bol¦ise (*cont.*)
  sym¦bol¦ises
  sym¦bol¦ised
  sym¦bol¦is¦ing
sym¦bol¦ism +s
sym¦bol¦ist +s
  (adherent of
  symbolism etc.
  △ cymbalist)
sym¦bol¦is¦tic
sym¦bol¦iza¦tion
sym¦bol¦ize
  sym¦bol¦izes
  sym¦bol¦ized
  sym¦bol¦iz¦ing
sym¦bol¦ogy
sym¦bol¦ology
sym¦met¦ric
sym¦met¦ric¦al
sym¦met¦ric¦al¦ly
sym¦met¦rise Br.
  (use symmetrize)
sym¦met¦rises
sym¦met¦rised
sym¦met¦ris¦ing
sym¦met¦rize
sym¦met¦rizes
sym¦met¦rized
sym¦met¦riz¦ing
sym¦met¦ro¦
       pho¦bia
sym¦metry
sym¦met¦ries
Sy¦mons, Ju¦lian
  (English writer)
sym¦path¦ec¦tomy
sym¦path¦
    ec¦to¦mies
sym¦pa¦thet¦ic
sym¦pa¦thet¦ic¦
      al¦ly
sym¦pa¦thise Br.
  (use sympathize)
sym¦pa¦thises
sym¦pa¦thised
sym¦pa¦this¦ing
sym¦pa¦thiser Br.
  +s (use
  sympathizer)
sym¦pa¦thize
sym¦pa¦thizes
sym¦pa¦thized
sym¦pa¦thiz¦ing
sym¦pa¦thizer +s
sym¦pathy
sym¦pa¦thies
sym¦pat¦ric
sym¦pet¦al¦ous
sym¦phon¦ic
sym¦phon¦ic¦al¦ly
sym¦pho¦ni¦ous
sym¦phon¦ist +s

sym|phony
  sym|phon|ies
sym|phyl|lous
sym|phys|eal
sym|phys|ial
sym|phy|sis
  sym|phy|ses
sym|po|dial
sym|po|di|al|ly
sym|po|dium
  sym|po|dia
sym|po|siac +s
sym|po|sial
sym|po|si|arch +s
sym|po|si|ast +s
sym|po|sium
  sym|po|sia *or*
  sym|po|siums
symp|tom +s
symp|tom|at|ic
symp|tom|at|ic|
      al|ly
symp|tom|
      atol|ogy
symp|tom|less
syn|aer|esis
  syn|aer|eses
syn|aes|the|sia *Br.*
  (*Am.* synesthesia)
syn|aes|thet|ic *Br.*
  (*Am.* synesthetic)
syna|gogal
syna|gogic|al
syna|gogue +s
syn|al|lag|mat|ic
syn|an|ther|ous
syn|an|thous
syn|apse +s
syn|ap|sis
  synap|ses
syn|ap|tic
syn|ap|tic|al|ly
syn|arth|rosis
  syn|arth|roses
sync +s +ed +ing
  (= synchronize;
  synchronization)
syn|carp +s
syn|carp|ous
synch +s +ed +ing
  (use syncing)
syn|chon|drosis
  syn|chon|droses
syn|chro|cyclo|
      tron +s
syn|chro|mesh
  syn|chro|meshes
syn|chron|ic
syn|chron|ic|al|ly
syn|chron|icity

syn|chron|isa|tion
  Br. (use
  synchronization)
syn|chron|ise *Br.*
  (use synchronize)
  syn|chron|ises
  syn|chron|ised
  syn|chron|is|ing
syn|chron|iser *Br.*
  +s (use
  synchronizer)
syn|chron|ism
syn|chron|is|tic
syn|chron|is|tic|
      al|ly
syn|chron|iza|tion
syn|chron|ize
  syn|chron|izes
  syn|chron|ized
  syn|chron|iz|ing
  syn|chron|izer +s
syn|chron|ous
syn|chron|ous|ly
syn|chrony
  syn|chron|ies
syn|chro|tron +s
syn|clinal
syn|cline +s
syn|co|pal
syn|co|pate
  syn|co|pates
  syn|co|pated
  syn|co|pat|ing
syn|co|pa|tion +s
syn|co|pa|tor +s
syn|cope +s
syn|cre|tic
syn|cre|tise *Br.*
  (use syncretize)
  syn|cre|tises
  syn|cre|tised
  syn|cre|tis|ing
syn|cre|tism
syn|cre|tist +s
syn|cre|tis|tic
syn|cre|tize
  syn|cre|tizes
  syn|cre|tized
  syn|cre|tiz|ing
syn|cyt|ial
syn|cyt|ium
  syn|cytia
syn|dac|tyl
syn|dac|tyl|ism
syn|dac|tyl|ous
syn|dac|tyly
syn|desis
syn|deses
syn|des|mosis
  syn|des|moses
syn|det|ic
syn|dic +s

syn|dic|al
syn|dic|al|ism
syn|dic|al|ist +s
syn|di|cate
  syn|di|cates
  syn|di|cated
  syn|di|cat|ing
syn|di|ca|tion +s
syn|drome +s
syn|drom|ic
syne (since. △ sine,
  sign)
syn|ec|doche +s
syn|ec|doch|ic
syn|ecious *Am.* (*Br.*
  synoecious)
syn|eco|logic|al
syn|ecolo|gist +s
syn|ecol|ogy
syn|ere|sis *Am.* (*Br.*
  synaeresis)
syn|er|get|ic
syn|er|gic
syn|er|gism +s
syn|er|gist +s
syn|er|gis|tic
syn|er|gis|tic|al|ly
syn|ergy
  syn|er|gies
syn|es|the|sia *Am.*
  (*Br.* synaesthesia)
syn|es|thet|ic *Am.*
  (*Br.* synaesthetic)
syn|gam|ous
syn|gamy
Synge, J. M. (Irish
  playwright)
syn|gen|esis
syn|gnath|ous
syn|iz|esis
  syn|iz|eses
synod +s
syn|od|al
syn|od|ic
syn|od|ic|al
syn|oe|cious *Br.*
  (*Am.* synecious)
syno|nym +s
syno|nym|ic
syno|nym|ity
syn|onym|ous
syn|onym|ous|ly
syn|onym|ous|
        ness
syn|onymy
  syn|ony|mies
syn|op|sis
  syn|op|ses
syn|op|sise *Br.* (use
  synopsize)
  syn|op|sises

syn|op|sise (*cont.*)
  syn|op|sised
  syn|op|sis|ing
syn|op|size
  syn|op|sizes
  syn|op|sized
  syn|op|siz|ing
syn|op|tic +s
syn|op|tic|al
syn|op|tic|al|ly
syn|op|tist +s
syn|os|tosis
syn|ovia
syn|ovial
syno|vitis
syn|tac|tic
syn|tac|tic|al
syn|tac|tic|al|ly
syn|tagma
  syn|tag|mas *or*
  syn|tag|mata
syn|tag|mat|ic
syn|tag|mic
syn|tax
synth +s
  (= synthesizer)
syn|the|sis
  syn|the|ses
syn|the|sise *Br.*
  (use synthesize)
  syn|the|sises
  syn|the|sised
  syn|the|sis|ing
syn|the|siser *Br.* +s
  (use synthesizer)
syn|the|sist +s
syn|the|size
  syn|the|sizes
  syn|the|sized
  syn|the|siz|ing
syn|the|sizer +s
syn|thet|ic +s
syn|thet|ic|al
syn|thet|ic|al|ly
syn|the|tise *Br.*
  (use synthetize)
  syn|the|tises
  syn|the|tised
  syn|the|tis|ing
syn|the|tize
  syn|the|tizes
  syn|the|tized
  syn|the|tiz|ing
syph|ilis
syph|il|ise *Br.* (use
  syphilize)
  syph|il|ises
  syph|il|ised
  syph|il|is|ing
syph|il|it|ic
syph|il|ize
  syph|il|izes

syph¦il¦ize (*cont.*)
  syph¦il¦ized
  syph¦il¦iz¦ing
syph¦il¦oid
sy¦phon *Br.* +s +ed
+ing (pipe for
transferring liquid.
Am. siphon.
⚠ siphon)
sy¦phon¦age *Br.*
(*Am.* siphonage)
sy¦phon¦ic *Br.*
(pertaining to a
syphon. *Am.*
siphonic.
⚠ siphonic)
Syra|cuse (port,
Italy; city, USA)
Syr Darya (Russian
name for the
Sirdaryo)
syren +s (use
siren)
Syria
Syr¦iac (language)
Syr¦ian +s (of
Syria)
syr|inga +s
syr|inge
  syr|inges
  syr|inged
  syr|in|ging
syr|in|geal
syr¦inx
  syr|inxes *or*
  syr|inges
Syro-Phoenician
  +s
syr|phid +s
syrup *Br.* +s (*Am.*
sirup)
syr¦upy
SYSOP (= system
operator)
sys¦sar|cosis
  sys¦sar|coses
sys¦tal¦tic
sys¦tem +s
sys¦tem|at¦ic
sys¦tem|at¦ic|al¦ly
sys¦tem|at¦ics
sys¦tem|atisa|tion
Br. (use
systematization)
sys¦tem|atise *Br.*
(use systematize)
  sys¦tem|atises
  sys¦tem|atised
  sys¦tem|atis¦ing
sys¦tem|atiser *Br.*
+s (use
systematizer)

sys¦tem|atism
sys¦tem|atist +s
sys¦tem|atiza|tion
sys¦tem|atize
  sys¦tem|atizes
  sys¦tem|atized
  sys¦tem|atiz¦ing
sys¦tem|atizer +s
sys¦tem|ic
sys¦tem|ic|al¦ly
sys¦tem|isa¦tion
Br. (use
systemization)
sys¦tem|ise *Br.* (use
systemize)
  sys¦tem|ises
  sys¦tem|ised
  sys¦tem|is¦ing
sys¦tem|iser *Br.* +s
(use systemizer)
sys¦tem|iza¦tion
sys¦tem|ize
  sys¦tem|izes
  sys¦tem|ized
  sys¦tem|iz¦ing
sys¦tem|izer +s
sys¦tem|less
sys|tole +s
sys|tol¦ic
syzygy
  syzy|gies
Szcze|cin (port,
Poland)
Sze|chuan
  (= Sichuan)
Sze|chwan
  (= Sichuan)
Sze¦ged (city,
Hungary)
Szi|lard, Leo
(Hungarian-born
American
physicist)

Tt

....

’t (= it)
ta (= thank you.
⚠ tahr, tar)
taal, the
  (Afrikaans)
TAB (= typhoid-
paratyphoid A
and B vaccine)
tab
  tabs
  tabbed
  tab|bing
(flap, bill, etc.; also
= tabulator)
tab¦ard +s
tab|aret +s
Tab|asco (state,
Mexico)
Tab|asco (sauce)
Propr.
tab|asco +s
(pepper)
tab|bou|leh +s
tabby
  tab|bies
tab|er|nacle +s
tab|er|nacled
tabes
tab|et¦ic
tab|inet +s
Tab|itha
tabla +s
tab|la|ture +s
table
  tables
  tabled
  tab¦ling
tab|leau
  tab|leaux
tab|leau viv|ant
  tab|leaux viv|ants
table|cloth +s
table d’hôte
  tables d’hôte
table|ful +s
table lamp +s
table|land +s
table-mat +s
Table Moun|tain
(in South Africa)
table|spoon +s
table|spoon|ful +s
tab¦let +s +ed
+ing
table ten¦nis
table top +s *noun*
table-top *attributive*
table|ware

tab|lier +s
tab|loid +s
taboo +s +ed +ing
tabor +s
tab|oret *Am.* +s
(*Br.* tabouret)
tab|ouret *Br.* +s
(*Am.* taboret)
Ta¦briz (city, Iran)
tabu +s +ed +ing
(use taboo)
tabu|lar
tab|ula rasa
  tabu|lae rasae
tabu|lar¦ly
tabu|late
  tabu|lates
  tabu|lated
  tabu|lat¦ing
tabu|la¦tion +s
tabu|la¦tor +s
tabun
taca¦ma|hac +s
tac-au-tac +s
tacet (*Music.*
⚠ tacit)
tach +s
(= tachometer.
⚠ tack)
tache +s (use tash)
Ta|ching
(= Daqing)
tach|ism
tach|isme (use
tachism)
tach¦is|to|scope +s
tach¦is|to|scop¦ic
tacho +s
(= tachograph,
tachometer.
⚠ taco)
tacho|graph +s
tach|om¦eter +s
tachy|car|dia
tach|yg¦raph¦er +s
tachy|graph¦ic
tachy|graph¦ic|al
tach|yg¦raphy
tach|ym¦eter +s
tach|ym¦etry
tach|yon +s
tacit (understood or
implied. ⚠ tacet)
Tacit|ean
tacit¦ly
taci|turn
taci|turn|ity
taci|turn¦ly
Taci|tus (Roman
historian)
tack +s +ed +ing
(senses except

tack (*cont.*)
'tachometer'.
  ⚠ tach)
tack¦er +s
tack¦ily
tacki¦ness
tackle
  tackles
  tackled
  tack¦ling
tackle-block +s
tackle-fall +s
tack¦ler +s
tack room +s
tacky
  tack¦ier
  tacki¦est
taco +s (food.
  ⚠ tacho)
tact
tact¦ful
tact¦ful¦ly
tact¦ful¦ness
tac¦tic +s
tac¦tic¦al
tac¦tic¦al¦ly
tac¦ti¦cian +s
tac¦tics
tact¦ile
tac¦til¦ity
tact¦less
tact¦less¦ly
tact¦less¦ness
tac¦tual
tad +s
Ta¦djik (use Tajik)
  plural Ta¦djik *or*
  Ta¦djiks
Ta¦djiki¦stan (use
  Tajikistan)
Tad¦mur (modern
  name for
  Palmyra)
tad¦pole +s
Ta¦dzhik (use
  Tajik)
  plural Ta¦dzhik *or*
  Ta¦dzhiks
Ta¦dzhiki¦stan
  (use Tajikistan)
tae¦dium vitae
Taegu (city, South
  Korea)
Tae¦jon (city, South
  Korea)
tae kwon do
tae¦nia *Br.*
  tae¦niae *or*
  tae¦nias
  (*Am.* tenia)
tae¦ni¦oid *Br.*
  (*Am.* tenioid)

Taff +s (*often
  offensive*)
taf¦feta +s
taff¦rail +s
Taffy
  Taf¦fies
  (*often offensive*
  Welsh person)
taffy
  taf¦fies
  (confection;
  insincere flattery)
tafia +s
Taft, Wil¦liam
  How¦ard
  (American
  president)
tag
  tags
  tagged
  tag¦ging
Taga¦log +s
Tag¦an¦rog (port,
  Russia)
ta¦getes
taglia¦telle
tag line +s
tag¦meme +s
tag¦mem¦ics
Tag¦ore,
  Rab¦in¦dra¦nath
  (Indian writer)
Tagus (river, Spain
  and Portugal)
Ta¦hiti (island, S.
  Pacific)
Ta¦hi¦tian +s
tahr +s (animal.
  ⚠ ta, tar)
tah¦sil +s
tah¦sil¦dar +s
Tai'an (city, China)
t'ai chi (ch'uan)
Tai¦chung (city,
  China)
Ta'if (city, Saudi
  Arabia)
Taig +s (*offensive*)
taiga +s (forest.
  ⚠ tiger)
tail +s +ed +ing (of
  animal; end;
  follow. ⚠ tale)
tail¦back +s
tail¦board +s
tail¦coat +s
tail-end +s
tail-ender +s
tail fea¦ther +s
tail fin +s
tail¦gate +s
  tail¦gated
  tail¦gat¦ing

tail¦gater +s
tailie +s
tail¦ing +s
tail lamp +s
Taille¦ferre,
  Ger¦maine
  (French
  composer)
tail¦less
tail light +s
tail-off +s *noun*
tailor +s +ed +ing
tailor-bird +s
tail¦or¦ess
tailor-made
tail¦piece +s
tail¦pipe +s
tail¦plane +s
tail-race +s
tail-skid +s
tail¦spin
  tail¦spins
  tail¦spun
  tail¦spin¦ning
tail¦stock +s
tail¦wheel +s
tail¦wind +s
Tai¦myr
  Pen¦in¦sula (in
  Siberia)
Tai¦nan (city,
  Taiwan)
taint +s +ed +ing
taint¦less
tai¦pan +s
Tai¦pei (capital of
  Taiwan)
Tai¦ping
  Re¦bel¦lion (in
  China)
Tai¦wan
Tai¦wan¦ese
  plural Tai¦wan¦ese
Tai¦yuan (city,
  China)
Tai Yue Shan
  (Chinese name for
  Lantau)
Ta'iz (city, Yemen)
taj +s
Tajik
  plural Tajik *or*
  Ta¦jiks
Ta¦jiki¦stan
Taj Mahal
  (mausoleum,
  India)
taka
  plural taka
  (Bangladeshi
  currency)
tak¦able

tak¦ahe +s
take
  takes
  took
  tak¦ing
  taken
take¦away +s
take-home
  attributive
take-in +s *noun*
take-off +s *noun
  and attributive*
take-out +s
  *attributive and
  noun*
take¦over +s
taker +s
take-up +s *noun
  and attributive*
takin +s
tak¦ing¦ly
tak¦ing¦ness
tak¦ings
Tak¦li¦ma¦kan
  Des¦ert (in NW
  China)
Tako¦radi (port,
  Ghana)
tala +s (*Music.
  ⚠ thaler*)
tala
  plural tala or talas
  (Western Samoan
  currency.
  ⚠ thaler)
Ta¦laing
  plural Ta¦laing *or*
  Ta¦laings
tala¦poin +s
tal¦aria
Tal¦bot, Wil¦liam
  Henry Fox
  (English
  photography
  pioneer)
tal¦bot +s
talc
  talcs
  talced *or* talcked
  talc¦ing
talc¦ose
talc¦ous
tal¦cum +s +ed
  +ing
talcy
tale +s (story.
  ⚠ tail)
tale¦bearer +s
tale¦bear¦ing
tal¦ent +s
tal¦ent¦ed
tal¦ent¦less

talent-spot
  talent-spots
  talent-spotted
  talent-spotting
talent-spotter +s
tales (writ for
  summoning
  substitute jurors)
ta¦les|man
  ta¦les|men
  (*Law.* ⚠ talisman)
tale|tell¦er +s
tali (plural of talus)
tal¦ion +s
tali|pes
tali|pot +s
tal¦is|man +s
  (lucky charm.
  ⚠ talesman)
tal¦is|man¦ic
talk +s +ed +ing
  (speak. ⚠ torc,
  torque)
talka|thon +s
talka|tive
talka|tive¦ly
talka|tive|ness
talk|back +s
talk¦er +s
talk|fest +s
talkie +s (film.
  ⚠ torquey)
talk|ing point +s
talk|ing shop +s
talking-to
  talkings-to
tall +er +est
tall|age +s
Tal¦la|has¦see
  (city, Florida)
tall|boy +s
Tal¦ley|rand,
  Charles
  Maur|ice de *in*
  full Talleyrand-
  Périgord
  (French
  statesman)
Tal|linn (capital of
  Estonia)
Tal¦lis, Thomas
  (English
  composer)
tall|ish
tall|lith
  tal|lith¦im
tall|ness
tal¦low +s +ed
  +ing
tal¦low|ish
tal¦low tree +s
tal|lowy

tally
  tal|lies
  tal|lied
  tally|ing
tally-ho +s *noun*
tally-ho
  tally-hoes
  tally-hoed
  tally-hoing
verb
tally|man
  tally|men
Tal¦mud
Tal¦mud¦ic
Tal¦mud¦ic¦al
Tal¦mud¦ist +s
talon +s
tal|oned
talus
  tali
  (ankle-bone)
talus
  tal|uses
  (slope of wall etc.)
TAM (= television
  audience
  measurement)
tam +s (= tam-o'-
  shanter)
tam¦able (use
  tameable)
tam¦ale +s
tam¦an|dua +s
tam¦an|oir +s
Tamar (river,
  England)
Tam¦ara (name)
tam¦ar|ack +s
tam¦ar|illo +s
tam¦arin +s
  (marmoset)
tam¦ar|ind +s
  (fruit; tree)
tam¦ar|isk +s
Tamau|lipas (state,
  Mexico)
Tambo, Oli¦ver
  (South African
  politician)
tam|bour +s +ed
  +ing
tam|boura +s
tam|bourin +s
  (drum; dance;
  music for this)
tam¦bour|ine +s
  (jingling
  percussion
  instrument)
tam¦bour|in|ist +s
Tam¦bov (city,
  Russia)

Tam¦bur|laine
  (alternative name
  of Tamerlane)
tame
  tames
  tamed
  tam¦ing
  tamer
  tam¦est
tame|abil¦ity
tame|able
tame|able|ness
tame¦ly
tame|ness
tamer +s
Tam¦er|lane
  (Mongol ruler)
Tamil +s
Ta¦mil|ian
Tamil Nadu (state,
  India)
Tamla Mo¦town
  (record company)
  Propr.
Tam¦many
  (benevolent
  society, New York
  City)
Tam¦muz
  Babylonian and
  Assyrian Mythology
Tam¦muz (Jewish
  month; use
  Thammuz)
tammy
  tam|mies
tam-o'-shanter +s
tam|oxi|fen
tamp +s +ed +ing
Tampa (port, USA)
tam|pan +s
tam|per +s +ed
  +ing
Tam|pere (city,
  Finland)
tam|per¦er +s
tam|per|ing +s
tamper-proof
Tam|pico (port,
  Mexico)
tam|pion +s
tam|pon +s +ed
  +ing
tam|pon|ade +s
tam|pon|age +s
Tam|sin
tam-tam +s
Tam|worth +s
  (town, England;
  pig)
tan
  tans

tan (*cont.*)
  tanned
  tan|ning
  (colour; make
  leather; become
  brown; also
  = tangent)
Tana, Lake (in
  Ethiopia)
tan|ager +s
Tan|agra +s
Tanak
Tana¦na|rive
  (former name of
  Antananarivo)
tan|bark +s
tan¦dem +s
tan|door +s
tan|doori +s
Tang (Chinese
  dynasty)
tang +s +ed +ing
Tanga (port,
  Tanzania)
tanga +s
Tan¦gan|yika
  (former name of
  Tanzania)
Tan¦gan|yika,
  Lake (in E. Africa)
Tan¦gan|yi¦kan +s
Tange, Kenzo
  (Japanese
  architect)
tan|gelo +s
tan|gency
  tan|gen|cies
tan|gent +s
tan|gen|tial
tan|gen|tial¦ly
tan|ger|ine +s
tan|ghin +s
tan¦gi|bil¦ity
tan|gible +s
tan|gible|ness
tan|gibly
Tan|gier (port,
  Morocco)
Tan|giers (older
  form of Tangier)
tangi|ness
tan¦gle
  tan|gles
  tan|gled
  tan|gling
tan¦gly
  tan|glier
  tan|gli|est
tango +s (dance
  (*noun*); colour)
tango
  tan|goes

tango (*cont.*)
tan|goed
tango|ing
  verb
tan|gram +s
Tang|shan (city,
  China)
tangy
  tang|ier
  tangi|est
tanh (= hyperbolic
  tangent)
Tania *also* Tanya
tan|ist +s
tan|ist|ry
Tan|jung|ka|rang
  (city, Indonesia)
tank +s +ed +ing
tanka +s (Japanese
  poem. △ tanker)
tank|age +s
tank|ard +s
tank|er +s +ed
  +ing (ship;
  aircraft; vehicle.
  △ tanka)
tank-farming
tank|ful +s
tank|less
tank top +s
tan|nable
tan|nage +s
tan|nate +s
tan|ner +s
tan|nery
  tan|ner|ies
Tann|häuser
  (German poet)
tan|nic
tan|nin +s
tan|nish
tan|noy (public-
  address system)
  Propr.
Tannu-Tuva
  (former name of
  Tuva)
tan|rec +s
Tan|sen (Indian
  musician)
tansy
  tan|sies
tan|tal|ic (of or
  pertaining to
  tantalus)
tan|tal|isa|tion *Br.*
  (use
  tantalization)
tan|tal|ise *Br.* (use
  tantalize)
tan|tal|ises

tan|tal|ise (*cont.*)
tan|tal|ised
tan|tal|is|ing
tan|tal|iser *Br.* +s
  (use tantalizer)
tan|tal|is|ing|ly *Br.*
  (use
  tantalizingly)
tan|tal|ite
tan|tal|iza|tion
tan|tal|ize
tan|tal|izes
tan|tal|ized
tan|tal|iz|ing
tan|tal|izer +s
tan|tal|iz|ing|ly
tan|ta|lum
Tan|ta|lus *Greek
  Mythology*
tan|ta|lus
  tan|ta|luses
tan|ta|mount
tan|tivy
  tan|tivies
tant mieux
tant pis
tan|tra +s
tan|tric
tan|trism
tan|trist +s
tan|trum +s
Tanya *also* Tania
Tan|za|nia
Tan|za|nian +s
Tao +s
Taoi|seach (Irish
  prime minister)
Tao|ism
Tao|ist +s
Tao|is|tic
Taor|mina (resort,
  Sicily)
Tao-te-Ching
tap
  taps
  tapped
  tap|ping
tapa +s (bark;
  cloth. △ tapper)
tapas (Spanish bar
  snacks)
tap-dance
  tap-dances
  tap-danced
  tap-dancing
  tap-dancer +s
tape
  tapes
  taped
  tap|ing
tape|able
tape|less
tape|like

tape-measure +s
taper +s +ed +ing
  (thin candle; make
  or become
  thinner. △ tapir)
tape-record
  tape-records
  tape-record|ed
  tape-record|ing
  verb
tape re|cord|er +s
tape re|cord|ing
  +s *noun*
taper|er +s
tap|es|tried
tap|es|try
  tap|es|tries
tap|etum
  tap|eta *or*
  tap|etums
tape|worm +s
tapho|nom|ic
taph|ono|mist +s
taph|onomy
tap-in +s *noun*
tapi|oca
tapir +s (animal.
  △ taper)
tapir|oid +s
tapis
  plural tapis
tap|less
tapote|ment
tap|pable
tap|per +s (person
  or thing that taps.
  △ tapa)
tap|pet +s
tap|ping +s
tap|room +s
tap root +s
tap|ster +s
tap-tap +s
tapu
tap water
tar
  tars
  tarred
  tar|ring
  (liquid; sailor.
  △ ta, tahr)
Tara (hill, Republic
  of Ireland; name)
ta-ra (goodbye)
tara|did|dle +s
tara|kihi
  plural tara|kihi
tara|ma|sa|lata
Tara|naki (region,
  New Zealand)
tar|an|tass
tar|an|tasses

tar|an|tella +s
tar|ant|ism
Tar|anto (port,
  Italy)
tar|an|tula +s
Tar|awa (atoll, S.
  Pacific)
tar|axa|cum +s
tar|boosh
  tar|booshes
tar-brush
  tar-brushes
Tar|den|ois|ian
tar|di|grade +s
tar|dily
tar|di|ness
tardy
  tar|dier
  tar|di|est
tare +s (weed;
  unladen weight.
  △ tear)
tare and tret
targa +s
targe +s
tar|get +s +ed
  +ing
tar|get|able
Tar|gum +s
Tar|gum|ist +s
tar|iff +s +ed +ing
Tarim (river,
  China)
tar|latan +s
tar|mac (*noun*)
  Propr.
tar|mac
  tar|macs
  tar|macked
  tar|mack|ing
  verb
tar|mac|adam
Tarn (river, France)
tarn +s (lake)
tar|na|tion
  interjection
tar|nish
  tar|nishes
  tar|nished
  tar|nish|ing
tar|nish|able
Tar|nów (city,
  Poland)
taro +s (plant)
tarot +s (cards)
tarp (= tarpaulin)
tar|pan +s (horse)
tar|paulin +s
Tar|peia (Roman
  Vestal Virgin)
Tar|peian Rock
  (cliff, Rome)

tar|pon +s (fish)

Tar|quin (= either
Tarquinius)

Tar|quin|ius
Pris|cus (king of
Rome)

Tar|quin|ius
Su|perb|us (king
of Rome)

tar|ra|did|dle +s
(use taradiddle)

tar|ra|gon

Tar|ra|gona (town
and province,
Spain)

tar|ras

Tar|rasa (city,
Spain)

tar|rier +s (person
who tarries)

tar|ri|ness (of tar)

tarry
tar|rier
tar|ri|est
(of tar)

tarry
tar|ries
tar|ried
tarry|ing
(linger)

tar|sal +s

tarsi

tar|sia (= intarsia)

tar|sier +s (animal)

Tar|sus (city,
Turkey)

tar|sus
tarsi

tart +s +ed +ing

tar|tan +s

Tar|tar +s (Turkic
people)

tar|tar +s (deposit
on teeth etc.;
violent-tempered
person; in 'cream
of tartar'.
⚠ tartare, ta-ta)

tar|tare (sauce.
⚠ tartar, ta-ta)

Tar|tar|ean (of
Tartarus)

Tar|tar|ian (of
Tartars)

tar|tar|ic

tar|tar|ise Br. (use
tartarize)
tar|tar|ises
tar|tar|ised
tar|tar|is|ing

tar|tar|ize
tar|tar|izes

tar|tar|ize (cont.)
tar|tar|ized
tar|tar|iz|ing

Tar|tarus Greek
Mythology

Tar|tary (historical
region, Asia and E.
Europe)

tart|ily

tarti|ness

tart|let +s

tart|ly

tart|ness
(sharpness,
acidity)

tar|trate +s

tar|tra|zine

tarty
tart|ier
tarti|est

Tar|zan +s
(fictional hero;
strong or agile
man)

tash
tashes
(= moustache)

Tashi lama +s

Tash|kent (capital
of Uzbekistan)

task +s +ed +ing

task force +s

task|mas|ter +s

task|mis|tress
task|mis|tresses

Tas|man, Abel
Jans|zoon (Dutch
navigator)

Tas|mania (island
and state,
Australia)

Tas|man|ian +s

Tas|man Sea
(between Australia
and New Zealand)

Tass (Soviet news
agency; now
ITAR-Tass)

tass
tasses
(cup)

tas|sel
tas|sels
tas|selled Br.
tas|seled Am.
tas|sel|ling Br.
tas|sel|ing Am.

tas|sie +s

Tasso, Tor|quato
(Italian poet and
dramatist)

taste
tastes
tasted
tast|ing

taste|able

taste bud +s

taste|ful

taste|ful|ly

taste|ful|ness

taste|less

taste|less|ly

taste|less|ness

taster +s

tasti|ly

tasti|ness

tast|ing +s

tasty
tasti|er
tasti|est

tat
tats
tat|ted
tat|ting

ta-ta (goodbye.
⚠ tartar, tartare)

tat|ami +s

Tatar +s (use
Tartar)

Tatar|stan
(republic, Russia)

Tate, Nahum (Irish
dramatist)

Tate Gal|lery (in
London)

tater +s (= potato)

Tati, Jacques
(French film
director)

Tati|ana

tat|ler +s (archaic;
= tattler)

tatou +s

Tatra Moun|tains
(in E. Europe)

Tat|ras (= Tatra
Mountains)

tat|ter +s

tat|ter|de|ma|lion
+s

tat|tered

Tat|ter|sall,
Rich|ard (English
horseman)

tat|ter|sall +s
(fabric)

Tat|ter|salls
(English horse
auctioneers)

tat|tery

tat|tie +s (= potato.
⚠ tatty)

tat|tily

tat|ti|ness

tat|ting (lace)

tat|tle

tat|tles

tat|tled

tat|tling

tat|tler +s

tattle-tale +s

tat|too +s +ed
+ing

tat|too|er +s

tat|too|ist +s

tatty
tat|tier
tat|ti|est
(tattered; tawdry.
⚠ tattie)

Tatum, Art
(American jazz
pianist)

tau +s (Greek
letter. ⚠ taw, tor,
tore, torr)

tau cross
tau crosses

taught (past tense
and past participle
of teach. ⚠ taut,
tort, torte)

taunt +s +ed +ing

taunt|er +s

taunt|ing|ly

Taun|ton (town,
England)

tau par|ticle +s

taupe +s (colour.
⚠ tope)

Taupo (town, New
Zealand)

Taupo, Lake (in
New Zealand)

Tau|ranga (port,
New Zealand)

Taur|ean +s

taur|ine

taur|om|achy
taur|om|achies

Taurus
(constellation;
sign of zodiac;
Stock Exchange.
⚠ torus)

Taurus
Moun|tains (in
Turkey)

taut +er +est (tight.
⚠ taught, tort,
torte)

taut|en +s +ed
+ing

taut|ly

taut|ness

tau|tog +s
tauto|logic
tauto|logic|al
tauto|logic|al¦ly
tau|tolo¦gise *Br.*
  (use tautologize)
    tau|tolo¦gises
    tau|tolo¦gised
    tau|tolo¦gis¦ing
tau|tolo¦gist +s
tau|tolo¦gize
    tau|tolo¦gizes
    tau|tolo¦gized
    tau|tolo¦giz¦ing
tau|tolo¦gous
tau|tol¦ogy
    tau|tolo¦gies
tauto|mer +s
tauto|mer¦ic
tau|to¦mer¦ism
tau|toph¦ony
    tau|toph¦onies
tav¦ern +s
tav¦erna +s
Tav¦ern|ers (in
  'Lord's
  Taverners')
taw +s +ed +ing
  (make into
  leather; marble.
  △ tau, tor, tore,
  torr)
taw|drily
taw¦dri|ness
taw¦dry
    taw|drier
    taw¦dri|est
tawer +s
taw¦ni|ness
tawny
    taw|nier
    taw¦ni|est
taws
  plural taws
  (use tawse)
tawse +s
tax
    taxes
    taxed
    tax¦ing
taxa (plural of
  taxon. △ taxer)
tax|abil¦ity
tax|able
tax|ation
tax col|lect¦or +s
tax-deduct¦ible
tax-efficient
taxer +s (person
  who levies a tax.
  △ taxa)
tax-exempt

tax-free
taxi +s *noun*
taxi
    tax¦ies
    tax¦ied
    taxi|ing *or*
    taxy|ing
    verb
taxi|cab +s
taxi|der¦mal
taxi|der¦mic
taxi|der¦mist +s
taxi|dermy
taxi driver +s
taxi man
    taxi men
taxi|meter +s
tax|ing¦ly
taxis (plural of taxi)
taxis
    taxes
    Surgery; Biology;
    Grammar
taxi|way +s
tax|less
tax¦man
    tax¦men
taxon
    taxa
taxo|nom¦ic
taxo|nom¦ic|al
taxo|nom¦ic|al¦ly
tax|onomy
    tax|ono¦mies
tax|pay¦er +s
tax|pay¦ing
tax-saving
Tay (river,
  Scotland)
Tay, Firth of
  (estuary,
  Scotland)
tay|berry
    tay|berries
Tay¦lor, Eliza|beth
  (American
  actress)
Tay¦lor, Jer¦emy
  (English
  churchman)
Tay¦lor, Zach|ary
  (American
  president)
Tay¦myr
  Pen|in¦sula (use
  Taimyr
  Peninsula)
Tay–Sachs
  dis|ease
Tay|side (region,
  Scotland)

tazza +s
T-bar +s
Tbil¦isi (capital of
  Georgia)
T-bone +s
T-cell +s
Tchai|kov¦sky,
  Pyotr (Russian
  composer)
te (*Music.* △ tea,
  tee, ti)
tea
    teas
    teaed *or* tea'd
    tea¦ing
    (drink; take tea.
    △ te, tee, ti)
tea bag +s
tea-ball +s
tea-bread +s
tea break +s
tea|cake +s
teach
    teaches
    taught
    teach|ing
teach|abil¦ity
teach|able
teach|able|ness
teach¦er +s
teach|er¦ly
tea chest +s
teach-in +s
teach|ing +s
Teachta Dála
    Teachti Dála
    (member of Irish
    parliament)
tea clip|per +s
tea cosy
    tea cos¦ies
tea¦cup +s
tea¦cup|ful +s
teak +s
teal
    plural teal *or* teals
tea leaf
    tea leaves
team +s +ed +ing
    (group; form a
    team. △ teem)
team-mate +s
team play¦er +s
team|ster +s
team-teaching
team|work
tea party
    tea par¦ties
tea plant|er +s
tea¦pot +s

tea¦poy +s
tear
    tears
    tore
    tear|ing
    torn
    (rip; pull; rush;
    etc. △ tare)
tear +s (fluid in
  eyes. △ tier)
tear|able
tear|away +s
tear|drop +s
tear duct +s
tear¦er +s
tear|ful
tear|ful¦ly
tear|ful|ness
tear gas
    tear gases
    noun
tear-gas
    tear-gasses
    tear-gassed
    tear-gassing
    attributive and verb
tear-jerker +s
tear-jerking
tear|less
tear|less¦ly
tear|less|ness
tear|like
tear-off *adjective*
tea|room +s
tea rose +s
tear sheet +s
tear-stained
teary
tease
    teases
    teased
    teas|ing
tea¦sel +s +ed
    +ing
tea|sel¦er +s
teaser +s
tea¦set +s
tea shop +s
teas|ing¦ly
tea|spoon +s
tea|spoon|ful +s
tea-strainer +s
teat +s
tea|time +s
tea towel +s
tea tray +s
tea-tree +s (shrub.
  △ ti-tree)
tea|zel +s +ed
    +ing (use teasel)

tea¦zle (use teasel)
  tea¦zles
  tea¦zled
  teaz|ling
Tebet (Jewish
  month)
tec +s (= detective;
  technical college)
tech +s (= technical
  college;
  technology)
techie +s
  (technology
  enthusiast.
  ⚠ tetchy)
tech|ne¦tium
tech|nic +s
tech|nical +s
tech¦ni¦cal|ity
  tech¦ni¦cal|ities
tech¦nic|al¦ly
tech¦nic|al|ness
tech¦ni¦cian +s
tech¦ni¦cist +s
Tech¦ni|color
  (cinematographic
  process) Propr.
tech¦ni|color Am.
  (vivid colour;
  artificial brilliance;
  Br. technicolour)
tech¦ni|colored
  Am.
tech¦ni|col¦our Br.
tech¦ni|col¦oured
  Br.
tech|nique +s
techno
tech|no|bab¦ble
tech|noc¦racy
  tech|noc¦ra¦cies
tech|no|crat +s
tech|no|crat¦ic
tech|no|crat¦ic|
          al¦ly
tech|no|logic|al
tech|no|logic|al¦ly
tech|nolo¦gist +s
tech|nol¦ogy
  tech|nolo¦gies
tech|no|phile +s
tech|no|phobe +s
tech|no|pho¦bia
tech|no|pho¦bic
techy (technology
  enthusiast; use
  techie)
  tech|ies
techy (irritable; use
  tetchy)
  tech|ier
  techi|est

tec|ton¦ic
tec|ton¦ic|al¦ly
tec|ton¦ics
tec|tor¦ial
tec|trix
  tec|tri¦ces
Ted +s (= Teddy
  boy; name)
ted
  teds
  ted¦ded
  ted|ding
  (turn hay etc.)
ted¦der +s
Teddy (name)
teddy
  ted|dies
  (teddy bear;
  garment)
teddy bear +s
Teddy boy +s
Te Deum +s
  (hymn. ⚠ tedium)
te|di|ous
te|di|ous¦ly
te|di|ous|ness
te|dium (boredom.
  ⚠ Te Deum)
tee
  tees
  teed
  tee¦ing
  (in golf etc. ⚠ te,
  tea, ti)
tee-hee
  tee-hees
  tee-heed
  tee-heeing
teem +s +ed +ing
  (be full; flow
  copiously.
  ⚠ team)
teen +s
teen|age
teen|aged
teen|ager +s
teens
teensy
  teen|sier
  teen|si|est
teensy-weensy
teeny
  teen|ier
  teeni|est
teeny-bop
teeny-bopper +s
teeny-weeny
tee¦pee +s (use
  tepee)
Tees (river,
  England)

tee shirt +s (use T-
  shirt)
Tees|side (region,
  England)
tee¦ter +s +ed +ing
teeth (plural of
  tooth)
teethe
  teethes
  teethed
  teeth¦ing
  verb
teeth¦ing ring +s
tee|total
tee|total¦er Am. +s
tee|total|ism
tee|total|ler Br. +s
tee|total¦ly
tee|totum +s
teff +s
TEFL (= teaching of
  English as a
  foreign language)
Tef¦lon Propr.
teg +s
Tegu¦ci|galpa (city,
  Honduras)
tegu|lar
tegu|lar¦ly
tegu|ment +s
tegu|men|tal
tegu|men|tary
te-hee (use tee-
  hee)
  te-hees
  te-heed
  te-heeing
Teh¦ran (capital of
  Iran)
Teil|hard de
  Char|din, Pierre
  (French Jesuit
  philosopher)
Te Kan¦awa, Kiri
  (New Zealand
  soprano)
tek|nonym|ous
tek|nonymy
tek|tite +s
tel|aes|the¦sia Br.
  (Am. telesthesia)
tel|aes|thet¦ic Br.
  (Am. telesthetic)
tela|mon
  tela|mo¦nes
Tel Aviv (city,
  Israel)
telco +s
tele-ad +s
tele|bank¦ing
tele|cam¦era +s

tele|cast
  tele|casts
  tele|cast
  tele|cast|ing
tele|cast¦er +s
tele|cine
tele|comms
  (= telecommunica-
  tions)
tele|com¦mu¦ni|
        ca¦tion +s
tele|com¦mute
  tele|com¦mutes
  tele|com¦muted
  tele|com¦mut¦ing
tele|com¦muter +s
tele|coms
  (= telecommunica-
  tions)
tele|con¦fer¦ence
  +s
tele|con¦fer|
        en¦cing
tele|cot¦tage +s
tele|cot¦ta¦ging
tel|edu +s (badger)
tele-evangel¦ism
  (use
  televangelism)
tele-evangel¦ist +s
  (use
  televangelist)
tele|fac¦sim¦ile +s
tele|fax
  tele|faxes
  Propr.
tele|fax
  tele|faxes
  tele|faxed
  tele|fax|ing
tele|film +s
tele|gen¦ic
tele|gon¦ic
tel|egony
tele|gram +s
tele|graph +s +ed
  +ing
tel¦eg|raph¦er +s
tel¦eg|raph|ese
tele|graph¦ic
tel¦eg|raph¦ic|al¦ly
tel¦eg|raph|ist +s
tel¦eg|raphy
Tel¦egu (use
  Telugu)
  plural Tel¦egu or
  Tel¦egus
tele|kin¦esis
  tele|kin¦eses
tele|kin¦et¦ic
Tel¦ema|chus
  Greek Mythology

Tele|mann, Georg
  Phil|ipp (German
  composer)
tele|mark +s +ed
  +ing
tele|mar¦ket¦er +s
tele|mar¦ket|ing
tele|mes¦sage +s
tel|em¦eter +s +ed
  +ing
tele|met¦ric
tel|em¦etry
teleo|logic
teleo|logic¦al
teleo|logic¦al¦ly
tele|olo¦gism
tele|olo¦gist +s
tele|ology
  tele|olo¦gies
tele|ost +s
tele|path +s
tele|path¦ic
tele|path¦ic|al¦ly
tel¦ep¦ath¦ise *Br.*
  (use telepathize)
  tel¦ep¦ath¦ises
  tel¦ep¦ath¦ised
  tel¦ep¦ath¦is¦ing
tel¦ep¦ath¦ist +s
tel¦ep¦ath¦ize
  tel¦ep¦ath¦izes
  tel¦ep¦ath¦ized
  tel¦ep¦ath¦iz¦ing
tel|ep¦athy
tele|phone
  tele|phones
  tele|phoned
  tele|phon¦ing
tele|phoner +s
tele|phon¦ic
tele|phon¦ic|al¦ly
tel¦eph|on|ist +s
tel¦eph|ony
tele|photo +s
tele|photo|
      graph¦ic
tele|photo|
    graph¦ic|al¦ly
tele|pho¦tog¦raphy
tele|point +s
tele|port +s +ed
  +ing
tele|por¦ta¦tion
tele|pres¦ence
tele|print¦er +s
tele|prompt¦er +s
tele|re¦cord +s +ed
  +ing
tele|re¦cord|ing +s
tel|ergy
tele|sales

tele|scope
  tele|scopes
  tele|scoped
  tele|scop¦ing
tele|scop¦ic
tele|scop¦ic|al¦ly
tele|shop¦ping
tele|soft¦ware
tel|es¦the¦sia *Am.*
  (*Br.* telaesthesia)
tel|es¦thet¦ic *Am.*
  (*Br.* telaesthetic)
tele|tex
  tele|texes
  (electronic text
  transmission)
  Propr.
tele|text (text and
  graphics
  transmitted to
  televisions)
Tele|text Ltd
  (teletext service
  on British
  Independent
  Television) *Propr.*
tele|thon +s
tele|type +s *Propr.*
tele|type|writer +s
tele|van¦gel|ism
tele|van¦gel|ist +s
tele|view +s +ed
  +ing
tele|view¦er +s
tele|vis¦able
tele|vise
  tele|vises
  tele|vised
  tele|vis¦ing
tele|vi¦sion +s
tele|visor +s
tele|vis¦ual
tele|visu¦al¦ly
tele|work +s +ed
  +ing
tele|work¦er +s
telex
  tel|exes
  tel|exed
  tel|ex|ing
Tel|ford (town,
  England)
Tel|ford, Thomas
  (Scottish civil
  engineer)
Tell, Wil|liam
  (legendary Swiss
  hero)
tell
  tells
  told
  tell|ing

tell|able
Tell el-Amarna
  (site of Akhetaten,
  Egypt)
Tel¦ler, Ed¦ward
  (Hungarian-born
  American
  physicist)
tell¦er +s
tell¦er|ship +s
tell|ing¦ly
telling-off
  tellings-off
tell-tale +s
tel¦lur|ate +s
tel¦lur|ian +s
tel¦lur¦ic
tel¦lur|ide +s
tel¦lur|ite +s
tel¦lur|ium
tel¦lur|ous
telly
  tel|lies
telo|phase +s
tel|pher +s
tel|pher|age
tel|son +s
Tel|star
Tel¦ugu
  plural Tel¦ugu *or*
  Tel|ugus
tem|blor +s
tem¦er|ari¦ous
tem¦er|ity
Temne
  plural Temne *or*
  Tem¦nes
temp +s +ed +ing
tem|peh
tem|per +s +ed
  +ing
tem|pera
tem|per|able
tem|pera|ment +s
tem|pera|men¦tal
tem|pera|
      men¦tal¦ly
tem|per|ance
tem¦per|ate
tem¦per|ate¦ly
tem¦per|ate|ness
tem|pera|tive
tem|pera|ture +s
tem|pered¦ly
tem|per¦er +s
tem|per|some
Tem|pest, Marie
  (English actress)
tem|pest +s
tem|pes¦tu|ous
tem|pes¦tu|ous¦ly

tem|pes¦tu¦ous|
        ness
tempi
Tem|plar +s (*Law.*
  △ Knight
  Templar)
tem|plate +s
Tem|ple, Shir|ley
  (American actress
  and diplomat)
tem|ple +s
tem|plet +s (use
  template)
tempo
  tem¦pos *or* tempi
tem|pora (in 'O
  tempora, O
  mores'.
  △ tempura)
tem|poral
tem|por¦al|ity
  tem|por¦al|ities
tem|por¦al¦ly
tem|por¦ar|ily
tem|por¦ari|ness
tem|por¦ary
  tem|po¦rar|ies
tem|por¦isa¦tion
  Br. (use
  temporization)
tem|por¦ise *Br.*
  (use temporize)
  tem|por|ises
  tem|por|ised
  tem|por|is¦ing
tem|por¦iser *Br.* +s
  (use temporizer)
tem|por¦iza¦tion
tem|por¦ize
  tem|por|izes
  tem|por|ized
  tem|por|iz¦ing
tem|por¦izer +s
tempt +s +ed +ing
tempt|abil¦ity
tempt|able
temp|ta¦tion +s
tempt|er +s
tempt|ing¦ly
temp|tress
  temp|tresses
tem|pura
  (Japanese dish.
  △ tempora)
ten +s
ten|abil¦ity
ten|able
ten|able|ness
ten|ace +s
ten|acious
ten|acious¦ly
ten|acious|ness

ten|acity
ten|acu|lum
   ten|acula
ten|ancy
   ten|an|cies
   (status or period
   of being a tenant.
   △tenency)
ten|ant +s +ed
   +ing
ten|ant|able
ten|ant|less
ten|ant|ry
tench
   plural tench
tend +s +ed +ing
ten|dance
ten|dency
   ten|den|cies
ten|den|tious
ten|den|tious|ly
ten|den|tious|ness
ten|der +s +ed
   +ing +er +est
ten|der|er +s
tender-eyed
ten|der|foot +s
tender-hearted
tender-
   hearted|ness
ten|der|ise *Br.* (use
   tenderize)
   ten|der|ises
   ten|der|ised
   ten|der|is|ing
ten|der|iser *Br.* +s
   (use tenderizer)
ten|der|ize
   ten|der|izes
   ten|der|ized
   ten|der|iz|ing
ten|der|izer +s
ten|der|loin +s
ten|der|ly
ten|der|ness
ten|din|itis
ten|din|ous
ten|don +s
ten|don|itis (use
   tendinitis)
ten|dril +s
Tene|brae
tene|brous
tene|ment +s
tene|men|tal
tene|men|tary
tene|ment house
   +s
ten|ency
   ten|en|cies
   (in 'locum

ten|ency (*cont.*)
   tenency'.
   △tenancy)
Ten|er|ife (Canary
   Islands)
ten|es|mus
tenet +s
ten|fold
ten-gallon hat +s
Teng Hsiao-p'ing
   (= Deng
   Xiaoping)
tenia *Am.* +s (*Br.*
   taenia)
Ten|iers, David
   (Flemish painter)
teni|oid *Am.* (*Br.*
   taenioid)
ten-iron +s
Ten|nant Creek
   (town, Australia)
tenné
ten|ner +s
   (banknote.
   △tenor)
Ten|nes|see (river
   and state, USA)
Ten|niel, John
   (English
   illustrator)
ten|nis
ten|nis play|er +s
tenno +s
tenny (use tenné)
Ten|ny|son,
   Al|fred, Lord
   (English poet)
Ten|ny|son|ian
Ten|och|ti|tlán
   (ancient city,
   Mexico)
tenon +s +ed +ing
ten|on|er +s
tenon saw +s
tenor +s (singer.
   △tenner)
ten|or|ist +s
teno|syno|vitis
ten|ot|omy
   ten|oto|mies
ten|pence +s
ten|penny
   ten|pen|nies
ten|pin +s
ten|rec +s
tense
   tenses
   tensed
   tens|ing
   tenser
   tens|est
tense|less

tense|ly
tense|ness
ten|sile
ten|sil|ity
ten|sim|eter +s
ten|sion +s +ed
   +ing
ten|sion|al
ten|sion|al|ly
ten|sion|er +s
ten|sion|less
ten|sity
ten|son +s
ten|sor +s
ten|sor|ial
tent +s +ed +ing
ten|tacle +s
ten|tac|led
ten|tacu|lar
ten|tacu|late
tent|age
ten|ta|tive +s
ten|ta|tive|ly
ten|ta|tive|ness
tent-bed +s
ten|ter +s
ten|ter|hook +s
tent-fly
   tent-flies
tenth +s
tenth|ly
tenth-rate
tent-like
tent peg +s
tent-pegging
tent stitch
   tent stitches
ten|uis
   ten|ues
tenu|ity
tenu|ous
tenu|ous|ly
tenu|ous|ness
ten|ure +s
ten|ured
ten|ur|ial
ten|uri|al|ly
ten|uto +s
ten-week stock +s
   (plant)
Ten|zing Nor|gay
   (Sherpa
   mountaineer)
ten|zon +s
teo|calli +s
teo|sinte
Teo|ti|hua|cán
   (ancient city,
   Mexico)
tepal +s
tepee +s
tephra +s

Tepic (city,
   Mexico)
tepid
tep|id|arium
   tep|id|ar|iums *or*
   tep|id|aria
tep|id|ity
tep|id|ly
tep|id|ness
te|quila +s
tera|flop +s
terai +s
tera|kihi
   plural tera|kihi
tera|metre +s
ter|aph
   ter|aph|im
ter|ato|gen +s
tera|to|gen|ic
tera|togeny
tera|to|logic|al
tera|tolo|gist +s
tera|tol|ogy
   tera|tolo|gies
tera|toma
   tera|to|mas *or*
   tera|to|mata
tera|watt +s
ter|bium
terce +s (time for
   prayer. △terse)
ter|cel +s
ter|cen|ten|ary
   ter|cen|ten|ar|ies
ter|cen|ten|nial +s
ter|cet +s
tere|bene
tere|binth +s
tere|binth|ine
tere|bra
   plural tere|bras *or*
   tere|brae
tere|brant +s
ter|edo +s
Ter|ence (name)
Ter|ence (Roman
   comic dramatist)
Ter|eng|ganu (use
   Trengganu)
ter|eph|thal|ate +s
ter|eph|thal|ic
Ter|esa *also*
   Ther|esa
   (name)
Ter|esa, Mother
   (nun and
   missionary in
   India)
Ter|esa of Ávila
   (Spanish saint)
Ter|esa of Lis|ieux
   (French saint)

Ter¦esh|kova,
  Val¦en|tina
  (Russian
  cosmonaut)
Tere|sina (port,
  Brazil)
ter¦ete
ter¦gal
ter|gi¦ver|sate
  ter|gi¦ver|sates
  ter|gi¦ver|sated
  ter|gi¦ver|sat¦ing
ter|gi¦ver|sa¦tion
  +s
ter|gi¦ver|sa¦tor +s
teri|yaki
term +s +ed +ing
Ter¦ma|gant +s
  (imaginary deity)
ter¦ma|gant +s
  (virago)
ter¦min|able
ter¦min|able|ness
ter¦min|al +s
ter¦min|al¦ly
ter¦min|ate
  ter¦min|ates
  ter¦min|ated
  ter¦min|at¦ing
ter¦min|ation +s
ter¦min|ation¦al
ter¦min|ator +s
ter¦min¦er (in 'oyer
  and terminer')
ter¦mini
ter¦min|ism
ter¦min|ist +s
ter¦mino|logic¦al
ter¦mino|logic¦
      al¦ly
ter¦min|olo¦gist +s
ter¦min|ology
  ter¦min|olo¦gies
ter¦minus
  ter¦mini
ter|minus ad quem
ter|minus ante
  quem
ter|minus a quo
ter¦mit|arium
  ter¦mit|aria
ter¦mit|ary
  ter¦mit|ar¦ies
ter¦mite +s
term|less
term¦ly
ter¦mor +s
term-time *noun*
  and attributive
tern +s (bird.
  ⚠ terne, turn)
tern|ary

tern|ate
tern|ate¦ly
terne (metal.
  ⚠ tern, turn)
terne-plate
tero|tech¦nol¦ogy
ter|pene +s
Terp|sich¦ore
  Greek and Roman
  Mythology
Terp|sich¦or|ean
terra alba
ter|race
  ter|races
  ter|raced
  ter|ra¦cing
terra|cotta +s
terra firma
terra|form +s +ed
  +ing
ter|rain +s
terra in¦cog|nita
terra|mara
  terra|mare
terra|mare +s
Terra|pin +s
  (prefabricated
  building) *Propr.*
terra|pin +s (turtle)
ter|raque|ous
ter|rar|ium
  ter|raria
terra sigil|lata
Ter|rassa (use
  Tarrasa)
ter|razzo +s
Terre Haute (city,
  USA)
ter|rene (of the
  earth; earthly,
  worldly.
  ⚠ terrine)
terre|plein +s
ter¦res|trial +s
ter¦res|tri|al¦ly
ter¦ret +s
terre-verte +s
ter|rible
ter|rible|ness
ter|ribly
ter|rico|lous
Ter|rier +s
  (member of the
  Territorial Army)
ter|rier +s (dog)
ter|rif¦ic
ter|rif¦ic|al¦ly
ter|ri|fier +s
ter|rify
  ter|ri|fies
  ter|ri|fied
  ter|ri¦fy|ing

ter|ri¦fy|ing¦ly
ter|ri¦gen|ous
ter|rine +s (coarse
  pâté; earthenware
  dish. ⚠ terrene)
ter|rit +s (use
  terret)
ter|ri|tor|ial +s
ter|ri|tori|al|
  isa|tion *Br.* (use
  territorialization)
ter|ri|tori|al|ise *Br.*
  (use territorialize)
  ter|ri|tori|al|ises
  ter|ri|tori|al|ised
  ter|ri|tori|al|is¦ing
ter|ri|tori|al|ism
ter|ri|tori|al|ity
ter|ri|tori|al|
      iza|tion
ter|ri|tori|al|ize
  ter|ri|tori|al|izes
  ter|ri|tori|al|ized
  ter|ri|tori|al|iz¦ing
ter|ri|tori|al¦ly
ter|ri|tory
  ter|ri|tor|ies
ter¦ror +s
ter¦ror|isa¦tion *Br.*
  (use
  terrorization)
ter¦ror|ise *Br.* (use
  terrorize)
  ter¦ror|ises
  ter¦ror|ised
  ter¦ror|is¦ing
ter¦ror|iser *Br.* +s
  (use terrorizer)
ter¦ror|ism
ter¦ror|ist +s
ter¦ror|is|tic
ter¦ror|is|tic|al¦ly
ter¦ror|iza¦tion
ter¦ror|ize
  ter¦ror|izes
  ter¦ror|ized
  ter¦ror|iz¦ing
ter¦ror|izer +s
terror-stricken
Terry (name)
Terry, Ellen
  (English actress)
terry
  ter|ries
  (fabric)
terse
  terser
  ters¦est
  (brief; curt.
  ⚠ terce)
terse¦ly
terse|ness

ter|tian
Ter|tiary *Geology*
ter|tiary
  ter|tiar¦ies
  (third; monk)
ter|tium quid
Ter|tul|lian
  (Carthaginian
  theologian)
ter|va¦lent
Tery|lene *Propr.*
terza rima
ter|zetto
  ter|zet¦tos *or*
  ter|zetti
TESL (= teaching of
  English as a
  second language)
Tesla, Ni¦kola
  (Croatian-born
  American
  electrical
  engineer; coil)
tesla +s (unit)
TESOL (= teaching
  of English to
  speakers of other
  languages)
Tess
TESSA +s (= tax
  exempt special
  savings account)
Tessa (name)
tes¦sel|late
  tes¦sel|lates
  tes¦sel|lated
  tes¦sel|lat¦ing
tes¦sel|la¦tion +s
tes|sera
  tes|serae
tes|seral
Tes|sin (French
  and German name
  for Ticino)
tes|si¦tura +s
test +s +ed +ing
testa
  tes¦tae
  (seed-coat.
  ⚠ tester)
test|abil¦ity
test|able
test|aceous
Test Act +s
tes¦tacy
  tes|ta|cies
tes¦ta|ment +s
tes¦ta|ment|ary
tes|tate +s
tes|ta¦tor +s *male*

tes¦ta¦trix

  tes¦ta¦tri¦ces
  female

Test-Ban Treaty

test bed +s

test case +s

test drive +s *noun*

test-drive

  test-drives

  test-drove

  test-driven

  test-driving

  verb

test¦ee +s

test¦er +s (person
or thing that tests;
sample; canopy.
△ testa)

tes¦tes (plural of
testis)

test flight +s

test-fly

  test-flies

  test-flew

  test-flying

  test-flown

tes¦ticle +s

tes¦ticu¦lar

tes¦ticu¦late

tes¦ti¦fier +s

test¦ify

  testi¦fies

  testi¦fied

  testi¦fy¦ing

test¦ily

tes¦ti¦mo¦nial +s

tes¦ti¦mony

  tes¦ti¦monies

testi¦ness

test¦ing ground +s

tes¦tis

  tes¦tes

tes¦tos¦ter¦one

test piece +s

test pilot +s

test tube +s *noun*

test-tube *attributive*

tes¦tu¦din¦al

tes¦tudo

  tes¦tu¦dos or
  tes¦tu¦di¦nes

testy

  test¦ier

  testi¦est

tet¦an¦ic

tet¦an¦ic¦al¦ly

tet¦an¦ise *Br.* (use
tetanize)

  tet¦an¦ises

  tet¦an¦ised

  tet¦an¦is¦ing

tet¦an¦ize

  tet¦an¦izes

  tet¦an¦ized

  tet¦an¦iz¦ing

tet¦an¦oid

tet¦anus

tet¦any

tetch¦ily

tetchi¦ness

tetchy

  tetch¦ier

  tetchi¦est

  (irritable.
  △ techie)

tête-à-tête +s

tête-bêche

tether +s +ed +ing

Te¦thys (*Greek
Mythology*; moon
of Saturn; former
ocean)

Tet Of¦fen¦sive (in
Vietnam War)

Té¦touan (city,
Morocco)

tetra +s

tetra¦chlor¦ide

**tetra¦chloro¦
        ethyl¦ene**

tetra¦chord +s

tetra¦cyc¦lic

tetra¦cyc¦line +s

tet¦rad +s

tetra¦dac¦tyl +s

tetra¦dac¦tyl¦ous

tetra¦ethyl

tetra¦gon +s

tet¦rag¦on¦al

tet¦rag¦on¦al¦ly

tetra¦gram +s

**Tetra¦gram¦ma¦
        ton**

tet¦ragyn¦ous

tetra¦he¦dral

tetra¦he¦dron

  tetra¦he¦dra

**tetra¦hydro¦
      canna¦binol**

tet¦ralogy

  tet¦ralo¦gies

tet¦ram¦er¦ous

tet¦ram¦eter +s

tetra¦morph +s

tet¦ran¦drous

tetra¦plegia

tetra¦plegic +s

tetra¦ploid +s

tetra¦pod +s

tet¦rapod¦ous

tet¦rap¦ter¦ous

tet¦rarch +s

tet¦rarch¦ate +s

tet¦rarch¦ic¦al

tet¦rarchy

  tet¦rarch¦ies

tetra¦stich +s

tetra¦style +s

tetra¦syl¦lab¦ic

tetra¦syl¦lable +s

tet¦rath¦lon +s

tetra¦tom¦ic

tetra¦va¦lent

tet¦rode +s

tet¦rox¦ide

tet¦ter +s

Teuton +s

Teut¦on¦ic

Teut¦oni¦cism

Tevet (use Tebet)

Texan +s

Texas (state, USA)

Tex-Mex

text +s

text¦book +s

text¦book¦ish

tex¦tile +s

text¦less

text¦ual

text¦ual¦ism

text¦ual¦ist

textu¦al¦ity

text¦ual¦ly

tex¦tural

tex¦tur¦al¦ly

tex¦ture

  tex¦tures

  tex¦tured

  tex¦tur¦ing

tex¦ture¦less

tex¦tur¦ise *Br.* (use
texturize)

  tex¦tur¦ises

  tex¦tur¦ised

  tex¦tur¦is¦ing

tex¦tur¦ize

  tex¦tur¦izes

  tex¦tur¦ized

  tex¦tur¦iz¦ing

**Thack¦eray,
Wil¦liam
Make¦peace**
(British novelist)

Thad¦daeus
(Apostle)

Thai

  plural **Thai** *or*
  Thais

Thai¦land

Thai¦land, Gulf of
(inlet of South
China Sea)

Thai¦land¦er +s

thal¦am¦ic

thal¦amus

  thal¦ami

thal¦as¦sae¦mia *Br.*

thal¦as¦semia *Am.*

thal¦as¦sic

**thal¦as¦so¦
        ther¦apy**

thaler +s (German
coin. △ tala)

Tha¦les (Greek
philosopher)

Tha¦lia (*Greek and
Roman Mythology*;
name)

thal¦ido¦mide

thalli

thal¦lic

thal¦lium

thal¦lo¦gen

thal¦loid

thal¦lo¦phyte +s

thal¦lous

thal¦lus

  thalli

thal¦weg +s

Thames (river,
England; shipping
area, North Sea)

Tham¦muz
(Jewish month.
△ Tammuz)

than

than¦age +s

thana¦tol¦ogy

Thana¦tos

thane +s (English
or Scottish
landholder.
△ thegn)

thane¦dom +s

thane¦ship +s

thank +s +ed +ing

thank¦ful

thank¦ful¦ly

thank¦ful¦ness

thank¦less

thank¦less¦ly

thank¦less¦ness

thank-offering +s

thanks¦giv¦ing +s

thank you (actual
utterance)

thank-you +s
(instance of saying
'thank you')

thar +s (use tahr.
animal. △ ta, tar)

Thar Des¦ert (in
India and Pakistan)

that

  those

thatch

  thatches

thatch (*cont.*)
thatched
thatch|ing
Thatch|er,
Mar|ga|ret
(British prime
minister)
thatch|er +s
Thatch|er|ism
Thatch|er|ite +s
thauma|trope +s
thauma|turge +s
thauma|tur|gic
thauma|tur|gic|al
thauma|tur|gist +s
thauma|turgy
thaw +s +ed +ing
thaw|less
the (*definite article.*
△ thee)
the|an|dric
the|an|throp|ic
the|archy
the|arch|ies
the|ater *Am.* +s
theater|goer *Am.*
+s
theater|going *Am.*
theater-in-the-
round *Am.*
the|atre *Br.* +s
theatre|goer *Br.* +s
theatre|going *Br.*
theatre-in-the-
round *Br.*
the|at|ric +s
the|at|ri|cal +s
the|at|ri|cal|
isa|tion *Br.* (use
theatricalization)
the|at|ri|cal|ise *Br.*
(use theatricalize)
the|at|ri|cal|ises
the|at|ri|cal|ised
the|at|ri|cal|is|ing
the|at|ri|cal|ism
the|at|ri|cal|ity
the|at|ri|cal|
iza|tion
the|at|ri|cal|ize
the|at|ri|cal|izes
the|at|ri|cal|ized
the|at|ri|cal|iz|ing
the|at|ri|cal|ly
Theban +s
thebe
plural **thebe**
(Botswanan
currency)
Thebes (cities,
ancient Egypt and
Greece)

theca
the|cae
the|cate
thé dan|sant
thés dan|sants
thee (*archaic* = you
△ the)
theft +s
thegn +s (English
landholder.
△ thane)
theine (caffeine)
their (of or
belonging to them.
△ there, they're)
theirs (the one(s)
belonging to them.
△ there's)
their|selves (*dialect*
or *nonstandard*;
use themselves)
the|ism
the|ist +s
the|is|tic
the|is|tic|al
the|is|tic|al|ly
Thelma
them
the|mat|ic
the|mat|ic|al|ly
the|mat|ics
theme
themes
themed
them|ing
theme park +s
The|mis *Greek
Mythology*
The|mis|to|cles
(Athenian
statesman)
them|self prefer
themselves)
them|selves
then
the|nar +s
thence
thence|forth
thence|for'ward
Theo
Theo|bald
theo|bro|mine
theo|cen|tric
The|oc|racy, the
(Jewish
commonwealth)
the|oc|racy
the|oc|ra|cies
(divine
government)
the|oc|rasy
(mingling of
deities into one;

the|oc|rasy (*cont.*)
union of the soul
with God)
theo|crat +s
theo|crat|ic
theo|crat|ic|al|ly
The|oc|ri|tus
(Greek poet)
theo|di|cean
the|odicy
the|odi|cies
the|odo|lite +s
the|odo|lit|ic
Theo|dora
(Byzantine
empress; name)
Theo|dor|akis,
Mikis (Greek
composer)
Theo|dore
Theo|dor|ic (king
of the Ostrogoths)
Theo|dos|ius
(Roman emperor)
the|ogo|nist +s
the|ogony
the|ogo|nies
theo|lo|gian +s
theo|logic|al
theo|logic|al|ly
the|olo|gise *Br.*
(use theologize)
the|olo|gises
the|olo|gised
the|olo|gis|ing
the|olo|gist +s
the|olo|gize
the|olo|gizes
the|olo|gized
the|olo|giz|ing
the|ology
the|olo|gies
the|om|achy
the|om|achies
theo|mania
the|ophany
the|opha|nies
theo|phor|ic
Theo|phras|tus
(Greek
philosopher)
theo|phyl|line
the|op|neust
the|or|bist +s
the|orbo +s
the|orem +s
the|or|em|at|ic
the|or|et|ic
the|or|et|ic|al
the|or|et|ic|al|ly
the|or|et|ician +s

the|or|isa|tion *Br.*
(use theorization)
the|or|ise *Br.* (use
theorize)
the|or|ises
the|or|ised
the|or|is|ing
the|or|iser *Br.* +s
(use theorizer)
the|or|ist +s
the|or|iza|tion
the|or|ize
the|or|izes
the|or|ized
the|or|iz|ing
the|or|izer +s
the|ory
the|or|ies
theo|soph +s
the|oso|pher +s
theo|soph|ic
theo|soph|ic|al
theo|soph|ic|al|ly
the|oso|phise *Br.*
(use theosophize)
the|oso|phises
the|oso|phised
the|oso|phis|ing
the|oso|phist +s
the|oso|phize
the|oso|phizes
the|oso|phized
the|oso|phiz|ing
the|oso|phy
the|oso|phies
Thera (Greek
island)
Theran
thera|peut|ic
thera|peut|ic|al
thera|peut|ic|al|ly
thera|peut|ics
thera|peut|ist +s
ther|ap|ist +s
ther|ap|sid +s
ther|apy
ther|ap|ies
Thera|vada
Buddhism
there (in that place
etc. △ their,
they're)
there|about
there|abouts
there|after
there|anent
there|at
there|by
there|for (*archaic*
for that purpose)
there|fore (for that
reason)

there|from
there|in
there|in|after
there|in|before
there|in|to
there|of
there|on
there|out
there's (= there is.
⚠ theirs)
Ther|esa *also*
Ter|esa
(name)
Ther|esa, Mother
(use Teresa)
Thérèse of
Lis|ieux
(= Teresa of
Lisieux)
there|through
there|to
there|to|fore
there|under
there|unto
there|upon
there|with
there|with|al
ther|iac +s
theri|an|throp|ic
therio|morph|ic
therm +s
ther|mae
ther|mal +s
ther|mal|isa|tion
Br. (use
thermalization)
ther|mal|ise *Br.*
(use thermalize)
ther|mal|ises
ther|mal|ised
ther|mal|is|ing
ther|mal|iza|tion
ther|mal|ize
ther|mal|izes
ther|mal|ized
ther|mal|iz|ing
ther|mal|ly
ther|mic
thermi|dor
ther|mion +s
thermi|on|ic
ther|mi|on|ics
ther|mis|tor +s
ther|mit
ther|mite
thermo|chem|ical
thermo|
        chem|is|try
thermo|cline +s
thermo|couple +s
thermo|dynam|ic

thermo|dynam|
            ic|al
thermo|dynam|ic|
            al|ly
thermo|dynami|
            cist +s
thermo|dynam|ics
thermo|elec|tric
thermo|elec|tric|
            al|ly
thermo|
        elec|tri|city
thermo|gen|esis
thermo|gram +s
thermo|graph +s
thermo|graph|ic
therm|og|raphy
thermo|labile
thermo|lumin|
            es|cence
thermo|lumin|
            es|cent
therm|oly|sis
thermo|lyt|ic
therm|om|eter +s
thermo|met|ric
thermo|met|ric|al
thermo|met|ric|
            al|ly
therm|om|etry
thermo|nuclear
thermo|phile +s
thermo|phil|ic
thermo|pile +s
thermo|plas|tic +s
Therm|opy|lae
(coastal pass and
battle, Greece)
ther|mos
ther|moses
Propr.
thermo|set
thermo|set|ting
thermo|sphere +s
thermo|stable
thermo|stat +s
thermo|stat|ic
thermo|stat|ic|
            al|ly
thermo|tac|tic
thermo|tax|ic
thermo|taxis
thermo|trop|ic
thermo|trop|ism
thero|pod +s
the|saurus
    the|sauri *or*
    the|saur|uses
these
The|seus *Greek
Mythology*

thesis
    theses
thesp +s
thes|pian +s
Thes|pis (Greek
poet)
Thes|sal|ian +s
Thes|sa|lon|ian +s
Thes|sa|lon|ica
(Latin name for
Thessaloníki)
Thes|sa|lon|iki
(port, Greece)
Thes|saly (region,
Greece)
theta +s
The|tis *Greek
Mythology*
the|ur|gic
the|ur|gic|al
the|ur|gist +s
the|urgy
thew +s
they
they'd (= they had;
they would)
they'll (= they will;
they shall)
they're (= they are.
⚠ their, there)
they've (= they
have)
thia|min (use
thiamine)
thia|mine
thia|zide +s
thick +er +est
thick|en +s +ed
+ing
thick|en|er +s
thick|en|ing +s
thicket +s
thick|head +s
thick|head|ed
thick|head|ed|
                ness
thick|ish
thick-knee +s
thick|ly
thick|ness
    thick|nesses
    thick|nessed
    thick|ness|ing
thick|ness|er +s
thicko +s
thick|set +s
thick-skinned
thick-skulled
thief
    thieves
thieve
    thieves

thieve (*cont.*)
    thieved
    thiev|ing
thiev|ery
thieves (plural of
thief)
thiev|ish
thiev|ish|ly
thiev|ish|ness
thigh +s
thigh bone +s
thig|mo|trop|ic
thig|mo|trop|ism
thill +s
thill|er +s
thill-horse +s
thim|ble +s
thimble|ful +s
thimble|rig
thimble|rig|ger +s
Thim|phu (capital
of Bhutan)
thin
    thins
    thinned
    thin|ning
    thin|ner
    thin|nest
thine
thing +s
thing|ama|bob +s
thing|ama|jig +s
thing|am|bob +s
thing|amy (use
thingummy)
thing|amies
thingum +s
thing|uma|jig +s
(use thingamajig)
thing|ummy
    thing|um|mies
thingy
    thing|ies
think
    thinks
    thought
    think|ing
think|able
think|er +s
think-tank +s
thin|ly
thin|ner +s
thin|ness
thin|ning +s
thin|nish
thin-skinned
thio-acid
thiol +s
thio|pen|tone
thio|sul|phate
thio|urea

Thíra (Greek name for Thera)
third +s
third-best
third-class *adjective*
third¦ly
third-party *attributive*
third-rate *adjective*
thirst +s +ed +ing
thirst¦ily
thirsti¦ness
thirst¦less
thirsty
  thirst¦ier
  thirsti¦est
thir¦teen +s
thir¦teenth +s
thir¦ti¦eth +s
thirty
  thir¦ties
thirty-first, thirty-second, etc.
thirty¦fold
thirty-one, thirty-two, etc.
thirty-second note +s
thirty-something +s
thirty-two-mo
Thirty Years War
this
  these
Thisbe *Roman Mythology*
this¦tle +s
thistle¦down
this¦tly
thither
thixo¦trop¦ic
thix¦otropy
tho' (use though)
thole
  tholes
  tholes
  tholed
  thol¦ing
thole-pin +s
tho¦los
  tho¦loi
Thomas (Apostle and saint; name)
Thomas, Dylan (Welsh poet)
Thomas, Ed¦ward (English poet)
Thomas à Kem¦pis (German theologian)

Thomas Aqui¦nas (Italian saint)
Thom¦ism
Thom¦ist +s
Thom¦is¦tic
Thom¦is¦tic¦al
Thomp¦son, Daley (English athlete)
Thomp¦son, Fran¦cis (English poet)
Thom¦son, James (two Scottish poets)
Thom¦son, Jo¦seph John (English physicist)
Thom¦son, Wil¦liam (Lord Kelvin)
thong +s +ed +ing
Thor *Scandinavian Mythology*
thor¦ac¦al
thor¦acic
thorax
  thora¦ces *or* thor¦axes
Thor¦eau, Henry David (American writer)
thoria
thor¦ium
thorn +s
thorn apple +s
thorn¦back +s
thorn¦bill +s
thorn¦bush
  thorn¦bushes
Thorn¦dike, Sybil (English actress)
thorn¦ily
thorni¦ness
thorn¦less
thorn¦proof
thorn¦tail +s
thorny
  thorn¦ier
  thorni¦est
thor¦ough
thor¦ough¦bred +s
thor¦ough¦fare +s
thor¦ough¦going
thor¦ough¦ly
thor¦ough¦ness
thorough-paced
thorough-wax (use thorow-wax)
thorow-wax
thorp +s
thorpe +s (use thorp)

Thors¦havn (use Tórshavn)
Thor¦vald¦sen, Ber¦tel (Danish sculptor)
those
Thoth *Egyptian Mythology*
thou (*archaic* you)
thou
  plural thou *or* thous
(thousandth of an inch)
though
thought +s
thought¦ful
thought¦ful¦ly
thought¦ful¦ness
thought¦less
thought¦less¦ly
thought¦less¦ness
thought-provok¦ing
thought-reader +s
thought-reading
thought-wave +s
thou¦sand +s
thou¦sand¦fold
Thou¦sand Is¦land (mayonnaise)
Thou¦sand Is¦lands (in St Lawrence River, N. America; in Indonesia)
thou¦sandth +s
Thrace (ancient country, part of E. Balkan Peninsula; region, Greece)
Thra¦cian +s
thral¦dom +s
thrall +s
thrash
  thrashes
  thrashed
  thrash¦ing
thrash¦er +s
thrash¦ing +s
thras¦on¦ical
thras¦on¦ic¦al¦ly
thrawn
thread +s +ed +ing
thread¦bare
thread¦er +s
thread¦fin +s
thread¦fish
  plural thread¦fish *or* thread¦fishes
thread-like

Thread¦nee¦dle Street (in London)
thread¦worm +s
thready
  thread¦ier
  threadi¦est
threat +s
threat¦en +s +ed +ing
threat¦en¦er +s
threat¦en¦ing +s
threat¦en¦ing¦ly
three +s
three-cornered
three-decker +s
three-dimension¦al
three¦fold
three-handed
three-iron +s
three-legged race +s
three-line whip +s
Three Mile Is¦land (site of nuclear power station, USA)
three¦ness
three¦pence +s
three¦penny
  three¦pen¦nies
three-phase
three-piece
three-ply
three-point
three-pronged
three-quarter +s
three¦score
three¦some +s
three-way
three-wheeler +s
threm¦ma¦tol¦ogy
thren¦ode +s
thren¦odial
thren¦od¦ic
thren¦od¦ist +s
thren¦ody
  thren¦odies
threo¦nine
thresh
  threshes
  threshed
  thresh¦ing
thresh¦er +s
thresh¦ing floor +s
thresh¦ing ma¦chine +s
thresh¦old +s
threw (past tense of throw. △through)

thrice
thrift +s
thrift|ily
thrifti|ness
thrift|less
thrift|less|ly
thrift|less|ness
thrifty
  thrift|ier
  thrifti|est
thrill +s +ed +ing
thrill|er +s
thrill|ing|ly
thrips
  plural thrips
thrive
  thrives
  thrived *or* throve
  thriv|ing
  thriven
thro' (use through)
throat +s
throat|ily
throati|ness
throaty
  throat|ier
  throati|est
throb
  throbs
  throbbed
  throb|bing
throe +s (pang;
  anguish. △ throw)
thrombi
throm|bin +s
thrombo|cyte +s
thrombo|cyto|
      penia
throm|bose
  throm|boses
  throm|bosed
  throm|bos|ing
throm|bosis
  throm|boses
throm|bot|ic
throm|bus
  thrombi
throne
  thrones
  throned
  thron|ing
  (chair of state;
  sovereign power.
  △ thrown)
throne|less
throng +s +ed
  +ing
thros|tle +s
thros|tle frame +s
throt|tle
  throt|tles

throt|tle (*cont.*)
  throt|tled
  throt|tling
throt|tler +s
through (from
  beginning to end
  etc. △ threw)
through|out
through|put +s
through|way *Br.*
  +s (*Am.* thruway)
throve
throw
  throws
  threw
  throw|ing
  thrown
  (propel etc.
  △ throe)
throw|able
throw|away +s
throw|back +s
throw|er +s
throw-in +s *noun*
thrown (past
  participle of
  throw. △ throne)
throw-off +s *noun*
throw-out +s *noun*
throw-over +s
  noun
throw|ster +s
thru *Am.* (use
  through. *Br.*
  through)
thrum
  thrums
  thrummed
  thrum|ming
thrum|mer +s
thrummy
  thrum|mier
  thrum|mi|est
thrush
  thrushes
thrust
  thrusts
  thrust
  thrust|ing
thrust bear|ing +s
thrust block +s
thrust|er +s
thru|way *Am.* +s
  (*Br.* throughway)
Thu|cydi|des
  (Greek historian)
thud
  thuds
  thud|ded
  thud|ding
  thud|ding|ly

Thug +s (member
  of Indian group)
thug +s (generally)
thug|gee
thug|gery
thug|gish
thug|gish|ly
thug|gish|ness
thug|gism
thuja +s
Thule (ancient
  northern land;
  Eskimo culture;
  settlement,
  Greenland)
thu|lium
thumb +s +ed
  +ing
thumb hole +s
thumb index
  thumb in|dexes
  noun
thumb-index
  thumb-indexes
  thumb-indexed
  thumb-indexing
  verb
thumb|less
thumb|nail +s
thumb nut +s
thumb|print +s
thumb|screw +s
thumb|tack +s
thump
  thumps
  thumped
  thump|ing
thump|er +s
thun|der +s +ed
  +ing
Thun|der Bay
  (city, Canada)
thun|der|bird +s
thun|der|bolt +s
thun|der|box
  thun|der|boxes
thun|der|bug +s
thun|der|clap +s
thun|der|cloud +s
thun|der|er +s
thun|der|flash
  thun|der|flashes
thun|der|fly
  thun|der|flies
thun|der|head +s
thun|der|ing +s
thun|der|ing|ly
thun|der|less
thun|der|ous
thun|der|ous|ly
thun|der|ous|ness
thun|der|storm +s

thun|der|struck
thun|dery
thunk +s +ed +ing
Thur|ber, James
  (American
  humorist)
Thur|gau (canton,
  Switzerland)
thur|ible +s
thuri|fer +s
thur|ifer|ous
thur|ifi|ca|tion
Thur|in|gia (state,
  Germany)
Thur|in|gian +s
Thurs|day +s
Thurso (port,
  Scotland)
thus
thus|ly
thuya +s
  (use thuja)
thwack +s +ed
  +ing
thwaite +s
thwart +s +ed
  +ing
thy
Thy|es|tean
Thy|es|tes *Greek*
  Mythology
thy|la|cine +s
thyme +s (herb.
  △ time)
thymi
thy|mi|dine
thy|mine
thy|mol
thy|mus
  thymi
thymy (like thyme)
thy|ris|tor +s
thy|roid +s
thy|rox|ine
thyr|sus
  thyrsi
thy|self
ti +s (tree. △ te,
  tea, tee)
ti (*Music*; use te.
  △ tea, tee)
Tia|mat *Babylonian*
  Mythology
Tian|an|men
  Square (in
  Beijing, China)
Tian|jin (city,
  China)
Tian Shan (= Tien
  Shan)
tiara +s
tiara'd (use
  tiaraed)

tiaraed
Tiber (river, Italy)
Ti¦ber¦ias, Lake
  (alternative name
  for the Sea of
  Galilee)
Ti¦ber¦ius (Roman
  emperor)
Ti¦besti
  Moun¦tains (in N.
  Africa)
Tibet
Ti¦bet¦an +s
tibia
  tib¦iae
tib¦ial
tibio¦tar¦sus
  tibio¦tarsi
Tib¦ul¦lus (Roman
  poet)
tic +s (twitch.
  ⚠ tick)
tic dou¦lour¦eux
tice +s
Tich¦borne
  (claimant)
Ti¦cino (canton,
  Switzerland)
tick +s +ed +ing
  (click; moment;
  mark; animal;
  credit; mattress
  cover. ⚠ tic)
tick-bird +s
tick¦er +s (heart;
  watch; tape
  machine. ⚠ tikka)
tick¦er tape +s
ticker-tape
  attributive
ticket +s +ed +ing
ticket col¦lect¦or
  +s
ticket-day +s
ticket-holder +s
ticket¦less
ticket-of-leave
  man
  ticket-of-leave
  men
tickety-boo
tick¦ing +s
tickle
  tickles
  tickled
  tick¦ling
tick¦ler +s
tick¦less
tick¦lish
tick¦lish¦ly
tick¦lish¦ness

tickly
  tick¦lier
  tick¦li¦est
tick-over noun
tick-tack
tick¦tack¦toe
tick-tock
tic-tac (use tick-
  tack)
tic-tac-toe (use
  ticktacktoe)
tidal
tid¦al¦ly
tid¦bit Am. +s (Br.
  titbit)
tiddle¦dy¦wink Am.
  +s (use
  tiddlywink. Br.
  tiddlywink)
tid¦dler +s
tid¦dly
  tid¦dlier
  tiddli¦est
tiddly¦wink +s
tide
  tides
  tided
  tid¦ing
  (of sea; trend etc.
  ⚠ tied)
tide¦land +s
tide¦less
tide¦line +s
tide¦mark +s
tide mill +s
tide-rip +s
tide table +s
tide¦wait¦er +s
tide¦water +s
tide¦wave +s
tide¦way +s
tidi¦ly
tidi¦ness
tid¦ings
tidy
  tidies
  tidied
  tidy¦ing
  tidi¦er
  tidi¦est
tie
  ties
  tied
  tying
tie-back +s noun
tie-bar +s
tie-beam +s
tie-break +s
tie-breaker +s
tie-breaking
tie-clip +s

tie-dye
  tie-dyes
  tie-dyed
  tie-dyeing
tie-in +s noun and
  attributive
tie¦less
tie line +s
Tien Shan
  (mountain range,
  China)
Tien¦tsin
  (= Tianjin)
tie¦pin +s
Tiep¦olo,
  Gio¦vanni
  Bat¦tista (Italian
  painter)
tier +s (layer.
  ⚠ tear)
tierce +s
tierced
tier¦cel +s
tier¦cet +s
tiered
tier¦ing +s
Tierra del Fuego
  (island off S.
  America)
tie-up +s
tiff
  tiffs
  tiffed
  tiff¦ing
Tif¦fany (name)
Tif¦fany, Louis
  Com¦fort
  (American
  glassmaker)
tif¦fany
tif¦fa¦nies
  (muslin)
tif¦fin +s +ed +ing
Tif¦lis (former
  name of Tbilisi)
tig +s
tiger +s (animal.
  ⚠ taiga)
tiger-cat +s
tiger-eye +s
  (stone; use tiger's-
  eye)
tiger¦ish
tiger¦ish¦ly
tiger lily
  tiger lil¦ies
Ti¦gers (Tamil
  military
  organization)
tiger's-eye +s
  (stone)
tiger¦skin +s

tiger-wood
tight +s +er +est
tight¦en +s +ed
  +ing
tight¦en¦er +s
tight-fisted
tight-fitting
tight-knit
tight-lipped
tight¦ly
tightly-knit
tight¦ness
tight¦rope +s
tights
tight¦wad +s
Tiglath-pileser
  (Assyrian kings)
tigon +s
Ti¦gray (province,
  Ethiopia)
Ti¦gray¦an +s
Tigre (province,
  Ethiopia; use
  Tigray)
Tigre (Semitic
  language)
Ti¦gre¦an +s (use
  Tigrayan)
tig¦ress
  tig¦resses
Tig¦rinya
Ti¦gris (river,
  Mesopotamia)
Tihwa (former
  name of Urumqi)
Ti¦juana (town,
  Mexico)
Tikal (ancient city,
  Guatemala)
tike +s (use tyke)
tiki +s
tikka +s (food.
  ⚠ ticker)
'til (use till)
til¦apia
  plural til¦apia or
  til¦apias
Til¦burg (city, the
  Netherlands)
Til¦bury (port,
  England)
til¦bury
  til¦bur¦ies
  (carriage)
Tilda (name)
tilde +s (accent)
tile
  tiles
  tiled
  til¦ing
tiler +s
til¦ing +s

till
  tills
  tilled
  till|ing
till|able
till|age
till|er +s +ed +ing
til|ley lamp +s
  Propr.
Til|lich, Paul
  Jo|han|nes
  (German-born
  American
  theologian)
Tilly
tilt +s +ed +ing
tilt|er +s
tilth
tilt-hammer +s
tilt-yard +s
Tim
Tim|aru (port, New
  Zealand)
tim|bal +s (drum)
tim|bale +s (dish)
tim|ber +s +ed
  +ing
timber-frame
  adjective
timber-framed
timber-getter +s
tim|ber|land +s
tim|ber|line +s
tim|ber|man
  tim|ber|men
timbre +s
tim|brel +s
Tim|buc|too (use
  Timbuktu)
Tim|buktu (town,
  Mali; any remote
  place)
time
  times
  timed
  tim|ing
  (progress of
  events; etc.
  △thyme)
time-and-motion
time bomb +s
time clock +s
time-consum|ing
time-frame +s
time-fuse +s
time-honored *Am.*
time-honoured *Br.*
time|keep|er +s
time|keep|ing
time lag +s
time-lapse
  attributive
time|less

time|less|ly
time|less|ness
time limit +s
time|li|ness
time lock +s
time-locked
time|ly
  time|lier
  time|li|est
time-out +s
time|piece +s
timer +s
time|scale +s
time-served
time-server +s
time-serving
time|share +s
time-sharing
time-shift
  time-shifts
  time-shifted
  time-shifting
time-span +s
time switch
  time switches
time|table
  time|tables
  time|tabled
  time|tab|ling
time travel
time trav|el|er *Am.*
  +s
time trav|el|ler *Br.*
  +s
time trial +s
time value +s
time warp +s
time-waster +s
time-wasting
time-work
time-worn
time zone +s
timid +er +est
tim|id|ity
tim|id|ly
tim|id|ness
tim|ing +s
Timi|şoara (city,
  Romania)
tim|oc|racy
  tim|oc|ra|cies
timo|crat|ic
Timor (island,
  Indonesia)
Ti|mor|ese
  plural Ti|mor|ese
tim|or|ous
tim|or|ous|ly
tim|or|ous|ness
Timor Sea
  (between Timor
  and Australia)

Tim|othy (early
  saint; name)
tim|othy
  tim|othies
  (grass; brothel)
tim|pani
tim|pan|ist +s
tin
  tins
  tinned
  tin|ning
tina|mou +s
Tin|ber|gen, Jan
  (Dutch economist)
Tin|ber|gen,
  Niko|laas (Dutch
  zoologist)
tinc|tor|ial
tinc|ture
  tinc|tures
  tinc|tured
  tinc|tur|ing
tin|dal +s
tin|der
tin|der|box
  tin|der|boxes
tin|dery
tine +s
tinea
tined
tin|foil
ting +s +ed +ing
  (bell-like sound;
  make this sound)
tinge
  tinges
  tinged
  tinge|ing *or*
  tin|ging
  (colour or affect
  slightly; slight
  trace)
tin-glaze +s
tin|gle
  tin|gles
  tin|gled
  tin|gling
tin|gly
  tin|glier
  tin|gli|est
tin|horn +s
tini|ly
tini|ness
tin|ker +s +ed
  +ing
tin|ker|er +s
tin|ker|ing +s
tin|kle
  tin|kles
  tin|kled
  tink|ling
tink|ling +s
tin|kly
tin|ner +s

tin|nily
tin|ni|ness
tin|nitus
tinny
  tin|nier
  tin|ni|est
tin-opener +s
tin plate *noun*
tin-plate
  tin-plates
  tin-plated
  tin-plating
  verb
tin|pot
tin|sel
  tin|sels
  tin|selled *Br.*
  tin|seled *Am.*
  tin|sel|ling *Br.*
  tin|sel|ing *Am.*
tin|sel|ly
Tin|sel|town
  (= Hollywood)
tin|smith +s
tin|snips
tin|stone
tint +s +ed +ing
tin-tack +s
Tin|tagel (village,
  England)
tint|er +s
tin|tin|nabu|lar
tin|tin|nabu|lary
tin|tin|nabu|
      la|tion +s
tin|tin|nabu|lous
tin|tin|nabu|lum
  tin|tin|nab|ula
Tin|tor|etto (Italian
  painter)
tin|ware
tiny
  tinies
  tini|er
  tini|est
tip
  tips
  tipped
  tip|ping
tip-and-run
tip|cat +s
tipi +s (use tepee)
tip|less
tip-off +s *noun*
tip|per +s
Tip|per|ary
  (county, Republic
  of Ireland)
tip|pet +s
Tip|pett, Mi|chael
  (English
  composer)

Tipp-Ex *noun*
  Propr.
Tipp-Ex
  Tipp-Exes
  Tipp-Exed
  Tipp-Exing
  verb
tip|ple
  tip|ples
  tip|pled
  tip|pling
tip|pler +s
tippy
  tip|pier
  tip|pi|est
tip|sily
tip|si|ness
tip|staff
  tip|staffs *or*
  tip|staves
tip|ster +s
tipsy
  tip|sier
  tip|si|est
tipsy-cake +s
tip|toe
  tip|toes
  tip|toed
  tip|toe|ing
tip-top
tip-up +s *adjective*
  and noun
tir|ade +s
tir|ail|leur +s
tira|misu +s
Tir|ana (use
  Tiranë)
Tir|anë (capital of
  Albania)
tire
  tires
  tired
  tir|ing
  (grow weary etc.
  △ tyre)
tire *Am.* (on
  vehicle; *Br.* tyre)
tired +er +est
tired|ly
tired|ness
Tiree (Scottish
  island; weather
  station)
tire gauge *Am.* +s
  (*Br.* tyre gauge)
tire|less
tire|less|ly
tire|less|ness
Tir|esias *Greek*
  Mythology
tire|some
tire|some|ly

tire|some|ness
Tîrgu Mureş (city,
  Romania)
Tir|ich Mir
  (mountain,
  Pakistan)
Tir-nan-Og *Irish*
  Mythology
tiro +s (use tyro)
Tirol (German
  name for Tyrol)
Tiru|chi|ra|palli
  (city, India)
'tis (*archaic* = it is)
Tisa (Serbian name
  for the Tisza)
tis|ane +s (infusion
  of dried herbs etc.
  △ ptisan)
Tishri (Jewish
  month)
Tis|iph|one *Greek*
  Mythology
Tisri (use Tishri)
tis|sue +s
tis|sue paper +s
Tisza (river, E.
  Europe)
tit +s
Titan (*Greek*
  Mythology; moon
  of Saturn)
titan +s (person of
  great strength,
  intellect, etc.)
ti|tan|ate +s (salt
  of titanic acid)
Ti|tan|ess
  Ti|tan|esses
  Greek Mythology
Tit|ania (fairy
  queen; moon of
  Uranus)
ti|tan|ic (of
  titanium; gigantic)
Ti|tan|ic (ship)
ti|tan|ic|al|ly
ti|tan|ium
tit|bit *Br.* +s (*Am.*
  tidbit)
titch
  titches
titchy
  titch|ier
  titchi|est
titer *Am.* +s (*Br.*
  titre)
tit|fer +s
tit-for-tat
tith|able
tithe
  tithes

tithe (*cont.*)
  tithed
  tith|ing
tith|ing +s
Tith|onus *Greek*
  Mythology
titi +s (monkey.
  △ titty)
Ti|tian (Italian
  painter)
Titi|caca, Lake (in
  Peru and Bolivia)
tit|il|late
  tit|il|lates
  tit|il|lated
  tit|il|lat|ing
tit|il|lat|ing|ly
tit|il|la|tion +s
titi|vate
  titi|vates
  titi|vated
  titi|vat|ing
titi|va|tion +s
tit|lark +s
title
  titles
  titled
  tit|ling
title deed +s
title-holder +s
title-page +s
tit|ling +s
tit|mouse
  tit|mice
Tito *born* **Josip
  Broz**
  (Yugoslav
  president)
Tito|grad (former
  name of
  Podgorica)
Tito|ism
Tito|ist +s
ti|trat|able
ti|trate
  ti|trates
  ti|trated
  ti|trat|ing
ti|tra|tion +s
titre *Br.* +s (*Am.*
  titer)
ti-tree +s (cabbage
  tree. △ tea-tree)
tit|ter +s +ed +ing
tit|ter|er +s
tit|ter|ing|ly
tit|ti|vate (use
  titivate)
  tit|ti|vates
  tit|ti|vated
  tit|ti|vat|ing
tit|tle +s

tittle|bat +s
tittle-tattle
  tittle-tattles
  tittle-tattled
  tittle-tattling
tit|tup
  tit|tups
  tit|tuped *or*
  tit|tupped
  tit|tup|ing *or*
  tit|tup|ping
tit|tuppy
titty
  tit|ties
  (nipple; breast.
  △ titi)
titu|ba|tion
titu|lar
titu|lar|ly
Titus (Roman
  emperor; Greek
  saint)
Tiv|oli (town, Italy)
tiz (use tizz)
  tizzes
tizz
  tizzes
tizzy
  tiz|zies
T-joint +s
T-junction +s
Tlax|cala (city and
  state, Mexico)
Tlem|cen (city,
  Algeria)
Tlin|git
  plural **Tlin|git** *or*
  Tlin|gits
T-lympho|cyte +s
tme|sis
  tme|ses
to (*preposition* in 'to
  London' etc.; with
  verb infinitives,
  e.g. 'to go'. △ too,
  two)
toad +s
toad-eater +s
toad|fish
  plural **toad|fish** *or*
  toad|fishes
toad|flax
toad-in-the-hole
  +s
toad|ish
toad|let +s
toad|like
toad|stone +s
toad|stool +s
toady
  toad|ies
  toad|ied

toady (*cont.*)
  toady|ing
  (sycophant; to
  fawn. ⚠ tody)
toady|ish
toady|ism
toast +s +ed +ing
toast|er +s
toastie +s (toasted
  sandwich.
  ⚠ toasty)
toasting-fork +s
toast|mas|ter +s
toast|mis|tress
  toast|mis|tresses
toast rack +s
toasty (like toast)
to|bacco +s
to|bac|con|ist +s
tobacco-stopper
  +s
To|bagan +s
To|bago (island,
  West Indies)
Toba|go|nian +s
To|bias
Tobit *Bible*
to|bog|gan +s +ed
  +ing
to|bog|gan|er +s
to|bog|gan|ist +s
To|bruk (port,
  Libya)
Toby
toby jug +s
Toc|an|tins (river
  and state, Brazil)
toc|cata +s
Toc H (Christian
  society)
Toch|ar|ian +s
toco|pherol +s
toc|sin +s (alarm.
  ⚠ toxin)
tod
today +s
Todd, Mark
  James (New
  Zealand
  equestrian)
tod|dle
  tod|dles
  tod|dled
  tod|dling
tod|dler +s
toddler|hood
toddy
  tod|dies
to-do +s
tody
  todies
  (bird. ⚠ toady)

toe
  toes
  toed
  toe|ing
  (on foot. ⚠ tow)
toe|cap +s
toe clip +s
toe|hold +s
toe-in
toe|less
toe|nail +s
toe-rag +s
toey
toff +s +ed +ing
tof|fee +s
tof|fee apple +s
tof|fee|ish
toffee-nosed
toft +s
tofu
tog
  togs
  togged
  tog|ging
toga +s
toga'd
togaed (use toga'd)
to|gether
to|gether|ness
tog|gery
tog|gle
  tog|gles
  tog|gled
  tog|gling
Togli|atti (city,
  Russia)
Togo (in W. Africa)
Togo|land (former
  region, W. Africa)
Togo|lese
  plural Togo|lese
To|hoku (region,
  Japan)
toil +s +ed +ing
  (work)
toile +s (cloth)
toil|er +s
toi|let +s +ed +ing
toi|let roll +s
toi|let|ry
  toi|let|ries
toi|lette +s
toilet-train +s +ed
  +ing
toil|some
toil|some|ly
toil|some|ness
toil-worn
toing and fro|ing
to|ings and
  fro|ings

Tojo, Hi|deki
  (Japanese prime
  minister)
toka|mak +s
Tokay +s (wine)
tokay +s (gecko)
Tok|elau (island
  group, W. Pacific)
token +s
token|ism
token|ist
token|is|tic
Toku|gawa
Tokyo (capital of
  Japan)
tol|booth +s (use
  toll-booth)
Tol|bu|khin
  (former name of
  Dobrich)
told (past tense and
  past participle of
  tell ⚠ tolled)
To|ledo (cities,
  Spain and USA)
tol|er|abil|ity
tol|er|able
tol|er|able|ness
tol|er|ably
tol|er|ance +s
tol|er|ant
tol|er|ant|ly
tol|er|ate
  tol|er|ates
  tol|er|ated
  tol|er|at|ing
tol|er|ation +s
tol|er|ator +s
To|lima (volcano,
  Colombia)
Tol|kien, J. R. R.
  (British novelist)
toll +s +ed +ing
  (charge; cost; ring.
  ⚠ told)
toll-booth +s
toll bridge +s
toll gate +s
toll-house +s
toll|road +s
Tol|lund Man
Tol|pud|dle
  mar|tyrs
Tol|stoy, Leo
  (Russian writer)
Tol|tec
  plural Tol|tec *or*
  Tol|tecs
Tol|tec|an +s
tolu
To|luca (de Lerdo)
  (city, Mexico)

tolu|ene
tol|uic
tol|uol
Tol|yatti (Russian
  name for
  Togliatti)
Tom (name)
tom +s (male
  animal)
toma|hawk +s +ed
  +ing
to|mal|ley +s
toma|tillo +s
to|mato
  to|ma|toes
to|ma|toey
tomb +s
tom|bac
Tom|baugh, Clyde
  Wil|liam
  (American
  astronomer)
tom|bola +s
tom|bolo +s
Tom|bouc|tou
  (French name for
  Timbuktu)
tom|boy +s
tom|boy|ish
tom|boy|ish|ness
tomb|stone +s
tom-cat +s
Tom Col|lins
  Tom Col|linses
  (drink)
tome +s
to|men|tose
to|men|tous
to|men|tum
to|menta
tom|fool +s
tom|fool|ery
  tom|fool|er|ies
Tomis (ancient
  name for
  Constanța)
Tommy
  Tom|mies
  (British soldier;
  name)
tommy bar +s
tommy-gun +s
tommy|rot
tommy ruff +s
tomo|gram +s
tomo|graph +s
tomo|graph|ic
tom|og|raphy
Tomor, Mount (in
  Albania)
to|mor|row +s

Tom|pion,
  Thomas (English
  clockmaker)
tom|pion +s
tom|pot +s
tom|pot blenny
  tom|pot blen|nies
Tomsk (city,
  Siberia)
tom|tit +s
tom-tom +s
ton +s (various
  units of weight;
  100. △tonne,
  tun)
ton +s (fashion)
tonal
ton|al|ity
  ton|al|ities
ton|al|ly
Ton|bridge (town,
  England.
  △Tunbridge
  Wells)
tondo
  tondi
tone
  tones
  toned
  ton|ing
tone arm +s
tone|burst +s
tone-deaf
tone-deafness
tone|less
tone|less|ly
ton|eme +s
ton|em|ic
tone|pad +s
tone poem +s
toner +s
tone-row +s
tong +s +ed +ing
Tonga (in S.
  Pacific)
Tonga
  plural Tonga *or*
  Ton|gas
  (member of
  African people;
  their language)
tonga +s (horse-
  drawn vehicle)
Ton|gan +s (of
  Tonga; person;
  language)
Tonga|riro, Mount
  (in New Zealand)
tong|kang +s
tongs
Tong|shan (former
  name of Xuzhou)

tongue
  tongues
  tongued
  tonguing
  (in mouth etc.
  △tung)
tongue-and-
  groove *attributive*
tongue-in-cheek
tongue-lashing +s
tongue|less
tongue-tie +s
tongue-tied
tongue-twister +s
Toni (woman's
  name. △Tony)
Tonia *also* Tonya
tonic +s
ton|ic|al|ly
ton|icity
tonic sol-fa
to|night
ton|ish
tonka bean +s
Ton|kin, Gulf of
  (between Vietnam
  and China)
Tonlé Sap (lake,
  Cambodia)
ton-mile +s
ton|nage +s
tonne +s (1000 kg.
  △ton, tun)
ton|neau +s
ton|om|eter +s
ton|sil +s
ton|sil|lar
ton|sil|lec|tomy
  ton|sil|lec|to|mies
ton|sil|litis
ton|sor|ial
ton|sure
  ton|sures
  ton|sured
  ton|sur|ing
ton|tine +s
Ton|ton Ma|coute
  Ton|tons
  Ma|coutes
ton-up +s
Tony (man's name.
  △Toni)
Tony
  Tonies
  (American theatre
  award)
tony
  toni|er
  toni|est
  (stylish)
Tonya *also* Tonia

too (*adverb*, in 'too
  much' etc. △to,
  two)
toodle-oo
took
tool +s +ed +ing
tool bag +s
tool|box
  tool|boxes
tool|er +s
tool hold|er +s
tool kit +s
tool|maker +s
tool|mak|ing
tool-pusher +s
tool shed +s
toot +s +ed +ing
toot|er +s
tooth
  teeth
tooth|ache +s
tooth-billed
tooth|brush
  tooth|brushes
tooth|comb +s
toothed
tooth-glass
  tooth-glasses
tooth|ily
toothi|ness
tooth|ing
tooth|less
tooth|like
tooth-mug +s
tooth|paste +s
tooth|pick +s
tooth|some
tooth|some|ly
tooth|some|ness
tooth|wort +s
toothy
  tooth|ier
  toothi|est
too|tle
  too|tles
  too|tled
  toot|ling
toot|ler +s
too-too (extreme,
  excessive;
  excessively.
  △tutu)
tootsy
  toot|sies
  (toe. △Tutsi)
Too|woomba
  (town, Australia)
top
  tops
  topped
  top|ping

topaz
  to|pazes
top|azo|lite +s
top-boot +s
top|coat +s
top-down
top-drawer
  adjective
top dress
  top dresses
top dressed
top dress|ing
tope
  topes
  toped
  top|ing
  (drink; grove;
  Buddhist shrine;
  fish. △taupe)
topee +s (use topi)
To|peka (city,
  USA)
toper +s
top-flight
top|gal|lant +s
top-hamper +s
top-hatted
top-heavily
top-heaviness
top-heavy
To|phet *Bible*
top-hole
to|phus
  tophi
topi +s
topi|ar|ian +s
topi|ar|ist +s
topi|ary
  topi|ar|ies
topic +s
top|ic|al
top|ic|al|ity
top|ic|al|ly
Top|kapi Pal|ace
  (in Istanbul)
top|knot +s
top|less
top|less|ness
top-level *adjective*
top-line *adjective*
top|lofty
top|man
  top|men
top|mast +s
top|most
top-notch
top-notcher +s
top|og|raph|er +s
topo|graph|ic
topo|graph|ic|al
topo|graph|ic|al|ly

top|og|raphy
  top|og|raph|ies
topoi (plural of
  topos)
topo|logic|al
topo|logic|al|ly
top|olo|gist +s
top|ology
topo|nym +s
topo|nym|ic
top|onymy
topos
  topoi
top|per +s
top|ping +s
top|ple
  top|ples
  top|pled
  top|pling
top|sail +s
top-sawyer +s
top se|cret
top-shell +s
top|side +s
top|slice (in tennis
  etc.)
top-slicing *Tax*
top|soil +s
top|spin +s
top|stitch
  top|stitches
  top|stitched
  top|stitch|ing
topsy-turvily
topsy-turviness
topsy-turvy
top-up +s *noun and*
  attributive
toque +s
to|quilla +s
tor +s (hill. △ tau,
  taw, tore, torr)
Torah
Tor|bay (resort,
  England)
torc +s (necklace.
  △ talk, torque)
torch
  torches
  torched
  torch|ing
torch-bearer +s
tor|chère +s
torch-fishing
torch|light
torch|lit
tor|chon +s
torch race +s
torch-thistle +s
tore +s (past tense
  of *tear*;
  Architecture;

tore (*cont.*)
  Geometry. △ tau,
  taw, tor, torr)
torea|dor +s
tor|ero +s
tor|eut|ic
tor|eut|ics
tor|goch
  plural tor|goch
tori (plural of *torus*
  △ Tory)
toric
torii
  plural torii
tor|ment +s +ed
  +ing
tor|ment|ed|ly
tor|men|til +s
tor|ment|ing|ly
tor|ment|or +s
torn
tor|nad|ic
tor|nado
  tor|na|does *or*
  tor|na|dos
Torne Älv
  (Swedish name for
  the Tornio)
Tor|nio (river,
  Scandinavia)
tor|oid
tor|oid|al
tor|oid|al|ly
To|ronto (city,
  Canada)
tor|ose
tor|pedo
  tor|pe|does
  tor|pe|doed
  tor|pe|do|ing
tor|pedo boat +s
tor|pedo bomb|er
  +s
torpedo-like
torpedo-net +s
torpedo-netting
tor|pefy
  tor|pe|fies
  tor|pe|fied
  tor|pe|fy|ing
tor|pid
tor|pid|ity
tor|pid|ly
tor|pid|ness
tor|por +s
tor|por|if|ic
tor|quate
Tor|quay (resort,
  England)
torque
  torques
  torqued

torque (*cont.*)
tor|quing
  (turning force.
  △ talk, torc)
Tor|que|mada,
  Tomás de
  (Inquisitor-
  General of Spain)
tor|quey
  (producing much
  torque. △ talkie)
torr
  plural torr
  (unit of pressure.
  △ tau, taw, tor,
  tore)
tor|re|fac|tion
tor|refy
  tor|re|fies
  tor|re|fied
  tor|re|fy|ing
tor|rent +s
tor|ren|tial
tor|ren|tial|ly
Tor|res Strait (N.
  of Australia)
Tor|ri|celli,
  Evan|ge|lista
  (Italian physicist)
Tor|ri|cel|lian
tor|rid
tor|rid|ity
tor|rid|ly
tor|rid|ness
torse +s
tor|sel +s
Tórs|havn (capital
  of the Faeroe
  Islands)
tor|sion
tor|sion|al
tor|sion|al|ly
tor|sion|less
torsk +s
torso +s
tort +s (*Law.*
  △ taught, taut,
  torte)
torte
  tort|en *or* tortes
  (cake. △ taught,
  taut, tort)
Tor|tel|ier, Paul
  (French cellist)
tor|telli
tor|tel|lini
tort|fea|sor +s
tor|ti|col|lis
tor|tilla +s
tor|tious
tor|tious|ly
tor|toise +s

tortoise-like
tor|toise|shell +s
Tor|tola (island,
  British Virgin
  Islands)
tor|trix
  tor|tri|ces
tor|tu|os|ity
tor|tu|ous
tor|tu|ous|ly
tor|tu|ous|ness
tor|tur|able
tor|ture
  tor|tures
  tor|tured
  tor|tur|ing
tor|turer +s
tor|tur|ous
tor|tur|ous|ly
tor|ula
  toru|lae
Toruń (city,
  Poland)
torus
  tori *or* tor|uses
  (*Architecture;*
  Botany; Anatomy;
  Geometry.
  △ Taurus)
Tor|vill, Jayne
  (English ice-
  skater)
Tory
  Tor|ies
  (Conservative.
  △ tori)
Tory|ism
tosa +s
Tos|ca|nini,
  Ar|turo (Italian
  conductor)
tosh
Tosk
  plural Tosk *or*
  Tosks
toss
  tosses
  tossed
  toss|ing
toss|er +s (*coarse*
  slang)
toss-up +s
tot
  tots
  totted
  tot|ting
total
  to|tals
  to|talled *Br.*
  to|taled *Am.*
  to|tal|ling *Br.*
  to|tal|ing *Am.*

to¦tal¦isa¦tion *Br.*
  (use totalization)
to¦tal¦isa¦tor *Br.*
  (use totalizator)
to¦tal¦ise *Br.* (use
  totalize)
to¦tal¦ises
to¦tal¦ised
to¦tal¦is¦ing
to¦tal¦iser *Br.* +s
  (use totalizer)
to¦tali¦tar¦ian +s
to¦tali¦tar¦ian¦ism
to¦tal¦ity
  to¦tal¦ities
to¦tal¦iza¦tion
to¦tal¦iza¦tor +s
to¦tal¦ize
  to¦tal¦izes
  to¦tal¦ized
  to¦tal¦iz¦ing
to¦tal¦izer +s
to¦tal¦ly
tote
  totes
  toted
  tot¦ing
  (carry; totalizator;
  lottery)
tote bag +s
totem +s
to¦tem¦ic
to¦tem¦ism
to¦tem¦ist +s
to¦tem¦is¦tic
totem pole +s
toter +s
tother (= the other)
tot¦ter +s +ed +ing
tot¦ter¦er +s
tot¦tery
totting-up
  tottings-up
totty
tou¦can +s
touch
  touches
  touched
  touch¦ing
touch¦able
touch-and-go
touch¦back +s
touch¦down +s
tou¦ché
touch¦er +s
touch-hole +s
touch¦ily
touchi¦ness
touch¦ing +s
touch¦ing¦ly
touch¦ing¦ness
touch-in-goal +s

touch judge +s
touch¦line +s
touch-mark +s
touch-me-not +s
  (plant)
touch-needle +s
touch¦paper +s
touch screen +s
touch¦stone +s
touch-type
  touch-typing
touch-typing
touch-typist +s
touch-up +s *noun*
  and attributive
touch¦wood +s
touchy
  touch¦ier
  touchi¦est
tough +s +er +est
  (durable; hardy;
  severe; etc. △ tuff)
tough¦en +s +ed
  +ing
tough¦en¦er +s
toughie +s
tough¦ish
tough¦ly
tough-minded
tough-
  minded¦ness
tough¦ness
Tou¦lon (port,
  France)
Tou¦louse (city,
  France)
Toulouse-Lautrec,
  Henri de (French
  artist)
tou¦pee +s
tour +s +ed +ing
tour¦aco +s
tour de force
  tours de force
Tour de France
  (cycle race)
tour¦er +s
Tour¦ette's
  syn¦drome
tour¦ism
tour¦ist +s
tour¦ist¦ed
tour¦is¦tic
tour¦is¦tic¦al¦ly
tour¦isty
tour¦ma¦line +s
Tour¦nai (town,
  Belgium)
tour¦na¦ment +s
tour¦ne¦dos
  plural tour¦ne¦dos

tour¦ney +s +ed
  +ing
tour¦ni¦quet +s
Tours (city, France)
tou¦sle
  tou¦sles
  tou¦sled
  tous¦ling
tousle-haired
tous-les-mois
  plural **tous-les-**
  mois
Tous¦saint
  L'Ouver¦ture,
  Pierre (Haitian
  revolutionary)
tout +s +ed +ing
tout court
tout de suite
tout¦er +s
to¦var¦ich (use
  tovarish)
to¦var¦iches
to¦var¦ish
  to¦var¦ishes
tow +s +ed +ing
  (pull; fibres.
  △ toe)
tow¦able
tow¦age
to¦ward
to¦ward¦ness
to¦wards
tow bar +s
towel
  towels
  tow¦elled *Br.*
  tow¦eled *Am.*
  tow¦el¦ling *Br.*
  tow¦el¦ing *Am.*
towel-horse +s
tow¦el¦ing *Am.* +s
tow¦el¦ling *Br.* +s
tower +s +ed +ing
tower block +s
tow¦ery
tow-head +s
tow-headed
tow¦hee +s
towing-path +s
towing-rope +s
tow¦line +s
town +s
townee +s (use
  townie)
Townes, Charles
  Hard (American
  physicist)
tow-net +s
town house +s
townie +s
town¦ish

town¦less
town¦let +s
town-major +s
town¦scape +s
towns¦folk
town¦ship +s
towns¦man
towns¦men
towns¦people
Towns¦ville (port,
  Australia)
towns¦woman
  towns¦women
Towns¦women's
  Guild +s
town¦ward
town¦wards
tow¦path +s
tow¦plane +s
tow rope +s
towy
tox¦ae¦mia *Br.*
tox¦aem¦ic *Br.*
tox¦emia *Am.*
tox¦em¦ic *Am.*
toxic +s
tox¦ic¦al¦ly
toxi¦cant +s
tox¦icity
  tox¦ici¦ties
toxi¦co¦logic¦al
toxi¦colo¦gist +s
toxi¦col¦ogy
toxi¦co¦mania
toxin +s (poison.
  △ tocsin)
toxo¦cara
toxo¦caria¦sis
tox¦oph¦il¦ite +s
tox¦oph¦ily
toxo¦plas¦mo¦sis
toy +s +ed +ing
toy-box
  toy-boxes
toy¦boy +s
toy¦like
toy¦maker +s
Toyn¦bee, Ar¦nold
  Jo¦seph (English
  historian)
toy¦shop +s
toy¦town
T-piece +s
trab¦eate
trabea¦tion
trab¦ecula
  trab¦ecu¦lae
trab¦ecu¦lar
trab¦ecu¦late
Trab¦zon (city,
  Turkey)
trac¦as¦serie +s

trace
  traces
  traced
  tra¦cing
trace|abil¦ity
trace|able
trace-horse +s
trace|less
tracer +s
tra¦cer|ied
tra¦cery
  tra¦cer|ies
Tra¦cey *also* Tracy
trachea
  trach|eae
trach|eal
trach|eate
trache|os¦tomy
  trache|os¦to¦mies
trache|ot¦omy
  trache|oto¦mies
trach|oma
trach¦oma|tous
trach¦yte +s
trach|yt¦ic
tra¦cing +s
tra¦cing paper +s
track +s +ed +ing
track|age
track|ball +s
track|bed +s
track|er +s
track|lay¦er +s
track-laying
trackle|ment +s
track|less
track|man
  track|men
track|side
track|suit +s
track|way +s
tract +s
tract|abil¦ity
tract|able
tract|able|ness
tract|ably
Tract|arian +s
Tract¦ar¦ian|ism
trac|tate +s
trac|tion +s
trac|tion|al
trac|tion en¦gine +s
trac|tion wheel +s
trac|tive
trac|tor +s
Tracy, Spen|cer
  (American actor)
Tracy *also* Tra¦cey
trad (= traditional
  jazz; traditional)
trad|able

trade
  trades
  traded
  trad¦ing
trade|able
trade-in +s *noun
  and attributive*
trade-last +s
trade|mark +s +ed
  +ing *verb*
trade mark +s
  noun
trade name +s
trade-off +s *noun*
trader +s
trad¦es|can¦tia +s
trades|man
  trades|men
trades|people
trades union +s
trades union|ism
trades union|ist
  +s
trade union +s
trade union|ism
trade union|ist +s
trade-weight¦ed
trad¦ing stamp +s
trad¦ing sta|tion
  +s
trad|ition +s
trad|ition|al
trad|ition|al|ism
trad|ition|al|ist +s
trad|ition|al|is¦tic
trad|ition|al|ly
trad|ition|ary
trad|ition|ist +s
trad|ition|less
tradi|tor
  tradi|tors *or*
  tradi|tor¦es
tra|duce
  tra|duces
  tra|duced
  tra|du¦cing
tra|duce|ment +s
tra|ducer +s
tra|du¦cian +s
tra|du¦cian|ism
tra|du¦cian|ist +s
Tra|fal¦gar (naval
  battle; shipping
  area)
traf¦fic
  traf¦fics
  traf¦ficked
  traf¦fick|ing
traf¦fic|ator +s
traf¦fic calm|ing
traf¦fick¦er +s
traf¦fic|less

traf|fic light +s
traga|canth +s
tra|gedian +s
  (writer of or male
  actor in tragedies)
tra|gedi¦enne +s
  (actress in
  tragedies)
tra|gedy
  tra¦ged|ies
tra¦gic
tra¦gic|al
tra¦gic|al|ly
tragi|com¦edy
  tragi|com¦ed|ies
tragi|com¦ic
tragi|com¦ic|al|ly
trago|pan +s
Tra|herne,
  Thomas (English
  writer)
trahi|son des clercs
trail +s +ed +ing
trail|blazer +s
trail|blaz¦ing
trail|er +s +ed
  +ing
trail-net +s
train +s +ed +ing
train|abil¦ity
train|able
train|band +s
train-bearer +s
train driver +s
train|ee +s
trainee|ship +s
train|er +s
train ferry
  train fer|ries
train|less
train|load +s
train|man
  train|men
train-mile +s
train-oil
train set +s
train-shed +s
train|sick
train|sick|ness
train-spotter +s
train-spotting
traipse
  traipses
  traipsed
  traips|ing
trait +s
  (characteristic.
  △tray, trey)
trai|tor +s
trai|tor|ous
trai|tor|ous¦ly

trai|tress
  trai|tresses
Tra¦jan (Roman
  emperor)
tra|jec¦tory
  tra|jec¦tor¦ies
tra-la
Tra¦lee (town,
  Republic of
  Ireland)
tram +s
tram|car +s
Tra|miner +s
tram|line +s
tram|mel
  tram|mels
  tram|melled *Br.*
  tram|meled *Am.*
  tram|mel|ling *Br.*
  tram|mel|ing *Am.*
tram|mie +s
tra|mon|tana +s
tra|mon|tane +s
tramp +s +ed +ing
tramp|er +s
tramp|ish
tram|ple
  tram|ples
  tram|pled
  tramp|ling
tramp|ler +s
tramp-like
tram|po|line
  tram|po|lines
  tram|po|lined
  tram|po|lin¦ing
tram|po|lin¦ist +s
tram road +s
tram|way +s
trance
  trances
  tranced
  tran¦cing
trance-like
tranche +s
tranny
  tran|nies
tran|quil
tran¦quil|isa¦tion
  Br. (use
  tranquillization.
  Am.
  tranquillization)
tran¦quil|ise *Br.*
  (use tranquillize)
  tran¦quil|ises
  tran¦quil|ised
  tran¦quil|is¦ing
  (*Am.* tranquilize)
tran¦quil|iser *Br.*
  +s (use

tran¦quill¦iser
(*cont.*)
tranquillizer. *Am.*
tranquilizer)
tran¦quill¦ity (use
tranquillity)
tran¦quill¦iza¦tion
Am. (*Br.*
tranquillization)
tran¦quill¦ize *Am.*
tran¦quill¦izes
tran¦quill¦ized
tran¦quill¦iz¦ing
(*Br.* tranquillize)
tran¦quill¦izer *Am.*
+s (*Am.*
tranquillizer)
tran¦quill¦lisa¦tion
Br. (use
tranquillization.
Am.
tranquilization)
tran¦quill¦lise *Br.*
(use tranquillize)
tran¦quill¦lises
tran¦quill¦lised
tran¦quill¦lis¦ing
(*Am.* tranquilize)
tran¦quill¦liser *Br.*
+s (use
tranquillizer. *Am.*
tranquilizer)
tran¦quill¦lity
tran¦quill¦liza¦tion
Br. (*Am.*
tranquilization)
tran¦quill¦lize *Br.*
tran¦quill¦lizes
tran¦quill¦lized
tran¦quill¦liz¦ing
(*Am.* tranquilize)
tran¦quill¦lizer *Br.*
+s (*Am.*
tranquilizer)
tran¦quil¦ly
trans¦act +s +ed
+ing
trans¦ac¦tion +s
trans¦ac¦tion¦al
trans¦ac¦tion¦al¦ly
trans¦act¦or +s
trans¦alpine
trans¦at¦lan¦tic
Trans¦cau¦ca¦sia
Trans¦cau¦ca¦sian
trans¦ceiver +s
tran¦scend +s +ed
+ing
tran¦scend¦ence
tran¦scend¦ency
tran¦scend¦en¦
cies

tran¦scend¦ent +s
tran¦scen¦den¦tal
tran¦scen¦den¦tal¦
ise *Br.* (use
transcendental-
ize)
tran¦scen¦den¦tal¦
ises
tran¦scen¦den¦tal¦
ised
tran¦scen¦den¦tal¦
is¦ing
tran¦scen¦den¦tal¦
ism
tran¦scen¦den¦tal¦
ist +s
tran¦scen¦den¦tal¦
ize
tran¦scen¦den¦tal¦
izes
tran¦scen¦den¦tal¦
ized
tran¦scen¦den¦tal¦
iz¦ing
tran¦scen¦
den¦tal¦ly (in a
visionary, abstract
manner)
Tran¦scen¦den¦tal
Medi¦ta¦tion
tran¦scend¦ent¦ly
(pre-eminently)
trans¦code
trans¦codes
trans¦coded
trans¦cod¦ing
trans¦con¦tin¦
en¦tal
trans¦con¦tin¦
en¦tal¦ly
tran¦scribe
tran¦scribes
tran¦scribed
tran¦scrib¦ing
tran¦scriber +s
tran¦script +s
tran¦scrip¦tion +s
tran¦scrip¦tion¦al
tran¦scrip¦tive
Trans¦dan¦ub¦ian
High¦lands (in
Hungary)
trans¦duce
trans¦duces
trans¦duced
trans¦du¦cing
trans¦ducer +s
trans¦duc¦tion
tran¦sect +s +ed
+ing
tran¦sec¦tion +s
tran¦sept +s

tran¦sep¦tal
tran¦sex¦ual +s
(use transsexual)
tran¦sexu¦al¦ism
(use
transsexualism)
trans¦fer
trans¦fers
trans¦ferred
trans¦fer¦ring
trans¦fer¦abil¦ity
trans¦fer¦able
transfer-book +s
trans¦fer¦ee +s
trans¦fer¦ence
trans¦fer¦or +s
(generally)
transfer-paper +s
trans¦fer¦ral +s
trans¦fer¦rer +s
Law
trans¦fer¦rin
trans¦fer RNA
trans¦fig¦ur¦ation
+s
trans¦fig¦ure
trans¦fig¦ures
trans¦fig¦ured
trans¦fig¦ur¦ing
trans¦finite
trans¦fix
trans¦fixes
trans¦fixed
trans¦fix¦ing
trans¦fix¦ion
trans¦form +s +ed
+ing
trans¦form¦able
trans¦form¦ation
+s
trans¦form¦
ation¦al
trans¦form¦ation¦
al¦ly
trans¦forma¦tive
trans¦form¦er +s
trans¦fuse
trans¦fuses
trans¦fused
trans¦fus¦ing
trans¦fu¦sion +s
trans¦gen¦ic
trans¦gress
trans¦gresses
trans¦gressed
trans¦gress¦ing
trans¦gres¦sion +s
trans¦gres¦sion¦al
trans¦gres¦sive
trans¦gres¦sor +s
tran¦ship (use
trans-ship)
tran¦ships

tran¦ship (*cont.*)
tran¦shipped
tran¦ship¦ping
tran¦ship¦ment +s
(use trans-
shipment)
trans¦hu¦mance
tran¦si¦ence
tran¦si¦ency
tran¦si¦ent +s
tran¦si¦ent¦ly
trans¦illu¦min¦ate
trans¦illu¦min¦
ates
trans¦illu¦min¦
ated
trans¦illu¦min¦
at¦ing
trans¦illu¦min¦
ation
tran¦sire +s
tran¦sis¦tor +s
tran¦sis¦tor¦
isa¦tion *Br.* (use
transistorization)
tran¦sis¦tor¦ise *Br.*
(use
transistorize)
tran¦sis¦tor¦ises
tran¦sis¦tor¦ised
tran¦sis¦tor¦lis¦ing
tran¦sis¦tor¦
iza¦tion
tran¦sis¦tor¦ize
tran¦sis¦tor¦izes
tran¦sis¦tor¦ized
tran¦sis¦tor¦iz¦ing
tran¦sit +s +ed
+ing
transit-circle +s
transit-compass
transit-
compasses
transit-duty
transit-duties
transit-
instru¦ment +s
tran¦si¦tion +s
tran¦si¦tion¦al
tran¦si¦tion¦al¦ly
tran¦si¦tion¦ary
tran¦si¦tive +s
tran¦si¦tive¦ly
tran¦si¦tive¦ness
tran¦si¦tiv¦ity
tran¦si¦tor¦ily
tran¦si¦tori¦ness
tran¦si¦tory
transit-theodo¦lite
+s
Trans¦jor¦dan
(region, Jordan)

Trans|jor|dan|ian +s
Trans|kei (former homeland, South Africa)
trans|lata|bil|ity
trans|lat|able
trans|late
  trans|lates
  trans|lated
  trans|lat|ing
trans|la|tion +s
trans|la|tion|al
trans|la|tion|al|ly
trans|la|tor +s
trans|lit|er|ate
  trans|lit|er|ates
  trans|lit|er|ated
  trans|lit|er|at|ing
trans|lit|er|ation +s
trans|lit|er|ator +s
trans|lo|cate
  trans|lo|cates
  trans|lo|cated
  trans|lo|cat|ing
trans|loca|tion +s
trans|lu|cence
trans|lu|cency
trans|lu|cent
trans|lu|cent|ly
trans|lunar
trans|lun|ary
trans|mar|ine
trans|mi|grant +s
trans|mi|grate
  trans|mi|grates
  trans|mi|grated
  trans|mi|grat|ing
trans|mi|gra|tion +s
trans|mi|gra|tor +s
trans|mi|gra|tory
trans|mis|sible
trans|mis|sion +s
trans|mis|sive
trans|mit
  trans|mits
  trans|mit|ted
  trans|mit|ting
trans|mit|table
trans|mit|tal +s
trans|mit|tance
trans|mit|ter +s
trans|mog|ri|fi|
        ca|tion +s
trans|mog|rify
  trans|mog|ri|fies
  trans|mog|ri|fied
  trans|
        mog|ri|fy|ing
trans|mon|tane

trans|mut|abil|ity
trans|mut|able
trans|mu|ta|tion +s
trans|mu|ta|tion|al
trans|mu|ta|tion|
        ist +s
trans|mu|ta|tive
trans|mute
  trans|mutes
  trans|muted
  trans|mut|ing
trans|muter +s
trans|nation|al +s
trans|ocean|ic
tran|som +s
tran|somed
tran|sonic
trans|pa|cif|ic
trans|pad|ane
trans|par|ence
trans|par|ency
  trans|par|en|cies
trans|par|ent
trans|par|ent|ly
trans|par|ent|ness
trans-Pennine
trans|per|son|al
trans|pierce
  trans|pierces
  trans|pierced
  trans|pier|cing
tran|spir|able
tran|spir|ation
tran|spira|tory
tran|spire
  tran|spires
  tran|spired
  tran|spir|ing
trans|plant +s +ed
        +ing
trans|plant|able
trans|plant|ation
trans|plant|er +s
tran|spon|der +s
trans|pon|tine
trans|port +s +ed
        +ing
trans|port|abil|ity
trans|port|able
trans|por|ta|tion
trans|port|er +s
trans|pos|able
trans|posal
trans|pose
  trans|poses
  trans|posed
  trans|pos|ing
trans|poser +s
trans|pos|ition +s
trans|pos|ition|al
trans|posi|tive

trans|puter +s
trans|sex|ual +s
trans|sexu|al|ism
trans-ship
trans-ships
trans-shipped
trans-shipping
trans-shipment +s
trans-Siberian
trans-sonic
tran|sub|stan|ti|
                ate
tran|sub|stan|ti|
                ates
tran|sub|stan|ti|
                ated
tran|sub|stan|ti|
                at|ing
tran|sub|stan|ti|
                ation
tran|su|da|tion
tran|su|da|tory
tran|sude
  tran|sudes
  tran|suded
  tran|sud|ing
trans|uran|ic
Trans|vaal (former province, South Africa)
trans|ver|sal +s
trans|ver|sal|ity
trans|ver|sal|ly
trans|verse
trans|verse|ly
trans|vest +s +ed
        +ing
trans|vest|ism
trans|vest|ist +s
trans|vest|ite +s
Tran|syl|va|nia (region, Romania)
Tran|syl|va|nian
trant|er +s
trap
  traps
  trapped
  trap|ping
trap-ball
trap|door +s
trapes (use traipse)
  trapeses
  trapesed
  trapes|ing
trap|eze +s
tra|pez|ium
  tra|pezia or
  tra|pez|iums
  tra|pez|ius
  tra|pezii
trap|ez|oid +s
trap|ez|oid|al

trap|like
trap|pean
trap|per +s
trap|pings
Trap|pist +s
Trap|pist|ine
trap-rock +s
trap-shooter +s
trap-shooting
trash
  trashes
  trashed
  trash|ing
trash|ery
trash|er|ies
trash-ice
trash|ily
trashi|ness
trashy
  trash|ier
  trashi|est
Trás-os-Montes (region, Portugal)
trass
trat|toria +s
trauma +s
trau|mat|ic
trau|mat|ic|al|ly
trau|ma|tisa|tion
        Br. (use traumatization)
trau|ma|tise Br. (use traumatize)
  trau|ma|tises
  trau|ma|tised
  trau|ma|tis|ing
trau|ma|tism
trau|ma|tiza|tion
trau|ma|tize
  trau|ma|tizes
  trau|ma|tized
  trau|ma|tiz|ing
trav|ail +s +ed
        +ing
travel
  travels
  trav|elled Br.
  trav|eled Am.
  trav|el|ling Br.
  trav|el|ing Am.
  trav|el|er Am. +s
  trav|el|er's check
        Am. +s
  trav|el|ling bag Am.
        +s
  trav|el|ling rug Am.
        +s
  trav|el|ler Br. +s
  trav|el|ler's
        cheque Br. +s
  trav|el|ling bag Br.
        +s

trav¦el¦ling rug *Br.*
+s
trav¦el¦ogue +s
travel-sick
travel-sickness
trav¦ers¦able
tra¦vers¦al
tra¦verse
  tra¦verses
  tra¦versed
  tra¦vers¦ing
tra¦ver¦ser +s
trav¦er¦tine +s
trav¦esty
  trav¦es¦ties
  trav¦es¦tied
  trav¦esty¦ing
tra¦vois
  plural tra¦vois
trawl +s +ed +ing
trawl¦er +s
trawler¦man
  trawler¦men
trawl net +s
tray +s (for
  carrying plates
  etc. △ trait, trey)
tray¦ful +s
treach¦er¦ous
treach¦er¦ous¦ly
treach¦er¦ous¦ness
treach¦ery
  treach¦er¦ies
trea¦cle +s
trea¦cly
tread
  treads
  trod
  tread¦ing
  trod¦den
tread¦ed (having
  tread)
tread¦er +s
treadle
  treadles
  treadled
  tread¦ling
tread¦mill +s
tread¦wheel +s
trea¦son +s
trea¦son¦able
trea¦son¦ably
trea¦son¦ous
treas¦ure
  treas¦ures
  treas¦ured
  treas¦ur¦ing
treas¦urer +s
treas¦urer¦ship +s
treas¦ury
  treas¦ur¦ies
treat +s +ed +ing

treat¦able
treat¦er +s
trea¦tise +s
  (written work)
treat¦ment +s
treaty
  treat¦ies
  (agreement)
Trebi¦zond (former
  name of Trabzon)
treble
  trebles
  trebled
  treb¦ling
Treb¦linka
  (concentration
  camp, Poland)
trebly
trebu¦chet +s
tre¦cent¦ist +s
tre¦cento
tree
  trees
  treed
  tree¦ing
tree¦creep¦er +s
tree fern +s
tree house +s
tree¦less
tree¦less¦ness
tree-like
treen
tree¦nail +s
tree stump +s
tree¦top +s
tree trunk +s
trefa
tref¦oil +s
tref¦oiled
trek
  treks
  trekked
  trek¦king
trek¦ker +s
Trek¦kie +s
trel¦lis
  trel¦lises
  trel¦lised
  trel¦lis¦ing
trellis-work +s
trema¦tode +s
trem¦ble
  trem¦bles
  trem¦bled
  trem¦bling
trem¦bler +s
trem¦bling +s
trem¦bling¦ly
trem¦bly
  trem¦blier
  trem¦bli¦est
tre¦men¦dous

tre¦men¦dous¦ly
tre¦men¦dous¦ness
trem¦olo +s
tremor +s +ed
  +ing
tremu¦lous
tremu¦lous¦ly
tremu¦lous¦ness
tren¦ail +s (use
  treenail)
trench
  trenches
  trenched
  trench¦ing
tren¦chancy
tren¦chant
tren¦chant¦ly
trench coat +s
trench¦er +s
trench¦er¦man
  trench¦er¦men
trend +s +ed +ing
trend¦ify
  trendi¦fies
  trendi¦fied
  trendi¦fy¦ing
trend¦ily
trendi¦ness
trend¦set¦ter +s
trend¦set¦ting
trendy
  trend¦ies
  trend¦ier
  trendi¦est
Treng¦ganu (state,
  Malaysia; also in
  'Kuala
  Trengganu')
Trent (river,
  England)
Trent, Coun¦cil of
tren¦tal +s
trente-et-quarante
Trentino-Alto
  Adige (region,
  Italy)
Trento (city, Italy)
Tren¦ton (city,
  USA)
tre¦pan
  tre¦pans
  tre¦panned
  tre¦pan¦ning
trep¦an¦ation +s
tre¦pang +s
treph¦in¦ation +s
tre¦phine
  tre¦phines
  tre¦phined
  tre¦phin¦ing
trepi¦da¦tion

tres¦pass
  tres¦passes
  tres¦passed
  tres¦pass¦ing
tres¦pass¦er +s
tress
  tresses
  tressed
  tress¦ing
tres¦sure +s
tressy
tres¦tle +s
trestle-tree +s
tret +s
Tret¦'ya¦kov
  Gal¦lery (art
  gallery, Moscow)
tre¦vally
  tre¦val¦lies
Tre¦vith¦ick,
  Rich¦ard (English
  engineer)
Trevor
trews
trey +s (three dice
  or cards. △ trait,
  tray)
tri¦able
tri¦acet¦ate +s
tri¦acid +s
Triad +s (Chinese
  secret society)
triad +s (three)
tri¦adel¦phous
tri¦ad¦ic
tri¦ad¦ic¦al¦ly
tri¦age
trial
  trials
  trialled *Br.*
  trialed *Am.*
  trial¦ling *Br.*
  trial¦ing *Am.*
trial¦ist +s
trial¦list +s (use
  trialist)
tri¦an¦drous
tri¦angle +s
tri¦angu¦lar
tri¦angu¦lar¦ity
tri¦angu¦lar¦ly
tri¦angu¦late
  tri¦angu¦lates
  tri¦angu¦lated
  tri¦angu¦lat¦ing
tri¦angu¦late¦ly
tri¦angu¦la¦tion +s
Tria¦non (palaces,
  France)
tri¦an¦te¦lope +s
Trias

Tri|as|sic
tri|ath|lete +s
tri|ath|lon +s
tri|atom|ic
tri|axial
trib|ade +s
trib|ad|ism
tri|bal +s
tri|bal|ism
tri|bal|ist +s
tri|bal|is|tic
tri|bal|ly
tri|basic
tribe +s
tribes|man
  tribes|men
tribes|people
tribes|woman
  tribes|women
trib|let +s
tribo|elec|tri|city
trib|olo|gist +s
trib|ology
tribo|lumin|
        escence
tribo|lumin|escent
trib|om|eter +s
tri|brach +s
tri|brach|ic
tribu|la|tion +s
tri|bu|nal +s
trib|un|ate +s
trib|une +s
trib|une|ship +s
trib|un|icial
trib|un|ician +s
trib|un|itial
tribu|tar|ily
tribu|tari|ness
tribu|tary
  tribu|tar|ies
trib|ute +s
tri|car +s
trice
  trices
  triced
  tri|cing
tri|cen|ten|ary
  tri|cen|ten|ar|ies
tri|ceps
tri|cera|tops
trich|ia|sis
trich|ina
  trich|inae
Trichi|nop|oly
  (former name of
  Tiruchirapalli)
trich|in|osis
trich|in|ous
tri|chlor|ide +s
tri|chloro|eth|ane
trich|ogen|ous

tricho|logic|al
trich|olo|gist +s
trich|ology
trich|ome +s
tricho|monad +s
tricho|mon|ia|sis
trich|op|athy
tri|chord +s
tricho|tom|ic
trich|ot|om|ise Br.
  (use
  trichotomize)
  trich|ot|om|ises
  trich|ot|om|ised
  trich|ot|om|is|ing
trich|ot|om|ize
  trich|ot|om|izes
  trich|ot|om|ized
  trich|ot|om|iz|ing
trich|ot|om|ous
trich|ot|omy
  trich|oto|mies
tri|chro|ic
tri|chro|ism
tri|chro|mat|ic
tri|chro|ma|tism
Tricia also Trisha
trick +s +ed +ing
trick|er +s
trick|ery
  trick|er|ies
trick|ily
tricki|ness
trick|ish
trickle
  trickles
  trickled
  trick|ling
trick|ler +s (thing
  that trickles.
  △tricolor,
  tricolour)
trick|less
trick|ly
trick|sily
trick|si|ness
trick|ster +s
tricksy
  trick|ier
  tricki|est
tri|clin|ic
tri|clin|ium
  tri|clinia
tri|color Am. +s
tri|col|ored Am.
tri|col|our Br. +s
  (flag etc.
  △trickler)
tri|col|oured Br.

tri|corn +s (use
  tricorne)
tri|corne +s
tri|cot +s
tri|coty|ledon|ous
tri|crot|ic
tri|cus|pid +s
tri|cycle
  tri|cyc|les
  tri|cyc|led
  tri|cyc|ling
tri|cyc|lic +s
tri|cyc|list +s
tri|dac|tyl
tri|dac|tyl|ous
tri|dent +s
tri|den|tate
Tri|den|tine +s
tri|digi|tate
tri|dimen|sion|al
trid|uum
tridy|mite +s
tri|ecious Am. (Br.
  trioecious)
tried
tri|en|nial
tri|en|ni|al|ly
tri|en|nium
  tri|en|ni|ums or
  tri|en|nia
Trier (city,
  Germany)
trier +s (person
  who tries)
trier|archy
  trier|arch|ies
Tri|este (city, Italy)
tri|facial
tri|fecta +s
trif|fid +s (fictional
  plant)
tri|fid (in three
  parts)
trifle
  trifles
  trifled
  trif|ling
trifler +s
trif|ling|ly
tri|focal +s
tri|foli|ate
tri|for|ium
  tri|foria
tri|form
tri|fur|cate
  tri|fur|cates
  tri|fur|cated
  tri|fur|cat|ing
trig
  trigs
  trigged
  trig|ging

trig (cont.)
  (wedge, tidy, etc.;
  trigonometry)
trig|am|ist +s
trig|am|ous
trig|amy
tri|gem|in|al
tri|gem|inus
  tri|gem|ini
trig|ger +s +ed
  +ing
trig|ger|fish
  plural trig|ger|fish
  or trig|ger|fishes
trigger-happy
Trig|lav (mountain,
  Slovenia)
tri|gly|cer|ide +s
tri|glyph +s
tri|glyph|ic
tri|glyph|ic|al
tri|gon +s
tri|gon|al
tri|gon|al|ly
tri|gon|eut|ic
trig|ono|met|ric
trig|ono|met|ric|al
trig|onom|etry
tri|gram +s
tri|graph +s
tri|gyn|ous
tri|he|dral
tri|he|dron
  tri|he|dra or
  tri|he|drons
tri|hy|dric
trike
  trikes
  triked
  trik|ing
tri|labi|ate
tri|lam|in|ar
tri|lat|eral +s
tril|bied
trilby
  tril|bies
tri|lemma +s
tri|lin|ear
tri|lin|gual
tri|lin|gual|ism
tri|lit|eral
tri|lith +s
tri|lith|ic
tri|lithon +s
trill +s +ed +ing
tril|lion
  plural tril|lion or
  tril|lions
tril|lionth +s
tril|lium +s
tri|lob|ate
tri|lo|bite +s

tri|locu|lar
tril|ogy
  trilo|gies
Trim (town,
  Republic of
  Ireland)
trim
  trims
  trimmed
  trim|ming
  trim|mer
  trim|mest
tri|maran +s
tri|mer +s
tri|mer|ic
tri|mer|ous
tri|mes|ter +s
tri|mes|tral
trim|eter +s
tri|met|ric
tri|met|ric|al
trim|ly
trim|mer +s
trim|ming +s
trim|ness
Tri|mon|tium
  (Roman name for
  Plovdiv)
tri|morph|ic
tri|morph|ism
tri|morph|ous
Tri|murti
tri|nal
Trinco|ma|lee
  (port, Sri Lanka)
trine +s
Trin|ian (in 'St
  Trinian's')
Trini|dad (island,
  West Indies)
Trini|dad and
  To|bago (country,
  West Indies)
Trini|dad|ian +s
Trini|tar|ian +s
Trini|tar|ian|ism
tri|nitro|tolu|ene
tri|nitro|toluol
trin|ity
  trin|ities
trin|ket +s
trin|ket|ry
tri|nomial
tri|nomi|al|ism
trio +s
tri|ode +s
tri|oe|cious Br.
  (Am. triecious)
trio|let +s
tri|ox|ide
trip
  trips

trip (cont.)
  tripped
  trip|ping
tri|par|tite
tri|par|tite|ly
tri|par|ti|tion
tripe +s
tri|pet|al|ous
trip-hammer +s
tri|phibi|ous
tri|phos|phate +s
triph|thong +s
triph|thong|al
triph|yl|lous
tri|pin|nate
Tri|pit|aka
tri|plane +s
triple
  triples
  tripled
  trip|ling
trip|let +s
Trip|lex (glass)
  Propr.
trip|lex (triple)
trip|li|cate
  trip|li|cates
  trip|li|cated
  trip|li|cat|ing
trip|li|ca|tion +s
trip|li|city
  trip|li|ci|ties
trip|loid +s
trip|loidy
triply
trip|meter +s
tri|pod +s
tri|pod|al
Trip|oli (capital of
  Libya; port,
  Lebanon)
trip|oli +s (stone;
  powder)
Trip|oli|tania
  (coastal region,
  Libya)
Trip|oli|tan|ian +s
tri|pos
  tri|poses
trip|per +s
trip|pery
trippy
trip|tych +s (set of
  three hinged
  pictures, writing
  tablets etc.
  △ tryptic)
trip|tyque +s
Trip|ura (state,
  India)
trip|wire +s

tri|quetra
  tri|quet|rae
tri|quet|ral
tri|quet|rous
tri|reme +s
tri|sac|char|ide +s
Tris|agion +s
tri|sect +s +ed
  +ing
tri|sec|tion +s
tri|sect|or +s
Trish
Trisha also Tricia
tri|shaw +s
tris|kai|deka|
        pho|bia
tri|skel|ion +s
tris|mus
tri|somy
trisomy-21
Tris|tan
Tris|tan da Cunha
  (island, S.
  Atlantic)
triste
trist|esse
tri|stich|ous
tri|stig|mat|ic
Tris|tram
tri|styl|ous
tri|sul|cate
tri|syl|lab|ic
tri|syl|lable +s
tri|tag|on|ist +s
trite
  triter
  trit|est
trite|ly
trite|ness
tri|tern|ate
tri|the|ism
tri|the|ist +s
triti|ate
  triti|ates
  triti|ated
  triti|at|ing
triti|ation
trit|ium
Tri|ton (Greek
  Mythology; moon
  of Neptune)
tri|ton +s (mollusc;
  newt; nucleus)
tri|tone +s (musical
  interval)
trit|ur|able
trit|ur|ate
  trit|ur|ates
  trit|ur|ated
  trit|ur|at|ing
trit|ur|ation
trit|ur|ator +s

tri|umph +s +ed
  +ing
tri|umph|al
tri|umph|al|ism
tri|umph|al|ist
tri|umph|al|ly
tri|umph|ant
tri|umph|ant|ly
tri|um|vir
  tri|um|virs or
  tri|um|viri
tri|um|vir|al
tri|um|vir|ate +s
tri|une
tri|un|ity
  tri|un|ities
tri|va|lency
  tri|va|len|cies
tri|va|lent
Tri|van|drum (city,
  India)
trivet +s
trivia
triv|ial
trivi|al|isa|tion Br.
  (use
  trivialization)
trivi|al|ise Br. (use
  trivialize)
trivi|al|ises
trivi|al|ised
trivi|al|is|ing
trivi|al|ity
  trivi|al|ities
trivi|al|iza|tion
trivi|al|ize
  trivi|al|izes
  trivi|al|ized
  trivi|al|iz|ing
trivi|al|ly
trivi|al|ness
triv|ium
trivia
tri-weekly
Trixie
Troad (ancient
  region, NW Asia
  Minor)
Tro|bri|and
  Is|lands (in SW
  Pacific)
tro|car +s
tro|cha|ic
tro|chal
tro|chan|ter +s
troche +s (tablet)
tro|chee +s (metric
  foot)
troch|lea
  troch|leae
  noun
troch|lear adjective

troch|oid +s
troch|oid|al
tro|chus
  tro|chi *or*
  tro|chuses
trod
trod|den
trog +s
trog'lo|dyte +s
trog'lo|dyt|ic
trog'lo|dyt'ic|al
trog'lo|dyt|ism
tro|gon +s
troika +s
troil|ism
Troi|lus *Greek*
  Mythology
Tro|jan +s
troll +s +ed +ing
troll|er +s
trol|ley +s
trol'ley|bus
  trol'ley|buses
trolley-car +s
trol|lop +s
Trol|lope,
  An|thony
  (English novelist)
trol|lop|ish
trol|lopy
trom|bone +s
trom|bon|ist +s
trom|mel +s
trom|om|eter +s
tromo|met'ric
trompe +s
trompe l'œil +s
Tromsø (port,
  Norway)
Trond|heim (port,
  Norway)
Troon (town,
  Scotland)
troop +s +ed +ing
  (assemblage;
  soldiers; to
  assemble or move
  in large numbers.
  ⚠ troupe)
troop car|rier +s
troop|er +s
  (soldier; police
  officer; troopship.
  ⚠ trouper)
troop|ship +s
tro|pae|olum +s
trope +s
troph|ic
tro|phied
tropho|blast +s
tropho|neur|osis
  tropho|neur|oses

trophy
  tro|phies
trop|ic +s (of
  Cancer or
  Capricorn)
trop|ic|al +s
trop|ic|al|ly
Trop|ics (region)
trop|ism +s
tropo|logic|al
trop|ology
  trop|olo|gies
tropo|pause +s
tropo|sphere +s
tropo|spher|ic
troppo
Tros|sachs, the
  (valley, Scotland)
Trot +s
  (= Trotskyist)
trot
  trots
  trot|ted
  trot|ting
  (run etc.)
troth +s
Trot|sky, Leon
  (Russian
  revolutionary)
Trot|sky|ism
Trot|sky|ist +s
Trot|sky|ite +s
trot|ter +s
trot|ting race +s
tro|tyl +s
trou|ba|dour +s
trouble
  troubles
  troubled
  troub|ling
trouble|maker +s
trouble-making
troub|ler +s
trouble|shoot
  trouble|shoots
  trouble|shot
  trouble|shoot|ing
trouble|shoot|er
  +s
trouble|some
trouble|some|ly
trouble|some|ness
trouble spot +s
troub|lous
trough +s +ed
  +ing
trounce
  trounces
  trounced
  troun|cing
troun|cer +s

troupe +s
  (company of
  actors etc.
  ⚠ troop)
trouper +s
  (member of
  troupe; staunch
  colleague.
  ⚠ trooper)
trou|ser *attributive*
trouser-clip +s
trou|sered
trou|ser leg +s
trouser|less
trou|ser press
  trou|ser presses
trou|sers
trou|ser suit +s
trous|seau
  trous|seaus *or*
  trous|seaux
trout
  plural trout *or*
  trouts
trout|let +s
trout|ling +s
trouty
trou|vaille +s
trou|vère +s
trove +s
trover +s
trow +s +ed +ing
Trow|bridge
  (town, England)
trowel
  trowels
  trow|elled *Br.*
  trow|eled *Am.*
  trow|el|ling *Br.*
  trow|el|ing *Am.*
Troy (ancient city,
  Turkey)
troy (weight)
Troyes (town,
  France)
Troyes, Chré|tien
  de (French poet)
tru|ancy
tru|ant +s +ed
  +ing
truce +s
truce|less
tru|cial
Tru|cial States
  (former name of
  the United Arab
  Emirates)
truck +s +ed +ing
truck|age
truck|er +s
truckie +s

truckle
  truckles
  truckled
  truck|ling
truck|ler +s
truck|load +s
trucu|lence
trucu|lency
trucu|lent
trucu|lent|ly
Tru|deau, Pierre
  (Canadian prime
  minister)
trudge
  trudges
  trudged
  trudg|ing
trudgen
trudger +s
Trudi *also* Trudy
Trudy *also* Trudi
true
  trues
  trued
  tru|ing *or* true|ing
  truer
  tru|est
true-blue +s
true-born
true-bred
true-hearted
true|ish
true love +s
true-love knot +s
True|man,
  Fred|die (English
  cricketer)
true|ness
Truf|faut,
  Fran|çois (French
  film director)
truf|fle +s
trug +s
tru|ism +s
tru|is|tic
Tru|jillo (city, Peru;
  in 'Ciudad
  Trujillo')
Tru|jillo, Raf|ael
  (Dominican
  president)
Truk Is|lands (in
  W. Pacific)
trull +s
truly
Tru|man, Harry S.
  (American
  president)
tru|meau
  tru|meaux
trump +s +ed +ing

trump|ery
  trump|er¦ies
trum|pet +s +ed
  +ing
trum|pet blast +s
trum|pet call +s
trum|pet¦er +s
trum|pet¦ing +s
trum|pet¦less
trum|pet play¦er
  +s
trun|cal
trun|cate
  trun|cates
  trun|cated
  trun|cat¦ing
trun|cate¦ly
trun|ca¦tion +s
trun|cheon +s
trun|dle
  trun¦dles
  trun¦dled
  trund|ling
trundle-bed +s
trunk +s
trunk|ful +s
trunk|ing +s
trunk|less
trunk|like
trunk line +s
trunk road +s
trun|nion +s
Truro (city,
  England)
truss
  trusses
  trussed
  truss|ing
truss¦er +s
trust +s +ed +ing
trust|able
trust|bust¦er +s
trust|bust¦ing
trust¦ee +s
  (administrator of
  trust. △ trustie,
  trusty)
trustee|ship +s
trust¦er +s
trust|ful
trust|ful¦ly
trust|ful¦ness
trust fund +s
trustie +s
  (prisoner; use
  trusty. △ trustee)
trust|ily
trusti|ness
trust|ing¦ly
trust|ing¦ness
trust|wor¦thily
trust|worthi|ness

trust|worthy
trusty
  trust|ies
  trust|ier
  trusti|est
  (trustworthy;
  prisoner.
  △ trustee)
truth +s
truth|ful
truth|ful¦ly
truth|ful|ness
truth|less
try
  tries
  tried
  try¦ing
try|ing¦ly
trying-plane +s
try-on +s noun
try-out +s noun
tryp¦ano|some +s
tryp¦ano|
  som¦ia¦sis
tryp|sin
tryp|sino¦gen
tryp|tic (of or
  pertaining to
  trypsin.
  △ triptych)
tryp¦to|phan +s
try|sail +s
try-scorer +s
try-scoring noun
  and attributive
try-square +s
tryst +s +ed +ing
tryst¦er +s
Tsao-chuang
  (= Zaozhuan)
tsar +s
tsar|dom +s
tsar|ev¦ich
  tsar|ev¦iches
tsar|evna +s
tsar|ina +s
tsar|ism
tsar|ist +s
Tsar|it¦syn (former
  name of
  Volgograd)
Tsavo Na|tion¦al
  Park (in Kenya)
tses|sebi +s
tse¦tse +s
T-shirt +s
Tsi¦nan (= Jinan)
Tsing|hai
  (= Qinghai)
Tsiol|kov¦sky,
  Kon|stan|tin
  (Russian

Tsiol|kov¦sky
  (cont.)
  aeronautical
  engineer)
Tsi¦tsi|kamma
  For¦est (in South
  Africa)
Tskhin|vali (capital
  of South Ossetia,
  Russia)
Tsonga
  plural Tsonga or
  Tson|gas
T-square +s
tsu|nami +s
Tsu|shima
  (Japanese island,
  Korea Strait)
Tswana +s
Tua|motu
  Archi|pe¦lago (in
  French Polynesia)
Tua¦reg
  plural Tua¦reg or
  Tua|regs
tua|tara +s
Tua¦tha Dé
  Dan¦aan
  (legendary Irish
  people)
tub
  tubs
  tubbed
  tub|bing
tuba +s
tubal
tub|bable
tub|bi|ness
tub|bish
tubby
  tub|bier
  tub|bi|est
tubby|ish
tube
  tubes
  tubed
  tub¦ing
tub|ec¦tomy
  tub|ec¦to¦mies
tube|less
tube|like
tuber +s
tu|ber¦cle +s
tu|ber¦cu|lar +s
tu|ber¦cu|late
tu|ber¦cu|la¦tion
tu|ber¦cu|lin
tuberculin-tested
tu|ber¦cu|losis
tu|ber¦cu|lous
tu|ber¦ose +s
tu|ber¦os¦ity

tu|ber¦ous
tube worm +s
tub|ful +s
tu|bico¦lous
tu|bi|corn +s
tu|bi|fex
tu|bi|fex worm +s
tu|bi|form
tu|bi|lin¦gual
tub|ing +s
tub-sized
tub-thumper +s
tub-thumping
Tu|buai Is|lands
  (in S. Pacific)
tu|bu|lar
tu|bule +s
tu|bu|lous
tuck +s +ed +ing
tuck-box
  tuck-boxes
tuck¦er +s +ed
  +ing
tucker-bag +s
tucket +s
tuck-in +s adjective
  and noun
tuck-net +s
tuck shop +s
Tuc¦son (city, USA)
Tudor +s (English
  royal house)
Tudor|bethan
Tudor|esque
Tues|day +s
tufa +s
tu|fa¦ceous
tuff (rock. △ tough)
tuff|aceous
tuf¦fet +s
tuft +s +ed +ing
tufty
  tuft|ier
  tufti|est
Tu Fu (Chinese
  poet)
tug
  tugs
  tugged
  tug|ging
tug|boat +s
tug|ger +s
tug of love
tug-of-war
  tugs-of-war
tu|grik +s
tui
  plural tui or tuis
Tuil|er¦ies
  (Gar|dens) (in
  Paris)
tu|ition

tu¦ition¦al
tu¦ition¦ary
Tula (city, Russia;
  ancient city,
  Mexico)
tu¦lar¦ae¦mia *Br.*
tu¦lar¦aem¦ic *Br.*
tu¦lar¦emia *Am.*
tu¦lar¦em¦ic *Am.*
tul¦chan +s
tulip +s
tulip-root +s
tulip tree +s
tulip¦wood +s
Tull, Jethro
  (English
  agriculturalist)
Tul¦la¦more (town,
  Republic of
  Ireland)
tulle (net)
Tulsa (port, USA)
Tul¦si¦das (Indian
  poet)
tul¦war +s
tum +s (= tummy)
tum¦ble
  tum¦bles
  tum¦bled
  tum¦bling
tumble¦down
tumble-drier +s
  (use tumble-
  dryer)
tumble-dry
  tumble-dries
  tumble-dried
  tumble-drying
tumble-dryer +s
tum¦bler +s
tum¦bler¦ful +s
tumble¦weed +s
tumbling-barrel
  +s
tumbling-bay +s
tum¦brel +s (use
  tumbril)
tum¦bril +s
tu¦me¦fa¦cient
tu¦me¦fac¦tion
tu¦mefy
  tu¦me¦fies
  tu¦me¦fied
  tu¦me¦fy¦ing
tu¦mes¦cence
tu¦mes¦cent
tu¦mes¦cent¦ly
tumid
tu¦mid¦ity
tu¦mid¦ly
tu¦mid¦ness

tummy
  tum¦mies
tummy ache +s
tummy bug +s
tummy but¦ton +s
tumor *Am.* +s
tu¦mor¦ous
tu¦mour *Br.* +s
tump +s
tum¦tum +s
tu¦mu¦lar
tu¦mult +s
tu¦mul¦tu¦ary
tu¦mul¦tu¦ous
tu¦mul¦tu¦ous¦ly
tu¦mul¦tu¦ous¦ness
tu¦mu¦lus
  tu¦muli
tun
  tuns
  tunned
  tun¦ning
  (cask. △ ton,
  tonne)
tuna
  plural tuna *or*
  tunas
  (fish. △ tuner)
tun¦able
tuna fish
  plural tuna fish
Tunb Is¦lands (in
  Persian Gulf)
Tun¦bridge Wells
  (officially Royal
  Tunbridge Wells;
  spa town,
  England.
  △ Tonbridge)
tun¦dish
  tun¦dishes
tun¦dra +s
tune
  tunes
  tuned
  tun¦ing
tune¦able
tune¦ful
tune¦ful¦ly
tune¦ful¦ness
tune¦less
tune¦less¦ly
tune¦less¦ness
tuner +s (person
  who tunes
  instruments; part
  of radio. △ tuna)
tung +s (tree; oil.
  △ tongue)
tung¦state +s
tung¦sten
tung¦stic

Tun¦gus
  plural Tun¦gus
Tun¦gus¦ian +s
Tun¦gus¦ic
Tun¦guska (two
  rivers, Russia)
tunic +s
tu¦nica
  tu¦nicae
tu¦ni¦cate +s
tu¦nicle +s
tun¦ing +s
Tunis (capital of
  Tunisia)
Tu¦nisia
Tu¦nis¦ian +s
tun¦nel
  tun¦nels
  tun¦nelled *Br.*
  tun¦neled *Am.*
  tun¦nel¦ling *Br.*
  tun¦nel¦ing *Am.*
tun¦nel¦er *Am.* +s
tunnel-kiln +s
tun¦nel¦ler *Br.* +s
tunnel-net +s
tun¦nel vi¦sion
tunny
  tun¦nies
tup
  tups
  tupped
  tup¦ping
Tupa¦maro +s
Tup¦elo (city, USA)
tu¦pelo +s
Tupi
  plural Tupi *or*
  Tupis
Tupi-Guarani
  plural
  Tupi-Guarani *or*
  Tupi-Guara¦nis
tup¦pence +s
tup¦penny
  tup¦pen¦nies
tuppenny-
  ha'penny
Tup¦per¦ware
  Propr.
tuque +s
tur¦aco +s
Tur¦an¦ian +s
tur¦ban +s
tur¦baned
tur¦bary
  tur¦bar¦ies
tur¦bel¦lar¦ian +s
tur¦bid
tur¦bid¦ity
tur¦bid¦ly
tur¦bid¦ness

tur¦bin¦al
tur¦bin¦ate
tur¦bin¦ation
tur¦bine +s
tur¦bit +s (pigeon.
  △ turbot)
turbo +s
turbo|charge
  turbo|charges
  turbo|charged
  turbo|char¦ging
turbo|char¦ger +s
turbo-diesel +s
turbo|fan +s
turbo|jet +s
turbo|prop +s
turbo|shaft +s
turbo|super|
  char¦ger +s
tur¦bot
  plural tur¦bot *or*
  tur¦bots
  (fish. △ turbit)
tur¦bu¦lence
tur¦bu¦lent
tur¦bu¦lent¦ly
Turco +s
Turco|man +s (use
  Turkoman)
Turco|phile +s
Turco|phobe +s
turd +s (*coarse
  slang*)
turd|oid
tur¦een +s
turf
  turfs *or* turves
  noun
turf +s +ed +ing
  verb
Tur¦fan
  De|pres¦sion
  (area, China)
turf|man
  turf|men
turfy
Tur¦genev, Ivan
  (Russian writer)
tur¦ges¦cence
tur¦ges¦cent
tur¦gid¦es¦cence
tur¦gid¦es¦cent
tur¦gid|ity
tur¦gid|ly
tur¦gid|ness
tur¦gor
Turin (city, Italy)
Tur¦ing, Alan
  (English
  mathematician;
  test; machine)

tur¦ion +s
Turk +s
Tur|kana
  plural Tur|kana
  (person; language)
Tur|kana, Lake (in
  Kenya)
Turk|estan (region,
  central Asia)
Tur|key (country)
tur¦key +s (bird;
  flop; stupid
  person)
tur¦key|cock +s
Turki +s
  (languages;
  person)
Turk¦ic
Turk¦ish
Turki|stan (use
  Turkestan)
Turk|men
  plural Turk|men
  or Turk|mens
Turk|meni|stan
Turko|man +s
Turks and Cai¦cos
  Is¦lands (in West
  Indies)
Turku (port,
  Finland)
tur|meric
tur|moil +s
turn +s +ed +ing
  (rotate; change;
  etc. △ tern terne)
turn|about +s
turn|around +s
turn|back +s
turn-bench
  turn-benches
turn-buckle +s
turn-cap +s
turn|coat +s
turn|cock +s
turn|down +s
Turn¦er, Jo¦seph
  Mal|lord
  Wil|liam (English
  painter)
turn¦er +s
turn¦ery
  turn|er¦ies
turn-in +s *noun*
turn|ing +s
turn|ing circle +s
turn|ing point +s
tur¦nip +s
turnip-top +s
tur|nipy
turn|key +s
turn-off +s *noun*
turn-on +s *noun*

turn|out +s
turn|over +s
turn|pike +s
turn|round +s
turn|sick
turn|side
turn|sole +s
turn|spit +s
turn|stile +s
turn|stone +s
turn|table +s
turn-up +s *noun*
  and adjective
tur¦pen|tine
  tur¦pen|tines
  tur¦pen|tined
  tur¦pen|tin¦ing
tur|peth +s
Tur¦pin, Dick
  (English
  highwayman)
tur|pi¦tude
turps (= turpentine)
tur|quoise +s
tur|ret +s
tur|ret|ed
tur¦tle +s
turtle-dove +s
turtle|neck +s
turtle|shell
  adjective
tur¦tle shell +s
  noun
turves
Tus¦can +s
Tus¦cany (region,
  Italy)
Tus¦ca|rora
  plural Tus¦ca|rora
  or Tus¦ca|roras
tush
  tushes
tusk +s +ed +ing
tusk¦er +s
tusky
tus¦sah *Am.* (*Br.*
  tussore)
Tus¦saud,
  Ma¦dame Marie
  (wax-modeller)
Tus¦saud's,
  Ma¦dame
  (waxworks)
tus¦ser (use
  tussore)
tus|sive
tus¦sle
  tus¦sles
  tus¦sled
  tus¦sling
tus|sock +s
tus|socky

tus¦sore +s
tut
  tuts
  tut¦ted
  tut¦ting
Tu¦tan|kha¦men
  (pharaoh)
Tu¦tan|kha¦mun
  (use
  Tutankhamen)
tutee +s
tu¦tel|age
tu|tel|ar
tu|tel|ary
tu|tenag
Tuth|mo¦sis
  (pharaoh)
tutor +s +ed +ing
tu|tor|age
tu|tor|ess
  tu¦tor|esses
tu|tor|ial +s
tu|tori|al¦ly
tu|tor|ship +s
tut¦san +s
Tutsi
  plural Tutsi *or*
  Tut¦sis
  (person. △ tootsy)
tutti +s *Music*
tutti-frutti +s
tut-tut
  tut-tuts
  tut-tutted
  tut-tutting
tutty (polishing
  powder)
Tutu, Des¦mond
  (South African
  archbishop)
tutu +s (dancer's
  skirt; plant. △ too-
  too)
Tuva (republic,
  Russia)
Tu¦valu
Tu¦va|lu¦an +s
tu-whit, tu-whoo
  +s
tux
  tuxes
  (= tuxedo)
tux¦edo +s
Tux¦tla Gu¦tiér¦rez
  (city, Mexico)
tuy¦ère +s
Tuzla (town,
  Bosnia)
Tver (port, Russia)
Twa
  plural Twa *or*
  Twas *or* Batwa

twad¦dle
  twad¦dles
  twad¦dled
  twad¦dling
twad|dler +s
twad|dly
Twain, Mark
  (American writer)
twain
twang +s +ed +ing
twan¦gle
  twan¦gles
  twan¦gled
  twan|gling
twangy
'twas (= it was)
twat +s (*coarse
  slang*)
tway|blade +s
tweak +s +ed +ing
twee
  tweer
  tweest
Tweed (river,
  Scotland and
  England)
tweed +s (cloth;
  clothes)
tweed|ily
tweedi|ness
Tweedle|dum and
  Tweedle|dee
tweedy
twee¦ly
'tween (= between)
'tween-decks
twee|ness
tweeny
  tween|ies
tweet +s +ed +ing
tweet¦er +s
tweez¦er +s +ed
  +ing
twelfth +s
twelfth¦ly
twelve +s
twelve-bore +s
twelve|fold
twelvemo
twelve|month +s
twelve-note
  adjective
twen¦ti¦eth +s
twenty
  twen|ties
twenty|fold
twenty-fourmo
twenty|
  some¦thing +s
twenty-twenty
'twere (= it were)
twerp +s

Twi
  plural **Twi** *or* **Twis**
twi|bill +s
twice
twicer +s
Twick|en|ham
  (district, London;
  rugby ground)
twid|dle
  twid|dles
  twid|dled
  twid|dling
twid|dler +s
twid|dly
twig
  twigs
  twigged
  twig|ging
twiggy
twi|light +s
twi|lit
twill +s +ed +ing
'twill (= it will)
twin
  twins
  twinned
  twin|ning
twin-cam
twine
  twines
  twined
  twin|ing
twin-engined
twiner +s
twinge
  twinges
  twinged
  twin|ging *or*
  twinge|ing
twink +s
twin|kle
  twin|kles
  twin|kled
  twink|ling
twink|ler +s
twin|kly
twin|ning +s
Twins, the
  (constellation;
  sign of zodiac)
twin-screw
twin|set +s
twirl +s +ed +ing
twirl|er +s
twirly
twirp +s (use
  twerp)
twist +s +ed +ing
twist|able
twist|er +s
twist|ing +s

twisty
twist|ier
twisti|est
twit
  twits
  twit|ted
  twit|ting
twitch
  twitches
  twitched
  twitch|ing
twitch|er +s
twitch|ily
twitchi|ness
twitchy
  twitch|ier
  twitchi|est
twite +s
twit|ter +s +ed
  +ing
twit|ter|er +s
twit|tery
twit|tish
'twixt (= betwixt)
twiz|zle
  twiz|zles
  twiz|zled
  twiz|zling
two +s (number.
  ⚠ to, too)
two-bit
two-by-four +s
two-dimension|al
two-edged
two-faced
two|fold
two-handed
two-iron +s
two|ness
two|pence +s
two|penn'orth
two|penny
  two|pen|nies
twopenny-
  halfpenny
two|penny|worth
two-piece +s
two-ply +s
two-seater +s
two-sided
two|some +s
two-step +s
two-stroke +s
two-time
  two-times
  two-timed
  two-timing
two-timer +s
two-tone
'twould (= it
  would)
two-up

two-way
two -wheeler +s
twyer +s
Ty|burn (former
  site of public
  hangings, London)
tych|ism
tych|ist +s
Ty|cho|nian +s
Tych|on|ic
ty|coon +s
tying
tyke +s (may cause
  offence in
  Australia and New
  Zealand)
Tyler, John
  (American
  president)
Tyler, Wat
  (English
  revolutionary)
ty|lo|pod +s
ty|lopo|dous
tym|pan +s
tym|pana
tym|pani
  (kettledrums; use
  timpani)
tym|pan|ic
tym|pan|ites
  (swelling of
  abdomen)
tym|pan|it|ic
tym|pan|itis
  (inflammation of
  eardrum)
tym|pa|num
  tym|pa|nums *or*
  tym|pana
tym|pany
  (= tympanites)
Tyn|dale,
  Wil|liam (English
  translator of Bible)
Tyn|dall, John
  (Irish physicist)
Tyne (river,
  England; shipping
  area)
Tyne and Wear
  (metropolitan
  county, England)
Tyne|side (region,
  England)
Tyne|sider +s
Tyn|wald
  (legislative
  assembly, Isle of
  Man)
typal
type
  types

type (*cont.*)
  typed
  typ|ing
type|cast
  type|casts
  type|cast
  type|cast|ing
type|face +s
type found|er +s
type foun|dry
  type foun|dries
type metal
type|script +s
type|set
  type|sets
  type|set
  type|set|ting
type|set|ter +s
type site +s
type size +s
type|writer +s
type|writ|ing
type|writ|ten
typh|lit|ic
typh|litis
ty|phoid
ty|phoid|al
ty|phon|ic
ty|phoon +s
typh|ous *adjective*
ty|phus *noun*
typ|ical
typ|ic|al|ity
typ|ic|al|ly
typi|fi|ca|tion +s
typi|fier +s
typ|ify
  typi|fies
  typi|fied
  typi|fy|ing
typ|ist +s
typo +s
typ|og|raph|er +s
typo|graph|ic
typo|graph|ic|al
typo|graph|ic|al|ly
typ|og|raphy
  typ|og|raph|ies
typo|logic|al
typ|olo|gist +s
typ|ology
  typ|olo|gies
typo|nym +s
Tyr *Scandinavian*
  Mythology
tyr|am|ine
tyr|an|nic|al
tyr|an|nic|al|ly
tyr|an|ni|cidal
tyr|an|ni|cide +s
tyr|an|nise *Br.* (use
  tyrannize)

tyr|an|nise(cont.)
  tyr|an|nises
  tyr|an|nised
  tyr|an|nis|ing
tyr|an|nize
  tyr|an|nizes
  tyr|an|nized
  tyr|an|niz|ing
tyr|an|no|saur+s
tyr|an|no|
  saur|uses or
  tyr|an|no|sauri
Tyr|an|no|saurus
  Rex
tyr|an|nous
tyr|an|nous|ly
tyr|anny
  tyr|an|nies
tyr|ant+s
Tyre(port,
  Lebanon)
tyre Br. +s (on
  wheel. Am. tire
  ⚠ tire)
tyre gauge Br. +s
  (Am. tire gauge)
Tyr|ian+s
tyro+s
Tyrol (state,
  Austria)
Tyr|ol|ean+s
Tyr|ol|ese
  plural Tyr|ol|ese
Tyr|one (county,
  Northern Ireland;
  name)
tyro|sine
Tyr|rhene+s
Tyr|rhen|ian+s
Tyr|rhen|ian Sea
Tyu|men (city,
  Russia)
tzar+s (use tsar)
Tzara, Tris|tan
  (Romanian-born
  French poet)
tzar|ina +s (use
  tsarina)
tzar|ist +s (use
  tsarist)
tza|tziki+s
tzi|gane +s
Tzu-po (= Zibo)

Uu

Ubaid
Ubanghi Shari
  (former name of
  the Central
  African Republic)
Über|mensch
  Über|mensch|en
ubi|ety
  ubi|eties
ubi|qui|tar|ian+s
ubi|qui|tar|ian|ism
ubi|qui|tous
ubi|qui|tous|ly
ubi|qui|tous|ness
ubi|quity
U-boat+s
UCATT (= Union of
  Construction,
  Allied Trades, and
  Technicians)
UCCA
  (= Universities
  Central Council on
  Admissions)
Uc|cello, Paolo
  (Italian painter)
udal+s
udal|ler+s
udal|man
  udal|men
udder+s
ud|dered
Ud|mur|tia
  (republic, Russia)
udom|eter+s
UEFA (= Union of
  European Football
  Associations)
uey+s
Ufa (city, Russia)
Uf|fizi (art gallery,
  Florence, Italy)
UFO +s
  (= unidentified
  flying object)
ufolo|gist+s
ufol|ogy
Uganda
Ugan|dan+s
Ugarit (ancient
  port, Syria)
Ugar|it|ic
ugh
ug|li|fi|ca|tion
ugli fruit
  plural ugli fruit
  (fruit. ⚠ ugly)
  Propr.

uglify
  ugli|fies
  ugli|fied
  ugli|fy|ing
ug|lily
ugli|ness
ugly
  ug|lier
  ugli|est
  (hideous etc.
  ⚠ ugli fruit)
Ugrian+s
Ugric+s
uh-huh
uhlan+s
Ui|ghur+s
Uigur+s (use
  Uighur)
Uist, North and
  South+s
  (Scottish islands)
Uit|land|er+s
uja|maa
Uji|ya|mada
  (former name of
  Ise)
Uj|jain (city, India)
Ujung Pan|dang
  (port, Indonesia)
ukase+s
ukiyo-e
Ukraine
Ukrain|ian+s
uku|lele+s
Ulala (former name
  of Gorno-Altaisk)
Ulan Bator (capital
  of Mongolia)
Ulan|ova, Gal|ina
  (Russian ballet
  dancer)
Ulan-Ude (city,
  Russia)
ulcer+s
ul|cer|able
ul|cer|ate
  ul|cer|ates
  ul|cer|ated
  ul|cer|at|ing
ul|cer|ation+s
ul|cera|tive
ul|cered
ul|cer|ous
Uleå|borg (Swedish
  name for Oulu)
ulema+s
Ul|fi|las (bishop
  and translator)
Ul|has|nagar (city,
  India)
uligin|ose
uligin|ous

ull|age
Ulm (city,
  Germany)
ulna
  ulnae
  noun
ulnar adjective
ulot|ri|chan+s
ulot|ri|chous
Ul|pian (Roman
  jurist)
Ulsan (port, South
  Korea)
Ul|ster (former
  province,
  Northern Ireland)
ul|ster+s (coat)
Ul|ster|man
  Ul|ster|men
Ul|ster|woman
  Ul|ster|women
ul|ter|ior
ul|ter|ior|ly
ul|tima+s
ul|tim|acy
ul|ti|mata
ul|tim|ate+s
ul|tim|ate|ly
ul|tim|ate|ness
ul|tima Thule
ul|ti|matum
  ul|ti|matums or
  ul|ti|mata
ul|timo
ul|ti|mo|geni|ture
  +s
ultra+s
ultra|cen|tri|fuge
  +s
ul|tra|dian
ultra|fil|tra|tion
ultra-high
ultra|ism
ultra|ist +s
ultra-left
ultra|mar|ine+s
ultra|micro|scope
  +s
ultra|micro|
          scop|ic
ultra|mon|tane+s
ultra|mon|tan|ism
ultra|mon|tan|ist
  +s
ultra|mun|dane
ultra-right
ultra|son|ic
ultra|son|ic|al|ly
ultra|son|ics
ultra|sound
ultra|struc|ture+s
ultra|vio|let

ultra vires
ulu|lant
ulu|late
  ulu|lates
  ulu|lated
  ulu|lat|ing
ulu|la|tion +s
Ul|undi (town,
  South Africa)
Uluru (Aboriginal
  name for Ayers
  Rock)
Ul|ya|nov (original
  surname of Lenin)
Ul|yan|ovsk
  (former name of
  Simbirsk)
Ulys|ses (Roman
  name for
  Odysseus;
  European space
  probe)
um
Umay|yad +s
umbel +s
um|bel|lar
um|bel|late
um|bel|lif|er +s
um|bel|lif|er|ous
um|bel|lule +s
umber +s
um|bil|ical +s
um|bil|ic|al|ly
um|bil|icate
um|bil|icus
  um|bil|ici *or*
  um|bil|ic|uses
um|bles
umbo
  umbos *or*
  umbo|nes
umbo|nal
umbo|nate
umbra
  um|bras *or*
  um|brae
um|brage +s
um|bra|geous
um|bral
um|brella +s
umbrella-like
um|brette +s
Um|bria (region,
  Italy)
Um|brian +s
Um|briel (moon of
  Uranus)
um|brif|er|ous
Umeå (city,
  Sweden)
umiak +s

um|laut +s +ed
  +ing
Umm al Qai|wain
  (state and city,
  UAE)
ump +s
um|pir|age +s
um|pire
  um|pires
  um|pired
  um|pir|ing
um|pire|ship +s
ump|teen
ump|teenth
umpty
umpty-doo
Um|tali (former
  name of Mutare)
'un (= one, as in
  'young 'un')
Una *also* Oona,
  Oo|nagh
un|abashed
un|abashed|ly
un|abated
un|abated|ly
un|able
un|abridged
un|absorbed
un|aca|dem|ic
un|accent|ed
un|accept|abil|ity
un|accept|able
un|accept|able|
          ness
un|accept|ably
un|accept|ed
un|acclaimed
un|accom|
         mo|dated
un|accom|
         mo|dat|ing
un|accom|pan|ied
un|accom|plished
un|account|
         abil|ity
un|account|able
un|account|able|
         ness
un|account|ably
un|account|ed
un|accus|tomed
un|accus|tomed|ly
un|achiev|able
un|acknow|ledged
un|acquaint|ed
un|adapt|able
un|adapt|ed
un|ad|dressed
un|adja|cent
un|adjust|ed
un|ad|mit|ted

un|adopt|ed
un|adorned
un|adul|ter|ated
un|ad|ven|tur|ous
un|ad|ven|tur|
         ous|ly
un|ad|ver|tised
un|ad|vis|able
un|ad|vised
un|ad|vised|ly
un|ad|vised|ness
un|aes|thet|ic *Br.*
  (*Am.* unesthetic)
un|affect|ed
un|affect|ed|ly
un|affect|ed|ness
un|affec|tion|ate
un|affili|ated
un|afford|able
un|afraid
un|aggres|sive
un|aid|ed
un|alarmed
un|alien|able
un|alien|ated
un|aligned
un|alike
un|alive
un|allevi|ated
un|allied
un|allo|cated
un|allow|able
un|alloyed
un|alter|able
un|alter|able|ness
un|alter|ably
un|altered
un|alter|ing
un|amazed
un|am|bi|gu|ity
un|am|bigu|ous
un|am|bigu|ous|ly
un|am|bi|tious
un|am|bi|tious|ly
un|am|bi|tious|
         ness
un|am|biva|lent
un|am|biva|lent|ly
un|amen|able
un|amend|ed
un-American
un-American|ism
un|ami|able
un|amp|li|fied
un|amused
un|amus|ing
un|ana|lys|able
un|ana|lysed
un|aneled
unan|im|ity
unani|mous
unani|mous|ly

unani|mous|ness
un|announced
un|answer|able
un|answer|able|
         ness
un|answer|ably
un|answered
un|antici|pated
un|apolo|get|ic
un|apolo|get|ic|
         al|ly
un|ap|os|tol|ic
un|appar|ent
un|appeal|able
un|appeal|ing
un|appeal|ing|ly
un|appeas|able
un|appeased
un|appe|tis|ing *Br.*
  (use
  unappetizing)
un|appe|tis|ing|ly
  Br. (use
  unappetizingly)
un|appe|tiz|ing
un|appe|tiz|ing|ly
un|applied
un|appre|ci|ated
un|appre|cia|tive
un|appre|hend|ed
un|approach|
         abil|ity
un|approach|able
un|approach|able|
         ness
un|approach|ably
un|appro|pri|ated
un|approved
unapt
un|apt|ly
un|apt|ness
un|argu|able
un|argu|ably
un|argued
unarm +s +ed
  +ing
un|arrest|ing
un|arrest|ing|ly
un|articu|lated
un|artis|tic
un|artis|tic|al|ly
un|ascer|tain|able
un|ascer|tain|ably
un|ascer|tained
un|ashamed
un|ashamed|ly
un|ashamed|ness
un|asked
unasked-for
un|assail|abil|ity
un|assail|able

un|assail|able|
    ness
un|assail|ably
un|assert|ive
un|assert|ive|ly
un|assert|ive|ness
un|assign|able
un|assigned
un|assim|il|able
un|assim|il|ated
un|assist|ed
un|associ|ated
un|assuage|able
un|assuaged
un|assum|ing
un|assum|ing|ly
un|assum|ing|ness
un|atoned
un|attached
un|attack|able
un|attain|able
un|attain|able|
    ness
un|attain|ably
un|attempt|ed
un|attend|ed
un|attest|ed
un|attract|ive
un|attract|ive|ly
un|attract|ive|ness
un|attrib|ut|able
un|attrib|ut|ably
un|attrib|uted
unau +s
un|audit|ed
un|authen|tic
un|authen|tic|al|ly
un|authen|ti|cated
un|author|ised *Br.*
 (use
 unauthorized)
un|author|ized
un|avail|abil|ity
un|avail|able
un|avail|able|ness
un|avail|ing
un|avail|ing|ly
un|avoid|abil|ity
un|avoid|able
un|avoid|able|
    ness
un|avoid|ably
un|avowed
un|awakened
un|aware
un|aware|ness
un|awares
un|awed
un|back|able
un|backed
un|baked

un|bal|ance
un|bal|ances
un|bal|anced
un|bal|an|cing
unban
un|bans
un|banned
un|ban|ning
un|bap|tised *Br.*
 (use unbaptized)
un|bap|tized
unbar
un|bars
un|barred
un|bar|ring
un|bear|able
un|bear|able|ness
un|bear|ably
un|beat|able
un|beat|ably
un|beat|en
un|beau|ti|ful
un|beau|ti|ful|ly
un|be|com|ing
un|be|com|ing|ly
un|be|com|ing|
    ness
un|be|fit|ting
un|be|fit|ting|ly
un|be|fit|ting|ness
un|be|friend|ed
un|be|got|ten
un|be|hold|en
un|be|known
un|be|knownst
un|belief
un|believ|abil|ity
un|believ|able
un|believ|able|
    ness
un|believ|ably
un|believed
un|believer +s
un|believ|ing
un|believ|ing|ly
un|believ|ing|ness
un|be|loved
un|belt +s +ed
 +ing
un|bend
un|bends
un|bent
un|bend|ing
un|bend|ing|ly
un|bend|ing|ness
un|biased
un|bib|li|cal
un|bid|dable
un|bid|den
un|bind
un|binds

un|bind (*cont.*)
 un|bound
 un|bind|ing
un|birth|day +s
un|bleached
un|blem|ished
un|blend|ed
un|blessed
un|blest (use
 unblessed)
un|blink|ing
un|blink|ing|ly
un|block +s +ed
 +ing
un|bloody
un|blown
un|blush|ing
un|blush|ing|ly
un|bolt +s +ed
 +ing
un|bon|net +s +ed
 +ing
un|book|ish
un|boot +s +ed
 +ing
un|born
un|bosom +s +ed
 +ing
un|bothered
un|bound
un|bound|ed
un|bound|ed|ly
un|bound|ed|ness
un|bowed
un|brace
 un|braces
 un|braced
 un|bracing
un|brand|ed
un|breach|able
un|break|able
un|break|ably
un|breath|able
un|brib|able
un|bridge|able
un|bridle
 un|bridles
 un|bridled
 un|brid|ling
un-British
un|broken
un|broken|ly
un|broken|ness
un|brother|ly
un|bruised
un|brushed
un|buckle
 un|buckles
 un|buckled
 un|buck|ling
un|build
 un|builds

un|build (*cont.*)
 un|built
 un|build|ing
un|bun|dle
 un|bun|dles
 un|bun|dled
 un|bund|ling
un|bund|ler +s
un|bur|den +s +ed
 +ing
un|bur|ied
un|burned (use
 unburnt)
un|burnt
un|bury
 un|buries
 un|buried
 un|bury|ing
un|busi|ness|like
un|but|ton +s +ed
 +ing
un|cage
 un|cages
 un|caged
 un|caging
un|cal|cu|lat|ing
un|called
uncalled-for
un|can|did
un|can|nily
un|can|ni|ness
un|canny
 un|can|nier
 un|canni|est
un|can|on|ic|al
un|can|on|ic|al|ly
uncap
 un|caps
 un|capped
 un|cap|ping
uncared for
uncared-for
 attributive
un|car|ing
un|car|pet|ed
un|case
 un|cases
 un|cased
 un|cas|ing
un|cashed
un|catch|able
un|cat|egor|is|able
 Br. (use
 uncategorizable)
un|cat|egor|iz|able
un|caught
un|caused
un|ceas|ing
un|ceas|ing|ly
un|cele|brated
un|cen|sored
 (uncut)

un|cen|sured
(uncriticized)
un|cere|mo|ni|ous
un|cere|mo|ni|
ous|ly
un|cere|mo|ni|ous|
ness
un|cer|tain
un|cer|tain|ly
un|cer|tainty
un|cer|tain|ties
un|cer|tifi|cated
un|cer|ti|fied
un|chain +s +ed
+ing
un|chal|lenge|able
un|chal|lenge|ably
un|chal|lenged
un|chal|len|ging
un|change|abil|ity
un|change|able
un|change|able|
ness
un|change|ably
un|changed
un|chan|ging
un|chan|ging|ly
un|chan|ging|ness
un|chap|er|oned
un|char|ac|ter|
is|tic
un|char|ac|ter|
is|tic|al|ly
un|charged
un|char|is|mat|ic
un|char|it|able
un|char|it|able|
ness
un|char|it|ably
un|charm|ing
un|chart|ed
un|char|tered
un|chaste
un|chaste|ly
un|chas|tened
un|chaste|ness
un|chas|tity
un|checked
un|chiv|al|rous
un|chiv|al|rous|ly
un|chosen
un|chris|tian
un|chris|tian|ly
un|church
un|churches
un|churched
un|church|ing
un|cial
un|ci|form
un|cin|ate
un|cir|cum|cised
un|cir|cum|ci|sion

un|civil
un|civ|il|ised *Br.*
(use uncivilized)
un|civ|il|ized
un|civ|il|ly
un|clad
un|claimed
un|clasp +s +ed
+ing
un|clas|si|fi|able
un|clas|si|fied
uncle +s
un|clean
un|cleaned
un|clean|li|ness
un|clean|ly
un|clean|ness
un|cleansed
un|clear
un|cleared
un|clear|ly
un|clear|ness
uncle-in-law +s
un|clench
un|clenches
un|clenched
un|clench|ing
un|climb|able
un|climbed
un|clinch
un|clinches
un|clinched
un|clinch|ing
un|clip
un|clips
un|clipped
un|clip|ping
un|cloak +s +ed
+ing
un|clog
un|clogs
un|clogged
un|clog|ging
un|close
un|closes
un|closed
un|clos|ing
un|clothe
un|clothes
un|clothed
un|cloth|ing
un|cloud|ed
un|clut|tered
unco +s
un|coded
un|coil +s +ed
+ing
un|col|lect|ed
un|col|ored *Am.*
un|col|oured *Br.*
un|combed
uncome-at-able
un|come|ly

un|com|fort|able
un|com|fort|able|
ness
un|com|fort|ably
un|com|mer|cial
un|
com|mer|cial|ly
un|
com|mis|sioned
un|com|mit|ted
un|com|mon
un|com|mon|ly
un|com|mon|ness
un|com|mu|ni|
ca|tive
un|com|mu|ni|
ca|tive|ly
un|com|mu|ni|
ca|tive|ness
un|com|pan|ion|
able
un|com|pen|sated
un|com|peti|tive
un|com|peti|tive|
ness
un|com|plain|ing
un|com|plain|
ing|ly
un|com|pleted
un|com|pli|cated
un|com|pli|
men|tary
un|com|pound|ed
un|com|pre|
hend|ed
un|com|pre|hend|
ing
un|com|pre|hend|
ing|ly
un|com|pre|hen|
sion
un|com|prom|
is|ing
un|com|prom|
is|ing|ly
un|com|prom|
is|ing|ness
un|con|cealed
un|con|cern
un|con|cerned
un|con|cern|ed|ly
un|con|cluded
un|con|di|tion|al
un|con|di|tion|
al|ity
un|con|di|tion|
al|ly
un|con|di|tioned
un|con|fi|dent
un|con|fined
un|con|firmed
un|con|form|able

un|con|form|able|
ness
un|con|form|ably
un|con|form|ity
un|con|gen|ial
un|con|geni|al|ly
un|con|gest|ed
un|con|jec|tur|able
un|con|nect|ed
un|con|nect|ed|ly
un|con|nect|ed|
ness
un|con|quer|able
un|con|quer|able|
ness
un|con|quer|ably
un|con|quered
un|con|scion|able
un|con|scion|able|
ness
un|con|scion|ably
un|con|scious
un|con|scious|ly
un|con|scious|
ness
un|con|se|crated
un|con|sent|ing
un|con|sid|ered
un|con|sol|able
un|con|sol|ably
un|con|soli|dated
un|con|sti|
tu|tion|al
un|con|sti|tu|tion|
al|ity
un|con|sti|tu|tion|
al|ly
un|con|strained
un|con|strain|
ed|ly
un|con|straint
un|con|strict|ed
un|con|struct|ive
un|con|sult|ed
un|con|sumed
un|con|sum|mated
un|con|tact|able
un|con|tain|able
un|con|tam|in|
ated
un|con|ten|tious
un|
con|ten|tious|ly
un|con|test|ed
un|con|test|ed|ly
un|con|tra|dict|ed
un|con|trived
un|con|trol|lable
un|con|trol|lable|
ness
un|con|trol|lably
un|con|trolled

un|con|trolled|ly
un|con|tro|ver|sial
un|con|tro|
    ver|sial|ly
un|con|tro|vert|ed
un|con|tro|vert|
    ible
un|con|ven|tion|al
un|con|ven|tion|al|
    ism
un|con|ven|tion|
    al|ity
un|con|ven|tion|
    al|ly
un|con|vert|ed
un|con|vert|ible
un|con|vict|ed
un|con|vinced
un|con|vin|cing
un|con|vin|cing|ly
un|cooked
un|cool
un|co|opera|tive
un|co|opera|
    tive|ly
un|co|opera|tive|
    ness
un|co|or|din|ated
un|copi|able
un|cord +s +ed
    +ing
un|cor|dial
un|cork +s +ed
    +ing
un|cor|rect|ed
un|cor|rel|ated
un|cor|rob|or|ated
un|cor|rupt|ed
un|cor|set|ed
un|count|abil|ity
un|count|able
un|count|ably
un|count|ed
un|count noun +s
un|couple
  un|couples
  un|coupled
  un|coup|ling
un|court|ly
un|couth
un|couth|ly
un|couth|ness
un|cov|en|ant|ed
un|cover +s +ed
  +ing
un|crack|able
un|cracked
un|creased
un|cre|ate
  un|cre|ates
  un|cre|ated
  un|cre|at|ing

un|crea|tive
un|cred|it|ed
un|crit|ic|al
un|crit|ic|al|ly
un|cropped
un|cross
  un|crosses
  un|crossed
  un|cross|ing
un|cross|able
un|crowd|ed
un|crown +s +ed
  +ing
un|crum|pled
un|crush|able
un|crushed
UNCTAD (= United
  Nations
  Conference on
  Trade and
  Development)
unc|tion +s
unc|tu|ous
unc|tu|ous|ly
unc|tu|ous|ness
un|culled
un|culti|vated
un|cul|tured
un|curb +s +ed
  +ing
un|cured
un|curl +s +ed
  +ing
un|cur|tailed
un|cur|tained
un|cus|tomed
uncut
un|dam|aged
un|damped
un|dated
un|daunt|ed
un|daunt|ed|ly
un|daunt|ed|ness
un|dead
un|dealt
un|deca|gon +s
un|deceive
  un|deceives
  un|deceived
  un|deceiv|ing
un|decid|abil|ity
un|decid|able
un|decided
un|decided|ly
un|de|cipher|able
un|de|ciphered
un|declared
un|de|cod|able
un|dec|or|ated
un|defeat|ed
un|defend|ed
un|defiled

un|defin|able
un|defin|ably
un|defined
un|deflect|ed
un|deformed
un|deliv|ered
un|demand|ing
un|demand|ing|
    ness
un|demo|crat|ic
un|demo|crat|ic|
    al|ly
un|dem|on|strable
un|dem|on|
    stra|ted
un|demon|stra|
    tive
un|demon|stra|
    tive|ly
un|
  demon|stra|tive|
    ness
un|deni|able
un|deni|able|ness
un|deni|ably
un|denied
un|denom|in|
    ation|al
un|dent|ed
un|depend|able
under
under|achieve
  under|achieves
  under|achieved
  under|achiev|ing
  under|achieve|
    ment
under|achiever +s
under|act +s +ed
  +ing
under-age
  attributive
under|appre|ci|
    ated
under|arm +s
under|belly
  under|bel|lies
under|bid
  under|bids
  under|bid
  under|bid|ding
under|bid|der +s
under|blan|ket +s
under|body
  under|bodies
under|bred
under|brush
under|cap|acity
under|cap|it|al|ise
  Br. (use
  undercapitalize)

under|cap|it|al|ise
  (*cont.*)
  under|cap|it|al|
      ises
  under|cap|it|al|
      ised
  under|cap|it|al|
      is|ing
under|cap|it|al|ize
  under|cap|it|al|
      izes
  under|cap|it|al|
      ized
  under|cap|it|al|
      iz|ing
under|car|riage +s
under|cart +s
under|charge
under|charges
under|charged
under|char|ging
under|class
  under|classes
under|clay +s
under|cliff +s
under|clothes
under|cloth|ing
under|coat +s +ed
  +ing
under|
  con|sump|tion
under|
  con|sump|tion|
    ist +s
under|cook +s +ed
  +ing
under|cover
under|croft +s
under|cur|rent +s
under|cut
  under|cuts
  under|cut
  under|cut|ting
under|devel|oped
under|devel|op|
    ment
under|do
  under|does
  under|did
  under|do|ing
  under|done
under|dog +s
under|drain|age
under|drawers
under|draw|ing
under|dress
  under|dresses
  under|dressed
  under|dress|ing
under|edu|cated
under|empha|sis
under|empha|ses

under|empha:sise
Br. (use
underemphasize)
under|
    empha:sises
under|
    empha:sised
under|
    empha:sis:ing
under|empha:size
under|
    empha:sizes
under|
    empha:sized
under|
    empha:siz:ing
under|employed
under|
    employ:ment
under|equipped
under|esti:mate
under|esti:mates
under|esti:mated
under|
    esti:mat:ing
under|esti:ma:tion
under|exploit:ed
under|expose
under|exposes
under|exposed
under|expos:ing
under|expos:ure
under|fed
under|felt +s
under|financed
under|finan:cing
under-fives
under|floor
under|flow +s
under|foot
under|frame +s
under|fund +s +ed
  +ing
under|fur
under-garden:er
  +s
under|gar:ment +s
under|gird +s +ed
  +ing
under|glaze
under|go
under|goes
under|went
under|go:ing
under|gone
under|grad +s
under|gradu:ate
  +s
under|ground
under|growth
under|hand
under|hand:ed

under|heat:ed
under|hung
under|lay
under|lays
under|laid
under|lay:ing
under|lease
under|leases
under|leased
under|leas:ing
under|let
under|lets
under|let
under|let:ting
under|lie
under|lies
under|lay
under|lain
under|lying
under|line
under|lines
under|lined
under|lin:ing
under|linen
under|ling +s
under|lip +s
under|lit
under-manager +s
under|manned
under|man:ning
under|men:tioned
under|mine
under|mines
under|mined
under|min:ing
under|miner +s
under|min:ing:ly
under|most
under|neath
under|nour:ished
under|nour:ish|
    ment
under-occupancy
under-occupy
under-occupies
under-occupied
under-occupy:ing
under|paid
under|paint:ing
under|pants
under|part +s
under|pass
under|passes
under|pay
under|pays
under|paid
under|pay:ing
under|pay|ment
  +s
under|per:form +s
  +ed +ing

under|per:form|
    ance
under|pin
under|pins
under|pinned
under|pin|ning
under|pin|ning +s
under|plant +s
  +ed +ing
under|play +s +ed
  +ing
under|plot +s
under|popu:lated
under|pow:ered
under-prepared
under|price
under|prices
under|priced
under|pricing
under|priv:il:eged
under|
    pro:duc:tion
under|proof
under|prop
under|props
under|propped
under|prop|ping
under-provision
under|quote
under|quotes
under|quoted
under|quot:ing
under|rate
under|rates
under|rated
under|rat:ing
under-read
under-reads
under-read
under-reading
under-rehearsed
under-report +s
  +ed +ing
under-represent
  +s +ed +ing
under-resourced
under|ripe
under|score
under|scores
under|scored
under|scor:ing
under|sea
under|seal
under-secretary
under-
  secretar:ies
under|sell
under|sells
under|sold
under|sell:ing
under|set
under|sets

under|set (cont.)
under|set
under|set|ting
under|sexed
under|sheet +s
under-sheriff +s
under|shirt +s
under|shoot
under|shoots
under|shot
under|shoot|ing
under|shorts
under|shrub +s
under|side +s
under|signed
under|size
under|sized
under|skirt +s
under|slung
under|sold
under|sow
under|sows
under|sowed
under|sow|ing
under|sown
under|spend
under|spends
under|spent
under|spend|ing
under|staffed
under|staff|ing
under|stairs
under|stand
under|stands
under|stood
under|stand|ing
under|stand|
    abil:ity
under|stand|able
under|stand|ably
under|stand:er +s
under|stand|ing
  +s
under|stand|ing:ly
under|state
under|states
under|stated
under|stat:ing
under|state|ment
  +s
under|stater +s
under|steer +s +ed
  +ing
under|stood
under|storey +s
under|strap:per +s
under|strength
  attributive
under|study
under|stud:ies
under|stud:ied
under|study|ing

under|sub|scribed
under|sur|face +s
under|take
  under|takes
  under|took
  under|tak|ing
  under|taken
under|taker +s
under|tak|ing +s
under|ten|ancy
  under|ten|an|cies
under|ten|ant +s
under-the-counter
  attributive
under|things
under|tint +s
under|tone +s
under|took
under|tow +s
under|trained
under|trick +s
under|use
  under|uses
  under|used
  under|using
under|util|isa|tion
  Br. (use
  underutilization)
under|util|ise *Br.*
  (use underutilize)
  under|util|ises
  under|util|ised
  under|util|is|ing
under|util|iza|tion
under|util|ize
  under|util|izes
  under|util|ized
  under|util|iz|ing
under|valu|ation
  +s
under|value
  under|values
  under|valued
  under|valu|ing
under|vest +s
under|water
under way
under|wear
under|weight
under|went
under|whelm +s
  +ed +ing
under|wing +s
under|wired
under|wood +s
under|work +s
  +ed +ing
under|world +s
under|write
  under|writes
  under|wrote

under|write (*cont.*)
  under|writ|ing
  under|writ|ten
under|writer +s
un|des|cend|ed
un|described
un|deserved
un|deserved|ly
un|deserv|ing
un|deserv|ing|ly
un|des|ig|nated
un|designed
un|design|ed|ly
un|desir|abil|ity
un|desir|able +s
un|desir|able|ness
un|desir|ably
un|desired
un|desir|ous
un|detect|abil|ity
un|detect|able
un|detect|ably
un|detect|ed
un|deter|mined
un|deterred
un|devel|oped
un|devi|at|ing
un|devi|at|ing|ly
un|diag|nosed
undid
un|dies
un|dif|fer|en|
  ti|ated
un|digest|ed
un|dig|ni|fied
un|diluted
un|dimin|ished
un|dimmed
un|dine +s
un|dip|lo|mat|ic
un|dip|lo|mat|ic|
  al|ly
un|dir|ect|ed
un|dis|cern|ing
un|dis|charged
un|dis|cip|line
un|dis|cip|lined
un|dis|closed
un|dis|cov|er|able
un|dis|cov|ered
un|dis|crim|in|
  at|ing
un|dis|cussed
un|dis|guised
un|dis|guised|ly
un|dis|mayed
un|dis|puted
un|dis|solved
un|dis|tin|guish|
  able
un|dis|tin|guished
un|dis|tort|ed

un|dis|trib|uted
un|dis|turbed
un|div|ided
un|divulged
undo
  un|does
  undid
  un|do|ing
  un|done
un|dock +s +ed
  +ing
un|docu|ment|ed
un|dog|mat|ic
un|do|ing +s
un|domes|ti|cated
un|done
un|doubt|able
un|doubt|ably
un|doubt|ed
un|doubt|ed|ly
un|doubt|ing
un|drained
un|dram|at|ic
un|draped
undreamed-of
  attributive
undreamt-of (use
  undreamed-of)
un|dress
  un|dresses
  un|dressed
  un|dress|ing
un|drink|able
un|driv|able
un|drive|able (use
  undrivable)
UNDRO (= United
  Nations Disaster
  Relief Office)
undue
un|du|lant
un|du|late
  un|du|lates
  un|du|lated
  un|du|lat|ing
un|du|late|ly
un|du|la|tion +s
un|du|la|tory
un|duly
un|duti|ful
un|duti|ful|ly
un|duti|ful|ness
un|dyed
un|dying
un|dying|ly
un|dynam|ic
un|earned
un|earth +s +ed
  +ing
un|earth|li|ness
un|earth|ly
un|ease

un|eas|ily
un|easi|ness
un|easy
  un|eas|ier
  un|easi|est
un|eat|able
un|eat|en
un|eco|nom|ic
un|eco|nom|ic|al
un|eco|nom|ic|
  al|ly
un|edify|ing
un|edify|ing|ly
un|edit|ed
un|educ|able
un|edu|cated
un|elect|able
un|elect|ed
un|embar|rassed
un|embel|lished
un|em|bit|tered
un|emo|tion|al
un|emo|tion|al|ly
un|emphat|ic
un|emphat|ic|al|ly
un|employ|abil|ity
un|employ|able
un|employed
un|employ|ment
un|emp|tied
un|en|closed
un|en|cum|bered
un|en|dear|ing
un|end|ing
un|end|ing|ly
un|end|ing|ness
un|en|dowed
un|en|dur|able
un|en|dur|ably
un|en|force|able
un|en|forced
un|en|gaged
un-English
un|en|joy|able
un|en|light|ened
un|en|light|en|ing
un|enter|pris|ing
un|en|thu|si|as|tic
un|en|thu|si|as|tic|
  al|ly
un|envi|able
un|envi|ably
un|envied
un|en|vir|on|
      men|tal
UNEP (= United
  Nations
  Environment
  Programme)
un|equable
un|equal

un|equaled *Am.*
(*Br.* unequalled)
un|equal|ise *Br.*
(use unequalize)
un|equal|ises
un|equal|ised
un|equal|is|ing
un|equal|ize
un|equal|izes
un|equal|ized
un|equal|iz|ing
un|equalled *Br.*
(*Am.* unequaled)
un|equal|ly
un|equipped
un|equivo|cal
un|equivo|cal|ly
un|equivo|cal|
    ness
un|err|ing
un|err|ing|ly
un|err|ing|ness
un|escap|able
UNESCO (= United
  Nations
  Educational,
  Scientific, and
  Cultural
  Organization)
un|escort|ed
un|essen|tial
un|estab|lished
un|esthet|ic *Am.*
(*Br.* unaesthetic)
un|eth|ic|al
un|eth|ic|al|ly
un|evan|gel|ic|al
un|even
un|even|ly
un|even|ness
un|event|ful
un|event|ful|ly
un|event|ful|ness
un|exact|ing
un|exam|ined
un|exam|pled
un|ex|ca|vated
un|ex|cep|tion|
    able
un|ex|cep|tion|
    able|ness
un|ex|cep|tion|
    ably
un|ex|cep|tion|al
un|ex|cep|tion|
    al|ly
un|ex|cit|abil|ity
un|ex|cit|able
un|ex|cit|ing
un|ex|clu|sive
un|ex|ecuted
un|ex|haust|ed

un|ex|pect|ed
un|ex|pect|ed|ly
un|ex|pect|ed|ness
un|ex|pi|ated
un|ex|pired
un|ex|plain|able
un|ex|plain|ably
un|ex|plained
un|ex|ploded
un|ex|ploit|ed
un|ex|plored
un|ex|port|able
un|ex|posed
un|ex|pressed
un|ex|pur|gated
un|face|able
un|fad|ing
un|fad|ing|ly
un|fail|ing
un|fail|ing|ly
un|fail|ing|ness
un|fair
un|fair|ly
un|fair|ness
un|faith|ful
un|faith|ful|ly
un|faith|ful|ness
un|fal|ter|ing
un|fal|ter|ing|ly
un|famil|iar
un|famil|iar|ity
un|fan|cied
un|fash|ion|able
un|fash|ion|able|
    ness
un|fash|ion|ably
un|fash|ioned
un|fas|ten +s +ed
    +ing
un|fathered
un|father|li|ness
un|father|ly
un|fath|om|able
un|fath|om|able|
    ness
un|fath|om|ably
un|fath|omed
un|favor|able *Am.*
un|favor|able|ness
    Am.
un|favor|ably *Am.*
un|favor|ite *Am.*
un|favour|able *Br.*
un|favour|able|
    ness *Br.*
un|favour|ably *Br.*
un|favour|ite *Br.*
un|fazed (not
  disconcerted.
  △ unphased)
un|feas|ibil|ity
un|feas|ible

un|feas|ibly
unfed
un|feel|ing
un|feel|ing|ly
un|feel|ing|ness
un|feigned
un|feign|ed|ly
un|felt
un|fem|in|ine
un|fem|in|in|ity
un|fenced
un|fer|ment|ed
un|fer|til|ised *Br.*
  (use unfertilized)
un|fer|til|ized
un|fet|ter +s +ed
    +ing
un|fil|ial
un|fili|al|ly
un|filled
un|fil|tered
un|finan|cial
un|fin|ished
unfit
un|fit|ly
un|fit|ness
un|fit|ted
un|fit|ting
un|fit|ting|ly
un|fix
un|fixes
un|fixed
un|fix|ing
un|flag|ging
un|flag|ging|ly
un|flap|pabil|ity
un|flap|pable
un|flap|pably
un|flat|ter|ing
un|flat|ter|ing|ly
un|fla|vored *Am.*
un|fla|voured *Br.*
un|fledged
un|fleshed
un|flexed
un|flick|er|ing
un|flinch|ing
un|flinch|ing|ly
un|flur|ried
un|flus|tered
un|focused
un|focussed (use
  unfocused)
un|fold +s +ed
    +ing
un|fold|ment
un|forced
un|for|ced|ly
un|ford|able
un|fore|cast
un|fore|see|able
un|fore|seen

un|fore|told
un|for|get|table
un|for|get|tably
un|for|giv|able
un|for|giv|ably
un|for|given
un|for|giv|ing
un|for|giv|ing|ly
un|for|giv|ing|ness
un|for|got|ten
un|formed
un|for|mu|lated
un|forth|com|ing
un|for|ti|fied
un|for|tu|nate
un|for|tu|nate|ly
un|found|ed
un|found|ed|ly
un|found|ed|ness
un|framed
un|free
un|free|dom
un|freeze
un|freezes
un|froze
un|freez|ing
un|frozen
un|fre|quent|ed
un|friend|ed
un|friend|li|ness
un|friend|ly
un|friend|lier
un|friendli|est
un|fright|en|ing
un|frock +s +ed
    +ing
un|froze
un|frozen
un|fruit|ful
un|fruit|ful|ly
un|fruit|ful|ness
un|ful|fil|lable
un|ful|filled
un|ful|fill|ing
un|fund|ed
un|fun|nily
un|fun|ni|ness
un|funny
un|fun|nier
un|funni|est
un|furl +s +ed
    +ing
un|fur|nished
un|fuss|ily
un|fussy
un|gain|li|ness
un|gain|ly
un|gal|lant
un|gal|lant|ly
un|gen|er|ous
un|gen|er|ous|ly
un|gen|er|ous|ness

un|gen|ial
un|gen|tle
un|gentle|man|li|ness
un|gentle|man|ly
un|gentle|ness
un|gently
unget-at-able
un|gift|ed
un|gild|ed
un|gird +s +ed
  +ing
un|glam|or|ous
un|glazed
un|gloved
un|god|li|ness
un|god|ly
un|gov|ern|abil|ity
un|gov|ern|able
un|gov|ern|ably
un|grace|ful
un|grace|ful|ly
un|grace|ful|ness
un|gra|cious
un|gra|cious|ly
un|gra|cious|ness
un|gram|mat|ical
un|gram|mat|ic|al|ity
un|gram|mat|ic|al|ly
un|gram|mat|ic|al|ness
un|grasp|able
un|grate|ful
un|grate|ful|ly
un|grate|ful|ness
un|green
un|ground|ed
un|grudg|ing
un|grudg|ing|ly
un|gual
un|guard +s +ed
  +ing
un|guard|ed|ly
un|guard|ed|ness
un|guent +s
un|guess|able
un|guicu|late
un|guided
un|guis
  un|gues
un|gula
  un|gu|lae
un|gu|late +s
ungum
  un|gums
  un|gummed
  un|gum|ming
un|hal|lowed
un|ham|pered

un|hand +s +ed
  +ing
un|hand|ily
un|handi|ness
un|hand|some
un|handy
un|hang
  un|hangs
  un|hung
  un|hang|ing
un|hap|pily
un|hap|pi|ness
un|happy
  un|hap|pier
  un|happi|est
un|har|bor *Am.* +s
  +ed +ing
un|har|bour *Br.* +s
  +ed +ing
un|harmed
un|harm|ful
un|har|mon|ious
un|har|ness
  un|har|nesses
  un|har|nessed
  un|har|ness|ing
un|har|vest|ed
un|hasp +s +ed
  +ing
un|hatched
un|healed
un|health|ful
un|health|ful|ness
un|health|ily
un|healthi|ness
un|healthy
  un|health|ier
  un|healthi|est
un|heard
unheard-of
un|heat|ed
un|hedged
un|heed|ed
un|heed|ful
un|heed|ing
un|heed|ing|ly
un|help|ful
un|help|ful|ly
un|help|ful|ness
un|her|ald|ed
un|hero|ic
un|hero|ic|al|ly
un|hesi|tat|ing
un|hesi|tat|ing|ly
un|hesi|tat|ing|ness
un|hid|den
un|hin|dered
un|hinge
  un|hinges
  un|hinged

un|hinge (*cont.*)
  un|hinge|ing *or*
  un|hin|ging
unhip
un|his|tor|ic
un|his|tor|ic|al
un|his|tor|ic|al|ly
un|hitch
  un|hitches
  un|hitched
  un|hitch|ing
un|holi|ness
un|holy
  un|holi|er
  un|holi|est
un|hon|ored *Am.*
un|hon|oured *Br.*
un|hood +s +ed
  +ing
un|hook +s +ed
  +ing
un|hoped
un|hope|ful
un|horse
  un|horses
  un|horsed
  un|hors|ing
un|house
  un|houses
  un|housed
  un|hous|ing
un|human
un|hung
un|hur|ried
un|hur|ried|ly
un|hurry|ing
un|hurt
un|husk +s +ed
  +ing
un|hygien|ic
un|hygien|ic|al|ly
un|hyphen|ated
uni +s
  (= university)
Uni|ate +s
uni|axial
uni|axial|ly
uni|cam|eral
UNICEF (= United
  Nations Children's
  Fund)
uni|cel|lu|lar
uni|color *Am.*
uni|col|ored *Am.*
uni|col|our *Br.*
uni|col|oured *Br.*
uni|corn +s
uni|cus|pid +s
uni|cycle +s
uni|cyc|list +s
un|idea'd
un|ideal
un|ideal|ised *Br.*
  (use unidealized)

un|ideal|ized
un|iden|ti|fi|able
un|iden|ti|fied
uni|di|men|sion|al
un|idiom|at|ic
uni|dir|ec|tion|al
uni|dir|ec|tion|al|ity
uni|dir|ec|tion|al|ly
UNIDO (= United
  Nations Industrial
  Development
  Organization)
uni|fi|able
uni|fi|ca|tion
uni|fi|ca|tory
uni|fier +s
uni|flow
uni|form +s +ed
  +ing
uni|formi|tar|ian
  +s
uni|formi|tar|ian|ism
uni|form|ity
  uni|form|ities
uni|form|ly
unify
  uni|fies
  uni|fied
  uni|fy|ing
uni|lat|eral
uni|lat|eral|ism
uni|lat|eral|ist +s
uni|lat|eral|ly
uni|lin|gual
uni|lin|gual|ly
uni|lit|eral
un|illu|min|ated
un|illu|min|at|ing
un|illus|trated
uni|locu|lar
un|imagin|able
un|imagin|ably
un|imagina|tive
un|imagina|tive|ly
un|imagina|tive|ness
un|imagined
un|im|paired
un|im|part|ed
un|im|pas|sioned
un|im|peach|able
un|im|peach|ably
un|im|peded
un|im|peded|ly
un|im|port|ance
un|im|port|ant
un|im|pos|ing
un|im|pos|ing|ly
un|im|pressed

un|im|pres|sion|
    able
un|im|pres|sive
un|im|pres|sive|ly
un|im|pres|sive|
    ness
un|im|proved
un|im|pugned
un|in|cor|por|ated
un|indexed
un|in|fect|ed
un|in|flamed
un|in|flam|mable
un|inflect|ed
un|influ|enced
un|influ|en|tial
un|in|forma|tive
un|in|formed
un|in|hab|it|able
un|in|hab|it|able|
    ness
un|in|hab|it|ed
un|in|hib|it|ed
un|in|hib|it|ed|ly
un|in|hib|it|ed|
    ness
un|initi|ated
un|in|jured
un|in|spired
un|in|spir|ing
un|in|spir|ing|ly
un|in|struct|ed
un|insu|lated
un|in|sur|able
un|in|sured
un|inte|grated
un|in|tel|lec|tual
un|in|tel|li|gent
un|in|tel|li|gent|ly
un|in|tel|li|gi|
    bil|ity
un|in|tel|li|gible
un|in|tel|li|gible|
    ness
un|in|tel|li|gibly
un|in|tend|ed
un|in|ten|tion|al
un|in|ten|tion|al|ly
un|inter|est|ed
un|inter|est|ed|ly
un|inter|est|ed|
    ness
un|inter|est|ing
un|inter|est|ing|ly
un|inter|est|ing|
    ness
un|in|ter|pret|able
un|in|ter|pret|ed
un|inter|rupt|ed
un|inter|rupt|ed|ly
un|inter|rupt|ed|
    ness

un|inter|rupt|ible
un|in|timi|dated
uni|nucle|ate
un|in|vent|ed
un|in|vent|ive
un|in|vent|ive|ly
un|in|vent|ive|
    ness
un|in|vest|ed
un|in|ves|ti|gated
un|in|vited
un|in|vited|ly
un|in|vit|ing
un|in|vit|ing|ly
un|in|voked
un|in|volved
union +s
union-bashing
union|isa|tion *Br.*
    (use
    unionization)
union|ise *Br.* (bring
    under trade-union
    organization; use
    unionize)
union|ises
union|ised
union|is|ing
un-ionised *Br.* (not
    ionised; use un-
    ionized)
union|ism
union|ist +s
union|is|tic
union|iza|tion
union|ize
union|izes
union|ized
union|iz|ing
    (bring under trade-
    union
    organization)
un-ionized (not
    ionized)
unip|ar|ous
uni|part|ite
uni|ped +s
uni|per|son|al
uni|planar
uni|pod +s
uni|polar
uni|polar|ity
unique +s
unique|ly
unique|ness
un|ironed
uni|ser|ial
uni|sex
uni|sex|ual
uni|sexu|al|ity
uni|sexu|al|ly

UNISON (trade
    union)
uni|son +s (sound;
    agreement)
unis|on|ant
unis|on|ous
un|issued
unit +s
UNITA (Angolan
    nationalist
    movement)
UNITAR (= United
    Nations Institute
    for Training and
    Research)
Uni|tar|ian +s
Uni|tar|ian|ism
uni|tar|ily
uni|tar|ity
uni|tary
unite
    unites
    united
    unit|ing
united|ly
unit|hold|er +s
uni|tive
uni|tive|ly
unit-linked
Unity (name)
unity
    uni|ties
    (oneness;
    harmony; etc.)
uni|va|lent +s
uni|valve +s
uni|ver|sal +s
uni|ver|sal|is|
    abil|ity *Br.* (use
    universalizabil-
    ity)
uni|ver|sal|isa|tion
    Br. (use
    universalization)
uni|ver|sal|ise *Br.*
    (use universalize)
uni|ver|sal|ises
uni|ver|sal|ised
uni|ver|sal|is|ing
uni|ver|sal|ism
uni|ver|sal|ist +s
uni|ver|sal|is|tic
uni|ver|sal|ity
uni|ver|sal|iz|
    abil|ity
uni|ver|sal|
    iza|tion
uni|ver|sal|ize
uni|ver|sal|izes
uni|ver|sal|ized
uni|ver|sal|iz|ing
uni|ver|sal|ly

uni|verse +s
uni|ver|sity
    uni|ver|sities
uni|vocal
uni|vocal|ity
uni|vocal|ly
Unix *Computing*
    Propr.
un|jaun|diced
un|join +s +ed
    +ing
un|joint +s +ed
    +ing
un|just
un|jus|ti|fi|able
un|jus|ti|fi|ably
un|jus|ti|fied
un|just|ly
un|just|ness
un|kempt
un|kempt|ly
un|kempt|ness
un|kept
un|kill|able
un|kind +er +est
un|kind|ly
un|kind|ness
un|king +s +ed
    +ing
un|kink +s +ed
    +ing
un|kissed
un|knit
    un|knits
    un|knit|ted
    un|knit|ting
un|knot
    un|knots
    un|knot|ted
    un|knot|ting
un|know|able
un|know|ing
un|know|ing|ly
un|know|ing|ness
un|known +s
un|known|ness
un|labeled *Am.*
un|labelled *Br.*
un|labored *Am.*
un|laboured *Br.*
un|lace
    un|laces
    un|laced
    un|lacing
un|lade
    un|lades
    un|laded
    un|lad|ing
    (unload. ⚠ unlaid)
un|laden
un|lady|like

un|laid (past tense
  and past participle
  of unlay.
  △unlade)
un|lam|ent|ed
un|lash
  un|lashes
  un|lashed
  un|lash|ing
un|latch
  un|latches
  un|latched
  un|latch|ing
un|law|ful
un|law|ful|ly
un|law|ful|ness
unlay
  un|lays
  un|laid
  un|lay|ing
un|lead|ed
un|learn
  un|learns
  un|learned or
  un|learnt
  un|learn|ing
  verb
un|learn|ed
  adjective
un|learn|ed|ly
un|leash
  un|leashes
  un|leashed
  un|leash|ing
un|leav|ened
un|less
unlet
un|let|tered
un|lib|er|ated
un|licensed
un|light|ed
un|like
un|like|able
un|like|li|hood
un|like|li|ness
un|like|ly
  un|like|lier
  un|likeli|est
un|like|ness
un|lim|ber +s +ed
  +ing
un|lim|it|ed
un|lim|it|ed|ly
un|lim|it|ed|ness
un|lined
un|link +s +ed
  +ing
un|liquid|ated
un|list|ed
un|lis|ten|able
unlit
un|lit|er|ary

un|liv|able
unlived-in
un|load +s +ed
  +ing
un|load|er +s
un|locat|able
un|located
un|lock +s +ed
  +ing
un|looked
unlooked-for
un|loose
  un|looses
  un|loosed
  un|loos|ing
un|loosen +s +ed
  +ing
un|lov|able
un|loved
un|love|li|ness
un|love|ly
un|lov|ing
un|lov|ing|ly
un|lov|ing|ness
un|luck|ily
un|lucki|ness
un|lucky
  un|luck|ier
  un|lucki|est
un|maid|en|ly
un|make
  un|makes
  un|made
  un|mak|ing
un|mal|le|able
unman
  un|mans
  un|manned
  un|man|ning
un|man|age|able
un|man|age|able|
                ness
un|man|age|ably
un|man|aged
un|man|eu|ver|
  able Am.
un|man|li|ness
un|man|ly
un|man|nered
un|man|ner|li|ness
un|man|ner|ly
un|man|oeuv|
  rable Br.
un|man|ured
un|mapped
un|marked
un|marked|ness
un|mar|ket|able
un|marred
un|mar|riage|able
un|mar|ried
un|mas|cu|line

un|mask +s +ed
  +ing
un|mask|er +s
un|match|able
un|match|ably
un|matched
un|mated
un|matured
un|mean|ing
un|mean|ing|ly
un|mean|ing|ness
un|meant
un|meas|ur|able
un|meas|ur|ably
un|meas|ured
un|me|di|ated
un|melo|di|ous
un|melo|di|ous|ly
un|melt|ed
un|mem|or|able
un|mem|or|ably
un|mend|ed
un|men|tion|
              abil|ity
un|men|tion|able
  +s
un|men|tion|able|
                ness
un|men|tion|ably
un|men|tioned
un|mer|chant|able
un|mer|ci|ful
un|mer|ci|ful|ly
un|mer|ci|ful|ness
un|mer|it|ed
un|meri|tori|ous
unmet
un|met|alled
un|meth|od|ical
un|meth|od|ic|al|ly
un|met|ric|al
un|mili|tary
un|mind|ful
un|mind|ful|ly
un|mind|ful|ness
un|miss|able
un|mis|tak|abil|ity
un|mis|tak|able
un|mis|tak|able|
                ness
un|mis|tak|ably
un|mis|take|
  abil|ity (use
  unmistakability)
un|mis|take|able
  (use
  unmistakable)
un|mis|take|able|
  ness (use
  unmistakable-
  ness)
un|mis|take|ably
  (use
  unmistakably)

un|mis|taken
un|miti|gated
un|miti|gated|ly
un|mixed
un|mod|ern|ised
  Br. (use
  unmodernized)
un|mod|ern|ized
un|modi|fied
un|modu|lated
un|mol|est|ed
un|moor +s +ed
  +ing
un|moral
un|mor|al|ity
un|mor|al|ly
un|mother|ly
un|moti|vated
un|mount|ed
un|mourned
un|mov|able
un|move|able
  (use unmovable)
un|moved
un|mov|ing
un|mown
un|muf|fle
  un|muf|fles
  un|muf|fled
  un|muf|fling
un|mur|mur|ing
un|mur|mur|ing|ly
un|music|al
un|music|al|ity
un|music|al|ly
un|music|al|ness
un|mutil|ated
un|muz|zle
  un|muz|zles
  un|muz|zled
  un|muz|zling
un|nail +s +ed
  +ing
un|name|able
un|named
un|nat|ural
un|nat|ur|al|ly
un|nat|ur|al|ness
un|nav|ig|abil|ity
un|nav|ig|able
un|neces|sar|ily
un|neces|sari|ness
un|neces|sary
un|need|ed
un|neigh|bor|li|
              ness Am.
un|neigh|bor|ly Am.
un|neigh|bour|li|
              ness Br.
un|neigh|bour|ly Br.
un|nerve
  un|nerves

un|nerve (*cont.*)
  un|nerved
  un|nerv|ing
un|nerv|ing|ly
un|nil|pen|tium
un|nil|qua|dium
un|notice|able
un|notice|ably
un|noticed
un|num|bered
UNO (= United
  Nations
  Organization)
un|ob|jec|tion|able
un|ob|jec|tion|able|
      ness
un|ob|jec|tion|ably
un|ob|li|ging
un|ob|scured
un|ob|serv|able
un|ob|ser|vant
un|ob|ser|vant|ly
un|ob|served
un|ob|served|ly
un|ob|struct|ed
un|ob|tain|able
un|ob|tain|ably
un|ob|tru|sive
un|ob|tru|sive|ly
un|ob|tru|sive|
      ness
un|occu|pancy
un|occu|pied
un|offend|ed
un|offend|ing
un|offi|cial
un|offi|cial|ly
un|oiled
un|open|able
un|opened
un|opposed
un|ordained
un|ordin|ary
un|organ|ised *Br.*
  (use
  unorganized)
un|organ|ized
un|ori|gin|al
un|ori|gin|al|ity
un|ori|gin|al|ly
un|orna|men|tal
un|orna|ment|ed
un|ortho|dox
un|ortho|dox|ly
un|ortho|doxy
un|ortho|dox|ies
un|osten|ta|tious
un|
  osten|ta|tious|ly
un|osten|ta|tious|
      ness
un|owned

un|oxi|dised *Br.*
  (use unoxidized)
un|oxi|dized
un|pack +s +ed
  +ing
un|pack|er +s
un|pad|ded
un|paged
un|paid
un|paint|ed
un|paired
un|pal|at|abil|ity
un|pal|at|able
un|pal|at|able|
      ness
un|pal|at|ably
un|par|al|leled
un|par|don|able
un|par|don|able|
      ness
un|par|don|ably
un|par|lia|
     men|tary
un|pas|teur|ised
  Br. (use
  unpasteurized)
un|pas|teur|ized
un|pat|ent|ed
un|pat|ri|ot|ic
un|pat|ri|ot|ic|
     al|ly
un|pat|ron|is|ing
  Br. (use
  unpatronizing)
un|pat|ron|iz|ing
un|pat|terned
un|paved
un|peace|ful
un|peeled
unpeg
  un|pegs
  un|pegged
  un|peg|ging
un|pen|al|ised *Br.*
  (use unpenalized)
un|pen|al|ized
un|people
  un|peoples
  un|peopled
  un|peop|ling
un|per|ceived
un|per|cep|tive
un|per|cep|tive|ly
un|per|cep|tive|
     ness
un|per|fect|ed
un|per|for|ated
un|per|formed
un|per|fumed
un|per|son +s
un|per|suad|able
un|per|suad|ed

un|per|sua|sive
un|per|sua|sive|ly
un|per|turbed
un|per|turb|ed|ly
un|phased (not in
  phases.
  ⚠ unfazed)
un|philo|soph|ic
un|philo|soph|ic|al
un|philo|soph|ic|
     al|ly
un|physio|logic|al
un|physio|logic|
     al|ly
un|pick +s +ed
  +ing
un|pic|tur|esque
unpin
  un|pins
  un|pinned
  un|pin|ning
un|pitied
un|pity|ing
un|pity|ing|ly
un|place|able
un|placed
un|planned
un|plant|ed
un|plas|tered
un|plas|ti|cised *Br.*
  (use
  unplasticized)
un|plas|ti|cized
un|plaus|ible
un|play|able
un|play|ably
un|played
un|pleas|ant
un|pleas|ant|ly
un|pleas|ant|ness
un|pleas|ant|ry
  un|pleas|ant|ries
un|pleas|ing
un|pleas|ing|ly
un|pleas|ur|able
un|pledged
un|ploughed *Br.*
un|plowed *Am.*
un|plucked
un|plug
  un|plugs
  un|plugged
  un|plug|ging
un|plumb|able
un|plumbed
un|poet|ic
un|poet|ic|al
un|poet|ic|al|ly
un|point|ed
un|polar|ised *Br.*
  (use unpolarized)
un|polar|ized
un|pol|ished

un|pol|it|ic
un|pol|it|ic|al
un|pol|it|ic|al|ly
un|polled
un|pol|lin|ated
un|pol|luted
un|pom|pous
un|popu|lar
un|popu|lar|ity
un|popu|lar|ly
un|popu|lated
un|posed
un|pos|sessed
un|post|ed
un|pow|ered
un|prac|ti|cal
un|prac|ti|cal|ity
un|prac|ti|cal|ly
un|prac|tised
un|pre|ced|ent|ed
un|pre|ced|ent|
     ed|ly
un|pre|dict|
     abil|ity
un|pre|dict|able
un|pre|dict|able|
     ness
un|pre|dict|ably
un|pre|dict|ed
un|pre|ju|diced
un|pre|medi|tated
un|pre|medi|
     tated|ly
un|pre|pared
un|pre|pared|ly
un|pre|pared|ness
un|pre|pos|sess|
     ing
un|pre|scribed
un|pre|sent|able
un|pressed
un|pres|sur|ised
  Br. (use
  unpressurized)
un|pres|sur|ized
un|pre|sum|ing
un|pre|sump|tu|
     ous
un|pre|tend|ing
un|pre|tend|ing|ly
un|pre|tend|ing|
     ness
un|pre|ten|tious
un|pre|ten|tious|ly
un|pre|ten|tious|
     ness
un|pre|vent|able
un|priced
un|primed
un|prin|cipled
un|prin|cipled|
     ness

un|print|able
un|print|ably
un|print|ed
un|priv|il|eged
un|prob|lem|at|ic
un|prob|lem|at|ic|
    al|ly
un|pro|cessed
un|pro|claimed
un|pro|cur|able
un|pro|duct|ive
un|pro|duct|ive|ly
un|pro|duct|ive|
    ness
un|pro|fes|sion|al
un|pro|fes|sion|al|
    ism
un|pro|fes|sion|
    al|ly
un|prof|it|able
un|prof|it|able|
    ness
un|prof|it|ably
Un|pro|for
    (= United Nations
    Protection Force)
un|pro|gres|sive
un|prom|is|ing
un|prom|is|ing|ly
un|prompt|ed
un|pro|nounce|
    able
un|pro|nounce|
    ably
un|prop|er|tied
un|proph|et|ic
un|pro|pi|tious
un|pro|pi|tious|ly
un|pros|per|ous
un|pros|per|ous|ly
un|pro|tect|ed
un|pro|tec|ted|
    ness
un|pro|test|ing
un|pro|test|ing|ly
un|prov|abil|ity
un|prov|able
un|prov|able|ness
un|proved
un|proven
un|pro|vided
un|pro|voca|tive
un|pro|voked
un|pruned
un|pub|li|cised *Br.*
    (use
    unpublicized)
un|pub|li|cized
un|pub|lish|able
un|pub|lished
un|punc|tual
un|punc|tu|al|ity

un|punc|tu|al|ly
un|punc|tu|ated
un|pun|ish|able
un|pun|ished
un|puri|fied
un|put|down|able
un|quali|fied
un|quan|ti|fi|able
un|quan|ti|fied
un|quench|able
un|quench|ably
un|quenched
un|ques|tion|
    abil|ity
un|ques|tion|able
un|ques|tion|able|
    ness
un|ques|tion|ably
un|ques|tioned
un|ques|tion|ing
un|
    ques|tion|ing|ly
un|quiet
un|quiet|ly
un|quiet|ness
un|quot|able
un|quote
un|quoted
un|raced
un|ran|somed
un|rated
un|rati|fied
un|rationed
un|ravel
un|ravels
un|rav|elled *Br.*
un|rav|eled *Am.*
un|rav|el|ling *Br.*
un|rav|el|ling *Am.*
un|reach|able
un|reach|able|
    ness
un|reach|ably
un|reached
un|re|act|ive
un|read
un|read|abil|ity
un|read|able
un|read|ably
un|read|ily
un|readi|ness
un|ready
un|real (not real.
    ⚠ unreel)
un|real|is|able *Br.*
    (use unrealizable)
un|real|ised *Br.*
    (use unrealized)
un|real|ism
un|real|is|tic
un|real|is|tic|al|ly
un|real|ity

un|real|iz|able
un|real|ized
un|real|ly
un|rea|son
un|rea|son|able
un|rea|son|able|
    ness
un|rea|son|ably
un|rea|soned
un|rea|son|ing
un|rea|son|ing|ly
un|re|bel|lious|
    ness
un|re|cep|tive
un|re|cip|ro|cated
un|reck|oned
un|re|claimed
un|rec|og|nis|able
    Br. (use
    unrecognizable)
un|rec|og|nis|able|
    ness *Br.* (use
    unrecognizable-
    ness)
un|rec|og|nis|ably
    Br. (use
    unrecognizably)
un|rec|og|nised *Br.*
    (use
    unrecognized)
un|rec|og|niz|able
un|rec|og|niz|able|
    ness
un|rec|og|niz|ably
un|rec|og|nized
un|rec|om|pensed
un|rec|on|cil|able
un|rec|on|ciled
un|re|con|
    struct|ed
un|re|cord|able
un|re|cord|ed
un|re|cov|ered
un|rec|ti|fied
un|re|deem|able
un|re|deem|ably
un|re|deemed
un|re|dressed
un|reel +s +ed
    +ing (unwind
    from a reel.
    ⚠ unreal)
un|reeve
un|reeves
un|rove
un|reev|ing
un|re|fined
un|re|flect|ed
un|re|flect|ing
un|re|flect|ing|ly
un|re|flect|ing|
    ness

un|re|flect|ive
un|re|formed
un|re|futed
un|re|gard|ed
un|re|gen|er|acy
un|re|gen|er|ate
un|re|gen|er|ate|ly
un|regi|ment|ed
un|regis|tered
un|re|gret|ted
un|regu|lated
un|re|hearsed
un|rein +s +ed
    +ing
un|re|inforced
un|re|lated
un|re|lated|ness
un|re|laxed
un|re|leased
un|re|lent|ing
un|re|lent|ing|ly
un|re|lent|ing|ness
un|re|li|abil|ity
un|re|li|able
un|re|li|able|ness
un|re|li|ably
un|re|lieved
un|re|lieved|ly
un|re|li|gious
un|re|mark|able
un|re|mark|ably
un|re|marked
un|re|mem|bered
un|re|mit|ting
un|re|mit|ting|ly
un|re|mit|ting|
    ness
un|re|morse|ful
un|re|morse|ful|ly
un|re|mov|able
un|re|mu|nera|tive
un|re|mu|nera|
    tive|ly
un|re|mu|nera|tive|
    ness
un|re|new|able
un|re|newed
un|re|nounced
un|re|pair|able
un|re|paired
un|re|pealed
un|re|peat|abil|ity
un|re|peat|able
un|re|peat|ed
un|re|pent|ant
un|re|pent|ant|ly
un|re|pent|ed
un|re|port|ed
un|rep|re|sen|
    ta|tive
un|rep|re|sen|
    ta|tive|ness

un¦rep¦re¦sent¦ed
un¦re¦proved
un¦re¦quest¦ed
un¦re¦quit¦ed
un¦re¦quited¦ly
un¦re¦quited¦ness
un¦re¦searched
un¦re¦serve
un¦re¦served
un¦re¦served¦ly
un¦re¦serv¦ed¦ness
un¦re¦sist¦ed
un¦re¦sist¦ed¦ly
un¦re¦sist¦ing
un¦re¦sist¦ing¦ly
un¦re¦sist¦ing¦ness
un¦re¦solv¦able
un¦re¦solved
un¦re¦solved¦ly
un¦re¦solved¦ness
un¦re¦spon¦sive
un¦re¦spon¦sive¦ly
un¦re¦spon¦sive¦
    ness
un¦rest
un¦rest¦ed
un¦rest¦ful
un¦rest¦ful¦ly
un¦rest¦ing
un¦rest¦ing¦ly
un¦re¦stored
un¦re¦strain¦able
un¦re¦strained
un¦re¦strain¦ed¦ly
un¦re¦strain¦ed¦
    ness
un¦re¦straint
un¦re¦strict¦ed
un¦re¦strict¦ed¦ly
un¦re¦strict¦ed¦
    ness
un¦re¦turned
un¦re¦vealed
un¦re¦veal¦ing
un¦re¦versed
un¦re¦vised
un¦re¦voked
un¦revo¦lu¦tion¦ary
un¦re¦ward¦ed
un¦re¦ward¦ing
un¦re¦ward¦ing¦ly
un¦rhymed
un¦rhyth¦mic¦al
un¦rhyth¦mic¦al¦ly
un¦rid¦able (use
  unrideable)
un¦rid¦den
un¦rid¦dle
  un¦rid¦dles
  un¦rid¦dled
  un¦rid¦dling
un¦rid¦dler +s

un¦ride¦able
unrig
  un¦rigs
  un¦rigged
  un¦rig¦ging
un¦right¦eous
un¦right¦eous¦ly
un¦right¦eous¦ness
unrip
  un¦rips
  un¦ripped
  un¦rip¦ping
un¦ripe
un¦rip¦ened
un¦ripe¦ness
un¦risen
un¦rivaled *Am.*
un¦rivalled *Br.*
un¦rivet +s +ed
  +ing
un¦road¦worthy
un¦roast¦ed
un¦robe
  un¦robes
  un¦robed
  un¦rob¦ing
un¦roll +s +ed
  +ing
un¦roman¦tic
un¦roman¦tic¦al¦ly
un¦roof +s +ed
  +ing
un¦root +s +ed
  +ing
un¦rope
  un¦ropes
  un¦roped
  un¦rop¦ing
un¦round¦ed
un¦rove
un¦royal
UNRRA (= United
  Nations Relief and
  Rehabilitation
  Administration.
  △ UNRWA)
un¦ruf¦fled
un¦ruled
un¦ru¦li¦ness
un¦ruly
  un¦ru¦lier
  un¦ruli¦est
UNRWA (= United
  Nations Relief and
  Works Agency.
  △ UNRRA)
un¦sack¦able
un¦sad¦dle
  un¦sad¦dles
  un¦sad¦dled
  un¦sad¦dling
un¦safe

un¦safe¦ly
un¦safe¦ness
un¦said
un¦sal¦ar¦ied
un¦sale¦abil¦ity
un¦sale¦able
un¦salt¦ed
un¦salu¦bri¦ous
un¦sal¦vage¦able
un¦sanc¦ti¦fied
un¦sanc¦tioned
un¦sani¦tary
un¦sapped
un¦sat¦is¦fac¦tor¦
    ily
un¦sat¦is¦fac¦tori¦
    ness
un¦sat¦is¦fac¦tory
un¦sat¦is¦fied
un¦sat¦is¦fied¦ness
un¦sat¦is¦fy¦ing
un¦sat¦is¦fy¦ing¦ly
un¦sat¦ur¦ated
un¦sat¦ur¦ation
un¦saved
un¦savor¦ily *Am.*
un¦savori¦ness *Am.*
un¦savory *Am.*
un¦savour¦ily *Br.*
un¦savouri¦ness
  Br.
un¦savoury *Br.*
unsay
  un¦says
  un¦said
  un¦say¦ing
un¦say¦able
un¦scal¦able
un¦scaled
un¦scarred
un¦scathed
un¦scent¦ed
un¦sched¦uled
un¦schol¦ar¦li¦ness
un¦schol¦ar¦ly
un¦schooled
un¦sci¦en¦tif¦ic
un¦sci¦en¦tif¦ic¦
    al¦ly
un¦scram¦ble
  un¦scram¦bles
  un¦scram¦bled
  un¦scram¦bling
  un¦scram¦bler +s
un¦scratched
un¦screened
un¦screw +s +ed
  +ing
un¦script¦ed
un¦scrip¦tural
un¦scrip¦tur¦al¦ly
un¦scru¦pu¦lous

un¦scru¦pu¦lous¦ly
un¦scru¦pu¦lous¦
    ness
un¦seal +s +ed
  +ing
un¦search¦able
un¦search¦able¦
    ness
un¦search¦ably
un¦searched
un¦sea¦son¦able
un¦sea¦son¦able¦
    ness
un¦sea¦son¦ably
un¦sea¦son¦al
un¦sea¦soned
un¦seat +s +ed
  +ing
un¦sea¦worthi¦
    ness
un¦sea¦worthy
un¦sec¦ond¦ed
un¦sect¦ar¦ian
un¦secured
un¦see¦able
un¦seed¦ed
un¦see¦ing
un¦see¦ing¦ly
un¦seem¦li¦ness
un¦seem¦ly
  un¦seem¦lier
  un¦seemli¦est
un¦seen
un¦seg¦re¦gated
un¦select
un¦select¦ed
un¦select¦ive
un¦self¦con¦scious
un¦self¦
    con¦scious¦ly
un¦self¦con¦scious¦
    ness
un¦self¦ish
un¦self¦ish¦ly
un¦self¦ish¦ness
un¦sell¦able
un¦sen¦sa¦tion¦al
un¦sen¦sa¦tion¦
    al¦ly
un¦sent
un¦sen¦ti¦men¦tal
un¦sen¦ti¦men¦tal¦
    ity
un¦sen¦ti¦
    men¦tal¦ly
un¦sep¦ar¦ated
un¦seri¦ous
un¦ser¦vice¦abil¦ity
un¦ser¦vice¦able
unset
un¦set¦tle
  un¦set¦tles

un|set|tle (*cont.*)
  un|set|tled
  un|set|tling
un|settled|ness
un|settle|ment
un|sev|ered
un|sewn (not sewn.
  ⚠ unsown)
unsex
  un|sexes
  un|sexed
  un|sex|ing
un|sexy
un|shackle
  un|shackles
  un|shackled
  un|shack|ling
un|shaded
un|shak|abil|ity
  (use
  unshakeability)
un|shak|able (use
  unshakeable)
un|shak|ably (use
  unshakeably)
un|shake|abil|ity
un|shake|able
un|shake|ably
un|shaken
un|shaken|ly
un|shape|li|ness
un|shape|ly
un|shared
un|sharp
un|sharp|ened
un|sharp|ness
un|shaved
un|shaven
un|sheathe
  un|sheathes
  un|sheathed
  un|sheath|ing
un|shed
un|shell +s +ed
  +ing
un|shel|tered
un|shield|ed
un|shift|able
un|ship
  un|ships
  un|shipped
  un|ship|ping
un|shock|abil|ity
un|shock|able
un|shock|ably
un|shod
un|shorn
un|shrink|abil|ity
un|shrink|able
un|shrink|ing
un|shrink|ing|ly
un|shriven

un|shut|tered
un|sight +s +ed
  +ing
un|sight|li|ness
un|sight|ly
  un|sight|lier
  un|sightli|est
un|signed
un|sign|post|ed
un|silenced
un|sim|pli|fied
un|sink|abil|ity
un|sink|able
un|sized
un|skil|ful *Br.*
un|skil|ful|ly *Br.*
un|skil|ful|ness *Br.*
un|skilled
un|skill|ful *Am.*
un|skill|ful|ly *Am.*
un|skill|ful|ness
  Am.
un|skimmed
un|slak|able (use
  unslakeable)
un|slake|able
un|slaked
un|sleep|ing
un|sleep|ing|ly
un|sliced
un|sling
  un|slings
  un|slung
  un|sling|ing
un|smil|ing
un|smil|ing|ly
un|smil|ing|ness
un|smoked
un|smoothed
un|snap
  un|snaps
  un|snapped
  un|snap|ping
un|snarl +s +ed
  +ing
un|soaked
un|soci|abil|ity
un|soci|able
un|soci|able|ness
un|soci|ably
un|social
un|social|ist +s
un|social|ly
un|soft|ened
un|soiled
un|sold
un|sol|der +s +ed
  +ing
un|sol|dier|ly
un|soli|cit|ed
un|soli|cit|ed|ly
un|solv|abil|ity

un|solv|able
un|solv|able|ness
un|solved
un|sophis|ti|cated
un|sophis|ti|
  cated|ly
un|sophis|ti|cated|
  ness
un|sophis|ti|
  ca|tion
un|sort|ed
un|sought
un|sound
un|sound|ed
un|sound|ly
un|sound|ness
un|soured
un|sown (not sown.
  ⚠ unsewn)
un|spar|ing
un|spar|ing|ly
un|spar|ing|ness
un|speak|able
un|speak|able|
  ness
un|speak|ably
un|speak|ing
un|spe|cial
un|spe|cial|ised
  Br. (use
  unspecialized)
un|spe|cial|ized
un|spe|cif|ic
un|speci|fied
un|spec|tacu|lar
un|spec|tacu|lar|ly
un|spent
un|spilled
un|spilt
un|spir|it|ual
un|spir|itu|al|ity
un|spir|itu|al|ly
un|spir|it|ual|ness
un|spoiled *Am.*
un|spoilt *Br.*
un|spoken
un|spon|sored
un|spool +s +ed
  +ing
un|sport|ing
un|sport|ing|ly
un|sport|ing|ness
un|sports|man|
  like
un|spot|ted
un|sprayed
un|sprung
un|stable
un|stable|ness
un|stably
un|staffed
un|stained

un|stall +s +ed
  +ing
un|stamped
un|stan|dard|ised
  Br. (use
  unstandardized)
un|stan|dard|ized
un|starched
un|stat|able
un|stated
un|states|man|like
un|stat|ut|able
un|stat|ut|ably
un|stead|fast
un|stead|ily
un|steadi|ness
un|steady
un|ster|ile
un|ster|il|ised *Br.*
  (use unsterilized)
un|ster|il|ized
un|stick
  un|sticks
  un|stuck
  un|stick|ing
un|stifled
un|stimu|lated
un|stimu|lat|ing
un|stint|ed
un|stint|ed|ly
un|stint|ing
un|stint|ing|ly
un|stirred
un|stitch
  un|stitches
  un|stitched
  un|stitch|ing
un|stocked
un|stock|inged
un|stop
  un|stops
  un|stopped
  un|stop|ping
un|stop|pabil|ity
un|stop|pable
un|stop|pably
un|stop|per +s +ed
  +ing
un|strained
un|strap
  un|straps
  un|strapped
  un|strap|ping
un|strati|fied
un|streamed
un|stream|lined
un|strength|ened
un|stressed
un|stretched
un|string
  un|strings

un|string (*cont.*)
un|strung
un|string|ing
un|stripped
un|struc|tured
un|stuck
un|stud|ied
un|stud|ied|ly
un|stuffed
un|stuffy
un|styl|ish
un|sub|dued
un|sub|ju|gated
un|sub|scribed
un|sub|sid|ised *Br.*
(use
unsubsidized)
un|sub|sid|ized
un|sub|stan|tial
un|sub|stan|ti|al|
ity
un|sub|stan|tial|ly
un|sub|stan|ti|
ated
un|subtle
un|subtly
un|suc|cess
un|suc|cesses
un|suc|cess|ful
un|suc|cess|ful|ly
un|suc|cess|ful|
ness
un|sugared
un|sug|gest|ive
un|suit|abil|ity
un|suit|able
un|suit|able|ness
un|suit|ably
un|suit|ed
un|sul|lied
un|sum|moned
un|sung
un|super|vised
un|sup|plied
un|sup|port|able
un|sup|port|ably
un|sup|port|ed
un|sup|port|ed|ly
un|sup|port|ive
un|sup|pressed
un|sure
un|sure|ly
un|sure|ness
un|sur|faced
un|sur|mount|able
un|sur|pass|able
un|sur|pass|ably
un|sur|passed
un|sur|prised
un|sur|pris|ing
un|sur|pris|ing|ly
un|sur|veyed

un|sur|viv|able
un|sus|cep|ti|
bil|ity
un|sus|cep|tible
un|sus|pect|ed
un|sus|pect|ed|ly
un|sus|pect|ing
un|sus|pect|ing|ly
un|sus|pect|ing|
ness
un|sus|pi|cious
un|sus|pi|cious|ly
un|sus|pi|cious|
ness
un|sus|tain|able
un|sus|tain|ably
un|sus|tained
un|swal|lowed
un|swathe
un|swathes
un|swathed
un|swath|ing
un|swayed
un|sweet|ened
un|swept
un|swerv|ing
un|swerv|ing|ly
un|sworn
un|sym|met|ric|al
un|sym|met|ric|
al|ly
un|sym|pa|thet|ic
un|sym|pa|thet|ic|
al|ly
un|sys|tem|at|ic
un|sys|tem|at|ic|
al|ly
un|tack +s +ed
+ing
un|taint|ed
un|taken
un|tal|ent|ed
un|tame|able
un|tamed
un|tan|gle
un|tan|gles
un|tan|gled
un|tan|gling
un|tanned
un|tapped
un|tar|nished
un|tasted
un|taxed
un|teach
un|teaches
un|taught
un|teach|ing
un|teach|able
un|tear|able
un|tech|nic|al
un|tech|nic|al|ly
un|tem|pered

un|tempt|ed
un|ten|abil|ity
un|ten|able
un|ten|able|ness
un|ten|ably
un|ten|ant|ed
un|tend|ed
un|ten|ured
Un|ter|mensch
Un|ter|mensch|en
Un|ter|walden
(canton,
Switzerland)
un|test|able
un|test|ed
un|tether +s +ed
+ing
un|thanked
un|thank|ful
un|thank|ful|ly
un|thank|ful|ness
un|thatched
un|theo|logic|al
un|the|or|et|ic|al
un|the|or|ised *Br.*
(use untheorized)
un|the|or|ized
un|thick|ened
un|think
un|thinks
un|thought
un|think|ing
un|think|abil|ity
un|think|able
un|think|able|ness
un|think|ably
un|think|ing|ly
un|think|ing|ness
un|thought
un|thought|ful
un|thought|ful|ly
un|thought|ful|
ness
unthought-of
unthought-out
un|thread +s +ed
+ing
un|threat|ened
un|threat|en|ing
un|threshed
un|thrift|ily
un|thrifti|ness
un|thrifty
un|throne
un|thrones
un|throned
un|thron|ing
un|tidi|ly
un|tidi|ness
un|tidy
un|tidi|er
un|tidi|est

untie
un|ties
un|tied
un|tying
until
un|tilled
un|timed
un|time|li|ness
un|time|ly
un|tinged
un|tipped
un|tired
un|tir|ing
un|tir|ing|ly
un|titled
unto
un|toast|ed
un|told
un|touch|abil|ity
un|touch|able +s
un|touch|able|
ness
un|touched
un|to|ward
un|to|ward|ly
un|to|ward|ness
un|trace|able
un|trace|ably
un|traced
un|tracked
un|trad|ition|al
un|train|able
un|trained
un|tram|meled
Am.
un|tram|melled *Br.*
un|tram|pled
un|trans|fer|able
un|trans|formed
un|trans|
lat|abil|ity
un|trans|lat|able
un|trans|lat|ably
un|trans|lated
un|trans|mit|ted
un|trans|port|able
un|trav|eled *Am.*
un|trav|elled *Br.*
un|treat|able
un|treat|ed
un|trendy
un|tried
un|trimmed
un|trod|den
un|troubled
un|true
un|truly
un|truss
un|trusses
un|trussed
un|truss|ing
un|trust|ing

un|trust|worthi|ness
un|trust|worthy
un|truth +s
un|truth|ful
un|truth|ful|ly
un|truth|ful|ness
un|tuck +s +ed +ing
un|tun|able
un|tuned
un|tune|ful
un|tune|ful|ly
un|tune|ful|ness
un|turned
un|tutored
un|twine
  un|twines
  un|twined
  un|twin|ing
un|twist +s +ed +ing
un|tying
un|typ|ical
un|typ|ic|al|ly
un|usable
un|use|able (use unusable)
un|used
un|usual
un|usual|ly
un|usual|ness
un|utter|able
un|utter|able|ness
un|utter|ably
un|uttered
un|vac|cin|ated
un|valued
un|van|dal|ised Br. (use unvandalized)
un|van|dal|ized
un|van|quished
un|var|ied
un|var|nished
un|vary|ing
un|vary|ing|ly
un|vary|ing|ness
un|veil +s +ed +ing
un|vent|ed
un|ven|til|ated
un|veri|fi|able
un|veri|fied
un|versed
un|viabil|ity
un|viable
un|vio|lated
un|visit|ed
un|viti|ated
un|voiced
un|waged

un|wak|ened
un|walled
un|want|ed
un|war|ily
un|wari|ness
un|war|like
un|warmed
un|warned
un|war|rant|able
un|war|rant|able|ness
un|war|rant|ably
un|war|rant|ed
un|wary
  un|wari|er
  un|wari|est
un|washed
un|watch|able
un|watched
un|watch|ful
un|watered
un|waver|ing
un|waver|ing|ly
un|waxed
un|weak|ened
un|weaned
un|wear|able
un|wear|ied
un|wear|ied|ly
un|wear|ied|ness
un|weary
un|weary|ing
un|weary|ing|ly
unwed
un|wed|ded
un|wed|ded|ness
un|weed|ed
un|weighed
un|weight +s +ed +ing
un|wel|come
un|wel|comed
un|wel|come|ly
un|wel|come|ness
un|wel|com|ing
un|well
un|wept
un|wet|ted
un|whipped
un|whitened
un|whole|some
un|whole|some|ly
un|whole|some|ness
un|wield|ily
un|wieldi|ness
un|wieldy
  un|wield|ier
  un|wieldi|est
un|will|ing
un|will|ing|ly
un|will|ing|ness

un|wind
  un|winds
  un|wound
  un|wind|ing
un|wink|ing
un|wink|ing|ly
un|win|nable
un|wiped
un|wired
un|wis|dom
un|wise
un|wise|ly
un|wished
un|with|ered
un|wit|nessed
un|wit|ting
un|wit|ting|ly
un|wit|ting|ness
un|woman|li|ness
un|woman|ly
un|wont|ed
un|wont|ed|ly
un|wont|ed|ness
un|wood|ed
un|work|abil|ity
un|work|able
un|work|able|ness
un|work|ably
un|worked
un|work|man|like
un|world|li|ness
un|world|ly
un|worn
un|wor|ried
un|wor|shipped
un|worth|ily
un|worthi|ness
un|worthy
  un|wor|thier
  un|worthi|est
un|wound
un|wound|ed
un|woven
un|wrap
  un|wraps
  un|wrapped
  un|wrap|ping
un|wrin|kled
un|writ|able
un|writ|ten
un|wrought
un|wrung
un|yield|ing
un|yield|ing|ly
un|yield|ing|ness
un|yoke
  un|yokes
  un|yoked
  un|yok|ing
unzip
  un|zips

unzip (cont.)
  un|zipped
  un|zip|ping
up
  ups
  upped
  up|ping
up-anchor +s +ed +ing
up-and-coming
up-and-over
up and run|ning
up-and-under +s
Upani|shad +s
upas
upas tree +s
up|beat +s
up|braid +s +ed +ing
up|braid|ing +s
up|bring|ing +s
up|build
  up|builds
  up|built
  up|build|ing
up|cast +s
up|chuck +s +ed +ing
up|com|ing
up-country
up|cur|rent +s
up|date
  up|dates
  up|dated
  up|dat|ing
up|dater +s
Up|dike, John (American writer)
up|draft Am. +s
up|draught Br. +s
upend +s +ed +ing
up|field
up|flow
up|fold +s
up|front adjective
up front adverb
up|grade
  up|grades
  up|graded
  up|grad|ing
up|grade|able
up|grader +s
up|grad|ing +s
up|growth
up|haul +s
up|heav|al +s
up|heave
  up|heaves
  up|heaved
  up|heav|ing
up|hill

up|hold
  up|holds
  up|held
  up|hold|ing
up|hold|er +s
up|hol|ster +s +ed
  +ing
up|hol|ster|er +s
up|hol|stery
up|keep
up|land +s
up|lift +s +ed +ing
up|lift|er +s
up|light|er +s
up|link +s +ed
  +ing
up|load +s +ed
  +ing
up|lying
up|mar|ket
up|most
upon
upper +s
upper case *noun*
upper-case
  attributive
upper-class
  adjective
upper|cut
  upper|cuts
  upper|cut
  upper|cut|ting
upper-middle-
  class *adjective*
upper|most
upper|part +s
Upper Volta
  (former name of
  Burkina)
up|pish
up|pish|ly
up|pish|ness
up|pity
Upp|sala (city,
  Sweden)
up|raise
  up|raises
  up|raised
  up|rais|ing
up|rate
  up|rates
  up|rated
  up|rat|ing
up|rat|ing +s
up|right +s +ed
  +ing
up|right|ly
up|right|ness
up|rise
  up|rises
  up|rose

up|rise (*cont.*)
  up|ris|ing
  up|risen
up|ris|ing +s
up|river
up|roar +s
up|roari|ous
up|roari|ous|ly
up|roari|ous|ness
up|root +s +ed
  +ing
up|root|er
up|rose
up|rush
  up|rushes
ups-a-daisy
up|scale
upset
  up|sets
  upset
  up|set|ting
up|set|ter +s
up|set|ting|ly
up|shift +s +ed
  +ing
up|shot +s
up|side down
  *adverb and
  adjective*
upside-down
  attributive
up|sides
up|sil|lon +s
up|stage
  up|stages
  up|staged
  up|staging
up|stair
up|stairs
up|stand +s
up|stand|ing
up|start +s
up|state
up|stater +s
up|stream
up|stretched
up|stroke +s
up|surge +s
up|swept
up|swing +s
upsy-daisy
up|take +s
up-tempo
up|throw +s
up|thrust +s
up|tick +s
up|tight
up|tilt|ed
up|time
up to date *adverb
  and adjective*
up-to-date
  attributive

up-to-the-minute
up|town
up|town|er +s
up|turn +s +ed
  +ing
up|ward
up|ward|ly
up|wards
up|warp +s
up|well +s +ed
  +ing
up|wind
Ur (ancient city,
  Iraq)
ura|cil
ur|ae|mia *Br.* (*Am.*
  uremia)
ur|aem|ic *Br.* (*Am.*
  uremic)
ur|aeus
  uraei
Ural-Altaic +s
Ural|ic +s
Ural Moun|tains
  (in Russia)
Urals (= Ural
  Mountains)
Ur|ania *Greek and
  Roman Mythology*
ur|an|ic
ur|an|in|ite
ur|an|ism
ur|an|ium
uran|og|raph|er +s
urano|graph|ic
uran|og|raphy
uran|om|etry
uran|ous
  (of uranium)
Ura|nus (*Greek
  Mythology*; planet)
urate +s
urban
ur|bane
ur|bane|ly
ur|bane|ness
ur|ban|isa|tion *Br.*
  (use
  urbanization)
ur|ban|ise *Br.* (use
  urbanize)
  ur|ban|ises
  ur|ban|ised
  ur|ban|is|ing
ur|ban|ism
ur|ban|ist +s
ur|ban|ite +s
ur|ban|ity
  ur|ban|ities
ur|ban|iza|tion
ur|ban|ize
  ur|ban|izes

ur|ban|ize (*cont.*)
  ur|ban|ized
  ur|ban|iz|ing
ur|ceo|late
ur|chin +s
Urdu
urea
urea-
  formal|de|hyde
ureal
ur|emia *Am.* (*Br.*
  uraemia)
ur|emic *Am.* (*Br.*
  uraemic)
ur|eter +s
ur|eter|al
ur|eter|ic
ur|eter|itis
ur|eter|ot|omy
  ur|eter|oto|mies
ur|eth|ane
ur|ethra
  ur|eth|rae
ur|eth|ral
ur|eth|ritis
ur|eth|rot|omy
  ur|eth|roto|mies
Urey, Har|old
  Clay|ton
  (American
  chemist)
Urga (former name
  of Ulan Bator)
urge
  urges
  urged
  ur|ging
ur|gen|cy
  ur|gen|cies
ur|gent
ur|gent|ly
urger +s
ur|ging +s
Uriah *Bible*
uric
urim
ur|inal +s
urin|aly|sis
  urin|aly|ses
urin|ary
urin|ate
  urin|ates
  urin|ated
  urin|at|ing
urin|ation
urine +s
urin|ous
urn +s (vase; vessel
  for tea etc.
  ⚠ earn, ern, erne)
urn|field +s
urn|ful +s

uro|chord +s
uro|chord|ate +s
uro|dele +s
uro|geni|tal
uro|lith|ia|sis
uro|logic
ur|olo|gist +s
ur|ology
uro|pygium
  uro|pygia
uros|copy
Ursa Major
  (constellation)
Ursa Minor
  (constellation)
ur|sine
Ur|sula (legendary
  British saint;
  name)
Ur|su|line +s
ur|ti|caria
ur|ti|cate
  ur|ti|cates
  ur|ti|cated
  ur|ti|cat|ing
ur|ti|ca|tion
Uru|guay
Uru|guay|an +s
Uruk (ancient city,
  Mesopotamia)
Urum|chi
  (= Urumqi)
Urumqi (city,
  China)
urus
  plural **urus**
us
us|abil|ity
us|able
us|able|ness
usage +s
us|ance +s
USDAW (= Union
  of Shop,
  Distributive, and
  Allied Workers)
use
  uses
  used
  using
  (bring into service;
  exploit. △ youse)
use|abil|ity (use
  usability)
use|able (use
  usable)
use|able|ness (use
  usableness)
use-by date +s
use|ful
use|ful|ly
use|ful|ness

use|less
use|less|ly
use|less|ness
user +s
user-friendli|ness
user-friend|ly
ushabti +s
U-shaped
usher +s +ed +ing
ush|er|ette +s
ush|er|ship +s
Ushu|aia (port,
  Tierra del Fuego)
Üskü|dar (suburb
  of Istanbul,
  Turkey)
Us|pa|llata Pass
  (in Andes)
usque|baugh
Us|ta|ba|kan|skoe
  (former name of
  Abakan)
Usta|sha +s
  (member of
  Croatian
  nationalist
  movement)
Usta|she (these
  collectively)
Us|ti|nov (former
  name of Izhevsk)
Us|ti|nov, Peter
  (British actor)
usual
usu|al|ly
usual|ness
usu|cap|tion
usu|fruct +s +ed
  +ing
usu|fruc|tu|ary
  usu|fruc|tu|ar|ies
Usum|bura (former
  name of
  Bujumbura)
us|urer +s
us|uri|ous
us|uri|ous|ly
usurp +s +ed +ing
usurp|ation
usurp|er +s
usury
Utah (state, USA; D-
  Day beach)
Uta|maro,
  Kita|gawa
  (Japanese painter)
Ute
  plural **Ute** *or* **Utes**
  (American Indian)
ute +s (utility truck)
uten|sil +s
uter|ine

ut|er|itis
uterus
  uteri
Uther Pen|dragon
  Arthurian Legend
utile
util|is|able *Br.* (use
  utilizable)
util|isa|tion *Br.*
  (use utilization)
util|ise *Br.* (use
  utilize)
  util|ises
  util|ised
  util|is|ing
util|iser *Br.* +s (use
  utilizer)
utili|tar|ian +s
utili|tar|ian|ism
util|ity
  util|ities
util|ity pro|gram
  +s
util|iz|able
util|iza|tion
util|ize
  util|izes
  util|ized
  util|iz|ing
util|izer +s
ut|most
Uto|pia +s
Uto|pian +s
Uto|pian|ism
Ut|recht (city, the
  Netherlands)
ut|ricle +s
ut|ricu|lar
Ut|rillo, Maur|ice
  (French painter)
Ut|sire (island,
  Norway)
Ut|sire, North and
  South (shipping
  areas, North Sea)
Uttar Pra|desh
  (state, India)
utter +s +ed +ing
ut|ter|able
ut|ter|ance +s
ut|ter|er +s
ut|ter|ly
ut|ter|most
ut|ter|ness
Ut|tley, Ali|son
  (English writer)
U-turn +s
U2 (Irish rock
  group)
uvea +s

uvula
  uvu|lae
  (part of throat)
uvu|lar +s
  (of the uvula;
  consonant)
ux|or|ial
ux|ori|cidal
ux|ori|cide +s
ux|ori|ous
ux|ori|ous|ly
Uzbek +s
Uz|beki|stan
Uzi +s (gun)

Vv

Vaal (river, South Africa)
Vaasa (port, Finland. △ Vasa, *Vasa*)
vac +s (= vacation; vacuum cleaner)
va¦cancy
　va¦can|cies
va¦cant
va¦cant¦ly
vac|at¦able
vac¦ate
　vac|ates
　vac|ated
　vac|at¦ing
vac|ation +s +ed +ing
vac|ation¦er +s
vac|ation|ist +s
vac|ation|land +s
vac|cinal
vac|cin|ate
　vac|cin|ates
　vac|cin|ated
　vac|cin|at¦ing
vac|cin|ation +s
vac|cin|ator +s
vac|cine +s
vac|cinia +s
vacil|late
　vacil|lates
　vacil|lated
　vacil|lat¦ing
vacil|la¦tion +s
vacil|la¦tor +s
vacua
vacu|ity
vacu|olar
vacu|ol|ation +s
vacu|ole +s
vacu|ous
vacu|ous¦ly
vacu|ous|ness
vac¦uum
　vac¦uums *or*
　vacua
　noun
vac¦uum +s +ed +ing *verb*
vacuum-clean +s +ed +ing
vac¦uum clean¦er +s
vacuum-packed
vade-mecum +s
Vado|dara (city and district, India)

Vaduz (capital of Liechtenstein)
vag
　vags
　vagged
　vag|ging
vaga|bond +s +ed +ing
vaga¦bond|age
vagal
va¦gari|ous
va¦gary
　va|gar¦ies
vagi
va¦gina +s
va¦ginal
vagin|is¦mus
vagin|itis
va|grancy
va|grant +s
va|grant¦ly
vague
　vaguer
　vaguest
vague¦ly
vague|ness
vaguish
vagus
　vagi
vail +s +ed +ing (doff; yield. △ vale, veil)
vain +er +est (conceited. △ vane, vein)
vain|glori¦ous
vain|glori¦ous¦ly
vain|glori¦ous|ness
vain|glory
vain¦ly
vain|ness
vair
Vaish|nava +s
Vai¦sya +s
Val
Val¦ais (canton, Switzerland)
val|ance +s (short curtain. △ valence)
val|anced
Valda
vale +s (valley; farewell. △ vail, veil)
val¦edic|tion +s
val¦edic|tor¦ian +s
val¦edic|tory
val¦edic|tor¦ies

val|lence +s (*Chemistry*. △ valance)
Val¦en|cia (city and region, Spain)
Val¦en|cian
Val¦en|ci|ennes (lace)
va|lency
　va¦len|cies
Val¦en|tia (weather station off Ireland)
Val¦en|tine (Italian saint; name)
val¦en|tine +s
Val¦en|tino, Ru|dolph (Italian-born American actor)
Val¦era, Eamon de (Irish statesman)
val¦er|ate +s
Val¦er¦ian (Roman emperor)
val¦er|ian +s (plant)
val¦er¦ic
Val|erie
Val¦éry, Paul (French writer)
valet +s +ed +ing
val¦eta +s (use veleta)
val¦etu¦din|ar|ian +s
val¦etu¦din| ar¦ian|ism
val¦etu¦din|ary
val¦etu¦din|ar¦ies
val¦gus
val|guses
Val|halla (*Scandinavian Mythology*)
vali|ant
vali|ant¦ly
valid
val¦id|ate
　val¦id|ates
　val¦id|ated
　val¦id|at¦ing
val¦id|ation +s
val¦id|ity
val¦id¦ly
val¦ine +s
val¦ise +s
Val¦ium *Propr.*
Val|kyrie +s (*Scandinavian Mythology*)
Valla|do|lid (city, Spain)

val|lec¦ula
　val¦lecu|lae
val¦lecu|lar
val¦lecu|late
Valle d'Aosta (region, Italy)
Val|letta (capital of Malta)
val¦ley +s (region between hills)
val¦lum
　valli
　(Roman rampart and stockade)
Val¦ois, Nin|ette de (Irish dancer and choreographer)
val|onia
valor *Am.* (*Br.* valour)
val|orem (in 'ad valorem')
val¦or|isa¦tion *Br.* (use valorization)
val¦or|ise *Br.* (use valorize)
　val¦or|ises
　val¦or|ised
　val¦or|is¦ing
val¦or|iza¦tion
val¦or|ize
　val¦or|izes
　val¦or|ized
　val¦or|iz¦ing
val¦or|ous
val¦our *Br.* (*Am.* valor)
Val|par¦aíso (port, Chile)
valse +s
valu|able +s
valu|ably
valu|ate
　valu|ates
　valu|ated
　valu|at¦ing
valu|ation +s
valu|ator +s
value
　val¦ues
　val¦ued
　valu¦ing
value added *noun and adjective*
value-added (*attributive* except of tax)
value added tax
value-based
value-for-money *attributive*

value judge|ment
+s

value judg|ment
+s (use value
judgement)

value|less

value|less|ness

valuer+s

val|uta+s

valv|ate

valve+s

valved

valve gear

valve|less

valvu|lar

valv|ule+s

valv|ul|itis

vam|brace+s

vam|oose

  vam|ooses

  vam|oosed

  vam|oos|ing

vamp+s +ed +ing

vam|pire+s

vam|pir|ic

vam|pir|ism

vamp|ish

vam|plate+s

vampy

  vamp|ier

  vampi|est

Van (name)

Van, Lake (in
Turkey)

van+s (vehicle)

van|ad|ate+s

van|ad|ic

van|adium

van|ad|ous

Van Allen (belt;
layer)

Van|brugh, John
(English architect)

Van Buren,
Mar|tin
(American
president)

Van|cou|ver (city,
Canada)

Van|cou|ver,
George (English
navigator)

Van|cou|ver
Is|land
(in Canada)

Vanda (Swedish
name for Vantaa)

Van|dal+s
(member of
Germanic people)

van|dal+s
(destructive
person)

Van|dal|ic

van|dal|ise Br. (use
vandalize)

van|dal|ises

van|dal|ised

van|dal|is|ing

van|dal|ism

van|dal|is|tic

van|dal|is|tic|al|ly

van|dal|ize

  van|dal|izes

  van|dal|ized

  van|dal|iz|ing

van de Graaff
(generator)

Van|der|bijl|park
(city, South
Africa)

Van|der|bilt,
Cor|ne|lius
(American
shipping and
railway magnate)

Van der Post,
Laur|ens (South
African explorer)

van der Waals
(forces)

van de Velde,
Adri|aen (Dutch
painter)

van de Velde,
Henri (Belgian
architect)

van de Velde,
Wil|lem ('the
Elder' and 'the
Younger', Dutch
painters)

Van Die|men's
Land (former
name of
Tasmania)

Van Dyck,
An|thony
(Flemish painter)

Van|dyke,
An|thony (use
Van Dyck)

Van|dyke+s
(beard)

van|dyke+s (lace
point; cape or
collar)

Van|dyke brown
noun and adjective

Vandyke-brown
attributive

vane+s
(weathervane;
blade of propeller
etc.; sight on
instrument; part of
feather. △ vain,
vein)

vaned

vane|less (without
vanes. △ veinless)

Vän|ern (lake,
Switzerland)

Van|essa (name)

van|essa+s
(butterfly)

Van Eyck, Jan
(Flemish painter)

vang+s

Van Gogh,
Vin|cent (Dutch
painter)

van|guard+s

van|illa+s

van|il|lin

van|ish

  van|ishes

  van|ished

  van|ish|ing

van|ish|ing point
+s

vani|tory

  vani|tor|ies
Propr.

van|ity

  van|ities

van Ley|den,
Lucas (Dutch
painter)

van|load+s

van|quish

  van|quishes

  van|quished

  van|quish|ing

van|quish|able

van|quish|er+s

Van|taa (city,
Finland)

vant|age+s

vant|age point+s

Vanua Levu
(island, Fiji)

Vanu|atu (in S.
Pacific)

vapid

vap|id|ity

vap|id|ly

vap|id|ness

vapor Am. +s (Br.
vapour)

vapor-check Am.
attributive (Br.
vapour-check)

va|por|er Am. +s
(Br. vapourer)

vap|or|etto

vap|or|etti or
vap|or|ettos

va|por|if|ic

va|por|iform

va|por|im|eter+s

va|por|ing Am. +s
(Br. vapouring)

va|por|is|able Br.
(use vaporizable)

va|por|isa|tion Br.
(use
vaporization)

va|por|ise Br. (use
vaporize)

va|por|ises

va|por|ised

va|por|is|ing

va|por|iser Br. +s
(use vaporizer)

va|por|ish Am. (Br.
vapourish)

va|por|iz|able

va|por|iza|tion

va|por|ize

  va|por|izes

  va|por|ized

  va|por|iz|ing

va|por|izer+s

va|por|ous

va|por|ous|ly

va|por|ous|ness

va|pory Am. (Br.
vapoury)

va|pour Br. +s +ed
+ing (Am. vapor)

vapour-check Br.
attributive (Am.
vapor-check)

va|pour|er Br. +s
(Am. vaporer)

va|pour|ing Br. +s
(Am. vaporing)

va|pour|ish Br.
(Am. vaporish)

va|poury Br. (Am.
vapory)

va|quero+s

var|ac|tor+s

Varah, Chad
(English founder
of the Samaritans)

Vara|nasi (city,
India)

Var|an|gian+s

varec

Var|ese (town,
Italy)

Var|èse, Ed|gard
(French-born

Var|èse (*cont.*)
American
composer)
Var|gas, Getú|lio
Dor|nel|les
(Brazilian
president)
Var|gas Llosa,
Mario (Peruvian
writer)
vari|abil|ity
vari|abil|ities
vari|able +s
vari|able|ness
variable-rate
attributive
variable-speed
attributive
vari|ably
vari|ance +s
vari|ant +s
vari|ate +s
vari|ation +s
vari|ation|al
vari|cella
vari|ces
vari|co|cele +s
vari|col|ored *Am.*
vari|col|oured *Br.*
vari|cose
vari|cosed
vari|cos|ity
var|ied
var|ied|ly
varie|gate
varie|gates
varie|gated
varie|gat|ing
varie|ga|tion +s
var|ietal
var|ietal|ly
var|iet|ist +s
var|iety
var|ieties
vari|focal +s
vari|form
vari|ola *noun*
vari|olar *adjective*
vari|ole +s
vari|ol|ite +s
vari|ol|it|ic
vari|ol|oid +s
vari|ol|ous
vari|om|eter +s
vari|orum +s
vari|ous
vari|ous|ly
vari|ous|ness
var|is|tor +s
varix
vari|ces
var|let +s

var|let|ry
var|mint +s
Varna (port,
Bulgaria)
varna +s *Hinduism*
Varne (lightvessel,
English Channel)
var|nish
var|nishes
var|nished
var|nish|ing
var|nish|er +s
Varro, Mar|cus
Ter|en|tius
(Roman scholar)
var|sity
var|sities
Var|so|vian +s
var|so|vi|ana +s
var|so|vi|enne +s
Var|una (Hindu
god)
varus
var|uses
varve +s
varved
vary
var|ies
var|ied
vary|ing
vary|ing|ly
vas
vasa
Vasa (Swedish
dynasty. △ Vaasa)
Vasa (ship.
△ Vaasa)
vasal
Vas|ar|ely, Vik|tor
(Hungarian-born
French painter)
Vas|ari, Gior|gio
(Italian painter
and biographer)
Vasco da Gama
(Portuguese
explorer)
vas|cu|lar
vas|cu|lar|isa|tion
Br. (use
vascularization)
vas|cu|lar|ise *Br.*
(use vascularize)
vas|cu|lar|ises
vas|cu|lar|ised
vas|cu|lar|is|ing
vas|cu|lar|ity
vas|cu|lar|iza|tion
vas|cu|lar|ize
vas|cu|lar|izes
vas|cu|lar|ized
vas|cu|lar|iz|ing

vas|cu|lar|ly
vas|cu|lum
vas|cula
vas def|er|ens
vasa def|er|entia
vase +s
vas|ec|tom|ise *Br.*
(use
vasectomize)
vas|ec|tom|ises
vas|ec|tom|ised
vas|ec|tom|is|ing
vas|ec|tom|ize
vas|ec|tom|izes
vas|ec|tom|ized
vas|ec|tom|iz|ing
vas|ec|tomy
vas|ec|to|mies
vase|ful +s
Vas|el|ine *noun*
Propr.
vas|el|ine
vas|el|ines
vas|el|ined
vas|el|in|ing
verb
vasi|form
vaso|active
vaso|con|stric|tion
vaso|con|strict|ive
vaso|con|strict|or
+s
vaso|dilat|ing
vaso|dila|tion
vaso|dila|tor +s
vaso|motor
vaso|pres|sin
vas|sal +s
vas|sal|age +s
vast +er +est
Väs|ter|ås (port,
Sweden)
vast|ly
vast|ness
vast|nesses
VAT (= value
added tax)
vat
vats
vat|ted
vat|ting
(tank)
VAT-free
vat|ful +s
vatic
Vati|can (pope's
palace)
Vati|can City
(papal state,
Rome)
Vati|can|ism
Vati|can|ist +s

va|ti|cinal
va|ti|cin|ate
va|ti|cin|ates
va|ti|cin|ated
va|ti|cin|at|ing
va|ti|cin|ation +s
va|ti|cin|ator +s
va|ti|cin|atory
VAT|man
VAT|men
(tax officer)
vat-man
vat-men
(paper worker)
VAT-registered
Vät|tern (lake,
Sweden)
Vaud (canton,
Switzerland)
vaude|ville +s
vaude|vil|lian +s
Vaud|ois
plural Vaud|ois
Vaughan, Henry
(Welsh
metaphysical
poet)
Vaughan, Sarah
(American jazz
musician)
Vaughan
Wil|liams, Ralph
(English
composer)
vault +s +ed +ing
(arch;
underground
chamber; jump.
△ volt, volte)
vault|er +s
vault|ing horse +s
vaunt +s +ed +ing
vaunt|er +s
vaunt|ing|ly
vava|sory
vava|sor|ies
vava|sour +s
Vav|ilov, Niko|lai
(Soviet plant
geneticist)
V-bomber +s
veal
vealy
Veb|len,
Thor|stein
(American
economist)
vec|tor +s +ed
+ing
vec|tor|ial

vec|tor|isa|tion *Br.* (use vectorization)
vec|tor|ise *Br.* (use vectorize)
vec|tor|ises
vec|tor|ised
vec|tor|is|ing
vec|tor|iza|tion
vec|tor|ize
vec|tor|izes
vec|tor|ized
vec|tor|iz|ing
Veda +s *Hinduism*
Ve|danta
Ve|dan|tic
Ve|dan|tist +s
Vedda +s (Sri Lankan aboriginal)
ved|ette +s
Vedic
vee +s
veep +s
veer +s +ed +ing
veery
veer|ies
veg
plural veg (= vegetable)
Vega (star)
Vega Car|pio, Lope Felix de (Spanish dramatist)
vegan +s
Vege|bur|ger +s (△ veggie burger) *Propr.*
Vege|mite *Propr.*
vege|table +s
vege|tal
vege|tar|ian +s
vege|tar|ian|ism
vege|tate
vege|tates
vege|tated
vege|tat|ing
vege|ta|tion
vege|ta|tion|al
vege|ta|tive
vege|ta|tive|ly
vege|ta|tive|ness
veg|gie +s
veg|gie bur|ger +s (△ Vegeburger)
vegie +s (use veggie)
vehe|mence
vehe|ment
vehe|ment|ly
ve|hicle +s
ve|hicu|lar

veil +s +ed +ing (cover. △ vail, vale)
veil|ing +s
veil|less
vein +s +ed +ing (blood vessel. △ vain, vane)
vein|less (without veins. △ vaneless)
vein|let +s
vein|like
vein|stone
veiny
vein|ier
veini|est
vela (plural of velum. △ velar)
ve|la|men
ve|la|mina
velar (of a veil or velum; *Phonetics.* △ vela)
Ve|láz|quez, Diego Rod|ríguez de Silva y (Spanish painter)
Ve|láz|quez de Cué|llar, Diego (Spanish conquistador)
Vel|cro *Propr.*
Vel|croed
veld +s
Velde, van de (see van de Velde)
veld|skoen
veld|skoens *or* veld|skoene
vel|eta +s
veli|ger +s
veli|ta|tion +s
vel|le|ity
vel|le|ities
Vel|leius Pat|er|cu|lus (Roman historian)
vel|lum +s (parchment etc. △ velum)
Velma
velo|cim|eter +s
vel|oci|pede +s
vel|oci|ped|ist +s
vel|oci|rap|tor +s
vel|ocity
vel|oci|ties
velo|drome +s
vel|our +s
vel|ours *singular* (use velour)
vel|outé +s

velum
vela (membrane. △ vellum)
velu|tin|ous
vel|vet +s
vel|vet|ed
vel|vet|een +s
vel|vety
vena cava
venae cavae
venal
ve|nal|ity
ve|nal|ly
ven|ation +s
ven|ation|al
vend +s +ed +ing
Venda +s (person; language; former homeland, South Africa)
ven|dace
plural ven|dace
Ven|dée (department, France)
vend|ee +s (buyer)
vend|er +s (use vendor)
ven|detta +s
vend|euse +s
vend|ible
vend|ing ma|chine +s
vend|or +s
ven|due +s
ven|eer +s +ed +ing
vene|punc|ture +s
ven|er|abil|ity
ven|er|able
ven|er|able|ness
ven|er|ably
ven|er|ate
ven|er|ates
ven|er|ated
ven|er|at|ing
ven|er|ation
ven|er|ator +s
ven|ereal
ven|ere|al|ly
ven|ereo|logic|al
ven|ere|olo|gist +s
ven|ere|ology
ven|ery
vene|sec|tion +s
Ven|etia (English name for the Veneto; name)
Ven|etian
ven|etianed

Ven|eto (region, Italy)
Vene|zuela
Vene|zuelan +s
ven|geance
venge|ful
venge|ful|ly
venge|ful|ness
ve|nial
veni|al|ity
veni|al|ly
veni|al|ness
Ven|ice (city, Italy)
Ven|ing Mein|esz, Felix An|dries (Dutch geophysicist)
veni|punc|ture +s (use venepuncture)
veni|sec|tion +s (use venesection)
ven|ison
Ven|ite +s
Venn dia|gram +s
venom +s
ven|omed
ven|om|ous
ven|om|ous|ly
ven|om|ous|ness
ven|ose
ven|os|ity
ven|ous
ven|ous|ly
vent +s +ed +ing
vent-hole +s
venti|duct +s
venti|fact +s
ven|til +s
ven|ti|late
ven|ti|lates
ven|ti|lated
ven|ti|lat|ing
ven|ti|la|tion
ven|ti|la|tive
ven|ti|la|tor +s
vent|less
Ven|to|lin *Propr.*
ven|touse +s
ven|tral
ven|tral|ly
ventre à terre
ven|tricle +s
ven|tri|cose
ven|tricu|lar
ven|tri|lo|quial
ven|trilo|quise *Br.* (use ventriloquize)
ven|trilo|quises
ven|trilo|quised
ven|trilo|quis|ing

ven|trilo|quism
ven|trilo|quist +s
ven|trilo|quis|tic
ven|trilo|quize
  ven|trilo|quizes
  ven|trilo|quized
  ven|trilo|quiz|ing
ven|trilo|quous
ven|trilo|quy
ven|ture
  ven|tures
  ven|tured
  ven|tur|ing
ven|turer +s
Ven|ture Scout +s
ven|ture|some
ven|ture|some|ly
ven|ture|some|
    ness
Ven|turi, Rob|ert
  (American
  architect)
ven|turi +s (tube)
venue +s
ven|ule +s
Venus (Roman
  Mythology; planet)
Venus de Milo
  (statue)
Venus fly|trap +s
Ven|us|ian +s
Venus's comb
Venus's looking-
  glass
Vera
ver|acious
ver|acious|ly
ver|acious|ness
ver|acity
Vera|cruz (city and
  state, Mexico)
ver|anda +s
ver|an|daed
ver|an|dah +s (use
  veranda)
vera|trine
verb +s
ver|bal
  ver|bals
  ver|balled
  ver|bal|ling
ver|bal|is|able Br.
  (use verbalizable)
ver|bal|isa|tion Br.
  +s (use
  verbalization)
ver|bal|ise Br. (use
  verbalize)
  ver|bal|ises
  ver|bal|ised
  ver|bal|is|ing

ver|bal|iser Br. +s
  (use verbalizer)
ver|bal|ism
ver|bal|ist +s
ver|bal|is|tic
ver|bal|iz|able
ver|bal|iza|tion +s
ver|bal|ize
  ver|bal|izes
  ver|bal|ized
  ver|bal|iz|ing
ver|bal|izer +s
ver|bal|ly
ver|bas|cum +s
ver|ba|tim
ver|bena +s
verb form +s
ver|bi|age
ver|bose
ver|bose|ly
ver|bose|ness
ver|bos|ity
ver|bo|ten
verb. sap.
ver|dancy
ver|dant
verd-antique
ver|dant|ly
ver|der|er +s
Verdi, Giu|seppe
  (Italian composer)
Verdi|an +s
ver|dict +s
ver|di|gris
ver|diter
Verdon-Roe,
  Al|li|ott (English
  engineer)
Ver|dun (town,
  France)
ver|dure
ver|dured
ver|dur|ous
Ver|eeni|ging (city,
  Transvaal)
Ver|ena also
  Ver|ina
verge
  verges
  verged
  ver|ging
ver|ger +s
ver|ger|ship +s
Ver|gil (Roman
  poet; use Virgil)
Ver|gil also Virgil
  (name)
ver|glas
ver|idi|cal
ver|idi|cal|ity
ver|idi|cal|ly
veri|est

veri|fi|able
veri|fi|ably
veri|fi|ca|tion
veri|fier
ver|ify
  veri|fies
  veri|fied
  veri|fy|ing
ver|ily
Ver|ina also
  Ver|ena
veri|sim|ilar
veri|sim|ili|tude
ver|ism
ver|ismo +s
ver|ist +s
ver|is|tic
ver|it|able
ver|it|ably
Ver|ity (name)
ver|ity
  ver|ities
  (truth)
ver|juice
Ver|khne|udinsk
  (former name of
  Ulan-Ude)
ver| krampte +s
Ver|laine, Paul
  (French poet)
ver| ligte +s
Ver|meer, Jan
  (Dutch painter)
ver|meil
ver|mian
vermi|celli
vermi|cide +s
ver|micu|lar
ver|micu|late
ver|micu|la|tion
  +s
ver|micu|lite
vermi|form
vermi|fuge +s
ver|mil|ion
ver|min
ver|min|ate
  ver|min|ates
  ver|min|ated
  ver|min|at|ing
ver|min|ation
ver|min|ous
ver|mivor|ous
Ver|mont (state,
  USA)
ver|mouth +s
ver|nacu|lar +s
ver|nacu|lar|ise Br.
  (use
  vernacularize)
  ver|nacu|lar|ises
  ver|nacu|lar|ised

ver|nacu|lar|ise
  (cont.)
  ver|nacu|lar|
    is|ing
ver|nacu|lar|ism
ver|nacu|lar|ity
ver|nacu|lar|ize
  ver|nacu|lar|izes
  ver|nacu|lar|ized
  ver|nacu|lar|
    iz|ing
ver|nacu|lar|ly
ver|nal
ver|nal|isa|tion Br.
  (use
  vernalization)
ver|nal|ise Br. (use
  vernalize)
  ver|nal|ises
  ver|nal|ised
  ver|nal|is|ing
ver|nal|iza|tion
ver|nal|ize
  ver|nal|izes
  ver|nal|ized
  ver|nal|iz|ing
ver|nal|ly
ver|na|tion
Verne, Jules
  (French novelist)
vern|icle +s
ver|nier +s
Ver|non
Verny (former
  name of Almaty)
Ver|ona (city, Italy;
  name)
ver|onal (drug)
Vero|nese, Paolo
  (Italian painter)
Ver|on|ica (early
  saint; name)
ver|on|ica +s
  (plant)
Ver|ra|zano
  Nar|rows Bridge
  (in New York)
ver|ruca
ver|ru|cae
ver|ru|cose
ver|ru|cous
Ver|sailles (town
  and palace,
  France)
ver|sant +s
ver|sa|tile
ver|sa|tile|ly
ver|sa|til|ity
verse
  verses
  versed
  vers|ing

verse (*cont.*)
(poetry etc.
⚠ verst)
verse|let +s
ver'set +s
vers|icle +s
ver'si|col'ored *Am.*
ver'si|col'oured *Br.*
ver'sicu|lar
ver'si|fi|ca'tion
ver'si|fier +s
vers|ify
  ver'si|fies
  ver'si|fied
  ver'si|fy|ing
ver'sin +s
ver'sine +s
ver|sion +s
ver|sion'al
vers libre
verso +s
verst +s (Russian
measure of length.
⚠ versed)
ver'sus
vert +s *Heraldry*
ver|te|bra
  ver|te|brae
ver|te|bral
ver|te|bral'ly
ver|te|brate +s
ver|te|bra|tion
ver|tex
  ver'ti|ces
ver'ti|cal
ver'ti|cal|ise *Br.*
(use verticalize)
  ver'ti|cal|ises
  ver'ti|cal|ised
  ver'ti|cal|is|ing
ver'ti|cal|ity
ver'ti|cal|ize
  ver'ti|cal|izes
  ver'ti|cal|ized
  ver'ti|cal|iz|ing
ver'ti|cal|ly
ver'ti|cil +s
ver'ticil|late
ver|tigin|ous
ver|tigin|ous|ly
ver|tigo +s
vertu (use virtu)
Veru|la|mium
(Roman city,
England)
ver|vain +s
verve
ver'vet +s
Ver|viers (town,
Belgium)
Ver|woerd,
Hen|drik (South

Ver|woerd (*cont.*)
African prime
minister)
Very (light; pistol)
very
  veri|est
(extremely; real;
etc.)
Vesa|lius,
An|dreas
(Flemish
anatomist)
ves|ica +s
vesi|cal
vesi|cant +s
vesi|cate
  vesi|cates
  vesi|cated
  vesi|cat|ing
vesi|ca'tion +s
vesi|ca'tory
ves|icle +s
ves|icu|lar
ves|icu|late
ves|icu|la'tion +s
Vespa +s (motor
scooter) *Propr.*
Ves|pa'sian
(Roman emperor)
ves'per +s
ves'per|tine
ves'pi|ary
  ves|pi'ar|ies
ves|pine
Ves|pucci,
Amer|igo (Italian
explorer)
ves'sel +s
vest +s +ed +ing
Vesta (*Roman
Mythology*;
asteroid; name)
vesta +s (match)
Ves|tal +s (of
Vesta; Vestal
Virgin)
ves'tal +s (chaste;
chaste woman)
vest|ee +s
Ves|ter|ålen
(islands off
Norway)
ves|ti|ary
  ves|ti|ar'ies
ves|tibu|lar
ves|ti|bule +s
ves|tige +s
ves|tigial
ves|tigial|ly
ves|ti|ture +s
vest|ment +s

vest-pocket
  attributive
ves|tral
ves'try
  ves|tries
vestry|man
  vestry|men
ves|ture
  ves|tures
  ves|tured
  ves|tur|ing
Vesu|vian
Vesu|vius
(volcano, Italy)
vet
  vets
  vet'ted
  vet|ting
vetch
  vetches
vetch|ling +s
vetchy
vet|eran +s
Vet|er|ans Day (11
November in
USA)
vet'er|in|ar'ian +s
vet'er|in|ary
  vet'er|in|ar'ies
veti|ver +s
veto
  ve'toes
  ve'toed
  veto|ing
veto'er +s
vex
  vexes
  vexed
  vex|ing
vex|ation +s
vex|atious
vex|atious|ly
vex|atious|ness
vex|ed|ly
vexer +s
vex'il|lo|logic'al
vex'il|lolo'gist +s
vex'il|lol'ogy
vex'il|lum
  vex|illa
vex|ing|ly
Vi (name)
via
Via Appia (Latin
name for the
Appian Way)
via|bil'ity
vi'able
vi'ably
via|duct +s

vial +s (glass
vessel. ⚠ vile,
viol)
vial|ful +s
via media
viand +s
vi'ati|cum
  vi'at|ica
vibes
vi'bracu|lar
  adjective
vi'bracu|lum
  vi'brac|ula
  noun
vi|brancy
vi|brant
vi|brant|ly
vi|bra|phone +s
vi|bra|phon|ist +s
vi|brate
  vi|brates
  vi|brated
  vi|brat|ing
vi|bra|tile
vi|bra|tion +s
vi|bra|tion|al
vi|bra|tive
vi|brato +s
vi|bra|tor +s
vi|bra|tory
vib|rio
  vib|rios *or*
  vibri|ones
vi|bris|sae
vi|bur|num +s
Vic
vicar +s
vic|ar|age +s
vicar-general
  vicars-general
vic|arial
vic|ari|ate +s
vic|ari|ous
vic|ari|ous|ly
vic|ari|ous|ness
vic|ar|ship +s
vice +s (depravity;
character defect;
vice-president
etc.; in the place
of; in succession
to. ⚠ vise)
vice *Br.*
  vices
  viced
  vi'cing
(clamp; *Am.* vise)
vice ad|miral +s
vice-captain +s
vice-captain'cy
  vice-captain'cies
vice-chair +s

vice-chairman
  vice-chairmen
vice-
  chairman¦ship
  +s
vice-chairwoman
  vice-chairwomen
vice-chamber¦lain
  +s
vice-chancel¦lor
  +s
vice-consul+s
vice-direct¦or+s
vice|ger¦ency
  vice|ger¦en¦cies
vice|ger¦ent+s
vice-govern¦or+s
vice|less
vice-like
Vice-Marshal+s
  (in 'Air Vice-
  Marshal')
vi¦cen¦nial
Vi|cente, Gil
  (Portuguese
  dramatist)
Vi|cenza (town,
  Italy)
vice-premier+s
vice-presidency
  vice-
  presiden¦cies
vice-president+s
vice-presiden¦tial
vice-princi¦pal+s
vice-provost+s
vice|regal
vice|regal¦ly
vice|reine+s
vice|roy+s
vice|royal
vice|roy¦alty
vice|roy|ship+s
vi¦cesi¦mal
vice versa
Vichy (town,
  France; water)
vichys|soise+s
vicin|age+s
vi|cinal
vicin|ity
  vicin|ities
vi|cious
vi|cious¦ly
vi|cious|ness
vi¦cis¦si¦tude+s
vi¦cis¦si¦tu¦din|ous
Vicki also Vickie,
  Vicky
Vickie also Vicki,
  Vicky

Vicks|burg (city,
  USA)
Vicky also Vicki,
  Vickie
Vico,
  Giam|bat¦tista
  (Italian
  philosopher)
vic¦tim+s
vic¦tim|hood
vic¦tim|isa¦tion Br.
  (use
  victimization)
vic¦tim|ise Br. (use
  victimize)
vic¦tim|ises
vic¦tim|ised
vic¦tim|is¦ing
vic¦tim|iser Br. +s
  (use victimizer)
vic¦tim|iza¦tion
vic¦tim|ize
  vic¦tim|izes
  vic¦tim|ized
  vic¦tim|iz¦ing
vic¦tim|izer+s
vic¦tim|less
Vic¦tor (name)
vic¦tor+s (winner)
Vic¦tor
  Em¦man|uel
  (Italian kings)
Vic|toria+s
  (British queen;
  name; carriage)
Vic|toria (state,
  Australia; port,
  Canada; capital of
  Hong Kong or the
  Seychelles;
  railway station,
  London)
Vic|toria, Tomás
  Luis de (Spanish
  composer)
Vic|toria and
  Al¦bert Mu¦seum
  (in London)
Vic|toria Falls (in
  central Africa)
Vic|toria Is|land
  (in Canadian
  Arctic)
Vic|tor|ian+s
Vic|tori|ana
Vic|toria Nile
  (river, E. Africa)
Vic|tor|ian|ism+s
Vic|toria Peak
  (mountain, Hong
  Kong)
vic|tori|ous

vic|tori|ous¦ly
vic|tori|ous|ness
vic¦tor lu|dorum
  male
vic|tory
  vic|tor|ies
vic|trix
  vic|tri¦ces
vic|trix lu|dorum
  female
vict¦ual
  vict¦uals
  vict¦ualled Br.
  vict¦ualed Am.
  vict¦ual|ling Br.
  vict¦ual|ing Am.
vict¦ual¦ler Am. +s
vict¦ual|ler Br. +s
vict¦ual|less
vi¦cuña+s
Vic-Wells Bal¦let
vid+s (= video)
Vidal, Gore
  (American writer)
vide
vi¦de|licet
video +s *noun*
video
  vid¦eoes
  vid¦eoed
  video|ing
  verb
video|con¦fer¦ence
  +s
video|con¦fer|
      en¦cing
video|disc+s
video|fit+s
video|phile+s
video|phone+s
video re|cord¦er
  +s
video re|cord¦ing
  +s
video|tape
  video|tapes
  video|taped
  video|tap¦ing
video|tape
  re|cord¦er+s
video|tape
  re¦cord|ing+s
video|tex
  video|texes
video|text+s
vidi|mus
  vidi|muses
vie
  vies
  vied
  vying
vi|elle+s

Vi¦enna (capital of
  Austria)
Vi¦enne (city,
  France)
Vi¦en|nese
  plural Vi¦en|nese
Vien|tiane (capital
  of Laos)
Viet|cong
  plural Viet|cong
Viet|minh
  plural Viet|minh
Viet|nam
Viet¦nam|ese
  plural
  Viet¦nam|ese
vieux jeu
view+s +ed +ing
view|able
view|data
view¦er+s
view¦er|ship
view|find¦er+s
view|graph+s
view|ing+s
view|less
view|point+s
view|port+s
view|screen+s
Vigée-Lebrun,
  Élisa|beth
  (French painter)
vi¦gesi|mal
vi¦gesi|mal¦ly
vigil+s
vigi|lance
vigi|lant
vigi|lante+s
vigi|lant|ism
vigi|lant¦ly
vi|gneron+s
vi|gnette
  vi|gnettes
  vi|gnet|ted
  vi|gnet|ting
vi|gnet|ter+s
vi|gnet|tist+s
Vi|gnola,
  Gia|como
  Bar|ozzi da
  (Italian architect)
Vigny, Al¦fred,
  Comte de
  (French writer)
Vigo (port, Spain)
Vigo, Jean (French
  film director)
vigor Am. (Br.
  vigour)
vig|or|ish
vig|or|less Am. (Br.
  vigourless)

vig|oro
vig|or|ous
vig|or|ous|ly
vig|or|ous|ness
vig|our *Br.* (*Am.*
  vigor)
vig|our|less *Br.*
  (*Am.* vigorless)
vi|hara +s
Vi|jaya|wada (city,
  India)
Vi|king +s
  (Scandinavian
  people; American
  space probes;
  shipping area,
  North Sea)
Vila (capital of
  Vanuatu)
vil|ayet +s
vile
  viler
  vil|est
  (loathsome.
  ⚠ vial, viol)
vile|ly
vile|ness
vili|fi|ca|tion
vili|fier +s
vil|ify
  vili|fies
  vili|fied
  vili|fy|ing
vill +s
Villa, Pan|cho
  (Mexican
  revolutionary)
villa +s
vil|lage +s
vil|la|ger +s
vil|la|gey
vil|la|gisa|tion *Br.*
  (use villagization)
vil|la|giza|tion
Vil|la|her|mosa
  (city, Mexico)
vil|lain +s (wicked
  person. ⚠ villein)
vil|lain|ess
  vil|lain|esses
vil|lain|ous
vil|lain|ous|ly
vil|lain|ous|ness
vil|lainy
  vil|lain|ies
Villa-Lobos,
  Hei|tor (Brazilian
  composer)
vil|lan|elle +s
vil|leggia|tura
  vil|leggia|ture

vil|lein +s (serf.
  ⚠ villain)
vil|lein|age
vil|li|form
Vil|lon, Fran|çois
  (French poet)
vil|lose
vil|los|ity
vil|lous *adjective*
vil|lus
  villi
  noun
Vil|nius (capital of
  Lithuania)
vim
vim|in|eous
Vimy Ridge (battle
  site, France)
vina +s
vin|aceous
vin|ai|grette +s
vinca +s
Vince
Vin|cent
Vin|cent de Paul
  (French saint)
Vin|cen|tian +s
Vinci, Leo|nardo
  da (Italian painter
  and designer)
vin|ci|bil|ity
vin|cible
vin|cu|lum
  vin|cula
vin|da|loo +s
vin|dic|able
vin|di|cate
  vin|di|cates
  vin|di|cated
  vin|di|cat|ing
vin|di|ca|tion +s
vin|di|ca|tive
vin|di|ca|tor +s
vin|di|ca|tory
vin|dic|tive
vin|dic|tive|ly
vin|dic|tive|ness
Vine, Bar|bara
  (pseudonym of
  Ruth Rendell)
vine +s
vine-dresser +s
vin|egar +s
vin|egared
vin|egar|ish
vin|egary
vin|ery
  vin|eries
vine|stock +s
vine|yard +s
vingt-et-un
vinho verde +s

vini|cul|tural
vini|cul|ture
vini|cul|tur|ist +s
vini|fi|ca|tion
vin|ify
  vini|fies
  vini|fied
  vini|fy|ing
vin|ing
Vin|land (region, N.
  America)
Vin|ney +s (in
  'Blue Vinney')
Vin|nitsa (Russian
  name for
  Vinnytsya)
Vin|nyt|sya (city,
  Ukraine)
vino +s
vin or|din|aire
  vins or|din|aires
vin|os|ity
vin|ous
vin rosé
  vins rosés
Vin|son Mas|sif (in
  Antarctica)
vint +s +ed +ing
vin|tage +s
vin|ta|ger +s
vint|ner +s
viny
  vini|er
  vini|est
vinyl +s
viol +s (musical
  instrument. ⚠ vial,
  vile)
Viola (name)
viola +s (flower;
  musical
  instrument)
viol|able
viol|aceous
viola da brac|cio
  +s
viola da gamba +s
viola d'amore
  violas d'amore
viola play|er +s
vio|late
  vio|lates
  vio|lated
  vio|lat|ing
vio|la|tion +s
vio|la|tor +s
vio|lence +s
vio|lent
vio|lent|ly
Vio|let (name)
vio|let +s
vio|lin +s

vio|lin|ist +s
viol|ist +s
vio|lon|cel|list +s
vio|lon|cello +s
vio|lone +s
viper +s
vi|peri|form
vi|per|ine
vi|per|ish
viper-like
vi|per|ous
viper's bu|gloss
viper's grass
vir|ago +s
viral
vir|al|ly
Vir|chow, Ru|dolf
  Karl (German
  physician)
vir|elay +s
vire|ment +s
vireo +s
vires (in '*ultra vires*')
vir|es|cence
vir|es|cent
virga (evaporating
  rain)
vir|gate +s
vir|ger +s (use
  verger)
Vir|gil (Roman
  poet)
Vir|gil *also* **Vergil**
Vir|gil|ian
Vir|gin, the
  (constellation;
  sign of zodiac)
vir|gin +s
vir|gin|al
vir|gin|al|ist +s
vir|gin|al|ly
vir|gin|hood
Vir|ginia (state,
  USA; tobacco;
  name)
Vir|gin|ian +s
Vir|gin Is|lands,
  Brit|ish and US
  (in Caribbean)
vir|gin|ity
Virgo
  (constellation;
  sign of zodiac)
Vir|go|an +s
vir|gule +s
viri|des|cence
viri|des|cent
vir|id|ian
vir|id|ity
vir|ile
vir|il|ism
vir|il|ity

vir|ino+s
vir|ion+s
vir|oid+s
viro|logic|al
viro|logic|al|ly
vir|olo|gist+s
vir|ology
virtu (knowledge of
  fine arts; in 'object
  of virtu'. △ virtue)
vir|tual
vir|tu|al|ity
vir|tu|al|ly
vir|tue+s (moral
  excellence etc.
  △ virtu)
vir|tue|less
vir|tu|osic
vir|tu|os|ity
vir|tu|oso
  vir|tu|osi or
  vir|tu|osos
vir|tu|oso|ship
vir|tu|ous
vir|tu|ous|ly
vir|tu|ous|ness
viru|lence
viru|lent
viru|lent|ly
virus
  vir|uses
visa
  visas
  visaed or visa'd
  visa|ing
vis|age+s
vis|aged
Visa|kha|pat|nam
  (port, India)
vis-à-vis
  plural vis-à-vis
Visby (port,
  Sweden)
vis|cacha+s
vis|cera
vis|ceral
vis|cer|al|ly
vis|cid
vis|cid|ity
visc|om|eter+s
visco|met|ric
visco|met|ric|al|ly
visc|om|etry
Vis|conti,
  Lu|chino (Italian
  film director)
vis|cose
vis|cos|im|eter+s
vis|cos|ity
  vis|cos|ities
vis|count+s

vis|count|cy
vis|count|cies
vis|count|ess
vis|count|esses
vis|count|ship
vis|county
vis|count|ies
vis|cous (sticky.
  △ viscus)
vis|cous|ly
vis|cous|ness
vis|cus
  vis|cera
  (internal organ.
  △ viscous)
vise Am.
  vises
  vised
  vis|ing
  (Br. vice; clamp.
  △ vice)
Vishnu
Vishnu|ism
Vishnu|ite+s
visi|bil|ity
vis|ible
vis|ible|ness
vis|ibly
Visi|goth+s
Visi|goth|ic
vi|sion+s
vi|sion|al
vi|sion|ari|ness
vi|sion|ary
  vi|sion|ar|ies
vi|sion|ist+s
vi|sion|less
vi|sion mixer+s
vi|sion mix|ing
visit+s +ed +ing
vis|it|able
vis|it|ant+s
vis|it|ation+s
vis|it|ator|ial
vis|it|ing+s
vis|it|ing card+s
vis|it|or+s
vis|it|or|ial
vis|it|ors' book+s
visor+s
vi|sored
vi|sor|less
vista+s
vis|taed
Vis|tula (river,
  Poland)
visu|al+s
visu|al|is|able Br.
  (use visualizable)
visu|al|isa|tion Br.
  +s (use
  visualization)

visu|al|ise Br. (use
  visualize)
visu|al|ises
visu|al|ised
visu|al|is|ing
visu|al|ity
visu|al|iz|able
visu|al|iza|tion+s
visu|al|ize
visu|al|izes
visu|al|ized
visu|al|iz|ing
visu|al|ly
Vita
vital+s
vi|tal|isa|tion Br.
  (use vitalization)
vi|tal|ise Br. (use
  vitalize)
vi|tal|ises
vi|tal|ised
vi|tal|is|ing
vi|tal|ism
vi|tal|ist+s
vi|tal|is|tic
vi|tal|ity
vi|tal|iza|tion
vi|tal|ize
vi|tal|izes
vi|tal|ized
vi|tal|iz|ing
vi|tal|ly
vita|min+s
vita|min|ise Br.
  (use vitaminize)
vita|min|ises
vita|min|ised
vita|min|is|ing
vita|min|ize
vita|min|izes
vita|min|ized
vita|min|iz|ing
Vi|tebsk (Russian
  name for
  Vitsebsk)
vi|tel|lary
vi|tel|li
vi|tel|lin (protein)
vi|tel|line (of a
  vitellus)
Vi|tel|lius, Aulus
  (Roman emperor)
vi|tel|lus
  vi|telli
viti|ate
  viti|ates
  viti|ated
  viti|at|ing
viti|ation
viti|ator+s
viti|cul|tural
viti|cul|tur|al|ly

viti|cul|ture
viti|cul|tur|ist+s
Viti Levu (island,
  Fiji)
viti|ligo
Vi|toria (town,
  Spain)
Vi|tória (port,
  Brazil)
Vi|tosha (ski resort,
  Bulgaria)
vit|re|ous
vit|re|ous|ness
vit|res|cence
vit|res|cent
vit|ri|fac|tion
vit|ri|fi|able
vit|ri|fi|ca|tion
vit|ri|form
vit|rify
  vit|ri|fies
  vit|ri|fied
  vit|ri|fy|ing
vit|riol
vit|ri|ol|ic
vitro (in 'in vitro')
Vit|ru|vian
Vit|ru|vius (Roman
  architect)
Vit|sebsk (city,
  Belarus)
vitta
  vit|tae
vit|tate
vi|tu|per|ate
  vi|tu|per|ates
  vi|tu|per|ated
  vi|tu|per|at|ing
vi|tu|per|ation+s
vi|tu|pera|tive
vi|tu|per|ator+s
Vitus (early saint;
  in 'St Vitus's
  dance')
Viv
viva
  vivas
  viv|aed or viva'd
  viva|ing
  (oral exam.
  △ vivers)
viva+s (shout; long
  live .... △ vivers)
viv|ace
viv|acious
viv|acious|ly
viv|acious|ness
viv|acity
Viv|aldi, An|tonio
  (Italian composer)
viv|ar|ium
  viv|aria

vivat
viva voce +s *noun*
viva-voce
  viva-voces
  viva-voced
  viva-voceing
  verb
vivax
Viv|eka|nanda,
  Swami (Indian
  spiritual leader
  and reformer)
vi|ver|rid +s
vi|ver|rine
vi|vers (food.
  ⚠ viva, *viva*)
Viv|ian *also*
  Vyv|yan
  (man's name.
  ⚠ Vivien,
  Vivienne)
vivid
viv|id|ly
viv|id|ness
Viv|ien *also*
  Vivi|enne
  (woman's name.
  ⚠ Vivian,
  Vyvyan)
Vivi|enne *also*
  Viv|ien
  (woman's name.
  ⚠ Vivian,
  Vyvyan)
vivi|fi|ca|tion
viv|ify
  vivi|fies
  vivi|fied
  vivi|fy|ing
vivip|ar|ity
viv|ip|ar|ous
viv|ip|ar|ous|ly
viv|ip|ar|ous|ness
vivi|sect +s +ed
  +ing
vivi|sec|tion
vivi|sec|tion|al
vivi|sec|tion|ist +s
vivi|sect|or +s
vivo (in *'in vivo'*)
vixen +s
vix|en|ish
vix|en|ly
Vi|yella (fabric)
  Propr.
viz.
viz|ard +s
viz|cacha +s (use
  viscacha)
viz|ier +s
viz|ier|ate +s
viz|ier|ial

viz|ier|ship +s
vizor +s (use visor)
Vlach +s
Vladi|kav|kaz
  (city, Russia)
Vlad|imir (city,
  Russia)
Vlad|imir ('the
  Great', Russian
  saint)
Vladi|vos|tok (city,
  Russia)
Vlam|inck,
  Maur|ice de
  (French painter)
vlei +s
Vlis|singen (port,
  the Netherlands)
Vlorë (port,
  Albania)
Vltava (river,
  Czech Republic)
V-neck +s
voc|able
vo|cabu|lary
vo|cabu|lar|ies
vocal +s
vocal cords
vo|cal|ese (singing
  to instrumental
  music.
  ⚠ vocalise)
vo|cal|ic
vo|cal|isa|tion *Br.*
  +s (use
  vocalization)
vo|cal|ise +s (vocal
  music written with
  no words.
  ⚠ vocalese)
vo|cal|ise *Br.* (form
  sound; use
  vocalize)
  vo|cal|ises
  vo|cal|ised
  vo|cal|is|ing
vo|cal|iser *Br.* +s
  (use vocalizer)
vo|cal|ism +s
vo|cal|ist +s
vo|cal|ity
vo|cal|iza|tion +s
vo|cal|ize
  vo|cal|izes
  vo|cal|ized
  vo|cal|iz|ing
vo|cal|izer +s
vo|cal|ly
vo|ca|tion +s
vo|ca|tion|al
vo|ca|tion|al|ise
  Br. (use

vo|ca|tion|al|ise
  (*cont.*)
  vocationalize)
vo|ca|tion|al|ises
vo|ca|tion|al|ised
vo|ca|tion|al|
        is|ing
vo|ca|tion|al|ism
vo|ca|tion|al|ize
vo|ca|tion|al|izes
vo|ca|tion|al|ized
vo|ca|tion|al|
        iz|ing
vo|ca|tion|al|ly
voca|tive +s
vo|cif|er|ance
vo|cif|er|ant +s
vo|cif|er|ate
  vo|cif|er|ates
  vo|cif|er|ated
  vo|cif|er|at|ing
vo|cif|er|ation
vo|cif|er|ator +s
vo|cif|er|ous
vo|cif|er|ous|ly
vo|cif|er|ous|ness
vo|coder +s
Voda|fone +s
  Propr.
vodka +s
voe +s
vogue
  vogues
  vogued
  vo|guing *or*
  vogue|ing
vogue word +s
vo|guish
voice
  voices
  voiced
  voi|cing
voice box
  voice boxes
voice|ful
voice|less
voice|less|ly
voice|less|ness
voice-over +s
voice|print +s
voicer +s
voi|cing +s
void +s +ed +ing
void|able
void|ance +s
void|ness
voile +s
Voj|vo|dina
  (province, Serbia)
vol|ant
volar
vola|tile +s

vola|tile|ness
vola|til|is|able *Br.*
  (use volatilizable)
vola|til|isa|tion *Br.*
  (use
  volatilization)
vola|til|ise *Br.* (use
  volatilize)
  vola|til|ises
  vola|til|ised
  vola|til|is|ing
vola|til|ity
vola|til|iz|able
vola|til|iza|tion
vola|til|ize
  vola|til|izes
  vola|til|ized
  vola|til|iz|ing
vol-au-vent +s
vol|can|ic +s
vol|can|ic|al|ly
vol|can|icity
vol|can|ism
vol|cano
  vol|ca|noes
vol|cano|logic|al
vol|cano|olo|gist +s
vol|can|ology
vole +s
volet +s
Volga (river, E.
  Europe)
Vol|go|grad (city,
  Russia)
voli|tant
vol|ition
vol|ition|al
vol|ition|al|ly
voli|tive
volk (Afrikaners)
Volk (Germans, in
  Nazi ideology)
Völker|
        wan|der|ung
Völker|
        wan|der|ung|en
völk|isch
vol|ley +s +ed
  +ing
vol|ley|ball
vol|ley|er +s
Vol|ogda (city,
  Russia)
Volos (port,
  Greece)
vol|plane
  vol|planes
  vol|planed
  vol|plan|ing
Vol|scian +s
volt +s (*Electricity.*
  ⚠ vault, volte)

Volta (river, Ghana)
Volta,
  Ales|san|dro
  (Italian physicist)
volt|age+s
Vol|ta|ic (language)
vol|ta|ic *Electricity*
Vol|taire (French
  writer)
volt|ameter+s
  (measures electric
  charge.
  △ voltmeter)
volte+s (*Fencing*;
  movement by
  horse. △ vault,
  volt)
volte-face
  plural volte-face
volt|meter+s
  (measures electric
  potential in volts.
  △ voltameter)
volu|bil|ity
vol|uble
vol|uble|ness
vol|ubly
vol|ume+s
vol|umed
volu|met|ric
volu|met|ric|al|ly
vo|lu|min|os|ity
vo|lu|min|ous
vo|lu|min|ous|ly
vo|lu|min|ous|ness
vol|un|tar|ily
vol|un|tari|ness
vol|un|tar|ism
vol|un|tar|ist
vol|un|tary
  vol|un|tar|ies
voluntary-aided
voluntary-
  controlled
vol|un|tary|ism
vol|un|tary|ist+s
vol|un|teer+s +ed
  +ing
vol|un|teer|ism
vo|lup|tu|ary
  vo|lup|tu|ar|ies
vo|lup|tu|ous
vo|lup|tu|ous|ly
vo|lup|tu|ous|ness
vol|ute+s
vol|uted
volu|tion+s
vol|vox
  vol|voxes
Volzh|sky (city,
  Russia)
vomer+s

vomit+s +ed +ing
vom|it|er+s
vom|it|orium
vom|it|ory
vom|it|or|ies
von Braun,
  Wern|her
  (German rocket
  designer)
V-1+s (German
  flying bomb)
Von|ne|gut, Kurt
  (American writer)
von Neu|mann,
  John (Hungarian-
  born American
  mathematician)
von Stern|berg,
  Josef (Austrian-
  born American
  film director)
voo|doo+s +ed
  +ing
voo|doo|ism
voo|doo|ist+s
Vopo+s
vor|acious
vor|acious|ly
vor|acious|ness
vor|acity
Vor|arl|berg (state,
  Austria)
Vor|on|ezh (city,
  Russia)
Voro|shi|lov|grad
  (former name of
  Lugansk)
Vor|ster, John
  (South African
  president.
  △ Forster)
vor|tex
  vor|texes *or*
  vor|ti|ces
vor|ti|cal
vor|ti|cal|ly
vor|ti|cella+s
vor|ti|cism
vor|ti|cist+s
vor|ti|city
vor|ti|cose
vor|ticu|lar
Vosges (mountains,
  France)
Vos|tok (Soviet
  spacecraft)
vot|able
vo|tar|ess
  vo|tar|esses
vo|tar|ist+s

vo|tary
  vo|tar|ies
vote
votes
voted
vot|ing
vote|less
voter+s
vot|ing ma|chine
  +s
vot|ing paper+s
vo|tive+s
vouch
vouches
vouched
vouch|ing
vouch|er+s
vouch|safe
vouch|safes
vouch|safed
vouch|saf|ing
vous|soir+s
Vou|vray+s
  (village, France;
  wine)
vow+s +ed +ing
vowel+s
vow|eled *Am.* (*Br.*
  vowelled)
vow|el|ise *Br.* (use
  vowelize)
vow|el|ises
vow|el|ised
vow|el|is|ing
vow|el|ize
vow|el|izes
vow|el|ized
vow|el|iz|ing
vow|elled *Br.* (*Am.*
  voweled)
vow|el|less
vowel|ly
vowel-point+s
vox an|gel|ica
vox hu|mana
vox pop+s
vox pop|uli
voy|age
  voy|ages
  voy|aged
  voy|aging
voy|age|able
Voy|ager
  (American space
  probe)
voy|ager+s
  (traveller)
voy|ageur+s
  (Canadian
  boatman)
voy|eur+s
voy|eur|ism

voy|eur|is|tic
voy|eur|is|tic|al|ly
vraic
vroom+s +ed
  +ing
V-sign+s
V/STOL (= vertical
  and short take-off
  and landing)
VTOL (= vertical
  take-off and
  landing)
V-2+s (German
  missile)
vug+s
vuggy
vugu|lar
Vuil|lard,
  Éd|ouard (French
  painter)
Vul|can *Roman*
  Mythology
Vul|can|ian+s
vul|can|ic
vul|can|is|able *Br.*
  (use
  vulcanizable)
vul|can|isa|tion *Br.*
  (use
  vulcanization)
vul|can|ise *Br.* (use
  vulcanize)
  vul|can|ises
  vul|can|ised
  vul|can|is|ing
vul|can|iser *Br.* +s
  (use vulcanizer)
vul|can|ism
Vul|can|ist+s
vul|can|ite
vul|can|iz|able
vul|can|iza|tion
vul|can|ize
  vul|can|izes
  vul|can|ized
  vul|can|iz|ing
vul|can|izer+s
Vul|cano (island off
  Italy)
vul|cano|logic|al
vul|can|olo|gist+s
vul|can|ology
vul|gar
vul|gar|ian+s
vul|gar|isa|tion *Br.*
  (use
  vulgarization)
vul|gar|ise *Br.* (use
  vulgarize)
  vul|gar|ises
  vul|gar|ised
  vul|gar|is|ing

vul|gar|ism+s
vul|gar|ity
  vul|gar|ities
vul|gar|iza|tion
vul|gar|ize
  vul|gar|izes
  vul|gar|ized
  vul|gar|iz|ing
vul|gar|ly
Vul|gate+s (bible)
vul|gate+s (other
  text)
vul|ner|abil|ity
  vul|ner|abil|ities
vul|ner|able
vul|ner|able|ness
vul|ner|ably
vul|ner|ary
  vul|ner|ar|ies
vul|pine
vul|ture+s
vul|tur|ine
vul|tur|ish
vul|tur|ous
vulva+s *noun*
vul|val
vul|var *adjective*
vulv|itis
Vyatka (town,
  Russia)
vying
Vyv|yan *also*
  Viv|ian
  (man's name.
  △ Vivian,
  Vivienne)

Ww

....

Waac+s (member
  of Women's Army
  Auxiliary Corps)
Waaf+s (member
  of Women's
  Auxiliary Air
  Force)
Waal (river, the
  Netherlands)
WAC (= Women's
  Army Corps)
wack+s (crazy
  person; familiar
  term of address.
  △ wacke, whack)
wacke+s (rock.
  △ wack, whack)
wack|ily
wacki|ness
wacko
  wackos *or*
  wack|oes
  (crazy. △ whacko)
wacky
  wack|ier
  wacki|est
wad
  wads
  wad|ded
  wad|ding
wad|able
wad|ding+s
wad|dle
  wad|dles
  wad|dled
  wad|dling
wad|dler+s
waddy
  wad|dies
  (club. △ wadi)
Wade, George
  (English field
  marshal)
Wade, Vir|ginia
  (English tennis
  player)
wade
  wades
  waded
  wad|ing
Wade–Giles
  (system for
  transliterating
  Chinese)
wader+s
wadg|ula+s

wadi+s
  (watercourse.
  △ waddy)
Wadi Halfa (town,
  Sudan)
wady
  wad|ies
  (use wadi
  watercourse.
  △ waddy)
WAF (= Women in
  the Air Force)
wafer+s +ed +ing
wafer-thin
wafery
waf|fle
  waf|fles
  waf|fled
  waf|fling
waffle-iron+s
waf|fler+s
waf|fly
waft+s +ed +ing
wag
  wags
  wagged
  wag|ging
wage
  wages
  waged
  wa|ging
wage bill+s
wage claim+s
wage cut+s
wage earn|er+s
wage-earning
wager+s +ed +ing
Wagga Wagga
  (town, Australia)
wag|gery
  wag|ger|ies
wag|gish
wag|gish|ly
wag|gish|ness
wag|gle
  wag|gles
  wag|gled
  wag|gling
wag|gly
wag|gon+s (use
  wagon)
wag|gon|er+s
wag|gon|ette+s
wag|gon|ful+s
  (use wagonful)
wag|gon|load+s
  (use wagonload)
Wag|ner, Rich|ard
  (German
  composer)
Wag|ner|ian+s
wagon+s

wag|on|er+s
wag|on|ette+s
wag|on|ful+s
wagon-lit
  wagons-lits
wag|on|load+s
wagon-roof+s
wagon train+s
wag|tail+s
Wa|habi+s
Wah|habi+s (use
  Wahabi)
wa|hine+s
wahoo+s (tree;
  interjection)
wah-wah+s
waif+s
waif|ish
waif-like
Wai|kato (river,
  New Zealand)
Wai|kiki (resort,
  Honolulu)
wail+s +ed +ing
  (cry. △ whale,
  wale)
wail|er+s (person
  who wails.
  △ whaler)
wail|ful
wail|ing+s (crying.
  △ whaling)
wail|ing|ly
Wain, John (British
  writer. △ Wayne)
Wain, the
  (constellation)
wain+s (wagon.
  △ wane)
wains|cot
  wains|cots
  wains|cot|ed *or*
  wains|cot|ted
  wains|cot|ing *or*
  wains|cot|ting
wain|wright+s
Waira|rapa
  (region, New
  Zealand)
waist+s (part of
  body etc.
  △ waste)
waist|band+s
waist-cloth+s
waist|coat+s
waist-deep
waist|ed (having a
  waist; in 'high-
  waisted' etc.
  △ wasted)
waist-high
waist|less

waist|line +s
wait +s +ed +ing
(delay action; etc.
△weight)
wait-a-bit (plant)
Wai|tangi (Day and
Treaty, New
Zealand)
wait|er +s
wait|ing list +s
wait|ing room +s
wait|per|son +s
wait|ress
  wait|resses
wait|ress|ing
waive
  waives
  waived
  waiv|ing
(forgo. △ wave)
waiver +s (act of
waiving. △ waver)
Wajda, An|drzej
(Polish film
director)
wake
  wakes
  wak|ing
  woken
Wake|field (town,
England)
wake|ful
wake|ful|ly
wake|ful|ness
waken +s +ed
  +ing
waker +s
wake-robin +s
wakey-wakey
Wa|khan Sali|ent
(strip of land,
Afghanistan)
Waks|man,
  Sel|man
  Abra|ham
(Russian-born
American
microbiologist)
Wal|ach +s (use
  Vlach)
Wal|achia (use
  Wallachia)
Wal|ach|ian (use
  Wallachian)
Wal|den|ses
Wal|den|sian +s
Wald|heim, Kurt
(Austrian
president)
Waldo
wale
  wales

wale (cont.)
  waled
  wal|ing
(ridge in fabric;
timber on ship etc.
△wail, whale)
wale-knot +s
Wales (part of
United Kingdom)
Wał|esa, Lech
(Polish president)
Waleses, the
(Prince and
Princess)
Wal|ian +s (in
'North Walian'
and 'South
Walian')
walk +s +ed +ing
walk|able
walk|about +s
walk|athon +s
Walk|er, Alice
(American writer)
Walk|er, John
(New Zealand
athlete)
walk|er +s
walk|ies
walkie-talkie +s
walk-in +s adjective
and noun
walk|ing boot +s
walk|ing frame +s
walking-on part
  +s
walk|ing shoe +s
walk|ing stick +s
walk|ing tour +s
Walk|man
  Walk|mans or
  Walk|men
  Propr.
walk-on +s
adjective and noun
walk|out +s
walk|over +s
walk-up +s
adjective and noun
walk|way +s
wall +s +ed +ing
(structure.
△ waul whor)
wal|laby
  wal|la|bies
Wal|lace (name)
Wal|lace, Al|fred
  Rus|sel (English
naturalist)
Wal|lace, Edgar
(English writer)

Wal|lace, Wil|liam
(Scottish national
hero)
Wal|lace
  Col|lec|tion
(museum,
London)
Wal|lace's line
Wal|lachia (former
principality,
Romania)
Wal|lach|ian +s
wal|lah +s
wal|la|roo +s
Wal|la|sey (town,
England)
wall-barley
wall|board +s
wall|chart +s
wall clock +s
wall|cover|ing +s
Wal|len|berg,
  Raoul (Swedish
diplomat)
Wal|ler, Fats
(American jazz
musician)
wal|let +s
wall-eye +s
wall-eyed
wall fern +s
wall|flower +s
wall-fruit
wall hang|ing +s
wall-hung
Wal|lis, Barnes
(English inventor)
Wal|lis and
  Fu|tuna Is|lands
(in Pacific Ocean)
wall-knot +s
wall-less
wall-mounted
Wal|loon +s
wal|lop +s +ed
  +ing
wal|lop|er +s
wal|low +s +ed
  +ing
wal|low|er +s
wall paint|ing +s
wall|paper +s +ed
  +ing
wall|plan|ner +s
wall plaque +s
wall-plate +s
wall plug +s
wall rocket
wall space
Wall Street (in
New York)
wall tie +s

wall-to-ceiling
wall-to-wall
Wally (name)
wally
  wal|lies
(foolish or inept
person)
wal|nut +s
Wal|pole, Hor|ace
(English writer)
Wal|pole, Hugh
(British novelist)
Wal|pole, Rob|ert
(British prime
minister)
Wal|pole, Rob|ert
  Penn (American
poet)
Wal|pur|gis night
  +s
wal|rus
  wal|ruses
Wal|sall (town,
England)
Wal|sing|ham
(pilgrimage town,
England)
Wal|sing|ham,
  Fran|cis (English
politician)
Wal|ter
Wal|ton, Er|nest
(Irish physicist)
Wal|ton, Izaak
(English writer)
Wal|ton, Wil|liam
(English
composer)
waltz
  waltzes
  waltzed
  waltz|ing
waltz|er +s
Waltz|ing Ma|tilda
(Australian song)
Wal|vis Bay (port,
Namibia)
wam|pum
WAN (= wide area
network)
wan
wan|ner
wan|nest
(pale. △ won)
wand +s
Wanda (name)
wan|der +s +ed
  +ing (go
aimlessly)
wan|der|er +s
wan|der|ing +s
wan|der|lust

wan|deroo +s
wan|der plug +s
wan|doo +s
wane
  wanes
  waned
  wan|ing
  (decline; decrease;
  defect in plank.
  ⚠ wain)
waney
wang +s +ed +ing
  (use whang)
Wanga|nui (port,
  New Zealand)
wan|gle
  wan|gles
  wan|gled
  wan|gling
wan|gler +s
wank +s +ed +ing
  (*coarse slang*)
Wan|kel, Felix
  (German
  engineer)
wank|er +s (*coarse
  slang*)
Wankie (former
  name of Hwange)
wanky (*coarse slang*
  worthless)
wanly
wanna (= want to)
wan|nabe +s
wan|ness
want +s +ed +ing
want ad +s
want|er +s
wan|ton +s +ed
  +ing (motiveless.
  ⚠ wonton)
wan|ton|ly
wan|ton|ness
wap|en|take +s
wap|iti +s
Wap|ping (district,
  London)
war
  wars
  warred
  war|ring
  (fighting. ⚠ wore)
wara|tah +s
warb +s
War|beck, Per|kin
  (Flemish
  pretender to the
  English throne)
war|ble
  war|bles
  war|bled
  warb|ling

war|ble fly
  war|ble flies
warb|ler +s
War|burg, Aby
  (German art
  historian)
War|burg, Otto
  Hein|rich
  (German
  biochemist)
warby
war cloud +s
war cry
  war cries
Ward, Mrs
  Hum|phry
  (English writer)
ward +s +ed +ing
war|den +s
war|den|ship +s
war|der +s
ward-heeler +s
ward|ress
  ward|resses
ward|robe +s
ward|room +s
ward|ship +s
ware +s (articles
  for sale; aware;
  beware. ⚠ wear,
  where)
ware|house
  ware|houses
  ware|housed
  ware|hous|ing
ware|house|man
  ware|house|men
war|fare
war|farin
war game +s
war gam|ing
war|head +s
War|hol, Andy
  (American artist)
war|horse +s
wari|ly
wari|ness
Warka (Arabic
  name for Uruk)
war|like
war|lock +s
war|lord +s
warm +s +ed +ing
  +er +est
warm-blooded
warm-
  blooded|ness
warmed-over
  attributive
warmed-up
  attributive
warm|er +s

warm-hearted
warm-hearted|ly
warm-
  hearted|ness
warming-pan +s
warm|ish
warm|ly
warm|ness
war|mon|ger +s
war|mon|ger|ing
warmth +s
warm-up +s *noun
  and attributive*
warn +s +ed +ing
  (inform;
  admonish.
  ⚠ worn)
warn|er +s
War|ner Broth|ers
  (American film
  company)
warn|ing +s
warn|ing|ly
warp +s +ed +ing
  (bend; pervert;
  haul; rope; threads
  in loom; sediment.
  ⚠ whaup)
warp|age
war|paint +s
war|path +s
warp|er +s
war|plane +s
war|ra|gal +s (use
  warrigal)
war|rant +s +ed
  +ing
war|rant|able
war|rant|able|ness
war|rant|ably
war|rant|ee +s
  (person.
  ⚠ warranty)
war|rant|er +s
  (person giving an
  assurance.
  ⚠ warrantor)
war|rant of|ficer
  +s
war|rant|or +s
  (*Law* person
  giving a warranty)
war|ranty
  war|ran|ties
  (undertaking.
  ⚠ warrantee)
War|ren (name)
War|ren, Earl
  (American judge)
War|ren, Rob|ert
  Penn (American
  writer)

war|ren +s (rabbits'
  burrows)
war|ren|er +s
war|ri|gal +s
War|ring|ton
  (town, England)
war|rior +s
war|rior king +s
war|rior queen +s
War|saw (capital of
  Poland)
war|ship +s
wart +s
wart|hog +s
war|time
war-torn
warty
  wart|ier
  wart|iest
war-weariness
war-weary
War|wick (town,
  England)
War|wick, Earl of
  ('the Kingmaker',
  English
  statesman)
War|wick|shire
  (county, England)
war-worn
war wound +s
war-wounded
wary
  wari|er
  wari|est
was
Wash, the (inlet,
  England)
wash
  washes
  washed
  wash|ing
wash|abil|ity
wash|able +s
wash-and-wear
wash|bag +s
wash|basin +s
wash|board +s
wash|day +s
washed-out
  attributive
wash|er +s
washer-drier +s
  (use washer-
  dryer)
washer-dryer +s
wash|er|man
  wash|er|men
washer-up
  washers-up
wash|er|woman
  wash|er|women

wash|ery
  wash|er|ies
wash|et|eria +s
wash-hand basin
  +s
wash-hand stand
  +s
wash-house +s
wash|ily
washi|ness
wash|ing
  ma|chine +s
wash|ing pow|der
  +s
wash|ing soda +s
Wash|ing|ton
  (state and capital
  of the USA; town,
  England)
Wash|ing|ton,
  Booker T.
  (American
  educationist)
Wash|ing|ton,
  George
  (American
  president)
washing-up *noun*
  and attributive
wash|land +s
wash-leather +s
Washoe
  (chimpanzee)
wash|out +s
  Geology
wash-out +s
  (failure; gap in
  road etc. caused
  by flood)
wash|room +s
wash|stand +s
wash|tub +s
wash-up *noun and*
  attributive
wash/wipe
washy
  wash|ier
  washi|est
wasn't (= was not)
Wasp +s (*usually*
  offensive; White
  Anglo-Saxon
  Protestant)
wasp +s (insect)
waspie +s (corset.
  ⚠ waspy)
Wasp|ish (*usually*
  offensive; of a
  Wasp)
wasp|ish (spiteful)
wasp|ish|ly
wasp|ish|ness

wasp|like
wasp-waist +s
wasp-waisted
Waspy (*usually*
  offensive; of a
  Wasp. ⚠ waspie)
waspy (wasplike.
  ⚠ waspie)
was|sail +s +ed
  +ing
wassail-bowl +s
wassail-cup +s
was|sail|er +s
Was|ser|mann
  (test)
wast
wast|able
wast|age
waste
  wastes
  wasted
  wast|ing
  (squander.
  ⚠ waist)
waste|bas|ket +s
waste bin +s
waste|ful
waste|ful|ly
waste|ful|ness
waste ground
waste|land +s
waste|less
waste paper
waste-paper
  bas|ket +s
waste pipe +s
waster +s
wast|rel +s
watch
  watches
  watched
  watch|ing
watch|able
watch|band +s
watch-case +s
watch-chain +s
watch|dog +s
watch|er +s
watch face +s
watch|fire +s
watch|ful
watch|ful|ly
watch|ful|ness
watch-glass
  watch-glasses
watch|keep|er +s
watch|maker +s
watch|mak|ing
watch|man
  watch|men
watch-night +s
watch spring +s

watch strap +s
watch|tower +s
watch|word +s
water +s +ed +ing
water-bag +s
water-based
Water-bearer, the
  (constellation;
  sign of zodiac)
water|bed +s
water|bird +s
water bis|cuit +s
water-bloom
water-boatman
  water-boatmen
water-borne
water bot|tle +s
water|brash
water-buck +s
water buf|falo
  plural **water**
  buf|falo *or* **water**
  buf|fa|loes
water-butt +s
water-cannon +s
Water-carrier, the
  (constellation;
  sign of zodiac)
water chute +s
water-clock +s
water closet +s
water|color *Am.* +s
water|col|or|ist
  Am. +s
water|col|our *Br.*
  +s
water|col|our|ist
  Br. +s
water-cooled
water-cooler +s
water-course +s
water|cress
water-diviner +s
water|er +s
water|fall +s
Water|ford (town
  and county,
  Republic of
  Ireland; glass)
water|fowl
water|front +s
Water|gate (US
  political scandal)
water|gate +s
  (floodgate; gate to
  river etc.)
water glass
  water glasses
  (tumbler)
water-glass
  (substance)
water ham|mer +s

water heat|er +s
water hen +s
water|hole +s
water ice +s
wateri|ness
water|ing +s
water|ing can +s
water|ing hole +s
water|ing place +s
water jug +s
water|less
water level +s
water lily
  water lil|ies
water|line +s
water|logged
Water|loo (battle,
  Belgium; railway
  station, London)
water|man
  water|men
water|mark +s
  +ed +ing
water-meadow +s
water|melon +s
water|mill +s
water nymph +s
water-pepper +s
water pipe +s
water pis|tol +s
water polo
water-power
water|proof +s
  +ed +ing
water|proof|er +s
water|proof|ness
water rat +s
water rate +s
water-repellency
water-repellent
water-resist|ance
water-resist|ant
Waters, Muddy
  (American blues
  musician)
water scor|pion +s
water|shed +s
water|side +s
water-ski +s +ed
  +ing
water-skier +s
water slide +s
water snake +s
water soft|en|er
  +s
water-soluble
water-splash
  water-splashes
water sport +s
water|spout +s
water-sprite +s

water supply
  water sup|plies
water-table +s
water taxi +s
water|thrush
  water|thrushes
water|tight
water tower +s
water vole +s
water|way +s
water|weed +s
water|wheel +s
water wings
water|works
watery
Wat|ford (town, England)
Watha|wur|ung
wa|tjin +s
Wat|ling Street (Roman road, England)
Wat|son, Dr (companion of Sherlock Holmes)
Wat|son, James D. (American biologist)
Wat|son, John B. (American psychologist)
wat|sonia +s (plant)
Watson-Watt, Rob|ert (Scottish physicist)
Watt, James (Scottish engineer)
watt +s (unit. △ what, wot)
watt|age +s
Wat|teau, Jean An|toine (French painter)
watt-hour +s
wat|tle
  wat|tles
  wat|tled
  wat|tling
watt|meter +s
Watts, George Fred|erick (English artist)
Watts, Isaac (English hymn-writer)
Wa|tusi
  plural Wa|tusi *or* Wa|tu|sis (person)
Wa|tusi (dance)

Wa|tutsi
  plural Wa|tutsi *or* Wa|tut|sis
Waugh, Eve|lyn (English novelist)
waul +s +ed +ing (cry like cat. △ wall, whorl)
wave
  waves
  waved
  wav|ing (gesture; on water; curve. △ waive)
wave|band +s
wave|form +s
wave|front +s
wave|guide +s
wave|length +s
wave|less
wave|let +s
wave|like
wave mo|tion +s
waver +s +ed +ing (falter. △ waiver)
waver|er +s
waver|ing|ly
wav|ery
wave|top +s
wavi|ly
wavi|ness
wavy
  wavi|er
  wavi|est
wa-wa +s (use wah-wah)
wawl +s +ed +ing (cry like cat. use waul. △ wall, whorl)
wax
  waxes
  waxed
  wax|ing
wax|berry
  wax|berries
wax|bill +s
wax|cloth +s
waxen
waxer +s
wax|ily
waxi|ness
wax|ing +s
wax-light +s
wax-like
wax myr|tle +s
wax-painting +s
wax-pod +s
wax-tree +s
wax|wing +s
wax|work +s

waxy
  wax|ier
  waxi|est
way +s (road etc.; method. △ weigh, wey, whey)
way|back (outback)
way|bill +s
way|bread +s
way|farer +s
way|far|ing
way|far|ing tree +s
way in (entrance. △ weigh-in)
Way|land the Smith *English Legend*
way|lay
  way|lays
  way|laid
  way|lay|ing
way|lay|er +s
way-leave +s
way|mark +s +ed +ing
way|mark|er +s
Wayne (name)
Wayne, John (American actor. △ Wain)
way out (exit)
way-out *adjective*
way|point +s
way|side +s
way sta|tion +s
way|ward
way|ward|ly
way|ward|ness
way-worn
wayz|goose +s
we (plural of I. △ wee, whee)
weak +er +est (feeble. △ week)
weak|en +s +ed +ing
weak|en|er +s
weak|fish
  plural weak|fish *or* weak|fishes
weak|ish
weak-kneed
weak|li|ness
weak|ling +s
weak|ly
weak|lier
weak|li|est (feebly. △ weekly)
weak-minded
weak-minded|ness

weak|ness
weak|nesses
weal +s +ed +ing (mark on skin; prosperity; in 'the common weal'. △ we'll, wheel)
Weald, the (region, SE England)
weald-clay +s
Weald|en
wealth
wealth|ily
wealthi|ness
wealthy
  wealth|ier
  wealthi|est
wean +s +ed +ing (accustom to food. △ ween)
wean|er +s (animal. △ wiener.
wean|ling +s
weapon +s
weap|oned
weapon|less
weapon|ry
  weap|on|ries
Wear (river, England; in 'Tyne and Wear')
wear
  wears
  wore
  wear|ing
  worn (have on (clothes etc.). △ ware, where)
wear|abil|ity
wear|able
wear|er +s
weari|less
wear|ily
weari|ness
wear|ing|ly
weari|some
weari|some|ly
weari|some|ness
Wear|side (region, England)
weary
  wear|ies
  wear|ied
  weary|ing
  weari|er
  weari|est
weary|ing|ly
weasel +s +ed +ing
weasel-faced

weas|el|ly

wea|ther +s +ed +ing (atmospheric conditions; expose to weather; survive. △ wether, whether)

weather-beaten

wea|ther|board +s +ed +ing

weather-bound

weather-chart +s

wea|ther|cock +s

wea|ther|girl +s

weather-glass

weather-glasses

wea|ther|li|ness

wea|ther|ly

wea|ther|man

wea|ther|men

wea|ther|most

wea|ther|proof +s +ed +ing

wea|ther|strip

wea|ther|strips

wea|ther|stripped

wea|ther|strip|ping

wea|ther|tight

weather-tiles

wea|ther|vane +s

weather-worn

weave

weaves

wove

weav|ing

woven or wove (make fabric or story. △ we've)

weave

weaves

weaved

weav|ing (move; zigzag. △ we've)

weaver +s (person who weaves. △ weever)

weav|ing +s

web

webs

webbed

web|bing

Webb, Bea|trice and Sid|ney (English economists and historians)

Webb, Mary (English novelist)

web|bing +s

webby

Weber, Carl Maria von (German composer)

Weber, Max (German sociologist)

weber +s (unit)

Web|ern, Anton (Austrian composer)

web-footed

Web|ster, John (English dramatist)

Web|ster, Noah (American lexicographer)

web-wheel +s

web|work +s

web|worm +s

wed

weds

wed|ded or wed

wed|ding

we'd (= we had; we should; we would. △ weed)

Wed|dell Sea (off Antarctica)

wed|ding +s

Wede|kind, Frank (German dramatist)

wedge

wedges

wedged

wedg|ing

wedge|like

wedge-shaped

wedge|wise

wedgie +s

Wedg|wood, Jo|siah (English potter)

Wedg|wood (pottery; colour). Propr.

wed|lock

Wed|nes|day +s

wee

wees

weed

wee|ing (urinate. △ we, whee)

wee

weer

weest (tiny. △ we, whee)

weed +s +ed +ing (plant. △ we'd)

weed|er +s

weed-grown

weedi|ness

weed|kill|er +s

weed|less

weedy

weed|ier

weedi|est

Wee Free +s

week +s (seven days. △ weak)

week|day +s

week|end +s +ed +ing

week|end|er +s

week-long

week|ly

week|lies (once a week; newspaper etc. △ weakly)

ween +s +ed +ing (think. △ wean)

weenie +s (sausage; use wienie)

weeny

ween|ier

weeni|est (tiny. △ wienie)

weeny-bopper +s

weep

weeps

wept

weep|ing

weep|er +s

weepie +s (film etc. △ weepy)

weep|ily

weepi|ness

weep|ing|ly

weepy

weep|ier

weepi|est (tearful. △ weepie)

weever +s (fish. △ weaver)

wee|vil +s

wee|vily

wee-wee

wee-wees

wee-weed

wee-weeing

weft +s

Weg|en|er, Al|fred Lothar (German meteorologist)

Wehr|macht

Wei (Chinese dynasties)

Wei|fang (city, China)

wei|gela +s

weigh +s +ed +ing (measure the weight of. △ way, wey, whey)

weigh|able

weigh|bridge +s

weigh|er +s

weigh-in +s (*noun*; weighing of boxer. △ way in)

weigh|ing ma|chine +s

weight +s +ed +ing (heaviness etc. △ wait)

weight gain

weight|ily

weighti|ness

weight|ing +s

weight|less

weight|less|ly

weight|less|ness

weight|lift|er +s

weight|lift|ing

weight loss

weight train|ing

Weight Watch|er +s (member of Weight Watchers)

weight-watcher +s (dieter)

Weight Watch|ers (organization). Propr.

weight-watching

weighty

weight|ier

weighti|est

Weih|sien (former name of Weifang)

Weil, Sim|one (French philosopher)

Weill, Kurt (German composer)

Weil's dis|ease

Wei|mar (town, Germany; Republic)

Wei|mar|aner +s

weir +s (dam. △ we're)

weird +er +est

weirdie +s

weird|ly

weird|ness

weirdo +s

Weis|mann,
Au|gust
Fried|rich
(German biologist)
Weis|mann|ism
Weiss|mul|ler,
Johnny
(American
swimmer and
actor)
Weiz|mann,
Chaim(Israeli
president)
weka+s
We|land
(= Wayland the
Smith)
Welch(in 'Royal
Welch Fusiliers'.
⚠ Welsh)
welch(default; use
welsh)
welches
welched
welch|ing
wel|come
wel|comes
wel|comed
wel|com|ing
wel|come|ly
wel|come|ness
wel|comer+s
wel|com|ing|ly
weld+s +ed +ing
weld|abil|ity
weld|able
weld|er+s
wel|fare
wel|far|ism
wel|far|ist +s
wel|kin
Wel|kom (town,
South Africa)
well
bet|ter
best
(satisfactorily etc.)
well+s +ed +ing
(shaft for water;
etc.)
well-(Unless given
below, phrases
beginning with
well, such as well
aimed and well
balanced, are
written as two
words when used
predicatively, i.e.
when they follow
a verb, as in That
shot was well

well-(cont.)
aimed, but with a
hyphen when used
attributively, i.e.
when they come
before a noun, as
in That was a
well-aimed shot.)
we'll(= we shall;
we will. ⚠ weal,
wheel, will)
well ac|quaint|ed
well ad|vised
Wel|land (Ship)
Canal(in Canada)
well-being
well-conditioned
well deck+s
well-dressed
well-dressing+s
Welles, Orson
(American actor
and director)
Wel|les|ley,
Ar|thur(Duke of
Wellington)
well-found
well-head+s
well-heeled
well|lie(use welly)
wel|lies
wel|lied
welly|ing
Wel|ling|ton
(capital of New
Zealand)
Wel|ling|ton,
Duke of(British
soldier and
prime minister)
wel|ling|ton +s
(boot)
well-knit
well-laid
well|ness
well-nigh
well pleased
Wells(town,
England)
Wells, H. G.
(English novelist)
Wells, Fargo &
Co.(American
transport
company)
well-spoken
well|spring +s
well-structured
well thought of
well-thought-of
attributive
well thought out

well-thought-out
attributive
well-to-do
well-traveledAm.
well-travelledBr.
well-trodden
well-wisher+s
well woman
welly
wel|lies
wel|lied
welly|ing
wels
plural wels
(fish)
Wels|bach, Carl
Auer von
(Austrian chemist)
Welsh(of Wales.
⚠ Welch)
welsh
welshes
welshed
welsh|ing
(default)
welsh|er+s
Welsh|man
Welsh|men
Welsh|ness
Welsh|pool(town,
Wales)
Welsh|woman
Welsh|women
welt+s +ed +ing
Welt|an|schau|ung
Welt|an|schau|
ung|en
wel|ter+s +ed
+ing
wel|ter|weight+s
Welt|schmerz
Welty, Eu|dora
(American writer)
Wemba-wemba
Wem|bley(district
and stadium,
London)
wen+s (runic
letter. ⚠ when)
Wen|ces|las ('Good
King Wenceslas',
Czech saint)
Wen|ces|laus(king
of Bohemia and
Germany)
wench
wenches
wenched
wench|ing
wench|er+s
Wen-Chou
(= Wenzhou)

Wend+s (Slavic
people)
wend+s +ed +ing
(go)
Wenda
Wend|ic
Wend|ish
Wendy
Wendy house+s
Wens|ley|dale+s
(region, England;
cheese; sheep)
went
wentle|trap+s
Wen|zhou(city,
China)
wept
were(in 'we were'
etc. ⚠ whirr)
we're(= we are)
weren't(= were
not)
were|wolf
were|wolves
Wer|ner,
Abra|ham
Gott|lob(German
geologist)
Wer|ner, Al|fred
(French-born
Swiss chemist)
wert(in 'thou wert'.
⚠ wort)
Weser(river,
Germany)
Wes|ker, Ar|nold
(English
playwright)
Wes|ley(name)
Wes|ley, John
(English founder
of Methodism)
Wes|ley|an+s
Wes|ley|an|ism
Wes|sex(region,
SW England)
West, Ben|ja|min
(American
painter)
West, Mae
(American
actress)
West, Re|becca
(British writer)
West, the(part of
country etc.;
European
civilization; non-
Communist states)
west(point;
direction)
west|about

west|bound
West Brom|wich
　(town, England)
west|er|ing
west|er|ly
　west|er|lies
West|ern (of the
　West)
west|ern +s (of or
　in the west;
　cowboy film etc.)
west|ern|er +s
west|ern|isa|tion
　Br. (use
　westernization)
west|ern|ise *Br.*
　(use westernize)
west|ern|ises
west|ern|ised
west|ern|is|ing
west|ern|iser *Br.*
　+s (use
　westernizer)
west|ern|iza|tion
west|ern|ize
west|ern|izes
west|ern|ized
west|ern|iz|ing
west|ern|izer +s
west|ern|most
West In|dian +s
west|ing +s
West|ing|house,
　George
　(American
　engineer)
West Irian
　(province,
　Indonesia)
West|mann
　Is|lands (off
　Iceland)
West|meath
　(county, Republic
　of Ireland)
West|min|ster
　(borough;
　London)
West|mor|land
　(former county,
　England)
west-north-west
Weston-super-
　Mare (resort,
　England)
West|pha|lia
　(former province,
　Germany)
West|pha|lian +s
west-south-west
west|ward
west|wards

wet
wets
wet|ted
wet|ting
wet|ter
wet|test
　(moist; make
　moist. △ whet)
weta +s (insect)
wet-and-dry
　attributive
wet|back +s
wether +s (sheep.
　△ weather,
　whether)
wet|land +s
wet-look *attributive*
wetly
wet|ness
wet-nurse
　wet-nurses
　wet-nursed
　wet-nursing
wet|suit +s
wet|table
wet|ting +s
wet|tish
wet-weather
　attributive
we've (= we have.
　△ weave)
Wex|ford (town
　and county,
　Republic of
　Ireland)
wey +s (unit.
　△ way, weigh,
　whey)
Wey|den, Ro|gier
　van de (Flemish
　painter)
Wey|mouth (town,
　England)
whack +s +ed
　+ing (strike.
　△ wack, wacke)
whack|er +s
whack|ing +s
whacko
　(*interjection.*
　△ wacko)
whacky
　whack|ier
　whacki|est
　(use wacky)
whale
　whales
　whaled
　whal|ing
　(sea mammal.
　△ wail, wale)
whale|back +s

whale|boat +s
whale|bone
whale-headed
　stork +s
whale oil
whaler +s (ship;
　person who hunts
　whales; shark;
　tramp. △ wailer)
whale-watching
whaling-master
　+s
wham
　whams
　whammed
　wham|ming
whammy
　wham|mies
whang +s +ed
　+ing
Whanga|rei (port,
　New Zealand)
whangee +s
whap (use whop)
　whaps
　whapped
　whap|ping
whare +s (Maori
　house)
wharf
　wharves *or*
　wharfs
wharf|age
wharfie +s
wharf|inger +s
Whar|ton, Edith
　(American writer)
wharves
what (which; which
　thing. △ watt,
　wot)
what-d'you-call-it
what|e'er
　(= whatever)
what|ever
what|not +s
what's-her-name
what's-his-name
whats|it +s
what's-its-name
what|so
what|so|e'er
　(= whatsoever)
what|so|ever
whaup +s (curlew.
　△ warp)
wheal +s +ed +ing
　(use weal
　△ we'll, wheel)
wheat +s
wheat belt +s
wheat|ear +s

wheat|en
wheat flour
wheat|germ
wheat|grass
wheat|meal
wheat|sheaf
　wheat|sheaves
Wheat|stone,
　Charles (English
　inventor; bridge)
whee (*interjection.*
　△ we, wee)
whee|dle
　whee|dles
　whee|dled
　wheed|ling
wheed|ler +s
wheed|ling|ly
wheel +s +ed +ing
　(on vehicle etc.
　△ weal, we'll)
wheel arch
　wheel arches
wheel-back
wheel|bar|row +s
wheel|base +s
wheel|chair +s
wheel clamp +s
　noun
wheel-clamp +s
　+ed +ing *verb*
wheel|er +s
wheeler-dealer +s
wheeler-dealing
wheel|house +s
wheelie +s
wheelie bin +s
wheel|ing +s
wheel|less
wheel lock +s
wheel|man
　wheel|men
wheel|slip
wheels|man
　wheels|men
wheel|spin
wheel|wright +s
wheely bin +s (use
　wheelie bin)
wheeze
　wheezes
　wheezed
　wheez|ing
wheezer +s
wheez|ily
wheezi|ness
wheez|ing|ly
wheezy
　wheez|ier
　wheezi|est
whelk +s

whelm +s +ed +ing
whelp +s +ed +ing
when (at what time.
  △ wen)
whence
whence|so|ever
when|e'er
  (= whenever)
when|ever
when|so'e'er
  (= whensoever)
when|so|ever
where (what place
  etc. △ ware,
  wear)
where|abouts
where|after
where|as
where|at
where|by
wher|e'er
  (= wherever)
where|fore +s
where|from
where|in
where|of
where|on
where|so|e'er
  (= wheresoever)
where|so|ever
where|to
where|upon
wher|ever
where|with
where|withal
wherry
  wher|ries
wherry|man
  wherry|men
whet
  whets
  whet|ted
  whet|ting
  (sharpen;
  stimulate. △ wet)
whether
  (*conjunction*.
  △ weather,
  wether)
whet|stone +s
whet|ter +s
whew
whey (from milk.
  △ way, weigh,
  wey)
whey-faced
which (*adjective and
  pronoun*. △ witch,
  wych)
which|ever
which|so|ever

whicker +s +ed
  +ing (noise of
  horse. △ wicker)
whi'|dah +s (bird;
  use whydah.
  △ wider)
whiff +s +ed +ing
whif'|fle
  whif'|fles
  whif'|fled
  whif'|fling
whif'|fler +s
whiffle|tree +s
whiffy
Whig +s (*Politics*.
  △ wig)
Whig|gery
Whig|gish
Whig|gism
while
  whiles
  whiled
  whil'|ing
  (period; during;
  pass time. △ wile)
whi'|lom
whilst
whim +s
whim|brel +s
whim|per +s +ed
  +ing
whim|per'|er +s
whim|per|ing +s
whim|per|ing|ly
whim|si'|cal
whim|si'|cal|ity
  whim|si'|cal|ities
whim|si'|cal'|ly
whim|si'|cal|ness
whimsy
  whim|sies
whim-wham +s
whin +s (gorse;
  rock or stone.
  △ win, wyn)
whin|chat +s
whine
  whines
  whined
  whin|ing
  (sound; complain.
  △ wine)
whiner +s
whinge
  whinges
  whinged
  whinge|ing *or*
  whin|ging
whinge|ing|ly
whin|ger +s
whin|gey
whin|ging|ly (use
  whingeingly)

whingy (use
  whingey)
whin|ing|ly
whinny
  whin|nies
  whin|nied
  whinny|ing
whin|sill +s
whin|stone +s
whiny
  whi'|nier
  whini|est
  (whining.
  △ winey)
whip
  whips
  whipped
  whip|ping
whip|bird +s
whip|cord +s
whip-cracking
whip-crane +s
whip-graft +s
whip hand
whip|lash
  whip|lashes
  whip|lashed
  whip|lash|ing
whip|less
whip-like
whip|per +s
whipper-in
  whippers-in
whip'|per|snap'|per
  +s
whip|pet +s
whip|pi|ness
whip|ping +s
whip|ping boy +s
whip|ping cream
  +s
whip|ping post +s
whipping-top +s
whipple|tree +s
whip|poor|will +s
whippy
  whip|pier
  whip'|pi|est
whip-round +s
whip|saw +s
whip snake +s
whip|ster +s
whip stitch
  whip stitches
whip|stock +s
whir (sound; use
  whirr. △ were)
whirs
whirred
whir|ring

whirl +s +ed +ing
  (swing round.
  △ whorl)
whirl|er +s
whirli|gig +s
whirl|ing|ly
whirl|pool +s
whirl|wind +s
whirly|bird +s
whirr +s +ed +ing
  (sound. △ were)
whisht
whisk +s +ed +ing
whis|ker +s
whis|kered
whis|kery
whis|key +s (Irish
  and American)
whisky
  whis|kies
  (Scotch)
whis|per +s +ed
  +ing
whis|per'|er +s
whis|per|ing +s
whis|per|ing
  gal|lery
  whis|per|ing
  gal|ler|ies
whist (game; hush.
  △ wist)
whis|tle
  whis|tles
  whis|tled
  whist|ling
whistle-blower +s
whistle-blowing
Whist|ler, James
  Mc|Neill
  (American artist)
whist|ler +s
Whist|ler|ian
whistle-stop
Whit (Whitsuntide.
  △ wit)
whit (least possible
  amount. △ wit)
Whitby (town,
  England)
White, Gil|bert
  (English
  naturalist)
White, Pat|rick
  (Australian
  novelist)
white
  whites
  whited
  whit|ing
  whiter
  whit|est

white (*cont.*)
(colour; person.
△ wight)
white|bait
  plural white|bait
white|beam +s
white|board +s
white|cap +s
white-collar
  attributive
white|cur|rant +s
white-eye +s
white|face
white|fish
  plural white|fish
  or white|fishes
  (lake fish of trout
  family)
white fish (plaice,
  cod, etc.)
white|fly
  white|flies
White|hall (street,
  London)
White|head,
  Al|fred North
  (English
  philosopher)
white|head +s
  (pimple)
White|horse (city,
  Canada)
white-hot
White House (in
  Washington D.C.)
white-knuckle
  attributive
white|ly
whiten +s +ed
  +ing
whit|en|er +s
white|ness
whiten|ing
white-out +s *noun*
White Sea (inlet,
  NW Russia)
white|smith +s
white|thorn +s
white|throat +s
white|wash
  white|washes
  white|washed
  white|wash|ing
white|wash|er +s
white|wood +s
whitey +s (*offensive*
  person. △ whity)
whither (to where.
  △ wither)
whith|er|so|ever
whith|er|ward

whit|ing
  plural whit|ing
  (fish)
whit|ing +s
  (substance)
whit|ish
Whit|lam, Gough
  (Australian prime
  minister)
whit|leather
whit|low +s
whitlow-grass
Whit|man, Walt
  (American poet)
Whit|ney, Eli
  (American
  inventor)
Whit|ney, Mount
  (in USA)
Whit|sun
Whit Sun|day +s
Whit|sun|tide
Whit|tier, John
  Green|leaf
  (American poet)
Whit|ting|ton,
  Dick (Lord Mayor
  of London)
Whit|tle, Frank
  (English
  aeronautical
  engineer)
whit|tle
  whit|tles
  whit|tled
  whit|tling
Whit|worth (screw
  thread)
whity (whitish.
  △ whitey)
whiz (use whizz)
  whizzes
  whizzed
  whizz|ing
whiz-bang +s
whiz-kid +s (use
  whizz-kid)
whizz
  whizzes
  whizzed
  whizz|ing
whizz-bang +s
  (use whiz-bang)
whiz|zer +s
whizz-kid +s
whizzo
Who, the (English
  rock group)
who
whoa (stop. △ woe)
who'd (= who had;
  who would)

who-does-what
  attributive
who|dunit *Am.* +s
who|dun|nit *Br.* +s
who|e'er
  (= whoever)
who|ever
whole (entire;
  entirety. △ hole)
whole|food +s
whole|grain +s
whole|heart|ed
whole|heart|ed|ly
whole|heart|ed|
           ness
whole-life
  attributive
whole|ly (fully; use
  wholly. △ holey,
  Holi, holy)
whole|meal
whole|ness
whole|sale
  whole|sales
  whole|saled
  whole|sal|ing
whole|saler +s
whole|some
whole|some|ly
whole|some|ness
whole-time
whole-tone scale
whole|wheat
whol|ism
whol|ly (fully.
  △ holey, Holi,
  holy)
whom
whom|ever
whom|so
whom|so|ever
whoop +s +ed
  +ing (shout.
  △ hoop)
whoo|pee
whoop|er +s
whoop|ing cough
whoops
whoosh
  whooshes
  whooshed
  whoosh|ing
whop
  whops
  whopped
  whop|ping
whop|per +s
whore
  whores
  whored
  whor|ing

whore (*cont.*)
  (prostitute.
  △ haw, hoar)
who're (= who are)
whore|dom
whore|house +s
whore|mas|ter
whore|mon|ger +s
whorer +s
whore|son +s
whor|ish
whor|ish|ly
whor|ish|ness
whorl +s (ring.
  △ wall,
  waul, whirl)
whorled (having
  whorls.
  △ whirled)
whortle|berry
  whortle|berries
who's (= who is)
whose (of or
  belonging to
  whom or which)
whose|so
whose|so|ever
whos|ever
whoso
who|so|ever
who's who
who've (= who
  have)
whump +s +ed
  +ing
why +s
Why|alla (town,
  Australia)
why|dah +s (bird.
  △ wider)
Whym|per,
  Ed|ward (English
  mountaineer)
wibbly-wobbly
Wicca
Wic|can +s
Wich|ita (city,
  USA)
wick +s
wicked +er +est
wick|ed|ly
wick|ed|ness
wicker (basket
  material. △ whicker)
wick|er|work
wicket +s
wicket|keep|er +s
wicket|keep|ing
wicket-taker +s
wicket-taking
wicki|up +s
Wick|low (town
  and county,

Wick|low (*cont.*)
  Republic of
  Ireland)
wid|der|shins (use
  withershins)
wide
  wider
  wid|est
wide-angle +s
  (*noun* lens;
  adjective)
wide|awake +s
  (hat)
wide awake (fully
  awake)
wide boy +s
wide-eyed
wide|ly
wide|ly ac|cept|ed
wide|ly based
wide|ly ex|pect|ed
wide|ly held
wide|ly known
widely-known
  attributive
wide|ly read
widely-read
  attributive
wide|ly
  re|spect|ed
wide|ly scat|tered
wide|ly spaced
wide|ly used
widen +s +ed +ing
widen|er +s
wide|ness
widen|ing +s
wide open
wide-open
  attributive (in
  sense 'fully
  opened')
wider (comparative
  of wide
  △ whydah)
wide-ranging
wide-screen
wide|spread
widg|eon +s
widget +s
widgie +s
wid|ish
Wid|nes (town,
  England)
widow +s +ed
  +ing
widow-bird +s
wid|ow|er +s
widow|hood
widow's cruse +s
widow's mite +s
widow's peak +s

widow's weeds
width +s
width|ways
width|wise
Wie|land,
  Chris|toph
  Mar|tin (German
  writer)
wield +s +ed +ing
wield|er +s
wieldy
Wie|ner, Nor|bert
  (American
  mathematician)
wie|ner +s
  (sausage.
  △ weaner)
Wie|ner schnit|zel
  +s
wie|nie +s (sausage.
  △ weeny)
Wies|baden (city,
  Germany)
Wie|sel, Elie
  (Romanian-born
  American
  authority on the
  Holocaust)
Wie|sen|thal,
  Simon (Austrian
  Jewish
  investigator of
  Nazi war crimes)
wife
  wives
wife|hood
wife|less
wife|like
wife|li|ness
wife|ly
wife-swapping
wif|ish
wig
  wigs
  wigged
  wig|ging
  (hair; rebuke.
  △ Whig)
Wigan (town,
  England)
wi|geon +s (use
  widgeon)
wig|ging +s
wig|gle
  wig|gles
  wig|gled
  wig|gling
wig|gler +s
wig|gly
  wig|glier
  wig|gli|est

Wight (shipping
  area, English
  Channel)
Wight, Isle of (off
  England)
wight +s (*archaic*
  person. △ white)
Wight|man Cup
  (tennis contest)
Wig|town|shire
  (former county,
  Scotland)
wig|wag
  wig|wags
  wig|wagged
  wig|wag|ging
wig|wam +s
Wil|ber|force,
  Wil|liam (English
  social reformer)
Wil|bur
wilco
Wil|cox, Ella
  Wheel|er
  (American writer)
wild +s +er +est
wild card +s *noun*
wild-card
  attributive
wild|cat +s
wild-caught
Wilde, Oscar (Irish
  writer)
wilde|beest
  plural wilde|beest
  or wilde|beests
Wilder, Billy
  (American film
  director)
Wilder, Thorn|ton
  (American writer)
wil|der +s +ed +ing
wil|der|ness
  wil|der|nesses
wild|fire
wild flower +s
wild|fowl
  plural wild|fowl
wild-goose chase
  +s
wild|ing +s
wild|ish
wild|life
wild|ly
wild|ness
wild|wood +s
wile
  wiles
  wiled
  wil|ing
  (trick. △ while)

Wil|fred *also*
  Wil|frid
Wil|frid *also*
  Wil|fred
wil|ful *Br.* (*Am.*
  willful)
wil|ful|ly *Br.* (*Am.*
  willfully)
wil|ful|ness *Br.*
  (*Am.* willfulness)
wilga +s
Wil|helm (German
  emperors)
Wil|hel|mina
Wil|helms|haven
  (port, Germany)
wili|ly
wili|ness
Wilkes Land (in
  Antarctica)
Wil|kie, David
  (Scottish painter)
Wil|kins, Maur|ice
  (New Zealand-
  born British
  biochemist)
Will (name)
will (*auxiliary verb.*
  △ we'll)
will +s +ed +ing
  (wish; impel;
  bequeath. △ we'll)
Willa (name)
Wil|lard, Emma
  (American
  educational
  reformer)
Wil|lem|stad
  (capital of the
  Netherlands
  Antilles)
will|er +s
will|let
  plural wil|let
will|ful *Am.* (*Br.*
  wilful)
will|ful|ly *Am.* (*Br.*
  wilfully)
will|ful|ness *Am.*
  (*Br.* wilfulness)
Wil|liam (English
  and British kings)
Wil|liam of
  Occam (English
  philosopher)
Wil|liam of
  Orange (William
  III of Great Britain
  and Ireland)
Wil|liam Rufus
  (William II of
  England)

Wil|liams, John
(Australian
guitarist)
Wil|liams, J. P. R.
(Welsh Rugby
Union player)
Wil|liams,
Ten|nes|see
(American
dramatist)
Wil|liams,
Wil|liam Car|los
(American writer)
Wil|liams|burg
(city, USA)
wil|lie +s (penis;
use willy)
wil|lies, the
(unease)
will|ing
will|ing|ly
will|ing|ness
will-less
will-o'-the-wisp
+s
wil|low +s
wil|low|herb +s
wil|low tree +s
wil|low warb|ler
+s
wil|low wren +s
wil|lowy
will-power
Wills, Wil|liam
John (English
explorer)
willy
  wil|lies
willy-nilly
willy wag|tail +s
willy-willy
  willy-willies
Wilma
Wil|son, Angus
(English writer)
Wil|son, Charles
Thom|son Rees
(Scottish
physicist)
Wil|son, Ed|mund
(American writer)
Wil|son, Ed|ward
Os|borne
(American social
biologist)
Wil|son, Har|old
(British prime
minister)
Wil|son, Thomas
Wood|row
(American
president)

wilt +s +ed +ing
Wil|ton +s (carpet)
Wilts. (= Wiltshire)
Wilt|shire (county,
England)
wily
  wili|er
  wili|est
Wim|ble|don
(district, London;
tennis
championship)
wimp +s +ed +ing
wimp|ish
wimp|ish|ly
wimp|ish|ness
wim|ple
  wim|ples
  wim|pled
  wimp|ling
Wimpy +s
(hamburger)
Propr.
wimpy
  wimp|ier
  wimpi|est
(feeble)
Wims|hurst
(machine)
win
  wins
  won
  win|ning
(gain through
effort etc. ⚠ whin,
wyn)
wince
  winces
  winced
  win|cing
win|cer +s
win|cey +s
win|cey|ette
winch
  winches
  winched
  winch|ing
winch|er +s
Win|ches|ter (city,
England)
Win|ches|ter +s
(rifle) *Propr.*
Win|ches|ter (disk;
drive)
win|ches|ter +s
(bottle)
win|cing|ly
Winck|el|mann,
Jo|hann (German
archaeologist)

wind +s +ed +ing
(moving air;
breath; scent; etc.)
wind
  winds
  wound
  wind|ing
(coil. ⚠ wynd)
wind|age
Win|daus, Adolf
(German organic
chemist)
wind|bag +s
wind-blown
wind|bound
wind|break +s
wind|break|er +s
wind|burn
wind|cheat|er +s
wind-chill
wind-cone +s
wind-down +s
  noun
wind|er +s
Win|der|mere
(town, England)
Win|der|mere,
Lake (in England)
wind|fall +s
wind|farm +s
wind|flower +s
wind force +s
wind gap +s
wind-gauge +s
Wind|hoek (capital
of Namibia)
wind|hover +s
wind|ily
windi|ness
wind|ing +s
wind|ing en|gine
+s
winding-house +s
winding-sheet +s
wind|jam|mer +s
wind|lass
  wind|lasses
  wind|lassed
  wind|lass|ing
(machine)
wind|less (without
wind)
windle|straw +s
wind ma|chine +s
wind|mill +s +ed
+ing
win|dow +s +ed
+ing
win|dow box
  win|dow boxes
win|dow clean|er
+s

win|dow clean|ing
win|dow dress|ing
win|dow frame +s
win|dow ledge +s
win|dow|less
window-pane +s
win|dow seat +s
window-shop
  window-shops
  window-shopped
  window-
  shopping
window-shopper
+s
win|dow|sill +s
wind|pipe +s
wind-rose +s
wind|row +s
wind-sail +s
Wind|scale (former
name of
Sellafield)
wind|screen +s
wind shear +s
wind|shield +s
wind shift +s
wind-sleeve +s
wind|sock +s
Wind|sor (city,
Canada; town,
England)
Wind|sor +s
(British royal
house)
wind speed +s
wind|storm +s
wind|surf +s +ed
+ing
wind|surf|er +s
wind|swept
wind-tossed
wind tun|nel +s
wind-up +s
(*adjective and noun*
clock; conclusion;
provocation)
wind|ward
Wind|ward
Is|lands (in E.
Caribbean)
windy
  wind|ier
  windi|est
wine
  wines
  wined
  win|ing
(drink. ⚠ whine)
wine bar +s
wine|berry
  wine|berries
wine|bib|ber +s

wine|bib|bing
wine box
  wine boxes
wine|glass
  wine|glasses
wine|glass|ful +s
wine-grower +s
wine-growing
wine|less
wine list +s
wine|maker +s
wine|mak|ing
wine|press
  wine|presses
wine red +s *noun and adjective*
wine-red *attributive*
win|ery
  win|eries
wine shop +s
wine|skin +s
wine taster +s
wine tast|ing +s
winey
  wini|er
  wini|est
  (like wine.
  ⚠ whiny)
wing +s +ed +ing
wing-beat +s
wing-case +s
wing chair +s
wing col|lar +s
wing com|mand|er +s
wing|ding +s
wing|er +s
wing for|ward +s
wing-game +s
wing-half
  wing-halves
wing|less
wing|let +s
wing|like
wing|man
  wing|men
wing nut +s
wing|span +s
wing|spread +s
wing-stroke +s
wing-tip +s
wing-walker +s
wing-walking
Wini|fred
wink +s +ed +ing
wink|er +s
win|kle
  win|kles
  win|kled
  wink|ling
winkle-picker +s
wink|ler +s

win|less
win|nable
win|ner +s
Win|nie
win|ning +s
win|ning|ly
win|ning|ness
win|ning post +s
Win|ni|peg (city, Canada)
Win|ni|peg, Lake (in Canada)
win|now +s +ed +ing
win|now|er +s
wino +s
Win|ona
win|some
win|some|ly
win|some|ness
Win|ston
win|ter +s +ed +ing
win|ter|er +s
win|ter|green +s
Win|ter|hal|ter, Franz Xav|ier (German painter)
win|ter|isa|tion *Br.* (use winterization)
win|ter|ise *Br.* (use winterize)
  win|ter|ises
  win|ter|ised
  win|ter|is|ing
win|ter|iza|tion
win|ter|ize
  win|ter|izes
  win|ter|ized
  win|ter|iz|ing
win|ter|less
win|ter|ly
win|ter sports
Win|ter|thur (town, Switzerland)
winter-tide
win|ter|time
winter-weight *adjective*
win|tery (use wintry)
win|trily
win|tri|ness
win|try
  win|trier
  win|tri|est
winy
  wini|er
  wini|est
  (like wine; use winey. ⚠ whiny)

wipe
  wipes
  wiped
  wip|ing
wipe|able
wipe-clean *adjective*
wipe-out +s *noun*
wiper +s
Wir|ad|huri
wire
  wires
  wired
  wir|ing
wire brush
  wire brushes *noun*
wire-brush
  wire-brushes
  wire-brushed
  wire-brushing *verb*
wire-cutter +s
wire|draw
  wire|draws
  wire|drew
  wire|draw|ing
  wire|drawn
wire-haired
wire|less
  wire|lesses
wire|man
  wire|men
wire|pull|er +s
wire|pull|ing
wirer +s
wire strip|per +s
wire-tap
  wire-taps
  wire-tapped
  wire-tapping
wire-tapper +s
wire-walker +s
wire|worm +s
wir|ily
wiri|ness
Wir|ral, the (peninsula, NW England)
wiry
  wiri|er
  wiri|est
Wis|con|sin (state, USA)
Wis|dom, John (English cricketer)
wis|dom +s
wise
  wises
  wised
  wis|ing

wise *(cont.)*
  wiser
  wis|est
wise|acre +s +ed +ing
wise|crack +s +ed +ing
wise|crack|er +s
wise|ly
wis|ent +s
wish
  wishes
  wished
  wish|ing
wish|bone +s
wish|er +s
wish|ful
wish-fulfil|ling
wish-fulfill|ment *Am.*
wish-fulfil|ment *Br.*
wish|ful|ly
wish|ful|ness
wishing-well +s
wish-list +s
wish-wash
wishy-washy
wisp +s
wisp|ily
wispi|ness
wispy
  wisp|ier
  wispi|est
wist (*archaic* knew. ⚠ whist)
wis|taria +s (use wisteria)
wis|teria +s
wist|ful
wist|ful|ly
wist|ful|ness
wit +s (intelligence; humour; person; in 'to wit'. ⚠ whit, Whit)
witan +s
witch
  witches
  witched
  witch|ing
  (sorceress; charm; lure. ⚠ which)
witch alder +s
witch|craft
witch doc|tor +s
witch elm +s (use wych elm)
witch|ery
witches' broom +s
witches' sab|bath +s

witch|etty
  witch|et|ties
witch hazel+s
witch-hunt+s
witch-hunter+s
witch-hunting
witch|like
wit|ena|gemot+s
with(in the
  company of; etc.
  △ withe)
withal
with|draw
  with|draws
  with|drew
  with|draw|ing
  with|drawn
  with|draw|al+s
  with|draw|er+s
  with|draw|ing
    room+s
withe+s (willow
  shoot. △ with)
wither+s +ed
  +ing (shrivel.
  △ whither)
wither|ing|ly
with|ers(on horse)
wither|shins
  adverb
with|hold
  with|holds
  with|held
  with|hold|ing
with|hold|er+s
with|in
with it adjective and
  adverb
with-it attributive
with|out
with-profits
with|stand
  with|stands
  with|stood
  with|stand|ing
with|stand|er
withy
  with|ies
wit|less
wit|less|ly
wit|less|ness
wit|ling+s
wit|loof+s
wit|ness
  wit|nesses
  wit|nessed
  wit|ness|ing
  wit|ness box
  wit|ness boxes
witness-stand+s
Wit|ten|berg
  (town, Germany)

wit|ter+s +ed
  +ing
wit|ter|ing+s
Witt|gen|stein,
  Lud|wig
  (Austrian-born
  British
  philosopher)
wit|ti|cism+s
wit|tily
wit|ti|ness
wit|ting
wit|ting|ly
witty
  wit|tier
  wit|ti|est
Wit|waters|rand,
  the(region, South
  Africa)
wi|vern+s (use
  wyvern)
wives
wiz noun (use
  whizz)
  wizzes
wiz|ard+s
wiz|ard|ly
wiz|ard|ry
  wiz|ard|ries
wiz|ened
wizzo(use whizzo)
wo(stop; use
  whoa △ woe)
woad
wob|be|gong+s
wob|ble
  wob|bles
  wob|bled
  wob|bling
wobble-board+s
wob|bler+s
wob|bli|ness
wob|bly
  wob|blier
  wob|bli|est
Wode|house, P. G.
  (British-born
  American
  novelist)
Woden
  Scandinavian
  Mythology
wodge+s
woe+s (grief.
  △ whoa)
woe|be|gone
woe|ful
woe|ful|ly
woe|ful|ness
wog+s (offensive)
wog|gle+s

Wöhl|er,
  Fried|rich
  (German chemist)
wok+s
woke
woken
Wo|king(town,
  England)
wold+s
Wolf, Hugo
  (Austrian
  composer)
wolf
  wolves
  noun
wolf+s +ed +ing
  verb
Wolf Cub+s
  (former name for
  a Cub Scout)
wolf cub+s
  (animal)
Wolfe, James
  (British general.
  △ Woolf, Woulfe)
wolf-fish
  plural wolf-fish or
  wolf-fishes
  (fish)
wolf|hound+s
wolf|ish(wolf-like)
wolf|ish|ly
wolf-like
wolf-man
  wolf-men
wolf pack+s
wolf|ram
wolf|ram|ite
wolfs|bane
Wolfs|burg(town,
  Germany)
wolf|skin+s
wolf's-milk(plant)
Wolf|son, Isaac
  (British
  businessman)
wolf spi|der+s
wolf whis|tle+s
  noun
wolf-whistle
  wolf-whistles
  wolf-whistled
  wolf-whistling
  verb
Wol|las|ton,
  Wil|liam Hyde
  (English scientist)
Wol|lon|gong(city,
  Australia)
Woll|stone|craft,
  Mary(English
  writer)

Wolof
  plural Wolof or
  Wol|ofs
Wol|sey, Thomas
  (English
  churchman and
  statesman)
Wol|ver|hamp|ton
  (city, England)
wol|ver|ine+s
wolves
woman
  women
woman|hood
woman|iseBr. (use
  womanize)
  woman|ises
  woman|ised
  woman|is|ing
woman|iserBr. +s
  (use womanizer)
woman|ish
woman|ish|ly
woman|ish|ness
woman|ist+s
woman|ize
  woman|izes
  woman|ized
  woman|iz|ing
woman|izer+s
woman|kind
woman|less
woman|like
woman|li|ness
woman|ly
womb+s
wom|bat+s
womb-like
women(plural of
  woman)
women|folk
women|kind
  (use
  womankind)
Women's
  In|sti|tute+s
womens|wear
won
  plural won
  (North or South
  Korean currency.
  △ wan)
won(past tense
  and past participle
  of win △ one)
Won|der, Stevie
  (American
  musician)
won|der+s +ed
  +ing
won|der|er+s
won|der|ful

won|der|ful|ly
won|der|ful|ness
won|der|ing +s
won|der|ing|ly
won|der|land +s
won|der|ment +s
wonder-struck
wonder-worker +s
wonder-working
won|drous
won|drous|ly
won|drous|ness
wonk|ily
wonki|ness
wonky
  wonk|ier
  wonki|est
wont
  wonts *or* wont
  wont|ed *or* wont
  wont|ing
  (accustom(ed);
  habit)
won't (= will not)
won|ton +s
  (dumpling.
  ⚠ wanton)
woo +s +ed +ing
woo|able
Wood, Henry
  (English
  conductor)
wood +s (timber;
  forest. ⚠ would)
wood|bind +s
wood|bine +s
wood|block +s
wood|carver +s
wood|carv|ing +s
wood|chat +s
wood|chip +s
wood|chuck +s
wood|cock
  plural wood|cock
wood|craft +s
wood|cut +s
wood|cut|ter +s
wood|cut|ting
wood|ed
wood|en
wood en|graver +s
wood en|grav|ing
  +s
wooden-head +s
wooden-headed
wooden-
  headed|ness
wood|en|ly
wood|en|ness
wood fiber *Am.* +s
wood fibre *Br.* +s
wood grain

wood-grain
  attributive
wood|grouse
  plural
  wood|grouse
woodi|ness
wood|land +s
wood|land|er +s
wood|lark +s
wood|less
wood|louse
wood|lice
wood|man
wood|men
wood mouse
wood mice
wood|note +s
wood nymph +s
wood|peck|er +s
wood|pie +s
wood pi|geon +s
wood|pile +s
wood pulp
wood rat +s
wood|ruff +s
wood|rush
wood|rushes
Woods, Lake of
  the (in Canada
  and USA)
wood|screw +s
wood|shed +s
woods|man
woods|men
wood|smoke
wood stain +s
Wood|stock (town,
  USA)
woodsy
wood|turn|er +s
wood|turn|ing
Wood|ward,
  Rob|ert Burns
  (American organic
  chemist)
wood|wasp +s
wood|wind +s
wood|work
wood|work|er +s
wood|work|ing
wood|worm +s
woody
wood|ier
woodi|est
wood|yard +s
wooer +s
woof +s +ed +ing
  (bark; weft)
woof|er +s
woof|ter +s
  (*offensive*)
wool +s

wool|en *Am.* +s
  (*Br.* woollen)
Woolf, Vir|ginia
  (English writer.
  ⚠ Wolfe, Woulfe)
wool-fat
wool-fell +s
wool-gather|ing
wool-grower +s
wool|len *Br.* +s
  (*Am.* woolen)
Wool|ley,
  Leon|ard (English
  archaeologist)
wool-like
wool|li|ness
wool|ly
wool|lies
wool|lier
wool|li|est
woolly-bear +s
  (caterpillar)
wool|man
wool|men
wool-oil
wool|pack +s
Wool|sack (in
  House of Lords)
wool|shed +s
wool-skin +s
wool-sorters'
  dis|ease
wool-stapler +s
Wool|worth,
  Frank Win|field
  (American
  businessman)
Woo|mera (nuclear
  testing site,
  Australia)
woo|mera +s
  (Aboriginal stick
  or thrown club)
woop woop
woosh (use
  whoosh)
wooshes
wooshed
woosh|ing
wooz|ily
woozi|ness
woozy
wooz|ier
woozi|est
wop +s (*offensive*
  Italian. ⚠ whop)
Wor|ces|ter (city,
  England; sauce)
Wor|ces|ter|shire
  (former county,
  England)
word +s +ed +ing

word|age
word-blind
word-blindness
word|book +s
word-class
word-classes
word-deaf
word-deafness
word div|ision +s
word end|ing +s
word|find|er +s
word game +s
word|ily
wordi|ness
word|ing +s
word|less
word|less|ly
word|less|ness
word list +s
word order +s
word-painting +s
word-perfect
word-picture +s
word|play
word-processed
word pro|cess|ing
word pro|ces|sor
  +s
word|search
word|searches
word|smith +s
word-square +s
Words|worth,
  Wil|liam (English
  poet)
Words|worth|ian
  +s
wordy
word|ier
wordi|est
wore (past tense of
  wear. ⚠ war)
work +s +ed +ing
work|abil|ity
work|able
work|able|ness
work|ably
work|aday
work|ahol|ic +s
work-bag +s
work-basket +s
work|bench
work|benches
work|boat +s
work|book +s
work|box
work|boxes
work camp +s
work|day +s
work|er +s
work|er priest +s
work|fare

work|force +s
work group +s
work|horse +s
work|house +s
work-in +s *noun*
work|ing +s
work|ing class
  work|ing classes
working-class
  attributive
work|ing man
  work|ing men
working-out *noun*
work|ing party
  work|ing par|ties
Work|ing|ton
  (port, England)
work|less
work|load +s
work|man
  work|men
work|man|like
work|man|ship
Work|mate +s
  (workbench)
  Propr.
work|mate +s
  (person)
work|out +s
work|people
work|piece +s
work|place +s
work-rate +s
work|room +s
work|sheet +s
work|shop +s
work-shy
work|site +s
work|space +s
work sta|tion +s
work sur|face +s
work table +s
work|top +s
work-to-rule +s
work-up +s *noun*
work|wear
work|woman
  work|women
work-worn
world +s
world-beater +s
world-class
worlde (in 'olde
  worlde')
world-famous
world-line +s
world|li|ness
world|ling +s
world|ly
  world|lier
  world|li|est
worldly-minded

worldly-wise
world order +s
world-shaking
World Trade
  Cen|ter
world-view +s
world-weariness
world-weary
world|wide
World Wide Fund
  for Nature
World Wide Web
worm +s +ed +ing
worm-cast +s
worm-eaten
worm|er +s
worm-fishing
worm-gear +s
worm|hole +s
wormi|ness
worm|like
Worms (town,
  Germany; Diet)
worm|seed +s
worm's-eye view
  +s
worm-wheel +s
worm|wood +s
wormy
  worm|ier
  wormi|est
worn (past
  participle of wear.
  △ warn)
worn out *adjective*
worn-out *attributive*
wor|ried|ly
wor|rier +s
wor|ri|ment
wor|ri|some
wor|ri|some|ly
wor|rit +s +ed
  +ing
worry
  wor|ries
  wor|ried
  worry|ing
worry-guts
  plural worry-guts
worry|ing|ly
worse
worsen +s +ed
  +ing
wor|ship
  wor|ships
  wor|shipped *Br.*
  wor|shiped *Am.*
  wor|ship|ping *Br.*
  wor|ship|ing *Am.*
wor|ship|able
wor|ship|er *Am.* +s
  (*Br.* worshipper)

wor|ship|ful
wor|ship|ful|ly
wor|ship|ful|ness
wor|ship|per *Br.* +s
  (*Am.* worshiper)
worst +s +ed +ing
  (most bad; get the
  better of. △ wurst)
worst|ed +s
wort +s (*Brewing*;
  plant. △ wert)
Worth, Charles
  Fred|erick
  (English couturier)
worth +s
wor|thily
worthi|ness
Wor|thing (town,
  England)
worth|less
worth|less|ly
worth|less|ness
worth|while
worth|while|ness
worthy
  wor|thies
  wor|thier
  wor|thi|est
wot (= know, e.g. in
  'God wot'. △ watt,
  what)
Wotan
  Scandinavian
  Mythology
wotcha (= what are
  you; what do you;
  what have you)
wotch|er (greeting)
would (*auxiliary*
  verb. △ wood)
would-be *attributive*
wouldn't (= would
  not)
wouldst
Woulfe (bottle.
  △ Wolfe, Woolf)
wound +s +ed
  +ing
Wound|ed Knee
  (battle site, USA)
wound|ed|ness
wound|ing +s
wound|ing|ly
wound|less
wound|wort +s
wove
woven
wow +s +ed +ing
wow|ser +s
WRAC (= Women's
  Royal Army
  Corps)

wrack +s +ed +ing
  (seaweed; a
  wreck. △ rack)
WRAF (= Women's
  Royal Air Force)
wraggle-taggle
wraith +s
wraith|like
Wran|gel Is|land
  (in Arctic Ocean)
wran|gle
  wran|gles
  wran|gled
  wran|gling
wran|gler +s
wran|gling +s
wrap
  wraps
  wrapped
  wrap|ping
  (envelop. △ rap,
  rapt)
wrap|around +s
wrap-over +s
  adjective and noun
wrap|page
wrap|per +s
wrap|ping +s
wrap|ping paper
  +s
wrap|round +s
wrasse +s
Wrath, Cape (in
  Scotland)
wrath (anger.
  △ wroth)
wrath|ful
wrath|ful|ly
wrath|ful|ness
wrathy
wreak +s +ed +ing
  (inflict. △ reek)
wreak|er +s
wreath +s
wreathe
  wreathes
  wreathed
  wreath|ing
wreck +s +ed +ing
  (destroy; ruin etc.
  △ rec, reck)
wreck|age
wreck|er +s
wreck-master +s
Wren +s (member
  of Women's Royal
  Naval Service)
Wren,
  Chris|to|pher
  (English architect)
Wren, P. C.
  (English novelist)

wren +s (bird)
wrench
  wrenches
  wrenched
  wrench|ing
wrest +s +ed +ing
  (wrench away.
  △ rest)
wrest-block +s
wres|tle
  wres|tles
  wres|tled
  wrest|ling
wrest|ler +s
wrest|ling +s
wrest-pin +s
wretch
  wretches
  (wretched person.
  △ retch)
wretch|ed
wretch|ed|ly
wretch|ed|ness
Wrex|ham (town,
  Wales)
wrick +s +ed +ing
  (use rick)
wrig|gle
  wrig|gles
  wrig|gled
  wrig|gling
wrig|gler +s
wrig|gly
  wrig|glier
  wrig|gli|est
Wright, Frank
  Lloyd (American
  architect)
Wright, Or|ville
  and Wil|bur
  (American
  aviation pioneers)
wright +s (maker
  or builder. △ right,
  rite, write)
wrily (use wryly)
wring
  wrings
  wrung
  wring|ing
  (squeeze tightly.
  △ ring)
wring|er +s
wrin|kle
  wrin|kles
  wrin|kled
  wrink|ling
wrin|kli|ness
wrin|kly
  wrink|lies
  wrink|lier
  wrink|li|est

wrist +s
wrist|band +s
wrist-drop
wrist|let +s
wrist-pin +s
wrist|watch
  wrist|watches
wrist-work
wristy
writ +s (written
  command; archaic
  past participle of
  write. △ rit.)
writ|able
write
  writes
  wrote
  writ|ten
  writ|ing
  (put words on
  paper. △ right,
  rite, wright)
write-down +s
  noun
write-in +s noun
write-off +s noun
writer +s (person
  who writes.
  △ righter)
writer|ly
writer's block
writer's cramp
write-up +s noun
writhe
  writhes
  writhed
  writh|ing
writh|ing +s
writ|ing +s
writ|ing desk +s
writ|ing pad +s
writ|ing paper +s
writ|ing room +s
writ|ten
WRNS (= Women's
  Royal Naval
  Service)
Wroc|ław (city,
  Poland)
wrong +s +ed +ing
  +er +est
wrong|doer +s
wrong|doing +s
wrong|er +s
wrong-foot +s +ed
  +ing
wrong|ful
wrong|ful|ly
wrong|ful|ness
wrong-headed
wrong-headed|ly

wrong-
  headed|ness
wrong|ly
wrong|ness
wrong'un +s
wrot (wrought
  timber. △ rot)
wrote (past tense of
  write. △ rote)
wroth (angry.
  △ wrath)
wrought (worked.
  △ rort)
wrought iron
  noun
wrought-iron
  attributive
wrung (past tense
  and past participle
  of wring. △ rung)
wry
  wryer
  wry|est or wri|est
  (contorted;
  mocking. △ rai,
  rye)
wry|bill +s
wryly
wry-mouth +s
wry-mouthed
wry|neck +s
wry|ness
Wu (Chinese
  dialect)
Wuhan (port,
  China)
Wu-hsi (= Wuxi)
Wul|fila (=
  Ulfilas)
wun|der|kind +s
Wundt, Wil|helm
  (German
  psychologist)
Wup|per|tal (city,
  Germany)
Wur|litz|er +s Propr.
wurst +s (sausage.
  △ worst)
Würz|burg (city,
  Germany)
wuss
  wusses
wussy
  wus|sies
wu-wei
Wuxi (city, China)
Wy|an|dot
  plural Wy|an|dot
  or Wy|an|dots
  (person)

Wy|an|dotte
  plural
  Wy|an|dotte or
  Wy|an|dottes
  (fowl)
Wyatt, James
  (English architect)
Wyatt, Thomas
  (English poet)
wych elm +s
Wych|er|ley,
  Wil|liam (English
  dramatist)
wych hazel +s
  (use witch hazel)
Wyc|lif, John
  (English religious
  reformer)
Wyc|liffe, John
  (use Wyclif)
Wye (river, England
  and Wales)
Wyke|ham|ist +s
wyn +s (runic
  letter. △ win,
  whin)
wynd +s (narrow
  street. △ wind)
Wynd|ham, John
  (English science
  fiction writer)
Wyo|ming (state,
  USA)
WYSIWYG (= what
  you see is what
  you get)
Wys|tan
wy|vern +s

Xx

Xan|kändi (capital of Nagorno-Karabakh)
xan|thate +s
Xan|the
Xan|thian
Mar|bles
xan|thic
xan|thin
xan|thine
Xan|thippe (wife of Socrates)
xan|thoma
xan|tho|mas or
xan|tho|mata
xan|tho|phyll
Xan|tippe (use Xanthippe)
Xav|ier
Xav|ier, St
Fran|cis (Spanish missionary)
x-axis
x-axes
xebec +s
Xen|akis, Ian|nis (French composer of Greek descent)
xen|og|am|ous
xen|og|amy
xeno|graft +s
xeno|lith +s
xenon
Xen|opha|nes (Greek philosopher)
xeno|phobe +s
xeno|pho|bia
xeno|pho|bic
Xeno|phon (Greek historian)
xer|an|the|mum +s
xeric
xero|derma
xero|graph +s
xero|graph|ic
xero|graph|ic|al|ly
xer|og|raphy
xero|phile +s
xer|oph|il|ous
xero|phyte +s
Xerox
Xer|oxes
noun Propr.
xerox
xer|oxes
xer|oxed

xerox (*cont.*)
xer|ox|ing
verb
Xer|xes (king of Persia)
Xhosa
plural Xhosa *or* Xho|sas
xi +s (Greek letter)
Xia|men (port, China)
Xian (city, China)
Xi|me|nes de Cis|neros (use Jiménez de Cisneros)
Xing|tai (city, China)
Xingú (river, S. America)
Xi|ning (city, China)
Xin|jiang (region, China)
Xiph|ias (old name for Dorado)
xiphi|ster|num
xiphi|sterna *or* xiphi|ster|nums
xiph|oid
Xmas (= Christmas)
xoa|non
xoana
X-rated
X-ray +s +ed +ing
xu
plural xu (Vietnamese currency. ⚠ sou, sue)
Xu|zhou (city, China)
xylem
xy|lene +s
xylo|carp +s
xylo|carp|ous
xylo|graph +s
xyl|og|raphy
Xy|lon|ite *Propr.*
xyl|opha|gous
xylo|phone +s
xylo|phon|ic
xyl|oph|on|ist +s
xys|tus
xysti

Yy

yab|ber +s +ed +ing
yab|bie +s (use yabby)
yabby
yab|bies
yacht +s +ed +ing
yacht club +s
yachtie +s
yacht ra|cing
yachts|man
yachts|men
yack +s +ed +ing (use yak)
yacka (work; use yakka. ⚠ yakker)
yacker (work; use yakka. ⚠ yakker)
yackety-yack +s +ed +ing
yaf|fle +s
Ya|gara
yager +s (use jaeger)
Yagi +s
yah
yahoo +s
Yah|veh (use Yahweh)
Yah|vist +s (use Yahwist)
Yah|weh *Bible*
Yah|wist +s
Yajur-veda
yak
yaks
yakked
yak|king (animal; chatter)
yaki|tori
yakka (work)
yak|ker +s (chatterer)
Yakut
plural Yakut *or* Ya|kuts
Ya|ku|tia (republic, Russia)
Ya|kutsk (city, Russia)
ya|kuza
plural ya|kuza
Yale +s (lock) *Propr.*
Yale (university, USA)
y'all (= you-all. ⚠ yawl, you'll)

Yalta (port, Ukraine)
Yalu (river, E. Asia)
yam +s
Yama *Hindu Mythology*
Yama|moto, Iso|roku (Japanese admiral)
Yama|saki, Min|oru (American architect)
Yamato-e (Japanese painting style)
yam|mer +s +ed +ing
Yam|ous|sou|kro (capital of the Ivory Coast)
Ya|muna (river, India)
Yan|cheng (city, China)
yandy
yan|dies
yan|died
yandy|ing
yang
Yan|gon (Burmese name for Rangoon)
Yang|shao (Chinese civilization)
Yang|tze (river, China)
Yank +s (*may cause offence*; American)
yank +s +ed +ing (tug)
Yan|kee +s (*may cause offence*)
Yan|kee Doo|dle +s
Yan|tai (port, China)
yan|tra +s
Ya|oundé (capital of Cameroon)
yap
yaps
yapped
yap|ping (bark; talk noisily)
yapok +s
yapp +s *Bookbinding*
yap|per +s

yappy
  yap|pier
  yap|pi|est
yar|bor|ough +s
yard +s +ed +ing
yard|age +s
yard|arm +s
yard|bird +s
Yardie +s
yard|man
  yard|men
yard|stick +s
yar|mulka +s (use yarmulke)
yar|mulke +s
yarn +s +ed +ing
Yaro|slavl (port, Russia)
yar|ran +s
yar|row +s
yash|mak +s
Yas|min
yata|ghan +s
yat|ter +s +ed +ing
yaw +s +ed +ing (deviate. △ yore, your, you're)
yawl +s (boat. △ y'all, you'll)
yawn +s +ed +ing
yawn|er +s
yawn|ing|ly
yawp +s +ed +ing
yawp|er +s
yaws (disease. △ yours)
y-axis
  y-axes
Yayoi
yclept
ye
yea +s *archaic*
yeah +s *colloquial*
yean +s +ed +ing
yean|ling +s
year +s
year|book +s
year-end +s
year in, year out
year|ling +s
year-long
year|ly
yearn +s +ed +ing
yearn|er +s
yearn|ing +s
yearn|ing|ly
year-round
yeast +s
yeast|ily
yeasti|ness
yeast|less

yeast|like
yeasty
yeast|ier
yeasti|est
Yeats, W. B. (Irish writer)
Yeats|ian
yegg +s
Ye|kat|er|in|burg (city, Russia)
Ye|kat|er|ino|dar (former name of the city of Krasnodar)
Ye|kat|er|ino|slav (former name of Dnipropetrovsk)
Ye|liza|vet|pol (former Russian name for Gäncä)
yell +s +ed +ing
yel|low +s +ed +ing +er +est
yel|low|back +s
yellow-bellied
yellow-belly
  yellow-bellies
yellow-bill
yel|low|cake
yel|low|fin
  plural yel|low|fin *or* yel|low|fins
yel|low|ham|mer +s
yel|low|ish
Yel|low|knife (city, Canada)
yel|low|legs
  plural yel|low|legs
yel|low|ness
Yel|low|stone (national park, USA)
yel|lowy
yelp +s +ed +ing
yelp|er +s
Yelt|sin, Boris (Russian president)
Yemen (in Arabian peninsula)
Yem|eni +s
Yem|en|ite +s
yen
  plural yen (Japanese currency)
yen
  yens
  yenned
  yen|ning

yen (*cont.*)
  (longing; feel a longing)
Yen-cheng (= Yancheng)
Yeni|sei (river, Siberia)
Yen-tai (= Yantai)
yeo|man
  yeo|men
yeo|man|ly
yeo|man|ry
  yeo|man|ries
Yeo|vil (town, England)
yep
yerba maté
Yere|van (capital of Armenia)
yes
  yeses
yes-man
  yes-men
yes|ter|day +s
yes|ter|eve
yes|ter|morn
yes|ter|night
yes|ter|year
yet
yeti +s
Yev|tu|shenko, Yev|geni (Russian poet)
yew +s (tree. △ ewe, you)
yew tree +s
Y-fronts *Propr.*
Ygg|dra|sil
Yi|chun (city, China)
Yid +s (*offensive*)
Yid|dish
Yid|dish|er +s
Yid|dish|ism +s
yield +s +ed +ing
yield|er +s
yield|ing|ly
yield|ing|ness
yikes
yin
Yin|chuan (city, China)
Yin|dji|barndi
yip
  yips
  yipped
  yip|ping
yip|pee
ylang-ylang +s
Ymir *Scandinavian Mythology*
yo

yob +s
yob|bish
yob|bish|ly
yob|bish|ness
yobbo
  yob|bos *or* yob|boes
yocto|meter *Am.* +s
yocto|metre *Br.* +s
yod +s
yodel
  yo|dels
  yo|delled *Br.*
  yo|deled *Am.*
  yo|del|ling *Br.*
  yo|del|ing *Am.*
  yo|del|er +s *Am.*
  yo|del|ler +s *Br.*
yoga
yogh +s
yog|hurt +s (use yogurt)
yogi +s
yogic
yo|gism
yog|urt +s
Yog|ya|karta (city, Java, Indonesia)
yo-heave-ho
yohi +s
yo-ho
yoicks
yoke
  yokes
  yoked
  yok|ing
  (neck-frame. △ yolk, yolked)
yokel +s
Yoko|hama (port, Japan)
Yo|landa
Yo|lande
yolk +s (part of egg; wool grease. △ yoke)
yolk-bag +s
yolked (having yolk. △ yoked)
yolk|less
yolk-sac +s
yolky
Yom Kip|pur
yomp +s +ed +ing
yon
yon|der
yoni +s
yonks
yoof (= youth)
yoo-hoo

yore (in 'of yore'.
△ yaw, your,
you're)
York (city,
England)
York, Cape (in
Australia)
York, Duke of
(Prince Andrew)
york +s +ed +ing
york¦er +s
York¦ist +s
York¦shire, North,
West, and South
(counties,
England)
York¦shire¦man
York¦shire¦men
York¦shire¦woman
York¦shire¦
      women
York¦town (town,
USA)
Yor¦uba
plural Yor¦uba
Yor¦vik (Viking
name for York)
Yo¦sem¦ite
(national park,
USA)
Yoshkar-Ola (city,
Russia)
yotta¦meter Am.
+s
yotta¦metre Br. +s
you (pronoun.
△ ewe, yew)
you-all
you'd (= you had;
you would)
youi +s (use yohi)
you-know-what
+s
you-know-who
you'll (= you shall;
you will. △ Yule)
Young, Brig¦ham
(American
Mormon leader)
Young, Thomas
(English physicist)
young +er +est
young¦ish
young¦ling +s
Young's modu¦lus
Young's mod¦uli
young¦ster +s
young 'un +s
youn¦ker +s
your (belonging to
you. △ yaw, yore,
you're)

you're (= you are.
△ yaw, yore,
your)
yours (the one(s)
belonging to you.
△ yaws)
your¦self
your¦selves
youse (you plural.
△ use)
youth +s
youth¦ful
youth¦ful¦ly
youth¦ful¦ness
you've (= you
have)
yowl +s +ed +ing
yo-yo +s noun
Propr.
yo-yo
yo-yoes
yo-yoed
yo-yoing
verb
Ypres (town and
battle site,
Belgium)
yt¦ter¦bium
yt¦trium
Yuan (Chinese
dynasty)
yuan
plural yuan
(Chinese
currency)
Yuca¦tán (state and
peninsula,
Mexico)
yucca +s
yuck
yucki¦ness
yucky
yuck¦ier
yuck¦iest
Yugo¦slav +s
Yugo¦slavia
Yugo¦slav¦ian +s
Yuit
plural Yuit or
Yuits
yuk (use yuck)
yukki¦ness (use
yuckiness)
yukky (use yucky)
Yukon (river, N.
America)
Yukon Ter¦ri¦tory
(in Canada)
Yule +s (Christmas.
△ you'll)
yule log +s
Yule¦tide +s

yummy
yum¦mier
yum¦mi¦est
yum-yum
Yun¦nan (province,
China)
yup
Yupik
yup¦pie +s
yup¦pie¦dom
yup¦pi¦fi¦ca¦tion
yup¦pify
yup¦pi¦fies
yup¦pi¦fied
yup¦pi¦fy¦ing
yuppy (use yuppie)
yup¦pies
yurt +s
Yu¦waa¦la¦raay
Yuz¦ovka (former
name of Donetsk)
Yv¦ette also Ev¦ette
Yv¦onne also
Ev¦onne

Zz

zaba¦gli¦one +s
Zabrze (city,
Poland)
Zaca¦tecas (city
and state, Mexico)
Zac¦chaeus Bible
Zach¦ary
Zack
zaf¦fer Am.
zaffre Br.
zag +s
Zaga¦zig (city,
Egypt)
Zag¦reb (capital of
Croatia)
Zag¦ros
Moun¦tains (in
Iran)
Zaire (country and
river)
zaire +s (Zairean
currency)
Za¦irean +s
Za¦irian +s (use
Zairean)
Zák¦in¦thos (Greek
name for
Zakynthos)
Zako¦pane (winter-
sports resort,
Poland)
Zak¦yn¦thos (Greek
island)
Zam¦besi (use
Zambezi)
Zam¦bezi (river, E.
Africa)
Zam¦bia
Zam¦bian +s
Zam¦bo¦anga (port,
Mindanao,
Philippines)
zam¦in¦dar +s
zan¦der
plural zan¦der
zani¦ly
zani¦ness
Zan¦skar (river and
mountain range,
India)
Zan¦skari +s
Zánte (alternative
name for
Zakynthos)
ZANU
(= Zimbabwe
African National
Union)

zany
  zanies
  zani|er
  zani|est
Zan|zi|bar (island, Tanzania)
Zan|zi|bari +s
Zao|zhuang (city, China)
zap
  zaps
  zapped
  zap|ping
Zap|ata, Emili|ano (Mexican revolutionary)
zapa|te|ado +s
Zapo|rizh|zhya (city, Ukraine)
Zapo|rozhe (Russian name for Zaporizhzhya)
Zapo|tec
  plural Zapo|tec or Zapo|tecs
Zappa, Frank (American rock musician)
zap|per +s
zappy
  zap|pier
  zap|pi|est
ZAPU (= Zimbabwe African People's Union)
Zaqa|ziq (use Zagazig)
Zara
Zara|goza (Spanish name for Saragossa)
zar|ape +s (use serape)
Zara|thus|tra (Avestan name for Zoroaster)
Zara|thus|trian +s
zar|eba +s (use zariba)
Zaria (city, Nigeria)
zar|iba +s
Zarqa (city, Jordan)
zar|zuela +s
Zato|pek, Emil (Czechoslovak runner)
zax
  zaxes
zeal
Zea|land (island, Denmark.
  ⚠ Zeeland)

Zealot +s (member of ancient Jewish sect)
zealot +s (fanatic)
zeal|ot|ry
zeal|ous
zeal|ous|ly
zeal|ous|ness
zebec +s (use xebec)
ze|beck +s (use xebec)
Zeb|edee
zebra
  plural zebra or zebras
zeb|rine
zebu +s
Zebu|llon (use Zebulun)
Zebu|lun Bible
Zech|ar|iah Bible
zed +s
Zed|ekiah Bible
zedo|ary
  zedo|ar|ies
zee +s
Zee|brugge (port, Belgium)
Zee|land (province, the Netherlands.
  ⚠ Zealand)
Zee|man ef|fect
Zef|fi|relli, Franco (Italian film and theatre director)
zein +s
Zeiss, Carl (German optical-instrument maker)
Zeit|geist
Zelda
zem|in|dar +s (use zamindar)
Zen
Zena
zen|ana +s
Zend +s
Zend-Avesta
Zener (card; diode)
Zen|ist +s
zen|ith
zen|ith|al
Zeno (two Greek philosophers)
Zen|obia (queen of Palmyra)
zeo|lite +s
zeo|lit|ic
Zepha|niah Bible
zephyr +s
Zep|pelin, Fer|di|nand,

Zep|pelin (cont.)
  Count von (German aviation pioneer)
Zep|pelin +s (airship)
zepto|meter Am. +s
zepto|metre Br. +s
Zer|matt (ski resort, Switzerland)
zero +s noun
zero
  zer|oes
  zer|oed
  zero|ing
  verb
zero hour
zero rate noun
zero-rate
  zero-rates
  zero-rated
  zero-rating
  verb
zero-sum
zer|oth
zest
zest|er +s
zest|ful
zest|ful|ly
zest|ful|ness
zesti|ness
zesty
  zest|ier
  zesti|est
Zeta (name)
zeta +s (Greek letter)
ze|tet|ic
zetta|meter Am. +s
zetta|metre Br. +s
zeugma +s
zeug|mat|ic
Zeus Greek Mythology
Zeuxis (Greek painter)
Zhang|jia|kou (city, China)
Zhan|jiang (port, China)
Zhda|nov (former name of Mariupol)
Zhe|jiang (province, China)
Zheng|zhou (city, China)
Zhen|jiang (port, China)

Zhito|mir (Russian name for Zhytomyr)
zho (use dzo)
  plural zho or zhos
Zhong|shan (city, China)
Zhou (Chinese dynasty)
Zhou Enlai (Chinese statesman)
Zhu|kov, Georgi (Soviet military leader)
Zhyto|myr (city, Ukraine)
Zia ul-Haq, Mu|ham|mad (Pakistani president)
Zibo (city, China)
zi|dovu|dine
Zieg|feld, Flor|enz (American theatre manager)
ziff +s
zig
  zigs
  zigged
  zig|ging
zig|gurat +s
zig|zag
  zig|zags
  zig|zagged
  zig|zag|ging
zig|zag|ged|ly
zilch
zil|lah +s
zil|lion +s
zil|lionth +s
Zim|babwe
Zim|bab|we|an +s
Zim|mer frame +s
  Propr.
zinc +s +ed +ing
zinc blende
zinco +s noun
zinco
  zin|coes
  zin|coed
  zinco|ing
  verb
zinco|graph +s
zinc|og|raphy
zinco|type +s
zincy
zing +s +ed +ing
Zin|garo
  Zin|gari
zing|er +s

zingy
  zing|ier
  zingi|est
Zin⌊jan¦thro⌊pus
zin¦nia+s
Zion
Zion|ism
Zion|ist+s
zip
  zips
  zipped
  zip|ping
Zip code+s
zip fas|ten¦er+s
zip¦per+s +ed
  +ing
zip|pily
zip|pi|ness
zippy
  zip|pier
  zip|pi|est
zip-up *adjective*
zir¦con+s
zir|co¦nia
zir|co¦nium
zit+s
zith¦er+s
zith¦er|ist+s
zizz
  zizzes
  zizzed
  zizz|ing
zloty
  plural zloty *or*
  zlotys *or* zlot¦ies
zo¦diac+s
zo¦di|ac¦al
Zoe *also* Zoë
Zoë *also* Zoe
zoe|trope+s
Zof|fany, Jo¦hann
  (German painter)

Zog (Albanian king)
zoic
Zola (name)
Zola, Émile
  (French writer)
Zöll|ner's lines
zoll⌊ver¦ein+s
zom¦bie+s
zonal
zon¦ary
zon¦ate
zon|ation+s
zonda+s
zone
  zones
  zoned
  zon¦ing
zonk+s +ed +ing
zoo+s
zoo|geo¦graph¦ic
zoo|
   geo¦graph¦ic¦al
zoo|geo¦graph¦ic|
   al¦ly
zoo|geog¦raphy
zo|og¦raphy
zooid+s
zo|oid¦al
zoo|keep¦er+s
zo|ol¦atry
zoo|logic¦al
zoo|logic¦al|ly
zo¦olo¦gist+s
zo|ology
zoom+s +ed +ing
zoo|mancy
zoo|morph¦ic
zoo|morph|ism
zoon|osis
  zoon|oses
zoo|phyte+s
zoo|phyt¦ic

zoo|plank¦ton
zoo|spore+s
zoo|spor¦ic
zo|ot¦omy
zoot suit+s
zori+s
zoril+s
zor|illa+s
Zoro|as¦ter
  (Persian founder
  of Zoroastrianism)
Zoro|as¦trian+s
Zoro|as¦trian|ism
Zou¦ave+s
zouk
zounds
Zsig|mondy,
  Rich|ard
  Ad¦olph (Austrian-
  born German
  chemist)
zuc|chetto+s
zuc|chini
  plural zuc|chini *or*
  zuc|chi¦nis
Zug (city and
  canton,
  Switzerland)
zug|zwang+s
Zui¦der Zee
  (former inlet, the
  Netherlands)
Zulu+s
Zulu|land (former
  name of
  KwaZulu)
Zur¦ba|rán,
  Fran|cisco de
  (Spanish painter)
Zur¦ich (city and
  canton,
  Switzerland)

Zür|ich (German
  name for Zurich)
Zwickau (city,
  Germany)
zwie|back
Zwingli, Ul¦rich
  (Swiss Protestant
  reformer)
Zwing|li¦an+s
zwit¦ter|ion+s
Zwolle (town, the
  Netherlands)
Zwory|kin,
  Vlad|imir
  (Russian-born
  American
  physicist)
zy¦deco
zygo|dac¦tyl+s
zygo|dac¦tyl|ous
zyg¦oma
  zyg|omata *or*
  zyg|omas
zygo|mat¦ic
zygo|morph¦ic
zygo|morph¦ous
zyg|osis
zygo|spore+s
zyg|ote+s
zyg|ot|ene
zyg|ot¦ic
zyg|ot¦ic|al¦ly
zym¦ase
zymo|logic¦al
zym|olo¦gist+s
zym|ology
zym|osis
zym|ot¦ic
zym|urgy